A HISTORY OF GERMAN LITERATURE

A HISTORY OF GERMAN LITERATURE

From the beginnings to the present day

Fourth edition

Wolfgang Beutin, Klaus Ehlert,
Wolfgang Emmerich, Helmut Hoffacker,
Bernd Lutz, Volker Meid, Ralf Schnell,
Peter Stein and Inge Stephan

Translated by Clare Krojzl

London and New York

English translation first published 1993
by Routledge
11 New Fetter Lane, London EC4P 4EE

Simultaneously published in the USA and Canada
by Routledge
29 West 35th Street, New York, NY 10001

First published in German by
J. B. Metzlersche Verlagsbuchhandlung in 1989

© 1989 J. B. Metzlersche Verlagsbuchhandlung
Translation © 1993 Routledge

The authors of individual sections of the book are as follows: pp. 60–105 by
Wolfgang Beutin; pp. 324–82 and 406–25 by Klaus Ehlert; pp. 573–660 and 761–9
by Wolfgang Emmerich; pp. 383–405 and 425–36 by Helmut Hoffacker; pp. 1–59
by Bernd Lutz; pp. 106–55 by Volker Meid; pp. 535–72 and 661–760 by Ralf
Schnell; pp. 248–323 by Peter Stein; pp. 156–93 and 436–503 by Inge Stephan.

Phototypeset in Garamond by
Intype, London

Printed and bound in Great Britain by
Mackays of Chatham Ltd, Kent

British Library Cataloguing in Publication Data
A catalogue record for this book is available from the British Library

Library of Congress Cataloging in Publication Data
Deutsche Literaturgeschichte. English
A history of German literature: from the beginnings to the present day/Wolfgang
Beutin . . . [et al.].—Fourth edn
p. cm.
Includes bibliographical references and index.
1. German literature—History and criticism. I. Beutin, Wolfgang. II. Title.
PT85.D369 1993
830.9—dc20 93–3381

ISBN 0–415–06034–6

CONTENTS

v

PREFACE

Starting point

When this book first appeared in 1979, the study of the history of literature was still under the sway of a type of account that had become prevalent in the 1950s under the banner of post-1945 'ideological freedom'. This had in turn developed out of an intellectual historical approach to German literary developments that had been the norm since Wilhelm Dilthey. The impact on German education of the authors and their generation, and the scholarly shortcomings of this fruitless approach, have been immense. This is attested by the sheer length of time it took for any discussion at all to arise on reasons for elaborating a new way of looking at the whole history of literature. Such a discussion did not even begin to manifest itself until the mid–1970s. The importance of social history as a dimension of literature, now a major area within the discipline besides that of aesthetic values, has since been accorded its rightful place among the subject matter proper to the discipline. The new awareness that has been brought to bear on this History of German Literature over the last decade is regarded by the authors as confirmation of their intention to make a complete break with customary guidelines for the presentation, classification and selection of material, and to bring this newly acquired self-perception of literary study into the clear light of day.

Two principles

It would be appropriate at this point to restate the two basic principles that have emerged from discussion as the authors' shared view of the overall conception and formal structure appropriate to this book. First, a socio-historical basis for the study of literature does not mean embedding it in political, social or ideological processes. What it definitely does mean, however, is interpreting the artistic autonomy of literary creation against this background, so as to be able to describe how literature both reconciles itself with and protests against 'human relations'. The conceptual marriage of literary and social change enables us to uncover the equally fundamental and productive contradiction between aesthetic illusion and social reality, and to conceptualise literature in terms of the dynamic of this contradiction as an 'organon of history' (Walter Benjamin), even in cases where it is ultimately subordinate to it. Second, it seemed only right to allow literature its own voice as a storehouse of historical experience, relating it to the contemporary situation, rather than treating it as a dead historical document that is 'over and done with'. It needs to be borne in mind, however, that knowledge is not lodged in literary works in the form of some 'fixed truth', 'concrete substance' or 'statement of meaning', but can only be derived from them through the mediation of the reader, becoming meaningful in terms of his or her own experiences in the present.

Guidelines for the account

The following guidelines consequently emerged for this account of the history of literature: a chronological approach, which nevertheless attaches varying weight to different periods, laying special stress on the concerns of the twentieth century, particularly the literature of both parts of Germany since 1945. The classification of periods has been made on the basis of upheavals in political history, taking into account the non-simultaneous relationship between material and creative productivity. Each section dealing with a different age begins by enumerating and pinpointing issues in the historical dimension of literature, elaborating the key issues and using them as examples with which to interpret the literary historical process. Writers and works are therefore selected on a functional basis, dispensing with the practice of a complete enumeration of authors and works and giving precedence instead to those that are in some way exemplary. Failure to mention an author or work should by no means be taken as a negative value judgement.

Like the second edition, the third has also been substantially revised and expanded. This concerns in the first instance the outward form of the book. The earlier format – a mixture of continuous narrative interspersed with original quotations and informative texts – seemed outdated. All chapters have been expanded and revised in terms of content and style, although the scope of this Preface precludes a detailed list of alterations. The most recent scholarly developments and research results have been taken into account.

September 1989

MEDIEVAL LITERATURE

A Romantic rediscovery

What do we know of the beginnings?

A survey of medieval German literature poses more problems than that of later ages. This is not least because of the time-span involved – several centuries from the earliest documents, dating from the middle of the eighth century, to the final echoes of the age in the fifteenth century – a span comparable with the period from early humanist literature until the advent of the modern age. The legacy of extant medieval literary material is particularly scant and random in character, precluding any accurate assessment of the scope and nature of what is now lost to historians forever. The scope and nature of German and other national literatures dating from the fifteenth century onwards is well-known to us by virtue of the greater number of copies and the chances of literature being preserved that accompanied the invention of printing. The drawback with literature of the early period (*Frühzeit*) is that it was an exclusively oral tradition. With the appearance of written records it was then used to serve the romantic propensities of subsequent generations: the deliberate compilation and authentic archiving of oral traditions was not the rule. Much more than with other periods, therefore, scholars of medieval literature are far more dependent on the resourceful reconstruction of presumed literary circumstances. A description of this literature, which took shape over several centuries, might give the impression that it stirred slowly and unfolded only gradually. This impression arises out of the assumptions of our own literate culture, which equates literature directly with written records. General statements about the form and function in pre- and early history of tribal and communal literature that was passed on and received orally can at best be only tenuous.

The sheer dearth of factual information, therefore, is a major cause of the unsure ground being trodden when evaluating medieval literature, particularly of the early period. A more decisive factor in the scholarly

1

interpretation of the Middle Ages and its literature, after the beginnings of philology in the Humanist period and the editorial endeavours of Bodmer and Breitinger over the Heidelberg song manuscripts and the Lay of the Nibelungs in the mid-eighteenth century, was the rediscovery of the Middle Ages by the German Romantics. For all the philological serious-mindedness the times allowed, an innate tendency towards speculative distortion nonetheless crept in. The creative concerns of the period around 1800 were marked by a polarisation between a classical-finite formal purpose, represented by pagan antiquity, and a romantic-infinite progression related to the Christian Middle Ages. The rediscovery of the Middle Ages by the Romantics took place at a time when, in the wake of the rationalist Enlightenment critique, a reflexive conception of history was taking shape, no longer concerned with facts alone, but with value-judgements related to notions of the 'progressive' and the 'backward'. Going beyond traditional Christian historical teleology with its ubiquitous tendency to interpret world history as a process of salvation, the Romantic view of the Middle Ages was to lead to the instigation of a national educational merger movement in the nineteenth century. What now appears a somewhat contrived resurgence of 'Occidental Catholicism' readily developed out of this view, and indeed the Romantic generation produced numerous conversions to Catholicism on the strength of their philosophy of history. In *Heinrich von Ofterdingen*, Novalis went as far as to denounce Protestantism as 'insurgence', thus circumventing the entire struggle between 'old' and 'new' faiths that had been waged during the Reformation.

The Romantic concept of the Middle Ages

The very term 'Middle Ages' as used by the Romantics now seems vague by modern philological and historical standards. It embraced a vast time-span stretching from early history to Dürer; only the age in which modern subjectivity began to emerge could lay claim to modernity. For contemporaries of the Romantic age, notably Tieck, Wackenroder, the two Schlegels and Novalis, the Middle Ages represented an age reconciled to the history of salvation, an age that by virtue of a social structure with clear-cut, unambiguous ranks and hierarchies, as well as the primacy of Christian religiosity, constituted the medium *par excellence* for understanding the relationship between God, Man and the world. Through the apparent inward and outward stability of the Hohenstaufen empire it seemed to offer a shining, timeless alternative scenario to the early nineteenth century scene – to the struggle against Napoleon and the first glimmerings of alienation (including the social impotence of art), to economic and social depression and unequivocal criticism of the Enlightenment. It was in this spirit that Friedrich Schlegel raised his voice: 'Der revolutionäre Wunsch, das Reich Gottes zu realisieren, ist der elastische Punkt der progressiven

2

Bildung und der Anfang der modernen Geschichte' ('The revolutionary desire to bring about the Kingdom of God is the elastic point of progressive education and the beginning of modern history.') In a similar vein, Novalis declares in his programmatic (*programmatisch*) book *Die Christenheit oder Europa* (1799):

> Es waren schöne glänzende Zeiten, wo Europa ein christliches Land war, wo Eine Christenheit diesen menschlich gestalteten Weltteil bewohnte; Ein grosses gemeinschaftliches Interesse verband die entlegensten Provinzen diesen weiten geistlichen Reichs. – Ohne grosse weltliche Besitztümer lenkte und vereinigte Ein Oberhaupt die grossen politischen Kräfte. – Eine zahlreiche Zunft, zu der jedermann den Zutritt hatte, stand unmittelbar unter demselben und vollführte seine Winke und strebte mit Eifer seine wohltätige Macht zu befestigen, jedes Glied dieser Gesellschaft wurde allenthalben geehrt, und wenn die gemeinen Leute Trost oder Hülfe, Schutz oder Rat bei ihm suchten und gerne dafür seine mannigfaltigen Bedürfnisse reichlich versorgten, so fand es auch bei den Mächtigeren Schutz. Ansehn und Gehör, und alle pflegten diese auserwählten, mit wunderbaren Kraften ausgerüsteten Männer wie Kinder des Himmels, deren Gegenwart und Zueignung mannigfachen Segen verbreitete. Kindliches Zutrauen knüpfte die Menschen an ihre Verkündigungen. – Wie heiter konnte jedermann sein irdisches Tagewerk vollbringen, da ihm durch diese heilige Menschen eine sichere Zukunft bereitet und jeder Fehltritt durch sie vergeben, jede missfarbige Stelle des Lebens durch sie ausgelöscht und geklärt wurde. Sie waren die erfahrnen Steuerleute auf dem grossen und unbekannten Meere, in deren Obhut man alle Stürme geringschätzen und unzuversichtlich auf eine sichre Gelangung und Landung an der Küste der eigentlichen vaterländischen Welt rechnen durfte.

> They were glorious times, when Europe was a Christian land, when a single Christendom inhabited this part of the world, created by human hands. A great communal interest bound the most distant provinces of this great spiritual empire. Without great worldly possessions, one leader steered and united its great political forces. A replete guild to which all had access stood directly under him, carrying out his every wish, seeking zealously to consolidate his benevolent power. Every member of this society was honoured everywhere, and when the common people sought comfort or succour, protection or counsel from him, gladly and generously meeting his every need in return, each member found protection with the more powerful. Deference and allegiance, and all men ensured the care of these chosen ones, these men blessed with wondrous powers, like children of heaven, whose presence and affection spread abroad manifold

3

blessings. A childlike trust was accorded by men to their promulgations. How cheerfully could every man fulfil his daily mundane tasks, ensured by these holy men of a secure future, every false step pardoned by them, every stain on the garment of life washed clean by them. They were their experienced helmsmen on the great unknown sea, in whose safekeeping one could afford to disdain all storms, confidently able to count on a safe arrival and landing on the shore of their true national homeland.

It was within such a scheme of art theory and the philosophy of history that the rediscovery of the Middle Ages was heralded – a backward-oriented utopia to be brought about as an alternative scenario to modern unease. Early German studies, represented by the Brothers Grimm, Karl Lachmann and Moriz Haupt among others, were the rationalist expression of this longing. Within this unearthing of the history of both national German literature and the language, these German studies were at first oriented towards an emphatic folk concept, so that for scholars such as Jakob Grimm the connection between German studies and history seemed an obvious one. It was to become a political issue when the historico-philosophical model crystallised into a set of principles aimed at achieving Prussian supremacy in Germany by national liberals such as A. Müller and J.G. Fichte. According to this model, the German people, by now a mythical category, constituted the irrational factor in the national propaganda of the wars of liberation. Such militant conceptual categories as 'France, Germany's traditional enemy' were derived from this conception, and were to continue to influence both the actual course of events and the ideological history of Germany up to World War II. Evidence of this continuity may be found not only in the introverted Romantic view of the Middle Ages, but above all in the imperial propaganda kitsch of the *Gründerzeit*, Richard Wagner and Bayreuth, as well as what the Nazis subsequently arrogated from the 'heroic' olden times of the German people.

European literature and the Latin Middle Ages

Given the nationalist background against which the study of philology and the ideological assessment of the German Middle Ages took place, it is hardly surprising that a sound all-European perspective was not to be brought to bear on medieval philology until the end of World War II. In his epoch-making book *Europäische Literatur und Lateinisches Mittelalter* (*European Literature and the Latin Middle Ages*) (1948), Ernst Robert Curtius drew attention to the extent to which the medieval literatures constituted a single all-European fabric – a view that was to bring him into frequent and uncompromising conflict with one of the foremost medievalists of his day, Gustav Ehrismann, a staunchly conservative proponent of nineteenth century national liberal German studies. The Anglo-Saxon, German, French and Italian literatures of the Middle Ages were all to some degree interconnected and influenced one another. They shared common roots in Greek and Roman antiquity, while the impact of Arab-Islamic cultural ideals and poetic forms in the cultural struggle with other religions, not least among which was Judaism, was likewise enormous. Autochthonous German literary development in the sense meant by the Romantics thus in fact never took place; this notion was born of historico-philosophical wishful thinking.

Philology and history – a manifesto

Ernst Robert Curtius attempted to carry this awareness over into philological practice:

> Im 20. Jahrhundert hat man vielfach der Altertumswissenschaft das wertsetzende Beiwort 'klassisch' entzogen, aber sie selbst ist dem Vermächtnis ihrer Gründer treu geblieben. Diese universale, Philologie und Geschichte vereinende Auffassung der Antike ist ein schönes Vorrecht der deutschen Altertumsforschung geblieben und hat reiche Frucht getragen. Von der Erforschung des Mittelalters kann das Gleiche leider nicht gesagt werden. Die Mittelalter-Forschung entstand im Zeichen der Romantik und hat die Spuren dieser Abkunft nie abgestreift. Altgermanisches Reckentum, Minnesang und Ritterzeiten – um sie wob die Romantik duftige Bilder. Die deutsche Erhebung von 1813 verschmolz sie mit dem nationalen Wollen einer neuen Jugend. Forscher, unter denen mancher zugleich Dichter waren, stellten die Texte her und wirkten am Bilde deutscher Vergangenheit. . . . Nur die Zusammenarbeit der verschiedenen Mittelalter-Wissenschaften kann das kulturhistorische Problem des höfischen und ritterlichen Ethos lösen, wenn es lösbar ist. Der mittelalterliche Philolog muss die mittelalterlichen Geschichtswissenschaft danach abfragen, was die über die mittelalterlichen Standesideale, ihre konkreten politischen, militärischen, wirtschaftlichen Bedingtheiten mitzuteilen weiss. . . . Diese Andeutungen genügen vielleicht, um zu zeigen, dass wir eine neue Mittelalter-Wissenschaft auf breitester Grundlage brauchen.

In the twentieth century, there have been frequent attempts to wrest the value-laden epithet 'classical' from antiquity studies, but these studies have remained true to the legacy of their founders. This universal concept of antiquity, uniting philology and history, is one of the more pleasant prerogatives of German research into antiquity, and has borne rich fruit. Unfortunately, the same cannot be said of medieval studies. This discipline came into existence under the banner of the Romantics, and has never managed to slough off the traces of its origin. Old German *Reckentum*, *minnesang* and the age of chivalry were all cloaked in rosy images by the Romantic age. The German Uprising of 1813 fused these images with the national aspirations of the up-and-coming generation. Scholars, who were often also poets, composed texts, thus shaping the perception of the German past. . . . Only cooperation between the various branches of medieval studies can resolve the cultural-historical problem of the courtly and chivalric ethos, if indeed it can be resolved. The medieval philologist needs to seek out the knowledge of medieval historians concerning medieval ideals of rank, and their respective political, military and economic aspects. . . . These suggestions should suffice to point out the need for a new kind of medieval studies on the broadest possible footing.

The thesis-ridden approach to medieval studies is unlikely to change now, and indeed is likely to become increasingly out of step with approaches to other periods. However, the universalist approach taken up so implacably by Ernst Robert Curtius, focusing on actual power relations in a syncretic European medieval period, has a far better chance than the nationalist-oriented one of shedding light on the specific conditions underpinning literature in its role among other cultural manifestations.

Germanic Pagan poetry, heroic lays

The earliest poetry to appear on German soil was pagan tribal and retainer poetry, of which few examples are extant. What little there is has been handed down from later times. It is a monument to vernacular dialect: on the basis of geographical linguistic analysis, comprising largely phonetics and orthography, the place or linguistic area in which it was recorded in written form can usually be pinpointed with accuracy. This earliest literature has to be evaluated outside the aesthetic strictures customary in the modern age. Early German studies treated this literature as a linguistic monument. The ceremonial spoken or sung word accompanied magic rituals designed to invoke the protection and assistance of tribal deities. We may deduce on the basis of what is known about tribally-organised communities outside Europe that sacrificial verse, oracular pronouncements and magic formulas were adjuncts to this literature. These magical textual forms pertain to the entire range of everyday concerns and aspirations of a bartering society characterised by a tribal political arrangement and a predominantly agrarian economic system.

Magic from the pre-literate period

The *Merseburger Zaubersprüche* (*Merseburg Incantations*), not recorded in written form until the tenth century, are the best-known testimony to this pre-literate period. The second incantation opens with an epic tale composed in two long lines in stave rhyme: Phol and Wodan are riding in the forest, when one of their horses sprains a leg. On another plane of speech, the attempt at magical incantation is made. This is repeated three times, as the first two attempts result in failure. Only when Wodan is addressed in his capacity as master of witchcraft is there a prospect of the horse being cured. The addressing of the illness and the command for a cure then ensue on a third, imperative plane of speech. The clear structure of the second *Merseburg Incantation*, and the alternation of a number of speech planes of equal weight in which magical forces are seen to be at work on the course of events, all point to its pre-literate German origin. Confidence in the efficacy and readiness to help of the Germanic world of gods was still alive and could still be declaimed with assurance. Later testimonies to magical incantation poetry that have since come to light are more equivocal in tone, and are partly overlaid with the Christian influence, in both diction and incantation: for example, the *Lorscher Bienensegen* (*Lorsch Blessing of the Bees*).

The migrations

The migrations both altered and expanded the magico-natural consciousness of the Germanic tribes. Their encounters with the alien and superior cultures of Spain, Italy and Africa altered their view of themselves, as the necessity for the warrior ethos came increasingly to the fore. A natural consequence of incessant combat and of migrational waves that often lasted for centuries was the emergence of a new kind of heroic or epic poetry. A number of legend cycles also appeared during this period, for example the Ostrogothic Dietrich and Hildebrand legends and the Lay of the Battle of Ravenna (*Rabenschlachtlied*), the Alemannic cycle with Walther and Hildegund, the Visigothic legend of the Battle of the Huns (*Hunnenschlachtsage*), the northern Germanic legends of Beowulf, Wieland the Smith, Hilde and Gudrun, and the Burgundian legend of the Nibelungs. These legend cycles were variously revised and altered over the course of time, even in the Middle Ages, and in some cases have completely lost their original form.

The most important literary testimony to the period is the *Hildebrandslied* or Lay of Hildebrand, which was discovered in a Fulda codex dating from the second half of the eighth century. The main contents of the codex are two books from the Old Testament, the Book of Proverbs and the Apocrypha. On the first and last pages, as far as space would allow, two different writers at the beginning of the ninth century then added the Lay of Hildebrand. They managed to add 68 stave rhyme long lines; the Lay is incomplete, as the end is missing. The Lay of Hildebrand stems from the Gothic-Langobardic legendary orbit. However, this extant record, obviously copied from an earlier version that itself is unlikely to have been original, is peppered with Upper and Lower German idiosyncrasies of speech. The history of the legend depicted in the Lay of Hildebrand points to Bavaria, so that its original linguistic form must have been Upper German. It is one of the epic poems dealing with the figure of Dietrich of Bern, which suggests an origin even further south. Bavaria, especially the monastery at Freising, was a literary emporium for poetry and both secular and specialist clerical prose (*Gebrauchsprosa*) on the way to the North. It is probable that the Lay was revised in Fulda into a new, Low German version. This suggests itself in view of the numerous monks of Bavarian origin of whom Fulda had the benefit in its early days, as well as the active links it cultivated with Regensburg as the literary importance of Freising gradually waned. The story of this uniquely extant, albeit fragmentary heroic epic poem – not only the end is missing, but apparently also some verses from the body of the text – is brief. A liegeman of Dietrich of Bern, Hildebrand had had thirty years earlier to leave his wife and son behind in his homeland during a retreat from Odoaker. On his way home at last, he meets a hero from the enemy side. Recognising the man as his son, he declares himself. His son distrusts him, however, suspecting an attempt on Hildebrand's part to evade combat, and intensifies his entirely legitimate anti-enemy invective. This touches Hildebrand at his most sensitive spot – his honour as a warrior. Combat between father and son thus becomes inevitable. The Fulda version is curtailed at this point. However, it is known from other sources that Hildebrand kills his son. Later versions have a more conciliatory conclusion, but these have little in common with the original form of the lay. It is precisely this tragic inevitability of the fateful encounter between father and son that ranks the Fulda version of the Lay of Hildebrand among the very earliest epic poetry. The basic rhetorical form is dialogue, an interchange brimming with the kind of bloodlust also typical for Nordic epic poetry. It is unlikely, however, to represent the very oldest epic poetry, clearly being based on the Dietrich legend cycle, the Lay of Hildebrand most probably being a late offshoot. It would appear that a seventh century Langobardic poet appropriated some migrant literary material with no apparent tribal origin, linking it in every detail with the primary pagan components of the Dietrich of Bern legend cycle. It portrays total allegiance and an unshakeable warrior ethic in a context of utmost moral dilemma.

Court minstrels and scholar-poets

The chief proponents of stave rhyme poetry were court minstrels, their poetry being one of rank, intended for the ears of the noble upper classes, whose war exploits they glorified. The displacement of the Germanic tribal kings and their retainers by more consequential exogenous social information entailed around the middle of the ninth century the rapid demise not only of the epic lay as such, but also of the very status of court minstrel. The new breed of poet and scholar was an exclusively monastic creature who was to exert a decisive influence over literature until the middle of the twelfth century. The minstrels of the tribes and noble entourages, the legacy of the Germanic pre-literate era, were thus replaced by intellectuals. It will be clear from this to what extent heroic poetry, quintessentially alien to Christian thought, was now nonetheless contingent upon it in terms of being handed down and disseminated. This marks the beginning of the crucial role of the medieval monasteries not only in teaching the German tribes to read and write, but also in determining what they should and should not read.

From the Carolingian Renaissance to the Hohenstaufen empire: cultural and political foundations

It would be difficult to exaggerate the importance of Charles the Great (Charlemagne) in promoting and propagating literate culture in the West and East Frankish kingdoms. A fervent proponent of education, literature, art and science, he decreed *inter alia* in 813 that every man should send his sons to school, either to a monastery or a priest. He likewise commissioned the compilation of a system of grammar for his mother tongue. His *Heldenliederbuch* (*Book of Heroic Lays*) is a compilation of the most important and earliest tribal literature and epic poetry. His cultural policy of *renovatio studii* was an integral part of his overall imperial policy of *renovatio imperii*, and was to lead to the first flowering of the study of antique classicism, later to lose all significance under the successors to the Holy Roman Empire. Art history in particular bears witness to the Carolingian or Ottonine Renaissance (Romanesque), that was to set the tone of the entire subsequent age under the Frankish-Carolingian and Saxon Emperors.

Educational reform

The reign of Charlemagne came too late to be shaped by the process of Christianisation that was for the most part long since complete. His interest focused on building up a strong, well-organised imperial church, albeit subordinate to his own imperial objectives. Inevitably, this imperial church was eventually to become a power in its own right, and hence also a political factor. In time it even came to constitute a separate sphere of dominion, oriented towards Rome. It was Charles's firm intention to place the laity under the authority of the Christian church and a classical-Christian system of education, thereby entrenching his own worldly claim to power. Nevertheless, the moment the Church laid claim to its own autonomy – declaring that it was not the Emperor, but Jesus of Nazareth, the promised Messiah and anointed Christ, who was Lord of the historical era – a profound sense of unease welled up among the laity, who were steeped in the Christian doctrine of salvation. An imperial ideological struggle between the worldly empire on the one hand and the kingdom of God represented by the Pope on the other was foreshadowed in this rivalry, and has persisted to the present day in the modern status quo between State and Church. This conflict was to be played out as a struggle of investiture (*Investiturstreit*) between the Pope and the kings of France, England and Germany, triggered by the vexed question of who was empowered to invest bishops: the Pope in Rome, or the worldly ruler. What began as a localised struggle of investiture rapidly proliferated; with his ontological proof of the existence of God, Anselm, Archbishop of Canterbury gave assurance not only of the Church's superiority to Islam, a palpable presence in Spain, as well as Judaism, likewise represented in numerous urban communities, but also to worldly power. The Church alone had a monopoly on eternal truth. Behind all this, however, lay a movement towards a massive expansion of the territory and the political power of the clergy. This power struggle, aimed at a substantial weakening of the European nobility, was to use even the Crusades as an instrument to achieve its ends, and was not to be resolved until the Concordat of Worms in 1122.

Monastic institutions undoubtedly played a crucial role in the Christian cultural mission envisaged by Charlemagne. They were therefore expanded, and their property augmented to the greatest possible extent. The monasteries were major landowners in the Middle Ages. Monastic life itself was conducted according to strict rules, mostly those of Benedict of Nursia, which governed the entire course of each day. This certainly made them from the outset a major influence on the surrounding Germanic tribes, symbolising through their exemplary high culture a break from time-honoured customs and technologies. Through their early attempt to form communities in the name of Christ – i.e. not of tribal chieftains – and to gather on a regular basis, they made one of the first substantial contributions to the urbanisation of Germanic tribal customs. Their implicit objective was the conversion of the feudal system to Christianity. However, the monasteries were not simply seats in which a new way of life was unfolding, but also major institutions of learning. Their responsibilities embraced the constant and strict subjection of both the community and the individual to the Christian faith, coupled with imparting the rudiments of culture, such as reading and writing skills. They were the mediators and guardians of a body of learning handed down from both early and late antiquity, the latter already imbued with early Christian thought.

The Cluniac monastic reforms that took place around 910 had one clear aim in view, an ascetic, hierarchical conception of Christianity and the Church that could only serve the newly-awakened militant spirit: autarchical monasteries unassailable by any worldly power, not unlike military bastions. These reforms were quick to take root, making the Cluniac monastic order a force to be reckoned with in the Empire. The spirit of Cluny spread in Germany also, making its presence clearly felt from 1070 (the Hirsau reform) onwards. The number of monasteries reformed in Germany is estimated at around 150. The literary repercussions of this were particularly apparent in Bavaria and Austria. By staking its claim to power, the Church not only directed the course of public debate, but in the wake of its original purpose also discovered an undogmatic and more spiritual way of addressing the laity, so as better to acquaint them with the ascetic monastic ideal. The advent of early Middle High German, a period informed by a spirit of 'enlightenment' and education, is likewise imbued with this purpose. Indeed, the period is sometimes referred to as the age of Cluny literature. Almost all its authors were clerics, although a few laymen may be found among them.

For a long time texts from the Latin translation of the scriptures by Hieronymus, probably dating from the end of the fourth or beginning of the fifth century, formed the core of monastic education. Considerable knowledge of Latin stylistics and rhetoric were needed for the scholar to draw full benefit from the wealth of the scriptures. This somewhat outmoded scholarship stemmed largely from late antiquity, dating back to the Neo-Platonist Martianus Capella. It was brought up to date at the end of the ninth and beginning of the tenth century by Alcuin of York, friend and tutor to Charlemagne, spiritual instigator of the Carolingian Renaissance. The outcome was a system known as the *septem artes liberales* or 'seven liberal arts'. This knowledge, which in its late classical meaning could only be obtained by a freeman, comprised *trivium* – grammar, dialectics as the capacity of logical reasoning and rhetoric, as well as *quadrivium* – knowledge of astronomy, arithmetic, geometry and music. Alcuin thereby laid the foundations for the later emergence of *studium*, a third faculty, as well as *sacerdotum* and *imperium*, which were complemented by the *artes mechanicae* or mechanical arts. The first faculties of arts, the core of the European universities, emerged from this basis. The system of the seven liberal arts was to shape the way universities organised the various branches of knowledge until the Renaissance. Not until then did the natural sciences, grouped under the heading of 'mechanical arts', gradually break free and begin to lead the life of their own that they have continued to do into the modern age.

The medieval concept of poetry was likewise subordinate to the seven liberal arts, being conceived as part of rhetorical education and practice, and incorporated in the didactic system of the liberal arts. In terms of descriptive and expressive technique, it was subordinate to purely theological approaches, by way of expounding on the Bible. A theory of poetry as a form in its own right for the interpretation of the world was hence lacking in this period. Scarcely any distinction was made between verse and prose: well into the late Middle Ages, poetry was regarded as a kind of controlled rhetoric. It was Alcuin, following on from Augustine, who first expanded the scope of the possible in poetry. Like the rest of the liberal arts, poetry was to be cultivated at the Carolingian court. Two approaches to poetry emerged: one was the *poetica divina*, which derived from the Paris school of theology and was compulsory for all sacred poetry of the Middle Ages. According to this approach, God is seen as the Creator of all beings and phenomena. The sole duty of Man, and hence also the poet, is to praise this great work of art. Another increasingly discernible approach was that of court poetry, which stresses the creative being of man. However, the development of these two was never so extreme as to obscure their common roots in the rhetorical aesthetics of antiquity, which recognised no distinction between rhetorical expression and the natural world order.

The monasteries as sources of written documents

Finally, the monasteries were responsible for the creation of substantial manuscript resources, partly in the simple form of direct copies, partly as revisions or adapted poetry texts, as well of course as magnificent, painstakingly written and richly illuminated manuscripts. The skill of writing was not the exclusive privilege of the clergy: lay scriveners were often also employed in monastic writing schools.

Medieval manuscripts were written on parchment. Since the manufacture of parchment was a costly and painstaking process, the drafting of a manuscript was often only possible with sponsoring from wealthy courts or monasteries. Scriveners and book illuminators were held in high esteem: a wide variety of skills, craftsmanship and care went into their work. The manuscript and the codex were revered in the Middle Ages to a degree that is no longer imaginable today. The commercial manufacture or distribution of manuscripts was unknown in that period.

Towards the end of the fourteenth century, however, paper replaced parchment, by now regarded as too costly. The increased demand for books certainly accelerated this process. The value of a manuscript derives from the care that has gone into the hand-written script in ink, from its initials, often decorated with gold or silver inlay, and its hand-coloured illuminations. One of the finest examples of medieval book art is the *Heidelberger Liederhandschrift* (*Heidelberg Lays Manuscript*), with its 137 miniatures of poets. It soon became an exhibition piece. The reason for this can be seen from the richly decorated pages, and the covers, which are partly ornamented with gold and precious stones. Notable manuscript artifacts worth seeing can be found in great libraries such as the Bavarian State Library in Munich (manuscripts of the *Heliand, Parzifal, Willehalm, Tristan,* the *Lay of the Nibelungs*), the Austrian National Library in Vienna and the Heidelberg University Library (*Kleine und Grosse Liederhandschrift – Minor and Major Song Manuscripts*).

Translations from the Latin and Greek

The prolific translation work issuing from monasteries was of incalculable importance in the maturation process of the Old High German literary language. The works of numerous classical authors were translated, often taking up the entire lifetime of a monk. One of the most inspiring figures in the translation of classical and Christian authors from the Latin was Hrabanus Maurus (died 856), an outstanding authority on Christian literature of late antiquity, author of an encyclopedia in several volumes on profane knowledge, founder and influential abbot of the monastery at Fuld, and pupil of Alcuin. Walahfried Strabo, a pupil of Hrabanus Maurus, abbot of the Reichenau monastery on Lake Constance and tutor to Charles the Bald, carried on this tradition. Around 1000, Notker of St Gallen, another of the many translator monks, also a learned commentator and philologist, was to become important in the history of literature and culture. It was he who introduced into the German-speaking world the core schoolroom authors of classical antiquity and the early Christian Middle Ages. Works included were by Augustine, the *Consolations of Philosophy* by Boëthius, the bucolic poetry of Theocritus and Virgil, Latin textbooks on rhetoric and poetics, parts of the Bible (the Psalms and the Book of Job), Aristotle's *Hermeneutics*, and one neo-platonist text that was to prove formative for the medieval conception of literature: the *Marriage of Mercury and Philosophy* by Martianus Capella. This curatorial, mediating and translating work of the monasteries could be found in all countries in Europe. It not only served to propagate and disseminate Christianity, however, but was also a suitable vehicle – later to be perfected in the form of near-professional translation schools such as that in Toledo in Spain (Gerard of Cremona), as well as around the Sicilian court of Frederic II – for Islamic and Arabic knowledge and thought.

The supremacy of Latin

This fundamental body of monastic educational work may help to explain why a deepening of vernacular Old High German, embracing both the spoken and written word, did not at first take place, and why medieval Latin continued to play a leading role. From the classical Latin of Roman antiquity ('golden and silver Latinity') a new combined form emerged displaying marked tendencies to absorb from the vernacular while still retaining a fundamental unity in grammar and rhetoric. The unbroken dominance of Latin was transferred to literature in the form of sacred poetry in medieval Latin. Although by the eighth century more vernacular proclivities were evident in the liturgy and the sermon – the only suitable vehicle for bringing the complex substance of the Christian faith 'among the people' – the Synod of Inden (817), no doubt mindful of the conflict then raging between mundane and clerical authority, saw to the reinstatement of Latin as the sole ecclesiastical language, thus prohibiting any exchange between priests and the laity in the vernacular.

The emergence of Old High German and Early New High German literature out of the spirit of translation

Bible translations and adaptations of biblical material were a key factor in the formation of Old High German writing and literary dialects. An early precursor of these was the Gothic Bible translation by Bishop Wulfila, who developed his own writing system in the process. A principal factor, however, were Old High German written dialects devised by commentators and philologists in equal measure from vocabulary books, marginal notes and glossaries. The German words for initially unknown Latin words used to be written into the text, either between the words or in the margins of texts of classical authors. This gave rise to what became known as interlinear, textual and marginal glosses. Interlinear glosses were often later expanded into appended translations known as interlinear versions, i.e. word-for-word translations. The oldest known translation into Old High German (originally Bavarian) is thought to be a compilation of synonyms, a kind of dictionary, which takes its name from the first word in the alphabet: the *Abrogans* (764–72). It was written in Freising and is based on a late ancient lexicon used for teaching in the *trivium*. It is the oldest extant 'book' in the German-speaking world.

Laity and clergy

The medieval Latin setback notwithstanding, an Old High German literary language did emerge from the encounter between the laity and the Christian clergy. In the second century AD Tatian the Syrian had combined the four gospels of Matthew, Mark, Luke and John into the unbroken narrative of the New Testament. This gospel harmony was translated in its entirety into Old High German at the Fulda monastery during the time Hrabanus Maurus was abbot. In this form it will certainly have played a crucial role in the instruction of the laity. An attempt to translate the life and passion of Christ into a Germanic Old German tribal composition, complete with the atmosphere of the local landscape and the contemporary period, resulted in the *Heliand* (*Saviour*), written around 830 in Old Saxon, which marks an attempt to create a Christian stave rhyme poem. The poet, basing himself on Tatian's *Gospel Harmony*, Hrabanus Maurus' commentary on St. Matthew's Gospel (dating from 821–2), as well as the Anglo-Saxon Christian stave rhyme epic, attempts to apply the stylistic principles of the heroic stave rhyme poem to this new Christian subject-matter.

Christian poetry

The *Gospel Harmony*, or *Krist* (*c.* 870) was a major Rhenish-Frankish end-rhyme poem. It was compiled by the Alsatian monk Otfrid of Weissenburg and consists of an independent selection by him from the gospels, furnished with scholarly commentaries and extracts from patrician writings. Each episode in the story is interpreted in three different senses (the mystical, moral and spiritual) using both exegesis and allegory. It is plain from this that Otfrid's intended readership was a narrow social stratum of educated nobles and clerics. His three dedications to King Ludwig the German, the Archbishop of Mainz and two fellow monks confirm this.

The complex structure of the *Gospel Harmony* is equally revealing of Otfrid's view of the role of literature. In a world view in which all things are interpreted in terms of their relationship to God, and regarded as created by him or having emerged from him in developmental stages, literature is no more and no less than allegory. The individual elements portrayed in it are more than they at first appear, since their reality is imbued with divine meaning. In other words, realities are fashioned in the form of allegories and symbols. Christian poetry, therefore, is praise to God in the form of allegory.

Otfrid's *Gospel Harmony*, an individual achievement by a writer known by name, represents one of the first major high points in German Christian poetry. Moreover, it can be seen from his dedication to King Ludwig the German, 'dessen Macht sich über das ganze fränkische Ostreich erstreckt', ('whose might extends over the entire Franconian eastern kingdom'), that Otfrid opens his work by paying homage to the Franks, who are seen by virtue of their boldness and wisdom to be as deserving as the Romans of being entrusted with the Christian message. Filled with pride, he explains his reasons for having written the book in German ('theodisce' – the first time the latter term is used in poetry). Having first lamented his inability to live up to the great authors of antiquity and Latin Christian poetry, he stresses the appropriateness of choosing this language by pointing out that God wishes to be praised in the language he has given to men, however arduous the task may be to him, Otfrid of Weissenburg. Otfrid took equally great pains with the rhyming verse of the *Gospel Harmony*, seeking regular alternation of unstressed syllables and accents, thus creating a highly rigorous form of rhyme in which sound liaison is carried out to the last stressed syllable. Where the Christian stave rhyme verse of the *Heliand* marked a mere episode in the history of poetry, Otfrid's rhyming verse was to become an archetype running through the history of German poetry from Wolfram's *Parzifal* to Goethe's *Faust*.

Clerics writing in Latin

Although the appeal of the *Gospel Harmony* to Christian poetry in the vernacular could not possibly be overlooked, the decades that followed until the middle of the eleventh century nevertheless continued to be dominated by clerics writing in Latin. Although the impetus towards the Carolingian reform of worldly power had started out as a matter of imperial policy, the Church, as the main proponent of these reforms, jealously guarded its distance from worldly power, sensing after the death of Charlemagne a chance to shift the balance of power in its own favour. The great objective of Carolingian reform in educational policy, to unite and integrate the eastern and western Frankish tribes under the banner of the Christian Church, had been achieved in outward form only. This resulted in a state of vacillation between Empire and Church; on the one hand there was an increasingly radical call for the true Christian to 'turn his back on the world', on the other the claim of the Empire over the laity. Against the background of this incessant struggle between *sacerdotum* and *imperium*, the Church made a self-confident and aggressive bid to win over the laity. This new line was preceded by internal reforms within the Church and the monasteries, designed to achieve a rigid concentration of power oriented towards Rome. The temporal supremacy of the Ottonine kings was subsequently challenged and laid open to question at every available opportunity. In the first instance, however, this threw the individual into a state of deep inner conflict, the echoes of which can still be found in the epigrammatic poetry of Walther von der Vogelweide.

As an example of the early phase of this literary development, which involved three generations, the *Ezzolied* (*Ezzo's Hymn*), dating from around 1060 in Bamberg, may be cited. Its aim is to depict the importance of Christ to the redemption of mankind and the world from the state of sin. Following the dogmatic scheme of the figure of the Redeemer, this account of the life of Christ focuses on his birth, baptism and passion, with the intention of portraying his exemplary life. The *Memento Mori* by

Notker of Zwiefalten, dating from around 1080, imparts the idea of certain redemption for the Christian man, also calling on him to follow in the footsteps of the monks. This is a clear Cluniac call to turn one's back on the world and adopt an ascetic lifestyle. The world itself is portrayed as repulsive; the true worth of a man is revealed not on Earth, but before the judgement seat of God. In his *Memento Mori*, Notker of Zwiefalten made use of the coercive tone of the penitential sermon, which was to form part of the basic rhetoric of the Church into the fifteenth and sixteenth centuries.

History of salvation

While the second 'cluniac' generation was occupied with reworking major biblical incidents concerned with the history of salvation (The *Wiener Exodus* [*Viennese Exodus*]: Moses' Exodus from Egypt), the development of sacred drama in Latin and the recording of sermons on the doctrine of salvation, along with incessantly reiterated laments over the sinful state of Man, conventional religious morphology inevitably predominated. However, a third generation of Christian poetry was in the meantime on the rise. Of particular note here is legendary poetry that developed out of the early *Annolied* (*Song of Saint Anno*) to become important in its own right. Beside this there were also Marian hymns, which grew out of cult veneration of the Mother of God and which can likewise be ranked among legend poetry. Transitional forms could already be observed: the *Marienleben des Priesters Wernher* (*Life of Mary by Wernher the Priest*) combines early Middle High German with early courtly stylistic elements.

Verse epics

In the aftermath of the penitent tenor and other-worldliness of early Middle High German poetry, verse epics, works composed by clerics in the service of noble patrons, such as *König Rother* (*King Rother*) (1150), *Herzog Ernst* (*Duke Ernst*) (1180) and the *Rolandslied* (*Lay of Roland*) (1170), or the early *Alexanderlied* (*Lay of Alexander*) (c. 1150), display an outlook and tone that points to the *aventuire* romance of the courtly age. Although the features typical for courtly poetry – the ideal of chivalric rank, chivalrous courtship, feudal loyalty and the Arthurian ideal – are not yet in evidence, knights are clearly in the forefront as protagonists in the action. This early courtly verse romance developed out of a number of narrative traditions, drawing richly on Crusade experience. The journey to the Orient thus occupies a central position, pointing the way to new directions in the literary portrayal of life in this world. A substantial part was played in this new development by French epic poetry, *chanson de geste*, which had found fertile ground under Charlemagne. Unlike the French version of the

Lay of Roland, that by the Regensburg cleric Konrad, commissioned by Duke Henry, the Lion of Bavaria, presents Charlemagne's realm as the fulfilment of the Kingdom of God, and bears full witness to the spirit of the Crusades.

The Crusades

The struggle of Christian knights against the heathen was a theme of poetry from the time of the Old French *Lay of Roland*, in both epic (e.g. *King Rother*) and lyric verse. Christian chivalry thus offers the ideal of the active, pugnacious Christian knight as a complement to the passive, contemplative, spiritual existence of monastic life. The motif of this poetry, like that of the historical events it portrays, is the liberation of the Holy Sepulchre in Jerusalem from the heathen.

A total of seven Crusades took place. The first (1096–9) ended with the capture of Jerusalem and the founding of the Kingdom of Jerusalem and the province of Edessa. After the recapturing of the province of Edessa by the 'heathen', Bernard of Clairvaux called for a second Crusade. This lasted from 1147 to 1149, failing to reach Jerusalem. The third Crusade was conducted as a campaign of the entire Empire after Sultan Saladin had taken Jerusalem. This Crusade, lasting from 1189 to 1192, and led by King Friedrich I, Phillip II of France and King Richard the Lionheart of England, also ended in failure. It was not until the fourth Crusade (1202–24) that Constantinople was captured, bringing down the Byzantine Empire. The fifth Crusade was undertaken by Friedrich II in 1228–9 with peaceful intentions after a papal edict had condemned it. After concluding a peace agreement with the heathen, Friedrich II had himself crowned king of Jerusalem, but the city was soon (1244) to be lost yet again. The sixth Crusade (1248–52) ended with the entire army being taken prisoner. In the seventh Crusade the army of knights reached no further than Tunis: the history of the Crusades and the Crusade states ended in 1291 with the capture of Acre. These latter failures were for internal reasons: the last Crusades had been used by the Church and Pope principally to check the military and political power of the Hohenstaufens. Noteworthy Crusade poets were the cleric Konrad, Friedrich von Hausen, Heinrich von Rugge, Albrecht von Johansdorf, Hartmann von Aue, Otto von Botenlauben, Walther von der Vogelweide, Rubin, Friedank, Niedhart and Tannhäuser. Whether these poets were all Crusaders themselves, or merely seized on generally available themes, motifs and material of the Crusades and reworked them into the form of poetry, is uncertain.

Ballads in the vernacular

In addition to the scant literary documents handed down in written form from Old and New High German poetry there must also have been a substantial body of ballads disseminated and passed on orally, partly in Latin, partly in the vernacular. Neither its scope nor its relationship to the written tradition can be ascertained today. The most striking witness to the subject-matter of this literature is to be found in *Vagantendichtung* (itinerant verse) dating back to the tenth century. Unlike sacred poetry, this form was characterised by an affirmation of the highs and lows of earthly existence. With its cheerful motto *memento vivere* ('remember to live'), this poetry of the street and tavern seems to offer the sensual experience of earthly existence as a counterbalance to the Christian doctrine of turning one's back on the world. Itinerant poets were former pupils, students and clerics of the cathedrals and monastic schools, the early universities of the Middle Ages, who had fled the spiritual rigours and asceticism of that life, preferring the precarious life of wandering, uninhibited revelling and earthly love to the celibate life in praise of the Virgin Mary. Their poetry took the form of hymn verses in medieval Latin. The most extensive knowledge of this form is owed to an anthology of lyric poems by goliards that has become well-known under the name of *Carmina Burana*. It dates from the thirteenth century, representing a collection of itinerant verse from the eleventh and twelfth centuries. An extract from the *Confessions of a Goliard* (*Vagantenbeichte*) by Archipoeta may serve as an example:

> Estuans interius
> ira vehementi
> in amaritudine
> loquor meae menti;
> factus de materia,
> cinis elementi,
> similis sum folio,
> de quo ludunt venti.
> Cum sit enim proprium
> viro sapienti
> supra petram ponere
> sedem fundamenti,
> stultus ego comparor
> fluvio labenti,
> sub eodem tramite
> nunquam permanenti.
> Feror ego veluti
> sine nauta navis,
> ut per vias aeris

vaga fertur avis;
non me tenent vincula,
non me tenet clavis,
quero mihi similes
et adiungor pravis.

Heisser scham und reue voll,
wildem grimm zum raube
schlag' ich voller bitterkeit
an mein herz, das taube:
windgeschaffen, federleicht,
locker wie von staube,
gleich' ich loser lüfter spiel,
gleich' ich einem laube!
Denn indes ein kluger mann
sorglich pflegt zu schauen,
dass er mög' auf felsengrund
seine Wohnung bauen:
bin ich narr dem flusse gleich,
der kein wehr darf stauen,
der sich immer neu sein bett
hinwühlt durch die auen.
Wie ein meisterloses schiff
fahr' ich fern dem strande,
wie der vogel durch die luft
streif' ich durch die lande.
hüten mag kein schlüssel mich,
halten keine bande.
mit gesellen geh' ich um –
oh, 's ist eine schande!

Fill'd with shame and bitter woe,
Wrathful and unfettered,
Hand I beat on heart and breast
To see I am no better.
Blown by breeze and light as air,
As dust in grave that festered
Go I first this way and then that,
Unanchored and unsettled.
Would I were a wiser man,
Foresight burn'd on his shield:
Taking care, his hearth and home
On firm good rock will he build.
Meanwhile, more like wilful stream
'fore which poor dams and weirs yield,

With nowhere to lay my head
Tramp I by inn and grain-field.
'kin to ship without a helm,
Wand'ring far from safe shore,
Or carefree bird on wayward wing,
I wander dale and heath moor.
Keys and locks will me not hold,
Nor chains nor ropes will curb more,
With my fellows on the rounds,
I'll drink to loss of honour!

Epic literature of the Hohenstaufen period

The Hohenstaufen era spanned a period between the peak, around 1180, of Emperor Friedrich Barbarossa's reign, beginning in 1152, and the death of Friedrich II in 1250. It was shaped by the struggle for control of the empire between the pro-emperor Ghibelline faction and the Guelph papal faction, and the ongoing struggle of the German emperors against papal and ecclesiastical tutelage, particularly against Pope Innocent II. Its end was marked by the untimely death of Heinrich VI (1197).

When Friedrich Barbarossa succeeded to the throne, poetry was still dominated by Latin and the clerics. Even early courtly verse romance was still firmly in clerical hands. It was Heinrich von Veldeke's *Eneit*, on which work began after 1170 and which was completed in 1185–7, that marked the breakthrough to a new courtly chivalrous literature of rank, which was to involve three generations of poets. The period from 1170 to 1250 was the most significant era in German medieval literature. A literary language evolved side by side with the Frankish-Alemannic spoken lingua franca, thus offering the first real challenge to the primacy of Latin, as well as achieving command of an immensely subtle wealth of expression. The Romance languages, on account of their close relationship to Latin which initially enabled them to develop much more rapidly, had up to this point enjoyed an advantage over German. However, a common German heritage now furthered the rise of a literary language that could at last take its place among the foremost of Europe. The dominant poetic forms were now the chivalrous epic and *Minnesang* lyricism. Confessional poetry was on the wane, and didactic poetry was not to make its appearance until the third generation of the Hohenstaufen era.

The term 'Hohenstaufen literary era' is no mere politico-historical label. Hohenstaufen literature was a quintessential expression of its time. Its verse was imbued in equal measure with the *rex iustus et pacificus* concept, embodied by Barbarossa in the eyes of so many of his contemporaries; the crusader ideal, of which Barbarossa, who died during the Third Crusade, was again a real and shining example, and with the new social status

21

accorded to poetry at court. Since the poetry of the Hohenstaufen era was the poetry of noble rank, it came to form a natural and obvious adjunct to the stately paraphernalia of court festivity. The 1184 court festival of Mainz, attested by numerous records, furnished an opportunity for Hohenstaufen imperial might to parade itself. Some 40–70,000 people are recorded as having gathered there, an unusually large number for the time. Of these, no fewer than 20,000 were knights, who competed against one another in a tournament. The attendance and performances of numerous poets and minstrels are also on record. The high point was the dubbing of Barbarossa's two eldest sons. The court festival came to be a demonstration of a unified European secular culture whose tone was set by knights, and of the universal Hohenstaufen empirehood and chivalry on which this imperial power rested. It is no coincidence that Hohenstaufen literature reached its peak at the turn of the century, just as the empire itself was in the grip of crisis. As a poetry of ideals and rank, Hohenstaufen literature was blind to the realities of imperial politics, which first impinged on it in the didactic poems of Walther von der Vogelweide in the early 1200s, by which time the contradictions of the age could no longer be ignored.

Medieval feudal society

Medieval feudal society was dominated by two classes, one of worldly and one of clerical rank, represented by the Emperor and the Pope respectively. The Emperor was answerable to God for his conduct in all worldly affairs, be they political, economic or cultural, but it was also incumbent on him to protect the Church. Together with the Pope, he was responsible for the weal and woe of Western Christendom. This was to prove a source of constant clashes with Rome. The Emperor, however, was at the same time the ideal representative of chivalric rank. Chivalric rank did not make its first appearance in the Hohenstaufen era: it was a European phenomenon. The knight was first and foremost a warrior, an armed rider, the decisive factor in the strength of an army. In economic terms, the knight ranked either with the landed nobility, or as a 'ministerial' (a status concerned with the execution of orders or law) possessing a fief that might take any one of a number of forms, but generally ensured him an income. The Hohenstaufen era was the age of knights 'on the make'. They rose to become able administrative officials, holding office at the imperial court, in the army or as regional governors, responsible for the administration of justice, minting coins, rights of way, collecting taxes, etc. Knights were not involved in the increasingly prevalent use of money. Nevertheless, commerce and crafts underwent a boom during the Hohenstaufen era, leading to the rise of an urban patriciate who sought to bring their influence to bear on the feudal forms of property and exchange. Medieval knights, whether they were freemen or ministerials risen from sub-freeman status, constituted a noble upper stratum with an unequivocal claim to rule. The third estate, the peasants and burghers, were unable at this stage to achieve self-awareness, either in literary terms or in relation to their estate. Even the first burgher in literature, the Cologne merchant in *Guter Gerhard* by Rudolf von Ems (1220–5), is portrayed as a nobleman of the court. It was this social background that shaped the ideal social order depicted in chivalrous courtly poetry. The chivalric estate comprised an ideal body of men among whom an insignificant crusader was the equal of the emperor. The prevailing system of land tenure in turn represented a common bond of mutual dependence, expressed in the ideal of loyalty, where chivalric honour consisted in safeguarding decency and the ordinances pertaining to the estate.

In the literature of the Hohenstaufen era the term 'knight' is used almost arbitrarily. Almost all male figures, even peripheral ones, are denoted in this way. These figures do not have an unequivocal or conventional social character imposed on them, however. Each new tale seeks through poetry to probe and redefine what a knight is. Only in this way could the reading public, who were of course fully cognisant of the identity of their station, continue to be surprised and entertained. The fact that events in chivalrous verse take place in an ideal realm beyond the realities of the everyday world has been stressed often enough. The adventures and intrigues encountered in that realm may be explained as arising out of the need to derive new ways of looking at what was in fact a static Arthurian verse form. However, a substantial part of the artifice in epic verse may be attributed, particularly in the case of the courtly romance (by authors such as Ulrich von Zazikhofen or Wirnt von Grafenberg), to the courtly proclivity for aesthetic exquisiteness. The designations 'chivalric' and 'courtly' are not interchangeable here. The term 'courtly' pertains to a human stylistic form embracing both intellectual and physical education, knowledge of languages and familiarity with foreign countries – in other words, those qualities requisite for courtly society. This stylistic form attached equal weight to both outer and inner education. What was outwardly beautiful also had to be inwardly beautiful: any deviation from this was unthinkable. All negative states, such as loneliness, despair or pain (for example in *Parzifal*) could only be permitted in the form of transitional phases on the road to becoming a chivalrous knight. Harmonious unison was the ideal, epitomized by the court festivity – the high point of social life in the Hohenstaufen age.

Arthurian epic verse

It is no longer certain exactly where in Germany the northern French Arthurian epic or romance first captured the imagination of the public and inspired adaptations. The Lower Rhine suggests itself not only because of its proximity to France, but also because of the more widespread knowledge of French there; or the court of the Palatinate Count Hermann von Thüringen, a known lover of art and literature. However, the Count did not exert any lasting influence as a patron of literature until after 1180, and at all events showed a predilection for adaptations of texts from classical antiquity (e.g. a translation of Ovid's *Metamorphoses* by Albrecht von Halberstadt, or the *Trojaroman* by Herbort von Fritzlar, which dates from around 1190). Meanwhile, however, the *Trier Floyris*, the *Strasbourg Alexander* and Eilhart von Oberge's *Tristrant* (1170–5) were already known in the Lower Rhine. The Lower Frank Heinrich von Veldeke, the foremost early court epic poet, had begun his Aeneas romance *Eneit*, based on the model of the Anglo-Norman *Roman d'Eneas*, in 1170, although in fact only completing it at the court of Hermann von Thüringen (1187–9).

Heinrich von Veldeke

Heinrich von Veldeke was born between 1140 and 1150, dying before 1210. His *Eneit* was an adaptation of one of the greatest classical educational texts of the Middle Ages, Virgil's *Aeneid*. Aeneas's flight from Troy, his sojourn with Dido, the journey into Hades and the landing in Italy, his struggle for the royal seat promised to him by prophesy, his marriage to Lavinia and the historically momentous vision of the founding and subsequent greatness of Rome are cornerstones of Veldeke's treatment of the plot, which he narrates in unembellished, dry, terse style with a complete absence of *aventuire*. The salient feature of Veldeke's version is his grasp of the Greek Trojan romance and the Roman Aeneas romance across the intervening ages, although ancient heroism is naturally shifted to the community of the contemporary chivalric order. No importance is attached to the contradiction between the Christian and heathen cultures. What is pertinent is the *Minne* description concerning Dido and Lavinia, which is presented in antithetical terms. The two women are seen as examples of ill-fated and fortuitous love, blessed by God. As the victor in this unequal struggle, Lavinia is conscious of being assured of her place in a higher order. She is depicted as a symbol of autonomous humanity to whom the knight must offer his service. Veldeke's overall conception was to prove a pointer for later authors, particularly since he employed pure rhyme, a hitherto uncustomary form that was to become the archetype for subsequent epic verse. The effects of his *Eneit* were still being felt into the fifteenth century, as can be attested by numerous manuscripts and fragments.

Chrétien de Troyes

The leading archetypes for chivalrous and courtly verse romance in the Hohenstaufen period came from the pen of Chrétien de Troyes, probably the best-known French epic poet. From 1160–90 he adapted tales from Celtic and Breton Arthurian sagas into verse romances such as *Erec*, *Yvain*, *Cliges*, *Lancelot* and *Perceval*, thereby creating a discrete poetic world outside the sphere of historical actuality. Transcending the boundaries of time and space, this Arthurian world established a style that was to exert an influence far beyond northern France, inspiring numerous adaptations of Chrétien's verse romances. This only serves to underline the European character of chivalrous and courtly verse, although Arthurian tales underwent significant changes and re-interpretations, especially in German verse romance form.

The Arthurian order

This ideal Arthurian order, which can only be briefly outlined here, has at its centre King Arthur himself, the incarnation of high court chivalry. It is from there and the Round Table that all the Arthurian exploits ensue, and there that all the knights eventually return. The Arthurian knights, who recognise neither national nor confessional boundaries, feel bound to one another as an order, and sit beside Arthur as equals at the Round Table. Although the actual royal seat is Nantes in northern France, as soon as the Arthurian knights leave the Round Table time and space lose all meaning and the fairy-tale *aventuire* begins, any real historical background to this verse completely obliterated. The Arthurian knights feel committed exclusively to *aventuire*, undertaken for its own sake, and to *Minne* – capturing the heart of a woman of superior rank. Their ethical driving force is the honour of the chivalric estate, which must be put to the test and proved again and again. *Aventuire* is undertaken in service of a lady, justified in terms of feudal law, with *Minne* as the reward for the test of chivalry, signified by the *aventuire*. In the *Minne* interpretation of the Arthurian epic, the barriers between the estates are insurmountable, the ethical focus of *Minne* being chivalric honour. As soon as an Arthurian knight returns home and King Arthur appears, a festive atmosphere takes over until the Arthurian circle is broken once again by another knight setting out on an *aventuire*.

Idealised poetry of rank

Whereas early courtly verse romance found suitable sources in ancient material and in Arthurian epic, epic verse of the Hohenstaufen age focused exclusively on the Arthurian world, which alone provided the necessary

25

creative inspiration for an elaborate fabric of fairy-tale exploits remote from the real world and for an idealised poetry of rank. The solutions for this rank ideal discovered in the epic poetry of Hartmann von Aue, Gottfried von Strassburg and Wolfram von Eschenbach surprised the reader by using established manners, conduct and meanings with which the courtly reading public could be assumed to be familiar. However, they do not deal with the commonplace, but rather with the unresolved aspects of these conventions. Nothing would have struck a more false note in this ideal poetry of rank than the bald illustration or factual presentation of an established pattern. An individual creative will is at work in this poetry, as well as an undogmatic inquiring quest for experience seeking conscious expression. Fittingly therefore, the hallmark for literature of the Hohenstaufen age is the way it uses convention to write against convention, thus allowing the poetry to blend into a mental horizon of constantly expanding experience.

Hartmann von Aue

A great deal in the work of Hartmann von Aue points to this chivalric intellectualism, although he concerns himself solely with the ethical problems of perfect chivalry, dispensing with any attempt at religious transcendence. In his *Erek*, which dates from 1180 to 1185, the plot at first proceeds according to the *aventuire* scheme laid down by Chrétien de Troyes: Erek rides out, wins his love and returns with honour to the court of King Arthur. At this point the aesthetic vehicles of the early courtly verse romance have been exhausted. However, in a continuation of the plot, Hartmann opens up a realm of spiritual trial and choice, thereby providing his courtly reading public with a major ethical experience. For Erek and his wife Enite the newly-experienced *Minne* is thrown into jeopardy since it has not yet become a conscious binding factor in the couple's relationship. When Enite one day expresses in a soliloquy her dissatisfaction and disappointment with Erek's idle life at court, Erek recognises this danger and acts immediately, riding out to restore his chivalric honour. Enite must follow him, since she herself is not without guilt, having failed to take him into her service and demand some 'labour' from him for the sake of *Minne*. During his adventures Erek sinks into a death-like sleep. Believing that he is really dead, Enite goes into mourning, during which a count courts and harasses her passionately. As she cries out, Erek awakes and slays the count. He thereby accomplishes his deed of chivalry, while she may now ride at his side, having made it possible for him to undergo this trial. Erek's development into a perfect knight is not yet complete, however. He must learn to lose honourably in a duel, since it is not enough to have a winner and a loser without considering the reasons behind a duel. Hartmann's examination of this question in itself shows that he has gone beyond the early courtly verse romance in which *aventuire* was undertaken purely for its own sake. On his final stage, Erek encounters Mabonagrin the Red Knight, who has sworn to his wife only to set out on another *aventuire* when he has been defeated in combat. Erek defeats Mabonagrin, who experiences his defeat as a release from enforced *Minne*, another early courtly model, represented by Dido in Heinrich von Veldeke's *Eneit*. Mabonagrin can be freed by Erek not least because the latter has experienced all the highs and lows of honour and *Minne*. Erek returns to the court of King Arthur with Enite a perfect knight and is welcomed with rejoicing.

Iwein, Armer Heinrich and Gregorius

Hartmann's *Iwein* (written after 1200) seems to have been conceived as a direct antithesis of *Erek*. Here it is not the immoderation of *Minne*, but the excess of *aventuire* that threatens to destroy the ideal courtly balance. Iwein's appetite for *aventuire* puts his *Minne* relationship with Laudine at risk. She has parted from him for a year, but he forgets about her return. When Laudine's servant Lunete scolds and curses him for this, Iwein breaks down into a state of madness and begins a new life as a hermit. A magical ointment restores him to his senses, and it is his firm intention to restore his honour and win back Laudine's *Minne*. He survives a series of adventures, at last fighting against Gawain who crosses his path and whom Iwein fails to recognise. Although neither emerges as victor from combat, Iwein's honour has been restored and he is accepted once again at King Arthur's Round Table. Still distressed, he hurries to Laudine, who admits that part of the guilt for his original loss of honour is hers. The couple are thus reconciled. *Iwein* was Hartmann von Aue's last verse epic and his most consummate in form. The constantly recurring chivalric schematism apparent in the work is a clear sign that the expressive potential of the courtly verse epic had been exhausted in the twenty years that had elapsed since *Erek*. Whereas *Erek* is marked by an ethical and moral distance from the early courtly verse romance that sets it apart as something innovative and unprecedented, *Iwein* works itself to a colourless conclusion that runs contrary to the conventions of chivalry and the courtly estate. Laudine shares none of the guilt for Iwein's loss of honour. The feudal relationship in the light of which *Minne* service is to be understood governs protection of the lady and service by the knight. In Hartmann's version, Laudine is not the wife but the lady, and therefore has the right to terminate the service of her knight if he fails to return in time to protect her. In this break with style, Hartmann displays clear indifference to the literary aim, which is to formulate the ethics of the chivalric estate; courtly convention is revealed here as something empty and divorced from reality.

Few details are known about Hartmann von Aue. He was born between

1160 and 1165, and lived as a liegeman; nothing is known about his patron. He did however lament the latter's death, taking the Crusader's vow. He probably took part in the third Crusade (1189–92), writing *Armer Heinrich* (*Poor Henry*) in 1195 after his return. This work has nothing in common with the Arthurian scheme, and is more akin to legendary poetry. As the plot develops, there is an interplay between love and the spirit of self-sacrifice existing between the fatally ill knight and the peasant girl, who is willing to sacrifice her life to bring about his cure. Hartmann's *Gregorius*, a legend of penitence, also steps beyond chivalrous courtly values. It is closely linked with the Crusade experience, thematising a clash between God and the world that would be unthinkable in poetry of the chivalric estate. The date of Hartmann's death is unknown, although it was certainly after 1210. On the one hand the resources of the chivalrous court epic were exhausted by Hartmann von Aue, despite the scope created for reflection and experience. The Arthurian world, too, had once again reached the limits of its potential, as it had in the early court romance. Wolfram von Eschenbach's *Parzifal*, however, was to open up fresh opportunities for self-experience within the order of knights.

Wolfram von Eschenbach

'Schildes ambet ist min art', writes Wolfram proudly, indicating his chivalric origins. He probably hailed from the Ansbach area, but was unpropertied and hence obliged to enter feudal service. His patrons included the Count von Wertheim, the Count von Dürne at Wildenburg in the Forest of Oden, as well as the Palatinate Count Hermann von Thüringen, who had been patron to early court poets such as Heinrich von Veldeke and later Walther von der Vogelweide. Wolfram was the most independently-minded of the three epic poets in Hohenstaufen literature. He thus considers the courtly knight to be untrue to type, rejecting both his own education, which was after all still controlled by the clergy, and chivalrous courtship, as can be seen from his remarks on Reinmar's poetry. Whereas none of Hartmann von Aue's works is untouched by reference to his literary erudition, particularly his knowledge of Latin, Wolfram von Eschenbach writes of himself with ironic derision: 'ich enkan keinen buchstaben', ('I know no letters'), asserting elsewhere that he is *kunstelos*, meaning that he lacks a clerical education in the seven liberal arts. His aim, however, is to present himself as unfettered by Latin studies rather than as uneducated *per se*, thereby dissociating himself entirely from subordination to the clergy – a self-assured chivalric layman.

Wolfram's *Parzifal* was one of the most widely-read medieval epic poems. Some 75 manuscripts and fragments testify to its unusually wide dissemination: in contrast, not a single fragment of Hartmann's *Iwein* is extant. Wolfram's *Parzifal* was likewise based on Chrétien de Troyes.

Although only a fragment of the latter's *Perceval*, begun in 1185, has survived, Wolfram's parallel treatment of Gawan and Parzifal is clearly based on Chrétien's version. Wolfram von Eschenbach also refers to another source, named as Kyot, possibly an ingenious device intended to fabricate a mysterious authority.

Parzifal's career is clearly described. He grows from guileless boy into Arthurian knight, ultimately becoming the Grail King, a path predestined for him but of which he is at first unaware – echoing the ancient scheme of tragedy. In Wolfram's version two narrative levels collide, the Arthurian cycle and the Grail legend. Whereas Parzifal and Gawan take equal part in the Arthurian cycle, the action of the Grail legend pertains exclusively to Parzifal. Wolfram conspicuously surpasses Hartmann von Aue in the new religious experience opened up for Parzifal by the Grail quest, as becomes apparent from the failure of the Arthurian knight on his first journey in search of the Grail.

Parzifal's 'career'

Parzifal is brought up by his mother in a remote forest region after the chivalrous death of her knight husband. She deliberately tries to keep the world of chivalry from her son so as to spare him his father's fate. However, a passing troop of knights arouses the boy's curiosity, and he decides to join them and see the world. Not even the fool's apparel given to him by his mother when he leaves home, in the hope of shielding him from serious harm, can prevent him from fulfilling this destiny. Parzifal passes through the first phase in his quest for the Grail entirely within the framework of the Arthurian world, albeit unwittingly, thereby incurring his first guilt. Thus, ignorant of the significance of *Minne* obligations, he seizes a ring and bracelet from Jeschute, wife of Duke Orilus. Orilus repudiates his wife and sets out in pursuit of the intruder. Parzifal meets Sigune, who is in mourning for her beloved, killed by Orilus. It is from her that Parzifal learns his name. Ither, the Red Knight, has struck camp outside the city gates at Nantes, and sends Parzifal into the city to challenge Arthur. Parzifal's brightly-coloured appearance attracts the court's attention. He requests the right to fight against the Red Knight Ither and obtains permission for a duel. He kills Ither with a pitchfork and dons his armour. He has passed his first test of valour. Without returning to King Arthur's court Parzifal continues on his quest, still wearing his fool's apparel under his armour. He learns from Gurnemanz all the rights and duties of chivalrous courtly life, chief among which are self-mastery and moderation. Gurnemanz gives him the fateful advice not to be too inquisitive: 'ir ensult niht vil gefragen'. Now a fully-fledged knight, Parzifal gives Condwiramur his support during the siege of her town, also winning her as his lady, thereby fulfilling one of the major aims of the Arthurian knight. Parzifal's soul craves more, however. Departing from Condwira-mur, he comes upon the Grail Castle, an arcane locality outside the real Arthurian world. He experiences the Grail and the Grail meal, but fails to inquire after the reason for mourning at court, having been warned by Gurnemanz not to be too inquisitive. The next morning Parzifal finds himself once again in front of the empty Grail Castle.

The perfect Arthurian knight has ventured beyond the boundaries of this world for the first time, and has failed. This is Wolfram's way of warning against the danger of rigidification of the notion of the chivalrous courtly class while also confronting his readership with an indeterminate religious experience that can no longer be subsumed within the conventional scheme of honour and *Minne*. Wolfram's consciously sought, outward-oriented path of development as autodidact only serves to underline this intention. Parzifal returns to the Arthurian world. He meets Sigune again, who informs him that his mother Herzeloyde is none other than the sister of the dying Grail King Amfortas. He also encounters Jeschute, whom he has unknowingly humiliated, defeats Orilus in combat and restores the marriage. Parzifal then returns to the court of King Arthur as a fully-fledged member of the Round Table. Once again, however, the as yet uncomprehended world of the Grail throws down another challenge to Parzifal. During the court festivities, the Lady Cundrie, Messenger of the Grail, enters and curses Parzifal in the name of the Grail, declaring that he has lost his honour as an Arthurian knight. He leaves court immediately, although in terms of Arthurian notions he is unaware of any guilt. He henceforth appears as a godless knight, justifying his alienation from God by his feudal relationship. His horse leads him to Trevrizent, to whom Parzifal presents himself as a repentant sinner.

The religious transcendence of the aventuire romance

This marks Parzifal's definitive step both towards a God-oriented existence and his departure from the Arthurian cycle, a fact that is made doubly clear to him by his loneliness and his yearning for the Grail and Condwira-mur. The Arthurian cycle is familiar with loneliness only in the course of the *aventuire*: it is not possible during court festivities. The Lady Cundrie, Messenger of the Grail, reappears, declaring that the curse on Parzifal has been lifted and that he is summoned to the Grail King. On this second journey towards the Grail Parzifal chooses Feirefiz as his companion. This time he asks King Amfortas the long-awaited sympathetic question: 'oeheim, waz wirret dir?' Amfortas is cured, and Parzifal becomes the Grail King. Feirefiz is drawn into the Grail story not without hesitation, the expression of a God-oriented chivalry embracing heathen and Christian alike. Such chivalry is necessary because in the day-to-day reality of the Hohenstaufen empire the questions 'God or the world?', and 'God or the Devil?' were constantly being reformulated. Wolfram's solution, in which Parzifal chooses God, acknowledges his sinfulness and experiences the grace of God through Trevrizent's priestly intercession, is an important link with Crusader chivalry, marked by a new pious movement. However, this link cannot be viewed as more than an ideal one, for papal power politics saw in the Crusades an effective means for weakening both imperial power and the chivalric estate that both epitomised and sustained it.

Tristan and Isolde

While two further works by Wolfram von Eschenbach are also known – *Willehalm* (around 1215, incomplete) and *Titurel* (around or after 1215) – Gottfried von Strasbourg left behind only one work: *Tristan and Isolde*. Eilhart von Oberge's *Tristant* was an early courtly version of this material. Gottfried, however, names as his model a version by Thomas von Britanje that is as significant as that of the Arthurian story by Chrétien de Troyes, and which adapted the material to suit the world of the chivalrous court. Gottfried's *Tristan and Isolde* was written some time around 1210, but remained unfinished. It was later continued by Ulrich von Türheim (around 1290) and Heinrich von Freiberg (around 1290). Gottfried was not of chivalric or ministerial, but of patrician origin, and from a restless town whose business was shaped by busy commerce between France and Germany. Gottfried is described as 'master' not as 'lord'. He was evidently highly educated, however, possessing extensive knowledge of ancient history and literature, theology and French courtly learning that was always a step ahead of that of his German counterparts. His dispute with Wolfram von Eschenbach is of some significance. Although he does not name him outright, it is clear whom he means, accusing Wolfram of sloppy handling of his Parzifal material, thereby ignoring Wolfram's innovative achievement in confronting the Arthurian world with that of the Grail. *Tristan and Isolde* is not in fact a genuine achievement in the same sense as the work of Hartmann von Aue or of Wolfram, being essentially a reworking of the various motifs with painstaking commentary and concentration. Gottfried von Strasbourg, an urban-educated man, treats Thomas von Britanje as an unimpeachable authority, while Wolfram the chivalric layman treats his fictive Kyot in an ironic, playful way. Gottfried undertakes no restructuring or fresh conceptualisation, adhering instead to the structural scheme of his original text, just as Eilhart von Oberge did. An account of Tristan's youth and first journey to Ireland is followed by the second journey, the love potion and the complications that arise out of it, ending with Tristan's banishment and his vain attempts to return to the court of King Marke. In his adaptation, Gottfried has unmistakably placed formal aspects such as rhyme harmony and the ingenious correspondence of words, terms and names at the forefront. Rhetorically the most adept and circumspect of all Middle High German epic poets, Gottfried calls Tristan and Isolde:

> ein senedaere und ein senedaerin
> ein man, ein wîp – ein wîp, ein man
> Tristan Isolt – Isolt Tristan.

Even these few lines reveal Gottfried's skill with words. He seeks at the level of verse and etymological harmony to symbolise the irreversible magic of the love potion, as if to render the music of enchantment that has joined Tristan and Isolde in love:

> Tristan and Isôt, ir und ich,
> wir zwei sîn iemer beide
> ein dinc ân underscheide.

The *Minne* notions of the chivalrous court world collapse in the face of this total union, and it is Gottfried's greatest achievement that he suppressed the legendary essence of the tale – the irreversible effect of the love potion – as little as Wolfram suppressed the compelling attraction of the Grail and the absolute nature of the crucial sympathetic question, which is never actually explained or thrown into doubt.

Tristan is wounded in combat with Morolt

The first high point in the Tristan story is his combat with Morolt, who wants to make Tristan's uncle, King Marke, obliged to pay tribute. He defeats Morolt, but sustains a wound in combat that can only be cured by Morolt's sister Isolde, Queen of Ireland. Tristan sets out in disguise and is cured. During his stay at court he meets the Queen's daughter, also called Isolde. On his return to King Marke he offers his services as a suitor to win the hand of the young Isolde in the King's name. Landing in Ireland secretly, he survives a furious battle with a dragon, collapsing unconscious after slaying it. He is discovered by courtiers and recognised in the bath by his scar. He succeeds in placating the Queen, who is incensed at him on account of Morolt, and in declaring his mission to seek Isolde's hand. He is permitted to attend Isolde on her journey to become the bride of King Marke. During the voyage, the two mistakenly drink the love potion intended by Queen Isolde for her daughter's wedding night with Marke.

The magic love potion

Tristan and the young Isolde are overcome by an irresistible longing for each other, to which they yield during the voyage. The marriage between Isolde and Marke takes place, but he is successfully deceived as to her virginity on the wedding night. Tristan and Isolde's insatiable desire for each other, their duplicity and discovery by King Marke result in the lovers being banished. This is followed by life in the forest and the blissful happiness of the love grotto. On their return to court Marke is forgiving, but he must also acknowledge the fateful union of the lovers, and forbids Tristan to stay at court. On his travels Tristan meets Isolde Weisshand, whose identical name seduces him into apparent renewed happiness in love. At this point Gottfried's account is cut short, but other Tristan sources indicate a continuation of the story in which Tristan marries Isolde Weisshand but is unable to resist the impulse to seek out the true Isolde and fulfil his love for her. One day Tristan is fatally wounded, and Isolde is sent for, as she is the only one who can cure him. Tristan dies before her arrival, however, and on learning of his death Isolde also dies.

The conception of Minne

This story-line and the evaluation of verse romance it implies is striking for its unusual treatment of *Minne*. All the threads of the plot lead towards both bodily and spiritual fulfilment. The very fact that *Minne* here includes physical union of the lovers runs counter to the chivalrous courtly notion, characterised by distance from the lady. The *aventuire* elements – Tristan's combat with Morolt and the dragon – are again outside the usually restrained field of tension between the chivalric pursuit of honour and the reward of *Minne* from the knight's lady. Here these elements are, rather, transitional stages, even obstacles, on the path to the union of the lovers. The regular alternation of farewell and return typical for Arthurian verse would be unthinkable for Tristan and Isolde. Although the *Minne* story resembles the conceptions of early court *Minne* lyric poetry in its emphasis on the bodily as well as the spiritual factor, the relationship between Tristan and Isolde nonetheless also possesses an absolute character that is alien to society, if not downright hostile to it. It constitutes a magical compulsion from a distant pre-courtly age, deliberately remote from the rational worldly wisdom of chivalrous court society. This is the message, partly a negative one, that Gottfried wishes to convey to his readers. Nothing is more indicative of his attitude than his treatment of the character of King Marke, who is declared to possess and comprehend Isolde only physically ('ze lîbe'), not spiritually ('z'êren'). As both the courtly and human representative of the *Minne* convention, he has no place in the magical-religious order that both creates this love relationship and in turn is only created for it. He either acts as intruder and disturber of peace, or arrives too late, as in the death of the two lovers. The very inclusion of death in the *Minne* concept is a further affront to the courtly interpretation, which revolves around rejoicing and feasting. It is for this reason that Gottfried of Strasbourg appeals in his prologue to *Tristan and Isolde* not to the courtly reading public, from whom he can expect little understanding, but to a socially vague, anonymous community of 'noble hearts' for whom life and death, love and suffering are inseparable.

Epic verse from the period of the migrations: the Nibelungenlied

Just as the Lower Rhine and Thüringen were the home of early courtly verse romance, and the Upper Rhine the home of the court epic, so Bavaria and Austria were the home of a body of epic verse whose origins go back to the Germanic heroic poetry of the migrations. This was handed down in the form of songs in which end rhyme gradually came to replace stave rhyme. There is no evidence of epics in book form until after 1200. The *Lay of the Nibelungs* is the only extant heroic epic from the Hohenstaufen age, in the form of some three dozen manuscripts from the thirteenth to the sixteenth centuries. Wolfram von Eschenbach was familiar with the Bavarian-Austrian version, although he does not name its author. The latter must however have been familiar with Hartmann von Aue's *Iwein*. It may be concluded from the dedication to the Bishop of Passau, Wolfger von Ellenbrechtskirchen, who was in office from 1194 to 1204, that the *Lay of the Nibelungs* was written some time between 1200 and 1210. Whereas West Frankish heroic verse soon lost its original character, rapidly developing into *aventuire* and *Minne* romance (*The Lay of Roland, Willehalm*), on German soil the tribal and retainer note of poetry and songs in praise of heroes persisted far longer. German heroic verse, much closer to the original form, was therefore also characterised even in later examples by the depiction of authentic heroes and exploits, whereas the West Frankish path tended towards the non-historical Arthurian world. German heroic verse therefore also kept its traditional storehouse: the tribe and retainer, combat for victory or to the death, fateful encounters and heroic verbal exchange – all features typical for the *Nibelungenlied*. Another striking difference is that whereas the West Frankish tradition went on to develop the rhyme pair type as a common element in epic recitation, German heroic poetry, stemming from a sung tradition, retained the stanza as its exclusive form. The Nibelungen stanza comprises four long lines, derived from the Old Germanic stave rhyme long line. Each long line is composed of a verse with four accents, divided by a caesura into a second verse with three accents, the last verse of each stanza having four accents:

Es wuohs in Burgonden	ein viel edel magedîn
daz in allen landen	niht shoeners mohte sîn
Kriemhilt geheizen	wart eine schoene wip
darumbe muosen degene	vil verliesen den lip.

The unknown poet-author of the *Nibelungenlied* may have lived somewhere between Passau and Vienna. This was a lively area for literature, and fortunate in its numerous patrons, who included the Bishop of

Passau and the Babenberg court in Vienna. It was this poet who imbued the *Nibelungenlied* with its chivalrous courtly atmosphere and succeeded in finding a language that would captivate his courtly reading public. More than the unusual subject matter itself must therefore have worked an exotic charm on them. Its heathen Germanic roots broke through its chivalrous patina again and again, while most importantly the subject-matter was skilfully harnessed into an uncluttered stanza work of striking clarity. The *Nibelungenlied* was not in fact the result of a single, definitive adaptation, but arose out of a juxtaposition of earlier and later layers. The core of the work is a combination of two song fables about Siegfried and his murder, and the fall of the Burgundians at the court of Etzel. The superficial common element is Kriemhild, but even she is not a unified figure: in the first half she appears as a lovely sought-after girl, while in the second she appears in the thrall of dark vengefulness. The author of the *Nibelungenlied* respects this disparity, preserving it faithfully in his account.

The heroes are likewise portrayed in various lights. While Hagen dies a hero without complaint, thereby demonstrating acceptance of his fate, the character of Rüdiger, like Dietrich von Bern a symbol of chivalrous humanity, shows how a foreboding of death leads to tragic conflict of a kind that is unknown in heroic song. Both Rüdiger and Dietrich are 'adjuncts' from a later age, shaped to conform to the creative will of the court poet. In this sense, stress should be laid mostly on Dietrich, who proves the superiority of the chivalrous knight on numerous occasions and who slows the tragic process.

However, Dietrich is not an Arthurian knight, being in possession of tragic insight into the fateful inevitability of events and himself bringing them to fruition. Hagen stands in stark contrast to him, an autochthonous figure from the early heroic age who callously, even sneeringly, admits to having murdered Siegfried. He also contrasts with the vengeful Kriemhild, whose actions arise out of her heartfelt obligations to the purity and honour of her house.

The way Hagen and Kriemhild act as equally-matched antagonists was also unusual for the reading public of that time. The Arthurian epic was only magnanimous to the positive hero: that which was evil and negative was declared as such and condemned from the outset. There is another substantial difference, however. While the Arthurian romance remained largely episodic in character, with one *aventuire* succeeding another, the tragic certainty of the fateful outcome runs through the *Nibelungenlied* as a unifying thread. Although the poet is fully conversant with the gamut of courtly glory, festive mood and rejoicing, these moments never appear in unclouded form, always being overhung with forebodings of the impending tragic outcome.

One last feature also needs to be stressed. The *Nibelungenlied* asserts that heroic events are historically authentic, unique events. The protagonists are not conceived as types, but individuals. A corresponding great significance is hence attributed to death. The deeds performed in this heroic Lay are likewise unrepeatable. They do not provide a pattern to which persons are essentially adjuncts, in the manner of Arthurian verse, as has been shown in the comparison between Hartmann's *Erek* and *Iwein*. The *Nibelungenlied* is only conceivable in the unrepeatable form in which it has been handed down. Despite being recorded in written form it had in fact no impact on subsequent style and literature. Its truly remarkable and all too apparent impact on the course of German history is a different matter altogether, and has nothing to do with the comparative level, which is concerned with the emergence of the Arthurian world out of Norman-Breton heroic poetry. Nor indeed does it have much to do with the form of the Lay itself around 1200.

Late court satire of rank

Wernher der Gärtner (*Wernher the Gardener*), whose exact social standing is unknown, came from the Bavarian-Austrian region. His epic poem *Meier Helmbrecht* (*Peasant Helmbrecht*, written between 1250 and 1280), represents a satirical response, albeit from the viewpoint of the declining hierarchical social order, to the changing reality lamented by Walther in his epigrammatic poetry. Wernher's story is a variation on the theme of the Prodigal Son, but with one significant change: when the Prodigal Son returns home he is not received with forgiveness, but rejected in anticipated correction of God's intended order and administration of justice. The son, and the secondary character of the daughter, have broken the fourth commandment. Of peasant origin, Helmbrecht despises his father and cherishes ambitions towards the loftier order of knights, which transcends inherited rank boundaries. This ambiguity of rank and Helmbrecht's open pursuit of higher rank are a sign of the times and the unsettled century. Meier Helmbrecht dons a splendid cap, which becomes a symbol of his presumed chivalric status. He ruthlessly pursues the life of a highwayman and robber knight, returning home after a year has elapsed and behaving like a loud-mouthed show-off. He is given a joyful reception, but makes his contempt of the peasant station quite plain, trying to pass himself off as the perfect knight. A week later he sets off again, courting his sister as bride for one of his accomplices. Peasant Helmbrecht's illegitimate pursuit of the orders of higher rank is revealed not only in his infraction of prescribed dress with his cap, but also in the way he throws a wedding feast, which is an embarrassingly precise imitation of the nobleman's table, complete with cupbearer, lord high steward, chamberlains, etc. The booty from his robberies is dissipated during the wedding banquet. Suddenly, the judge appears with his hangman. Peasant Helmbrecht's companions are condemned to death and hanged, and he himself is blinded and maimed in the hand and foot. This completes the earthly judgement on him. Laboriously and in great distress he manages to limp home. Here he is cursed by his father: 'the plough is thy office'. He wanders helplessly, seeking refuge with a peasant he had once plundered. Instead of bread and wine, however, the peasant Helmbrecht is given the rope, meeting his end, like his friends, on the gallows. His cap, once a symbol of his new-found rank identity, lies in tatters, trodden underfoot in the dust. Wernher's *Meier Helmbrecht* is a rare and trenchant example of the capacity of politico-social observation in epic poetry to shift, as the latter seeks to free itself from its courtly orientation towards the social realities taking shape in the late Middle Ages.

Minnesang

Beside court epic verse, *Minnesang* was another part of the Hohenstaufen literary age, likewise the province of the chivalric estate and a major vehicle for its self-expression. Unlike epic verse, however, *Minnesang* was a solo performance for one voice with instrumental accompaniment, such as the fiddle, harp, flute, bagpipes or shawm. It played a central role during court festivities, with minnesingers not infrequently competing against one another in a sublime form of chivalrous tournament. Minnesingers came from all social classes, including kings such as William IX of Aquitaine, Henry VI, Frederic II and Alphonse of Castille. Numerous burgraves were also well-known *Minne* poets, and although in reality an immense social gulf existed within the chivalric estate the body of minnesingers contained knights of noble birth and property and low-ranking impoverished ministerials side by side with people of the humblest social rank.

Given its preferred venue, the court festivity, *Minnesang* is a quintessentially social art, presupposing a gathering of knights and ladies. The core of *Minnesang* has most often been described as a paradox: the minnesinger sings a song of courtship and praise to one of the ladies present, knowing all the while that he can never win her. He will never experience the thing of which he sings – one of the basic reasons for the introverted diction of *Minnesang* and its resignatory congelation in social convention. Since *Minne* precludes physical encounter it must be viewed as an entirely ethical and educational phenomenon.

The stollen strophe emerged as the classic *Minnesang* form. This was a three-part form with the first two metrically equal verses forming the first stolle and the next two identical ones forming the second. This *Aufgesang* canto is balanced by an *Abgesang* canto, which differs both in metrical structure and in the number of verses. The melody to which the *Minnesang* was sung was added, although this is no longer extant for the vast majority of *Minne* lyrics. Where they have survived from the closing phase of the age, such as in the case of Neidhart, whose work was the most widely disseminated, particulars concerning long and short syllables and time are usually missing.

Development

Minne lyrics developed in several distinct phases in the Hohenstaufen literary epoch. Between 1150 and 1170 a group in the Danube lands composed *Minne* lyrics independently of contact with southern French troubadour poetry (Meinloh von Sevelingen, the Burgrave of Regensburg, Kürnberger, Dietmar von Aist, the Burgrave of Rietenburg). The period from 1170 to 1190 saw a group in the Middle and Upper Rhine with distinct points of contact with the Provençal tradition, but which rapidly developed a body of work in a form of its own. Rudolf von Fenis, Heinrich VI, Bernger von Horheim, Heinrich von Rugge, Bligger von Steinach, Heinrich von Veldeke, Frederic von Hausen, Albrecht von Johansdorf, Hartmann von Aue, Heinrich von Morungen and the classic author Reinmar were major representatives of 'high *Minnesang*'. Walther von der Vogelweide is regarded as having both perfected and surpassed high *Minnesang*. The hungriest for experience, the most open to the world and the most critical poet of his day, above all in his late lower *Minne* songs and his epigrammatic poetry, he discovered a new form of expression oriented towards reality. The crisis of *Minnesang* – the danger of rigidification in conventionalism – was already evident from the summer and winter songs of Neidhart, whose deliberate principle of breaking with style won the approbation of a public soon wearied by the sterility of *Minnesang*. Finally, a late group appeared at the court of Heinrich VII (1220–35) with Burkhart von Hohenfels and Gottfried von Neufen, essentially marking the completion of the transition from high *Minne* poetry to the *Gesellschaftslied* of the late Middle Ages. New forms were evolving in addition to the chivalrous courtly verse of the chivalric estate: Marianic verse and hymns, and the *pastourelle* with its erotic tenor and theme of encounters between knights and simple country girls. By the end of the thirteenth century *Minnesang* had lost its social relevance. Hadloub heralded the completion of the transition to mastersong, ushering in the era of the compiler.

Illuminated manuscripts

A considerable number of illuminated manuscripts commissioned as collections of *Minne* lyrics are extant. The most important of these are the minor Heidelberg song manuscript, compiled towards the end of the thirteenth century in Strasbourg; the Weingarten manuscript dating from around 1300, probably from Konstanz, which also contains miniatures of poets, and may have been commissioned by Bishop Henry of Klingenberg; and the major Heidelberg manuscript. The latter dates from 1300 to 1330, was compiled in Zurich and is also known as the Manesse song manuscript, one of the most splendid and valuable of its kind. It has a hierarchical arrangement starting with the Emperor Henry, spanning the period from Kürnberger to Frauenlob and Hadloub. It contains 137 miniatures of poets and is a compilation of 140 texts. It owes its existence to the Manesse patrician family of Zurich, whose extensive library contained a huge collection of songs.

Origins of Minnesang

With regard to the origins of *Minnesang* it must be stressed that despite the efforts of Erich Köhler and Norbert Elias, our present-day understanding can at best be only superficial, particularly in the case of the Bavarian-Austrian early period. Early *Minne* lyrics were not collected as songs to be sung, there being no reason to do so at the time. The majority of songs that could have provided information about the genres involved, such as folk songs, chorales, love poetry, goliardic lyrics, etc., have been lost. The only lyric form extant from the period up to 1200, therefore, is the *Minne* lyric. It is known, however, that after originating in southern France, troubadour lyrics moved northward, continuing to press forward into the Upper Rhine.

> Ich zôch mir einen valken mêre danne ein jâr
> dô ich in gezamete als ich in wolte hân,
> und ich im sîn gevidere mit golde wol bewant,
> er huop sich ûf vil hôhe
> und floug in anderiu lant.

Chivalrous art

These lines open one of the best-known early *Minnesang* poems, the *Falkenlied* (*Falcon Song*) by Kürnberger, an Austrian knight who composed it between 1160 and 1170. Everything about the Song is chivalrous; even before troubadour lyric poetry was known, *Minne* poetry from the Bavarian-Austrian region showed itself capable of developing sublime forms of courtly love out of the chivalrous milieu. Falcon-rearing was the privilege of knights, and the care with which the falcon was adorned expressed longing for the distant beloved. Another poet from this same Bavarian-Austrian German-speaking area, Dietmar von Aist, seems to be responding directly to Kürnberger, writing some time around 1150:

> Es stuont ein frouwe alleine
> und warte uber heide
> und warte ir liebes,

39

> so gesach si valken fliegen.
> 'sô wol dir, valke, daz du bist!
> du fliugest, swar dir liep ist.
> du erkiusest dir in dem walde
> einen boum, der dir gevalle.'
> alsô hân ouch ich getân:
> ich erkôs mir selbe einen man,
> den erwelton mîniu ougen.
> daz nîdent schoene frouwen.
> owê wan lânt si mir mîn liep?
> jo engerte ich ir dekeiner trûtes niet.

Here again the falcon becomes a symbol of longing. Even in this early phase, *Minnesang* was imbued with loneliness and longing, albeit with one major difference from high *Minnesang*: this longing could still be satisfied. *Minnesang* is not a poetry of experience, but an expression of homage or a lament of absence. In classical *Minnesang* only the man speaks, the role of the woman, as in the example from Dietmar, remaining undefined to avoid depriving her of her ideal abstract quality. She cannot display any emotion, and indeed is not even present. Early *Minnesang* is characterised by a more realistic notion of *Minne*. Kürnberger, for example, continues:

> Wîp unde vederspil diu werdent lîhte zam:
> swer sî rehte lucket sô suochent sî den man.
> als warb ein schoene ritter um einen frouwen guot.
> als ich dar an gedenke, sô stêt wol hôhe mîn muot.

The courting knight can still hope that his dream will come true, since he can assume that his lady shares the same inclination towards love.

Classical Minnesang

The three outstanding poets of classical or high *Minnesang* are Friedrich von Hausen, Heinrich von Morungen and Reinmar. Friedrich von Hausen lived in the vicinity of the Emperor Frederic. He was born in the Middle Rhine region and died during the Third Crusade shortly before Barbarossa on 6 May 1190, as a result of a fall from a horse. His poems are permeated with lamentation for the coldness of his adored lady and her unattainability. Ultimately he holds *Minne* itself responsible for his suffering:

> Wâfenâ, wie hât mich minne gelâzen,
> diu mich betwanc, daz ich lie mîn gemüete
> An solhen wân, der mich wol mac verwâzen,
> ez ensî, daz ich genieze ir güete,
> Von der ich bin alsô dicke âne sin.

mich dûhte ein gewin, und wolte diu guote
wizzen di nôt, diu mir wont in mîn muote.

Minne is described here as *wân* (madness). Friedrich von Hausen feels smitten as if by a sickness, even if his beloved, on learning of his condition, were to take pity on him and accept his courtship. However she does not even stop to greet him, but passes him by proudly. He is deeply wounded by this, although he remains convinced that she is the only lady he can serve: 'seht dest min wan'.

Excess

He repeats his inner lamentation, turning over in his mind the phenomenon of *Minne* that has robbed him of all reason and racked his body with torment. Finally he rebels:

Minne, got müeze mich an dir gerechen!
wie vile mînem herzen der fröuden du wendest!
Und möhte ich dir dîn krumbez ouge ûz gestechen,
des het ich reht, wan du vil lützel endest
An mir solhe nôt, sô mir din lîp gebôt.
und waerest du tôt, sô dûhte ich mich rîche.
sus muoz ich von dir leben bétwungenlîche.

God should come to his aid in his struggle with *Minne*, which has used him so badly. He would gouge out her eye, even if it meant that she met her end in suffering. This would only be just revenge and he would count himself fortunate. As it is, however, he must resign himself to his fate as the loser.

Suffering through Minne

It is important to remember that these images are an antithetical social game. It was a question of finding the boldest and most daring comparisons in order to give fresh poetic facets to what was in fact a very straight-forward *Minne* scheme.

Heinrich von Morungen was a liegeman of the Margrave of Meissen and is assumed to have died in 1222 at the Thomas monastery near Leipzig. He too presents *Minne* as a magical power by which he is gravely threatened:

Mirst geschên als einem kindelîne,
daz sîn schônez bilde in einem glase ersach
Unde greif dar nâch sîn selbes schîne
sô vil, biz daz ez den Spiegel gar zerbrach.
Dô wart als sîn wünne ein leitlich ungemach.
alsô dâhte ich iemer frô ze sîne,

> dô'ch gesach die lieben frouwen mîne,
> von der mir bî liebe leides vil geschach.

The power of *Minne* causes his beloved to appear to him in a dream, and the author gives this dream an erotic undertone by telling of her inviting red mouth. This allusion has to be withdrawn immediately, however, once again using the same image of the red mouth, this time antithetically: suddenly he is seized with the fear that his beloved might die ('grôze angest hân ich des gewunnen/ daz verblîchen süle ir mündelîn sô rôt'). In the face of this fear he feels as helpless as a little child seeing its own reflection in a well and wanting to embrace it with love. Only death can release him from his insatiable longing. There is no lack of religious allusion in Heinrich von Morungen's poetry. He speaks of the salvation of men and women alike, chivalrous courtship being seen as effecting the soul's acceptance among the blessed. *Minne* is supplanted by *herzeliebe* and hence placed in direct contact with the soul's relationship with God. The most conspicuous symptom of crisis here, however, is that *Minne* can essentially no longer be articulated in a social context. This was to demolish the dialogue-seeking status of *Minnesang* as a performance during court festivities.

Reinmar the classic poet

Reinmar was probably of Alsatian origin. Gottfried von Strasbourg expressed his heartfelt grief at Reinmar's death in 1210. While perhaps the least inwardly committed to the genre, Reinmar was of all the high *Minnesang* poets the most skilled exponent of its wealth of form and expressive potential, and therefore provides the clearest illustration of them. His attitude to *Minnesang* is a seamless one, while his tone of lament commands the full register of the poetry of rank. It involves no religious transcendence, nor is his concept of *Minne* reconcilable with reality.

> Ich waen, mir liebe geschehen wil:
> mîn herze hebet sich ze spil,
> ze fröuden swinget sich mîn muot,
> als der valke enfluge tuot
> und der are ensweime.

The eagle and the falcon, symbols of chivalric self-assurance and self-confidence, are brought into harmony with openness to the *Minne* experience, which is experienced as joyful.

> Die werlt verswîge ich miniu leit
> und sage vil lützel iemen, wer ich bin.
> Ez dunket mich unsaelikeit,
> daz ich mit triuwen allen mînen sin

Bewendet hân, dar ez mich dunket vil,
und mir der besten eine
des niht gelouben wil.

Reinmar's poetry betrays an exhaustive, almost mechanical enumeration of *Minnesang* stereotypes. Nowhere is there a trace of the personal perplexity characteristic of Friedrich von Hausen and Heinrich von Morungen. Indeed, Reinmar even goes so far as to shield courtly society from the signs of suffering, which is incompatible with the conceptual world of rank. His lament for the unattainability of the beloved thus scarcely grazes the conventional boundaries of *Minnesang*.

Und wiste ich niht, daz sî mich mac
vor al der welte wert gemachen, ob sie wil,
Ich gediende ir niemer mêre tac:
sô hât sie tugende, den ich volge unz an daz zil,
Niht langer, wan die wîle ich lebe.
noch bitte ich sî, daz sî mir liebez ende gebe.
waz hilfet daz? ich weiz wol, daz siez niht entuot.
nu tuo siz durch den willen mîn
and lâze mich ir tôre sîn
und neme mîne rede für guot.

European *Minne* poetry is generally regarded as the initial phase of personal lyric poetry, concerned with pursuit of the experience of self. Although this holds good with regard to form, the heart of the dispute between Walther von der Vogelweide and Reinmar concerning the substance of *Minne* poetry – the most famous literary feud of the Middle Ages – revolved around the expressive potential of personal inner experience. Individual experience did not begin to assert itself in lyric poetry until the appearance of Walther's *Minne* and epigrammatic poetry.

Walther von der Vogelweide was born in 1170. In 1190 he was under the protection of Leopold V at the Babenberg court in Vienna. After the death of Leopold V in 1194 his son Friedrich assumed patronage; when this ended in 1198 Walther lost his feudal claim. Whether this was brought about by an altercation with Friedrich's successor Leopold VI is now immaterial. At all events it marked for Walther the beginning of a time of wandering and material insecurity which he repeatedly laments in his Lays. In the summer of 1198 he was already in the service of Phillip of Swabia, later becoming retainer to Otto IV and Friedrich II. In 1203 he returned to Vienna as a retainer of Wolfger von Ellenbrechtskirchen, Bishop of Passau, in time for the wedding feast of Leopold VI. By this time Walther's definitive break with classical *Minnesang* was complete. The two following years saw a breakthrough to a new and unmistakable poetic style. While in the service of Friedrich II he was rewarded around 1220 with a fief near

Würzburg that secured him an income. This brought his life as a wandering minstrel to an end. One of Walther's later poems is dedicated to the Crusade of 1228–9 – the last historical date in his life that can now be deduced. He died around 1230 and was buried in Würzburg. During the century that followed his grave was frequently sought out and its location attested, as well as forming a growing source of legends.

Walther's realism

Walther von der Vogelweide started as a pupil of Reinmar, although his own lyric poetry was permeated by a brighter, more joyous tone from the very outset. There are echoes of the early poetry of the Danube lands, such as that of Kürnberger and Dietmar von Aist, who must have been part of his immediate cultural milieu. From the literary viewpoint Walther can only be comprehended in terms of his dispute with Reinmar. ('Herr got, gesegene mich vor sorgen/ daz ich vil wünnecliche lebe') ('God preserve me from a sad life'), he declares, thereby challenging the sorrow and lamentation dominating the paradoxical nature of *Minne* lyric poetry (with its adoration and unattainability of the beloved) with a new *joie de vivre*. Another significant distinction, however, is the way women are portrayed in his poetry. Whereas in classical *Minnesang* the lady is always absent, in Walther's poetry she takes shape again in the form of a direct encounter.

> Al mîn fröide lît an einem wîbe:
> der herze ist ganzer tugende vol,
> und ist sô geschaffen an ir lîbe
> daz man ir gerne dienen sol.
> ich erwirbe ein lachen wol von ir.
> des muoz sie gestaten mir:
> wie mac siz behüeten,
> in fröwe mich nach ir güeten.
> Als ich under wîlen zir gesitze,
> sô si mich mit ihr reden lât,
> sô benimt sie mir sô gar die witze
> daz mir der lîp alumme gât.
> swenne ich iezo wunder rede kan,
> gesihet si mich einest an,
> sô han ichs vergezzen,
> waz wolde ich dar gesezzen.

Chivalrous courtship

Walther's poetry is also *Minnesang* with chivalrous courtship at its heart. He, too, loses reason, but he loses it when he sees his beloved or sits talking by her. Walther's work differs from classical *Minnesang* in its new *Minne* principle, based on reciprocity. There is no stress on hierarchy, therefore, such as might suggest itself for poetry addressed to a courtly audience, but an open approach to an individual woman who is no longer the 'abstract' embodiment of a courtly representative type. Walther developed this approach during his travels after 1198, giving it straight-forward expression:

Praise of sensual love

Ich wil einer helfen klagen,
der ouch fröide zaeme wol,
dazs in alsô valschen tagen
schoene tugent verliesen sol.
hie vor waer ein lant gefröut um ein sô schoene wîp;
waz sol der nû schoener lîp?
Swâ sô liep bî liebe lît
gar vor allen sorgen frî,
ich wil daz des winters zît
den zwein wol erteilet sî.
winter unde sumer, der zweier êren ist sô vil
daz ich die beide loben wil.
Hât der winter kurzen tac,
sô hât er die langen naht,
dazu sich liep bî liebe mac
wol erholn daz ê dâ vaht.
wâz hân ich gesprochen? wê jâ het ich baz geswigen,
sol ich iemer sô geligen.

This praise of sensual love is familiar in early *Minnesang*, folk song, dawn songs (*Tagelied, aubades*), *pastourelles* and goliardic verse. Walther incorporates it into his conceptual framework – note his feigned dismay when he states that he would rather remain silent if direct experience were to be denied him – but does not make it his exclusive subject-matter. Walther is not merely opposing here the injustice, and indeed hollowness, of the classical *Minne* concept, but also abasement and humiliation of the man, which he perceives as entirely unchivalrous and the mark of courtly decadence. This constitutes the justification in rank terms for the inclusion of 'lower *Minne*'. Hartmann von Aue clearly felt much the same way when he declared his rejection of high *Minne*:

Ze frouwen habe ich einen sin:
als sî mir sint, als bin ich in;
wand ich mac baz vertrîben
die zît mit armen wîben.

swar ich kum, dâ ist ir vil,
dâ vinde ich die, diu mich dâ wil;
diu ist ouch mînes herzen spil:
waz touc mir ein ze hôhez zil?

These poets do not shrink from criticising the conduct of the courtly lady. She abuses the high rank accorded to her in poetry with her haughty indifference to the man. Like Hartmann von Aue, Walther distinguishes between the *frouwe* or lady and the *wîp* or woman, meaning the lady preferred by virtue of her rank as distinct from women in general. Again like Hartmann, he does not choose the woman of lower status, rather seeking to change the courtly model. His portrayal of women should be understood as a universal one. From the rank viewpoint it is neither inside nor outside worldly nobility.

Walther's dawn songs, *pastourelles* and crusade poetry comprised a smaller proportion of his work than his *Minne* poetry. However, his epigrammatic poetry, appearing from 1198 onwards, made him the first political poet in the German language. Epigrammatic poetry, as represented by the moral *didache* of the *Spervogel*, may be classified as didactic poetry. However, the aim of Walther von der Vogelweide was to function as a Hohenstaufen philosopher of rank ethics, not as a moralist.

Walther as a Hohenstaufen philosopher of rank ethics

Walther was directly affected by the 1197 imperial crisis. As a poet with the ear of noble circles, he naturally expressed his concern at events in the empire and at the machinations of the Pope aimed at bringing down secular authority. In his three *Reichssprüche* or imperial epigrams he makes an outspoken call for the coronation of Phillip as the new King:

Ich hôrte ein wazzer diezen
und sach die vische fliezen
ich sach swaz in der welte was,
velt walt loup rôr unde gras.
swaz kriuchet unde fliuget
und bein zer erde biuget,
daz sach ich, unde sage iu daz:
der keinez lebet âne haz.
daz wilt und daz gewürme
die strîtent starke stürme,
sam tuont die vogel under in;
wan daz si habent einen sin:
si dûhten sich ze nihte,
si enschüefen starc gerihte.
sie kiesent künege unde reht,

sie setzent hêrren unde kneht.
sô wê dir, tiuschiu zunge,
wie stêt dîn ordenunge!
daz nû diu mugge ir künec hât,
und daz dîn êre alsô zergât.
bekêrâ dich, bekêre.
die cirkel sint ze hêre,
die armen künege dringent dich:
Philippe setze en weisen ûf, und heiz si treten hinder sich.

Walther never actually doubts the concordat between secular and clerical power, as is clear from the first imperial epigram, *Ich saz uf eime steine*. He was nevertheless the first German layman-poet ever to attack the papal curia, accusing it of simony (the sale of ecclesiastical preferment). The Interregnum period and the greed for power of Pope Innocent III proved to Walther that the Hohenstaufen cosmos that had shaped his view of the world since his youth was now shattered. He relates this realisation to the social as well as the political situation. The days of self-assured Hohenstaufen chivalry sustaining and epitomising the Empire were over. His elegy gives despairing expression to this realisation, far removed from either chivalric-Christian or rank-religious self-assurance, or indeed the prevailing tone of his day:

Elegy

Owê war sint verswunden alliu mîniu jâr!
ist mir mîn leben getroumet oder ist ez wâr?
daz ich ie wânde ez wœre, was daz allez iht?
dar nâch hân ich geslafen und enweiz es niht.
nû bin ich erwachet, und ist mir unbekannt
daz mir hie vor was kündic als mîn ander hant.
liut unde lant, dar inn ich von kinde bin erzogen,
die sint mir worden frömde reht als ez sî gelogen.
die mine gespilen wâren, die sint trœge unt alt.
bereitet ist daz velt, verhouwen ist der walt:
wan daz wazzer fliuzet als ez wîlent flôz,
für wâr mîn ungelücke wânde ich wurde grôz.
mich grüezet maneger trâge, der mich bekande ê wol.
diu welt ist allenthalben ungenâden vol.
also ich gedenke an manegen wünneclîchen tac,
die mir sint enpfallen als in daz mer ein slac,
iemer mêre ouwê.

Owê wie uns mit süezen dingen ist vergeben!
ich sihe die gallen mitten in dem honege sweben:

47

diu Welt ist ûzen schœne,   wiz grüen unde rôt,
und innân swarzer varwe,   vinster sam der tôt.
swen si nû habe verleitet   der schouwe sînen trôst:
er wirt mit swacher buoze   grôzer sünde erlôst.
dar an gedenkent, ritter: ez ist iuwer dinc.
ir tragent die liehten helme   und manegen herten rinc,
dar zuo die vesten schilte   und diu gewîhten swert.
wolte got, wan wœre ich   der sigenünfte wert!
sô wolte ich nôtic armman   verdienen richen solt.
joch meine ich niht die huoben   noch der hêrren golt:
ich wolte sœlden krône   êweclîchen tragen:
die mohte ein soldenœre   mit sîme sper bejagen.
möht ich die lieben reise   gevaren über sê,
sô wolte ich denne singen wol,   und niemer mêr ouwê,
niemer mêr ouwê.

An outline of late medieval literature

The decline of Hohenstaufen chivalry

One should not be misled by Walther von der Vogelweide's repeated lamentation of the moral decline among knights and people alike, or of the generally uncertain situation in the country and the visible decline of Hohenstaufen imperial power. His is essentially a lament of rank, however much it may appear to be made in the name of humanity. Ideologically it is addressed to a now politically redundant body of Hohenstaufen imperial knights, not to the people of Christendom. For all the perspicacity and diversity this poetry of rank can offer, it must ultimately be classified in the conservative camp. As its authoritarian, typologically constricted late phase in the thirteenth century clearly shows, it inevitably lacked by its very nature either the willingness or the capacity for a receptive view of changing reality. Although the epic and lyric poetry of the Hohenstaufen era survived into the thirteenth century, it was merely reproducing a time-honoured pattern, and was clearly oriented towards the past.

The literary background to the German late medieval period is difficult to ascertain. Even extensive accounts of that century, which was characterised by a transformation of literary forms and major social shifts, frequently complain on the one hand of the daunting welter of material, and on the other of inadequate or even totally lacking literary research. The reasons for this situation are many and various, but only the most important can be enumerated here.

Middle-class literature?

The literature of the thirteenth and fourteenth centuries cannot yet be designated middle-class literature in the modern understanding of the term. At the same time, however, it is no longer, as in the eleventh to mid-twelfth centuries, either a literature of clerical poets or the later art form of knights. Burgher families such as the patrician Manesse family of Zurich did strive to preserve and obtain chivalrous poetry of the Hohenstaufen era, acting as patrons and ensuring its custodianship. However, this was a matter of prestige for an urban upper stratum that had achieved wealth and social standing. It was in essence a backwards-looking attempt at 'aristocratising' themselves, and by no means an independent literary expression on the part of the increasingly powerful urban patrician class. Similarly, the two favourite figures portrayed in literature of the thirteenth to fifteenth centuries, the peasant and the journeyman, are hardly indicative of a middle-class appropriation of literature, since they invariably appear in the context of comic verse (*Schwank* – anecdote), satire and Shrovetide plays), and even there could assume diametrically opposed roles. The volume of written works, as well as of handed-down works, rose sharply in this period. There are indications of a social deepening of education, as well as an increased demand for literary products of all kinds, with a great preponderance of specialised literature. Despite these shifts, however, the medieval concept of literature continued to hold sway even in these newly-emerging forms. The reproduction of literary patterns and the formation of typological series of original work continued to be preferred. The creation of manuscript copies or the adaptation of medieval Latin or Middle High German material was still tantamount to a new edition. Concepts such as intellectual property, originality or genius had yet to appear, even in this late medieval period. A general tendency towards the anonymous production of art persisted.

Innovative aspects

There were nevertheless some literary innovations and pointers to future development. The prose romance was in its infancy and gradually replacing traditional rhyme-paired epic verse. Religious and secular drama alike were evolving into an autonomous dramaturgy. Both secular and religious specialist literature could now offer a substantial body of written material, ranging from theology through philosophy to the mathematical and natural sciences, thereby proving to be more decisive than poetry in laying the foundations for the New High German written language. Princely courts, towns and universities were the centres of this new development.

Collapse of the concept of empire

The political and economic situation after the death of Heinrich VI in 1197 made the inward and outward collapse of the empire ever more glaringly apparent. The great early medieval concept of the empire as a continuation of the ancient *imperium romanum*, restructured in Christian form and legitimised by the donation of Constantine, collapsed during the Interregnum in the face of French supremacy and the Roman Curia. Within the empire itself, the struggle for supremacy on German soil between the Wittelsbachs, Habsburgs and Luxemburgs fostered political developments in what proved in subsequent centuries to be a fatal direction. From an imperial state characterised by an association of people it became a territorial principality. Whereas the imperial state had delegated control and protection by means of a complex feudal system, the territorial princes now began to consolidate all power in their own hands. Executive authority, taxation and the administering of justice were all reorganised, creating empires within the empire. The imperial reforms of Maximilian I were ultimately powerless to check the arbitrary political power of electors, the mundane and clerical princes and the lesser and minor landowners and counts. In Germany, the princes began to pursue an 'inwardly-directed foreign policy'. Particularism penetrated political, social and cultural life, creating fateful trends that were to persist until the nineteenth century.

Clerics, knights, the middle classes, peasants

The medieval social order changed along with the political system, acquiring a more universal significance. Formerly a distinction had been made only between the clergy and the laity. Late medieval social ranks, however, comprised clerics, knights, the middle classes and the peasantry. The burgeoning towns in particular became points of attraction and integration for the various ranks. Rank boundaries were no longer regarded as insuperable. Towns became havens for knights and landless peasants alike. The increased urban demand for labour can be accounted for by the rise in skilled trades and crafts and by growing national and international trade relations. Foreign trade embraced the Mediterranean and the colonised East. A market based on supply and demand was taking shape. As a result of this, traditional agricultural production, accustomed to trade based on bartering goods, found itself in considerable difficulties that affected the majority of the peasantry and the landed chivalric gentry. This situation was exacerbated by poor harvests and catastrophes such as the plague years of 1347–51, which wiped out half the German population. As a result of the agrarian crisis and the fall in prices, the ground rents of the landowners were lost. This shifted the conflict between peasants and landowners into the political arena.

The urban patrician class

Towards the end of the fourteenth century the first signs of peasant unrest began to appear in southern and south-western Germany. In the towns it was the patricians, merchants who had acquired wealth, who set the tone in matters of urban prestige, public and commercial law, the regulation of the market and of weights and measures, prices and tolls, the police and the lower levels of jurisdiction. It was some time before master craftsmen, organised in corporations or guilds, managed to gain seats and votes on town councils. In the middle of the fourteenth century, towns such as Cologne, Frankfurt, Zurich, Ulm and Augsburg even saw armed uprisings to bring this about. The guilds in turn waged a marked 'downward' struggle against journeymen, immigrants and servants. The demography of the urban population at that time reveals the necessity for this: although only an average of 10 per cent were patricians, 50 per cent were craftsmen, and 40 per cent belonged to the lower classes. Craftsmen were thus over-represented in the social pyramid, and had to resist the upwardly mobile.

The Church

In the daily life of town and country alike the Church enjoyed clear intellectual supremacy, although it too underwent numerous crises. Religious poetry formed a major part of late medieval literature. The exemplary life and Crucifixion of Christ were the key elements in this literature, which conveyed the idea of certain redemption in the next world to counter the confusion of the age, the contrast between material poverty and good fortune and the conflict raging among all social strata. It included collections of legends for evening reading to accompany the religious calendar and religious dramas such as the Passion or the Day of Judgement, freed from a narrow liturgical context and performed on cathedral squares in the vernacular, often with many changes of scene, and sometimes lasting for several days. In all cases, however, these literary forms sought to permeate the everyday level of experience of the Christian, lending an immediately recognisable allegorical Christian meaning to his fortunes and misfortunes. Christian poetry of the late Middle Ages was of a practical, moral character.

Religious drama

Religious drama, the most notable genre of religious poetry, comprised a wide range of themes, including Easter plays, Passion plays, Marian laments, Nativity plays, lives of Jesus, prophet plays, paradise plays, procession plays and legend dramas. Latin versions of these dramas are known, and can therefore be compared with new vernacular versions, in contrast to secular drama. Religious dramas were staged and directed in the first instance by urban clerics, with burghers and students as actors. Although biblical events formed the basis, adapters had a free hand in the shaping of scenes and characters. A tendency towards the use of increasingly large numbers of characters and lavish scenes forced plays out of the church and on to the market place. This brought about a certain secularisation in the creation of scenes and characters. Shopkeepers and knights appear, while scenes with the devil and the uneducated acquired elements of humour to amuse the audience. Religious dramas were widespread throughout the German-speaking world. They were stationary, often calling for an extensive stage for several levels of simultaneous action, so that performers could not leave until the play was over. Occasionally, especially in the case of Passion plays, religious drama took the form of a procession from one scene to the next. The mummers could not lend any individuality to their roles, having to concentrate on achieving a mask-like form of representation.

The popular pious movement

Late medieval religious drama formed an important part of a new, popular pious movement at the heart of which was the figure of the Virgin Mary as gracious helper of sinners and of people made anxious by the numerous perils around them. The Mother of God became the subject of numerous legends, at first in the form of an oral tradition. In this way she also found her way into painting and the pictorial arts, as well as into minor epics, lyrical hymns and drama poetry. This development marks a link with the second and third Cluniac generations of legendary and Marian poetry, underlining the astonishing continuity in religious poetry from the eleventh–thirteenth and fourteenth centuries. It also makes one aware of just how limited the sphere of influence of courtly chivalrous poetry really was. Whereas religious poetry found popular forms at the broadest possible level, courtly verse remained restricted to a ruling class of nobles, clerics and, to a limited extent, the urban patriciate. The period from the eleventh to the thirteenth century witnessed the assertion and upholding of fundamental Christian emphasis on the certainty of death, the transitory nature of all earthly phenomena, and the uncertain fate of the soul after death. Indeed, these elements took root in the parallel allegorical form of *Dame World*, whose portrayal is a blend of beauty and decay, life and death, that was soon to permeate the courtly chivalrous poetry of Walther von der Vogelweide, Konrad von Würzburg and Frauenlob, for example.

Didactic poetry, moralism

However, this tradition was no longer appropriate for a medieval cosmos characterised by discord between the Pope and the Emperor. The intellectual uncertainty of the times demanded more pragmatic models. This is what made didactic, moral poetry, composed by clerics and laymen alike, of such importance in the late Middle Ages. It is a verse form concerned with instructing the Christian how to conduct himself in this world without falling victim to it. It appeals to astuteness in the Christian who is aiming to live at peace with God and the world, squaring the circle of the Christian and the profane. It is not a manifestation of a middle-class *didache* of the middle classes, instead taking as its starting-point a Christian universalism. In the light of the Day of Judgement and the Ten Commandments, beggar and king, burgher and knight are all equal. The preferred genres of this verse were *Schwank* (anecdote), fable and *Beispiel* (archetype). Traditional genres stemming from late classical verse, such as biblical verse, the spiritual didactic poem, the doctrine of Christian virtue, epigrammatic poetry, the beast epic and chronicle verse continued in parallel. An all-embracing casuistic way of looking at virtue and vice evolved in which narrative was linked in the first instance with instruction. Didactic, moralistic verse did not begin to display traits of the urban middle-class world until towards the end of the fifteenth century, when it abandoned the dichotomy between this world and the next characteristic of Christian verse, becoming instead a vehicle of the urban intelligentsia, the patriciate and the craftsman class, whose *Meistersang* is clearly informed by this development.

Secular literary forms

The secular literary forms of the late Middle Ages may be envisaged as *Schwank* (anecdote) and Shrovetide plays of an entertaining character. Both genres enjoyed great popularity, and an important reason for the broad appeal of religious drama among such a diverse public derives from the fact that religious verse adopted theatrical and character elements from comical verse. While *Schwank* has a tradition dating back to antiquity, the Shrovetide play did not appear in written form until the fifteenth century. The comic *Schwank* genre does not derive from a genuine literary form, but from a universal human desire for diversion, comedy, satire and irony. It is thus akin to the fairy-tale, anecdote, fable, wit, the example, and humoresque. *Inter alia* it includes such widely treated themes of the day as the *Wettlauf des Hasen mit dem Igel* (The Race between the Hare and the Hedgehog). Medieval short verse tales in Latin had a direct influence on the forms and themes emerging in the fourteenth and fifteenth centuries. As the *Kleinepik* developed, *Schwank* became a separate narrative form contingent on a punch-line. Its primary targets were the nobility and the patriciate. Popular prose tales did not appear until the sixteenth century.

Schwank literature

From the welter of extant *Schwank* literature, Heinrich Wittenwiler's *Ring* may serve as an example. This work has been handed down in the form of a single copy, dating from 1410, in which it is stated that the author is still alive aged fifty. He probably came from Thurgau. Wittenwiler's intention in the *Ring*, which comprises 10,000 verses, is to elucidate the ways of the world, and how a person is to conduct himself in the face of its various encumbrances and complications in such a way as not to come to any harm. In part one the peasant lad Bertschi Triefnas of Lappenhausen courts the peasant girl Mätzli Rüerenzumpf. His '*Minnebrief*' letter, whose complete divergence from *Minnesang* in both form and content is immediately striking, reads: 'Got grüess dich, lindentolde! / Lieb, ich bin dir holde. / Du bist mein morgensterne; / Pei dir so schlieff ich gerne./ Mich hat so ser verdrossen, / Daz du bist so verschlossen/ In dem speicher über tag, / Daz ich nit geschlaffen mag. / Dar zuo han ich mich vermessen, / Daz ich fürbas nit wil essen / Noch gedrinken dhainer stund, / Mich trösti dann dein roter mund. / Dar umb so sag mir an oder ab! / Daz got dein lieben sele hab!' The betrothal and wedding continue the plot in logical sequence. Before the wedding takes place, however, there is a long-winded disputation among the peasants on the pros and cons of married life, the male and female ideals of beauty, etc. A brawl breaks out during the wedding dance, resulting in war between the villages of Lappenhausen and Nissingen. Allies are sought: the Turks and Russians appear, giants and heroes from the Dietrich epic, witches and dwarves from Heuberg. Lappenhausen is razed to the ground, and when Bertschi, the sole survivor, finds Mätzli dead among the rubble, he resolves to spend his life as a hermit in the Black Forest. The three stages of the *Ring* plot are devoted respectively to instruction in the chivalric and musical arts (with *Minne* parody as a courtship motif), the development of tenets of virtue, the portrayal of a pupil, Christian tenets, tenets of household management and tenets concerning health (the parodied subjects of the 'learned disputation' before the wedding), farcically caricatured table manners during the wedding feast, and tenets of war and siege during the concluding battle action. Wittenwiler sets this didactic structure against the background of peasant village life, but in so doing by no means implies criticism of the fourth estate. His 'peasants' are comically caricatured burghers, who were probably also his intended audience, since they would have been the only people capable of grasping all his allusions to the contemporary educational horizon. 'Das Werk enthält ... die Synthese der Möglichkeiten spätmittelalterlicher Dichtung. Wir haben damit ein Epos vor uns von inneren Dimensionen, wie es

die Zeit schon lange nicht mehr aufzuweisen hatte. Weltbild und Wirklich-
keitsauffassung des Dichters ermöglichen seinem eminenten Gestaltungs-
vermögen die enge Verbindung von kräftigem Naturalismus und
willkürlich-grotesker Phantastik, Übersteigerung und Verzerrung.' ('The
work contains a synthesis of the potential in late medieval poetry. It
constitutes an epos of inner dimensions such as had not appeared for a
long time in that era. The poet's world-view and perception of reality
enable his eminent creative capacity to combine an earthy naturalism with
deliberately grotesque fantasy, hyperbole and caricature.' (H. Rupprich)

The culture of laughter

Mikhail Bakhtin, the most outstanding theorist of this late medieval culture
of laughter, writes:

> Medieval laughter is neither a subjective and individual, nor a biologi-
> cal sense of the endless nature of life. It is a social sense, embracing
> the entire people. A person sensed the endless nature of life in the
> public square and the carnival crowd, in physical contact with people
> of all ages and social stations. Here he felt part of a people that was
> constantly increasing and renewing itself. The festive laughter of the
> people therefore embraces not only the moment of victory over fear
> of the horrors of the next world, of the sanctified, or of death, but
> also the moment of victory over all forms of violence, over mundane
> rulers, the mighty of this world, and everything that enslaves and
> restricts. Inasmuch as medieval laughter overcame the fear of mystery,
> the world and power, it fearlessly exposed the truth about the world
> and power. It confronted lies, adulation, flattery and hypocrisy. The
> truth of laughter dethroned power, taking its place alongside cursing
> and invective. Among the proponents of this truth was the medieval
> Fool.

The Shrovetide play had an influence on this culture of laughter. The first
evidence of such plays dates from 1430, and they lost their importance
soon after 1600. The distinction from clerical poetry is easier to discern
here than in the case of *Schwank*, for the simple, superficial reason that
the ecclesiastical calendar that informed urban everyday life was almost
completely interrupted at Shrovetide.

The ecclesiastical year – Shrovetide

Shrovetide is the festival that precedes the forty days of Lent, the period
of fasting before Easter, which begins on Ash Wednesday and derives
from the forty days that Christ fasted in the wilderness. Lent has been
observed since the seventh century. Shrovetide itself, which begins on the

Feast of Epiphany or Candlemas, is intended as a conscious emphasis of earthly sensual pleasure, feasting and uncouth exuberance, in contrast with the asceticism and inner composure of Lent itself. This at least constitutes the inner ecclesiastical reasoning behind Shrovetide. In addition, however, this feast also coincides with pagan traditions of the battle of the seasons, spring festivals and the battle between winter and summer. Although these festivals had long since lost their pagan mythical character by the late Middle Ages their merry and expectant mood had nevertheless been retained, and indeed can still be seen today in the masks and costumes of the Allemannic and south German carnival processions.

Shrovetide play

Social companionship between men and women is fundamental to this situation, and the Shrovetide play touches on this. The intention is not to break through this situation, but by wit, parody and riddle to increase the relaxed mood. Solo performances by masks dominate, usually with the intention of comic self-representation. Rhymed pair verse with four accents, totalling from four to at most thirty verses, are the rule:

From Wittenwiler's 'Ring'

Herr der wirt, ich heiss der Tiltapp.
Ich bin gar ein einveltiger lapp,
Ich nutz die frauen lieber unten zu zeiten,
Dann solt ich an einem wilden beren streiten.
So trink ich lieber Wein, dann sauers bier,
so leck ich lieber honig, dann wagensmir.
So fleuhe ich grosse erbeit, wo ich sie weiss.
So verhalt ich unten nimmer keinen scheiss.
Si iss ich zuckermus für hebrein brei.
Nu bruft, ob ich icht ein einveltiger lapp sei!

Company of fools

Whereas the call of the last verse, 'Nun gebt zu, dass ich ein grosser Trottel bin!' draws the audience into the situation, groups of strolling players began to appear in addition to solo performers. These groups would travel from one festival to another, and in some respects already had the autonomous character of a theatre group. They did not, however, seek a rigid separation between themselves and their audience. Rather than performing before an audience, they would move in among the public, forming *inter alia* a company of fools. Unlike religious drama, Shrovetide plays were not yet performed on stage, nor were they arranged in scenes. The limit of dramaturgical design was marked by the narrator, who gave the reciters their cue and to whom they deferred after they had finished. Their recitations formed an open-ended sequence; like solo reciters they made frequent appeals to bystanders, calling for their opinions and pleased to be interrupted by them. The aim of the Shrovetide play is to create as much laughter and merriment as possible among those present within the immediate context of the Shrovetide festivities, finishing with the reciters and audience joining together in a dance.

The example given above shows that reciters were not exactly prudish in their choice of means of expression or in their allusions. Uncouthness, scatological language and sexual obscenity are elementary components of a world of instinct seeking to free itself from narrow urban rules of conduct. The deliberate flouting of taboos, and a basic delight in uttering the forbidden is its highest principle. To this it may be added that the reciters, who for the most part composed their texts themselves on the basis of contemporary models, were journeymen with extremely limited contact with the opposite sex. Such contact only became legal with marriage, a status that was achieved with that of 'master'. The most popular figure of the Shrovetide plays from Nuremberg, one of the mainstays of this literary form, was the peasant. Somewhat remote from the urban sphere of experience, he was a logical vehicle for projecting urban alienation and a comic affirmation of existence. The peasant figure serves both a passive and an active purpose in the late medieval culture of laughter. He allows himself to be made into a figure of fun, and at the same time makes fun of others.

The role of specialist literature

Late medieval specialist literature in the vernacular, whether of secular or religious content, was of greater significance than poetry for the emergence of a New High German written language – identical with the New High German literary language. The preceding account has repeatedly stressed how narrow the social strata responsible for the development of poetry in Germany were. The ability of Germany to mature into a reading and writing cultural nation would therefore be impossible to explain without reference to the function of specialist literature in disseminating education and expert knowledge. Whether these were theological *summae*, world chronicles, systematised theories of the world, falconry or remedies for wounds, their distribution was at all events greater than that of poetry, and their social effect many times more complex. One indication of this may be surprising, although it should not be: the first German book, the *Abrogans*, was just such a practical reference book. It was in fact a Latin–German glossary, and pre-dates the *Hildebrandslied*. Needless to say, specialist literature also far exceeded poetry in terms of quantity, not only in the number of titles, but also in the number of editions or copies and the number of extant texts.

We use the number of extant manuscripts of particular literary works as an aid in estimating their former level of distribution and impact. Of courtly poetry, Wolfram von Eschenbach's *Parzifal* is top of the list in view of the number of manuscripts that have survived: 86. Of early humanist literary works, Johannes von Tepl's *Ackermann aus Böhmen* is in first place with 15 manuscripts and 17 printed editions. By way of comparison, some 400 manuscripts of the *Schwabenspiegel* are documented, some 270 of the *Sachsenspiegel*, some 250 of Seuse's *Büchlein der ewigen Weisheit*, 205 of Albrant's *Rossarzneibuch*, 136 of Heinrich von St. Gallen's *Leben Jesu*, and likewise over a hundred of Master Bartholomew's *Praktik*. This literature was furthermore not restricted to a few small circles of literature enthusiasts: they were in the hands of all ranks. Whether ten or a thousand manuscripts have been lost to every one that has survived, or around 150, as seems most likely, the proportion remains the same: specialist literature was by far the most widely distributed and read literature in those centuries in which the written language was emerging.

(G. Eis)

Some reference to the medieval educational system will be necessary in order to describe the scope and structure of specialist literature. This system essentially rested on the scholastic theory of knowledge, distinguishing three basic *artes*: the seven liberal arts that formed university propaedeutics, introductory studies for all faculties that had to be studied by all students; the 'mechanical arts', comprising crafts, military science, navigation and geography, commerce, agronomy and housekeeping, forestry and zoology, medical science and the courtly arts, and law; and a third series comprising the 'forbidden arts', which came under the jurisdiction of the Church. These latter were the pseudo-sciences of magic and divination, professional imposture, and fraudulent practice as craftsman or merchant.

The system of knowledge

Whereas the seven liberal arts constituted worthy employment for a free burgher and were the elementary subjects of the cathedral and monastery schools, as well as the urban schools and arts faculties of the newly-emerging universities of the late Middle Ages, the mechanical arts, which were based on numerous ancient foundations, became the fixed asset of urban scholarly literature, exerting a strong influence on the deep economic and cultural structure of towns. The reverse process is documented for advances in medicine, astronomy, town planning, commerce, architecture, fortifications, natural science and much besides in this literature. Their diverse professional vocabulary seems only in part to have been made accessible to the development of the German language. The volume of specialist literature is highlighted by the fact that, unlike poetry, it evolved uninterruptedly from the eighth century onwards with no gaps or backward steps. On the contrary, it was in many instances translated into other European languages, just as German specialist literature was in turn fed by countless translations that appeared in the service of disseminating knowledge. The significant date of 1250, which marks a watershed in the Hohenstaufen literary age, does not exist for specialist literature.

Late medieval universality

Wittenwiler's *Ring* provides poetic evidence of a well-documented propensity for universalism and the encyclopedic in the late Middle Ages that was at first curbed in secular specialist literature. One of the earliest examples of this is the *Summarium Henrici*, which appeared in 1010 near Worms, written in Latin but glossed in German. It is extant in a number of manuscripts, and comprises the jargon of the mechanical arts and law. Commissioned by Henry the Lion, the *Lucidarius* appeared between 1190 and 1195, a comprehensive theory of the world comprising the Kingdom of God (human beings, animals, the elements, constellations, etc.), the Kingdom of Christ (the Church and the expectation of grace) and the Kingdom of the Holy Spirit (the Day of Judgement, the Last Things). Like other theories of the world, the *Lucidarius* also provided a welcome quarry for poetic allusion. Familiarity with this literature is often indispensable to interpretation of the poetry of the period. The impact of *Lucidarius* may be judged from the fact that it has survived in the form of 66 manuscripts and 85 printed editions.

The most important German encyclopedia of the late Middle Ages is the *Buch der Natur* by the Regensburg canon Konrad of Megenburg, which appeared around 1349–50. It is a systematic account of nature in eight volumes: Man and his nature, the sky and planets, animals, trees, herbs, precious stones, metals, and wonderful springs. However extraordinary, haphazard and occasionally incomprehensible this specialist literature may appear as the product of a syncretic, cosmologically Christian world-view, it did nonetheless form, in conjunction with the increasing importance of the universities and of urban scholarship, the historical roots of modern specialist literature. Without it – despite the huge debt it owed to a long Graeco-Latin, Islamic and Judaic tradition – our own scientific age could hardly have come about.

HUMANISM AND THE
REFORMATION

O Jahrhundert, o Wissenschaften! (Oh Century! Oh Sciences!)
Renaissance Humanism

Ulrich von Hutten was one of the most outstanding German Humanists.
A letter of his dated 25 October 1518 to the Nuremberg patrician Willibald
Pirckheimer amounts to a summing-up of the contemporary situation. In
it Hutten gives expression to the Humanist feeling for life, representing a
whole generation in an age whose intellectual and artistic flowering could
be seen as a decisive breakthrough and a departure from the Middle Ages:
'O Jahrhundert, o Wissenschaften! Es ist eine Lust zu Leben, wenn auch
noch nicht in der Stille. Die Studien blühen, die Geister regen sich. Barba-
rei, nimm dir einen Strick und mache dich auf Verbannung gefasst.' ('O
century! O sciences! It is a delight to be alive, even if not yet in tranquillity.
Study is burgeoning, the mental faculties are stirring. Barbarity, take a rope
and prepare yourself for banishment.')

What Hutten could not know was that at the very moment he was
singing the praises of his century Renaissance Humanism was already
reaching its zenith, only a short while later to lose its resonance – in some
cases rapidly, in others more gradually. The year 1527 saw the 'Sacco di
Roma', the dreadful ravaging of Renaissance Rome by the mercenary army
of the German emperor Karl V – an event that is customarily regarded as
marking the end of the Renaissance.

The Italian model

The beginning of the Italian Renaissance is generally set in the thirteenth
century, with the end of Hohenstaufen rule. This created a power vacuum
in which the towns and a new urban culture could begin to develop. The
first stirrings of Renaissance Humanism in Germany were discernible
around 1400, and the first signs of the Humanist movement in the second
half of the fifteenth century. Among the innovations evident prior to the

shift towards the Renaissance in the empire, some of those concerning world-view and art in particular may be mentioned here.

Mysticism and the official Church

Late medieval German mysticism coincides with the first high points in the Italian Renaissance. Research has revealed links between this mysticism and Italian poetry, such as those between Dante and the mysticism of nuns in Helfta (near Magdeburg). Like Renaissance Humanism the *unio mystica*, the sought-after union with God in innermost saintliness, the soul of the believer, was disquieting to the clergy. The official Church and its hierarchy found itself threatened with superfluousness, a danger that was not lost on them (hence the Inquisition proceedings against and conviction of the most important of the German mystics, Meister Eckhart, in 1329). With the *devotio moderna* the fourteenth century saw the rise of a new form of piety, documented in literary form in the work *De imitatione Christi* by Thomas à Kempis. Printed in 1470, it remains one of the most widely disseminated devotional books in the Christian world next to the Bible itself. Erasmus of Rotterdam, later regarded as the leading figure of northern European Humanism, gained his knowledge of classics and Humanism at the schools of the 'Brothers of the Common Life'. New developments in the arts, particularly in architecture and painting (mural painting, altar-pieces and the appearance of panel painting), became known by the art-historical terms 'Gothic' or 'Late Gothic'. A special development in Western Europe (France, the Netherlands and England) was *ars nova*, involving an attempt to adopt and cultivate ancient subject-matter, as well as nature studies (hence the development *inter alia* of history painting, portraits, and landscape and genre painting in old Dutch painting).

Italian Renaissance Humanism

The introduction of Italian Renaissance Humanism into the unsettled world of the late Middle Ages was the result of deliberate intervention on the part of Italian and other Humanists. Foremost among these Italians from the German viewpoint was Enea Silvio Piccolomini (after 1458 Pope Pius II), who tirelessly expounded and propagated the principles of Renaissance Humanism in both his letters and instructional works. His Renaissance novella *De duobus amantibus historia* (*A Tale of Two Lovers*, 1444), a story of adultery, influenced the rise of the short prose genre in Germany. The same is true of *Facetien*, by another Italian author of the time, Poggio, which had a marked impact on the rise of the *Schwank* genre. The *Facetien*, published in 1452, are very short prose texts, each with a surprise ending. Secretary to a number of popes, Poggio was also well-known for rediscovering classical works. C.F. Meyer paid tribute to him in his novella

Plautus im Nonnenkloster. The frivolity of Enea's novella was a vexation to the Church, and was later to vex the author himself when he came to seek the highest office in the Church. Despite its origins in the back chambers of the Vatican, however, all the derision and scorn of Poggio's *Facetien* is directed at the highest clerical ranks. Other Humanists of the period made similar attacks on the old faith and the old Church.

The Donation of Constantine

Critical probing of one of the cornerstones of the Papacy – worldly rule – was made by the Italian humanist Lorenzo Valla, who in 1440 succeeded in exposing what was known as the Donation of Constantine as a fake. This fictitious deed of donation implied that the Emperor Constantine had ceded the western Roman Empire to Pope Sylvester. Valla's work became one of Luther's main items of documentary evidence in his argument against the papacy. He used it in his 1520 reformation programme pamphlet *An den christlichen Adel* after seeing Valla's work in a printed edition commissioned by the German Humanist Ulrich von Hutten in Basle in 1518–19.

The Ploughman from Bohemia

The history of Renaissance poetry in Germany begins with an isolated – because early – experiment that nonetheless marks a first-rate literary achievement and a piece of avant-garde art whose essential features put it at least a hundred years ahead of its time. At some time in 1400–1 an author named Johann von Tepl, a municipal clerk presumed to have belonged to the Prague chancery Humanist circle, wrote a prose poem in the form of a disputation: *Der Ackermann aus Böhmen* (*The Ploughman from Bohemia*), printed in Bamberg around 1460. The protagonists in this disputation are the ploughman, actually the 'author' since he says of himself 'Von vogelwat ist mein pflug', meaning that a quill, or feather, is his working tool, and Death. The use of prose is itself significant: it is the new modern form of expression. Verse and rhyme were now commonplace and identified with the Middle Ages. Another significant feature is that this is not a confrontation between two abstract principles, Death and Life in allegorical form, but between an allegory of Death and a human being, an individual of particular profession and social standing. Death is on the one hand defender of the medieval clerical world-view, propounding the notion of the futility of life and of the suffering inherent in earthly existence. On the other hand he also upholds the standpoint of those who rule: 'Doch glauben wir, dass ein Knecht Knecht bleibt, ein Herr Herr' ('Still we believe that a bondsman remains a bondsman and a lord a lord'). This lends the dialogue its social accent. Outraged, the author sets out to counter

Death, this herald of human futility and subjection. He brings Death, who has robbed him of his beloved wife, before the judgement seat of God. What he confronts his adversary with amounts to a modern notion of human life and happiness. The idea with which he starts out is that man is the greatest, most ingenious and free of all God's creatures ('Das grossartigste, das kunstreichste und der allerfreieste Werkstück des Schöpfergotts'). The main contributors to earthly happiness are love, marriage and the family. Man is said to be characterised not least by being the sole creature in possession of reason, 'den edlen Schatz' – 'that noble treasure'. On account of his courageous tackling of Death, God finds in favour of the plaintiff. Victory nonetheless remains with Death, since no rebel can be allowed to conquer Death – Death to which all life must succumb at last. The *Ackermann* poem forms part of the Humanist confrontation both with the old faith and the medieval view of man.

Itinerant Humanists

Around the middle of the fifteenth century, the so-called 'itinerant Humanists', such as Peter Luder and Samuel Karoch of Lichtenberg, appeared in Germany. As students and later as university teachers they sometimes changed the location of their employment from one semester to another, partly to avail themselves of the *studia humanitatis*, partly in order to teach other students. To find any foothold at all at German universities, Humanist teaching usually had to overcome opposition from established, scholastically-imbued traditional disciplines. The chief Humanist disciplines were classical languages, above all Latin, rhetoric, poetry and history. The lawyer and writer Gregor Heimburg was a contemporary of the itinerant Humanists. At first in the service of Enea Silvio as a secretary, he was later to become the Italian's most relentless German opponent in his period of office as Pope. Enea himself gives a most revealing miniature portrait of his antagonist:

> Es war aber Gregor ein schöner Mann, hochgewachsen, mit blühendem Gesicht, lebhaften Augen, kahlköpfig. Seine Redeweise wie seine Bewegungen hatten etwas Unbeherrschtes. Eigenwillig wie er war, hörte auf keinen anderen und lebte nach seiner Art, die Freiheit über alles stellend, so denn auch anstössig im Betragen, ohne Schamgefühl und zynisch. In Rom pflegte er nach der Vesper am Monte Giordano sich zu ergehen, schwitzend und als verachte er zugleich die Römer und sein eigenes Amt. Mit überhängenden Stiefelschäften, offener Brust, unbedecktem Haupt, aufgekrempelten Ärmeln kam er missvergnügt daher, ständig auf Rom, den Papst und die Kurie wie auf die Hitze Italiens schimpfend.'

But Gregor was a handsome man – bald, tall with a radiant expression and eyes full of vitality. There was something slightly out of control about his speech and movements. Wilful as he was, he paid no heed to what others said and went his own way, valuing freedom above all else. This made his manner offensive, without shame and cynical. When in Rome, it was his habit to take a stroll up the Monte Giordano after Vespers, sweating as if in contempt both of the Romans and his own office. Bare-chested, head uncovered, sleeves rolled up and with the legs of his boots hanging over, he would return in ill temper, giving out a stream of invective against Rome, the Pope, the Curia and the heat of Italy, all at the same time.

Humanists as translators

Another circle of German Humanists is known from its outstanding work as the 'early Humanist translators'. This work still largely revolved around the popularisation of Humanist ideas in Germany by making them accessible to a German readership. From 1461 onwards, for example, Niclas von Wyle compiled his *Translationen* (or *Translatzen*), editing them as an anthology in 1478. The total of eighteen documents attests once again that Humanism did not have to connote a pre-eminent concern with antiquity. Besides a medieval text and one by a contemporary Swiss author, they contain only one piece from the classical period, a story by Lucian called the *Eselsgeschichte* (*The Tale of the Ass*, dating from the second century). The impressive remainder comprises no less than 15 pieces by Italian Renaissance authors. Two derive from lesser-known authors, two from Boccaccio, two from Petrarch, four by Enea Sylvio and as many as five by Poggio. Heinrich Steinhöwel similarly translated Boccaccio among others, in particular his famous collected edition *De claris mulieribus* (*On Famous Women*, 1360–2). He also produced a German version of the hundredth novella of the *Decamerone*, *Griseldis*, which made the work popular in Germany under the title of the *Volksbuch*. It continued to appear in a series of revised versions (including one by Hauptmann) into the present century. Albrecht von Eyb supplied skilful translations of Plato as well as original works incorporating above all classical source material, including three treatises on a problem that is also topical today: that of women (the best-known remains *Das Ehebüchlein*, printed in Nuremberg in 1472).

Konrad Celtis

Konrad Celtis is regarded as the most profoundly gifted poet of the subsequent generation, and indeed of the whole of German Renaissance Humanism. He was the first German to be crowned as poet, by Emperor

Friedrich III in Nuremberg in 1487. His first major poetry work was the *Quattuor libri amorum*, (*Four Volumes of Love Poetry*, 1502). The editing accomplishments of this German 'arch-Humanist', as he has been styled, include the rediscovery of such seminal works as the *Germania* by Tacitus, as well as the tenth century oeuvres of the first German poetess, Hrotsvith of Gandersheim (the Celtis edition appeared in 1501). Celtis also proved himself as an organiser of cultural politics. Following the model of the Italian academies, for example that in Florence, he founded around 1490 a number of scholarly societies for the promotion of education and the arts, calling them 'Sodalitates', i.e. associations. Two of these were located in Vienna and Heidelberg respectively.

The Dunkelmännerbriefe

In 1517, the year of Luther's thesis on indulgences, the second part of the *Dunkelmännerbriefe* (*Epistolae obscurorum virorum*) by the German Humanist Ulrich von Hutten appeared, the first, written mainly by Hutten's tutor Crotus Rubeanus, having been published two years earlier. The work as a whole, therefore, is a joint effort, a brilliant satire on the life of a degenerate clergy that ranks among world literature. It comprises over a hundred invented letters, ostensibly from representatives of the clergy, exposing their narrowness of mind, hypocrisy, corruption and scant self-knowledge. Both in his person and in his works, Ulrich von Hutten symbolises the shift among parts of the Humanist movement to the Reformation cause. It was a fundamental conviction of this knight that Germany was in need of a Reformation: 'Dass Teutschland einer Reformation bedürfe'. This is expressed, in the viewpoint of the papal nuncio Alexander: 'Schon hat er sich einen Umsturz der gesamten deutschen Verhältnisse vorgesetzt' ('He has resolved to overthrow the entire German order'). For a time, Hutten's impact came close to that of Luther in terms of historical developments, perhaps even exceeding it. Hutten had the gift of giving expression to the feelings and needs of broad sections of society. Hutten's themes were the struggle against 'tyrants', who 'all belonged in Hell after all' ('doch alle in die Hölle'), against Rome, its wealth and its machinations, and against the crimes and wars of the popes. Subject-matter of this kind clearly came into its own in German. Hutten's move from the Latin of the Humanists to writing in German proved to have significant repercussions. Not only did other major authors also change over to German, but at the same time public opinion acquired a revolutionary character. The whole German nation was now, as it were, being addressed face to face, since, as Hutten explained, Latin was not known to all ('einem jeden nit bekannt'). Important texts originally written in Latin he now either translated himself or had translated, above all the *Gesprächbüchlein* (*Book of Dialogues*, 1521). His view of the world, the perspective of a nobleman, did make itself felt up to a point in terms of the position and prejudices of the class from which he originated, but class barriers could be overcome, not least by Hutten the Humanist. He asserted that only 'eigene Leistung', ('one's own accomplishment') could justify the privilege of regarding oneself as noble. All other forms of nobility were valueless. 'Diejenigen, die das Zeug zum Ruhm haben and nutzen, was wir geringschätzen, müssen uns in der Tat vorgezogen werden, selbst wenn sie Söhne von Webern und Schumachern sind' ('Those who have the makings of fame and make use of that which we despise must indeed be preferred over us, even if they are the sons of weavers and shoemakers'). The watchword that runs through all his writings in the years of struggle was 'freedom'. 'Ich sehe, dass an allen Orten an Freiheit gedacht und Bündnisse zu ihrer Verwirklichung gemacht werden' ('I see in all places people thinking of freedom and joining together to bring it about'), he concludes with satisfaction, himself hoping to urge 'aller Gemüt zur Wiederbringung allgemeiner Freiheit' ('all people to the restoration of general freedom'). In his mind these efforts included the use of force: 'Unser Vorsatz kann aber nit wohl ohne Schwertschlag und Blutvergiessen Fortschritte machen' ('Our purpose can probably not be furthered without the wielding of swords or the shedding of blood').

Polemics and satire

Another wing of the Humanists did not join the Reformation, rather opposing it and its representatives, for example Erasmus of Rotterdam, often in a polemical manner. And yet he too criticised both the dogma and the institution of the old Church hardly less vehemently than Luther and his followers. In the crucial year of 1517 he published his polemic treatise *Querula pacis* (*Plea for Peace*). It is the first comprehensive modern peace programme, and is presented in the form of a monologue by Peace. Peace is pilloried by wars and the warmongering policies of the popes and princes of the Church. War is seen not as a matter of fate, but as a human affair, something brought about by men: 'Although life brings so many almost intolerable hardships with it, men in their madness bring the overwhelming majority of their troubles upon themselves'. The perpetrators of war are without exception the 'princes, who know full well that peace among the people threatens their power'. 'A factual examination of the causes of war would show that all wars are started by princes for their own advantage and to the disadvantage of the people.' He objects to the establishment of 'nurseries of war', recommending that war be proscribed: 'All men must forswear war and defame it together. In public life and private circles alike, however, they should preach, praise and hammer home the cause of peace.'

'Die Grundsuppe des Wuchers, der Dieberei und Räuberei': ('The fount of all usury, theft and robbery') – social criticism and the Reformation programme From *Reformatio Sigismundi* to Hans Sachs

Perhaps the most famous passage of social criticism in German literature prior to the *Communist Manifesto* is contained in Thomas Müntzer's lampooning rejoinder to Luther, the *Hochverursachte Schutzrede* (1524). It contains some extremely resolute statements:

> Sieh zu, die Grundsuppe des Wuchers, der Dieberei und Räuberei sind unsere Herren und Fürsten. Sie nehmen alle Geschöpfe zum Eigentum. Die Fische im Wasser, die Vögel in der Luft, die Pflanzen auf Erden, ihnen muss alles gehören. Darüber lassen sie dann Gottes Gebot ausgehen unter die Armen und sagen: Gott hat befohlen, du sollst nicht stehlen. Aber selber halten sie sich nicht daran. Indem sie nun alle Menschen peinigen und den armen Ackermann und Handwerksmann und alles, was lebt, schinden und schaben, so muss, wenn einer von diesen sich dann am Allergeringsten vergreift, er hängen. Dazu spricht dann der Doktor Luther: Amen. Die Herren machen das selber, dass ihnen der arme Mann feind wird. Die Ursache des Aufstands wollen sie nicht beseitigen. Wie kann es dann auf die Dauer gutwerden?

> See, the fount of all usury, theft and robbery is our lords and princes. They take all creatures for their own possession: the fish in the water, the birds of the air, the plants on the earth, everything has to belong to them. They then have the idea put about among the poor, saying 'God has commanded you not to steal'. But they do not hold to this themselves. While they themselves then torment people and ill-treat and do harm to the poor ploughman and journeyman and everything that lives, any of these latter who misappropriates the smallest trifle must hang for it. Doctor Luther's answer to all this is 'Amen'. It is the nobility themselves who make the poor man their enemy. They do not want to do away with the cause of rebellion. So how can it be put right in the long run?

The age of the Reformation was not the first to hear complaints of this kind: they had been voiced centuries earlier. When opposition tendencies were asserting themselves forcefully in the middle of the thirteenth century, which witnessed the first glimmerings of resistance to the social constraints of the Middle Ages, Freidank had written: 'Die Fürsten unterwerfen mit Gewalt/ Feld, Gebirge, Wasser, Wald, / dazu an Tieren alles, wild und zahm. / Verführen mit der Luft sehr gern auch so. / Die aber muss uns allen gemeinsamen bleiben: / Und könnten sie uns den Sonnenschein entwenden, / desgleichen Winde und den Regen, / sie liessen sich die

Steuer dafür in Gold aufwiegen' ('By force do princes subdue / Field, mountains, water, woods, / Adding to them the animals, wild and tame. / Gladly would they treat the very air the same. / But that must remain common to all: / Could they purloin the sun from us, / and do the same with wind and rain, / they would weigh out the taxes for them in gold').

Opposition movements

Nevertheless, whereas in previous centuries complaints and accusations of this kind had been thin on the ground, after 1500 they gained both in weight and in importance. The painter Albrecht Dürer acknowledged 'dass man uns unser Blut und unseren Schweiss raubt und abstiehlt, und dass das Gestohlene den Müssiggängern verzehrt wird, was eine Schande und ein Verbrechen ist. Arme kranke Menschen müssen deshalb Hungers sterben' ('We are robbed of our very blood and sweat, and what is stolen from us is consumed by the idle, which is a scandal and an outrage. Poor sick people are therefore obliged to perish of hunger'). The printer, writer and martyr Hans Hergot, who rejected both worldly and clerical authorities, wrote: 'Ihr Schriftgelehrten lehrt den Adel, dass er der Kuh nichts in dem Euter lasse und die Milch gänzlich aussauge, auf dass die Jungen keine mehr vorfinden. Wirklich, es ist der Punkt erreicht, dass sie alles ausgesogen haben, weder Milch noch Blut ist mehr da, Frauen und Kinder müssen vor Hunger sterben' ('You men of letters teach the nobility to leave nothing in the cow's udder and to extract every drop, so that the boys find nothing left. Indeed, the point has now been reached where all has been sucked out of them: neither milk nor blood remains, and women and children are having to die of hunger').

The exploited, therefore, were peasants and journeymen, especially peasants, since the entire nation lived on their produce as depicted in the 'tree of ranks' of the day, which represented the social hierarchy in the form of a tree. At the bottom of the tree, portrayed as the roots and interwoven among them, were the peasants. Above them, on the overhanging branches closest to the ground, were journeymen and tradespeople. Above them were the clergy and princes of the Church, the nobles and the secular princes. Close to the crown were emperors, kings and the Pope. Finally, at the very top, there were two more peasants, one playing music, the other sleeping – partly in irony, partly implying that peasants are the alpha and omega of all things. The fact that peasants were the most enslaved and oppressed of all social classes is attested and lamented again and again by contemporary authors – from the 'Upper Rhenish revolutionary' to Hutten, and from Thomas Müntzer to Hans Sachs.

The hierarchy of ranks is set in motion

Just how clearly the social structure of the time was discernible to contemporaries themselves is demonstrated by Hans Sachs in his Shrovetide play *Ein Bürger, Bauer, Edelmann, die holen Krapfen*. Here the peasant, speaking to the burgher and the nobleman, declaims: 'O ihr tut euch alle beide ernähren, / Gott weiss wohl wie: Ich darfs nicht nennen', meaning that in order to obtain their livelihood they employ any means, ranging from exploitation to violent pillage. The peasant describes his own tasks as follows: 'Ackern, Säen, / Schneiden, Dreschen, Heuen und Mähen, / Pferdepflege und andere Arbeit mehr. / Hiermit ich euch alle beide ernähr.' Although the burgher also carries out productive work, he does so in a less arduous manner: 'Meinen Unterhalt erwerbe ich in der Ruh, / brauche nicht solch grobe Arbeit zu tun.' The nobleman, however, in contrast to the other two, declares that he is fully occupied at his princely court: 'ohne Arbeit, aber mit Rente und Zins'. Speaking to the peasant, he declares: 'Wir haben die Regierung inne, / alle Macht liegt in unseren Händen. / Du musst uns liegen unter den Füssen.' This is how the facts of exploitation in oppression are presented, seen through the eyes of an urban shoemaker-poet.

The old order and progress

Besides the deplorable state of affairs described by the authors of the time as the *Grundsuppe* or fount of all ills, another more recent factor was becoming apparent, even to contemporaries. This was progress, which was breaking down the old order and beginning to superimpose itself on the key medieval conflict between the peasant and noble ranks, threatening to dismantle the entire social structure. A new sovereign had made its entrance, in the words of Hans Sachs: 'das Geld', money, which 'jetzunder in ganzer Welt regiert' ('now rules the whole world'). In Sach's perception money essentially divided humanity into grand and petty thieves and nothing else. The conditions that permitted this development were created by the separation of commercial from agrarian production, and by the rise of an urban culture, with its concomitant concentration of the production of goods and of trade. Money, or the tradespeople, shopkeepers and usurers who controlled it, contributed to a breakdown of the traditional economy, characterised by small-scale trade and bartering.

Criticism of tradespeople

Johann Eberlin of Günzburg, proponent of the Reformation, wrote: 'Nachdem die Händler und Kaufleute derart überhand genommen haben, ist der Adel verdorben, die Bürger in den Städten haben nichts, das Landvolk geht betteln' ('With this proliferation of tradesmen and merchants, the nobility is ruined, the burghers in the towns have nothing, and the country folk go begging'). The pass to which things had come by that time is described as follows: 'Die ganze Menschheit ist auf Kaufen und Verkaufen ausgerichtet' ('The whole of humanity is bent on buying and selling'); 'Solche Kaufleute und Händler schaffen nichts als die Zerstörung der Länder und der Christenheit' ('Such merchants and tradesmen will accomplish nothing except the destruction of the nations and of Christendom'). Eberlin was thus fully aware of the implications of this new phenomenon, a society based on buying and selling that was also manifesting a new kind of conflict between the traders and shopkeepers on the one hand and the 'burgher in the towns' on the other. A new relationship of dependancy was arising between the tradespeople and shopkeepers, then also termed *Verleger* (lit. 'publishers' of goods of all kinds, although nowadays only books), and the journeyman or wage worker. This explains the hardship of plying crafts and trades in those days; as Hans Sachs expresses it: 'Mit meinem Handwerk, das ich treibe, / Damit gewinne ich kaum das Brot. / Im Haus ist nichts als Sorge und Not. / Ich arbeite hart Tag und Nacht. / Meine Arbeit wird mir gänzlich verachtet. / Mein Verleger beugt mich aufs äusserste. / Der Kaufmann drückt mir den Preis meines Produkts' ('The work of my hands that I ply, / Hardly earns me my daily bread. / There is nothing but want and distress in the house. / I work hard day and night. / My work is utterly despised. / My buyer oppresses me in the extreme. / The merchant keeps down the price of my product').

Reaction among writers

Contemporary writers could respond to this state of affairs in various ways, with bitter complaint or resignation, irony, satire, sarcasm, and derision, or with discussion of reforming issues. Politico-social revolution was not yet on the cards in fifteenth century Germany as it was in Bohemia, where Hussite church reforms combined cultural renewal with political revolution, and revolution with military expansion. The name derives from Jan Huss, the Czech reformer burned at the stake during the Council of Constance (1414–18) after being promised safe conduct. The Council of Constance was one of the political events on which people at that time pinned their hopes for reform of their intolerable conditions, and particularly for church reform, hence the name 'reform council'.

The 'reformations'

In fifteenth and sixteenth century German literature a literary genre combining social analysis with discussion of reforming issues came to be known as the *Reformationen*. The best-known piece of its kind is the *Reformatio*

Sigismundi, or *Reformation of the Emperor Sigismund* of 1439, whose author used the name of the Emperor Sigismund to lend his ideas greater weight. It was a widely disseminated work: 17 post-1439 manuscripts are known, as well as a number of printed editions dating from 1476 until shortly before the peasants' war. Generations before the peasant revolution of 1525, therefore, an author was voicing the need to abolish serfdom, the cornerstone of the entire feudal means of production.

> Es ist eine unerhörte Sache, dass man in der frommen Christenheit das grosse Unrecht eigens enthüllen muss, welches vor sich geht, wenn einer, obwohl Gott zuschaut, so gierig ist, dass er es wagt, zu einem Menschen zu sprechen: 'Du bist mein eigen!' Es ist daran zu denken, dass Gott... uns befreit und von allen Banden löst.... Darum wisse jedermann, der lebt, der seinen Mitchristen als Eigentum erklärt, dass er nicht Christ ist.

> It is a disgrace in pious Christendom to have to expose the ultimate great injustice being perpetrated when, in the full sight of God, a man is so full of greed that he can dare to say to another 'You are my property!' It behooves us to recall that God... will loose us from all our chains.... Let everyone who lives, and declares his fellow Christian to be his property, therefore be mindful that he is no Christian.

This meant putting an old Saxon legal tradition into effect. The *Sachsenspiegel* of Eike von Repgow had already proscribed serfdom. The author of the *Reformation of Emperor Sigismund* further declared the right of serfs to resist lords who refused to grant them their freedom. It was permitted to 'do away with them completely' ('ganz abtun'), and if a monastery refused such a claim, it would have to be destroyed.

'Property is theft'

Another anonymous author, known as the 'Upper Rhenish revolutionary', compiled a comprehensive reform strategy between 1498 and 1510: *Das Buch der hundert Kapitel und vierzig Statuten (The Book of the Hundred Chapters and Forty Statutes)*. He, too, started from the assumption that serfdom had to be abolished: 'Das ist Diebstahl und schlimmer als jeder andere Diebstahl wegen der damit verbundenen Machtausübung. Der Adlige sagt: 'Du bist mein Eigenmann!' Aber die Wahrheit lautet: Wir Deutschen sind frei, frei nach dem Gesetz Kaiser Karls des Grossen, alle edel' ('That is theft, and worse than all other forms of theft on account of the exercise of power associated with it. The nobleman says 'You are my liegeman!' But the truth is that we Germans are free – free according to the law of Emperor Charles the Great, all noble'). This author was no less clearly aware of the other deplorable factor in the contemporary situation, brought about by the goods–money relationship: 'Ein Wucherer... ist böser als ein Mörder' ('A usurer... is worse than a murderer'). The principle he sets against the deplorable state of affairs he is criticising, against self-interest, is 'der gemeine Nutzen' ('the common interest'). The conceptual opposition of self-interest and the common interest is a ubiquitous one in the socially critical literature of the day, a key word-pair that recurs again and again in the pamphlets of the peasant war period as well as in Hans Sachs, in the *Schildbürgerbuch* (*Chapbook of the Gothamites*) through to Enlightenment literature.

It also shaped the world-view of the foremost contemporary critic of German literature at the end of the fifteenth century: Sebastian Brant. His outstanding work, *Das Narrenschiff* (*Ship of Fools*, 1494), composed in rhyming couplets in the old style, presents all social groupings as fools voyaging to the land of Narragonian. The literary satire derives from a lament on the decline of faith and the concomitant decline of the Empire. The example of ancient Rome is put forward to the reader as a warning: 'Zur Freiheit wardst du hingeführt, / Als dich gemeinsamer Rat (Nutzen) regiert. / Doch als auf Hoffart man bedacht, / Auf Reichtum und also grosse Macht, / Und Bürger wider Bürger stritt, / Und des gemeinen Nutzens man gedachte nit, / Da fing die Macht zu verfallen an....' ('You were led to freedom, / As long as the common interest reigned. / But when thoughts turned to the ways of court, / To wealth and great power, / And burgher fought with burgher / And no thought more given to the common interest, / So power began to crumble....')

Brant could see no way out in his own time, and cherished little hope for improvement. He puts forward no suggestions for reform. Despite this, his poetry, for all its conservative tenor, displays a disposition towards typical burgher thinking, for example in his rejection of hereditary nobility in favour of inner nobility, 'Aus Tugend ist aller Adel gemacht' ('All nobility derives from virtue'), thus making nobility accessible to the burgher. Brant's *Ship of Fools* was reprinted no less than 25 times within a century, as well as undergoing numerous adaptations and translations.

'Derhalben musst du, gemeiner Mann, selber gelehrt werden' ('Therefore, common man, you yourself must be taught'): the discovery of the word as weapon

Pamphlet literature

The triumphal procession of both religious and political renewal in the sixteenth century that was known as the Reformation was contributed to in no small measure by literature, and one literary medium in particular that was experiencing an early flowering: the pamphlet. As a result of shifts in social structure from about 1400 onwards, the consciousness of broad sections of society was undergoing a transformation, contributing in turn to the processes at work in society. This overall mechanism came to fruition in the language through the written and the spoken word, and above all in literature having the widest possible sphere of influence – primarily specialist and commercial non-fiction (*Gebrauchsprosa*) and didactic and pamphlet literature. What was new about this was the sheer power of the word. This entailed a newly-emerging consciousness, involving the imparting of ideas in conjunction with social reality – ideas arising and being formulated in the specific conditions of the age – thoughts, conceptions, suggestions and plans. Literature began to exert an influence on the will of large sections of the population through the dissemination of ideas, arguments, demands and calls to struggle, as well as through utopias and fantastic dreams. In other words, literature was becoming a call to action. In this sense, therefore, it was qualitatively different from what had gone before.

Popular literature

This rising new literature thus depicted reality in a hitherto uncustomary manner, reflecting it in such a way that it was found wanting and in need of change by the broadest sections of the people – the 'common man'. This new portrayal of reality was accompanied by a new image of man himself. The 'common man', the peasant and the journeyman, made his entrance into literature where formerly his existence had either not been acknowledged at all or where he had had at best a peripheral role shaped by the exigencies of rank. Now he stood on equal terms with knights, clerics and princes, sometimes even appearing to arbitrate as a judge of the nobility and clergy. Literature now found itself entrusted with the new mission of mediating intellectual and political discussion. The preconditions for this were provided by the recently increased capacity for dissemination arising from the invention of letterpress printing and the appearance of reasonably priced specialist and commercial works. Not the least of these new conditions was the surmounting of barriers of locality and rank. Writers – journeymen, clerical and secular scholars, knights and even princes – were now addressing not merely a single, rigidly-defined rank, but a general public repeatedly defined by Hans Sachs as the 'common man'. The result was a cultural revolution that went hand in hand with a literary one.

The literary revolution

The literary revolution that took place around 1520 was part and parcel of a far-reaching religious and political upheaval involving virtually the entire German nation fighting either for or against it. However, this religious and political revolution from 1517 to 1526 – from the date Luther nailed his controversial theses to the door of All Saints' Church at the castle in Wittenberg to the end of the peasant war – should not be treated as an illustration or literary commentary. Reformation writing cannot be properly understood by interpreting it merely as proof of an otherwise separate movement. It was an integral part of that historical movement, contingent on practice.

Although contemporary authors were in fact protagonists of a literary revolution, this was not made explicit. They did, however, knowingly convey the substance of the revolution, not unmindful of the effects of their pamphlets. Luther notes: 'Es meinen etliche, ich hätte dem Papst ohne alle Faust (i.e. Gewaltanwendung) mehr Schaden getan, als ein mächtiger König tun könnte, mit Reden und Schreiben' ('Some assert that I have done the Pope more harm without raising a finger against him than a mighty king could have done, merely by speaking and writing'). Similarly, although the literary revolution was part and parcel of a general upheaval, authors did not state this in so many words. Using the concept of the 'Reformation', their writings were neither more nor less than plans and slogans, testimonies and demands for a religious and political revolution. Where authors resisted or actively attempted to fend off revolution, this only served to underline its existence.

'Dass wir frei sind und es sein wollen' ('That we are free and wish so to be'): pamphlet literature

Pamphlet literature

Pamphlet literature of the first third of the sixteenth century is an outstanding area of study for anyone interested in the potential effects of literature, and in particular in the realisation of revolutionary goals by means of the word. The number of pamphlets published during the period in question is estimated at several hundred, and may even have exceeded a thousand. They were small printed works ranging from three or four to up to 50 or even 60 pages, seldom more. Considerable numbers of copies were printed, often a thousand or more, and a significant number of texts attained several reprints. The revolutionary dialogue *Karsthans* (then a popular term for 'peasant'), for example, was reprinted ten times in a single year. As far as can be ascertained today, the best-known catalogue of revolutionary demands, the *Twelve Articles* (1525), was reprinted 24 times in only a few weeks, as well as being reproduced in manuscript form. The *Twelve Articles* was disseminated within a very short time from the west of Germany to East Prussia, and from the Tyrol to England.

Literary genres

The literary genre of pamphlets embraced sermons and treatises, chronicles, tracts, bulletins, dialogues, and even drama, verse and song. Of these the treatise and dialogue were preponderant. The former, a sub-genre of the letter, differed from the private letter in that the matters addressed in them were taken to be of general interest. The dialogue was related to the spoken speech, thereby enshrining in literature the numerous discussions and conversations being conducted on the streets and squares and in private houses and taverns. The language used was shaped by the desire of authors for maximum power of expression and ease of understanding to achieve greater impact. Three particular stylistic means to this end stand out: lavish peppering with biblical verses, the extensive employment of idioms and proverbs and the use of vulgar vocabulary intended to insult and offend the opponent.

Religious discourse

There were numerous discussions and discourses, often conducted in the presence of thousands. The 'religious discourses' of those days would be comparable with the podium discussions of today, except that religious discourses were often continued over several weeks. Besides these, pamphlets made a substantial contribution towards creating what we would understand today as the first appearance of free public opinion. Created through arguments and words, it was a force to counteract religion and the ruling political powers. Looked at another way, the views and declared will of the oppressed in Germany for the first time in world history won the upper hand over the conceptual world of the ruling classes. The subjugated classes were journeymen and peasants, 'common men' involved throughout the country in religious and political controversy. There was no lack of hasty attempts at censorship. The 1521 Edict of Worms banned the penning, printing, sale and dissemination of books declaring war on the old Church and the old secular authorities, since such books were 'full of evil teaching and example'. The persecution of authors, printers and booksellers was severe, including exile, deprivation of civil rights, imprisonment and even execution. For this reason printers often lived outside the law and authors remained anonymous. Since German people in the Reformation period were oppressed by fundamental abuses, these inevitably constituted the main themes of the entire body of pamphlets. Suggestions as to how to bring about change, coming from authors themselves and during the 1524–6 period from spokesmen of the rebellion, may be summed up in various ways. The demand for freedom for the lower classes is to be found in almost all programmatic literature. The rebels fought for nothing more vehemently than for the abolition of serfdom. The third of the *Twelve*

Articles, denied most firmly by Luther and Melancthon, insisted 'we are free and wish so to be', amounting to a refusal to be 'owned' at all.

The revolutionary programme

Besides the demand for freedom, there was also a call for equality. The Taubertaler revolutionary tract, for example, contains the passage: 'Es sollen auch die Geistlichen und Weltlichen, Adligen und Nichtadligen in Zukunft sich an das allen gemeinsame Bürger- und Bauernrecht halten und nicht mehr sein als jeder andere' ('In future, the clerical and the secular, the noble and the non-noble should all adhere to one common law for burghers and peasants, and not be more than any other'). Inequality of rank, like serfdom in the Middle Ages, was largely upheld by force. The visible signs of this were the castles and monasteries, whose owners, the nobility and the clergy, consequently had to be parted from their estates. This implied either demolition or burning for all fortifications of this kind.

The call to brotherhood was another clarion call. In the *Neu-Karsthans* dialogue, for example, one of the minor orators declares: 'In der Kirche Christi soll Gleichheit bestehen, und wir sollen uns all untereinander als Brüder begegnen' ('There should be equality in the Church of Christ, and we should all meet one another as brothers'). Rebels of the 1524–6 period set up associations known as 'brotherly unions'.

Egalitarian principles

The modern character of the social and the political movements alike is attested by the significance that increasingly accrued to egalitarian principles during these years of struggle. One such principle was that of the *Wahl* or election, for example the right to free election of ministers of religion proclaimed in virtually all reform literature. Besides the right to free election a right was also claimed to dismiss holders of office who failed to fulfil their duties adequately – a right found today in all democracies. The chief concern of the pamphlet *An die Versammlung gemeiner Bauernschaft* is 'ob die Versammlung aller die Obrigheit absetzen darf' ('whether the assembly is permitted to remove all ruling representatives from office'), finally agreeing that it does. The author further raises the question of whether this was not the right time to elect tailors, shoemakers and peasants to positions of authority who would have to govern 'in brotherly fidelity' in order to uphold the 'Christian brotherhood'.

Criticism of the Church

Foremost among the many and diverse reflections aimed at removing the medieval conditions of exploitation, and one constantly reiterated in pamphlets, was the demand for the abolition of the plundering practices of the Church. 'Alles den Armen geraubte Gut ist im Hause der Reichen oder der Priester' ('All the wealth plundered from the poor is in the houses of the rich or of the priests'). Together with this demand, another call arose in contemporary literature, for example by Luther, to abolish the great trading companies, which he called 'monopolies'. In the *Reichsreformentwurf* (also known as the *Heilbronn programme sheet*), which is generally regarded as moderate in its demands, he called for the abolition of 'die Handelsgesellschaften, z.B. die Fugger, Höchstetter, Welser u. dergl., beseitigt werden, weil durch diese jedermann im Warenverkehr nach ihrem Gefallen entmündigt und bedrückt wird' ('the trading companies, for example the Fuggers [a family of Augsburg merchants in the fifteenth–sixteenth centuries who became a byword for underhand dealing, *Translator's note*], Höchstetters, Welsers and the like, since it is through them that everyone is impeded and oppressed in the traffic of his merchandise'). Pamphlet authors of the day now and then perceived the real motives behind ostensibly religious controversies, for example the case of Eck, a prominent opponent of the Reformation: 'Mein Lieber, der Eck ist kein Narr, er verteidigt die ökonomischen Machenschaften Fuggers' ('My dear man, Eck is no fool: he is defending the economic designs of Fugger').

Two reformers, one Reformation propagandist

In calling for tailors, shoemakers and peasants to be appointed to positions of authority, the author of the radical pamphlet *An die Versammlung gemeiner Bauernschaft* was merely putting forward what had already been convincingly urged in July 1524 by Thomas Müntzer in his formula that power now had to be passed into the hands of the common people. In the months that followed, Müntzer reiterated this declaration or view, which became something of a leitmotif, in a succession of letters and manifestos. The language in which these are couched marks the most radical form of revolutionary expressive force of which the times were capable. On 13 May 1525 during the weeks of fighting, once again from a military camp, he repeated the call that all creatures must be free and that 'power be given to the common people'. The principle of sovereignty of the people is being proclaimed here – the first declaration in German history of the intention to achieve democracy.

'God's lansquenet'

Like Luther and other major writers of the time, Müntzer was a theologian, although he also styled himself 'Landsknecht Gottes' ('lansquenet [mercenary soldier] of God'). Although starting out as a follower of Luther, Müntzer soon ceased to rely on 'Grace' and 'Scripture', speaking instead in terms of 'God's revelation' ('Offenbarung Gottes'), in which man was obliged to involve himself. Whereas for Luther the Bible was, as the Word of God, to be the guide for the Christian, for Müntzer the 'innerliche Wort', 'the inner word' of God was the proper basis for the Christian life. However, this 'inner word' could not be achieved without a concerted search for Truth, which the Christian could only hope to approach 'with a solemn heart'. All Müntzer's writings are imbued with this spirit and with his constant search for truth. They bear witness to Müntzer's conviction that the struggle for truth was inseparable from the struggle for outward living conditions that would enable everyone, and above all the common man, to begin living a Christian life. Müntzer's principle of revelation also differed from Luther's teaching in asserting that non-Christians, the 'heathen', even if they did not accept the Gospel, were still capable of receiving revelation, the 'inner word', through 'human reason'. In developing the concept of reason, Müntzer was preempting the Enlightenment and the Age of Reason.

The struggle for truth

The link between the struggle for truth and that for the creation of outward conditions that alone would ensure that the truth would be heard by all and put into practice in daily life was forcibly argued in Müntzer's theological-political writings. The three most significant of these all date from the first year of the peasant war, 1524: *Auslegung des andern Unterschieds Danielis* (an exegesis of Chapter Two of the Book of Daniel), *Ausdrückte Entblössung des falschen Glaubens* (*The Exposure of False Faith*) and the *Hochverursachte Schutzrede und Antwort wider das geistlose, sanftlebende Fleisch zu Wittenberg* (on Luther).

Spokesman for the lower classes

Müntzer the political thinker was spokesman for a struggling radical faction within an urban lower class that was the most extreme wing of the contemporary popular movement. It would be a misnomer categorically to label him a peasant leader because he led sections of the rebellious peasants side by side with members of the urban lower classes. Some modern accounts of his politics and personality occasionally even categorise him as a 'visionary' or 'utopian'. It was the leftist Protestant faction, reviled in the person of Müntzer, which, even in Luther's view, brought to fruition a process that the *Reformator* had merely set in motion. Müntzer's conviction that religious reform, the transformation of faith and changes in the intellectual sphere, was unthinkable without concomitant political and social reform, showed him to be far ahead of his time and extraordinarily modern.

Revolutionary mobilisation

Müntzer consequently propounded the idea of a complete transformation of the entire social order, probably envisaging something based on common property. In hoping to eliminate princely power, however, it was by no means his intention to abolish all states and governments, but purely and simply to achieve the sovereignty of the people and armed populist power. Acknowledgement of the fact of exploitation and oppression of the common people by princes, the nobility and the clergy was for him the starting-point for a fundamental transformation of the political and social order that for him meant 'eine vortreffliche, unüberwindliche Reformation' ('a superior, invincible Reformation'). The question that posed itself was whether in the given conditions the common man could reasonably expect to be guided by more learned people out of his position of dependency, brought about through no fault of his own. Müntzer was realistic enough to recognise that most of the intellectuals of his day did not see themselves as having been educated '[so] dass der gemeine Mann ihnen, indem sie ihn lehren, gleich werde' ('by teaching the common man to make him equal to themselves'). They were for the most part 'gottlose Heuchler und Schmeichler, die da redeten, was die Herren gern hören' ('godless hypocrites and bootlickers who say what their masters want to hear'), 'Schriftgelehrte, die gern fette Brocken essen am Hofe' ('scriveners fond of eating tasty morsels at court'). The way out in Müntzer's view was: 'Derhalben musst du, gemeiner Mann, selber gelehrt werden, auf dass du nicht länger irregeführt werdest' ('Therefore, common man, you yourself must become learned, so that you are no longer misled'). The common man being addressed, however, may lack the wherewithal to become learned, 'vorm Bekümmernis der Nahrung' ('weighed down by the cares of keeping body and soul together'). Change could not be instigated as long as the 'masters' still had power in their hands. That power therefore had to be wrested from them. Müntzer indeed regarded 'die Gewalt des Schwertes' ('the might of the sword') as lawful for 'eine ganze Gemeine' ('a whole community'). During those critical months, Müntzer was to reiterate like a leitmotif a quotation from Luke, Chapter 1, Verse 52: 'He has brought down monarchs from their thrones but the humble have been lifted high'.

Luther against the peasants

Martin Luther's hostile response to the peasant movement is well-documented. Equally well-known, indeed notorious, is his 1525 pamphlet *Wider die räuberischen und mörderischen Rotten der Bauern* (*Against the Murdering, Thieving Hordes of Peasants*), where he states that people now 'have the power to earn a place in Heaven with murder and bloodshed. . . .

Therefore, good lords, liberate here, rescue here, help here, take pity on the poor! Stab, slay, strangle here, who can!' ('mit Morden und Blutvergiessen den Himmel zu verdienen.... Darum, liebe Herren, befreit hier, rettet hier, helft hier, erbarmet euch der armen Leute! Steche, erschlage, würge hier, wer da kann!') Catholic opponents saw in this pamphlet, and in others against the peasants, an attempt on the part of the *Reformator* to distance himself from the popular peasant movement and to disclaim all responsibility or complicity. They pointed to other works by Luther in which he had not only failed to rule out the use of force, but had even condoned it, even against superiors and ecclesiastical authorities, quoting in particular the passage: 'Warum greifen wir sie nicht mit allen Waffen an und waschen unsere Hände in ihrem Blut?' ('Why then do we not attack them with all the weapons at our disposal and wash our hands in their blood?')

Thomas Murner

In the supreme satire on Luther, *Von dem grossen Lutherischen Narren* (1522) by Thomas Murner, the most gifted poet among Catholic counter-Reformationists, can therefore be found among the statutes of the 'Lutheran Order': 'Das is unser Plan und unser Mut, / Die Hände zu waschen in dem Blut, / Das wäre eine stolze Lutherei!' ('This, then is our plan and our resolve, / To wash our hands in blood, / What a proud Lutheran act!') From 1520 onwards Murner was a vigorous opponent of Luther, publishing *inter alia* in 1520 a rejoinder to Luther's pamphlet *An den christlichen Adel* with the same addressee as Luther's. He warned insistently that Luther would become the instigator of a peasant uprising, a modern Catilina. The call to freedom implicit in Luther's demands was indeed more far-reaching than that of anyone else: *Von der Freiheit eines Christenmenschen* (1520). Luther did not, however, declare the whole man free, but only man as a spiritual individual, the *Christenmensch*, not man as an entity with a body and a soul. As a subject, he owed obedience to governmental authority. The common man was not capable of sustaining such a split, however. 'Freedom' meant both political and religious freedom to him. This was condemned by Luther as an abomination: 'Das heisst christliche Freiheit ganz fleischlich machen' ('That would mean making Christian freedom a thing of the flesh'). His associate Melanchthon echoed loyally: 'Es ist auch ein Frevel und Gewalttat, dass sie nicht wollen leibeigen sein!' ('It is a sacrilege and an atrocity, that they do not want to be serfs!') The real meaning of this sacrilege and atrocity was the translation of the *Freedom of a Christian* into a form in this world – its manifestation in social reality.

The equality of all Christians

In going on to proclaim all Christians 'equal', Luther made equality, like freedom, merely an equality of souls. In his 1520 pamphlet *An den christlichen Adel deutscher Nation*, the main theme of which is the equality of all Christians, he pledges to tear down the three 'walls' behind which the Papists have entrenched themselves. The first of these, inequality, signifies the separation of clerical from secular rank, 'denn alle Christen sind wahrhaftig geistlichen Stands' ('since all Christians are in fact of clerical rank'). Since, however, this 'spiritual' demand by Luther did have one implicitly worldly aspect – the wresting of worldly power from the clerical estate – it was only a short step from equality in terms of spiritual demands to the question that Luther himself indeed directly posed: 'Warum ist dein Leib, Leben, Gut und Ehre so frei und nicht das meine, obgleich wir doch in gleicher Weise Christen sind, Taufe, Glauben, Geist und alle Dinge gleich haben? Wird ein Priester erschlagen, so liegt ein Land im Interdikt; warum nicht auch, wenn ein Bauer erschlagen wird?' ('Why is your body, life, property and honour so free and not mine, although we are both Christians in the same way, having the same baptism, faith, spirit, and all things in common? If a priest is slain, the land is under interdict; why not then also if a peasant is slain?') In terms of its justification, equality could equally well be extended to questions of theology. This demolished the second wall: the monopoly of the Pope on matters of doctrine. Anyone should have the right to his say, 'ein geringer Mensch' ('lowly man') being after all, argued Luther, sometimes even more judicious than the Pope ('der gemeine Mann verständig') The Bible could therefore be entrusted to him.

Luther's translation of the Bible

Luther began translating the Bible during his Wartburg period from 1521 onwards, the New Testament appearing in 1522. In 1534 he published the Old Testament, completing his German version of the entire text of the Bible. It was his greatest literary achievement and linguistically the most creative opus not only of Luther personally, but of his age. Its impact is comparable with the poetry and linguistic creativity of German Classicism around 1800. Although Luther did not create a new language, he did create a new High German literary language. He himself states that his style of speech was that of the Saxon chancery, 'welcher nachfolgen alle Fürsten und Könige in Deutschland, alle Reichsstädte' ('emulated by all German princes and kings and all imperial towns'). The basis for Saxon chancery German, however, was the speech of the East Middle German colonial region, 'East Middle German'. In order to make the German Bible accessible to a broad popular readership, however, Luther had to expand this chancery language by blending it with colloquial German, using words and idioms that would give expression to the imaginative and conceptual world of the common man. Explaining the theoretical principles of translation into German (*Treatise on Translation*, 1530), he wrote: 'Man muss die Mutter im Hause, die Kinder auf der Gasse, dem gemeinen Mann auf dem Markt darum fragen und denselbigen auf das Maul sehen, wie sie reden, und danach dolmetschen' ('We must consult the mother at home, the children on the street and the common man in the marketplace, looking to see what is on their lips, and then translate accordingly'). As a consequence of its rapidly acquired and enduring popularity, the Lutheran Bible made a substantial contribution to the development of a New High German written language based on East Middle German.

Checks on papal power

The third wall, papal autocracy, also came tumbling down. The community of all Christians, the Council, had greater authority than the Pope. In villages and towns, now even among the lower classes, the community of believers, the 'common people', had the right to elect and dismiss their ministers, as had initially been demanded in the first of the *Twelve Articles* of the peasants in 1525. The right to elect and dismiss a minister and all clergy up to the level of the Pope was one of Luther's demands, representing a democratising element, albeit one that he himself only recognised as appropriate to the clerical estate. His treatises clearly place established authority in general, with the possible exception of urban authorities, in a highly dubious light. Having proclaimed in 1520 that the Pope could be removed from office, he called on Christians in 1523 to remove or drive from office all rulers 'die an uns unchristlich gehandelt haben' ('who have treated us in an un-Christian manner') and who were therefore 'tyrants', a duty which he again hastily limited to the clergy: 'solche Bischöfe, Äbte, Klöster und was zu Regierungen dieser Art gehört' ('those bishops, abbots, monasteries and all that pertains to authorities of that kind'). Did this mean, however, that the rebels should not apply this to secular rulers, when Luther himself had designated them as established authorities of equal status with the clergy, more criminal than 'thieves and scoundrels' ('Räuber und Spitzbuben')? Luther was unmistakably increasing the chances of concerted action against the status quo and established authority with every such statement – quite apart from Müntzer's attempts to expose Luther's radicalism as a radicalism of words alone, and to demonstrate that Luther, who donated monasteries and churches to princes, was merely trying to make it up to the peasants.

Luther's work and doctrine alike exhibit two different faces, both to his contemporaries and to us – one looking back to rekindle aspects of medieval times, the other looking and pointing forward to the modern age. By effectively abolishing the gulf between the clerical and the secular estates and elevating what had previously been regarded as lowly professions, he further helped to create a new social ethos characterised by a particularly high regard for working people, and indeed for work itself. His was a truly revolutionary doctrine, although in many respects it was not carried to fruition. Together with the work of his contemporaries, his writings laid the foundations for a new world-view, and for the first genuinely serious social, spiritual, intellectual and political movement in Germany – a movement that had grown out of the destitution and penury of the lower classes. By selecting Rome and the Catholic Church, the most powerful feudal lords in Europe, as his main target for attack, he helped shift the *de facto* balance of power in favour of secular rulers and the urban upper classes, and to a future expansion of burgher power. This was his legacy to future generations.

Hans Sachs

'Jetzt müssen euch die Schuster lehren' ('Now the cobblers will have to teach you'), declared Hans Sachs in his prose dialogue *Disputation zwischen einem Chorherren und einem Schuhmacher* (*Disputation between a Choirmaster and a Shoemaker*, 1524), in which he depicts himself as 'der toller Schuster' ('the mad cobbler'). The thirty-year-old author acquired this appellation through his support for the Reformation. His epigrammatic poem *Die Wittenbergisch Nachtigall* (*The Wittenberg Nightingale*, 1523) proved to be one of the most powerful propaganda instruments of the religious resurgence. He had his share of difficulties when it came to writing and publishing, including the censorship and banning of his works. They were the difficulties of a political poet who dared to cultivate a rabble-rousing genre. The times he lived in gave him enough cause. Hans Sachs, whose work is most often associated with *Knittel* (doggerel verse in regular four-bar form) proved himself in 1524 at the height of these political events to be a prose writer of considerable stature. Four prose dialogues, whose significance was later to be rediscovered by Lessing, take the burning issues of the day as subjects for reflection. He resorted to this form on only two further occasions, in 1546 and 1554, at the time of the Schmalkal war, resulting in two more prose dialogues. In addition to prose dialogues his works include over 4,000 master songs, some 2,000 poems, epigrams, fables, rhymed *Schwänke*, both secular and religious songs, and 208 dramas. With its clear preponderance of secular subjects over religious ones, his choice of material marked a decisive step towards the secularisation of German verse, especially in drama.

Hans Sachs was Germany's finest middle-class poet. A three-fold set of barriers circumscribed the life and work of the lower middle classes in those days: the barrier of the guild, barriers connected with urban life as opposed to rural and the social barriers associated with the transition from the medieval to the modern age. These three-fold limitations help to explain his narrow lower-middle-class morality, such as when he puts forward the Tristan and Isolde tragedy as an example of 'unordentlicher Liebe' ('illicit love') on the grounds of pre-marital sex and adultery, or when Siegfried (Seufried) appears as an example of disobedient son and apprentice:

Seufried: Ei, warum gibst du mir so einen kleinen Hammer? Einen grossen will ich führen. (Der Schmied gibt ihm einen grossen Hammer.)

Seufried: Ja der tut meiner Stärke gebühren. (Seufried tut einen grauenerregenden Schlag auf den Amboss.)

Schmied: Ei, das Aufschlagen taugt gar nicht.

Seufried: Aber ihr habt mich doch zuvor unterrichtet, Ich sollte nicht faul sein, weidlich darauf schlagen? Das habe ich getan, warum tust du klagen!

Knecht: Mich dünkt, du bist recht bei Sinnen.

Seufried: Halt, halt, dessen sollst du werden innen! (Er schlägt mit dem Hammerstiel Meister und Knecht hinaus.)

Such a rebellion in the workshop was horrendous conduct in the eyes of a master craftsman of the day. Honouring the marriage bond, filial obedience, and above all obedience at the workplace and similar moral qualities were regarded as vital necessities to guild burghers. Lower-middle-class guild morality was nothing less than a precondition for existence. Without the iron laws to which they themselves submitted, they would have been unable to survive. Nevertheless, the narrowness of his moral code and the threefold barriers of his class by no means prevented this master shoemaker–poet from gaining a clear insight into the economic and political mechanisms of the day. His works mirror the social tensions of his age.

The literary legacy of Hans Sachs is an accurate picture of the society he lived in – a fact which remains an inestimable merit of his writings to this day. Seeing the exploitation of peasants, he was equally vigorous in deploring the conditions of the urban lower classes: 'Weiter regiert die Profitsucht gewaltiglich unter den Kaufherren und Verlegern. Sie drücken ihre Arbeiter und Stückwerker, wenn diese ihnen ihre Arbeit und Ware bringen oder neue Arbeit heimtragen. Da tadeln sie ihnen ihre Arbeit aufs Schärfste. Dann steht der arme Arbeiter zitternd bei der Tür, mit geschlossenen Händen, stillschweigend, damit er des Kaufherrn Huld nicht verliere' ('The craving for profits continues to rage among the chief merchants and tradesmen. They oppress their labourers and piece-workers when they bring the results of their labours and their wares, or take fresh work home. That is when they censure their work most bitterly. Then the poor unfortunate artisan stands trembling at the door, silent, his hands obediently folded so as not to lose favour with his merchant master'). Sachs' voice was that of the simple people, the craftsmen, artisans and peasants. This did not preclude him, however, from depicting the same simple people, above all peasants, in a comical light in his *Schwänke* and Shrovetide plays. He wrote and composed for the 'common man' and no-one else: even his *Wittenberg Nightingale* was intended to make the Reformation accessible to the 'common man'. It was likewise the part of the common man he took when he depicted the devastation wrought by war: 'Es geht über den armen Mann. / Der muss das Haar herlangen schon, / Wenn sich die Fürsten raufen.'

'Sie hand gemacht ein Singschul' – *Meistersang*, popular song, congregational hymns, confessional lyric poetry

Just as Humanism may be grasped as a new spiritual medium coming into its own beside the Church, so by looking at German poetry between the medieval and modern periods it is possible to discover a remarkable phenomenon that was no less a new spiritual medium in its own way. A companion piece to Humanism as it were, this poetry – *Meistersang (Mastersong)* - cannot be explained without linking it to the European Renaissance. There have been frequent attempts to dismiss *Meistersang* as trivial and moralising, and even as artistically worthless by comparison with *Minnesang*, from which its form originates, as if it were no more than a waste product of it. Consequently not a single example of *Meistersang* is contained in the body of earlier German literature, although today it is assured of at least some attention on account of its educational value. Even the best-known exponent of the *Meistersang* form, Hans Sachs, has survived in the modern memory chiefly as a writer of Shrovetide plays. General knowledge of *Meistersang* usually derives from Richard Wagner's *Die Meistersinger*.

Collective art form

Whereas *Minnesang* could still be termed 'high literature' in terms of having given rise to individual creative personalities, for the most part of noble birth, *Meistersang* is an entirely different phenomenon. The *Meistersang* heritage contains not *individuelle hohe Kunst* ('individual high art') so much as *kollektiv geprägte Durchschnittsleistung* ('average achievements of a collective character') (B. Nagel). However, the term 'average' should not be taken too hastily at face value. *Meistersang* artistic creativity was rooted in a particular concept of the nature of artistic accomplishment that was entirely different from our own, measured by the standard established in the aftermath of the classical literary age. A struggle for poetry of genius, for highly-developed individuality or unique creativity was not at all the main concern. Instead a poetic form and a valid catalogue of rules were pursued that were completely appropriate for all artistic contemporaries, the 'masters'. Mastersongs were the product of communities known as *Singschulen* (song schools) which served the dual purpose of instructing and entertaining both their own community and the wider community that was the town.

Art for the laity

This made *Meistersang* a product of the late medieval and early modern urban culture of a burgher laity – as opposed to clergy – asserting a definite place for itself in a society of rank. Opposition to Christianity as a set of institutions, but certainly not as a doctrine of faith, was an inherent part of it from the very outset. Proof of this is the legend of its origin that traces *Meistersang* back to the time of the Ottonine kings and tells of the hostility of the Papal Church to the first mastersingers. It is no coincidence that one song about the founding of the first song school, in Mainz, contains the words: 'Sy hand gemacht ain singschuol, / Vnd setzen oben vff den stuol, / Wer übel redt vom pfaffen.' Polemics against the clergy are as ubiquitous in *Meistersang* as in Humanism, and particularly against clerical *geitigkeit* (greed, avarice). This polemic was later taken up by the Reformation and absorbed into its anti-papal doctrine. Similarly in harmony with Renaissance Humanism (Boccaccio and others), the counterbalance offered in *Meistersang* to the secular nobility is less a question of openly conducted opposition to the economic and ruling practices of nobles and princes than of undermining their basic legitimising positions. One of the convictions upheld by the song schools was that their profession consisted of handing down *guter* (meaning 'noble') *gesanges kunst* (song art), after the appreciation of poetry had been lost among the nobility. In their view there was nothing more noble than the art of song, since 'Der ist wahrhaft adligen Geschlechts, wer sich mit der Dichtkunst beschäftigt' ('he who is employed with the art of making verse is truly of noble birth') (Michel Beheim, mid-fifteenth century). The mastersinger thus proved himself a member of a new nobility, the nobility of the mind (or *Tugendadel*). A new yardstick had been established. The epigrammatic poet Frauenlob wrote around 1300: 'Schaz unt geburt gên lîbes adel biegen, / sô wil der geist kunst mir der tugend wiegen' (meaning that nobility of blood or that bought with a purse are phenomena of the corporeal world, whereas in the world of the spirit personality and ability are all that count).

86

Meistersang persists for half a millennium

Of all traditions in German literature *Meistersang* has the longest history. Song schools where *Meistersang* was cultivated are documented from the fifteenth century onwards, and the last one closed in 1875. Thus *Meistersang* spans some five hundred years. The number of works produced (the majority of which were never published) is impossible to calculate. The golden age of *Meistersang*, however, was the fifteenth and sixteenth centuries, the age when guild burghers, the class most closely involved with it, still enjoyed high status. Extant documents testify to the fact that the majority of mastersingers were craftsmen. However, the urban artisan of the late Middle Ages and the early modern age was not the same person as the socially oppressed artisan of the twentieth century. Financial prosperity and considerable self-confidence were not uncommon. Enclosed within the world of the old German towns, he often combined his particular trade with broad religious and venturing interests, but above all with the arts. The German Renaissance artist (for example Dürer and Riemenschneider, or the builders of cathedrals and burgher town palaces) did not grow out of this class by chance.

Both a spiritual and a secular education were preconditions for working within a song school. The degree of erudition was indeed often astounding; scholars could become members, as for example the first German translator of the *Iliad*, the teacher, jurist, textual editor and translator Johannes Spreng in Augsburg in the sixteenth century. It is not surprising, therefore, that in these song schools the seeds of an attitude formed that was later to be expressed in the formula: 'Wer immer strebend sich bemüht...' He who 'works and studies' in the song school will be rewarded at last with supreme happiness, as the mastersinger Daniel Holtzmann expressed it around 1600.

Particular schools

Quite a substantial body of information has been handed down concerning the history of *Meistersang*, particular song schools and their premises, as well as about particular mastersingers. This information on the one hand takes the form of historical and theoretical accounts in verse, composed by mastersingers themselves (known as *Schulkünste*), and on the other of documentary reports, all of which date from the closing phase of the period (*inter alia* by Puschmann, Spangenberg and Wagenseil): the end of the sixteenth to the end of the seventeenth centuries). All these accounts agree that the oldest, and hence foremost song school was that in Mainz, whose fame and importance was nevertheless later eclipsed by the Nuremberg school in the sixteenth century. This represented a removal of 'golden Mainz', which had experienced its golden age in the late Middle Ages, to

Nuremberg, the leading German city of the early modern age, which occupied first place in German cultural life. Otherwise there were song schools scattered all over western and southern Germany; no song schools are documented in northern Germany, the Low German-speaking area, apart from a few minor exceptions.

Formal principles

The formal principles of *Meistersang* remained essentially unchanged through the many centuries of its existence, giving it a continuity unmatched by any other poetic form in history. Obligatory elements included rhyme, syllable numbers, etc., compiled in a register of all rules known as the 'Tabulator'. This contains the entire terminology that gave *Meistersang* its formal character: the *Bar* (the entire song), the *Gesätz* (the strophe or stanza), the *Gebänd* (rhyme scheme), *Ton* (overall metrical and musical form), directions for incorporating each strophe in three parts (two *stollen* of equal structure and one *Abgesang* canto). Virtually anything might form the theme of the *Meistersang* – the comprehensive store of religious doctrine and opinion was drawn on as well as the micro- and macrocosm, classical, medieval or contemporary themes, morality or anecdotal *Schwank*. As the *Schulkünste* unanimously document, however, the accent was mainly on religious themes including God, the Virgin Mary and the Holy Trinity. There was also social criticism of issues such as the increasing dominance of money.

After Luther's nailing of his theses to the church door in Wittenberg, the mastersingers had another great theme, the Reformation, and became in fact mediators of Reformation thinking through their songs. New song schools sprang up in the aftermath of the Reformation. In Austria, *Meistersang* only became possible at all as a result of the growing swell of popular support for the Reformation, although this was to come to an end in the seventeenth century with the counter-Reformation. Luther's own songwriting, influenced by *Meistersang* in form, indeed ensured him the accolade 'unter die allerberühmtesten Meistersinger gezählt' ('numbered among the most famous of all mastersingers' – Spangenberg).

Women mastersingers

As in the guilds of former times, so too in the song schools women were accepted as mastersingers. Apart from some noblewomen-poets, early medieval German women poets are unknown. By contrast, the names of early German women poets of non-noble origin are known from the song schools; Katharina Holl from the Munich song school, for example. Unlike examples of *Meistersang*, folk songs of previous centuries are still known, although one does not directly perceive the age of their verses and melodies.

'All mein Gedanken, die ich hab', and 'Innsbruck, ich muss dich lassen' are among many examples of folk songs dating from the fourteenth to sixteenth centuries – a period of transition from the medieval to the modern age, and generally regarded as a golden age of popular lyricism in works on the history of literature. This period coincided with that of the first great compilations (a second ensued in the eighteenth century, led by Herder and Goethe). This resulted in comprehensive compilations of songs preserving the folk songs of previous ages, such as the *Lochamer-Lieder-buch* (1452–60), the *Rostocker Liederbuch* (around 1460), Georg Forster's five-volume anthology *Frische teutsche Liedlein* (1539–56), and the *Ambr-aser Liederbuch* (1582) – all of which contained a substantial number of songs (Forster, for example, collected 380). The period after 1512 also saw the first printed songbooks.

Folk songs

Seen in context, folk songs constitute one section within the broad sphere of 'popular poetry'. It is important to point out, therefore, that it does not constitute a distinctly separate body of literature to be set against creative poetry. The folk song is no less a work of art than creative poetry, just as it usually also has a particular, if not always traceable author. What distinguishes the two categories, therefore, is not so much whether they are art or not, but simply the different way in which each of the genres is handed down. The folk song 'lives' through being handed down. The mediators of the tradition come from all walks of life (peasants, artisans and artisans' associations, and the middle and lower urban classes in general, as well as miners and sailors, soldiers, students and, later, workers). The life of the folk song in handed-down tradition nonetheless entails a process of variation. The variability that is the law of the folk song tradition, in contrast with the preservation of canonical text typical for 'high' literature, is hence a productive process: 'Die produktive, schöpferische Überlieferung durch die Gemeinschaft, durch das Kollektiv also ist das Primäre, was das Volkslied von anderen Lied- (und Dichtungs-)arten unterscheidet und in seinem Wesen bestimmt' ('The productive, creative handing down by the community, the collective body, is therefore the primary factor distinguishing folk song from other song and poetry genres, and lending it its particular character' – H. Strobach).

The penury of the lower classes

Folk songs of earlier centuries provide deep insight into the social conditions and privations of the people. The penury of the lower classes was a constant song theme, for example the life of the journeyman depicted by the author of the Book of *Eulenspiegel*: 'Der Winter war kalt und gefror hart, und es kam eine Teuerung hinzu, also dass viele Dienstknechte ledig gingen' ('The winter was a cold one with severe frosts, and with the price rises, many servants were without work'). A song about Augsburg weavers' apprentices having to put up with harsh conditions in winter is in similar vein: 'Im Winter, wenn die weissen Mücken fliegen / So müssen sich die Webergesellen schmiegen' ('In winter, when the gnats fly / The weavers' apprentices must huddle together'). Similarly, the everyday life of country folk left traces in songs of the *Bauernklage* (peasant lament) type. The tone always to be found in these songs is as follows: 'Ach, ich bin wohl ein armer Baur / Mein Leben wird mir mächtig saur' ('Oh, I am but a poor peasant / My life is mighty unpleasant'). Peasant laments may be classified together with bondsman's laments, for example the Low German *Dat ole Leisken van Henneke Knecht*, which declares at the start: 'Eck will neinen Buren deinen fort, / Solk Arweit will eck haten' ('From now on I will serve farmer no more, / I will disdain such drudgery'). In the form of rapidly reproduced and disseminated pamphlets the folk song also constituted a musical accompaniment to the peasant war. However, the majority of songs dating from the peasant war period are hostile to peasants, taking rather the part of the enemy. The reason for this is that after the defeat of the peasant army, songs sympathetic to peasants fell under the official censorship of the sovereign. Only a handful have been preserved from sources such as contemporary torture records. The defiant *Bündische Lied*, for example, dates from the peasant war period. Information about how this song came about is relatively detailed. It begins: 'Ein Geier ist ausgeflogen, / Im Hegau am Schwarzwald' ('A vulture has flown out, / In Hegau near the Black Forest'). The vulture is here a symbol of the rebels. The author makes his meaning amply plain: 'Die Bauern sind einig geworden / Und kriegen mit Gewalt / Sie haben einen grossen Orden / Sind aufständig mannigfalt / Und tun die Schlösser zerreissen / Und brennen Klöster aus: / So kann man uns nicht mehr bescheissen. / Was soll ein bös' Raubhaus?' ('The peasants have united / And make mighty war / They have amassed great numbers / And are rebelling on all sides / And are tearing down the castles / And burning down the monasteries: / They're not going to shit on us any more. / What good an evil den of thieves?')

Love and death

The overwhelming majority of extant earlier songs are concerned with everyday events in the lives of simple people, in the main the constantly recurring theme of love and how it comes to an end, with farewells and death. There is another type, somewhat hesitantly confirmed by research, of explicitly erotic folk song, represented by the full gamut as far as obscene song. Other folk songs are concerned with the seasons, with festivals, dancing and drinking, while some are religious in character or joking songs. Another component of the early folk song genre was the ballad, including some about knightly heroes (Hildebrand, 'Der edle Moringer'), although these are equally imbued with the folklore tone: 'Nun will ich aber heben an / Von dem Tannhäuser zu singen' ('Now would I rise up / To sing of the Tannhäuser').

Congregational hymns

The Reformation saw the congregational hymn rise to become a new creative genre. Previous centuries had, of course, been familiar with sacred song, *geistliche Lied*, as well as chant, but had lacked congregational song in the form of participation by lay believers in worship. The first to attempt to redress this situation was Thomas Müntzer in Allstedt. This made him the initiator of the Protestant congregational hymn, just as Martin Luther was the founder of Protestantism as such. Chroniclers of *Meistersang*, like the mastersingers themselves, not only ranked Luther among their number, but also revered him as an outstanding mastersinger. The fact that the Reformer gave pride of place to music above all other arts has not been forgotten to this day. His congregational hymns, many of which remain popular, are still to be found in modern hymn books of the Lutheran (*evangelische*) church, of which they form the core.

Luther the hymn- and songwriter

The status accorded to Luther by the mastersingers points to one source of Lutheran congregational hymns. Another was the folk song of his day. However, it was neither his knowledge of *Meistersang* nor his love of music that made the Reformer a poet and songwriter. It was the contingencies of religious reform that led him to direct his considerable poetic gifts to express themselves in the congregational hymn. It was in other words the Reformation that made the Reformer a poet. In the sixteenth century, however, poetry or verse-writing was not the strictly distinct literary activity that it is today – separate from translation, adaptation or variation (using texts from earlier times or reworking texts by contemporary authors). Among the forty or so hymns written by Luther, for example, there are German translations of Old Church and medieval Latin hymns and chants; adapted and expanded German *Leisen* and strophes have been added to some hymns; hymns on liturgical pieces; catechism hymns; children's hymns; a few specimens of 'free' verse (the number of 'original' hymns was small) and festival hymns ('Vom Himmel hoch'). This did not detract at all from the impact of Luther's hymn writing, especially since in the context of the confessional controversies of the day it acquired functions that no longer attach to it today (in this connection Heine compared Luther's 'Ein feste Burg' with the 'Marseillaise' of the French

Revolution). This should therefore be a warning to the modern reader: the powerful congregational hymns of the sixteenth century cannot be compared with their pale twentieth-century counterparts.

Confessional poetry

The struggles of the age produced some outstanding confessional poetry. It now became possible to express personal confession in song form. Those involved in Reformation controversies left behind confessional lyric poetry, of which some is of a contemplative, even solitary and reflective nature, some militant, some explicit personal statement, some implicit, blended with the substance of religious notions. Explicit personal statement of the most militant kind derives from the pen of Ulrich von Hutten: 'Ein neu Lied' ('Ich habs gewagt mit Sinnen') is a piece of lyric poetry that some would wish to see ranked beside the personal statements of Walther von der Vogelweide and Goethe. Luther's 'Nun freut euch lieben Christen gmein' (with the lines: 'Dem Teufel ich gefangen lag / Im Tod war ich verloren') is both personal confession (autobiography) and religious at the same time. Ulrich Zwingli, the Zurich Reformer, composed his plague hymn ('Hilf, Herr Gott, hilf') in 1519 with the three sections: 'Im Anfang der Krankheit', 'Inmitten der Krankheit', and 'In der Besserung' ('At the beginning of the Sickness', 'During the Sickness' and 'During Recovery'). Sebastian Franck, in his confessional poem 'Von vier zwieträchtigen Kirchen' was making a conscious and overt break with the confessions taking shape in his day by using the parallel structured strophes: 'Ich will und mag nicht Päpstlich sein', '... nicht Luthrisch sein', '... nicht Zwinglische sein', 'Kein Wiedertäufer will ich sein', in order at the end to decide in favour of his own individual religious approach. A tragic variation of this confessional lyric poetry was contributed in the same epoch by Thomas Murner, the Catholic poet and controversial theologian. Against the background of his break with the Reformation he revealed visibly and perceptibly in his life confession 'In Bruder Veiten Ton' the isolated position of an author standing by the Old Church to the bitter end against the onslaught of the new. Not unmindful of the faults and wrongs perpetrated by the old establishment, indeed denouncing them, he is not making his statement on anyone else's behalf, but on the strength of his own legitimation: 'ich red' das alles für meine Person, / Und mein' ich, ich tu damit Recht, / Dass ich beim alten Glauben stohn.'

'Der Jugend Gottes Wort und Werk mit Lust einzuprägen' ('To instil enjoyment of God's word and works into youth'): Reformation drama

During the transition from the medieval to the modern age changes took place in all spheres of literature that accelerated after the onset of the

Reformation. The same holds good for changes taking place in drama, in which the first high point can be discerned in new developments of the sixteenth century. Neither baroque drama nor that of German Classicism takes precedence in this regard. At all events, however, only a handful of Shrovetide plays by Hans Sachs have remained of sixteenth-century drama, although Bertolt Brecht did attempt to revive a sixteenth-century German drama: *Hans Pfreim* by Martin Hayneccius. A typological grasp of pre-Reformation drama is aided by dividing it into three genres: the medieval religious play, the 'secular' play, represented mainly by the Shrovetide play, and Humanist drama in Latin. It was the latter, although chronologically the most recent, that created the preconditions for later developments in German drama.

Jakob Wimpfeling

Playwrights in Humanist circles imitated the ancient, in particular the Latin model of Terence, adopting its structure and verse treatment etc. The first Humanist drama by a German author is held to be *Stylpho* by the Alsatian playwright Jakob Wimpfeling. This one-act play (six scenes, prologue and epilogue) was written in 1480. Wimpfeling, Dean of the Heidelberg Faculty of Liberal Arts, awarded licentiate degrees to sixteen Bachelors on behalf of the Chancellor. Instead of the conventional eulogy he read out a dramatic text – unless he had it read out by the students – *Stylpho*. The play describes the careers of two budding scholars, presented side by side: the fluent Vincentius, who is drawn to a university, and the idle Stylpho, who goes to study with the Curia in Rome. Since Stylpho's efforts at studying prove inadequate, he has no choice but to accept the office of village swineherd from the Bishop of Schultheissen. The author sums up:

> Welch erstaunlicher Schicksalswandel! Vom Höfling ward er zum Dörfler, vom Freund von Kardinälen zum Bauernknecht, vom Hohen zum Erniedrigten, Vom Seelenhirten zum Sauhirten. Solch Elend bringt Unwissenheit. Dem Vincentius halfen seine Eltern aus, er ging zurück zur Universität, studierte eifrig die Rechte und wurde dann zuerst in des Fürsten Kanzlei aufgenommen und darauf durch dessen Fürspruch zum Domherrn befördert; schliesslich wurde er einstimmig zur Bischofswürder erhoben und regierte glücklich.

What an extraordinary twist of Fate! The courtier became a villager, the friend of cardinals a peasant bondsman, the high-born became lowly, the shepherd of souls a swineherd. It is ignorance that brings one to such a sorry pass. Vincentius was helped by his parents, returned to the university, studied law diligently and was first employed in the prince's chancery, later through the latter's recommendation being promoted to canon. At last he was unanimously elected to the office of bishop and reigned happily.

The stage as weapon

An overview of the drama emerging from the 1520s onwards as the Reformation spread across broad areas of Germany and the bordering countries reveals a multiplicity of models with such a degree of overlapping and interconnectedness of form and content that it would seem to defy order or classification. In the nineteenth century the literary historian K. Goedeke recognised the impetus behind these new developments, formulating his perception in the oft-quoted sentence: 'The idea of making the stage a weapon brought forth hundreds of plays and involved thousands of performers and spectators alike through three human ages'. Drama became an active agent in the service of Reformation doctrine to such a degree that it became the preferred vehicle for proponents of Protestantism in situations of conflict, even in cases where it constituted, in the words of Creizenach, no more than 'reckless dramatic rabble-rousing' ('rücksichtslose dramatische Agitation'). Two general features rapidly materialised as typical for literature promoting the Reformation: the setting forth of a 'purified' (Protestant) doctrine, and polemical attacks on the old Church and its adherents insofar as they opposed the Reformation. The preaching of the Gospel and militant confrontation with Rome were core themes of Reformation drama of all hues.

Humanist drama

Biblical Humanist drama, or the religious instruction play, first appeared in the 1630s. Its development was accompanied by theoretical reflection, having been positively inspired by some lines by Martin Luther concerning his interpretation of the Apocrypha (in his prefaces to the Books of Judith and Tobias and the 'plays' Esther and Daniel), where he designated these books religious writings, possibly plays that could be performed. In the 1640s a debate flared up to which Luther contributed by means of a testimonial. The point at issue was whether stories from the Bible could be presented to the public in the form of drama. This question had already been answered realistically by Johann Ackermann in 1536 when he said that people preferred seeing a play to reading the Bible themselves. This was in fact the decisive factor: the point was to mediate what was beneficial (i.e. Biblical teaching) in a pleasant way – as Paul Rebhun, the pace-setting dramatist of this genre, expressed it in 1535: 'der jugent gottes wort und werck mit lust [einzuprägen]' ('to [instil] enjoyment of God's word and works into youth'). The result in the Protestant region was a flood of plays based on biblical themes within a few decades, most of them in

German: the Old Testament including the Apocrypha (*inter alia* the Fall from Grace, Cain and Abel, Noah, Abraham, Jacob, Joseph, Judith, Susanna), and the New Testament (including the Nativity, the wedding at Cana, Lazarus, Judas, the Prodigal Son and the Acts of the Apostles).

Paul Rebhun

Paul Rebhun's work *Geistlich Spiel von der Gotfürchtigen und keuschen Frauen Susannen* (1536) has long been regarded as a classic of its genre, not least because of its formal structure. The work is divided into consistent acts and scenes, and is composed in verse characterised wherever possible by an integration of verse and word accents, as opposed to the principle of syllable count. It has a topical theme derived from a biblical story: a clash between the homely middle-class (*bürgerlich*) world, where Susanna attends chastely to her duties as housewife, and the world of the powers that be (*Obrigkeit*), seen here in the form of two judges. (Comparable perhaps with the classic conflict in the age of the struggle of the burghers against the feudal powers, as depicted in *Emilia Galotti* and *Kabale und Liebe*). It is no coincidence that the key concept running through the text is *gewalt*: power. The plot follows that of its biblical source – an attempt on the part of the judge to seduce Susanna, and when this fails, to denounce her and condemn her to death. She is saved by a *deus ex machina*, by Daniel the servant of God, who exposes the villainy of the judge. It is a eulogy to persecuted innocence vindicated in times of privation with deliverance to be expected from God alone. However, Rebhun's admixture of worldly problems is not sparing, as is attested by the accusation of criminal worldly authority together with corrupt justice, a call for competent justice that pays some regard to the accused and passes judgement on the basis of evidence rather than suspicions. Daniel's exposure of the judge is a minor detective story in its own right, with Daniel himself acting the detective and proceeding on the basis of rational deduction.

Rebhun's work had been preceded in 1532 by *Susanna* by Sixt Birck, a work in which several major differences from Rebhun's may be discerned. Birck was a headmaster in Basle. He attached great importance to formal democratic procedure in collective bodies such as the college of judges, making this the focal point of his presentation.

The legend of Joseph

Another popular theme of the period, perhaps the best-loved of all, was the story of Joseph (one that was to be taken up again by Thomas Mann even in the twentieth century). This offered a similar opportunity to present a story of how persecuted innocence is vindicated, complete with subsequent deliverance and improvement in fortune. In some ways this is a reversal of the Susanna story: here it is the man who is subjected to a seduction attempt and who suffers as a result of rebuffing it. The fact that an additional worldly dimension is likewise derived here from the Joseph story is attested to by the history of sixteenth century drama. Thomas Brunner states, for example, in the epilogue to his play *Jacob und seine zwölf Söhne* (1566), in which Joseph appears as an unequivocal hero: 'Was David in den Psalmen spricht / Den armen thut erheben Gott / Vnd reist in mitten aus dem kott / Das er jn alles leids ergetz / Vnd neben grossen Fürsten setz / Wie denn Josephus ward zuhand / Ein Fürst uber Egypten land / Dem Pharaoni gleich an gwalt. . . .' ('As David says in the Psalms / Who lifts the weak out of the dust / And raises the poor from the dunghill, / Giving them a place among princes, / Among the princes of his people / As happened with Joseph, / A prince over the land of Egypt, / Equal to Pharaoh in power. . . .') These verses would have been unthinkable without the example set by Luther in 1530 in his sermon *Predigt, dass man Kinder zur Schulen halten solle*, a detailed interpretation of Psalm 113 quoted above. Even in the early phase of the age the aim was to conquer not so much the place of the prince himself, so much as the place next to him.

Thomas Naogeorg

The most important German play in the sixteenth century was regarded as the *Tragoedia nova Pammachius* by Thomas Naogeorg (1538). Today the title would read something like 'The New Tragedy of the Opponent of All', i.e. the papacy. Several German translations of the Latin original by different authors appeared almost simultaneously, one of them with a preface by Paul Rebhun. The work is a forceful piece of historical verse, depicting the conflict between Protestantism and the Papacy. There is virtually no plot, but an abundance of intense disputation with a noteworthy open ending: the fifth act, according to the playwright, would be written by history itself. In line with Luther's teaching, the Papacy is treated as the Antichrist, its 'catalogue of sins' being presented in the 'Twelve Articles of the Christian Faith'. This allowed the (Protestant) author to enumerate the chief aspects of the Catholic Church that in the Protestant view constituted the main crimes of the Papacy. The literary technique used was to present the disputed view of the opponent using the latter's own, albeit distorted, monologue account. This technique was in evidence elsewhere in contemporary literature, for example in a satire by Murner in which Luther exposed his own aims, seen by Murner as criminal.

European comparison

With rare exceptions, German drama of the Reformation period is no longer performed today. The reason for this is that it was mostly too much the captive of confessional controversy to be capable of the artistic heights reached only a little later in Spain (Lope de Vega, Calderón) or in England (Shakespeare and his contemporaries). A familiar quotation has it that the Muses are silent amid the clash of arms. In fact the drama Muse of the Germans was not silent during the Reformation: she was unusually vociferous, but her voice was hoarse with polemical zeal and her literary substance bound by the system of confessional doctrine. An additional factor was the confined character of German territorial state life in a nation still hidebound by rank. This prevented the expansion of horizons to which the theatre was then opening up in Spain and England – nations whose outlook was being shaped by the spirit of discovery, overseas expansion and booming participation in world trade. Admittedly, a backlash was not long in coming: in Spain with the subjugation of the Inquisition, and in England with the rise of Puritanism, so hostile to the arts. Not least, however, German Reformation drama was deprived of the discoveries and lessons of the Italian Renaissance from which the Spanish and English profited. It was the embracing of the Renaissance that enabled the theatre in Spain and England to reach the heights discernible in the period around 1600. Shakespeare's works would not be what they are without his willingness to embrace Renaissance Humanism, philosophy and anthropology, fed *inter alia* by the art of the Italian novella. It was not until the eighteenth century that classical German drama made up some of this lost ground by adopting the Renaissance through the medium of Shakespeare. It was this that made it possible for the substance of Renaissance literature, in terms both of form and content, to bear fruit in the development of drama writing in Germany.

Schwank and the pre-novel romance

German literature suffered no lack of epic literature – lengthy verse narratives – in the age of Humanism and the Reformation. However, it was written in new Latin, which has so far impeded thorough scholarly research into the genre. Apart from a mere handful of works, a substantial body of epic literature comparable with Italian epic poetry (e.g. by Bojardo, Ariosto or Tasso) was lacking. Notable exceptions include the verse works of Sebastian Brant and Thomas Murner. The term 'verse epic' is most appropriate for a Dutch copy of anonymous works entitled *Reynke de Vos*, published in Lübeck in 1498. Here, however, didactic and satirical elements are in the forefront, narrative being of secondary importance.

Facetie

Minor literary genres to some extent still betrayed their derivation from medieval narrative forms (such as *Exempel* and *Schwank*), although also reflecting Italian Renaissance influence (again *Schwank*), while the *Facetie* genre was a pure Italian import. In Germany its chief representative was Heinrich Bebel's anthology *Libri facetiarum iucundissimi* ('The most entertaining books of the Facetie', 1509–14). The *Exempel* genre was epitomized by Johannes Pauli's substantial anthology of preachers' homilies, *Schimpf und Ernst* ('Jest and Earnest', 1522). These two works inspired a spate of *Schwank* authors in the second half of the century following the Augsburg Religious Peace of 1555. The result was that *Schwank* volumes now became collections of *Facetie* and preachers' homilies (*Predigtmärlein*) with additional material of various origin, such as the medieval verse novella (re-written in prose), the French fable and the Middle High German *Märe* or tale – a motley assortment of amusements. This was still possible in the absence of an idea of *Schwank* as a distinct genre. Besides fables, tales, novellas, facetie and homilies, anthologies also contained narrative texts that would later be classified as fairy tales, for example *Das tapfere Schneiderlein*, ('The Brave Little Tailor').

Jörg Wickram, author of what is arguably the best-known *Schwank* anthology *Das Rollwagenbüchlein* ('The Coach-Traveller's Companion'), informs us that the work has the sole purpose of entertaining: 'Denn dies Büchlein ist allein von guter Kurzweil wegen an den Tag gegeben, niemand zur Unterweisung noch Lehre, auch gar niemand zu Schmach, Hohn oder Spott' ('Since this humble book has been brought forth solely for the sake of pleasant diversion, not with the intention of instruction or teaching, or with affronting, scorning or deriding anyone'). This explanation need not be taken at face value, however. A notable proportion of *Schwank* anecdotes, including those by Wickram, did contain a moral, lesson or element of instruction. *Schwank* thus resembled other literature in general in the second half of the sixteenth century in having a element of indirect political or social opposition: 'Hingegen aber is mancher Herr, der sich solcher seiner Gewalt überhebt und sie missbraucht, seine armen, ja auch frommen Untertanen mit Brandschatzen einen um den anderen plagt, ihnen das Mark aus den Knochen saugt, dass Gott vom Himmel herabsehen möchte' ('In contrast some lords and masters who presume on their power and abuse it, torment their poor and indeed pious vassals by plundering them one by one, sucking the very marrow out of their bones, so that God himself might look down and see from Heaven').

Schwank as a form of anti-clericalism

As an overall phenomenon, *Schwank* literature of the sixteenth century formed part of urban burgher culture, a genre focused on this world, one of its striking features being an absence of the metaphysical, accompanied by the anti-clericalism that was the hallmark of the genre. Problems concerned with the next world were on the whole omitted, since narrative was almost exclusively preoccupied with everyday human life and community, usually portrayed in a comic light. There are nevertheless *Schwank* anecdotes with tragic endings (in Wickram, for example), a fact that serves to underline once again the lack of a clear definition of the genre.

The beginnings of the novel?

Locating the beginning of the great prose genre poses considerable difficulties in the history of recent German literature. It has yet to be satisfactorily explained, for example, whether we may speak of a continuous development in the history of the genre, or rather of a recasting of the baroque novel from which the novel of the Enlightenment followed on together with its successors. The readiness with which the term 'baroque novel' springs to mind would nevertheless seem to suggest the establishment of the 'novel' as the great prose genre, at least from the seventeenth century onwards – *de facto*, although poetry studies initially paid no heed to it at all (Opitz, *Buch von der Deutschen Poeterey*, 1624).

Chapbooks (Volksbücher)

An examination of the romance prior to the emergence of the modern novel (both 'romance' and 'novel' are termed *Roman* in German) poses even more difficulties – the 'pre-' or 'early' forms of the modern novel, or its 'pre-' or 'early' history. Forms include chapbooks (small pamphlets – *Volksbücher* – of tales, ballads, tracts, etc., hawked by chapmen), as well as French, Italian and Spanish literary models (the knightly romance, the romance of heroic gallantry, as well as pastoral and fantastic romances), *Schwank* anecdotes and *Schwank* cycles in no less measure than novellas and novella anthologies. Literary historians have not infrequently seized on the shorthand definition of the 'chapbook' as *the* beginning of the German prose novel. There have even been occasional attempts at simply 'planting' a sub-genre, by raising for example the *Schwank* cycle to the status of *Schwankroman*, anecdotal novel. In reality, however, such juggling with terminology is as unhelpful as the opposite procedure recommended by other literary historians of wielding the term 'chapbook', whatever that may in fact mean, as a means of disputing the term 'novel', speaking instead of an 'early form of the novel-like design' ('Frühform der romanhaften

Gestaltung'), or 'early New High German narrative prose' ('frühneuhochdeutscher Erzählprosa'). The problem with both these approaches, the use of circuitous terms such as 'novel-like' (*romanhaft*) and deliberate avoidance of the term 'novel', is their retention of the concept of the novel as a point of reference.

At that time authors used neither 'chapbook' nor 'novel' as defining terms, employing *Historia* (for example the *Historia von D. Johann Fausten*, 1587) to cover all eventualities. The author of *Eulenspiegel* (*Ein kurzweilig Lesen von Dil Ulenspiegel*, probably first published around 1510) used the same term, but as an equivalent for the modern term 'chapter' (1, 2, etc.). In 1587 Bartholomew Krüger published a comparable anthology entitled *Hans Clawerts Werckliche Historien*. It would appear that here the term *historia* refers to the historical authenticity of the narrative. He used works of various origin and in different languages as his sources. In addition to medieval German texts (courtly verse epics broken down into prose, hence *Prosaauflösungen*), French and Latin were the most frequent source languages. 'Histories' with no demonstrable alternative source (although particular chapters, sections and motives might be borrowed from other literature) were treated as original German compositions (*Originalschöpfungen*): for example the *Eulenspiegel* Book, the *Lalebuch* (1597, a second version appearing under the title *Die Schildbürger* a year later), and the *Historia von D. Johann Fausten*.

Of the *historia* anthologies, Eulenspiegel achieved the largest number of editions, translations and adaptations, including one by Hans Sachs and a rhymed version by Johann Fischart. The main motifs were later used in the nineteenth century by Charles de Coster, and children's editions included one by Erich Kästner. The text is a blend of extended and short prose in the form of a *Schwank* cycle. The term *Schwank* (anecdote) denotes a form of short tale, either rhymed or in prose, of a humorous nature and often ending with a punch-line. *Schwank* cycles were formed from an accumulation of well-known tales and anecdotes, either attributed to a specific person such as the figure of Till Eulenspiegel, who is scarcely verifiable in historical terms, or a historically verifiable figure such as Faust. Alternatively a cycle focused on a real or invented locality (e.g. Laleburg, or Schilda). The homogeneousness characteristic of the modern novel was not aimed for.

The *Eulenspiegel* anthology hence remained essentially a series of episodes of indefinite sequence. The author declared no interest in giving a detailed account of the hero's life. All we are given is a few facts about his birth and death. Aside from the detail that Till has parents, we learn nothing either of his relations and friends or other human ties such as love, or of the spiritual forces that motivate him. He is conspicuously lacking in any emotion apart from his lust for revenge and his penchant for gloating (*Schadenfreude*). Moral scruples of any kind are alien to him.

Eulenspiegel plays tricks on all ranks

The substance of the stories is astonishingly straightforward: Eulenspiegel plays tricks on his peers. It is not even as if he aims at any specific group of people: peasants, artisans, nobles and the clergy all fall victim to his ploys. Admittedly master guildsmen are his most frequent objects, but he does not restrict himself to the well-off. On one occasion only does Till assert that he must expose a particular grievance 'damit der Irrtum aus dem Volke komme' ('to wrest error from among the people') (story no. 65). Eulenspiegel gives the impression of identifying himself solely with his own actions, belonging to no-one and to no class, so that society as a whole presents itself to him only from the outside, an object of his derisive trick-playing as an outsider. Till's conduct is that of individual opposition to an entire society through the medium of cunning. The aim of his opposition, however, is to win material wealth through idleness – the least likely aim of a progressive character or freedom fighter. For all that, Till is strikingly modern in one respect: although himself without property, penniless, and without workshop or tools, he avails himself of the new, then most modern form of human interchange, the exchange of goods for money. He is much more than a common thief. He neither begs nor uses violence to achieve his ends. His expertise consists in achieving a superior performance as buyer or seller, always with the intention of bartering other people's money and goods. He frequently sells no more than his own labour, which he then however renders valueless for the purchaser, for example, a master craftsman, by taking literally the conditions of his working contract.

The burgher as fool

The end of the sixteenth century brought another example of attempted opposition by means of cunning in the *Schwank* cycle of Lalen or the Schildbürger (the Gothamites). The foolishness of the citizens of Laleburg, the Schildbürger, was not innate or learned, but a foolishness acquired by dissimulation and cunning arising out of necessity. The citizens of Laleburg were once regarded as the wisest and cleverest. Princes and lords craved their services to such a degree that the life of their families and community, indeed their entire existence, was thereby jeopardized. The only thing that could save them in the face of such circumstances, so they believed, was folly or foolishness.

All Laleburg citizens therefore expressly relinquished their wisdom in the interests of the common good, and each made haste to become a fool. This attempt to secure their own survival through cunning, however, proved even more dangerous than their former circumstances, which had given cause enough for concern. It was certainly not the intention of the unnamed author (Fischart?) to reveal opposition *per se* as foolishness. His work is punctuated with traces of opposition, for example his express criticism of the exploitative practices of usurers, 'die den Armen, welche ohnedies bedrängt und notleidend sind, nicht anders als die Zecken auch das Blut aus dem Leib, ja das Mark aus den Knochen saugen' ('who are no better than ticks sucking the blood out of the bodies and the very marrow out of the bones of the poor, who are oppressed and poverty-stricken enough as it is'). The protesting attitude of the citizens of Laleburg, however, gradually begins to shift in the direction of its unreasoning opposite. What began as a measure aimed at self-protection comes to deprive them of power, and what was once feigned foolishness becomes genuine 'second nature'. Having stripped themselves of their own power, they ultimately slide into self-destruction, the result of an opposition that had originally been a justifiable protest against an intolerable burden. Not only does it fail to salvage the endangered common good, it completely obliterates it. Encapsulated in their own foolishness, they are doomed to extinction. The citizens of Laleburg have in fact merely wronged the common good in the real sense of the term: 'Denn es ist ja nicht ein Geringes, sich selber zum Narren zu machen: sintemalen hierdurch dem allgemeinen Nutzen, welchem wir auch unser Leben schuldig sind, soweit sich dasselbe erstreckt, das seine geraubt und entzogen wird' ('Since it is no trifling thing to make a fool of oneself: since one thereby robs and deprives the common good, to which we all owe our life, as long as it may endure, of that which rightfully belongs to it').

The *Historia von D. Johann Fausten* (1587) was to have worldwide impact. Not only was it subsequently translated into virtually every European language (as well as into contemporary Low German and rhymed versions), it also formed the basis for various strands of tradition, comprising both narrative and drama. A sequel appeared as early as 1593 in the form of an allegedly 'other' (i.e. second) part, in which the main role fell to Famulus Wagner, from whom the book therefore also derived its name (the *Wagner* Book). In addition there were also constantly altered prose versions in a rapid succession of editions: by G.R. Widman (1599), C.N. Pfitzer (1674) and a 1725 version by an anonymous author who styled himself *Christlich Meinende* ('One with Christian intentions'). Dramatised versions were based on the *Tragic History of Doctor Faust*, by Christopher Marlowe, a contemporary of Shakespeare, probably dating from 1588–9, first performed in 1594 and first published in 1604. The popular play (*Volksschauspiel*) Doctor Faust and the puppet theatre adaptation also derive from the Marlowe version. Goethe's *Faust* reveals influences from both strands of the tradition, since the poet was inspired by the narrative and the dramatic versions. Thomas Mann also used the 1587 *Historia* as the basis for his *Doktor Faustus*.

Faust – one of the great figures in world literature

The Faust story is arguably the most successful in modern world literature. Few stories, perhaps taken from ancient mythology or the Bible, can compete with it. It gives pause for thought to realise that a few decades around 1600, as the Renaissance was waning, gave rise to no less than four literary figures who have since been dubbed human archetypes by scholarship. Apart from Faust, these were Hamlet (Shakespeare, 1600–1), Don Quixote (Cervantes, 1605–15) and Don Juan (Tirso de Molina, 1630).

What is the secret of the story's success? The *Historia* text presents Faust as a warning – an example to others not to act as Faust did. The reader is warned against the career of a scholar focused too much on worldliness – a sorcerer and lecher. Hailing from Weimar, he becomes a student in Wittenberg (like Hamlet), but soon abandons his theology studies (his faith and God) to live the life of an 'Epicurean' (a cipher for an atheist and libertine). He makes a pact with the Devil to obtain the means to fathom the world, heaven and hell and live a life of pleasure. After undergoing a series of adventures and playing tricks on some of his peers, while giving others a helping hand, towards the end of his life he obtains Helen of Greece as his 'concubine'. As the period of twenty-four years agreed on with the Devil draws to a close, Faust awaits a bloody demise and descent into Hell. What the (so far still unknown) author managed to assemble in this work proved to be a highly explosive mixture. He conjures up the figure of one who played a decisive role in shaping what was modern: the Renaissance scholar, doing so in order to issue a healthy warning against a career à la Faust. This produced a special dynamic, a tension between circumstances (the scholarly life) and inclination (wickedness from the orthodox Protestant viewpoint), so that the reading public was bound to feel two contradictory forces at work in the book, identical with the dominant forces of the epoch, an age 'in the midst of revolutions'.

The great prose works of Jörg Wickram and Johann Fischart's *Geschichtklitterung* have been recognised for over a century as forming part of the 'pre-' or 'early' history of the novel. They represent individual works of major stature whose authors rank beside Hans Sachs among the great representatives of the burgher class in German literature of the early modern period.

From 1539–57, around the middle of the sixteenth century, Wickram published his five major prose works, in addition to his *Schwank* anthology. Of these, three contain plots revolving either entirely or predominantly around a courtly milieu: *Ritter Calmy, Gabriotto und Reinhard* and *Der Goldfaden*. The two remaining works depict either exclusively or predominantly events from burgher life, the scenes of action thus being mostly burgher towns and trading establishments: *Der jungen Knaben Spiegel*

('Mirror of Boys') and *Von guten und bösen Nachbarn* ('Of Good and Bad Neighbours'). The extent to which Wickram missed the mark with his reading public in these two works is attested by their limited sales. This contrasted sharply with that of the first three titles, which enjoyed great popularity, parts of them even being included in sought-after chapbook anthologies (e.g. *Das Buch der Liebe*, 1587). Their motifs and language are closer to those of the chapbook, whereas works like *Der jungen Knaben Spiegel* are variations on themes such as that of the Prodigal Son. This notwithstanding, none of the five works can be denied the accolade of being included in the great prose genre (*Grossprosa*) with regard to composition, character or plot.

Early burgher ideology

All five works have a striking common element in the contemporary 'sociology' they offer, irrespective of differences between the courtly and burgher milieux. They provide a comprehensive compendium of early burgher ideology. Key features include the high esteem in which work was held and the conviction that 'trouble' (*Unruhe*) is the lot of humankind: 'Wie denn das ganze menschliche Geschlecht zur Unruhe geboren und erschaffen ist: ein jeder muss nach Gottes Ordnung, Arbeit und Lebenslauf vollbringen' ('Since then all mankind was born and created to trouble, each must perform his task and live out his life as God has ordained'). This ideology places love above differences in rank or class (with fortunate results in *Ritter Calmy* and *Goldfaden*, with tragic results in *Gabriotto und Reinhard*) and eulogises the family, marriage and bringing up children, neighbourliness and not least friendship. Another key aspect of Wickram's work and that of other pioneers of burgher thought from the late Middle Ages onwards is the way it sets nobility of virtue against nobility of birth. The disparagement and ultimate rejection of nobility of birth and its replacement by a nobility of virtue is the ideological counterpart of the process of social change that formed the main substance of early modern history until 1789. This transvaluation is depicted by Wickram in symbolic form in *Der jungen Knaben Spiegel* when the son of a nobleman, Wilbald, becomes subordinate to a burgher, who significantly bears the name of Fridbert, and recognises the latter as his 'lord' – the nobleman hence rendering obedience to the burgher and taking his orders.

Johann Fischart

Fischart's major prose work, generally cited in the abbreviated form of *Geschichtklitterung* (there were three editions during the author's lifetime, in 1575, 1582 and 1590), has an original title of 'baroque' length that takes up a good dozen lines or so. It contains *inter alia* the information that the book has been translated from the French, the original work being the romance *Gargantua and Pantagruel* by François Rabelais (1532–), or to be precise the first part, *Gargantua*. Rabelais in turn had based his version on a 1532 chapbook telling of the giant Gargantua, which contained blended elements of the Arthurian epic as well as medieval folk tales – fairy tales about giants. Fischart's adaptation of Rabelais' *Gargantua* does not, however, constitute what we would understand as a translation, being rather an extended version of it. Fischart was clearly more concerned with conveying his own additions and appendages – an abundance of stories which nevertheless remained in the spirit of Rabelais: his derision of the old nobility and the senior clergy, all governmental authority, scholastic obscurantists and the new monied nobility (what Fischart terms *Pfeffersecklichkeit*, *Pfeffer* referring to the exorbitant prices from which the *nouveau riche* derived their wealth). Fischart similarly preserved the character of the original work as a 'triumph of the flesh' and the bodily functions ('Triumph der Leiblichkeit' – E. Auerbach). New elements in the Fischart version include reformed Bible faith along with Calvinist educational doctrine – both in intransigent contrast with Fischart's high-spirited derision and his colourful depiction of physicality and bodily functions. This deprives his version of the resolute and homogeneous character typical of the Renaissance. Despite this, however, the *Geschichtklitterung* stands out among all other sixteenth-century German literary works for its 'eminently poetic and incomparable virtuoso language' ('eminent dichterische und unvergleichlich virtuose Sprache' – Sommerhalder).

BAROQUE LITERATURE

Seventeenth-century Germany

The Thirty Years War: a European conflict

By the seventeenth century the ailing Holy Roman Empire was under
threat from both within and without. As France evolved towards a more
territorially unified state in the aftermath of religious and civil wars, the
Empire was still reeling from the devastating political and economic setback
of the Thirty Years War. Seen as a European conflict, this war was a
regional power struggle between the Habsburgs and the Bourbons, with
the French at first entirely on the defensive. In time, however, French
political manoeuvring managed to break through Spanish and Austrian
encirclement tactics. By the end of the war France had emerged as the
dominant European power, the threat of a universal Habsburg monarchy
banished with the aid of Sweden.

The struggle for supremacy within the Empire

Within the Empire itself, however, the war took the form of a power
struggle between the Emperor and the imperial estates. While the latter
sought to uphold the rights they had gained over the centuries, the conduct
of Emperor Ferdinand II revealed a modern absolutist view of the state.
Like Karl V before him, he tried to halt or reverse centrifugal tendencies,
which had gained momentum through religious schism. The Augsburg
Religious Peace of 1555 that put an end to conflict in the age of the
Reformation, granting religious freedom to the territorial princes ('cuius
regio eius religio'), proved little more than a fleeting truce. It was the
peace treaties of Münster and Osnabrück that brought about a definitive
settlement of the various disputes. For the imperial constitution these
treaties meant a confirmation of the rights of those estates without whom
imperial affairs would virtually have ground to a halt. They were granted
the freedom to make alliances, hence effectively resolving the struggle

106

between the Emperor and the imperial estates. The history of the Empire from then on shows only modifications to this balance of power, becoming instead the history of its major territories.

Pufendorf: the German Empire as a 'monster'

Samuel Pufendorf, Professor of Natural Law and Politics, describes the state of the Empire after the Peace of Westphalia in precise terms:

> All that remains, therefore, if we wish to classify the German Empire by the standards of political science, is to call it an abnormal, monster-like entity that, as a result of the neglectful complacency of the Emperor, the ambition of princes and the machinations of the clergy, has developed from a normal monarchy into such a disharmonious form of government that it can no longer be described as a constitutional monarchy, although outward appearances might seem to suggest this, but is not yet a federation of a number of states, being something between the two. This deplorable state of affairs is the abiding source of the fatal malaise and inner upheavals taking place within the Empire, as the Emperor strives on the one hand to restore the supremacy of the monarchy, and the estates on the other strive for absolute freedom.
>
> (*De statu imperii Germanici* 1667)

Although the Thirty Years War had dissimilar effects on different regions, and for various spans of time, it left the country as a whole devastated. Whereas prior to the war the population had numbered some 15–17 millions, by 1648 it had been reduced to 10–11 millions, although losses as a direct result of war were relatively low. Neither the number of fallen nor abuse of the civil population can account for these losses, or at least for the major losses. The chief culprit was the ravages caused by the plague, although war conditions greatly exacerbated its effects. The risk of contamination was increased by towns teeming with refugees from the war. Recovery from this demographic decline and restoration of pre-war demographic levels were not achieved until well into the eighteenth century. Economic recovery was equally slow, particularly as the immediate postwar period began with an agrarian crisis and a depression in trade and commerce that were not overcome until towards the end of the century. States and their rulers intervened actively in economic life through the instrument of mercantilism, if only to ensure themselves of an income and thereby strengthen their own positions.

The end of the Thirty Years War put paid to all efforts at achieving absolute imperial power in Germany, where such power was synonymous with territorial absolutism. With the decline of central imperial power, the territories widened their sphere of jurisdiction, seeking to bolster internal government activities and wherever possible reduce the rights of the landed estates. State parliaments were no longer assembled, taxes were raised arbitrarily, former privileges abrogated and religious pressure was brought to bear. These measures were aimed not solely at the nobility, however, but equally against towns and cities, which were more or less forcibly subjugated to the will of their landed rulers.

A steady expansion in the jurisdiction of the state necessitated the reorganisation of regional administration. Intensive state activity with the aid of a growing administrative apparatus brought about territorial standardisation, enabling the state to influence a wide range of social spheres. The judiciary, education system, social welfare, social security, the economy and ecclesiastical affairs were all now regulated by numerous decrees. Hardly any aspect of human life was exempt from this official planning or welfare activity. The urge on the part of state and municipal government to instruct and control – aimed at the 'social discipline' of their subjects (Gerhard Ostreich) – knew, in theory, no bounds.

Absolutist court culture found tangible expression in the ostentatious castle- and palace-building that took place from the 1690s onwards. After the Thirty Years War the French model came to dominate more and more, typified by the Versailles of Louis XIV (built between 1661 and 1689), although in Vienna, the most important royal household in the Empire, it was the Spanish court style that took hold. Imitation of the celebrated luxurious court style at Versailles, as well as the public display of absolute power through sumptuous design and festivities, obviously overstretched the finances of less powerful German territories. This led in some cases to a grotesque incongruity between the claim to rule and the actual political and economic capacity that upheld it. The burden of this was borne in the main by the subjects. The essence of court ceremonial lay in the public display of princely power and the disciplining of court society, chiefly the nobility. The court social system, with the prince at its hub, regulated social conduct, imposed constraints and provided employment, placing people in a world fraught with tension and rapacious for status and rank. Court pageantry, ceremonial, banquets and festivities also served to sustain the unbridgeable gap between the court and its subjects. The perceived need for a separate social space, apart from the rest of the world, may be discerned among other things in the design of baroque castles and their stylised gardens.

The bourgeois intellectual as ideal public servant

The expansion of state jurisdiction, with a concomitantly increased need for academically trained officials, resulted in an improvement in the status of Humanist-educated intellectuals, who were now able to achieve privileged positions in the rank hierarchy and even establish themselves as pillars of the state. The Humanist intellectual came to see himself as the ideal public servant, and was now competing with the nobility. In the sixteenth century principalities particularly, numerous posts at court, in the judiciary and in financial administration were filled by intellectuals of burgher origin, either because the nobility lacked the necessary competence for these new duties, or because they refused to enter public service. It would be wrong, however, to picture this as an alliance between Humanist intellectuals and princes with a view to depriving the nobility of their power. The existing rank hierarchy was not being challenged at this stage; it was simply a matter of denying the nobility their political aspirations. As a result of the need for a body of officials with a Humanist education, which found expression among other things in rebellion among the official aristocracy, princes succeeded in confronting the old aristocracy with a rival, at the same time pointing the way to new realities of princely service. This development was reversed during the seventeenth century. As absolutist rule entrenched itself the nobility regained some of their former privileges by availing themselves of Humanist knowledge, acquiring through university education the qualifications required for these expanding official professions.

Internal strife

However, the seventeenth century was not only the age of the Thirty Years War, wars against the Turks (with the siege of Vienna in 1683), conflicts with France (the Dutch war of 1672–9, the Palatinate War of 1688–97), or with Sweden (the Swedish-Brandenburg War of 1675–9). It was also a period of internal strife and social unrest. These issues may at first sight seem less spectacular than the major political and religious confrontations of the day, but they do point to areas of conflict within an apparently well-ordered hierarchical rank society. Numerous cities underwent constitutional conflicts and social upheaval: there were repeated peasant uprisings and wars in rural Germany, while witch hunts reached epidemic level over wide areas.

Persecution of the Jews

The roots of conflict in the towns and cities, besides militant Reform and counter-Reform measures, may be seen from clear indicators of economic crisis, such as inflation, and from conflicts between the ruling upper class and the guilds. During a period of unrest in the imperial city of Frankfurt am Main (the Fedtmilch uprising of 1612–14) the *Judengasse*, the Jewish ghetto, was stormed and plundered by a furious mob, the entire community of some 2,500 being expelled from the city. In 1616 they returned to Frankfurt under the protection of imperial troops. This plundering and expulsion was the culmination of a series of acts against Jews instigated by the guilds. In an age of economic decline, unemployment and pauperisation, the blame was once more laid at the door of the Jews, who were moreover also under the protection of the loathed patriciate and council, who used them for profitable financial transactions. Since 1460 the Frankfurt Jewish community, which had already been subjected to pogroms in the thirteenth and fourteenth centuries, had lived in a ghetto, restricted in personal and economic development alike by a wide range of discriminatory regulations. *Der Juden zu Franckfurt Stättigkeit und Ordnung* of 1613 stipulated fines for all manner of offences, decreeing for example, under the heading 'Juden sollen Zeichen tragen' ('Jews should wear symbols'):

> Damit auch die Christen vor den Juden zuerkennen seyen / so sollen alle und jede Juden und Jüdinnen / sie seyen frembt oder Ingesessen / ausserhalb der Judengassen / in und zwischen den Messen / ihr gebührlich Zeichen / als mit nahmen ein runden gelben Ring / offentlich und mit ihren Mänteln unverdeckt an ihren Kleidern tragen / bey Vermeidung den Ingesessen der Bussen / nemblichen 12. Schilling. Und den Frembden ein Gulden unablösslich zubezahlen / so offt und dick das noth geschieht / darnach sich ein jeder wisse zurichten.

> So that Christians might be told apart from Jews / each and every Jew and Jewess / be he foreign or resident / both outside the *Judengasse* and in and between the markets / should wear his proper mark / namely a round yellow circle / openly and uncovered by the coat, on their clothing / in case of non-compliance, the resident shall be fined / the sum of 12 shillings. And the foreigner should pay one guilder, from which he cannot be absolved / As often and as frequently as the need may arise / may each and everyone act accordingly.

Although no more serious persecutions or massacres of Jews, such as those of the Late Middle Ages, took place, the position of the Jews in the Empire remained extremely precarious. In the sixteenth century they were expelled from a number of territories (Bavaria, the Palatine and Brandenburg), and in 1670 from the Austrian *Erblanden*. Luther's hostility to the Jews fuelled anti-semitism in Protestant regions.

Witch-mania

A decline in the persecution of Jews in the sixteenth and seventeenth centuries compared with the late medieval period went hand in hand with a steady rise in the persecution of so-called witches, which came to a horrendous climax in the first half of the seventeenth century. According to the historian Hugh Trevor-Roper, 'in the sixteenth century the witch gradually replaces the Jew, and in the seventeenth the reversal is almost complete. If the universal scapegoat of the Black Death in Germany had been the Jew, the universal scapegoat of the Wars of Religion will be the witch'. Witch trials were exploited as an instrument of discipline in the religious and political power struggle. Another more deeply-rooted motive behind witch-hunts is mirrored in the fact that most of their victims were women. Although some men were brought to trial, women seemed much more prone to this crime. The statement: 'Also schlecht ist das Weib von Natur, da es schneller am Glauben zweifelt, auch schneller den Glauben ableugnet, was die Grundlage für die Hexerei ist' ('The female of the species is thus evil by nature, quicker to doubt the faith and quicker to disavow it, which is the root of witchcraft') corresponds to the image of women propounded by the medieval church and its theology. It is a quotation from the *Hexenhammer*, written around 1487 by Heinrich Institoris and Jacob Sprenger; the work, disseminated in no less than 29 editions in the fifteenth, sixteenth and seventeenth centuries, became a handbook for the conduct of witch trials.

Criticism of the witch trials

Some voices were raised against this organised persecution mania, the principles underlying it and its spurious legal proceedings, but at first they were unable to make themselves heard. Critics included the Jesuit Friedrich Spee, who severely denounced the practices of the witch trials of the day from his own viewpoint in *Cautio Criminalis*, published anonymously in 1631. Success in opposing witch trials came only later with Christian Thomasius, who quotes Spee, although by this time persecution was already beginning to wane of its own accord.

Literature and society

Social and occasional poetry

Despite broad differentiation, seventeenth-century poetry is essentially typified by its social character: 'Prior to the emancipation of the subject, Art, in a certain sense, was unquestionably more social than thereafter' (Theodor W. Adorno). This fundamentally social character of seventeenth-century literature is most clearly apparent in occasional poetry, *Casualcarmina*, which despite being severely criticised by contemporary poets nevertheless flourished on a massive scale, accompanying the course of human life from the cradle to the grave. Martin Opitz wrote: 'Es wird kein buch / keine hochzeit / kein begräbnüss ohn uns gemacht; und gleichsam als

111

niemand köndte alleine sterben / gehen unsere gedichte zuegleich mit ihnen
unter' ('Not a book can be made / nor a wedding / or funeral held without
us; and as if no-one could even die alone / our poems go into the very
grave with him'). While the problems associated with such mass production
– written to order and often for a fee – are not difficult to discern, this
did not detract from a practice that revolved around social convention.
The idea of a commission preceding the creation of a work of art was after
all already accepted without question in fine art and music. It nevertheless
lay behind not only *Casualcarmina*, but all literary genres, albeit not
always so directly – be it religious verse written for a special occasion,
pedagogically or religiously motivated school and Jesuit drama or verse
composed for court festivities.

The 'utility' of poetry

The fundamentally rhetorical character of seventeenth-century literature,
and the continued upholding of the Horatian requirement that the poet
'mit der Liebligkeit und schöne den Nutzen [verbinde]' ('[combine] usefulness with the delightful and beautiful' – Augustus Buchner) serve to underline its public character. Poetry was intended for didactic purposes – to
foster the virtuous life. Using examples from poets and story-writers,
Buchner, a Professor in Wittenberg, describes how this didactic effect could
best be achieved in his *Poetik (Poetics)*, published in the 1730s: 'Lehren
also beyde / was zu thun oder zulassen sey; nicht zwar durch gebiethen
und verbiethen / oder durch scharfsinnige Schlussreden... / sondern durch
allerley Exempel und Fabeln / welches die alleranmuthigste Art zu lehren
ist / und bey denselben / die sonst nicht so gar erfahren sind / zum meisten
verfängt: in dem Sie hierdurch ohn allen Zwang und mit einer sondern
Lust / fast spielend zur Tugend / und dem was nützlich ist / angeführet
werden' ('Therefore teach both / what is to be done and what is to be left
undone; and not through directions and prohibitions / or sagacious closing
speeches... / but through all manner of examples and fables, / which is
the most charming way of all to teach, / and with those who are not yet
so experienced the most effective: whereby without any coercion and with
an uncommon delight, / almost playfully, you will lead them to virtue and
that which is useful').

Poetry as a means of imposing discipline

Teaching 'what is to be done and what is to be left undone' encompassed
more than general ethical norms or a catalogue of Christian virtues. Imparting ethical norms and leading the student to virtue also embraced social
and political conduct: '[so] dass sich die Poesie, indem sie ihren ethischen
Auftrag erfüllte, unmittelbar auf gesellschaftliches und politisches Ges-

chehen bezog' ('[so] that poetry, by performing its ethical function, might relate directly to social and political events' – Wolfram Mauser). The principle of serving virtue presented itself as a powerful means for imposing discipline on the people. By upholding virtue, poetry could assist in maintaining peace and order in a hierarchically stratified society: 'Hüte dich für fressen und sauffen', 'Förchte Gott', 'Ehre vater und mutter' as well as 'Sey der Obrigkeit unthan' ('Keep watch over your eating and supping', 'Fear God', 'Honour thy Father and thy Mother', 'Be subject to your rulers') are some of the headings in an anthology of sonnets by Johann Plavius (1630), which provides an illuminating example of how virtue, society and politics could be combined.

Poets as intellectuals

With few exceptions, of which Grimmelshausen was one, all middle-class German poets were intellectuals. Their university education had taken them through the faculty of arts, acquainting them with rhetoric and poetics and equipping them with a sound philological training that was regarded as indispensable for engaging in the art of poetry. More and more nobles were becoming involved in literary activity, sharing the same educational and intellectual background as middle-class authors. Although aristocrats in particular tended to designate their poetry-writing as *Neben-Werck* (a 'sideline', or subsidiary profession), poetry was by no means the main profession even for non-aristocratic writers. Authors made their living as clerics, university professors, physicians, or as municipal, *Land* or court officials; they were certainly not autonomous writers of independent means.

The Fruchtbringende Gesellschaft: aims and conflicts

Princes relied on the output of intellectuals and poets not only on account of their 'Begiehr der Unsterblichkeit' ('desire for immortality' – Martin Opitz) or even their conviction that 'die herrlichkeit der wörter' ('the splendour of words') could talk the rebellious 'common man' into compliance ('zur ruhe' – Jakob Horst, 1558). There was also the matter of *kulturpatriotische* aims, concerned with safeguarding the German language and culture. These were shared by many princes in common with poets, without whose specialist qualifications they would remain unfulfilled. A glance at the *Fruchtbringende Gesellschaft* (The Fruitbearing Society), the first and most important German language society of the seventeenth century, should suffice to show this. It was founded in 1617 on the model of academies elsewhere in Europe, with the stated aims of the 'erbawung wolanstendiger Sitten' ('inculcation of decent mores') and the cultivation of the German language. The society was to be open to any man, 'so ein liebhaber aller Erbarkeit, / Tugend' und Höfliggkeit / vornemblich aber des Vaterlands' ('who is a lover of all honourableness, / virtue and good manners / but above all of the Fatherland' – Ludwig von Anhalt-Köthen). Middle-class poets and intellectuals were indeed received into this predominantly aristocratic society. In fact, were it not for the accomplishments of the Humanist middle classes, who had little difficulty standing out from other, largely unproductive noble members, the Fruitbearing Society would hardly be worth noting. Despite this, however, the opening up of the society in this way struck some aristocrats, sensitive to rank distinction and more concerned with the social aspects of the endeavour, as going too far. Their attempt to transform the Fruitbearing Society into an order of knights nonetheless ran into opposition from Prince Ludwig von Anhalt-Köthen, who presided over the Society until his death in 1650: 'Der Zweck ist alleine auf die Deutsche sprache und löbliche tugenden, nicht aber auf Ritterliche thaten alleine gerichtet, wiewohl auch solche nicht ausgeschlossen' ('Our purpose is solely towards the German language and laudable virtue, not towards knightly deeds, howsoever the latter are not excluded').

Nobilitas litteraria?

Like other societies of its kind, the Fruitbearing Society introduced the custom of bestowing social appellations on its members, such as 'the Nurturing', 'the Sweet-smelling', 'the Tasteful', the Crowned ('der Nährende', 'der Wohlriechende', 'der Schmackhafte', 'der Gekrönte'). There is some controversy as to whether these designations may be interpreted as a playful nullification of class distinctions, and whether the idea of the *nobilitas litteraria* may therefore be regarded as having suffered at least an initial defeat. Although Ludwig did not deliberately set out to promote the middle-class intelligentsia, his social politics did achieve this indirectly, which may account for the resistance he encountered in aristocratic circles. At all events these efforts on the part of Ludwig, Humanist intellectuals and men of letters to carry out their patriotic cultural aims did improve their social standing, while they themselves, not entirely against their will, were taken into the service of the state and state administration.

Emphasis on class distinctions

Substantial as the achievements of the Fruitbearing Society and its middle-class members initially were, the death of Ludwig von Anhalt-Köthen in 1650 altered the picture, so that the association came more and more to adopt the character of an order of knights. This shift manifested itself not only in its membership policy, and in a consequent decline in its literary and scholarly accomplishments, but also in the social sphere. Some words by Georg Neumark, the (middle-class) secretary of the Society, concerning the social practice of 'restoring the privileges' of the nobility (1668) are significant:

> Es hat aber die Meinung allhier gar nicht / das grosse Herren und hohe Fruchtbringende Gesellschafter / sich mit den Niedrigern / in verächtliche und allzugemeine Kundschaft einlassen: oder die Niedrigere / weil Sie auch Ordensgenossen / denen vornehmen Standespersonen / wie Etliche aus unbescheidener Kühnheit und thörichter Einbildung / sich unterstanden / alzu nahe treten; Sondern vielmehr erheischender Nohtdurft und Umstände nach / in unterthänigster Aufwartung und geziehmender Demuht verharren sollen.

> By no means all here share the view that great nobles and highborn Fruitbearing associates are permitting themselves to fraternise with lowborn people in mean contemptuous patronage: or even that the lowborn, being likewise members of the order, are too familiar with distinguished persons of rank, as some of them are, out of immodest boldness and foolish conceit; it is rather that in accordance with necessity and circumstance they should abide in the most subservient attendance and becoming humility.

Membership of the Fruitbearing Society was, at least under Ludwig, a distinction worth striving for (under his leadership some 527 members were received into it, and by 1680 the number had increased to 890). Outstanding men of letters among the *Gesellschafter* included Johann Valentin Andreae, Anton Ulrich von Braunschweig-Wolfenbüttel, Sigmund von Birken, Augustus Buchner, Georg Philipp Harsdörffer, Friedrich von Logau, Johann Michael Moscherosch, Martin Opitz, Justus Georg Schottelius, Diederich von dem Werder, Johann Rist and Philipp von den Zesen. The active promotion of literature in translation was another of the undisputed accomplishments of the 'Order of Palms' (*Palmenorden*), as the Society was also known. Other societies modelled on the Fruitbearing Society were founded from the 1640s onwards, including the 'Deutschgesinnigte Genossenschaft' ('The German-Minded Association' – 1643), which reflected the ideas of Zesen and the 'Pegnesische Blumenorden' ('The Pegasean Order of Flowers' – 1644), both of which also accepted female members. Given the territorial fragmentation of Germany, these language societies may be regarded as 'the real literary centres of the seventeenth century' (Ferdinand van Ingen).

Limited readership, expensive books

The literature produced under these conditions (censorship was an additional factor) was only available to a very limited readership – one equipped with the appropriate educational background, but whose open-mindedness to secular literature could by no means be taken for granted. Access to literature also presumed a certain degree of affluence, since books were relatively costly: reading circles or libraries open to the public were still a thing of the future. The lengthy court-history novels of the day, for example, were only within reach of the purses of the well-off, for example high-ranking officials or the aristocracy: the price of eight imperial dollars set for Lohenstein's *Arminius* (1689–90), for example, represented something like the monthly income of a minor official. Adrian Beier's *Kurtzer Bericht von der Nützlichen und Fürtrefflichen Buch-handlung* (1690) contains the laconic statement: 'der gemeine Hauffe den Buchladen nicht viel kothig machet' ('the common herd doth not much besmirch the bookshop').

Literary reform

The time-lag in Germany

At the beginning of the seventeenth century, when Shakespeare's masterpieces were being written, the secretary of a Bohemian magnate posed a question that troubled more than himself:

> Warumb sollen wir den unser Teutsche sprachen,
> In gwisse Form und Gsatz nit auch mögen machen,
> Und Deutsches Carmen schreiben,
> Die Kunst zutreiben,
> Bey Mann und Weiben.

The poem from which this verse is taken is quoted in *Von Art der Deutschen Poeterey*; both its content and awkward form are indications of the poor standard of German poetry around the end of the sixteenth and beginning of the seventeenth centuries. Theobald Hock, its author, as well as other educated contemporaries, were struck by the discrepancy between Renaissance literature in the vernacular in southern and western Europe and the hidebound Late Medieval models still prevalent in German verse. Writing in 1624, Opitz declared himself, in characteristic patriotic vein, 'mightily' (*heftig*) amazed 'dass / da sonst wir Teutschen keiner Nation an Kunst und Geschicklichkeit bevor geben / doch biss jetzund niemandt under uns gefunden worden / so der Poesie in unserer Muttersprach sich mit rechten fleiss und eifer angemasset [habe]'. Stress is laid on poetry 'in the mother tongue', where German literature indeed lagged, having failed to take the decisive step to which the literatures of southern and western European countries owed their recent flowering, namely the revitalisation of poetry in the vernacular on the basis of Humanism.

National Humanist aspirations in other countries

Italy led the field in national Humanist aspirations. Poetry in Italian had first burgeoned in the fourteenth century with Dante, Petrarch and Boccaccio, reaching a second peak in the sixteenth century with Ariosto and Tasso. In France the Pléiade poets set themselves the task of reviving both the French language and literature using ancient and Italian Renaissance models. Poets in Spain, England and Holland likewise followed the Italian, and later French example, thereby ushering in a 'Golden Age' in their respective literatures. In Germany, however, the early Humanism of the waning fifteenth century, and its attempts to translate seminal Italian Renaissance texts into German with the aim of revitalising German literature in the spirit of the Renaissance, was no more than a passing phase. Latin remained virtually the sole language of Humanist scholars and poets. As a result, two literatures continued to exist side by side, one in Latin and the other in German, each feeding on its own traditions: one on Humanism, the other on the unlearned folklore heritage.

Latin and German in the sixteenth and seventeenth centuries

Italian Humanists, who fancied themselves surrounded by barbaric lands, were not alone in dismissing the Germans as barbarians and German as a barbaric language. German Humanists themselves shared these sentiments. Latin was the language of the major German lyric poets of the sixteenth century, and Latin the language in which works of a European standard, far above what was then possible in German, were written. The creators and consumers of neo-Latin poetry were for the most part identical. The educated Humanist class saw itself as an intellectual elite, but was also striving to establish itself as a social class in its own right. It therefore made a point of sharply distinguishing itself from the classes below it, the mass of non-Humanist intellectuals. This social chasm grew no narrower in the seventeenth century, since the new *Kunstdichtung* in German then being propounded and promoted with such patriotic cultural enthusiasm was scholarly poetry on a Humanist basis. For Opitz and other reformers it was quite obvious that the shift to the use of German precluded a return to the forms and themes of sixteenth-century German vernacular poetry: 'Und muss ich nur bey hiesiger gelegenheit ohne schew dieses erinnern / das ich es für eine verlorene arbeit halte / im fall sich jemand an unsere deutsche Poeterey machen wolte / der / nebenst dem das er ein Poete von natur sein muss / in den griechischen und Lateinischen büchern nicht wol durchtrieben ist / und von ihnen den rechten grieff erlernet hat; das auch alle die lehren / welche sonsten zue der Poesie erfodert werden ... / bey ihm nichts verfangen können.'

The only possible exponents of the new German 'art poetry'

(*Kunstdichtung*) were Humanist intellectuals. German was usurping Latin, but the Humanist intellectual arsenal of poetic language, and the very prerequisites for poetic creativity, remained one and the same: even in the vernacular, poetry was still the privilege of an elite. The revival of German poetic language and German verse entailed a decisive break with indigenous tradition: there was no path leading from Hans Sachs to Martin Opitz or Andreas Gryphius. There was nonetheless continuity of a kind, albeit not linked to language as such: the Latin poetic tradition was an essential prerequisite for German seventeenth century art poetry (*Kunstdichtung*).

Antiquity and the Renaissance as models

In the more advanced countries of southern and western Europe, it was Renaissance poetry, besides the Latin tradition, that became the model and example, although these countries had already achieved what was still waiting to be done in Germany: a revival of poetry in the vernacular on a Humanist basis. The capacity of German culture to accomplish this was argued by pointing to the venerable age of German poetry, as well as to evidence from the Middle Ages. Clearly, however, only poetry from antiquity and the Renaissance could provide suitable models for the development of a sophisticated poetic language.

The reform of German poetry in the seventeenth century is associated by contemporaries and literary historians with the name of Martin Opitz. The launching of his concerted efforts was marked by declarations of his vision and his recipes for poetry. These were followed, with no less success, by models for nearly all genres and forms: drama, opera libretti, court novels, as well as didactic, biblical and lyric poetry. His *Buch von der Deutschen Poeterey (Book of German Poesy)* (1624) was the first work on poetics in the German language. Aside from rules on language and the art of verse-writing, this concise work contains nothing that had not already appeared in previous studies of Renaissance poetics. The decisive passage in terms of the future development of German verse deals with rhymes, their words and forms of poetry, as well as elaborating on the basic aspects of reform with respect to poetic technique. These include the following metric rules: 'Nachmals ist auch ein jeder verss entweder ein iambicus oder trochaicus; nicht zwar das wir auff art der griechen unnd lateiner eine gewisse grösse (i.e. length) der sylben können inn acht nemen; sondern das wir aus den accenten unnd dem thone erkennen / welche sylbe hoch unnd welche niedrig gesetzt soll werden.' Opitz thus required German poetry to respect the principle of alternating verse (iambs and trochees) and, in contrast to the quantity-based procedures of ancient metre, laid down laws of stress. This rule of alternation was soon abandoned, but the second principle, that of respecting natural word stress, was to persist. In addition to the concise delineation of the various literary genres, poetics further

118

comprised recommendations for specific verse forms: the Alexandrine and *vers commun* (an iamb with five stresses and a caesura) were classified with the sonnet and epigram, whereas trochaic verse (or a mixture of iambic and trochaic lines) continued to be classified with the freer song form – the 'ode' in the terminology of the day.

Limits of reform

Scholarly verse-writing in German did not assert itself in all regions. Catholic areas in southern and western Germany, for example, were largely averse to reforms in language and verse-writing, pursuing instead their own traditions, both Latin and German. Social differences were involved besides confessional and regional ones. The gulf between the educated Humanist classes and the people, which in the sixteenth century had found its clearest expression in the use of different languages – Latin and German – now manifests itself within the same language. The traditions of sixteenth-century literature in German, opposed by the scholar-poets, were consequently by no means entirely superseded. Although the scholarly tendency did make considerable headway in terms of art poetry, anthologies such as the *Venusgärtlein* (1656), with its blend of old and new *Lieder*, show that the folk song was still very much alive. Similarly, the art of *Meistersang* was still cultivated in some cities. Even in Breslau, a veritable bastion of baroque poetry, there was a song school until 1670. The scholar-poets, however, had nothing but contempt for artistic creation of this kind, which inevitably in their eyes was a classic example of behind-the-times, inept verse composition. By the same token, even handbills publishing rhymed commentaries on political and religious events, social problems and miraculous occurrences by no means invariably adhered to the norms of art poetry, as may be seen from the following satirical epitaph (1634):

Wallenstein's Epitaph

Hie liegt und fault mit Haut und Bein
    Der Grosse KriegsFürst Wallenstein.
Der gross Kriegsmacht zusamen bracht /
    Doch nie gelieffert recht ein Schlacht.
Gross Gut thet er gar vielen schencken /
    Dargeg'n auch viel unschuldig hencken.
Durch sterngucken und lang tractiren /
    Thet er viel Land und Leuth verliehren.
Gar zahrt war ihm sein Böhmisch Hirn /
    Kont nicht leyden der Sporn Kirrn.
Han / Hennen / Hund / er bandisirt /
    Aller Orten wo er losirt.

Doch musst er gehn des Todtes Strassen /
D'Han krähn / und d'Hund bellen lassen.

Those groups who were precluded from enjoying modern art poetry (i.e. large sections of the rural population and the urban lower and middle classes) were thus not starved of poetry altogether. It was among them that *Volkspoesie* (folk poetry) thrived in its various forms, passed on mainly orally in the form of songs that were sung and pamphlets intended to be read aloud. These phenomena exerted no influence on the development of German literature in the seventeenth century, however.

Poetry and rhetoric

The categories of the poetry of experience are not applicable to seventeenth-century literature. The fact that they are nevertheless occasionally applied to it even today is evidence of how deeply-rooted the classical-romantic conception of poetry is in the tradition of German literary scholarship. It likewise highlights the difficulty of devising an appropriate conceptual framework for dealing with pre-classical literature – or at least one amounting to something more than the mere antithesis of categories familiar from the aesthetics of experience.

Of those concepts that have so far been introduced into discussion for the purposes of defining baroque poetry and its distinctness from other forms, i.e. its maintenance of distance, ostentation, objectivity and courtly character, only rhetoric is specifically linked with language. The idea of poetry as *gebundene Rede* (metrical speech) and hence its status as part of rhetoric, was undisputed in the seventeenth century. Harsdörffer writes in *Poetischer Trichter* (1647–53): 'Diesem nach ist die Poeterey und Redkunst miteinander verbrüdert und verschwestert / verbunden und verknüpftet / dass keine sonder die andre gelehret / erlernet / getrieben und geübet werden kan' ('Therefore poetry and rhetoric are brother and sister one to the other / bound together and joined, / so that the one can be neither taught / learned / practised nor exercised without the other'). This approach is part of the ancient heritage, and is fundamental to any understanding of poetry and poetics in the early modern era. In seeing the prime objective of poetry as 'uberredung und unterricht auch ergetzung der Leute' ('the persuasion, instruction and edification of men'), Opitz is simply availing himself of the categories of rhetoric – *persuadere, docere, delectare* – defining 'the art of rhetoric as the art of intention' (Wilfried Barner). Poetry, of whatever genre, is intended to achieve effects – it has 'purpose'.

It was from the art of rhetoric that poetics also adopted the essential distinction between *res* and *verba*, i.e. things (the subjects or themes of poetry) and words, and the arrangement of words that follows from them, whereby only the art of setting to verse has no parallel in rhetoric: 'Weil die Poesie / wie auch die Rednerkunst / in dinge und worte abgetheilet wird; als wollen wir erstlich von erfindung und eintheilung der dinge / nachmals von der zuebereitung und ziehr der worte / unnd endtlich vom masse der sylben / Verse / reimen / unnd unterschiedener art der carminium und getichte reden' ('Since poetry / like rhetoric / is divided into things and words; we wanting to speak firstly of the invention and arrangement of things / then of the preparation and adornment of words / and lastly of the measure of syllables / Verse / rhymes / And the various forms of carminium and poem').

With these words, Opitz begins the fifth chapter of his Poetics, as he commences its more specific part. Whereas the introductory chapters deal with the nature of poetry, defending the vocation of poet and the venerable age of German poetry, there now ensues a systematic account of the principles and 'rules' of poetry, in the same order to be found in textbooks on rhetoric: *inventio, dispositio* and *elocutio* (the invention, arrangement, and preparation and adornment of words respectively). Harsdörffer elaborates on the logic of this sequence: 'Wann ich einen Brief schreiben will / muss ich erstlich wissen / was desselben Inhalt seyn soll / und bedencken den Anfang / das Mittel / das End / und wie ich besagten Inhalt aufeinander ordnen möge / dass jedes an seinem Ort sich wolgesetzet / füge: Also muss auch der Inhalt oder die Erfindung dess Gedichts erstlich untersucht / und in den Gedancken verfasset werden / bevor solcher in gebundener Rede zu Papier fliesse. Daher jener recht gesagt: *Mein Gedicht ist fertig / biss auf die Wort*' ('If I wish to write a letter / I must first know / what the content of the same is to be / and think of the beginning / the middle / the end / and how I may so order the said content together / so that each is put in its rightful / place: Thus the content or invention of the poem must first be considered / and conceived in thought / before the same can flow on to paper in the form of metrical speech. Hence the apt saying: *My poem is finished, but for the words*').

Aptness

Things and words are thus chosen to suit one another: poetry is always related to its subject-matter. Harsdörffer's observation that speech should be 'verständlich-zierlich und den Sachen gemäss' ('intelligible, elegant and befitting the subject') indicates that the relationship between the two cannot be arbitrary, and that words must be chosen to suit their subjects. Moreover, in line with the intentional character of poetry, stylistic expression focuses on the effect being aimed for in the reader or hearer. It is hence remote from the subjective, the poet distanced both from the subject and the word. Enquiry after experience is anachronistic and inappropriate to this rhetorical understanding of verbal expression.

Contradiction between theory and practice

Although the integration of subject and words is not arbitrary, having been governed from ancient times by a theory of decorum, there is always a chance that the bond between subject and word will loosen, rendering creative form a goal in its own right. There is considerable evidence to suggest the existence of a contradiction between seventeenth-century poetic theory, based on the tradition of classical rhetoric, and poetry in practice. Whereas most poets deviated only slightly from time-honoured guidelines, poetic practice became increasingly removed from theory, and began to take on mannerist features. The reason for this is that rhetorical tradition is not confined to theory alone, being a discipline based 'on the trinity of *doctrina* (or *praecepta*), *exempla* and *imitatio*' (W. Barner). Any shift in poetic models in an age when the whole notion of poetry rested on the principle of *imitatio* was therefore bound to have far-reaching consequences for poetic practice.

Imitatio

Here, *imitatio* signifies the emulation not of nature, but of literary models and patterns. Modern concepts such as plagiarism or originality have no place in this way of thinking. To avail oneself of 'frembder Poeten Erfindungen' ('the inventions of other poets') is 'ein rühmlicher Diebstal bey den Schülern / wann sie die Sache recht anzubringen wissen' ('a laudable form of theft in pupils, if they know how to go about it' – Harsdörffer). This notwithstanding, such statements are based on the assumption that the *imitatio* of works from the past and present that are worthy of emulation will result in something new and distinctive.

Lyric poetry

With the advent of literary reform the themes and forms of European Renaissance poetry also came to govern the German lyric. German poets upheld the traditions of both lamenting and humorous love poetry, convivial song (*geselliges Lied*), eulogy (*Lobdichtung*) and satire, at the same time adopting the formal canon of Humanist art poetry. The sonnet, the protracted Alexandrine poem (elegy), the epigram and the ode – in the form both of the great tripartite Pindaric ode and the song – were the predominant forms. These were accompanied by attempts at ingenious forms such as the sestina [a rhymed or unrhymed poem with six stanzas of six lines and a final triplet, each stanza having the same words to end its lines but in different order – *translator*], as well as experiments with other ancient ode forms (e.g. rhymed Sapphic odes). Lastly, the immense popularity of pictographic poems (*Figurengedichten*) is an indication of the new-found aesthetic potential of the German language.

Religious lyricism also adopted new verse and strophe forms, although the hymn remained largely bound to indigenous traditions, its function in congregational singing offering limited potential for development. Despite, or perhaps even because of this, hymns are among the few seventeenth-century poetic works that have been kept alive to this day. Besides the conventional type of hymn, intended for singing at public services, another hymn form emerged in the seventeenth century intended for private services or devotions at home. The musical composition and artistic nature of the texts of this new sacred song (*geistliches Lied*) form show that it was aimed at a public familiar with the rudiments of Humanist art poetry.

Opitz

As the Schleswig-Holsteiner Johann Rist writes in the poetry anthology *Musa Teutonica* (1634), which introduced the regularised German lyric to the Low German-speaking regions, Opitz had broken the ice 'und uns Teutschen die rechte Art gezeigt / wie auch wir in unsrer Sprache / Petrarchas, Aristos, und Ronsardos haben können' ('and shown us Germans the right way / to have Petrarch, Aristotle and Ronsard / in our own language'). This vision of reform was brought to bear throughout Protestant Germany, the models laid down by Opitz being emulated and varied. His works, both his book of rules and examples of his own poetry, laid the foundations for the great lyric compositions of the ensuing decades.

The poetry of Paul Fleming, who regarded himself as an Opitz adherent, marked the first high point in the seventeenth-century German lyric. It is generally viewed in the light of Petrarchism, the motifs of which had been introduced into German literature by Opitz, Georg Rudolf Weckherlin and others, although Fleming embraced it in its entirety, allowing it to dominate the character of his lyric love poetry. His love poetry, published posthumously in 1646 in *Teutschen Poemata*, is concerned with the praise and beauty of the beloved (meticulously divided up into her several bodily parts), and with the objects and localities associated with her, treating of the nature of love and its effects, and to this end making use of the entire antithetical and hyperbolic arsenal of the traditional language of love, occasionally bordering even on parody. Apart from the traditional motifs of lamenting love, loss of self and the death wish, however, another theme, that of fidelity, also asserts itself. It is no coincidence that Fleming's finest compositions are to be found among his odes. While the sonnet and Alexandrine offered suitable forms for conveying the antithetical nature of the Petrarchan concept of love, the ode – a form of song – allowed a less pretentious tone reminiscent of folk song and *Gesellschaftslied* ('Ein getreues Herze wissen / hat dess höchsten Schatzes Preiss' – 'To know a true heart / is worth the greatest treasure').

Fleming's great ideological-philosophical sonnets offset the image of the Petrarchian lover, torn between conflicting emotions, portrayed in some of his love poetry. In the sonnet *An Sich* Fleming gives voice in trenchant imperatives to the maxims of a practical philosophy – a vision of virtue based on the doctrines of neo-Stoicism. As befits the expanded conception of the sonnet as epigram, it culminates in a concluding aphorism in the form of a proverb setting the autonomy of the individual above all external constraints:

> Sey dennoch unverzagt. Gieb dennoch unverlohren.
> Weich keinem Glücke nicht. Steh' höher als der Neid.
> Vergnüge dich an dir / und acht es für kein Leid /
> hat sich gleich wider dich Glück' / Ort / und Zeit
> verschworen.
>
> Was dich betrübt und labt / halt alles für erkohren.
> Nim dein Verhängnüss an. Lass' alles unbereut.
> Thu / was gethan muss seyn / und eh man dirs gebeut.
> Was du noch hoffen kanst / das wird noch stets gebohren.
>
> Was klagt / was lobt man doch? Sein Unglück und sein Glücke
> ist ihm ein ieder selbst. Schau alle Sachen an.
> Diss alles ist in dir / lass deinen eiteln Wahn /
>
> und eh du förder gehst / so geh' ich dich zu rücke.
> Wer sein selbst Meister ist / und sich beherrschen kan /
> dem ist die weite Welt und alles unterthan.

Gryphius

While Fleming's approach reflects the ideals of Renaissance individualism (see also the *Grabschrifft / so er ihm selbst gemacht*), Andreas Gryphius places suffering and consciousness of the transience and fragility of life at the centre of his work, which transcends the limitations of Opitzian Classicism through an intensification of rhetorical style that remains unparalleled in German lyricism to this day. Even Gryphius, however, built on foundations laid by Opitz, as is clear from quite specific features: one of the most renowned poems of the era, the *Trawrklage des verwüsteten Deutschlands* (later *Thränen des Vaterlands / Anno 1636*) uses motifs and formulations drawn from the *Trostgedichte in Widerwertigkeit dess Krieges* (1633) by Opitz. This work provides the model not only for the 'grawsamen Posaunen' ('terrible trumpets') and 'fewrigen Carthaunen' ('fiery cannons'), but also for the antithetical Alexandrines of the *amplificatio*: 'Die Mawren sind verheeret / Die Kirchen hingelegt / die Häuser umbgekehret'. These elements, scattered throughout Opitz's lengthy epic poem over hundreds of verses, are condensed by Gryphius into a symbolic image of a land racked by the horrors of war, transforming it into an apocalyptic vision.

Thränen des Vaterlandes/Anno 1636

Wir sind doch nunmehr gantz / ja mehr denn gantz verheeret!
Der frechen Völcker Schaar / die rasende Posaun
Das vom Blutt fette Schwerdt / die donnernde Carthaun /
Hat aller Schweiss / und Fleiss / und Vorrath auffgezehret.

Die Türme stehn in Glutt / die Kirch ist umgekehret.
Das Rathauss ligt im Grauss / die Starcken sind zerhaun /
Die Jungfern sind geschänd't / und wo wir hin nur schaun
Ist Feuer / Pest / und Tod / der Hertz und Geist durchfähret.

Hir durch die Schantz und Stadt / rinnt allzeit frisches Blutt.
Dreymal sind schon sechs Jahr / als unser Ströme Flutt /
Von Leichen fast verstopfft / sich langsam fort gedrungen.

Doch schweig ich noch von dem / was ärger als der Tod /
Was grimmer denn die Pest / und Glutt und Hungersnoth
Das auch der Seelen Schatz / so vilen abgezwungen.

Vanitas

Gryphius' first collection of poems (*Lissaer Sonette*, 1637) takes up the theme that was to typify all his work. Titles such as *Vanitas, vanitatum, et omnia vanitas, Trawklage des Autoris / in sehr schwerer Kranckheit, Der Welt Wollust ist nimmer ohne Schmertzen*, and *Menschliches Elende* cover the whole range of notions of the futility of earthly human existence that are constantly varied in his lyric poetry, tragedies and funeral orations. The sonnets *An Gott den Heiligen Geist*, on the beginning of all things and the four Last Things (*Der Todt, Das Letzte Gerichte, Die Hölle, Ewige Frewde der Ausserwehlten* – Death, the Last Judgement, Hell, The Eternal Joy of the Elect), at the end of the first two volumes of sonnets (1643, 1650) make it clear that these themes are rooted in a wider context: the history of salvation. Between the beginning and the end, the poems on 'irdische Dinge' ('earthly things') are not fortuitously prefaced by the Vanitas sonnets – a placing that highlights the relative importance of life in this world, characterised by frailty and transience. A concomitant relationship is suggested with the suffering of Christ, pointing to the necessity for suffering and privation in the earthly life, but also to the way to eternal life that leads through suffering. Poems dealing with the vain nature of the world and the transience of all earthly things are set beside a sonnet devoted to 'Menschliches Elende' ('Human Misery') as examples of the nature and destiny of man ('Was sind wir Menschen doch? ein Wohnhauss grimmer Schmertzen' – 'For what are we men? An abode for agonised anguish'). They speak in stark terms of the frailty of men – the sonnet *An sich selbst* – (*To Myself*) begins: 'Mir grauet vor mir selbst / mir zittern alle Glider ('I shudder at myself / all my members tremble').

Even where Gryphius appears to be speaking of the world, for example of nature, he is still preoccupied with its significance for the history of salvation and the salvation of the individual. Thus neither the sonnet *Einsamkeit* (*Loneliness*) nor the sonnets of the times of the day are nature or *Landschaft* poems. Their observation of the things of this world leads the mind back to man and his destiny of salvation. Natural phenomena and elements are portrayed as having a referential character, being 'Sinnenbilder' ('sensory images') the meaning of which may often be sought in the allegorical Christian interpretation of nature. A background of traditional biblical exegesis is clearly discernible here, while the form of some of the sonnets resembles that of the emblem with its tripartite structure: title (*inscriptio*), picture (*pictura*) and epigram (*subscriptio*). However, this tripartite structure is not always as marked as it is in the sonnets *Einsamkeit, Morgen, Mittag* or as in the following poem, whose traditional subject-matter (the voyage metaphor) typifies the allegorical interpretation of the emblematic poem:

> *An die Welt*
> Mein offt bestürmbtes Schiff der grimmen Winde Spil
> Der frechen Wellen Baal / das schir die Flutt getrennet /
> Das über Klip auff Klip' / und Schaum / und Sandt gerennet.
> Komt vor der Zeit an Port / den meine Seele wil.
>
> Offt / wenn uns schwartze Nacht im Mittag überfil
> Hat der geschwinde Plitz die Segel schir verbrennet!
> Wie offt hab ich den Wind / und Nord' und Sud verkennet!
> Wie schadhafft ist Spriet / Mast / Steur / Ruder / Schwerdt
> und Kill.
>
> Steig aus du müder Geist / steig aus! wir sind am Lande!
> Was graut dir für dem Port / itzt wirst du aller Bande
> Und Angst / und herber Pein / und schwerer Schmertzen loss.
>
> Ade / verfluchte Welt: du See voll rauer Stürme!
> Glück zu mein Vaterland / das stette Ruh' im Schirme
> Und Schutz und Friden hält / du ewig-lichtes Schloss!

Intensification of rhetorical devices

Gryphius' lyrics strive for pathos-laden language. The repetition of words, asyndetic sequences of words, parallelisms and antitheses are among the most important rhetorical devices employed. They are subsidiary to the insistent naming of and circling around the object, which is described either by enumerating its several parts (*enumeratio partium*), or by means of a series of definitions. Through an intensification of rhetorical devices, a predilection for asymmetry, and by exaggerating the rigidity of existing forms (metre and verse forms), Gryphius achieves an incisiveness of language whose impact is further enhanced by his selection of stark, harsh expressions (*Zentnerworte* – 'hundredweight words'). It is in his frequent repetition of words in particular, which carries to extremes the device of insistent naming, that Gryphius shows where he transcends the moderate language of Classicism for the sake of achieving the rhetorical aim of *movere*:

> Ach! und weh!
> Mord! Zetter! Jammer / Angst / Creutz! Marter! Würme! Plagen.
> Pech! Folter! Hencker! Flamm! Stanck! Geister! Kälte! Zagen!
> Ach vergeh!

The expansion of expressive potential (Zesen and the Nurembergers)

Philipp von Zesen and the Nuremberg poets Georg Philipp Harsdörffer and Johann Klaj chose a different means of expanding the expressive potential of poetic language. The dactyl, which Opitz was only prepared to tolerate in exceptional cases, was reinstated, and together with onomatopoeia and internal rhyme helped in the 1640s to create verse forms of a vitality and rhythmical animation hitherto unknown in German literature. Harsdörffer's work moreover contains numerous signs of an intensification of metaphorical language that prepared the ground for subsequent developments.

C. R. von Greiffenberg: Gotteslob (praise of God) and the mannerist art of language

These stimuli from the Nuremberg poets also had their impact on Catherina Regina von Greiffenberg, the foremost woman poet of the seventeenth century (*Geistliche Sonnette / Lieder und Gedichte – Religious Sonnets / Songs and Poems*, 1662). The first sonnet in her volume of poems *Christlicher Vorhabens-Zweck* defines the 'Spiel und Ziel' (aim and purpose) she has set herself in her life and writing: the praise of God, praise of divine Providence, the grace and goodness of God, praise of God in Nature and – a distinct paradox – in the experience of suffering. She prefers the

127

ingenious sonnet form as a means of expression appropriate to her way of thinking and religious experience. The aesthetic effect of the poems derives here largely from the musicality of the language used ('Jauchzet / Bäume / Vögel singet! danzet / Blumen / Felder lacht!') as well as from the abundant use of unusual compounds: *Herzgrund-Rotes Meer, Herzerleuchtungs-Sonn', Anstoss-Wind, Himmels-Herzheit, Meersands-Güt', Anlas-Kerne, Schickungs-Aepffel.* Although this gives some poems a mannerist veneer, the technique has a deeper significance than mere aesthetic appeal. The juxtaposition of words reveals hidden analogies – Man, Nature and God are related one to another and the world is visibly shown to be a place in which the various spheres of existence find a mutual relationship.

Genre-bound poetry

Despite this expansion of expressive potential, the history of seventeenth-century German lyricism cannot be described as a continuous process developing from a classicist style of the Opitzian variety via an intensifying or experimental, playfully artistic rhetorical style into a mature phase in which artistry was finally reinstated as a goal in itself. Evidence against construing literary history in this way may be found above all in the genre-bound nature of seventeenth-century poetry, the continued observance of hidebound genre rules, and the persistent link between 'things', i.e. the subjects of poetry, genre and words.

Protestant hymns

The hymn proved to be a particularly genre-bound form. The outstanding Protestant hymn writer of the seventeenth century was Paul Gerhardt, whose hymns were republished again and again in numerous editions of Johann Crüger's *Praxis Pietatis melica – The Practice of Piety*, 1648–; complete edition, *Geistliche Andachten – Religious Devotions*, 1667). Like other religious poets, Gerhardt set to verse the Passion story and Sunday gospel readings. *O Haupt vol Blut und Wunden – Oh Sacred Head Sore Wounded*, one of his best-known hymns, comes from the Latin hymn tradition (*Salve caput cruentatum*). He made his name with hymns such as *Befiehl du deine Wege, Geh aus mein Hertz und suche Freud* or *Nun ruhen alle Wälder*, i.e. with texts that answered the need for inner piety. Despite this, however, the oft-propounded contrast between the 'We' hymns of Luther and the 'I' hymns of Gerhardt does not (in itself) signify a breakthrough to subjectivity. The 'I' in the verse

Geh aus mein Hertz und suche Freud
In dieser lieben Sommerzeit
An deines Gottes Gaben:

Schau an der schönen Garten-Zier /
Und siehe wie sie mir und dir
Sich aussgeschmücket haben.

does not signify a unique individual, but rather, as was almost exclusively the case in seventeenth-century religious song, the human being as member of the confessional community. Gerhardt's treatment of nature is a further indication that a subjective mode of experience has yet to appear. Although half this lengthy hymn comprises an enumeration of images from nature, nature itself has no more than a symbolic function. The (transitory) beauty of 'this poor Earth' is intended to lead us to the Creator, to the *Christi Garten* (the Garden of Christ) and to faith. Natural and genre images thus have no purpose in themselves, serving rather a referential context. This is the meeting-point, for example, between some of Andreas Gryphius' sonnets and Gerhardt's hymns. There are further parallels in emblematic structure. Where Gryphius' title, natural images and interpretation combine to create a formal unity, this corresponds to Gerhardt's procedure of making the natural image subordinate to religious interpretation.

Not being bound by liturgical constraints, Catholic confessional song was freer than the Protestant hymn, which allowed it to develop closer links with the popular German song style. Independently of Opitz, the Rhineland Jesuit Friedrich Spee moved towards art poetry with the hymns, written in the 1620s, that appeared in *Trutz Nachtigal* (1649). The Jesus *Minne*, marked by expressive devices typical of Petrarchan love poetry, became a central feature of hymn-writing ('O süssigkeit in peinen! O pein in süssigkeit!'). In addition, Spee had a particular eye for the beauty of nature – for landscape, times of day and seasons – yet, despite this love for detail, his concept of nature is no different from that of Paul Gerhardt. Nature is of symbolic importance only, representing the love of God, while praise of nature is a song of praise to the Creator: 'O Mensch ermess im hertzen dein, wie wunder muss der Schöpffer sein.' Another motif cycle derives from the pastoral masquerade. Some of the lyric poems collected in the *Trutz Nachtigal* are religious bucolic verses, which Spee calls eclogues or pastoral songs or dialogues, linking them with a likeness to the Good Shepherd.

Catholic hymn-writing in southern Germany

An independent form of Catholic hymn-writing also developed in southern Germany. Here there was little inclination either to relinquish the indigenous Upper German linguistic tradition, or to incorporate the ideas of reform in language and literature associated with Protestant Central Germany. A hymn school thus formed in Munich around the priest Johannes Khuen, who had an even closer association with poets of the Jesuit order than the Neo-Latin poet Jacob Balde, exerting an influence, through his solo hymn form, on the Jesuits Albert Curtz (*Harpffen Davids*, 1659) and the Capuchin Laurentius von Schnüffis (*Mirantisches Flötlein*, 1682).

Mysticism

Discussion of faith among poets inspired by mystical and chiliastic traditions took place on a different level. This kind of poetry was not popular preaching by other means, but rather an expression of religious enthusiasm and intense contemplation. A defining aspect of the mystical trends of the period was the link between concepts of medieval German mysticism on the one hand and contemplation of nature and natural philosophy, such as had emerged in conjunction with Renaissance Platonism and Neoplatonism, on the other. The leading figure of this group was Jacob Böhme (Behmen), whose influence extended far beyond Germany, despite opposition from orthodox Lutheran clergy and a ban on his writings. Böhme's circle included Abraham von Franckenberg, who published Böhme's work in Holland, himself contributing substantially to the dissemination of mystical thought in the seventeenth century through his own writings and missionary journeys. Besides contacts with a number of German poets, he was the author of hymns and religious epigrams.

Angelus Silesius

Johannes Scheffler, who called himself Angelus Silesius after his conversion to Catholicism, was likewise introduced to mystical literature, as well as religious epigrammatic literature, by Franckenberg (Daniel Czepko). His *Geistreichen Sinn- und Schlussreime* appeared in 1657, although this volume is better known by the title of the extended 1675 edition, *Cherubinischer Wandersmann*. The mention of cherubim refers to the traditional hierarchy of angels, indicating that an attempt to describe the mystical road to God is to be undertaken in an intellectual manner, comprehensible to the faculty of reason. The form deemed suitable for this purpose is the epigram, the 'ingenious' (*geistreich*) quality of which is alluded to in the subtitle. The focal point of the book is the relationship between man (*Ich*) and God, which Scheffler formulates in constantly new paradoxes:

> Ich bin wie GOtt / und GOtt wie ich
> Ich bin so gross als GOtt / Er ist als ich so klein:
> Er kann nicht über mich / ich unter Ihm nicht seyn.

> GOtt lebt nicht ohne mich
> Ich weiss dass ohne mich GOtt nicht ein Nun kan leben /
> Werd' ich zunicht Er muss von Noth den Geist auffgeben.

Die Liebe zwinget GOtt
Wo GOtt mich über GOtt nicht solte wollen bringen /
So wil ich Ihn dazu mit blosser Liebe zwingen.

I am as God / and He as me
I am as great as God / And he as small as me
He cannot be above me / Nor I below Him.

Without me God liveth not
I know that without me He liveth not a jot
Come I to nought, so must He too give up the ghost.

'Tis love that moveth God
So should God not wish to place me above Himself /
Then will I move Him with pure love to do it.

The reader is referred in these epigrams to the prologue, where he is told
that they are concerned with the *unio mystica*, the condition reached 'after
this union' ('nach dieser Vereinigung') and which Scheffler, drawing on
quotations from earlier mystical literature describes thus: 'Wenn nu der
Mensch zu solcher Vollkommner gleichheit GOttes gelangt ist / dass er
ein Geist mit Gott und eins mit ihm worden / und in Christo die gäntzliche
Kind- oder Sohnschafft erreicht hat / so ist er so gross / so reich / so
weise und mächtig als GOtt / und GOtt thut nichts ohne einen solchen
Menschen / denn Er ist eins mit ihm.' ('When a man has thus attained
such perfect likeness with God / that he is one spirit with God and one
with Him / having achieved the state of being the complete child or son
in Christ / then is he as great / as abundant / as wise and as mighty as
God himself / and God undertakes nothing without such a man / for He
is one with him').

The poet as prophet: Quirinus Kuhlmann

With Quirinus Kuhlmann religious poetry took quite a different direction.
Striking as mannerist features in his style may be, the decisive factor is the
new function of poetry itself. Kuhlmann's magnum opus, the *Kühlpsalter*
(1684–6), is conceived as a holy book, the author seeing himself as prophet
– the youth anticipated by Böhme as coming to overthrow the Antichrist
and usher in the kingdom of a thousand years. His whole life and his
visions were bound to legitimise his status as chosen one. The political
interpretation placed on his chiliastic vision was to cost him his life in
Moscow. Overreaction though this must now seem in relation to
Kuhlmann's scarcely practicable ideas, it is hardly possible to dispute that
his *Kühlmonarchie*, a union of true believers in a Kuhlmann empire of
Jesuelites, left no room for the existing authorities ('Auf, Kaiser, Könige!
Gebt her Kron, hutt und Zepter!').

Satire

The lyric confrontation with the world proceeded on a number of levels. Depending on starting-point and method, the results range from complete negation (in extreme cases, of the prophet of the kingdom of heaven on earth) through the general Christian verdict of *vanitas*, to criticism of specific social and political injustices. It was in this latter area that the satirists' interest was engaged. Some held up a mirror to a social order in disarray, criticising moral perversities or reprehensible social trends. Others, since this was, after all, the time of the Thirty Years War and of Franco-German antagonisms, indulged in partisan attacks on the politics of the day, frequently disregarding in the process the maxim that satire aims to condemn vice but spare individuals.

Logau: the critique of social and political developments

'Die Welt ist umgewand' – 'The world is upside-down', we read in Friedrich von Logau (*Deutscher Sinn-Getichte Drey Tausend*, 1654), whose body of satirical epigrammatic poetry depicts a disordered, perverse world. Logau draws the criteria for this critical confrontation of contemporary social reality from an idealised past – a static, hierarchically-ordered world in which the old German virtues of fidelity, integrity and piety still held sway, and the German language, style of dress and national character had not yet fallen prey to foreign influence. Against this background of a glorious, time-honoured society of rank, he censures the events, institutions and human conduct of the present, rejecting innovation and defending that which has been superseded. The innovative spirit, which threatens to obliterate the old ways, manifests itself first and foremost at court and in court organisation, which was subjected to radical changes as absolutist rule was established. Elements of traditional court criticism, e.g. 'Wer will, dass er bey Hof fort kom, Der leb als ob er blind, taub, stum' – 'He who would further his own cause at court lives as though he were blind, deaf and dumb' – Weckherlin) are combined with attacks on specific abuses. The absolute ruler, his court and courtiers are set here against the ideals of a patriarchal style of government, requiring a relationship of personal fidelity between the ruling prince and his advisers. The world in which such an outlook on life is possible, however, is seen by Logau as under threat:

> *Heutige Welt-Kunst*
> Anders seyn / und anders scheinen:
> Anders reden / anders meinen:
> Alles loben / alles tragen /
> Allen heucheln / stets behagen /
> Allem Winde Segel geben:
> Bös- und Guten dienstbar leben

Alles Thun und alles Tichten
Bloss auff eignen Nutzen richten;
Wer sich dessen wil befleissen
Kan Politisch heuer heissen.

To be one thing / and appear another:
Say one thing / and mean another:
Praise all things / endure all things /
To feign all / ever keen to please /
To give wind to every sail:
To serve both good and ill:

To do all and strive for all
Above all to serve one's own interest;
He who seeks after this end
Can call himself politically 'in'.

Logau sees the new aristocracy of officials, on whom the ruler now depended, as encroaching on the position of the old landed aristocracy – a new type of courtier, representing 'political' morality, usurping the role of the 'redlicher Mann' (the 'honest man'), and a new court culture dominated by French fashion, language and literature, obliterating the old ways. Life at court is now a morass of ambition, hypocrisy, envy, jealousy and ingratitude. His lament on 'Hofe-Leben' is set topically against the old nostalgia for rural life:

O Feld / O werthes Feld / ich muss es nur bekennen /
Die Höfe / sind die Höll; und Himmel du zu nennen.

O field / O goodly field / I must but profess it /
To be in court is to be in hell, and heaven to use first names.

Mannerism and Classicism

It is difficult to form a clear overview of German lyric poetry in the final decades of the seventeenth century. Mannerist features grew stronger in both religious and secular poetry, while there was also evidence of a counter-movement seeking to restore metaphorical style to a classicist medium. This left untouched the whole basis of poetry – the rhetoric-based notion of the art of verse-writing. There was, however, variation in the models or *exempla* around which verse-writing focused. Whereas Opitz had taken as his archetype the Renaissance poetry of western and southern European countries, the second half of the century saw, with an equal time-lag, the adoption of baroque and mannerist tendencies from Italian and Spanish literature. For its part the counter-movement found itself focusing on the French classicist approach.

Hoffmannswaldau

The leading exponent of late baroque lyric poetry was Christian Hoffmanswaldau. Although the major part of his work was written in the 1640s, it was decades later before it became available to a wider readership, first in a selected anthology edition (*Deutsche Übersetzungen und Getichte – German Translations and Poems*, 1679) and then in the first volumes of Benjamin Neukirch's anthology *Herrn von Hofmanswaldau und andrer Deutschen auserlesene und bissher ungedruckte Gedichte (Herr von Hofmannswaldau and other select and hitherto unpublished poems*, 1695–). Like that of Daniel Casper von Lohenstein, Hoffmanswaldau's work, too, was regarded by pro-Enlightenment critics as the quintessence of the unnatural.

Enlightenment criticism

Whereas Opitz 'durch seine natürliche und vernünftige Art zu denken... uns allen ein Muster des guten Geschmacks nachgelassen [habe]' – 'through his natural and reasonable way of thinking... bequeathed us all a model for good taste', Hoffmannswaldau and Lohenstein had, according to Johann Christoph Gottsched, brought disgrace on German poetry with 'ihre regellose Einbildungskraft, durch ihren geilen Witz und ungesalzenen Scherz' ('their undisciplined imaginative faculty, their wanton wit and tasteless quips'). Johann Jacob Bodmer is specific in his criticism only in taking exception to Hoffmanswaldau's metaphorical style and Lohenstein's sombre similes. The fundamental objection to this 'hochgefärbte Schein' (gaudy phenomenon), lies in the way it debunks the regulative function of the *iudicium*, the faculty of judgement, that should properly govern the poetic genius: 'Ihm fehlt' es an Verstand, den Geist geschickt zu lencken' ('He lack'd the power of reason with which to steer the spirit adroitly'), writes Bodmer of Hoffmannswaldau, who is held responsible for having contaminated all Germany with this affliction.

Contemporaries viewed the situation differently, however: for them, it was this ingenious wit that made a poet one of standing. Mannerist poets of the day write of aiming to arouse *stupore* or *meraviglia*, stupefaction or astonishment, in their hearers or readers. Giambattista Marino, who starts from the assumption that poetry should thrill 'the ears of the reader with all the allure of novelty', sums up this approach in an epigram:

> E del poeta il fin la meraviglia
>
> . . .
>
> Chi non sa fa stupir, vada alla striglia!

> The proper aim of poetry being to astonish
> Let him who knows not how
> To horse-grooming be banish'd!

Concetti

It is in *concetti*, puns and plays on words, that the poet reveals his *acutezza*, his penetrating wit. Hoffmannswaldau for example, who appreciates the 'good inventions' of the 'southerners', takes as his theme, in an epigram not intended for publication, the Duke of Alba. He puts into verse a terse epitaph certainly not lacking in bluntness, but at the same time rises to an opportunity to do justice to subtlety by linking the name (*albus* = 'white') with fate (*erbleichen* = 'to grow pale'):

> Hier liegt der wüterich / so nichts von ruh gehört /
> Biss ihm der bleiche tod ein neues wort gelehrt;
> Er brach ihm seinen hals / und sprach: du must erbleichen /
> Sonst würd ich dir noch selbst im würgen müssen weichen.

> Here lies the tyrant / so of peace was nothing heard /
> Till pale Death taught him a new word;
> He broke his neck / saying: you must now grow pale
> Or else must I needs step aside for your death-dealing hail.

Erotic poetry

Despite a number of sacred songs, epitaphs and lyric discourses, Hoffmannswaldau's predominant theme is sensual love, showing 'was die Liebe vor ungeheure Spiele in der Welt anrichte' – ('what extraordinary dramas love works in the world'), and celebrating sensual pleasure with religious imagery. The Petrarchan tradition forms the backdrop to these poems, its basic concepts, motifs and images being modified and treated with irony in virtuoso playfulness. The charm of the poems does not lie in these basic models themselves, however, such as lamentation of the hard-heartedness of the beloved, or the requiting of love in a dream, but in the ingenious frivolous playfulness and ironic stance with which this adopted body of motifs is treated. This is further enriched by the elegance and unfettered virtuosity that characterises such sonnets as *Vergänglichkeit der schönheit* (*The Transience of Beauty*), which combines two of the central poetic themes of Hoffmannswaldau and his day, *carpe diem* and *memento mori*, using a metaphorical style that borders on light parody:

> Es wird der bleiche tod mit seiner kalten hand
> Dir endlich mit der zeit umb deine brüste streichen /
> Der liebliche corall der lippen wird verbleichen;
> Der schultern warmer schnee wird werden kalter sand /

> Der augen süsser blitz / die kräffte deiner hand /
> Für welchen solches fällt / die werden zeitlich weichen /
> Das haar / das itzund kan des goldes glantz erreichen /
> Tilgt endlich tag und jahr als ein gemeines band.

Der wohlgesetzte fuss / die lieblichen gebärden /
Die werden theils zu staub / teils nichts and nichtig werden /
Denn opfert keiner mehr der gottheit deiner pracht.

Diss und noch mehr als diss muss endlich untergehen /
Dein hertze kan allein zu aller zeit bestehen /
Dieweil es die natur aus diamant gemacht.

At last pale Death in fullness of time
Will stroke thy fair breasts with his cold hand /
The lovely coral colour of thy lips forever bann'd
The warm snow of thy shoulders cold as lime.

The sweet brightness of thy eye / the zest of thy hand /
Those who now pursue them / will in time recoil
The hair that now attains the glitter of gold royal
Will be erased by days and years into a meagre band.

The well-turned foot / the lovely mien /
Will turn part to dust / and part to nought and vain /
Then none will offer to the divinity of your glory.

All this and more must one day come to pass /
Only thy heart can all time outlast /
Made by Nature's hand of a diamond.

A re-orientation in lyric poetry

Opposition to this art form, at first sparing the great names of Hoffman-swaldau and Lohenstein, came from two quarters: the so-called 'gallant' poets and theoreticians, concerned at a decline in the sharp-witted, ponderous baroque style; and, more radically, the classicists, who sought to set the ideal style founded by Nicolas Boileau (*L'Art poetique*, 1674), based on Reason and Nature, against what they perceived as this excessive and unnatural symbolic language. The classicist trend, best exemplified by the (*Freiherr*) von Canitz (*Neben-Stunden Unterschiedener Gedichte*, 1700) did not prevail until after a lengthy period of transition and the appearance of the works of Gottsched.

Between epochs: Johann Christian Günther

The work of Johann Christian Günther was part of this period of transition, marked by tension between the advent of subjectivity and the traditional notion of the poet's role. This has led to numerous attempts to draw Günther forward into the time of Goethe, interpreting his poems largely as evidence of a genius whose life was nevertheless licentious, ending in poverty and privation: Goethe wrote of him, 'er wusste sich nicht zu zähmen, und so zerran ihm das Leben wie sein Dichten' ('He was unable to tame himself, so that his life became as out of hand as his poems'). Günther saw himself as following the tradition of the Humanist-oriented scholar-poet: 'Vielleicht wird Opiz mich als seinen Schüler kennen' ('Perhaps Opitz may acknowledge me as his pupil'). Tradition also defined the poetic role with which he identified: as the 'German Ovid', he sees his destiny as being that of the exiled Roman poet, or another Job (see *inter alia* his poem *Gedult, Gelassenheit, treu, fromm und redlich seyn* – Patience, Tranquillity, to be true, pious and honest). There is no doubt that autobiographical events were of great importance in Günther's creative writing, whether in his love poetry, songs of lament or the conflict he had with his father over poetry. This cannot, however, be viewed as a break-through to a poetry of experience in the sense understood in the late eighteenth century, since even the 'impression of a quality of immediate encounter and of suffusion with experience' in Günther's poetry arises out of rhetorical ways of thinking and procedures (Wolfgang Preisendanz). Günther came at the end of a long tradition, able to avail himself of it and the forms of expression and roles that it offered him. He was a professional poet with a profound awareness of the high calling of poetry and his vocation as a poet. He therefore engaged his own person in his poetry more forcefully than any other poet of his day, and in so doing prepared the way for later developments, although himself leaving the fabric of traditional poetic art untouched. He attained fame only posthumously when in 1724, a year after his death, the complete four-part edition of his poems first began to appear (the last part appeared in 1735).

On tragedies and comedies

The world as a theatre

The idea of the whole world as a stage was ubiquitous in seventeenth-century literature. The theatre metaphor was clearly nothing new, having been known from antiquity, but no age made it its own in quite the same way as the baroque: 'Die Welt / ist eine Spiel-büne / da immer ein Traur- und Freudgemischtes Schauspiel vorgestellet wird: nur dass / von zeit zu seit / andere Personen auftretten' ('The world / is a stage / on which a tragi-comic play is always being acted out: only that / from time to time / different characters appear'), wrote Sigmund von Birken in 1669. The world is a theatre, man an actor who plays the role assigned to him – an image that penetrated all European literatures. In his *Great Theatre of the World* (1675), Calderón extended it into an all-embracing allegory of human life, aptly summed up by the satirist Francisco de Quevedo:

137

Forget not that life is a play,
and the whole wide world a great farce,
changing scenes in the twinkling of an eye
and treating us as actors all the while.
Forget not either that God has arranged
this whole play and its long-protracted theme
into acts according to his scheme. . . .
The assignation of scripts and roles,
How long, how high our action is to unfold
Lies with the one great Dramatist to disclose.

Obviously poets in the theatre drew particularly heavily on this meta-phor. Nevertheless, Germany had little to set against the flower of the European theatre – Shakespeare, Lope de Vega, Calderón, Monteverdi, Corneille, Racine, Molière, or Joost van den Vondel. In the theatrical sphere, as in others, a new beginning was much needed, and the way to a German national theatre proving protracted.

Theatre in Germany

'Theatre' in seventeenth-century Germany had many meanings: amateur plays (e.g. the Oberammergau Passion play from the middle of the century onwards), professional travelling theatre companies, Protestant school thea-tre, drama performed by Catholic orders, court theatre and opera. There were clear links among these various genres: wandering groups of players would play under the patronage of a prince; the Jesuit theatres in Munich or Vienna took on the function of court theatres; plays originally written for the school stage by Gryphius and Lohenstein were performed at court, as well as being adapted for travelling theatre stages.

Travelling theatre: English 'comedians'

Travelling theatre companies from abroad performed in Germany from the middle of the sixteenth century onwards. The influence of Italian *Commedia dell'arte* companies remained, for language reasons, largely restricted to southern German and Austrian courts. Groups known as English 'com-edians' were of greater significance for the development of German theatre. These professional English actors, first documented in Dresden in 1586, brought to Germany a new style of acting whose vividness and naturalism made it diametrically opposed to the declamatory style of the Humanist school theatre. The outlandish quality of the performances of the English 'comedians', as well as their musical interludes and acrobatic scenes, were all the more appropriate in Germany since up to the beginning of the seventeenth century they did not perform in German. Only in the second half of the century did German companies of any importance begin to form.

It was through these English 'comedians' that Germany gained its first impression of contemporary Elizabethan drama (including Marlowe and Shakespeare), albeit adapted so as to reduce the originals to a sequence of scenes of maximum effect. Besides blood-curdling, swash-buckling theatre, clown comedy and *Pickelhäring* humour, the repertoires of these companies also included biblical plays and works by German authors. They were further expanded in the second half of the century to include Italian, Spanish and French plays. The company of Master Johannes Velten, who was in the permanent employ of the Prince of Saxony from 1685, special-ised in French comedy as well as the traditional repertoire. There are records of performances of ten plays by Molière. Female roles, moreover, were by now no longer played by men – a progressive step that did nothing to allay opposition to theatrical performances, from the Protestant clergy in particular.

Jesuit drama

Despite advances in the professional theatre, schools continued to be the leading dramatic exponents. Drama by Catholic orders, chiefly the Jesuits, grew to become a major rival to the Protestant school theatre. Education in Jesuit colleges, and public performances at festivals at the end of the school year, were placed at the service of the Counter-Reformation – the defence of the 'true faith', the refutation of heretics and the reclamation of the lapsed.

Missionary impact: report on a production

A report on the impact of a 1609 Munich production of *Cenodoxus* by Jacob Bidermann reveals how missionary success was envisaged (the text can hardly be evaluated as a record of actual events, since it dates from a preface, written over fifty years later in 1666, to an edition of Bidermann's dramas):

> It is thus known that *Cenodoxus*, which was able like virtually no other play to rock the auditorium with mirthful laughter so great that it nearly broke the benches, nonetheless called forth in the spirits of the audience a wave of true piety of such magnitude that the few hours devoted to this play achieved what a hundred sermons could not. Namely, the most distinguished persons of the Bavarian Resi-dence and the city of Munich, a total of fourteen men, were so seized by holy fear of God, who is the stern judge of all the deeds of men, that not long after the conclusion of the play they withdrew to

Ignatian [religious] exercises, most of them proceeding to a miraculous conversion.

Bidermann's *Cenodoxus* (first performed in 1602), the story of a famous, arrogant and hypocritical doctor of Paris, is a tendentious play directed against the Humanism of the Renaissance and the emancipation of the individual. As in morality plays such as *Jedermann*, a person, although not here an Everyman, is confronted as death approaches by a decision between Heaven and Hell, just as in morality plays a struggle for the soul is waged by unnatural beings and allegorical figures. This work represents an extended form of Jesuit drama; another variant is the martyr drama. Whether the plays involve stories about saints or martyrs, biblical or historical themes, however, there is a fundamental concern with the Church triumphant. This permitted further expansion into the political dimension. In Vienna, for example, school theatre evolved into festival performances for the purposes of court pageant. Nicholas von Avancini's *Pietas Victrix* (1659) uses the example of Constantine the Great to show the victory of a ruler who is true to the Church over all hostile forces, glorifying the Austrian monarch as the successor to Constantine.

Latin was the *lingua franca* of Jesuit drama. To facilitate understanding a type of programme, or *Perioche*, was produced for each performance. It contained a detailed account of the contents of the play in German and/ or Latin, divided into acts and scenes.

Kunstdrama in German: Opitz

The impetus towards *Kunstdrama* in the German vernacular originated again with Opitz, whose efforts to supply models for the various literary genres also embraced the theatre. He translated Italian opera libretti: *Dafne* (1627) after Ottavio Rinuccini and Jacopo Peri, to music by Heinrich Schütz, was the first German-language opera, as well as two ancient tragedies – Seneca's *The Women of Troy* (1625), and Sophocles' *Antigone* (1636). His theoretical reflections on drama include the well-known rank proviso (*Ständeklausel*) that tragedy in the high style should deal with the fate of high-ranking persons, whereas comedy is concerned 'in schlechtem wesen unnd personen' ('[with] mean and lowly characters and persons'). The effect aimed for in tragedy is defined as follows:

> Solche Beständigkeit aber wird uns durch Beschawung der Missligkeit dess Menschlichen Lebens in den Tragödien zuforderst eingepflanzet: dann in dem wir grosser Leute / gantzer Stätte und Länder eussersten Untergang zum offtern schawen und betrachten / tragen wir zwar / wie es sich gebüret / erbarmen mit ihnen / können auch nochmals auss Wehmuth die Thränen kaum zurück halten; wir lernen aber darneben auch durch stetige Besichtigung so vielen Creutzes und

Ubels das andern begegnet ist / das unserige / welches uns begegnen möchte / wenige fürchten unnd besser erdulden.

However, such perseverance is instilled in us in the first instance by observation of the vicissitudes of human life in tragedies: since in frequently beholding and discerning the extreme downfall of great persons, entire cities and countries, we are moved, as is only proper, to pity them, often scarcely able to hold back the tears for sheer pathos. Through this continuous sight of so much affliction and calamity that befalls others, however, we may also learn to fear less and endure better that which may befall ourselves.

The significance of (neo)-Stoical ideas

Recent theorists have tended to disavow in these ideas any evidence of the stoical control of the emotions, referring as a rule to Aristotle and the arousal of 'terror and sympathy' as the aim of tragedy. Stoical ideas (the Christian stoical ideal of fortitude, control of the emotions, the supremacy of individual reason) were nonetheless of great significance for the characterisation and mode of conduct of baroque dramatic heroes. Besides Seneca, Jesuit drama and dramas by the Dutchman Joost van den Vondel exerted an influence on baroque tragedy.

Gryphius: martyr drama

Kunstdrama in German, after the preparatory groundwork of Opitz, begins with Andreas Gryphius, who had acquired theatrical experience in Holland, France and Italy. In his first tragedy *Leo Armenius / Oder Fürsten-Mord (Leo Armenius / Or the Murder of a Prince*, written in 1646, published 1650), he expresses his aim as 'die vergänglichkeit menschlicher sachen in gegenwertigem / und etlich folgenden Trawerspielen vorzustellen' ('to set forth the transience of human affairs in the present tragedy and sundry more to follow'). This aim is most impressively accomplished in his martyr dramas, where the transience and vanity of human life – most often exemplified by court life with its intrigues and cabals – are set against the stance of the martyr, who overcomes the world by emulating the Passion of Christ through his acceptance of suffering. The counterpart of the martyr is the tyrant, who offends against the divine order and only apparently remains the victor : 'Tyrann! der Himmel ists! der dein Verderben sucht' ('Tyrant! 'Tis Heaven itself that seeks thy destruction') cries out the soul of Catherine to the desperate Chach Abas (*Catherina von Georgien. Oder Bewehrete Beständikeit – Catherine of Georgia: Or Perseverance Rewarded*, first performed 1651, published 1657).

At the same time the martyr plays have a political significance. Catherine

141

dies for 'Gott und Ehr und Land' ('God and Honour and Country'). Papinianus in the 1659 play of the same name steadfastly opposes the unreasonable imperial demand to justify the unjustifiable, while the 'Trauer-Spil' (topical tragedy), *Ermordete Majestät. Oder Carolus Stuardus König von Gross Britanien* (*Murdered Majesty: Or Charles Stuart King of Great Britain*), written soon after the execution of Charles I on 30 January 1649, is a consummate Lutheran defence of the divine right of kings:

> Herr der du Fürsten selbst an deine stat gesetzet
> Wie lange sihst du zu?
> Wird nicht durch unsern Fall dein heilig Recht verletzet?
> Wie lange schlummerst du?
>
> O Lord who thyself settest princes in Thy stead
> How long wilt Thou look on?
> Does not our downfall injure Thy holy law?
> How long wilt Thou slumber?

Lohenstein: politics and morality

This perspective changed with Daniel Casper von Lohenstein, the foremost dramatist after Gryphius. Lohenstein's plays are exclusively concerned with pagan themes: the clash between Roman military might and the declining African empires (*Cleopatra*, 1661; *Sophonisbe*, first performed 1669, published 1680), episodes from Roman history in the era of Nero (*Agrippina*, 1665; *Epicharis*, 1665), and from sixteenth- and seventeenth-century Turkish history (*Ibrahim Bassa*, 1653; *Ibrahim Sultan*, 1673). The choices to be made are no longer between time and eternity, this world and the next: conflicts are now of an entirely mundane character, although without completely excluding transcendence. Another major theme is the question, much discussed from the Machiavellian era onwards, of the extent to which political conduct can, or is obliged to, dissociate itself from religious and moral norms. This includes the clash between human reason and human passions. The victor in the struggle for political supremacy is he who is best able to control his own emotions: 'Ich bin ein Mensch wie du / doch der Begierden Herr' ('I am a man as you are, but master of my desires'), proclaims Scipio to the erratic Massinissa in *Sophonisbe*. Inner conflicts – as of Massinissa in *Sophonisbe* or Marcus Antonius in *Cleopatra* – are provoked by women, the heroines of these plays, who use all possible means to retain their supremacy, ultimately in vain:

> Ein Fürst stirbt muttig / der sein Reich nicht überlebt.
> Es ist ein täglich Todt / kein grimmer Ach auf Erden /
> Als wenn / der / der geherrscht sol andern dinstbar werden.

A prince dieth courageously / who does not survive his kingdom.
It is a daily death / no more wrathful cry on earth /
Than when / he / who should rule must serve others.

Portrayal of history

Sophonisbe and Cleopatra fail with a degree of culpability, but in grand style. The course of history, steered by Fate, is against them. Lohenstein hints on the one hand at an inexorable course of history, while on the other also indicating a connection between political reason and successful political dealings. At the end of *Sophonisbe* he proclaims the aim of history to be the 'Reyen Des Verhängnüsses / der vier Monarchien', the traditional portrayal of history as a sequence of four world monarchies now being complemented by a fifth. 'Fate' (*Verhängnüs*) leads the eye beyond the victory of Rome towards the future, when 'Teutschland wird der Reichs-Sitz sein' ('Germany shall be the seat of Empire'):

> Mein fernes Auge siehet schon
> Den Oesterreichschen Stamm besteigen
> Mit grösserm Glantz der Römer Thron.

> My far-seeing eye already spies
> How house of Austria with great glory
> To the throne of Rome will rise.

Reyen

The Alexandrine was the metre used in German tragedies by Gryphius and Lohenstein. An exception to this rule were *Reyen*, which placed the action on a higher plane by changing the metre and performing through the medium of song. Harsdörffer writes in the *Poetischer Trichter* of the chorus: 'Dieses Lied sol die Lehren / welche aus vorhergehender Geschichte zuziehen / begreiffen / und in etlichen Reimsätzen mit einer oder mehr Stimmen deutlichst hören lassen' ('The aim of this song is to comprehend the lessons to be drawn from the preceding history and to render them audible as clearly as possible, in one or more voices, in sundry rhymed sentences'). Lohenstein frequently develops these *Reyen* into allegorical mythological *Singspiele* in which the 'Lehren' ('lessons') are emblematically encoded. Lohenstein's poetic style is generally characterised by an excessive use of the figurative, surpassing Gryphius in its mannerist metaphorical language. Both brought the high rhetorical style to fruition.

Christian Weise's Masaniello: a revolution play

Christian Weise's attempt at a tragedy in prose marks a trend in a different direction. *Trauer-Spiel Von dem Neapolitanischen Haupt-Rebellen Masaniello (The Tragedy of the Neapolitan Rebel Leader Masaniello)*, first performed by students of the Zittau grammar school in 1682, is a dramatisation of a popular uprising in 1647. The play is divided into numerous short scenes permitting the depiction of a broad spectrum of social strata (the substantial cast numbers up to eighty-two). Comic scenes and figures are reminiscent of travelling theatre plays. The theme of the tragedy, which was appreciated by Lessing for its 'freien Shakespearschen Gang' ('unrestrained Shakespearean pace'), is the rebellion by an oppressed people against their corrupt authorities and restoration of the *ancien régime*. Linked with this is the rise and fall of the poor fisherman Masaniello, who comes to lead the rebellion and who struggles selflessly for the people's cause, until he eventually loses his mind, his rule degenerating into raging tyranny. His antagonists are the viceroy and a brutal, egotistical nobility. Their machinations, violations of the law and repressive measures are depicted in all their horror – not so much out of sympathy with revolution, but rather as a warning to rulers not to allow matters to come to such a pass. The work was also intended as a didactic play for schoolchildren, whom Weise hoped to prepare for practical experience with his plays, of which there are some sixty.

Capitano: or The Man in Love

The court is the main scene of action in baroque tragedy, although even comedies performed among the lower social classes did not at first dispense with a court backdrop. Here, however, the court served a different function: it represented the social norm against which incorrect social conduct could be measured. Comedy consisted in failing to recognise one's proper place in the social hierarchy – in the discrepancy between social pretension and social reality, between appearance and fact. This holds good for braggart plays in the style of *Miles gloriosus*, or Capitano in the Italian *Commedia dell'arte* (Gryphius: *Horribilicribrifax*, 1663), for plays of the 'king for a day' type (Christian Weise: *Ein wunderliches Schau-Spiel vom Niederländischen Bauer – A Wonderful Play about the Dutch Peasant*, 1685, published 1700), and for *Peter Squentz* (1658) by Gryphius, in which the device of a theatre within a theatre heightens the contrast between court society and dilettantish artisans and the petty bourgeoisie, who overestimate both their social standing and their artistic skills. These plays are all designed to entertain the higher social ranks: they confirm the prevailing order and the courtly world-view.

Towards the end of the century, however, a type of comedy was emerging in which morality was more closely related to burgher practice: Weise's play *Vom verfolgten Lateiner* (*On the Persecuted Latin*) (1693) and Christian Reuter's *L'Honnête Femme Oder die Ehrliche Frau zu Plissine* (*The Honest Woman at Plissine*) (1695). Both plays criticise bourgeois or petty bourgeois social arrogance, and in both cases social presumption is exposed by the superior intelligence of a student antagonist. The skeleton of the plot, rendered more topical by autobiographical features, derives from Molière's *Les Précieuses ridicules* (1659). This is not coincidental, but an indication of the major place that French drama by then occupied in the repertoire of theatre companies. Whereas collections of plays from the 1620s and 1630s were entitled *Engelische Comedien und Tragedien* (1620, 1630), the title of a 1670 volume is *Schaubühne Englischer und Frantzösischer Comödianten*. It contains five plays by Molière. The popularity of French comedy may be seen from a 1695 three-volume prose translation of Molière's works. The admission of Molière into the German theatrical repertoire eventually led to the Saxon *Verlachkomödie*.

The novel

The proportion of novels in relation to poetic works in seventeenth-century literature was not yet very high: there was still no sign of the rapid upsurge in novel-writing and the increase in the reading public that accompanied it in the post-1740 period. When in 1698 the Calvinist novel critic Gotthard Heidegger wrote of 'an infinite sea' of novels washing over the reader, he meant that 'one or more novels' were appearing at quarterly intervals. More recent estimates have confirmed this assumption, reaching the conclusion that towards the end of the seventeenth century no more than six or eight novels (including translations) were being published a year.

Other prose genres

Aside from the novel, however, a diverse prose literature was evolving. The European novella tradition was made accessible to a German readership in moralistic translations and adaptations (including G. P. Harsdörffer's *Der Grosse Schau-Platz jämmerlicher Mordgeschichte* – *The Great Show-Case of Terrible Tales of Murder*, 1649–50). Interpretations of historical works and travelogues in journalistic or popular scientific and edifying vein point to a growing craving for novelty in the 'curious' reader that was being satisfied by the burgeoning number of newspapers appearing (and disappearing) in this period. The first documented newspapers appeared in 1609 in the form of weeklies. Besides these, the traditional genres continued to hold their own: literature for edification, moral satire and entertaining *Gebrauchsliteratur* (*Schwank* and other small epic forms). Even the

Volksbücher of the fifteenth and sixteenth centuries lingered on for some time. Although dismissed by leading *literati* with contempt and derision, they saw a considerable number of editions in the seventeenth century.

The court-history novel

The three main genres of the German baroque novel, the court history, the pastoral novel and the picaresque novel, were oriented towards the European novel tradition. As these basic models were adopted, however, deviations and hybrid forms evolved. German court-history novels in their own right were late in appearing – long after the genre had been introduced into Germany by means of numerous translations, mainly from the French, but also from Latin, Italian and English. Among the novels finding their way into Germany during the first half of the seventeenth century, *Argenis* by John Barclay (Latin 1621, French 1623, German translation by Opitz 1626) occupies a particular place. In this work, Barclay revived an ingenious technique used in Heliodorus' *Aithiopika* (third century AD), which is characterised by an abrupt opening, a gradual illumination of previous history affecting the present in the novel and a limiting of the length of the plot. Also adopted with the form is the love-story framework – the story of a young couple separated against their will and then reunited after a series of perils, both psychological and physical, when they are rewarded for remaining steadfast. The fact that the love story of *Argenis* unfolds almost exclusively among characters of high rank, for whom the private and public spheres are identical, enables the former novel structure to be expanded to include a political dimension – the glorification of Absolutism – which subsequently imbued the seventeenth-century court-history novel. As the happy ending can be postponed at will by introducing an unlimited number of mishaps and complications, so the simple basic structure of Heliodorus' *Aithiopika* or Barclay's *Argenis* can be almost incalculably complicated by bringing in more pairs of lovers. The baroque *Grossromane* which, although not very numerous, shape the usual idea of the seventeenth-century court-history novel, came about in this way.

The novel and Absolutism

The German court-history novel was a product of court and burgher-intellectual culture. Its affinity to the prevailing political doctrine of its day, Absolutism, is manifest, although emphasis varies depending on the social status and particular interests of the various authors. These novels relate to the contemporary scene, regardless of whether the histories being related are Germanic, Roman or biblical. Lohenstein's *Arminius* (1689–90), for example, is in its way a key novel, involving events and persons of the contemporary age in disguised form, and intended as a commentary on the current political situation and a warning against the consequences of discord among Germans.

Zesen

Philipp von Zesen's *Assenat* (1670), presented in biblical guise, as it is a Joseph novel, is concerned with the carrying out of an Absolutist reform programme. Joseph is portrayed as 'ein rechter Lehrspiegel vor all Stahts-leute', and as 'lehrbild [aller] Beamten der Könige und Fürsten' ('a true object lesson for all statesmen', a 'model [for all] officials of kings and princes'), whose entire ambition is directed towards the establishment of a rationally organised, powerful Absolutist welfare state. If Zesen articulates the interests of an educated burgher class who see prospects for their own advancement within an Absolutist system of government, there is a shift of perspective when a Lutheran minister seeks to ensure a morally blame-less, i.e. edifying prose literature (Andreas Heinrich Bucholtz in his novels *Herkules*, 1659–60, directed against *Amadis*, and *Herkuliskus*, 1665).

Anton Ulrich

Finally, in the novels of Duke Anton Ulrich von Braunschweig-Wolfen-büttel (*Die Durchleuchtige Syrerin Aramena* – Aramena, The Sagacious Syrian Woman, 1669–73, and *Octavia Römische Geschichte* – Octavia, A Roman History, 1677–.) we see reflected the exclusive world of a princely Absolutism that is able to claim unquestioned universal validity both for itself and its laws, since the author is assuming a readership who will share his values. The fact that the *Fürstliche Geschichten* ('Princely Histories') of Anton Ulrich occupy a special place in the history of the German court novel is largely owing to this thoroughly intentional exclusivity, and to the high standing of an author who can vouch for the authenticity of the world he depicts. Whereas in other court-history novels the Absolutist state ideal is disputed, or portrayed while being implemented in practice, Anton Ulrich is concerned with presenting an idealised self-portrait of the Absolutist world of princes.

The novel as theodicy

This aim is not without its philosophical or theological aspect. The com-plex, bewildering structure of novels – *Aramena*, for example, contains a mesh of no less than 36 biographies – becomes meaningful only in the light of the conclusion: behind the apparently chaotic sequence of events the working of Providence is revealed. That 'künstliche zerrütten / voll schönster ordnung ist' ('this artificial disorder is full of the loveliest order') was acknowledged at the time by such contemporary readers as Catharine

Regina von Greiffenberg, who describes the novel as a likeness of the divine order in the world. Her thoughts on the novel as a poetic theodicy were later carried further by Leibniz who, in letters to the Duke, spoke of the parallel relationship between the ingenious structure of the novel and history, between the author of a novel and God. Alluding to the Peace of Utrecht (1713), he likens the 'Roman dieser Zeiten' ('novel of this age'), for which he would like to see 'eine bessere entknötung' ('a better dénouement'), to Anton Ulrich's work on his second novel, which spanned some decades without being brought to a conclusion: 'Und gleichwie E. D. [Eure Durchlaucht] mit Ihrer Octavia noch nicht fertig, so kan Unser Herr Gott auch noch ein paar tomos zu seinem Roman machen, welche zuletzt besser lauten möchten. Es ist ohne dem eine von der Roman-Macher besten künsten, alles in verwirrung fallen zu lassen, und dann unverhofft herauss zu wickeln. Und niemand ahmet unsern Herrn besser nach als ein Erfinder von einem schöhnem Roman' ('And just as Your Grace is not yet done with his *Octavia*, so the Good Lord can also add another couple of volumes to his novel, which might in the end have a better ring to it. It is in any case one of the novel-writer's finest arts to allow everything to collapse into confusion, so as then to unravel the whole to unhoped-for satisfaction. And none imitates Our Lord better as an inventor of fine novels').

Zigler's Asiatische Banise

The *Asiatische Banise* (1689) by Heinrich Anshelm von Zigler und Kliphausen saw the return of the court-history novel to a more manageable plot structure. Its thrilling plot, set in exotic Indochina, its extreme characters and rhetorical brilliance ensured a readership for the work well into the eighteenth century. Nevertheless, the *Banise* provided the eleven-year-old Anton Reiser 'zum ersten Male das unaussprechliche Vergnügen verbotner Lektüre' ('for the first time [with] the unutterable pleasure of forbidden reading') (Karl Philipp Moritz, *Anton Reiser*, 1785).

The galanter Roman (gallant novel)

Towards the end of the seventeenth century a development occurred that was to lead the novel away from the court history to what came to be known as the gallant novel. This term comprises works that owe their form to court-history novel, but modify its ethical, theological-philosophical bases (such as perseverance or theodicy), also suppressing 'heroic' elements (such as chivalry or affairs of state) in favour of the depiction of romantic entanglements. One of the first exponents of the genre was August Bohse with novels such as *Der Liebe Irregarten* (*The Maze of Love*) (1684), or *Liebes-cabinet der Damen* (*The Ladies' Love Chamber*) (1685). The gallant novel reached its purest form with Christian Friedrich Hunold (among other works the author of *Die Liebens-Würdige Adalie – The Charming Adalia*, 1702). Johann Gottfried Schnabel's work already marks a deviation from this tradition (*Der im Irr-Garten der Liebe herum taumelnde Cavalier – The Cavalier Hopelessly Lost in the Maze of Love*, 1738).

The Schäferroman: a specifically German phenomenon

Whereas, despite all modifications of detail, the models for the court-history novel taken from other European literatures were preserved in Germany, the German *Schäferroman* came to occupy a particular place. Although the great Renaissance pastoral novels – Jorge de Montemayor's *Diana* (1559) and Honoré d'Urfé's *Astrée* (1607–27) – were translated into German from 1619 onwards, the adoption of these pastoral novels of court pageantry, depicting and discussing supra-individual romantic conflicts and ideas of love, bore no direct fruit in Germany. German literature saw instead the development of separate forms, short novels with the theme of love as *Privat-werck* and giving expression to the personal that nonetheless sought to conceal this circumstance, indicative of things to come, under the veil of conventional, cliché-ridden style and moral zeal. The first and most successful of these novels, which was published under a pseudonym, was the *Jüngsterbawete Schäferey / Oder Keusche Liebes-Beschreibung / Von der Verliebten Nimfen Amoena, Und dem Lobwürdigen Schäffer Amandus* (*The Lately Built Sheep-pen / Or The Chaste Love Story / of the Enamoured Nymph Amoena and the Commendable Shepherd Amandus*) (1632). The narrative is in fact more moral example than love story: love, bursting as an irresistible force into the stylised courtly pastoral world, is portrayed as sinful passion and remains unrequited. Victory goes to 'kluge Vernunft' ('clever Reason'). This model was adhered to throughout a series of pastoral novels, even affecting the sensitive melancholy atmosphere of Philipp von Zesen's *Adriatische Rosemund* (1645), which combines elements of the court-history and pastoral novels. A noteworthy exception to the general rule of the unhappy ending is Johann Thomas's novel *Damon und Lisille* (1663), which is strikingly unconventional in its depiction of the happy relationship of two people in marriage.

'Lesser prose': opposition to the court-history novel

Authors of the *niederer Roman*, or 'lesser prose', the third major baroque prose genre, viewed their works as a counterbalance to the 'high' court-history novel, from which they differed in their essential aspects: the figure of the hero and his world, and the structure and mode of the narrative. Fundamental opposition manifested itself in the express aspiration of 'lesser prose' towards authenticity, where 'high prose' required no more than a 'plausible' link between history and fiction. Such is the aim of Hans Jacob Christoph von Grimmelshausen in his *Simplicissimus* (1669), in which he deliberately sets the value of 'rechten Historien' ('real histories') and 'warhafften Geschichten' ('true stories') against that of 'Liebes-Büchern' ('love-books') and 'Helden-Gedichten' ('heroic poems'). Likewise Johann Beer, Grimmelshausen's leading adherent, who sought to combine authenticity with utility. In his *Teutsche Winter-Nächte* (*German Winter Nights*) (1682) he refers to a 'Jugendgeschichte' ('tale of youth') with the words:

> Natürliche Sachen sind endlich nicht garstig, und deswegen werden solche Sachen erzählet, damit wir uns in der Gelegenheit derselben wohl vorsehen and hüten sollen. Ich habe vor diesem in manchen Büchern ein Haufen Zeuges von hohen und grossen Liebesgeschichten gelesen, aber es waren solche Sachen, die sich nicht zutragen konnten noch mochten. War also dieselbe Zeit, die ich in Lesung solcher Schriften zugebracht, schon übel angewendet, weil es keine Gelegenheit gab, mich einer solchen Sache zu gebrauchen, die in demselben Buche begriffen war; aber dergleichen Historien, wie sie Monsieur Ludwigen in seiner Jugend begegnet, geschehen noch tausendfältig und absonderlich unter uns. Dahero halte ich solche viel höher als jene, weil sie uns begegnen können und wir also Gelegenheit haben, uns darinnen vorzustellen solche Lehren, die wir zu Fliehung der Laster anwenden und nützlich gebrauchen können. Was hilft es, wenn man dem Schuster eine Historia vorschreibet und erzählet ihm, welchergestalten einer einesmals einen göldenen Schuh gemachet, denselben dem Mogol verehret, und also sei er hernach ein Fürst des Landes worden? Wahrhaftig, nicht viel anders kommen heraus etliche gedruckte Historien, welche nur mit erlogenen und grossprahlenden Sachen angefüllet, die sich weder nachtun lassen, auch in dem Werke selbsten nirgends als in der Phantasie des Scribentens geschehen sind.

> Natural things are not after all vile, wherefore such things should be told, that we might have an opportunity to foresee and forearm against them. I have before today read in such books a great deal of high and great love stories, but these were such things as could never come to pass. The time employed in the reading of such writings was therefore used ill, having provided no opportunity to make use of such things as were contained in the book in question; however, histories of the kind encountered by Monsieur Ludwig in his youth are such as occur a thousandfold and in strange fashion among ourselves. I would therefore hold the latter to be far higher than the former, since we can encounter them and we thus have an opportunity to envisage in them such lessons as may be employed to escape the vice and make good use of. What good can come of writing a *historia* for a cobbler and telling him of someone who once made a golden

shoe, the same being admired by the Mogul, the cobbler then rising to become a prince of the land? In truth, not much else comes of the sundry published histories that are full of nought but fabricated and fustian things as cannot be emulated, or which in the work have occurred nowhere aside from the imagination of the scribbler himself.

Writing elsewhere that he sees his 'Entwurf mehr einer Satyra als Histori ähnlich' ('brief as being more akin to that of the satirist than the historian'), Beer reveals that authors of 'lesser prose' classify their works with satirical writings.

Translations

Like other baroque prose genres, indigenous lesser prose was also preceded by translations and adaptations of foreign works. The two leading trends in lesser prose are both represented: the Spanish picaresque novel, modified to suit the Counter-Reformation taste (*Lazarillo de Tormes*, 1554, German 1617; Mateo Aleman: *Guzman de Alfarache*, 1599–1605, German 1615), and the French *roman comique* (Charles Sorel: *Histoire comique de Francion*, 1623–33, German 1662 and 1668) were already available in translation when Grimmelshausen's *Simplicissimus Teutsch*, the first lesser prose work in German, appeared. Among Grimmelshausen's numerous other sources is the work of the Alsatian satirist Johann Michael Moscherosch, traces of whose view of the soldier's life may be discerned in the *Geschichten Philanders von Sittewalt* (1640–50) in *Simplicissimus*.

Unlike the court-history novel, the picaresque novel views the world from below, from the perspective of the oppressed and the community of outcasts. This effect is achieved through the form of fictional autobiography, which helps lend authenticity to the story. The retrospective style of narrative employed makes it possible for the narrator to compare his various developmental phases with one another, and hence comment on his or her own mode of conduct:

> zuletzt als ich mit hertzlicher Reu meinen gantzen geführten Lebens-Lauff betrachtete / und meine Bubenstück die ich von Jugend auff begangen / mir selbsten vor Augen stellte / und zu Gemüth führete / dass gleichwohl der barmhertzige GOtt unangesehen aller solchen groben Sünden / mich bissher nit allein vor der ewigen Verdambnuss bewahrt / sonder Zeit und Gelegenheit geben hat mich zu bessern / zubekehren / Ihn umb Verzeyhung zu bitten / und umb seine Gutthaten zudancken / beschreibe ich alles was mir noch eingefallen / in dieses Buch. . . .

When at last I surveyed with heartfelt remorse my entire life's course, seeing before my eyes the knavery committed since my youth, making me mindful that the merciful God, nonetheless, disregarding all such grave sins, has thus far not only preserved me from eternal damnation, but has even granted me time and occasion to improve, repent, ask his forgiveness, and give thanks to him for His mercies, I describe all that has befallen me here in this book. . . .

Thus proclaims the narrator of *Simplicissimus* at the end of the novel after finding peace from the temptations of the world on an island. What he begins to write there on palm leaves is at first a 'story of repentance' ('Bekehrungsgeschichte': the 'Entwicklung' (development) category is inappropriate to the content). The story nevertheless expands into a trenchant depiction of an unholy world, the world of the Thirty Years War.

The plot of Grimmelshausen's Simplicissimus

The novel opens with the outbreak of war in the idyllic forest of Spessart, where the hero has grown up innocent and unknowing. He finds refuge with a recluse, his father as it later transpires, in whose care he changes 'auss einer Bestia zu einem Christenmenschen' ('from a beast into a Christian man') and who gives him three lessons to serve him along the way: 'sich selbst erkennen / böse Gesellschafft meiden / und beständig verbleiben' ('to acquire self-knowledge, to avoid bad company and to remain steadfast'). He falls finally into the clutches of war, first as a victim, later as a protagonist, incurring guilt and allowing himself to be swept along, apart from occasional attempts at self-betterment – until finally achieving self-knowledge and the certainty of faith 'auss sonderlicher Barmhertzigkeit' ('by the special grace') of God and seeking to live a life pleasing to God as a recluse. He only succeeds at his second attempt, however.

The recluse scenes form the framework of the novel, rounding it off and suggesting a kind of cyclical structure by returning to the beginning. Rejection of the world is portrayed as the inevitable outcome of the life depicted. Appearances are deceptive, however. The return of a changed Simplicissimus in *Seltzamer Springinsfeld* (1670), one of the 'sequels' to the novel, with its emphasis on active practical Christianity, makes it clear that shunning human society is not intended to be the last word.

Satire

Grimmelshausen, who sets out to 'tell the truth with laughter' in the Horatian manner, takes as the theme of his novels the state of the world and of humanity in his day. He regards them as satirical novels. The very monster depicted on the title page of *Simplicissimus* reveals the satirical intention of its contents: the half-animal, half-human figure with its gesture of scorn and derision (see the left hand) is an allusion to the satyr, and hence to 'Satyre', satire (from a theory, widespread in the seventeenth-century, on the origin of satire). The monster is likewise an embodiment of fable, as depicted by Horace at the opening of his *Art of Poetry*, using it as a warning against violation of classicist rules of art (e.g. the emulation of nature and plausibility). This tradition also formed the basis of the dominant seventeenth-century theory of high prose, with its requirements of plausibility and organic unity of plot. In contrast satire, even in antiquity, freed itself from the fetters of too narrow an adherence to rules. Grimmelshausen himself observes anti-Aristotelian and anti-classicist laws of structure, using them to fly in the face of the aestheticisation of reality in high prose. The title page, a substitute for an absent preface, hence refers to a satirical, realistic literary tradition that had existed side by side with idealising literary genres, as a corrective to them, since at least the late Middle Ages. Johann Fischart's conception of grotesque realism in his German translations of Rabelais ('überschrecklich lustig in einen Teutschen Model vergossen') falls especially into this tradition, leading to Grimmelshausen: prose as 'ein verwirretes ungestaltes Muster der heut verwirrten ungestalten Welt' ('a muddled, unfashioned model of today's muddled, unfashioned world') (*Geschichtklitterung*, 1582).

Allegory and reality

Various hints by Grimmelshausen of a hidden 'core' to the novel suggest an allegorical interpretation. On the other hand, the major allegorical 'inserts' – including the allegorical tree of rank, 'Mummelsee' episode, and shearing knife discourse, are not so much derived from the concrete world of appearances, but rather draw a vivid picture of contemporary society and its conflicts. This ambivalence is typical of the whole novel. The moral and religious requirement of edification, invoked by the depiction of an exemplary or allegorical course of life through the world, a place of inconstancy and transience, is in constant tension with an elemental delight in narration and a satirical, realistic concept of narration that Grimmelshausen was able to draw from Charles Sorel and the French *roman comique*. In this way *Simplicissimus* transcends the limited perspective of the fate of one individual, to give a harsh portrayal of the world of the Thirty Years War, and a society in which all values are topsy-turvy and whose unwholesome condition is made all the more starkly apparent by setting it against the background of Christian teaching and various spiritual ('innerweltlich') utopias. It is only through its release from the kind of one-dimensional Christian instruction that characterised German translations of Spanish picaresque novels that the world portrayed in *Simplicissimus* acquires the breadth that distinguishes it from all other seventeenth-century German novels.

The success of Simplicissimus

Grimmelshausen's other 'Simplician' works, including *Courasche* (1670), *Springinsfeld* (1670) and the two parts of the *Wunderbarliches Vogelnest* (1672–5), were not nearly as popular as *Simplicissimus itself*, of which six editions were published within only a few years. There was no lack of attempts to exploit this success. The terms 'Simplicissimus' and 'simplicianisch' were quickly put to advertising purposes, while even Johann Beer had his first work published under the title of *Simplicianischen Weltkucker* (1677–9).

The 'political' novel

Within the lesser prose genre, which was gradually acquiring burgher traits, a separate sub-genre established itself in the 1670s and 1680s under the influence of Christian Weise (*Die drey ärgsten Ertz-Narren In der gantzen Welt – The Three Wickedest Arch-Fools in the Whole World*, 1672) and Johannes Riemer (*Der Politische Maul-Affe – The Political Gaper*, 1679), known as the 'political' novel (in the sense of 'politic', or 'worldly-wise'). It propounded an educational ideal for the man-of-the-world, based on experience, cleverness and self-knowledge, as the prerequisite for a happy life and successful career in the Absolutist state. The form used in the 'political' novel – a scant epic framework and a journey as a vehicle for instruction – offered little scope for development, however. At the most it was open to parody: in Christian Reuter's story of duplicity and adventure, *Schelmuffsky* (1696), for example, the loud-mouthed hero learns nothing at all. The lesser prose scene was otherwise dominated by adventure stories. Most of the *Robinsonaden* that appeared following the publication of Daniel Defoe's *Robinson Crusoe* (1719, German 1720) fall into this category, making use of the name Robinson purely for publicity. The *Wunderlichen Fata einiger See-Fahrer (The Wonderful Fates of some Seafarers)* (1731–43) by Johann Gottfried Schnabel towers above the bulk of these. The *Insel Felsenburg*, as the work soon became named, combines the Robinson type of adventure with the model of a utopian common life, based on fear of God, Reason and Virtue, shared by men weary of Europe. The novel, a complex web of interlocking autobiographies, sets the narration of the emergence and continued development of this island republic against the life-stories of the people who have found peace there. Unlike Robinson Crusoe and the heroes of many Robinsonian works, who can hardly wait to return to Europe, the inhabitants of this idyllic island do not have the slightest desire to return to their home country, or to see a single European place ('oder nur einen eintzigen Ort von Europa') ever again. This earthly utopia, the dream of escape from the oppressive social conditions of the contemporary era, mark the advent of the *bürgerlicher Roman* – the domestic and private, as opposed to courtly and public, burgher novel of the German Enlightenment.

AUFKLÄRUNG: THE ENLIGHTENMENT

What is new politically and socially?

The eighteenth century was rightly perceived by contemporaries and later historians alike as the end of an era – the beginning of the modern age. After the Thirty Years War the German empire had splintered into a multitude of small and minute territories, and was by now more akin to a 'monster' (Pufendorf) than a modern state. Imperial territory had become a hopeless tangle of over 300 sovereign territories and a welter of semi-autonomous provinces and towns. Although supreme imperial power in the Holy Roman Empire (*das Heilige Römische Reich Deutscher Nation* was the official title) remained in the hands of the German Emperor until 1806, it had by then dwindled to a few rights of largely symbolic value. Major political decisions were made by the states, which wielded power of legislation, the judiciary, national defence, police (including censorship), etc. independently of imperial power.

The German Empire – a 'monster'

The empire was thus by now little more than a 'formal clamp', barely holding the 'monster' together. Virtually no contemporary writer failed to poke fun at the 'square-mile monarchs' and miniature courts, or deplore the 'horrors of plural German government' ('die Greuel der deutschen Vielherrschaft'). This welter of small and minute principalities can indeed only be described as a grotesque mosaic of petty princelings – lingering on, it should not be forgotten, to the detriment of the people. These innumerable miniature potentates were only able to maintain their costly courts by ruthless exploitation of their subjects. The living conditions of the people themselves were meagre to say the least. Oppressed by the burdens of feudalism and princely despotism, and for the most part still the bondsmen of their respective lords, peasants possessed scarcely more than the bare essentials for life – less, if there was a poor harvest. A sad picture is obtained of the eighteenth century if one visualises the living

156

conditions of the lower classes, who constituted over two-thirds of the total population. Conditions were not much better even in larger states such as Prussia or Saxony. Any notion of the 'good old days' simply collapses in the face of the calamitous conditions in the Germany of the day, yielded by the facts and figures of historical inquiry.

The economy and society

On what basis, therefore, do historians justify their statements about the advent of the modern age? If one examines the plight of the lower classes separately from overall social developments, it is easy to overlook the fact that new economic forces were stirring in the lap of feudal society, and that a new social class of a distinctly modern stamp was taking shape: industrial capitalism and the mercantile and capital-owning middle class. In towns especially, a growing middle class was acquiring wealth and social prestige through trade, banking and manufacturing. Although still weak and few in number, the members of this middle class were nonetheless a clear sign that feudalism had been consigned to history. Shifts in the balance of power among the various ranks caused tensions to arise in the rank pyramid as a whole, which had had a hierarchical arrangement since the Middle Ages. This led to the eventual collapse of the society of rank, and the formation of a middle-class egalitarian society. In the eighteenth century these tensions were most apparent in clashes between the nobility and the middle classes. The latter were no longer prepared to accept as God-given and unalterable the political and cultural supremacy of the aristocracy, who only made up an infinitesimal part of the population as a whole. They staked their own claim to sovereignty, appealing in so doing to the ideas of the Enlightenment, which sought to replace the feudal view of a world 'by the grace of God' with a new body of thought based on Reason.

The Enlightenment was a pan-European movement that differed very widely in character in different countries, and was also very diversely defined by its various proponents. The basic principles of the Enlightenment, however, were: an appeal to Reason as the yardstick for personal and social conduct, a focus on this world rather than the next, a positive image of man, human equality and a call for human rights for all. Criticism of religion and a more progressive faith were relatively late in arriving in Germany, although eventually forming a coherent body of thought on which the middle classes could base their sovereignty.

Changes in the reading public – the 'free' writer makes his appearance – the emergence of a literature market

Seventeenth-century court-style literature had been typified by remoteness from the people, a dearth of realism, artificiality and poverty of motifs.

Court poetry had ossified into a sterile, functionless body of literature incapable of the artistic comprehension, let alone expression, of recent developments. Its dramatised 'Haupt-und Staatsaktionen' (fussy theatrical productions), muddled pastoral and heroic novels and utterly torpid erotic poetry were appealing to fewer and fewer readers and spectators. Even princes themselves were finding their court poets an increasingly dispensable commodity. The last court poet in Prussia was dismissed, as part of an economy drive, in 1713 with the accession of Friedrich Wilhelm I.

Court poetry was most readily superseded in major mercantile cities, subject directly to the Emperor, which had grown to a position of cultural rivalry with the courts and were able to educate a literary public of their own. Leipzig, for example, was among the first cities to have its own municipal theatre, while Hamburg even had a municipal opera. The princely Maecenas (patron) was similarly replaced here and there by middle-class sponsor organisations such as the *Patriotische Gesellschaft* ('Patriotic Society') in Hamburg, which commissioned authors to write literary works. The theme and aim of this new poetry was no longer the praise of princes and the entertainment of court society, but the appreciation of middle-class life and the enlightenment of the middle-class reader.

This shift both in the function of poetry and the readership to whom it was addressed could only proceed in the face of difficulties, since a broad reading public had yet to evolve. At the beginning of the eighteenth century the vast majority of the population was still unable to read or write, while the few middle-class people who were literate tended to restrict their reading to the Bible and texts for religious edification. By 1770 the percentage of the total population who could read could not have been more than 15 per cent; it had reached only some 25 per cent even by 1800. Obviously the numbers of people interested in polite literature were even smaller. At the end of the eighteenth century, Jean Paul was undoubtedly overestimating in presuming a readership of 300,000: in reality the proportion out of the total of 25 million inhabitants who read polite literature cannot have been above 1 per cent. A broad readership and a public interested in literature had, in other words, still to be fostered.

Moralische Wochenschriften ('Moral weeklies')

Moral weeklies played a major role in bringing this about. Periodicals such as *Der Biedermann* (The Honest Man), *The Patriot* and *Die vernünftigen Tadlerinnen* (The Judicious Lady Censors), which mushroomed on the English model in the first half of the eighteenth century, fulfilled a major function in cultivating a middle-class reading public. Moral weeklies, themselves a product of the Enlightenment with their reasoning and informative style, had as their object popularising the ideas of the Enlightenment. This made them an important link between court circles and middle-class society. Their concise popular scientific treatises, analyses and essays on moral philosophy, as well as their innovative literary practices and methods of dissemination, all awakened a readiness in the public for new form and content. They cleared the way for a broader readership, thus creating the first prerequisites for literary education and the emergence of a market for literature.

Reading societies

Reading societies, which were organised in diverse ways and pursued a variety of aims, were a crucial factor in fostering a middle-class readership. The aim of reading *circles*, which had been in existence in Germany since the end of the century, was to alleviate the cost of reading newspapers, journals and books, whereas reading *societies* saw themselves as companionable social circles in which private reading matter was accorded a social status. The huge number of reading associations – some 430 were founded between 1760 and 1800 – shows how enormous the social need for reading matter was, and for discussion about it. The majority of reading societies felt indebted to the Enlightenment. Their Enlightenment objectives were reflected both in their selection of reading matter and in the organisational statutes that regulated their self-government according to democratic principles. Acceptance into a reading society was open in theory to any man of education and taste (women and students were excluded), although high membership fees restricted the circle to an affluent middle-class and aristocratic membership. The lower middle and working classes remained excluded. If they could read at all, they had to rely on lending libraries, which did not begin to exist in any number until towards the end of the eighteenth century. These, together with the commercial libraries that were likewise established in the same period, marked a provisional end to social reading. They concluded the first phase in the evolution of the middle-class reading public, and prepared the ground for a re-privatisation of reading.

Structural change and the public

A shift away from poetry rooted in court life not only brought about a structural change in the reading public, but also had an impact on the situation of the writer. The age of the salaried court poet was drawing to a close; he was being replaced by the 'free' writer endeavouring to make a living from his poetic works. The advantage of the 'free' writer's existence – his intellectual independence from princely or clerical sponsors – was offset by the huge disadvantage of the precariousness of his income. Given the limited number of editions and the low fees of the time, hardly any writer in the eighteenth century could afford to live on the income brought in by his works.

An edition of 1,000–3,000 copies was then regarded as the norm for a work by a well-known author. In 1779 Lessing had 2,000 subscribers to his *Nathan*, while some 6,000 copies were printed of Klopstock's *Gelehrtenrepublik (Republic of Scholars)*; Goethe's *Schriften (Writings)* were published in 1789–90 in an edition of 4,000. Even newspapers and journals had only small circulations. Wieland's *Teutscher Merkur (The German Mercury)*, one of the best-known journals of the eighteenth century, was published in editions of 2,000 copies, although of course the number of readers may have been much higher. Only popular handbooks for the masses were ever published in really substantial numbers: for example, Becker's *Noth- und Hülfsbüchlein für Bauern (The Book of Exigencies and Assistance for Farmers)*, of which over a million copies were printed between 1788 and 1811, and purposely distributed free of charge by many princes to their subjects as anti-revolutionary propaganda.

Fees

Fees were calculated per sheet ('Bogen'), the usual fee being 5–7 talers per sheet. Highly-paid authors such as Klopstock, Wieland and Lessing received paid fees amounting to the annual income of an official for their books. They were exceptions, however. It should also be borne in mind that not even these authors wrote a book every year, so were consequently obliged to live from their fees for lengthy periods.

Patronage

Most writers, therefore, if not from a wealthy household, had to look for additional sources of income, go into service as private tutors at court (*Hofmeister*), officials, etc., or once again seek noble benefactors at court. Penury compelled many writers to pin their hopes on princes, from whom they hoped to obtain material support, and in some cases even the entire organisation and economic funding of literature. Wieland, Klopstock and Herder, for example, devised detailed plans whereby the promotion of literature and authors would be taken over by charitable institutions known as academies. These in turn were to be protected and financed by princes. None of these plans came to fruition, however, owing to lack of interest on the part of the princes. Only a handful of writers, Klopstock among them, received an allowance without having to perform any services in return, whereas Wieland and Goethe in Weimar were expected to act as tutors and advisers to princes. Other writers felt compelled to find an additional livelihood, writing only in their meagre free time. Others again endeavoured to improve their financial situation as the publishers of journals, or as journalists.

Censorship

The new-found freedom of the writer was not impeded solely by his precarious financial situation, however, but also by rigid repression in the form of the censorship that prevailed in most German states. In 1761, a member of the Vienna Book Commission (Wiener Bücherkomission) in charge of censorship in Austria defined censorship as: 'die Aufsicht, dass sowohl im Lande keine gefährlichen und schädlichen Bücher gedrucket, also auch, dass dergleichen Bücher nicht aus andern Landen eingeführet und verkaufet werden' ('Supervision to ensure both that no dangerous or seditious books are published in the land, and that no such books are introduced from other countries and sold'), and wanted to make sure that only such books were printed as 'nichts Gefährliches vor die Religion, nichts zu offenen Verderb der Sitten, und nichts wider die Ruhe des Staats, und wider die, denen Regenten schuldige, Ehrerbiethung in sich enthalten' ('contain nothing to endanger religion, nothing openly to offend morals, and nothing to endanger the peace of the state, and those that contain due deference to rulers'). Just how far censorship impinged on public life is revealed by a celebrated (or notorious) controversy between Lessing and the orthodox Pastor Goeze over the publication of writings critical of religion. The Duke of Braunschweig initially exempted Lessing from censorship, later withdrawing these dispensations at Goeze's instigation. Subsequent rulings by the Duke banned Lessing both from publishing his critiques of religion and from continuing his controversy with Goeze. Goethe's *Werther* was also a victim of censorship in some parts of Germany – Goeze once again excelled himself – as well as Wieland's *Agathon*, whose sales success was considerably hampered by censorship in Zurich and Vienna. Although censorship procedures were implemented with great disparities between territories, so that for example a book banned from publication in Prussia or Saxony might still appear in Hanover, Braunschweig or Altona, the marketing and sale of books in general was hampered by the very existence of censorship. One consequence of censorship, the self-censorship of the author during writing, was a severe impediment to the development of the 'free' writer's existence. In order to avoid censorship by the authorities, some writers would take the precaution of avoiding altogether any potentially objectionable areas or lines of thought and argument they deemed risky, thereby entirely preempting censorship. Some chose the alternative course of seeking refuge in the anonymous publication of their works.

Freedom of the press

The existence of censorship was recognised as a serious problem by most writers, and opposed. A number of writers of the day argued for freedom of the press, i.e. the abolition of censorship. In 1785, Wieland wrote:

Freyheit der Presse ist Angelegenheit und Interesse des ganzen Menschen-Geschlechtes. Dieser Freyheit hauptsächlich haben wir den gegenwärtigen Grad von Erleuchtung, Kultur und Verfeinerung, dessen unser Europa sich rühmen kann, zu verdanken. Man raube uns diese Freyheit, so wird das Licht, dessen wir uns jetzt erfreuen, bald wieder verschwinden; Unwissenheit wird uns wieder dem Aberglauben und dem tyrannischen Despotismus preisgeben; die Völker werden in die scheusliche Barberey der finstern Jahrhunderte zurücksinken; wer sich dann erkühnen wird, Wahrheiten zu sagen, an deren Verheimlichung den Unterdrückern der Menschheit gelegen ist, wird ein Ketzer und Aufrührer heissen, und als ein Verbrecher bestraft werden.

Freedom of the press is an issue and concern for the whole of humankind. We owe this freedom chiefly to the present degree of enlightenment, culture and refinement of which our continent of Europe can boast. If we are robbed of this freedom, the light that we now enjoy will soon disappear; ignorance will once more abandon us to superstition and tyrannical despotism; the peoples will sink back into the foul barbarism of the dark ages; he who would dare to speak those truths whose concealment is in the interests of the oppressors of mankind will be denounced as a heretic and a subversive, and punished like a criminal.

The political function of censorship, and the connection between freedom of publication and social progress was most explicitly emphasised by writers who felt indebted to the Enlightenment. Opposition to censorship did not succeed in abolishing it, however. On the contrary, anxiety to avert revolution after 1789 in the aftermath of the French Revolution led to a massive tightening of censorship all over Germany, anticipating the censorship measures of the *Vormärzzeit*.

The literary market

Penury and censorship were only two of the factors restricting the freedom of the writer. A third was the market for literature that had been growing in Germany since the mid-eighteenth century. Two developments were largely responsible for this. The first was a boom in book production, the second an equally dramatic burgeoning of the number of writers. Between 1740 and 1800 annual book production figures rose from 755 to 2,569.

Polite literature accounted for the bulk of this boom. In absolute terms literary output increased sixteenfold between 1740 and 1800, increasing from 5.8 per cent to 21.5 per cent of total book production. In 1766 there were 2,000–3,000 authors; by the year 1800 there were over 10,000, of whom 1,000–3,000 endeavoured to live mainly or exclusively from their earnings as writers.

This boom in the sheer numbers of books necessitated the organisation of production and marketing along market economy lines. The existing book trade, conducted according to the laws of bartering, the principal method of trading between 1564 and 1764, was now replaced by modern publishing and bookselling institutions. Hitherto, the *Verleger* (publisher) had combined the functions of both publisher and retailer. These functions were now separated, production and sales specialising into mutually independent spheres. This period thus saw the birth of the modern publisher and bookseller. For the first time there were fixed prices. Books were no longer on sale once a year at fairs, but were obtainable all year round from a bookseller. The purchaser now had the enormous advantage of being able to buy a book at any time, like any other type of goods.

How authors saw themselves

This expansion and organisation of the literature market according to the laws of commodity manufacture had its impact on the situation of the author and how he saw himself, as well as on literary output. Writers were obliged, as one afflicted author bitterly complained: 'sich in manche Verhältnisse der bürgerlichen Gesellschaft fügen, die ihnen wehe thun' ('in certain respects to submit to the very middle-class society that harms them'). This meant for the most part adapting themselves to the market and the literary taste of their reading public. Literature, as contemporaries had recognised quite clearly, had become *Kaufmannsware*, merchandise, the writer a *Lohnschreiber*, a wage-earning writer. Gradations in the economic status of writers ranged from paid worker to independent producer. In his novel *Sebaldus Nothanker*, Nicolai writes of a publisher 'der in seinem Hause an einem langen Tische zehn bis zwölf Autoren sitzen hat und jedem sein Pensum fürs Tagelohn abzuarbeiten gibt' ('who has ten to twelve authors all sitting at a long table in his house, and who gives each his quota to work on for his day's wages').

Renowned authors such as Schiller and Goethe were able to deal with their publishers from a more dignified position. Schiller, for example, negotiated with his publisher a fixed allowance in return for everything he wrote in a year. Goethe offered his publisher the finished article.

Dependence on publishers was generally regarded as a bad thing, and a frequent object of bitter censure. Many an anxious writer asked what was to become of German literature if authors were to acquiesce to the will of booksellers. Lessing (*Leben und Leben lassen. Ein Projekt für Schriftsteller und Buchhändler – Live and Let Live. A Project for Writers and Booksellers*) and Wieland (*Grundsätze, woraus das mercantilische Verhältnis zwischen Schriftsteller und Verleger bestimmt wird – Principles for Defining the Mercantile Relationship between Writers and Publishers*) consequently made efforts to regulate the relationship between authors and publishers in such a way as not to burden authors alone. Other authors, such as Klopstock, tried to circumvent the resented intermediary of publishing altogether by publishing their books themselves.

The degree to which such measures were by that time already anachronistic is apparent from the bankruptcy of the Dessauer Gelehrtenbuchhandlung (Dessau Scholars' Bookshop) established in 1781 by the authors of central Germany as a cooperative publishing enterprise. Even attempts by authors to free themselves from publishers by means of subscriptions and advance fees proved fruitless, since, as one contemporary complained: 'das Herausgeben der Bücher auf Subskription und Pränumeration hat tausend Beschwerlichkeiten, die man sich vorher nicht hat träumen lassen, und am Ende gewinnt der Verfasser selten so viel, als ihm ein Verleger gegeben haben würde' ('the publishing of books on the basis of subscriptions and advances is fraught with a thousand difficulties that one would not even have dreamed of beforehand, and in the end the author rarely obtains even as much as a publisher would have paid him').

Copyright

Authors found it particularly galling not to be owners of their own writings. Property rights lay instead with publishers, who could do what they liked with manuscripts. The issue of intellectual property was made more acute by the evil of pirated editions. Flouting authors' and publishers' rights alike, resourceful booksellers pirated popular books for their own pockets, thereby detracting both from the profits of the original publisher, and, indirectly, from the income of the author. It was 1835 before legislation by the *Deutscher Bund* banned the publication of unauthorised editions. The debate over the protection of intellectual property and copyright, however, continued throughout the nineteenth century.

In the eighteenth century, the legal situation of the writer was still totally precarious, and utterly at the mercy of market forces. This was exacerbated by fierce competition among authors themselves. Only those authors who could largely adapt to public taste were able to survive on the literature market – or those authors whose works were of such originality in form and content that they spontaneously attracted the interest of the literary connoisseur. In the light of this, the concept and the publicising of the poet as 'original genius' had sound reasoning behind it.

Literary theories of the Enlightenment:
From Gottsched through Lessing to *Sturm und Drang*

The demise of the court poet also entailed the demise of court literature. It was succeeded by a new literature that tried to adopt all the central categories of the Enlightenment: Reason, utility, and humanity, in all literary genres. Johann Christoph Gottsched was the first to implement this long overdue shift in both theory and practice, and set the pace for the emergence of the new literature. His seminal theoretical work *Versuch einer Critischen Dichtkunst vor die Deutschen* (*An Essay on Critical Art of Poesy Before the Germans*) (1730) broke with the formalistic regulatory and directive poetics of the Baroque, which were still rooted in feudal society. He censured baroque poetry from the standpoint of the Enlightenment, calling for a literature that would serve the Enlightenment, disseminate the ideas of the Enlightenment in a generally comprehensible and pleasing manner, combining utility with pleasure (*prodesse et delectare*), and reach broad sections of middle-class society. The linchpins of Gottsched's poetics were the Aristotelian principle of the emulation of nature, and the Horatian requirement that *prodesse et delectare* be the proper tasks of poetry. For Gottsched, the laws of Reason were synonymous with the laws of nature, compliance with these rules therefore being identical with emulation of nature. By the emulation of nature Gottsched understood not the realistic reproduction of reality, but 'Ähnlichkeit des Erdichteten mit dem, was wirklich zu geschehen pflegt' ('similarity of the literary invention to what really tends to occur'). Gottsched used this principle of probability as the basis for his insistence on strict observance of the three Aristotelian unities (time, place and action) in drama – which Lessing was to criticise vehemently only a few years later. Gottsched even sought to organise the process of poetic creation according to the laws of Reason: 'Zu allererst wähle man sich einen lehrreichen moralischen Satz, der in dem ganzen Gedichte zum Grunde liegen soll, nach Beschaffenheit der Absichten, die man sich zu erlangen vorgenommen. Hierzu ersinne man sich eine allgemeine Begebenheit, worin eine Handlung vorkömmt, daran dieser erwählte Lehrsatz sehr augenscheinlich in die Sinne fällt' ('First of all one selects an instructive moral tenet on which to base the whole poem, depending on the nature of the objectives that one has undertaken to achieve. One then devises a general incident in which an act occurs such as to render this selected moral tenet very readily apparent').

Of no less significance was Gottsched's adherence to the so-called rank proviso (*Ständeklausel*), according to which only princes and nobles could be the protagonists in tragedy, *Staatsromanen* and heroic poems, while in comedy, pastoral poems and novels only middle-class and peasant protagonists could appear.

The charging of poetry with moral and pedagogical aims was to have an impact on the status of poets. They now became tutors and educators of the public, thus rising in moral and intellectual status while at the same time becoming more restricted in artistic scope.

Significant and pioneering as Gottsched's efforts in the spheres of journalism, drama and poetics were, they soon revealed the limitations of his ideas. His mechanistic view of the creative process in the poet, his no less mechanical notion of an emulation of nature that was true to reality and his rigid insistence on observance of the three unities and the rank proviso soon showed themselves to be impeding factors in the growth of a new middle-class literature, and they became the object of criticism from his contemporaries.

The leading critic of Gottsched's literary theory and practice was Lessing. In his *Briefwechsel mit Mendelssohn und Nicolai über das Trauerspiel* (*Correspondence on Tragedy with Mendelssohn and Nicolai*) (1756–7) he stood out against the three unities and the rank proviso, as well as the principle of mechanical emulation and the moral and didactic function of literature propounded by Gottsched, although of course without rejecting Enlightenment aims. Within the Enlightenment movement Gottsched represented an early middle-class stance that had not yet freed itself from concessions to the feudal intellectual universe, whereas Lessing adopted a progressive middle-class position that was ultimately to prevail conclusively over feudal literary theory and practice in Germany. He drew support for his standpoint from developments taking place on the literary scene that in France had led to the creation of a middle-class comedy genre (derisively described by opponents as 'weinerliches Lustspiel' – 'weepy comedy'), and in England to a middle-class tragedy genre. In these French and English dramas Lessing saw how abandonment of the feudal rank proviso, offensive to growing middle-class self-awareness, had already been implemented in practice: the middle classes had become capable of tragedy. Lessing exploded the feudal rank proviso by seeking to make a person's action separate from his rank: 'Die Namen von Fürsten und Helden können einem Stück Pomp und Majestät geben; aber zur Rührung tragen sie nichts bei. Das Unglück derjenigen, deren Umstände den unsrigen am nächsten kommen, muss natürlicherweise am tiefsten in unsre Seele dringen; und wenn wir mit Königen Mitleiden haben, so haben wir es mit ihnen als mit Menschen und nicht als mit Königen' ('The names of princes and heroes may lend a play of pomp and majesty, but they add nothing to the emotional effect. The misfortune of those whose circumstances are most like our own will naturally penetrate our soul most deeply, and if we feel sympathy for kings, we feel for them as men and not as kings'). Lessing's appeal to the human was closely associated with his efforts to create a new, more differentiated definition of the function of literature. His aim was ethical commentary rather than moral instruction in the Gottschedian sense. In his view the aim of tragedy was to instil fear and sympathy into his audience or reader. Through these emotions, tragedy was to lead to a cleansing of passion, or catharsis. The spectator was to identify with the hero, feel sympathy for him, but at the same be seized by fear of the same misfortune befalling himself. Such an objective could only be achieved if the hero was other than the ideal type envisaged by Gottsched; he had to come over realistically as a 'mixed character', i.e. a man 'weder nur gut noch völlig böse angelegt' ('a man disposed neither wholly to good nor evil').

Lessing's psychological realism is also apparent in his concept of poetic emulation. The aim of the poet was not a naturalistic representation of things, but rather poetic truth. The poet was to achieve this by omitting everything superfluous, coincidental and of secondary importance, concentrating wholly on representing the essential and the typical: 'Auf dem Theater sollen wir nicht lernen, was dieser oder jener einzelne Mensch getan hat, sondern was ein jeder Mensch von einem gewissen Charakter unter gewissen Umständen tun werde' ('At the theatre we should not learn what this or that individual has done, but what any individual of a certain character would do under certain circumstances').

Lessing's 'naturalness'

Lessing's definition of the function of literature opened up new artistic possibilities. The principle of poetic emulation, with which he countered the principle of emulating nature, made artistic creation in the modern sense possible for the first time. His definition also entailed a reassessment of the poet himself, who was, again for the first time, perceived and legitimated as an artistic subject.

No less significant than Lessing's achievements as a theoretician, which were most apparent in his work *Laokoon oder über die Grenzen der Malerei und Poesie* (*Laokoon, Or On the Limitations of Painting and Poetry*) (1766), were his accomplishments as a critic. His critical writings *Briefe, die neueste Literatur betreffend* (Letters Concerning the Latest Literature) (1759), published together with his friends Nicolai and Mendelssohn, and *Hamburgische Dramaturgie* (Hamburg Dramaturgy) (1767–9), are a model of 'constructive criticism', as the Romantic Friedrich Schlegel was to proclaim them decades later. Lessing's works of literary criticism ushered in a new era of literary debate in Germany, and a flowering of literary activity.

Many of Lessing's ideas were ahead of their time. His rejection of normative poetics in the Gottschedian sense, his concept of poetic truth and the accompanying notion of differentiated realism, which allowed the poet creative license, were all crucial for the coming generation of authors. The *Stürmer und Dränger* especially, a group of young poets who derived their name from Klinger's drama *Sturm und Drang*, took up Lessing's ideas, combining them with their own views to form a new conception of literature. The focal point of these new aesthetic perceptions was no longer regulated poetics, but genius, i.e. the creative power of the poetic individual. The *Geniekult*, the cult of the genius, of the *Stürmer und Dränger* raised the poet above the mass of humanity. Art was no longer something that could be learned ('Schädlicher als Beyspiele sind dem Genius Principien' – 'Principles are more harmful to the genius than examples' – Goethe): the artist creates out of his own genius. The notion of genius was enhanced by the growing acquaintance with Shakespeare's works taking place at that time. Whereas Gottsched had rejected Shakespeare for his lack of regulation, the discovery of Shakespeare from the 1750s onwards in Germany opened up a new world for the *Stürmer und Dränger*, allowing French classicist poetry to be replaced. Goethe's visionary essay *Zum Shäkespears Tag* (1771), influenced by Herder, emphatically paved the way for an enthusiasm for the English poet and for his psychological creation of characters: 'Ich erkannte, ich fühlte aufs lebhafteste meine Existenz um eine Unendlichkeit erweitert' ('I perceived, and felt in the most vital manner, my existence expanded by an infinity'). Shakespeare became a symbol of the poet of genius, and a model for indigenous poetic practice. This may be discerned, for example, in Goethe's *Götz von Berlichingen* (1773), which is as much influenced by Shakespeare as Klinger's drama *Die Zwillinge* (*The Twins*) (1776).

The cult of genius

The excesses of the cult of genius among some *Stürmer und Dränger* become understandable when seen against stiffening competition on the literature market. The stress placed on the element of genius and the subjective in the creative process was not least a consequence of the increasing number of writers and of the competitive struggle among them. In this situation, genius could be a 'weapon in the competitive struggle', and subjectivity a 'form of self-advertisement' (Hauser).

Negative aspects of the cult of genius should not be overlooked, however. The irrational element in the notion of genius stood in remarkable, and unresolved, contrast to the Enlightenment principle of rationality. Genius, spontaneity, individuality, emotion, sensitivity, naturalness and originality were the watchwords of the new literary movement. They were used by it to attack the normative requirements of Gottsched and his adherents and, notwithstanding their appreciation of Lessing's achievements, equally against the more normative concepts of Lessing and his adherents. Just as it is false to view Lessing and Gottsched as irreconcilable adversaries, even if they saw themselves as such, it is equally false to see the struggle of the *Stürmer und Dränger* against Gottsched and Lessing in terms of irreconcilable hostility. The *Stürmer und Dränger* simply took into a new phase the

Enlightenment movement that had been introduced by Gottsched and brought to its zenith with Lessing. The prevailing element of the early Enlightenment movement, the somewhat one-sidedly stressed principle of rationality, was not so much replaced as complemented by the *Sturm und Drang* cult of emotion. The two poles of the Enlightenment, Reason and Emotion, were combined, not without difficulty, into a single unity.

The *Sturm und Drang* conception of literature clearly reveals that it was not a countermovement to the Enlightenment, but rather a continuation, enrichment and partly a radicalisation of it. In *Die Schaubühne als eine moralische Anstalt betrachtet* (*The Stage Viewed as a Moral Institution*) (1784), for example, Schiller takes a step further those elements of social criticism already discernible in Lessing's theory of middle-class tragedy and his call for a national middle-class theatre. He calls on the stage to take over the 'sword and scales', bringing the vices and crimes of the powerful before the 'judgement seat' of Reason.

Such a conception of literature also changed the role of the writer. He became the custodian of oppressed Reason, and champion of the rights of the middle class. Once assigned, such a function could only be fulfilled by a literature that confronted current obstacles to the middle-class emancipation movement. Interest in the problems of the so-called 'common man' ('gemeiner Mann') indicate that the *Stürmer und Dränger* sought to include the lower middle class in the middle-class struggle for emancipation. Lenz states that it is to the advantage of the poet to go 'in die Häuser unserer sogenannten gemeinen Leute . . . auf ihr Interesse, ihre Leidenschaften Acht geben' ('into the homes of so-called common German people . . . to pay heed to their interest and their passions'), while Herder urged the poet to place himself in the service of the 'ehrwürdigsten Theils der Menschen, den wir Volk nennen' ('that worthiest portion of mankind, whom we call the people').

In practice this entailed a move away from the kind of poetry that was only intelligible to a narrow circle of intellectuals. The middle classes required art, 'die zwar von Gelehrten, aber nicht für Gelehrte als solche, sondern für das Volk ausgeübt werden muss' ('which must be practised *by* the educated, but is not intended for the educated as such, but for the people'). The popularity of a poetic work would now be for the poet 'das Siegel seiner Vollkommenheit' ('the seal of its perfection'). The poet was now to be a *Volksdichter*, a poet of the people, and poetry to be *Volkspoesie*. The *Volkspoesie* concept is a clear indication of how far Enlightenment literary theory had come in the mere fifty years from Gottsched and then Lessing to the *Stürmer und Dränger*.

169

The application of Enlightenment ideas in drama

Drama, having been credited with a more distinct educative potential, capable of transforming society, had pride of place among literary genres in the Enlightenment. Seen as a 'weltliche Kanzel' ('secular pulpit' – Gottsched), a 'Schule der moralischen Welt' ('school of the world of morals' – Lessing), and a 'moralische Anstalt' ('moral institution' – Schiller) by proponents of the Enlightenment, in only a few years the theatre rapidly became the leading institution of education and guidance, enjoying in the eighteenth century a degree of esteem and a flowering that has never been witnessed either before or since. The intelligentsia was positively seized by 'theatremania'. Many offspring of the middle classes gravitated towards the theatre to try their hand at acting. The novels *Anton Reiser* (1785–90) by Karl Philipp Moritz, and *Wilhelm Meisters theatralische Sendung* (1776–85) by Goethe are clear evidence of the passion of the younger generation for the theatre. Middle-class intellectuals sought to play in the theatre the role they were still denied in society at large.

From Harlequin to middle-class hero

The breathtaking rise experienced by the theatre in only a few years is all the more astonishing if one bears in mind that it started from literally nothing. 'Lauter schwülstige und mit Harlekins=Lustbarkeiten unter-mengte Haupt= und Staatsaktionen, lauter unnatürliche Romanstreiche und Liebesverwirrungen, lauter pöbelhafte Fratzen und Zoten waren das-jenige, so man daselbst zu sehen bekam' ('Nothing but the dreariest fuss and nonsense peppered with Harlequin diversions, nothing but unnatural romantic escapades and entanglements, nothing but vulgar grimaces and ribaldry were all one could see there') was how Gottsched had described the theatrical life of Leipzig in 1724. His derisive statement refers to touring theatre companies, which according to the famous actor Konrad Ekhof comprised 'itinerant troops of jugglers ... who wander through all Germany from one fair to another, entertaining the masses with smutty buffoonery'. Besides these there were also respectable and privileged court theatres for the entertainment of aristocratic court society, with perform-ances by permanent French and Italian theatre companies. Neither the so-called *Pöbeltheater*, nor the feudal court theatre were compatible with the Enlightenment vision of literature. It does credit to Gottsched's breadth of vision and instinct, therefore, that he began his attempts at reform with the despised *Pöbeltheater*.

Working with troops of actors, he endeavoured to raise the standard of touring companies and to make the theatre interesting to a middle-class audience. The yardstick for his reform efforts was French classicist drama, which he sought to adapt using his own 'regelmässigen' ('regular') plays, i.e. plays that conformed to his rules (metrical speech, a fixed number of acts, observance of the three unities of place, time and space, the rank proviso, etc.).

His tragedy *Sterbender Cato* (*The Dying Cato*) (1732) is an attempt by Gottsched to provide a practical example of his own dramatic theory. Using, as Gottsched's severest critic Bodmer later commented bitingly, 'scissors and paste', and basing his work on Cato plays by Addison and Deschamps, he wrote 'the first original German tragedy'. Substantial passages, however, are in fact translated: only 174 of the total 1,648 Alexandrines in the 'original drama' were penned by Gottsched himself. It would be wrong to condemn him for this, however. He saw himself not as an 'original poet' in the sense understood by the later *Stürmer und Dränger*, but rather as paving the way for a new type of 'regulated drama' ('regelmässiges Drama'). By translating existing plays, chiefly from the French- and also from the English-speaking world, he aimed to devise a model that could serve other authors in practice.

The play *Sterbender Cato*, however, is not interesting solely for the model of 'regulated tragedy' it seeks to provide, but also as documenting the anti-feudal tendencies already apparent in the early Enlightenment era. In his elucidation and defence of *Cato* against contemporary critics, Gottsched particularly stressed the political components of the play, writing, 'dass die wahre Grösse eines Helden in der Liebe seines Vaterlandes und einer tugendhaften Grossmuth bestehe; die Herrschucht aber und die mit einer listigen Verstellung überfirniste Tyrannei unmöglich eine rechte Grösse sein könne' ('that the true greatness of a hero lies in his love for his country, while it is impossible for the lust for power, or for tyranny veneered with a cunning disguise, to be truly great'). Using the confrontation between Caesar and Cato, Gottsched elaborates the distinction between a tyranny and a republic, his sympathies obviously lying with Cato.

Numerous reprints and repeated performances made *Cato* the most successful play of the next few decades – a huge success for the times. The publisher of the tenth edition of *Cato*, one of Gottsched's many pupils and admirers, acknowledged: 'So viel ist gewiss, dass nicht leicht eine Residenz, Reichs- oder andre ansehnliche Handelsstadt, von Bern in der Schweiz und Strassburg an bis nach Königsberg in Preussen und von Wien her bis nach Kiel im Holsteinischen, zu nennen ist, wo nicht *Cato* vielfältig wäre aufgeführt worden' ('This much is certain; it is no easy matter to name a capital, imperial or other sizeable mercantile city, from Bern in Switzerland to Königsberg in Prussia, or from Vienna to Kiel in Holstein, where *Cato* has not been performed many times').

A woman author: Kulmus

What Gottsched pioneered for tragedy through his plays, his wife Luise Adelgunde Victorie Kulmus accomplished for comedy. Kulmus was one of the leading women authors of the eighteenth century. *Pietisterey im Fischbein-Rocke* (*Pietism in a Whalebone Skirt*) (1736), based like Gottsched's *Cato* on foreign models, and her other comedies (*Die ungleiche Heyrath – The Unequal Marriage; Die Hausfranzösin – The Gouvernante; Das Testament – The Will; Der Witzling – The Jester*), evince 'an extraordinary satirical vein, wit and overall literary talent', as recent research has increasingly found. Her plays are important not only for presenting the formal aspects of a new comedy form, but also in documenting the anti-clerical struggle of the early Enlightenment. She takes the pietism of her day to task with derisive irony, condemning all the obscurantist and mystical traits she discerns in this movement. She uses characters such as Herr and Frau Glaubeleicht (Mr and Mrs Gullible), Magister Scheinfromm (Master Feign-Pious), the young Herr von Muckersdorff (Lord Bigotton) and many others with suggestive names to lampoon false piety and religious fanaticism, mounting a criticism of pietism that was unmatched for conviction and pungency even by later novels such as *Der redliche Mann am Hofe* (*The Honest Man at Court*) (1740) by Michael von Loen, or *Leben und Meinungen des Magisters Sebaldus Nothanker* (*The Life and Opinions of Master Sebaldus Nothanker*) (1773) by Friedrich Nicolai. Not least, its wicked satire against German pietism of the Francke and Spener varieties made it controversial, and outraged the authorities. In a cabinet decree of 1737 King Friedrich Wilhelm I called the *Pietisterey* 'an utterly godless lampoon' ('eine recht gottlose Schmäh Schrift'). It was banned in Berlin and Königsberg; booksellers were interrogated and numerous copies confiscated. The author herself was spared, however. Whether out of false modesty or on account of the politically explosive nature of the play, she published it anonymously, using false names both for the publisher and place of publication. Her husband, who had a high regard for the play as a major document in the struggle against the anti-Enlightenment movement, cautiously omitted to include the controversial and suppressed *Pietisterey* in his six-volume work *Deutsche Schaubühne* (*The German Stage*) (1740–5), a collection of model plays.

Orientation towards French classicism

Although orientation towards foreign prototypes and classical French drama in particular, typical for Gottsched, his wife and their adherents, did noticeably improve the standard of repertoires, it also greatly restricted poets in their creative freedom. Opposition to the rigid regulatory dogmatism of Gottsched and his associates was not long in arising. Lessing even went so far as to deny that Gottsched could take any of the credit for the creation of a German theatre (*17. Brief, die neueste Literatur betreffend – 17th letter, On recent literature*), lamenting the situation of the theatre in the 1760s with the not entirely apt words: 'Wir haben kein Theater. Wir haben keine Schauspieler. Wir haben keine Zuhörer' ('We have no theatre. We have no actors. We have no audience').

In fact, the differences between Gottsched's and Lessing's conceptions of the theatre were so enormous that Lessing was unable to appreciate Gottsched's achievements. Whereas Gottsched, on the basis of a moderate Enlightenment standpoint that was not always able to liberate itself from feudal ideas (for example, the rank proviso) focused his reforming efforts first and foremost at improving the repertoire, Lessing stood for a thorough-going anti-feudal literary vision.

The idea of a German national theatre

Lessing had set himself the task of creating a national theatre, i.e. a theatre for the entire nation, not for the privileged few. This theatre was to be free of all constraining foreign influences, and was to deal with the topical problems of the nation itself. In Lessing's view, only a middle-class theatre was capable of meeting these demands. In Lessing, as later with Schiller and the *Stürmer und Dränger*, the idea of a national theatre and the concept of middle-class drama formed an indivisible unity.

With the establishment of a permanent company and theatre in Hamburg (1765), Lessing's hopes for a national theatre seemed to have been fulfilled. In fact, however, essential aspects of his theatrical vision were still omitted. The initiative to establish a theatre had come not from the middle classes, but from private individuals, and the theatre was not subsidised from public funds. Not surprisingly, therefore, it failed as a result of financial difficulties after only two seasons.

The idea of a national theatre was subsequently commandeered by princes. In 1776 Emperor Joseph II appointed the Vienna court theatre as the national theatre; in 1778 the Mannheim national theatre was founded. Although unsuccessful in his attempt to implement his vision of a national theatre as a purely middle-class institution at the organisational level, however, Lessing was still able to foster the growth of middle-class drama. His *Emilia Galotti* (1772), *Minna von Barnhelm* (1776) and *Nathan der Weise* (1779) successfully pointed the way forward for eighteenth century middle-class drama. Together with dramas of the *Sturm und Drang* era and with Schiller's *Räuber* (1781) and *Kabale und Liebe* (1784), Goethe's *Götz von Berlichingen* (1771–3) and Lenz's *Hofmeister* (1774), Lessing's dramas form a body of plays that are still part of the permanent repertoire. Two decades saw the emergence of the German theatre from provincial narrowness. It could now stand comparison with the theatre in France and England.

Certain common features may be discerned in all these dramas, above all their middle-class character. These dramas were not *bürgerlich* in the modern, 'middle-class', sense of the term, however. In the eighteenth century the term *bürger* was not a designation of class in the modern meaning, but closer to the word 'civil'. It was thus used polemically as a counterpart to the public sphere of court to denote a private, domestic sphere outside the constraints of rank. This contrasting opposition between the civil, private sphere and a public sphere of court, however, also implied a strong element of social criticism. This entailed the private sphere of the family being reclaimed as 'generally humane' ('allgemeinmenschlich'), as opposed to the court sphere, which was seen as impersonal, cold and hostile to human attributes.

What made these dramas 'bürgerlich' or 'civil', therefore, was the way they propounded virtues such as humanity, tolerance, justice, the capacity for sympathy, morality, richness of feeling etc., not that 'burgher' heroes in the narrow sense of the word were portrayed in them. Lessing's Emilia Galotti, for example, comes from the minor nobility, but embodies through her morality the *bürgerlich*, or 'civil' idea of virtue that will not allow itself to be corrupted by immorality at court. Karl Moor in Schiller's *Die Räuber*, although again the son of the current Count von Moor, is an anti-feudal rebel, like Goethe's Götz von Berlichingen, who although also from the nobility despises court life and fights on the side of the socially oppressed. A truly 'middle-class' heroine does not appear until Schiller's *Kabale und Liebe*, in the person of Luise, the daughter of Miller the municipal musician. *Kabale und Liebe* deals with a similar theme to that of *Emilia Galotti* and *Miss Sara Sampson* (1755). With these two plays, which borrow from Lillo's *The London Merchant* and Diderot's *Le père de famille*, Lessing laid the foundations for German *bürgerlich* tragedy – a tradition that was to endure through to Hebbel's *Maria Magdalene*.

These dramas by Lessing, as well as Schiller's, all deal with the motif of 'seduced innocence'. All three have women as the focus of the confrontation between nobility and the middle classes, and all three end with the death of the heroine.

Miss Sara Sampson succumbs to the charm of the libertine Mellefont, who abducts her from her father's home, promising her marriage. Not wishing to jeopardise his freedom, however, he recoils from legalising the relationship. The virtuous Sara is torn between pining for the father she has left and love for her abductor and seducer Mellefont. Eventually she dies, taking poison that belonged to Mellefont's former lover. At the sight of the dead Sara, Mellefont also takes his own life. Mr Sampson concludes the drama with a forgiving assessment of the seducer: 'Ach, er war mehr unglücklich als lasterhaft' ('Ah, he was more unhappy than vicious.')

'Mixed characters'

The anti-feudal conflict in *Emilia Galotti* is more pointed. Here the Prince of Guastalla, the epitome of unfettered arbitrary tyranny and erotic profligacy, attempts to bring the virtuous Emilia into his power, not shrinking even from murdering Emilia's bridegroom Appiani. For her part, Emilia is not unreceptive to the erotic attractions of the prince, in stark contrast to the 'good Appiani'. 'Verführung ist die wahre Gewalt! – Ich habe Blut, mein Vater, so jugendliches, so warmes Blut als eine. Auch meine Sinne sind Sinne. Ich stehe für nichts' ('Seduction is true power! – I have blood, father, young and warm as any. My senses are senses too. I stand for nothing'): with these words, which incidently struck contemporaries as scandalous in the extreme, Emilia asks her father for the dagger with which to kill herself. Yet it is ultimately her father who takes her life, unable to face the idea of his daughter committing suicide.

The characters of the father Odoardo and the Prince of Guastalla represent the harsh and irreconcilable opposition between prince and private gentleman. Odoardo despises court life, and lives in self-imposed isolation in the country in Rousseauesque seclusion, far from the enticements of court. In the virtue of his daughter he sees the guarantee of his moral superiority over the feudal lord he despises.

In *Kabale und Liebe* this conflict is given a different nuance. Luise Millerin, after whom Schiller originally named his drama, is of middle-class origin. The story depicted by Schiller is, moreover, set in contemporary Germany, whereas Lessing sets his *Sara* in England and *Emilia* in a minor Italian state in a remote and vague past. This shift clearly indicates the development of *bürgerliches Drama* from relative abstractness to a precise delineation of the political and social spheres of conflict. Luise is nevertheless comparable with her predecessors Sara and Emilia in her virtue, which is an indestructible part of her being. Her lover Ferdinand is no longer an unscrupulous seducer, but is trying to overcome class barriers and marry Luise. In so doing, however, he is assailing the very foundations of feudal society, thereby incurring the fatal 'Kabale' ('cabals') of the court. Deceived by intrigue as to the virtue and fidelity of Luise, he poisons her, drinking from the poison cup himself on learning that she is 'innocent'.

Fathers and daughters

As in *Emilia Galotti* and *Miss Sara Sampson*, so, too, in *Kabale und Liebe* the father–daughter relationship is of crucial importance. It is depicted not simply as a tender familial tie, but also as a state of ownership. Daughters are the 'property', 'wealth' and 'goods' of their fathers. Virtue is not merely an ideal, but also a material asset. The vocabulary, drawn from middle-class business life, gives this away, showing the 'economisation' of relationships within the newly-forming mercantile society, whose propagation of paternal authority likewise betrays the inclination of middle-class society to reinstate a patriarchal order. The virtue of the daughter is the power of the father. Like 'goods and chattels', daughters are a commodity of exchange between men, and a focus of conflict between the nobility and the middle classes. Daughters are victims in a dual sense: they do not kill themselves once, as men do, they are killed. Long before their death on stage at the end of the drama they perish as victims of a fetishist notion of virtue that stylises them in the name of middle-class morality. Desensualised, pure beings, in short angels in the true sense of the word, they are incapable of life, being consecrated to death.

The confrontation between the nobility and the middle classes is thus not conducted on the political level here, but is privatised and moralised, acted out on stage as a conflict between middle-class rectitude and absolute arbitrary power. The sphere of social conflict becomes noticeably more concrete and precise. Whereas in the early phase of *bürgerlich* drama the concept of a private humanity was still connected with persons from the nobility, only a few years later the *Stürmer und Dränger* were transferring it to the middle classes themselves.

This shift had consequences for the direction of social criticism in the genre. A more accurate focus on social subject, the make-up of the cast and the sphere of conflict led to social criticism taking on a more concrete aspect. What had been moral criticism of feudalism now became political.

The plight of the intelligentsia

This and the more concrete aspect of social criticism are particularly discernible in the dramas of Jakob Michael Reinhold Lenz. In his *Hofmeister (The Private Tutor)*, Lenz portrayed the difficulties of the contemporary intelligentsia in finding a place for themselves in the rank society of the time, taking up a topical problem of his day. Läuffer, the son of a *Stadtprediger*, a preacher, is forced after his studies to make his living as a private tutor in the house of a noble major, where he is treated scarcely better than the rest of the servants. His humiliating position as private tutor is made all the more acute by his love affair with the daughter of the house. Läuffer finally sees no other way out than to castrate himself. The social equilibrium is thus only restored by his maiming himself.

Die Soldaten (The Soldiers) similarly stresses the element of social criticism much more than, for example, Lessing's early *bürgerlich* drama. Lenz sets his dramas in the present, his conflicts arising out of social tensions in the contemporary social order. Having dealt in the *Hofmeister* with the problem of the tutor's existence, in which not only he himself, but numerous other intellectuals and authors of the day were obliged to suffer, Lenz dealt in *Die Soldaten* with another topical issue of the day: the dangers to the virtue of middle-class girls inherent in the 'unmarried state of commissioned officers' ('ehelosen Standes der Herren Soldaten').

What makes Lenz's dramas so fascinating is not only the consistency of his commitment to social issues, expressed in his realistic and differentiated portrayal of characters and conflicts, but also his blend of the tragic and comic. The formerly rigid separation of comedy and tragedy propounded by Gottsched, and still practised by Lessing, was abandoned by Lenz in favour of a new dramatic form permitting a blend of the two, of the satirical and the serious. It is in this, rather than in the political thrust of his dramas, that Lenz's modernity lies, and which inspired nineteenth- (see Büchner's novella *Lenz*) and twentieth-century authors (see Brecht's adaptation of the *Hofmeister*, and Kipphardt's adaptation of *Die Soldaten*) to repeated productive grappling with this author, who was entirely unappreciated in his own time.

The ideal portrayal of characters customary in early *bürgerlich* theatre was likewise abandoned by Lenz. Although Lessing had developed the pioneering concept of the 'mixed hero' in his theory of tragedy, the heroes and heroines of his plays were more akin to representatives of some abstract ideal of *bürgerlich* virtue than to realistically portrayed characters. This is particularly apparent in *Nathan der Weise*: the noble Jew Nathan is an embodiment of the Enlightenment ideals of tolerance and humanity. It was the *Stürmer und Dränger* who first created real, living characters in their dramas, although Goethe in *Götz* and Schiller in *Die Räuber* both tended to exaggeration in their heroes. The traits of powerful genius found in Götz and Karl Moor, which still make them interesting to modern audiences, had no counterpart in reality. They were the products of wishful thinking in their authors.

Lenz, in contrast, dispensed not merely with 'mixed' heroes, but with heroes altogether. Although there are main and subsidiary characters in his plays, they are not embodiments of virtue, stylised portrayals of powerful genius or villains, but people whose characters and conduct are shaped by the social conditions in which they live.

The theme of the family

A major linking theme in *bürgerlich* drama at that time, and one fraught with problems, is the portrayal of and focus on the middle-class nuclear family, set as a private sphere against the public sphere of court. The discovery of the middle-class nuclear family by eighteenth-century dramatists is linked with far-reaching social change. The emergence of middle-class society in the course of the eighteenth century led to the demise of formerly dominant feudal family types such as the noble family association or the peasant extended family, which had survived as a common household

177

for the purposes of production and common ownership. As the division of labour proceeded, the former link between production and reproduction was severed, separating them into two spheres. Production was now an activity conducted outside the family, which was in turn consigned to reproductive functions, the role of the wife being confined to the household and child-rearing.

This new lifestyle and organisation of the middle-class nuclear family was based on a strict division of labour between men and women. Male work was recognised and paid, while women worked unpaid at home, thus becoming financially dependent on men and receiving recognition solely in the form of praise and esteem. So strong was the position of the man in the middle-class nuclear family that he was practically the owner of his wife.

The theme of marriage

This state of ownership, provided for in law, was apparent from the monogamous structure of marriage. Research has frequently spoken of the creation of the family as one of the 'great achievements of the middle classes', the nuclear family being based on a 'perfect spiritual union and the most far-reaching possible intellectual union' between men and women (Schücking). In reality, however, this literary stylisation of the family as a stronghold of *bürgerlich* sensitivity and virtue was an ideal image advanced by authors who were only too sensible of the destructive effects of capitalist middle-class trends on the individual. The family was therefore hailed as a refuge against feudal tyranny, and stylised as an enclave of feeling to counter the principle of rationality that was taking increasing hold in economic and social life. The idyll is misleading, however, and the cost paid for it a high one.

Bürgerlich dramas in particular show that the family was not at all the perfect spiritual community suggested by research. In many of these dramas, the family is either incomplete, the mother having died young, or relations between the marriage partners are notoriously poor, as, for example, in *Kabale und Liebe*, where the father's behaviour towards the mother is decidedly uncouth: he reviles her, for example, as 'a vile procuress' ('infame Kupplerin'). Alternatively, relations between the father and children may be extremely tense, or even completely broken down. Daughters involve themselves in fatal conflicts in seeking to reconcile their love for their fathers with that for their lovers, while sons find themselves in fatal rivalry for the love and inheritance of their fathers. Besides *bürgerlich* tragedies dealing mainly with father–daughter relationships, therefore, there are also dramas treating the bloody consequences of father–son conflicts, such as for example, *Julius von Tarent* (1776) by Leisewitz, *Die Zwillinge* (*The Twins*) (1776) by Klinger and *Die Räuber* (*The Robbers*) by Schiller.

The theme of insurrection and crime

In *Die Räuber* the dramatic conflict arises out of rivalry between two dissimilar brothers, Franz and Karl. 'Warum bin ich nicht der Erste aus Mutterleib gekrochen? Warum nicht der Einzige? Warum musste sie [die Natur] mit diese Bürde von Hässlichkeit aufladen? gerade mir?' ('Why was I not first to crawl from my mother's womb? Why not the only one? Why did she [nature] have to place this burden of ugliness upon me? Why me?'). With these words Franz, the second-born son, rages against the fate that has condemned him. He uses all available means to usurp the place of the 'Schooskind', the favourite Karl in the hearts of his father and lover Amalia.

Die Räuber is more than a family drama, however. Anti-feudal and revolutionary elements are even more apparent in this play than in *Emilia Galotti* or *Kabale und Liebe*. The robber plot of the play allows the social reality of the eighteenth century, pauperism and organised banditry, to be stressed more than ever before in literature. More even than an accurate depiction of social reality, however, it is also a sweeping 'fantasy of unqualified negation of the prevailing order' (Scherpe), although this is retracted in the play and denied by the action of the plot.

Images of men and women

Concentration on the middle-class family for setting and plot was accompanied by the propagation of a new image of men and women. Virtue, fidelity, acquiescence and emotionality were proclaimed as female attributes, while men were portrayed as strong, courageous and active. This assignation of roles, which was becoming more and more marked, particularly in tragedy, was to foster a subsequent formation of clichés, still prevalent today, of male and female 'nature'. It also prepared the way for a 'polarisation of gender character' (Hauser) that was enshrined in philosophy at the end of the eighteenth century by Fichte and Humboldt *inter alia*. The demand of the early Enlightenment, led by writers such as Gottsched, for middle-class equality applicable to men and women alike had led to the emergence of a new type – the educated, worldly-wise woman. Under the influence of Rousseau and his *Emile* and *Nouvelle Heloise* in particular, these attributes were now reclaimed, and henceforth applied to the middle-class male only. Women were no longer seen as independent, autonomous beings, but defined solely in relation to men and their happiness. Woman 'hat aufgehört, das Leben eines Individuums zu führen, ihr Leben ist Teil seines Lebens geworden' ('has ceased to live the life of an individual; her life has become part of his life'), as Fichte was to argue in his *Grundriss des Familienrechts*.

This new assignation of roles was somewhat delayed in *bürgerlich* comedies, however. Lessing's Minna, for example, is portrayed as a strong, confident, resolute woman who successfully dissuades Major von Tellheim from his exaggerated notion of marriage, which stands in the way of their union, and wins him over to her point of view. This reversing of roles – Minna is the active, Tellheim the passive protagonist – was only possible in comedy. In tragedy women remained in the background, like Amalia in *Die Räuber*, or Maria in *Götz;* even when they are the main or central characters, such as Emilia, or Luise in *Kabale und Liebe*, they are confined to the role of victim.

The dramas of Lenz represent something of an exception to this, the author at least dispensing with the idealisation and disembodiment of women. In *Die Soldaten*, Marie is shown as a frivolous, seducible, sexually active creature ('Soldatendirne'), and Lenz blames society rather than his heroine for her tragic fate.

The theme of 'seduced innocence'

For the *Stürmer und Dränger* the motif of seduced innocence now acquired new weight. Their interest shifted from a criticism of feudalism (the feudal lord as seducer of middle-class innocence) to a criticism of middle-class morality – which held up the idea of pre-marital virginity in women as a moral commodity of the highest value, but at the same time regarded the sexual activity of men both before and outside marriage as entirely normal, or at least tolerable. The *Stürmer und Dränger* were fully aware that this double standard persisted to the detriment of women. In Wagner's drama *Die Kindermörderin* (*The Child-Murderess*) (1776), and in Goethe's *Urfaust* (1775), Evchen and Gretchen, women seduced and then abandoned, murder their new-born children because they are unable to face the social disgrace incurred by having a child born out of wedlock. Instead of thereby avoiding disgrace, however, they incur it in double measure. As unmarried mothers they were 'only' ostracised and outcast; as child-murderesses they are utterly spurned by society, condemned to the scaffold. These stories, moreover, are no product of literary license, but an accurate reflection of eighteenth-century reality. Goethe drew his ideas for the Gretchen plot of *Faust* from the trial records of the convicted child-murderess Susanna Margaretha Brandt, who was executed on 14 January 1772.

Middle-class resignation?

However, the limitations of *bürgerliches Drama* are not only apparent from what is today seen as a questionable division of gender roles, but also from its underlying attitude of resignation. *Minna von Barnhelm*, in which the conflict is resolved happily, is one of the few comedies in the drama of the day. Tragedies were in a distinct majority. Emilia Galotti is

killed by her father Oduardo at her own wish; Karl Moor kills his fiancée
Amalia and gives himself up to the feudal henchmen; Götz dies of his
injuries and his lack of courage in the face of entrenched social conditions;
Ferdinand and Luise die of poison in *Kabale und Liebe*, and Läuffer
castrates himself in the *Hofmeister*. Murder, suicide and self-maiming lie
at the end of *bürgerlich* tragedies: the hero and heroine fail in the face of
prevailing social conditions, and can only preserve their identity through
self-destruction. The anti-feudal point of *bürgerliches Drama* finds no
revolutionary solution, ending instead in self-destruction, resignation and
submission. A clear example of this is the anti-feudal rebel Karl Moor,
who ultimately gives himself up for trial, and hence submits to the very
order against which he has struggled in vain. Even in drama, the objective
social conditions did not admit a positive solution to the conflict between
the middle-class desire for emancipation and the institutions of feudal
dominance. The spirit of rebellion in the *bürgerliches Drama* of that time
is nonetheless unmistakable, and has been perceived as such by contemporary and later audiences alike. French revolutionaries made Schiller an
honorary citizen for *Die Räuber*, Piscator staged it in the Weimar Republic
as a model for the Russian October Revolution and the play was re-read
by the post-1968 student movement in the context of extra-parliamentary
opposition (*Das Räuberbuch*). This continuous revolutionary tradition was
able to draw especially on the powerful and inspired language of the play,
which gives forlorn vent to horror at the 'Tintenkleksenden Sekulum' ('age
of scribbling') and the 'Kastraten-Jahrhundert' ('the century of castrates').
'Warum sind Despoten da? Warum sollen sich tausende und wieder tausende unter die Laune Eines Magens krümmen und von seinen Blähungen
abhängen? – Das Gesetz bringt es so mit sich – Fluch über das Gesetz,
das zum Schneckengang verderbt was Adlerflug worden wäre!' ('Why are
there despots? Why should thousands upon thousands squirm under the
humour of one stomach, hanging on its every belch? – 'Tis the law makes
it so – A curse on the law that condemns to a snail's pace what should
have been an eagle's flight!') These words, spoken by Karl in *Die Räuber*,
assail the very foundations of Absolutist feudal government, and government in general. The legitimacy of government and law is just as much a
theme as the issue of the form the state takes: 'Stelle mich vor ein Heer
Kerls wie ich, und aus Deutschland soll eine Republik werden, gegen die
Rom und Sparta Nonnenklöster seyn sollen' ('Show me an army of fellows
such as myself, and I'll show you how to make a republic out of Germany
that will make Rome and Sparta look like nunneries'). These pithy lines
read like a harbinger of the events that were to shape the post-1789
European scene.

Individual experience in the novel

Besides drama, the novel was the other genre that burgeoned in the eighteenth century, and was also closely linked with awakening self-awareness. Like drama, it too was still frowned upon as an inferior literary form at the beginning of the century. Unlike drama, however, the novel lacked even the status of being part of poetics. The epic poem, based on ancient traditions (Homer's *Iliad* and *Odyssey*), was regarded as the sole legitimate form.

Despite this, however, the period did witness a multitude of novels that deviated from the epic tradition, seeking to satisfy the craving for entertainment. Torpid love novels, gallant pastoral novels, intricate adventure novels and a great number of translations from the Spanish, English and French had a predominantly aristocratic readership, but were dismissed by contemporary critics as 'Lugen=Kram' ('lies and trash') and also censured on moral grounds.

Not even novels of literary merit such as Grimmelshausen's *Der Abentheuerliche Simplicissimus Teutsch* (1669), which is in the tradition of Cervantes' *Don Quixote*, or Schnabel's *Insel Felsenburg* (1731–43), the outstanding German *Robinsonade*, influenced by Daniel Defoe's *Robinson Crusoe*, were spared the strict censure of the critics. 'Wer Roman list, list lügen' ('He who reads novels, reads lies') was how contemporaries summed up their revulsion at the new genre.

Pro-Enlightenment authors were the first to recognise the potential of the genre, seeking to give a new direction to this hitherto despised form in the spirit of *prodesse et delectare* (utility and pleasure). This could only be achieved by changing novel-writing practices. The *höfischer Roman*, the court romance or novel, would have to be replaced by a *bürgerlicher Roman*, a private, domestic novel, involving similar aims to those applied to *bürgerliches Drama*. The nobleman-adventurer or gallant lover would likewise be supplanted by a *bürgerlicher* hero who, like the 'mixed character' of *bürgerliches Drama*, would be depicted in a psychologically credible way. The torpid, over-intricate narrative style of the court novel would give way to a 'natural narrative style' (Gottsched). Novelists were to leave behind ancient or contemporary foreign models in favour of dealing with topical everyday problems and issues of the present-day and their own nation. The call for a national *bürgerliches Theater* thus had its parallel in a plea for a national *bürgerlicher Roman*. In both cases the objective was to co-opt literature into the service of *bürgerlich* self-realisation.

Literary models from abroad

German authors had major sources of inspiration in their efforts, chiefly from English and French novels (Richardson's *Pamela*; Fielding's *Tom*

Jones; Rousseau's *Confessions* and *Nouvelle Heloise*) – novels of high literary merit deriving from the advanced development of the middle classes in those countries.

A brief period saw a positive boom in novel-writing. From 1700 to 1770 some 1,287 novels were published, including translations. The ratio of new novels to overall production increased continuously and, after 1764, dramatically. By around 1770 the new *bürgerlicher Roman* had completely dislodged other forms of the novel. Translations from the English and the French took up a major proportion of this rapid upsurge – accounting in some years for almost half of all new publications – as did borrowed foreign literary models.

This orientation towards English and French models was not always without its drawbacks. Although Wieland's *Agathon* (1766–7), which relates the development of the Greek youth Agathon, was hailed by contemporaries as an example of a 'new class of novel', the author himself being celebrated as the 'first novelist' in Germany, he was nevertheless also criticised for being 'too much of an imitator, sometimes of Fielding, sometimes of Rousseau, sometimes of Cervantes'. Similarly, Gellert's *Leben der schwedischen Gräfin von G* (1747–8) and Sophie von La Roche's *Geschichte des Fräuleins von Sternheim* (1771), both influenced by the English sentimental novel, despite evincing clear signs of major progress towards the *bürgerlicher* novel still failed to meet the need felt by contemporaries for an 'original German novel'.

The *Bürgerlichkeit* (the private, domestic and moral attributes) of these novels, as in the case of drama, manifests itself chiefly in the moral and emotional character of their heroes and heroines, who in the early stages of the form could still be nobles. Goethe's *Werther* marked the real advent of the *bürgerlicher* novel as such in Germany.

The integration problems of the intellectual

In his *Leiden des jungen Werthers* Goethe portrays the archetype of the disenchanted young middle-class intellectual who fails to find a niche for himself in society, faced both with the rigid hierarchy that still characterised the social order of rank, and no less his high estimation of his own worth. Goethe's novel shows the impossibility of the middle-class individual defining a place or finding an identity for himself within the feudal system. Werther's suffering, culminating in his suicide, caused by society and his failure, makes him akin to those heroes of *bürgerliches Drama* who are likewise broken by the social order, such as Karl Moor in *Die Räuber* or Läuffer in the *Hofmeister*.

The impact of Goethe's *Werther* was enormous. 'Da sitz ich mit zerflossnem Herzen, mit klopfender Brust, und mit Augen, aus welchen wollüstiger Schmerz tröpfelt, und sag Dir, Leser, dass ich eben die Leiden des jungen Werthers von meinem lieben Göthe – gelesen? – Nein, verschlungen habe' ('Here I sit with melted, pounding heart, with eyes dripping tears of bewitching sorrow, and I tell you, Reader, that I have just read the *Sufferings of Young Werther* by our dear Goethe? Nay, I have devoured it'), writes one contemporary of how he experienced the book. There was a veritable outbreak of Werther-mania, sparked off by the novel's depiction of the dilemma of the middle-class self-view in the feudal state. Responses ranged from enthusiastic agreement to fanatical rejection. Orthodox theologians in particular denounced the work for its alleged glorification of suicide as a 'lure of Satan', calling for it to be censored. The sale of *Werther* was indeed banned in Leipzig in 1775.

Two of the major reasons for the epoch-making impact of *Werther* lay in its depiction of the problems inherent in the relationship between the individual and society, and in its sensitive portrayal of the love story between Lotte and Werther. This new form was to set the tone for the nineteenth and twentieth centuries. The appearance of *Werther* marked the birth of the modern novel in Germany. It was not morally tendentious like, for example, *Die schwedische Gräfin* or *Das Fräulein von Sternheim*, but a highly subjective confession in letter form. Goethe drew on his own trials and experiences, and on the suicide of a friend, blending these with the experience of the young burgher intelligentsia, typical for the age, to create what was perceived by readers of the day as a highly unusual form. Previously accustomed to being given a clear moral evaluation of events, they were now left to arrive at their own assessment of *Werther*. The monologue form taken by this letter-novel – there are no answers to Werther's letters – rendered the perspective of the hero absolute, virtually forcing the reader to identify with him. His suicide at the end must leave the reader in a state of deep turmoil. A considerable number of suicides did indeed occur among *Werther*-readers, leading Goethe to preface the second edition with the warning: 'Sei ein Mann, und folge mir nicht nach!' ('Be a man, and do not follow my example!').

The repercussions of the novel were not restricted to the eighteenth century, however. As an attempt to deal with the theme of self-realisation in the middle-class individual, Goethe's *Werther* posed a challenge to following generations. Many nineteenth- and twentieth-century authors had recourse to the novel, and were inspired by its content and form (see, for example, Ulrich Plenzdorf, *Die neuen Leiden des jungen W*, 1973).

Autobiography as a form of self-reflection

The highly subjective form of Goethe's *Werther* has to be viewed in the context of a general rise of the autobiographical in eighteenth-century literature. Liberation from the constraints of court and clergy was not without its repercussions. For the first time the middle-class individual began to see himself as a unique personality in his own right, and was obliged to shape his own identity independently of external influences and authorities. Literature became a significant form of experience and self-portrayal in this search for identity. A major source of inspiration for German authors in this regard was Rousseau, whose *Confessions* (1765–70) was a story of education and development written with unflinching candour and enormous insight into human psychology. *Anton Reiser* (1785–90) by Karl Philipp Moritz, still well worth reading today, is one of the most interesting examples of the new form. The reader will not only gain insights into the typical educational career and developmental of a young lower-middle-class person, but will also gain valuable information about the times and conditions in which the literary intelligentsia lived.

Autobiographical documents dating from the period, regardless of their overall differences, clearly show how difficult it was for the literary intelligentsia either to define themselves as autonomous individuals, or to find a recognised niche for themselves. This was owing in no small measure to the miserable social prospects of authors such as Bräker, Laukhard or Seume, who either found themselves unable to rise into the middle class at all, or had to pay a high price for their rise. Even authors who started out as middle-class sons, and whose positions were hence more favourable, still felt their developmental potential restricted by the 'fatal middle-class conditions' that eventually bring about Werther's downfall.

It was this experience of constraint that lay behind the melancholy and hypochondria that were to become the social diseases of the eighteenth century. The self became a refuge into which the individual could withdraw, giving rise to the contemplative, subjective qualities that were to become typical of the eighteenth-century middle-class individual. There was a distinct preference for solitude, and in the aftermath of Rousseau a sentimentalisation of the experience of nature that was reflected in the nature lyric of the period. The rejection of society by the individual and his turning towards nature were two complementary forms of escape from society. Autobiography was a major, if not the only possible, form for the eighteenth-century *bürgerlicher Roman*.

Besides the subjective and the autobiographical, however, there were also satirical forms, emulating Swift's *Gulliver's Travels* (1726) and Voltaire's *Candide* (1759), which were openly critical of society. Wezel's *Belpheghor* (1776), the 'German Candide', marked the advent in Germany of a tradition of political and social satire that was to diagnose and lampoon the contradictions of the day with startling clarity and lack of compromise. One master of the genre was Georg Christoph Lichtenberg. In his *Sudelbücher* he sets down his reflections on state and society, art and literature, philosophy, religion and psychology, giving them added pungency by presenting them in the form of aphorisms. The result is not a work in the traditional sense, but rather a wealth of ideas and thoughts, transcending the horizons of Enlightenment thought with its sceptical and pessimistic view of German social conditions.

Subjectivity and social criticism in lyric poetry

In lyric verse, the displacement of court poetry was already under way by the end of the seventeenth and beginning of the eighteenth centuries. Effete poetry steeped in convention was replaced by a new lyricism with form and content drawn from the Enlightenment. The astonishing multitude of themes and diversity of means of expression make it impossible to reduce eighteenth-century lyric poetry to a common denominator. A mere 60 years saw the emergence of a highly creative poetic language of great expressional power – in a matter of a few decades a level hitherto unknown was attained. Besides theoretical didactic poetry and contemplative lyrics, conveying Enlightenment ideas in more or less abstract form, there were also mournful odes and hymns treating of religious and philosophical themes. Apart from ballads, some of which depicted events from everyday middle-class life with epic breadth, there were experiential and nature poems in which the lyric self of the poet expressed itself in a highly personal manner, governed by emotion.

It was this release of the poet's subjectivity, the articulation of individuality in poems, that made the lyric of that time so innovative and epochmaking. By articulating his own subjectivity, the poet was anchoring in the lyric sphere the middle-class aspiration for freedom and personal happiness. Lyric poetry became a private form of self-experience and selfportrayal, although its political link with the Enlightenment movement was ever-present, albeit in indirect, encoded form.

However, in addition to personal lyric forms, for which the love and nature poems of the young Goethe are exemplary (e.g. *Willkommen und Abschied*, 1771; *Mailied*, 1771; *Ganymed*, 1774), there also emerged more forceful lyric verse, militant and critical of society, pointing out social injustices and taking a stand. Bürger's poem *Der Bauer an seinen durchlauchtigen Tyrannen* (*The Peasant to His Grace the Tyrant*) (1773) and Schubart's *Fürstengruft* (*The Prince's Tomb*) (1779), for example, are trenchant indictments of feudalism. They initiated a tradition of provocative political lyric poetry extending from the German *Jakobiner* through *Vormärz* writers to the political lyric of the modern age. Even poems that at first glance seem apolitical, such as Goethe's ode *Prometheus* (1773) are revealed on closer examination to be documents of the awakening self-awareness of the middle class and the creative artist.

Besides attempts to treat the subjectivity of the individual and his perception of his age in highly creative forms, there were also efforts to make lyric poetry *volkstümlich*, i.e. accessible to the people. Bürger thus urged lyric poets to seek material 'unter unsren Bauern, Hirten, Jägern, Berg-leuten, Handwerksburschen, Kesselführern, Hechelträgern, Bootsknechten, Fuhrleuten' ('among our [German] peasants, herdsmen, huntsmen, miners, journeymen, tinkers, hatchel-carriers, boatsmen, and waggoners'), and to write and compose 'nicht für Gottessöhne' ('not for children of the gods'), but for human beings. 'Steiget herab von den Gipfeln eurer wolkigen Hochgelahrtheit und verlanget nicht, dass wir vielen, die wir auf Erden wohnen, zu euch wenigen hinaufklimmen sollen' ('Come down from the peaks of your great erudition up there in the clouds, and do not expect us, the many who live here on Earth, to climb up to you few up there'). In Bürger's view, a *Nationalgedicht*, a national poetic form (compare aspirations towards a national theatre and a national novel form), could only come about when poets began to focus on the interests and powers of perception of the people in terms both of theme and form.

This 'plebeian' conception went beyond, at least in its initial stages, the framework of eighteenth-century middle-class creativity. Popular poets were to draw their models mainly from folk songs current among the people. Efforts on the part of the *Stürmer und Dränger* to rescue the folk song repertoire, buried in obscurity, formed part of this drive. Herder and Goethe, for example, collected folk songs in Alsace and published them as part of a wider intention (1778–9). Not only did they regard the songs they had discovered as proof of the creative abilities of the people, they also made use of them as models for their own lyric poetry. This popular lyricism, in reality reshaped with great artistic skill, can be found in numerous love and nature poems by Herder and Goethe, and even more so in the work of Schubart, Bürger and Voss, who combined a popular approach and social criticism to create a potent form of political lyric.

Didactic fables

In the eighteenth century, fables attained the high point of a process of development spanning two millennia. It was the sixth century BC when the Greek slave Aesop wrote the first fables, still of relevance today, that became the pattern for all subsequent fable-writers. From its very beginnings the fable was a militant literary form. According to Phaedrus, who revised Aesop's fables in the first century AD, Aesop saw in it 'a suitable medium for saying the truth in disguised form when one dare not do so openly'. In Germany, fables were written from the Middle Ages onwards, enjoying a first flowering during the Reformation, when Luther in particular employed them as a vehicle for political and religious discourse. Seventeenth-century baroque writers showed little interest in the genre, looking down on it as literature for the 'common people' and a pastime 'for children and old women'.

In stark contrast to these contemptuous assessments was the high esteem fables enjoyed in the Age of Enlightenment. From 1730 to 1800 over 50 fable compilations were published, including one by an author of no less stature than Lessing, who even put forward his own theory of fable (1759). As 'an example of practical ethics' (Lessing), the fable struck eighteenth-century writers as a particularly felicitous genre for achieving the objectives of the Enlightenment, having the virtues of a didactic character, simple structure and an easily remembered, metaphorical style. No other genre could offer the reader such a combination of pleasure and utility.

Themes, structure and form

The themes, structure and form of fables were extremely diverse. Besides fables criticising human frailty, there were some denouncing political injustices of the day in a more or less direct fashion. Some fables featured animals, some did not. Some were composed in verse, others in prose. Some fables were of great length, while others were terse. Some concluded with an overt moral for the reader, others omitted to provide one. And yet despite these differences the structural principles were always the same. By means of a transference of human conduct or social injustices to animate and inanimate nature, a generally acknowledged truth was illustrated in either a witty and satirical or moral and didactic way. Many fable-writers drew on ancient models (Aesop, Phaedrus), re-telling them for the contemporary period or modifying them. Another major influence was La Fontaine, who had raised fable to a recognised art form, and whose narrative style became the archetype for many German fable-writers. Apart from translations, revisions and modified versions, there was also a wealth of original work.

The various developments of eighteenth-century fable literature are clearly discernible. In the early Enlightenment, fable was largely a vehicle for moral lessons and innovative Enlightenment principles. After 1750, moral criticism expanded to include social criticism. A further shift towards the end of the century aimed at the political criticism of Absolutist feudal rulers and their institutions of power (see the dancing-bear motif in Gellert, Bock, Lessing, Burmann, Kazner and Pfeffel).

The emergence of children's and young people's literature

Fables were always a genre for adults, developing into a children's genre only in the nineteenth century. In his *Thoughts on Education*, which soon became accessible in Germany through the *Moralischen Wochenschriften* (moral weeklies), John Locke recommended Aesop's fables and *Reineke Fuchs* as easily comprehensible for children, but his suggestions were only taken up by a few. Not even Richardson's *Ethics for the Young in Select Fables*, translated by Lessing in 1757, did much to alter this. Locke's second recommendation, however, that 'light, amusing books', appropriate to the ability and level of comprehension of children, should be written and disseminated, was widely heeded in Germany. A literature emerged written expressly for children and the young.

Written works for children had already existed in the sixteenth and seventeenth centuries, such as primers on good behaviour and ABC spelling books similar to the *Orbis pictus* of Comenius, but these did not amount to a separate literature for children and the young. This did not emerge until the eighteenth century, and it was no coincidence that it did so in connection with the Enlightenment movement. A popular philosophical movement concerned with the 'education of humankind' (Herder), the Enlightenment had an a priori interest in moral and intellectual instruction, elaborating a diversity of didactic forms of which the fable may be regarded as the most popular. Not without reason, the eighteenth century has gone down in history as the 'century of pedagogy', in which children and the young were discovered as a distinct, clearly defined readership.

This had been preceded by a change in the concept of childhood in general. Since Rousseau, childhood had been recognised as a separate and non-interchangeable state. In fact Rousseau had warned in *Emile* of the dangers of putting books in the hands of children ('reading is the scourge of childhood'), and had rejected tract literature such as Enlightenment fables as unsuitable reading for children ('fables can serve to instruct adults, but children must be told the naked truth').

Rousseau's German adherents, however, did not share this extreme view. On the contrary, using Rousseau's concept of childhood as their yardstick they elaborated a form of their own in an attempt to adapt to children's ways of thinking and disposition. They pursued a children's readership with such devices as copper plates, charts and playful entertaining elements. This soon opened them to the allegation of *Kindertümelei*, child-aping. Another no less serious accusation was that of trivialising the genre with mass-produced writing and dilettantism. One contemporary spoke of the 'vast swarm of scribblers' hurling themselves on the new genre like 'hungry locusts'. The proportion of children's books did indeed increase enormously, especially in the second half of the eighteenth century, accounting for a substantial proportion of total book output.

One of the leading children's authors was J.H. Campe, who was a key influence on pedagogical discussion and practice with his 16-volume *Allgemeinen Revision des gesamten Schul- und Erziehungswesens* (*General Revision of the Entire School and Education System*) (1785–92). With Rochow, Basedow, Salzmann and Weisse he ranked among the most successful authors in the new genre. His books, above all his adaptation of *Robinson Crusoe*, were reprinted many times, well into the nineteenth century.

Childhood becomes an object of pedagogy

The expansion of the literary market to include a new readership, children and the young, was not without its negative aspects. These pertained less to the trivialisation alluded to in the admonitions of contemporaries than to the overall tendency for childhood as a whole to become an object of pedagogy. Once acknowledged as a distinct group, children became the preferred objects of educational fervour. It is clear from the innumerable ethics pamphlets of the time, as well as from the books and other writings of Campe himself, that the main object was to curb sensuality. 'O pfui! ich wollte, dass wir den Trieb nicht hätten!' ('Oh fie! Would that we did not have the urge!'), exclaims Campe in his *Kleinen Seelenkunde für Kinder* (1780). The preservation of innocence in children was a prime objective among educators of the Enlightenment, and literature fully acquiesced. There was a veritable literary crusade against the so-called 'vice of self-abuse', masturbation.

No less problematic than this hysterical hostility to sex is the manner in which gender roles are put over in literature for children and the young. A separate girls' literature evolved with the aim of preparing girls for their later role as housewives and mothers. Sentimental didactic novels and stories pointed out what happened to girls who strayed from the path of virtue, while sermons and ethics instruction inculcated their duties. Campe's *Väterlicher Rath an meine Tochter* (*Fatherly Advice to My Daughter*) (1789) and Ewald's *Die Kunst ein gutes Mädchen, eine gute Gattin, Mutter und Hausfrau zu werden* (*The Art of Becoming a Good Girl, A Good Wife, Mother and Housewife*) (1798) are striking examples of a literature of moral and social adjustment that enjoyed its first golden age around the end of the eighteenth century.

Rationalism and *Empfindsamkeit* (Sensibility): the dialectic of the Enlightenment movement

The various stages through which the literary and philosophical movement of the Enlightenment passed between the beginning of the eighteenth century and the French Revolution did not amount to a continuous, linear development towards ever-increasing rationality. They are better likened to a series of controversies, adjustments and divergent tendencies. Lessing continued the literary Enlightenment that had begun with Gottsched, as well as being its severest critic. The *Stürmer und Dränger* were in turn the continuation of a tradition that had originated with Lessing, just as the latter followed on from Gottsched. They were also the founders of a new tradition, dominated by genius and emotion.

Research once tended to stress the way the *Stürmer und Dränger* saw themselves as being the antithesis of Enlightenment thought. Nowadays they are seen rather as a continuation of it. The sensibility that acquired a new quality in *Sturm und Drang* literature is likewise now seen less as a protest against an increasingly entrenched and rigid Enlightenment, and more as a complementary phenomenon, attempting to combine reason with emotion. It is evident from contemporary definitions that sensibility was viewed as an integral part of the all-embracing Enlightenment movement. K.D. Küster wrote in 1773, for example:

> Der Ausdruck: ein empfindsamer Mensch, hat in der deutschen Sprache eine sehr edle Bedeutung gewonnen. Es bezeichnet: die vortreffliche und zärtliche Beschaffenheit des Verstandes, des Herzens und der Sinnen, durch welche ein Mensch geschwinde und starke Einsichten von seinen Pflichten bekömmet, und einen würksamen Trieb fühlet, Gutes zu thun. Je feiner die Nerven der Seele und des Cörpers sind, je richtiger sie gespannet worden, desto geschäftiger und nützlicher arbeitet er; und desto grösser ist die Erndte des Vergnügens, welches er geniesset, wenn er nicht nur gerecht, sondern auch wohlwollend, oder gar wohlthätig handeln kann. Solche empfindsame Fürsten und Princessinnen, solche empfindsamen Minister, Helden, Rechtsgelehrte, Prediger, Ärzte, Schulmänner, Bürger und Landleute zu bilden, ist das angenehme und wichtige Geschäft eines jeden selbst empfindsamen Erziehers.

> The expression 'a sensible man' (i.e. a feeling man) has acquired a noble meaning in German. It denotes a superior and delicate constitution of the faculty of reason, heart and senses, whereby a man receives prompt and distinct insights as to his obligations, and feels a strong desire to do good. The finer the nerves of body and soul, and the more finely-tuned they are, the more zealously and usefully he is employed, and the greater the harvest of pleasure he enjoys when he acts not only justly, but also with good will, or even good deeds. It is the pleasant and important office of an educator who is himself a sensible man to instruct similarly sensible princes and princesses, ministers, heroes, scholars of law, preachers, physicians, schoolmasters, burghers and yeomen.

The discovery of *Empfindsamkeit* obviously involved a shift of emphasis: emotion now asserted itself on the side of reason, as a complement to it. Sensibility and tenderness were the watchwords of a movement focused inwardly on the self and on emotion. This naturally involved some protest against raising the rationalist principle to the status of an absolute – a tendency that was considered, probably not without justification, as being discernible in some Enlightenment authors.

In the wake of Sterne's *Sentimental Journey* (1768) and Richardson's novels a new kind of literature, and an accompanying social trend, soon appeared in Germany, for which the term *Empfindsamkeit* soon became established, remaining part of the language to this day. The movement was able to draw on tendencies towards sentiment in *bürgerlich* tragedy, as well as on the cult of emotion of the *Stürmer und Dränger*. The thesis that *Empfindsamkeit* was a secularised form of pietism is only of limited explanatory value if one fails to see it in the context of influences from its contemporary English and French equivalents, *sensibility* and *sensibilité*. Warning voices were instantly raised, however, against this so-called *Empfindeley*, nor was scorn spared for the 'grassierende empfindsame Seuche' ('rampant sentimental epidemic') associated chiefly with Miller's *Siegwart* (1776) and the works of Schummel and Thümmel. Attempts were made to distinguish 'true' from 'false' sensibility, and to restore the balance between 'head' and 'heart' that was one of the central requirements of the Enlightenment.

Human affect

Wherever sensibility was able to give a voice to neglected or suppressed domains of emotion, it led to an enrichment of literary potential in terms both of form and content, as is shown by the example of Goethe's *Werther*, as well as by his experiential and nature lyrics. Wherever it became morbidly inward-looking, however, it led to debasement. *Empfindsamkeit* was a double-edged sword: in the form of sensibility, it supplied a necessary complement and enrichment to rationalism, opening up the horizon of human affect in the sense meant by the 'Erfahrungsseelenkunde' of Karl Philipp Moritz. In the form of sentimentality, however, it found itself in conflict with the central tenets of the Enlightenment. *Empfindsamkeit* made two things apparent: first, that the Enlightenment left gaps in the individual's awareness, and second, that a stress on emotion and subjectivity sank into the trivial when it departed from the Enlightenment as a movement for political and social emancipation.

The clash between head and heart

What was described by Horkheimer and Adorno as the dialectic of the Enlightenment may also be observed in the juxtaposition and contradiction between rationalism and *Empfindsamkeit*. A paradoxical movement by the very nature of its social and political assumptions and demands, the Enlightenment was unable to resolve the 'head–heart' conflict. This led to an unintended fermenting of the obverse aspects of applied reason, resulting in that 'Andere der Vernunft' ('Other than Reason' – Böhme) that it was futile to reject and exclude on the grounds of its irrationality. More than this, however, it also revealed the price to be paid by each and every individual for his emergence from political minority: the stunting and mutilation of human emotional and sensual potential for the sake of realising the middle-class capitalist social and economic order. The conquest of nature and emotion are two sides of one coin, the necessary consequences of the 'process of civilisation' (Elias). *Empfindsamkeit* and the *Sturm und Drang* gave expression to those frustrated desires for holistic development that had been awakened by the Enlightenment, but remained unfulfilled by it. Certain forms of sensibility writing, like certain forms of pastoral writing (*Schäferdichtung*) (Gessner) and idyll writing (Maler Müller), cherish dreams of a better life, which the writer sets against the poverty of existing reality in an attempt to come to terms with the experience of alienation. The fact that this proved to be so unexplosive a social mixture is the result not only of the overpowering nature of existing social forces, but also of the premature dilution of these 'wild desires' (*Kabale und Liebe*) into the idyllically sentimental, the agreeable and the noncommittal.

Emotion as a commodity

Emotion rapidly became a saleable commodity, subjected to the same marketing process that was extending, to a greater or lesser degree, to all products of the world of letters in the eighteenth century. Novels of sensibility soon became tear-jerking 'fashionable novels' (*Moderomanen*), preparing the way for the entertainment literature that was to flood the market in the nineteenth and twentieth centuries.

THE *KUNSTEPOCHE*

Between revolution and restoration

In Heinrich Heine's view the *Kunstperiode* was the period up to about 1830, dominated above all by the towering figure of Goethe and his works. If one accepts Heine's view of the special importance of Goethe, the end of the *Kunstperiode*, which is mentioned among others by Hegel in his *Vorlesungen über die Ästhetik*, and which runs like a motif through the writings of the *Jungdeutschen* after 1830, is marked by Goethe's death in 1832. Heine associates the term *Kunstperiode* among other things with the idea of an epoch in which art and the creative artist enjoyed a particularly high status, and in which the issue of the relationship between art and life was decided in favour of art. The special role of art between the 1789 and 1830 revolutions has also frequently been stressed by research, leading to formulations such as 'the age of German classicism and Romanticism', 'the age of Goethe and Schiller', 'the golden age of German poetry', etc. Compared with these, the term *Kunstperiode* seems more neutral and less value-laden. To delineate more precisely than Heine, our *Kunstepoche* will be taken to be the period between two European revolutions that oscillated between the two poles of revolution and restoration.

Specifically German developments

Unlike its neighbour France, Germany did not experience revolution, and yet for good or ill revolution remained a point of reference for specifically German developments. Instead of a revolution, there was a reform movement of enlightened absolutism, which sought to achieve cautious changes in state and society through a number of major measures (the 'Allgemeines Landrecht' of 1794 and the Stein-Hardenberg reforms from 1806 onwards), drawing heavily on developments in neighbouring France in these reform gestures. Historically, the period between 1789 and 1830 was not merely an epoch torn between revolution and restoration, but also one characterised by spectacular military conflicts (the divisions of Poland, coalition wars, the Napoleonic Wars, wars of liberation), as well as by the run-up to the industrial age. The emancipation of peasants, the gradual introduction of freedom of trade, the transformation of the old cottage industries into branches of industry, the emergence of 'free' entrepreneurs and manufacturers, and the proletarianisation of increasingly broad sections of the population were aspects of a reshaping of the economy and society that can only be depicted sketchily by using such terms as 'modernisation' or 'dynamisation'. These changes in economic structure took place under the auspices of what Heine termed an 'abgelebten alten Regimes' ('decrepit *ancien régime*') still rooted in the history of the Holy Roman Empire. The Empire was not reorganised until the Congress of Vienna (1815), leaving only 39 individual states, including four free imperial cities, out of the former 314 independent territories and over 1,400 imperial knightly fiefs. Compared to adjacent nation-states Germany was hopelessly fragmented, but at least the prerequisites had been created for its development into a nation-state, brought to a premature end in 1871 when Bismarck founded the Reich.

These structural shifts and changes in the economic and political fabric went largely unnoticed by contemporaries, and are only discernible with the hindsight provided by the historical events of the nineteenth and twentieth centuries. Despite this they are no less significant in their way than the spectacular revolutions and counter-revolutions, or wars of conquest and liberation that rocked Europe at the time and gave contemporaries the impression of a 'new epoch' (Goethe). The drama and fever of events in neighbouring France were indeed overpowering. In a matter of a few years France passed from monarchy to republic, reverting after eventful intermediary phases to monarchy under Napoleon, and finding itself after a brief respite again in the grip of revolutionary change.

The vagaries of French history – revolution, restoration and again revolution – were bound to exert an influence on Germany, particularly since the German Empire was directly involved in the concomitant military conflicts. First it participated in the coalition against the French Revolution, then fell victim to the Napoleonic policy of conquest. The Napoleonic wars of conquest unleashed a first great wave of national outrage. This and the wars of liberation fostered the growth of a nationalist literature, represented by authors such as E.M. Arndt and Theodor Körner, whose thought was ambivalent in its blend of nationalist and emancipation sentiment.

Responses to the French Revolution: Classicism – Romanticism – Jacobinism

The French Revolution was more than a central event in the political history of Western Europe. It was also of fundamental importance for the development of literary theory and convention after 1789. The relative homogeneity of the literary period from Gottsched to the *Stürmer und Dränger*, arising from the common function of Enlightenment of literature, was now lost in the process of coming to terms with the French Revolution and its impact on Germany.

In 1789, when the revolution broke out, the literary intelligentsia of Germany initially hailed it enthusiastically, extolling it as the 'noblest deed of the century' (Klopstock). Sympathy abated, however, after the execution of the King and the September massacres, or at the latest after the onset of Jacobin rule, instilling a deep abhorrence of the 'terror' in neighbouring France.

Rejection of the Revolution

The experience acquired at that time as a result of the French Revolution led to some serious rethinking concerning the degree to which a society could be changed, and also concerning the legitimacy of revolutionary changes and the use of force for revolutionary ends in general. This entailed some fresh reflection on the role of literature. Questions such as whether Enlightenment led to revolution, or whether violent revolutions were fostered by writers, were among the most widely discussed problems of the 1790s. While many intellectuals considered the influence of literature to be minimal, assessing the potential effects of the writer relatively pessimistically, others maintained that Enlightenment literature was of immense importance for revolution and for social transformation. This controversy was waged across the political board, and must form the background to any account of the efforts of writers in the 1790s to develop a new literary theory and practice.

Literature as a vehicle for historical progress

Within this redefinition of the function of literature, the self-confident stance typical of the Enlightenment – that Truth would prevail and that literature merely performed an intermediary function in this process – was considerably deflated. The former basic consensus of the Enlightenment as to the particular pedagogical value of literature was replaced by a diversity of new positions. Three main trends may be distinguished: the classical, most decisively formulated by Goethe and Schiller, the Romantic, elaborated especially by the Schlegel brothers and Novalis, and the Jacobin, put forward by a number of revolutionary democrats.

Germany not ready for revolution

The starting-point for the classical conception of literature was its rejection of revolution. Goethe and Schiller took a vehement stand against the French Revolution, and most particularly against attempts 'artificially to bring about similar scenes in Germany' (Goethe), on the grounds that the German people was not sufficiently politically mature. This apart, however, they were basically in favour of social change, and indeed regarded middle-class reform as urgently necessary in Germany. Their aim was to see these changes brought about gradually, and not by the revolutionary path.

They attributed a major role to literature in this process: it should improve the morality of the population, and raise the ethical standard to a point where social and political change would occur of their own volition, and above all without the use of force. Ethical improvement, both of the individual and of the people in general, was regarded as an essential precondition. This was to be achieved through classical poetry, the principles of which were laid down by Schiller in his seminal work *Über die ästhetische Erziehung des Menschen* (*The Aesthetic Education of Man*) (1794–5). Such a moral improvement in the individual seemed possible to Schiller only by achieving a balance between his sensual and rational natures. The gulf between the two was seen as the real cause of all social injustice and the excesses of the French Revolution. The task of the writer was to anticipate this balancing process in ideal typical form in the work of art, presenting the reader with the person of the 'classical hero', the epitome of this balance between sensuality and rationality, as a model for the process of his own ethical perfection.

Idealisation of reality

Applying these principles in creative writing largely entailed dispensing with a portrayal of the realities of the day, and its prevailing conflicts and incongruities, in favour of an idealisation of reality that anticipated a utopia. In view of the level of education among the population at large, writing imbued with such idealisation and refinement of human nature could only ever be grasped by an extremely narrow elite among the educated middle classes. The masses remained unreached. Given this dilemma, the hope of changing political conditions by achieving a general moral improvement of humanity was an illusory one. Schiller was mindful of this when he wrote that 'the ideal of political equality' which the French revolutionaries had tried to make a reality could only ever be fulfilled in the sphere of aesthetic appearances.

Romantic opposition

The Romantics reacted as negatively as classical writers both to the revolution in France and to half-hearted revolutionary ventures in Germany (the Mainz Republic). They, too, started from the assumption that revolution was undesirable in Germany, and reprehensible from the ethical standpoint. This position did not exclude criticism of existing conditions in Germany, however. As regards social criticism the Romantics found themselves in agreement with classical authors on many issues, tending however to draw different conclusions for literary theory and practice. The Romantic vision of literature broke with the idea of the social function of art that had been prevalent in the Enlightenment, and which was still retained by classical authors, at least as an aspiration. In its stead they formulated the idea of the autonomy of literary creation. Now without function, or at least neutral in function, literature was disengaged from social context, both for the author who wrote it and the reader who obtained and read it, correlating instead to the subjectivity of both. The solutions to existing social and political conflicts, or the road to those solutions, were no longer to be sought through the medium of art. The author and reader were to find a substitute for them through the medium of poetry – a freedom that was denied them in real life.

The call for autonomy, employed polemically in the Enlightenment against the co-option of art by clerical and feudal authorities, and now playing a progressive role in the formation of a new *bürgerlich* art, was handled ambivalently by the Romantics. Although continuing to embrace *bürgerlich* protest, both against the use of art as a vehicle for politics, and its subjection to the laws of the literary market, Romantic notions of autonomy now supported no more than a retreat into the sphere of subjectivity, fantasy, playful experimentation with form and ironic improvisation. The Romantic writer withdrew into his own private world and artistic creativity. Reflection on the nature of poetry was now inevitable, and produced a highly ambitious conception.

Art and life

The goal of Romantic poetry was to remove the distinction between art and life, the finite and the infinite, the present and the past – in short the 'poeticisation' rather than politicisation of life. Through recourse to the German Middle Ages and the imaginative spheres of religion and mythology, another world was to be conjured up to counter the dreaded here and now. The focusing by Romantic poets on the Middle Ages, and their accompanying glorification of precapitalist means of production and ways of life, could never amount to a viable alternative to the realities of early capitalism. It should rather be seen as a nonconformist escape.

This new conception of poetry had repercussions on the way writers saw themselves. The Romantics followed in the footsteps of the *Stürmer und Dränger* concept of genius, magnifying subjective and irrational elements to the point of deifying art and the creative artist: 'Dichter und Priester waren im Anfang Eins, und nur spätere Zeiten haben sie getrennt. Der ächte Dichter ist aber immer Priester, so wie der ächte Priester immer Dichter geblieben ist' ('In the beginning, poets and priests were one: only in recent times have these functions been separated. The true poet, however, has always remained a priest, just as the true priest has always remained a poet' – Novalis, 1798).

In reality, the stylisation of art as religion and the creative artist's exaggerated sense of his own importance were both an expression of and compensation for actual political impotence. It was no coincidence that the portrayal of the creative artist's predicament, precipitated by the painful disparity between his view of himself and the workaday middle-class world, was a central theme of Romantic writing.

The Jacobin position

Jacobin authors had a different reaction to the French Revolution than classical and Romantic authors: they strove for a revolutionary reshaping of Germany. They were called *Jakobiner* either because they truly resembled the French Jacobins in their political views, or because they did so in the opinion of contemporary reactionaries. In fact they were a small group of predominantly intellectual opponents who, while scrutinising events in France critically, nevertheless still sought to take up the revolutionary option for Germany. They attributed a major role to literature in this process.

A literature for political commitment

Distancing themselves critically both from the classical theory of idealisation and the Romantic notion of autonomy, the Jacobins elaborated a concept of a politically committed literature that went decidedly further than the *prodesse et delectare* concept of the pre-1789 Enlightenment. They saw it as the task of literature to provide insight into the injustice of the social and hierarchical order, and to awaken in the people both political consciousness and the readiness for revolutionary activity. In the Jacobins' understanding, this could not be achieved by a literature in the classical or Romantic sense, but only by one capable of making a connection in both form and content with the level of awareness of their target readership.

Partiality

The concept of *Volkstümlichkeit*, already elaborated in the prerevolutionary period by the *Stürmer und Dränger*, was now politically refined by the German Jacobins, who linked it with the principle of partiality, i.e. with the partisanship of Jacobin authors for suppressed and exploited sections of the population. Political orations, pamphlets, appeals to rise up, propagandist poems, satirical novels and political journals with fabricated places of publication were the literary forms best suited to the Jacobin author's frame of mind. Although these are now scarcely intelligible to the modern reader on account of their extreme topicality, this detracts nothing from their value as examples of politically committed literature.

The Kunstepoche – a surprising diversity

The period from 1789 to 1815, between the outbreak of the French Revolution and the conservative reordering of Western Europe by the Congress of Vienna, was one of the most prolific in the history of German literature. This span of 25 years saw the creation of a literature that is impressive both for its quantity and its quality. The classical works of Goethe and Schiller, those of the Romantics and the extensive literature of the Jacobins together form a bewildering complex of diverse themes and forms that can hardly be reduced to a common denominator.

This impression of diversity conveyed by the *Kunstepoche* is heightened by two facts. The first is that aside from those authors who can be classified with relative confidence in one of the great 'camps' of literary theory – the classical, Romantic or Jacobin – there are also authors such as Hölderlin, Kleist and Jean Paul, who were 'mavericks'. Although keeping themselves largely apart from the literary constellations of the day, they did nonetheless react in their own ways to the particular configuration of the age, producing literature that is more widely acknowledged today than ever before. The second of these facts was the copious output of trivial literature that strove on the one hand to meet the mounting demand for reading material towards the end of the eighteenth century, and on the other to lead the anti-revolutionary offensive, using literature as a vehicle.

Trivial literature

The gradual divergence and eventual separation of literature into the categories of serious and trivial was a distinction that did not yet exist in the Age of the Enlightenment. The latter's objectives had tended merely to distinguish between good and less good literature. Trivial genres inevitably flourished where literature itself was increasingly losing its social roots, or choosing to dispense with them, thereby rendering it comprehensible only to a narrow stratum of the educated middle classes. The emergence of trivial literature was history's answer first to a concept of aesthetic education that had bypassed the 'common herd', and second to the endeavours of Romantic writing to achieve autonomy. Third, it was also a reaction to the concept of politically committed literature put forward by the Jacobins. Politically conformist, and therefore unencumbered by fear of censorship or persecution, authors of trivial literature had no difficulty reaching a mass reading public. Trivial literature was directed against the seriousness of classical, Romantic and Jacobin authors alike, and hence also against the substance of political opposition that their works contained.

The sense of diversity that can only roughly be conveyed by the catchphrases 'Weimarer Klassik' on the one hand and 'trivial literature' on the other is enhanced still further if one expands the 1789–1815 period to include the years from 1815 to 1830, i.e. from the Congress of Vienna to the outbreak of the July Revolution. This second phase saw the publication of the chief works of E.T.A. Hoffmann, Eichendorff and others, usually grouped together in literary history terminology under the collective term of Late Romantic. The same period, however, also saw the early works of Heine and Mörike, *inter alia*, which are usually classified in the *Vormärz* period.

The span from 1815 to 1830 is thus a time of overlapping and parallels, of ends and new beginnings. Countless literary trends and schools existed side by side. Classical and Romantic authors continued to be published – albeit in a different way from the end of the eighteenth century. Goethe died in 1832, Brentano in 1842 and Tieck in 1853. New authors such as Platen, Rückert, Immerman and Hebel came into the field of public vision without causing any friction with the classical and Romantic authors who were still alive. The world of letters at that time, however, was shaped less by those writers and works who are today regarded as part of the literary canon than by names such as Kotzebue or Iffland. With over two hundred dramas to his name, Kotzebue was the most successful and widely acclaimed playwright of his day.

The Weimar classical period

The idea evoked by the term classicism is inextricably bound up with the figures of Goethe and Schiller, and with Weimar, the place that in the minds of contemporaries and posterity alike is invariably associated with their literary activities. The term 'Weimarer Klassik' denotes a clearly distinguishable literary trend in terms of the people, place and time it refers to, and has become a yardstick of literary merit, for the nineteenth and twentieth centuries especially. The ideological reference-point for the emergence of Weimar classicism was the French Revolution and its impact on German public life.

Change after 1789

However, the prerequisites for the change wrought by Goethe and Schiller after 1789, in the case of Goethe at least, extend to the period before 1789. Goethe set himself on the path towards those future developments with his decision to go to Weimar in 1776, making a break with his own *Sturm und Drang* period and with many of the friends who had thus far accompanied him. His attempt to attract earlier companions such as Lenz to the court at Weimar proved unfruitful. 'Was Teufel fällt dem Wolfgang ein, in Weimar am Hofe herumzuschranzen und zu scherwenzen. . . . Gibt es denn nichts *Besseres* für ihn zu tun?' ('What devil has possessed Wolfgang to play the slimy courtier and bow and scrape at Weimar. . . . Is there nothing *better* for him to do?') Behind these alarmed inquiries by his friend Merck lies the fear that at Weimar Goethe might succumb to the role of court poet, and thereby risk forfeiting the 'poetic individuality' that had only recently become possible in the middle-class Age of Enlightenment.

Goethe himself, however, saw his decision to move to Weimar as an attempt to expand his field of operations – to break out of the 'Unverhältniss des engen und langsam bewegten bürgerlichen Kreyses' ('lack of proportion of the narrow, cumbersome middle-class circle') under which his hero Werther had suffered. He hoped in doing so to obtain sufficient breathing space for the 'Weite und Geschwindigkeit' ('breadth and swiftness') of his nature.

To this extent his decision to go to Weimar was also an expression of the middle-class desire for upward mobility. Goethe was fully aware that the position of privy councillor to which he was appointed in 1779 was the highest honour that could then be accorded to a middle-class man in Germany, as he wrote in a letter at the time.

The residential town of Weimar

Weimar was not just another obscure German royal seat, but one in which the Duchess Anna Amalia enjoyed a high reputation among intellectuals and art lovers in Germany. In 1772 Anna Amalia had sent for Wieland to come to Weimar as tutor to her son, thereby initiating a chain of events that was to transform Weimar into a cultural centre in a country that lacked a capital of the calibre of Paris or London. By the time Goethe was called to the Weimar court in 1776, by Ernst August, son of Anna Amalia, who had recently come of age, he found a modest cultural life flourishing there that was qualitatively different from that of other royal seats.

Goethe rapidly became the close friend and confidant of the young Duke, and as a member of the privy council he was directly involved in affairs of state. From 1779 he was in charge of the mining commission, which involved him in a sphere of practical politics to which he devoted considerable attention until 1788. He was also entrusted with the task of establishing the University of Jena, to which Schiller, Fichte, and Humboldt among others were also brought. He thus acquired a detailed knowledge of various branches of public service, which he came in retrospect to see as an advantage, by making his poetry more in touch with reality.

In addition to his official duties, Goethe had numerous cultural responsibilities. He had a decisive voice in the 'Weimarer Liebhabertheater' as playwright, director and actor, later running the Weimar Court theatre for many years, where he staged not only his own plays, but also those of other playwrights. Aside from all this he also built up a literary and cultural community with the *Freitagsgesellschaft* ('Friday Society'), a society of highly-educated men that was later expanded to comprise other, similar circles.

Although Weimar remained his home and workplace until his death, Goethe interrupted his stay there many times with some brief and other more protracted stays in the Harz mountains (*Harzreise im Winter*, 1777), Switzerland (1779 and 1797), and Italy (1786–8 and 1790). From 1792 to 1793, as attendant to the Duke of Weimar, Goethe was involved in the first Coalition War. Goethe drew inspiration not only from his journeys, however, which took him less far afield after 1800, but also from the people already making their mark in Weimar, such as Wieland. As publisher of the *Teutscher Merkur*, the latter exerted an influence equal to Goethe's own in shaping German public opinion, as did his former colleague and Weimar resident Bertuch, who was later to make a name for himself as publisher of the *Allgemeine Literaturzeitung* and the *Journal des Luxus und der Moden*. Besides these two, there were other writers and intellectuals who were attracted to Weimar to a greater or lesser extent by the personality and works of Goethe. In 1776, for example, Goethe enabled Herder to move to Weimar by intervening to obtain the post of General Superintendent for him. It was during his Weimar years that Herder wrote such seminal works on the history of philosophy and cultural criticism as the *Ideen zur Geschichte der Philosophie der Menschheit* (*Ideas on the History of Philosophy*) (1784–91) and the *Briefe zur Beförderung der Humanität* (*Letters on the Furtherance of Humanity*) (1793 onwards). The subsequent addition of Fichte and Humboldt formed the circle that has gone down in history as Weimarer Klassik.

Life at court

Although Goethe was later to assert that his life at court had widened his horizons, especially with regard to practical social issues, in his first years there he found cause to complain of the constraints imposed on him by his position. He grumbled constantly about the 'Tagewerk', his daily chores, and yet he carried them out so meticulously, at least in his first ten years in Weimar, that his literary work suffered as a result. Apart from some minor contributions to the Weimar Court theatre, the first decade of Goethe's residence in Weimar produced no major works. This led to a slow but steady deterioration in his reputation as a writer, which had first swept him to fame with *Werther* and *Götz*. 'Was er gegeben hat, das hat er gegeben – und jetzt ist er fürs Publikum so unfruchtbar wie eine Steinwüste.... Seine meiste Zeit und Kraft schenkt er itzt den ersten Geschäften des Staates' ('What he has given, he has given – and now he is as sterile for the public as a desert of stone.... He devotes most of his time and energy to affairs of high state') is how a contemporary traveller describes his impression of Goethe (1783–4). Goethe himself, however, felt exhausted and distracted not merely by the sheer volume of his responsibilities, but also by the contradictions he was obliged to confront.

Resignation

Sentences such as: 'Es gehört immer viel Resignation zu diesem ekeln Geschäft, indessen muss es auch sein' ('Much resignation is always a part of this loathsome business, and yet it must be so') show that he was soon obliged to shelve his plans of reform ('Die Disharmonie der Welt in Harmonie zu bringen' – 'To bring the disharmony of the world into harmony'). 'Resignation', 'distance' and 'alienation' are words that appear frequently in his letters of that time, revealing the difficulty he was having in adapting to his new way of life. The 'continual sheer alienation from human beings' of which he writes is a sign of his efforts to be different from the 'base people' who surrounded him, and to achieve that 'separation' that Schiller declared a few years later in his *Ästhetischen Briefe* to be the precondition for the life of a true poet.

Iphigenie

An early literary expression of this need for separation is Goethe's drama *Iphigenie auf Tauris*, which has been understood as a 'paradigm of that division between art and life' (Bürger) that Goethe achieved in the 1780s and 1790s at the Weimar court. His progression from *Sturm und Drang* to classical author can easily be traced from the three stages in which the work was produced (1st version 1779, 2nd version 1780, 3rd version 1786). The disappointment of many friends in the play led Goethe to assume that they had expected 'something Berlinguesque', which *Iphigenie* certainly was not. Though the substance of the play, the Tantalus myth, is brimming with drama, Goethe tried to tame it in his adaptation, not only by reshaping the content, as had already been done by Euripides, Racine and Gluck before him, but also and chiefly though its form. Goethe was dissatisfied with the first 'sloppy' prose version, although even the 'more measured' blank verse version failed to please him. It was only the third version in iambic metre, composed after being inspired by K.P. Moritz's *Versuch einer deutschen Prosodie* (*Attempt at a German Prosody*) (1786), that met his demands for 'more harmony of style'.

His deliberate separation from reality found expression in the aspiration towards both 'pure form' and 'fine humanity' ('schöner Humanität') in content that was typical of Goethe's early Weimar years. Goethe retells the myth: he endeavours to break the barbaric chain of violence and guilt derived from passion, murder, revenge and repeated murder that hangs like a dreadful fate over the Tantalid house. This involves first and foremost a complete reshaping of the character of Iphigenie. Goethe styles her into a representative of 'pure humanity'. Through this she achieves a reconcili- ation between the male protagonists and the conquest of barbarism (the abolition of human sacrifice). The price she has to pay is high, however. In order to become a redeeming figure, she must be deprived of vitality ('Entlebendigung'), so as to transform her into a 'beautiful soul'. She thus heralds the 'sacrificial woman' ('Frauenopfer') that was later to play a central role in the classical dramas of Schiller.

The dilemma of the creative artist

Goethe's dramas *Egmont* (1789) and *Tasso* (1790) likewise clearly bear the stamp of the new Weimar environment. *Egmont*, to which Goethe similarly returned again and again, is concerned with the relationship between the individual and history, taking up the predicament depicted in *Götz*, only this time on a more refined, differentiated level. In *Tasso*, Goethe portrays the conflicts of the middle-class creative artist of his day, using the example of the Italian Renaissance poet of the same name. The original version, no longer extant, was completed by 1780–1, but Goethe was able to return to the material on his journey to Italy, which gave him the benefit of distance from conditions at Weimar. *Tasso* is a drama in which Goethe comes to terms with his own position as a middle-class creative artist at the court of a prince, dealing with insults to himself and his own disappointments through Tasso's rejection by court society. The more resigned parts of the drama, as well as the open-ended conclusion, show clearly that Goethe was still having difficulty adapting to conditions at Weimar.

Goethe's crisis

The personal crisis in which Goethe found himself plunged after ten years at Weimar was overlapped by the huge crisis of state brought on by the French Revolution in 1789, which drew the whole of Europe along in its wake. Scarcely had he completed work on *Tasso* before 'the present-day of world history captured my entire spirit', as Goethe wrote in 1822, looking back on those years. He was indeed more than a mere onlooker. In the service of his Duke he took part in the Coalition War against France in 1792, and was present at the siege of Mainz. Although written with the distance of old age, his two travelogues *Campagne in Frankreich* (*Campaign in France*) and *Belagerung von Mainz* (*The Siege of Mainz*) give a good idea of the difficulties he had as a middle-class intellectual coming to terms with the Revolution. A number of satirical plays (*Der Gross-Cophta* – *The Great Cophte*; *Der Bürgergeneral* – *The Burgher General*; *Die Aufgeregten* – *The Inspired*), written between 1792 and 1793, mark a direct effort to analyse the revolution in neighbouring France and attempts to stage a revolution in Germany itself. The Revolution also remained a focal point for a number of other plays, being taken up, for example, in the drama *Das Mädchen von Oberkirch*, (*The Maid of Oberkirch*) (1795–6), the verse epics *Reineke Fuchs* (*Reynard the Fox*) (1793) and *Hermann und Dorothea* (1797), and in the tragedy *Die natürliche Tochter* (*The Natural Daughter*) (1803). *Hermann und Dorothea*, a *bürgerlich* epopee in hexameters, influenced in form by hexameter epics by J.H. Voss (*Luise*, 1781) as well as his translations of Homer (*Odyssee*, 1791 and *Ilias*, 1793), depicts the mood swing of Germans west of the Rhine from initially euphoric revolutionary fervour to ultimate horror and opposition. The enthusiasm of Dorothea's first bridegroom for the Revolution proves to be a fatal illusion: he dies on the scaffold in Paris, the victim of his own revolutionary fervour. Her second bridegroom finds happiness with her in a deliberate restriction to domestic life, the family being the only place that can offer refuge from the dark forces of the Revolution. As in *Iphigenie* before it, the 'pure form' of *Hermann und Dorothea* lends the material a timeless, classical quality. 'Ich habe das reine Menschliche der Existenz einer kleinen deutschen Stadt in dem epischen Tiegel von seinen Schlacken abzuschneiden gesucht, und zugleich die grossen Bewegungen des Welttheaters aus einem kleinen Spiegel zurück zu werfen getrachtet' ('In the epic crucible, I tried to divest of its dross the purely human in small-town German life, while at the same time striving to reflect the majestic motions of international theatre with a small mirror'), wrote Goethe in a letter in 1796. Unlike *Iphigenie*, however, this verse epic was acclaimed by a broad public. The idyllic traits, as well as the idealisation and stylisation of petty bourgeois life in archetypes, raised *Hermann und Dorothea*, together with Schiller's poem *Die Glocke*, which similarly aspires to avert revolution, to the level of one of the seminal educational works of the nineteenth century.

Friendship between Goethe and Schiller

Their rejection of the revolution constituted an area of common ground that enabled Goethe and Schiller to form a close bond in the 1790s that was eventually to lead to that much-celebrated 'bond of friendship' that has shaped the picture of classicism held by subsequent generations. After some troubled years wandering from place to place, Schiller had moved to the cultural centre of Weimar in 1787 in the hope of finding material security. The two authors were not close in these early years, however. This lengthy process, which was not without its disagreements, was to lead to a close and intensive cooperation in various spheres. A keen interchange of literary and philosophical work was the result, in which Schiller's sound criticism particularly assisted and encouraged Goethe in his work on the *Lehrjahre*. The friendship also produced their joint publication of the journal *Horen* (*Horae*) – for some years a major authority in the German world of letters. It was intended as a platform for all authors who felt committed to the 'ideal of ennobled humanity' theoretically formulated by Schiller in his *Ästethischen Briefen*, and put into practice by Goethe in his *Iphigenie*. *Wohlanständigkeit* (decency), *Ordnung* (order), *Gerechtigkeit* (justice) and *Frieden* (peace) were the rallying-calls for these authors. Other colleagues, apart from the two publishers themselves, included chiefly Wilhelm von Humboldt, Herder and August Wilhelm Schlegel. Schiller published a list of 25 authors who had promised to contribute regularly. Others, such as Hölderlin and Sophie Mereau, joined the contributors later, although the journal was not representative from the latter's point of view. The esteem in which *Horen* was held was great at first, and sales considerable. The first year brought some 1,800 subscribers, although this figure was to decline steadily in later years. The fact that Schiller, Humboldt and Fichte were represented by seminal works in *Horen* (*Horae*) did nothing to change this, nor that Goethe contributed his *Unterhaltungen deutscher Ausgewanderter* (*Diversions of German Emigrés*), nor even that numerous poems by Schiller were published there for the first time. Unlike Wieland's *Teutscher Merkur* or Bertuch's *Allgemeiner Literaturzeitung*, both also edited in Weimar, *Horen* was unable to hold its own in the market.

Another area that Goethe and Schiller held in common was their joint work on the *Xenien-Almanach*. Following the example of Martial, they composed in a few months well over 600 epigrams, which took satirical and polemic issue with rival journals and authors of different viewpoints. Only a small proportion of these epigrams ever appeared in the almanach, and some were even published anonymously, since by this time there was such a convergence of thought and writing in Goethe and Schiller that crediting their names hardly seemed necessary in all cases. The *Xenien* (donated contributions) was the joint manifesto through which they passed judgement on 'Philistines', 'fanatics' and 'hypocrites', seeking also to strengthen their bond by distinguishing it from outside influences. The 'German revolutionaries' Reichardt and Forster were the particular objects of their often unjustified scorn and derision.

The public acclaim aroused by the *Xenien* was enormous. The embittered objects of their attacks sought to defend themselves, accusing Goethe and

Schiller of elitism, arrogance and inhumanity, thereby formulating the beginnings at least of those points of criticism that were later to be directed against classicism.

1797 – year of ballads

The 'bond' between Goethe and Schiller was made possible not least because Weimar was spared the vagaries of the coalition wars, making it a peaceful island in a hostile environment. It was not dissipated, however, in the efforts to distinguish it from outside influences, or even in mutual encouragement. It also led to a burst of creativity in both authors in the lyric sphere. Schiller designated 1797 the 'year of ballads'; this was the year in which his *Musenalmanach* (*Almanach of Muses*) was published. It contained numerous ballads by both authors that were later to become seminal works for broad sections of the population. In contrast to the ancient or imitation ancient genres they otherwise preferred, they selected for the first time a popular form for their ballads in order to give expression to their view of the world. With its blend of lyric, epic and dramatic elements, the ballad had been a highly popular folk form even in the pre-revolutionary time of Bürger. This adoption of the ballad form, which was to bear such celebrated fruit as *Die Bürgschaft* (*Surety*), *Die Kraniche des Ibykus* (*The Cranes of Ibycus*), *Der Ring des Polykrates* (*The Ring of Polycrates*), *Die Braut von Korinth* (*The Corinthian Bride*), *Der Zauberlehrling* (*The Sorcerer's Apprentice*) and *Der Gott und die Bajadere* (*The God, The Bayadère*), went hand in hand with a thoroughgoing elimination of the popular political elements still prevalent in ballads in Bürger's time. This brought it much closer to the philosophical worldview form of poem that was the purest expression of Goethe and Schiller's new classical understanding of their role as poets (*Grenzen der Menschheit* (*The Limits of Humanity*); *Das Ideal und das Leben* (*The Ideal and Life*); *Die Götter Griechenlands* (*Gods of Greece*); *Lied von der Glocke* (*Song of the Bell*)). These poems subject both characters and events to a dominant idea, stylising them to make them convey an ethical lesson.

Apart from ballads, Schiller also wrote in his Weimar years an extensive body of dramatic works on the strength of preparatory historical research. Unlike Goethe, he never directly took up the theme of revolution in his dramas, although the latter do respond in a variety of ways to the dominant event of the age.

The most striking evidence of Schiller's changed understanding of himself as a playwright is seen in his departure from the *bürgerlich* tragedy in which he had once excelled. His conviction that the poet should 'withdraw from the sphere of the real world' and 'direct his efforts towards the most rigorous separation' could no longer be reconciled to the form and demands of *bürgerlich* tragedy. The latter had consisted in the creative capturing of German reality, bringing about change by affecting the audience. Where, therefore, his 1784 play *Die Räuber* had been an excursion into German reality, his post-1789 dramas reached far back into history. The *Wallenstein* trilogy (1798–9) is set in the seventeenth century, *Maria Stuart* (1800) deals with a theme from sixteenth-century English history, while the *Jungfrau von Orleans* (1801) depicts fifteenth-century France.

The concept of aesthetic education

At the same time, Schiller was departing from that form of *bürgerliches Drama* whose theory and practice had been elaborated by Lessing, through taking up the French *tragédie classique*. Schiller's aim in resorting to the formerly proscribed, rigorous, closed *tragédie classique* form was to bring about 'aesthetic education' by using a 'pure artistic form'. The revival of an aristocratic, court form of tragedy that had been so vehemently decried by Lessing involved more than literature alone. It was also a fact of significance for society as a whole. It signified the beginning of a phase of restoration in German middle-class society, at a time when neighbouring France was suffering the ravages of post-revolutionary conflict. The rebellious undertone of Schiller's pre-1789 dramas had now almost completely disappeared. Whereas in 1787 the Marquis de Posa had called for freedom of thought in *Don Carlos*, by the time of *Maria Stuart* in 1800 this call is fully internalised, and resides in the subjectivity of the heroine. In the struggle portrayed between the two Queens, Elizabeth and Mary, the moral and political controversies are treated at such a lofty level that their relationship to contemporary German reality is scarcely discernible. The link between *bürgerlich* motifs, to which Schiller continued to adhere, and the new aristocratic form, led moreover to an inconsistency and woolliness that seems to herald the historical compromise between the middle and aristocratic classes that was to characterise nineteenth-century German history.

This was especially apparent in Schiller's conception of the hero. Wallenstein, Mary Stuart and the Maid of Orleans are all stylised, according to the laws of classicist tragedy, into individuals who transcend the constraints of the middle class, and indeed history itself. The *bürgerlich* morality represented by Mary Stuart against her adversary Elizabeth – in the teeth of historical fact – is thus disengaged from its political function, shedding the former anti-feudal qualities that it had still retained in pre-1789 *bürgerlich* tragedy.

Wilhelm Tell (1804), in which the liberation struggle of the Swiss people at the beginning of the fourteenth century is made into a thrilling theme, is something of an exception here. Despite the historical distance of the material, its relationship to the German present was still apparent. It nevertheless differs from Schiller's other classical dramas in that the latter deal with the issues of middle-class emancipation in encoded, artificial form, whereas *Wilhelm Tell*, like Kleist's *Hermannsschlacht* (1808), represents, even in terms of form, a dramatic attempt to treat the issues of national consciousness and foreign domination in the folk-popular vein. The restoration policy of France after 1799 and the Napoleonic wars of conquest, which threatened the integrity of the German empire, pushed the national question to the fore. Schiller was thus less concerned in this play with the middle-class aspects of the liberation struggle, than with national issues.

'Vaterland' – a German metaphor

In *Wilhelm Tell* the disagreements between the people and the nobility are resolved through a common reference to the 'fatherland' and the struggle against foreign rule. The aged Baron (*Freiherr*) von Attinghaus is thus on the side of the people and his nephew Ulrich von Rudenz joins Wilhelm Tell, the man of the people, in resisting Gessler, the High Bailiff (*Landvogt*). The tyrannicide (Tell kills Gessler) lacks true revolutionary character, being an act of national resistance based on a common social consensus. A retention of *bürgerlich* elements is nonetheless still discernible even in this conception of national resistance against foreign rule, elaborated by Schiller in *Wilhelm Tell* as a model for the German present. When the delegates from the three Swiss cantons take the oath: 'Wir wollen sein ein einzig Volk von Brüdern' ('We would be a single people of brothers'), Schiller is making a clear reference to the call to *fraternité* of the French Revolution.

Wilhelm Tell is one of the most frequently staged of Schiller's plays. Depending on the historical context, the accent shifts from social to nationalist issue. A witty recent version of the Tell story is Max Frisch's *Wilhelm Tell für die Schule* (*William Tell For Schools*) (1971). He treats Schiller's interpretation with heavy irony, as well as taking to task the nationalist myth of the Swiss liberation struggle connected with him.

The road to the *Bildungsroman* (the novel of education)

The reinstatement of the novel as a recognised literary genre had been the achievement of the Enlightenment, but it was not until the *Kunstepoche* that the novel took its place alongside drama in the great literature of the world.

Middle-class identity?

Goethe's *Werther* (1774) and Wieland's *Agathon* (1766–7) marked the first attempts to capture the experience and development of the middle-class individual in epic form, but neither of these novels even remotely matched the lofty expectations that Blanckenberg had cherished for the *bürgerlich* novel in his *Theorie des Romans* (1774). *Werther* at best offered only a highly subjectively portrayed section of society, while *Agathon* was veiled in ancient garb, and obscured rather than illuminated the predicament of middle-class identity. Even Wilhelm Heinse's *Ardinghello* (1787), which Goethe contemptuously regarded, according to his own testimony, as 'garbage', and which Schiller unjustly dismissed as a 'sensual caricature with neither truth nor aesthetic merit', was in fact set in sixteenth century Italy. Further steps on the road to the novel of education and development came in the wake of *Werther* with the novels *Aus Eduard Allwills Papieren* (*From Eduard Allwill's Papers*) (1775) and *Woldemar* (1779) by Friedrich Heinrich Jacobi, and *Anton Reiser* (1785–90) by Karl Philipp Moritz. *Anton Reiser* in particular, like the works of Jung Stilling (*Heinrich Jung Stillings Jugend – Heinrich Jung Stilling's Youth*, 1777) and Ulrich Bräker (*Lebensgeschichte und natürliche Abentheuer des armen Mannes in Tockenburg – The Life and Natural Adventures of the Poor Man in Tockenburg*, 1789), belong to the autobiographical genre that gave impetus to the novel after 1789. Like *Wilhelm Meisters theatralische Sendung*, *Anton Reiser* was a theatre novel, in which Moritz uses the theatre as a symbol of flight from an insupportable here and now.

With *Wilhelm Meisters Lehrjahre* (1794–6), Goethe was the first to capture a representative sample of German reality and to treat the contemporary experience of the middle-class intelligentsia without clothing it in historical guise. This makes *Wilhelm Meister* the first effective example of the novel of education and development, i.e. a novel that 'in deliberate and meaningful composition and with psychological consistency follows both the inner and outer progress of a man from its beginnings to a certain maturity of personality, portraying the development of existing traits in constant confrontation with influences from the environment in a broad cultural context' (Wilpert).

It should be noted that the hero of the novel of education and development is always a man. This may have something to do with the fact that the authors were themselves men coming to terms through the medium of a new genre with their own socialisation as individuals and on a wider stage, as well as with their own aspirations and fantasies. The most important likely reason, however, was that women in the eighteenth century had such a subordinate social rank that they were unthinkable as suitable heroines for a novel of education and development, playing no more than a subsidiary role in the careers of men.

Like the Faust theme, the Wilhelm Meister theme was another that preoccupied Goethe for virtually the whole of his life. Having found himself unable to complete the novel *Wilhelm Meisters theatralische Sendung*, also known as *Urmeister*, on which he had worked from 1777 to 1785, he took up the theme again from 1794 to 1796, reducing the six volumes of *Urmeister* to the four of the *Lehrjahre*. The theatre ceased to be the culmination of the developmental process, becoming instead just one educational phase among others. A quarter of a century later, Goethe took up the Meister theme yet again, revising the *Lehrjahre* and writing a second part, *Wilhelm Meisters Wanderjahre* (1821), in which he portrays Wilhelm's integration into an active, socially responsible life. Having sought to realise himself through the theatre in *Urmeister* and remained without either satisfactory professional or social prospects in *Lehrjahre*, Wilhelm becomes a physician in the *Wanderjahre*, thereby arriving at a profession that is both socially useful and fulfilling. He progresses, as Schiller aptly wrote concerning the *Lehrjahre*, 'from a hollow, vague ideal to a clearly-defined professional life, but without forfeiting his capacity to idealise'.

Wilhelm Meister became the model for all subsequent novels of education and development, its literary impact extending into the twentieth century. The influence of the novel on Goethe's writing contemporaries is transparent. Tieck's novel *Franz Sternbalds Wanderungen* (*The Travels of Franz Sternbald*) (1798), described at the time as an 'ill-conceived Wilhelm Meister' and dismissed by Goethe himself on account of its 'inner hollowness and tendency to falseness', portrayed the predicament of middle-class individuality in manifest dependence on Goethe. Wilhelm's passion for the theatre is replaced by Franz Sternbald's love of painting, the predicament of the creative artist becoming the focal point of the novel, as was originally the case in *Wilhelm Meisters theatralische Sendung*. Its fundamental divergence from the Goethe model lies first in setting the plot in the fifteenth century, and second in the failure to integrate the hero into middle-class life. The journey to Italy undertaken by both Wilhelm Meister and Franz Sternbald for the sake of finding their own identity becomes in Tieck's novel a romantic excursion into the vague and mysterious. The fragmentary character of the novel and its open-ended conclusion are further indications of the romantic notion of the impossibility of fulfilling human longings in middle-class life. Goethe's novel must, therefore, have seemed to the Romantics a disputable compromise with an inadequate reality. Wilhelm's shift away from an artistic and towards a professional middle-class existence was unacceptable to the Romantics. For Novalis, for example, *Wilhelm Meister* was 'fundamentally an unfortunate and absurd book – unpoetic in the extreme as far as spirit is concerned – however poetic the manner of presentation may be'.

'Anti-Meister'

The avowed intention of Novalis in his own novel *Heinrich von Ofterdingen*, published in 1802 by Tieck as a 'fragment', was to 'outstrip' Goethe, 'but only in the way that the aged can be outstripped, in capacity and strength, diversity and profoundness – not as a creative artist'. Novalis aimed in his 'Anti-Meister' to relate how a young man matures into a poet: 'The whole is intended as an apotheosis of poesy. In the first part Heinrich von Ofterdingen matures into a poet, and in the second is transfigured as a poet'. As with Tieck's *Sternbald*, only a fragment of the novel, the second part, is extant.

Heinrich von Ofterdingen differs from Goethe's *Wilhlem Meister* in more ways than its concentration on the predicament of the creative artist and its shift away from contemporary German reality (the novel is set in the Middle Ages, like Tieck's *Sternbald*). It is also different in the symbolic, fairy-tale structuring of the plot, which has proved a source of fascination to more readers than those of the author's day. The blue flower is a symbol of the true, authentic poetry that Heinrich aspires to. The fairy-tale narrated by the poet Klingsor contains the key to the novel: poetry alone is able to redeem the world, and therefore men. For the Romantics, the concept of the redeeming nature of poetry replaced the classical concept of aesthetic education as a precondition for social activity and change, as elaborated in epic form in a highly creative way in *Wilhelm Meister*.

The middle classes and creative artists – agreement or opposition?

A late Romantic response to *Wilhelm Meister* came from E.T.A. Hoffmann with his novel *Kater Murr* (*Tom-Cat Murr*) (1820–2), which differs substantially from early Romantic novels in its satirical and pessimistic features. The ingenious and witty interweaving of Kater Murr's life story with the biography of the *Kapellmeister* Kreisler conceals a double-edged criticism. The pompous, voluble autobiography of Kater Murr parodies the educational career of the middle-class individual, denouncing it as philistine (anti-Meister). The fragmentary character of the Kreisler biography moreover brings to light the failure of the Romantic creative artist in the face of the conflict between ideals and real life (anti-Ofterdingen). The middle-class world and the world of the creative artist are irreconcilable. The integration of the creative artist in middle-class life is as impossible as the redemption of the middle classes through art. The middle-class representative comes to an arrangement with reality and survives as a Philistine, while the creative artist is crushed by the contradictions he is forced to confront, and ultimately ousted from the world.

The predicament of middle-class identity is also a theme in novels by Jean Paul and Hölderlin, whose literary practice placed them outside the established schools of thought in literary theory. In contrast to the classical and Romantic novel of education and development, where the search for and finding of identity are central, in the novels of Jean Paul (*Hesperus*, 1795; *Titan*, 1800–3; *Flegeljahre*, 1804–5) and *Hyperion* (1797–9) by Hölderlin the individual is much more an integral part of the social and political context of his day, his identity crisis arising out of this very social anchoring, bringing middle-class individuality into conflict with society.

213

The blending of the dramatic and the epic in the novella

As a major epic form the novel made great demands on author and reader alike. *Wilhelm Meister* preoccupied Goethe for nearly fifty years, and was understood by only a narrow social stratum of intellectuals, being a highly thought-out, painstakingly composed and artistically extremely refined product of Goethe's attempts to come to terms with the dilemma of middle-class identity. Very few authors, furthermore, were in a position, even financially, to invest so much creative effort in a single work. Goethe's financial security as advisor to the Duke of Weimar was a key factor here. It gave him the time and leisure to persevere with such a major literary project.

Journals – purchasers of short prose works

Authors who were more dependent on the literary market, i.e. the sale of their books, were compelled to pay greater heed to the tastes of their readers and the chances of their works being sold. In somewhat different form, this applied even to authors such as the Jacobins, who on the basis of their socio-political convictions sought to achieve a direct impact on the public with their literary works. Minor epic forms such as the novella seemed ideal for this purpose. The sharp increase in the output of short narrative prose works towards the end of the eighteenth century was fostered by numerous literary journals, which were avid purchasers of short prose works. Circumventing publishers, authors found quite favourable opportunities for publication in such journals, although these were rapidly reduced by the enormous number of competing authors. The link between the advent of short prose works and the emergence of literary journals is so complex that it is difficult to discern cause and effect.

The appearance of the novella as a separate form can be traced back to the Italian Renaissance, although the name of the genre did not appear in Germany until much later. Clear distinction between the novel and this lesser narrative form was not made until towards the end of the eighteenth century. In 1772, Wieland defined the novella as 'a type of tale ... which differs from the major novel in the simplicity of its plan and the limited scope of the fable, or which bears the same relationship to the latter as the minor comedy does to the major tragedy or comedy'. Significant developments in the theory and practice of the novella did not take place until the *Kunstepoche*. This was the expression of an altered situation in the literary market, now characterised by a complex interrelationship between the financial interests of the author on the one hand and the growing demand for reading material and entertainment among broader sections of the population on the other.

Theory of the novella

Friedrich Schlegel made a substantial contribution to the theory of the novella in his essay *Nachricht von den poetischen Werken des Johann Boccaccio* (1801), in which he sought to construct a bridge between the father of the novella, Boccaccio (*The Decameron*, 1353), and the Romantic novella convention. The novella was acclaimed as a typically Romantic genre, eminently capable of uniting other forms within itself: it is 'fragment, study, and sketch in prose; – one of these, or all at the same time'. An important feature of the novella for Schlegel was that it should be, 'in every point of its being and making, new and surprising', and composed with careful attention to form: 'The art of good narration is intrinsic to the novella form'. Ludwig Tieck, one of the most prolific novella authors of the *Kunstepoche*, added a new category: the turning-point. He asserted that every novella should have a 'distinctive, striking turning-point . . . distinguishing it from other narrative genres' – a point 'from which it turns about, quite unexpectedly, and yet naturally, and out of which the rest develops, contingent on the characters and circumstances'. The theoretical exertions of Romantic authors, especially with regard to the 'nature of the novella', derived from their perceived need for poetic legitimacy. Their postulates should not, therefore, be understood as normative, timeless categories.

The legitimation of the novel as a genre had been achieved in the Age of the Enlightenment, and was secured through literary convention. The status of short prose works as a separate form of equal artistic merit to the novel and other genres had yet to be justified. The objective reasons for the emergence of a short narrative prose genre towards the end of the eighteenth century can be discerned only indirectly from theoretical efforts to capture the nature of the genre and contain it within the term 'novella'. Without doubt, however, deference to the reading public played some part in Tieck's category of the turning-point, as well as in Schlegel's requirement that the novella should above all be well told.

The constantly reiterated kinship of the novella to drama indicates another major connection. Its epic art form and dramatic structure placed the novella somewhere between the 'public' drama and the 'private' novel, the differing reactions of audiences and readers corresponding to the divergent intended effects of the author and the playwright. The novella thus blended the intended effects of the author and the reaction of the reader in a telling form. As a pseudo-dramatic form that could nevertheless be read or 'experienced' by an individual, the novella enabled the reader to stage the action being related in the form of private reading. This marked a decisive step along the road towards the reprivatisation of reading at the end of the eighteenth century. On another level, however, it marked a response to the miserable situation of the theatre. Kleist, who was both a playwright and a novella-author, thus embodying the close link between the two genres, was virtually without an audience as a playwright. Of his eight dramas, only two were ever performed in his own lifetime, whereas he was able to publish the bulk of his novellas either in his own journals or as separate publications. In addition to Kleist, E.T.A. Hoffmann and Eichendorff, Tieck, Brentano, Fouqué and Hauff with their fairy-tale novellas were the most prolific short prose writers. Tieck and Eichendorff continued to write and publish long after the *Kunstepoche* was over: Tieck wrote his two major late novellas *Der junge Tischlermeister* (*The Young Master Joiner*) (1836) and *Des Lebens Überfluss* (*Abundance of Life*) (1839) in the 1830s. The short prose works of these two authors are a particularly clear example of how socially accessible the novella was as an entertaining form, for which the need persisted beyond the *Kunstepoche*. There was indeed a sharp increase in short prose works in the nineteenth century: German novella writing did not actually reach its height until the period of middle-class Realism (Keller, Storm, Stifter, Meyer, Raabe, Fontane).

Romanticism as a way of life and of writing

The term 'Romantic' contains as many layers as the term 'classicism', and is equally open to a broader or a narrower interpretation. As a category spanning several epochs, the term Romantic is used to distinguish trends of aesthetic opposition to 'classical' and 'realistic' literary positions. Definite thematic priorities are associated with the term. Derived from the genre designation *roman* or 'romance', it denotes the wonderful, exotic, adventurous, sensual, and the weird, a shift away from modern civilisation and a turning towards the inner and outer natures of man, obsolete social forms and past times, especially the Middle Ages. In the narrower, historical sense, the term Romantic denotes a literary tendency that evolved during the *Kunstepoche* side by side with classicism and Jacobinism, as a counter-trend to them.

Whereas classicism had the single focal point of Weimar, the urban centres of Romanticism shifted. The Berlin group led by Tieck was distinct from the Jena group of the Schlegel brothers, and both were substantially different again from the Heidelberg group around Arnim and Brentano. The Dresden and Munich groups distinguished themselves from the so-called 'Swabian School' of Uhland, Schwab and Kerner, which was in turn inspired by the Heidelberg group. Unlike Weimar classicism, which was shaped by the two towering figures of Goethe and Schiller, the spectrum of Romanticism was broader, and involved a larger number of authors who felt part of it. What united the various groups and authors was the common conviction that 'only a *romantic* revival of literature and the arts would be able to surmount the global crisis in the social order and individual lifestyles manifest since the French Revolution' (Ribbat).

Early Romantic enthusiasm for the Revolution among such writers as Tieck ('Oh, to be a Frenchman now! I would not wish to sit here now, for ... France is now my only thought, day and night') was soon swept away by the conviction that social transformation could only be effected through a 'revolution' in thought and writing. Speaking in this context, Novalis asserted that the world must be 'romanticised' in order to overcome alienation and rediscover the original meaning of life. Friedrich Schlegel expressed this vision in 1798: 'Romantic poetry is a progressive, universal poetry. Its objective is not merely to reunite all the separated poetic genres and to bring poetry into contact with philosophy and rhetoric. It aims for, and should achieve a rapid blending and melting together of poetry and prose, genius and criticism, *Kunstpoesie* and nature poetry, rendering poetry lively and accessible, and life and society poetic.... Poetry alone is infinite, just as it alone is free, and the highest law acknowledges that the will of the poet will suffer no law to be above itself.' Although individual authors combined divergent ideas with the call for romanticisation, there were still priorities of content and stylistic features in common.

The revival of mythology

Among the central requisites of Romanticism was a new mythology. This was a crucial distinction between the early Romantic movement and the Enlightenment, with which there were otherwise still common links. Scepticism towards myth was indeed one of the central aspects of the Enlightenment view. The aim of the early Romantics was now to reunite poetry and mythology, 'since that is the beginning of all poetry, to abolish the progress and laws of reasoning, and to remove us back into the delightful confusion of the imagination, that primeval chaos of human nature for which I have yet to know a more beautiful symbol than the colourful throng of the ancient gods', as Friedrich Schlegel expressed it in his *Gespräch über die Poesie* (*Discourse on Poetry*) (1800). In his *Philosophie der Kunst* (*Philosophy of Art*) (1802–3), Schelling details the relationship between poetry and mythology, while Friedrich Schlegel, in his *Über Sprache und Weisheit der Inder* (*On the Language and Wisdom of India*) (1808) refers to the huge wealth of mythology and poetry of the Far East.

Irony

Another central feature of the early Romantic view of poetry is its distinctive aesthetic practice, for which Friedrich Schlegel coined the term 'romantic irony'. This denotes a specific manner of reflection and perception, which he described as 'agility' of the imaginative and reflective faculties. Irony 'springs from a communion between the sense for the art of life and the spirit of inquiry, from a convergence of natural philosophy and consummate philosophy of art. It both contains and arouses a sense of the inextinguishable struggle between the conditional and the unconditional, between the impossibility and the necessity for complete communication.' Irony was a central poetic principle to which Friedrich Schlegel returned again and again without ever defining it unequivocally, the definitions being themselves an expression of a Romantic irony that is unable to settle on anything unequivocal: 'Irony is the form of paradox. Paradox is everything that is good and great at one and the same time.'

The unconscious

A third major common feature lay in the Romantic discovery of the unconscious and the irrational, which had been suppressed and taboo in the Enlightenment. The latter had set out to devise for the middle-class individual a model of subjectivity and identity, demarcated from both the inner and outer natures, through the medium of literature. The Romantics, by contrast, gave voice to archaic structures of aspiration and desire. They opened themselves to experiences such as madness, sickness, enthusiasm, sensuality and idleness, which had been 'policed' in the Enlightenment. This nevertheless makes Romanticism less an opposing force than a complement to the Enlightenment: it augmented those dimensions that had remained blind spots in the discourse on rationality. It would therefore be false to dismiss Romanticism as an irrational, elite movement remote from reality, although there is ample evidence of such traits. Romanticism was rather the historically necessary response to a Enlightenment that had grown rigid. It criticised and complemented it, at the same time taking it a step further.

Volkslied, legend, fairy-tale

Efforts by Arnim and Brentano to preserve and revive the body of German *Volkslieder* and by the Brothers Grimm to record German legends and fairy-tales, the recourse to popular folk forms in poetry by Eichendorff, and the development of satirical poetry by E.T.A. Hoffmann are clear proof of the complexity of the Romantic literary movement, at the same time making the persistence of ties with Enlightenment writing abundantly clear. Creative literary activity was extremely diverse, some of it much more in touch with reality, and more straightforward, than might be expected in the light of ambitious, esoteric Romantic literary theory. The reasons for this lie in the Romantic notion of the autonomy of art, which in turn rests on the principle of poetic licence. Open forms, such as the fragment, the creative playful handling of traditional forms and genres, and formal experiments involving self-irony are all worthy of note here. The common feature of Romantic literature was an expansion in creative modes of expression and a liberation of the imagination, which in both the Enlightenment and in classicism had been subordinated to rationality and the classical rigours of style respectively.

The truly innovative and pioneering aspect of Romanticism, and indirectly also the element of social criticism it contained, lay in its liberation of the imagination. The call for a free creative space for author and reader in the sphere of literary creation was bound to collide with the realities of the historical situation around 1800, in which the potential for liberty and happiness of the individual was being increasingly constrained by political oppression and control, and by alienating conditions of work and production. The recourse to imagination and the creative human faculties under these circumstances posed a potential threat to middle-class society and its morality wherever it was united with the humanity of the Enlightenment. It lost its social critical function wherever it ossified into elitism. Utopia and illusion, social criticism and affirmation were the poles between which Romantic writing oscillated.

Among the best-known Romantic authors was Friedrich Schlegel, who together with his brother August Wilhelm Schlegel was a leading theoretician of the early Romantic period. Their jointly published journal *Athenäum* (1798–1800) was as central to disseminating the vision of the Romantic movement as *Horen* was for Weimar classicism. The two brothers were exceptionally prolific in the history and theory of literature. A.W. Schlegel's Berlin and Vienna lectures *Über schöne Literatur und Kunst* (*On Belles Lettres and Art*) (1802–4) and *Über dramatische Kunst und Literatur* (*On Dramatic Art and Literature*) (1808) were held up as the epitome of Romantic literary criticism, and his translation of Shakespeare, begun alone and then continued with Tieck, became the basis for his fame in Europe.

Shakespeare

The Schlegel–Tieck Shakespeare translations marked a temporary conclusion to the efforts to acquaint the German public with Shakespeare and his works that had accompanied the whole of the eighteenth century. A translation of *Julius Caesar* had appeared in 1741, arousing vehement criticism from Gottsched for failing to observe 'one single rule of the stage'. A relaxation in Gottsched's regulated poetics brought with it a new view of Shakespeare and his works. Through the mediation of Gottsched's opponents, the Swiss authors Bodmer and Breitinger, the young Wieland became acquainted with Shakespeare's works. His subsequent prose translation of *Shakespeares theatralischen Werken* (*Shakespeare's Theatrical Works*) (1762–6) then formed the textual basis for an enthusiastic discovery of Shakespeare in the *Sturm und Drang* period. This was also preceded by

J.E. Schlegel's work *Vergleichung Shakespeares und Andreas Gryphs* (*A Comparison of Shakespeare and Andreas Gryph*) (1741) and Lessing's seventeenth literary letter (1759), through which Shakespeare's name reached a broad literary public. Shakespeare and his works became a focus for *Sturm und Drang* endeavours towards literary reform. Goethe's essay *Zum Schäkespears Tag* (*For Shakespeare's Day*) (1771), Herder's *Shakespeare* (1773), and the essay *Anmerkungen übers Theater* (*Observations on the Theatre*) (1774) by Lenz were high points in this new discovery of the English dramatist, encapsulated in the watchwords 'emulation of nature' and 'original genius'. It was in this recourse to Shakespeare and his works that the shift away from French classicist tragedy and the turn towards *bürgerliches Drama* was completed.

Discussion of Shakespeare went far beyond the *Sturm und Drang* era, however, and also extended to lower-class authors such as Ulrich Bräker, who adopted Shakespeare in a highly individual manner (*Etwas über Shakespears Schauspiele – Something on Shakespeare's Plays*, 1780). In *Anton Reiser* by Karl Philipp Moritz the name of Shakespeare is associated with a new way of thinking and feeling that bursts out of the narrowness of lower-middle-class life; in Goethe's *Wilhelm Meister* Shakespeare proves an increasingly fruitful point of reference in the hero's search for his own identity. Like his hero Wilhelm Meister, Goethe reflected on Shakespeare throughout his life. In retrospect (*Shakespeare und kein Ende – Shakespeare and No End*, 1815) he came to the conclusion that any discussion of Shakespeare was bound to fall short because Shakespeare was simply 'too rich and too powerful': 'Eine productive Natur darf alle Jahre nur ein Stück von ihm lesen, wenn sie nicht an ihm zugrunde gehen will. Ich that wohl, dass ich durch meinen "Götz von Berlichingen" und "Egmont" ihn mir vom Halse schaffte.... Shakespeare ... giebt uns in silbernen Schalen goldene Äpfel. Wir bekommen nun wohl durch Studium seiner Stücke die silberne Schale, allein wir haben nur Kartoffeln hineinzuthun, das ist das Schlimme!' ('A creative nature should only read one play by him every year, if he would not perish as a result. I did well in ridding myself of him through my "Götz von Berlichingen" and "Egmont".... Shakespeare ... gives us golden apples in silver bowls. But although by studying his plays we obtain the silver bowls, the trouble is we have only potatoes to put in them!')

Of equally crucial importance were the writings of Friedrich Schlegel on literary theory and criticism. His *Fragmenten* and *Ideen* (*Ideas*) are a penetrating formulation of the Romantic approach to art and life. It was his novel 'fragment' *Lucinde* (1799), however, that propelled him to fame. This text incurred an allegation of obscenity against Schlegel, which Schleiermacher in his *Vertrauten Briefen über Lucinde* (*Confidential Letters about Lucinda*) (1800) tried in vain to defend. It unleashed a literary scandal that was to bring the Romantic movement as a whole into the firing-line. Schiller held *Lucinde* to be the 'height of modern disproportion and unnaturalness'. He discerned in the novel all the tendencies that he and Goethe were most against. *Lucinde* was indeed an attempt by Schlegel to put his theory of aesthetics into practice in a text.

The focus of the novel is the career of the hero, Julius. His letters to his lover Lucinde and his friend Antonio, as well as his conversations, notes and reflections, are used by Schlegel to elaborate the 'learning years of manhood', which are presented in the form of a series of romantic involvements on the part of the hero with various types of woman. This structural principle incidentally makes it very similar to the novel *Wilhelm Meister*, against which Schlegel polemicised vehemently. Unlike Goethe, however, Schlegel reflects openly and directly on the physical aspects of love, thereby breaking with a prevailing taboo and opening himself to allegations of immorality by prudish literary critics. Other, more liberal-minded critics, however, gave him credit for having written a manifesto for liberated love and a non-alienated life.

Ideas of role reversal and androgyny, and the postulate of free love, are not as revolutionary, however, as Schlegel and his supporters would have had their readers believe. These ideas and demands are linked to a portrayal of women that excludes the ideas of development and progression. The feminine is still not liberated, but mythologised and co-opted into an aesthetic function, just as in classical texts. Schlegel criticises the dichotomy in the portrayal of women typical of classical authors. His Lucinde is 'sensual' lover and 'intellectual' partner all in one – the sum of all the qualities that the hero Julius has elsewhere come to know in different women. Lucinde is 'one and indivisible', and yet ultimately she is still only another product of male projection. A natural being, she is as organic and perfect as a plant and superior in her wholeness to inwardly torn, alienated man. At the same time, however, this fixes her as a static being, excluding her from the processes of infinite progression. Female growth and male development form the polar structure of the novel, which once again takes up the classic polarisation of the sexes found in authors such as Humboldt (*Über männliche und weibliche Form*) on another level.

The plea for free love

What was regarded at the time as even more scandalous than the erotic passages in the novel, however, was the fact that Schlegel and his friends attempted to live out in their daily lives what is celebrated in the novel as 'free love'. The early Romantics associated with the Schlegel brothers experimented with new forms of living together. They did not feel bound by the middle-class conventions extolled by Schiller, for example, in his poems *Männerwürde* (*The Dignity of Men*), and the *Würde der Frauen* (*The Dignity of Women*). They thus sought, even in their daily lives, to lead an anti-middle-class, bohemian life. In friendly circles they also tried out a form of social companionship along the lines of the French *salons* – hitherto unknown in German public life.

An alternative type to these versatile, gregarious, restless intellectuals, exemplified by the Schlegel brothers, is that of Novalis (Friedrich von Hardenberg). Although a close friend of Friedrich Schlegel and Tieck, Novalis remained an outsider and a loner. He was the only early Romantic to come of noble parentage, although he pursued a middle-class profession. His few works: *Die Christenheit oder Europa* (*Christendom or Europe*) (1799, published 1826), the novel fragments *Die Lehrlinge von Sais* (*The Apprentices of Sais*) (1798–1800) and *Heinrich von Ofterdingen* (1802), and his *Hymnen an die Nacht* (*Hymns to the Night*) (1800), set him apart from other early Romantic authors. The 'dark' language of his prose and lyric poetry incorporates a wealth of mythical and mystical imagery that have come to shape the image of the Romantic held by subsequent generations. His *Hymns* celebrate the night as a creative mystery of life and death, in the form of free rhythmic songs in which the transitions between prose and lyric are fluid. He was thus touching here on ideas that were to be further elaborated a little later by Schubert in his *Ansichten von der Nacht-seite der Naturwissenschaften* (*Views on the Dark Side of the Natural Sciences*) (1808), and by Klingemann in his *Nachtwachen des Bonaventura* (*The Night Watches of Bonaventura*) (1804). His death at a young age helped make him an object of legend.

Tieck's Kunstmärchen

One of the most prolific authors of the Romantic movement was Ludwig Tieck. He continued to publish into the middle of the nineteenth century, his works thereby exerting a strong influence over a period spanning the Early to the Late Romantic. His novels *Die Geschichte des Herrn William Lovell* (*The Story of Mr William Lovell*) (1795–6) and *Franz Sternbalds Wanderungen* (*The Travels of Franz Sternbald*) brought him into the *Wilhelm Meister* debate, which he entered yet again in 1836 with his novella *Der junger T.* (*The Young Master Joiner*). He was also very interested in theatre (*Der gestiefelte Kater* – *Puss-in-Boots*, 1797), as well as trying his hand at the new *Kunstmärchen* genre.

It was in these fairy-tales that Tieck found a form to suit his interest in the fantastic. His *Blonder Eckbert* (*The Blond Eckbert*) (1796) and *Runen-berg* (*The Rune Mountain*) (1802) were forays into the imaginary world of the Unconscious and of Desire, enabling him to deal with the theme of sensuality in coded fairy-tale form. In *Runenberg* the hero Christian oscillates between life in the mountains and life in the lowlands. These are symbolic landscapes representing the opposing forces of the patriarchal middle-class order and the primeval wilderness. The Rune Mountain, with its enticing Venus figure, symbolises all the desires that have to be suppressed in the lowlands. The socialisation of the hero takes place in a process of movement between these symbolic spheres. During his first journey into the mountains Christian grows up, preparing for his future life as a husband in the lowlands. Obviously this does not make him happy. He is forced back to the mountains, where he loses himself in his erotic imaginings, and falls victim to madness. The metaphor of the Venus cult also appears in other Romantic texts: in Tieck's *Der Getreuer Eckart und der Tannenhäuser* (*The Faithful Eckart and Tannenhäuser*), in Eichendorff's *Marmorbild* (*Image of Marble*), and in E.T.A. Hoffmann's *Bergwerke zu Falun* (*The Mines at Falun*). Here too there is antagonism between the heathen, demonic figure of Venus, the paternal, spiritual, Christian God and the often fatal attraction of demonic femininity for the male heroes.

Soon after 1800 Early Romantic circles dissolved, entailing an increase in the number not only of people involved in the movement, but also of their centres. One of the larger of these formed in Heidelberg, led by Clemens Brentano and Achim von Arnim. Although following on from Early Romanticism, their works reflected the changed historical conditions, fraught with the confusion of the Napoleonic Wars and wars of liberation. The response of the coming Romantic generation to this external threat, which was experienced as an inner peril, was to intensify their recourse to religion. The turn to religion to some extent anticipated tendencies towards restoration that were to become increasingly manifest after 1815. The search for fixed points in an age of internal strife and chaos, however, also led to a renewed embracing of legend and fairy-tale, in turn based on a modified concept of childhood.

The Romantic concept of childhood

Early Romantic authors had broken with the customary didacticism prevalent in Enlightenment literature for children and young people. Childhood had acquired a value in its own right, the child being stylised into a perfect being. This notion of childhood as epitomising a primeval stage of development, naturalness and wholeness was overlaid with a reverence for ancient poetic forms and an admiration of times past (the cult of the Middle Ages) which can be traced back to the influence of Herder's philosophy of history. For Schlegel and Novalis especially, childhood became a central theme of moral and aesthetic reflection, as well as a focal point for their far-reaching concepts of leisure and play. The recourse of Romantics to fairy-tale needs to be seen in this context. In the process, however, these somewhat over-zealous notions of childhood rapidly hardened into idealised projections of 'innocent childhood'. In practice they became every bit as repressive in their way as Enlightenment notions of the intrinsically 'evil nature' of children that had to be nipped in the bud through judicious education. Even these idealising models of the Romantics thus tended to suppress the psychological and historical realities of child-hood (e.g. child labour).

Arnim and Brentano collected German *Volkslieder* and old folk poems, publishing them under the title *Des Knaben Wunderhorn* (1806 and 1818). In 1812 the Brothers Grimm published their *Kinder- und Hausmärchen* (*Fairy-tales for Children and Home*), and in 1816 their *Deutsche Sagen* (*German Legends*). All three compilations are documents of the patriotic struggle against the threat of national fragmentation, as well as against inner and outer alienation arising from modern civilisation. Social contra-dictions were obliterated by their concept of *Volkspoesie*, through resort to an alleged primeval nature of man in a utopian manner. Following on from Herder's efforts to collect *Volkslieder* (1778–9), they felt able to recapture this primeval state through fairy-tales, and to set it against modern class society.

Ancient poetry of the Germans?

Even in the Enlightenment there had been efforts to revive the fairy-tale. Wieland, for example, had sought to vindicate the Wonderful as an aesthetic category with his compilation of fairy-tales *Dschinnistan* (1786–9), and Musäus had published a compilation of *Volksmärchen der Deutschen* (*Folk Fairy-tales of the Germans*) (1782–7). Neither of these authors, however, even remotely sought to discern in fairy-tales some kind of ancient poetry in the Romantic sense. The treatment of 'raw' fairy-tales was only deemed justifiable by Enlightenment authors in adapted aesthetic form.

The fairy-tale genre continued into the classical and Early Romantic periods. Among the more famous volumes were Goethe's *Märchen* (*Fairy-Tales*) (1795), in which he elaborated a utopia of harmonious social con-ditions to offset the French Revolution, and the fairy-tales of Novalis and Tieck. Novalis in particular raised the fairy-tale to the ultimate Romantic form: 'Das Mährchen ist gleichsam der Canon der Poesie – alles poetische muss märchenhaft seyn' ('The fairy-tale is at one and the same time the canon of poetry – everything poetic must have a fairy-tale quality'). Bren-tano and Arnim continued in the vein of Novalis' Romantic vision by attempting to eradicate in their own literary creation the distinction between *Volksmärchen* (folk fairy-tale) and *Kunstmärchen* (invented fairy-tale). They did this both by adapting folk fairy-tales to suit the Romantic mould, and by trying to achieve the tone of the folk fairy-tale in their own invented tales.

Women authors of the Romantic age

Contrary to the self-perception of some adherents of the Romantic age, and that of their uncritical female admirers, Romanticism, too, failed in its vocation as a revolutionary movement that would eradicate the alienation of human beings, making them free individuals. However, it did succeed in generating a creative space in which women could participate in the world of letters. There had, of course, been women authors in the Age of the Enlightenment. Luise Adelgunde Victorie Kulmus, later Gottsched's wife, and Anna Louise Karsch were two exceptional and greatly admired women whose work was widely acknowledged.

The discovery of *Empfindsamkeit* (sensibility) and the *Briefroman* (letter novel) form particularly favoured increased participation by women in the world of letters. Sophie von La Roche's novel *Die Geschichte des Fräulein von Sternheim* (*The Story of Miss von Sternheim*), published by Wieland in 1771, instigated a veritable flood of *Frauenromane*, whose women authors (including Benedikte Naubert, Elisa von der Recke, Frederike Helene Unger, Karolina Wobeser and Karoline von Wolzogen) were often obliged by economic considerations to forfeit their own aspirations, both aesthetic and emancipatory, in order to supply the literary market with ideologically inoffensive products.

Women often reproduced in their novels the reactionary portrayal of women propounded by male authors. It was extremely difficult for them to liberate themselves as authors from the conception of women laid down in the prevailing male discourse, according to which the dignity of woman lay above all in 'being unknown', her source of happiness lying 'in the esteem of her husband' and 'in the joy of her family' (Rousseau). The dream of 'the quill in the hand and the dagger in the fist' that could still be confidently entertained by Gottsched's pupil Sidonie Hedwig Zäunemann at the beginning of the century had become a fearful prospect by the end of the century. By way of admonition to his fiancée Caroline Flachsland, Herder, for example, cites the warning Arab proverb: 'A hen that crows and a learned female are bad omens: both should be beheaded', exhorting her as a Muse to restrict herself to the 'refinement', 'animation' and 'encouragement' of her husband.

Salon culture

Women were central to Romantic circles, exerting a powerful influence on the social life of the era with their spirit, their education, their art of conversation, their letters, and not least their erotic attraction. Among the best-known were Caroline Böhmer, who married A.W. Schlegel, and later the philosopher Schelling, Dorothea Veit, who married Friedrich Schlegel after her divorce, and on whom Schlegel based the character of *Lucinde*;

Sophie Mereau, who married Brentano after her divorce, Karoline von Günderode, who took her own life, Bettina Brentano, the sister of Clemens Brentano, who later married von Arnim, Sophie Tieck, who was regarded as a particularly gifted poet, and lastly Henriette Herz and Rahel Levin, who were famous for their salons.

Each of these women strove in her own way to break out of the narrow confines of femininity, and all eventually lived to see the dominant role conceptions catch up with them. Caroline Schlegel-Schelling and Dorothea Veit-Schlegel sacrificed themselves to the manifold activities of their husbands, which were indeed only made possible by their self-denying cooperation. Caroline Schlegel, for example, worked with her husband on his Shakespeare translations, also writing reviews and critical articles, some of which were published under a pseudonym, others included in her husband's works without her name being credited. Dorothea Schlegel translated Madame de Staël into German for her husband, also working on a large number of omnibus volumes for which Schlegel was credited as editor. Sophie Mereau at first published anonymously (*Das Blüthenalter der Empfindung* (*The Blossoming Age of Sensibility*)), although she later gained confidence and published under her own name (*Amanda and Eduard*, 1803), even publishing a journal for women (*Kalathiskos*). Her husband Brentano, however, showed no regard for the literary work of his wife, and compelled her to give up the independence she had fought so hard for after her divorce from her first husband, Mereau, whom she had not loved. She died, just 36 years old, giving birth to their fifth child.

Karoline von Günderode was destroyed not by marriage – that 'anvil of the middle classes', as Rahel Levin called it – but by the contradictory nature of her own aspirations, which nevertheless only reflected the ambivalence of prevailing demands on her as a woman. In letters to her friend Gunda Brentano, Günderode wrestled with her fate:

> How often have I had the unwomanly desire to throw myself into the thick of furious battle and die – why was I not born a man! I have no taste for female virtues, or for feminine bliss. Only the wild, the great and the glorious pleases me. This is an accursed, but irreparable incongruity in my soul. And it must be and remain so, for I am a woman, and have the desires of a man without the strength of a man. This is why I am so volatile and so ill at ease with myself.

She published little. Her lyrics (*Gedichte und Phantasien* – *Poems and Fantasies*, 1804; *Poetische Fragmente* – *Poetic Fragments*, 1805) were published under the pseudonym Tian. Her book *Melete*, discovered among the papers she left, was not published until 1906. Her dramas have yet to have an audience. A memorial volume, *Die Günderode* (1804), written by Bettina Brentano, is an authentic and sensitive monument to her, despite its tendencies to stylise both Günderode and herself.

Another woman who felt cheated of her life and work was Rahel Levin-Varnhagen. For her, the experience of being 'only a woman' was coupled with the humiliating sense of being a pariah. Like Dorothea Veit-Schlegel, the daughter of Moses Mendelssohn, and Henriette Herz, she was from a Jewish family, and therefore suffered all her life from the dual stigma of being both woman and Jew, despite the official emancipation of the Jews. She left no work in the true sense of the word: her letters were her work. As for many women of the Romantic movement, letters were for Rahel the only permitted form of self-expression within a half-open literary world hedged round with social convention.

The Mainz Republic and the literary practice of the Jacobins

Affirmation of the French Revolution

An alternative model to those of classical and Romantic literature, albeit only in incipient form, may be found among those authors who were defamed by reactionaries as Jacobins. They saw themselves, however, rather as an embodiment of that type of political writer never given its due in Germany and almost always discredited. The political views of these authors were in any case far from homogeneous, ranging from fairly moderate reformist stances to radical concepts aimed at the revolutionary transformation of Germany. Apart from being shaped by the social and political origins of authors themselves, these concepts were also affected by the places in which they lived. The feasibility of exerting political influence in Mainz, southern Germany, or west of the Rhine, for example, was incomparably greater than in northern Germany or Prussia, where the reform movement of 'enlightened Absolutism' tended to take the wind from the sails of revolutionary-minded itellectuals.

A literature of intervention

In contrast, Jacobin ideas concerning the role of literature in the social process were more homogeneous than their political concepts, which were contingent upon factors of time, personal biography and timing. As a counter to Schiller's vision of aesthetic education, Jacobin authors set their model of a literature for intervention. Laukhard, for example, criticised Schiller's preface to *Horen*, denouncing its idealistic core by asserting that 'the hungry stomach . . . can have no ears and no eyes for idealising works of art'. As a rule, Jacobin authors tended to be sceptical about the power of literature to exert influence, giving preference instead to direct political action. They wanted to 'make poems, not compose them' (Rebmann). This notion of a tension between 'word' and 'deed' anticipates stances that were to play a major role in the authors of the *Junges Deutschland* movement.

Their sceptical view of the political potential of literature is an expression of their conviction that the situation would be changed not by literature, but by revolutionary acts. It is at the same time, however, a reflection of their having been compelled by circumstances to forfeit concrete revolutionary practice, and of frustrating experiences with their own literary practice.

Word and deed

The fact that, nevertheless, literature did occupy such a crucial place in German Jacobinism conflicts neither with the Jacobins' overall sceptical stance, nor with their specific opposition to the classical concept of 'aesthetic education'. Their repeated contrasting of 'word' and 'deed', i.e. of literary and political practice, should be understood not as an antonymous relationship, but rather as one that resolves itself through the dialectic of history. It derives from the specific social situation that prevailed in Germany at the end of the eighteenth century, and can be surmounted by a form of writing that is consciously political and places itself in the service of enlightening underprivileged sections of the population. This is not 'aesthetic education' in the classical sense, but political education, i.e. the enlightenment of the population as to their rights and duties through the medium of literature. This is the answer of Jacobin authors to the prevailing social situation. Unlike the classical concept, which seeks to avoid revolution, the Jacobin concept of education seeks to awaken in the population a sense of the necessity for revolution. Writing is thus transformed into a direct aspect of revolution. It either loses its importance or changes character as soon as a transformation of social conditions has occurred, and the *bürgerliche Republik* has been established.

The break with classical and Romantic notions of literature had three aspects: the way the creative artist saw himself; a reformulation of the form–content issue; and finally a new relationship between artistic creation and the process of living in society. Following on from notions developed by the poetics of the Enlightenment, and above all the *Sturm und Drang*, pertaining to the functions attributable to literature, the Jacobins assigned to literature the tasks of criticising prevailing conditions and exposing the dominant ideology. Through literature, the population at large was to be helped to acquire social and political knowledge, and insights into the ability of social conditions to be changed. Literature was also to help bridge the gulf between the small band of Jacobin intellectuals, who saw themselves as a revolutionary avant-garde, and the mass of the population, who were seen as the real champions of the revolution. Literature was intended to appeal not only to the intellect, but also to the emotions of the reader.

The Mainz Republic

The Mainz Republic was a crucial event in German history. In 1792–3, in the aftermath of the Coalition War, a revolution occurred whose reverberations were to be felt even in Goethe's writings. It also unleashed a spate of counter-revolutionary propaganda in a wide variety of forms. The short-lived republic set up in Mainz was the first of its kind on German soil. Although the cultural and political significance of Mainz can in no way be compared with the Weimar of Goethe and Schiller, it is nonetheless associated with its own distinctive brand of literary practice and convention, which flourished on a different soil from that of Weimar, the locus of classicism.

Among other things, Mainz spawned an indigenous revolutionary press (*Der Bürgerfreund – The Citizen's Friend; Der fränkische Republikaner – The Franconian Republican; Der kosmopolitische Beobachter – The Cosmopolitan Observer; Der Volksfreund – The People's Friend*), which was a world apart from classical and Romantic journals. Like the numerous pamphlets produced in connection with the Mainz Revolution, this journalism also pre-empted the 1848 revolution in both structure and content.

Another feature peculiar to the Mainz scene was the founding of a *National-Bürgertheater* (National Citizens' Theatre) – a politically more radical extension of the Enlightenment idea of a national theatre. Formed after the disbanding of the Elector's theatre company, it was sustained by an amateur ensemble and run by a collective. Innovation was not restricted to the organisational level alone, however, but affected the repertoire as well. Some socially critical plays of the *Sturm und Drang* period were revived by the Jacobins, for example. They also strove to win the population over to ideas of revolution and the Republic with plays of their own, tailor-made for the Mainz situation (*Der Freiheitsbaum – The Tree of Freedom*, 1796).

A leading light of the Mainz Republic was Georg Forster, who became a particular target for reactionary spleen. Even Goethe and Schiller passed harsh judgement on him in *Xenien*, their journal. Only Schlegel made a bid to salvage Forster's reputation in a lengthy essay of 1797, but was unable to prevent him from being treated like a 'dead dog' (Engels), both in the contemporary world of letters and by subsequent generations.

Forster's literary work was highly diverse. As a travel writer (*Ansichten vom Niederrhein – Views from the Lower Rhine*, 1791–2; *Parisische Umrisse – Contours of Paris*, 1793), essayist (*Über die Beziehung der Staatskunst auf das Glück der Menschheit – On the Bearing of the Art of Statesmanship on the Happiness of Mankind*), political orator and journalist (*Der Volksfreund – The People's Friend*), he was committed to the ideal of humanity. He defended this ideal not only against growing counter-revolution in his own country, but equally against the cynical and inhumane post-1793 revolutionary practices of the French. Following the collapse of the Mainz Republic Forster was compelled to flee to Paris where, again a forerunner of the *Vormärz* generation, he lived in exile until 1794, unrepentant but disillusioned.

Two other authors who may be classified beside Forster as political writers are Rebmann and Knigge. Where Rebmann was first and foremost a journalist and travel writer, Knigge's literary work focused largely on satire.

The travel novel (Reiseroman)

The travel novel was an appropriate vehicle for conveying in a personal and authentic manner the private individual's experience of self and reality. It was thus a counterpart to the novel of education and development, in which experience was imparted with such a literary overlay and so heavily objectivised that it could only hope to address a narrow readership. Having his horizons broadened to include foreign countries, people, political institutions, cultures and literature, however, enabled the individual to break out of the constraints of his middle-class lifestyle and open himself up to a wider spectrum of experiences. These experiences were presented in widely differing literary styles. While some travel novels were highly fictionalised accounts, other travel books and descriptions had almost the character of news reports.

Experience of the foreign

The task of these travel reports was to provide the public with information about foreign lands and the conditions prevailing in them. Inasmuch as they were seen as helping to inform the literary public about political conditions, therefore, they were a continuation of the Enlightenment tradition. A thorough knowledge of conditions in other countries was intended to develop the reader's faculties of critical judgement with regard to conditions in his own country. It was not by chance that a high percentage of these travel books were accounts of revolutionary events in France (Campe: *Briefe aus Paris* – Letters from Paris, 1790; Halem: *Blicke auf einen Teil Deutschlands, der Schweiz und Frankreich* – Glimpses at Parts of Germany, Switzerland and France; Kerner: *Briefe über Frankreich* – Letters about France, 1797). Jacobin authors such as Forster, Rebmann and Knigge saw it as their duty to inform the German public about political developments in neighbouring France, in the hope of providing an impetus to revolutionary changes in Germany.

The satirical novel

A readership-oriented, popular form, the satirical novel was another domain of Jacobin authors. Here, too, they were following in the footsteps of the Enlightenment, while making the genre explicitly political. The didactic and yet amusing character of satire made it an eminently suitable medium, rooted in Enlightenment morality, for establishing a bond between the author and his readership. This tacit mutual understanding in turn facilitated the initiation of a learning process in the reader.

Some outstanding examples of social criticism in the satirical novel are Knigge's novels *Joseph von Wurmbrand* (1792) and *Des seligen Herrn Etatsraths Samuel Conrad von Schaafskopf hinterlassene Papiere* (*The Papers Left by the Late Sir Samuel Conrad of Sheepshead, Privy Councillor*) (1792), and Rebmann's *Hans Kiekindiwelts Reisen in alle vier Weltheile* (*Hans Kiekindiewelt's Travels to All Corners of the Globe*) (1795). These novels lampoon the current state of German society with extreme ruthlessness, rigour and candour, especially targeting the German aristocracy and their policy of opposing the humanitarian ideals of the French Revolution.

Lyric verse within the popular concept (Volkstümlichkeit)

Lyric verse occupied a central position in Jacobin literary practice, where it was used to radicalise Bürger's concept of the popular (*Volkstümlichkeit*). The bulk of this lyric verse consists of political poems, some published anonymously and in pamphlet form, specifically for use in political discourse. The explicit political lyric of the German Jacobins (*Freiheitslieder* – Songs of Freedom; *Liederlese für Republikaner* – A Selection of Songs for Republicans, etc.) marked the advent of a tradition on which the authors of the *Vormärz* era would build.

Klopstock built up his post-1789 lyric works in a similar political vein, although his poetry shows marked formal deviations from Jacobin lyric verse. This acclaimed but little-read author of the monumental religious lyric poem *Der Messias* (*The Messiah*) (1748–73) and *Oden* (*Odes*) (1771) matured into a major lyric poet critical of his age, as his own relationship with the French Revolution – an event which he had initially welcomed – changed and developed. His poems *Die Etats Généraux, Kennet Euch selbst* (*Know Thyselves*), *Der Freiheitskrieg* (*The War of Liberation*), and *Der Eroberungskrieg* (*The War of Conquest*), are examples of a poetry of topical social criticism, a rare genre in Germany, that combines aesthetic beauty with a commitment to topical issues.

231

On the periphery of classicism, Romanticism and Jacobinism: Jean Paul – Kleist – Hölderlin

Outside the major literary groupings already mentioned, there were authors who deliberately kept themselves apart, adhering to no particular grouping and going their own unique ways. This special position condemned each of them to the onerous life of the outsider. It also makes it difficult for scholars to formulate an adequate assessment of their role in the *Kunstepoche*.

Johann Paul Friedrich Richter, who wrote under the *nom de plume* of Jean Paul, managed in his own lifetime to acquire an equal and acknowledged place beside classical and Romantic authors, becoming an authority in the world of letters. His origins had been anything but conducive to such success. The son of a poor teacher and organist, he was soon acquainted with poverty. He suffered great personal distress under the stern discipline of his father. It was indeed his early family experiences, in many respects comparable with those of Moritz (*Anton Reiser*), that laid the foundations for his 'pathological impulsive character' and that 'narcissistic self-obsession' (Minder) from which Jean Paul was never able to free himself, and which condemned him early on to the life of an unconventional loner. Like many authors from a petty bourgeois milieu, he was forced against his will to study theology. Later, he was obliged to earn his living as a private tutor for many years before finally escaping from his financial insecurity via a modest income as a 'free' writer.

Jean Paul made his debut with satirical writing, clearly in the Enlightenment tradition. His acerbic, caustic brand of irony, however, was hardly calculated to warm many hearts (*Grönlandische Prozesse* – *Greenland Trials*, 1783; *Auswahl aus des Teufels Papieren* – *A Selection from the Devil's Papers*, 1789). Not until the 1790s did he succeed in expanding this satirical style to include elements of sensibility, emotion and humour, thereby establishing that particular blend of styles that was to make him famous. His novel *Hesperus* (1795) proved an enduring success, inspiring an awe among his readership previously achieved only by *Werther*.

The new author indeed attracted the attention of Goethe and Schiller, who invited him to Weimar, but were unable to win him over. Jean Paul turned down an offer pressed on him by Schiller to work on *Horen*, instead becoming an adherent of Herder, who had broken with Goethe definitively in 1796. Jean Paul was particularly repulsed by Goethe, in whom he saw what he called the 'egotism of genius': 'Goethe's character is horrendous; genius without virtue is bound to fail'. He also had political grounds for his abhorrence of Goethe, however. Himself a fervent Republican, Jean Paul admired in the Weimar circle only Herder, Wieland and Reichardt, who were in his opinion the 'most passionate Republicans'.

Jean Paul's novel *Titan* (1800–3) explicitly takes to task Weimar classicism, to which he was vehemently opposed as an aesthetic trend. The two negative figures of Roquairol (the 'pseudo-genius') and Gaspard are endowed with the character traits of Goethe and Schiller, while the material for the many passages in the novel is drawn from his experiences in Weimar. *Titan* is a novel of education in conscious opposition to *Wilhelm Meister*. Jean Paul criticises the classical educational ideal by dealing with themes concerned with the social and ideological prerequisites for education. His *Titan* is in fact an 'Anti-Titan', and as such is aimed against what he calls the 'general licentiousness of the age'. In *Titan*, together with two of his other works, *Hesperus* and *Unsichtbarer Loge* (*The Invisible Theatre Box*) (1793), Jean Paul not only paints a picture of the ideal German revolutionary, but also offers a bold political vision for the transformation of Germany.

Despite these ideals, he persistently adhered to the concept of a harmonious universal education, in this respect showing an unwitting affinity to Goethe, whom he claimed to oppose. In addition to what were probably reluctant tendencies towards classicism, he also reveals numerous areas of common ground with Jacobin and Romantic convictions. Aside from his Republican fervour, he also shared with the Jacobins their sceptical view of the political potential of literature, giving precedence to deed over word: 'Vorzüglich handle! O in Taten liegen mehr hohe Wahrheiten als in Büchern!' ('Better by far to act! Oh, in deeds there are more high truths than in books!')

After 1800 Jean Paul moved to Berlin, where he improved his acquaintance with leading exponents of the Berlin Romantic group on the basis of a shared estimation of the role of the fantastic. Although participating in the salon life of Rahel Levin-Varnhagen and Henriette Herz, however, he never felt one of the Romantics. He came closest to the 'Romantic School' (Heine) in his *Vorschule der Ästhetik* (*Preparatory School of Aesthetics*) (1804), although some Romantic authors completely failed to perceive this affinity. Tieck, for example, reproached the work as being no more than 'an artisan's account of his work'. In fact, Jean Paul's aim in the *Vorschule* was to lay down his aesthetic principles and procedures. To this end he adopted elements from a variety of literary trends, creatively modifying those he was able to employ in his own literary practice.

Social criticism of the restoration

A constantly recurring theme in Jean Paul's novels is the conflict between poetry and reality – an experience characteristic of all intellectuals for the period around 1800. In his *Flegeljahre* (*The Awkward Age*) (1804), the dissimilar twin brothers Walt and Vult are more than embodiments of contrary orientations in the history of the age: Jean Paul also uses them to work through two divergent aspects of his own experience of himself.

His move to Bayreuth (1804), where he lived until his death in 1825, was accompanied by an entrenchment of the more prosaic side of his character. He was by now a recluse, and took on those traits typical of the eccentric characters in his works. One reason for this was undoubtedly that his lofty political aspirations had been dashed, leaving him no choice but to play the role of impotent spectator as restoration proceeded apace.

His late works, which deliberately take up the thread of his early ones, were a return to satire. His *Komet* (1820–2), a 'socially critical portrait of the German age of restoration' (Harich), was permeated by a deep scepticism towards literature in general. A fragment, it was a 'born ruin', like *Die unsichtbare Loge* and *Flegeljahre*.

Another outsider: Kleist

Heinrich von Kleist was another outsider in the world of letters of his day. Intended by his family for a career as an army officer, the sensitive, musical and literary-minded Kleist soon abandoned the military life. With support chiefly from his sister Ulrike he led a restless, itinerant life fraught with self-doubt. It ended in 1811 with his suicide since, as he wrote in a farewell letter to his sister, there was 'no help [for him] on Earth'. He took his own life together with that of the seriously ill Henriette Vogel, who volunteered to die with him. Their dramatic deaths caused a huge public sensation, highlighting as they did in a dramatic way the difficulties of living outside the establishment.

Kleist's strength was in the sphere of drama: even his novellas are dramatic masterpieces. His first play, *Die Familie Schroffenstein* (*The Schroffenstein Family*) (1803) was still fully in accord with *Sturm und Drang* dramaturgy. His later works for the stage, however, evince a distinctive, unique tone. Despite his gift he was denied public acclaim: of his eight dramas only two were performed in his lifetime. A production of the *Zerbrochener Krug* (*The Broken Jug*) (1805–6) staged by Goethe at the Weimar Court theatre was a huge flop, which Kleist took badly. The reasons for this lack of acclaim are manifold: aside from the catastrophic state of German theatre at the time, his off-beat themes and his eccentric execution of them told heavily against him.

Kleist's anti-classical drama

Kleist's *Penthesilea* (1807), first performed in 1876, depicts with great psychological skill the relationship in a mythical pre-history between the Amazon queen Penthesilea and the Greek king Achilles. The fantastic element elaborated both in the plot and its execution was far ahead of the technical potential of the theatre of his day, and indeed the capacity of audiences to appreciate it. A counterpart to *Penthesilea* was created by

Kleist in *Kätchen von Heilbronn* (1807). He himself called Kätchen 'the obverse of the Amazon queen, her opposite pole – a being who is as powerful in acquiescence as the other was in action'. Unlike Penthesilea, Kätchen epitomises the image of women held up by the social consensus of the day. The fairy-tale-like, Romantic execution of the plot was also calculated to be well-received by contemporary audiences. It is no coincidence that *Kätchen* and *Der zerbrochene Krug* were the only two plays performed in Kleist's lifetime. His most interesting play, however, and one that has made a deep impression on twentieth-century audiences, returned to again and again by famous directors and actors, is *Prinz Friedrich von Homburg* (1809–11, published 1821). Never taken up by any theatre in Kleist's own time, the play's rejection was probably due less to its political stance than to its heavy emphasis on the Unconscious, emotion, dream and fantasy as forces shaping action.

A reflection of the wars of liberation

With his *Hermannsschlacht* (1808), Kleist produced a quintessentially political drama, intended to stir his contemporaries to rise up against Napoleon by inspiring them with the example of the struggle of the Teutons against the Romans. Like his *Katechismus der Deutschen* (*Catechism of the Germans*) (1809), this drama is part of the literature of the wars of liberation whose anti-Napoleonic feeling gave impetus to later nationalist sentiments. The same two plays may also be classified among a range of other more or less problematical texts dedicated to the struggle against Napoleon, which displayed a clear preference for national liberalism over finding solutions to social issues.

The myth of national orientation

Only a few authors, such as J.G. Seume (*Mein Sommer 1805, 1806 – My Summer* 1805, 1806; *Apokryphen – Apocryphas*, 1807–8), showed any attempt to combine these two tendencies. Fichte, in his *Reden an die deutsche Nation* (*Speeches to the German Nation*) (1807–8), and later E.M. Arndt (*Katechismus für teutsche Soldaten – Catechism for German Soldiers*), Rückert (*Katechismus für den deutschen Kriegs- und Wehrmann – Catechism for the German Military and Armed Men*) and Theodor Körner (*Leyer und Schwert – Lyre and Sword*), all preached hatred of the French, and therefore provided the ideological basis for what was later described as the 'traditional enmity' between Germany and France. E.M. Arndt's visionary piece *Der Rhein, Deutschlands Strom, aber nicht Deutschlands Grenze* (*The Rhine: Germany's River, but not its Boundary*) (1813) contains all those expansionist elements that were later to be invoked in subsequent altercations with France.

Finding his dramas unsuccessful, Kleist turned to publishing in an effort to make a living. Both the journals he founded – *Phöbus* (1807–8) and the *Berliner Abendblätter* (1810–11) – enjoyed little success. The publication of a third planned journal, the *Germania*, was thwarted by political circumstances. Although these journals brought him no financial success, however, they did at least provide him with a chance to publish his own texts. His *Erzählungen* (*Tales*) (1810–11), some of which were published in his own journals, again took up the theme of the tension between psychological and social reality, already broached in his dramas and elaborated theoretically in his essay *Über das Marionettentheater* (*On the Puppet Theatre*) (1810). Kleist's prose is marked by a terse, dramatic style and apparent objectivity anticipating narrative strategies that were later to become famous as distinctive features of Franz Kafka's prose.

Force and counter-force

One of Kleist's best-known stories is *Michael Kohlhaas* (1808). This novella portrays the correlation between social forces and individual force, or violence. Finding himself the victim of a series of arbitrary procedures, Michael Kohlhaas, described at the beginning of the text as 'one of the most law-abiding and yet repulsive of men', feels his sense of justice to have been offended. He suffers both personal and financial loss. This rouses him to fight back with an increasing violence that eventually brings him into conflict with state authority. The execution of Michael Kohlhaas at the end of the novella is the culmination of his own uncompromising conduct, which places him outside the accepted norms of society. The conciliatory, utopian note of the novella's conclusion (Kohlhaas has the satisfaction of seeing all his demands met before his death: both his black horses are paraded, well-fed, before him, and his sons are dubbed knights by the Elector of Brandenburg) cannot obscure the fact that the problem of force is unilaterally foisted here on to the individual, or that the social order can only be restored at the expense of the individual. The Kohlhaas story rapidly became the myth of a man who seeks to enforce justice by means of force, thereby incurring guilt – a myth that has attracted authors time and again. In the nineteenth century alone Kleist's novella was dramatised several times. In the modern period, Stefan Schütz (*Kohlhaas*, 1977), Elisabeth Plessen (*Kohlhaas*, 1982) and Yaak Karsunke (*Des Colhaas letzte Nacht – The Last Night of Colhaas*, 1979) have all returned to the theme. In his novella *Ein Mann namens Kohlhaas* (*A Man Named Kohlhaas*) (1982), freely adapted from Kleist's work, Dieter Eue deals with the entanglement of the individual in the machinery of society.

Conscious–Unconscious

The *Marquise von O* ... (1808) also deals with the use of force, this time against a marchioness. During the seizure of her father's home in an onslaught by Russian troops, the marchioness is saved from being raped by 'brutish murderous cut-throats' ('viehische Mordsknechte'). Her rescuer, Count F., however takes advantage of her fainting-fit to ravish her himself. The marchioness finds herself pregnant without knowing how or by whom. Showing self-assurance in this respect, she sets about finding the unknown father by placing an advertisement in the press. After many convoluted twists in the plot the Count is finally forgiven and a happy reconciliation arrived at, with due reference to the 'delicate mechanisms of the world'. Kleist narrates the rape scene as a combined stream of thoughts in whose place he presents the symbols of warfare. This leaves in limbo, as it were, the question of what the fainting-fit of the Marchioness is really about. 'In Ohnmacht? Schamlose Posse! Sie hielt, weiss ich, die Augen bloss zu' ('In a faint? What shameless farce! She is, I know, merely keeping her eyes closed'): with this ironic epigram, Kleist plays with the voyeuristic interest that the text evoked among his readers at the time, and which Eric Rohmer was later to make the starting-point of his film production of the *Marquise von O* ... (1976). The marchioness thus appears as a woman who chooses not to know what the reader knows, and for whom a fainting-fit is the only means of breaking out of sexual taboos and giving in to her own desires. This reinstatement of the Unconscious and of secret desires, however, does not lead to a model of female emancipation. On the contrary, the ambivalent conduct of the marchioness affirms the dichotomy in the portrayal of women that Kleist had presented in his two dramas *Penthesilea* and *Kätchen von Heilbronn*.

Most of Kleist's stories do not have utopian endings, like *Kohlhaas*, or reconciliatory ones as in the *Marquise*. They deal with force, desire, sexuality and struggle, emotions and deception, more often than not ending in murder and slaughter, as for example in *Der Findling* (*The Foundling*), *Der Zweikampf* (*The Duel*), *Das Erdbeben in Chili* (*The Earthquake in Chile*) and *Die Verlobung in St. Domingo* (*The Engagement in St Domingo*). At the level of content Kleist shows much common ground with Romanticism, although he differs fundamentally from the latter in his laconic, and yet emphatic language.

Kleist's topicality

Kleist's own dramatic life and death have inspired present-day authors to attempt to come to terms with him. Helma Sanders-Brahms, in her film *Heinrich* (1977), depicts a disjointed, internally fraught life, in which one scene follows another as in a dream sequence. It is not a historical film, endeavouring rather to understand Kleist as our contemporary. Christa Wolf has also drawn attention to the contemporary affinity for and fascination with an author described in his day by Goethe as 'sick', and for a long time left beyond the pale of literary scholarship in the GDR, with its fixation on classicism. The title of her story *Kein Ort, Nirgends* (*No Place, Nowhere*) (1979) refers to the homelessness of writers whose sex, as in the case of Günderode, or atypical literary practices, placed them outside the socio-political consensus. Karin Reschke approaches Kleist from a different angle. In her *Findebuch der Henriette Vogel* (1982), consisting of fictitious notes in the form of a diary, she gives a voice to the woman who is usually only referred to in Kleist biographies as his 'companion in suicide' ('Selbstmordgevatterin'), thereby expanding our view of the poet and his political and literary milieu to include a number of important new facets.

Greece as an ideal

Like Novalis, who met an early death, Friedrich Hölderlin is an author whose life and work have become a focus of legend. His poetry, impressive for its immense density of style, wealth of ideas, richness of imagery and symbolic power, stands apart from classical, Romantic and Jacobin lyric verse as belonging to a different order. Sensibility and melancholy are fused with hope for a restoration of devastated human and social harmony, making his a form of political poetry that lacks any trace of political agitation but is nevertheless convincing in the depth of its sensitivity, morality and political integrity, style and aesthetic form. It was in an idealised Greece, propounded to contemporaries by Winckelmann (*Gedanken über die Nachahmung der griechischen Werke* – *Thoughts on the Imitation of Greek Works*, 1755; *Geschichte der Kunst des Altertums* – *History of the Art of Antiquity*, 1764), that Hölderlin found a focal point for his conception of Humanism. His use of ancient strophic forms, for example, was no mere adoption of traditional models, but an expression of his sense of inner kinship with antiquity and a desire to manifest it in the contemporary era. Besides rigorous ancient verse forms, there are later hymns and elegies, by now transferred into freer rhythms, that give voice to his longing for a long-lost Greece (*Archipelagus, Mnemosyne, Patmos*). Even his numerous nature poems are permeated with longing for the lost kinship between man and nature.

The painful experience of alienation is a pervasive motif in Hölderlin's poetry that was little understood by his contemporaries. The importance of Hölderlin and the humanitarian, political approach of his work was not recognised and appreciated until our own century. The reception of Hölderlin's work into the canon was also impeded by the fact that many of his poems, particularly his later ones, are in the form of barely decipherable hand-written manuscripts, posing the would-be publisher with almost insuperable problems. The Stuttgart edition (1943–) by Friedrich Beissner and Adolf Beck – a pioneering achievement in the field of modern editing techniques – documented for the first time the stages in which texts were written, thereby attempting a new and authentic approach to the author's work. The Frankfurt edition by D.E. Sattler dispenses entirely with ideal texts, offering instead a typographical representation of the drafts from the first to the last beside a facsimile of the original manuscript.

Hölderlin a Jacobin?

What isolated Hölderlin most of all from his contemporaries was his persistent adherence to the ideals of the French Revolution. Together with Hegel and Schelling, he had first shown enthusiasm for it as a student at the Tübingen seminary. 'Bete für die Franzosen, die Verfechter der menschlichen Rechte' ('Pray for the French, the defenders of human rights'), he wrote in 1792 to his sister. Hölderlin, however – through his friend Isaac Sinclair, who planned a coup against the Duke of Württemberg and was therefore charged with high treason in 1805 – was to remain involved in revolutionary efforts in the southern German region even after 1800, long after the majority of German intellectuals had rejected the revolutionary option. The extent to which Hölderlin was involved in his friend's plans to overthrow the Duke is disputed. There can be no doubt, however, that Sinclair's trial for high treason, involvement in which Hölderlin only escaped because a medical certificate had declared him unfit to be interrogated, was a major factor in bringing on his mental illness. It was eventually necessary, from 1807 onwards, for him to spend the remaining 36 years of his life in the 'Tübingen Tower' in the care of a carpenter.

Hölderlin's enthusiasm for the Revolution, for a long time regarded by scholarship as incidental, has recently led to a fresh assessment of the author. The thesis of Pierre Bertaux, however, that Hölderlin was a Jacobin, and that his entire work should be read as a 'pervasive metaphor' for the Revolution (*Hölderlin und die Französiche Revolution*, 1969), is undoubtedly a polemical exaggeration prompted by reaction against traditional Hölderlin research. This largely excluded the political implications and background of social experience from analysis of Hölderlin's writing. A similar sensation to that of the Jacobin thesis was created by Bertaux's later thesis that Hölderlin was not mentally ill, but chose to stay in the Tübingen Tower as a form of self-imposed exile – and that his later poems are therefore not the documents of a madman, but encoded messages from a man who was outside the political consensus of his day and was only able to sustain his political and moral integrity in isolation. Obviously this later thesis of Hölderlin as the 'noble dissimulator' received as many rebuffs as Bertaux's earlier Jacobin thesis. Subsequent research has either refuted it entirely, or at the very least modified it, e.g. Adolf Beck (*Hölderlins Weg zu Deutschland* – *Hölderlin's Road to Germany*, 1982).

Nevertheless, although the radical approach of Bertaux's theses does not stand up to scrutiny, and his use of terms such as Jacobinism and madness leave him open to criticism, his polemical remarks have at least served to focus attention on the previously neglected political aspects of Hölderlin's works. His *Hyperion* (1797–9), for example, is a political confession dealing with the process whereby the author comes to terms with the French Revolution and the potential for revolutionary transformation in Germany. Hyperion's sophisticated political awareness, which distinguishes him from the heroes in novels of education and development, as well as his demand for freedom, both for himself and others – he takes part in the Greek war of independence – come up against entrenched lines of defence in his society, and fail to evoke a response or bring success. Hyperion's attempt to combine the private with the political in his life fails in the face of existing social structures. He is able to retain his identity only through isolation.

Underlying Goethe's *Wilhelm Meister* is the naive conviction of the author 'dass der Mensch trotz aller Dummheit und Verwirrungen, von einer höhern Hand geleitet, doch zum glücklichen Ziel gelange' ('that a man, despite all his stupidity and confusion, led by a higher hand, will ultimately arrive safely at his goal'). Hölderlin, by contrast, yielded to the painful insight, based on political experience, that the desire of the individual for happiness could not be fulfilled in the society of his day. Hölderlin shares his hero Hyperion's disillusionment with the potential of political action to achieve political change. He was unable to fulfil in his own life the hope he expresses at the end of the novel for a balance between Man, nature and society, based on happiness and harmony.

His unfinished tragedy *Empedokles* (1797–1800) is another reflection by Hölderlin on the alienation of human beings from both one another and nature. Empedokles, who represents an attempt by Hölderlin to come to terms with his own position as a poet, hopes to give a signal through his own sacrificial death, preparing the way for 'better days'. Empedokles' struggle against a priesthood remote both from nature and the gods is coded criticism by Hölderlin of the political circumstances of his day: 'This is no longer the age of kings'.

The Late Romantic period

Just as the end of the eighteenth century had been shaped by the experience of the French Revolution, so the beginning of the nineteenth century was dominated by the restoration. Hopes that the premises of freedom and equality would be transformed into political reality had been doubly dashed – on the one hand, by the path from the French Revolution back to monarchy, and the accompanying pan-European process of restoration, and on the other by the increasingly glaring social contradictions ensuing from socio-economic development towards middle-class capitalism. The prevailing reaction to this tide of restoration and increasing social contradictions was one of alienation. The mood of awakening of the Early Romantic period now gave way to a sombre, sarcastic and fragmented view of current conditions.

A classic example of this new phase in the Romantic movement is the work of E.T.A. Hoffmann, which soon attracted attention beyond Germany and was to exert a major influence on authors such as Gogol, Baudelaire and Poe. Like many of his characters, Hoffmann himself led a double life. His irksome daytime profession as a lawyer at the Supreme Court was exchanged at night for his 'real' life. Hoffmann's talents were so versatile that it was difficult for him to settle on one creative sphere. He drew, both played and composed music (he set Fouqué's *Undine* to music and was a successful composer and theoretician of music), and wrote again and again about the schism between the 'creative artist' and the 'Philistine' – a theme which other Romantic authors besides himself felt compelled to deal with. His *Fantasiestücke* (*Fantasy Pieces*) (1814) and *Nachtstücke* (*Night Pieces*) (1817) portray above all the 'dark side' of civilisation, with the unearthly, the demonic, madness and lawlessness as their focal point. His novel *Die Elixiere des Teufels* (*The Elixirs of Satan*) (1815–16) particularly highlights the fluid transition between mainstream and *Schauerromantik* (Romanticism of Horror).

The dark side of human existence

The interest of *Schauerromantik* in the 'dark side' of human existence – the unfathomable, the bizarre and the mysterious – distinguished it from the Enlightenment, which had taken upon itself the task of 'illuminating' darkness and shedding light. Although an element of the Wonderful had been in evidence in the Enlightenment, therefore, it had always been subordinate to 'pleasure' and 'utility'. The legitimation of the Wonderful as a poetic category (Bodmer, *Critische Abhandlung von dem Wunderbaren in der Poesie – A Critical Essay on the Wonderful in Poetry*, 1740) was integral to Enlightenment strategy. The beginnings of *Schauerliteratur*, with its stereotyped arsenal of ghostly apparitions, underground vaults, mysterious ruins, murder, inbreeding, rape, torture, *Doppelgängers*, satanism and black masses can thus be traced back to the Age of the Enlightenment, where it was nevertheless kept firmly inside the framework of rationality, lacking the autonomous status it acquired later in 'black Romanticism'.

Hoffmann depicts his own experience as a musician and writer in the character of the *Kapellmeister* (band-master) Kreisler, who appears both in *Kater Murr* (*Tom-Cat Murr*) (1820–2) and in the *Kreisleriana* stories

(1814–16). Hoffmann is concerned here not only with the clash between the world of the creative artist and that of the middle classes, and its destructive effects on the creative individual, but also with the whole problem of artistic creativity and existence as such. The plight of the creative artist is seen as a dual one – both as the result of his social isolation, and arising out of the demonic character of art and artistic creativity. This existential plight is sometimes resolved through fairy-tale, as in *Der Goldene Topf* (*The Golden Pot*) (1814). Elsewhere it ends in madness or self-destruction, as in *Kreisleriana*, or even murder, as in *Das Fräulein von Scuderi* (*Madame de Scuderi*) (1819), in which the goldsmith Cardillac is so attached to the jewellery he makes that he murders the people who purchase it so as to bring it back into his possession. One of Hoffmann's most famous tales is *Der Sandmann* (*The Sandman*), from his *Nachtstücken* (1817), in which he gives voice to the suppressed fears, dreams, desires and fantasies of the middle classes.

Hoffmann was one of the first to show an interest in the so-called 'dark side', recognising that social pressure to conform sometimes resulted in serious psychological deformation. Split personality, the phenomenon of the *Doppelgänger*, loss of the sense of identity or reality, as well as persecution mania, are all depicted in Hoffmann's tales as reactions symptomatic of a failure in social integration. The destruction of individuality is not restricted solely to the male individual. The tendency, already discernible in the classical novel of education and development, to reduce women to nothing more than stages in the development of men, and to define female identity purely in terms of a self-sacrificing devotion to men, takes on grotesque form in Hoffmann. Olympia, the understanding beloved of Nathanael in the *Der Sandmann*, is in reality no more than an automaton into whom Nathanael pours his desires and fantasies. The relationship between the sexes is thus depicted through an image that reveals it for what it is: as a male quest for identity that obliterates female individuality.

Romantic alienation

The problem of alienation is also the theme of the story *Peter Schlemihls wundersame Geschichte* (*The Wonderful Story of Peter Schlemihl*) (1814) by Adalbert von Chamisso. Schlemihl, the man without a shadow, is made into an allegory of an age in which it is questionable to have one's own identity. Peter Schlemihl sells his shadow to a stranger, receiving in return a sack of money that always fills up again. His wealth does not make him happy, however, because the loss of his shadow makes him an outsider, spurned by his fellow men. With the aid of seven-league boots he finally succeeds in fleeing from these painful circumstances. Chamisso worked some of his own experiences into this story: as a French emigrant who had come to Berlin with his family in 1792, he had difficulty making his way socially and politically in his new homeland. Not until a world tour (*Reise um die Welt*, 1836) opened up new experiences for him was he able to develop a moderate degree of middle-class optimism and a belief in progress. This ultimately enabled him to look on the French Revolution as a historically necessary event, and to follow the ensuing process of industrialisation with interest.

The melancholy quest for harmony

A third representative of the Late Romantic period besides Hoffmann and Chamisso was Joseph Freiherr von Eichendorff (Baron Eichendorff). His lyric poetry repeatedly evokes a long-lost harmony in images full of mood and melancholy. Lakes, mountains, forests, the song of nightingales, mysterious castles, moonlit nights, etc. are constantly recurring facets in his distinctive portrayal of nature, which reflects not real landscapes, but an ideal – the manifestation of an inner landscape of the soul and the emotions. His novel *Ahnung und Gegenwart* (*Intuition and the Present*) (1815) severely criticises the modern era, which for him is inextricably linked with the loathed figure of Napoleon, pointing out its destructive effects on the individual: 'Überall von der organischen Teilnahme ausgeschlossen, sind wir ein überflüssig stillstehendes Rad an dem grossen Uhrwerk des allgemeinen Treibens' ('Shut out on every side from organic participation, we are a useless, motionless wheel in the great clockwork mechanism of general activity'). The danger to human beings derives not only from the 'geschäftgen Welt' ('world of business'), however, but also from their own sensual nature and the enticements of the 'powers of darkness'. In the *Marmorbild* (*Image of Marble*) (1819) Eichendorff picks up the thread of the cult of Venus that is so central to Tieck's *Runenberg*, stressing even more strongly than Tieck the antagonism between the heathen, demonic Venus and the Christian, spiritual father God. The marble image of Venus, like the stone image of the mother in Brentano's *Godwi*, (1801), incorporates the secret desire to live out sensuality freely, which is depicted in the text as a wild and satanic power. The image of marble, contrasted in the text with the image of Mary the Mother of Jesus, is transformed into the terrible face of the Medusa. The hero Florio's choice of the virginal Bianka at the end of the tale also completes his rejection of the powers of darkness that have sought to gain mastery over him. Eichendorff saw the unleashing of sensuality not only as a psychological problem, however, but also as a social one. The warning that appears at the end of the tale *Das Schloss Dürande* (*Castle Dürande*) (1817) – 'Du aber hüte dich, das wilde Tier zu wecken in der Brust, dass es nicht plötzlich ausbricht und dich selbst zerreisst' ('Take care not to rouse the wild beast in your breast, lest it suddenly break free and destroy you') – refers not merely to the French Revolution, but more generally to the unleashing of sensuality.

The only thing that can offer a 'firm, secure hold' in the 'world of business' and against the 'powers of darkness' is a deliberate return to society by the individual, out of his alienated lifestyle. The tale *Aus dem Leben eines Taugenichts* (*From the Life of a Good-for-Nothing*) (1826) portrays a hero who withdraws cheerfully and without concern from the middle-class life of trade, finding happiness in the life of a vagabond. Despite its core of social criticism, this particular tale displays idyllic and escapist traits that pre-empt the Biedermeier era. Eichendorff is not, however, the sentimental idyll-writer or precursor of the *Wanderbewegung* that he was presented as until the twentieth century. His work manifests an immense sensitivity to the social contradictions of his age. Eichendorff's sadness at the lost integrity of humanity enriches his work with an additional layer of meaning. Behind the naïveté and overt cheerfulness of his texts we can discern a genuine striving to live life in the here and now.

A stock-taking of the age: Goethe's late works

Goethe was the towering figure in the world of letters in the first 30 years or so of the nineteenth century. In the period after the death of Schiller (1805), the suicide of Kleist (1811) and Hölderlin's decline into derangement (1807), no other author succeeded in winning such a prominent position in the public awareness. This is even true with respect to Jean Paul, who from the hindsight of the *Vormärz* era was upheld as a counterpart to Goethe, but whose resigned attitude after 1804 precluded him from being a counterpart to Goethe, the universal man. Hoffmann and Eichendorff were likewise far more one-sided than Goethe, both by temperament and aspiration. The latter, in his incomplete autobiography *Dichtung und Wahrheit* (*Poetry and the Truth*) (1814) saw his own life as exemplary, casting himself in the mould of a personality representative of his age. Hoffmann and Eichendorff's ironic and grotesque, or idyllic and resigned works are no more than component aspects taken up by Goethe in his later works, where he raised them to a new symbolic order either by subordinating or eradicating them.

A glance into the modern age

In his later works Goethe deals with themes concerned with the problems of the age, of which he had already formed a vision together with Schiller in his classical period. This was now subjected to a fresh, expanded and deeper approach. The sheer length of Goethe's life enabled him to perceive connections between experiences that were denied to other authors. He was not only a spectator of the post-Napoleonic era, but also a contemporary observer of the advent of the modern age, complete with steam engines, stocks and shares, industrialisation and road construction. *Gespräche mit*

Goethe (*Conversations with Goethe*) (1836–48), recorded by his close and trusted assistant Eckermann, reveal just how closely Goethe followed the changes taking place, and how concerted were his efforts to come to terms with them.

Goethe's *Wilhelm Meister* and *Faust*, on which he worked for the best part of a lifetime, were the outstanding products of his post-classical phase, and occupy a central place in the works of his old age. Work on *Wilhelm Meister*, which he left for over a decade after completing the *Lehrjahre*, was taken up again in 1807. Fourteen years later in 1821 the first version of the *Wanderjahre* appeared with the addendum 'oder die Entsagenden' ('or the years of resignation'). In the *Wanderjahre* Goethe expands the original framework of his story not only in terms of content – he sends Wilhelm off on new travels to discover new spheres of experience (the society of the resigned, pedagogy, a colonisation project, an emigration enterprise, the nature of machinery, etc.) – but also by greatly extending the structure far beyond the traditional boundaries of the novel. Its blend of epic and lyric passages, the complex interaction between the overall plot and inserted component novellas ('Der Mann von fünfzig Jahren' – 'The Man of Fifty Years'; 'Die neue Melusine' – 'The New Melusine'), and its juxtaposition of documentary and fictional passages make the *Wanderjahre* an experiment in narrative that anticipates modern writing in its complex symbolic arrangement.

The Wahlverwandschaften (*Elective Affinities*)

Goethe's novella *Die Wahlverwandschaften*, originally intended for inclusion in the *Wanderjahre*, grew so lengthy that he developed it into a novel in its own right (1809). It thus acquired structural similarities with the *Wanderjahren*, likewise containing inserted novellas, passages of reflection and maxims. It also treats of the theme of 'resignation', but differently from *Wilhelm Meister*, with the latter's universal scope. Instead, it contains space, time and the protagonists within the intimacy of a private story. With the title *Elective Affinities* Goethe, who was both interested and well-versed in the natural sciences, plays on a term from chemistry. It originally refers to the process whereby particular chemical elements attract and repel one another. Here, however, Goethe transposes the term to moral and social life. Eduard and Charlotte, who have found happiness in marriage somewhat late in life, and who live in self-imposed isolation, have their peaceful life disturbed by the arrival of a friend, Otto, and his foster-daughter Ottilie. This arrival sets in motion a process of attraction and repulsion akin to that in the test-tube, causing the original couples to split and new ones to form. Although this 'double adultery' never goes beyond the mind, the harmony that had prevailed is lost for ever. The two men leave their estates, the child of Eduard and Charlotte drowns because of

Ottilie, who thereupon refuses to eat and dies of exhaustion, and Eduard himself dies shortly afterwards. Charlotte has the two lovers buried in a common grave. This conciliatory conclusion cannot obscure the fact that the conflict between sensuality and the moral order can have fatal consequences unless those involved work their way towards resignation, abiding by the prevailing moral order of their own free will. The demonic element that can break into marriage like a natural force has its counterpart in the political sphere. These traits are encoded in the text by motifs such as boredom and idleness, which characterise the aristocratic milieu. Goethe confided to Riemer in 1808 that his aim in the novel had been to portray 'social conditions and the conflicts caused by them in a symbolic way'.

The 'crown' not only of Goethe's old age, but of his life's work, is his *Faust*, which was his 'major enterprise', occupying him for a period of over 50 years. The first scenes were written before 1775, but were not published until after his death, when they became known as *Urfaust*. He took up work on *Faust* again during his journey to Italy (1786–8), publishing *Faust, ein Fragment* (*Faust, a Fragment*) in 1790. Inspired by Schiller, he took up the Faust theme again around the turn of the century, publishing *Faust, Der Tragödie erster Teil* (*Faust the Tragedy Part One*) in 1808. It is clear that Goethe had by no means finished with the theme, not only from the 'Part One' in the subtitle, but also from the fact that he was already working on the Helena act. It was 1824, however, before he resumed work in a concentrated way, this time with the support of Eckermann, to develop a scheme for Part Two, which he managed to finish in 1831, shortly before his death. *Faust, der Tragödie, zweiter Teil* (*Faust, the Tragedy Part Two*) was not published until after his death, in the *Nachgelassene Werke* (*Unpublished Works*).

Faust, a German story that lives on

Goethe's two works stem from a long historical tradition that in turn inspired a new tradition. The story itself is derived from a *Volksbuch*, the *Historia von D. Johann Fausten, dem weitbeschreyten Zauberer und Schwarzkünstler* (*The History of D. Johann Faust, the Notorious Sorcerer and Black Magician*) (1587). This story had already been dramatised by Christopher Marlowe as *The Tragic History of Doctor Faustus* (1604). In the eighteenth century, Lessing (*Faust-Fragmente* – *Faust Fragments*, 1755–81), Maler Müller (*Faust Leben dramatisiert* – *A Dramatised Life of Faust*, 1776–8) and Klinger (*Fausts Leben, Taten and Höllenfahrt* – *The Life, Deeds and Descent into Hell of Faust*, 1791, *Der Faust der Morgenländer* – *The Faust of the Orient*, 1797) had all attempted to tackle the Faust story. It was nevertheless Goethe's adaptation of Faust, with its first and second parts, that took hold as the 'classic' interpretation used for the subsequent endeavours of later generations. Major texts in the post-Goethe tradition are Grabbe's *Don Juan und Faust* (1829), Lenau's *Faust* (1836), Heine's dance poem *Faust* (1847), Vischer's *Faust, der Tragödie dritter Theil* (*Faust, the Tragedy Part Three*) (1862), a parody on the failed revolution of 1848, Lunacharski's *Faust und die Stadt* (*Faust and the City*) (1918), a socialist Faust model on the basis of revolutionary experiences in the vanguard of the Russian October Revolution, Valéry's subjective adaptation of the story as *My Faust* (1946), and Thomas Mann's 'artist novel' *Doktor Faustus* (1947). There are many other texts, as well as adaptations for the opera (Schumann, Berlioz, Gounod, Busoni, Eisler), showing that the Faust story continues to be relevant in the present day.

The theme of *Faust* is the aspiration of the middle-class individual towards recognition, personal happiness and meaningful social activity. Whereas in the original version Faust was a unique and unrepeatable personality of genius, after the French Revolution he became more a representative of humanity and a symbol of the human struggle towards higher development. The course of his development through various phases – the middle-class sphere of existence of Gretchen, the demonic witches' sabbath and the classical *Walpurgisnacht*, the medieval imperial court and the world of antiquity – culminates, as in *Wilhelm Meister*, in the practice of a profession for the general good. The attempt by the devil to bring Faust down from his higher aspirations into the *gemein* – the base – ultimately fails. Although incurring a great deal of guilt in his passage through the world, Faust is saved at the end of the drama, just as his lover Gretchen is in Part One. The divine plan for the world has made allowance just as much for failure and error on the part of the individual as for his positive attributes. The harmony of the whole remains undisturbed. The issue of middle-class individuality is in this way objectivised and transposed into timeless dimensions. Part Two has placed considerable demands on audiences, both then and now, with its elegant dovetailing of the various spheres of symbolism, as well as in its blend of the ancient (the Helena scene), the Middle Ages (the imperial court) and the modern age (the colonisation project). Part One of *Faust* was first performed in 1829, Part Two in 1854, and both were performed together for the first time in 1876. *Faust II* did not become part of the fixed repertoire of the German stage until the twentieth century, however.

The impact of Faust

This incorporation of *Faust* into the German repertoire is only comprehensible against the background of political developments in Germany during the nineteenth and twentieth centuries. In particular, the founding of the Reich in 1871, accompanied by the ideological need for a confirmation of national identity, created the first preconditions for a positive reception of *Faust*. Faust became increasingly stylised into an ideal figure, the 'essence of Germanness' that was to 'heal the world'. The Faustian aspect, as an allegedly typical German trait, thus became increasingly removed from the Goethe text, developing into a 'freely disengaged general concept' (Schwerte) and a vogue word that could be exploited for various ideological ends. By declaring Faust to be a representative of the entire Western culture, Oswald Spengler, a cultural philosopher whose ideas gave him an affinity with National Socialism, laid the foundations in 1918 for a co-opting of Goethe's text into an imperialist power struggle and the national-socialist policy of hegemony. This abuse of German classicism by fascism is undoubtedly one of the reasons why Goethe became a difficult author to approach after 1945, and also why the evaluation of his work has been subject to such wild swings. Goethe himself spoke of the 'incommensurability' of the work as a whole, and of the relative self-sufficiency of its 'mutually reflecting structures' – thus anticipating the difficulties that interpretation of the text would pose. Whereas earlier philological research into Goethe tended to attribute the symbolism in *Faust II* to timeless *Urphänomene*, primeval phenomena in the sense meant by Goethe, more recent research has tended to elaborate on the social aspects of the work, interpreting *Faust II* as an 'allegory of the nineteenth century' (Heinz Schlaffer).

Interpretation

Although some controversy still persists concerning the interpretation both of the work as a whole and its individual parts, critics are nevertheless of one mind as regards their positive assessment of its form and metrical diversity. *Faust II* is not a tragedy in the classical sense, but rather a blend of all the basic essential forms of European drama – 'from Attic tragedy, through medieval mystery play, sixteenth-century folk drama and court theatre to the Romantic *Gesamtkunstwerk* of the present day' (Borchmeyer). The metrical form of the work is no less richly diverse. Here, too, Goethe has adapted the entire Western tradition, incorporating the metre of doggerel, the Alexandrine, trimeters and iambs, to mention only a few, but always in a way relevant to the situation and evocative of the various protagonists. In *Faust II*, therefore, Goethe embraces the entire gamut of poetic diction in a way never seen before, thereby expanding the potential for dramatic expression in a way comparable to the innovations he created in the lyric sphere with his poem anthology *West-östlicher Divan* (1819, expanded edition 1827), and for the novel with the *Wanderjahre*.

The admiration of the classics and the impact of classicism in the nineteenth and twentieth centuries

It is no easy matter to establish definitively what 'classicism' really is. At one level it may be understood as a timeless ideal of life and art created by exceptional artists and geniuses, as an ultimate norm and pattern radiating from a long-distant past and into the future. This was how Humanists understood the 'classical' from the Renaissance until the end of the eighteenth century. For them, the historical manifestation of the classical was antiquity, specifically the golden age of Periclean Greece in the fifth century BC and the flowering of Rome in the Augustan era around the time of the birth of Christ. The same 'classical' appellation, however, was variously accorded – by the Italians to the fifteenth century AD, the age of Leonardo da Vinci and Raphael, by the English and Spanish to the sixteenth century, the age of Shakespeare and Cervantes, by the French to the seventeenth century in honour of Corneille, Molière and Racine, and finally by the Germans to the age of Goethe. These designations are symptomatic of a changed understanding of the term that needs to be seen in the context of the formation of the modern nation-state.

Classicism as a universal human attribute?

By this time the 'classical' typically expressed not only the humanist element of universal humanity, but also the specific factor of national identity, which is so modern that there is a complete divergence not only between ancient and modern classicism, but even between one national manifestation of classicism and another. This brings varying interpretations of classicism into play, as becomes particularly clear in any discussion of German classicism. One interpretation reads classicism as a phenomenon of two opposite poles (contrasting with the baroque, the Romantic, or the modern), while another sees it as a synthesis of two opposing forces (e.g. the ancient and the modern, the cosmopolitan and the national, or nature and spirit). One interpretation thus sees classicism as a cultural heritage that continues to live on, a contemporary mindfulness, as it were, of previously attained consummate standards and works. A unique example of this, apart perhaps from Shakespeare or Homer, would be the story of Goethe's impact on the nineteenth and twentieth centuries. The classical is nevertheless also capable of deteriorating into an oppressive dominance of accepted standards, exerting a cold, marble-like effect, impeding change and ossifying into classicism for its own sake. In a country with a blighted political history like Germany, classicism can be accorded the status of myth and legend in its cultural life. The fact that this did indeed occur to an unusual degree in nineteenth century Germany was not without significant consequences for the cultural and political self-image of the nation. As a contemporary of German classicism, albeit one of different views, the Romantic Friedrich Schlegel asserted: 'Most people are unable to conceive of the classical without thinking in terms of a radius of several miles, weight in hundredweights, or a time-span stretching into aeons.'

Madame de Staël

When at the beginning of the nineteenth century Madame de Staël, a fierce opponent of Napoleon, uttered the often quoted *mot* that the Germans were a 'nation of poets and thinkers', her words were directed largely against France. Since up to that time France's history had made it the leading European nation of culture, this accolade was perhaps most due to France herself. In fact the unforeseen flowering of philosophy and poetry in Germany after 1770 was, strictly speaking, more a question of catching up with the cultural level that was already a tradition in France and England – despite the fact that the latter at that time had no writers of the stature of Goethe or Hegel. The all too avid predisposition of many Germans for cultural veneration, rooted in the stunted political growth of a Germany that had splintered into small states and nervous 'great powers', led to more than the harmless but ridiculous kind of local intellectual patriotism discernible in the Swabian verses: 'Der Schiller und der Hegel, der Uhland und der Hauff, / Das ist bei uns der Regel, fällt gar nicht weiter auf' ('Schiller, Hegel, Uhland, Hauff, the authors that we prize, / Are just the usual stuff with us, they can no more surprise'). Backed by the declarations of the very classic authors on whom the intellectual greatness of Germany was built, a view came to prevail of Germans poor in deeds and rich in ideas, their dignity a 'moral greatness', 'chosen by the spirit of the world to work during the struggle of the age on the eternal edifice of human education' and whose day will come as 'the harvest of all time' (Schiller). Only a little later Fichte asserted that 'the world will be healed by the essence of Germanness'. From 1850 onwards this classical idea of the special cultural vocation of the Germans was to have fatal consequences, disguised in the cloak of a cosmopolitan tendency towards nationalist and imperialist messianism.

'Germany's vocation'

This trend was writ large in Geibel's poem *Deutschlands Beruf* (*Germany's Vocation*) (1861), in which he styles Germany as the 'core' of the world and the 'heart of Europe', and expresses a longing for a unifying, powerful emperor who will put the French, English and Russians in their places:

> Macht und Freiheit, Recht und Sitte,
> Klarer Geist und scharfer Hieb
> Zügeln dann aus starker Mitte
> Jeder Selbstsucht wilden Trieb,
> Und es mag am deutschen Wesen
> Einmal noch die Welt genesen.

Might and Freedom, Law and Ethic
Clear spirit and a strong blow
Will then bridle from a strong centre
All the self-seeking of wild desires,
And once again the world may be healed
Through the essence of Germanness.

Dating from the *Vormärz* era, Hoffmann von Fallersleben's *Lied der Deutschen* (1841), written in exile in English Heligoland, extols a united Germany as the highest good. This was to take on a new, more sinister and imperialist meaning after the founding of the Reich in 1871, in the context of the new, powerful, but nonetheless still *kleindeutsch* entity: 'Deutschland, Deutschland über alles, / über alles in der Welt!' (the German national anthem since 1922). German writers and thinkers have subsequently notoriously excelled in their endeavours to provide on the basis of classical and Romantic ideas chauvinistic, and later fascist justifications for the uniqueness of German culture, German politics and the German race, sometimes distorting those ideas, at other times drawing logical conclusions from them. By that time, however, the familiar words concerning the nation of writers and thinkers (*Dichter und Denker*) had long been supplemented by the 'nation of the judge and hangman' (*Richter und Henker*) (K. Kraus).

The Kunstperiode

Shortly before Goethe's death, Heine coined the term *Kunstperiode* to designate the immediately preceding phase of German literature and intellectual growth that had begun in about 1780. For Heine, this was bound up with the life and work of Goethe, and for that reason its conclusion would also be marked by Goethe's death. Long after the *Vormärz* era, this view continued to be shared by many others. Historians of literature, for example, would end their accounts of German literature in 1832. All literature that came after Goethe was hence deemed 'modern'. Although this designation was not left unchallenged, works by certain isolated 'classic' authors of the Goethe era found their way into the post-1830 canon, especially from 1850 onwards. This process was accompanied by a parallel tendency not to recognise other literature that failed to conform to the criteria of classic authors, and that was now relegated to the category of 'trivial literature'. A body of minority 'polite' literature deemed to constitute literary tradition was thus distinguished from a more substantial body of popular 'lesser' literature, which was deprived of a history. Lessing, Herder and Jean Paul were rapidly moved into the 'classic' camp to take their places beside Goethe and Schiller, soon to be followed by a few authors from the second half of the eighteenth century (e.g. Wieland and

Klopstock) and even to a limited extent from among the Romantics (e.g. Eichendorff). Forster, Hölderlin and Kleist were at this stage unrecognised, overlooked, or even completely unappreciated as 'classic' authors. This exclusivity, characteristic of the classic literary heritage, derived in no small measure from the fact that with the exception of Jean Paul all the major authors of the Goethe era were published by the leading publishing house of the day, Cotta Verlag. Until 1867, the so-called 'Year of Classic Authors', when the term of copyright protection ran out for all authors who had died before 9 November 1837 ('The classic authors are free!'), Cotta enjoyed a publishing monopoly on the elite of German literature, exploiting it to the full with high prices and not always accurate editions.

The boom in the classics

In the *Vormärz* period a certain amount of cheaper competition to Cotta appeared in the form of pirated editions, volumes of selected works and series (e.g. C. J. Meyer's *Miniaturbibliothek deutscher Classiker*, which attained well over 100,000 copies in several editions). The real boom in the classics did not occur until after 1867, however. A flood of new, cheap and *de luxe* editions of the classics now enticed purchasers even from the lower middle classes. The only extant example of these is Reclam's *Universalbibliothek*, whose first volume was Goethe's *Faust*. Commercialisation brought with it a fresh extension of the term 'classic literature'. There was now a tendency to extend the category from the intellectual giants of the turn of the century to include writers who had died before 1837. From the middle of the nineteenth century onwards there was also an increase in public celebrations for writers of the acknowledged canon (especially Schiller, for whom celebrations reached their high point in 1859, the centenary of his birth). Statues (formerly an accolade reserved for heads of state and generals) of famous writers and thinkers were now erected in public places (to Luther in Wittenberg in 1821, at Walhalla near Regensburg in 1842, to Lessing in Brunswick in 1853, the Goethe–Schiller monument in Weimar in 1857, etc.). This practice was soon augmented to include the naming of streets and squares after esteemed writers. The classics even began at last to feature in the German teaching syllabuses of grammar schools.

This official and public celebration of classic authors was to develop incalculable ideological functions. In addition to continuously feeding the irrational German 'we are somebody' complex, this harping on the intellectual unity of the nation propounded by (select) classic authors – after the failed democratic revolution of 1848 – undoubtedly helped prepare the ground for, and legitimate, the revolution from above that led to the conservative imperial Reich. Critical contemporaries were nevertheless fully aware even then that this renewed and expanding recognition of classic

authors (and of the category itself) was hardly conducive to deeper understanding, let alone true education. A full century earlier, Lessing had
foreseen:

> Wer wird nicht unsern Klopstock loben?
> Doch wird ihn jeder lesen? – Nein!
> Wir wollen weniger erhoben,
> Doch fleissiger gelesen sein!

> Who will not praise Klopstock indeed?
> But will they deign his works to read? – No!
> We would rather be less extolled
> And more avidly read!

The impact of the classics

In order to answer the question of how avidly the classics were read, by
whom, and what else may have been read, possibly more avidly, instead,
it will be necessary to call to mind some of the circumstances that were
important for the dissemination of classic literature and its impact. In 1820,
for example, Perthes the Hamburg bookseller was the first of his profession
to display bound books for sale in his shop. Until then, and long afterwards, it was customary to supply books only to order, and in the form
of uncut, unbound printed sheets – not a convenient or cheap means of
access to literature. Moreover, until the middle of the nineteenth century
the major public libraries kept specialist literature only, but no *belles-
lettres*. If one did not wish, or could not afford to buy literature, it was
only available by subscribing to the wide variety (especially after 1815) of
pocket-books, almanacs, and literary magazines or, above all, through cheaper lending libraries, which became much more widespread after the end
of the eighteenth century. These had substantial stocks at their disposal,
and poor and rich alike availed themselves of their facilities. In fact these
libraries, often denounced as 'dens of iniquity' as they specialised mainly
in supplying novels for mass entertainment, only rarely kept books by
classic authors, and then usually only their few commercial successes.
Goethe's *Werther* and *Götz*, Schiller's *Geisterseher*, a little of Jean Paul and
later Chamisso's *Schlemihl* were among these few works.

Added to the sheer unavailability of many works by classic authors was
the fact that a considerable proportion of their works had been mutilated
by censorship until 1848. Some were not published at all in the author's
lifetimes, but only posthumously (e.g. Goethe's *Urfaust*, which was not
published until 1887).

The concept of Humanist education

The dissemination of drama by classic authors was scarcely more favourable. To cite a few examples: the Weimar stage, run personally by Goethe and Schiller, staged only 17 works by Goethe, with a total of 156 performances (most frequently *Die Geschwister* – *The Siblings*), only 14 works by Schiller, with 174 performances (most frequently *Wallenstein*), three works by Lessing in 42 performances, and only one work by Kleist (*Der zerbrochene Krug* – *The Broken Jug*, a flop at the time). In contrast, playwrights who are virtually unknown today, but who were famous in their own day, enjoyed ever more resounding successes: Iffland, for example, had 31 works performed 206 times, and Kotzebue had 69 works performed 410 times. Raupach, acclaimed dramatist of the Royal Theatre (*Königlicher Schauspiel*) in Berlin, with his 120 dramas, was even more extensively performed: by royal command his 14 Hohenstaufen dramas were performed no less than 1,837 times in succession.

The Romantics, revered in histories of literature since the late nineteenth century, had little scope for making their works well-known in their own day. Brentano's works, for example, published only sporadically in his own lifetime, first appeared in collected form after 1850, and only then began to exert influence in the modern age. His anthology of folk songs, *Des knaben Wunderhorn*, edited with Arnim, was his sole success. Arnim's other works, like those of Novalis, Wackenroder and even Friedrich Schlegel, were largely ignored in the nineteenth century.

Recognition and esteem were most readily granted to those Romantic writers who sold out, more or less, to diluted or degraded notions of the Romantic, such as *Zauberromantik, Schauerromantik* and so-called German *Waldromantik*. Hence the popularity of Tieck (according to Hebbel the 'King of the Romantics'), who invented the key word *Waldeinsamkeit* – 'the solitude of the forest', E. T. A. Hoffmann ('Hoffmann of the ghosts'), and Eichendorff, whose *Taugenichts* (1826) was published in no less than 100 new editions and reprints between 1850 and 1925.

The substantial number of classical-Romantic also-rans, descendants and imitators who overtook classic authors with their domestic family dramas, melodramas, dramas of destiny, knight-errant romances, *Schauerromanen*, love novels, and even their lyric verse of 'sensibility', conserved, popularised and trivialised the original ideas and forms. Although in one respect their work is a mockery of the achievements of authors such as Schiller or Novalis, they are nevertheless in another respect the obverse of that classical high-mindedness and Romantic awareness of the artistic whose absolutist approach and holistic tendencies were all too apt to leave the contemporary reader alone with his limited potential and his day-to-day needs. 'My thoughts can never be popular', affirmed Goethe to Eckermann in a discussion of the troublesome relationship between the classical writer and his readership. 'They are not written for the masses, but for individuals who want and are searching for something similar, and who share similar approaches.' The question is not broached as to who or what was supposed to make the individual capable of wanting 'something similar'. The great writers of the Goethe era were thus something akin to a 'lodge of freemasons'. As Humboldt put it: 'You have to be an initiate'.

Instruction in German

It was in fact the new conception of educational institutions (grammar schools and universities) developed by Humboldt in the nineteenth century that sought to universalise the principle of initiating students into something higher and of timeless validity – particularly in German instruction and in the study of German philology. Immense importance was attached in this process to the study of the classics, from ancient times until the eighteenth century. Unfortunately, however, this new brand of humanitarian education through classic works, on the model of the former catechism classes ('collecting pennies in the little purse of faith, so as to draw from this treasure in later life' – H. J. Frank) misfired from the outset. What remained in practice was a strictly regulated 'going through' of texts in the canon, and the learning by rote of the best passages, which remained with the student for a lifetime. The result was simply a sterile capacity to churn out intimidating familiar passages. From the middle of the nineteenth century onwards, literary education in grammar schools, what was performed in the middle-class *Bildungstheater* (theatre of education) and various agencies of cultural pedagogy and policy – ranging from literary criticism to poets' associations – all promoted a brand of literary education that held up the 'classics' as an unassailable elite order. Since, therefore, 'higher education' was itself the privilege of an elite, as distinct from 'popular (*volkstümlich*) education', the bulk of the population was excluded from it, even though it was provided at their expense. The 'classics' and their dissemination were thus something decidedly exclusive within national, middle-class culture. Viewed overall, therefore, it should be pointed out that the real impact of the 'classical' message being put over consisted not in the humanitarian ideal in the wider sense, but in the latent 'inhuman influence of what amounted to a particular humanity' (C. Bürger).

There has not so far been any attempt in any phase of the dissemination of the classics to deduce the lessons to be learned from this dilemma concerning the origin and crisis of middle-class cultural development. Faced with the very real poverty of the classical humanitarian ideal in the twentieth century, one is left with Alfred Andersch's question in *Der Vater eines Mörders* (*The Father of a Murderer*) (1980): 'Does Humanism then preserve us from nothing at all? This question is calculated to drive one to despair.'

Wilhelminism

The dissemination of the classics in Wilhelmine Germany was in crisis in the final years of the Weimar Republic. Schoolmasters such as W. Schön-brunn and J. Frankenberger protested against what they saw as a dead cult of the classics, calling for a more realistic approach to written works, and more realistic, modern texts. They soon found themselves with support from an unwanted quarter. The 'modernity' of the National Socialists consisted in following this very tendency, albeit under fascist watchwords: Germanic-Nordic, homeland-oriented poetry 'of the people' now supplanted 'comfortable' classic, middle-class Humanist texts as compulsory reading matter. The inherent conservatism of this process should be clear. The former principle of adhering to a canon, closely linked with what was by this time the meaningless term 'classical', was left unchallenged. The sheer power of this educational cliché, unwholesomely bound up with the teaching of the history of literature from the very outset, becomes clear when one realises that it was scarcely broken even after 1945 and after necessary adjustments to the previous canon had been made. This is equally true of German instruction in the Federal Republic (particularly in the restoration period of the 1950s and 1960s), as it is of the rather different German instruction of the former German Democratic Republic, where it persisted largely in the guise of a theory of cultural heritage. 'An injustice is being done, after all, and not only to him who is on the receiving end of the works of the past,' (as E. Schmalzriedt described in 1971 the inhuman consequences of this late phase in the history of the classics from antiquity up to the Goethe era) 'but also to those past works themselves. Not only because *all* works of the past and present, from whatever age, culture or intellectual discipline, are, as products of the human spirit, documents of the process by which human beings come to terms with the world in which they live, therefore constituting models for a rich source of instruction. More than this, it is injustice because as soon as these works are divorced from their historical dimension in terms of ideals they become vulnerable to arbitrary political manipulation. If Plato and Thucydides, Caesar, Tacitus (!) and Horace could be distorted into crown witnesses for fascism and its cultural and political ambitions, this was not least because of the unhistorical glorification of the "classical". This process brutally disfigured into their very opposite the humanising effects inherent in a venerated work that was held up as a model.'

The legitimate heritage of classicism

Despite all this, another foray into the nineteenth century, chiefly the first half, is still worthwhile. Here there were already a number of 'initiated' (in the classical sense) and important (as part of the process of German

256

literary history) writers. On the other hand, they were not exactly popular, and their work would have been unthinkable without the model of classical-Romantic creative achievements. Worthy of note, apart from those writers of the classical-Romantic generation who were still living and writing beyond 1815, or even 1830 (Goethe, Jean Paul, E. T. A. Hoffmann, Tieck, Eichendorff, etc.), were first and foremost writers such as Grillparzer, Mörike, Droste, Stifter, Immermann and Hebbel. Divergent though these authors were in their political awareness, aesthetic conceptions and literary techniques, they all nevertheless share one fundamental tenet in their understanding of themselves as creative writers. They were unanimous in the conviction that, in view of the growing gulf between the classical idea of art and humanity on the one hand and middle-class capitalist reality on the other, their primary duty was one of preservation – of standing, in other words, 'where Goethe and Schiller stood' (Grillparzer). Inasmuch as they continued, even in the face of increasing adversity, to adhere to the idea that art should be distinct from 'life', in order that life should in turn be perfected by art, they were initially able to follow on from classicism and Romanticism in their literary practice. Thus they directly adopted existing forms, techniques and themes (e.g. the novel of development, historical drama, song, the concepts of the tragic and the symbolic, the middle-class hero, the portrayal of women, etc.).

At the same time, however, they also inherited the troublesome relationship so typical of classicism and Romanticism between the creative artist and the public. 'In these days,' Stifter could now write, 'let no-one to whom God has lent the strength for artistic creativity lose heart. Let him work bravely on in higher spheres, enlivened by his spirit, though recognition come only from other initiates, and his reward lie in his awareness alone.'

We can discern here the early formulation of a perception of the creative artist's role, and indeed of art itself, that was to have repercussions into late nineteenth century Germany and beyond. This formulation was by now devoid of the earlier Enlightenment proclivity for practical contact with day-to-day life and constructive effects. Post-classical, post-Romantic art is viewed as a form of contemplation that deliberately separates itself from the real world, establishing its own resigned, inward-looking world of the mind, a world in which consolation and utopia, reconciliation and education (as a manifestation of the aesthetic) are possible in a way they could never be anywhere in middle-class life.

In contrast with this, the literature of the German *Vormärz* era strove to achieve a new vision of literature through a critical analysis based on further elaboration of the basic aesthetic positions of the *Kunstepoche*. The connection that had been asserted by the Enlightenment between literary and political action was to be revived and developed in practice under the new social conditions.

VORMÄRZ: THE RUN-UP TO 1848

The dawn of the Industrial Revolution

By June 1848 there was a virtually direct railway network running from Munich to Berlin, from Stettin to the Rhine and on to Paris. The steamship, gaslight and telegraph were in operation; factories and child labour had been introduced. Middle-class political parties had crystallised into the conservatives, liberals and democrats, and Marx and Engels published the *Communist Manifesto*.

And yet the first half of the nineteenth century, especially the period from 1815 to 1848, is still associated in most minds with mail coaches, the Brothers Grimm, the spinning wheel and the night-cap, Spitzweg's *Armer Poet in der Dachstube* (*The Poor Poet in the Garret*), Eichendorff's *Taugen-ichts* (*Good-for-Nothing*) between the mill and the castle and the night watchman with halberd and horn. The era conjures up the Romantic *Biedermeier*: a rural, pre-industrial, still 'poetic' Germany.

The image of an epoch

This distortion of the past tends to overlook one crucial fact: that in a time of seeming peace a civil war was brewing that was to culminate in revolution. This was an era of far-reaching structural changes in both the political and social spheres, an era of new inventions and discoveries in the natural sciences and technology – changes that were sweeping aside centuries of tradition with increasing momentum. Finance capital, the anonymous capitalist society and the world of investment and speculation all made their appearances in Germany, too, and with them came new social types: the entrepreneur and the factory-owner. These in turn improved the social status of the middle classes as a whole. Politically, however, the middle class was still without representation.

Political and economic factors

The process of transformation from an inherited feudal order to middle-class capitalism taking place across Europe is commonly referred to as the Industrial Revolution. In Germany, a phase of accelerated change was set in motion towards the end of the eighteenth century, and brought to fruition around the mid-1830s. A similar process had been at work in England from 1780.

The reasons for the relative time-lag between Germany and the rest of Western Europe may be traced far back into its previous history. They include territorial fragmentation, limited economic resources and the 'enlightened Absolutism' of German rulers. The result was that the German middle classes remained politically dependent and passive. Until 1815 the loosening and removal of feudal chains in Germany was a process driven not by massive political pressure from a middle class in the process of winning political emancipation, as in France, but from the outside. It was achieved either indirectly through French dominance of the Rhine federation states, or from above, as in the case of state reforms in Prussia. The defeat of Napoleon in 1813 and 1815 was accompanied by a political regrouping of conservative feudal elements, both within the Holy Alliance (Russia, Austria and Prussia) and the German federation (*Deutscher Bund*: 34 hereditary monarchies and four city republics) at the Congress of Vienna in 1815. This heralded a new phase of political restoration.

Side by side with this, however, tension was mounting between the increasingly furious pace of the industrial revolution and middle-class aspirations for political emancipation. The latter were forcibly suppressed in an endeavour to restore the pre-revolutionary balance of power.

Liberalism

The middle-class opposition movement to reactionary feudal elements found its first political expression in early liberalism, whose main aspiration was for middle-class freedom. This aspiration was expressed in advocacy of a constitutional monarchy with a constitution allowing for representation, separation of powers, independence of the judiciary, guarantees for human and civil rights (including freedom of movement, freedom of the press and freedom of assembly), free trade and national unity.

As the political influence of the lower middle classes and, after the 1840s, of the rural and urban working classes increased, the anti-feudal movement split into a number of factions, expanding to include democratic republican and socialist/communist groups. The latter's revolutionary demands for a republic and for social equality went substantially beyond those of liberalism. Opposition manifested itself, more vociferously in western and southern Europe than in Germany, in a spate of protests, revolts and revolutionary struggles. The first wave broke out all over Europe in the revolutions of 1830, and culminated in the revolutions of 1848–9.

The central demand for restoration of national unity on a democratic basis for Germany remained unfulfilled. The liberal middle class, and still more radical democratic and socialist opposition, were massively suppressed and persecuted by the highest feudal authorities from the outset. The sheer force of this suppression, and the still relatively weak position of the middle classes (let alone the working class) were crucial factors in the failure of the democratic revolution, and in the decision on the part of the upper middle classes from 1848–9 onwards to work towards a political compromise with leading feudal elements.

Repression and revolution

Both the civil pro-constitution movement and the movement for national unity, a university-centred professor and student movement (e.g. the *Deutsche Burschenschaft, Wartburgfest 1817*, comprising men who had returned disappointed from the wars of liberation against Napoleon) were outlawed and to some degree forced underground by the 'persecution of the demagogues'. The latter was a set of repressive measures instigated by the Carlsbad Resolutions of 1819, passed by a body known as the Central Commission of Investigation, established in Mainz for this purpose. After 1830 liberal and democratic protests and uprisings were put down even more mercilessly (ranging from rebellions by Poles, by 'Fatherland' associations, the Hambach festival of 1832, the Frankfurt *Wachensturm* (Watch-Tower) of 1833, artisans' associations and secret societies of the German People's Association (*Deutscher Volksverein*) to the Federation of the Just (*Bund der Gerechten*)). Many of those involved were either imprisoned or sent into exile. The authorities had no qualms about exercising arbitrary power, such as in the case of the 'seven professors of Göttingen', who included the Brothers Grimm. When the latter publicly protested against a breach of the constitution by the Hanoverian king, they were dismissed from their posts.

After 1840 conflicts between the feudal police state and the rebellious population increased on all sides, particularly since increasing destitution among the lower classes was stepping up pressure for organised political protest (e.g. the weavers' uprising of 1844 and the hunger revolts of 1847). Given what preceded it, therefore, the 1848 revolution was hardly unexpected. People at the time saw it as a fight for their very survival, and a crisis of the traditions and values that had held sway until that time. As such, it was more than a revolution in the narrow sense of the word – more than mere political change. This insight was an early response to the capitalist mode of production that was revolutionising the familiar social conditions, even though the full effects of it were not to be felt until the second half of the nineteenth century. Shared to a greater or lesser extent by all politically aware people living at the time, it was an insight in itself marking the move into a new age.

Detailed analysis of the causes of this move, however, reveal that most politicians, intellectuals and writers, whether conservative or progressive, were still largely helpless. Some looked to the future with concern, while others looked to the past with nostalgia. It was not only defenders of the old order, however, but also middle-class people who recoiled from the implications of being liberated from the chains of feudalism. Many withdrew nervously into a world of their own to avoid facing social change.

On the eve of the 1848 revolution, the 'spectre of communism' was evoked and the end of the reign of the middle classes was predicted – a reign into which they had not yet even entered. This brought to the surface a concept that has been making history ever since – the recognition 'that the old Europe has reached the beginning of the end' (Metternich).

The role of literature

What was the specific role and function of literature in this replacement of the old by the new? It will not suffice here simply to consider the distinctive achievements of literary trends during the *Vormärz* era purely, or even mainly, in terms of the political struggle going on at the time between feudalism, the middle classes and the emerging working classes.

The ability of *Vormärz* writers to give expression to the political process in their work, and thereby to involve themselves in that process in a practical way, was undoubtedly a hallmark of the age. From 1830 and even more so from 1840 onwards, glaring conflicts between reactionary, conservative, liberal, democratic and socialist elements in society were aired both in and through literature to an extent hardly ever seen before in the history of German literature. This is one reason why *Vormärz* literature has recently received closer attention in accounts of the history of literature than was formerly the case. This is not to say, however, that writers who showed a less active involvement in the burning social issues of their day – either by a declared lack of interest, or simply by choosing to write about other themes and problems – should consequently be dismissed as less interesting or behind the times. The contribution of literature to the growing realisation that the old Europe had reached the beginning of the end cannot be simplistically reduced to the function of portraying the political process and taking part in shaping it. Another more important function must take precedence over this definition – one that ultimately even encompasses it. It may be summed up as follows: the literature of the *Vormärz* period documents in a highly ambivalent manner a fundamental restructuring process taking place in the social perception of time and space, in which inherited modes of perception were assuming new forms, both in line with, and in response to, the industrial revolution.

A change in the perception of history

Implicit in the changes being wrought in social and economic realities by the shift to middle-class capitalism was a concomitant change not only in the perception of reality, but also in the perception of change *per se*. The social historians W. Kaschuba and C. Lipp comment:

> Within a new, critical perceptual view of concrete reality the absolute validity of existing rules of conduct in the spheres of production and reproduction began to be questioned. The historical logic of tradition and custom was no longer sufficient: *viability* and *efficiency* now asserted themselves as the norms of economic activity. Much that had formerly been held up as eternally valid now appeared virtually manipulable at will with machinery and industrial production methods – the relationship between a product and labour costs, the technical rules governing manufacturing procedures, the way human labour was utilised, the management of the working day, and the speed of travel and transportation. It becomes clear that, within the transformational process of the 'industrial revolution', structures of experience and perception were also coming into existence behind the more obvious adjustments in social stratification, the formation of industrial capital and technical innovation. At the root of this lay an awareness of 'the relativity of all things'. Mechanical and machine manufacturing, railways, steamships and the telegraph are not merely symbols of the modern technological age that changed the procedures for working and business life. They also wrought a change in the whole *experience of time and space, social relationships and individual prospects*.

Although linked to processes of material change, therefore, this new experience is not bound to them in any determinist sense. The fact is that *Vormärz* experience of the industrial revolution was only occurring directly in major industrial centres such as Westphalia, or major commercial cities such as Hamburg and Frankfurt, and yet it also caught up people living in the far more numerous regions still outside the spheres of heavy industry and commerce.

Art as a means of achieving re-orientation

The arts can serve as a specific medium in the process of reorientation within structures of experience and perception. It both gives aesthetic expression to, and helps to shape modes of perception – particularly when creative communication enjoys a respected position as part of social education, as was the case in the *Vormärz* period. The history of *Vormärz* literature is for this reason an outstanding source of historical experience in the form of aesthetic symbolism – even in what appear to be apolitical or 'non-strategic' accounts such as were most prevalent in the years leading up to 1830. It was in this period that writers were able to respond to and/or deal strategically with themes concerning the process of change already described.

This became possible not least because the capitalisation of the relations of production in general created a market for literature in which writers were able to figure for the first time as 'active agents'. The *Vormärz* period saw the emergence of a literature market that continues to function on the same principle to this day, except that nowadays it reaches a wider readership. This, combined with analysis of its variously liberating and constraining consequences on the literary output of the 'free' writer, poses fundamental questions regarding the increasingly controversial question of the role of art in the class struggle.

The literature market, professional authorship and censorship

The literature market

In the aftermath of the Napoleonic Wars, which had been disastrous for trade and the economy, the scale on which goods were produced and exchanged began to enlarge, despite multifarious economic and political obstacles. This process entailed an ongoing process of restructuring and reorganisation within production and exchange to cope with the requirements of a capitalist economy.

Hand in hand with growth in the volume of commercial exchange went a steadily rising demand for up-to-date information. This concerned not only the market and the latest trends (with a view to gaining an advantage over less well-informed competitors), but also possible changes concerning existing political impediments to profitable expansion. Hard-headed economic interest, aimed at immediate exploitation, was supplemented by more long-term political interests, articulated mainly through critical, and later more overtly propagandist economic literature and poetry. The invention of the paper-machine and the high-speed press (in operation from the 1820s onwards) made it possible for the newspaper and book-printing industries to step up production levels in leaps and bounds, especially after 1830. They were thus able to meet the equally massive increase in the demand for information. Journals, newspapers, books, brochures and pamphlets were distributed on a scale never seen before. Between 1821 and 1838 annual book production rose by 150 per cent to over 10,000 titles. This was a stunning rate of increase compared with the two other great waves of expansion in the book trade, which had required twice that period of time: to approximately 4,000 titles from 1770 to 1805, and to approximately 25,000 titles from 1868 to 1901. Interestingly, the greatest growth occurred in two areas: in applied sciences directly exploitable in production and distribution, and in the sphere of overt ideology (theology). Fiction was an area of stagnation in the period up to 1830 – a fact that was to have major repercussions on the process of politicisation through literature.

This rise in production was accompanied by a proliferation of the distribution network (to some 1,350 booksellers by 1840). Prices fell as editions were produced in greater numbers of copies. Growth in the retail market led to the capture of new readership markets (with penny magazines and cheap editions, etc.). The result of all this, and the consequent increase in potential profits (estimated as 4–6 million *talers* in the year 1844), was an economically stable, steadily expanding publishing and book retailing industry.

From 1825 onwards, publishers were organised into a Market Association of German Booksellers (*Börsenverein der Deutschen Buchhändler*). Publishers wielded considerable political influence during the *Vormärz* period in the battle for copyright protection and freedom of the press. The capital wealth of individual publishing firms was moreover able to guarantee improved financial security for many writers, enabling them at last to turn to full-time professional writing.

Paradoxically, the veritable army of authors writing custom-made literature for the entertainment market were not the only ones to profit from this new-found stability in the publishing industry. Politically committed authors also benefited. The growing market for literature of political opposition – an expression of the conflict of political interests between the middle classes and their feudal rulers – became part of the overall politicisation process. The state administration tried to combat this with censorship, thereby drawing into the fray publishers who were making good profits from literature that was now under the threat of a ban. Although they faced high financial risks, therefore, publishers had a material interest in this literature. In this way, the profit motive of middle-class capitalists worked to a large extent in favour of opposition writers, journalists and intellectuals. This situation, which persisted until at least the 1840s, helped to bolster critical literature for a time, enabling it to be used as an instrument of political strategy. This literary and political success in turn formed a commercial base for those publishers who dealt in (and with) books purely as merchandise, and who were not afraid to operate on the very fringes of legality (e.g. Campe).

It is also worth mentioning that this short-lived and historically unique phase in the relationship between middle-class capitalists and critical literature was to exert a lasting influence on attitudes. Publishers and booksellers came to be thought of as selfless stewards of the highest cultural values, rather than as market-oriented entrepreneurs dealing with literature as a commodity. Similarly, the writer came to be seen as addressing and influencing his reader irrespective of markets, rather than as someone increasingly dependent on circumstances outside his control. Such attitudes tended to obscure the tension between the purposes of the market and the freedom of the arts.

The first signs of such contradictions are already discernible in the *Vormärz* period – in Heine's complaints about exploitation, and his publisher Campe's censoring interference; in the difficulties made for progressive publishers by the Marketing Association and in the problems socialist authors had in finding publishers at all. Viewed overall, however, these conflicts were relatively minor compared to the all-eclipsing battle against state censorship on the one hand and, initially at least, the even more pressing problem of combating pirated editions and winning copyright protection on the other.

Pirated editions

After 1815, an eye to profits led publishers to press more and more vehemently for an extension of the concept of middle-class property to include intellectual property. They also urged a nationwide codification of copyright protection law to stem the swelling tide of pirated editions that were affecting their most profitable titles on the growing market – informative literature, fiction, conversation lexicons and the like. At Metternich's prompting, however, the National Assembly in Frankfurt procrastinated over this demand for so long that it was 1845 before a final and binding ban on the practice of pirating editions was on the statute book. His motives were clear: a book retailing industry hampered in its further expansion by the practice of pirating would be in no position to disseminate subversive ideas on a large scale. Economic constraints were thus intended to act as a substitute for inopportune political repression by means of overt censorship. After 1830, however, it soon became clear that the flow of literature being produced, and the growth of political consciousness accompanying it, were not to be curbed by economic measures alone. Realising this, the feudal state stepped up its censorship measures.

Censorship

For publishers, booksellers and writers, censorship was an incomparably greater threat than the practice of pirating, whose advocates' arguments were ultimately as anti-feudal as they were anti-capitalist. Against privilege and monopoly, 'pirates' saw themselves as fostering what was still an exclusive book culture on the basis of cheap production for mass distribution and popularisation.

In order to survive in face of repressive state censorship in the *Vormärz* period, however, opposition writers needed more capital from wealthy publishers than was brought in by the wider distribution of pirated editions – fame without money. The price they paid for this was not without its complications. From now on writers of critical publications were tied to publishers whose progressiveness was limited by their concern for the economic viability of publishing – in other words, the profit motive.

The practice of censorship reintroduced in 1819 by means of general regulations applicable to all states in the German federation (although practised differently in different places) was a form of 'pre-censorship'. Applicable to all publications under 20 sheets in length (i.e. 320 pages), it was directed mainly at newspapers, journals, brochures and other short works with a broad potential readership on account of their size and price. The effect of this type of censorship up to 1830 was to curb the growth of a significant critical press, and to contain political criticism firmly within the confines of high-priced scholarly works.

From the 1830s onwards, however, publishers, editors and writers grew bolder and more resourceful at evading the muzzle of censorship. They printed abroad, where the law was more liberal; they expanded the length of books to 21 sheets; newspapers that were banned were rapidly re-established or sold. Branches of knowledge such as theology, philosophy, philology and economics were, moreover, becoming increasingly political and popular. The grip of censorship was tightened accordingly. 'Pre-censorship' was now augmented by the subsequent confiscation or banning of already published works, particularly those exempt from pre-censorship. Before long the works of specific authors (for example Heine's *Junges Deutschland*), and even whole publishing houses, were banned in advance.

Another aspect to be considered is that censorship was but one facet, that pertaining to the writer, of a far-reaching state security and secret-police apparatus aimed at destroying the entire communications network of the political opposition – its various associations, clubs and groups, etc. This apparatus facilitated the penalisation of those not already affected by the collective measures of the 'persecution of the demagogues' in operation since 1819, i.e. by various instances of political persecution, imprisonment, the *Berufsverbot* (a law banning members of certain political parties from practising their profession) and the power to exile. A contemporary student song proclaimed: 'Wer die Wahrheit kennet und sagt sie frei, / der kommt nach Berlin auf die Hausvogtei!' ('He who knows the truth and says it out loud, / Will find himself in Berlin at the Hausvogtei!' – i.e. the Prussian interrogation prison).

The police and censorship authorities had their work cut out for them. All positive mention of the 'demagogical' was banned, effectively covering any criticism of prevailing conditions or general approval of the principles of progress and change. Hoffmann von Fallersleben was thus able to denounce with irony even the season of spring as an 'eternal demagogue'. The ban also covered any criticism of ruling houses, government, the nobility, military, Christian institutions and morality.

This effectively condemned as immoral virtually every scene in Goethe's *Faust I*, and much of it was denounced as blasphemy. Kleist was seen as defaming the noble Prussian officer by having his Prince of Homburg weep. *Egmont* was seen as too liberal, and Schiller's *Wilhelm Tell* was positively revolutionary. At theatres entirely dependent on princely courts these dramas therefore remained either more or less banned, or were performed only in mutilated, censored form.

The position was no different with books and the press. Narrow-minded, prudish and nervous censors 'defused' texts according to whim and their level of education. At first they contented themselves with prescribing 'corrections' for deleted passages, but soon they simply struck them out. Deleted passages were initially indicated to the reader by means of so-called censorship gaps or strike-outs. This practice inspired Heine in the twelfth chapter of *Ideen. Das Buch Le Grand* to write the satirical lines: 'Die deutschen Zensoren —— Dummköpfe —— ' ('The German censors —— blockheads —— '). From 1837 onwards, however, even the printing of censorship gaps was banned in Prussia.

On the one hand it is true that even this most rigorous form of censorship by a feudal regime still proved powerless to prevent a general politicisation of the population that was eventually to lead to revolution. This was in no small measure because of the impossibility of achieving the uniform implementation of censorship legislation throughout the 38 states of the federation, and because the existence of so many frontiers made the 'smuggling of ideas' practically unstoppable. On the other hand, however, the deforming effects and far-reaching harm done by censorship to German authors should not be overlooked. The relegation of literary opposition to the realm of criminality by political snoops, and the 'jurisdiction of suspicion' (Marx) had repercussions that have persisted to the present day in terms of the role of German literature in the ongoing class struggle. Literature split into a movement towards rebellion on the one hand, and a retreat into a private inner world on the other.

Viewed as a whole, however, the period from 1815 to 1848 can be described as one in which German writers were both helped and hindered by the increasingly capitalist stamp of the social conditions governing literature, although there was still an overwhelming continuation of existing aesthetic traditions. Both hampered and shaken into action at the same time by state repression, and with a growing political consciousness, writers were able to become active in a particular way. This process of activation was closely linked to a resumption of the debate concerning the role of literature and the writer – a debate first sparked off by the French Revolution.

What is literature good for now?

The concept of Vormärz literature

To arrive at an accurate appraisal of the character and significance of *Vormärz* literature, the modern reader must be aware of a number of basic differences between the world of letters at that time and now. The first is that the body of German literature was perceived as something new. In the minds of post-1815 readers it was above all a contemporary phenomenon because of its eighteenth-century origin. The themes and styles of German literature were viewed as 'modern' compared to the 'classical' literature of the Greeks and Romans, which was equated with poetry – so modern, in fact, that it was not yet an established feature of the curriculum in educational institutions. Until 1848 there was no distinct discipline of German literary studies (*Deutsche Literaturwissenschaft*) at German universities, if indeed it was taught at all. Those scholars described as *Germanisten* were concerned with Old German law, Old German history and Old German as a language (e.g. figures such as the Brothers Grimm, Uhland, Gervinus, Hoffmann von Fallersleben). In a particularist Germany even they were regarded with suspicion on account of the pan-German, rather than Prussian or Bavarian nature of their subject-matter. They consequently often fell victim to what were in some cases severe disciplinary measures.

The prevailing character of lectures and published works (some 50 by 1848) on the history of German literature by such German scholars, other academic outsiders, writers, or simply lovers of literature, was one of 'parliamentary speeches, as Goethe says of Byron's poems' (T.W. Danzel, 1849). They were, in other words, an expression of political opposition. Ancient authors still dominated the literature curriculum in grammar schools.

An increasingly spirited debate was raging, however, between educators, progressive teachers and education ministries on the educational value of 'classical' German literature for schools. Authorities feared that schoolchildren might be incited to rise up against the feudal state and the Christian religion by middle-class oppositional, national and liberal literature since Klopstock and Lessing. Syllabuses and school library stocks were therefore subject to strict control and censorship. If even 'classical' German authors were viewed with suspicion, then contemporary literature was doubly suspect and was not taught at all.

Literary society in the Vormärz period

The outcome was that recent and modern German literature, before attaining its post-1848 status as the Muse of apolitical educational authority, grew from below. Through the market, the reader and the texts themselves, literature became a powerful catalyst, affecting the political and ideological issues of the day. Not only was it of considerable commercial value, but it was also gaining more and more potential scope actively to influence affairs.

Reading was becoming an ever more popular activity, not simply because increased literacy and prosperity were enlarging the circle of readers, but because reading had become a vehicle for the aspirations of an upwardly mobile class with only limited scope for actual achievement. Women, for example, who were barred from educational institutions, and severely handicapped in their intellectual development by stubborn prejudice, were particularly avid readers, and themselves began to write.

The numbers of reading circles, associations and lending libraries rose steadily, and the number of bookshops doubled between 1820 and 1840. Admittedly only 5 per cent of the 23 million total population of the German states could be described as regular readers at the beginning of the nineteenth century. And yet this was still enough soon to justify speaking in terms of a 'deluge of literature', and to accuse the Germans of reading-fever and fostering graphomania. The literary critic W. Menzel wrote in 1829, for example:

> The Germans don't do very much, but they write all the more for that. . . . We have become a nation of writers: we should put a goose on our national coat-of-arms instead of the double eagle. Here, it is the quill that reigns and serves, works and remunerates, fights and nourishes and brings fortune or punishment. We have left the Italians to their heaven, the Spaniards to their saints, the French to their deeds and the English to their money-bags and we sit over our books.

Metternich, however, saw things differently: he saw this traffic in literature not as de-politicising, but as politicising, and ordered censorship to be stepped up accordingly. Writers were to be spied on and persecuted, and publications to be banned.

The social importance of literature

Literature, whether in the form of fiction and poetry, scientific or journalistic texts, was taken seriously in the *Vormärz* era, both by readers and the rich and powerful alike. Its importance arose not least out of mounting tension between the entrenchment of the middle classes on the one hand and their political suppression on the other. This resulted in a shift in the class struggle from the political to the ideological level and a concomitant increase in the importance of philosophy, science and literature. This in turn intensified the already fervent debate on the roles and functions of these disciplines – a level of discussion in which the political character of criticism was becoming ever more apparent. Writing in 1820 in Berlin, where he taught, Hegel was still in full accord with long-standing Western tradition in asserting that philosophies, the thought of the world, invariably appeared too late, 'after the reality of the educational process has been completed' ('The owl of Minerva does not launch its flight until twilight'). A good 25 years later, Marx wrote the trenchant lines: 'Philosophers have only ever variously interpreted the world. The problem is how to change it.'

The *Vormärz* period saw an equally radical change in the function assigned to the writer, who was now no longer a mere '(his)story-writer' ('Geschichtsschreiber'), but a 'maker of history' ('Geschichtstreiber': Börne). This new definition of literature in terms of practical politics first made its mark after 1830 with the appearance of the *Jungdeutschen* (New Germany) writers, as well as with an upsurge in journalism and pamphlet literature that reached its zenith after 1840 with a new agenda for political writing.

However, this redefinition found itself up against not only the police, but also the traditionally defined functions of literature and the writing profession handed down from classicism and Romanticism. The debates on literary theory that arose out of this encounter were not the mere literary 'potato fights' of earlier days, as Heine described them in 1830. They were the beginnings of an endeavour that has continued to the present day to come to terms with the duties and responsibilities of middle-class or post-middle-class art. As Heine went on to comment, what was at stake now were 'the highest interests of life itself; revolution has made its entrance in literature, and war is going to be waged more fiercely'.

Biedermeier or Junges Deutschland?

Writers such as Heine, the *Jungdeutschen* and political lyric poets were on the offensive in this discussion, looking to the future positively with hopes for a new art form. Writers such as Immermann, Grillparzer and the *Biedermeier* poets, in contrast, took a more sceptical view, defining themselves negatively in a retrospective light compared to the literature of Goethe and Schiller: 'Things were better for the two of them: they could still shut themselves off and concentrate on the pure-spirited and the ideal, whereas in our times of realistic politics this is no longer remotely possible, and the poet is constantly being sucked into the vortex of practicality, far removed from everything poetical' (Immermann).

Here we can see the two main reactions to one and the same experience of post-1815 social reality. Reality is seen and experienced as changing radically in relation to conditions hitherto: the present is perceived as a crisis, a watershed. Previous attempts at aesthetic solutions continued to be practised up to 1830, but hesitantly, desperately and with a spirit of resignation. After 1830 they were criticised with ever greater boldness, and from the 1840s onwards either expanded or replaced to make way for new conceptions.

The concept of Biedermeier

Many histories of literature, particularly earlier ones, define the Biedermeier era as covering the literary period from 1815–30 to 1848. Recently one expert on the period, F. Sengle, even put forward an interpretation of 'the specific German form of late European Romanticism' as the 'Biedermeier period'. This must be refuted, however, along with associated attempts to sum up the dominant movement in literature – by analogy with the politics of the Metternich system – under the heading of 'restoration'. Such attempts must be regarded as an untenable generalisation from a single aspect of this highly complex era, which culminated in 1848 with a virtually all-European revolution. Any overall conception of an age in which the criticism of tradition took on a bewildering number of ambivalent forms needs to be presented as a dialectic interplay between old traditions being upheld in vain on the one hand and still impracticable attempts to implement the new on the other. The part played by conservative antagonists in all this cannot of course be overlooked, but terms such as 'the age of Biedermeier' or 'restoration' are quite simply inadequate here.

This may clearly be seen by glancing at the various forms that literature took in the *Vormärz* era. The most extreme wing is represented by what is known as 'the militant clerical restoration', marking an attempt to reinstate the authority of the Church and the Christian religion, which had been under attack since the eighteenth century. This wing includes journalists such as the former *Burschenschaftler* and influential literary critic W. Menzel, Hengstenberg, editor of the *Evangelische Kirchenzeitung* (Journal of the Lutheran Church) and J. Görres with his Catholic journal the *Historisch-politische Blätter* (Historico-Political Pages). This camp included writers such as Friedrich Schlegel, Eichendorff, Spitta and Gotthelf, and in certain respects the later Tieck, Droste and Stifter, who were all in their various ways in favour of a Christian approach and in perpetuating the inherited political order.

The term 'classicism' is an attempt to define the literary tendency that was to lead to the era of German classicism. It also refers to the desire to defend the artistic ideals and formal regulations that were elaborated within that tendency – albeit for the most part in resigned rather than overtly aggressive form – in conscious opposition to a middle-class world that was

271

hostile to art. This trend would include mainly Platen and Rückert, as well as some of Mörike's and Grillparzer's works. Offshoots of this trend were still in evidence in the *Nachmärz* era, in the imitative *Goldschnittlyrik* and epic verse of poets such as Geibel and Heyse.

Traditions of 'sensibility' (*Empfindsamkeit*) and anti-classical Romanticism still persisted in various forms, for example in so-called 'Swabian Romanticism' represented by writers such as K. Mayer and G. Schwab, and in modified form by such authors as Mörike and Lenau. These traditions were also subjected to ruthless criticism by authors such as the young Heine. The trend towards political acquiescence was stronger than that towards the liberal political commitment of such authors as W. Müller, Hauff, Uhland, Chamisso, Lenau. Authors such as the story-writer Immermann and the dramatist Hebbel, however, can scarcely be classified in terms of antagonism between the preservation of political and aesthetic tradition and the desire to change it.

Junges Deutschland – The Young Germany movement

It would be equally unacceptable to present authors of the *Junges Deutschland* movement as the exclusive representatives of their age. This group of liberal writers, first brought together by a ban on the publication of their works by the German Federal Assembly in Frankfurt in 1835, included the banned Heinrich Heine, Ludolf Wienbarg, Heinrich Laube, Theodor Mundt and Karl Gutzow. They underwent various fallings-out among themselves, and were far from being of one mind either with, or on the subject of their spiritual mentors, Ludwig Börne and Heinrich Heine, from whom they nevertheless learned both the pungent writing style that proved so effective in the media, as well as their themes (i.e. political, religious and moral emancipation), their concept of literature (the supplanting of rigid genres and the precedence of prose) and their interpretation of the vocation of the author as poet and prose writer, journalist and critic. As emigrants, Börne and Heine were unable either to found, publish or edit critical literary journals (*Journale sind unsere Festungen – Journals are our Bastions*, 1828), but the writers of *Junges Deutschland* did so, and were able to use these journals to popularise their modern ideas. The *Deutsche Revue* (*German Review*) (Gutzkow/Wienbarg), the *Phönix* (*Phoenix*) (Gutzkow), *Aurora* (Laube), the *Literarischer Zodiacus/Dioskuren* (*The Literary Zodiac/Dioskuri*) (Mundt), the *Telegraph für Deutschland* (*Telegraph for Germany*) (Gutzkow), and the *Zeitung für die elegante Welt* (*Journal for the Elegant World*) (Laube) are among the most noteworthy titles.

Carrying on the criticism initiated in the 1820s by Börne (mainly in the *Dramaturgische Blätter – Dramaturgical Pages* and *Briefe aus Paris – Letters from Paris*) and by Heine (mainly in *Reisebilder – Pictures from a*

Journey), *jungdeutsche* writers pushed the criticism of literature, culture and politics into the forefront of literary activity. In 1833 Laube wrote: 'A world in the making is now turning. Experiment is its flag, and judgement its sceptre. In such periods of development the warming sun seldom appears. Everything is in search of the guiding moon – criticism'. The 'blood-red daughter' of criticism, revolution, as Laube phrased it, soon loomed on the horizon, and before long made the *Jungdeutschen* seem tame by comparison, as younger and more radical critics such as D.F. Strauss, a critic of religion, R. Prutz and A. Ruge, critics of science, and not least Marx and Engels, critics of ideology, appeared on the scene. A federal assembly ban on the *Jungdeutschen* accused them of 'attacking the Christian religion in the most impudent manner, denigrating existing social conditions, and making a mockery of all propriety and morality in works of fiction accessible to all classes of readers'. This ban applied mainly to the following works: Laube's *Die Poeten* (*The Poets*, 1832: Part One of the *Das junge Europa* – *The Young Europe* trilogy), Mundt's *Madonna, Unterhaltungen mit einer Heiligen* (*Madonna: Conversations with a Saint*) (1835) and Gutzkow's *Wally, die Zweiflerin* (*Wally, the Woman Who Doubted*) (1835).

Volkstheater and working-class literature

Analysis of the function of art in capitalism cannot be restricted to the narrow sphere of 'polite' literature, which has been put forward as the sole criterion for evaluating literary developments in traditional accounts of the history of literature. There is a need to pay attention to the forms and consequences of this analysis within those literary areas that were becoming important and influential in the *Vormärz* period. This is all the more vital since the people to whom these works were largely addressed were not so much the educated middle classes as the rapidly swelling ranks of the urban lower-middle and working classes. Genres worthy of note in this connection are *Volksliteratur* (folk literature), which had traditions of varying length in different regions (the *Lokalstück*, the folk calendar, songs, etc.) and nascent working-class literature (artisans' and workers' songs, pamphlets, etc.).

In their *Vormärz* form, both these types of literature were a product of and at the same time a factor influencing the changing definition of the function of literature. It must above all be borne in mind, however, that besides the above literary activities within philosophy, scholarship, science, *Kunstdichtung*, journalism, *Volksdichtung* and working-class literature, there was a steady stream of unacknowledged but widely-read literature that had come about with the growth in the literature market from the end of the eighteenth century onwards. This literature – a literature of entertainment, often also derisively called 'trivial literature' – was mass-produced for the first time during the *Vormärz* period.

Only a handful of *Vormärz* literary critics, such as R. Prutz, recognised this new type of literature as 'a necessary product of our times, and actually a reflection of it' , and understood that the claims and assessment of what was known as 'polite' literature would therefore have to be rethought in terms of their real significance for the times. For the *Vormärz* period itself, this rethinking process entailed a reassertion of the creative artist's view of himself (accompanied by a fresh coming to terms with Romanticism, especially in the 1820s and 1830s), criticism of the *Kunstepoche* (mainly in the 1830s), and picking up the threads of Jacobin and Enlightenment approaches.

The curse of being a poet, or: from history-writer to maker of history

Since the eighteenth century there had been a steady change in the situation of writers, from writing as a sideline to another profession or in the service of a feudal patron, to becoming a 'free' creative artist – although, on the other hand, also a producer for the literature market. As it moved into the nineteenth century, therefore, the writing profession found itself enjoying the utmost esteem. This greater recognition was expressed not only in considerably better payment and in the greatly multiplied publication of literary works, but also in an improvement in the social status of 'writers and thinkers' to the level of celebrated representatives and intellectual leaders of the nation, and leading critics. The cult surrounding the personality of Goethe and the fame he enjoyed both in his own lifetime and after his death for his epoch-making works is clear evidence of this new status.

There was another side to this coin, however. Not every writer was able to follow in the footsteps of the Weimar Olympian in being able to unite fame and recognition so happily by transforming them into 'greatness'. Flawed talent or genius now sometimes lay at the root of success. Since the advent of the 'free' writer with the emergence of the literature market, the correlation between individual talent and social recognition, and between artistic aspirations and real importance, was now much less clear-cut. Opportunities for the mass distribution of literature had opened up avenues for achieving wealth and fame with aesthetically mediocre or ideologically conformist works, while more ambitious creative artists went unacknowledged, or were even denounced.

This state of affairs became increasingly prevalent in the nineteenth century, especially in Germany. Being an author was by its very nature a positive thing, ripe with opportunity. The prospects of a 'classical' writer, entertainment author or journalist were entirely secure as far as recognition and livelihood were concerned. Nevertheless, being a creative artist, writer or poet was also becoming more and more synonymous with, on the one hand, setting oneself apart from a middle class in the process of establishing itself and, on the other, with catering to the trivial artistic tastes of a broad readership. What, in other words, became the central aspect of the creative artist's view of himself among most post-Romantic German writers was the feeling of being homeless and on the edge of society.

The crises of the creative artist

In the novel *Nachtwachen des Bonaventura* (*The Night Watches of Bonaventura*) (1804), the night watchman calls up to the poet in his garret: 'Friend, he who would live nowadays cannot write poetry.' In Brentano's novella *Geschichte vom braven Kasperl und dem schönen Annerl* (*The Story of Good Kasperl and Pretty Annerl*) (1815), the poet is ashamed of his vocation and says: 'He who lives from poetry has lost his balance . . .'. In E.T.A. Hoffmann's work, creative artists have completely lost their balance: they are torn apart, sick, crazy and mad. Until Grillparzer's *Der arme Spielmann* (*The Poor Street-Player*) and after, creative artists and writers are depicted as abnormal and eccentric, part unappreciated genius, part degenerate genius, preserving true human values, but ostracised from society and paying the price for this of a life in ruins. The *malheur d'être un poète* ('the misfortune of being a poet' – Grillparzer) is manifest not only in literature. Writers of noble origin such as Kleist or Droste were regarded as blots on the reputations of their families. Jean Paul and Grabbe consoled themselves with alcohol; Schlegel, Brentano and Droste took refuge in religion, Mörike and Lenau in illness. Some, such as Platen and Grillparzer, set their art on a higher plane, and were thereby compelled to forfeit fame and a wide readership, while others fell silent or retracted, or even gave up writing (some for periods, some gradually, others all at once). Some dissipated their energies, some went over to the other camp, some committed suicide (e.g. Kleist, Raimund, Stifter). Musicians and painters met similar fates. Suffering for art had a number of faces in the *Vormärz* period. It expressed itself in desperation at a world that had turned to middle-class philistinism and inhumanity, in Romantic anti-capitalism and *Weltschmerz*. It surfaced as aristocratic derision of the public, and as artistic Titanism, as well as in doubts about the potential of art, and (self-)criticism of the abilities of the creative artist himself (the problem of being an 'imitator').

Suffering at the hands of a society that was hostile to art always implied a latent criticism of that society, and hence an expression of the aspiration towards a different relationship between art and society. This nevertheless took on highly different perspectives, as will be seen from the careers, work and public reception experienced by Mörike and Herwegh.

The example of Mörike

Eduard Mörike was born in 1804, lost one of his parents early in life and lived in poverty. He was regarded as average at school, managing only with some difficulty to obtain the required grades to enter the famous Tübingen seminary to study theology. Like Hegel, Hölderlin and others both before and after him, including Herwegh and other major figures from Swabian German intellectual history, he studied free of charge, 'lured into the mouse-trap of theology by the bacon of charitable endowments' (D.F. Strauss). The years from 1826 after qualifying found him living the irksome wandering life of a parish assistant and curate in Swabian villages, punctuated by a failed attempt to become an independent writer (1828) and by unrequited love. In 1834 Mörike finally became a rector. *Maler Nolten*, a novel of art and development, appeared in 1832, followed in 1836 by a novella and in 1838 by his first volume of poetry. He became increasingly disenchanted with his ministry and his sickliness increased. He retired early in 1843, marrying late but unhappily. From 1850 onwards Mörike's fame and public acclaim grew, but his poetry-writing declined in the same period (occasional poems were published and in 1855 appeared his novella *Mozart auf der Reise nach Prag – Mozart on the Way to Prague*, a revised edition of *Maler Nolten*). He became more and more isolated, was incessantly ill and constantly took trips for spa treatment. Visiting him in 1862, Hebbel described Mörike as 'languishing in the most miserable and heart-breaking circumstances imaginable'. Mörike died in 1875. Five years later a monument was erected to him in Stuttgart.

Provincialism and the inner life

It is striking that not once in his life did Mörike ever leave the region of Swabia-Franconia. Stuttgart, with some 40,000 inhabitants in 1840, was the largest town he knew. He never saw the Rhine, industrial Westphalia, the North Sea, Berlin or Vienna, let alone London, Paris or Italy. Up to 1850 (his most prolific writing period) he had only scant contacts with other writers, mainly Swabians. With not a single literary dispute or even a public appearance to his name, he lived for the most part alone. Major political events are hardly touched on in his works, and only a few are even mentioned in his letters, although he was personally affected by some of them. One of his teachers in Urach was dismissed as a 'demagogue' in 1822; his brother was convicted of 'revolutionary subversion' in 1831, and his friend H. Kurz was a radical democrat in the period before and after the 1848 revolution. Both his correspondence and his personal attitudes revealed time and again that Mörike preferred to avoid political issues, retreating instead to safe conformist viewpoints and adopting from a distance a nervous defensive posture when matters took a serious turn.

This road leading inwards into seclusion, neurotic infirmity, and an art absorbed in psychological detail is above all the expression of a resignation typical for broad sections of the literary intelligentsia in nineteenth-century Germany, and which had its counterpart in apolitical tunnel vision. At the same time, however, it is also an expression of voluntary exile from the middle-class world on the part of the artist of sensibility, an act of protest that was becoming increasingly common since the Romantic era. Although Mörike and others like him had effectively passed a death sentence on modern progress, they did not dare criticise it politically. Instead they had to make do with expressing their views on the level of art in the form of a heightened alienation from the self. It goes without saying that the price they paid for this in their lives was high, and by no means recompensed by the false reward of posthumous fame.

The example of Herwegh

The son of an inn-keeper, Georg Herwegh was born in 1817, beginning his theological training at the Tübingen seminary. From the first he showed an interest in contemporary *junges Deutschland* literature, as well as in the modern left-wing Hegelian critique of religion. He was expelled from the seminary in 1836 for insubordination, turning to independent writing. In 1839 he deserted from forced military recruitment in Switzerland. In 1841 his *Gedichte eines Lebendigen* (*Poems of a Living Soul*) were published – an anthology of liberal and even radical democratic lyric poetry that managed to become a bestseller despite a censorship ban. Herwegh achieved instantaneous fame, which brought with it the acquaintance of Heine, Victor Hugo, Feuerbach, Marx, Bakunin, Weitlin and other socialists, communists and anarchists. He married a wealthy merchant's daughter, thereby acquiring financial independence. Herwegh's fame was at its height in 1842 during a triumphant tour of Germany when he was received by the King of Prussia. Soon, however, there was mounting criticism of his extravagant behaviour, both personal and political. He was banished from Germany and settled in Paris. In 1848 he became leader of a German legion of emigrants that marched on Baden from Paris in support of the revolution. Following their defeat he lived in exile in Switzerland. From that time his poetry-writing came to a virtual standstill, apart from the federal song he composed in 1862 for the General German Workers' Association (the *Allgemeiner Deutscher Arbeiterverein*, a forerunner of the Socialist Party of Germany, the SPD): 'Mann der Arbeit aufgewacht! / Und erkenne deine Macht! / Alle Räder stehen still, / Wenn dein starker Arm es will' ('Man of work arise / And know thy power! / All the wheels will stand still / If 'tis thy sovereign will'). Herwegh returned to Germany in 1866. He died in Germany, but was buried in Switzerland, and no monument was erected to him in Germany.

The striking aspect of Herwegh's career is the meteoric success of his first work – which was reprinted six times in the first two years and had sold some 15,000 copies by 1848. To compare: Mörike's poems of 1838 were published in 1,000 copies, and the second edition was not published until ten years later in 1848. Lyric poetry no longer fled 'into the heart of holy quiet places' ('in des Herzens heilig stille Räume' – Schiller). It had made its entrance into political life, and was proving effective and successful in its partisanship. It was as rare then in the nineteenth century as it is now for a German (and non-Jewish) writer to win and retain a place in European centres of political and intellectual life, and to possess close international contacts with the critical intelligentsia. What makes Herwegh unusual is the popularity and publicity he enjoyed, albeit only briefly, in the *Vormärz* period, and above all the fact that he was a poet-spokesman for the political opposition.

Herwegh is associated with the image of the lyric poet who 'smashes his harp', becoming politically active in the pursuit of his moral commitment, but who succumbs 'to arrogance, as if literature were the whole of life' (Prutz) and as if he saw himself as only able to accomplish something as a revolutionary. As we know, success eluded him. The outcome of his stance was personal denunciation as a bad poet and a cowardly revolutionary, and ideological exploitation as proof of the impossibility of combining poetry with politics. Above all, however, he was consigned to oblivion, exiled and deprived of citizenship. Like other writers before and contemporary with him, Herwegh's life and eventual fate show how a middle class in the process of abandoning its revolutionary aspirations was beginning to treat its revolutionary critics, thereby closing the road to the political use of literature in future. Development of the self-perception of writers who adhered to what were by now the conservative views of the German (Late) Romantics (e.g. Eichendorff, Grillparzer, Geibel, Hebbel) was now hopeless, and often ended in elitist or reactionary attitudes.

Elsewhere, however, the German standpoint was broadening its scope, linking up ideologically with continuing Western European development in the Romantic movement towards political liberalism (Victor Hugo, Béranger, Byron). This process was not infrequently assisted by journeys or political activity, etc. Here German post-Romantic writers arrived as early as the 1820s not only at an anti-feudal position, but also at a stable perception of themselves as creative artists (e.g. Uhland, Heine, Chamisso, Platen; after 1830 Lenau and after 1840 Freiligrath). This position involved the adoption of a critical distance from Romanticism. The process of disengagement, typical of *Vormärz* literature, is particularly clear in the work and maturation process of Heinrich Heine from the 1820s to the 1840s.

Enfant perdu: Heinrich Heine

Heinrich Heine, who styled himself the 'last pensioned-off king of fable' of German Romanticism, was a follower of Byron, who represented liberal Western European Romanticism and took active part in the Greek war of liberation. In Byron we find the literary position of *Weltschmerz* that was widespread throughout Europe in the 1820s – a characteristic combination of radical subjectivity and afflicted emotion. Associated with these we can also find manifestations of the inner turmoil of Hamlet-like figures and of 'problematical natures', which may be interpreted as an expression of the first serious fundamental crisis in social identity among opposition intellectuals in the age of the Holy Alliance and Metternich's restoration. These intellectuals, at war with themselves, and yet resigned, are also – within the dialectic cloak of emotion – in revolt against existing reality, although without at first encompassing social causes in their view of the world (compare Grabbe and Immermann). On Byron's death in 1824, Heine described him as his 'cousin', also drawing attention to the political core of Byron's attitude of *Weltschmerz*: 'er hat im Schmerze neue Welten entdeckt, er hat den miserablen Menschen und ihren noch miserableren Göttern prometheisch getrotzt' ('he discovered new worlds in pain; he took vengeance in Promethean style on insufferable people and their even more insufferable gods'). In so doing Heine was taking on himself and pushing into the forefront the task of political protest – albeit a radically subjective and indeed provocatively private and religiously couched one – against a non-aristocratic, but nonetheless feudal and philistine middle-class world. Admittedly Heine did this at first without Byron's defiant spirit, but the force of his irony grew steadily (compare *Reisebilder – Pictures from a Journey*, 1826–; *Buch der Lieder – The Book of Songs*, 1827). The third poem in his anthology *Die Heimkehr* (*The Homecoming*) contains the lines: 'Mein Herz, mein Herz ist traurig, / Doch lustig leuchtet der Mai. . . .' ('My heart, my heart is sorrowful, / But May is sparkling merrily . . .'). This poem concludes his depiction of a peaceful idyll by the ramparts of old Lüneburg with an observation about the Hanoverian guards, and the wish:

> Er spielt mit seiner Flinte,
> Die funkelt im Sonnenrot,
> Er präsentiert und schultert –
> Ich wollt', er schösse mich tot.

> He toys there with his musket,
> It gleams in sunlight so red,
> His arms he presents and shoulders –
> I wish he'd shoot me dead.

The present-day, wrote Heine in 1831, calls for the 'poignant celebration of pain of those modern songs that refuse to fabricate a catholic harmony of feeling, but rather in ruthless Jacobin style dissect feelings for the sake of truth'.

Living in exile in Paris from 1831 onwards, Heine completed the critique he had begun of Romanticism as the 'poetry of impotence'. He based this critique on theory (*Die Romantische Schule – The Romantic School*, 1836; *Zur Geschichte der Religion und Philosophie in Deutschland – On the History of Religion and Philosophy in Germany*, 1834), thus giving a new quality both to his perception of himself as a writer and his assessment of the function of literature within the totality of social relationships.

Art and politics

Heine was now a leading figure in the literary avant-garde, whose ranks also included *junges Deutschland* writers such as Gutzow and Laube. According to Heine's words, and agenda, they were writers who now wanted to make 'no distinction between life and writing, never more to separate politics from science, art and religion, and who are at one and the same time artists, tribunes and apostles'.

Although sceptical at first about translating it into poetry, Heine set about elaborating a more precise theory of a literature of political strategy in the 1830s, beginning with a vigorous polemic analysis of Börne (*Ludwig Börne. Eine Denkschrift – Ludwig Börne: a Memorial*, 1840). Here he also categorically distanced himself from calls on the part of the republican opposition to place his artistic genius at their service. In his view of the political creative artist, Heine insisted on a position 'between parties'. This led him to be completely misunderstood by his critics, and to accusations of 'lack of principle', and even betrayal. The analytical trenchancy, and linguistic and stylistic mastery evinced by his contemporary history of polite literature (his 'bellestristische Gegenwartshistorie' – Briegleb), written and published as a series of articles for the *Augsburger Zeitung* (1840–, revised and republished in 1854 as *Lutetia*), nevertheless make it difficult to categorize him as a political writer entirely within his own proclaimed position. He was able, for example, to predict revolution as the outcome of reactionary entrenchment, 'communism' as the consequence of a liberal 'money aristocracy', and nationalist reaction as the response to patriotic revolutionaries. From 1844 onwards he was on the offensive again as a lyric poet with topical satirical poems, mainly his verse epic *Deutschland. Ein Wintermärchen (Germany: A Winter's Tale)* (1844), arguably the most important satirical work of the nineteenth century.

Deutschland. Ein Wintermärchen (Germany: A Winter's Tale)

The poem cycle *Deutschland: Ein Wintermärchen* was written in 1843, immediately following a visit to Germany – Heine's first after twelve years' exile in Paris. Travel accounts had existed in prose since the eighteenth century (e.g. Goethe: *Italienische Reise – A Journey to Italy*; Forster: *Ansichten vom Niederrhein – Views of the Lower Rhine*; Seume: *Spaziergang nach Syrakus – A Walk to Syracuse*; Heine: *Die Harzreise – A Journey to the Harz Mountains*). During the *Vormärz* period the lyric cycle form (e.g. Heine: *Reisebilder – Pictures from a Journey*; Grün: *Spaziergänge eines Wiener Poeten – Walks by a Viennese Poet*; Dingelstedt: *Lieder eines kosmopolitischen Nachtwächters – Songs by a Cosmopolitan Night-Watchman*) was often resorted to in order to describe the enlightened political life of a foreign country and criticise one's own. Heine was able to make this vehicle more potent. As a 'foreign' German visiting his homeland from exile he was able to strike at 'the old, official Germany, the festering land of the Philistines' (Heine, 1852) by confronting it with his image of the 'real Germany, the great, mysterious, as it were anonymous Germany of the German people'. This confrontation gave rise to a critique of Germany of such devastating penetration that it helped launch a prolonged process of coming to terms with the 'German calamity'. This was already in evidence in the *Vormärz* period in the work of Marx and Engels, and continued during the imperial era of Heinrich Mann (*Der Untertan – The Subject*, 1916), the Weimar Republic of Kurt Tucholsky and John Heartfield (*Deutschland, Deutschland über alles*, 1929), the fascist era of Bertolt Brecht (*Furcht und Elend des Dritten Reiches – The Fear and Misery of the Third Reich*, originally published under the title: *Deutschland – Ein Greuelmärchen – Germany: A Tale of Horror*, 1938), and in the present day with writers such as Wolf Biermann (*Deutschland. Ein Wintermärchen – Germany: A Winter's Tale*, 1972).

At the same time, however, this heterogeneous work also contains something that has tended to be overlooked since the *Vormärz* era and the vociferous reaction it evoked among German nationalists. It gives voice to a love for the real (future) Germany a love born out of suffering under the prevailing conditions in Germany and a kind of hymnic patriotism that could not be misappropriated by the 'pharisees of nationality' (Heine). This was from the very outset something quite different from the black-red-and-gold and much less the 'brown' invocations of German greatness – from Hoffmann von Fallerleben's *Deutschland, Deutschland über alles* to Baumann's *Denn heute gehört uns Deutschland und morgen die ganze Welt* (*For Today Germany is Ours, and Tomorrow the Whole World*).

The 'revolutionary spring'

This is the Germany of the 'Winter's Tale' – an anachronistic country that has ossified into permanent winter with no growth, 'an absence of political present constituted into a world of its own' (Marx, 1843). It is also the German people, standing on the threshold of a great revolutionary spring – their future – when as the almost hymn-like words of the preface express it:

> We bring to fruition what the French began, when we surpass this in deeds, as we have already done in our thoughts, when we soar to the very last consequences of it, when we destroy servitude to the very last nook and cranny, Heaven, when we rescue the God who resides on Earth in men from his degradation, when we become the saviour of God, when we restore the dignity of the impoverished people, disinherited of their fortune and happiness, and of derided genius and besmirched beauty, such as was spoken of and sung by our great masters, and as we ourselves desire, we the young. . . .

This satire on a Germany of the past without a present (a satire still subject to censorship), represented by the 'ghosts' of Prussia, empire, the military, teutonic nationalism, the Church and Christianity, Romanticism, the Middle Ages and Barbarossa, just as much as a Hamburg rebuilt in the image of middle-class philistinism, thus amounts to a prophetic vision of the future Germany. Here, Heine is close to the ideas of the young Marx, whose acquaintance he had made shortly after his return from Germany. This dual character is in evidence from the very first chapter, in which the poet offsets a song of resignation by the harp-girl with another 'better song', which praises a happiness on Earth that is liberated both from intellectual servitude and economic exploitation. It continues to the very end, where war is declared by the poet on the ruling classes in the name of the 'new breed' of men.

Political poetry

Heine himself saw *Deutschland. Ein Wintermärchen* as an exemplary contribution to political poetry, and as a 'better song' with which to counter the 'tendentious poetry' of his day. This self-assurance is based on the one hand on the ideological radicalism of his political critique – from the 'standpoint of the theory that declares man to be the highest essence of man' (Marx) – and on the other on the conviction that this standpoint required a new artistic technique. This technique was intended to replace the aesthetic and social isolation of classical artistic creation with a creative and effective blend of formal elements drawn from journalistic prose and popular folk lyric, from satire, hymn, irony and utopia, from comedy and tragedy.

This type of political writing, rooted in a commitment to a changed relationship between thought and deed, artistic creation and social change (on this see also Chapters 6, 7 and 27 of the *Wintermärchen*, as well as the poem *Doktrin*), set Heine apart in the *Vormärz* period, aside from some initial signs in Herwegh and echoes in Weerth. After the 1848 revolution Heine, bedridden from then until his death, looked to the future with gloom, but undeterred in his principles. *Enfant perdu*, the final poem of the *Lamentationen* from the *Romanzero* anthology (1851), opens with the lines: 'Verlorner Posten in dem Freiheitskriege, / Hielt ich seit dreissig Jahren treulich aus. / Ich kämpfte ohne Hoffnung dass ich siege, / Ich wusste, nie komm' ich gesund nach Haus' ('Faithfully for over thirty years, / On positions already long-lost I held my ground, / Fought on with no hope of victory, / Knowing I'd ne'er return safe and sound'). The final strophe reads: 'Ein Posten ist vakant! – Die Wunden klaffen – / Der eine fällt, die andern rücken nach – / Doch fall ich unbesiegt, und meine Waffen / Sind nicht gebrochen – nur mein Herze brach' ('A post is vacant! – The wounds are gaping – / One falls, and the others move up – / And yet I fell unconquered, and my weapons / Are not broken – only my heart broke'). Politically, there were no doubts in his mind: 'Sentence was passed long ago; this outmoded society stands condemned. May justice come to pass! May it be dashed to pieces, this archaic world where innocence has gone to ruin, where self-seeking has flourished, where man has been exploited by man!'

Heine predicted that this archaic world would be swept aside by 'communism'. He was concerned, however, that in this necessary process of removing injustice, what was beautiful (art and sensuality) would be preserved – those things that the middle-class inheritors of the archaic world had already begun to do away with and degrade.

Weltschmerz

Heine's development from *Weltschmerz* poet to political poet mirrors the course taken by German literature from 1815 to 1848, although obviously the latter suffered many more massive breaks in continuity. Heine found a way out of the creative depression of the Late Romantic era, arriving at a realistic appraisal of the fresh potential to be tapped in a literature of political strategy in the *Vormärz* and making a personal political commitment on that basis. This made Heine even in his own lifetime the only German writer of the period to achieve European status, as Goethe and E.T.A. Hoffmann had done before him. Despite this, it did not occur to any German historian of literature at that time to give him the accolade of 'the greatest German poet since Goethe', as Marx and Engels did in accordance with the overall European appraisal of him. Even since then, Heine's association with Marx and Engels for a long time induced mainstream history to banish contemptuously for a second time this all too disturbing and atypical Franco-German writer. Following persistent preparation of the ground by chauvinistic and anti-socialist German studies from the end of the nineteenth century onwards, Heine was finally declared a non-person by the National Socialists. His name was erased, so that even his most popular and hence irrepressible poem, the *Lorelei* ('Ich weiss nicht, was soll es bedeuten, dass ich so traurig bin'), was attributed to an anonymous author as a folk song.

A central aspect of Heine criticism, and one that began to emerge even in his own lifetime, particularly after his emigration to Paris, was the problem of reconciling the tortured isolation of Heine the man, the political and moral views of Heine the poet and his creative talent. The latter aspect of the man could hardly be denied, and a grudging acknowledgement of him as a lyric poet was the result. His person and his views, however, invoked a torrent of criticism and abuse. He was variously defamed as a Jew, a subversive influence, an 'un-German' intellectual, a 'revolver' journalist, a characterless libertine, a communist, etc. Obviously, therefore, attempts in Düsseldorf, Frankfurt and Hamburg towards the end of the nineteenth century to have a monument erected to him were shot down in the crossfire of German-studies experts and journalists.

The absorption of Heine's work

From the end of the nineteenth century onwards, liberal, social-democrat and socialist advocates ensured that Heine's work was able to exert an influence during the Weimar Republic and among emigrant German writers. The fact remains, however, that Heine remained for the most part excluded from German teaching in schools. As late as 1936, a certain Lutz insisted: 'Heine has no place in the study of German literature or in any reader or textbook. No research on Heine. No publishers for new editions of Heine'. This intransigence is hardly more radical than the failure to appreciate Heine that preceded it. As late as 1966 it was ascertained in a report on Heine's work in German teaching in the German Federal Republic: 'To anyone who had acquired his knowledge of German literature in a West German school after 1945, even one who has had the benefit of unusual teaching material, Heine is scarcely more than a name. In school syllabuses, readers and anthologies, Heine's place (where he has one at all) lags far behind those of authors such as Eichendorff, Hauptmann or Kafka' (E. Becker).

Things have improved somewhat since the 1960s. Heine is now a respected figure in the Federal Republic, albeit more in the sphere of scholarly research than among the public. This has been accompanied by an increasing tendency to see in Heine an aesthetically 'modern', politically non-partisan poet, in contrast with the idea of the socialist Heine cultivated at first, a view that later obviously took a particularly strong hold in the German Democratic Republic. This shift of emphasis has made him palatable to all political persuasions, especially right-wing liberals and conservatives, enabling them moreover to declare proudly that the injustices done to the long-defamed writer Heine have now at last been put right.

The end of art, or a new age and new art

The end of art?

Protestations by young writers against time-honoured ways of thinking and writing, and declarations that the old art and literature are dead, accompanied by visions and works purporting to mark a new beginning, are propounded to the observer of twentieth-century art almost *ad nauseam*. The struggle between various trends, and the quickening pace with which they succeed one another and are promptly commercialised as the new fashion, are themselves proof of 'modernity', which always sets itself up with claims of progressiveness compared with outmoded forms that seem too old or 'classical'. In reality, however, modernity is older than any particular latest fashion. With its attachment to the market and its claims of progressiveness it also embraces the 'old–new', which could become modern again. As Brecht expresses it through Me-ti, there are many for whom the old is quite new.

This brand of modernity can be traced far back into the crisis-ridden history of the middle class and the conflicts it underwent in the process of emancipation from feudalism in the eighteenth and nineteenth centuries. These crises and conflicts may be understood as the origin, driving force and substance of modern art, and of its permanently reiterated attempts at revolutionisation. Since that period, the constant theme, transformed to suit each particular historical situation, has been that 'the world is out of joint' (Brecht). This theme is debated in terms of the development of the relationship between poetry and reality, art and the class struggle – a debate posing questions such as: is art above reality, or part of it? Does art withdraw from or participate in reality? Does it transfigure or enlighten? Is it pointless or committed? After the revolutionary literary movements of the *Sturm und Drang* and the early Romantics and Jacobins, this theme became topical again in the *Vormärz* era, when discussion took on a radical hue.

An uncertain notion of art

The increasing sense of urgency in the discussion surrounding the function and significance of classical and Romantic literature in the *Vormärz* era may be attributed to a number of coinciding causes. The first of these was a general crisis in politics and *Weltanschauung* that erupted in the Paris revolution of July 1830, and which may be seen as an expression of the Europe-wide process of transformation from a feudal to a middle-class capitalist order. The second was an increasing consciousness among many contemporaries from the 1820s onwards of standing 'at a critical cross-roads from one period of world history to another' (Schlegel, 1827). A third factor was that the decade between 1825 and 1835 saw the deaths of a number of the most important figures of the previous epoch, including Jean Paul, Friedrich Schlegel, Goethe, Hegel, and Wilhelm Von Humboldt.

On the other hand there was a resurgence in the middle-class liberal and democratic protest movement from the 1830s onwards. Younger writers who were politically committed to this movement were coming increasingly to realise that the methods and principles of classical and Romantic art were no match for the new issues of the day. The controversy of the era, therefore, was whether the inadequacy of this time-honoured principle of art made it unequal to the reality of a new epoch, or whether the inadequate conditions of these turbulent new times now made it impossible for the idea of art expressed in earlier masterpieces, and which was still the correct idea, to find full expression. This debate proliferated out of a controversy over Goethe, the chief representative of this notion of art.

The Goethe controversy

Goethe's life and work were at the same time extraordinary and yet typical of his era. They won him an early acclaim that bordered on cult veneration, but also incurred opposition and protest on account of the 'despotism of fame' (Gutzow) and the influential, normative power of his works. The fact above all that the Weimar 'prince of poets' had adopted after 1815 a reserved or even critical stance towards the middle-class emancipation movement, as well as speaking out against the use of poetry in topical issues, provoked discussion.

Goethe's advocates argued that the true creative artist has a duty 'to belong to no people or time' and 'to be a contemporary of all times' (Schiller). Goethe, the creative artist *par excellence*, they argued, had conducted himself consistently, and those who could not or would not follow him must give up art, but not criticise its principle. This standpoint was adopted by traditionalists and *Biedermeier* writers alike, and is still to some extent discernible in literary appraisal to this day.

Even then, however, it was augmented by one contemporary historian of literature, Gervinus, with a liberal and provocative variation. For him, the book of German national literature had been closed with the death of Goethe, and for the time being at least could not be reopened. The nation, therefore, would now have to turn from books to political action in order to restore its outward unity. Only when this had been achieved could a new flowering of literature take place. This variation has also resurfaced in various guises up to the present day.

Those who criticised Goethe, however, although by no means unanimous among themselves, arrived at quite opposite conclusions. Their criticism, and the broad discussion that arose out of it, prepared the ground in the 1830s for a fundamental reorientation in the theory of literature with regard to the task of literature and the modern writer, within both literary tradition and contemporary politics.

Wolfgang Menzel as a critic of Goethe

This major debate was sparked off by the most influential literary critic of the day, the former *Burschenschaftler* Wolfgang Menzel. His provocative work *Die deutsche Literatur*, published in 1828, declared that Goethe had not been a genius, but merely a talent who had wasted his potential in the treatment of themes directed against morality, religion and his fatherland. Menzel's schoolmasterly critique was based on an attitude that purported to be liberal but was in fact reactionary. It set up as the measure of all things a widely-held, narrow-minded brand of Christian morality, an openly anti-semitic patriotism and a vaguely Romantic-oriented notion of the creative artist. This obtuse, public-prosecution approach to literary criticism has reared its head again and again up to the present day in poisonous, denunciatory 'criticism', inciting readers to outlaw, burn and banish writers like Goethe, as well as Jews such as Heine, Humanists like Heinrich Mann, socialists such as Brecht or 'sympathisers with terror' such as Böll.

Interestingly, Menzel's critique, which is in fact of non-intellectual origin, does agree on one major point with the journalist and literary critic Börne's attack on Goethe. This is the indictment levelled against Goethe that he was politically indifferent to the major issues of his day. Börne, however, couched this indictment in terms of the issue of 'freedom', whereas Menzel saw the issue as that of the 'nation'. From the very beginning of his literary and journalistic career in 1818, when he published the journal, soon to be banned, *Die Wage*, until his death in 1837 as an emigrant in Paris, Börne strove for a politically-minded journalism that would pay heed to the interests of freedom and progress. He did this through argument and polemic, reviews and his own creative work, through criticism of other authors, and through the example he tried to set in his own life. In Börne's view it had been the duty of Goethe, the leading German poet, to use his artistic authority in the service of middle-class emancipation and the struggle against oppression of the middle class by princes, thereby offering an encouraging example both to the nation and to other writers. Instead, Börne argued, Goethe had chosen to remain a *Stabilitätsnarr*, 'a fool for stability' in the service of a prince.

Genius and social calamity

This critique, originally based on moral grounds, was later shifted to the political level by Engels in 1846–7. Engels was less interested in the degree of personal failure in face of historical duty than in the extent of social calamity that impeded genius:

> Goethe's works reveal an ambivalent attitude towards the German society of his time. Sometimes he is hostile to it, seeking to flee from what is repugnant to him. . . . At others, however, he is well-disposed to it and 'sends' himself into it . . . , even defending it against the imminent progress of history. . . . Goethe is thus at times colossal, and at others petty; sometimes the defiant, derisive world-despising genius, sometimes the respectful, frugal, narrow Philistine. Not even Goethe was able to rise above the German calamity. On the contrary, it rose above him, and this victory of that calamity over the greatest German of all is the best proof that it cannot be overcome at all 'from the inside out'.

In his critique of Goethe, Börne likewise supported ideological disengagement from what was regarded as the ultimate literature – classical literature. It was Heine who then gave theoretical form to this idea. Whereas Börne had focused predominantly on the person of Goethe and his alleged failure, and Engels had accentuated the calamitous state of German society, Heine's critique of Goethe urged a focus on principles, and hence an overall analysis of the 'Goethe school of art' and of Romanticism as the *Kunstperiode*.

Art as a Scheinwelt (false world)

In his *Romantische Schule (Romantic School)* (1836), Heine asserts that the adherents of Goethe view 'art as a separate, other world, placing it so high that the entirety of human activity, religion and morality ebbs and flows below it'. Even before the July Revolution, Heine was of the opinion that such an art, devoid of political consequence, was

> doomed to failure. Its roots lie buried in the obsolete *ancien régime* of the Holy Roman Empire, and are thus awkwardly at odds with the present, like all other faded remnants of that past. It is this state of being at odds, not the movement of time itself, that is so damaging to art. . . . And yet, the new age will give birth to a new form of art

in enthusiastic harmony with itself. It will not need to borrow its symbolism from a faded past, and will inevitably bring forth a new technique, different from the previous one.

The critique of the old and the demand for new, up-to-date art forms and techniques was probably most broad-based in Heine. It held good up to the time of Benjamin and Brecht, but was first followed by writers of the *junges Deutschland* movement, such as Gutzow, Wienbarg, Laube and Mundt, albeit with some difficulty. The political character of their initial revolutionary aspiration waned rapidly for a number of reasons. They were theoretically somewhat weak, shocked by an 1835 ban on their publications arising out of the denouncing critique of Menzel, and caught up in petty critical squabbles, both among themselves and with their opponents on the Right – and later also with those on the Left. 'We are struggling for the way to the goal, but do not even recognise the goal ourselves', acknowledged Gutzow. He thereby aptly summed up how the struggle for a new literature relevant to the age must, on the one hand, be seen from the first as the beginning of a sought-after literary renewal. On the other hand, it was the fate of the modern writer himself to remain an intellectual precursor, embodying the transition between the past-in-the-present and the future.

Through their paradoxical reconciliation with the previously criticised principle of the *Kunstepoche*, however, the *Jungdeutschen* soon came to see themselves as preparing the way for an intellectual emancipation that was to be brought about purely by literature. They furthermore sought their readership precisely where the old literature had done: among intellectuals, as distinct from the populist movements of the 1830s and 1840s, which were now regarded as raw, uneducated and criminal.

The example of Georg Büchner

The achievement of the *Jungdeutschen* in breaking out of the exclusivity of the classical-Romantic book culture, and thereby greatly enriching literature itself, can hardly be disputed. This was done, first, through their themes: these demonstrated a commitment to civil liberties, the emancipation of the Jews and of women, cosmopolitanism, the abolition of rank distinctions, religious freedom, etc. Second, they did this through their practical work as writers and journalists. It would be equally difficult, however, to dispute Georg Büchner's political criticism of what he saw as the half-baked literary revolution of the Young Germans. In 1836 he wrote to Gutzow: 'To reform society through the Idea, starting with the educated class? Impossible! Our time is a purely material one; had they addressed themselves to the task in a more directly political way, they would soon have arrived at the point where reform would have stopped of its own accord.' In his own literary work, Büchner drew radical conclusions from criticism of the *Kunstepoche*, long before the 1840s agenda of politically strategic literature made a further attempt, by abolishing the 'dead pseudo-phenomenon of the old art' (Heine) to generate a new literature that would 'address itself to the task in a directly political way'.

Hardly a German writer of the last two centuries, aside from Hölderlin, is so difficult to place in the developmental process of literary history as Büchner. A few years younger than the Young German authors, he began like them to write in the period after the 1830 July Revolution and to distance himself critically from the *Kunstepoche*. His own literary theory and practice nevertheless went considerably beyond theirs in consequence of his more progressive (early socialist-materialist) world-view. He never made the acquaintance of Heine, whose views were closest to his own, nor did he live to see the social-revolutionary literature of the 1840s and the beginnings of scientific socialism. Adherents of the latter were likewise almost completely deprived of an acquaintance with Büchner's few works, most of which were destroyed or confiscated, mutilated by censors or published after long delays. It was the beginning of this century before he reached a wider readership with a first critical edition of his works in 1879 and the premieres of his dramas between 1885 and 1913.

Since that time, Büchner has been ranked beside Lenz, Kleist and Grabbe as one of the classic 'modern' authors who were ahead of their times, variously claimed by the naturalists, expressionists and theatres of politics and the absurd.

Literature and revolution

A further aspect of Büchner that distinguishes him from both typical *Vormärz* political writers and others is that he was first and foremost a materialist researcher of nature, and a politically aware revolutionary. His work as a writer arises in the first instance out of the connection between research into the natural sciences and philosophy (anatomy) and political revolutionary practice (the founding of the subversive *Gesellschaft für Menschenrechte*, the Society for Human Rights, in Giessen). The *Gesellschaft* played a role of some significance in republican and early working-class publicity work after the July Revolution. Büchner's first publication was the pamphlet *Der Hessische Landbote* (*The Hessian Messenger*) (1834), which was edited by Weidig, a Butzbach pastor and one of the leading south German democrats of the 1830s. Intended for revolutionary publicity purposes, the pamphlet goes into considerable detail, including statistics, without losing its overall sense of proportion. It exposes in biblically simple, and yet rhetorically powerful language the ruthless exploitative practices of the feudal Hessian Grand Duchy and its beneficiaries. Writing in 1878 of the *Hessische Landbote*, Karl Emil Franzos, the first publisher, asserts: 'For the first time in Germany a democrat made a stand not for the intellectual property of the intellectual, but for the material property of the poor and uneducated. For the first time we see discussed not the issues of freedom of the press, the right to associate and electoral consensus, but "the basic need for bread". Instead of democratic political publicity we see here social democratic indictment and arraignment.'

Realistically, and without a shred of liberal illusion, Büchner came to the conclusion, even as a student in the French town of Strasbourg in 1833, that: 'If anything is going to help in these times, then it is force. We know what to expect of our princes. Everything they have consented to has been forced out of them by necessity. And even what they consented to has been tossed to us like mercy to a beggar, or like some miserable children's toy, to make the ceaselessly gaping people forget that their swaddling bands were tied too tight'.

At the same time, however, Büchner also wrote that he refrained from all forms of practical participation in revolutionary activities, 'since at the present time I regard all revolutionary movements as doomed to failure, and do not share the delusion of those who see in the Germans a people ready to fight for their rights'.

The concept of force

On the one hand, therefore, stood Büchner's essentially momentous perception of the prevailing balance of power and the necessity for the use of force to counteract it, including an active role for the people (his focus was on the suffering peasants exclusively). On the other stood his resigned acknowledgement that 'there is nothing to be done', since the present balance of power precluded action. The tension between these two perceptions was to remain a hallmark of Büchner's work. Following the failure of the actions planned through the *Hessische Landbote*, he withdrew from underground work and tried to apply his political awareness in some other way. Within five weeks he had written the drama *Dantons Tod* (*Danton's Death*), which deals with a central theme of the French Revolution at a turning-point. Since a warrant for his arrest had been issued, however, he fled to Strasbourg, and later to Zurich. It was in exile, when he was primarily concerned with securing his professional life (he graduated and became an unsalaried university lecturer), that the rest of his literary works were written within a relatively short time. These were the comedy *Leonce und Lena*, the unfinished social drama *Woyzeck*, the also unfinished story *Lenz*, and some translations.

A week after Börne's death, on 19 February 1837, Büchner died of typhus. His grave bore an inscription written three years later by Herwegh, another emigrant to Zurich: 'Ein unvollendet Lied sinkt er ins Grab / Der Verse schönsten nimmt her mit hinab' ('He takes an unfinished song into his grave / The loveliest of his verses he takes with him').

The ideal of art

Unlike the critique of the *Kunstepoche* elaborated by Heine and the Young Germans, that of Büchner is not theoretically broad-based. It develops in a more pragmatic form out of his immediate interest in achieving political effects, as well as from problems in his own literary work as a dramatist and narrator. He held Goethe in high esteem, but showed scarcely any interest in Hegel. He severely criticised the Romantics, and above all Schiller, as 'Idealdichter' ('ideal poets'), whose aesthetic principles he objected to for their idealism and their 'most outrageous contempt for human nature', as he phrased it in *Lenz*.

Against their work and theory he set his own writings as the practical implementation of his concept of a realistic art that was relevant to society. The anti-idealist code of life and art, which is linked to his basic outlook in a thought-provoking, action-oriented way, is summed up in one sentence, written as a vindication of *Danton*: 'The poet is no instructor in morality; he invents and creates characters and makes times past live again, so that people can learn from them just as well as from the study of history and from the observation of what goes on in human life'. In the well-known discourse on art in *Lenz*, Büchner has his main character draw the aesthetic conclusions from this basic outlook in a more precise way, once again directed against 'transfiguring' idealism:

> What I look for in everything is – life, the potential for existence, and then it is good; then it is not for us to ask whether it is beautiful or ugly. The feeling that that which has been created has life, should stand above both beauty and ugliness and be the sole criterion in matters of art. . . . One must love humanity in order to penetrate to the real substance of anything. No-one can seem too low, or too ugly: only then can one understand. The most insignificant of faces makes a deeper impression than the mere perception of the beautiful, and one is able to allow characters to come out of oneself without having to copy anything from the outside world, where there is no life, no muscle and no pulse throbbing in response to oneself.

The aesthetics of ugliness

Following his study of the idealistic individual hero in *Dantons Tod*, and a satire on 'obsolete modern society' in *Leonce und Lena*, in *Lenz*, and even more so in *Woyzeck*, Büchner turned to this despised reality of the low and the ugly. In the character of Woyzeck he puts on stage the same poor and oppressed people and poverty-stricken peasants he had earlier addressed in his first written work *Der Hessische Landbote*. His expressive technique of 'allowing characters [to] come out of himself without copying anything from the outside' meant allowing the situation portrayed on stage to speak for itself, thereby provoking thought. This distinguished him not only from the practice of idealist drama, which involved a proclamation of the dramatic solution through the active speech of the hero, but also from the Young German manifestation of liberal-minded strategy, and later also many political lyricists, with the exception of Heine and Weerth.

The agenda of political poetry

Writers and politics

From the very earliest times, but most of all since the Reformation and the early middle-class revolution, writers have seen it as both their right and duty to express themselves in their works on major philosophical issues and the politics of their day. Since the earliest times, therefore, but most of all since the eighteenth century, writers have been praised and rewarded or penalised and persecuted by those in power, depending on their political standpoint and the trenchancy of their criticism. Luther, author of what Engels called the 'Marseillaise of the sixteenth century', the hymn *Ein feste Burg ist unser Gott* (*A Mighty Fortress is Our God*), and of many other religious songs and writings, was persecuted, and Thomas Müntzer, pamphlet author and active participant in the Peasant War, even more so. Luther compromised and survived; Müntzer remained radical and was beheaded. Criticism of religion was a political act of the first order, even after the Reformation, since it invariably concerned the feudal, and later the middle-class state, both of which were bound up with the Church. Lessing discovered this in his public altercation with the pastor Goeze (he was forbidden to continue the dispute); Fichte was dismissed from his chair as Professor of Philosophy in 1799, accused of atheism. Gutzow was sentenced to ten weeks imprisonment in 1835 for allegedly having propounded an anti-Christian 'emancipation of the flesh' in his novel *Wally, die Zweiflerin* (*Wally, the Woman Who Doubted*).

Direct political stances, even loyal and patriotic ones, were not without their perils, either. Gleim's *Grenadierlieder* (*Grenadier Songs*) (1758) in honour of the Seven Years War brought the author fame and public acclaim. For glorifying the idea of middle-class emancipation in their writing Klopstock and Schiller were made honorary French citizens by the Paris National Assembly, but this was rather detrimental to them in feudal Germany. Goethe had an audience with Napoleon that proved fruitless. Prussian patriots in the struggle against Napoleon (Kleist, Körner, and Arndt *inter alia*) were far from popular at court in Berlin, where they were regarded, if anything, as demagogues. The sole recipients of royal honours and pensions were tame monarchist or apolitical writers such as Geibel.

Suppression of opposition

All opposition to the ruling authorities and their policies was openly and brutally suppressed. Schubart was imprisoned for ten years from 1777 on the Hohenasperg before his release, physically and mentally broken. Schiller was obliged to flee Württemberg in order to escape the same fate ('*Die Raüber* cost me my family and homeland'). Jacobin authors also suffered persecution. In 1806 Napoleon had Palm the book dealer shot as a warning to all German writers. From 1819 onwards Metternich ordered the persecution of opposition intellectuals as 'demagogues', oppressing them after 1830 with increased censorship, banning them from their professions and imposing prison sentences. The Prussian Minister of the Interior, von Rochow, decreed: 'It is not seemly for subjects to apply the measure of their limited insight to actions by the head of state, or in their conceited insolence to pass public judgement on the rightness of the same.'

As a result, in 1830–48 the numbers of Germans emigrating to France rose from 30,000 to 170,000, to Switzerland from 20,000 to 40,000, and to Belgium from 5,000 to 13,000. The stepping-up of persecution of opposition writing in the *Vormärz* period appeared successful at first. It seemed to confirm Goethe's often quoted polemical words from *Faust*: 'Ein garstig Lied! Pfui! ein politisch Lied / ein leidig Lied' ('A foul song! Fie! a political song / a tiresome song'). Goethe's meaning had been that to allow politics into literature brings only trouble on the author and reader alike. It is always cleverer to sing some innocuous 'song of the latest stamp'.

The fact remains, however, that particularly from 1830 onwards there was no stopping many writers and intellectuals not only from direct reference to politics in their works (ranging from constitutional issues to social deprivation), but also from practical involvement, both as parliamentarians (including Uhland, Grimm, Arndt, and Blum) and in the underground (including Follen, Pastor Weidig, Büchner and Herwegh). This begs the question of how it was possible.

The politicisation of literature

The growth and expansion of the literature market facilitated a speedier and more effective distribution of the printed word among broad sections of the population in the *Vormärz* period. This emergence of an avid, interested readership with considerable purchasing power furthermore enabled the politically committed writer to free himself from the dependence on feudal service and patronage that had prevailed in the Germany of petty states. This in turn enabled him to express criticism openly. Between 1789 and 1848 censorship crushed many incipient signs of political activism on the part of writers, leading to an enduring distortion of the relationship between politics and literature. It nevertheless failed to achieve its purpose, restoration of the former obedience, which was coming under more attack in the 1840s than ever before in the history of German literature. This last decade before the outbreak of the 1848 revolution saw a radical increase in the politicisation of literature, and it was at this time that the agenda of political poetry found its first theoretical vindication.

Political poetry

The agenda of political poetry – a term first used as a challenge and to indicate a completely new literary direction in the *Vormärz* era – as well as the issues surrounding it, developed against the background of intensified conflict between feudalism and the middle classes on the one hand, and between the liberal moneyed aristocracy and the radical lower middle and working classes on the other. Another aspect of this background was more fervent discussion of the aesthetic heritage of the *Kunstperiode*. Given the deliberate withdrawal by classical and Romantic writers from the immediate political scene (the beginnings of class conflict), and their turning towards a moral and aesthetic world set above it, the first contingency of the *Vormärz* era was to fix the sphere of politics and the state not merely as an indispensable, but indeed as a central theme of art and literature.

Legitimated by a long-standing tradition concerning the relationship between writing and politics that stemmed from the 1790s, and further entrenched by Goethe in the last years of his life, the thesis that poetry and politics were irreconcilable on aesthetic grounds possessed considerable dogmatic force. It continued to carry considerable weight in the *Vormärz* era, especially among poets who felt an aesthetic affinity with classicism and Romanticism.

However, even writers who subsequently developed into political poets during the *Vormärz* period were at first explicitly behind this thesis. Börne, for example, who from 1819 was firmly committed to political writing, still applied it to journalists and prose-writers only, not to poets. Wienbarg, theoretician of the *junges Deutschland* movement, went a step beyond this in assigning to the lyric poet a degree of political participation in current affairs. He immediately restricted this licence, however, by seeing it in the form of a reflection of events in lyric verse – not as direct partisan involvement, or as an attempt 'to influence the political sense of the reader'. Up to the beginning of the 1840s Heine likewise explicitly excluded poetry from furthering the political interest ('we want to further this, but only in good prose'). Even Herwegh and Freiligrath asserted only a few years before their appearance as celebrated political lyricists that the proper substance of poetry was the 'eternal'. It was not its task to recreate the 'accursed filth and trash of our pitiful, miserable human and political life' (Freiligrath, 1841).

It was to take until the 1840s for a standpoint to crystallise from which it would become possible to make a clean break with time-honoured aesthetic dogma. This reformulation took the following form: 'Where there is political consciousness in a nation, this consciousness will also find political expression, and hence there will be political poetry. Furthermore, where there is truly political poetry, then politics must already have become part of the educated individual. The one points to the existence of the other; politics is justified in poetry and poetry in politics.' Seen in this light, political poetry was not merely another variant of poetry, but the historically determined expression of an expansion in the sphere of poetry itself, which consciously possesses a political quality by its very nature.

Partiality

The next task was to demonstrate that the inevitable partiality and 'tendency' of the political poet did not signify the end of his artistry, but was on the contrary its real vindication. This crucial question of the role of poetry in the class struggle sparked off in the *Vormärz* era for the very first time a debate whose central aspects have persisted to this day and which continue to be relevant – albeit differentiated according to the particular period in question. For *Vormärz* contemporaries the lyricist Georg Herwegh, however short-lived his fame, provided the first convincing example of the possibility of combining the aesthetically beautiful with the politically trenchant in the same work. Up to that time 'tendentious poetry' had tended to be criticised. In Herwegh's view of poetry, beauty and political tendency were closely interlinked, because the true poet had a duty not only to the 'supreme law of aesthetics', but at the same time to his people and his times, which he called the 'Madonna of Poetry' in one of this poems.

An die deutschen Dichter (1840)

Seid stolz! es klingt kein Gold der Welt
Wie eurer Saiten Gold;
Es ist kein Fürst so hoch gestellt,
Dass ihr ihm dienen sollt!
Trotz Erz und Marmor stürb er doch,
Wenn ihr ihn sterben liesset;
Der schönste Purpur ist annoch
Das Blut, das ihr als Lied vergiesset!
. . . .
Dem Volke nur seid zugetan,
Jauchzt ihm voran zur Schlacht,
Und liegt's verwundet auf dem Plan,

So pfleget sein und wacht!
Und so man ihm den letzten Rest
Der Freiheit will verkümmern,
So haltet nur am Schwerte fest
Und lasst die Harfen uns zertrümmern!

To German Poets (1840)

Stand proud! No gold on this earth
Sounds as golden as your pages;
Nor is any prince of such noble birth
That you must be his pages!
For all his bronze and marble he must perish,
If you would have it so;
The loveliest purple still to cherish
Is the blood that in your songs doth flow!
. . . .
To the people alone your fealty yield
To battle give them the call,
And lie they wounded on the field,
So tend and care for them withal!
And if any their freedom would stunt,
Be it only the very last speck,
Then let our swords be not blunt,
And let the harps our bodies wreck!

The democratic tendency

The poet had to walk with the people. The principle behind this new
literature (meaning above all the growing body of political lyrics from
1840 onwards, of which Herwegh himself was the outstanding exponent)
was a 'democratic' one. As Herwegh reiterated many times, the poet is
bound to find himself in opposition as a consequence of this position –
both to the undemocratic social conditions that prevailed in the *Vormärz*
era, and to classical-Romantic literature, which was now seen as aristocratic. For him, the political poetry that arose out of this opposition was
tendentious poetry in a higher sense, on the one hand because the involvement of the poet in his own age was for Herwegh 'an integral part' of
eternity, and on the other because he saw eternity itself as a 'tendency'. In
this way political poetry lent expression to the 'eternal tendency' towards
freedom. The generality of this formula, heavily laden with an over-simple
rhetoric, made it politically explosive enough, but also led to its being
adopted as the tendency of the liberal and democratic opposition. On the

other hand, Herwegh was one of the first writers consciously to face up to the consequences of unequivocal political partiality.

In his dispute with Ferdinand Freiligrath, who had declared in his poem *Aus Spanien* (*Out of Spain*) (1841): 'Der Dichter steht auf einer höhern Warte, / als auf den Zinnen der Partei' ('The poet stands on a loftier vantage-point, / than the battlements of the party'), Herwegh resolutely asserted that the poet, with a view to the political situation, must become involved and represent 'unilateral direction . . . since our universality keeps holding us back from action'. In his famous and highly controversial poem *Die Partei (The Party)*, Herwegh replies to all indifferent poets with the assertion:

> Ihr müsst das Herz an *eine* Karte wagen,
> Die Ruhe über Wolken ziemt euch nicht;
> Ihr müsst euch mit in diesem Kampfe schlagen,
> Ein Schwert in eurer Hand ist das Gedicht.
> O wählt ein Banner, und ich bin zufrieden,
> Ob's auch ein andres, denn das meine sei;
> *Ich* hab gewählt, ich habe mich entschieden,
> Und *meinen* Lorbeer flechte die Partei!

> Set your hearts on but *one* card,
> The calm above the clouds is not your right;
> Throw yourselves into battle hard,
> Let poems be the swords with which you fight.
> Choose one banner, and I'll not complain,
> Though it be a different one than mine,
> *My* choice is made without refrain,
> *My* laurel will I round the party's head entwine!

Herwegh is here by no means recommending poets to place themselves in the service of propaganda for a particular political party. Political parties were still only in their very earliest stages in the *Vormärz* era, and party organisations in the modern sense did not yet exist at all. What Herwegh had in mind in a very general way was the taking up of a position. He was throwing doubt on the traditional posture of political impartiality adopted by Freiligrath and many poets in the aftermath of Goethe ('Inasmuch as a poet seeks to be politically active, he must give himself over to one party, and inasmuch as he does this, he is lost as a poet' Goethe, 1832). Gottfried Keller, a passionate admirer of Herwegh's in the *Vormärz* era, is even more severe in his condemnation of impartiality: 'Wer *über* den Partein sich wähnt mit stolzen Mienen, / Der steht zumeist vielmehr beträchtlich *unter* ihnen' ('He who fancies himself *above* parties in his conceit, / Is most often indeed some way beneath their feet').

Not long afterwards in 1843, Freiligrath stepped down from his 'loftier vantage-point' to the battlements of the party, conceding in the preface to his latest collection of political poems, *Ein Glaubensbekenntnis* (*A Confession of Faith*): 'Firmly and unshakeably, I place myself on the side of those who set themselves squarely against the forces of reaction.' Soon, however, even this stand on the side of political opposition to the forces of reaction, which was opposed from a number of political quarters, was not enough for him. He now felt compelled to state the specific groups for which he wished to take a stand. It was in this profession of allegiance to a particular party, in his case communism, that Freiligrath went considerably beyond Herwegh's call for political partiality.

Criticism of political poetry: the antagonism between political tendency and literary practice

Art or occasional writing?

In the *Vormärz* period, as now, political poetry was seen as a contradiction in terms. Conservative criticism held it to be something 'which, being impossible, does not exist, or, being unjustified, should not exist' (Prutz, 1843). However, there was also criticism which, despite accepting the principle of a poetry of political strategy, still doubted whether the political poetry written by such as Herwegh, Freiligrath, and Hoffmann von Fallersleben was something to be applauded. The first objection raised concerned its political tendency as such, the second the literary technique used – the two being closely related.

The political lyric of the young Herwegh was liberal, being based on middle-class aspirations towards emancipation, national unity, a constitution and law. Liberal lyric poets sought to release the necessary energy for this struggle by mobilising emotions (love, hate, enthusiasm, indignation). In so doing, however, they unwittingly widened the gulf between the writer and political reality by tending to treat politics like a religion. Given that the actual political knowledge of most political lyric poets was scant, this poetry gave rise to a tendency to replace inadequate political education by passion, enthusiasm and *Gesinnung*, a vague term suggesting a loyalty and patriotism that required no further justification.

As political occasional poetry, it was written predominantly in the form of a subjective dialogue with the self, i.e. initially as an extension of Goethe's conception of experience as a profession of political awakening, with the aim of 'giving voice to one's own enthusiasm and keeping alive that of others' (Freiligrath). In the form of collective professions of feeling or a demonstration of loyalty on the part of a 'community', songs, patriotic pieces and hymns (including what was to become the national anthem *Deutschland, Deutschland über alles* by Hoffmann von Fallersleben, which was also written at that time) became part of a popular movement that made political folk singers out of many lyric poets.

Heine's critique

Heine's severe criticism of the tendentious poets of the 1840s, which opened him to the unjust accusation of betraying the cause, probably penetrates to the heart of the matter. He takes issue with Herwegh's political enthusiasm, for example, saying that it blinded him to political and social reality and created harmful illusions. He likewise arraigns the *Freiheitssänger* (freedom singers) for the generality of their protest, which he claims opened the way for hypocrites and dilettanti. What he is giving voice to here, therefore, is the concern that by treating the weapon of political poetry, one which Heine himself used, in such a manner, they were running the risk that it would become blunt (compare Heine's poems *An Georg Herwegh – To Georg Herwegh; Die Tendenz – The Tendency; An einen politischen Dichter – To a Political Poet*). This concern included grave doubts on the part of Heine the creative artist that this popular, but politically illusory poetry, based on the traditional principle of enthusiasm, was the right precursor for a strategic creative procedure that would facilitate a 'new technique'. Such a technique, he was convinced, was necessary to be able both to perceive and to intervene in changing social reality. Heine himself tried to practise this new way of writing in his topical poetry, political verse epics and prose texts, endeavouring to combine elements of the subjective with the distanced, the sensual with the ironic and the associative with the open in a single combination. This made him a contributor to the 'prehistory of the modern', which was characterised from the outset by a tense and to some extent ambivalent relationship between the revolutionising of aesthetic means (i.e. technique) and political partiality (i.e. tendency).

Political agitation

However, criticism was to be levelled even at the later lyric poetry of Herwegh, and above all that of Freiligrath, by now more politically precise because of its commitment to a specific party. In his poem *Wie man's macht! (How to Go About It!)* (1846), Freiligrath suggests first storming the arsenal of the territorial army in this hour of greatest need, taking arms there and marching on the capital with the newly-deserted local military:

Anschwillt ihr Zug lawinengleich!
Umstürzt der Thron, die Krone fällt, in seinen Angeln
    ächzt das Reich!

Aus Brand und Glut erhebt das Volk sieghaft sein lang zertreten
   Haupt!
Wehen hat jegliche Geburt! – So wird es kommen, eh ihr glaubt!

March on in rising, swelling ranks!
Topple the throne and crown on which empire hangs!
Out of fire and flame the conquering people raises its long down-
   trodden head!
There is no birth without pain – 'Twill be upon us sooner than they
   dread!

What made this poem so totally unprecedented was not only the fact
that it came from a hitherto respectable German middle-class poet such as
Freiligrath, but also that it painted a picture of a viable working-class
revolution purely on the basis of its technical feasibility, and even openly
recommended it. All the same it was arraigned by Marx and Engels for
what they saw as its unstated assumption that the seizure of power was
no more than a question of the courage and will of a single group. Concerning the revolution anticipated in the poem (which did indeed break out
only two years later), they commented ironically that 'throughout the
entire proceedings certainly not a single member of the proletarian battalion
suffered the inconvenience of his pipe going out'. Their idea of revolution,
as Arnold Ruge, later opposed by Marx, wrote in 1838, was: 'revolutions
are not made, they make themselves, i.e. when they occur it is because
the force of progress makes them historically necessary'. Socialist pro-
revolutionary publicity material was based on this view of the historical
necessity of revolution. Its aim was to deepen awareness of the inevitability
of this process to dismantle resistance to the revolutionary act.

Revolutionary literature?

This entailed extensive changes to the strategic writing style. Taken to their
logical conclusion, they led to 'smashing of the harps', or the political act
itself. What made political poetry, collected into bound books and offered
for sale on the literature market, so inadequate was the fact that it remained
a substitute for politics proper. It continued to be a product of art, although
aspiring beyond it aesthetically. It was still a commodity destined to be
the prisoner of commercial interests, although politically it opposed them.
   Socialist publicity material managed to break out of this predetermined
mould, most markedly in the case of Georg Weerth. The striking aspects
of this breakthrough were a change in the form in which literature was
distributed, and an expansion of the readership being addressed. Bound
books in the form of anthologies of lyric poetry, novels or closet dramas,
etc. now gave way to pamphlets, posters and newspapers and major literary

forms and to short journalistic forms such as the *feuilleton*, gloss, commentary, essay, satire, joke, caricature and song.

Literature and socialism before and after the 1848 revolution
(Vor- und Nachmärz)

The beginnings of socialist literature

The isolation of this as a theme is a new phenomenon. The most widely consulted histories of literature are generally concerned only with the relationship between literature and the middle classes, and hence omit socialist literature (the core of political writing and politically partial literature) altogether from the canon of work worthy of being preserved. Its significance has only begun to be recognised in recent decades as part of research into the history of literature in the former German Democratic Republic (where there was an interest in the socialist heritage), and since the 1970s in the Federal Republic (where there was an interest in the interrupted democratic revolutionary tradition). It is difficult to give a straightforward answer, however, to the question of whether or not the *Vormärz* period had its own socialist literature or not, and which authors and texts form part of it.

On the eve of a middle-class revolution

On the one hand there can be no doubt that Germany in the first half of the nineteenth century was on the eve of a middle-class revolution (hence the German term *Vor-März*, i.e. pre-March 1848), nor that the driving force behind the anti-feudal movement was the middle classes. The working classes were only beginning to become politically aware as a class in the few decades before this, and then in the 1848 revolution itself.

On the basis of these historical facts the central aspect of this era must be regarded as the politicisation process taking place in middle-class literature. Early socialist literature must consequently be regarded first and foremost as an extremely radicalised form of middle-class philosophy and writing. This found expression in the close reference made by developing socialist theory to the Enlightenment and to Hegel (by Marx in the *Frühschriften* – *The Early Writings*), to criticism of the idealist *Kunstepoche* (in Heine), and to the agenda of political poetry among political lyricists. It is also expressed in the middle-class origins of most writers who were committed to socialism, and who by a more or less complicated process of ideological disengagement 'had worked towards a theoretical understanding of the movement of history as a whole' (Marx).

On the other hand, however, nothing would be more calculated to distort the picture than to divorce the emergence of the literature associated with the working classes from its beginnings in the *Vormärz* period. Within the broad process of radicalisation taking place within middle-class philosophy and literature there were distinct changes and the first signs of a socialist literature that sought to serve the theoretical self-understanding of the working class, both as a political force and as a creative phenomenon. These must therefore be taken into account in a history of literature, even when the texts in question are of a predominantly theoretical, scientific or journalistic nature, or when they originate in the so-called sub-literary sphere of folk literature.

Important theoreticians

A substantial role was played by theoretical writings (analyses, pamphlets, and journalism) in the growing self-understanding of the democratic revolutionary German intelligentsia, as well as in the mobilisation of the early German workers' movement. The first major documents of early socialist (communist) propaganda and lyric verse came in the 1830s with pamphlets and songs by German artisans and workers, who formed both in exile (in Paris and Switzerland), and in the German territories a number of secret societies (including the *Frankfurter Männerbund, Gesellschaft der Menschenrechte, Deutsche Volksverein, Bund der Geächteten* and the *Bund der Gerechten*).

The most important theoretician of these still highly differentiated early socialist movements was the tailor's apprentice Weitling with the political agenda contained in his piece on the self-emancipation of the working classes: *Die Menschheit, wie sie ist und wie sie sein sollte (Humanity As It Is, and As It Should Be)* (1842). This was later proclaimed by Marx to be the 'immense and brilliant literary debut of the German workers'. The political poetry and song written in connection with what came to be known as *Handwerkercommunismus* (artisan communism) was distributed both in special songbooks (e.g. the *Deutsche Volksstimme* – *Voice of the German People*, 1833; *Volksklänge* – *Sounds from the People*, 1841), and orally by journeymen themselves ('propaganda on foot').

The 1840s saw the development of the theory of 'true socialism' in line with French and English utopian socialism. The moral improvement of capitalists and the working classes was now to replace class struggle and social revolution. This, and the increasing social destitution afflicting major urban centres, industrial and rural areas, gave rise in Germany to a substantial literature of social criticism. This included Beck's *Lieder vom armen Mann (Songs from the Poor Man)*, 1846; novels dealing with factory workers and industry, such as Willkomm's *Eisen, Gold und Geist (Iron, Gold and Spirit)*, 1843, and *Weisse Sklaven (White Slaves)*, 1845, and commentaries such as Wolff's *Die Kasematten (The Casemates)*, 1843, which is about a poorhouse, Dronke's *Polizeigeschichten (Police Stories)*, 1846, and his account of the capital city, *Berlin*, 1846. This literature, most of which appealed for sympathy and advocated reform, was still nevertheless addressed to an enlightened middle-class readership.

Marx, Engels and the socialist writers

This literature was intended to rouse the middle classes emotionally on the one hand and to alter their consciousness and appeal to their reason through argument on the other. The middle class was assigned the task of setting in motion in a non-violent way the process whereby the working and middle classes would be emancipated to become 'human'. Seeing a further exacerbation in social tensions after the 1844 uprising of Silesian weavers, Marx and Engels, in their joint criticism of left-wing Hegelianism and the theory of 'true socialism' (*Die heilige Familie* – *The Holy Family*, 1844–5; *Die deutsche Ideologie* – *German Ideology*, 1845–6; *Das Elend der Philosophie* – *The Poverty of Philosophy*, 1847) also laid the foundations of scientific socialism as a historical materialistic theory of class struggle. Soon after, in February 1848, with the outbreak of the 1848 Revolution, this was brought together in the *Communist Party Manifesto*. By committing themselves to the revolutionary interests of the working class and addressing themselves directly to workers as the subject of history ('Workers of the world unite'), Marx and Engels won the friendship and support of many writers, ranging from Heine and Herwegh to Freiligrath, Wolff, Dronke and Weerth. Most of these were actively involved in the 1848 Revolution as journalists and writers in the most important mouthpiece of the Left, the *Neue Rheinische Zeitung* (*The New Rhenish Journal*). A number of Freiligrath's best texts (*Trotz alledem, Abschiedswort an die Neue Rheinische Zeitung* – *For All That: A Farewell to the New Rhenish Journal*) and especially Weerth (e.g. the satirical *feuilleton* novel *Leben und Taten des berühmten Ritters Schnapphahnski* – *The Life and Deeds of the Famous Sir Schnapphahnski*) appeared in this journal up to 1849.

Georg Weerth

Despite being heralded by Engels in 1883 as 'the first and most important writer of the German working class' Weerth remained virtually unknown in the history of literature until well into the twentieth century. Having spent many years in England, and as a result of his intellectual exchange with Engels, he became a convinced socialist. He wrote at the end of 1844: 'All we need here is two successive bad harvests and some kind of bad luck in the commercial world, and the revolution will be upon us. A revolution not against royal power, parliamentary foolishness or religion, but against property.' As a journalist, public speaker (at the Brussels free trade congress in 1847, for example), and not least as a political lyricist he showed commitment to this conviction. His poem *Die Industrie* states unequivocally:

> Doch Tränen fliessen jedem grossem Krieg,
> Es führt die Not nur zu gewisserm Sieg;
> Und wer sie schmieden lernte, Schwert und Ketten,
> Kann mit dem Schwert aus Ketten sich erretten!

> Yet in all great wars the tears must flow,
> Till Want to certain victory grow;
> And he who sword and chain did make
> Can set with sword his chains to break!

Weerth refers at the end of his poems again and again to the imminent revolution. By heralding it, he strengthens in the minds of his readers the conviction that it is drawing inexorably closer. Unlike Herwegh, he rarely rouses the reader to acts of revolution. Instead he allows the working class to speak menacingly of the impending revolution. Elsewhere, as in his *Lieder aus Lancashire* (*Songs from Lancashire*), he allows destitution to speak for itself without going into its political implications. In this way, Weerth is propagating a working-class revolution that he sees as being in the making and 'historically necessary'.

Weerth used a descriptive approach and quotations with commentary to develop a consummate diatribe technique in his minor prose works, particularly in his contributions to the *Neue Rheinische Zeitung* from June 1848 to May 1849. His greatest piece in this connection was his title (borrowed from Heine's *Atta Troll*) *Leben und Taten des berühmten Ritters Schnapphahnski* (*The Life and Deeds of the Famous Sir Schnapphahnski*). The allusions that this contains to Prince Felix Lichnowski, who was shot in Frankfurt in September 1848, brought him a prison sentence despite his assertion in his own defence: 'I was not offering persiflage of any one person, no, I was describing a whole social class.'

Adolf Strodtmann

In interpreting revolution as 'historically necessary', Weerth was following on from a young socialist lyric poet who propounded the class struggle in his poetry – Adolf Strodtmann. His poem *Kasematten-Parlament in Rastatt* (*The Casemate Parliament in Rastatt*) (1849) is a successful portrayal, using the example of uninterrupted protest by incarcerated revolutionaries, of the plight of the working class and the necessity of fighting against oppression and exploitation. Exhausted by heavy forced labour, the prisoners still voice their certainty that in spite of the failed revolution those 'by whose hand humanity lives', 'who though they manufacture endlessly never profit' will one day be victorious over the 'profiteering urge' of the 'retinue of shopkeepers', for whom the whole world is no more than an 'emporium of goods'. Strengthened by this certainty, Strodtmann remains unshaken even by the final collapse of the Revolution. Freiligrath, with an eye more to political revolution, declared at the beginning of 1848: 'We put it briefly: "Us or You / The people or the Crown!".' Strodtmann and other socialist writers were striving more after a social revolution: 'Us or them! / T'will never be otherwise!'

The Arbeiterlied (The Song of the Workers)

In 1851 this idea was further expanded:

> Hinaus zum Kampf! Die Freiheit führt uns an!
> Fortan gehört die Welt dem Arbeitsmann!

> Go out and fight! Liberty leads us on!
> From now on the world belongs to the working man!

This core idea of socialist political publicity is also particularly stressed by Herwegh in his *Bundeslied für den Allgemeinen Deutschen Arbeiterverein* (*Fraternity Song for the General German Workers' Union*), which was in fact written in 1863, but belongs in spirit more to the post-*Vormärz* period:

> The Bundeslied
> Mann der Arbeit aufgewacht!
> Und erkenne deine Macht!
> Alle Räder stehen still
> Wenn dein starker Arm es will.

> Working man, Oh clear thy sight
> And know the fullness of thy might!
> The wheel and cog would cease to go
> If thy strong arm would have it so.

In addition to this, there was a diverse and largely anonymous critical, satirical and lyric pamphlet literature during the Revolution, written by and for workers, especially in Berlin and Vienna. Luise Otto-Peters, who later founded the General German Women's Union, was the first to voice the demands of the working-class woman with her piece *Die Adresse eines deutschen Mädchens* (*The Address of a German Girl*) (1848).

Socialist literature in the Nachmärz period

The defeat of the middle-class democratic revolution of 1848–9 had major repercussions for the subsequent development of socialist literature. Economic destitution, the immediate impetus for revolution, had not been alleviated either during or after a year of it, and was now exacerbated by political persecution on the part of the victorious forces of reaction.

A wave of emigration in the aftermath of 1848

As a result, between 1848 and 1855 around a million Germans emigrated, including many political refugees. From Baden, where the people had risen up earlier, a tenth of the total population emigrated. The material and mental privations endured by these emigrants, victims of political persecution and disappointed people, is documented in many contemporary autobiographical accounts, although the fate of the working class is greatly under-represented (Carl Schurz: *Lebenserinnerungen – Memoirs*, 1906–12; Malwida von Meysenburg: *Memoiren einer Idealistin – Memoirs of an Idealist*, 1876; Stephan Born: *Erinnerungen eines Achtundvierzigers – Memoirs of an 1848-er*, 1898).

Domestic suppression of democratic socialist organisations and their means of publication and communication soon brought working-class literature, which had only just started, to a complete standstill. The process of political consciousness-raising among (predominantly middle-class) writers who had been on the side of socialism during the Revolution underwent severe crises in exile.

Heine, who was isolated by his illness, remained true to his principles, both in his aesthetic practice and in his political views, despite doubts and scepticism (see the French preface to *Lutetia*, 1855). The little that Herwegh published after 1848 showed him to be both a resolute democrat (from 1869 he was a member of the Social Democratic Workers' Party) and a staunch opponent of nationalism and Prussian militarism. In London, Freiligrath at first worked closely with Marx and Engels. He distanced and isolated himself increasingly from socialism, however, returning to Germany following an amnesty in 1868. In the Franco-Prussian war he composed the chauvinistic song *Hurra, Germania!* Weerth fell completely silent after 1849, not only because the political situation and future prospects had changed, but also because it was by now largely impossible to continue writing in the old satirical style. Problems connected with producing written works after 1849, to which Weerth reacted so radically, were accompanied by the problems writers now experienced with their political self-perception. These two factors together in fact constituted the particular plight of post-1849 socialist writing.

Besides their ongoing political work in the running of day-to-day politics and the party organisation, Marx and Engels were also able to deepen their theoretical study of history and the capitalist economy (*On the Criticism of Political Economy*, 1859; *Capital*, Volume 1, 1867). While they were able, therefore, to make a huge contribution to strengthening the workers' movement, both ideologically and in terms of organisation, the contribution of democratic socialist writers was sparse from then until the *Gründerzeit*.

Revitalising the failed revolution?

Literary attempts were made to revitalise the failed revolution of 1848. One by Lassalle, later leader of the General German Workers' Union, in his historical drama *Franz von Sickingen* (1859), unleashed what became known as the Sickingen debate, in which Marx and Engels levelled criticisms in letter form at its alleged ideological and aesthetic shortcomings. Not only did these literary attempts fail, however, but it proved impossible even to build on early *Vormärz* signs of a realistic literary portrayal of the working class. A major contribution was admittedly made, however, by lyricists and song-writers with their revolutionary and festive songs. Apart from the *Bundeslied* by Herwegh, which was written for Lassalle's General German Workers' Union, the best-known of these was the so-called 'Workers' Marseillaise' by Jakob Audorf: *Lied der deutschen Arbeiter* (*Song of the German Workers*) 1864). These songs continued relatively unbroken the style of traditional revolutionary songs.

Improvements were made in the organisational structure of the workers' movement (associations for workers' education and the founding of the General German Workers' Union in 1863, the International Workers' Union in 1864, and the Social Democratic Workers' Party in 1869). As these were established, so too were their journalistic mouthpieces (including *Der Social-Demokrat, Deutsche Arbeiterhallen, Demokratisches Wochenblatt*), which provided a suitable platform for articulating working-class consciousness in literary form. The manner in which these newspapers commented on events such as the Franco-Prussian War, the Paris Commune and the founding of the Reich in 1870–1 (Liebknecht styled the latter ironically a 'royal insurance institution against democracy') points to growing self-confidence among socialist authors. This was to find expression in the 1870s and 1880s in the context of the heightened class conflict brought about by the socialist laws of 1878–90. This resulted above all in new forms of satire and *feuilleton* prose, which was able to draw on the writing styles of *Vormärz* literature (compare the satirical journals *Der Süd-deutsche Postillon – The South German Postillion*, 1882–; *Der Wahre Jakob – True Jacob*, 1884–).

Review of an age: new writing styles in prose, lyric poetry and drama

Radical changes in literary technique

The decisive factors affecting developments in literature during the *Vormärz* period were the process whereby it came to terms with the legacy of the *Kunstepoche* (whether in the form of critical attack or an attempt to conserve) and the endeavour to define contemporary literature in terms of its practical political function (whether accepting or rejecting such a function). All this gave rise to a strong impulse towards an experimental breaking with traditional genre forms and writing styles, accompanied by a re-evaluation of the status of each.

Both these tendencies must be seen as inseparable from the parallel experience of the *Vormärz* writer himself: a reality changing so fundamentally could now only be encompassed with innovative literary techniques.

The most striking and far-reaching of these changes occurred in the relationship between verse-writing (with its traditional genres of lyric, epic and drama) and prose (with the 'modern genres' of *feuilleton*, travel report, letter, narrative prose, etc.). In the course of this debate surrounding the redefinition of the function of literature, and on the basis of an expanding press and publishing industry, the status of prose greatly improved in relation to verse, which was still highly regarded.

The new literary forms that evolved as part of this process concerned not only the genre type itself, but also the manner and style of writing. The latter were increasingly characterised by a media-oriented approach concerned with purpose and effect (including popularity and success), and precisely aimed at a largely new reading public. Heine rightly claimed credit for himself and *junges Deutschland* authors for having developed this new writing style (once described by Laube as 'literary gunpowder'): 'Not for the dangerous ideas that "Young Germany" took to market, but for the popular form in which those ideas were clothed was the famous anathema pronounced over the evil brood [mankind] and specifically its ringleader, the master of language, persecuting not the thinker himself, but the stylist. No, I modestly insist, my crime was not the thought, but the manner of writing – the style.'

'Modern' prose: feuilletonism

This writing style, known even then as *feuilletonism*, had a subjectivity and an elastic feel for the topical that distinguished it sharply from the more esoteric poetic 'style' of classical-Romantic art. It was typical not only of *Vormärz* writers of the political opposition, however. To some extent it was even adopted by authors aiming to preserve tradition. This should give some idea of the diversity of 'modern' prose forms in the *Vormärz* period.

Modern authors of the Young Germany movement and political poets, for whom journalism was an integral aspect of their understanding of themselves as writers, dominated this rapidly flourishing, specifically journalistic genre. They included, for example, Börne with his socially critical literary and theatre reviews of the 1820s, Börne and Heine with their political correspondences (*Briefe aus Paris* – *Letters from Paris*, 1832–4; *Französische Zustände* – *The State of Affairs in France*, 1833), Heine's *feuilletons* in the *Augsburger Allgemeiner Zeitung*, and the Young Germans in their many journals, particularly Weerth in the *Neue Rheinische Zeitung* (1848–9).

Feuilletonist forms of presentation in the press were adopted in scientific and theoretical literature with the aim of making it more practically effective. This led to a burgeoning in essay-writing (e.g. Heine's *Die Romantische Schule* – *The Romantic School*, 1836), treatises (e.g. Wienbarg's *Ästhetische Feldzüge* – *Aesthetic Campaigns*, 1834, which in many respects outlined the vision of new Young German literature), as well as pamphlet and polemical literature, most of which appeared in response to the many major pioneering and thought-provoking new works in theology, philosophy, politics and aesthetics).

The increased importance in the political debate of instructive pieces and political publicity material – tracts, pamphlets, proclamations and manifestos – derives not least from the fact that they presented criticism in a modern literary style. This applies not only to such famous documents in the genre as Büchner's *Der Hessische Landbote* (1834) or *The Communist Manifesto* (1848), but equally, albeit to a more limited degree, to the surge of feudal and clerical counter-propaganda that rose to meet it, which was quick to pick up the style.

Feuilletonism similarly exerted a wide-ranging influence in creative prose. Here it manifested itself in the form of heightened subjectivity (cf. the rising tide of letter and travel literature, for which the young Heine had significantly set the tone in 1826 with his *Harzreise*) and realistic conception (cf. the emergence of the critical topical novel from the tradition of the classical novel of development in Immermann's *Die Epigonen*, 1836 and Weerth's *Skizzen aus dem deutschen Handelsleben* – *Sketches from German Commercial Life*, 1845).

This brought critical narrative prose, and the novel, a form energetically championed by the Young Germans, into centre stage as a modern art form. This occurred, however, without linking up with developments towards the topical and social novel taking place outside Germany in the work of authors such as Balzac (*The Human Comedy*, which was available in German from 1829 in 14 volumes), Stendhal (*Le Rouge et le noir* – *Scarlet and Black*, 1830) and Dickens (*The Pickwick Papers*, 1836). In addition to Büchner, whose novella *Lenz* (1835) offers a visionary and realistic portrayal of what was at that time a psychologically sick human nature, liberal democratic writers such as Bettina von Arnim, Willkomm (*Weisse Sklaven* – *White Slaves*, 1845), Wolff (*Das Elend und der Aufruhr in Schlesien* – *Poverty and Uprising in Silesia*, 1844, 1845) and Dronke (*Berlin*, 1846) were the first to move towards realistic depiction by giving detailed descriptions in their novels of social deprivation, exploitation and oppression. By resorting to these new spheres of realism (provincial regions, local landscapes and history, and the psyche), even conservative and Humanist authors, such as Immermann (*Münchhausen*, 1838), Gotthelf (*Uli der Knecht – Uli the Farm Labourer*, 1841–6), Droste-Hülshoff (*Die Judenbuche – The Jews' Beech*, 1842), Stifter (*Studien – Studies*, from 1844) and Grillparzer (*Der arme Spielmann – The Poor Street-player*, 1848) helped to expand the scope of previous literary themes. This expansion is sometimes referred to as 'poetic realism'. With these authors, however, it was accompanied by a suppression of topical social issues that brought with it the danger of obscuring rather than illuminating them, or of skating over areas of conflict.

Crime fiction (*Kriminalgeschichte*)

A good example of this process is the crime fiction genre. This arose out of an interest in elucidating the world of law and crime in general (cf. the many reforms in criminal law from the end of the eighteenth century), and in particular the phenomenon of criminality, a thought-provoking topic to the progressive middle-class mind. Crime fiction developed from the second half of the eighteenth century onwards, drawing its material from legal case files and trial records (*Pitaval*, German edition 1747; *Richer*, German edition 1792; Feuerbach: *Merkwürdige Criminalrechtsfälle – Remarkable Cases from Criminal Law*, German edition 1808; Hitzig/ Alexis: *Der Neue Pitaval – The New Pitaval*, German edition 1842). The explicit authenticity of early crime fiction gave it a compelling truthfulness compared to the many invented penny dreadfuls and blood-curdling tales of the day.

Beginning with Edgar Allen Poe's *The Murders in the Rue Morgue* (1841), however, it was superseded by the detective story, a highly inventive genre that suggested the authentic and the factual to the reader in what was in fact invented.

The small degree to which the factual aspect itself (the incident, the deed, the denouement, the punishment, etc.) constituted the interesting and fascinating aspect of this genre is shown by the variations in crime fiction by authors ranging from Schiller (*Der Verbrecher aus verlorener Ehre – The Criminal from Lost Honour*, 1786), through A.G. Meissner, Kleist, Brentano and E. T. A. Hoffmann's *Das Fräulein von Scuderi* (1819), to *Die Judenbuche* (*The Jews' Beech*) (1842) by Droste and on to Fontane's *Unterm Birnbaum* (*Under the Pear Tree*) (1885). All these works deal with the ever-topical problems of justice, injustice, guilt, atonement and the origin and power of evil, in highly diverse fictional adaptations of factually documented material. Schiller seeks to demonstrate 'the unalterable structure of the human soul' by analysing the criminal himself and the causality of the deed; Kleist seeks to show the freedom of the individual to choose in a fragile world, and E.T.A. Hoffmann 'how the worm may come into existence with the seed of the loveliest flower, poisoning it to death'; Droste points to the social and historical constraints on the individual in an age in which a pre-capitalist idyll is coming to an end – a period of transition in which the inherited order is no longer valid and the new has not yet come into effect.

In her 'moral portrait from mountainous Westphalia', the subhead of her novella *Die Judenbuche* (*The Jews' Beech*), Droste sets against the background of this particular region and its history, including the people who live in it and their social condition, her portrayal of the origins, career and eventual fate of Friedrich Mergel. A series of exemplary episodes arranged in five narrative phases deals with events from Friedrich's ninth, twelfth, eighteenth, twenty-second and sixtieth years, unfolding the story of a crime, and the psychology of the man who becomes a criminal. Friedrich, already an accomplice to the murder of the forester Brand, slays under a beech tree the Jew Aaron, to whom he owes money. He flees, spends twenty-six years as a slave to the Turks, and returns at the end of his life in the pitiful guise of his alter-ego Johann Niemand ('John Nobody'). Drawn at last by some magical power to return to the scene of his crime, he hangs himself from the 'Jews' Beech'. The culprit thus becomes the victim of his deed, the deed itself the result of a crisis-ridden time of change in which concepts 'of right and wrong are somewhat muddled'. There are a number of contradictions in *Die Judenbuche* that need to be deciphered on the interpretive level and which derive from what is for Droste the characteristic conflict between the fusion of Christianity with conservatism on the one hand (cf. the opening poem) and efforts to arrive at a realistic notion of reality on the other. What for the narrator is the 'lost' authentic world of the eighteenth century in which the story takes place is contrasted with the topically important and precisely depicted socio-economic transition of nineteenth century *Vormärz*, with the social contradiction of the wood dispute, proletarianisation of the peasants, money and luxury, etc. Contradictions emerge with respect to evaluation of the main character, the importance of nature and the adoption of a position with regard to social conflict. These contradictions arise between the somewhat riddle-like interpretations of a narrator who has turned her back on the historical process and the meaning to be derived from the subtly depicted realities of a crystallising middle-class capitalist society. At all events, however, Droste does not go so far as Bettina von Arnim, who wrote in *Dies Buch gehört dem König* (*This Book Belongs to the King*) in 1845: 'The criminal is the most particular crime of the state!' and 'Why has the criminal not become the hero of virtue? Because he was unable to fence his extensive faculties into a narrow, peculiar culture!'

Goldschnittlyrik

The 'modern prose' that made its first spectacular appearance in the *Vormärz* period may be described as the art form of urban centres. It was not without influence, as may be seen from the work of authors such as Gotthelf or Droste, on 'regionalist' writers who had settled within the still agrarian structures of the provinces. In the latter, however, art forms that gave precedence to verse proved far more tenacious. Conflicts arising out of the claims of modern prose also produced greater tensions in the provinces. This is most clearly apparent in the lyric. It should first be pointed out here that poetry-reading, reciting and verse-writing played an important part in the middle-class life of that time, in the form of occasional poetry for celebrations, albums, letters, etc. Everyone from the well-brought-up daughter in middle-class families to the King of Bavaria was an avid poet. Against the background of the use of lyric verse for almanacs, journals and pocket-books in the widespread *Goldschnittlyrik* of poets such as Rückert, Geibel and the like, lyric poets such as Mörike or Droste were scarcely heeded, with their experiential poetry of sensibility, or their epic lyric cycles and ballads. It may be discerned here that the process of renewal taking place *vis-à-vis* traditional lyric poetry was not without elements of the 'modern' for the further development of middle-class literature. This poetry was characterised by a stylistically highly differentiated and subtle depiction of the experience of nature, and analytical accounts of the anxiety-ridden psychological impulses of a self that was systematically smothered in private, in a changing world (Mörike: 'Lass, O Welt, O lass mich sein': 'Leave, Oh world, Oh leave me alone'). It thus opened up new perspectives on the problems of middle-class subjectivity, which were only to be treated as themes in the arts and sciences much later.

By the end of the 1830s there were increasingly urgent calls to make 'that most unpractical of all things, poetry, practical' (L. Schücking). Within a few years a new, politically strategic type of poetry had appeared, making a resolute break with the constraints on the genre that had been common since the *Kunstepoche*. The lyric verse that had been a kind of formally immaculate personal plea now gave way to lyrics that focused more and more sharply on socio-political reality.

The lyric spectrum

The first signs of this had been in evidence soon after 1815 in the *Vormärz* era with Uhland, arguably the lyricist who was closest to the popular folk form. In a number of political poems, he had urged that what the constitution promised after the liberation war was long overdue. Similarly Chamisso, and to a greater extent Platen and Lenau, had participated after the

July Revolution of 1830 in freedom movements in Europe (Poland). This was of not insignificant help after 1840 in encouraging young political lyric poets in Germany to stand up for their political poetry agenda and speak openly about conditions in Germany.

As the masses became increasingly involved, a process that went hand in hand with both a stepping up and differentiation in political protest that extended to democratic revolutionary objectives, political lyric poetry inevitably became more direct. There were numerous patriotic songs (e.g. *Die Wacht am Rhein – The Watch on the Rhine*), whose tone and political consciousness drew on patriotic songs from the anti-Napoleonic era (Körner, Arndt), fraternity songs, festive songs and national anthems, anonymous bloodcurdling ballads (e.g. *Das Lied vom Tschech – The Song of the Czech*), revolutionary songs (e.g. *Das Blutgericht – The Court of Blood*) and political folk songs by authors such as Hoffmann von Fallersleben. In addition to these, however, there also appeared in pamphlets and journals, or through rapid oral dissemination, political poems as rallying calls (Herwegh), professions of belief (Freiligrath), social indictments, satires and parodies (Herwegh, Heine, Weerth).

Notwithstanding the often abstract pathos of topical liberal lyric poetry, or the delusions apparent in some democratic revolutionary poems, political lyric poetry was nevertheless the dominant literary genre of the 1840s. More than this, it was undoubtedly a major mobilising factor for political revolution. In satirical topical poetry, especially, a type of criticism can be discerned ranging from the subversive to the explicitly polemical. It is to this that the genre owes the undiluted pungency it commands to this day. A diversity of literary caricatures of German life that combine to give a picture of a somnolent, dopey German 'Michel' originated in this period. They are presented, for example, as a catalogue of German 'virtues' in Heine's *Deutschland. Ein Wintermärchen* (*Germany: A Winter's Tale*) (1844): the delight of Germans in singing, rejoicing in song over that which cannot be brought about in political life; piety and an allegiance to royalty that are devoid of all political consciousness; speculative calculation, smugness, a nostalgia for the days of empire and teutonism combined with a Philistine brand of domesticity that had no taste for public life or work.

'Modern' drama

Even in the *Vormärz* period it was probably true of most writers that their greatest ambition was to write a drama. This is in itself an indication of the inertia both of drama as a literary genre and the theatre as an institution in the nineteenth century. In royal seats the stage continued to function under the auspices of ruling princes, and hence at the beck and call of their taste and whim. There were nevertheless growing numbers of commercially run theatres subsidised by middle-class patrons, meeting the needs of audiences with the greatest spending power. Besides these there was also the relatively new phenomenon of suburban theatres in larger cities. These performed (often in dialect) cheap productions for rapid consumption – farces, plays of moral edification and comedies. They were patronised by lower middle-class and semi-working-class suburban audiences and were the only place where they could still find what was known as *Volkstheater*, and where its subversive and critical tradition persisted (Nestroy and Raimund in Vienna, and also in Frankfurt, Hamburg and Munich).

The exclusivity of the theatre in this period gave it what Grillparzer called the character of a secularised form of 'public worship'. It was typified by conservative repertoire, an eye to the rulers of the day, a proclivity for amusement among audiences, and not least by strict police surveillance. All this conspired to ensure that the passion for theatre served to divert attention from politics; realistic and critical tendencies were far less in evidence in drama than in lyric and narrative prose. Of the four or so major dramatists of the time, for example, Grabbe and Büchner and their dramas were virtually unknown until the beginning of the twentieth century, with the exception of Grabbe's *Don Juan und Faust*. Grillparzer enjoyed only limited success and none of his plays was performed after 1838. Hebbel was the only one of the four to find great success from the beginning of his drama-writing career (*Judith*, 1840), which took a further upward turn after 1848.

The work of Grabbe, and even more so of Büchner, was dedicated to realistic contemporary and historical drama. It depicted prevailing circumstances with authenticity, in contrast with idealistic drama of the Schiller type. In his play *Napoleon oder die hundert Tage* (*Napoleon, or the Hundred Days*) (1831, first performed 1869), Christian Dietrich Grabbe, a loner and non-conformist, portrayed recent history and his own period in terms of a historical process in which the material interests of the people were beginning to assert themselves against the great epoch-making individual. Grabbe thereby pre-empted modern political drama, but the political revolutionary Büchner went further than this, both in theory and practice.

Büchner based his work on two premises: first, that the distinction between rich and poor constituted 'the sole revolutionary element in the world', and second, that the supreme duty of the dramatist was 'to come as close as possible to history as it really happened'. In *Dantons Tod* (*The Death of Danton*) (1835, first performed 1902) he takes the example of the French Revolution and its protagonists Danton and Robespierre to show what he sees as the inevitable failure of middle-class attempts to revolutionise the historical process. Büchner bases his analysis on experience of the *Vormärz* period, which saw the establishment of a middle-class, capitalist order – a process triggered by the French Revolution. In his political drama *Dantons Tod*, as well as his social tragedy *Woyzeck* (1836–7, published 1879, first performed 1913), he used hindsight to expose the ever more absurd and brutal divergence between the ideals of 1789 and actual social reality, which was governed by quite different forces.

What follows from this analysis is a denial of the middle-class, idealist concept of freedom, and hence also of the great 'hero' held up in the figures of Egmont, William Tell or Wallenstein. At first sight this seems a nihilistic stance; in fact, however, it represents the first step towards a materialist-based perspective, which views history as determined by the 'imperative needs of the masses' (Büchner). This process is not yet conceived of as the history of class struggle, however. With this theoretical starting point, as well as his innovations in the spheres of dramatic technique, such as his epic treatment, his use of prose rather than verse, his documentary approach and his expressiveness in both language and scene, Büchner anticipates Wedekind, Brecht and present-day political drama.

Christian Friedrich Hebbel's *Maria Magdalene* (1843) is a (lower-) middle-class tragedy and a completely contemporary and topical play. His objectives with this drama were not in the direction of Büchner, however, but in conscious imitation of the idealistic approach of classical dramatists. This perspective is clear from his *Mein Wort über das Drama* (*My Word on Drama*) (1843), in the now famous preface to *Maria Magdalene* and in other pieces, where he outlines his vision of a historical (ideal) drama that was intended to exert an influence on the further development of the drama genre, especially after 1848.

Entertainment literature, literature for children and young people, women's literature

Entertainment literature

By way of conclusion, some account should be given here of a literature whose origins were older than the *Vormärz* era, but which flourished then as a result of the rapid commercialisation of literature. Entertainment literature has already been touched on as the obverse of a 'polite' literature written 'by literati, for literati'. This 'other' literature, which was bound to emerge in the form of entertainment literature for the masses, 'has need of no other stimuli than [the] curiosity and boredom' (Prutz) arising out of the monotony of the arduous daily task of earning a living.

Contemporary discussion of entertainment literature is conflicting. On the one hand it is difficult to hedge the moralising and aesthetic evaluation of this literature, which saw it as having been fabricated by 'vulgar writers' for 'vulgar readers' (Eichendorff), and as a disreputable source of profit for unscrupulous booksellers. On the other hand, inspired by a number of successful titles from abroad, from authors ranging from the Young Germany movement to conservative 'folk', writers made a concerted effort in this period to write readable, entertaining, easily understandable works that would appeal to the masses.

What is clear is that in the *Vormärz* era there was no sharp dividing-line between 'polite' and 'lesser' literature, but rather a fluid transition. This applies both to works by specific authors (especially the Young Germans), to genre forms (especially the novel), and to the manner in which it was presented to the reading public (a blend of 'polite' and 'lesser' literature was offered by journals and paper-bound books).

With the steadily increasing demand for popular reading-matter, and the market for it, novels became sub-divided into recognised fixed categories and special genres, such as the 'historical novel' (Alexis), the 'adventure novel' (Sealsfield), the 'salon novel', the novel of society on the model of the French bestseller by Eugène Sue: *Les Mystères de Paris* (1842), the 'village story' (*Dorfgeschichte*) and so on. During the second half of the nineteenth century this process became even more marked. This period saw the entertainment novels of Gustav Freytag (*Die Ahnen – The Forebears*, 1872), Felix Dahn (*Ein Kampf um Rom – A Battle for Rome*, 1876), Karl May, Eugenie Marlitt (whose romance novels appeared from 1867 in the family journal *Die Gartenlaube – The Bower*), Ludwig Ganghofer, Hedwig Courths-Mahler and many others. These were augmented by new genres such as the detective novel on the model of Edgar Allan Poe's *The Murders in the Rue Morgue* (1841) and Conan Doyle's Sherlock Holmes stories (1887 onwards), the science-fiction novel modelled on the works of Jules Verne and horror literature in the tradition of the so-called 'black Romanticism', such as the novels of Mary Shelley (*Frankenstein*, 1818), Poe and Bram Stoker (*Dracula*, 1897).

Children's and young people's literature

Besides the genres already mentioned there were two further literary forms that had first taken shape as major forms in the eighteenth century: children's and young people's literature and women's literature. It is possible to speak of a special literature for children and young people from the time when the first pedagogical efforts to teach and amuse the coming generation ceased to treat adults and children as a single group, and to concentrate specifically on children. It was not long before this group was further sub-divided into developmental stages.

This occurred in the last third of the eighteenth century as the middle-class family was in the process of forming, and the changed manner in which adults and children lived together necessitated a more systematic approach to educating children. This period thus witnessed factual and illustrated books on nature and work, such as Basedow's *Elementarwerk* (*Basic Mechanisms*) (1774), instructive adventure books such as Campe's

Robinson der Jüngere (*The Young Persons' Robinson*) (1779), the first German children's journal, F.C. Weisse's *Der Kinderfreund* (*The Children's Friend*) (1775 onwards) and many other children's books. Most of these took the form of moral tales, intended to inculcate useful knowledge and the middle-class way of thinking and conception of morality.

This children's and young people's literature, which had been markedly oriented towards utility and didacticism, was now from the beginning of the nineteenth century augmented by fairy tales collected and written by Romantic authors such as the Brothers Grimm, Bechstein and Andersen, and by other popular forms such as humorous tales and old legends (Schwab). The more sophisticated school system of the nineteenth century began to release children's and young people's literature from the burden of direct didacticism, allowing it to become more entertaining. Despite this, however, it remained a major vehicle of socialisation for the inculcation of middle-class virtues, such as a sense of order, cleanliness, obedience, diligence and piety, etc. During the *Vormärz* period the picture-book *Struwwelpeter* (1845) by the Frankfurt physician Hoffmann became famous. This depicts a wayward child, equated at a deeper level with the political revolutionaries of the day, who is brought to reason and taken to task with overtly brutal force. In a less overt manner the same message is evident in Busch's *Max und Moritz* (1865), where narrow-minded morality is exposed by cheeky youthfulness, which nevertheless is also ultimately punished.

The imperial period was characterised by an increasing tendency to idealise the middle-class domestic world of the family and children. Rooted in this was a propagation of subservience, piety, and patriotism. The same period saw the publication of young people's books that are still famous today, such as Mark Twain's *Tom Sawyer* (1876), Stevenson's *Treasure Island* (1884), and Kipling's *Jungle Book* (1894–5). From the 1890s onwards the first socialist books for children and young people were published (e.g. the *Märchenbuch für die Kinder des Proletariats* – Book of Fairy Tales for the Children of the Working Class).

Women's literature

The term 'women's literature' is not precise. It is generally taken to mean literature for women, by women and about women's issues. Since, however, the above definition also comprises literature bound up with a patriarchalism that depicts women in subservient roles as the wives, mothers or mistresses of men, it needs to be more specifically defined. It is therefore generally taken to mean only literature both dealing with the issue of female emancipation and seeking to further it.

This issue became particularly urgent in the Enlightenment and during social changes taking place towards the end of the eighteenth century. This process exacerbated the existing inequality of women: the capitalist form of production was beginning to emerge, and with it an increasing separation between the sphere of work and public life for which men were responsible, and the domestic, family sphere ('Kinder, Küche, Kirche' – 'Children, Kitchen, Church') to which women were finding themselves increasingly relegated.

In the eighteenth century protest was possible only for isolated women of privilege (such as enlightened aristocrats, or teachers' wives and daughters). Despite the example set by independent women of the Romantic movement, such as Caroline Schlegel-Schelling, Rahel Varnhagen and Bettina von Arnim), such protest was almost impossible to convert into viable alternative ways of living. In this situation women's literature served an important function in correcting and criticising women's male-defined understanding of themselves (represented by such ideal literary figures as the girl Gretchen, the 'beautiful soul' Natalie, Helen, the heroine Joan of Orleans, the Amazon woman Penthesilea, the virago Orsina, mothers, virgins, elves, fairies, water-nymphs and witches, etc.), and in articulating a female-defined self-perception. This did not occur without massive opposition from men, who dominated the guild of writers, as well as from women.

In the eighteenth century women writers were still few, but their numbers rose during the *Vormärz* period, not least because it had become possible for them to make an independent living from writing, and hence to demand on their own account, as the early French socialist Fourier had declared, that the degree of female emancipation be taken as the natural measure of overall emancipation in a society. The 1840s, when women could be observed to make a more confident appearance as writers, nevertheless also marked the point when 'women's literature' as a category in its own right became questionable. It was not the fact that women were writing that was remarkable from this point onwards, but what they were writing.

Sophie von La Roche's *Geschichte Fräuleins von Sternheim* (*The Story of Miss von Sternheim*) (1771) is generally regarded as the first German women's novel, outlining a modern type of woman equal in rank to men. Since the French Revolution, in which politically active women had interpreted the declaration of human rights more precisely to include a 'declaration of the rights of women and female citizens', literary practice had seen a steady extension of the scope of what women should be emancipated from and for. This was also being perceived as more and more provocative by men. Mary Wollstonecraft was calling for women to be given the opportunity to practice a profession. In her novel *Die Ehelosen* (*Single Women*) (1829), Therese Huber criticised the traditional ideal of marriage, portraying it as a yoke for women. In his novel fragment *Lucinde* (1799), Friedrich Schlegel had already shocked his contemporaries by

319

portraying an intellectually and sensually independent woman as the true marriage partner.

The French writer and feminist George Sand, whose novels from 1831 onwards advocated free love and condemned men as incapable of love, influenced a spate of women's novels from the end of the 1830s. The Young Germans, who had also dealt with the issues of female emancipation, meanwhile turned to drama. These writers included Luise Mühlbach, Ida Hahn-Hahn, Fanny Lewald, Louise Aston and many others. The focal point of these texts, now forgotten, was discussion presented in a variety of ways about the equality of men and women, opposition to sex-specific prejudices, encouragement of the female will, complaints over the double (male) standard of morality, the sexual oppression of women in the context of prevailing social conditions and, in the case of Lewald and Aston, propagation of political and social revolution as the basis for female emancipation. The journalists Louise Otto-Peters and Franziska M. Anneke argued in a similar vein.

Bettina von Arnim is a clear example of the degree of general emancipation in prospect for a society, had what she achieved in terms of female self-realisation both as a woman and a writer not remained an exception. She was not a women's writer in the mould of her grandmother, Sophie von La Roche, or even in the same way as the *Vormärz* precursors of women's emancipation. She was a highly independent and self-confident woman (this is attributable not least to her privileged social rank). In her own life and the work that is inseparable from it she lived out a quality of female emancipation that makes Enlightenment and early Romantic definitions of the human redundant. She was not like the wives of Romantic writers, who 'served' their husbands by inspiring them in their creative work. She was no less different from the women writers of the *Vormärz*, who were competing with men. Her unique writing style (associative language, authentic letters edited into 'novels', dialogues, etc.) allowed her an independent expressive potential that retained her own vital subjectivity.

Misunderstood from her earliest childhood and even beyond the grave by men and women alike, she was beset alternately by perverse hostility and false praise (as a child-woman, the eternally feminine, as feminist, etc.). From the beginning her family were somewhat at a loss at what to do with the lively little girl Bettina, who was unwilling to conform in her behaviour, and even less in her thinking, to the relatively enlightened and liberal expectations of her well-off Frankfurt merchant family. She had contact with her brother Clemens's circle of friends (young writers, philosophers and women in Jena, such as Novalis, Schlegel, Tieck, Schelling, Schleiermacher, Caroline Schlegel-Schelling, Dorothea Veit-Schlegel, and Karoline von Günderode), whose 'modern' Romantic views on love, marriage, friendship, culture and society were quite at odds with prevailing opinion. Even here, however, the not yet twelve-year-old Bettina tried their patience with her impish, anarchic, spontaneous ways as a 'child of nature'. As the daughter of his former sweetheart Maximiliane Brentano, Bettina pestered the old and famous Goethe in Weimar with letters, gifts and finally her own misbehaving person, offering herself in the same role until the wife of the Privy Councillor became jealous. In 1811 she married the circumspect and mild-mannered Achim von Arnim, friend of Clemens and co-editor of the folk song anthology *Des Knaben Wunderhorn*. Although they had seven children between then and 1827 and these all had to be brought up, her husband found her restless and active, always eager to leave their estate in Wiepersdorf for the life of the Berlin salon.

It was after Arnim's untimely death in 1831 that she made her own debut as a writer. Her letter-novel *Goethes Briefwechsel mit einem Kinde* (*Goethe's Correspondence with a Child*) (1835) threw down a literary gauntlet, particularly to modern Young Germany writers, some of whom now numbered her in their ranks. In a review of the book, Grabbe wrote acerbically of Bettina von Arnim: 'If the writer continues in the same vein, she should not be treated as a lady, but as an author.'

As it turned out, however, it was but the first step in the process of literary and political self-realisation of this woman, by now over fifty. In an age in which her brother Clemens and Friedrich Schlegel had long made their uneasy peace with Catholicism and the forces of political reaction, this 'sibyl of the Romantic literary period' was beginning to put early Romantic anti-capitalism into practice. In so doing she went far beyond the objectives of the Young Germany movement. As a small girl she had had the self-assurance to defy the admonitions of her brother and to treat a Jewish girl, Veilchen, with respect rather than contempt. She continued to preserve this unerring principle even more resolutely after 1830, as a woman active in public life and as a writer. She showed her solidarity with the poor, the persecuted and the oppressed – with people sick with cholera in Berlin, exiled Poles, the poor in Vogtland, Silesian weavers, and victims of political persecution such as the Brothers Grimm, Hoffmann von Fallersleben and Kinkel.

Her family was critical of this more radical approach: one son broke with her, while her daughter Maxe wrote: 'It is disgraceful of you to believe that politics is your sphere. You bring suffering on all your children with it.' In 1842 Bettina von Arnim made the acquaintance of Karl Marx. In 1843 her book *Dies Buch gehört dem König* (*This Book Belongs to the King*) was published – a critique of the Prussian feudal state from the viewpoint of a liberal woman citizen of Frankfurt. A second more radical volume entitled *Gespräche mit Dämonen* (*Conversations with Demons*) was not published until 1852.

In 1844, the year of the Silesian weavers' uprising, she advertised in the major German newspapers for information about the situation of the poor in Germany. She did not dare publish the resulting material and commentary (known as the *Armenbuch – The Book of the Poor*). In the meantime she had been charged by the Berlin magistrate with defamation of the state; in 1847 she was sentenced to two months imprisonment. Disappointed by the outcome of the 1848 revolution, which she had greeted with high hopes and publications (*An die aufgelöste Preussische Nationalversammlung – To the Dissolved Prussian National Assembly*), she retired to Wiepersdorf. Having hardly known a day's illness in her life, Bettina von Arnim suffered a stroke in 1854 and had to be nursed. She died in 1859 in a state of mental confusion.

A setback for emancipation

The defeat of 1848–9 was also a major setback for the cause of women's emancipation, as well as for the women's literature that had championed it. The subsequent period saw 'women's literature' dominated by writers of the Ottilie Wildermuth and Marlitt ilk, whose women were portrayed as passive heroines. The women's movement remained in abeyance until the turn of the century, with the formation and consolidation of the workers' movement, and the publication of Bebel's *Die Frau und der Sozialismus* (*Women and Socialism*) (1879). It then enjoyed both a political and a literary revival, this time with both a middle-class and a working-class accent.

1848 and the shattering of the Enlightenment perspective

The more resolutely formulated the agenda for political writing, and the more determined individual writers such as Herwegh and Freiligrath, Heine and Weerth were to contribute as creative artists towards bringing about a revolutionary transformation of existing conditions, the more questionable their creativity became, newly revived as it was by this very struggle for revolution. This needs to be explained. Until the end of the *Goethezeit*, middle-class progressive writers had had to forgo becoming political writers in order to achieve the authority that was to make them the intellectual leaders and educators of the nation. Politically-committed writers of the *Vormärz* did maintain an uneasy claim to leadership, even in everyday political life, but were only permitted to do so inasmuch as their activity was perceived as being a continuation or even true fulfilment of classical literature. On an individual level writers were able to sustain an understanding of themselves in this vein for quite some time. Objectively speaking, however, their explicitly affirmed desire to make poetry an active political and practical force was bound to lead to a break with the traditional notion of poetry, and hence ultimately to the collapse of their own understanding of themselves as creative artists. As these writers were to realise during and after the failed revolution, not even the ultimate exertion of the active force of their art was enough to overthrow the conditions against which their political consciousness rebelled. If, as Heine had critically observed, Goethe and the literature of the *Kunstepoche* had been a tree whose wood was useless for building barricades, the wood of *Vormärz* political writers was of some use in building barricades, but those barricades were no match for the enemy. The alternatives were either to remain a middle-class creative artist and bury one's political aspirations, or to become politically active and bury one's creative ideas. It was not (yet) possible to be both at the same time, but nor was it possible to be only one or the other. Both alternatives brought grave human and creative crises in their wake.

In a surprising manner, albeit via a quite different route, politically committed writers around 1848 reached the same point as that reached by post-Romantic and Biedermeier authors. During the *Vormärz* the latter resolutely renounced political writing, and hence found themselves in a serious crisis of creative self-understanding. In other words the *Vormärz* endeavour to preserve poetry without breaking with tradition, or to make writing practical, thus redefining the relationship between middle-class literature and the ruling classes, resulted in both cases in a negation of creative activity – the shattering of the Enlightenment perspective.

What remained after 1848 was, on the one hand, a restorational, de-politicised, idealistic theory of literature. In the ensuing period this literary production was under the aegis of middle-class 'realism'. It sought to retain its middle-class character within a restricted national framework with less of its former regional slant, while at the same time picking up the emancipatory threads of its Enlightenment origins (Keller, Raabe, Spielhagen).

On the other hand stood the revolutionary perspective, articulated in Marxist theory and in an incipient socialist literature. Up to 1848 this should be seen predominantly as the result of political radicalisation of an idealistic philosophy and literature (Marx, Engels, Weerth, and to some extent Heine). To this extent, therefore, it was also marked by a negative estimation of the importance of art in the political struggle (in this case against the middle class). Socialist literature, however, which was separate from *Kunstdichtung*, drew on the pre- and sub-literary production of a working class in the making (anonymous or collective texts written by journeymen and members of the working class from the 1830s up to the revolution). The connection between literary and political activity formulated by a once revolutionary middle class was thus consciously preserved, enabling socialist and critical middle-class literature to take up the threads later.

REALISM AND THE
GRÜNDERZEIT

The contradictory overall situation

Looking at this era from the standpoint of writers and their works, one is struck by how many authors rapidly fell into obscurity between the 1848 revolution and World War I, despite having been among the most widely-read in their own day. The Nobel prize-winner Paul Heyse and the 'national' writers Gustav Freytag and Ernst von Wildenbruch would all fall into this category. The question this poses in terms of arriving at a comprehensive assessment of the literature of that time revolves around the texts that may be deemed representative of an era: those acclaimed from the perspective of the era itself (and possibly written against it), or those that really captured the attention, and with which a broad reading public was able to identify.

An atypical evaluation

By the beginning of the twentieth century a canon of great nineteenth-century narrative writers (Stifter, Meyer, Raabe, Keller, Storm, Fontane) and dramatists (Hebbel, Grillparzer) was beginning to form. Despite being held up as representative of the age, however, this canon in fact had nothing at all in common with either contemporary literary history or of the reading habits of the public in the previous century. The fifteenth (1884) edition of Kluge's history of literature for schools, for example, totally bypasses the names of Otto Ludwig, Storm, Keller, Meyer or Raabe. Even the thirty-fourth (1903) edition devotes more space to one now completely obscure contemporary author (Ebers) than to all these authors together. Kluge suggests that work on modern literature focus on Gustav Freytag's *Die Ahnen*.

Even contemporaries themselves were aware that the average reader's knowledge of German literature was limited to a few familiar quotations. Parody, allusion and plays on words were popular forms of showmanship in the second half of the nineteenth century in a society that preferred formal effect to searching analysis of content.

Discussion of form, content or literary tendencies, when present at all, was conducted less among the public at large than in groups such as 'circles' and 'associations'. During the years before and after the 1848 revolution, for example, discussion in the Berlin poets' circle known as the 'Tunnel over the Spree', founded in 1827, was chiefly concerned with the preservation of traditional ideas. When Fontane read two scenes from his one and only drama (it remained incomplete) *Charles Stuart*, it was not difficult for 'tunnel' members to discern parallels with the current King of Prussia Friedrich Wilhelm IV. Merkel, the secretary who kept the minutes, warned the young Fontane against writing a tendentious play: 'That which makes the journalist pious is beneath the poet. He should serve art, not the party!'

An aristocratic middle class?

Fontane's shift of focus to the historical ballad (H.H. Reuter speaks of 'aristocratisation' and de-topicalisation') brought about his breakthrough as a poet into 'elementary school readers, calendars and anthologies'. Fontane's 'change' was thus widely endorsed by the public.

Literature in Germany seemed in increasing danger of becoming a mere backdrop or distorted recollection behind which the middle classes could conceal the insecurity they felt after 1848. The subject-matter of literature scarcely touched on major issues concerning the structure and development of society. In the post-1790 period, with celebrated contributions by writers ranging from Forster to Laube and Heine, travel literature had tried to shed light on social conditions from the angle of the astonished or critical gaze of the observer. This genre now slid into contemplative observation, which was now in demand for its very noncommittal quality. Imitation and trivial idealism had by this time done more than find major support in higher girls' schools: they had become the hallmark of the age.

The cultivation of German feeling

Literature was now assigned a function that ran counter to its original aims: it was to serve in sentimental education and artistic instruction in 'the male-dependent role of the woman, which was restricted to the household' (R. Wittmann). Texts to this end were expected of the poets of the day; they were given preference, and above all published in numerous newly-emerging journals. Since ever greater numbers of authors were dependent on being published, they were often obliged to make literary compromises and put up with 'revised' pre-published versions of their pieces in journals such as the *Gartenlaube*. This was bound to have fatal consequences. It would be no exaggeration to say that apart from a few isolated forays into naturalism not a single literary text between 1850 and 1900 gave even an outline of the economic and social conditions of the new fourth estate, as Schiller had done for the third estate with his drama *Kabale und Liebe* (1793).

It cannot be disputed that Keller, Raabe, Storm and Fontane depicted characters from among the 'ordinary people'. However, they did not permit the people to appear in their works as a working class – only dissociated from it as individuals. The latter more or less discernibly developed into middle-class heroes, such as Hans Unwirrsch in Wilhelm Raabe's novella *Der Hungerpastor* (*The Hunger Pastor*) (1864), or Hauke Haien in Theodor Storm's novella *Der Schimmelreiter* (*The Ghost Rider*) (1888). In the latter example, however, the middle-class ideal becomes overlaid with the almost aristocratic power calculations of the young dyke-master, who perceives himself in a constant position of power, and under this mental strain loses touch with reality, tradition and all constraints. The new dyke, a symbol of the new age, must not be viewed in isolation, however, but needs to be seen as a single entity together with the old dyke. When Hauke Haien concentrates solely on the new, catastrophe results. She exposes as an illusion the idea of permanent middle-class success in a world of progress: Humanist ideals, or even simple humanity, seem to have been irrevocably lost in the ruthless lust for power.

Sometimes the human element is rescued from this blind faith in power and progress in the subtlest possible way. In Fontane's novel *Effi Briest* (1895), the title comes from the name of the main female character, whose express wish it is to have this name put on her gravestone, as if her marriage to the Baron von Innstetten had never taken place. Effi's return to the insular world of her parents' house is only one indication of her failure in a society of success, and of distance from it. Effi, a character invented by the writer, achieves less of a new start than the woman on whom she was modelled, the Baroness of Ardenne, who lived to be almost 99 years old and outlived the publication of the novel by nearly sixty years. Fontane's intention was to restructure completely this 'story from life' (letter to Marie Uhse, 1895), since the author harmonised and idealised the ways of society. This can be seen from the collapse of Effi's health, which loosens the rigid forms of social convention a little without, of course, threatening its underlying foundations. Similarly Wüllersdorf, Innstetten's colleague, and shortly before her death even Effi herself, both approve of Innstetten's conduct towards Major von Crampas, whom he shoots in a duel on account of an affair with Effi some seven years previously. He justifies this on the grounds that things cannot be 'as we want them, but as others want them' ('[nicht] wie wir wollen, sondern wie die andern wollen'). This begs the question, however, of who these 'others' are, who must be so uncritically obeyed. It suggests that the paradigm for the continuing supremacy of former power structures, now enriched with a new 'modern' brand of power, may have suppressed human values altogether. Were those values then permitted to surface during the reading of a novel, but to remain utterly impotent in terms of social effect – a form of participation demarcated by literature instead of a general solidarity?

The weakness of the middle class

The next question to be posed is whence this weakness in the self-understanding of the middle class derived. It had clearly suffered a heavy defeat in the revolution of 1848, but had not been without its share of the blame for this. Lending support to a revolution in one's thoughts and becoming part of it were in fact two quite different things, in Berlin as in other German cities. As former feudal elements reasserted themselves under the leadership of two so dissimilar siblings, Prussia and Austria, middle-class activities diversified in three directions. In social terms the middle class wanted to emulate the aristocracy; politically they wanted to shield themselves from the working class, and above all to prevent their rise to power; economically they wanted to boost the dynamic momentum of the entrepreneurial trend in the broadest sense of the term. These aspirations left little room either for ideals or for any concerted efforts to put them into practice. Again and again this was to lead to a substantial degree of insecurity within the middle class. The stuff of social life thus consisted not of decision-making related to the political and social spheres, but of idle chit-chat and moral catastrophes blown up out of all proportion – a failure that as often as not pertained to literature as well.

Although a broad-based literature relevant to society at large was thus becoming possible for the first time during the nineteenth century, the literature of 'realism' maintained a careful distance from the everyday life of society. The overall trend of literature in this era was a large-scale shift towards diversion and entertainment. To this extent, therefore, the age of realism and the *Gründerzeit* may be regarded as an age in which the masses were provided with entertainment literature.

Mediocrity in literature

The ground for this simplified literary diet was prepared by increasing numbers of journals that catered to mass tastes, such as the *Gartenlaube*, but equally also by German primers and readers, and therefore also by the curriculum and instruction in the native language. Since literature could not be converted into profit, it was cultivated predominantly by groups who for one reason or another were unable independently to shape their own lives, such as schoolchildren, women, the aged, and later salaried employees. Some slight change in this pattern began to occur among the lower classes around 1890, but this did not make them into a readership markedly influenced or affected by literature.

These unfavourable overall conditions for literature led to the rise of a writing style stamped with a spirit of compromise that was characteristic for a literary *juste milieu*. There was simplicity both in form and content, 'objectivity', an avoidance of drastic stylistic devices, and a striving after balance and a tranquil 'middle' way. None of this was calculated to broaden the horizons of the readership: instead it presented them with carefully selected aspects of the world at large as if they constituted reality.

The middle class greatly appreciated sketches of sweeping landscapes such as were provided by Raabe, Meyer or Storm. Some of these were depicted with such palpable force, e.g. the opening passage of Meyer's *Jürg Jenatsch* (1876), that the reader is 'caught up' in the scenario before the action itself begins. In an age before photography and film, the spectator was presented with a backdrop in which people and landscapes were blended together to form a unity. This made the interpretation of one in terms of the other appear self-evident, which in turn helped to cultivate an impression of overall harmony, often when this effect was not even being aimed for, as in the case of Theodor Storm. The almost tangible imagery of his work is often a dominant *leitmotif*, giving it character and force.

Literary trends and the intellectual life of the era: national and liberal education instead of general freedom?

The mass distribution and mass impact of literature did not arise simply out of the fresh potential opened up by innovative printing technology and publishing legislation within the German Federation, and later the North German Federation. The wider issue at stake here was who had an interest in freedom for the purposes of literary exchange in order for literature to become a serious contender on the commodity market – whether, in other words, a public existed that had a marked need to read. The high prices asked for modern literature, in contrast with editions of the classics, rendered it for the most part inaccessible to the bulk of the population, thereby forcing the reading public to read entertainment literature. For 'the same sum of money that a one-volume novel costs one can have a daily newspaper and a polite literature journal; in other words in addition to the now indispensable news one can now have three novels, a half dozen novellas and three "shock" feuilletons' (E. Peschkau, 1884).

Another question to be asked is whether literature still had in this era, as it had had in the eighteenth century, the 'function of a testing-ground for social reasoning', or whether it was witnessing instead the rise of an anonymous mass culture-consuming middle class for whom literature was no more than a vehicle for entertainment and the mediation of ideologies.

What may be discerned is the clear departure of modern literature from the models of the *Goethezeit* – a departure that was developing some remarkable aspects.

This process of departure is a stunning illustration both of how much literary awareness had changed since 1780, and of the repercussions of this change. A departure from abstract stylisation entailed, for example, relinquishing large-scale, *a priori* lines of thought to stress the individual and the specific. A sense of the whole thus tended to be lost in diversity and abundance. And yet at the same time there was the stated aim of propounding and presenting the whole to the people, whether in real or surrogate form. This may be seen in the backward-looking utopian character of the Goethe–Schiller memorial erected in 1857 in Weimar. 'Goethe facing life and Schiller gazing upwards to the realm of ideals' was the commentary on this 'witness to German history' in one illustrated children's book.

The 'nationalisation' of education

The state was gaining ground generally in the post-1848 period, and particularly so in schools and teacher training. Here too the age of idealism was over. As late as 1843 the post of German language teacher was still described by Wackernagel as a 'royal, high priestly' one, but the duties of the German teacher were now to be considerably expanded from now on: 'The German teacher is not only paramount in the sphere of ideals and mediator of the pure poetic word; he is at the same time the guardian of the spirit of the nation', it being his duty to exert a strong influence against 'subversive reasoning', to promote 'love' and 'feeling', and 'a warming force in the heart'. His vocation, in other words, was that of character-builder.

What makes this educational agenda new is, first, that it marks the earliest formulation of German irrationalism, which 'conceives of and combats the intellect as the antagonist of the soul', and, second, that this agenda was implemented in schools by order. This meant that it exerted a massive influence on both the general penetration and overall conception of literature in the second half of the nineteenth century. This poses the question of whether it is more appropriate to speak here of censorship or education. Government agents and parliamentarians were at times quite candid regarding what they expected of literature. In their view it was to provide innocuous entertainment and artistic inspiration – an argument that was used in the 1895 debate surrounding the scandalous performance of Gerhart Hauptmann's drama *Die Weber* (*The Weavers*) in the Prussian House of Representatives. This debate culminated in the statement:

How long are we to stand idly by while all the most sacred possessions of the nation, which are still truly sacred to the people, are denigrated and dragged through the mud in the most ignominious manner possible? There is still time: we still have the power behind us, we still have the authority, built and based on the sound sense of the people, who are not yet polluted and depraved; and as long as we, the government, have authority behind us, we will not hesitate to use it. . . .

The symbol of Prussia

Prussia was a symbol of military and economic might, not of literature, in which official interest was slight. All talk of progress focused on economic and scientific issues. In social terms the guiding principles were God, King, Fatherland, discipline, order and hard work. Theodor Storm spoke of Potsdam as one 'great officers' mess'. He realised during his very first visit in 1852–3 'that in the educated circles of Berlin the emphasis is laid not on personality, but on rank, title, medals and other such trinkets' – as if no development of middle-class notions had ever taken place. Fontane complements Storm's view in graphic terms: 'Everything suggested the impression that the court and the persons connected with it had slept through the last half century at least' (*Von Zwanzig bis Dreissig – From Twenty to Thirty*). Concerning this lag, Prussia was but the 'hard core' of Germany, the paradigm: other federal states deviated from Prussia in nuance, but not in principle, and were able at all times to refer to Prussia as their authority.

One of the greatest blunders perpetrated by German teaching in schools was its collusion in this narrowing of what qualified as literature. In so doing it contributed in no small measure to perpetuating literary immaturity among students. The 'Stiehl regulations' pertaining to the education of elementary school teachers in Prussia (1854) were a well-known model of how authorities pulled all the strings in the last century in the interests of reducing literary education to a minimum. The overall aim was to create a 'Lutheran Christian community' with a single-class elementary school as the standard school. There was thus to be 'nothing of German national literature, nothing of Lessing, Goethe and Schiller' (Nyssen), and nothing at all of contemporary literature.

German literature as a 'national duty'

At higher institutions of learning in 1859, a delight in unfettered and thoughtless enjoyment was presented as a fundamental aim of literature studies. It was further regarded as a 'national duty' for grammar school (*Gymnasium*) students 'to preserve what was particularly precious in the classical writing of [our] own nation as a treasure not to be lost to memory'. The dangers inherent in this kind of education should be self-evident. They included distortion of international problems and the way they were dealt with in literature – in other words, a tendency towards provincialism; and a failure to appreciate modern foreign literature in schools, which ignored both the dramas of Scandinavian literature, and Russian, French and English novels, thereby encouraging what was without doubt an unjustifiably high estimation of German literature. Here also was the cultivation of the German mass cliché of character-building, which sought to paper over the many cracks of uncertainty or questioning on the part of the reading public with a facile appearance of harmony, casting aspersions on the slightest self-criticism by condemning it as 'subversive'. Educational policy strove to impart a sense of self-worth based on an ill-thought-out sense of the collective German nation that bore no relation whatever to the individual. The effect of all this on literature itself may be discerned in the abundance of war poems in the 1870–1 and 1914 periods, in its formal and esoteric tendencies, its discipleship, and its 'schools'. The names of H.S. Chamberlain, Langbehn, Nietzsche, Wagner or George are representative of many, and the effect on literature of some of these has yet to be fully clarified. Another repercussion was a tendency to retreat into history as a way of taking flight from the present, instead of undertaking a rational analysis of the past.

The political failure of the middle class in the 1848–9 revolution was publicly discussed, as in the derision of Julian Schmidt as early as 1850: 'But the German revolution had something unique about it that enabled it to compete with the poetry of its prophets in lyric pathos, a dream-like quality and dim, vague longings. That is all over now. The abdication of their creation, the vice-regent with no kingdom, was its last act.'

Departure from the ideals of liberalism

Instead of striving after ideals, the middle class now strove after passable routes and some way of nevertheless attaining power. In relation to the degree of departure from the former ideals of liberalism (humanity, liberty, solidarity, progress) it is possible to distinguish at least three major middle-class groupings. These were the economically-oriented liberal upper middle class, the *Oberklasse* (Schmoller), 'a considerable proportion of whom [like the aristocracy] were non-literary, or even anti-literary' (Wittmann); the spiritual conservatives (often characterised by strong religious tendencies or resignation); and the progressive democratic middle class. The latter were open to literature, particularly those employed in independent and upwardly mobile professions, or as officials in administration, education and science. For groups such as these literature was integral to their understanding of themselves. Most officials, however, thought conservatively, in terms of loyalty to the king. Their contact with culture was limited to national events or those that they were obliged socially to attend.

The 'character' of the German nation

All this raises the question of the subject-matter of literary creation under such circumstances, and the value attached to it by the public. The potential of literature in an age of growing dependence on the 'market' was related to the wider social and political situation of the country. This applied to all literature, not only the specifically political. Personal liberty and freedom of thought, social development, ideas pertaining to the social order, political tolerance and political interests all play an important part in the creation and distribution of literature. The question here, therefore, is whether it was possible for literature to be significant in an age that hailed as 'progress' the shift from a politics of conviction to a politics of pragmatism (*Realpolitik*).

In the literary sphere the reconciliation of idealism with realism was propounded in the form of a 'study of the character and traits' of the nation 'without one form of the German character being obliged to be subordinate to the others'. Literature was thus conceived of as showing 'the right way towards the political unity of Germany'. In this process, 'more individuality, and hence more reality' was often attributed to characters associated with rural areas. Hebbel's praise of the Austrian Emperor and the Vienna Constitution of 1862, Geibel's work at the Munich court, and Freytag's affiliation with the Meiningen Court Theatre reveal among other things that many courts sought out poets and writers as aides and publicity agents or as the focal points of a cultural circle. The danger for literature in all this, of course, was that it could be relegated to the level of decoration, like the awarding of medals.

The Prussian spirit of the Gründerzeit

As Prussia rose to become the leading power in Germany after 1866, it began to act as a model in virtually all spheres of life. To this extent it also exerted a major influence on the spirit of the *Gründerzeit*.

> If it had really been anyone's intention at that time to depict wielded power and the increase of power achieved through war, and to depict it as a true expression of the age, that is at the highest artistic level, then the creation of the new German Reich and the instruments of power enshrined within it, such as the Kaiser and the Chancellor, would have been the appropriate starting-point for this heroic monumental portrayal. Where could Nietzsche have found a better model

for his *Übermensch* than Bismarck – a man who both domestically and internationally was the most powerful man in Europe? The evidence on all sides points to the fact that less interest was taken in the problems of the state as such than in the prerogative and will of the great individual.

(Hamann/Hermand 1965–)

'German greatness'

The manner in which great individuals and their deeds were depicted in post-1848 German literature was a problem that could hardly be over-estimated. Since there was a desire not to show mere abstractions or types, the great man had to be depicted as an individual, i.e. as a fellow creature, but set apart with numerous outstanding characteristics corresponding to the aspirations of the middle-class reader and hence enabling him to ident-ify with the character. An initially vague notion of an idol or *Übermensch* came about in this way, stylistically suited to the particular author, but brought to completion over the head of the reader. The dream of 'German greatness' seemed in this grotesque manner to become reality.

Freytag was close to the ideal of the 'great individual', even if at first he seemed to be striving after something different: he sought to disperse, at least on the literary level, 'the despondency and weary slackness of the nation', since the Germans had already experienced an excess of 'despon-dency, unfulfilled aspirations and zealous wrath'. It was not granted to every age 'to give expression to the beautiful in the noblest form', but in all things 'the creative writer should be true to his art and to his people', he wrote in the dedication to the Duke of Sachsen-Coburg-Gotha of his novel *Soll und Haben* (*Debit and Credit*) (1855). Freytag's view of realism can be found in the closing sentence of the dedication, as well as in the motto of the novel. The two together constitute an agenda. The closing sentence of the dedication reads: 'I shall be happy, if this novel gives Your Highness the impression that it was created true to the laws of life and the art of writing, and yet never written in imitation of the chance events of reality.' The motto is a quotation from Julian Schmidt's *Geschichte der deutschen Literatur* (*History of German Literature*), Volume 3 (1855), which reads: 'The novel should seek the German people where they are to be found in that at which they excel, namely at work.'

We might ask at this point whether German novel literature after 1848 may therefore be said to have had a tendency or an agenda. Freytag's friend Julian Schmidt gave numerous indications in the journal the two of them edited, *Die Grenzboten* (*The Frontiersman*), of what he meant by this requirement. In one analysis entitled *Wilhelm Meister im Verhältniss zu unserer Zeit* (*Wilhelm Meister in Relation to Our Day*) (1855), for example, he writes: 'However, now we miss among the classes he [Goethe]

333

depicts in the first instance the most important element of German national life, the middle class. Werner, a representative of this class, provides a poor and distorted picture. Work devoted to a specific purpose and which exerts every effort towards that end appears as a contradiction of the ideal, because it contradicts the liberty and versatility of the desire for education.'

Soll und Haben (Debit and Credit)

Schmidt's objection to Goethe is that 'the truly human, the individual life, is lost'. *Soll und Haben*, however, was well received by the reading public, appearing in numerous reprints until well into this century. Realistic literary presentation was clearly widely accepted, and middle-class readers in particular identified themselves with the businessman Anton Wohlfahrt, who ultimately achieves success. In an 1855 review, Fontane spoke of an 'internal fusing of three dramas'. He sees the focal point of the novel as the middle-class drama of the hero Anton Wohlfahrt, who matures from a young apprentice through various vicissitudes and 'trials', ultimately becoming a respectable shareholder in the family business of his master and marrying the boss's daughter. Set around this middle-class novel of development, in Fontane's view, are two tragedies reflecting historical conditions as Freytag saw them and, as Fontane freely admits, as the middle class liked to view them. The Baron von Rothsattel fails because of his desire to conserve at any price; Veitel Itzig and Hirsch Ehrenthal because of their desire to win at any price.

Das Volk

However, *Soll und Haben* provided no account of the people at work, as numerous critics were quick to point out – Karl Gutzkow with devastating sarcasm, Hermann Marggraf with wit and irony. It scarcely troubled the contemporary reader to see business coupled with a vigorous defence of self-interest, although it was widely criticised in the conflict with the Poles, and undoubtedly had some bearing on the Prussian–Polish conflict of 1848. At all events, however, Fontane did criticise the overwhelming anti-semitism underlying the novel. This attitude was widely held in the nineteenth century among figures ranging from Raabe to Bismarck, long before Stoecker and Treitschke made it clear with their anti-semitic campaign of 1877 that the days of liberalism were over and *Gründerzeit* imperialism had made its entrance. By that time, a good twenty years after the appearance of the novel *Soll und Haben*, the characters depicted in it were already *Bilder aus der deutschen Vergangenheit* (*Pictures from the German Past*), if there had ever been such a thing. This raises the question of whether the ideal of Anton Wohlfahrt did not perhaps lie in the very lack of credibility of his success – whether in fact the real issue here was not reality or the problem of work, but rather success, regardless of how it was achieved.

'Attitudes' as a literary response to social developments: 'spirituality' (*Innerlichkeit*), 'distance' and the danger of 'restorative utopia'

Middle-class optimism

More than any of Freytag's other works, *Soll und Haben* presupposed not only an educated reader, but also one interested in society, in the sense of being prepared to greet the booming economy actively and optimistically. He was more likely to live among an urban than a rural population, since success was a crucial goal of urban dwellers. Freytag was certainly no poet for men living in the shadows and stillness of the land, who tended to view recent developments with some scepticism. On a closer examination of the term, therefore, Freytag cannot be regarded as a popular (*Volks-*) writer. As early as 1849 indeed, Gottfried Keller had rightly enquired in his *Blätter für literarische Unterhaltung* (*Pages for Literary Entertainment*) whether it was possible for a 'popular' writer to reach the entire people: 'We have no report at all as to whether popular German writers are as well known in the cottages of the rural people as they are in literary pages and among the urban middle classes, and if they are as well known, what effect they have had there.' The rural population, he argued, remained as poor as ever, and anyone familiar with rural life must be aware 'how long it takes before a farmer had four gulden to spare to buy any book that is not the Bible'.

Gotthelf

The Swiss writer Albert Bitzius, a parson at Lützelflüh in the canton of Bern, described the poverty of the rural population with some force, in both his sermons and his numerous tales, which he wrote under the pseudonym of Jeremias Gotthelf. *Die schwarze Spinne* (*The Black Spider*) (1842); *Elsi, die seltsame Magd* (*Elsie, the Strange Girl*) (1843); *Uli der Knecht* (*Uli the Farm Labourer*) (1846), and *Uli der Pächter* (*Uli the Tenant Farmer*) (1849) are the best known of these. In 1854 Gotthelf's novel *Erlebnisse eines Schuldenbauers* (*The Experiences of a Mortgaged Farmer*) was published. In the foreword the author explains: 'Out of pity for the honest and hard-working men who would gladly escape the morass of poverty, was this book written, and written in anguish, for one does not breathe easily in this cheerless air. If anything at all then, this book may be accused of not presenting the whole truth in its full breadth and depth.' Gotthelf made no secret of the fact that he saw his writing in a didactic light, intended to influence and improve – another form of pastoral care. His works consequently divided the critical camp more sharply than was usually the case. Conservatives praised his closeness to the people, his simple narrative style and his religious tendency: 'the wholesome power of simple family life and the quiet fulfilment of duty'. Liberals, on the other hand, were put off by what they perceived as a lack of style, a tendency towards 'demagogy', false and sweeping generalisations, and what they perceived in the author as a reactionary attitude, hostile to education. Keller took issue with Gotthelf time and again, and not always in the friendliest way, even in the case of Bitzius' last work.

A dam against the tide of progress

Gotthelf managed to assuage the fear many people had of not being equal to the new developments taking place. As a result of this, however, his works tended to be misinterpreted as a bulwark against the modern age – a dam against the tide of a 'progress' that seemed mainly to menace people living on the land. The fact that Keller's criticism was directed largely against the invitation to misinterpretation in Gotthelf's work becomes clear when one takes into account his subsequent conduct. No sooner had Keller completed his review of the *Erlebnisse eines Schuldbauers* than he learned of Gotthelf's death in October 1854. His immediate response was to attempt, by way of an addendum, an overall assessment of the Swiss theologian and writer: Gotthelf had never sought to stand above the contrasts among his own people, but had immersed himself deeply in the problems of his compatriots, and felt for them. Despite all his anti-liberal 'vehemence' he had not been a reactionary in the 'negative sense of the word', had never supplied fodder to 'reactionaries' and had never betrayed his innate republicanism. He had been a 'popular writer in the more specific and usual sense of the word', with a gift for shaping his writings in such a way 'that we can share in completely sated perception the enjoyment of all that is sensual, visible and palpable', because 'appearances and events are fused together'.

German literature in comparison with the rest of Europe

In the major epic works of other European nations the maturation process of the main characters had long since been depicted in terms of a close interaction with social conditions, the latter being described in as much detail as possible (examples would be Charles Dickens: *David Copperfield*, 1849; or Fyodor Dostoyevsky: *Crime and Punishment*, 1866). Compared to this the social scope of the German nineteenth century epic seems very limited. Until about 1855, the composition of society was either not dealt with as a theme at all, or was idealised and stylised by authors such as Wilhelm Raabe. It is therefore not a coincidence, but entirely explicable in the light of these developments, that only a year after the publication of Freytag's *Soll und Haben* Gustave Flaubert's *Madame Bovary* appeared in France. This novel reveals the tenuousness of middle-class notions of marriage and morality in virtually every character, portraying the main character more as the victim of her own false assumptions than as a heroine. *Madame Bovary* exposes the mendacity and crisis of middle-class society on all sides, whereas the German hero of *Soll und Haben*, Anton Wohlfahrt, believes in the sense of vocation and cultural superiority of the businessman.

An important factor in this connection is that until the age of naturalism all art, including literature, was thought of as autonomous, and hence obliged to set forms and subjects as a counter to 'reality' – to be raised above everyday life, in other words. Art was not concerned, therefore, with showing the reader the real world – this could be experienced daily without any mediation – but with enabling the reader to perceive meanings that were far above political or economic concerns. Since the rise of the middle class, the meaning conveyed by literature was no longer concerned with recognising or fulfilling a given (divine) order, but with developing the 'personality' of the main characters. This included the capacity to act with moral responsibility, and the ability to take social decisions in the light of a general humanity, which was seen as the foundation of human society. Where the basic consensus and fabric of society were no longer stated, however, perpetuation of the traditions of the novel of education or development was a dubious enterprise. Since a basic social consensus was absent, the nineteenth century was a time of crisis in middle-class consciousness that affected Germany not only in its politics, but also in its literature.

The Land as a theme

From among the many sketches, stories and novels dealing with themes of rural life, the works of two writers in particular merit particular attention, albeit for completely different reasons: Gottfried Keller for his many novellas, but chiefly for *Romeo und Julia auf dem Dorfe* (*Romeo and Juliet in the Village*), and Adalbert Stifter for his various stories, among which *Bergkristall* (*Rock Crystal*) is especially noteworthy. It is important to point out that these two texts are not going to be neatly 'catalogued' according some criterion of classification already mentioned. The quality of both works places them far beyond any such classification. What will be undertaken is an attempt to discern the particular tendencies and perspectives that they represent.

Both texts were published in anthologies: Keller's novella in the first volume of stories about *Die Leute von Seldwyla* (*The People of Seldwyla*) (1856), and Stifter's story in a volume entitled *Bunte Steine* (*Brightly-*

coloured Stones) (1853). As readers may be aware, neither author put these anthologies together merely for the sake of producing a thicker volume: the stories were intended to be taken collectively as contributions on a single theme.

The six stories collected in the volume *Bunte Steine* were revised by Stifter many times before finally receiving this overall title, which is intended to express their common focus. In the preface to the book, Stifter expounds in a few pages both his literary aims and some of the basic principles of his world-view. The sense of structure and precision evinced in his line of thought are virtually unsurpassable. He begins with a three-fold denial, stating that he is not an artist or *Dichter*, that he does not wish to preach on virtue or morals, and that he is aiming neither for the 'greater' nor the 'lesser'. This effectively demarcates Stifter and his friends from the outside world. His stated aim is merely to contribute to 'conviviality among friends' and a grain of good to the edifice of the world – and, of course, also to reject false prophets. Not until he has dispatched this almost intimate declaration does Stifter proceed to explain what he means by 'greater' and 'lesser'. There was no doubt in his mind that man was not equal to the great forces of nature, and that the latter must therefore be unsuitable models for human conduct. Stifter regards a conservative rational position as feasible, and after 1848 as necessary, in order to exert an enduring counter-balance to human force – and for him a revolution was nothing other than an act of human force. His aim was to see men achieving through a series of small steps the ability to act responsibly. His transfer of nature into the hands of man was cautious, but still represents a clear rejection of revolutionary developments wherever they might appear. For Stifter, a convinced Christian, revolutions could have no part in the divine plan for the world and represented an interference by men in this plan, with the aim of subverting the whole.

The balance of nature

Stifter's conclusion, which he largely leaves to the reader to draw for himself, is that only men who lack reverence for the whole are capable of revolutionary acts against the true balance of nature (as a creation of God). They commit these acts out of lack of piety. In perpetrating them, men endanger themselves, since the true balance of nature is also set within man himself, although he all too easily tends to 'overlook' it. This means that revolutionary men are unbalanced: the individual shows contempt for the whole, for quiet development, in 'pursuit of his desire and his depravity'. Peril and confusion are the inevitable consequences for the people. What Stifter intimates in the preface to *Bunte Steine* is then transposed into the six stories of the anthology – perhaps most consummately in *Bergkristall*. In this story the writer leads the reader gently but firmly from the external (the mountains, representing the massive forces of nature) to the internal sphere – towards the miraculous rescue of two children who, because they have lost their way, have had to spend Christmas Eve amid the eternal ice.

Landscape

Stifter describes the monumental landscape of the high Alps in a detail that is at first glance almost pedantic. The reason for this becomes clear later, however. The Alps are an ominous scene of action and miraculous events. They are even mute protagonists in the action, an age-old divider of men. The mother of the two main characters, the children Konrad and Susanna, for example, has always remained an outsider in the village of Gschaid where she has lived since her marriage, because she comes from the other side of the mountain, from Millsdorf. The two children themselves are likewise drawn to the other side, to their grandparents, making the trip over the mountain more often 'than all the other villagers put together'. Christmas Eve thus finds them taking presents over the mountain. On the return trip, however, they are caught in driving snow. Despite their familiarity with the route they lose their way, straying on to the glacial ice. They take shelter in a cave, keeping themselves awake with the drink intended as a present for their mother from their grandmother. In this miraculous, and yet fully explicable manner they manage to survive the night of Christmas Eve and are rescued the next morning. There is no scope to go in detail here into the finer points of the story, most especially the relationship between the two children in their hour of greatest danger. Stifter's description of the driving snow is undoubtedly one of the most remarkable achievements in German prose, worthy of being set beside Thomas Mann's chapter on snow in his novel *Der Zauberberg* (*The Magic Mountain*). The story as a whole is alive with a palpable and evocative language that allows the reader to follow closely every step the children take, and at last even to understand their silences and the pauses brought on by their great fear.

Restorative utopia

The *Bunte Steine* anthology has been described as an 'agenda for separation and for inward retreat'. Stifter, however, wanted to go even further than this. Virtually all critics are agreed that his novel *Der Nachsommer* (*The Indian Summer*) (1857) is an attempt to elaborate a 'restorative utopia' (H.A. Glaser). Stifter seems himself to have seen it like this. He wrote to his publisher Heckenast on 11 February 1858: 'Ich habe ein tieferes und reicheres Leben als es gewöhnlich vorkommt, in dem Werk zeichnen wollen und zwar in seiner Vollendung und zum Überblicke entfaltet daliegend

.... Dieses tiefere Leben soll getragen sein durch die irdischen Grundlagen bürgerlicher Geschäfte ... und [die] überirdischen' ('I wanted to portray a deeper and richer life in this work than is usually to be found, setting it forth in its perfection, unfolded in its full scope.... This deeper life should be sustained by the earthly substructures of civic affairs and by supernatural ones'). Stifter mentions in this connection art, morality, pure humanity and religion. To illustrate his purpose he chose as the main character of the novel an average, inconspicuous, but also extraordinarily educable young man, Heinrich Drendorf, who does not so much 'mature' as move towards deeper understanding through a succession of encounters with contrasted spheres such as 'nature', history and religion.

Looking inward for an open space

Unlike Stifter, Gottfried Keller does not see spirituality as an end in itself, but as a last resort offering an open space that should not be denied even to the social outcast. In the preface to the first volume of *Die Leute von Seldwyla*, Keller calls his stories 'peculiar oddities (sonderbare Abfällsel) that happened from time to time, as it were exceptionally, and yet which could still only have occurred in Seldwyla'. The fact is that the *People of Seldwyla* are easily recognisable as average citizens. It is 'das Wahrzeichen und sonderbare Schicksal derselben, dass die Gemeinde reich ist und die Bürgerschaft arm, und zwar so, dass kein Mensch zu Seldwyla etwas hat und niemand weiss, wovon sie seit Jahrhunderten eigentlich leben. Und sie leben sehr lustig und guter Dinge, halten die Gemütlichkeit für ihre besondere Kunst' ('the hallmark and special destiny of the same being that the parish is rich and the citizenry poor, in such a manner that no man in Seldwyla possesses anything, and no-one knows what in fact they have been living on for all these centuries. And what is more they live with great gusto and with the good things of life, regarding cosiness as an art peculiar to themselves'). At first sight, the second of the five stories in the first volume seems to be the very image of the comfortable living touched on in the introduction. The sweeping panorama of the landscape depicted in it positively radiates peace, security and sedateness.

Selfishness

However, Keller then proceeds to show through the two ploughmen, Manz and Marti, what becomes of men who defend their respectable, hard-earned positions out of 'private economic interest'. What starts out as avarice develops into hatred, escalating into violence. Blind selfishness causes them to forget their true interests. Two men who have failed to understand the system to which they have submitted – not without hardship – become deadly enemies, dragging their families into the abyss with them.

Sali, Manz's son, and Vreni, Marti's daughter, become victims of this strategy of cheating, and yet it is the senseless dispute between their fathers that brings them together and forces them into each other's company. Their love for each other sets in motion a disastrous chain of events. They cannot declare their love openly, because their fathers would immediately learn of it. They come to realise that there is no chance for them to be together in the middle-class world. Since, however, they are quite certain of their love for each other, they sell what few possessions they have, and spend the proceeds on a day together in seeming middle-class bliss. Now, however, they are no longer in the society in which they still actually live and move: they are only with each other. Turning inward in this way enables them to do no more than spend a single day of their lives as they would wish. The middle-class world they inhabit is now a mere backdrop for their self-realisation. This is enhanced by fine food and dancing – showing their surrender to middle-class mores, while at the same time they disengage themselves from them to create their own personal bliss.

Lovers portrayed as lost

This day in the lives of the two lovers comes to an end. The dance at a late hour becomes an act of freedom for outcasts and loners – a world in which Sali and Vreni cannot live for long, as their brief sojourn with the black fiddler's band shows. Neither of them is able or willing to seize life and freedom at any price: their sense of honour will not permit them to do so. It is not middle-class honour they are fulfilling now, but the honour dictated by their own inner world. They are wedded for themselves alone, a relationship denied them by middle-class society. They have not heeded the offer by the black fiddler 'gleich hier Hochzeit' ('wedding right here'). They both know that such a wedding would not be followed by any enduring bond. They decide in favour of their personal form of honour and, unlike the fiddler, against life, 'once more a sign of creeping demoralisation and degeneracy of the passions', as Keller states by way of conclusion to the novella.

The bitter irony of this conclusion shows the difficulties inherent in realistic portrayal. Keller himself was, of course, fully aware of these, as numerous letters reveal. For a long time he regarded it as difficult, if not impossible, to make this realism flow into his works. His more than thirty years of work on the novel *Der Grüne Heinrich* (*Green Henry*) (planned in 1842–3; first version 1846–50; first publication 1854–5; revised edition 1879–80) illustrate this. One of the characters in the novel, the Dutch painter Ferdinand Lys, for example, realises in Italy that the ideal of great historical tableaux 'has no experience of time and life'. Clearly, however, he does not yet know how to find his own way among the bewildering mass of models before him. This problem also troubled Keller personally

341

for some considerable time. Despite its trenchant analysis, *Der Grüne Heinrich* was unable to provide the means for creating a counter-image, at first within himself and then for the benefit of society. As his *Künstlerroman* and his *Romeo und Julia auf dem Dorfe* show, Keller strove throughout the 1850s and 1860s to achieve some degree of equilibrium in his relationship with society.

In literary terms, however, Keller moved beyond an attitude of resignation in the second volume of *Leute aus Seldwyla* (1874), especially in the story *Kleider machen Leute* (*Clothes Maketh the Man*). This story has a main character, but not a real hero in the sense created by C.F. Meyer in *Jürg Jenatsch* or Theodor Storm in *Der Schimmelreiter*. In some respects this sets the story apart from other outstanding tales of the century. The tailor Wenzel Strapinski is poor, and a foreigner in Switzerland. Unwittingly at first, he finds himself passed off as a Polish count as a result of a coachman's prank. This practical joke, however, forces the tailor into a role that goes against his nature. He becomes more and more embroiled, partly because he lacks the courage to declare his true identity. The high point of this comedy of alienation is the engagement of the would-be count to Nette, daughter of the town clerk. Strapinski finds reality catching up with him, however, at a masked ball. The citizens of Seldwyla envy the golden raiment of their 'count', plucking to pieces the sole source of his noble existence. At this point in the plot the character of Nette comes more to the forefront. She shows herself to be a woman of outstanding middle-class virtues. She does not allow herself to be carried away by her feelings, but trusts her judgement of human character. Having taken the trouble to find out Wenzel's true life and background, she comes to the conclusion that it seems to offer her sufficient basis for a solid middle-class existence, and decides to stand by him: 'So feierte sie jetzt ihre rechte Verlobung aus tief entschlossener Seele, indem sie in süsser Leidenschaft ein Schicksal auf sich nahm und Treue hielt' ('And so now she celebrated her true engagement within a deeply resolved heart, by taking a destiny on herself in sweet ardour, and remaining faithful').

The agenda of the Seldwyla citizens

This faithfulness is more than a mere coming to terms with a given situation, as one might suppose. It is an agenda: 'Nun wollen wir gerade nach Seldwyl gehen und den Dortigen, die uns zu zerstören gedachten, zeigen, dass sie uns erst recht vereinigt und glücklich gemacht haben!' ('Now let us go to Seldwyl and show the people there who sought our destruction that they have made us more united and happy than ever!') For similar reasons, Nette refuses to move with Wenzel 'into unknown parts and live there secretly in tranquil bliss', as Wenzel would like to do: 'Keine Romane mehr! Wie du bist, ein armer Wandersmann, will ich mich zu dir bekennen und in meiner Heimat allen diesen Stolzen und Spöttern zum Trotze dein Weib sein!' ('No more fancies! I would acknowledge you as you are, a poor journeyman, and live with you as your wife in spite of all these proud and scoffing people!') The daughter of Seldwyla's town clerk has indeed acquired such a degree of self-confidence that she is able to share in deciding the future with her future husband: 'Wir wollen nach Seldwyla und dort durch Tätigkeiten und Klugheit die Menschen, die uns verhöhnt haben, von uns abhängig machen!' ('We shall go to Seldwyla and there through our deeds and resourcefulness make those people dependent on us who have scorned us!') This goes beyond the realm of middle-class attributes into those of the entrepreneurial. The latter also show themselves when Nette explains to local dignitaries why she intends to turn down the offer to 'rescue her honour' made by the respectable citizen Melchior Böhni, whose far from altruistic motives she has been quick to see through: 'Sie rief, gerade die Ehre sei es, welche ihr gebiete, den Herren Böhni nicht zu heiraten, weil sie ihn nicht leiden könne, dagegen dem armen Fremdem treu zu bleiben, welchem sie ihr Wort gegeben habe und den sie auch leiden könne' ('She cried that it was no less than honour which forbad her to marry Mr Böhni, since she could not abide him, and on the contrary to remain true to the poor foreigner to whom she had given her word, and who incidentally she could abide!'). This astonishing female character is not the only aspect of Keller's story that offers something of a vision or agenda, leaving a number of men in the story quite at a loss in the process. It becomes clear that here Keller has moved beyond the constraining notions of middle-class honour that had still played a fateful role in *Romeo und Julia auf dem Dorfe*. It may be asserted that Keller had democratised the concept of middle-class honour, thereby enabling him to add some positive aspects to literary middle-class realism.

Two masterpieces as differing representatives of the age: *Mozart auf der Reise nach Prag* (*Mozart on the Way to Prague*) and *Der Heilige* (*The Saint*)

The fulcrum in Mörike's creative life lay before 1848. Between the revolution and his death he published few texts, all of which had already been drafted or begun before 1848. The most important of these are the stories *Das Stuttgarter Hutzelmännlein* (*The Wizened Little Man of Stuttgart*) (1853) which, although Mörike was unaware of it, went back to an old Swabian legend, as Uhland and other writers were able to assure him; *Die Hand der Jezerte* (*The Hand of Jezerte*), which appeared in the same year, and his great novella *Mozart auf der Reise nach Prag* (*Mozart on the Way to Prague*) (1855). Two great poems were to follow these works: *Erinna an Sappho* (*Erinna to Sappho*) (1863), and *Bilder aus Bebenhausen* (*Pictures from Bebenhausen*) (dating from September 1863, while the author was on a prolonged visit to Bebenhausen).

Remarkable as it may sound to the modern reader, it would scarcely be an exaggeration to say that Mörike used up his strength in holding out against the vicissitudes of everyday life. His was a constant exertion to achieve distance between himself and the world around him, and in general the time in which he lived. Mörike aspired to an ideal world, 'in which one could not only write, but also live' (F. Sengle). He tried to be open towards the world, but was unable to withstand this openness. Life and writing no longer seemed possible to him in the form of a living unity. In the 1830s and 1840s he wrote many poems on the themes of 'things' or 'situations', e.g. *Auf eine Lampe* (*To a Lamp*) (1846), *Inschrift auf eine Uhr mit den drei Horen* (*Inscription on a Watch with the Three Horae*) (1846), *Die schöne Buche* (*The Lovely Beech*) (1842) and *Auf das Grab von Schillers Mutter* (*On the Grave of Schiller's Mother*) (1835). These may all be regarded as minor masterpieces, but in the meantime the middle-class fixation on the world around him and on things as possessions had taken a complete hold, degrading them to purely utilitarian objects. This made it increasingly difficult for Mörike to 'salvage' the view of life that formed the basis for his writing. The poet was thus no longer able to enliven and extol things by means of an empathetic penetration of their nature. This may be argued as a case of alienation in poetry.

Threat

Just once, in his story *Mozart auf der Reise nach Prag*, which first appeared in Cotta's *Morgenblatt für gebildete Stände* (*Morning Paper for the Educated Classes*), Mörike managed to break free of this constant inner threat by transferring it to his main character. He visibly moves Mozart towards the rococo, thereby exposing him to that potential for playfulness that so often and so severely plagued the real Mozart. At the same time, however, the author is confronting his own age. In the character of this musician of genius whom he studied for many years, Mörike is also presenting his own ideal character. 'After two decades of neurotic self-preservation, he had realised that greatness is associated with "dissipation", i.e. with the audacious surrendering of the self to life and society, and that the poet who is not prepared to commit himself in this way can never attain the artistic richness of a Mozart' (F. Sengle).

Threatened by art

Mörike thus felt threatened by art whenever, as he himself put it 'harmony with the world, with myself, with everything' was threatened. This harmony was for him 'the truest possible criterion of any work of art' (letter to L. Rau, 10 December 1832). Art should moreover be able to 'ward off and isolate all kinds of contamination'. Mörike brought these ideas and experiences into his Mozart novella. As many contemporaries recognised at the time, in this novella Mörike was able sympathetically to portray play and art, absentmindedness and conviviality, cheerfulness and a premonition of death, social restraints and how to overcome them in art.

He did not simply fabricate the situation of a particular journey to Prague. It arose out of his deepest feeling and his whole approach towards Mozart's music. As the following letter shows, he lived and breathed the music of this great composer:

> With incredible speed the weather was over our heads. White, powerful streaks of lightning, such as I have never seen by day, fell like showers of roses into our white chamber, and flash after flash. During these moments with the baton of the *Kapellmeister*, old Mozart himself must have been standing behind and touching me on the shoulder, for the overture to *Titus* burst like a bat out of hell into my soul, so unstoppable and so glorious, so penetrating with that oft-repeated resolute cry of the Roman tuba that my two fists were clenched with delight.
>
> (Letter to Mährlen, 5 June 1832).

Stamped as Mörike's approach to Mozart was by his Biedermeier feeling for life and art, his creative will goes far beyond the boundaries of this limitation. He gives us a Mozart whose 'genius [is based] as much on human attributes as on his soaring artistic gifts. . . . The artist is thus not left outside society, although his gaze penetrates more deeply than that of his fellow men; he is a part of the society in which he lives and works, and his work unites the members of that society with a common bond' (E. Sagarra). This puts Mörike's achievement on the same level as Beethoven's setting to music of Schiller's *Ode to Joy*.

Mörike himself was fully aware that this capacity for empathy had led to an astonishing heightening of linguistic form (W. Höllerer), pointing the way to innovative developments. He took pains to point out to his publisher Cotta, for example, that the fee for such writing could not be calculated on the basis of its being mere 'prose'. The author had achieved here a 'depth of expression all his own' (Storm to Mörike) and a 'distinct individualisation of language' (F. Sengle), combining several layers of thought and discourse in sentences that on the surface appeared to be quite banal. These were achievements that extended far beyond the brief of a mere story – however much the 'episodic, and apparently or actually improvised structure' (F. Sengle) may at first have been misunderstood and censured by critics.

Der Heilige (The Saint)

In his Mozart novella, Mörike cultivates a sense of distance less out of historical removal from the events as from a certain timidity in approaching the unusual world of thought of this composer of genius, and yet it is through this very timidity that he penetrates to the heart of Mozart's feelings. In contrast with this, Conrad F. Meyer in his story *Der Heilige* (*The Saint*), on which he worked for over a decade (1870–80), makes no attempt whatever to explain the main character of his work – Thomas Becket, first Chancellor of England and then Archbishop of Canterbury and Primate of the Church of England. On the contrary, the more we are told about the actions of this man, the more our doubts grow as to his motives. The truth does not emerge from the sum total of the facts, an approach which makes this finely differentiated story run entirely contrary to the *Zeitgeist* of the nineteenth century. Neither King Henry II (1154–89) nor Thomas Becket is portrayed as a hero or superhuman person in the manner of the day: they evince both their own character flaws and the effects of their respective offices. Indeed, Meyer gives a penetrating exposition of how 'character' and 'office' exert a constant mutual influence, each bringing about corruption in the other and making allowances for misdeeds possible. The moodiness, tactlessness and brutal acts of the king, as well as his seduction of the under-age Grace Becket, form a kind of screen through which the nature and character of his chancellor can be reflected.

The whole story revolves around an evaluation of the first man behind the throne at the English court. Since the character Jack (Hans) was always only a peripheral figure at court, the depiction offered cannot be a complete one. It is rather a not quite finished mosaic that paradoxically makes the dubious sides of Thomas Becket's nature even more obvious. 'Armbruster' ('crossbowman') is able to report many events, but is not really able to classify them. This leaves doubts not only in the mind of Burkhard the choirmaster, but also in that of the reader.

Love as a world religion?

There are many such doubts. Is Thomas not only of Saracen origin (a child born of an illicit love affair between the English crusader Gilbert Becket and the daughter of an Arab prince: see Meyer's poem *Mit zwei Worten – With Two Words*), but also deeply permeated by the Islamic faith, or even perhaps secretly a Muslim? Is it possible for him to be a Christian at all? Could he be the 'Prince Moonshine' who so impressed the Caliph in Cordoba that he gave his own daughter to him in marriage, the prince then disappearing with his baby daughter following the untimely death of his wife and barbaric treatment by the Caliph? Why does the disciplined and superior Thomas serve the erratic and vital, but frequently brutal king as his chancellor and tutor to his son?

There are still further areas of doubt: can Thomas ever forget the death of his daughter Grace, a death for which the king himself carries the burden of guilt? When Thomas repeatedly warns the king of the possible consequences of his conduct, is he serving him truly, telling the king what he wants to say not only so that he will hear, but also so that he will understand it – or does he tell the truth in form only, knowing that the king is unable to believe it? The answer to this latter question leads to the very heart of the story – the question of whether Thomas is ultimately martyred for his faith, or is simply so obsessed with power that he plans his own destruction in the certainty that it will drag the king down in its wake.

Conrad Ferdinand Meyer narrates the story through a 'witness', the armoury smith and personal servant of the King of England, a man of sound formal education. In critical situations 'Armbruster' is able to win over the Chancellor of England with an Arab greeting or a verse from the Koran. He understands Arabic and is able to read documents. His craftsman's skill and circumspection have made him indispensable to his lord. He is no match, however, for the character of Thomas Becket, nor does he even attempt to explain doubtful circumstances, simply passing them on to his listener, the Zurich choirmaster, with manifest suspicion. In the author's view Meyer's device of a mediating figure works more successfully here than it did for Siegfried Lenz with Sigi in his novel *Die Deutschstunde* (*The German Lesson*) (1966), because 'Armbruster' is able to move freely and credibly in the court milieu, being himself so closely bound up with it. 'Armbruster''s narrative leaves open the question of whether a conflict of interests gives rise to enmity, or whether it is the other way round, although he himself inclines to the latter view. His own observations would seem to suggest that Thomas is unable to forget the death of his daughter.

The struggle between the king and the primate becomes more and more unequal. Outwardly it appears that Henry is having his own way. He has Becket condemned and rejected by a court of nobles, forcing Thomas to flee to France, 'aber während so seine Leiblichkeit in Frankreich abnahm und schwand, wuchs seine Macht und geistige Gegenwart in Engelland und stand über den trauernden Sachsen wie der Vollmond in der Nacht' ('but while his bodily presence diminished and waned in France, his power and spiritual presence waxed in England, hanging over the mourning Saxons like a full moon in the night').

In 1170 'Armbruster' is a witness to the murder in Canterbury cathedral. He is also present some years later when the king repents at the grave of his former opponent. 'Armbruster' has lost his desire to serve the king, however, and leaves England. It might be supposed that this puts him on the side of the saint. In fact, however, he is suspended somewhere between doubt and faith, outward piety and the lust for power, openness and calculation, wild emotion and shrewd distance – a confused 'Armbruster' standing back from it all and wondering at the confusion wrought by 'great men'.

This crowns an unusually 'modern' theme with a perplexingly 'modern' conclusion, albeit in medieval guise. It also leaves open the question of whether Meyer's masterly story is to be regarded as a contribution to the *Kulturkampf* in Germany. Meyer was clearly breaking new ground with this apparently completely unbiased portrayal of his characters, who often bear a disconcerting resemblance to modern power politicians. It is not human beings, but figures without hearts who determine the course of events, and there is no way of knowing whether the things they do conform to any overall scale of values, or what such a value scale might be. The same subject-matter was dealt with again on two occasions in the twentieth century: first by T.S. Eliot with his verse drama *Murder in the Cathedral* (1935), and then by Jean Anouilh with *Becket ou l'Honneur de Dieu* (1959).

How can politically committed writers write and whom can they reach?

Literature in competition with everyday middle-class life

The economic crisis from 1846 onwards and the revolution of 1848 set the literary scene in motion. Many middle-class writers wrote letters to their friends giving voice to their expectations and joy at the changes that at last seemed to be happening. Most authors, however, maintained a careful distance from political events. Apart from a few isolated exceptions, such as the aging Uhland, or examples of courageous involvement, such as that of Fanny Lewald or Louise Otto, most authors kept themselves apart from the events of the day, the uniqueness of which inspired for the most part astonishment (and sometimes dismay). Louise Otto wrote a famous letter, the *Offener Brief an den sächsischen Innenminister* (*Open Letter to the Saxon Ministers of the Interior*), in April 1848 with the motto of her agenda: 'Do not forget working women!' She set out clearly in this letter what she saw as her duty: 'I regard it as my most sacred duty to lend my voice to those who lack the courage to represent themselves. They will not be able to accuse me of presumption, for history has taught us throughout the ages, and recent history most particularly, that those who forget to think of their rights will be forgotten. I will therefore admonish you in the name of my poor sisters, the poor working women!'

Gnashing of teeth in parody

This kind of direct and specific tone was not the rule even for left-wing writers. Understandable as this may be, writers were at the same time aware of the necessity of reaching, arousing and winning over the 'people' in support of their arguments. The frequently hectic, but ill-directed discussions taking place in associations and clubs were by no means approved by all. Most politically committed writers on the Left were all too aware of the huge distance between themselves and the consciousness of the 'people' they were aiming to reach and change. It was clear to them, therefore, that only appeals related to everyday events had any chance of immediate success. During the revolution itself, and to a lesser extent before and after it, many songs were written as commentaries on all manner of revolutionary events. Catchy texts, often filled with pathos, were also distributed in pamphlet form. Songs caught on more quickly when they were set to already familiar tunes, such as a song by Ludwig Pfau which was set to Becker's famous *Wacht am Rhein* (*Watch on the Rhine*), or Franz Dingelstedt's parody of Goethe's *Lied Mignons* (*Song of Mignon*):

> Kennst du das Land, wo Einheits-Phrasen blühn:
> In dunkler Brust Trennungsgelüste glühn,
> Ein kühler Wind durch Zeitungsblätter weht,
> Der Friede still und hoch die Zwietracht steht?
> . . . .
> Kennst du das Haus? Auf Säulen ruht sein Dach,
> Es hallt der Saal, die Galerie hallt nach,
> Und Volkvertreter stehn und sehn sich an:
> Was haben wir fürs arme Volk getan?

> Know'st thou the land where unity phrases grow:
> In darkened breasts the lusts for separation glow,
> Where cool winds do blow through journal leaves,
> Of tranquil peace where reigns the spirit that cleaves?
> . . . .
> Know'st thou this house? Its roof on pillars stands,
> The hall doth echo, the gallery, answering, resounds,
> The people's representatives are lined up one by one:
> And what have we for these poor people done?

The emotional tone of many of these songs is often insufferable to the modern taste, and yet it has its precursors. On the one hand these songs were swept along by the tide of the *Marseillaise*, and on the other served to bridge the gap between aspiration and reality – or as one critic somewhat maliciously put it: 'Solidarität soll herbeigeredet werden' ('Solidarity is to be talked into existence'). This is clear from the many subversive ballads, which were by no means all complimentary to the revolutionary. The revolutionary from Baden enjoyed huge popularity, however, as both songs and many cartoons show. Those German writers who stood on the side of the revolution were also expected to stand on the side of armed struggle where necessary.

These responses show that political writing was measured by different criteria than 'other' writing. The fact is, however, that Heine had long been living as an exile in Paris, while Herwegh, Freiligrath and Strodtmann were obliged to flee into exile in 1849. Pfau and Schanz were incarcerated for many years, and others (such as Richard Wagner, who was at that time mainly employed in the world of letters) were only spared as a result of adapting their position to new conditions after the revolution. Adolf Glassbrenner, the popular Berlin poet, presented the potential and the reality of popular political activity:

Der Messias
Hofft den Messias ihr noch? Nicht kommt er vom Himmel! Ihr Völker,
Reicht euch zum Kampf die Hand und – der Messias ist da.

The Messiah
You hope for him still? Not from Heaven will he come! You peoples
Reach out your hands to fight and – the Messiah is there.

The isolation of literature

The post-1849 period was one of a total social and political deadlock spanning some ten years and, on account of the reading public on whom it depended, also embracing political writing. Three problems to which no satisfactory answers were found were to persist until the end of the century for radical democrats and the writers who sympathised with them. First, they were too conscious of themselves as writers, therefore tending to place aesthetic problems above political ones. Second, they were unable to find a new form of writing appropriate to their political aspirations. Third, they continued after the revolution to find themselves exerting an insignificant effect on the periphery of society. In the ensuing years they developed into a major source of competition to the swelling tide of trivial literature, in that both the latter and their own writing were aimed at a mass readership. The thesis of the apolitical German writer was thus not merely middle-class ideology, but equally the result of ongoing capitalist conditions in publishing that were giving rise to a literature of entertainment for the apolitical masses. This literature both required and tirelessly pursued the semblance of harmony.

Marx's coalition of the lower middle class and the workers

In the aftermath of the seizure of power in France by Napoleon II, Marx commented in 1852 that the coalition between the lower middle class and the workers, which sought to achieve democratic republican institutions through opposition, did not do so in order to abolish capital and wage labour, those two opposite extremes, but in order to soften this opposition and transform it into harmony. Marx drew this conclusion on the basis of his observation that even lower-middle-class writers were unable to 'escape in their minds the categories' laid down by their class, and 'are hence driven to seek the same tasks and solutions' that the lower middle class has always striven for socially (*Der achtzehnte Brumaire des Louis Bonaparte – The Eighteenth Brumaire of Louis Bonaparte*). It should be added that the lack of innovative forms and of working-class writers forced politically committed authors back into the middle-class camp again and again.

For this and other reasons, Friedrich Theodor Vischer became one of the most influential and possibly the most typical aesthete of the nineteenth century with his *Kritische Gänge* (*Critical Sallies*), first published in 1846 and then reprinted from 1860 to 1870 in six volumes. Vischer provided the following explanation for the impossibility of political poetry in his day, justifying it with the widely-accepted view: 'It is useless, since it expresses an idea that is still disembodied and yet to be embodied, an idea which is thus still abstract.'

As scholars and writers in Germany began to devise categories of liberty in the arts and sciences, they soon realised that liberty and the intellect were attributes of the people and of the world of learning, but that writers were caught 'between the fronts'. Sinecures provided by princes, and increasingly by middle-class capital investors, were scarcely compatible with a literature of liberty.

During the eighteenth and first half of the nineteenth century a number of intrepid authors, in a line stretching from Lessing and many of his contemporaries up to Heine, had striven after progress in literary theory and practice. There was little evidence of similar efforts after 1848. Indeed, Fontane's treatise on *Realism* dating from 1853 is an exemplary piece of retrogressive thinking. Fontane was deliberately propounding an aesthetics that would act as a purifying filter for all perception of life by authors. He himself searched some considerable time before finding a new middle-class critical form. This was because of an increasingly unmistakable desire among the middle class for a clearly-structured and palpable unity between the individual and society. The less evidence there was of such unity in reality, the more aversion there was to the differentiated disclosure of human individuality in literature, which was perceived as weakness. A 'democratisation process of character' was no more wanted in literature than in real life. The counter-model to differentiation was the strong character of a hero who was able to bend reality to his will, and this not merely with great effort, but almost playfully. This could be accomplished in literature, if not in life.

Nietzsche's aristocratic ideal

Nietzsche was quick to recognise this desire for unity, giving repeated descriptions of it and exploiting it theoretically. He wrote in 1872:

> What has been demonstrated here as an isolated example is valid in the most general sense: every man, together with the sum of his work, only possesses dignity to the extent that he, consciously or unconsciously, is the instrument of genius. The ethical conclusion immediately to be drawn from this is that 'man in himself', or absolute man, possesses neither dignity, rights, nor duties. The sole justification for his existence is as a being who is completely determined, serving unknown ends.
> (*Fünf Vorreden zu fünf ungeschriebenen Büchern* – *Five Prefaces to Five Unwritten Books*)

A 'realistic' literary direction would undoubtedly have pursued a different course. The times, however, were marked by totally thwarted social and political aspirations, which made these deficiencies all too apparent when the gaze was directed at the real world and the very real lack of liberty that was spreading in it. Inevitably, therefore, a literature that bowed to the prevailing body of aesthetics developed into an apology for existing conditions. As a result, the post-1848 period became a stamping-ground for large numbers of prolific trumped-up writers of decorative literature whose ranks swelled in inverse proportion to the quality of their works.

In 1862 Ferdinand Lassalle began to press for a new working-class party, which finally came into being in 1863 with the aim of pursuing social democracy. Lassalle's early speeches are permeated by flowery figures of speech. In a speech to workers at the Borsig machine factory in Oranienburg, for example, he declared that in 1789 the fourth estate had still been concealed in the heart-strings of the third estate, but that now it had to 'raise its principle to be the guiding principle of society and with it penetrate all its institutions'.

The 'Bundeslied'

On the occasion of the founding of the party, Herwegh sent Lassalle what was later to become his famous *Bundeslied*, based on a text by Shelley. The last three verses of a total of twelve read:

Mann der Arbeit, aufgewacht!
Und erkenne deine Macht!
Alle Räder stehen still,
Wenn dein starker Arm es will.

Deiner Dränger Schar erblasst,
Wenn du, müde deiner Last,
In der Ecke lehnst den Pflug,
Wenn du rufst: es ist genug!

Brecht des Doppeljoch entzwei!
Brecht die Not der Sklaverei!
Brecht die Sklaverei der Not!
Brot ist Freiheit, Freiheit Brot!

Man of work arise
And know thy power!
All the wheels will stand still
If 'tis thy sovereign will.

Thy oppressors will turn pale
If thou, tired of thy burden,
Wilt put thy plough away
And 'Enough!' to them wilt say.

Break the double yoke in twain!
Break the poverty of slavery!
Break the slavery of poverty!
Bread is freedom, and freedom bread!

'Lassalle recited this poem at many rallies, always with the same stirring effect – a success that has remained faithful to this day to the emphatic hammer beats of the verse' (W. Grab). Before turning to practical political work, Lassalle attempted in his drama *Franz von Sickingen* (1858) to give literary expression to the experience of the 1848 defeat. He did not do this directly, however, but by analogy, setting the plot in the time of the peasant wars. His drama unleashed a mighty controversy, especially among committed democrats – a debate that has gone down in history as the 'Sickingen debate'. The central aspects of this controversy revolved around whether literary writing was capable of solving political problems, and whether contemporary problems clothed in the past did not sacrifice their topicality as a result and hence inevitably seem 'unrealistic'. Lassalle was unable to withdraw from this debate, having conceded at an early stage that his *Sickingen* had been intended as a general statement of position, concerning not only the German revolution in particular, but revolution *per se*. His stated aim was to devise a model for which Sickingen himself served merely as a vehicle. Lassalle believed in the 'eternally recurring conflict of revolutionary action', and intended his play as a 'tragedy of the formal revolutionary ideal *par excellence*'.

What does 'representativeness' mean?

Marx at once discerned the 'error' that Lassalle was bound to make in connection with this aspiration, and informed the author accordingly: 'Sickingen . . . did not flounder because of his shrewdness. He went under because he posed as the champion and representative of a floundering class against the prevailing class, or rather the new form of the prevailing class.' This is not made clear at any point in Lasalle's text itself, however. Despite the radicalism of Sickingen's ideas, the author was unable to detach him from middle-class aesthetics, and hence presented him as a hero. This compelled him to seek solutions to historical and political issues by aesthetic means. Lassalle's copious 'vindication' to Marx is hence rather a theoretical attempt to salvage a failed work. This reveals just how far the literary accommodation of political problems was from its theoretical aspirations. This deficiency had three causes: a lack of literary skill; the (middle-class) notion that the state could be developed into a guarantor of liberty, if only, by such means as people's tribunes, it could be reshaped or 'purified'; and the absence of an effective, progressive aesthetics. Sickingen was to become the mouthpiece of modern political rhetoric; in other words, the didactic tradition of much German prose fiction (E. Sagarra) was extended to drama. This made the champion of the peasant wars a people's hero without a people, while in real life the people were being degraded into the masses.

'A morass of triviality'

Rarely did early socialist literature in Germany succeed in hauling itself 'out of the morass of triviality' (F. Mehring) and offering the reader subjects, plots and characters conveying a new image of man in a new art, thereby developing and shaping a new consciousness. Unlike the Age of Enlightenment, there was virtually no literary anticipation of political change to come in the period between 1850 and 1900. There were, however, many texts full of sympathy for suffering humanity among the lower classes and the industrial working class, but which did not portray them as a class in action. Friedrich Engels recognised this and issued vigorous warnings against the didactic bombast of tendentious poetry, as his letter to Minna Kautsky shows:

> You obviously felt a need in this book to take a firm stand on one side, and bear witness before the world of your convictions. This has now been accomplished; it is behind you and there is no need for

you to repeat it in this form. I have no objection to tendentious poetry as such. The father of tragedy, Aeschylus, and the father of comedy, Aristophanes, were both markedly tendentious poets, and no less Dante and Cervantes; indeed the finest aspect of Schiller's *Kabale und Liebe* is that it represents the first German politically tendentious drama. The modern Russians and Norwegians, who have produced excellent novels, are all tendentious poets. In my opinion, however, tendentiousness should arise out of the plot itself without being explicitly pointed out. Likewise the writer has no need to hand the reader on a plate the future historical solution to the social conflicts he depicts. Moreover, under present circumstances the novel is predominantly addressed to readers from middle-class circles who do not belong to us directly. The socialist tendentious novel is hence in my opinion entirely fulfilling its function by the faithful depiction of actual circumstances, sweeping away prevailing conventional illusions, undermining the optimism of the middle-class milieu, and leading the reader to an inexorable doubt as to the eternal validity of presently prevailing conditions, without itself directly offering a solution, and indeed under certain circumstances without overtly displaying any bias at all.

(Engels to Minna Kautsky, 26 November 1885)

Clearly this letter also exudes a degree of resignation at the fact that so little change was evident in either the literary or political spheres. At all events, however, Engels sought to avoid a dovetailing of social themes with middle-class morality and professions of sympathy, having realised that this made the resulting literature scarcely distinguishable from mass literature for middle-class entertainment, as well as excluding the potential for change in political consciousness. This may also be the reason behind Engel's 'retreat' into tendentious poetry of a documentary character that facilitated political consciousness-raising through the descriptive.

Lyric poetry in the age of realism

Ihr starrt dem Dichter ins Gesicht
Verwundert, dass er Rosen bricht
Von Disteln, aus dem Quell der Augen
Koral und Perle weiss zu saugen;
Dass er den Blitz herniederlangt,
Um seine Fackel zu entzünden,
Im Wettertoben, wenn euch bangt,
Den rechten Odem weiss zu finden:
Ihr starrt ihn an mit halbem Neid,
Den Geisteskrösus seiner Zeit,

Und wisst es nicht, mit welchen Qualen
Er seine Schätze muss bezahlen.

You gaze the poet in the face,
Amazed that he the rose can pluck
From thistles, from the well of the eyes
From coral and pearl the blood to suck;
That he summons lightning's glare
To set aflame his burning flare,
When stormy weather you doth 'fright
The poet knows how to capture the right breath;
You gaze at him, some part in rage,
The cerebral Croesus of his age,
But know not of the mental torture
Expended for this precious treasure.

(Annette Droste-Hülshoff: *Der Dichter – The Poet*)

Doubling of reality through metaphor

The poem from which this extract is taken may be regarded as a representative sample of pre-1848 lyric verse. There is a rapid succession of metaphors showing the contrast between the readership ('You') and the poet. Droste is above all at pains to express the torment of artistic creation, to this end using metaphors or allowing the poet to be treated metaphorically ('that he the rose can pluck from thistles'). In the second half of the text Annette von Droste-Hülshoff proceeds to an attempt, using carefully selected metaphors, to influence the everyday world (as if she were describing real things), or at least a world comparable with this everyday world. She asks:

Meint ihr, das Wetter zünde nicht?
Meint ihr, der Sturm erschüttre nicht?
Meint ihr, die Träne brenne nicht?
Meint ihr, die Dornen stechen nicht?

Think you the weather stirreth not?
Think you, the storm quaketh not?
Think you, that tears burn not?
Think you, that thorns pierce not?

Assuming that the phenomena enumerated in the metaphors developed above are 'realistic', then the weather, storm, tears and thorns are metaphors for the poet and for endured reality alike. He can hardly survive this 'duality', however much he may wish to. The poem thus draws to a close in overly laconic brevity, almost abruptly:

Ja, eine Lampe hat er entfacht,
Die nur das Mark ihm sieden macht;
Ja, Perlen fischt er und Juwele,
Die kosten nichts – nur eine Seele.

Yes, a lamplight hath he set aflame
That marrow alone will soothe and warm;
He fishes for pearls and jewel-shoal,
They cost him nothing – save his soul.

The texts written by this poet clearly go far beyond the 'ingenious imagery' pinpointed by Eduard Engels in his widely-read *Deutsche Stilkunst (The German Art of Style)* as 'the common vice of baroque and Young German poets'. Eduard Mörike's lyric verse, most of which was written before 1848, and was often dismissed as 'Biedermeier', is a convincing example of a consummate language form in a rich tradition (*Er ist's – 'Tis Him*, 1829; *Im Weinberg – In the Vineyard*, 1838; *Die schöne Buche – The Lovely Beech*, 1842). Mörike had a facility not only for playing with ancient models virtually at will for the creative purposes of his work (*An eine Aolsharfe – To an Aeolian Harp*, 1837, based on an ode by Horace), but also succeeded in finding a humorous popular lyric narrative tone (*Der alte Turmhahn – The Old Weathercock*, final version 1852). Here he set an example that has never since been followed: humour blended with pietist tone – a swan-song for a fading society? Obviously it came easily to Mörike the pastor to match the melody of a famous hymn to the structure of his poem (*In der Frühe – In the Early Morning*, 1828). His famous *Septembermorgen – September Morn* anticipated as early as 1827 the development towards realism in lyric poetry nearly twenty years before it emerged.

'Playing with metaphors'

Hebbel made an early and concerted effort to move beyond 'playing with metaphors' in his lyric poetry, in order to make his lyric themes able to stand more in their own right as symbols and keep his poetry as free as possible from rhetorical formulation. He had good reason to adopt this approach: there were still many texts overladen with metaphors, including some of Droste's. The severe criticism directed after 1848 at this metaphorical excess was justified, therefore. The language of lyric verse was far removed from that of everyday life, often being perceived as a 'filter' for the platitudes censured in village stories. This withdrawal from everyday life in metaphors was derided by Heinrich Heine in one of his poems, entitled *Entartung (Decadence)*:

Ich glaub nicht mehr an der Lilie Keuschheit
. . . .

Von der Bescheidenheit der Veilchen
Halt' ich nicht viel
. . . .
Ich zweifle auch, ob sie empfindet,
Die Nachtigall, das, was sie singt,
Sie übertreibt und schluchzt and trillert
Nur aus Routine, wie mich dünkt.

I believe not in the lily of chastity
. . . .
Of the modesty of the violet
I think little
. . . .
I doubt also, whether the nightingale
Feels all that she sings;
She embellishes and sobs and trills
Out of mere routine, it seems to me.

'Ich und Du' ('Thou and I')

Hebbel's early poem *Ich und Du* (*Thou and I*) (1843) already shows the huge transformation that had taken place in the portrayal of love relationships during the restoration era. He opens the poem in an apparently entirely 'real' way, then expands the theme he has broached, allowing it to culminate in an aphoristic statement of such terseness it could easily be mistaken for lack of feeling:

Wir träumten voneinander
Und sind davon erwacht,
Wir leben, um uns zu lieben,
Und sinken zurück in die Nacht.

We dreamed one of the other
Until our dream took flight,
We live to love and be loved
And sink back into night.

The inner contradiction between the first two and final two lines fills the entire second verse, finally being raised in the third verse into a symbolism displaying a density of language that can scarcely be surpassed:

Auf einer Lilie zittern
Zwei Tropfen, rein and rund,
Zerfliessen in eins und wollen
Hinab in des Kelches Grund.

On lily petal trembling,
Two drops so round and chaste;
But fused they seek, descending
The lily-cup's base to taste.

Other poems by Hebbel reveal the continuous steady development from metaphor to the concrete graphic quality sought in realistic concepts. Examples would be *Ein Bild aus Reichenau* (*A Picture from Reichenau*) (July 1848) and *Liebesprobe* (*Test for Love*) (1854). A typical specimen of pure and total concentration on close scrutiny in order to achieve a total internal image is the *Herbstbild* (*Picture of Autumn*) of 1852. Hebbel's new-found objectivity in lyric did not aspire to 'realism' in the general sense, however. Hebbel, Keller, Storm, Meyer and many others were instead making a concerted effort to offer a poetic world to counter the rising positivism that was accompanying the natural scientific conquest of the earth. Initially, therefore, the central feature of their work was conservative, believing as they did that the calling of the poet was to create or point to refuges in which people could sense a higher meaning in their lives and conduct.

Nature 'aestheticised'

Other well-known examples of a natural world that was perceived idealistically and recreated aesthetically, apart from Hebbel's *Herbstbild*, are Storm's many 'homeland' ('Heimat') poems, such as *Abseits* (*The Other Side*), *Meeresstrand* (*The Beach*), *Über die Heide* (*Across the Heath*), and his love poems: *Dämmerstunde* (*Twilight Hour*), *Abends* (*In the Evening*), or *Im Volkston* (*In the Tone of the People*). Storm invariably achieved consummate results when he was able to bring nature and man into a parallel relationship (as in *Über die Heide*), enabling the outsider to share in the sense of a lyrical self as an integral part of nature. Storm's ultimate achievement in this regard is his total blending of the two, man and nature, in *Die Nachtigall* (*The Nightingale*). Here the third verse, which is in fact identical with the first, takes on a completely new meaning in relation to the girl in the second verse, promoting a mutual interpretation that unites them into a symbolic whole. Consummate texts such as these seem to indicate that after the middle of the nineteenth century poets were for perhaps the last time capable of such a relationship with nature. Mörike and Keller were aware of this fact, and Conrad Ferdinand Meyer even more acutely so. The latter's poem *Der schöne Tag* (*The Lovely Day*), first drafted as the end of the century approached, and *Zwei Segel* (*Two Sails*), *Auf dem Canal Grande* (*On the Grand Canal*), and *Der römische Brunnen* (*The Roman Fountain*) (final version completed in 1882 after at least two preliminary drafts: there is evidence of at least twenty years work on the text) were capable of a precise sensual apprehension of 'reality' while at the same time combining it with declarations that went far beyond that apprehension. Should such texts be looked on as 'attempts to salvage the soul?'

The cult of the ballad

The cult of the ballad was first pursued by the 'Swabian School', with the support of the publisher Cotta and led by the poet Ludwig Uhland, in the Biedermeier period. One contemporary critic asserted that this 'cult' was in great danger of being debased into the 'factory-like manufacture' of ballads, characterised by a blend of lyric and epic in the dramatic – the model most frequently employed. Ludwig Uhland's *Des Sängers Fluch* (*The Singer's Curse*) and *Das Glück von Edenhall* (*The Fortune of Edenhall*) represent such attempts to meet the appetite for harmony that was characteristic of their day. These texts showed history making its way through excess and arrogance as if these attributes were not integral to every age.

Uhland, however, was to influence whole generations of schoolchildren with his humour in poems such as the ballad *Roland Schildträger* (*Roland the Shieldbearer*). His *Siegfrieds Schwert* (*Siegfried's Sword*) has a laconic simplicity about it, while his song *Der gute Kamarad* (*The Good Comrade*) is still topical to this day in its continuing function for public mourning, albeit a largely unconscious one, since the lyrics are absent.

Schauerballade (horror ballads)

The Biedermeier era was both familiar with and passed on a wide range of ballad styles, by far the best-known of which at the time was the *Schauerballade* (Droste-Hülshoff: *Der Knabe im Moor* – *The Boy on the Moor*; Mörike: *Der Feuerreiter* – *The Fire-Rider*; G. Schwab: *Das Gewitter* – *The Thunderstorm*). 'Realistic' ballad poets lent the portrayal of nature a magical omnipotence that on occasion cloaked an ill-thought-out hostility to technology (Fontane: *Die Brücke am Tay* – *The Bridge on the Tay*), but contributed nothing to foster the horror ballad tradition. Instead they portrayed headstrong heroes who could be set beside those of middle-class domestic novels. Social criticism was rare (Heine: *Das Sklavenschiff* – *The Slave-Ship*, or in historical guise *Donna Clara*), as were critical ballads concerning the issues of the day. Heine's *Die schlesischen Weber* (*The Silesian Weavers*) and Dronke's *Das Weib des Webers* (*The Weaver's Wife*) competed with the heart-rending genre scenes and appeals for sympathy of their various contemporaries (e.g. Luise Otto or Ferdinand Freiligrath). As a rule, however, the human capacity for sacrifice tended to conceal the shortcomings of contemporary conditions, particularly social ones: in *John Maynard*, Fontane selects such a tiny piece of reality to indicate that the circumstances are difficult to make out. He also 'ennobles' the conduct of the helmsman, producing an ambivalent image of his hero: his death becomes a celebration, but the circumstances remain unchanged.

'Great men'

A much more popular and widespread trend in realism was the depiction of great men in a human light (e.g. Fontane: *Herr von Ribbeck auf Ribbeck im Havelland* – *Herr von Ribbeck on Ribbeck in Havelland*). Alternatively, recollection of great men was perceived as a symptom of their greatness (Freiligrath: *Prinz Eugen* – *Prince Eugene*). Virtually all realist ballad poets conjured up scenes from history, most of all perhaps Conrad Ferdinand Meyer (*Bettlerballade* – *The Beggars' Ballad; Die Füsse im Feuer* – *The Feet in the Fire; Mit Zwei Worten* – *With Two Words; Der gleitende Purpur* – *The Slipping Purple Mantle*). In so doing, however, Meyer by no means always depicted the great historical moment, often showing the moment of greatness of insignificant or obscure people. Since the increase in realist lesser narrative prose was unsuited to the ballad as an art form, ballad-writing after 1850 grew away from the *Zeitgeist* so often invoked by Heine, and towards an ideally viewed, more abstract form of 'ballad objectivity'. This art form was characterised by greater density and a maintenance of distance both from the subject-matter itself and the contemporary era. Obviously this does not apply to the numerous 'clapper ballads' by Geibel or Freiligrath that were soon to fill reading-books. Even great poets made concessions to the age in which they lived. Fontane, who had a sharp eye for the social dimension, thus also developed a sense for dynamic moments, questions of power and for 'characters' – that is, for heroes.

At the end of the century, Detlev von Liliencron found a new tone. For all its brevity, his narrative poem *Die Musik kommt* (*The Music Comes*) (1892) is a masterpiece in the humorous depiction of milieu, as well as maintaining ironic distance from a presentation that is perceived as an illusion. Liliencron, a trained officer, was in fact no militarist. In presenting, for example, the crushing defeat of Friedrich II, King of Prussia, at Kolin in terms of individual destiny, he omits both the customary sentimentality and any future perspective (*Wer weiss so* – *Who Knows Where?*):

> Doch einst bin ich, und bist auch du,
> Verscharrt im Sand zur ew'gen Ruh, –
> Wer weiss wo.

> Yet one day will I, and you too be
> Hastily laid to eternal rest in the sand, –
> Who knows where.

Idea and reality in the drama of realism

'Inwardly torn literature'

Like the *Gründerzeit*, the phase between the revolution and German unification came to be regarded as one in which politically committed literature
was either morally or ideologically overladen, and hence lacking in credibility – an 'inwardly torn' literature, as F.T. Vischer termed it. It went
against the idealistic notion of the day, since 'realism led in all spheres to
finite, indeed closed entities that were as inaccessible to universal tendencies
as to particularist ones, and whose character was hence more technical than
organic, more inclined to close off than to lead to further development' (F.
Sengle). This came to apply to the middle-class dramatic tradition, where
it did not slide into genre or history-painting, far sooner than has previously been supposed.

This becomes clear from the example of Friedrich Hebbel. Born in 1813,
like Büchner, Hebbel had not written a single drama by the time Büchner
died. When he finally began to adapt dramatic themes, from 1837 onwards,
the universalist function of drama had become of major importance. He
did not wish, therefore, to follow in the footsteps of historical dramatists
like Grabbe or Büchner (even when adapting historical themes).

Incongruity between idea and phenomenon

Hebbel devised a comprehensive conception of tragedy that was unrelated
to the topical. It was based on a 'concept of tragic culpability [derived]
from life itself, from the primeval incongruity between idea and phenomenon, and ultimately expressed as excess, which is the natural consequence
of the urge towards self-preservation and self-justification, the first and
most justified urge of all' (Paris, June 1844). As contemporary audiences
discerned, this conception tended to lead to a static, determinist quality.
Hebbel was of the view 'that the conflicts that are brought to an overall
resolution should [not] also be brought to this point in the individuals
who represent them. This would entail . . . bending them and disintegrating
them, and thereby destroying the very basis of the drama' (to A. Ruge, 15
September 1852).

Despite being remote from his own times, Hebbel avoided the difficulties
experienced by Lassalle by lacking any desire to make veiled references to
the contemporary period. He dropped the theme of Napoleon, for example,
on the grounds that it was still too 'immediate' and 'topical'. In contrast,
Hebbel constantly sought an intensive examination of the models offered
by the authors he revered: Lessing, Schiller, and above all Kleist, a tendency
that often led to his being misunderstood. As a result, a number of his
plays were successful in terms of public acclaim by virtue of their dramatic

qualities, but were unable to achieve enduring effects. Hebbel was far from happy with the idea that his drama *Maria Magdalene* (1843) was interpreted as a social tragedy of the lower classes: not once in the language of the play had he condescended to the popular level. The strict tradition with regard to the style of speech upheld at the Vienna Burgtheater, with which Hebbel was linked from 1846 through his wife, the actress Christine Enghaus, was at pains to avoid 'penetrating individualism' (F. Sengle) and to be a 'purifying element of the universal'. In upholding this tradition, however, the Burgtheater was verging on anachronism, and Hebbel with it. While the age of realism was seeking to 'undermine rhetoric' and 'denigrate the high, emotional style', as well as to go beyond a lesser, witty, cynical style of writing towards an articulate stylistic unity (F. Sengle), Hebbel was pursuing quite different aims.

The individual–society dialectic

Hebbel was the last German dramatist to attempt a thorough-going solution to the challenges offered by dramatic art. For him the focal point of dramatic tension lay in the dialectic between the individual and society in the broadest sense (for which he used the term 'universe'). The stage was for him, therefore, neither a peep-show into reality, nor an institution of entertaining diversion, but a poetically created world or counter-world:

> Artistic imagination is the organ with which those depths of the world are plumbed that are inaccessible to the other faculties. In my view, therefore, it is appropriate to set against a false realism, which confuses the part with the whole, only a true realism, which also encompasses that which is not on the surface. . . . Geography knows no groves of the gods, Shakespeare's tempest, because there is no magic, or Hamlet and Macbeth, because only a fool is afraid of ghosts, etc.
>
> (to Siegmund Engländer, 1 May 1863)

Once Hebbel's figures were on stage, however, nothing was left to chance. They are inescapably exposed to the tension with the world, and have to conduct themselves according to the 'laws' of this tension. Here, Hebbel was seeking to remove the emphasis upon, indeed to eliminate what he regarded as the 'pathological requirement [of contemporary plays], namely the circumstance that the individual is their starting-point' (*Ein Wort über das Drama – A Word On Drama*, 1843). He was not interested, therefore, in topicality of subject-matter, since his emphasis was on the universal. He wrote in his diary in 1840: 'All life is the struggle between the individual and the universe.'

Hebbel's Judith

Hebbel was already endeavouring to put these ideas into effect in the first drama he completed, *Judith* (1884). In his dramatic work the idea or thought was always transmitted by means of a polished language form, however hard he strove after language as a means of achieving distance. It is not even certain that Hebbel actually intended all his dramas for the stage: they may have constituted a concerted effort to become clear in his own mind about the nature of tragedy. In *Judith*, for example, the first two acts are taken up with introducing the two main characters, Judith the Jewess and the Assyrian ruler Holofernes, more in terms of their conditions than their surroundings. 'Only a virgin soul is capable of a courage that feels equal to the most heinous.' When Judith pleads with the young Ephraim to liberate the Jewish people from Holofernes out of love for her, the young man shrinks back in horror – the deed is inconceivable to him in every respect. At this, the boundless individual Judith resolves to accomplish herself that which she has called on Ephraim to do. She approaches Holofernes with the clear-cut objective of murdering him. This triggers a 'dramatic concentration' that Hebbel himself judged as being 'here and there too rigid', as he wrote to Ludwig Tieck on 17 February 1840. A second attempt is required before the atrocious deed itself is finally accomplished. By then, however, it is no longer out of nationalist or religious grounds, i.e. 'noble' motives. The girl Judith has sworn revenge on the 'heinous individual' who is Holofernes, who usurps all authority as if he were a god, for having raped her – an act that Holofernes himself views as no more than an enthusiastic manifestation of lust. He wanted finally to possess this object who gave herself such airs. Later he falls asleep smiling. In the excess of her wounded pride, however, Judith does not feel herself to be a single being, but a symbol of the entire Jewish nation, suffering under the yoke of Holofernes' power. At the same time, however, Judith is acting as a wronged woman. She returns to the sphere of the universal by coming to the aid of her people and steeling herself for her own destruction. Judith's act of murder thus goes far beyond the scope of the deed originally envisaged. It is a representative act on behalf of one world order against another: the meaningful life of the entire nation is 'saved'.

Other 'classics'

Maria Magdalene (1843) and *Agnes Bernauer* (1851) both exerted a strong influence into the twentieth century that is all the more remarkable since they were included in scarcely a single school reader. There has naturally been a repeated tendency to perform and interpret them in a modern light, which goes against what Hebbel himself would have wished. He wrote in isolation from society, as the famous example of his tragedy *Herodes und Mariamne* (first performed at the Burgtheater in April 1849) shows. From his window in Vienna he was able to follow the events of the 1848 revolution while working on this drama. He was observing the advent of a new age, but all that interested him was the transition towards a new era in *Herodes*. This deliberate distance undoubtedly partly accounts for the lack of success of many productions of his plays. Farces, genre plays and *Historien* took precedence with theatre directors over his plays: they were more representative of the age.

Maria Magdalene could be described as a drama dealing with the short-comings of all the characters.

> My specific intention in this play was for once to construct a middle-class tragedy out of those elements that are original and peculiar to the middle-class milieu, which in my view consist solely in a profound, wholesome and hence so easily injured feeling, and a body of ideas that cannot be penetrated by any form of dialectic, and scarcely even by destiny itself. If therefore, aside from the greater chain of which it forms but one link, this play is only of partial merit, this may be because here the tragic element derives not from the conflict between the middle-class world and the aristocratic one . . . , but quite simply from the middle-class world itself – from its tenacious and self-motivated insistence on traditional patriarchal views, and its inability to help itself in complex situations.
>
> (letter to Auguste Stich-Crelinger, 11 December 1843)

Agnes Bernauer

In *Agnes Bernauer*, a drama that he managed to complete in a few short months in 1851 after lengthy preliminary planning, Hebbel was pursuing quite different objectives. The story of the barber-surgeon's daughter from Augsburg is documented. In 1342 she was married to Albrecht, son and heir to Ernst, Duke of Bavaria. In Hebbel's tragedy Albrecht is at first 'only' disinherited, and the marriage acceded to, although immediately after the wedding ceremony Duke Ernst has his legal advisers issue a death sentence on his low-ranking daughter-in-law. At this stage there is still the possibility of a nephew succeeding to the throne – an unwelcome, but nonetheless feasible solution. Destiny takes a hand after the death of this nephew. Agnes now stands in the way of 'legal' descendants, and is drowned in the Danube for reasons of state. After a period of protest, Albrecht is at the disposal of the state, if less of his father.

Hebbel's drama has often been interpreted politically, but he himself did not see it as such, regarding it as 'politically and socially entirely innocuous', as he wrote to Dingelstedt. Hebbel realised 'that the subject-matter [could only appear] tragic if the writer was able to depict her [Agnes Bernauer] as the modern Antigone' (to his wife Christine, 3 March 1852). It was not the tragedy of the heroine as such that Hebbel wished to stress here, however, but rather the 'imperative ... of perpetuating the world; what happens to individuals in the world, however, is a matter of indifference' (diary entry, Paris, November 1843). The 'relationship between the individual and society' is presented 'in two characters, one of whom came from the highest social sphere, the other from the lowest'. As the tragedy takes its course it becomes clear that the individual, 'no matter how glorious and great, noble and fine he may be, is bound under all circumstances to bend before society, because all of humanity lives within it and its imperative formal expression, the state, in which, however, but one aspect of the same can unfold'.

The totality of tragedy

The older Hebbel became, the more what was now a fully matured totality of the tragic event precluded all other potential perspectives. It thus came to act almost as an impediment, and certainly did nothing to further his contact with contemporary dramatists. There is considerable evidence documenting how Hebbel disputed again and again with the latter over new concepts of tragedy; conversely, no evidence suggests that he altered his own position. In a famous letter to S. Engländer written on 27 January 1863 (only a few months before his death), in which he takes up the question of 'social tragedy', he writes:

> The detailed description of your concept of social tragedy interested me enormously.... I am familiar with the horrendous abyss you disclose to me; I know the incalculable sum of human suffering that fills it. It is not as though I take a bird's eye view either; I have been familiar with it since childhood, since although my parents were not directly affected by it, they teetered on the edge of it, and only just managed to hold on to that edge by the skin of their teeth. This, however, is the general misery to which human beings are exposed, not least as a result of the tortuous course of history. It is a misery that admits the question of guilt and forgiveness as little as that of death – that second universal evil that strikes blind, and which, therefore, leads no more to tragedy than the former. From this viewpoint, one is more likely to arrive at a complete dissolution of tragedy – at satire, which throws the glaring inconsistencies of the moral world right in our faces, and not least the tragic form itself. It either ignores the the writer of tragedies ..., or turns a blind eye to him. ...
> The Indian caste system, the Roman slave war with Spartacus, or the German peasant rebellion that you cite to me can only produce

tragedy from the religious or communist standpoint, since the religious man recognises the guilt of all mankind, for which an individual does penance, while the communist believes in a balancing-out process. I am unfamiliar with the former and do not believe in the latter.

The modernity of woman

Earlier in his life, Hebbel had been at ease with different perspectives: in particular the uncontemporary manner in which he distinguished his female characters above all, such as Judith, Mariamne and Agnes Bernauer, and which enables us to feel more comfortable with them than with their male counterparts. This apparent modernity in his female characters was unintended by Hebbel, however. They simply provided vehicles for his dramatic action. What we today find remarkable about Judith, Mariamne or Agnes – the absolute power of their pure feeling – was for Hebbel no more than a building-block for his tragic plot. When Mariamne objects to Herodes treating her as an object, Hebbel is undoubtedly himself treating this character, like his other female characters, as an object to be subordinated to his notion of tragedy. In terms of the radicalism of his consistency in subordinating all parts to the whole, Hebbel as an author of tragedies in no way lagged behind the s me qualities displayed by Marx as a political philosopher, however much they lived and moved in entirely different 'worlds'.

Folk literature and the village story

Realist criticism and the literary history associated with it have reproved the diversity of pre-realistic writing both for its structure and its tone. This criticism has not omitted to point out that the 'folk' tone often gave a contrived impression and sometimes missed the mark altogether (see, for example, the assessment by Heyse and Kurz in their anthology *Deutsche Novellenschatz* of Brentano's *Geschichte vom braven Kasperl und dem schönen Annerl – The Story of Good Kasperl and Pretty Annerl*, 1817).

The question to be asked at this point is why the village story came to enjoy such high regard in the nineteenth century. It has often been seen as the successor to the idyll and related narrative forms: 'the motive for idealising rural life [is] to be seen in the context of the European tradition of idyllic writing and the rustic epic in general' (J. Hein). These initial trends towards the idyllic were being built on by the time of the Biedermeier era at the latest, as may be seen from the following extract:

Nothing from America! The soil and the homeland are everywhere: as to oases we come to wonderfully peaceful houses. . . . Without being asked who I am or what I want, the table is pulled up. The arrival of a guest seemed to be nothing unusual in this household. Everything breathed order and that cleanliness of German dairy farms that one can see is achieved through seriousness and hard work. The aroma of the freshly-scrubbed room, the white sand still wrinkled under one's feet, the crockery symmetrically arranged over the doorway and on the window-sill, the green birch branches behind the mirror in order to have a piece of the forest inside the house. I felt as if I were stepping into an idyll.

(Karl Immerman, *Die Papierfenster eines Eremiten* – *The Paper Windows of an Eremite*, 1822)

The exotic homeland?

This type of narrated experience stands in clear contrast to historical narrative and to the salon novel, reflecting a dialectic relationship to the homeland and to the increasingly manifest degree of exoticism that was creeping into travel descriptions and novels and being passed on to the reader. In the village story, the exotic element is suddenly no longer 'beyond a fixed horizon... , but in the midst of the immediate world ... , since what pertains to the homeland is by no means restricted to one's own homeland sphere' (H. Bausinger). What had originally been contradictory elements are thus now blended into a kind of 'inland exotic'.

> Social assumptions clearly played a part in the village story, especially with Immermann and Gotthelf, who showed a preference for well-off farmers. At the same time they also show that these stories are never solely concerned with familiarity with the land and the influence of the farmer class, but are in fact mainly concerned with what links them to specific values and ideals that the land embodies or should embody. As on an island in a distant ocean, it seems, an ideal, reasonable or pious community of men is more easily achieved in a village than in urban civilisation. The utopian and the pedagogical are thus integral to the village story.
>
> (F. Sengle)

Art and homeland – a contradiction?

Perhaps at first unintentionally, Altvater's definition strikes at the heart of the matter: 'In terms of subject-matter, "homeland art", preponderantly a narrative form, at first shared the characteristic features of its entire mental attitude and presentation in common with incipient realism.' At the same time, however, a cultural agenda was concealed in this new form, summed up by Höfig: 'Constituent for homeland fiction... is in fact the closed nature of its view of the world, which is cultivated pedagogically with an eye to the concurrent dissolution of such a world in reality'. In this way, for the reading individual, above all the urban middle-class reader, 'the homeland [becomes] a timeless, idyllic image of pristine reality itself. Attachment to the homeland is no longer based on an active relationship with objective circumstances, but is the expression of an irrational internal attitude.'

It should be stressed from the first, as contemporaries such as Freiligrath did at the time, that the village story stems from time-honoured traditions, particularly in Swiss literature, and can be traced by a process of extensive exegesis as far back as Wernher der Gärtner, and by intensive exegesis at least to Albrecht Haller's *Die Alpen* (*The Alps*) (1729), through Pestalozzi's *Lienhard and Gertrud* (1779) and Zschokke's *Das Goldmacher-Dorf* (*The Village of Goldsmiths*) (1817) to Gotthelf's *Bauernspiegel* (*The Farmers' Almanac*) (1837). The true cause of this rapid upsurge in village stories, which cannot be attributed simply to imitation of Berthold Auerbach's 'breakthrough' in 1843, most probably lies in the literary transition towards a mass society.

> The village story is not addressed to any particular readership, but at people with simple feelings and thoughts in general. Its readership embraces relatively broad sections of society, since its themes are as comprehensible to the reader who is uneducated in literature as they are to the educated reader. In general, therefore, the village story is to be responded to as a popular genre. As a sphere in its own right, the village story is characterised by *Volkstümlichkeit* (simplicity and clarity), a rustic narrative perspective and a pedagogical tendency. Its principal motifs are (1) the farmstead; (2) the village community; (3) town and country; (4) moral criticism (vices and passions).
>
> (J. Hein)

The popularity of the village story

These motifs are nevertheless peripheral to the popularity of the genre, which was engendered by a specific situation within society, namely the insecurity created by the abolition of the former commercial order, the emancipation of peasants and the onset of the industrial revolution. The idea behind the village story was to harness the 'advantages of a simple community way of life and the potential for rectifying social ills without revolution, by means of moral exertion and under the leadership of the Church' (F. Sengle). In the light of this interpretation, the village story becomes of eminent socio-political importance: 'The aim of educating the people into an ideal condition', as was to be reiterated by writers from

Haller to Zschokke, obviously inclined more towards the village idyll than to realistic depiction.

> The village story replaces the idyll as soon as the latter is no longer able to sustain the interest of the readership in the rustic world.... The village story takes up the contradictions between the 'ideal picture of the land and the nightmare image of the city' (F. Sengle) that was frequently treated in idyll. It only makes an appearance of shifting the political *topos* towards reality, then seeks to set against industrial, economic and social changes that pose a threat to rural existence an unchanging homeland offering a stable order characterised by nature, the landscape, tradition and mores.
>
> (J. Hein)

The picture of this rural life, in other words, is painted with ideal figures and plots which only appear authentic to the extent of the reader's remoteness from real rural life.

Berthold Auerbach achieved a sensational success with his four-volume *Schwarzwälder Dorfgeschichten* (*Village Stories from the Black Forest* (1843–54). It was indeed through him that the village story came to be recognised as a genre definition, uniting 'high' and 'folk' literature into a single 'national literature'. Auerbach's tales, set in his home village of Nordstetten in the Black Forest, are striking for their precision of detail. In his tale *Tolpatsch*, for example, the road from Nordstetten to Stuttgart is described with a precision that would have enabled the description to be used as a guide. Auerbach's objective in the tales, however, was not the 'representation, but mythologisation of real locations' (F. Sengle). This is made possible both through the distortion of perspectives and through his outstanding feel for symbolic plots, in addition to which there is evidence of folklore 'decoration'.

'Ideal realism'

Auerbach aspired, therefore, not to a 'poetry of the negative, of alienation', but to an 'ideal realism' (L. Widhammer), such as was advocated by Friedrich Theodor Vischer on the theoretical level. He censured the Romantics for having had 'no heart for the people' and for having amused themselves 'with the locally alien' aspects of rural life, claiming for themselves the right to an 'unshackled subjectivity', while expecting 'total subordination and acquiescence to authority' from the people. In the light of this criticism, Auerbach sought a compromise. Since the 'freedom of the individual ... [was] the predominant characteristic of our age', it was not possible to 'summarise and capture everything in overall concepts' since 'everyone creates his inner and outer worlds more or less for himself'. The task of the writer, in Auerbach's view, was to order 'the world he has constructed from reality according to higher considerations', leading moods and characters to conclusions 'that they have not perhaps reached outwardly'. All this can only be achieved, however, 'if he has arrived on ground that already has a degree of stability, not loose soil that only yesterday was flooded' (*Schrift und Volk*, 1846). This clearly reveals a conservative bent for arrangement and order: the village story is seen to stand on stable ground, making the depiction of 'existing circumstances' a secure enterprise. It then becomes easy 'to disentangle the so-called masses into individuals in their own right. Those with a high level of education or power are not alone in representing the life of the day or its conflicts' (Auerbach to J.E. Braun, 1843).

Nature as salvation

The tendency to regard nature as a source of salvation from civilisation, to stress a community of manageable size and to lend it an almost religious power did not first appear in village stories. It arose more as a result of their effect on readers, triggering an 'awareness of the fragmentary', as one contemporary critic acknowledged: 'Not an outward, spatial restriction . . . , but an inward, moral one' separated the (educated) reader from the persons depicted. This reader was irritated by the 'poetry of rank . . . propounded by *Dorfgeschichte*'. When F. Kürnberger wrote this in 1848, he was of course not speaking on behalf of the substantial readership who felt deeply but thought little about what they were reading.

Despite this, he still managed to unleash a vigorous controversy that was to touch on a dangerous tendency in German *Dorfgeschichte*. This was the question as to whether the village, as intellectuals maintained, was backward in terms of rank, or whether the farmer was more real, more religious and more moral by virtue of his uncontrived natural feeling – even if he himself was completely unaware of the fact. Was there such a thing as the 'simple life' of which Ernst Wiechert still dreamed in 1936 – possibly even as a form of resistance? By the time discussion of the *Dorfgeschichte* theme had arrived at this point, if not before, it was so far removed from the reality of village life that there was nothing to prevent it from being completely idealised. Sengle observes in this regard: 'Once the idea of a rigorous, pan-German, middle-class, popular-national narrative art form had receded into the background again, the rustic epic was able to enjoy a revival. This time, however, it was no longer idyllic, but elemental and wild in the sense of Nietzsche's "vitalism" (Anzengruber), a prelude to the literature of blood and earth.'

The homeland as refuge

In fact, however, the fashion for the *Dorfgeschichte* also masked the problem of many Realist writers who wanted to present their subject-matter more vividly, and hence sought a close link with the 'homeland', but not necessarily in the form of the *Dorfgeschichte*. Such a link was indeed achieved in the positive sense by writers such as Storm, C.F. Meyer or Raabe, although others such as Spielhagen or Wildenbruch rarely managed it. However, these great writers found themselves being commandeered in the name of that 'vitalism' even in their own century, and were powerless to defend themselves. This applies both to Meyer's *Jürg Jenatsch* and to Storm's *Der Schimmelreiter*. Indeed it was precisely because Storm had succeeded in creating a literary character of such compactness, despite all the contradictory aspects, that the *Schimmelreiter* was misunderstood only a few years after publication in 1888 as a homeland-loving 'man of the *Gründerzeit*': 'A man all burning energy, all public spirit, a man born for struggle, vigorous to the point of cruelty – and to boot a nature [that was] entirely the product of the Holstein seashore!' (Clara Lent, 1899)

The false quest for 'reality' in literature, particularly of the homeland-loving type, often led it to lapse into landscape description in the style of a good travel guide. This negative trend was encouraged by formal inducements, such as the drawing of parallels between man and nature, or the explanation of human actions and character in terms of the landscape, local custom or 'mores' alone (Ganghofer's novels are full of examples of this).

In isolated cases these stylistic features may achieve outstanding effects, but with cumulative or excessive use rapidly deteriorate into cliché, to which mass literature is inclined as a result of its pursuit of immediate and effortless impact. Nature and landscape become an ever-available backdrop and the set piece of epic drama, as the dreary monotony of *Heimatfilme* (homeland films) demonstrates. Did the *Heimat* regress to the status of a *topos* for the conservative view of the world? In Wilhelm Raabe's novel *Der Hungerpastor* (1864), for example, the homeland has a distinct value for all the characters in terms of status and a sense of direction, because here the term has an emotional meaning: homeland is history, tradition and obligation, and is able to overcome class conflicts. To this extent, therefore, it is a fundamentally constructive concept that fosters a sense of belonging. Raabe deals with a particular relationship to the homeland in his two contrasting main characters, the shoemaker's son Hans Jacob Nikolaus Unwirrsch and the son of the Jewish junk dealer, Moses Freudenstein (who later calls himself Dr Theophile Stein). The characters of the two boys, who are the same age, are measured according to their relationship to nature. The often drastic comparisons used not only shed light on them, but also evaluate them, both positively and negatively.

Overall, however, Raabe succeeded in this and other novels in going far beyond the themes of the *Dorfgeschichte* or of *Heimatliteratur*, despite his repeated use of essential elements from both. The same may be said of numerous realist fiction writers, and most especially of Storm, whose novellas *Pole Poppenspäler* (1874), *Aquis submersus* (1883–4), *Hans und Heinz Kirch* (1875–6) and *Zur Chronik von Grieshuus* (*On the Chronicle of Grieshuus*) (1883–4), as well as *Der Schimmelreiter* (1888), greatly transcended the previous limitations of *Heimatkunst*. Storm opened narrative perspectives which Thomas Mann was later to take up gratefully – the homeland as a formative substance in general human modes of conduct, which people reveal regardless of rank or class. Hans and Heinz Kirch are no less shaped by the narrowness of their town than Thomas Buddenbrook. Both works also show the first destructive effects of capitalism, which do not spare the provinces, but change people everywhere.

The evolution of mass literature after 1848 and its objectives

The novel as weapon

'The novel is indeed the greatest literary weapon of the present day; it is that which the stage was in the last century, being today mightier than the daily press, since it penetrates sections of society that a newspaper never does.' With these words Georg Hesekiel sought to demonstrate the necessity of the conservative novel, by which he meant not the salon novel widespread hitherto, but rather a 'popular form of narrative'. Sengle interprets this as follows: 'This ideal of the *Volksroman* (the German national novel) is more easily achieved by the conservative than the liberal novel. The fourth estate that has emerged as part of the growth of high capitalism is viewed as the natural ally against a too powerful finance capitalist.' Georg Hesekiel, who became Editor of the *Neuer Preussischer Zeitung* (*The New Prussian Daily*) in 1849, had already made his name in 1848 as a specialist on the social 'novel of nobility'. During the 1850s he wrote historical novels modelled on the works of Willibald Alexis, which were intended as a retreat from the social problems of the day. In general Hesekiel deliberately aspired to conservative, tendentious writing, so that there was a harmony of views between author and editor.

Lifestyle and literature

It was characteristic of the post-1848 period that lifestyle and literature grew increasingly apart. Clearly the 'Realism meant by the realistic critic of literature [was] a reflection not of social totality, but of liberal ideology' (L. Widhammer). It was in this vein that Julian Schmidt wrote in the *Grenzboten* (*The Frontiersman*) in 1855, citing Goethe, but also including his own period in the criticism:

The work that is dedicated to a specific aim and expends every last shred of strength to achieving that aim manifests itself as counter to that ideal since it runs counter to the freedom and diversity of the desire for knowledge. Modern writing displays an urge to extract middle-class life from its proper sphere – an urge that threatens the overall stability of our society. The very class that is required to constitute the firm foundation of society has lost faith in itself.

With a progressive liberalism in mind that would be manifestly capable of action, Theodor Vischer observed in 1842: 'We live in an age of discontent, and the thing now is to act; only when action has been taken can we begin to write again' (*Shakespeare in seinem Verhältnis zur deutschen Poesie, insbesondere zur politischen – Shakespeare in Relation to German Poetry, Particularly Political*). In 1844 the same author asked provocatively: 'What is it with this Freiligrath, this Lenau, this Herwegh? How contrived, how self-absorbed and vain, how inwardly sick and obsolete and, even if inspired by youthful indignation, how rhetorical it all is! Where are the novels that gave poetic form to the spirit of our time?'

The art of the restoration period

In 1850 Julian Schmidt labelled the art of the restoration period 'devoid of content, principle and form' and called on modern writing to aspire to 'an expansion and deepening of the moral ideal in the detail of real life' that could form the 'sole basis for true and great writing'. Despite this, however, he felt bound to observe in the same essay: 'Even revolutionary poetry (*Märzpoesie*) has so far done no more than profit from the deprivations of the public. It has presented them with heroic deeds and sentiments of liberty because they were goods that sold well.' This condemnation, issued from the standpoint of an educated middle class with a highly-developed critical sense, was far removed from the movements and needs of those newly-adopted into the ranks of the middle class, or even those who had found themselves able to fit into it quite comfortably but who lacked a traditional 'educational background', having achieved their new social position through hard work or the effects of capitalism. A literary example of this would be Fontane's *Frau Jenny Treibel* (published in book form in 1892). This distinguished businesswoman finds herself unable to jettison her lower-middle-class prejudices even when she begins to see clearly that she is harming her own interests by not doing so.

Prosperity increases

The middle class thus began to surround itself with capital, and to make a show of its assets and wealth. As a result of industrialisation, prosperity gradually spread. Not until the end of the century did the working class begin to experience a modest improvement as part of this general trend, however. Accompanying this process, the cultural requirements of the expanding middle class also changed: they wanted to be entertained and learn of new things from all over the world. They attended mass events such as horse races and went to the opera, or preferably operetta, but less often to concerts. They also read the new journals, periodicals and books, although perceiving them largely in terms of fashion. What were they reading? Obviously the reading habits of the German reading public, inasmuch as such a generalising term is valid at all, had been greatly divergent, in terms both of social strata or classes and interests, since the Age of the Enlightenment. *Rinaldo Rinaldini* (1799) the blood-curdling novel by Goethe's brother-in-law Vulpius, had been enjoyed by a substantially wider readership than even *Werther*, for all Thomas Mann's desire to have us believe that Mager, the barman at the Elephant Inn in Weimar had a detailed knowledge of Goethe's book (*Lotte in Weimar*, 1939).

Musical culture comes to the fore

As already shown, operetta became a vibrant symbol of the modern 'non-culture', especially in Berlin, which was dominated not by the 'revolutionary operetta of Jacques Offenbach' (S. Kracauer), but rather by those that take place in some fantastical realm. On the other hand, the opera style of Richard Wagner was readily received not only by virtue of its musical quality, but also because it was so much in tune with the mentality of the *Gründerzeit*. This allows one to speak of a fashion, a refined mass culture whose repercussions are still being felt today, and which undoubtedly also continues to be strongly tinged with ideology.

In a number of his novels, Fontane portrays the insecurity of the society of the day through the medium of salon chit-chat: 'All is fun and prosperity I say, side by side with an infinite dearth of inspiration, of thoughts, and above all of great creative ideas. . . . Acts based on no idea, or on duplicitous or disguised ideas, have something coarse and brutal about them. . . . I hate such acts. I hate them most of all when they confuse terms and blend contradictions, and when we have to stand by and watch while, lurking behind the time-honoured forms of our state-preserving principle, behind the mask of conservatism, is a revolutionary radicalism.' This greatly abbreviated extract from a conversation about the 'concealed radical element in society and the blending of contradictions' gave total expression to the middle-class fear of insecurity.

The literature of entertainment for these 'well-to-do circles' was able to exploit this fact, offering fixed points of reference in both form and content. Formalism, symbolic and constantly recurring 'attitudes', and established modes of conduct and a social tone and characters who despite their

375

wealth showed concern for others, were all part of the repertoire. More 'sophisticated' trivial literature was dominated by a tendency towards the allegorical, occasionally towards the kind of rigidity to be found in the images of Feuerbach, Böcklin or Markart. The expression of these images and the effect of some of the many novels by Paul Heyse (Nobel prize-winner of 1910) manifest parallel qualities. In them 'the characters are always noble, the women invariably beautiful and passionate, and the men admirable, clever and forceful' (E. Sagarra). Their similarity to the figures depicted in modern advertising is as unmistakable as it is to fairy-tale fantasies, which were later to become a welcome component of modern literature in the *Jugendstil*.

Theodor Fontane

Theodor Fontane demonstrated that a modern literature of entertainment could be both socially critical and ambitious. In his story *L'Adultera* (*The Adulteress*) (written 1879–80), he transmutes an ostensibly completely non-partisan rendition of salon chit-chat into a vehicle for social criticism. Using the personification form, he was able to portray and discuss the voices, ideas, and attitudes of the society immediately around him – which did not lend themselves to presentation in the form of a great character or extraordinary decisions. Using this device, Fontane became a poetic eye-witness of his age, a painter of the subtler influences and changes going on underneath the surface of society, an 'affectionate subversive' ('Verunsicherer') and opponent of all that tended towards the rigid and inhuman in social convention. During a dinner conversation at the home of the *Kommerzienrat* (the very title is an agenda for Fontane) van der Straaten, it is, of all people, the officer in the company who utters his despair at the prospect of another war (the novel is set in Berlin in the 1870s, i.e. the time of the 'imminent war' crisis). He expresses his concern, however, in the statement: 'Brother-in-law, you are too absorbed with stock-exchange rumours, not to mention the influence of stock-exchange speculation.' Through the ensuing reaction of the two wives, Fontane applies a gentle irony that is later taken up and spiced into satire in a declaration by the Chief-of-Police: 'The two ladies, who were most ardent advocates of peace, the brunette because she was loath to lose her fortune, the blonde because she was loath to lose her husband, cheered the speaker, while the Chief-of-Police, looking smaller and smaller, remarked: "Please allow me to express my most obedient assent to the Herr Major, from the bottom of my heart and soul".' To this should be added that he had a predilection for speaking of his soul. 'In general', he continued, '[there is] nothing more false or insane than presenting his Highness the Prince, in truth a peace-loving man, as if he were a cannoneer with an ever-burning slow-match, ready at a moment's notice to set light to Krupp's monstrous artillery to launch a European war and blow it to kingdom come. . . . Risk-taking is the craving of those who possess nothing, neither wealth nor fame. And the prince possesses both.' At this point the insecurity emerges that is always present in latent form in well-off middle-class circles. The Chief-of-Police goes on: 'The Prince is a very well-read man, and doubtless familiar with the tale of the *Fisher and his Wife*.' This passage gives us a better insight into the expectations and fears of the middle class than any trivial novel could ever do.

During the nineteenth century books became a major 'status symbol of the educated middle classes' (R. Schenda). The true level of education in Germany did not correspond to this prestige, however. 'In the German-speaking world (excluding Austria and Switzerland) in 1871 at least 10 per cent [of the population] were still illiterate. . . . By 1882 working-class people and their family members numbered 17.3 million and by 1907 this had risen to 25.8 million. The majority of these lower classes, almost half the total population, did not count as readers of any kind of literature at all, until well into the second half of the century' (R. Schenda). When they read at all, it was rarely the large and extremely expensive trivial novels, but rather the new 'mass literature for the working class', the *Heftchenromane* that appeared in serial form, series or sequels and enjoyed a boom after 1860. One contemporary source in 1887 states the motivation for reading: 'No progress is being made, and one must have entertainment.' As a rule, newspapers were the privilege of middle-class circles. Such living conditions, of course, shattered hopes for an intellectual flowering of the 'nation of poets and thinkers', showing that this compliment had been illusory from the first in the form that Madame de Staël had made it famous. Germany had never been a truly literary country, and had in fact always had two distinct literatures. As Arno Schmidt derisively put it: '(1) the universally popular printed drivel – a good 99 per cent – the delight of knitting females and lantern-lighters, and further "up" through "salaried commercial employees" to the mellifluous reading rabble who straddled ministerial chairs, (which even with the benefit of distance is the most revolting type of all). And (2) real "great literature".'

Public taste: literature as commodity

After the 'classics' boom had smoothed the path (Reclam's *Universal-Bibliothek* is a famous example), publishing entrepreneurs were quick to recognise literature for the masses as a promising commodity. All they did, in fact, was to exploit an existing situation in a systematic way. Once the new market presented itself, their idealistic ideas receded in the face of economic calculation, and the market proved them right. The concept behind the *Die Gartenlaube* (*The Bower*) (a periodical founded in 1853) should be recounted here as an example of mass literature and its rapidly growing influence on the literary taste of the day. It omitted direct political commentary, providing reports on culture as entertainment (the theatre, opera, art and arts and crafts), society and social life (the military, sport, major cities, female emancipation; articles on the family, fashion and medicine), as well as accounts of journeys to distant lands, up-to-date commentaries – and literature. *Die Gartenlaube* thus set up affluent middle-class life as its yardstick, like virtually all family magazines to this day. This chosen backdrop also determined the position of literature as the editors intended it to be understood. The aim of the founder and first editor, Ernst Keil, was to combine scientific instruction, reportage and useful commentary for the whole family with 'literature'. In this way the journal took over the 'function of adult education classes' (M. Zimmermann) by providing many people with their first information on biology, physics, technology and chemistry, of which they had learned nothing in their schooldays. On the other hand, it linked literature with domestic harmony, assigning it the role of entertainment, thereby cashing in on the free time, the individual leisure, that was then an entirely new phenomenon. The number of copies issued in 1870 (270,000, later to rise to nearly half a million) would be remarkable even today: at that time it was sensational. A 'side-effect' of the magazine, therefore, was its power to shape public taste. The reduction of this sphere to family-oriented utilitarianism in the broadest sense evidently fulfilled the expectations of rising (lower) middle class.

Prior to this clear stylisation into 'Bower literature', however, other types of entertainment fiction began to emerge, specifically adventure and travel fiction, and a little later utopian technological fiction (e.g. Max Eyth: *Hinter Pflug und Schraubstock – Behind the Ploughshare and the Workman's Bench*, 1899; Bernhard Kellermann: *Der Tunnel*, 1913). Travel and adventure literature in Germany has a tradition going back to the Enlightenment. Later, after the founding of the Reich, Friedrich Gerstäcker brought the ethnological novel of entertainment to its zenith, and was also responsible for the latter's breakthrough in the form of *Jugendbuch* (books for adolescents, e.g. *Die Flusspiraten des Mississippi – The River Pirates of the Mississippi*, 1848, which was followed by many others). At the same time, however, the rush of interest among the adult reading public in travel and adventure literature was evaporating – undoubtedly as a result of the increasing number of journals that offered similar material. Gerstäcker was familiar with America, and had even worked there for a number of years, writing his books on the basis of his view of actual conditions. He had also visited Hawaii, Australia and Haiti. Gerstäcker's success as an author of books for adolescents was continued by Sophie Wörishöffer (*Der Natur-forscherschiff – The Ship of the Naturalist*, 1881). Up to her death in 1890 her publishers knew only that the author of seventeen thrilling books was a woman who had never left northern Germany, and who prepared her material solely from the specialist literature they provided her. Despite this, however, she thrilled young readers well up to the time of World War II.

The personal amid the foreign

The culmination of adventure literature in the German-speaking world for almost a century, combining travel, foreign culture and thrills, was Karl May. All his life, with the exclusion of many exaggerations, May perceived the world as a prison, while at the same time developing a deep longing for light. This dualism was stylised by May into a myth that was to shape all other perspectives during his later life, particularly making their mark in the imagery of his writing. He also purported to be able to interpret his own spiritual and developmental crises as crises of humanity, setting against them his longing for harmony, and attempting to retrieve for his readers a realm of harmony and humanity. Even his very last lecture, given to 2,000 people in Vienna only a week before his death, was devoted to this theme. The various forms of imprisonment May himself experienced were stylised into an allegory of imprisoned humanity, out of which arose the urge to bring freedom to all men. His many novels and stories (the number of copies published was estimated at 50 million in 1893), far surpassed in popularity all other German-language literature. Nevertheless, they brought the author himself an interminable spate of court cases that persisted until his death. His works are pulp fiction propounding these longings and wishful thinking, punctuated by his ideas on philosophy, politics, theology and above all medicine, a profession he would dearly have loved to follow. A facility for giving medical assistance is one of the foremost attributes of his heroes. In his later years this crushed man, still a child, figuratively added a fantasy Djinistan to the Ardistan he had experienced: the swamp of a mountain landscape.

If one views Ardistan and Djinistan as dialectical opposites, then the adventure set in Märdistan represents, 'as a new, richer life', the beginning of a movement towards a synthesis to replace the dialectic of these two spheres,

> since all these various functions are in pursuit (the heroes Kara ben Nemsi, Old Shatterhand, Winnetou, Old Surehand) of but one aim: the overthrow of the unwholesome in a wholesome world. At the root of this idea is a medical futuristic chiliasm such as was pro-pounded by many physicians in the nineteenth century.... Unlike many of his fellow writers, Karl May dissolved the static image of the still-concealed identity of the human heart in the history of his stories, which all have one thing in common: they both represent and go beyond the time in which they were written, because they

379

are witnesses to a purposeful and steadfast fable-making aimed at freedom.

(G. Ueding)

As far as attitudes towards the propertied, educated middle class is concerned, the gap between the *Gartenlaube* and journals of literary theory (*Die Grenzboten, Blätter für die Literarische Unterhaltung; Preussische Jahrbücher*) was not nearly as wide as these journals were wont to suppose. 'It becomes clear just how closely linked literary self-perception and the theoretical vision of literary historians were bound up with the internal political situation of the post-revolutionary era. The latter was dominated by a "futuristic reference to German unification and liberty" that permeated the entire body of literary criticism to such a degree that one can only speak with reservations of a specifically literary vision' (H. Aust). A characteristic feature of the situation outlined here by Aust was that *Die Grenzboten* and the *Preussischen Jahrbücher* represented a general shift by liberalism towards a policy of pragmatic (*realpolitisch*) accommodation, and ulti- mately towards national liberalism. Widhammer coined the term 'illusion realism' to describe these developments. The 'value code of the liberal middle class became a central consideration' (H. Steinecke).

Gartenlaube literature was intended to deal with moral, entertaining, harmonious and simple themes, the plots and story-lines of texts being subordinated as far as possible to these aims. In itself, this was not enough to banish quality literature from the journal. However, there was the additional requirement of being able to reach as many readers as possible (as a rule they were subscribers). One way to achieve this end was to resort to tried-and-tested, familiar subjects, directions and forms, and since most of the short stories were written 'to order', this was not difficult to achieve. This effectively excluded periodical literature from positive development in its own right. It could, after all, have acted as a trendsetter, but chose not to. The new medium pursued a market-oriented 'practical consensus that manifests itself solely in success', as Keil the editor affirmed, instituting with these words the one-way street of triviality.

What enjoyed literary success?

Eugenie Marlitt-John's novel *Goldelse*, published in *Die Gartenlaube* in 1867, doubled the periodical's circulation within a few months. The novel itself became a model for successful periodical literature. Marlitt's view of humanity was tailor-made to touch the heart of the simple man, either avoiding conflict altogether, or else depicting black-and-white characters in Cinderella fashion. It was also hostile to both the privileges of the aristocracy and the often work-shy arrogance of upper middle-class circles. Her sympathies were on the side of tolerant, dutiful, hard-working people who were making a positive contribution in middle-class professions. In her stories the characters often went astray at first, or were seduced by false glamour. The attentive reader, however, was often aware even before the characters themselves who 'belonged' to whom, thereby becoming involved in the emotionally stirring texts, particularly since the basic structure of the novel was bound to conclude in a happy ending. In the process, however, the author developed an above-average linguistic creativity that struck even Gottfried Keller.

Pulp fiction

At least seven novels by Marlitt appeared in the *Die Gartenlaube*, and one uncompleted fragment was finished by her successor, Wilhelmine Heimburg, after her death. Heimburg, too, was catapulted to success with her first title (also to be followed by six more): *Lumpenmüllers Lieschen* (1879). All these 'little moral tracts' (F. Mehring) were evidently devoured with enthusiasm, setting the seal on the taste of this particular periodical. On the rare occasions when the text of a great writer was published, which the periodical could quite easily afford to do, the editors took it upon themselves to make 'extraordinarily far-reaching changes and abbreviations' (C. Jolles): for example, with Fontane's novel *Quitt* (1890). Henceforth the editors alone determined the content and form of *Gartenlaube* literature: the writers were mere suppliers of raw material.

Cosiness

Besides this literature for the well-placed and sophisticated middle classes, pulp fiction published in parts also rapidly began to make its presence felt as reading matter for the lower classes. Even Karl May achieved his first really great success with a novel published in one hundred (!) parts of 24 pages each (*Das Waldröschen* – *The Wild Rose*, from 1883). Novels published in parts found a market because they seemed to offer the public something that it was missing: relaxation and recreation in a fictional world of harmony. Eugenie Marlitt expressed this expectation trenchantly in a number of her works, as when a derisive, intellectual, 'subversive' woman from a wealthy home is juxtaposed with a simple 'more realistic' (!) girl. Of the latter, we are told:

> She writes no verses or novellas of her own – she has too little time, and yet she writes.... She writes, though, in the same way as she approaches life, always knowing how to make the most of a page from which an illuminating light proceeds, just as she decorates her simple home – a lovely thought peeps out of every corner – and just as she also understands how to make the home inexpressibly cosy,

and yet aesthetically pleasing for her good husband and me, silly old ass that I am, and for the few choice friends of the household.

(Im Hause des Kommerzienrates)

The perniciousness of such texts may not be overtly apparent. However, they seek to retreat from reality into the cosiness of a lovely home, and 'since they do not confront the objective reality of ... society, they fall into the trap of clever manipulation or collective stupidity. They cling to tradition, surrendering will and thought alike to be led by the here and now, instead of shaping it' (Schenda). This is characteristic of the expectant attitude of the reading public, apart from some 'extreme' situations – seen from the standpoint of middle-class taste! Trivial literature was making headway indeed if serialised novels such as Victor Falk's *Der Scharfrichter von Berlin* (*The Executioner of Berlin*) (1890) were achieving over a million copies. Here we find the following statement about the work of the executioner: 'I carry out the sentences passed by the judges and my Kaiser; certainly there is no disgrace in obeying the orders of such men.'

It is illuminating to consider that literary structures of this kind must both have corresponded to the codes of conduct of the time, and constantly reinforced them. The danger inherent in these texts, therefore, is the vicious circle of expectation and confirmation, conduct and counterpart, instead of a free development of alternatives and independent judgement. Is it pure coincidence that in 1889 the Editor-in-Chief of *Die Gartenlaube*, Carl Wald, sought with his article *Sozialdemokratie und Volksliteratur* (*Social Democracy and National Literature*), to form an 'alliance against progress'? He summarised his ideas on *Volksliteratur* (popular folk literature) as follows:

Only by a concerted effort on the part of the hereditary, moneyed and so-called intellectual aristocracies alike to cultivate both among and beneath themselves a genuine, vigorous, German folk literature, only in this way will it be possible to gain influence among the broadest sections of the people, the workers and their families, through a truly wholesome and cogent German folk literature. . . . It should contain national, Christian humanist and monarchical ideas! It should, in other words, want what Kaiser Wilhelm wants!

UNDER THE BANNER OF IMPERIALISM

The world of letters between 1890 and World War I

Industrial capitalism

The founding of the Reich, accompanied by the culmination of the growth of modern capitalist industrial production, including the emergence of centralised businesses and major banks, also saw at last the coming-of-age of a working class. This new class sought to gain increasing influence on political, social and literary life through its diverse organisational forms. Despite all these efforts, however, the literature of the period remained an entirely middle-class one, even where it took on anti-middle-class attributes. Artistic creativity was to some extent 'exiled' from mainstream official cultural life in this period. Meanwhile, individual authors took refuge in *Innerlichkeit*, the inner spiritual world, and the stylisation of artistic and poetic creative processes into an act of quasi-consecration: the contrast being sought between 'art and life', 'the self and the world'. The explanation often put forward for all these symptoms is that during the course of the century the middle class was in the process of shedding its former ideals of progress, based on an optimism of Reason, and entering into a 'phase of stagnation or decadence'.

A balance-sheet of the political economy

This interpretation is an erroneous one. Wherever the middle class and middle-class public spirit were active there was steady and even illustrious progress and advancement. In the last third of the nineteenth century the German Reich overtook the United Kingdom step by step in terms of its overall economic balance-sheet. By 1900 it had worked its way up to second place behind the United States. Since the *Gründerkrach*, the slump of the *Gründerzeit*, industry and trade had had their sights set on expansion. The class truce between the aristocracy and the middle class had

383

proved useful in the second half of the century, and was to continue to shape political and social conditions up to World War I.

Likewise German arts and sciences, also the domain of the 'educated middle class', who commanded far more than musical and literary education, were the finest the age had to offer anywhere in the world. German classical philology and history, chemistry and theoretical physics (e.g. Planck and Einstein), including their application in technology, are all evidence of this. Viewed as a whole, therefore, the middle class at that time had little overt trouble in coming to terms with the world.

Exceptions to this rule, as far as the horizon of values and questions of adjustment in existing conditions were concerned, were contemporary philosophy (Nietzsche), psychoanalysis (Freud) and men of letters, who might be viewed in retrospect as seismographers of their age, although for this very reason they were not among those who were widely acclaimed at the time. All this is particularly true of those trends in literary history between 1890 and 1914 that are to be dealt with in this chapter. Naturalism, for example, highlighted social ills and the discrepancies between Humanist ideals and social reality. Symbolism and aestheticism escaped into the rarefied existence of an artistically fabricated ideal world. Expressionism protested against art and reality alike – not merely by attacking their themes and traditional form, but also by anticipating the imminent debacle and its historical alternatives.

However, the historical alternative in the age of imperialism, socialism and social democracy, made scarcely any mark at all on the literature of the day. This is not to be wondered at, since imperialism, the world-wide expansion of the capitalist pursuit of gain, was not the concern of literature, which either chose not to oppose it, or failed when it did.

Following the abrogation of the Socialist Act (*Sozialistengesetz*) in 1890, it became clear that this law had had considerable repercussions on those affected by it, therefore fulfilling the function that the opponents of social democracy had hoped it would. During two decades, the course of the social-democratic workers' movement, which saw itself as the alternative to the conservative nationalist mood of Wilhelmine Germany, was characterised by a successful step-by-step process of integration, both theoretically in the form of revisionism, and practically in terms of reformism. Meanwhile, the social-democrat focus on activity in trade unions and parliament led to substantial neglect of the task of building an 'alternative culture'. The loan statistics of workers' public libraries around the turn of the century reveal, for example, that the reading habits of organised workers did not differ from those of non-organised or lower-middle-class sections of society. Their interest in political material was minimal, focusing instead on entertaining *belles lettres* (Emile Zola, Friedrich Gerstäcker and Jules Verne). Marxist classics, with the exception of Bebel's *Die Frau und der Sozialismus*, which was widely read out of respect for the party leader, went virtually unread.

Franz Mehring, the leading social-democrat theorist on art and literature, had made a study of the democratic tradition in middle-class literature in works such as *Lessinglegende* (*Legend of Lessing*). He himself was a man of brilliant education, and the readership he was addressing consisted of Humanist middle-class intellectuals who were sympathetic to the workers' movement. The most fruitful attempts to encourage a familiarity with literature and art among working people were the folk theatre (*Volksbühne*) movement and the workers' education programme. Even these efforts to create an indigenous working-class culture to set against the middle-class one failed as the social-democratic movement itself became increasingly middle-class in character. The active part played by German social democracy in cultivating the middle-class heritage at a time when it was still the party of the German working class reveals that it lacked the vision to develop anything new and innovative long before it had to face such historical moments of truth as the approval of war credits in the German Reichstag of 1914.

A single body of literary history?

The years between 1890 and the outbreak of World War I do not constitute a seamless body of literary history. Distinct phases – Naturalism, Symbolism and Expressionism – coexisted and overlapped, with divergent themes and styles. There were also outstanding authors who defy unequivocal classification. Fontane, for example, transcends the beginnings of Realism; Thomas and Heinrich Mann were to continue to shape literary history into the mid-twentieth century; Gerhart Hauptmann enjoyed an untarnished reputation in the Kaiserreich, republican and fascist periods, and even briefly in that of the four Allied powers after World War II. The Expressionist generation for the most part bled on the battlefields of World War I. Those who survived (Döblin, Becher, Benn, etc.) went down in literary history without having the label of the early Expressionist years firmly pasted on them. Only the nationalist–conservative literary trend, which had its beginnings in the nineteenth century and its end in the literature propounded by the fascists, may be regarded as having reached a final conclusion. Workers' literature spans the Weimar Republic to the literary history of the GDR, partially even that of the Federal Republic, where it was known as 'literature of the working world' ('Literatur der Arbeitswelt').

Workers' literature

The first appearance of working-class lyric verse in Germany is marked by the anonymous weavers' song *Das Blutgericht* (*Court of Blood*) (1844). This text is extant in a number of different versions, and also inspired a spate of weavers' poems, of which the best-known are by Freiligrath, Pfau, Weerth and Heine. The range of approaches in these poems extends from sentimental sympathy for the destitution of weavers to Heine's revolutionary appeal ('Deutschland, wir weben dein Leichentuch' – 'Germany, We Are Weaving Your Shroud'). Gerhart Hauptmann made the original weavers' song the leitmotif of his *Die Weber*.

Early workers' lyric poetry went hand in hand with modes of authorship and distribution that differed from those of middle-class lyricism. It did not appear in book form, for example, but in journals, and was intended for public recitation and communal singing. Being occasional poetry written for topical political purposes, it is class poetry addressed exclusively to a working-class public, and was therefore closely linked with the organisational forms of the workers' movement.

The first anthology of early workers' lyric poems to appear was the 1900 volume *Stimmen der Freiheit* (*Voices of Freedom*). Some twenty-four of the sixty-eight authors were worker-poets. They are accorded no special role in the anthology, but are placed on a par with those authors of middle-class origin who were committed to the working-class cause, such as Herwegh, Weerth and Freiligrath. The main themes of the songs and poems contained in it are not the working world and the social problems of the working class. Instead, they are dominated by an optimistic confidence concerning the mutability of their conditions. Everyday misery is raised into a social perspective of the future. Where this lyric poetry refers to nature at all, such as the seasons of the year, valleys and peaks, the weather, growing crops, the harvest, etc., this is not done in the Romantic manner of portraying a symbolic unity of the individual, nature and the world, but is concerned with using nature as an allegory of a particular political situation or perspective. Even Christian festivals are utilised with this in mind: Christmas becomes a symbol of the birth of socialism, Easter of the resurrection of the working class, and Whitsuntide of a celebration of solidarity. Even the world of Greek mythology, the allegories of battles, flags and colours, or technical inventions of the day acquire a functional political meaning intended to convey the socialist perspective to the authors' own class.

Early workers' lyric thus deliberately steered clear of descriptions of poverty and suffering such as dominated the middle-class social poetry of the day, playing a particularly dominant role in Naturalism. Whereas in the latter the poetic self, including the socially critical self, stood in the forefront, workers' lyric brought a collective self to the fore. This not only made it anti-subjective and anti-individualistic, but also gave it commitment both to class and party. In terms of form, it rests on classical models. The ode, stanza and sonnet, for example, were all adopted for these new themes and purposes, the language being of an impersonal character. It is always the language of the collective, the political class, never the individual language of a particular worker. Vocabulary is drawn from two main sources: on the one hand from socialist terminology, and on the other from the vocabulary of middle-class idealism that had developed in poetry, particularly of the *Vormärz* era. Overall, this new political and poetic consciousness developed no genuine lyrical forms of its own, having recourse instead to earlier forms and utilising them for this new function, as in J. Audorf's *Lied der deutschen Arbeiter* (*Song of the German Workers*):

> Wohl an, wer Recht und Freiheit achtet,
> Zu unsren Fahnen steht zu Hauf!
> Wenn auch die Lüg' uns noch umnachtet,
> Bald steigt der Morgen hell herauf!
> Ein schwerer Kampf ist's, den wir wagen,
> Zahllos ist unsrer Feinde Scharr,
> Doch ob wie Flammen die Gefahr
> Mög über uns zusammenschlagen,
>   Nicht zählen wir den Feind,
>   Nicht die Gefahren all':
>   Der kühnen Bahn nur folgen wir,
>   Die uns geführt Lassalle!

> Heads up, all you who right and freedom would extol
> Beneath our banner gather for the fight!
> For though yet swathed in falsehood's cowl,
> The light of day will soon dawn bright!
> Ours a bitter struggle that we dare,
> For countless are the hostile ranks,
> And yet despite the risk of battle's glare
> And flames' attack on all our flanks,
>   Count we neither cost nor foe,
>   Nor number we the perils all:
>   Along his dauntless path we go,
>   Led by our leader, Lassalle!

Kampfdrama (*Struggle plays*) – *Maifestspiel* (*May Day plays*)

The theatre was a more suitable literary vehicle for both portraying and furthering the interests of the working class. As such it began to develop a functional form that was at first separate from the middle-class theatre in workers' associations. When in 1878 the Act against the Public Danger of Social-Democratic Efforts (*Gesetz gegen die gemeingefährlichen Bestre-bungen der Sozialdemokratie*) forced the workers' movement into illegality, the function and form of working-class theatre also changed. Whereas up to that point it had been dominated by unequivocally tendentious plays for the purposes of political agitation, it was now compelled instead to resort to oblique allegorical forms, often in historical guise. The literary technique of allegory lent itself to this purpose as a more suitable medium for communicating collective historical processes and their topical signifi-cance than the portrayal of unique, personal destinies. The abrogation of the Socialists' Act (*Sozialistengesetz*) in 1890 led to a sharp rise in the number of plays being published. Since the oblique mode of speech was now no longer necessary, working-class theatre was able to shed its alle-gorical cloak and openly commit itself to the socialist perspective.

Workers against entrepreneurs

Kampfdrama (struggle drama) and *Maifestspiel* (May Day plays) emerged as forms peculiar to working-class theatre after 1890. One example of the former is Friedrich Bosse's strike drama *Im Kampf* (*In the Struggle*). Published in 1892, it depicts in four acts the conflicts between industrial workers and the entrepreneur. By employing strike action as a political weapon, the workers succeed in freeing their leader and upholding their right to political activity. The plays reveals some structural parallels to Schiller's *Kabale und Liebe*, albeit with the decisive difference that the struggling working class replace the rising middle class. When the Inter-national Congress of Workers held in Paris in 1890 declared 1 May to be International Day of Struggle for the workers' movement, this gave working-class writers an opportunity to articulate their new-found opti-mism in the form of *Maifestspielen*. The story-line of Andreas Scheu's *Frühlingsboten* (*Heralds of Spring*) has two strands, one for May Day and one for the setting-up of manufacturing cooperatives, linked by a love story. Despite its fairy-tale conclusion, complete with a musical comedy-like finale dedicated to the 'Spirit of the Brotherhood of Nations' and the marriage vows of the hero and heroine, it nonetheless concludes on a note of warning against all illusions:

> Enough, Comrades! . . . The competition of the market, which we as a cooperative manufacturing goods must submit ourselves to, will be a constant reminder to us that millions of our brothers are still languishing under the yoke, and that we owe them, those yet to be liberated, the better part of our ability. And therefore more truly still, and with more zeal than ever, with more towering strength and trained conviction, we will struggle for that great world revolution that will make our people masters of their own labour, making out

of the murderous wrestling of all against all an alliance of stronger, nobler men. Let us return to our labours and our struggle, comrades, with renewed vigour!'

Turning professional

As the product of amateur writers whose plays were addressed to audiences of their own class within associations for workers' education, working-class theatre was far-removed from middle-class theatre, both in form and in institutional character. Gradually, however, there was an increasing move towards professionalisation among both writers and journalists, who were now ambitious to find recognition and acclaim within mainstream middle-class cultural life as well. This wing of working-class theatre had strong leanings towards the dominant middle-class form, Naturalism. Formally, therefore, plays written after the turn of the century may be classified as Naturalist drama, both in terms of their depiction of milieu and in their use of language – aside, that is, from those directly emulating the genre of middle-class folk and entertainment theatre. The tendency to accommodate working-class literature to middle-class norms, expressed in reformism and revisionism thus also had its repercussions on working-class theatre.

A working-class novel?

The narrative prose of the workers' movement never achieved the stature of its lyric poetry or theatre. It proved especially difficult for the novel to rid itself of the shackles attaching it to the middle-class realm of ideas and its approach to life, and thereby free it to articulate a new working-class view of the world. Since 1876, the organised workers' movement had been publishing an illustrated newspaper for the people entitled *Die neue Welt* (*The New World*). The aim of this newspaper was 'by means of truth and writing to arouse, instruct and inspire, to set up a memorial to the pioneers of humanity in the hearts of the people, to defend the beautiful, the noble, and the good, to disseminate true education, to educate German youth, and to help the German people to become intellectually mature and free'. The paper published travel reports, popular science news, novellas, novels of entertainment and memoirs. However the authors published here, such as Minna Kautsky, hardly departed at all from the models put forward by the middle-class entertainment literature of the period. Minna Kautsky's novel *Die Alten und die Neuen* (*The Old and the New*) is set almost entirely in the milieu of the higher nobility, represented in the worn-out clichés of the decadent, the distinguished and the influential. The working-class milieu, in the few places where it was portrayed at all, was painted in exotic colours. The middle-class intellectual author, who was outside both the classes depicted in her novel, seems to have been guided by an assumption that workers as readers would allow themselves to be fascinated by this alien milieu in order to pursue their daydreams of the 'big wide world' after their daytime toil. In this respect, therefore, Minna Kautsky comes perilously close to the writing notions cherished by Eugenie Marlitt on the opposite side of the political spectrum. Engels criticised the idealistic and distorting character of the novel with the comment that it did not meet the criteria required of a novel with a socialist tendency.

In fact, however, no prose author met Engels's criteria, so that before 1918 only workers' autobiographies may be regarded as a 'socialist' form of narrative literature. These autobiographies were largely uninfluenced by middle-class literary traditions. Since working-class authors generally lacked an interest either in accommodating themselves to the middle class or in literary acclaim, they were under no compulsion to emulate middle-class models, seeking simply to narrate their own life-stories and struggles. Karl Fischer's *Denkwürdigkeiten und Erinnerungen eines Arbeiters* (*Memoirs and Recollections of a Worker*), published by Paul Göhre in 1903, relates not simply the life of the uneducated working-class author, but through confrontations with his class comrades and fellow sufferers makes the biography exemplary of his entire class. The book was published by a middle-class publishing house in a bibliophile edition (with vignettes, borders and initials by Heinrich Vogeler), thereby putting it well out of reach of the readership for whom the author had intended it. Other workers' autobiographies published by Göhre were robbed of their effect in similar manner. With their accounts of the persecution and exploitation, unemployment and destitution, Bromme, Rehbein and Holek were regarded as 'material for contemporary ethnography'. As well as workers' autobiographies a number of confessional accounts and novels of education and development were published before World War I, all sharing the common feature of a commitment to socialism as the course chosen for their lives. Many of these authors, such as Adelheid Popp, Josef Peukert and Heinrich Georg Dikreiter, later rose to become functionaries in the social-democratic party. Reading and writing were essential aspects of this rise. Their memoirs are related in the form of the middle-class novel of education and development. The end result, however, is not the 'universally educated man' in the classical Humanist sense, but the socialist who is conscious of class – admittedly with a transcendent aspect, in that socialism is presented as something purely intellectual, a tenet of faith. Before a change in subject-matter was even discernible, this recourse to the forms of the middle-class literary tradition already revealed the departure from revolutionary positions that had come about in the workers' movement. Wherever working life was depicted as a process of education in the middle-class idealistic sense, it was bound to appear as a lower condition from which one could be freed by socialist education and a career in the organisations of the workers' movement.

What is Naturalism?

Perspectives on the term

In broad terms, Naturalism is generally understood as that artistic direction that strives for direct emulation of nature and the particular aspects of natural or social reality that the creative artist is seeking to reflect, in a manner 'true to nature', in his or her own literary, visual or musical medium. Specifically, it refers to that particular literary trend that arose in the decade between 1890 and 1900, a trend that perceived itself as 'modern' in the artistic sense and was heralded by the younger generation in particular as a 'revolution' in art and literature. One aspect of this that should not be overlooked is that for the first time since the days of Realism a European dimension entered the field of vision in artistic theory. The young generation of intellectuals, aware of the coming 'turn of the century' were actively involved in this.

'Wilhelminism'

The economic, social and intellectual facets of the Wilhelmine age form the background against which this new movement needs to be seen. Following the final replacement of German particularism by the second German Imperial Reich there was, from 1871, a rapid and massive growth in capital, with a concomitant absorption of large sections of the population into the working class. This brought momentous social problems in its wake. Whereas only a few years earlier the majority of people had still been living on the land, there now began a wave of urban migration that the cities could scarcely absorb. Within four decades Berlin, the centre of the Naturalist literary movement, had been transformed from a Prussian royal seat with hardly half a million inhabitants into an imperial capital with a population of a million and a half. All these additional residents had been attracted by industrialisation, i.e. the income made possible through labour.

The Naturalists turned their entire attention to these realities of capitalism in the new Prusso-German Reich, making the newly-emerged poor quarters, the neighbourhoods of factory-workers, street-walkers and taverns, into the main subject-matter of their literature. In the novel *Adam Mensch* (*Adam Man*) (1889) by Hermann Conradi, for example, we are told: 'Better to get used to expecting ... filth, putrefaction, sweat, dust, vomit, slime and other fragrances as the most matter-of-course things in the world'. This milieu, in terms both of the social plight of those affected as well as of Naturalist literary theory, was all the more unsettling a concept because it was more deterministic. Its ugliness, repulsiveness and pathological nature put it beyond the pale of traditional aesthetic norms. On the strength of its choice of subject-matter alone, Naturalism was able to take on an anti-middle-class character and gain a 'revolutionary' reputation.

Positivism

Naturalism centred around both the philosophical and anthropological findings of Positivism, most emphatically represented by the French sociologist Hippolyte Taine. Positivism required that findings about nature be based on empirical inquiry. It then proceeded to transfer this methodological ideal, drawn from the natural sciences, to the question of human existence and the social environment of man. Purporting to be averse to all forms of idealistic speculation, like the natural sciences, Positivism itself was nevertheless ultimately a philosophising approach, despite its stated aim of discerning specific and predictable inherent laws, cause and effect and causal relationships, both in the behaviour of individuals and in society. On the basis of these ideas, however, the individual was thought to be determined by the three factors: *race*, *milieu* and *temps* (race, environment and contemporary influences). This anthropological determinism was then transposed unmodified and used to demonstrate a related theory of art and literature. This explains the reluctance of Naturalism to develop any perspective of change that went beyond the portrayal of social destitution.

A glance at Europe

As a literary movement, Naturalism was not an isolated German phenomenon; in fact, it followed other European models. Writers such as Dostoyevsky and Tolstoy, Jakobsen and Ibsen, Maupassant and the Goncourt brothers, and above all Zola all exerted an influence on Naturalists in Germany. In his twenty-volume magnum opus *Les Rougon-Macquart*, for example, Zola recounted the story of a family living in the second empire period in France (1852–70). In both method and presentation the novel gives a precise description of reality in faithful detail. The literary agenda on which this is based was to influence German and other Naturalists. Zola had declared: 'L'oeuvre d'art est un coin de la nature, vu à travers un tempérament' ('A work of art is a little sample of nature viewed via a temperament'). The Naturalist Arno Holz had a similar formula: 'Art has a tendency to return to nature, doing so according to its particular conditions of reproduction and application', or expressed as an equation: 'Art = nature − x.' In practice, this gave rise to the requirement to reproduce phenomena from reality as closely as possible. All 'x' factors, such as artistic subjectivity and the shortcomings of the artistic medium, had to be kept to a minimum so as to eliminate differences between reality and likeness. The 'first commandment' for literary technique was precision of description, which called for a quasi-scientific observation of reality and a focus on factual material. Intuition and imagination, the creative handling of facts supplied by reality and their artistic arrangement into a new, fictional reality were as much an anathema to the Naturalists as an artistic language that had nothing in common with spoken language. In order to achieve naturalness of effect and adhere to reality, Naturalists showed a marked preference for everyday language and dialect and incomplete, or even badly formulated statements.

Milieu

As regards the selection of subject-matter and characters, pursuit of the natural led to a rejection of out-of-the-ordinary story-lines and 'noble heroes'. Instead, authors sought normality, indeed what was by traditional standards ugly, beyond the pale and vulgar: street-walkers, alcoholics, the mentally disturbed and the lower social classes became the characters around which plots were arranged. Their milieu was interesting to Naturalists precisely because it was on the periphery of, indeed outside, the middle-class world from which they sought to distance themselves.

Naturalist literature sought to enlighten the reader by means of the objective depiction of reality, and if possible to bring about a change in its negative aspects and further social progress. This called for a literature serving the interests of a perception of reality that was both free of prejudice and opposed to the outmoded idealistic character of other literature, past and contemporary. The extent to which these aspirations were met in literary practice may be demonstrated using a particular work as an example.

Die Weber (The Weavers)

Gerhart Hauptmann's play Die Weber (The Weavers) was published in 1892, originally in the Silesian dialect, although a High German version followed almost immediately. The first performance was at the Freie Bühne (Free Stage) theatre in Berlin in 1893. Further performances of this 'subversive drama' were banned by the police. Considerable legal wrangling followed before the play could be performed again at the German Theatre in Berlin, or elsewhere.

The playwright drew his subject-matter for the drama from three sources. The first of these were stories told by his grandfather, who had himself worked as a weaver in Silesia. These stories were to form the core of the work, as Hauptmann himself stated. In addition to this, however, he made a trip to the weaving district in the Eulengebirge region in 1891. Lastly, he was also able to refer to contemporary accounts of the Silesian weavers' uprising of 1844: Zimmerman's *Blüte und Verfall des Leinengewerbes in Schlesien* (*The Rise and Fall of the Linen Trade in Silesia*) (1885) and Wolff's *Das Elend und der Aufruhr in Schlesien* (*Destitution and the Revolt in Silesia*) (1845).

Form

As regards the form of the play, it must be conceded that despite its traditional five-act arrangement it abandoned classical dramatic structure, replacing it with a loose sequence of complementary images with no rigid common context. Likewise, there is no individual hero as a focal point around which the plot and its dénouement revolve. The main focus and vehicle of the plot is the group or class. The events portrayed in the play more or less correspond to the historical course taken by the weavers' uprising. Nevertheless the emphasis of the action, the depiction of the main characters and the literary reconstruction of the milieu must all be credited as the creative achievement of the author and his Zola-esque *tempérament*.

The first act sets the overall scene with a description of working conditions and the destitution that accompanied them. The second act brings this situation into closer focus with an account of the destitution of the weavers, using one affected family as an example. Whereas up to this point the weavers themselves have appeared in a passive light, as down-trodden petitioners, the seeds of the revolt are nonetheless sown in these two opening acts by bakers and huntsmen. The banning of the weavers' song, which runs through the play as a leitmotif, taking on a parenthetic function, triggers a wider protest among those affected in the third act, culminating in revolutionary fervour and action in Act Four, where the rebels plunder and destroy the villa of the factory owner. The action is brought to a conclusion in Act Five, partially in documentary form. We are told that the rebels wanted to drive out the entrepreneurs, and that the military are on the alert ready to intervene and suppress the uprising. The final outcome of the conflict is left open in the play. Old Hilse, who had spoken out against the uprising, is hit by a stray bullet.

The message

In order to understand the message or substance of the play, it is necessary to take into account the history of how it was received, since it has been estimated differently by each subsequent era. Unfortunately the scope of this book does not permit such a historical analysis. However, perhaps some light may be shed here and there on its impact at the time, comparing this in turn with present-day evaluations. Public performance of *Die Weber* was banned by the Berlin Chief-of-Police on the grounds that it was a potential 'rallying point for that section of the Berlin population inclined towards demonstration'. Following prolonged legal wrangling, permission was finally granted to perform the play. In view of the explosive nature of its theme, however, the Kaiser felt compelled to forgo his box in the German Theatre on account of the play's 'demoralising tendency'. When the ban on the play was lifted, it became the subject of a debate by the Prussian House of Representatives during its session of 21 February 1895, in which Representative Baron von Heereman declared:

> I should like in general to request the Minister if possible to have the police make more stringent and concerted efforts than they have undertaken hitherto to combat certain theatrical performances that either pour utter contempt on morality and religion, or encourage other questionable tendencies liable to arouse the passions. . . . In my view, one cannot act stringently enough in this regard, since the purpose of theatre, which is to provide people with harmless entertainment, or to inspire them with literature and art, is not being discharged with these plays. [Instead], they encourage and foster frivolous notions of morality and order, an absence of all religious sense, and on many occasions incite to disaffection, revolt and [public] disorder in the state.

Contemporary criticism

Press reactions of the day reveal a spectrum of opinion that bears some resemblance to that of the present day. The reviewer for the conservative *Neue Preussische Zeitung* (*Kreuzzeitung*), for example, makes tacit use of current obscurantist categories such as 'objectivity' and 'balance' while asserting:

> The spectator is gripped by the profound human destitution depicted in graphic manner, while also revolted by the accumulation of ugliness, unpleasantness and tendentiousness. One is bound to acknowledge the talent of the author for creating folk types, for depiction drawn directly from life and for saturating powerful mass scenes with the authentic throb of life. On the other hand, one is also bound to shake one's head in astonishment at the clumsiness, conventionality and exaggerated tendentiousness in his portrayal of the 'upper classes'. . . . The political tendentiousness of his plays, especially *The Weavers*, is neither served by their provocative, inflammatory collisions between individual classes of people, nor by their attribution of all light to the side of the 'people', and all shadow to the side of

the 'upper classes'. The police were right, therefore, to ban the public performance of *The Weavers*. If the partisan passion of a theatre play were intended to incite, than no play would be more calculated to suit the purpose than *The Weavers*.

Franz Mehring's assessment

This may be contrasted with the contentions of Franz Mehring, the leading literary social-democratic critic of the day:

The Weavers by Gerhart Hauptmann is the only theatrical work of the present day that stands at the summit of modern life, and can therefore claim to have similar import for the end of the nineteenth century as Schiller's *Robbers* had for the end of the eighteenth century. . . . No literary achievement of German Naturalism can be measured on its own merits, separately from the *Weavers*. On the contrary, this play has become something of a touchstone for discerning what is true and what is false in modern Naturalism. *The Weavers* stands in stark contrast to the kind of 'scribbling genius' who tries to pass off some popular play about banal and brutal reality presented with photographic fidelity, and thinks the world of himself for it. *The Weavers* is brimming with life of the most authentic kind, but only because it has been worked with the concerted effort of a finely-tuned sense of art. Painstaking shading and balancing were necessary to infuse dramatic tension into this colourful mosaic of genre scenes! What earnest thought was required to create that wealth of vital, mostly exquisite, and on occasion consummately worthwhile characters of which the protagonist masses had to consist if they were really to be set in motion in a dramatic sense. With this play, Hauptmann has corroborated an old adage that no Naturalist change of terminology can ever usurp: not only talent, but also hard work make a true artist.

Fontane's opinion

Fontane wrote a carefully weighed review of his fellow writer's play, blending sagacious praise with censure:

This is a drama about a people's revolt that concludes by revolting against revolt, something like the Old Berliner saying: 'das kommt davon' ('I told you so!'). What attracted Gerhart Hauptmann to the subject-matter was its revolutionary theme. Nonetheless, it was not a calculating politician who wrote the play, but a real poet, who was drawn by its elemental aspect, the image of force and counter-force.

The Weavers was felt and conceived as a revolutionary drama, and it would have been more beautiful, and perhaps even of more immediate and powerful impact, had it been possible to maintain this unity throughout the play. This was not possible, however, and Gerhart Hauptmann felt it necessary, on his own account, to turn what had started out as a revolutionary play into an anti-revolutionary one. He had no alternative – not only for state and the government reasons, but also, as has already been suggested, for artistic reasons. Atonement by death and the ruin of a guilty man is a tragic con-clusion: mere rumpus and the smashing of mirrors is not. On the one hand it is too petty, on the other it is pure negation. We want to see injustice defeated, but we also want to see justice (not neces-sarily in the absolutist sense) triumph and find stability as a *rocher de bronce*. That which triumphs must be seen to be worthy of triumph. In this case, however, at the end of Act Four, revolutionary victory would have meant nothing but the victory of revenge – which is too little. It was the realisation of this that created Act Five. Here too, inasmuch as it is not merely a product of reason, but also and even of denial, Gerhart Hauptmann does justice to his great writing talent, albeit with the proviso arising out of the old 'once you give yourself up to poets, it is poetry that commands'. Act Five is a makeshift affair, but nonetheless a constraint that must comfort us, being rooted not simply in clever calculation or contingent upon purely external influences, but in a personal realisation of the inevita-bility of such an adjunct. We must therefore accept the result as something at one and the same time both revolutionary and anti-revolutionary, granting it our ultimate approval, despite a sense that the play is thereby weakened. It is better that way, since being permeated by these two aspects it also serves as a double warning: one directed upwards and the other downwards, speaking to the consciences of both parties. The way Act Five serves the function of a balancing-pole to the preceding four acts is reminiscent of Schiller's *Tell*.

Why the open end in The Weavers?

In addition to broaching the question of how representative this play was of its literary trend, a present-day analysis of both the play and Naturalism might also ask why the author omitted to stage the historical failure of the weavers' uprising, leaving the conclusion open, and also why Hilse in particular, an opponent of the uprising, is fatally wounded. The fact is that, contrary both to historical fact and hence the principles of Naturalism, the conclusion of the play gives the impression that the uprising is proceeding towards a successful conclusion ('se treiben de Soldaten zum Dorfe naus' – 'they're herding the soldiers out to the village'). On the basis of this and the death of old Hilse, we might come to the conclusion that at the end of the day, despite the dominant portrayal of lamentable conditions, positive prospects are being opened up for the audience being addressed, even if in a noncommittal way. The criticism may be levelled against the play that it displays poor conditions in the manner of simple, photographic reproduction, without explaining the cause of those conditions or how they are to be overcome in practice.

It is clearly greatly to Hauptmann's credit that he made the story the subject of a literary adaptation at all. Despite the limitations of his account (the uprising peters out in acts of revenge against the factory-owner and the smashing of machines – in line with historical record), the play does deal with the underlying class conflict as more than a natural event and, it should be noted for the sake of critical accuracy, both vividly and in a comprehensible manner.

The Naturalism debate

It is hardly surprising that the party of the German workers' movement, if somewhat belatedly, involved itself in the debate on Naturalism. The positions put forward in the party were neither homogeneous, nor did they differ from those of middle-class literary criticism of the day, with its pro- and anti-Naturalist views. On the one hand was the approval of Edgar Steiger, Editor of the journal *Die Neue Welt*, an entertainment supplement to social-democratic newspapers. With an eye to the subject-matter, themes and characters of Naturalism, which were often set in a working-class, folk-like milieu, he spoke of the democratic substance of the play as an example to party members. Many party functionaries, however, rejected Naturalism out of narrow-minded middle-class prejudice, accusing it of depicting destitution in too crass a manner, proffering 'stinking filth' and violating the laws of decency. This notwithstanding, the 1896 party conference at Gotha records the holding of a literature debate on this theme that lasted for a full one and half days. Naturalism in fact remained the only literary movement about which there was any extensive discussion in the party.

Realism versus Naturalism

Naturalists were later accused, both by Franz Mehring and Georg Lukács, of being decadent *Spätbürger* enthralled by their own decline, dealing with the theme of poverty in a downtrodden class out of exotic titillation, but in a manner revealing no prospects for change. Brecht may have based his comparison of the principles and shortcomings of the Naturalist and

Realistic methods on a similar assessment. His schematisation is equally applicable to neo-Naturalist modes of presentation in contemporary literature:

the difference between Realism and Naturalism still remains unclear

Naturalism	Realism
society viewed as a segment of nature	society viewed historically
sections of society (the family, school, military unit, etc.) are micro-worlds in themselves	micro-worlds are sectors of the front in major confrontations
the milieu	the system
reaction of individuals	social causal relationships
atmosphere	social tensions
sympathy	criticism
processes should speak for themselves	processes are made comprehensible
detail as characteristic	set against the whole
social progress recommended	taught
emulation	stylisation
the spectator as fellow-man	the fellow-man as spectator
audience addressed as a unity	unity destroyed
discretion	indiscretion
man and the world from the standpoint of the individual	of the many

Naturalism is a substitute for Realism
(by 'Realism', Brecht means his own way of writing)

Documentation of social calamity

The main point Brecht is raising against Naturalism here is that it describes social ills as they are without showing how they came about in terms of cause and effect, what should be criticised about them or how they can be changed. Naturalism is a substitute for Realism because although it is prepared to penetrate reality (which makes it more progressive than those literary trends that either ignore or suppress it), it does so in a way that precludes change. To achieve the latter, in Brecht's view, calls for a realistic way of writing that gives Naturalism its due, by revealing things as they are, but which also strives to offer criticism, explanation and change.

Did the middle class have room for art and literature?

Fontane's anti-feudalism

Theodor Fontane's letters to Georg Friedlaender in the period between 1884 and his death (1898) are a limitless storehouse of social and cultural criticism, and thoroughly debunk the legend of Fontane's alleged blithe insouciance. In these letters, he calls for what he anticipated in his late novels (e.g. in *Stechlin*, 1897): 'Fontane sets a warning sign over the social structure of his day in the knowledge that a reshaping will ensue' (K. Schreinert). In one letter dated 1897 the writer confides to his friend: 'Prussia – and indirectly all Germany – is sick from eating its *Ostelbirn* (a pun in German, meaning "produce from the East"). But our aristocracy must be shrugged off; they can be visited like the Egyptian museum . . . , but to govern the country for their sake, in the insane idea that this aristocracy *is* the country – that is our misfortune' (5 April 1897). Fontane named the aristocracy specifically, but meant the entire feudal system that offered its willing subjects an opportunity for economic advancement as long as they remained loyal to the system. This subjection was personified in the notion of loyalty to the Kaiser, as if such bonds could possibly still exist in a mass society. Ultimately, however, this early form of mass insanity worked, and could still be stabilised through the administration, police and armed forces. It therefore seemed that the problem of power in the state had largely been resolved, since the parties of the Left and the trade unions were unable to push through any fundamental change in the political situation between 1890 and World War I, however much social tensions repeatedly escalated beyond the threshold of tolerance. In leading social circles major scandals such as the *Daily Telegraph* affair caused little stir beyond replacement of the Chancellor, as Helene von Nostitz was astonished to discover during a visit to Berlin in November 1908: 'There was some political excitement, but it was [expressed] in such a tepid, tame manner, the whole affair being a matter of such deplorable indifference as to its cause. Comme des petits écoliers qui ont fait une faute d'orthographe' (to Hugo von Hofmannsthal, 6 November 1908).

Violence as a matter of course?

The sad fact that violence was accepted as a matter of course, as has been outlined here in simplified form, had far-reaching consequences for cultural life, which was only able to exist at all with permission, or at the very least indulgence from the highest level. Otherwise it was adjudged as being an affront to the honour of the fatherland. In a power-conscious state such as this, art was required to bring glory and fame, to fortify and to amuse – in other words divert attention from real tensions and propound the

400

ideology of German might. Reactionary ideologues such as Nietzsche (*Unzeitgemässe Betrachtungen – Untimely Reflections*, 1873–6), and Langbehn (*Rembrandt als Erzieher – Rembrandt as Educator*, 1890, the 'epitome of an obsolete, ideal condition representing life in wholeness . . . : an anti-modern model', U. Ketelsen), the writings of Adolf Bartels (who acquired dubious fame as an anti-semitic scholar of literature) and Friedrich Lienhard (*Wege nach Weimar – Roads to Weimar*, 1905–8) all exerted a lasting impact on the German middle class, as well as acting as a powerful complement to the already active political influence of the Naval Club (*Flottenverein*) and the Pan-German Union (*Alldeutscher Verband*).

Aesthetic opposition

Not unexpectedly, many creative artists in all spheres rejected these leading-strings. Their reactions, however, were varied. Anyone who sought to avoid sliding into the ruling camp, with its nationalistic, power-conscious, self-assertive lines of argument, had no choice but to refuse. This refusal sometimes manifested itself in the form of apolitical aestheticism with a traditionalist stamp. In this case the ruling system was held to be not liberal enough, not sufficiently aware of culture or insufficiently humane by artists who then withdrew into those cultural havens that still remained. Even in those days, the complexity of modern life provided creative artists of all kinds with numerous opportunities for conveying an impression of diversity to the cursory observer.

An alternative strategy was that of a deliberate aesthetic opposition that chose to ignore the models put forward by society, setting against them the free artist as a utopian demand for free men. Numerous secessions by painters (*Die Brücke – The Bridge*, 1905) and men of letters (Berlin and Munich), the founding of journals (*Freie Bühne/Die neue Rundschau – The Free Stage/The New Review*, 1890; *Blätter für die Kunst – Artistic Pages*, 1892; *Pan*, 1895; *Simplizissimus*, 1896; *Jugend – Youth*, 1896; *Die Fackel – The Torch*, 1899; *Die Insel – The Island*, 1899) and publishing houses (S. Fischer, 1886; Insel Verlag, 1902), as well as those international movements, exhibitions and shows that went on without the aid and approval and often even without the knowledge of the state, remain to this day unforgettable examples of these activities. The fact remains, however, that all this was going on largely unnoticed on the periphery of society. Although today we look upon these activities as guiding stars, at the time they were supplementary highlights at best.

Defiance, irony and attitudes of protest

At first almost all literary opposition took place in the minds of the authors themselves. With no small degree of arrogance, these mostly still young men of letters adopted a critical stance towards to the world, responding with defiance and irony to what they termed the *Lebensdurchschnitt*, the 'run-of-the-mill' and the middle-class order, 'the unlimited realm of possibilities' (H. Wysling) before them. They experienced as a 'schizoid catastrophe of consciousness' the yawning gulf between the intellectual and spiritual sophistication being imparted by philosophy and the coming science of psychology on the one hand, and political and social reality on the other (from which they were largely excluded). Increasing familiarity with the works of Nietzsche helped the young generation of the 1890s to develop an attitude of personal independence: 'We had joyful confidence in the individualist, the opposer of the state to the most extreme degree. . . . In this way we prepared ourselves for our own achievements, and this philosopher was most welcome. He set a proud spirit on the summit of the society he envisaged – why should we not do the same?' (Heinrich Mann). Commenting ironically on the 'modish mass effects' of Nietzsche's philosophy, Thomas Mann listed 'Renaissance-ism, the cult of the superman (*Übermensch*), "Cesare Borgia" aestheticism, as well as the loud-mouthed language of blood and beauty that was current at the time, writ both large and small.' He termed these manifestations 'bellows poetry' (*Blasebalg-Poesie*). The process whereby ideas, subject-matter and texts that already had literary form were blended together to create a new whole, resulting in such impressive works as Hofmannsthal's *Das Erlebnis des Marschalls von Bassompierre* (*The Experience of Marshal de Bassompierre*), 1900, Thomas Mann's *Tristan* (published in book form in 1903), or Heinrich Mann's entire early works (1898–1914), must undoubtedly be understood partly as an attempt to carve a constructive path out of literary opposition. These early prototypes of the montage technique also show the delight authors took in experimenting and seeking a deliberately subjective direction. In the process, intellectual faculties that were sensitive to stimuli and constantly open to reflection (e.g. Tonio Kröger in conversation with Lisaweta Iwanowna) resulted in a change of mood (e.g. in *Tristan*, when Gabriele Klöterjahn and Detlev Spinell play the Tristan score), thereby making literature an intoxicating experience.

The question remains, however: what kind of literature was this? A literature of departure, modification, positive acquisition, parody or a counterfeit of reality? Could the heightened sensitivity of these creative artists ever be contained in language that could be comprehensible to a wider readership? Did the declarations of indignation, distance and disgust that appeared in literary criticism not confirm the unbridgeable gap between art and life? What further paths needed to be explored to find ways of making literature effective?

Aestheticism, nihilism

The condemnations of Heinrich Mann and his pre-1914 works (as cold, soulless, profligate aestheticism, aesthetic nihilism, false emotions, a dreamer of impotence) clearly show how unwilling the established world of letters was to accept his radical presentation of decadence in his novels (*Im Schlaraffenland – In the Land of Cockaigne*, 1900; *Die Göttinnen – The Goddesses*, 1902; *Die Jagd nach Liebe – The Hunt for Love*, 1903). The growing tension already discernible between the brothers Heinrich and Thomas Mann at the beginning of the century developed not least as a result of this new subject-matter and the new modes of presentation appearing in literature. Put simply and succinctly, the problem at that time was 'the conflict between the artistic creative artist and the moral man of letters' (H. Wysling). In fact, however, the two brothers had tendencies towards both these aspects within themselves. Especially as a young man, Thomas Mann sought to ward off such aspersions, liking to see in the artist the actor and the charlatan, 'the morbid hybrid species of the artist'. He goes into this 'hybrid species' in some considerable depth in *Tonio Kröger*. He is unmistakably describing both his brother Heinrich and himself during their early Munich period (1894–6) and visit to Italy (1896–8):

> Ein Ekel und Hass gegen die Sinne erfasste ihn und ein Lechzen nach Reinheit und wohlanständigem Friedem, während er doch die Luft der Kunst atmete, die laue und süsse, duftgeschwängere Luft eines beständigen Frühlings, in der es treibt und braut und keimt in heimlicher Zeugungswonne. So kam es nur dahin, dass er, haltlos zwischen krassen Extremen, zwischen eisiger Geistigkeit und verzehrender Sinnenglut hin und her geworfen, unter Gewissensnöten ein erschöpfendes Leben führte, ein ausbündiges, ausschweifendes und ausserordentliches Leben, das er, Tonio Kröger, im Grunde verabscheute. Welch Irrgang! dachte er zuweilen. Wie war es nur möglich, dass ich in alle diese exzentrischen Abenteuer geriet? Ich bin doch kein Zigeuner im grünen Wagen, von Hause aus. . . . Aber in dem Masse, wie seine Gesundheit geschwächt ward, verschärfte sich seine Künstlerschaft, ward wählerisch, erlesen, kostbar, fein, reizbar gegen das Banale und aufs höchste empfindlich in Fragen des Taktes und Geschmacks. Als er zum ersten Mal hervortrat, wurde unter denen, die es anging, viel Freude und Beifall laut, denn es war ein wertvoll gearbeitetes Ding, was er geliefert hatte, voll Humor und Kenntnis des Leidens.

A loathing and hatred of the senses seized him, and a longing for purity and modest peace, even while he yet breathed the atmosphere of art, the warm and sweet atmosphere, pregnant with fragrance, of constant spring – an atmosphere full of germination, hatching and budding in the secret delight of creation. And so it came about that he, Tonio Kröger, found himself vacillating between crass extremes, tossed here and there between an iron intellect and the consuming fire of the senses, leading a dissipated life with pangs of conscience, the kind of prodigal, directionless and bizarre life that he basically abhorred. 'What aberration!' he would think to himself now and then. 'How do I manage to get into all these eccentric scrapes? I'm no gypsy in a green caravan by nature' ... And yet in the same degree as his health failed, his artistic faculties were heightened. They became choosy, select, sumptuous, refined, irritated by the banal, and hypersensitive with regard to matters of tact and taste. The first time he performed, the attending audience responded with elation and thunderous applause, for the performance was the precious result of careful preparation, full of humour and the knowledge of suffering.

'Betrayal of the mind': social criticism

Whereas the author of this work continued to show scarcely any interest at all in politics, regarding it as a 'betrayal of the mind', and looking down with contempt on all struggles by the middle class to achieve power or further its own interests, his brother manifested an early interest in social criticism. Heinrich Mann rejected with increasing vigour his early ideal of Flaubertian aestheticism, as his essays from about 1910 onwards reveal, showing a growing preference for cultural and political responsibility. A spirited republican, he also set great store by liberal traditions aimed at preventing the misuse of power. He was a vehement champion of progress, bringing the political essay to consummate form and becoming active in the pursuit of the idea of peace in Europe.

Thomas Mann's position was in contrast bolstered by the success of his novel *Buddenbrooks*, as well as his marriage into the upper middle class of Munich. As he himself repeatedly stressed, his regard for family ties alone had shifted him into the camp of the successful man of substance, who now began to seek moral rationalisations for his success. It was this situation that unwittingly brought the rift between the brothers to a head and made it part of German history. Whereas Thomas held the view that the world of letters could, 'with involvement in politics, lead to an almost trivial, almost infantile radicalism' (1909), Heinrich declared in his famous essay *Geist und Tat* (*Mind and Deed*) (1910):

'Niemand hat gesehen, dass hier, wo so viel gedacht wird, die Kraft der Nation je gesammelt worden wäre, um Erkenntnisse zur Tat zu machen. Die Abschaffung ungerechter Gewalt hat keine Hand bewegt. Man denkt weiter als irgendwer, man denkt bis ans Ende der reinen Vernunft, man denkt bis zum Nichts: und im Lande herrscht Gottes Gnade und die Faust. Wozu etwas ändern. Wo anderswo geschaffen, hat man in Theorien schon überholt. Man lebt langsam und schwer, man ist nicht bildnerisch genug begabt, um durchaus das Leben formen zu müssen nach dem Geist. Mögen neben und über den Dingen die Ideen ihre Spiele aufführen. Wenn sie hinuntergelangten und eingriffen, sie würden Unordnung und etwas nicht Absehbares stiften. Mann klammert sich an Lügen und Ungerechtigkeit, als ahnte man hinter der Wahrheit einen Abgrund. Das Misstrauen gegen den Geist ist Misstrauen gegen den Menschen selbst, ist Mangel an Selbstvertrauen. Da jeder einzelne sich lieber beschirmt und dienend sieht, wie sollte er an die Demokratie glauben, an ein Volk von Herren. Die angestammten und bewährten Herren mögen manchmal, unbeleckt wie sie sind, der hochgebildeten Nation auf die Nerven fallen: mit ihnen aber ist sie gewiss, zu leben, sicherer zu leben als die, die nur der Geist führt.... Die Monarchie, der Herrenstaat ist eine Organisation der Menschenfeindschaft und ihre Schule. Die Masse der Kleinen, die hier wie überall die grössere Wärme des Geschlechts enthält, wird zu entlegenen Hoffnungen verdammt und verdorben für die tätige Verbrüderung, die ein Volk gross macht. Kein grosses Volk: nur grosse Männer.

No-one has ever seen that here, where there is so much thinking, that the energy of the nation was ever mustered to convert ideas into deeds. The redressing of misused power has not stirred a single hand to action. We go on thinking, whoever we are, thinking to the limits of pure reason, thinking ourselves into oblivion, while the country is ruled by the grace of God and the fist. Why change anything? Whatever has been made has long since been superseded in theory. We live slowly and ponderously, lacking the imagination to feel any compulsion to conform our lives entirely to our minds. Let ideas play their games beside and above the world of things. If they were to come down and become involved, they would wreak disorder and something unpredictable. We cling to lies and injustice, as if we sense an abyss behind truth. Mistrust of the mind is mistrust of what is human, mistrust of oneself. Since as individuals we prefer to see ourselves protected and in servitude, why should we believe in democracy, in a nation of rulers? Our ancestral time-honoured rulers may sometimes, scarcely civilised as they are, get on the nerves of our highly educated nation. But with them our continued existence is secure – more secure than that of those who are guided by the mind.... The monarchy and the ruling state is an organisation of hostility to man and its school. The mass of small men, who here as everywhere else embrace the greater warmth of the species, are condemned to unrealisable hopes, and spoiled for the active process of brotherhood that makes a nation great. Not a great nation: just a nation of great men.

For Heinrich Mann, the lines were already clearly drawn, but not so for Thomas. As late as 1913 the latter confessed to his brother his inability 'really to focus myself mentally and politically, as you have been able to do' (letter dated 8 November). Thomas Mann, and together with him Dehmel, Hesse, Kerr, Rilke, Schaukal, R.A. Schröder and Werfel, all saw their writing as a sacrifice for their own nation when World War I broke out in 1914, writing essays and verses in the spirit of the Fatherland. In Thomas Mann this resulted in a dubious position arising out of falsely perceived duty – i.e. his defence of the 'Protestant-Romantic, apolitical and anti-political Germanness that I felt to be the basis of my life'. This self-delusion on the part of many otherwise open-minded writers may be described as a second, sublime phase of German imperialism.

Was there a 'literary revolt'?

The 'literary revolt' did not spring from some sudden impulse on the part of a few unruly young people. It was simply the most radical formal step in a tendency that had long been in evidence. The 'revolution' itself, however, took place solely on the surface, i.e. more in form than content. It was 'without a substantial basis', often presenting indications of resignation and animosity as positive signals.

Bismarck as critic

Despite Fontane's brilliant response, Bismarck's statement of the lack of economic productivity of men of letters hit home – the issue of 'usefulness to society' had thus far never been so clearly put to literature. There was nevertheless good reason to broach this issue. By around 1890 it had become clear that even most Naturalists were losing touch with society. After their brief period of public sympathy, they neither had a 'base' among the people, nor had they joined ranks with working-class literature, but were pursuing individual paths. This was because they continued to believe in the creative function of the writer within society, as a consequence of which they were neither willing nor able to allow – as the Naturalist thesis had in fact demanded – 'the artist to become absorbed in the work of art'. Similarly, the writer as an individual also wanted to continue to combine art and life. With this objective in mind, the editors of the *Freie Bühne für modernes Leben* (*The Free Stage for Modern Life*) were of one accord with the ideal notions of social democrats of a cultural turn of mind who, on founding their journal *Die Neue Zeit* (*The New*

Age) (1883) had started from the assumption that 'only by marriage with practical life can art and science become vehicles for the salvation of mankind'.

The road to modernity

The swift demise of Naturalism in both theory and practice in the early 1890s, and the movement that rose up to counter it, are generally seen as the turning-point marking the advent of 'modern literature' (H. Kaufmann). This turning-point is characterised by 'the now unbridgeable gap between art and the existing society' – in other words, the exact opposite of the Naturalist objective. Art was now seen as having to renew its efforts to win for itself a legitimate place and a humane function within society. Within this struggle, loneliness and distance, the states of alienation and isolation and the bewildered search for meaning and context were to become the defining themes of literature. The reader was spellbound by a language infused with powerful emotions, contradictions and polemics that made no effort to be precise, thus confirming the reader's own 'dark premonitions'. Crisis literature made an impact on a wide readership, although the mannered style of many authors met with severe criticism.

Fin de siècle

The *fin de siècle* mood was thus characterised by the 'anticipatory fine feeling' of decadence, by 'ingenious aphorisms scattered unsystematically', 'fascinating gestures of a hyper-revolutionary appearance', and 'deep dissatisfaction with contemporary culture' (G. Lukács), accompanied by lavish indulgence in it. This non-productive affectation was derided by Arno Holz in 1898 in an 'advertisement for himself' of *Phantasus*:

> Nur wenig Getreue, die ein vorsorgliches Geschick mit begüterten Vätern gesegnet, folgten ihr in die Einöde, wo der Mond sich in ihren Brillantringen spiegelte; und unter seltsamen Pappeln, die unter seltsamen Himmeln ein seltsames Rauschen vollführen, trieb nun ein seltsamer Kult ein seltsames Wesen. Ich kondensiere nur, ich übertreibe nicht. Das Kleid dieser wohlhabenden Jünglinge war schwarz vom schweren Violett der Trauer, sehnend grün schillerten ihre Hände, und ihre Zeilen – Explosionen sublimer Kämpfe – waren Schlangen, die sich wie Orchideen wanden. . . . Noch nie waren so abenteuerlich gestopfte Wortwürste in so kunstvolle Ornamentik gebunden. Half nichts. Ihr Dasein blieb ein submarines, und das deutsche Volk interessierte sich für Lyrik nur noch, insofern sie aus den Damen Friederike Kempner und Johanna Ambrosius träufelte.

Only a few faithful retainers, blessed by a providential knack with prosperous fathers, followed them into that wilderness where the moon was reflected in their diamond rings, there where under strange poplars that made a strange rustling noise under a strange sky, a strange cult now pursued a strange existence. I am merely condensing, not exaggerating. The raiment of these well-to-do young people was black from the heavy violet of mourning, craving green their hands dazzled, and their lines – the explosions of sublime battles – were snakes which were twisted like orchids. . . . Never had such adventurously stuffed sausages of words been tied together in such artful ornamentation. But all to no avail. Their existence remained submarine, and the German people were now only interested in the kind of lyric that trickled from the pens of such ladies as Friederike Kempner and Johanna Ambrosius.

Clearly the stylisation of every sphere of life pursued by the arts around 1900 was in part to conceal a deep bewilderment and insecurity whose lack of perspective could not be eradicated even by bold declarations. Such documents of social misdemeanour, however, were evidently apt to exert a profound impact. Rilke's *Briefe an einen jungen Dichter* (*Letters to a Young Writer*) (written between 1902 and 1908) was a favourite presentation volume from the famous *Inselbücherei* (*Insel Library*) that had begun in 1912 with Rilke's *Weise von Liebe und Tod des Cornets Christoph Rilke* (*The Way of Love and Death of Cavalry Officer Christoph Rilke*) (1890). Concerning the predicament of writers, Rilke wrote to Franz Xaver Kappus: 'That is no cause for anxiety or gloom [to be an outsider in society]: if there is nothing in common between people and yourself, try to remain close to those things that will not abandon you: the nights are still there, and the winds that travel through the trees and over many countries: among things and animals a great deal is still occurring of which you can be a part; and children are still as you were when you were a child, so sad and so happy' (23 December 1903).

The beginnings of his many so-called 'thing poems' are clearly discernible here and are to be understood as a way of repudiating a human society that was perceived as being no longer intact. Human understanding and the artistic feeling that the poet develops *vis-à-vis* the thing or animal in question are meant to build an emotional bridge to enable his fellow men to escape from their everyday situation.

'We are lonely'

This helps to explain why generations of middle-class citizens cultivated the art of feeling. It enabled them to raise their feeling of social isolation into a cult of loneliness that is already presaged by Rilke:

How could it not be hard for us? And when speaking again of

loneliness, it becomes increasingly clear that this is not something one can simply take or leave. We are lonely. One can try to delude oneself and pretend that it is not so. That is all. How much better, though, to admit that we are lonely, and indeed to accept it as a given thing. Admittedly, what will then happen is that we become giddy, for all those fixed points on which our eye once rested are taken from us. There is no longer anything new, and all that was remote is now infinitely remote. . . . For him who is affected by loneliness, all distances and proportions change. Of these changes, many occur rapidly, giving rise to strange fancies and odd sensations, like the experience of a man on a mountain-top.

(2 August 1904)

The 'alienation of men from their fellow-men' described here is the other side of a society under threat from the growth of capitalism. Literature sought to respond to this crisis in various ways.

The writer as society's fool

In his autobiographical sketch *Im Spiegel* (*In the Mirror*, 1907), Thomas Mann made the first response: the writer as society's fool:

Those who have leafed through my works will recall that I have always regarded the lifestyle of the creative artist and the writer with the utmost suspicion. Indeed, the honours heaped on this species by society never cease to amaze me. I know what a writer is, since I am demonstrably one myself. A writer is, to put it succinctly, someone who is absolutely useless in all spheres of significant activity, with his mind set solely on frivolity, not only of no use to the state, but indeed a rebellious-minded fellow who does not even need to possess special reasoning faculties, but can be as ponderous and woolly-minded as I myself have always been – and moreover an inwardly childish charlatan inclined to excess, and disreputable in every respect, who should expect nothing more from society, and basically does not expect anything more, than mute contempt.

Thomas Mann nevertheless drew the conclusion from his remarks: 'The fact is, however, that society affords this kind of people the opportunity to bask in the highest esteem and the lap of luxury in its midst.' This is because society gratefully misinterprets and rewards the writer as the protector of its harmonies. The character of the impostor Felix Krull is already here in outline.

The intellectual aristocracy

The second response to the situation described above comes in the form of the literary esoteric who despises society – such as Stefan George – and maintains a distance from it, as did Hofmannsthal when he formed a 'circle' with Borchardt, Schröder and others, however loose and internally contradictory its structure. But this fundamentally spurious defensive posture towards life, inclined towards the esoteric, can also be found in some of the literary characters of Thomas Mann, such as Gustav von Aschenbach in his novella *Der Tod in Venedig* (*Death in Venice*) (1911). Exposed to reality as he sets out on a trip to Venice, he is unable to hold his ground because he has been snatched from his habitual artificial world. His brush with reality is the ultimate in feeling from the subjective point of view – but objectively it proves fatal.

The third and final response is represented by the Expressionist attempt at a radical humanity outside society. This approach is put in exemplary form in Wolfenstein's poem *Städter* (*Town-dwellers*), where humanity is nonetheless reduced to observation and feeling:

> Nah wie die Löcher eines Siebes stehn
> Fenster beieinander, drängend fassen
> Häuser sich so dicht an, dass die Strassen
> Grau geschwollen wie Gewürgte sehn.
>
> Ineinander dicht hineingehakt
> Sitzen in den Trams die zwei Fassaden
> Leute, wo die Blicke eng ausladen
> Und Begierde ineinander ragt.
>
> Unsre Wände sind so dünn wie Haut,
> dass ein jeder teilnimmt, wenn ich weine,
> Flüstern dringt hinüber wie Gegröhle:
>
> Und wie stumm in abgeschlossner Höhle
> Unberührt und ungeschaut
> Steht doch jeder fern und fühlt: alleine.
>
> Close as the holes in a sieve press
> The windows on one another, side by side,
> The houses so crammed together that the streets
> Look grey and swollen like strangled men.
>
> As if densely knitted together
> Two rows of people sit in the frame –
> People, where glances shoot across a narrow space
> Mingling their desire.

Our walls are thin as human skin,
So that all hear and know when I weep,
And whispers pass through them like bawling:

And yet how mute is each in his sequestered cave,
Untouched and unseen,
Standing and feeling – alone.

Fontane again

The attitude of well-to-do youth towards culture prompted criticism from all sides. The aging Fontane, for example, was pleased not to be blinded by possessions: 'It almost brings me more pleasure to look at things than to possess them.... Always merely an onlooker.' He also conferred this attribute of patient observation on his characters. Fontane neither wanted, nor was he able to depict 'great heroes'. With his amiable doubters, sceptical observers and irresolute Humanists he was probably deliberately distancing himself and making particularly clear the contrast between his characters and the loud declaimers of the 'modern age' – be they the powerful men of the *Gründerzeit* or avaricious traders. The 'conflict between verbal claims and real existence' (C. Jolles) runs through all Fontane's later novels, from *Frau Jenny Treibel* (1892) to *Effi Briest* (1895) and *Der Stechlin* (1898) and including his unfinished novel *Mathilde Möhring* (1906). In this way Fontane gained a reputation among discerning contemporaries for being a writer with a sense of proportion, enabling him to depict a wide variety of characters in this very confrontation with the society of his day. Fontane's masterly skill exerted a profound influence on Thomas Mann, as the latter himself affirmed.

Folk-monumental and aesthetic-decorative trends

Im Frühtau zu Berge (In the Early Morning Mountain Dew)

The folk-monumental and aesthetic-decorative trends discernible in the visual arts of the period were equally manifest in its literature (Hamann/ Hermand). The folk-monumental trend was marked by a vehement resurgence of literature about rural life that sang the praises of the native soil and extolled folk art, regional mores and customs and the unspoiled man. Carl Carlsson's well-known picture-book *Das Haus in der Sonne* (*The House in the Sun*) (1899) may be cited as an example of the genre. Journals such as *Die Rheinlande* (published by W. Schäfer from 1900), *Heimat* (*Homeland*) (published by Meyer, Bartels and Lienhard), *Eckart* (from 1906) and *Blätter für deutsche Art und Kunst* (*Paper for German Ways and Art*) (published by R. Benz from 1915), in addition to numerous journals of a religious character, helped shape 'theory'. Those who worked 'practically' along these lines included Michael Georg Conrad, who had at first been influenced by Zola, but in 1902 claimed to find the secret of art in 'blood and earth', and Adolf Bartels, whose novel *Die Dithmarscher* (1898) was a pioneer in this literary trend, while the writer himself, both in his personal life and his thoughts, became completely committed to fascism. Lulu von Strauss und Torney, Helene Voigt-Diederichs, Timm Kröger, Gorch Fock and Hermann Löns all to some extent exerted a lasting influence as writers – Gorch Fock with the propagandist pro-imperialist title of his book *Seefahrt ist not!* (*We Must Set Sail!*) (1913), as well as his early death in the Skagerrak (1916). Hermann Löns was influential through his animal stories (*Mümmelmann*, 1909) and songs (*Der kleine Rosengarten – The Little Rose Garden*, 1911).

These works became the mass literature of smart people, the rising middle classes and urban youth. They dreamed of the country, and made Sunday forays into the 'early morning mountain dew', as they were exhorted to do by the *Wandervogel* youth movement. Writers linked with this movement, such as Hermann Löns, were offering them compensation, thereby opening up realms in the imagination of their readers to which they were inevitably denied access in the reality of their day.

A renaissance of the ballad

The revival of the ballad form by *Heimatdichter* (homeland poets) such as Börries von Münchhausen and Agnes Miegel likewise needs to be seen as compensatory in character. As early as 1916, Soergel condemned Münchhausen on the grounds that his 'gentleman's pride has eyes only for those of his own rank; he is quite socially unaware', and with Fontane summed him up thus: 'All dat Tüg ist to spektakolös. . . . Dat allens bummst und klappert to veel' ('All that stuff is way too spectackler. . . . The old caper bangs and clatters too much').

At all events, however, Münchhausen and his friends were responding to the problems of their society by their very exclusion of them as themes for their works (Kaufmann). They substituted for these days lost in dim distant time, legends, mythology and superstition. The true creative potential of the ballad, in terms of the individual and social worlds (Fontane), the dramatisation of an idea and the potential for human action (Schiller) or of social tensions in specific cases (Brecht) is scarcely tapped at all in their work.

Jugendstil

Stylistically and thematically quite distinct from this 'folk literature', a concomitant aesthetic-decorative trend was often summed up as the *Jug-*

endstil (youth style), a term borrowed from the visual arts. It was marked by an enthusiasm for the dark side of nature and the magically unreal (unicorns, nymphs and naiads), combining ecstatic religious experience with erotic hysteria. A famous example would be Oscar Wilde's *Salome* (1893). The trend was apt to exaggerate superficial effects by such devices as stylising sensory stimuli into 'gestures', further heightening this effect with a blatant cult of beauty that is particularly discernible in lyric poetry. Deliberate lack of precision with regard to detail, coupled with an incantation-like style, lent lyric verse a 'vividness' that could no longer be duplicated in everyday life, but called instead for a pseudo-sacred attitude of 'artistic feeling':

> Ich lebe mein Leben in wachsenden Ringen
> die sich über die Dinge ziehn. . . .

> I live my life in expanding rings
> that draw across the world of things. . . .

(Rilke, 1899)

This associative technique sometimes led to such loose connections with the subject-matter of a text that the words themselves were relegated to the function of ornament, mere scrollwork that shut out the real and the essential, the latter being 'isolated', as, for example, in Rilke's poem *Die Gazelle* (*The Gazelle*) (1907). Here the overall impression is composed in such a way that it cannot yield a complete poem without additional help from the reader. Like many writers of his day, Rilke presumed both knowledge and the possession of a highly sophisticated sensibility on the part of his readers. This inevitably restricted the scope of his readership and tended to foster *Gemeindebildung* (the formation of elites).

The 'aesthetics of the lie'

When the themes and forms of literature around the turn of the century are set against their historical background, their remoteness from all everyday reality immediately becomes apparent. An anti-Naturalist tendency was raised to the status of an agenda in Oscar Bie's *Ästhetik der Lüge* (*The Aesthetics of the Lie*) (1903): 'The truth of nature must be suppressed so that the lie of art can be revealed in its radiance. Imitative art, poor man's art and the art of reality are all vulgar. They pay far too much homage to nature.' Once again, the poet or writer became mediator, priest and leader. This assessment of the writer's role was raised to a cult in the circle of Stefan George, and even Hofmannsthal and Rilke liked to assert a special leading or mediating role for the poet. Examples of this attitude are Rilke's poems *Gesang der Frauen an den Dichter* (*Song of Women to the Poet*) (1907) and *Der Tod des Dichters* (*Death of a Poet*) (1906). There is much evidence of this attitude in George's work, a famous example being *Des sehers wort is wenigen gemeinsam* (*The Word of the Prophet is Common to Few*) (from *Das Jahr der Seele – The Year of the Soul*, 1897).

Aesthetic plays

Playfulness in general and the play form were characteristic of the anti-Naturalist tendency in style, approach, perspective and character make-up. Since fixed roles were assigned, there was a certitude in this playfulness, whose rules shaped the theme in hand, raising it above the everyday, and thereby preventing an 'incursion' of nature and life into the realm of art. The art of play-writing thus signified a deliberate exclusion of reality combined with a heightening of experience. An esoteric tendency was frequently to be found in lyric verse, as in George's poems *Wir schreiten auf und ab im reichen flitter* (*We Strode and Clamoured in the Gaudy Spangle*) and *Komm in den totgesagten park und schau* (*Come to the Park Declared Dead and Look*), both in the *Jahr der Seele* anthology. The power of suggestion intrinsic to the magic of words may have given the reader the impression of a more wholesome world than many authors would have liked. The two Austrian writers Hugo von Hofmannsthal and Arthur Schnitzler, who had tested the thematic potential of the play in nearly all its conceivable variations, as well as working on it at the theoretical level, ultimately pushed back its boundaries so far that it prevailed over the mental reality of their audiences and readers, opening up perspectives that were mostly closed to them in everyday life.

Hofmannsthal's experimentation begins with his *Prolog zu dem Buch 'Anatol'* (*Prologue to the Book 'Anatol'*) (by his friend Schnitzler, 1892) and ends with the play *Sterben des reichen Mannes* (*The Dying of a Rich Mann*) and *Jedermann* (*Everyman*) (1911). His two late comedies *Der Schwierige* (*The Awkward Man*) (1921) and *Der Unbestechliche* (*The Unbribable Man*) (1923) are not even remotely comparable with this notion of the play, although they did seek to break into new dimensions of dramatic representation and, at least in the case of *Der Schwierige*, fulfilled that aim. In this play, for example, we see the representation of 'speechlessness', and the performance of a character without representing him. Following a number of initial attempts, Schnitzler's plays achieved their first high point with his play *Reigen* (*La Ronde*) (1896–7). To say that the middle-class response to this piece, which shows characters dancing in a round-dance of sexual contact, was one of 'outraged protest' would be putting it mildly. Yet it is the very form of the play, which Schnitzler certainly intended as food for thought for society, that makes his treatment of the theme possible. There is an equilibrium and a criterion of character that consists in love. Schnitzler's stories *Leutnant Gustl* (*Lieutenant Gustl*) (1900) and *Fräulein Else* (1924) share that play's closed form, in this case as a result of a scrupulously maintained internal monologue – a device that led to the breaking of entirely new ground by James Joyce in his *Ulysses* (1922). Offering no explanation whatsoever, Schnitzler narrates entirely through the perceptions of his main character. The appearances of other people are dealt with inside the head of the main character. The verbatim words of others are reported, but in a different script. This radically subjective style of presentation compels the reader to 'play along', first of all identifying him or herself with the main character, since 'reality' can only be experienced (or more accurately reconstructed) through this subjective form of monologue. This propels the stories into a realm of intimacy that cannot be achieved through other modes of presentation. 'Closeness' is not the result of this process, however, since the speaking character is at the same time totally isolated in himself and utterly 'consigned' to his fate. There is no respite. By their very nature, texts of this kind are also obliged to maintain strict observance of the unity of time. It is the inner world, the substance of the character, that is the real vehicle for action. In *Fräulein Else* the reader is given over to catastrophe even more helplessly than the character herself, being denied even so much as a contrary thought. This kind of subjectivity is thus also unsurpassed in its pitilessness. With his novella *Spiel im Morgengrauen* (*Play at Twilight*) in 1927, Schnitzler succeeded in demonstrating that the hermetic unity of a play did not have to be an escape from reality, but could offer a peculiar capacity for the oppressive symbolism of a closed model with an impact that is hard to erase.

Aesthetic utopia

The tendency of *Jugendstil* to reshape and stylistically suffuse all aspects of everyday life through art also encompassed the wider sphere of literature. Each text or work was taken as a work of art – even criticism and memoirs of youth (a late example would be Walter Benjamin's *Berliner Kindheit um 1900 – A Berlin Childhood Around 1900*, 1933). Rilke's account of Worpswede and its people in his introduction to the monograph of the same name (1902) on the young artists' colony became well-known. In this piece, Rilke clearly recognised the idealistic, utopian nature of such secessions, aand attempted to rescue it:

> They [the artists] are neither helping, instructing, nor improving these people. . . . They contribute nothing to their lives, which remain lives of poverty and darkness, but they retrieve from the depth of this life a truth that helps them to grow, or, without asserting too much, a probability that one can be loved. . . . Because this is all art: love that has poured itself over riddles. And these are all works of art: riddles, surrounded, adorned and deluged with love. And here lay before the

young people who had come to find themselves the many riddles of this land. The birch trees, the moorland cottages, the sweeping heaths, the people, the evenings and the days of which no two are alike, and in which not even two hours could be confused one with another. And now they set about loving these riddles.

Much more energetically than Hofmannsthal, George submitted his entire writing to an overall order in which each piece had a fixed place and was contingent on its respective context. In addition to this he also saw to it that the punctuation, orthography and typography of the book format accorded with his wishes. He was only prepared to work with people who accepted his ideas about art. It is difficult to reach an accurate estimate of George's importance. Admiration is due for his early maturity (as with Hofmannsthal), for his poetry (*Die Bücher der Hirten- und Preis-gedichte, der Sagen and Sänge und der Hängenden Gärten – The Books of the Pastoral and Prize Poems, Legends and Songs of the Hanging Gardens*, 1895; *Das Jahr der Seele – Year of the Soul*, 1897; *Der siebente Ring – The Seventh Ring*, 1907), as well as for his translations from Baudelaire, Dante and Shakespeare. From 1892 he was also publisher of a journal for his circle of friends, the *Blätter für die Kunst* (*Newspaper for Art*). He lived apart from public life, however, and worked for many years far from any book market. For him 'writing' was irreconcilable with the 'daily scribbling' on which Hofmannsthal, for example, was dependent. He was equally far removed both from the 'sickly-sweet middle-class retinue' and the 'formless plebeianism of the apostles of reality'. His aim was to assist 'beauty and taste to a fresh victory' over 'the undistinguished rumblings of the day'. To this end he made use of his position as leader and master of his circle 'in a wholesome dictatorship', but also created a pseudo-religious dependence in such figures as Wolfskehl, Klages and Wolters. He maintained a resolute distance from all the political events of the day, although without undergoing any severe conflicts with his time. Hardly any poet can be said to have lived less in or with the society of his own age in the pre-1914 period than George. The unbridgeable gulf between art and existing society scarcely interested him.

The complex self and its relationship to the 'world'

Protestantism versus Catholicism?

The post-1890 period witnessed two fundamentally divergent trends in the development of young German intellectuals: a Protestant 'north German' one focused around Nietzsche, and a more Catholic-oriented south German and Austrian trend. Despite the fact that adherents to both trends were open to exchanges (e.g. Hofmannsthal and R.A. Schröder, or the brothers Mann, who both soon moved to Munich and Italy) and were by no means ill-disposed to each other, their responses to the intellectual crisis around the turn of the century were nevertheless fundamentally different. As has already been mentioned, the young Heinrich Mann not only read Nietzsche (like most intellectuals of his day), but almost 'used' him, although with the fastidiousness of a certain youthful conceit. Nevertheless, this philosopher exerted a far more momentous and far-reaching effect on the young generation, as has been graphically described by Count Harry Kessler. These effects comprised that 'imperialism of the intellect' that was soon to abandon toying with the idea of power and degenerate into a weapon against any free-thinking mind. Hugo von Hofmannsthal, who like Rilke, Musil and Schnitzler grew up in the late phase of the Habsburg monarchy, was imbued with a total view that strongly influenced his relationship with the world in the early phase of his writing in particular (1890–1905). Two maxims that were later captured in his *Buch der Freunde* (*Book of Friends*) (1922) vividly express that relationship: 'Man only becomes aware in the world of that which is already in himself, but he needs the world in order to become aware of what is in himself. But it requires work and suffering.... There is a qualitative difference between people who are able to conduct themselves towards others as spectators, and those who suffer, rejoice and become culpable with them: only the latter are truly alive.'

Hofmannsthal's Ein Brief (A Letter)

In 1902 Hugo von Hofmannsthal published an essay under the unassuming title *Ein Brief* (*A Letter*) in a Catholic Berlin daily – hardly in the spotlight. Written in historical guise, this essay sets forth highly personal experiences. In an imaginary letter dated 1603, Hofmannsthal writes as Philip Lord Chandos apologising to Francis Bacon for his 'total abandonment of literary activity'. In this way, the once famous Hofmannsthal seeks to explain his own experience of life and the world, and why he no longer believes himself capable of commanding his own poetic faculties.

A crisis of language

In his letter to Bacon, Chandos writes that he had once been able to fashion a supposed unity between himself and the world: 'The mental and physical worlds seemed no contradiction to me, ... the one was like the other ... ; everywhere I myself was in the thick of things'. Now, however, he finds he has lost the faculty of 'thinking and talking about anything coherently.... The abstract words which it is after all natural to the tongue to utilise in order to voice opinion in the course of the day disintegrated in my mouth like mouldy fungi.' The exchange between the self and the world was disrupted. All attempts to interpret this situation as personal insecurity and thereby overcome it have failed, the disturbance spreading 'like corrosive rust' to affect his everyday life:

> Even in familiar humdrum conversation, all the opinions I once used to air so casually with the assuredness of a sleepwalker, now became so ambiguous to me that I had to cease taking part in such conversations. . . . Everything fell to pieces, and then the pieces into more pieces. Nothing could be held together with a concept any longer. Isolated words swam around me, turning into eyes that were staring at me and forcing me in turn to stare back at them. They are maelstroms that make me dizzy to look into them, revolving ceaselessly and sucking me down into oblivion.

Having lost his ability to relate to the world and discovered that not even reading the classics offered any hope of retrieving his former balance, he became as a result more and more conscious of his loneliness. At last, after great exertions, he discovered something 'unknown that can hardly be named' breaking into his imagination, and even into his everyday life, appearing to him like catastrophes from times past (known to him from stories). It was not from the past, however, but the 'here and now, the fullest and most sublime here and now', an 'overflowing' into the totality of existence that can in no way be classified by man. 'Everything that exists, everything I can recollect, everything ever touched on by my most confused thoughts, seems to me to be something. Even my own ponderousness and the former dullness of my mind seems to me to be something.'

The sense of the unfathomable

Hofmannsthal summed up this new experience of reality in the statement 'It seems to me then as if my body were made up of nothing but numbers that open up everything for me. Or as if we could enter on a new portentous relationship with all of existence, if we began to think with the heart. But once this strange enchantment passes, I am unable to say anything about it.'

The state described here might be termed static utopia, or an inadvertent departure to the other shore of the self that had lost its perspective on society and the future. This is what brings about the gulf between the new-found intensity of inner experience and the potential for creativity. It is impossible to describe what has been experienced, as if it were no more than intoxication or a dream: 'No more, therefore, could I represent in meaningful words the substance of this harmony permeating myself and the whole world, or what it made me feel like.'

Chandos experiences this state of being thrown back on himself as a void to which he finds himself unable to respond: 'Aside from these strange events, of which incidentally I scarcely know whether they are attributable to the mind or the body, I live a life of almost unbelievable emptiness, and can only conceal the numbness of my heart . . . with great effort'. It is hard to imagine that Hofmannsthal ever sensed such a numbness. It is clear, however, that his earlier phase of light, sensual and extraordinarily harmonious-sounding spontaneous lyric poetry was over.

Harmonisation of the world

And yet Hofmannsthal never gave up his fundamental creative form. Even when his theatrical work and major essays called for an intensive application of rational, and indeed organisational faculties, he never became a writer of modern society, seeking instead other ways running outside the bounds of society that still permitted him to live out his ideal (his opera libretti for Richard Strauss and his contribution to the Salzburg festivals being cases in point). For him it was the ceaseless preoccupation of the writer 'to seek after harmonies in himself, a harmonising of the world he carries in himself. In his finest hours he needs only to combine, and what he juxtaposes becomes harmonious' (*Der Dichter und diese Zeit* – *The Writer and This Era*, 1907). However, this also meant that the more reality pressed in upon him, as it were, the more his creative phases tended to contract.

Appropriation of the world

This harmonious juxtaposition of the exterior and interior worlds, and hence of completely diverging phenomena, was achieved by many lyric poets to an astonishing degree: for example Rainer Maria Rilke (*Der Panther*, 1903; *Das Karussel*, 1906). The creative technique was a simple one. The poetic self was fully submerged in the object to be described, putting into words the sensations experienced in this process of assimilation, uniting observation, sensation, imagination, association and expression into a highly artificial symbiosis. Nevertheless, the starting-point remains the 'partnership relationship' between the poetic self and the object. Society at all events encroached on the sensations experienced by the poet with regard to the object. There was hardly any real relationship of exchange or tension between society and isolated objects. Where such a relationship had to appear at all, it was reduced to an experience of isolation, the 'remainder' always being guessed at. It is 'like a dance of power around the centre, / in which a great will stands stunned' (Rilke, *Der Panther*). If, therefore, the poet has not represented 'the substance of some industries and the like', he has not yet discovered the new rhythm, his own form of life in these enterprises, having been unable to adopt them as his own, or discover 'the infinite pregnant symbolism of matter' in order 'to bring into relationship everything that is there'.

This offers an exemplary clarification of what anti-Naturalist poets around the turn of the century sought to avoid. Hofmannsthal, for example, did not always choose to risk his own hard-won harmony with the world every time he was assailed by some new subject-matter. His creative principle rested on an aesthetic that mediated between the poetic individual (with his psyche) and the exterior world in such a way that this mediation is confirmed by a complete and sensually apprehensible form. If this fails, the poet is left with no access to the exterior world, or alternatively absorbs so much of it that he is unable to accommodate it in formal terms, leaving him struck dumb.

Reitergeschichte (A Rider's Story)

For Hofmannsthal and his generation, the poetic goals to aim for were to be able to perceive the world with the senses and accommodate that world on the aesthetic level. These two aspects together constituted poetic power. In his novella *Reitergeschichte* (*A Rider's Story*) (1899), Hofmannsthal sought to demonstrate, using the example of the cavalry sergeant Anton Lerch, how a man is bound to fail if he lacks this opportunity to accommodate reality, although able to perceive reality with his senses, and indeed being completely at its mercy. Gradually he falls victim not to perception itself, but to the unaccommodated ideas brought about through it, until his inner confusion eventually comes to match the outward confusion. The three extraordinary events that shape the last day in the cavalry sergeant's life are all marked by the use of force, to which Anton Lerch has exposed himself without realising it. The reader is compelled to follow with unease the course of these events, realising how an order of a dubious nature loses more and more 'beauty' – 'so ritt die schöne Schwadron durch Mailand' ('And so the beautiful squadron rode through Milan') – ultimately decaying into brutal violence – 'der Offizier ... wendete dem Wachtmeister ein junges, sehr bleiches Gesicht und die Mündung einer Pistole zu, als ihm ein Säbel in den Mund fuhr' ('the officer ... turned to the cavalry sergeant a young, very pale face and the muzzle of a pistol, when a sabre ran him through the mouth').

The perception of force

Anton Lerch has two occasions during this day to exploit the use of force apparently for his own ends: during his short exchange with Vuic and his brief combat with the cavalry officer. Both occasions prove to the advantage of the cavalry sergeant. The tables are turned on him within seconds, however – far too short a span for this obsessed man to grasp what is happening. He becomes a model of 'ordering' force, and yet while still alive he is no more than an object. The cavalry captain shoots Anton Lerch lackadaisically in order to restore the discipline of his troops. The fine squadron of the outset finishes as the fear-ridden order of death that also threatened the Habsburg monarchy, as Hofmannsthal clearly realised. Aside from his writings and efforts in the realm of ideas, however, there was nothing he could do about it, however much he suffered under the menace.

Out of place in the world

The sense of alienation felt by middle-class people in their world is portrayed in masterly fashion by Rainer Maria Rilke in his story *Die Turnstunde* (*The Gymnastics Class*) (final version 1902), as well as in frequently most revealing passages in his *Aufzeichnungen des Malte Laurids Brigge* (*Chronicles of Malte Laurid Brigge*) (1910), such as the following:

Die Zeit ging unberechenbar schnell, und auf einmal war es schon wieder so weit, dass der Prediger Dr Jespersen geladen werden musste. Das war dann für alle Teile ein mühsames und langwieriges Frühstück. Gewohnt an die sehr fromme Nachbarschaft, die sich jedesmal ganz auflöste um seinetwillen, war er bei uns durchaus nicht an seinem Platz; er lag sozusagen auf dem Land und schnappte. Die Kiemenatmung, die er an sich ausgebildet hatte, ging beschwerlich von sich, es bildeten sich Blasen, und das Ganze war nicht ohne Gefahr. Gesprächstoff war, wenn man genau sein will, überhaupt keiner da; es wurden Reste veräussert zu unglaublichen Preisen, es war eine Liquidation aller Bestände. Dr Jespersen musste sich bei uns darauf beschränken, eine Art von Privatmann zu sein; das gerade aber war er nie gewesen. Er war, soweit er denken konnte, im Seelenfach angestellt. Die Seele war eine öffentliche Institition für ihn, die er vertrat, und er brachte es zuwege, niemals ausser Dienst zu sein, selbst nicht im Umgang mit seiner Frau, 'seiner bescheidenen, treuen, durch Kindergebären seligwerdenden Rebekka', wie Lavater sich in einem anderen Fall ausdrückte.... Dr Jespersen gegenüber konnte Maman beinah ausgelassen sein. Sie liess sich in Gespräche mit ihm ein, die er ernst nahm, und wenn er dann sich reden hörte, meinte sie, das genüge, und vergass ihn plötzlich, als wäre er schon fort. 'Wie kann er nur', sagte sie manchmal von ihm, 'herumfahren und hineingehen zu den Leuten, wenn sie gerade sterben.' Er kam auch zu ihr bei dieser Gelegenheit, aber sie hat ihn sicher nicht mehr gesehen. Ihre Sinne gingen ein, einer nach dem andern, zuerst das Gesicht. Es war im Herbst, man sollte schon in die Stadt ziehen, aber da erkrankte sie gerade, oder vielmehr, sie fing gleich an zu sterben,

langsam und trostlos abzusterben an der ganzen Oberfläche. Die
Ärzte kamen, und an einem bestimmten Tag waren sie all zusammen
da und beherrschten das ganze Haus. Es war ein paar Stunden lang,
als gehörte es nun dem Geheimrat und seinen Assistenten und als
hätten wir nichts mehr zu sagen. Aber gleich danach verloren sie das
Interesse, kamen nur noch einzeln, wie aus purer Höflichkeit, um
eine Zigarre anzunehmen und ein Glas Portwein. Und Maman starb
indessen.

Time passed with unpredictable speed, and all at once it was time for
the preacher Dr Jespersen to be invited. It proved an onerous and
long-drawn-out breakfast for all concerned. Accustomed to very
pious neighbours who would not flinch from dissolving entirely on
every occasion for his sake, he felt quite out of place with us, floundering as it were like a fish gasping on the shore. The gill-breathing
that he had taught himself was fatiguing for him, forming bubbles,
and was an enterprise not without its perils. The topics of conversation, to be precise, were non-existent, leaving no choice but to sell
off remnants at incredible prices and liquidate all assets. Dr Jespersen
was obliged at our house to restrict himself to being a kind of private
man, but in reality he had never been such a thing. Insofar as he
could think at all, he was employed in the business of souls. For
him, the soul was a public institution which he represented, and he
managed never to be off duty, not even in his relations with his wife,
'his modest, faithful Rebecca, glorified by child-bearing', as Lavater
expressed it in a different context.... In relation to Dr Jespersen,
Maman could virtually be excluded. She began conversations with
him that he took seriously, and when he then heard himself speaking,
she would say that that was enough, and suddenly forget him, as if
he had already left. 'How can he', she would sometimes say of him,
'travel around and go in to people who are dying?' He came to her
too on the same occasion, but by then she could certainly no longer
recognise him. It was in autumn, time to move into town, but she
fell ill just then, or rather began straight away to die, dying away
slowly and without comfort over her whole surface. The doctors
came, and on one day were all there together, taking over the whole
house. For a couple of hours it was as if the place belonged to the
Privy Councillor and his assistants, and as if we were completely left
out of it. Soon after that, however, they lost interest and came only
individually, as if out of pure politeness, to take a cigar and a glass
of port. And *Maman* died meanwhile.

It is clear from numerous letters written by Rilke that after the completion of this work he was in even greater despair than ever, and was
considering undergoing psychoanalysis and giving up writing. In this soli-

tary biographical moment we see a repetition of the 'I' and 'It', conscious–unconscious, individual–society dialectic that ultimately leads to neurosis. Hofmannsthal's *Chandos* crisis has at all events its counterpart in Rilke's resigned and broken outcome.

Robert Musil

The crisis in the relationship between the writer and reality was most clearly expressed by Robert Musil in his story *Die Verwirrungen des Zöglings Törless* (*The Confusions of the Pupil Törless*) (1906). The outward structure of Musil's story is almost that of an intimate psychological play. Straightforward, clear, intelligible and almost sparse, its style is often one of sober distance. At the same time, it corresponds to the outward order of the military academy: the pupils live in a microcosm that is almost hermetically sealed off from the outside world, 'probably to protect the coming generation from the corrupting influences of the city', as the author comments ironically. The contradictions between social reality and the ostensible pedagogical objectives of the parents and educators become even more apparent when the function of the educational institution is stated: 'Since here the sons of the best families in the country received their education, so as on leaving the institution to proceed to higher education or enter the military or civil services. At all events it was regarded as a particular recommendation for moving in the circles of good society to have grown up in the boarding school at W.' Here, in other words, people are deliberately separated from society and subjected to regular discipline, so that later they will be better able to assume leading positions. Elitist attitudes are unmistakable in some of the pupils (e.g. Beineberg and Reiting), but evidently go unnoticed among the staff. Parents, staff and cadets all have very different ideas about what the institution should be providing. As a consequence of this, the pupils are left without advice and help in all difficult situations, so that each finally pursues his own interests, or what he perceives to be his own interests. The result is an all-out struggle of each against the other. Role-playing and vying for power develop, each seeking to bolster his own position using the attributes, experiences and encounters that the others lack – such as with the prostitute Božena.

It is against this more sociologically and psychologically interesting background that the story of the young Törless unfolds. The contradiction between overt claims and reality among his fellow pupils does not escape his keen powers of observation, and yet he is caught up in it himself. He cannot find a solution, and as a result is insecure, often confused, and regarded as a dreamer.

Everyday sadism

Matters come to a dramatic head when Törless finds himself caught in the crossfire of sadistic interests between two cadets. The cause of this is an everyday event in a residential academy of this kind. Basini steals money from Beineberg in order to pay his debts to von Reiting. The latter sees through the ploy and manages to force a confession out of Basini. Törless learns of these circumstances in the 'red chamber', the secret meeting-place at the boarding school, and realises the everyday character of the crime: 'What Reiting said of himself and Basini seemed to him, when he thought it over later, to be inconsequential. A frivolous act and cowardly badness on the part of Basini, soon no doubt to be followed by one of Reiting's foul moods . . .'.

Törless is nevertheless overwhelmed by the import of this reality. He is unable to adopt any stance, despite a number of attempts, and finally even finds himself embroiled in the plot against Basini, which escalates into loathsome scenes of enslavement: 'Er [Basini] hat sich mit dem Gehorsam, den er uns schuldet, abgefunden und leidet nicht mehr darunter. . . . Es ist also an der Zeit, mit ihm einen Schritt weiterzugehen. . . . Wir müssen ihn noch weiter demütigen und herunterdrücken. Ich möchte wissen, wie weit das geht' ('He [Basini] has come to terms with the obedience he owes us, and it no longer causes him pain. . . . The time has come, therefore, to go a step further. . . . We must humiliate and oppress him even more. I want to see how far we can go'). The numerous outrages now proposed are, as German history after the publication of the novel has shown, by no means restricted to the realm of literature. The reader is shocked by the realisation that Musil is depicting patterns of behaviour that were to become all too deadly a reality. In this general sense, therefore, his story contains truths that have still not been fully digested. Musil highlighted the social background of perversion through the use of force with far greater clarity than did, for example, Kafka.

Confusions

Compared with the magnificent composition of the story, with its inner dramatic quality, the conclusion is something of a disappointment. The author finds a solution that is 'merely' individual, leaving all more general problems unresolved. Even in this respect, therefore, the story is not entirely alien to the outside world. By virtue of extreme mental and spiritual exertion, Törless finally succeeds in drawing the attention of those responsible for running the school to these sadistic excesses, as a result of which he is taken away from the school. It soon transpires, however, that the staff are not remotely equal to dealing with the situation even now. When Törless attempts for the first time in his life to speak openly and make sense of his feelings and basic ideas, he is assumed to be 'confused'. Törless asserts that it is not possible to achieve every goal through thought alone, and that some other kind of supporting certainty is necessary. The problem is that he does not yet know what it is. Since, however, he is unwilling to turn away from science towards religious points of reference, the world of the teachers and educators is thrown into question, and they refuse to permit a philosophical discussion with their pupil. The school administrators ward off the risk of having to face their own self-doubt, even though it could be potentially productive, and Törless is returned home to his parents. Although, therefore, his personal liberty is thereby restored, the problem of the use of force and of aggression is by no means solved. The military academy system remains intact.

The literary revolt of Expressionism

Expressionism refers to a trend in literature, painting, music, theatre and film that roughly from 1906 to 1923 shaped modern literary and artistic life in Germany and other European countries. It was represented by a generation of men of letters and artists born between 1880 and 1895 who began from the turn of the century onwards to sense the growing crisis in middle-class imperial society, and sought to make use of it in art. The unity that lay behind this thoroughly contradictory movement made up of divergent tendencies was rooted in a common rejection of a society regarded as crisis-ridden, doomed to collapse and in need of renewal. The dominant ideas in Expressionist art, therefore, were of decay, decline, war, the end of the world and depression, although there were also concepts of awakening, revolution, revelation and happiness. The reasons for this contradictory attitude in Germany are to be sought in the socio-economic and cultural circumstances of the Wilhelmine period, which was at the same time a golden age of imperial expansion while proceeding towards its demise with World War I.

By the time Expressionist authors were starting to write around 1910 the imperial system of Wilhelmine Germany was fully-fledged. Modern industry was concentrated in large-scale enterprises, banking had become a major economic factor and small businesses and artisans were competing in large numbers. The mass of workers in cities had helped the social-democratic movement achieve increasing political influence.

Young Expressionist writers were for the most part of middle-class intellectual origin, and almost all of them had attended grammar school and university. At home and school they had come face to face with a traditional culture and education steeped in convention whose maxims contrasted sharply with social reality. This contradiction was the root of their self-doubt regarding both their middle-class values and personal prospects. A career based on a profession requiring academic study was consequently held not to be worth pursuing, although in fact a stable profession was necessary to provide a material base for many writers. Art was seen as the medium for coming to terms with the middle-class world – rarely the political sphere. This focus of interests likewise determined the function of art, which was to act as a vehicle for moving society towards liberty, humanity, naturalness and happiness. It was equally capable, however, of constituting an autonomous field of aesthetic creation of a resigned and depressive character – a world unto itself, of art for art's sake. Similarly, the creative artist himself was either a herald, precursor and representative of a new age, or someone in the process of liberating himself through the medium of art. Both attitudes implied a radical anti-middle-class approach in the light of the aesthetic norms of the day.

Hopes for salvation

The Expressionist world-view was thus coloured, in relation to established moral and cultural norms, by impotence and despair on the one hand and ecstatic awakening and hopes for salvation on the other. Despite a number of diverging propensities and positions, certain common features are clearly discernible. It was not, for example, the outward realities of life that were to be reflected in art, but the inner experience of the artist, whose reality takes shape within the work of art and is thereby made manifest. The criterion of whether this process of externalising the inner world had succeeded or not was not beauty or artistic mastery in the traditional sense, but power of expression (hence the term Expressionism), which drew the reader or spectator along on the strength of emotion and pathos. The hallmark of the Expressionist work of art, whose impact was achieved through intensity of feeling, plaintiveness and intoxicating effect, was an unfettered language that knew no rules or syntactical constraints. Haunting pathos escalated to ecstasy, to the Expressionistic 'shout' in an orgiastic style couched in free rhythms and fresh lyric forms. Writing sustained by such a degree of subjectivity and individuality favoured themes related to the decline and rebirth of the world, new men and the father–son generation conflict. The concern was not to objectivise these problems, however, by presenting them in the context of their historical genesis. Accounts focused on what was seen as the unchanging essence of a phenomenon, and on man as such.

Lyric poetry

At the beginning of the Expressionist era lyric poetry was the preferred form as best suited to voicing plaintive, proclamatory and herald-like exuberance of feeling. As men of letters became more and more involved in politics during World War I, however, drama came to the fore. A call for the authentic voicing of human feelings of poverty, suffering and denial was combined with the anti-war effort. Pacifism became an outstanding feature of Expressionist thought, which found nationalistic patriotism repugnant and called for reasoning based on humanity. War was declared on those things which caused suffering – capitalism and militarism – which Expressionist men of letters had ample and horrifying opportunity to experience through their involvement in World War I. Against these two enemies, however, they set largely vague and emotive notions of anarchism, pacifism and socialism.

Personal experience of war, which hurled many Expressionist authors into personal crisis, also opened up new dimensions of reality. The process of coming to terms with these new dimensions was now no longer primarily focused on cultural and intellectual matters, but on social and political phenomena. Instead of cultivating rational insights into social and economic circumstances, however, appeals were made on a more emotional basis to humanity, national reconciliation, peace and love of one's fellow men on the one hand, and against war and national hatred on the other. A fundamentally pacifist position that had crystallised quite spontaneously among most men of letters out of the sufferings caused by war developed during the war itself into an anti-imperialist stance, and to some extent even to involvement in revolution.

Drama

Drama was the medium best suited to the representation of these attitudes and stances. Expressionist scene-sequences whose composition also marked a departure from classical dramatic structures were modelled stylistically on such archetypes as Büchner's *Woyzeck*, then being discovered for the stage for the first time (1911). Lyric monologue and ballad styles were preferred. These dramas dispensed both with the Naturalist depiction of milieu, and with the in-depth psychological portrayal of characters. The central character was often a 'young person' intended to be a nameless type in revolt against the overwhelming forces of destiny, his own father or a narrow-minded world.

The artistic and political agenda and aims of Expressionists were also documented in a number of journals, the most important of which included *Der Sturm* (*The Storm*), edited by Herwath Walden and published in Berlin from 1910; *Die Aktion* (*Action*), edited by Franz Pfemfert and published in Berlin from 1911; *Die Weissen Blätter* (*The White Journal*), published in Leipzig in 1913 and in Zurich from 1914–15, edited by René Schickele; *Die Schaubühne* (*The Stage*) (1905–1918), later *Die Weltbühne* (*The World Stage*), published by Siegfried Jacobsohn, later by Carl von Ossietzky and Kurt Tucholsky; and *Der Brenner* (*The Brenner Pass*), published in

Innsbruck from 1919 by Ludwig von Ficker (in cooperation mainly with Georg Trakl).

'The lonely self'

The crisis of middle-class society and the decline of its moral values and world perspectives led in the early work of Gottfried Benn to a radical nihilism and an irrationality that shifted the 'lonely self' – a monomaniacal subjectivity – to the centre of literary creation. His first anthology *Morgue* (1912) comprises poems about medical life, dealing with the more repulsive horrors of the world: a rats' nest in the abdomen of a drowned girl, a tiny aster between the teeth of a drayman who has drunk himself to death, a visit to a cancer ward, etc. These verses, written in a sober, prosaic tone, often with flippant cynicism, are a departure both in form and content from the romantically transfigured, idealistic lyric output of the mainline culture of the day, and shocked Benn's readership ('Die Krone der Schöpfung, das Schwein, der Mensch' – 'The crown of creation, the pig, and Man'). Bodily functions and ruin were depicted in a matter-of-fact way to counterbalance alleged 'ideological prattle' about human beings as 'higher beings'. Morbidity of theme was matched by a style characterised by associative word combinations – a blend of medical jargon and philosophical or natural science terminology.

However, this stylistic and thematic affront to middle-class artistic norms, also manifest in the *Rönne* stories which appeared in 1915–16, was not intended as a way of overcoming conditions perceived as desolate. It was rather a way of articulating apathy and resignation in an alienated world in which only hallucinations and intoxicated states could offer an escape to the liberated individual. Typically, refuge was sought in unconscious and pre-conscious states, or in southern regions and paradise-like parts of the Pacific island world, where the self, freed from the constraints of society and civilisation, could commune with nature. This magically-invoked world has nothing of the utopia of better social conditions about it, being resolutely anti-social, a metaphor for the happiness of being released from the lonely self for a brief moment of intoxication. This outlook was accompanied by a denial of the potential for development, of either the individual or society. It was a static world-view that denounced the evolution of the human brain as an 'aberration' and propagated instead a return to the 'spinal cord', prehistory and the unconscious. In his essays, which are as aggressively polemical and stylistically brilliant as his poetry, Benn reveals himself as the most intelligent representative of a movement of literary reaction whose significance extends far beyond the Expressionist phase in the narrower sense.

Georg Trakl

Georg Trakl's poetry gives expression to universal feelings of impotence, fatalism and despair, which he gives form through images of menace and destruction. In a mediated, indirect way they reflect the declining pre-World War I Danube monarchy, whose decadence, social tensions and state of crisis find their structural counterparts in Trakl's lyric. The lyric subject hardly appears at all, being screened by his pictorial visions, and articulating itself in penetrating images of melancholy and horror. At the same time it absorbs the outward manifestations of decline into itself in order to externalise them again as compromised lyric concretions. The state of the world is identical with the state of the poetic subject, and vice versa. The underlying feelings of missed vocation and loss that have shaped the author are of direct bearing on the world of imagery in his lyrics. Feelings connected with the chaos of the world and notions of the loss of social coherence are matched by a lyric form and method that, line by line, takes individual image components to create a new image, which draws its expressional intensity from the fact that the poet is giving direct voice to a spontaneous experience of reality. This in turn gives rise to a lyric imagery that ascribes words a new function over and above their everyday one as conventional signs. They are made into signs representing individual moods and visions by means of which a hitherto unknown poetic reality can be constructed beyond that of the empirically apprehensible. The reality perceived by the author, who is suffering unwittingly from perceived portents of impending ruin, was to find its affirmation in the historical reality of the Great War, whose atrocity and chaos Trakl's poetry had anticipated with prophetic vision. This gives his poetry realistic moment. Its importance, therefore, lies not in its contribution to a new apprehension of reality through an indirect reflection of individual moods and social trends, but in the structure and message of the lyric image itself.

Johannes R. Becher

When Johannes R. Becher embarked on his literary career, his work was shaped by themes and motives similar to those of other Expressionists: on the one hand by notions and perceptions of the repulsiveness of life and the end of the world, on the other by protest and a desire for awakening. The author was convinced that his own suffering and desires were identical with those of his time. This gave him the certitude of finding an appropriate resonance with the anguish he invested in both his literary and public work. The inner conflicts of the poetic subject were understood by him to be identical with those of society. The function of poetry was to capture both the form and content of the poet's own life and to explain it, thereby ultimately furthering his own liberation. However, this focus on self, unlike the case of the monomaniac Benn, was not an end in itself. Rather it was intended to set an example to the reader of a socially relevant strategy for a comprehensive overpowering of conflict and for liberation. By giving voice to his sufferings and hopes in lyric form, the poetic subject aimed to document in exemplary form those of his era. The poet proceeding in this way was at the same time in search of forces capable of preparing for and carrying out the impending and overdue social transformation. Behind this was an idea that the new poetry was no longer addressed to a select circle of *cognoscenti*, but was a fanfare trumpeted from a tribune to reach the masses and serve them as a mobilising 'watchword'. The lyric subject anticipated social transformation and liberation in order to liberate his readers.

'Erlebnis, Formulierung, Tat' ('Experience, Formulation, Deed')

This process was to be accomplished on three levels: 'O Trinität des Werks: Erlebnis, Formulierung, Tat' ('Oh Trinity of the work [of art]: experience, formulation, deed') – i.e. from the subjective experience of the poet, via the composition of the poem to the deed articulated in the work as a model of concrete change. Becher's desire for change was not aimed at any specific group of people, nor was it able to offer keys for dealing with practical tasks in hand or political action. It appealed instead to a general emotional readiness for change. Individuals were often put before a particular cause, understanding being distorted by stylistic eccentricity. Becher's poetry did nevertheless confront the contradictions of his age in a different and clearer manner than his Expressionist contemporaries. Driven by a 'hunger for action', he had grasped that this alone could bring about a solution to social conflicts. His support for the revolutionary changes taking place in 1917 and 1918–19 was the logical outcome of his process of literary maturation up until the end of the *Kaiserreich*.

Parallels with Sturm und Drang?

If one cares to classify Expressionism as a literary movement within German tradition as a whole, one will find a number of features in common with the *Sturm und Drang* revolt of the eighteenth century. Just as in this earlier movement, for example, disaffection on the part of the middle-class literary intelligentsia with the prevailing feudal absolutist conditions found expression in lyric and dramatic protest, so with the literary revolt of Expressionism at the beginning of the twentieth century. The two literary trends also share an anticipation of major historical and political transformations, such as the French and Russian Revolutions – without, however, exerting any direct political impact. Inasmuch as they restricted themselves to bringing about a revolution of form and content, they were both typically German phenomena. As a rule, Expressionists neither understood the root causes of the crisis they experienced and wrote about, nor did they come up with any ideas on how to resolve it. Commenting in a letter of 1918 on Fritz von Unruh's drama *Geschlecht* (*Race*), for example, Karl Liebknecht notes that the author gives an immensely serious account of problems,

> but nevertheless only as a member of middle-class society accomplishing some skilful 'ragging', shaking his fist at the stars, arraigning the cosmos and tearing himself to pieces, who sees no way out – would like to escape and cannot – collapsing into idle despair instead of taking positive combative action to create a new world. He is blinded to primary problems by secondary ones, cannot see causes for effects, and fails to see either the social origins of the horrific things that surround him, or the power that can root them out. This work is a drama issuing from a bourgeoisie torn out of the madness of the sanctity of its own world order. And yet this exceptionally concentrated and intensive composition is imbued with a spirit seething with revolution. Let us wait and see whether the light of day follows this dawn glow.

What ensued in 1918–19 was only dim daylight. Radicalised writers lacked a political direction, having been unable to find one in the social-democratic workers' movement, which was by now hopelessly diluted with reformism. This is seen particularly clearly in the journal *Die Aktion*'s criticism of the social-democratic agenda, rejecting its opportunistic parliamentarianism and seeking to replace it with an anarchist agenda. The activities of this journal were largely aimed at changing social and political conditions, a process to which literature could contribute both by giving voice to the need for change and advancing change itself.

This succeeded only to a very limited degree. Few men of letters involved themselves in the 1918–19 revolution in any practical way (Ernst Toller), while others died young (Trakl, Heym). Most of them matured in entirely diverging directions: Becher towards socialism, Döblin towards Christianity, Benn to some extent towards fascism. Some became successful and prolific writers, such as Werfel, others starving emigrants, such as Else Lasker-Schüler. Expressionism as a homogeneous literary movement thus underwent a rapid demise in the early 1920s. The heterogeneity of its starting-points and perspectives had been held together only as long as protest was able to focus on common opposition to the imperialist conditions prevailing in Wilhelmine Germany. It fell apart as soon as the new parliamentary republic appeared to offer a constitutional guarantee of freedom in art and literature, and hence the personal liberty of the writer himself.

A review of the age of the middle class (Thomas Mann, Sternheim, Heinrich Mann)

This section will explore sample authors whose works are difficult to classify within a particular literary period or trend. They share a common core in giving a critical picture of the age of the middle class. Whether this criticism was expressly intended by these authors, however, or whether it is merely perceived by the reader on the basis of the literary objectivity of the work itself is immaterial.

Thomas Mann's dilemma: art and life

An examination of Thomas Mann's works before World War I reveals that four of his main characters (Hanno in *Buddenbrooks*, Spinell in *Tristan*, *Tonio Kröger* in the novella of the same name, and Gustav von Aschenbach in *Der Tod in Venedig – Death in Venice*) are all artists who either suffer or perish as a result of their tension-ridden relationship with the society of their day (the distinction between art and life). Mann depicts these conflicts and problems from the perspective of a particular individual's life. The complex of social causes remains in the background, and the apparent separation between the individual and society is treated as insuperable. The crucial factor in Mann's pre-1914 works is their descriptive principle – irony. As a stylistic principle, irony assumes a detached, distanced stance in relation to the object being described. Experienced reality is still regarded as worth describing, but is no longer taken entirely seriously. Instead it is revealed and exposed through an emphasis of its contradictions, peculiarities, and the cracks in the surface of the outward appearances focused on in the narrative.

Tonio Kröger

The theme of the tension-ridden relationship between middle-class life and art that runs through Mann's works is most clearly broached in his novella *Tonio Kröger* (1903). Extensive discussion of this problem in the second part of the story between the main character and his friend Lisaweta give it almost an essay form. Half a century later the author looked back on this work as his favourite. Tonio Kröger, like many of Mann's characters, has marked autobiographical features. He oscillates between condescending contempt of the middle-class world and a yearning for the normality and security it offers: as he himself puts it, 'a middle-class man who has gone astray in art, a Bohemian who is homesick for his cosy nursery, an artist with a bad conscience'. He is aware of having been shaped by the spirit of the middle-class world, despite his flight from it on account of its banal bustle and 'wholesomeness'. Clearly, however, this dilemma cannot be

432

resolved: 'I stand between two worlds, am at home in neither, and suffer somewhat as a result.'

Buddenbrooks

Buddenbrooks (1901) is the story of the 'decline of a family' of upper-middle-class people in Lübeck in the nineteenth century. It is based on biographical material from the Mann family which the author adopted down to the finest details for his epic work. It is the chronicle and review of an era, presented critically and sceptically in the form of the rise and fall of a patrician family over four generations. It was based on a conviction that he only needed to write about himself 'in order to loosen the tongue of the era and of universality'. He did not entirely achieve this aim, however, since the career of the Buddenbrook/Mann family is not representative of the nineteenth-century German middle-class family. The novel does nevertheless depict with the utmost precision and razor-sharp analytical intelligence the world of the Hanseatic merchant classes, revealing a wealth of common traits, such as middle-class consciousness, political conservatism, and the virtues of integrity and honesty that made the middle class great. Although the author's narrative style evinces pride at his middle-class patrician origins and the norms of his class, the love directed at himself in this way nonetheless pertains to that particular morbid late fruit of the middle-class way of life who no longer possesses the right abilities and aptitudes for middle-class business, and who therefore consigns himself to the life of a dilettante in art – Hanno Buddenbrook. Hanno is the only figure in the novel who is spared the ironic descriptive approach and is able to bask in the full sympathy of the author.

Buddenbrooks is a novel in the nineteenth-century German realistic, critical narrative tradition. The author reiterated frequently enough the debt he felt to authors such as Storm and Fontane on the one hand, and Tolstoy, Dostoyevsky and Turgenev on the other. From the publication of *Buddenbrooks* up until his death, Mann was among the most successful writers of his century, even internationally, winning the Nobel Prize in 1929. The brilliant irony and wealth of nuance in his writing style represent one of the high points in epic creation in terms of his use of the potential of the German language.

Carl Sternheim's comedy cycle *Aus dem bürgerlichen Heldenleben* (*From the Heroic Middle-Class Life*) appeared between 1909 and 1915. It describes the rise of the German bourgeoisie in the age of imperialism, with an eye to the economic and political roots of these developments. This fundamental realism makes Sternheim's work the most significant German drama in the first half of the present century apart from Brecht's. The creative use and composition of contemporary history as a process, brought about dramatically through a unity of economic, political, ideological and personal factors affecting individual representatives of middle-class life, is supported by the stylistic device of satire. Unlike irony, which is ultimately conciliatory, satire exposes its object to direct criticism and demolition. The 'heroes' are no longer heroes, and where they triumph it is a triumph of hollowness, narrow-mindedness and boasting. In the comedies of this cycle (*Die Hose – Trousers*, 1911; *Die Kassette – The Cash Box*, 1911; *Bürger Schippel – Citizen Schippel*, 1912; *Der Snob – The Snob*, 1913; *1913*, 1913–14), for example, the delusory notions that the middle class holds about itself are subjected to ridicule, and exposed through a confrontation of these notions with reality. The result is a satirical and realistic chronicle of pre-World War I lower-middle-class and middle-class society. The most important structural element in the cycle is the fact that the comic hero, the father Theobald, and his son Christian Maske (the middle-class 'character mask') develop on three levels, thereby bringing about on an individual plane within the family what is representative for social development as a whole. Maske is a member of the lower middle class in *Die Hose (Trousers)*, becomes a capitalist in the *Der Snob*, and a monopoly capitalist wielding power over the economy and politics of the country in *1913* at the height of his career. Similar rises in society are described for the middle-class 'hero' Krull in *Die Kassette*, and the working-class man Schippel whose acceptance into the middle class is described in *Bürger Schippel*. He makes a further appearance in *tabula rasa* as director of a firm. The modes of conduct and outlooks represented by the 'heroes' are to be understood as variations of a single basic pattern. It is less important to see their personal, individual structure than to see them as representatives of an objective socio-economic process. The overall picture produced by the comedy cycle offers a differentiated account of the era encompassing the various strata of the middle class. The demise of the *Kaiserreich* and the outcome of the November revolution were anticipated in the play *1913*, which was completed in 1914. The 'revolutionary' Krey allies himself with the capitalist class and wins Maske's daughter Ottilie. His bogus revolutionary reformism rescues the capitalist and middle class in their hour of greatest danger. The play was intended as a satirical contribution to the jubilee of the Hohenzollern monarchy. By passing political and moral judgement on the German society of the day through its dramatic design, it also constitutes a critical review of the era.

Heinrich Mann

Heinrich Mann's novel *Der Untertan* (*The Subject*) (1916) is characterised by similar aesthetic and political objectives, and likewise shows parallels of form and content. As Sternheim did with his comedy cycle, Mann attempted in this novel trilogy to review the Wilhelmine *Kaiserreich*. *Die Untertan* was later followed by *Die Armen* (*The Poor*) (1917) and *Der*

Kopf (*The Head*) (1925). Actual contemporary processes and events from social and political life form the foundation of the fictional plot treated in these novels. *Der Untertan* depicts the career of paper-mill owner and local politician Diederich Hessling. In form, the novel is a parody of the classical-Romantic and realistic novel of education and development of the eighteenth and nineteenth centuries that dominated German novel-writing. The ostensible outward rise of Diederich Hessling is thus depicted as a fall. With each succeeding step he adopts with a hearty tone of conviction the value-judgements and norms that he had once indignantly rejected, finally reaching a point where nothing remains of the individuality of the 'hero' and he emerges as no more than a representative of the reactionary *Zeitgeist*. With no less satirical fervour than that used to target the conservative, reactionary middle class in the guise of Hessling, Mann also lampoons the parliamentary political opportunism of the German social democrats. The conduct of the workers' leader Napoleon Fischer, revolutionary in word and opportunistic in deed, is held up as an example of the development of the social democrats and the trade union movements from the 1890s onwards. In contrast, the sympathy of the author is with the middle-class liberals of 1848, whose political influence waned steadily after the foundation of the second *Reich*, that national 'revolution from above'. In the novel they and their demise are depicted in old Buck. Economic processes (Hessling's rise from small to large entrepreneur), socio-political conditions (the Kaiser, the nobility, the military, the conservative and liberal middle class, working class and social democrats), and the specific conditions of socialisation prevailing in the authoritarian *Kaiserreich* (education for subject status) and its ideological and moral norms, form a whole that comprises several planes. In this way a creative literary portrait of the rotten totality of society emerges in microcosm. Although conceived before World War I, the novel is not content with mere satirical criticism of the state of society in Mann's own day, but instead becomes a prelude to the ultimate overthrow and demise of the era. Lightning strikes metaphorically over the jubilee celebrations and the inauguration of the Emperor's memorial, pointing unequivocally to the downfall both of the subject himself, and the social conditions that gave rise to him.

LITERATURE IN THE WEIMAR REPUBLIC

After the defeat in World War I

The oft-invoked image of the 'Golden Twenties' is misleading. The 1920s began with the military and political collapse of the *Kaiserreich* after a world war that had been embarked on with eagerness, but had brought about a shattering of traditional values and norms, and the debacle of the November revolution. The decade ended with a complete breakdown of democracy and the Nazi takeover. A crucial factor in all this was that the new democratic forms of government replacing the ruined monarchic social order were not rooted in any clear development of political will among the population at large, appearing only to fill the vacuum left by military calamity. This was to prove a heavy encumbrance in terms of future political prospects. Another equally serious obstacle was the fact that the break with the old order had not been as radical in fact as it was codified in the constitution. In reality, the anti-democratic traditions of the *Kaiserreich* and the former authoritarian state lived on in the Weimar Republic in far greater measure than may have been apparent at first glance to contemporary witnesses.

During the fifteen years of its existence, the first republic on German soil (aside from the brief episode of the 1792–3 Mainz Republic) was rocked by one major crisis after another. The Kapp *putsch* (1920), the *Ruhrkampf* (1920), the Hitler–Ludendorff *putsch* (1923), inflation, the international economic crisis and the growing army of unemployed after 1929 were all outward signs of the structural crisis to which the Weimar Republic was eventually to fall victim. The phase of relative stabilisation from 1924 to 1929 that was to give rise to the myth of the Golden Twenties was no more than a brief interlude. Underlying the process of democratisation introduced with the founding of the Weimar Republic and the republican constitution was an increasingly aggressive movement towards fascism.

The weakness of the Republic

The absence of a basic democratic consensus among the German people made those democratic groupings the constitution sought to foster vulnerable to suppression, and ultimately complete eradication. The workers' movement was split into a social-democrat and a communist wing. The growing internal division of the Left into factions made it incapable of offering any resistance to the united ranks of fascist forces in their forward march. The Republic was not worn down by the struggle between Left and Right, i.e. fascists and communists, but rather collapsed in the face of a lack of decisive unified action by the democratically-minded wing. Instead of waging an all-out struggle against their common enemy, the Left dissipated its strength in ideological and factional squabbles. The communists attacked the social democrats for being 'social fascists', while the social democrats defamed the communists for being an anti-democratic group as dangerous in its way as the National Socialists. The imminent danger of a Nazi takeover, present since the international economic crisis of 1929, was lost to view.

Rapid fluctuation in fashions

In the literary sphere this era, rocked by class conflict and structural crises, was a period of extreme contradictions defying conceptual containment. The collapse of the Wilhelmine *Reich* was seen by many writers as the demise of traditional literary techniques and themes. A rapid succession of different trends and fashions – Expressionism, Dadaism, new objectivity and Americanism – indicates the difficulties the literary intelligentsia were having in finding their bearings within the new era. Some authors responded to the ordeals of war and revolution with a politicisation of their artistic work, while others derived from the same experience an agenda that rejected any inclusion of politics in art. Between these two extreme reactions lay a diversity of intermediate positions in which a far-reaching sense of social responsibility in the writer was set against individualism, traditionalism, nihilism, extreme subjectivism, or contemplation (*Innerlichkeit*).

Literature as a commodity

Art in pursuit of money

The Weimar Republic was more than a period of upheaval that compelled writers to clarify their ideological and artistic positions. It completely changed the conditions in which literature itself originated. Authors became increasingly dependent on the alien and unfathomable machinery of production and distribution which was organised according to market forces and saw art strictly in terms of its own commercial interests. Even those writers who liked to see their literary creation as an act of 'pure' artistic creation, and themselves as 'autonomous creators of eternal cultural values', were now no longer able to evade this view of literature as a commodity. Writers had already realised by the end of the eighteenth century that literature was a saleable commodity, but it was not until the twentieth century that this realisation penetrated the consciousness of their contemporaries.

The lawsuit brought by Brecht in the 1920s against Nero-Film AG for their alleged falsification of his work through their film version of it has gone down in the history of literature as the *Dreigroschenprozess* (*The Threepenny Opera Trial*). This lawsuit clearly showed that once a work of art has reached the marketplace it can be commercialised at will. Brecht himself described the version of his *Dreigroschenoper* by Nero-Film AG as a 'breakdown production' (*Abbauproduktion*) in which his original work was dissected, destroyed and disfigured beyond recognition. In Brecht's view the dismantling of works of art followed the same laws of the marketplace as those governing the dismantling of cars ready for the scrapheap. 'A work of art can be taken to pieces, and particular parts removed. It can be mechanically dismantled, in accordance with the economic and law-enforcement view' (*Dreigroschenprozess*).

Original versus reproduction

In his *Das Kunstwerk im Zeitalter seiner technischen Reproduzierbarkeit* (*The Work of the Art in the Age of its Reproducibility*) (1936), Walter Benjamin gives a perceptive account of the changes wrought by this division of labour in the production process. The author changes from being a 'free' producer to become more and more a mere supplier to the middle-class culture 'business'. The quality of literature, in terms of the aesthetics and content that give it its artistic character as such, thereby comes into a contradictory relationship to its economic value. This in turn is determined by such factors as public interest, taste, reading habits and fashions. However, since the aesthetic quality of a work can only be mediated through the market, the economic aspect markedly outweighs the aesthetic. 'This [aspect] thereby imprints the entirety of literary production with its stamp, by exerting its authority on literary production in its own interests and modifying literary products, whether by bringing its influence to bear overtly, or through a process whereby the author consciously or usnconsciously anticipates the expectations of his contractors or purchasers' (F. Kron).

The author/entrepreneur

Only in exceptional cases did aesthetic quality and economic success coincide in a work, opening up for the author a relatively broad field of literary self-realisation. In general, market forces led to a levelling process between what was held to be 'higher' literature and trivial literature. This accelerated an already existing development towards the bestseller phenomenon, the destructive effects of which can clearly be seen in such authors of the day as Carl von Ossietzky:

> The publisher, however, under pressure, needs success at any price. He orders, injects ideas, or what he calls ideas, forces an author inclined to darkness to write brightly, confuses him and robs him of his personal attributes. Alternatively he encourages an author swept to fame by unexpected success to continue ploughing in the same field, rejecting other proposals as unpopular. In this way he robs his people of the right to develop, deprives literature of the charm of diversity, and displays his standardised authors side by side like pinned butterflies. . . . If a book that is innovative in form or motif acquires importance in a few days, a hundred publishers' offices will immediately resound with the words: 'We must have something like that too' (1929).

The assimilative capacity of the market

It would nevertheless be wrong to conclude that the entire production of literature in the Weimar Republic was standardised to the same degree, or that authors who deviated from the norm had no chance on the market at all. On the contrary, it was to a limited degree possible to deal via the market with themes and techniques that distanced themselves from the dominant literary fashions, or even challenged them. Benjamin himself made the baffling discovery 'that the middle-class machinery of production and publication is able to assimilate, and even propagate, astounding quantities of revolutionary themes without thereby seriously opening to question either its own existence or that of the propertied class that owned it' (1934). The successful marketing of Expressionism and the Dada literary revolt in the first years of the Weimar Republic were clear evidence of this, as was the war novel in the Republic's final years. The latter can be most clearly discerned from Remarque's bestseller *Im Westen Nichts Neues* (*All Quiet on the Western Front*) and the war novel fashion that followed its publication. Between 1928 and 1932 over 200 war novels were published. The effect of this mass production was to neutralise the war novel's capacity for effective social criticism.

Concentration of the press media

Writing was also influenced by the growing concentration of the press media, a process likewise dictated by market forces. In order to make a living, writers even in the eighteenth century had written contributions for journals, or alternatively offered their works to journals for pre-publication. The concentration of the press in the Weimar Republic greatly restricted publication opportunities for critical intellectuals in particular. The press empire of Alfred Hugenberg, the German nationalist and former managing director of Krupp, was financed by German heavy industry. Its columns were only accessible to authors who were prepared to fall in line with the overall ideological direction of the conglomerate, which was anti-semitic, anti-democratic and hostile to intellectuals.

Contrasted with the mass press apparatus of the Hugenberg conglomerate, which controlled newspapers and journals, its own press agency, printing presses and a typesetting service for the provincial press, the influence of democratic, liberal or socialist newspapers was small and rapidly waning. Leading journals such as *Die Weltbühne* (*The World Stage*) edited by Ossietzky and Tucholsky, or the *Fackel* (*Torch*) published by Karl Kraus enjoyed a high reputation among critical intellectuals, even achieving a degree of political impact and weight as opposition newspapers. Nevertheless, they were in no better position to provide an alternative to the mass press than the numerous left-wing newspapers with their small circulations.

Press media concentration was accompanied by the emergence of large publishing houses such as Ullstein, Mosse and Scherl, and by the consolidation of a rapidly proliferating entertainment industry complete with its own structures and internal organisations, such as book clubs. These developments exerted a massive pressure on writers to conform that only those already prominent or successful, or whose chances for publication were with left-wing publishing houses and journals were able to resist. Left-wing authors soon realised the danger inherent in this concentration, responding with the establishment of their own publishing houses (such as Malik-Verlag), their own press and their own book clubs. All of these were intended as an alternative to the middle-class literature business, and it was hoped to both create an alternative reading public and provide publication opportunities for authors of like mind. During the Weimar period the accelerated spread of literature for the masses took on a new quality, and acted as a further constraint on the work of authors. Scherl-Verlag, part of the Hugenberg conglomerate, churned out serialised fiction in editions of millions, flooding the market with cheap trivial literature. Writers of entertainment fiction were hard pressed to hold their own against this kind of competition. The *Rote-Eine-Mark-Romane* (*Red One-Mark Novels*) published by Malik-Verlag and written by the Union of Proletarian Revolutionary Writers (*BPRS: Bund proletarisch-revolutionärer*

Schriftsteller) represented one attempt to counteract this custom-made conformist literature.

Writers organise themselves

The formation of writers' unions

Reaction to dependence on the market and its forces in the Weimar Republic came in the form of writers' organisations, founded with a view to protecting the economic interests of authors. Some disposition towards this had already been evident by the end of the eighteenth century, but it was 1842 before the Leipzig Association of Literati (*Leipziger Literatenverein*) marked the founding of an organisation that was to acquire importance as a professional writers' body. 'Pirated editions, the legal and illegal state of the press, and the practice of censorship' were the three points declared by the statutes of the Leipzig Association of Literati to be 'topics for continuous discussion and resolution'. The pirate editions issue touched on the provisions of copyright and publishing legislation, but the issue of censorship touched on more general political questions that the association in fact hoped to avoid, according to its statutes.

After the failure of the 1848 revolution, the Leipzig Association of Literati became a virtually irrelevant body. It was replaced in 1878, again in Leipzig, by the General Federation of German Writers (*Allgemeiner Deutscher Schriftsteller-Verband*), a body which sought the 'energetic representation of the interests of the writing profession, both internally and externally', and in particular an improvement in the social position of writers. Within a few years, a diversity of supra-regional organisations were founded: the German Writers' Association (*Deutscher Schriftsteller-Verein*), 1885; the German Writers' Federation (*Deutscher Schriftstellerverband*), 1887; the Federation for the Protection of German Writers (*Schutzverein deutscher Schriftsteller*), 1887; the Union of German Writers (*Deutscher Schriftstellerbund*), 1888, and the General Association of Writers (*Allgemeiner Schriftstellerverein*), 1901.

These various bodies to some extent overlapped and to some extent competed. Attempts to create a homogeneous organisation with real political strength failed as a result of the individualist way writers saw themselves, as well as their divergent ideas on social policy. The question as to whether writers' organisations should restrict their activities to the representation of purely economic interests, or whether they should also seek to represent the political interests of writers remained a constant bone of contention, and led to disbandment and splintering.

The SDS (Schutzverband deutscher Schriftsteller – *The Federation for the Protection of German Writers*)

The first writers' organisation of any real consequence was the Federation for the Protection of German Writers (the SDS), founded in Berlin in 1909. Its members included virtually all the leading authors of the day, and it was established with the aim of protecting, representing and furthering 'the economic, legal and intellectual professional interests of its members'.

The SDS was to become an authoritative professional writers' body. It had detailed ideas regarding representation of the professional, legal, economic and social interests of its member writers, and its statutes also guaranteed 'legal protection in case of the confiscation of books or other instances of intervention or encroachment by executive power on the activities of federation members'.

Almost all the leading authors of the Weimar Republic were members of the SDS. In 1924, for example, Alfred Döblin became Chairman of the federation, followed by Theodor Heuss, later the first President of the German Federal Republic. Together with the SDS, the International Pen Club, founded in 1921 in the aftermath of World War I and committed to world peace and fighting against national and racial hatred, was another important body enabling writers to express a clear position on issues. Their concern here was not to represent economic interests, but to achieve a socio-political object arising out of the international composition of the membership. The SDS and the Pen Club were thus complementary rather than competing bodies. It was not unusual for writers to hold membership of both bodies.

The BPRS (Bund Proletarisch-Revolutionärer Schriftsteller – *The Union of Working-Class Revolutionary Writers*)

The Union of Working-Class Revolutionary Writers (BPRS), founded in 1928, was of a different character from the two writers' organisations already mentioned (the Pen Club exists to this day). This union consisted predominantly of a workers' cooperative of communist and socialist writers within the SDS, also constituting the German section of the International Association of Revolutionary Writers, founded in 1927, which saw itself as a counterpart of the Pen Club. The BPRS Union, whose membership included such prominent authors as Erich Weinert, Johannes R. Becher, Anna Seghers, Willi Bredel, Karl Grünberg and Hans Marchwitza, conceived of literature as an 'important component of the ideological superstructure within society'. In contrast with the Federation for the Protection of German Writers (SDS), it claimed a politically representative role. The beginnings of a working-class literature appearing in the Weimar Republic as a repercussion of the Russian October Revolution, as well as an increase

442

in social tensions, were seized on by the BRPS Union in the hope of 'creating a leading role for working-class revolutionary literature and turning it into a weapon of the working class within literature as a whole' (Political Action Agenda, 1928).

Völkisch associations

Socialist and communist authors were not alone in organising themselves into political pressure groups. *Völkisch*-oriented, conservative, reactionary and fascist writers also began to form their own pressure groups during the Weimar Republic. The National Federation of German Writers (Nationalverband deutscher Schriftsteller) and the Wartburg Circle of German Poets (Wartburger Kreis deutscher Dichter), for example, were both of an unequivocally *völkisch* tendency. The Action Union for German Culture (Kampfbund für deutsche Kultur), founded in 1927 by Alfred Rosenberg as a 'National Socialist Association for German Culture', was closely allied to the Nazi Party, being to all intents and purposes a fascist cultural organisation.

'Censorship is not practised' (*Eine Zensur findet nicht statt*): the persecution of writers

Freedom of expression

Article 118 of the Constitution of the Weimar Republic contains the important statement: 'Within the limits laid down by general legislation, every German has the right to freedom of expression by the spoken, written and printed word, by the visual image or other means.' Also: 'Censorship is not practised.' The reality, however, was different. The freedom of expression guaranteed under the Constitution existed on paper only, and in the final years of the Republic was eroded by special acts of parliament. The Weimar Republic is indeed a clear example of the step-by-step abolition of civil liberties. This process began in 1922 with the Act for the Protection of the Republic (*Gesetz zum Schutz der Republik*), a bill first brought in after the assassination of Rathenau as a measure to curb the nationalist right wing, but in fact almost exclusively invoked against liberal, left-wing middle-class, socialist and communist authors. Writers who were openly committed to conservatism, or even National Socialist views, and who glorified the use of force, murder and atrocities, such as the authors of numerous right-wing radical paramilitary novels, were as a rule spared from the impact of this legislation. Some of them were even publicly praised and encouraged, such as the former Expressionist, later National Socialist Arnolt Bronnen, whose paramilitary novel *O.S.* (1929) was a clear breach of the laws of the Republic in effect at the time. Another former Expressionist, Johannes R. Becher, however, whose experiences of World War I had led him to support the workers' movement in the November Revolution (he joined the German Communist Party in 1919), was hard hit by the Protection of the Republic Act. In 1925 a volume of his poetry was confiscated, and the author found himself in prison for a time. In 1927 he was brought to trial, charged with high treason on the basis both of his volume of poetry and other writings published after it. No criminal offence could be proved against Becher, but no such offences were even discussed. The prosecution based its arguments solely on Becher's literary statements. The affair provoked considerable public indignation, the protest involving numerous authors and other intellectuals who did not share Becher's political or literary views. Alfred Kerr, for example, an influential critic of the day, wrote the thought-provoking statement: 'Johannes R. Becher, that's you and you and you, and tomorrow all of us', making it clear that the measures being taken by the Public Prosecutions Office were in fact directed against all critical intellectuals in the Weimar Republic. Partly as a result of this public pressure, the case against Becher was dropped in 1928. Nevertheless, the persecution of critical intellectuals continued.

The Trash and Filth Act (*Schund- und Schmutzgesetz*) passed in 1926 proved an even more effective vehicle than the Protection of the Republic Act for suppressing authors who were out of favour. The true political objective of the Act was recognised by Thomas Mann, who wrote: 'The necessity of protecting the young German generation from trash and filth – this necessity on which the draft bill, unfortunately already at the debate stage, purports to be based, is for anyone who reads or is educated no more than a threadbare screen for its own authors, intended to provide them with a powerful legislative instrument against the mind itself and its liberty.' Strong public protest was unable to prevent the bill from being passed. Numerous bans on books and films were imposed on the strength of these two special acts passed in 1922 and 1926. Eisenstein's film *Battleship Potemkin*, the working-class revolutionary film *Kuhle Wampe* and *All Quiet on the Western Front*, based on Remarque's novel, all fell victim to these bans, as did Brecht's plays *Die Mutter* (*The Mother*) and *Die heilige Johanna der Schlachthöfe* (*St Joan of the Stockyards*). These bans affected authors whose works were perceived as a threat and political affront. Heinrich Mann's ironic statement 'There is mention in the Constitution of freedom of speech and writing. This refers to middle-class speech and middle-class writing', precisely captures the character of official banning policy. An exacerbating factor, however, was that these measures were directed not only against the authors and their works, but also against publishers and booksellers, who were likewise charged with high treason before the High Court.

Pressenotverordnung: the Emergency Press Decree

Despite the fact that existing special legislation gave the political administration of justice a free hand to persecute and suppress out-of-favour authors, it was still seen as too liberal by conservative and reactionary groups. In 1930 a revised, more stringent draft of the Protection of the Republic Act was passed. In 1931 a so-called Emergency Press Decree (*Pressenotverordnung*) was enacted, enabling the authorities to confiscate printed matter without a court order, and to ban the publication of newspapers and journals for up to eight months. On the basis of this stricter legislation Willi Bredel, author of the famous working-class revolutionary novels *Rosenhofstrasse* and *Maschinenfabrik N & K*, and also editor of the *Kommunistische Volkszeitung* (*The Communist People's Newspaper*), was sentenced to two years imprisonment for literary high treason and treason against the state. In contrast with the Becher case, public protest was unable this time to put a stop to the trial. Other working-class novels were also banned, such as *Sturm auf Essen* (*The Storming of Essen*) by Hans Marchwitza, and *Barrikaden am Wedding* (*Barricades in Wedding*) by Klaus Neukrantz. The surveillance of authors regarded as sympathetic to the German Communist Party was common practice by the end of the Weimar Republic. By May 1930 more than thirty editors of communist journals were under arrest. The number of editors and writers under arrest rose to over sixty-five during 1931. In the same year, forty-four communist newspapers and journals were banned from publication. In 1932, even the social democrat journal *Vorwärts* (*Forwards*) was banned for several days.

The general stringency and stepping-up of repression are particularly apparent in the trial of Carl von Ossietzky for high treason in 1931. Editor of the reputable *Die Weltbühne*, Ossietzky later died as a result of the torture he underwent in a concentration camp. On this occasion, however, he was brought to trial for an article revealing details of rearmament within the air force: this was in fact prohibited by the Constitution. Instead of bringing criminal charges against the anti-constitutional practices of the state ministry of defence, however, as was their duty, the judges condemned Ossietzky for having brought this infringement of the law to light. He was sentenced to eighteen months imprisonment.

A split in the Federation for the Protection of German Writers (SDS)

Faced with this situation, the resolve of the SDS crumpled almost entirely. A rift appeared in the Federation during its confrontation with the 'Filth and Trash Clauses'. Whereas a majority of members were vehemently opposed to these new clauses, seeking to draw public attention to them, the Chairman of the Federation, Theodor Heuss, who was also a representative in the *Reichstag* (state parliament), voted in parliament in favour of passing the disputed law. The arguments that this caused within the Federation led to even greater polarisation between the board and its members. Behind this dispute lay the deeper unresolved controversy as to whether the task of the SDS was purely to represent the interests and profession of writers, or whether it was also to involve itself in political issues. This controversy eventually led in 1932 to a split into a left-wing Berlin association, comprising prominent literary figures, and right-wing provincial associations, comprising conservative and National Socialist members and excluding left-wing authors.

In the latter phase of the Weimar Republic hostility towards left-wing authors reached such a pitch that the *Völkische Beobachter* (*The People's Observer*), official mouthpiece of the Nazis, went unpenalised in August 1932 for publishing a list of authors denounced for being 'representatives of a decadent period of baseness', who were threatened with the imposition of a ban on their books in the event of a Nazi takeover of power. Among the names on the list were many authors whose books were indeed banned and burned in 1933, and who themselves were driven into exile.

Literature in media competition

The capitalist structure of the literature business and the phenomena of suppression and censorship are not essentially unique to the twentieth century. They were already present in embryonic form in the eighteenth century. A new factor in the twentieth-century Weimar Republic, however, was the appearance of film and radio. Just as the discovery of photography in the nineteenth century had revolutionised painting, so these new media also changed literature, without those affected at the time being entirely aware of the transformation in its full implications.

What these new media did was to challenge the former claim of written literature and the theatre to a monopoly in cultural representation, thereby introducing an element of competition. The response to this from writers was varied. Some simply tried to ignore the new media, or, like Thomas Mann, to dismiss them as 'unartistic'. Others, like Kafka, not without some justification, feared a 'standardisation' of consciousness. Others again sought to set the 'soulless mechanism of film' against the 'immortality of theatre' (Max Reinhardt). Most authors thus involved themselves in what was, given the meteoric growth and success of these new media, the somewhat futile and anachronistic debate as to whether radio and film were art forms or not. A few, however, realised that through these new media the character of art was beginning to change: 'The earlier forms of communication, in other words, do not remain unchanged by the newly-emerging ones, and cannot persist beside them. The film-goer reads stories in a different way. But even one who writes stories is for his part also a film-goer' (Brecht, *Dreigroschenprozess*). Brecht and Benjamin were among the first authors to try to grasp the implications of this new situation in theoretical terms. From these insights Brecht immediately drew conclusions in terms of his literary work, experimenting with the new media (*Der Dreigroschenfilm – The Threepenny Opera Film; Ozeanflug – Ocean Flight*).

The film and radio industry

The basic problem was the subjection of film and radio to the laws of commodity production. The exploitation of the new media with a view to maximising profits, and the employment of film as an instrument of reactionary propaganda (the UFA, Germany's largest and most successful film company, belonged to the right-wing radical Hugenberg conglomerate) effectively excluded socially critical authors from the opportunity to work creatively with the new media. Brecht's experiences with the filming of his *Dreigroschenoper* (*Threepenny Opera*) by Nero-Film AG are symptomatic. Despite having negotiated a contract guaranteeing him a right of consultation over the screenplay prior to shooting, the film company failed to abide by this agreement, making a film that was diametrically opposed to Brecht's artistic and political intentions. Brecht's experience was that the writer was powerless in the face of the 'apparatus', and degraded himself to the level of a mere supplier as long as the media remained in the chains of capitalist exploitation. Given that cinemas had a mass attendance (the International Press Conference estimated in 1926 that some 800,000 working people attended film performances on a daily basis, there being over 8,000 large or medium-sized film theatres in the industrial areas alone), left-wing and communist authors saw it as a matter of great urgency to free the new media from this process of capitalist exploitation, and wherever possible set up alternative film and radio-programme production facilities, to be able to make use of the latent revolutionary potential they contained (see Willi Münzenberg, *Erobert den Film! – Conquer Film!*, 1925). Despite the severe production difficulties attached to working outside the mainstream middle-class film business, some success was achieved in making major, socially critical films, based on the avant-garde Russian model (Eisenstein), such as *Kuhle Wampe* and *Mutter Krausens Fahrt ins Glück* (*Mother Krause's Journey to Happiness*). *Kuhle Wampe*, however, was immediately banned, and showings were only allowed of a cut version.

In addition to a working-class film movement, in which prominent authors took part both theoretically and practically, a workers' radio movement also arose with the support of various left-wing parties and groups. This aimed to go beyond programme criticism and an influence on programme planning to develop a democratic alternative radio in the form of workers' broadcasts.

Changes in perception

Like film, radio too became a hotly disputed stronghold, not least because it opened up new employment opportunities for financially hard-pressed authors, as well as offering them a way out of the traditional production of art, which they now experienced as sterile. At a workshop entitled 'Writing and Radio' held in 1929, for example, in addition to radio producers numerous writers also took part, including Alfred Döblin, who pointed out the potential being opened up for literature by the new medium. He regarded this retrieval of the acoustic medium, the 'actual mother earth of all literature', as an enormous advantage of which writers should make full use. 'That means we must now write things intended to be spoken and heard. Anyone who writes knows that this will bring about changes affecting the very substance of the work.... Changes of form must or should be accepted by literature to make it suitable for radio.' Döblin himself wrote a radio version of his novel *Berlin Alexanderplatz* in an attempt to put into effect his own requirement that texts be made suitable for radio.

The radio play

Within a few years a new art genre developed – the radio play. The German radio station *Deutsche Rundfunk*, having opened its programme on 29 October 1923 with musical entertainment and poetry recitations, immediately followed this with brief dramatic scenes, one-act plays and *Schwänke* (farce), moving on to broadcast major dramatic adaptations known as *Sendespiele* (broadcast plays) across the ether. In 1926 alone some 500 dramatic adaptations were broadcast, mostly classical plays. All this formed the foundation for the radio play, which was able to establish itself in the ensuing years as an art form in its own right, although not reaching its heyday until after 1945 in the Federal Republic.

Attempts were soon made to comprehend this new form theoretically and determine its possible functions. Whereas Hermann Pongs (*Das Hörspiel – The Radio Play*, 1930) classified the radio play together with film as 'mouthpieces of the modern collective spirit', seeing its chief value as lying in the 'creation and reinforcement of a supra-partisan sense of community', Richard Kolb (*Das Horoskop des Hörspiels – The Horoscope of the Radio Play*, 1932), understood the radio play as a form more inclined 'to show us the movement in men than men in movement'. Both these concepts shaped radio-play production during the Weimar Republic and the Nazi era. While Pongs's concept was further elaborated by Gerhart Eckart in 1941 with a view to making use of the genre for the Nazis (*Der Rundfunk als Führungsmittel – Radio as a Vehicle for Leadership*, 1941), Kolb's concept smoothed the way for an artistic internalisation running parallel to concepts of *Innerlichkeit* (contemplation) current at that time in the literary sphere, thereby also auguring the 'internal emigration' that was to take place in the radio play as well (Eich, Huchel).

Brecht's radio theory

An attempt to harness the potential of radio in a socially critical way was undertaken by Brecht in his theory of radio, which is closely related to his *Lehrstücktheorie* (theory concerning the didactic play). Brecht proposed changing radio from an 'instrument of distribution' to an 'instrument of communication': 'Radio would conceivably be the most magnificent communication apparatus in public life, an immense channel system, which means it could, if it knew how, not only broadcast, but also receive, allowing the listener not only to hear, but also to speak, not isolating him, but opening up relationships for him. Radio would therefore have to leave off being a supplier and organise the listeners as suppliers' (*Rede über die Funktion des Rundfunks* – *Speech on the Function of Radio*, 1932). In his radio play *Ozeanflug* (*Ocean Flight*), in which he turns the much-celebrated flight of Charles Lindbergh across the Atlantic into a dialectic *Lehrstück* on the potential of modern technology, Brecht wanted to use radio in a different sense. '*Ocean Flight* is not intended to serve the uses of present-day radio, but to change them. The increasing concentration of mechanical means, as well as increasing specialisation in education – processes that should be accelerated – call for a kind of rebellion in the listener, activating him and reinstating him as producer.' Brecht was nevertheless aware of the utopian nature of his proposal to make a 'communication-apparatus' out of radio:

> This is an innovation, a proposal that appears utopian, and which I myself term utopian by stating that radio could, or the theatre could [do this or that]. I know that major institutions cannot do everything that they could do, any more than they can do everything they want to do. They want to have some input from us, to be revived and kept alive with innovation. It is not our task, however, to revive an ideological institution with innovations on the basis of the given social order. Instead we should shift that basis through our innovations. So we are for innovation, but against revival! By means of a continuous process of ceaseless proposals for the better use of this apparatus in the general interest, our task is to shake the social basis of these apparatuses and to dispute their use in the interests of the few. Unrealisable in this social order, realisable in another, these proposals, constituting no more than the natural consequence of technological development, serve to propagate and create that other order.

The first signs of a working-class revolutionary literature

A lost war, a failed revolution, an intensified class struggle, and splits and polarisation within the workers' movement, on the one hand, and movements towards concentration and media competition, on the other, created a sense of crisis that compelled writers to think about their own literary activity. The experience that literature as a whole had proved unable to offer any substantial contribution towards solving the major problems of the day was not confined to authors on the Left, although among them it did lead to the most far-reaching changes in literary practice, as well as to a highly fruitful debate on the usefulness of literature. The debate conducted on the Left was provoked, or inspired, by the example of the Russian *Proletcult*, of the working-class art that had emerged in revolutionary Russia and was a source of immense fascination to the left-wing literary intelligentsia in the Weimar Republic.

The Proletcult

The *Proletcult* was based first and foremost on the concepts of Bogdanov (*The Art of the Proletariat*), Lunacharsky (*The Cultural Responsibilities of the Working Class*), and Kershentsev (*The Creative Theatre*), which diverged substantially in terms of their ideas of working-class art, but were in agreement as to their working-class objectives. Bogdanov placed great emphasis on the collectivist character of working-class literature, and its distinct status from individualist middle-class literature. In Bogdanov's view, this collective character was linked with the collective consciousness of workers, which arose out of the capitalist working process. The aim of a working-class literature understood in this way is to integrate the reader into a sense of belonging to the working-class community. There was no problem about intellectuals creating art in the working-class sense, or even of their becoming 'artistic spokesmen of the proletariat', or 'organisers of its forces and consciousness in artistic form', provided they were 'truly and honestly saturated with the aspirations and ideals of the collective and its way of thinking'.

In contrast with Bogdanov, Lunacharsky distinguished between socialist art (which could only come about in socialism) and proletarian art, which he saw as class art in the phase of class struggle. Proletarian art had to reflect working-class consciousness and be in accordance with the interests of the working class, without, however, paying any heed to 'backward' proletarians. As regards cultural heritage, Lunacharsky held a modified version of Bogdanov's view. He saw the alliance between proletarians and the progressive middle class as a necessity, since in his view the working class needed support both in the process of making traditional art its own, and in developing its own literary practice. Utilising works of art from previous ages in a dialectic sense for the purposes of proletarian art was seen as part of this process.

Of particular importance for German intellectuals were the theories of Kershentsev, which related specifically to the theatre. Kershentsev abolished the distinction between players and spectators: anyone who felt like it should be able to act. Working-class actors should definitely in his view remain amateur, in order not to lose touch with reality. Performances should raise the class struggle to heroism and make direct contact with the people. Kershentsev regarded participation by progressive intellectuals in proletarian theatre as, if anything, detrimental. He believed they would infect the germinating working-class notion of art with purely middle-class categories of art. The use of bourgeois plays was for Kershentsev only a last resort, in the event that suitable proletarian production had not yet come about. Where middle-class plays were performed, they were to be brought up to date, modified and removed from their traditional context.

Traditional lines?

A central issue for the German intelligentsia and Russian writers alike was the question of how to handle their own relationship with tradition, i.e. discovering middle-class literature, its themes and techniques, and learning from them for present-day practice. Behind the ferocious attack by George Grosz and John Heartfield on the Expressionist painter Kokoschka in the *Kunstlump* debate of 1919–20, for example, lay what Heartfield described as 'a politically-motivated rejection of art, namely Expressionism, that after some initial resistance was made palatable for the salon by the bourgeoisie even during the War, and completely so after the November overthrow'. Applied to literature, a rejection of art of this kind begs the fundamental question of whether it is at all possible to follow on from the bourgeois middle-class heritage, and of what stance the creative artist should adopt in the class conflicts of his time. When a Rubens painting was damaged by a stray bullet, Kokoschka appealed to the inhabitants of Dresden to conduct themselves in such a manner during their revolutionary street fighting that 'human culture is not endangered'. This was seen by Grosz and Heartfield as the manifestation of a cynicism marked by a contempt for humanity, more concerned that works of art remain unscathed than human life.

Grosz and Heartfield were both seeking to break new ground in their own art – Grosz in drawing, Heartfield as a creator of political photomontage. For them, bourgeois art and the declining bourgeois avant-garde represented by Kokoschka were no more than means of diversion for the ruling classes of the day, with no 'essential value' (*Lebenswert*) for the mass of the population. Behind the provocative question 'What is the worker to do with art?' lay another question concerning the class character of art. It was their experiences of World War I that had brought Grosz and Heart-field to the conviction that 'it was complete insanity to believe that the spirit or some great human spirits ruled the world. Goethe in the barrage, Nietzsche in the field pack, Jesus in the trenches – there were still people who held the spirit and art for a self-evident power' (1925).

The anti-art movement

By way of reaction to the 'cloud-wandering tendencies of so-called sacred art, whose adherents mused on cubes and gothic while the generals painted in blood' (Grosz/Heartfield), Dadaism came about in the revolutionary phase of the post-war crisis in the Republic. This was an anti-bourgeois artistic and literary tendency whose 'revolutionary strength' lay, according to Benjamin, in 'testing art for its authenticity'. The revolutionary élan of this anti-art movement proved productive wherever it was linked with insight into the class character of literature and was oriented towards a new working-class literature. It became sterile, degenerating into the merely iconoclastic and into futile gestures of protest wherever it practised its own notion of art without elaborating a social function for it and seeking to legitimise it.

The negation of bourgeois art contained in the *Kunstlump* pamphlet ('We hail with joy the fact that the bullets are whistling into the galleries and palaces and the masterpieces of Rubens, instead of into the houses of the poor in the working-class quarters!'), and the fierce tone found in other Dadaist manifestos of the time, evoked criticism among the Left. The *Rote Fahne* (*Red Flag*, literary mouthpiece of the German Communist Party) in particular branded it as incitement to vandalism. In contrast with Grosz and Heartfield, Gertrud Alexander, the most influential literary critic of *Rote Fahne*, who set the course of literary policy for the German Communist Party during the first years of the Weimar Republic, still held firm to the 'essential value' of middle-class art for the working class. In the classical literature of the eighteenth century especially she saw a heritage from which the working class of the Weimar Republic should draw. The high esteem in which classical German literature was held, as is clear from numerous reviews of performances of the classics in *Rote Fahne*, was accompanied by an outright rejection of avant-garde literary trends such as Expressionism and Dadaism. Regardless of the enmity between the two movements, both were regarded as manifestations of decadence and as the degenerate products of middle-class society, and hence to be criticised.

This focus on classical literature was also the reason for the extreme mistrust with which the Communist Party responded during the early years of the Weimar Republic to tentative efforts towards a working-class literature. *Rote Fahne* responded to Piscator's project for a working-class theatre, for example, with the words: 'Let us not then choose the word theatre, but call the child by its proper name: propaganda. The name "theatre" is committed to art and to artistic performance! ... Art is too sacred a thing to surrender its name to a concoction of propaganda! ... What the worker needs today is powerful art ... , such art may even be of middle-class origin, but let it be art'.

The communist concept of the literary heritage

The German Communist Party's concept of the literary heritage was derived from Franz Mehring's epoch-making works of literary criticism on the German Enlightenment and classical literature of the nineteenth century. This conception was to play a part in the so-called Expressionism debate during the period of exile, and continued, in modified form, to be of major significance for literary theory and practice in the German Democratic Republic. The problem with this conception was that it raised a specific historical form of literary practice to the level of an absolute, invoking it against what was modern, and hence making it an impediment both to the growth of working-class art, and to creative experimentation with new literary techniques.

The high esteem in which early middle-class literature was held in the official cultural views of the Communist Party, and its under-estimation of the potential of working-class literature under capitalist conditions, evoked severe criticism from artists and writers who had acquired more radical views as a result of the November Revolution, and who had joined various party organisations to the left of the communists. The literary journal *Die Aktion*, for example, hailed the *Kunstlump* pamphlet with the words: 'One cannot destroy enough "culture" for the sake of culture. One cannot destroy enough "works of art" for the sake of art.... Comrades! Away with deference to all this bourgeois culture! Overturn the old idols! In the name of the coming working-class culture!' (1920).

The art of the proletariat?

During the crisis years of 1919–23, anarchist and left-wing communist authors in particular conducted a lively debate on the potential for working-class literature in the context of bourgeois society. During the course of this debate a modest working-class literature came into existence, but more than this there was also an attempt to define what working-class literature could and should be in Germany.

> Working-class art is the art of the working class as the ruling class. Until the working class exists as a ruling class, working-class art is the artistic expression of an oppressed class, and is therefore also oppressed, i.e. silenced, persecuted, banned, outlawed and lacking the

means of dissemination. At the present time of marked intensification of class conflicts, this art, drawing from the experiences of this transitional stage of the working class, will be an expression of the class struggle and the strongest influence affecting the working class at present.

(Kanehl)

The Union for Proletarian Art

In 1919 a Union for Proletarian Art (*Bund für proletarische Kunst*) was formed, comprising writers, visual artists and works councils seeking to 'prepare for a new proletarian culture ... so as to intellectualise and further the Revolution'. Following a brief period of tension-ridden cooperation with the trade union-oriented Expressionist *Tribüne*, the Union founded its own Proletarian Theatre of the Union for Proletarian Culture, which folded after only a few months as a result of internal discord. What had been intended as a spontaneous conversion of art into revolutionary action in the proletarian theatre ('The theatre should be the mouthpiece of the masses, calling to itself through it. They want to give a signal to action in it, and to proclaim the poverty of their situation and the hope behind their efforts') proved illusory, as well as being contradicted by theatrical practice. *Die Freiheit* (*Freedom*), for example, a play by Herbert Kranz produced by the Union, treats the theme of eight workers and sailors condemned to death for pacifism. Instead of seizing a chance to escape, they choose 'inner' freedom and acceptance of their execution instead, a conclusion that had more of an inhibiting effect on the audience than the revolutionary impact being sought. The elaboration of a working-class literary theory and practice was still in its infancy. *Die Kanaker* (*The Kanakas*) and *Wie lange noch?* (*How Much Longer?*) by Franz Jung, the lyric verse of Oskar Kanehl (*Steh auf, Prolet, Strasse frei! – Stand Up, Proletarian, the Way is Open!*), as well as the reflections of Erich Mühsam, Erwin Piscator, Gustav Wangenheim, Georg Grosz and John Heartfield, were the first signs of a working-class literary theory and practice, but the authors were still far from putting their ambitious literary concept into effect.

Bühne revolutionärer Arbeiter (The Stage of Revolutionary Workers)

In the autumn of 1919 another theatre was founded by Piscator and Schüller. It is clear from the theatre's alternative title, Stage of the Revolutionary Workers of Greater Berlin, that it was not an autonomous cultural institution, which the Union for Proletarian Culture remained despite all efforts to the contrary, but was part of the workers' movement and the political organisation associated with it. From October 1920 until it was banned in April 1921 the Proletarian Theatre put on over fifty performances. As an organisation with members, with regular meetings at which decisions were taken on the work of the theatre, the Proletarian Theatre, which played in association clubhouses and deliberately avoided a house of its own, competed with the social-democratic Volksbühne (People's Theatre). The Proletarian Theatre not only did away with the traditional hierarchical theatre organisation, replacing it with collective work, but also innovatively abolished the division between actors and spectators.

Piscator's idea of a proletarian theatre was that it should 'break with capitalist traditions as an enterprise, creating a relationship of equal rights, a common interest and a will to work collectively among the board of directors, performers, set technicians and all other technical and administrative employees, as well as between these collectively and the consumers (i.e. theatre-goers)'. The Proletarian Theatre saw its primary responsibility to lie in putting on the first contemporary attempts at working-class revolutionary drama. However, Piscator and Schüller also hoped to win over workers to the position of the revolutionary working class by adapting middle-class (bourgeois) dramas such as Büchner's *Dantons Tod* (*Danton's Death*) and Hauptmann's *Die Weber* (*The Weavers*). 'The utilisation of established literature' by means of 'deletions, amplification of certain parts, possibly also with the addition of a prologue and epilogue' was an attempt to make functional use of the bourgeois drama heritage. 'In such plays the old world is still found with which the most backward person is familiar, and here it will also be seen that all propaganda must start by showing what should be on the basis of what already is.'

After the Proletarian Theatre was banned, it was some considerable time before Piscator managed to set up a theatre of his own again. Following a number of years during which he worked as a producer for the People's Theatre he had once opposed, and where he developed his production style, it was 1927 before he opened a new theatre, known as the first Piscator Stage (Piscator-Bühne). An independent political theatre, it was fundamentally different from the Proletarian Theatre of the early twenties. Piscator used directorial techniques, film and projection, etc. in an attempt to bring about a form of political *Lehrtheater* (didactic theatre) that appeared to do away with the distinction between bourgeois and proletarian theatre. It soon became apparent, however, that the Piscator Stage was a social event to be savoured even by 'smart' people. Piscator's theatre work did nevertheless further the development of technical devices, making use of new media to an astonishing degree, and setting new standards for a modern production style. In the long term, however, he was unable to compensate for the shortcomings of his dramatic texts. Piscator's view that form alone could never be revolutionary, and that it was the content of a play that made it so, had originally been directed as a criticism of the bourgeois theatre business of his own day, but in fact aptly identifies the dilemma he himself shared with other directors.

The large crowds of Berlin workers drawn to Piscator's Proletarian Theatre had repercussions in the attitude of the German Communist Party. Where Gertrud Alexander had once dismissed the Proletarian Theatre as no more than a 'propaganda concoction', the Communist Party subsequently revised its disagreement with the practices of the Theatre:

The theatre movement has emerged spontaneously from among the masses and is part of the overall working-class movement. It is necessary to note that the interest is there, and there because the performances offered to audiences by reformist associations for workers' education no longer satisfy the working class. From this opposition to the bureaucratic practices of associations for workers' education the working-class theatre movement is emerging. It is hence the duty of the Communist Party to strengthen this opposition, which has recognised that these performances of the classics serve only to weaken the working-class struggle, but which is no yet clear as to what should replace this theatre practice. It is hence the duty of the Communist Party to come to these associations with a clear, revolutionary theatre agenda in order to make them centres of the class struggle whose ultimate aim is to revolutionise workers from the stage and to combat ideological influences from social-democratic educational bigwigs.

(Reimann)

A change in the conception of the literary heritage

Even among writers in the Communist Party, opposition was making itself felt against the restrictive classicist literary policy of the party and its stubborn insistence on traditional bourgeois art forms. Johannes R. Becher, for example, was at pains to develop a new conception of literature that would abolish through dialectic the contradiction between propaganda and art on the one hand and bourgeois and working-class art on the other. 'Art is a weapon of the classes in the class struggle. Just as great bourgeois poetry once served as a weapon of the then progressive bourgeoisie against feudalism, working-class revolutionary poetry now has to serve as the weapon of the working class in its struggle against the bourgeoisie.' This objective had implications for the conception of the literary heritage: 'Our relationship to middle-class literature is the question of our relationship to the past. This relationship is a dialectical one. We eliminate the worthless and preserve the valuable, adopting it and making use of it.'

A model for Agitprop?

The changed relationship of the Communist Party to working-class literature revealed itself in various spheres. It coincided with a phase of relative stability from 1924 to 1929, in which the party also adopted a more offensive posture. One effect was the party support for a German *Agitprop* theatre based on the Russian model, and the planning of political revues derived from Piscator's *Revue Roter Rummel* (*Red Racket Revue*) of 1924. Countless *Agitprop* groups sprang up within a few years: *Das rote Sprachrohr* (*The Red Speaking-Tube*), *Die roten Raketen* (*The Red Rockets*), etc. By 1929 there were over 300 *Agitprop* groups in Germany, and numerous revues, such as the *Roter Rummel* or the *Hände weg von China* (*Hands off China*) revue, which opened up new forms of theatrical expression for working-class theatre, and fostered working-class literary practice.

In 1925, Becher and other authors succeeded in obtaining the permission of the Communist Party to form a Working Group of Communist Writers (AKS – Arbeitskreis kommunistischer Schriftsteller) within the SDS, the Federation for the Protection of German Writers. From 1927 onwards Becher edited and published a *Proletarian Feuilleton Correspondence*, in which workers, known as workers' correspondents, reported their experiences in the workplace, etc., thereby being inspired to literary work of their own. These workers' correspondents, who were the link between the rank and file and the party, were an important source of stimulus. A new breed of writing workers was recruited from among them, including Bredel, Daudistel, Kläber, Lorbeer, and Grünberg.

The starting-point for these workers' correspondents was their own experience, conveyed in autobiographical form. This was a medium better suited to expressing and conveying authenticity and affliction than fictional forms, for example. A fine specimen of the workers' autobiography genre is Ludwig Turek's *Ein Prolet Erzählt* (*A Proletarian Tells his Story*) (1930). We see here the beginnings of a link between the private and political spheres in working-class literature that was incomparably more difficult to bring about in the closed form of the novel.

The new novel: a question of organisation?

In 1928 the Working Group of Communist Writers (AKS), together with workers' correspondents, directors and co-workers from communist publishing houses, formed the Union of Proletarian Revolutionary Writers (BPRS: Bund Proletarisch-Revolutionärer Schriftsteller). This was a literary and political organisation that sought to develop and put into practice a concept of working-class literature. The BPRS thereby ushered in a new phase in the development of literature in which the transition from short reportage forms and autobiographical chronicles would be completed. It was in this phase, which coincided with the disintegration of the Republic, that such important novels appeared as Willi Bredel's *Maschinenfabrik N & K* (1930) and *Rosenhofstrasse* (1931), Karl Grünberg's *Brennende Ruhr* (*The Burning Ruhr*) (1928), Hans Marchwitza's *Sturm auf Essen* (*The Storming of Essen*) (1930), Franz Krey's *Maria und der Paragraph* (*Maria and the Paragraph*) (1931), Klaus Neukrantz's *Barrikaden am Wedding* (*Barricades in Wedding*) (1931), and Walter Schönstedt's *Kämpfende Jugend* (*Struggling Youth*) (1932), all of which appeared in the *Rote-Eine-Mark* (*Red-One-Mark*) series. These novels told the story either of the recent past of the Weimar Republic from the viewpoint of struggling workers (the Kapp *putsch* in the case of Marchwitza, of conflicts in the Ruhr in the case of Grünberg), or described topical conflicts at the workplace (*Maschinenfabrik N & K*) and in street cells (Neukrantz, Schönstedt, or Bredel's *Rosenhofstrasse*), alternatively dealing with such central social and political themes as that of Paragraph 218, referring to the law against abortion. All that these novels had in common was their class commitment, their concern to create a simple, comprehensible language and narrative style and their militancy.

Proletarian critique of Germany: the BPRS

The Union was founded as the German section of the Moscow International Union of Revolutionary Writers, and in view of the cautiousness of the German Communist Party at the time was dependent on Moscow. It was thus the office of the International Union that bore the costs of the *Linkskurve* (*Left Curve*), published from 1929 to 1932 by the German Communist Party's own International Workers' Publishing House in Berlin as the official mouthpiece of the Union. The basis of the Union's activities was its programme of action, which comprised the following aims: the practical development of working-class revolutionary literature; the formulation of a working-class revolutionary theory of literature; criticism of bourgeois literature; the organisational gathering of working-class revolutionary writers; and the defence of the Soviet Union. There was lively disagreement both over the programme of action and the aims of the Union, which failed to pass a binding programme acceptable to all members. The conception of what working-class literature in fact was, and its relationship towards bourgeois literature was discussed – in accordance with communist policy at the time – in the national or international context. This left unexplained the issue of

> what the class character of literature in general, and working-class literature in particular, consists of, or in what it shows itself. Should it be a literature of the working class, as Gábor asserts? Or should it be a literature for the working class, as recommended by *Agitprop*

groups in favour of the creation of a new public? Or both? Should the 'working-class revolutionary' find expression in new literary forms and/or only in the subjects (*sujet*) of literature? Should this literature depict the lifestyle, struggles and viewpoints of the working class? Or should any and every subject be seen through the eyes of a member of the revolutionary working class?

(H. Gallas)

The position of the Linkskurve

Despite continuing lack of clarity on these key issues, the *Linkskurve* distanced itself vehemently from left-wing middle-class intellectuals from 1929 to 1930, thereby antagonising important Union members. Döblin, Toller, Tucholsky, and even BPRS member Piscator were all criticised for their refusal to join the German Communist Party. Döblin's novel *Berlin Alexanderplatz* was condemned because the hero Franz Biberkopf sought no contact with communist workers, the author presenting only a type – the unenlightened, disorganised worker, thereby giving a false picture of the revolutionary power of the German workers' movement. No less damaging than this mania for demarcation was the so-called 'midwife thesis' (*Geburtshelferthese*) that prevailed in the Union at that time. According to this thesis, intellectuals had the sole task of encouraging workers to write on their own, teaching them writing techniques and providing them with publishing openings. This conception drove a wedge between intellectuals and workers.

Marxist aesthetics

In the Union's final years the question of the relationship between bourgeois and proletarian art shifted increasingly to questions relating to Marxist aesthetics. Literary developments in the Soviet Union – the eradication of the *Proletkult* – seemed to endorse the implementation in the Union (BPRS) of a traditionalist concept of literature that ran counter to the Union's original intention. Georg Lukács became its authoritative theoretician, developing his concept of Realism in polemical opposition to the first signs of a working-class revolutionary literature (*Tendenz oder Parteilichkeit?; Reportage oder Gestaltung – Party Commitment or Shaping? Reportage or Creation?*). This was to play a significant part in the debate over literary theory during the period of exile. In fact the implementation of Lukács's concept of Realism within the Union and in the *Linkskurve* marked the end of working-class revolutionary literature as a category in its own right – a movement that had begun with such hope and enthusiasm. Working-class literature was subordinated by Lukács to the model of nineteenth-century middle-class Realist literature, and hence ultimately robbed of its revolutionary character. He likewise resolved the issue of literary heritage in favour of tradition and against modernity. With Lukács' concept of Realism the contradiction that had emerged in the Weimar Republic between bourgeois and proletarian literature was smoothed over and defused before it could even become a viable alternative, either in theory or in practice.

Developmental tendencies in prose

Politicisation versus Innerlichkeit (contemplation) again

The experience of World War, revolution and class conflict similarly led to a process of reorientation in the middle-class literary camp. Whereas a majority of writers were gripped by a process of politicisation, existing pre-war tendencies towards escape and retrogression intensified among a small minority to become a deliberately non-political agenda. Authors such as Gottfried Benn, for example, saw their position confirmed in a notion of the 'special nihilism of art', seeing the greatness of art in the very fact that it was 'historically ineffective and without practical consequences'. Benn called on poets to 'shut themselves off from contemporaries', to sweep aside all ethical and political scruples and henceforth to seek only 'individual perfection' (*Können Dichter die Welt verändern? – Can Poets Change the World?*, 1930). This escapist attitude, the problematic nature of which became apparent after 1933 with Benn's intermittent cooperation with the National Socialists, was combined with a recourse to experimentation in artistic forms that gave an appearance of revolutionary character in the Expressionist demolition of middle-class notions of form.

Similarly, the conception of *Innerlichkeit* or contemplation put forward by Werfel (*Realismus und Innerlichkeit – Realism and Contemplation*, 1931) to counter the 'Realism' and 'materialism' of his time was a reaction to the particular set of circumstances of the age, which compelled writers to decide where they stood. Werfel set against the trend towards the politicisation of literature his position of *Innerlichkeit* (contemplation), which at the theoretical level anticipated virtually all the various later forms of 'inner emigration'. Calling for a 'saturation of the world with intellectualism' and the creation of a counter-balance to both socialism and capitalism through the 'intensification of the inner life' (see also Hesse's *Der Weg nach innen – The Way Inwards*, 1931), he took up ideas such as 'creative restoration' put forward elsewhere with varying emphasis by Hofmannsthal (*Der Schwierige – The Difficult Man*, 1921), Rilke (*Duineser Elegien – The Duino Elegies*, 1923), George (*Das neue Reich – The New Realm*, 1928) and others. All these concepts were essentially varieties of the political concept of 'conservative revolution' that was to become the common ground for various trends opposed both to the newly-created Republic and efforts to achieve a socialist revolution.

In other writers the sense of crisis manifested itself in the form of reflection on traditional literary techniques and as a search for new forms (internal monologue, the montage principle, reportage forms, parable structure, etc.). In terms of content, it showed itself in a critical dissection of the assumptions of their own age and of their own existence as writers. The newly-acquired relationship to the times asserted itself predominantly in the form of more conspicuous social criticism.

Heinrich and Thomas Mann

A good example of the acquisition of a socially critical dimension in the novels of the Weimar Republic can be discerned in the work of the brothers Thomas and Heinrich Mann. The novels *Der Zauberberg* (*The Magic Mountain*) (1924) by Thomas Mann and *Der Untertan* (*The Subject*) (1916) by Heinrich Mann were attempts to come to terms with recent German history. Both authors started out with the claim of having written a 'novel of the epoch', i.e. a novel about pre-war Germany. Heinrich Mann styled his novel, written during the war years (the first notes being made in 1906), the 'story of the public soul under Wilhelm II'. Thomas Mann later described his novel as a 'contemporary novel' that 'seeks historically . . . to draw an inner picture of an epoch, the age of pre-war Europe'. Clearly, however, these analogous claims were dealt with very differently by the two authors.

Der Untertan, with its aggressively ironic tendency, and *Der Zauberberg*, with its restrained, ironic style, are two major documents of the age and represent diverging ways of assessing it from the middle-class perspective. Heinrich Mann succeeded in unravelling the social psychological structures and mechanisms of the authoritarian state, revealing the connection between the authoritarian individual character and the authoritarian state. In so doing he anticipated at the poetic level insights that would only be confirmed later with the social-psychological research of Adorno and Horkheimer into the authoritarian character. At the same time he succeeded in writing one of the most important social satires of his day. His novels *Die Armen* (*The Poor*) (1917) and *Der Kopf* (*The Head*) (1925), which form an inner unity with *Der Untertan*, as well as his novel *Ein Ernstes Leben* (*A Serious Life*) (1932), are all contributions to a genre that has hardly any roots in Germany.

By contrast, in *Der Zauberberg* Thomas Mann's analytical grasp of contemporary problems wavers and scarcely has a hold on anything concrete. The Humanist conception of the novel is very vague, revealing that the author was only just beginning to free himself from the national conservative positions of his youth (*Betrachtungen eines Unpolitischen* –

Reflections of a Non-Political Man, 1918). He had greatly clarified his stance by 1930 with his novella *Mario und der Zauberer* (*Mario and the Magician*), in which he lends symbolic form through the figure of the magician Cipolla to the sadism and suggestive demagogy of fascism.

Apart from their contemporary content, *Der Untertan* and *Der Zauberberg* are also significant as manifestations of the different directions of the twentieth-century middle-class novel. The satirical, socially critical novel of Heinrich Mann represents one possible line of development for the modern novel. The reflective, ironic and highly fragmented novel type of Thomas Mann, with its extremely refined narrative style, points in a different direction. The cultivation and refinement of traditional narrative procedures must have exerted enormous fascination on many writers living in an age in which old values were being destroyed. For this reason, aesthetic refinement and conscious social criticism often stood in a tense, problematic relationship to each other.

The novels of Hermann Broch (*Die Schlafwandler* – *The Sleepwalkers*, published 1931–2) and Robert Musil (*Der Mann ohne Eigenschaften* – *The Man Without Qualities*, published 1930–52) clearly reveal the limits of traditional narrative. Broch's novel is a large-scale attempt to depict the demise of German bourgeois society. The first book in the trilogy, *Pasenow oder die Romantik 1888* (*Pasenow or Romanticism 1888*), draws a picture of pre-war Germany in which the destruction of Humanist values is augured. The second book, *Esch oder die Anarchie 1903* (*Esch or Anarchy 1903*), depicts the unscrupulous seizure of power by the lower middle class, while the third book, *Hugenau oder die Sachlichkeit 1918* (*Hugenau or Realism 1918*) shows the final triumph of amorality and mediocrity over the old Humanist values. The decline of middle-class culture is commented on by essay-like digressions that punctuate the text. These express both the historical pessimism of the author, and his inability to grasp the driving forces behind social processes in an analytical way. The inserts tend to separate themselves from the body of the novel, interrupting the action. Broch thus heralds the passing of the epic form, a trend that is even more marked in the case of Musil. In *Der Mann ohne Eigenschaften* (*The Man Without Qualities*) the reflective, discursive element finally gains the upper hand over the narrative plot. The traditional novel form bursts its banks into a flood of reflections, comments, discourse and digressions. This makes a narrative conclusion to the work impossible. The novel, on which Musil worked for over twenty years, and only two volumes of which were published in his lifetime, therefore necessarily remains a fragment. Musil's theme is the identity crisis and loss of social orientation of the middle-class intellectual during the upheaval of the war and revolution.

Alienation

Musil himself saw the novel as a 'contemporary novel developed out of the past'. The middle-class individual perceives himself as alienated, and is no longer able to adopt the role and identity society expects of him. This brings in its wake a disintegration of identity, psychological deformation and loss of social competence. Musil sought to capture in the ironic formula of *The Man Without Qualities* an awareness of alienation in relation to society and his own subjectivity, which Musil saw as the effect of a highly organised society with a division of labour. Alienation was a principal experience of middle-class intellectuals at that time.

The problem of alienation also occupied a central position in the works of Franz Kafka, where it arguably also found its most convincing expression. Although most of Kafka's works were written either before or during the war (*Die Verwandlung* – *Metamorphosis; Das Urteil* – *The Judgement*, 1912; *Der Prozess* – *The Trial; In der Strafkolonie* – *In the Penal Colony*, 1914), his major works *Brief an den Vater* (*Letter to My Father*) and the novel *Das Schloss* (*The Castle*) were not written until 1919 and 1920 respectively. Kafka exerted only a modest influence after his early death in 1924, when his friend and executor, the writer Max Brod, published against Kafka's will the manuscripts that had been entrusted to him to be destroyed. It was not until World War II that Kafka began to make an impact on a wider readership with the publication in Germany of his collected works and letters (1950–). Kafka's work was then seen and reclaimed as a paraphrase of their own bleak post-war situation. Only a few of Kafka's prose pieces were ever published in his own lifetime, making him the private 'candidate for fame' of a small circle of literary connoisseurs. Alfred Döblin said of Kafka's texts that they were 'reports of total truth . . . , not at all as if invented, being blended together in a strange way, but ordered around a totally true and very real centre'. 'Some have said of Kafka's novels that they were written in the manner of dreams – and one can agree with that. But what is this manner of dreams? Their uncontrived, at all times highly illuminating, transparent course, our feeling and knowledge of the profound rightness of these things and the feeling that these things deeply concern us.' The sense of relevance evoked among Kafka's contemporaries and many of his readers in the years that followed is bound up with the manner in which Kafka poetically transforms apparently private experiences to make them generally visible. Kafka's conflict with his father, which made him incapable of leading the middle-class life envisaged by his parents and shaped both his psychological and social development, was a reaction to the authoritarianism that dominated the lower-middle-class nuclear family. Although Kafka suffered from this to an extreme degree, it was nevertheless both experienced and depicted in similar form by numerous other middle-class intellectuals, such as Heinrich

Mann in *Der Untertan*, Werfel in his story *Nicht der Mörder, der Ermordete ist schuldig* (*Not the Murderer, but the Murder Victim is Guilty*) (1920), Hasenclever in his *Sohn* (*Son*) (1913), von Unruh in his drama *Ein Geschlecht* (*A Race*) (1918) and Bronnen in *Vatermord* (*Patricide*) (1920).

In Expressionist father–son pieces, sons rebel against authoritarian fathers and wage war on the rigid traditions and anachronistic values and notions of middle-class family and sexual morality, which are usually explored with great pathos and the striking of pseudo-revolutionary attitudes. It is when set against these that the particular quality and achievement of Kafka becomes apparent. In contrast with the plays of Hasenclever, von Unruh and Bronnen, which focus on overtly middle-class taboos with an eye to effect and a spectacular violation of them, Kafka's texts represent a contribution towards understanding the generation conflict, highlighting its deforming consequences on the individual with the precision of a 'psychogram' and thereby rendering his line of analysis accessible to the reader.

The reality of dreams?

Just as Kafka's *Brief an den Vater* (1919) is an astonishing document of self-analysis in which the essential discoveries of Freud's psychoanalysis appear as if as a matter of course, so, too, his other texts are attempts to come to terms with and objectivise his experience of the authority conflict. Actual experiences are encoded in such a way that the texts themselves have the effect of 'hermetic records' (Adorno) that can only be deciphered with great effort and interpreted as what they are – the nightmares of a middle-class individual staging his own downfall in masochistic fashion. In *Der Prozess* (written 1914, published 1925), and the novel fragment *Das Schloss* (written 1922, published 1926), the deforming and injurious influence of the family seen, for example, in *Die Verwandlung* (*Metamorphosis*), in which the son becomes a species of vermin, is replaced by unknown laws or forces that reduce the individual to a mere object, ultimately destroying him both psychologically and physically. Here Kafka dealt not only with his own family experiences, but also with fear-generating social developments such as the increasing bureaucratisation of his time. In *Der Prozess* (*The Trial*), Josef K. suddenly finds himself being prosecuted and involved in a trial, with no knowledge either of the charges against him or the plaintiff. The trial itself takes place in secret, the court with jurisdiction over him remaining veiled in mysterious darkness. After a few feeble initial attempts to influence the course of events, Joseph K. resigns himself to his execution and offers no more resistance. The moral of the novel is contained in the doorkeeper legend related to Joseph K. by a priest, although Joseph K. fails to understand the lesson it contains: the trial being conducted against Joseph K. takes place within the individual, and its course can only be influenced by someone who has grasped this and learned how to free himself from his authoritarian fixation on external forces.

Similarly, the surveyor K. in *Das Schloss* feels that mysterious laws are at work against him whose violation is punished with the utmost severity by the castle bureaucracy. The attempt to lead a life of his own choosing and to create a modest degree of personal happiness fails. K. remains a foreign body within the village, wearing himself out in a protracted, dogged struggle against invisible, anonymous bureaucracy. The novel, which remains a fragment, was intended to end with the death of the utterly exhausted K.

All Kafka's works are marked by an impressively created sense of hopelessness and an absence of a more optimistic future. Nowhere is the individual able to escape the authoritarian and hierarchical structures of family and society, thereby overcoming the alienation from himself and others that these have caused. These qualities were particularly condemned by Marxist critics, as 'irrationalism' and 'decadence', so that for a long time Kafka's works were hardly published, let alone discussed in the socialist bloc. It was a Kafka conference in Liblice in 1963 that first heralded a change of attitude. Kafka's works were no longer seen and dismissed as 'irrational images of the world', but were found to contain a socially mediated psychic reality.

Hermann Hesse

The problem of alienation was an equally key issue in the writing of Hermann Hesse. Unlike Kafka, whose fame was slow to evolve, Hesse was soon a bestselling author, and has remained so to this day, apart from a few lapses. His work is particularly popular in modern Japan and the United States, where his sales have reached over eleven and eight million copies respectively. His *Siddharta* and *Steppenwolf* were hailed as prophetic books by the hippies of the 1970s.

Hesse's narrative works are admittedly a great deal more accessible than the 'hermetic records' of Kafka and also offer younger readers in particular greater opportunities for identification. Kafka had portrayed the problem of alienation through the coherent image of the metamorphosis of Gregor Samsa into a beetle in *Die Verwandlung* (*Metamorphosis*). Hesse deals with the same problem through a personality split into a human and beastly nature in the person of Harry Haller, who feels he is the Steppenwolf. Hesse thereby restricts the problem to the psychological level and stylises it into a metaphysical dualism between intellect and instinct. This perspective leaves social causes and structures almost entirely out of the picture. The roots of his inwardly torn state and melancholy lie, as Hesse has the fictitious publisher surmise, in the fact 'that he was brought up by loving, but strict and very pious parents and teachers according to a philosophy that made the "breaking of the will" the basis of education. . . . Instead of destroying his personality, it had only succeeded in teaching him to hate himself . . . , so that his entire life was an object lesson in how love for one's neighbour is impossible without the ability to love oneself'. Harry Haller's attempts to break out of the middle-class world and live out his 'wolfish nature' are no more than an illusory alternative, criticised by the author, to the hated middle-class world. Even in negation he remains captive to it and stamped by it. In contrast to *Steppenwolf*, in which Hesse directly treats the themes of the crippling and deformation of the individual and the decline of culture, he shifts to the Far East in *Siddharta* (1922), seeking to offer his readers assistance in coming to terms with life intellectually by means of Buddhist ideas.

Hesse proposes various solutions to these problems in his novels: a romantic anti-capitalism, a revival of classical middle-class culture to counter the modern, the retrieval of lost identity by means of inward-looking reflection (*Innerlichkeit*) and contemplation, changes and expansions of consciousness, eradication of the split personality by achieving a balance between sensuality and intellect in the human being, etc. All these nonetheless proved powerless to remove in any effective way the alienation that had come about, because they left the root causes of the problem quite untouched. In Hesse's work the problem of alienation appears first and foremost as an intellectual problem, limited moreover to intellectuals and creative artists. In reality, however, the problem pertained to the age as a whole, being one to which all sections of the population were exposed in one form or another and to a greater or lesser extent. In his novel *Berlin Alexanderplatz* (1929), for example, Alfred Döblin showed that alienation was a problem of the lower classes too, and that it had social and economic causes.

The hero of *Berlin Alexanderplatz*, Franz Biberkopf, is a one-time cement and transport worker who has gone off the rails. Following his release from jail, he resolves to go straight and to 'demand more from life than bread and butter'. However, he finds obstacles strewn in his path in this endeavour. He becomes embroiled in fresh crimes and is for a time placed in a mental institution. Finally discharged by court order, he looks for a fresh start – 'changed, battered, but nonetheless straightened out' by his ordeal. The fascination of Döblin's novel lies not so much in the plot itself, as in the innovative narrative style of montage technique with which Döblin, following the example of film, sought to capture the totality of the modern conurbation. He is not so much concerned with recreating the course of a personal destiny ('I am the enemy of the personal. There is nothing but false lyricism with it. Individual persons and their so-called destinies are unsuitable for the epic. Here they are the voice of the masses, which is the real and natural, and hence epic person'), as with presenting a totality in a way never previously attempted in the middle-class novel.

By means of association and montage, the insertion of documents such as songs, election campaign speeches, prison regulations, weather forecasts, advertisement texts, population statistics, and extracts from books, etc., he achieves a simultaneity and complexity that demanded of the reader the utmost in concentration and the ability to take an overall view.

The new technique of the novel

Döblin's new technique of the novel was variously received by his contemporaries. Communist authors belonging to the *Gruppe 25*, (the 25 Group), of which Döblin himself was a member, accused him of 'atomising' the plot. In Franz Biberkopf they saw only the 'battered self of a complex lower-middle-class man dressed up in proletarian guise'. Other critics accused him of 'chucking material around' (*Stoffhuberei*), and even of plagiarism. In fact, Döblin's montage and association technique had its precursors in Joyce's *Ulysses* (1922) and Dos Passos's *Manhattan Transfer* (1925). *Berlin Alexanderplatz* nonetheless remains an achievement in its own right, both as a creative appropriation of the narrative modes of non-German authors, and as an autonomous transfer of psychoanalytical procedures and film devices to the sphere of literature. Walter Benjamin was one of the few to appreciate Döblin's 'radical epic' achievement, seeing the novel as a creative progression of the middle-class novel. He did level some criticism at the plot, however: 'F.B.'s progress from pimp to petit bourgeois merely describes the heroic metamorphosis of bourgeois consciousness.'

The novel of documentary and reportage

Other authors in the Weimar Republic also experimented with the methods of montage, the use of documents and the adoption of reportage forms. Many authors felt that the traditional novel form was no longer a suitable vehicle for capturing the new reality in epic form, and no longer a match for the new media. The reportage form, developed into an art form by such writers as Egon Erwin Kisch, the 'raving reporter', was under these circumstances a source of enormous fascination to many authors, convinced they had found a directness and authenticity of experience and observation that traditional narrative forms could not provide. Out of a need 'to press close to reality' (Döblin), there soon arose a regular fashion for reportage and documentary style. For many authors the reportage or documentary novel was the only possible form for dealing with the burning issues of the day – war, revolution, technology, social injustice, militarisation and the growth of fascism, etc. Behind this conviction was the idea that the presentation of reality would have the greatest impact on a reader swamped with diverse stimuli. The documentary and reportage forms met the need for objectivity and realism that was now felt in reaction both to the excessive subjectivity of Expressionism and other varieties of 'contemplation', and to the politicisation of literature by working-class revolutionary authors that had come to be known as the *Neue Sachlichkeit*, the 'new objectivity'.

The 'new objectivity'

The 'new objectivity' that became intellectually modish between 1924 and 1933 offered authors shaken by the war and the post-war era a new ideological basis characterised by raising Americanism and technology to a fetish ('Technology is beautiful because it is real.... It embodies to a very high degree the style of our time, which is our lifestyle'). The enthusiasm for America, the 'land of unlimited opportunities', where the social issue seemed to have been solved and class conflicts reconciled, was an explicit counterposition to the enthusiasm for Russia that prevailed among many left-wing intellectuals.

As an expression of the new objectivity we may cite the industrial reportage work of Heinrich Hause (*Friede mit Maschinen* – Peace with Machines, 1928) and Erik Reger (*Union der festen Hand* – Union of the Firm Hand, 1930). While these texts purport to provide an exposition of the production sphere, they in fact treat technology as myth, in stark contrast with the 'realistic' claims of their authors. Their stance of objectivity and non-partisanship ('Nothing has been written about that has not been seen or experienced. These records are apolitical'; Hauser) proved as empty as the view that reportage penetrated and analysed reality like an X-ray film. Powerful analysis was the one thing critics found lacking in the reportage and documentary novels of the 'new objectivity'. Siegfried Kracauer, for example, who took issue with the ideological assumptions behind reportage, doubted the analytical capacity of the new genre: 'A hundred reports from a factory add nothing to the value of that factory, but remain for all eternity a hundred views on the factory. Reality is a construction.' Béla Balázs similarly took to task the superficial notion of reality among authors of the new objectivity: 'For the facts in themselves will not produce reality. Reality resides in the meaning of the facts, which need to be interpreted.'

As a 'strategy for circumventing the political state of affairs' (Benjamin) the 'new objectivity' reportage novel avoided taking sides in the way that working-class revolutionary authors did in their reportage novels, seeking instead a noncommittal approach. The struggle against poverty and destitution, Benjamin asserted, was degraded into an object for consumption. Objectively speaking it served only to amuse and divert the reader. Through its denial of social conflicts and its refusal to take sides, the 'new objectivity' created a vacuum into which fascism could then step, with its revival of ostensibly lost 'values' such as the homeland, the people and the nation, etc.

Erich Kästner, Hans Fallada

The novels of Kästner and Fallada, which became bestsellers in the last years of the Weimar Republic, were more influenced by the ideological positions of the 'new objectivity' than its formal concepts. *Fabian* (1931) by Erich Kästner is a novel about the impossibility of moral existence in declining bourgeois industrial society. Fabian is an intellectual who belongs to no political group and is not committed to any, being equally critical of all and suspicious of their ideologies. This makes him the epitome of the 'new objectivity' type of noncommittal intellectual. He distances himself from all forms of social involvement in order to preserve his 'purity'. The moment he jumps into the water in an attempt to save a child from drowning, the first time in his life he has done anything useful, he is unable to keep his head above water: 'The small boy swam crying to the bank. Fabian drowned. Unfortunately he could not swim.' The underlying mood of the novel is one of a 'left-wing melancholy' (Benjamin) that often spills over into sentimentality and lacks any critical capacity.

The same is true of Hans Fallada's novel *Kleiner Mann, was nun?* (*What Now, Little Man?*) (1932), which describes how a white-collar worker becomes a member of the working class during the international economic crisis. The worker, Johannes Pinneberg, reacts to this class demotion with fear and dismay. Unable to find a sense of solidarity with his fellow sufferers, he finds a degree of compensation only in the love of his wife and his family life. Social problems are in this way made private.

Topicality and relevance to the times were characteristic of all 'new objectivity' novels. The problem was that they could hardly be worthwhile for the reader, since in the case of Kästner and Fallada these attributes were combined with a refusal to become involved, with melancholy and a retreat into the private sphere, whereas in the case of Hauser and Reger they led to the raising of technology and management to fetishes, which allowed equally few prospects for change.

The war novel was the most prevalent form of contemporary novel in the Weimar Republic, and the one with the greatest impact on the masses. Remarque's *Im Westen Nichts Neues* (*All Quiet on the Western Front*) (1929) was published in eight million copies and translated into thirty languages. Other forms of the contemporary novel, such as the provincial novel (*Provinzroman*), had little chance in the face of such competition.

Among the best-known exponents of provincial literature was Oskar Maria Graf, who treated the designation as a title of honour, having his visiting cards printed with the words 'Oskar Maria Graf, provincial writer. Speciality – rural affairs.' Critical analysis of the provinces was an adjunct to the literary treatment of major conurbations, such as Döblin's *Berlin Alexanderplatz*. The provincial literature of Graf, Feuchtwanger or Fleisser was worlds apart from the *Heimatliteratur* of such authors as Rosegger, Ganghofer or Löns, or the glorification of the rural idyll propounded by the 'blood and soil' literature of conservative and pre-fascist authors.

Lion Feuchtwanger

In his novel *Erfolg* (*Success*) (1930), for example, which formed part of the *Wartesaal* (*Waiting-Room*) trilogy with the novels *Die Geschwister Oppenheim* (*The Oppenheims*) (1933) and *Exil* (1940), both written in exile, Feuchtwanger depicts 'three years in the history of a province'. The book draws a highly critical picture of the 'mores and customs of the Old Bavarian people' during the crisis years of 1921–4 in Munich. The theme of the novel is the political 'success' of the National Socialists, made possible through secret backing by a number of major industrialists and mass support from the lower middle class. A political law case reveals the corruption in judicial, political and economic life. This is attributed by Feuchtwanger to specifically Bavarian conditions, but in fact had a more general application, as the course of history subsequently showed.

The growth of fascist tendencies in the provinces is also dealt with in the works of Marieluise Fleisser, whose novel *Mehlreisende Frieda Geyer* (*Frieda Geyer the Travelling Flour Rep.*) (1931) and volume of stories *Echt Ingolstädter Originalnovellen* (*Genuine Original Novellas of Ingolstadt*) (1929) have remained, like her dramas, relatively unknown. Fleisser recreates the staleness, narrowness and constraints of the provinces using her home town Ingolstadt as an example. With great penetration she reveals the deformation of its inhabitants wrought by repressive provincial life. Fleisser's work shows, as Benjamin emphasised in praise of her, 'that one can have experiences in the provinces that are on a par with the large-scale life of the metropolis'.

Oskar Maria Graf

Oskar Maria Graf's novels and stories differ from the satirical novels of Feuchtwanger and Fleisser in their lively, popular-realistic narrative style. His narrative practice closely resembled Brecht's idea of popularity (*Volkstümlichkeit*) and realism, although his works lack the militant character that Brecht looked for. Graf was a popular writer who saw himself as a committed, socially critical author: 'My interest as a writer in the farm-worker was and is always to depict him as a man like any other, who simply happens to have been born into rural life. Aside from the kind of existence forced on him by his environment, he is just the same dubious poor wretch as the rest of us, driven by profit and instinct.' Graf's realism, evinced in his *Chronik von Flechting* (*The Chronicle of Flechting*) (1925), *Kalendargeschichten* (*Calendar Stories*) (1929), and *Bolwieser* (1931) was based on experiences that turned Graf himself into a social climber, as he claims in his autobiography *Wir sind Gefangene* (*We Are Prisoners*) (1927). After a period of Bohemian political activity in the early years of the Republic, when he vacillated between actionists, anarchists, socialists and spartacists, also sympathising with the Munich *Räterepublik*, he arrived in the later years of the Republic at a consistent socialist stance which was to form the basis of his distinctive popular writing style. In exile he developed into a major anti-fascist writer, whose novels *Der Abgrund* (*The Abyss*) (1937) and *Anton Sittinger* (1937) are among the most penetrating literary analyses of the relationship between the lower middle class and fascism.

Drama – *Zeitstück* (the contemporary play), *Volksstück* (the popular play) and *Lehrstück* (the didactic play)

In drama, too, contemporary criticism became sharper. In the first years of the Weimar Republic, war and above all revolution were the dominant themes in drama. In particular, those authors influenced by Expressionism, such as Toller, Mühsam, Kaiser, Hasenclever, Wolf, Rubiner and Feuchtwanger, dealt in their dramas with the experiences of the November Revolution, earnestly taking up issues such as the use of force in revolution, the relationship between leaders and the nation, and how to define the position of the poet-writer during a time of revolution. During the War there had been the first organisational contacts among writers seeking a link between political and literary practice along the lines indicated by Heinrich Mann in his pioneering essay *Geist und Tat* (*Mind and Deed*) (1916).

The Rat Geistiger Arbeiter (Council of Intellectual Workers)

The founding of the Council of Intellectual Workers (1918), with the support of such prestigious authors as Heinrich Mann, Rainer Maria Rilke and Robert Musil, was a short-lived effort to create a link between poets and writers and the revolutionary working class. The idea of the poet-writer as a leader of the revolutionary working class is most clearly expressed in Gustav Landauer's *Ansprache an die Dichter* (*Address to Poets*) (1918):

> The poet is the lead-singer in the choir, but also – like the solo tenor who in Beethoven's Ninth stubbornly insists on rising and singing his own way above the unified singing of the mass of the choir – gloriously isolated, asserting himself against the crowd. He is the

eternal rebel. In times of revolution he can be the foremost rebel, so much so that he is the first to press again for conservation, both of what has been newly achieved and of that which eternally remains. . . . Philistines and wizened systematicians dream the unutterably dreary dream of introducing a patent socialism which, with its established mechanisms and methods will, they say, once and for all do away with and – we may be permitted here the *mot* of the democratic bureaucrat – render impossible all injustice and social wrongs. What we need in truth, however, is a constant process of renewal, the willingness to be jolted out of our complacency . . . we need spring, delusion, intoxication and madness, we need – again and again and again – revolution, we need the poet.

Landauer stood by this position in practice as well as theory, embodying it in his person and paying for it with his life. In May 1919 he was executed without trial for his activities within the Munich *Räterepublik*.

This close link between politics and literature is also found in Toller and Mühsam who, like Landauer, were also active in the Munich *Räterepublik*. Toller was Chairman of the Bavarian Council of Workers and Soldiers, as well as Chairman of the Independent Social Democrats in Munich. As a member of the *Räte* government and one of its military leaders, he was sentenced like Erich Mühsam to five years confinement in a fortress. It was during this time that the dramas *Masse Mensch* (*Masses and Man*), *Die Maschinenstürmer* (*The Machine Wreckers*) and *Hinkemann* were written, which were so successful in the Weimar Republic.

Politics and literature

In *Masse Mensch* (1919), dedicated to the working class, Toller depicts the relationship between the poet and the working class as a conflict between the intellectual revolutionary, who is committed to non-violence, and the masses, who press for the use of revolutionary force. These ideas make him akin to Friedrich Wolf (*Der Unbedingt* – *The One Who is Wholly Committed*, 1919), Ludwig Rubiner (*Die Gewaltlosen* – *The Non-violent*, 1919), Erich Mühsam (*Judas*, 1920), Walter Hasenclever (*Die Entscheidung* – *The Decision*, 1919) and Lion Feuchtwanger (*Thomas Wendt*, 1919), who also deal with the problems of being a revolutionary intellectual. The central character of Wolf's drama is a 'whole-hearted' (*unbedingte*) young poet, who wants to convert the masses to his ideal of the simple, anti-capitalist life. At first the masses follow him, but later, misled by opposing influences, they turn against the 'whole-hearted' poet. The poet is only able to convince the masses of the sincerity of his motives through his own sacrificial death. Likewise in Rubiner's play the people are only won over to the ideal of non-violence by the sacrificial death of the *Gewaltlosen*, the non-violent ones. In *Judas*, Mühsam dealt with his experiences in the November Revolution, and in particular the struggles surrounding the Munich *Räterepublik* in which he himself was deeply involved. In Hasenclever's drama *Die Entscheidung*, the poet is unable to find a place in the republic. Condemned to death by the former government for his anti-war poetry, he is freed by the revolution, but is unable to join it because he disagrees with the revolution and the republic. Seeing no role for himself in society, he wants to commit suicide, but is in fact hit by a stray bullet.

The poet and the masses

In Feuchtwanger's drama *Thomas Wendt*, originally entitled *1918* – the poet-hero becomes a popular leader during the revolution – the poet is caught in the antagonistic relationship between the working and middle classes. His abstract Humanism proves useless in these concrete circumstances. Feuchtwanger's résumé at the end of the drama, in which he states that intellectuals have 'bungled the revolution', indicates not only his criticism of the role of intellectuals in the revolution, but also his disappointment at the failed attempt by left-wing Expressionist authors to build a bridge between politics and literature.

Georg Kaiser, whose drama *Von morgens bis mitternachts* (*From Morning to Midnight*) (1916) made him famous even during the war, combines problems concerning revolution and intellectuals with the typically Expressionist themes of father–son conflict, hostility to technology and criticism of capitalism. In *Gas* (written 1917–18), a sequel to his drama *Koralle* (*Coral*) (1917), the son of a millionaire rebels against his father. He breaks off contact with his own class and takes sides with the workers, trying to change them into 'new men' in line with his vision. He gives the workers a share of the profits, improves working conditions and gives the workers the feeling that they are producing for themselves. The socialist experiment fails, however, when the factory is destroyed by a huge gas explosion caused by the feverish increase in production. Thousands of workers are killed. Because another catastrophe could occur at any time, the son does not want to reconstruct the works, and intends to resettle his workers in land communes. Besotted with technology, however, the workers refuse to go along with his plans. Together with government representatives they remove the son of the millionaire, rebuild the factory and set the dangerous gas production going again. The introduction of socialism by a far-sighted capitalist fails through the lack of far-sightedness of the workers and the interests of the ruling class. The sequel, *Gas II* (1919), shows the rule of unfettered, inhuman technology. By now the workers have become totally depersonalised beings ruled by outside forces, 'blue figures' and 'yellow figures' moving around and performing their tasks like robots. The millionaire's son with his Humanist ideals occupies a position that has been lost.

Expressionist Menschheitsdrama ('human drama')

Kaiser's dramas clearly reveal the limitations and problems of post-war Expressionism. Abstract Humanism, the pathos-ridden ideal of the 'new man' and the 'new life', the demonisation and rejection of technological progress, the rigid separation of the 'individual' from the 'masses', and deep suspicion towards both middle and working classes alike had inhibiting effects on the artistic and political development of authors, as well as preventing them from analysing contemporary problems effectively: 'Expressionism, which greatly enriched the expressive resources of the theatre, bringing forth a hitherto untapped aesthetic yield, proved quite incapable of explaining the world as an object of human practice' (Brecht).

Authors who did not want to founder either in their claims to social criticism or their hopes for effective political action were thus faced with the historical necessity of turning away from Expressionist human drama. The pathos-ridden Expressionist drama of the revolutionary transition phase thus gave way in the relative stability of the Weimar Republic to a new form, the *Zeitstück* or contemporary play. In line with developments in novel-writing, this form similarly made use of reportage and documentary techniques.

Something of a forerunner of the documentary play was Karl Kraus's satirical anti-war drama *Die letzten Tage der Menschheit* (*The Last Days of the Human Race*) (first version 1918–19, first published as a supplement in the journal *Die Fackel – The Torch*, then in book form in 1922). The play's 220 scenes anticipate later forms of documentary theatre, revealing how stupidity, malice, brutality, unscrupulousness and careerism prevail over human attributes in war. The more than thousand protagonists in the drama include numerous figures from contemporary history, as well as types and fictitious characters. The writer, embodied in the character of the 'grumbler' (*Nörgler*), a self-portrait of Kraus, is powerless in face of the overwhelming stupidity and baseness of the times. The central theme of this monumental drama, intended solely for reading, is criticism of the press, a focus which also set its stamp on *Die Fackel* (1899–1936), the journal of which Kraus was editor. In this journal, the costs of which were borne almost entirely by Kraus alone, social criticism was presented primarily in the form of criticism of the press. An 'anti-newspaper' journal, the aim of *Die Fackel* was to expose the untruthfulness, empty clichés and corruption of the bourgeois press. Both in *Die Fackel* and in his dramas, Kraus's satirical method consists of taking a cliché at face value and exposing and making a nonsense of it using brief commentary, headlines, exclamation or question marks, ingenious montage, or bald quotation. For

Kraus, the cliché was not merely a symbol, but the cause of the contamination of the political and cultural life of his day.

Critique of technology, and the cult of technology

Plays dealing with technology and technological progress posed even more complex problems than the numerous *Justizdramen*, dramas on questions of justice. In contrast to the hostility to technology found in Expressionist dramas, where technology was for the most part presented as a 'Moloch' (see, for example, Kaiser's *Gas*), in *Zeitstücke* as in 'new objectivity' novels (Hauser, Reger), here technology was raised to a fetish. In Max Brand's play *Maschinist Hopkins* (*Hopkins the Machinist*) (1929), for example, productivity, objectivised in the form of machines, is made into an expression of progress, with technology appearing as fate. Hopkins represents not the interests of the workers, but the 'spirit' of work when justifying pay rises and strike slogans to his employers: 'I serve the machine alone. In it resides the spirit I must follow.' In a manner similar to the New Materialist industrial novel, the technology cult and Americanism are blended into an ideology of progress that sweeps aside traditional middle-class values and skates over existing social conflicts. These technology plays evoke an image of a 'new society' in which former social structures are retained side by side with utilisation of new production methods (the conveyor-belt and piece-work wages). Technology is made to appear as an instrument of liberation, and America is put forward as the model of a new and better lifestyle. The illusion of a 'material' solution to all social conflicts in a rationalised, industrialised society of the future is only one aspect of a comprehensive ideology of the 'material state' in which all problems can be solved by appropriately qualified experts, serving as an imaginary counterimage to the true condition of the Weimar Republic, torn apart by class conflict.

It is only a small step from the raising of technology to a fetish in contemporary dramas influenced by 'new objectivity' ideology to the mystification of technology by pre-fascist authors. The inhuman character of the technology cult became immense wherever it was combined with a glorification of war: 'Today we write poems of steel, and we struggle for power in battles in which the action interlocks with the precision of machines. There is a beauty here that we are able to appreciate in these battles on land, at sea and in the air, in which the scorching will of the blood is harnessed and expressed through the dominance of the technological wonders of power' (Ernst Jünger). In the drama *Flieger* (*Airmen*) (1932) by Hermann Reissmann, the new weapons technology of World War I becomes the basis for a new heroism, and the starting-point for a new spirit of cooperation. Airmen are seen as a homogeneous international community, bound together by the machinery of war. Technology opens the way for a new kind of heroism that was to be amplified into a national myth by Erwin Guido Kolbenheyer in his dramas *Die Brücke* (*The Bridge*) (1929) and *Jagt ihn, ein Mensch* (*Hunt Him, A Man*) (1932). We see here the forerunners of 'steely Romanticism' (Joseph Goebbels) and the 'heroic objectivity' (*heroische Sachlichkeit*) (Alfred Rosenberg) that were to become integral to the official ideological agenda after 1933.

Ödön von Horváth

The *Volksstück*, or popular folk play, was a countertype to the New Materialist *Zeitstück* in the Weimar Republic. The dramatic equivalent of the provincial novel, it deliberately departed from contemporary literary fashions, drawing instead from the nineteenth-century *Volksstück* tradition, and developing a new form of social criticism through a process of coming to terms with it. In his plays written in the Weimar Republic, therefore (*Italienische Nacht* – *Italian Night*, 1931; *Geschichten aus dem Wiener Wald* – *Tales from the Vienna Woods*, 1931 and *Kasimir und Karoline*, 1932), Ödön von Horváth drew on this tradition in order to modify it to meet the needs of his time: 'I would therefore like to continue the *Volksstück* today, naturally taking modern persons from among the people, and what is more from the leading, typical sections of the people today, bringing them on to the stage.'

The chronicler of the lower middle class

Horváth, who enjoyed something of a renaissance in the sixties as the dramatic antithesis of Brecht, departed from the typical nineteenth-century *Volksstück* depiction of farmworkers and a rural milieu such as still persisted with minor modifications in the folk play *Der fröhliche Weinberg* (*The Jolly Vineyard*) (1925) by Carl Zuckmayer. He turned instead to portraying the lower middle class: 'Now, however, ninety per cent of Germany, like all the other European states, consists of a fully-fledged or would-be lower middle class, but at all events a lower middle class. If, therefore, I wish to portray the people, I naturally cannot portray the ten per cent, but must as a true chronicler of my age [portray] the mass.'

This shift had far-reaching consequences above all on the language of his plays. In Horváth's plays, the characters do not speak in dialect, as in the earlier folk play, but in the new 'jargon of education': 'The lower middle class has brought about a disintegration of dialects as such through the jargon of education. In order to portray modern people realistically, I must make them speak the jargon of education.' This jargon was a style of speech used by the lower middle class to disavow its true social situation in an attempt to participate in the middle-class life of which they had *de facto* long ceased to be a part. It is thus an expression of their false consciousness, and prevents language from becoming a means of communication. Horváth uses the jargon with the explicit aim of exposing the speciousness of the middle-class mentality and the attitudes of the demoted lower middle class.

Criticism of the mythological category of the Volk

All Horváth's folk plays are concerned with presenting in dramatic form the gulf between socio-economic position and the false consciousness that unmasks itself in the 'jargon of education'. *Geschichten aus dem Wiener Wald* (*Tales from the Vienna Woods*) shows a middle-class nuclear family threatened with a lowering of its social status. The patriarchal, repressive structures that persisted largely at the expense of women are cloaked in sentimental and moral clichés through which brutal self-interest repeatedly breaks out against the will of the speaker. When the father pursues the engagement of his daughter, for example, with the words: 'This engagement must not fold, not even for moral reasons', he unwittingly betrays by the word 'even' that his economic motives are paramount. In the *Italienische Nacht* (*Italian Night*) Horváth depicts the political problems posed by the lower-middle-class mentality. While the lower-middle-class, for the most part solidly respectable social democrats prepare for a rally of the Association for the Protection of the Republic, the fascists are organising their 'German Day', demonstrating a militant nationalism the danger of which the lower middle class fails to perceive. Provincial narrow-mindedness and political apathy are concealed behind their talk of freedom and democracy, which has long been reduced to mere clichés. In this play (*The Italian Night*) Horváth succeeded in revealing this inherent menace, and in revealing the points of contact available to the fascists in the lower middle class. Since, however, his criticism is directed at all political groupings across the board, the play lacks a political counterforce to act as a check on the fascists. This made Horváth's play a warning that no-one could take up.

Marieluise Fleisser

Criticism of the lower middle class even more searing than Horváth's is found in the folk plays of Marieluise Fleisser. Her dramas *Fegefeuer in Ingolstadt* (*Purgatory in Ingolstadt*) (1924) and *Pioniere in Ingolstadt* (*Pioneers in Ingolstadt*) (1928) depict in all their brutality the constraints and repression of the provinces that led to a stifling staleness. Instead of Horváth's jargon of education, her characters articulate their deformed nature without disguise. This exposes the determining social factors behind it, since the behaviour of the characters derives from their specific social condition. The depersonalisation of the characters is the dramaturgical consequence of the process whereby the individual's personality is destroyed by exploitation, proletarianisation, a state of dependence and subordination. As a result, sexuality is depicted by Marieluise Fleisser not as a form of human communication, but as an instrument of repression, expressing the alienation of the human being both from himself and others.

The high esteem in which Brecht and Benjamin held Fleisser's plays (*Pioneers* was written at Brecht's instigation and performed for the first time under his direction in Berlin in 1929) derives from her realistic approach, in which the presentation of reality is combined with social criticism in a way that was innovative and pioneering for the traditional folk play.

Brecht

Despite the high esteem in which Brecht held the plays of Marieluise Fleisser, however, his own dramatic work in the Weimar Republic did not follow in the *Volksstück* tradition. It was not until his exile that he wrote the folk play *Herr Puntila und sein Knecht Matti* (*Mr Puntila and his servant Matti*) (1940). Brecht likewise rejected the contemporary play (*Zeitstück*) as a dramatic form. Both seemed to him different forms of a show theatre (*Schautheater*) that could not have a mobilising effect on the spectator. There were even aspects of the political theatre developed by Piscator, for all the high estimation in which Brecht held it, which prevented him from using it as a model. Brecht's chief criticism of Piscator was his strong proclivity for things technical, and his employment of new media and technology, arising out of dependence on the bourgeois theatre business:

> Since I am of the opinion that they are in possession of a machine which in reality is in possession of them, they are defending a machine over which they no longer have any control, which is no longer, as they persist in believing, a device for the producers, but has become a device against the producers, in other words against their own production staff (specifically where producers pursue new directions of their own which do not fit in with the machine, or are even opposed to it).

Brecht learned first and foremost from the working-class revolutionary *Agitprop* Theatre, which he felt embodied a didactic theatre that broke with the traditional artistic character of the bourgeois theatre, used amateurs instead of professional actors and was inclined to remove the barrier between performer and spectator.

478

Lehrstück: the didactic play

Brecht's recourse to the didactic play coincides with the period in which he took up the cause of the working class and accepted Marxism as the philosophical foundation for his future creative work. In his early plays, still influenced by Expressionism (*Baal*, 1918; *Trommeln in der Nacht* – *Drums in the Night*, 1920; *Im Dickicht der Städte* – *In the Jungle of the Cities*, 1921; *Aufstieg und Fall der Stadt Mahagonny* – *The Rise and Fall of the City of Mahogany*, 1928–9) he had by his own admission been mainly concerned with a 'nihilistic criticism of bourgeois society'. He now sought to put his socio-political insights to productive use. The starting-point of his didactic play theory, put into practice in the plays *Ozeanflug* (*Ocean Flight*) (1929), *Badener Lehrstück vom Einverständnis* (*The Baden Didactic Play on Consent*) (1929), *Der Jasager* (*The Yes-Man*) and *Der Neinsager* (*The No-Man*) (1929–30), *Die Massnahme* (*The Measures Taken*) (1930) and *Die Ausnahme und Die Regel* (*The Exception and the Rule*) (1930), is the assumption 'that the player, by carrying out particular modes of conduct, adopting certain attitudes, reproducing certain speeches and so on, can be socially influenced'. 'The *Lehrstück* or didactic play instructs by being performed, not by being seen. In principle no spectator is necessary for a didactic play, although he can be utilised as well.' Theatre-acting thus becomes a learning process characterised by 'imitation' and 'criticism'. The player has not only simply to reproduce the given patterns in the play, but also to criticise them. This can even give rise to a complete negation of the given patterns and the conception of new texts. The use of equipment such as radio or film in the performance of a didactic play differs fundamentally from the use of new media in either the traditional theatre or on the Piscator Stage. It serves not to create an entertainment-oriented theatre of illusion or to perfect a politically didactic theatre, but is part of a 'sociological experiment' being carried out through the performance of the didactic play. Radio and film enable the play to be objectivised. Whenever required, the players can technically reproduce their play, monitoring both it and themselves. They acquire a distance from themselves and from what they are performing, and are thereby stimulated to reflect on the new media and their creative use. Similarly, they realise that when they attempt to organise technical equipment for the purposes of their work with the didactic play, they come into conflict with social and economic commercialisation interests. In this way, rehearsal of the didactic play provides the player with direct social insights that are not merely mediated by the communally performed play.

Besides didactic plays (*Die Rundköpfe und die Spitzköpfe* – *The Round-heads and the Pointedheads*; *Die Horatier und die Kuratier* – *Horatii and Curatii*) and drafts for further didactic plays that were either written or prepared during Brecht's period of exile, he also wrote other plays. *Der*

Dreigroschenoper (*The Threepenny Opera*) (1928), *Die heilige Johanna der Schlachthöfe* (*St Joan of the Stockyards*) (1929–30) and *Die Mutter* (*The Mother*) (1930) were conceived in Brecht's words partly 'in the style of the didactic plays ... but requiring [professional] actors'. The didactic play and the show play (*Schaustück*) were two divergent forms of epic theatre that Brecht combined during his exile to produce the didactic political theatre.

Between artistry and political commitment – lyric poetry

In lyric poetry the old contradiction between so-called 'pure' and 'political' poetry gained renewed urgency in an age shaped by war, revolution and intensified class conflict. It soon became apparent that Expressionism, with its lavish stylistic gestures and its 'Man, world, brother, God' emotionalism was no basis for further literary work. Kurt Pinthus's volume of poetry *Menschheitsdämmerung* (*Twilight of Humanity*) and Ludwig Rubiner's volume *Kameraden der Menschheit* (*Friends of Humanity*), both published in 1919, document the Expressionist crisis of disintegration. Pinthus's now famous anthology is a showcase of Expressionist lyric verse. Pinthus saw the actual 'supra-political significance' of Expressionist poetry in the fact 'that with glowing finger and stirring voice it pointed to man himself again and again, recreating in the sphere of the mind the lost connection of men with one another and to one another, the link between the individual and the infinite, and encouraging it to come into effect'. The volume comprises poems by twenty-three authors, including Becher, Benn, Hasenclever, Heym, Lasker-Schüler, Lichtenstein, Stadler, Stramm, Trakl, Werfel and Zech, under the headings *Sturz und Schrei* (*Fall and Cry*), *Erweckung des Herzens* (*Awakening of the Heart*), *Aufruhr und Empörung* (*Rebellion and Revolt*), and *Liebe den Menschen* (*Love for Mankind*). The very fact that many of the authors presented in the *Twilight of Mankind* were no longer alive at the time of publication (Heym, Stadler, Trakl, Stramm and Lichtenstein all died either before or during the war), is itself an indication that Pinthus's volume was not a document of a living movement, but more an echo of one.

In contrast to Pinthus, Rubiner presented Expressionism as a militant movement, selecting supporters of the movement's left-wing activist wing and poems 'which confess the poet's struggle against an old world and his march into the fresh human territory of social revolution'. War and revolution are central themes in the volume: 'And here the poet was finally on the side of the working class: the working class liberates the world from the economic past of capitalism; the poet liberates it from the emotional past of capitalism. Friends of humanity raise the call to world revolution.' Statements of this kind voiced more the wishful thinking of the editor than reality. With only few exceptions (e.g. Hasenclever's *Die Mörder sitzen in der Oper – The Murderers are at the Opera*) the poems are trapped within their sense of human pathos and the hope of brotherhood. The 'power of the spirit' as set against the 'fury of the hangman' (Becher) is an illusory contrast. The call to revolution was meant as a call for the soul to revolt (see Werfel's *Revolutionsaufruf – Call to Revolution*). Both Rubiner's and Pinthus's volumes demonstrate that Expressionism as a literary movement was not able to cope with the new experiences of the age.

Benn and Becher as antitheses

Two of the leading Expressionist authors, Gottfried Benn and Johannes R. Becher, disengaged themselves early on from their Expressionist beginnings, becoming bitter literary and political opponents. They had been harmoniously included together in Pinthus's volume, although Benn was absent from Rubiner's. The courses taken by these two authors during the Weimar Republic were so diametrically different that during the period of exile they inspired a comprehensive debate on how to assess Expressionism. Becher joined the Communist Party, while Benn was for a time a sympathiser with the fascists. They set out their divergent standpoints in a 1931 radio dialogue on the relationship between poetry and politics. Opposing Becher, Benn insisted that political tendency was not poetic tendency, but one relating to class struggle: 'If it seeks to express itself in poetic form that is either coincidence or private fancy.' Benn categorically refused to involve himself politically through his writing. As he stated in his essay 'Können Dichter die Welt verändern?' 'Can Poets Change the World?' (1931), he could discern neither development nor sense in history:

There have always been social movements. The poor always wanted to rise, and the rich never wanted to sink. A horrendous world, a capitalist world, since Egypt first monopolised the incense trade and Babylonian bankers began money transactions... , a horrendous world, a capitalist world, and always there were countermovements. There were the hordes of helots in the Cyrenian tanneries, the slave wars in Roman times, the poor wanted to rise and the rich did not want to sink, horrendous world, but after three thousand years of this process, the thought might occur to one that all this is neither good nor evil, but purely phenomenal.

In Benn's view, the poetic form alone was capable of harnessing this chaos and giving meaning to the meaningless. The poem *Leben – niederer Wahn* (*Life, Base Delusion*) contains Benn's creed with regard to form: 'Form alone is faith and deed, / The first touched by hands, / But then snatched from the hands / Statues conceal the seed.'

Montage is a principle used throughout in Benn's lyric, in which elements of reality, often only key or emotive words, are juxtaposed as adjuncts or

contrasts, so that reality appears 'purely phenomenal'. The montage principle adhered to in this way, however, ultimately proves to be no more
than the consistent expression of a reality that has not been grasped.

J.R. Becher

Benn had espoused formalism with an aristocratic mien and a self-imposed
artistic exile from the political conflicts and social realities of his day ('He
who is alone also retains mystery'). Becher, however, was distinguished
from him by his clear avowal of political poetry in support of the revolutionary workers' movement:

> In my poetry I follow that tendency which in my view all poetry
> today must possess that makes any claim to be a living poetry – that
> is a poetry rooted in the decisive forces of our time, and which is
> capable of creating a true and self-contained picture of the world. In
> my writings I serve solely and exclusively that historical movement
> on which the fate of all mankind depends for forging a path into the
> future. As a poet I also serve the liberation struggle of the proletariat.

Becher endeavoured to put this ambitious agenda into poetic practice.
In his poetry volumes *Die hungrige Stadt* (*The Hungry City*) (1927–8),
Im Schatten der Berge (*In the Shadow of the Mountains*) (1928), *Graue
Kolonnen* (*Grey Columns*) (1930) and *Der Mann, der in der Reihe geht*
(*The Man Who Walks in Line*) (1932), he dealt with the current issues of his
day. World war, revolution, street and barricade fighting, unemployment,
rationalisation, the destitution of the working class, organisation of the
workers and so on are the themes of his poems. In his lengthy verse epic
Der grosse Plan (*The Great Plan*) (1931), he hailed the first Five Year Plan
of the Soviet Union as the 'beginning of a new age', in the tradition of
famous classical epics. Minor lyric forms such as the ballad and chronicle,
however, were the real mainstay of his work, being best suited to his idea
of *Volkstümlichkeit* (popularity).

Erich Weinert

In reality, however, Becher's poetry was a great deal less 'popular' than
that of Erich Weinert, who made political lyric verse, as Becher himself
ungrudgingly acknowledged, 'accessible to meetings, and hence accessible
to society in a new way': 'His poems, recited at meetings, appeared concurrently with political speeches, competing with and complementing them in
the most effective possible way from the poetic viewpoint. In this way,
not only were the poems of Erich Weinert heard by hundreds of thousands
of people, but poetry itself became the property of the people again.'
Weinert, whose background was in political cabaret, was the true represen-

tative of the popular political lyric in the Weimar Republic. As cabaret artist, reciter at party political events, collaborator on the *Revue Roter Rummel* (*The Red Racket Revue*), and declaimer of his own poetry at the legendary 'Weinert Evenings' that were banned in 1931, he achieved a degree of popularity that was denied to Becher. Weinert drew on the poetry of the *Vormärz* era (Heine, Herwegh, Weerth), creatively combining different traditions, such as cabaret lyrics, street songs (*Bänkelsang*), folk song (*Volkslied*), militant workers' songs and ballads. In this way he created a form of satirical poetry that he himself said was 'folk poetry in terms of its origin' (*Politische Satire*, 1926). This popular folk quality was the reason Weinert exerted such a huge fascination on his contemporaries. Poems such as *Sozialdemokratisches Mailiedchen* (*A Social Democratic May Day Ditty*); *Denke Daran, Prolet* (*Think of It, Working Man*); *Der rote Feuerwehrmann* (*The Red Fireman*), or *Wie hetze ich erfolgreich* (*How Can I Stir Up Trouble Successfully*) document a militant applied lyric poetry (*Gebrauchslyrik*) that took the part of the politically oppressed and socially disadvantaged masses. Weinert, who later in exile was involved as a lyric poet in the Spanish civil war, also supporting the Red Army with pamphlet poetry in its struggle against Nazi Germany, laid no claims to 'art' in the traditional sense. It was enough for him if his poems

> enlightened, convinced and gave direction to the vacillating. If when recited they met with the clamorous assent: Yes, that's it! Quite right!, then they had fulfilled their political mission. Not infrequently I recited a poem only once or twice before what motivated it was overshadowed by subsequent events. Had I been able to allow everything I wrote and recited to mature at the necessary leisure for it to stand up to the [scrutiny of] 'academics' like decorative crystal, I would have deprived myself of a thousand up-to-the-minute, direct effects. And it was these effects I was aiming for, far more than presenting my hearers with works of art.

Two other authors influenced by political cabaret, which was enjoying a boom in the Weimar Republic, were Kästner and Tucholsky. Weinert's 'tribune lyrics' were brought to life mainly by recitation; many of his poems were set to music by Eisler and sung by Ernst Busch. They thus acquired their function in the political context of a particular event. Kästner and Tucholsky, on the other hand, developed a form of social satire that was directed first and foremost at the reader. In Kästner's volumes of poetry *Herz auf Taille* (*Heart Made to Measure*) (1928) and *Gesang zwischen den Stühlen* (*Song Between Two Stools*) (1932) his socially critical tendency is far more marked than in his novel *Fabian*. His now famous poem *Stimmen aus dem Massengrab* (*Voices from the Mass Grave*) is a ferocious attack on the militarism of his day, but documents no less the resignation of the author, who both doubted the ability of those left alive to learn, and mistrusted the capacity of his verses to rouse the reader: 'Doch wir starben ohne Zweck / Ihr lasst euch morgen, wie wir gestern, schlachten' ('And yet we died to no purpose / Tomorrow you will let yourselves be slaughtered, as we did yesterday').

Without ever committing himself to a particular political party, Tucholsky was more decisive in taking up a position than Kästner, who rightly saw himself as someone between classes. In his 'devotional book' *Deutschland, Deutschland über alles* (1929), Tucholsky developed a form of political contemporary poetry that permitted him to launch vehement attacks on the Weimar judiciary, social oppression and exploitation and the imminent danger of fascism. His poem *Monolog mit Chören* (*Monologue with Choirs*) (1925) caricatures with self-irony the conflicting nature of 'pure' and 'political' poetry, which was very real for him.

Wir haben keine Zeit (We have no time)

To the poet's monologue 'Ich dichte leis und sachte vor mich hin. / Wie fein analysier ich Seelenfäden, / zart psychologisch schildere ich jeden / und leg in die Nuance letzten Sinn' ('I write my verses softly and gently. / How finely I analyse the threads of the soul, / Tenderly and psychologically I depict them one by one / And place ultimate meaning in the nuance'), the 'choirs' of unemployed, working-class mothers and tuberculosis-sufferers reply: 'Wir haben keine Zeit, Nuances zu betrachten! / Wir müssen in muffigen Löchern und Gasröhren übernachten! / Wir haben keine Lust, zu warten und immer zu warten! / Unsre Not schafft erst deine Einsamkeit, deine Stille und deinen Garten' / ('We have no time to consider nuances! / We have to spend the night in fusty holes and gas-pipes! / We have no taste for waiting and more waiting! / Our poverty is what makes your loneliness, your quietness and your garden!'). The choirs respond to such poetry, its back turned to the world, with a song of their own, the *International*.

In reality, however, Tucholsky was never the soft and gentle type of poet, his poetry being far more concerned with the problems of his time (e.g. *Prolet vor Gericht* – *A Working-Class Man in Court; Ruhe und Ordnung* – *Law and Order; Liebesfrucht* – *The Fruits of Love; Fragen an eine Arbeiterfrau* – *Questions to a Working Woman; Bürgerliche Wohltätigkeit* – *Middle-Class Charity Work*), but he was unable to arrive at the revolutionary assurance of poets committed to a particular political party. Resignation and melancholy, which increased with the rise of fascism, run through all of Tucholsky's lyric poetry. Faced with overt fascism, he finally capitulated as a satirist: 'Satire also has a bottom line. In Germany, for example, [it's] the ruling fascist authorities. It doesn't do any good – it's impossible to shoot so low.'

Bertolt Brecht

The lyric poetry of Bertolt Brecht was more richly layered and diverse than that of any of the above. Like Becher and Benn, Brecht, too, started as an Expressionist, but soon broke free from Expressionist models and began to experiment with a variety of lyric forms. The *Hauspostille* (*Book of Home Devotions*) (1927) discloses this difficult and not always consistent process of liberation. The title, relating to the internal arrangement of the volume, was drawn from the tradition of the devotional book for church and home that began with Luther and the books of religious edification that followed. Brecht's intention, however, was not to strengthen faith in God, but on the contrary to disillusion and destroy that faith. His satirical reference to Christian models was moreover based on his intention of creating a modern book of edification that would have a similar utility to the old Christian devotional books: 'This book of home devotion is intended for the use of the reader.' Brecht's devotional book was also intended as an attack on the widespread fashion among lyric poets at that time, based on Rilke's *Stundenbuch* (*Book of Hours*) (1905), to publish poetry in the form of prayer books.

The *Hauspostille* contains a diversity of lyric forms (ballads, songs, chronicles, etc.), and a wealth of poetic metaphors capturing the personal and political experiences of the poet in highly encoded form. The impotence, suppression and suffering of the individual as a result of the coldness of the world (*Von der Kindsmörderin Maria Farrar – On the Child Murderess Maria Farrar*), the inability to achieve friendly and supportive mutual relationships, as well as aggressive and in some cases cynical sexuality (*Ballade Von Liebestod – Ballad of a Love Death*), and the anarchic protest against family constraints (*Apfelböck*) are all expressions of the brutality of society. With few exceptions, however, the class conflicts of the day are nowhere explicitly dealt with. On the contrary, Brecht to a large extent avoided topical references.

Ballads: a grieving commemoration of history

From his poem *Vom ertrunkenen Mädchen* (*On the Drowned Girl*), for example, he erased the original title *Vom erschlagenen Mädchen* (*On the Girl Beaten to Death*), which was intended to refer to the murdered Rosa Luxemburg. In his poem about Apfelböck, a man who murders his parents, based on a true case, Brecht refrained from all direct explanatory references to the familial and social situation of the murderer, thereby refraining from a harsh psychological treatment of the murder, such as was the rule among Expressionist authors. The matter-of-course way in which Brecht presumes the innocence of this murderer of his parents (*Apfelböck oder die Lilie auf dem Felde – Apfelböck, or the Lily of the Field*), must have struck the

485

reader as a provocation. The reasons behind the deed are only revealed by a thorough examination of the logic of the text, taking its metaphors seriously.

The metaphorical nature of Brecht's texts places heavy demands on the reader, however. His poems *Vom Schwimmen in den Seen und Flüssen* (*On Swimming in Lakes and Rivers*) and *Vom Klettern in Bäumen* (*On Climbing Trees*) are private texts involving a confusing and complex combination of early childhood experiences and sexual fantasies.

Elegaic age tones

In the poems *Liturgie vom Hauch* (*Liturgy on Breath*); *Das Schiff* (*The Ship*); *Ballade auf vielen Schiffen* (*Ballad Aboard many Ships*) and *Lied am schwarzen Samstag* (*Song on Black Sunday*), Brecht takes issue in a self-critical way with poetry-writing and its potential in general. The unequivocal, overtly militant and socially critical character of the *Legende von toten Soldaten* (*Legend of the Dead Soldier*) sets it apart from the remaining poems in the volume, provoking the reader with its 'subversive lowness' and presenting 'anti-authoritarian lessons in manners of speech and reading' (H. Lethen). *The Legend of the Dead Soldier*, in which a long-buried soldier is exhumed, declared fit for military service by army doctors and sent to the front again, led Brecht's publisher to reject the volume in 1922, so that the *Hauspostille* did not appear until 1927 in modified, supplemented form, published by another house. The 'utilitarian standpoint' (*Nützlichkeitsstandpunkt*) already adopted by Brecht in the foreword to the *Hauspostille*, but which at that stage still gave an ironic impression, was the result of his changed political position. With his acceptance of Marxism in 1926–7, Brecht said goodbye to the 'anarchic nihilism' (C. Pietzcker) of his youth.

LITERATURE IN THE THIRD REICH

The National Socialist seizure of power

There was a latent process of radicalisation in social and political life during the Weimar Republic that was experienced by liberal and left-wing intellectuals and writers as an increasing constraint on their political and literary liberties and room for manoeuvre. With the Nazi takeover on 30 January 1933 this previously latent process changed to overt fascism, taking many of its later victims by surprise. The implications of this process for intellectuals, writers and creative artists would have been realised by alert contemporaries by 1929 at the latest. This was when the Nazi Frick took over the Ministry of the Interior and National Education (*Innen- und Volksbildungsministerium*) in Thüringen, providing a foretaste of Nazi cultural policy in miniature.

General underestimation of the Nazis is all the more astonishing given the clear signs of their ambitions for power, manifested in the Hitler–Ludendorff *putsch* in Munich in 1923, the establishment of the SA and SS combat units, and Hitler's creed *Mein Kampf* (1924). Election results at the end of the Weimar Republic era showed that the Nazis were on the way to becoming a party of the masses. In the 1930 elections to the Reichstag (parliament) they managed to increase their seats from 12 to 107.

Underestimation of the danger

Apolitical thinking and lack of insight into the nature and structural fabric of National Socialism contributed to this underestimation of its inherent dangers. In fact Hitler's seizure of power took German writers almost completely unawares. However, a certain degree of blindness is natural in witnesses to historical processes: one is always wise after the event. Only a handful of authors, such as Brecht, Feuchtwanger and Heinrich Mann, were alert to the imminent danger, and correctly assessed the subsequent course of events. Most lacked the 'imagination for what-has-not-yet-been' (Marcuse) – either convinced, like Klaus Mann, that 'someone [like Hitler] [would] never come to power', or that even if the Nazis did take over they would not last for long. Social democrat, 'left-wing' and communist authors in particular allowed themselves to be lulled into a fantasy that the Revolution was at the door, and that National Socialism was no more than a brief interlude on the road to socialism.

Potential escape routes for authors

This radical upheaval in the whole political frame of reference was bound to have repercussions for the working conditions and political stance of authors. For those who were not prepared to submit to the new literary conditions there were 'three possibilities', as the Prague exile journal *Neue Deutsche Blätter* (*New German Newspaper*) had already realised by September 1933. 'They can remain in Germany and launch a camouflaged attack on fascism by way of verbal ambush and artistic disguise, knowing that sooner or later they will be silenced and the pen snatched out of their hands. They can work anonymously for illegal literature within the country and for the anti-fascist press outside it. And finally, they can cross the border and address the Germans from abroad.'

Night escapes

Many authors were forced to flee Germany, often by night. Since these were without exception prominent writers still acknowledged and known today, there is a tendency to assume that the entire literary intelligentsia left the country at that time. In fact, however, the majority of authors remained in Germany, either sympathising or reaching a *modus vivendi* with fascism, or alternatively trying to survive psychologically and morally in a state of 'internal emigration'. A few went underground, putting their literary work to use in political support of the anti-Nazi resistance.

A wide spectrum of literature was written in Germany during the fascist era, ranging from political doctrine, through various modes of pro-fascist and indirectly non-fascist literature and literary forms of disguised opposition, to militant underground literature. This makes it in its way as wide-ranging as the literature written in exile, which can by no means be straightforwardly equated with anti-fascist literature, since here, too, there was a diversity of political and literary attitudes. Despite a partial formal congruence between exile literature and that of the Third Reich, evinced, for example, by a shared preference for certain literary genres such as the historical novel and the sonnet, a distinction between exile literature and literature of the Reich is nevertheless meaningful. It is particularly helpful to separate the literature of 'internal emigration' from the rest, since the working conditions for 'those who remained at home'

(*Daheimgebliebenen*) were fundamentally different from those of 'emigrants'.

Nazi cultural policy

Only days after the Nazis came to power emergency decrees were promulgated, severely limiting freedom of the press, freedom of assembly and the freedom to demonstrate. Any printed matter whose contents were deemed 'likely to endanger public security or order' could be confiscated. In February 1933 Heinrich Mann and Käthe Kollwitz were expelled from the Prussian Academy of Arts for having demanded an SPD (German Socialist Party)/KPD (German Communist Party) coalition in a written and signed election demand. Following the fire in the Reichstag parliament building on 27 February 1933, an event which was, to say the least, convenient to the Nazis, if not actually staged by them, the fascist nature of the new incumbent government was revealed in the full light of day. A 'presidential decree for the protection of the nation and state' dated 28 February abrogated certain key paragraphs of the constitution, marking the *de facto* 'irreversible replacement of the constitutional state by the police state' (Bracher).

The principal victims of this new legislation of terror were communists. The arrest of over 10,000 during the night of the Reichstag fire alone was without legal basis, also rendering subsequent Communist Party involvement in the parliamentary elections of 5 March a farce. During the night of 28 February numerous writers were arrested, by no means all of them Communist Party members. Carl von Ossietzky, Erich Mühsam and Ludwig Renn were among the first, followed a few days later by Willi Bredel, Anna Seghers and Klaus Neukrantz. Some only escaped arrest by chance, able to go underground or flee abroad just in time.

Following the parliamentary elections of 5 March, in which the Nazis managed to increase their representation to 44 per cent, they felt strong enough to reorganise cultural life in conformity with their own ideas. In his inaugural speech on 23 March 1933, Hitler summed up the cultural objectives of his government as follows: 'Side by side with the political decontamination of German public life, the government of the Reich will also carry out a thorough moral prophylactic treatment of the body of the nation. The entire educational system, theatre, film, literature, press and radio will all be means to this end.' Following an earlier ban on the communist and social-democrat press, this in practice meant that the bourgeois press was now to move into the firing line of the new dictatorship. Newspapers and journals that failed to conform to the new policy were banned at a moment's notice, the rest forced to toe the line with threats, dismissals, arrests and economic sanctions.

Gleichschaltung ('Bringing into line')

The process of bringing the press into line was soon followed by measures against writers' organisations. The Federation for the Protection of German Writers (SDS) was the first to be 'purged'. Here the Nazis were able to rely on followers within the association itself, who had already crystallised into an internal opposition during the Weimar era. Members of the Working Group of National Writers (Arbeitsgemeinschaft nationaler Schriftsteller), a body in existence since 1931, thus took over the leading role in the SDS and set about the process of 'decontamination' (*Entgiftung*) Hitler had called for. All members were vetted for their political reliability *vis-à-vis* the new dictatorship. Liberal and left-wing members were summarily expelled. In May the Editor-in-Chief of the *Völkischer Beobachter* (*The People's Observer*) became the new Chairman of the SDS, whose members were compelled to sign a declaration of allegiance to the Nazi state. In July 1933 the SDS was absorbed into the Association of German Writers of the Reich (Reichsverband Deutscher Schriftsteller), founded a month earlier.

At the same time the literary section of the Prussian Academy of Arts, whose Chairman Heinrich Mann had been forced to resign on what was obviously a thin pretext, was also brought into line. Only those prepared to submit a declaration of allegiance to the fascist state drafted by Gottfried Benn were permitted to remain members. Thomas Mann and Ricarda Huch immediately resigned, while others were expelled, either for refusing to sign the declaration, or because they were Jews and therefore now considered undesirables. The places of resigned or expelled members were taken by convinced Nazis, such as Grimm, Blunck, Johst, Kolbenheyer and Vesper. A similar reshuffle took place in the membership of the German section of the International Pen Club. The previous board was forced to resign, replaced by a new 'reliable' one, and political *personae non gratae* summarily expelled. When authors living in exile founded an alternative German section, the domestic German sectionresponded by leaving the International Pen Club. The Union of National Writers, founded under the leadership of Johst and Benn as a counter-platform for authors, was nevertheless only limited in its success.

The burning of books

The wave of terror against dissident writers now reached a new pitch with the burning of books. On 26 April 1933 the Berlin evening paper the *Nachtausgabe*, published by the Hugenberg conglomerate that had played a key role in Hitler's seizure of power, published a list of 'books fit for burning'. This was the prelude to a spate of so-called black and white lists containing the names of authors either in or out of favour. On 10 May an unprecedented burning of books took place all over Germany. Contrary to popular opinion, this was no *ad hoc*, spontaneous event on the part of the German population, but a 'synchronised, precisely orchestrated campaign' (H.A. Walter). The works of many major and prominent authors were 'consigned to the flames' at ceremonious, ritual meetings, accompanied by speeches from leading Nazis such as Goebbels, and prominent professors of literature. Heine's aphorism 'Where books are burned, men will ultimately also burn' was soon to come terribly true. A few days later the *Financial News for the German Book Trade* (*Börsenblatt für den deutschen Buchhandel*) published the first official list of books to be removed from public collections. It comprised 131 authors, and was regularly brought up to date.

Oath of allegiance

The regimentation of German cultural life was finally provided with a legislative basis in the form of the Reich Chamber of Culture Act (*Reichskulturkammergesetz*) of 22 September 1933. From then on, the Reich Chamber of Culture, inaugurated on 15 November 1933, met at the Reich Ministry of National Enlightenment and Propaganda (Reichsministerium für Volksaufklärung und Propaganda) under Goebbel's supervision to discuss who was allowed to be active in cultural life. Their work was backed by the Reich Chamber of Literature (Reichsschrifttumskammer), initially chaired by Blunck and later Johst, which demanded of its members both proof of 'Aryan' descent and an oath of allegiance to the Nazi state. This effectively banned Jewish and dissident authors from practising their profession. The work of state supervision was augmented by no less than three censorship bodies: the Literature Department of the Ministry of Propaganda (Schrifttumsabteilung/ Propagandaministerium), the Reich Agency for the Promotion of German Literature (Reichsstelle zur Förderung des deutschen Schrifttums), headed personally by Rosenberg, and the Party Bureau Board of Examiners for the Protection of National Socialist Literature (Parteiamtliche Prüfungskommission zum Schutz des NS-Schrifttums). A formal ban on criticism on 27 November 1936 and the administrative replacement of 'subversive criticism' (*zersetzende Kritik*) by 'promotional review' (*fördernde Betrachtung*), sounded the final death knell for German literary life.

The 'aestheticisation of politics', or fascist politics as a total work of art

A Nazi literature in its own right?

The view that German fascism produced no art or literature of its own, rather 'an eclectic synthesis of all reactionary tendencies' (Lukács), is only accurate up to a point. It holds good for traditional literary genres, which National Socialists did indeed adopt in a highly eclectic and imitative manner without adding any specific slant of their own. They drew on the existing body of literature, cannibalising bourgeois art and literature for their own purposes. Their arrogation of classical authors and brutal distortion of authors with clear-cut political views, such as Hölderlin, Kleist and Büchner, in order to present them as pre-fascist representatives of 'heroic pessimism' is one of the sorriest chapters in the history of German literature.

The charge of imitation cannot reasonably be levelled against propaganda art, however, where National Socialism was both highly original and creative, giving the new media – film, radio and the radio play – a special status within cultural policy and propaganda beside which literature had a decidedly subordinate role.

The Nazi world-view found fitting artistic expression in the *Thingspiel*, a genuinely fascist theatre form. Conceived as a new form of German national theatre, *Thingspiel* was intended as a devotional or cult play, abolishing the traditional separation between actors and audience, addressing the 'body, mind and soul of the German national comrade (*Volksgenosse*)', and fusing all protagonists into a single mystical community. The stated aim of *Thingspiel* was to produce a communal experience in which the individual 'national comrade can allow the power of his conviction, constantly strengthened by a steady repetition of the creed of community, to flow into the community of the nation, thereby conquering the half-heartedness of his surroundings and permitting the energy of the nation to grow stronger and stronger' (from an official party announcement in the journal *Neue Gemeinschaft – New Community*).

The theme of *Thingspiel* was first and foremost to propound German history from 1918 to 1933 as the run-up to the 'National Socialist Revolution'. Its principal character was the German nation itself, presented in the manner of a Greek chorus, individual players appearing as chorus leaders or representatives of rival groups from the chorus. The number of performers could go into the thousands, and of spectators into tens of thousands. In October 1933 there was a performance for 60,000 spectators in the Berlin Grünewald involving a cast of some 17,000 SA personnel.

Mass theatre of this kind was impossible to organise within the traditional theatre, and hence required new premises, new plays and a new dramaturgy. Within a short time gigantic *Thingspiel* arenas were constructed, intended to be a synthesis of the open-air theatre and the Greek amphitheatre. Only a small number of the 400 planned *Thingspiel* theatres was completed, however. Despite official backing – Goebbels had formed a working group of some forty *Thingspiel* authors – the repertoire remained relatively small. Some 10,000 *Thingspiel* entries were intended for submission to a competition arranged by the Reich Labour Front, but few of them met high-flown official expectations and hence found approval and backing. They included Eggers's *Job der Deutsche* (*Job the German*) (1933), Euringer's *Deutsche Passion* (*German Passion*) (1933), and Heynicke's *Der Weg ins Reich* (*The Road to the Reich*) (1935). Möller's *Frankenburger Würfelspiel* (*The Frankenburg Dice Game*) (1936) was performed at the 1936 Olympics, and was one of the most widely performed of all *Thingspiele*.

All these plays shared a dramatic form comprising various literary traditions, fusing elements of Greek tragedy, the medieval mystery play, baroque and classicist festival performance and modern forms of Expressionist and proletarian theatre from the Weimar Republic. The result was a form of fascist self-portrayal and celebration in which Lessing's and Schiller's Enlightenment ideal of a national theatre was perverted with the utmost cynicism. The adoption of elements from the revolutionary proletarian theatre of the Weimar Republic (Piscator) was a ruse to deceive audiences into perceiving a pseudo-socialist, pseudo-revolutionary content in Nazi policy, even in its literary forms.

The penchant of fascist art for monumental, ornamental and cult features became even more marked at Reich party congresses, which were staged with the precision of mass theatre, ultimately overshadowing even the *Thingspiel* by the consummate manipulation of mass audiences to fit in with Nazi ideology. The truly 'artistic' achievement of the Nazis, therefore, lies in the way they staged these party congresses. Even today, for example, Leni Riefenstahl's film about the 1934 Nuremberg party congress (*Triumph des Willens – Triumph of the Will*) exerts a huge aesthetic fascination.

Politics and art

As early as 1936, Walter Benjamin pointed out that the real aesthetic and artistic achievements of German fascism were to be found in its politics, thereby exposing the relationship between politics and art in fascism. This perversion of art and politics, and the fascist contempt for humanity that lay behind it, was unequivocally stated by Goebbels: 'Even politics is an art, perhaps the highest and most far-reaching there is, and we, we who are now shaping modern German politics have a sense of being artistic men entrusted with the onerous task of shaping a firm and contoured national structure out of the raw material of the masses.'

The way fascist politicians saw themselves as creative artists was treated as a theme by Brecht in a number of his exile poems, for example '*Die Regierung als Künstler* (*The Government as Creative Artist*); *Verbot der Theaterkritik* (*The Ban on Theatre Criticism*), as well as in his many poems about Hitler, in which the Nazi *Reichskanzler* appears as a pseudo-artist, a 'painter and decorator' (*Anstreicher*) who 'studies nothing but colour' and who had 'daubed all of Germany'. Similarly, Walter Benjamin's statements about Nazi propaganda art read like a commentary on the mass staging of a *Thingspiel* or of party congresses: 'Fascist art is an art of propaganda. It is thus carried out for the masses.' Art of this kind puts both 'the executor and the receiver under a spell which makes them appear monumental to themselves, i.e. incapable of well thought-out, independent action. In this way, art strengthens the suggestive energy of its impact at the expense of intellectual and enlightening energy. The raising of existing conditions to eternal values in fascist art is accomplished by disabling (the persons executing or receiving the art) who might be able to change those conditions.' The masses are unable to think about themselves and their needs, having been extinguished as individuals so that they are no longer equipped to deal with manipulation and abuse. Although the forming of the masses according to the laws of beauty provides them with a brief interlude of 'expression', it does not help them fulfil their 'rights' (Benjamin). The necessary shaping of society according to the principles of liberty, equality and justice was usurped by the aesthetic illusion of a national community (*Volksgemeinschaft*) in which the masses were duped into believing that their political and social problems had been solved.

Benjamin likewise pinpointed the true goal behind this fascist 'aestheticisation of politics': 'All efforts towards the aestheticisation of politics culminate at a single point. That point is war. War, and only war, enables a purpose to be found for large-scale mass movements while still retaining the inherited conditions of property ownership.'

Völkisch literature

Set beside the aestheticisation of politics and the aesthetic formation of the masses in the 'mass work of art' (*Gesamtkunstwerk*) that was the Reich party congress, *völkisch* literature, for a long time regarded as the true literature of Nazism, seems almost lightweight and innocuous. In fact, however, this literature was not a product of Nazism, however much the Nazis encouraged and feted it. With few exceptions, the 'literature of the Third Reich', i.e. that literature that was held up as exemplary Nazi writing, was written in the preceding Weimar period, in some case even prior to 1918. Bartels's *Volk wider Volk* (*Nation against Nation*) and Burte's *Wiltfeber der Deutsche* (*Wiltfeber the German*) were both published in 1912, Grimm's bestseller *Volk ohne Raum* (*Nation without Domain*) in 1926, Blunck's three novels *Hein Hoyer*, *Berend Fock* and *Stelling Rotkinnsohn* in 1922, 1923 and 1924 respectively, later being collected into a single volume entitled *Urvätersaga* (*Saga of the Ancestors*); Kolbenheyer's trilogy *Paracelsus* was published between 1917 and 1926, and finally Vesper's *Das harte Geschlecht* (*The Tough Breed*) in 1931.

Völkisch-nationale Literatur is a collective term embracing a number of literary trends. Besides 'blood and soil literature', for a long time a byword in *völkisch* literature, there was also *Heimat* (homeland) and provincial art in the style of Ludwig Ganghofer, Hermann Stehr and Hermann Löns, the historical novel in the Freytag and Dahn tradition, the colonial novel, most successfully exemplified by Grimm's *Volk ohne Raum* (*Nation without Domain*) and so-called 'soldier nationalism' (*Soldatischer Nationalismus*), i.e. war, paramilitary and civil-war fiction of the Weimar Republic.

What all these works have in common is their anti-democratic, anti-modern, and anti-semitic stance, as well as their glorification of the 'Germanic race' – qualities that made them extremely useful to the Nazis. It is not surprising, therefore, that the several varieties of *völkisch* literature, prior to 1933 only one literary strand among many, were raised to the level of a state literature when the Nazis came to power.

Literature of 'internal emigration'

Who were the real emigrants?

'Internal emigration' as opposed to exile is a concept that was already taking shape in the 1930s, but did not acquire a political connotation until after 1945 in the crossfire between 'those who had remained at home' (*Daheimgebliebenen*) and 'emigrants'. The well-known controversy over external and internal emigration between Thomas Mann on the one hand and Walter von Molo and Frank Thiess on the other (1945–6) introduced the term 'internal emigration', which was brought to play by von Molo and Thiess against authors who had been in exile. The argument was put forward that those authors who had 'stuck it out' in Germany had thereby gained a 'wealth of insight and experience' under the fascist dictatorship, making them 'richer in knowledge and experience' compared to those who had left. They also argued that it had been 'more difficult . . . to preserve one's personality intact here than to send the German nation messages from abroad'. All this was in fact no more than a heavy-handed bid by such authors to brush their own entanglement in fascism under the carpet, using the tactic of landing the first blow to defame emigrants indirectly as traitors to their country. Frank Thiess's statements in 1946 ooze cynicism: 'We expect no reward for not having left Germany', and 'I would not blame anyone for fleeing'. It was probably this that provoked Thomas Mann to an uncharacteristically forthright response. He flatly denied the literature of 'internal emigration' the moral right to see itself as a literature of resistance: 'It may be superstition [on my part], but in my eyes books that could be printed at all from 1933 to 1945 in Germany are less than worthless and not fit to be handled. There is a stench of blood and shame to them. They should all be pulped.'

As a result of these maladroit complaints by authors who would have

495

done better to remain silent, the term 'internal emigration' not only fell into disrepute, but was even discredited as a meaningless myth (Schonauer). Meanwhile, however, fresh research has revealed that there really was an 'internal emigration' in Germany, i.e. a dissident literature that was not brought into line and that was aimed at criticism of the regime. What this term really meant, however, and to which authors it could be applied, is still a subject of debate.

The first authors to be discussed in this connection are Gottfried Benn and Ernst Jünger, who have repeatedly been declared members of the 'internal emigration' and who, after 1945, also liked to see themselves in this light. For a time Benn had gone along with the Nazis. After the Nazi takeover he had given his open support, contributing energetically to the persecution of Jewish and other authors who were politically out of favour. His later disillusionment with Nazism, discontinuation of his literary work and joining of the *Wehrmacht* as a surgeon-major – presented by him as an 'aristocratic form of emigration' – nevertheless lack all trace of anti-fascist feeling. Ernst Jünger's disenchantment with the Nazis was similarly more out of aristocratic snobbery than political conviction. His works (e.g. *Auf den Marmorklippen – On the Marble Cliffs*, 1939) have so much in common with fascist ideology that it would be quite wrong to interpret his rejection of an appointment in the Academy of Arts and his strong letter to the *Völkischer Beobachter* as an act of resistance against German fascism. By his own admission, Jünger watched from a 'higher vantage-point' while the 'bugs devoured one another'.

Ricarda Huch and Ernst Barlach

The designation 'internal emigration' can nevertheless be justly applied to authors such as Ricarda Huch and Ernst Barlach. In a courageous letter of 1933, Ricarda Huch refused to sign the oath of allegiance required of its members by the Prussian Academy of Arts, adopting a clear position *vis-à-vis* the Nazis: 'That which the present government has put forward as the German character is not my idea of Germanness. I regard their centralisation, coercion, brutal methods, defamation of dissidents and boastful self-praise as both un-German and unwholesome.' Ricarda Huch was regarded as an undesirable author on account of her defence of Jews and others persecuted by the regime. Few of her works were allowed to appear.

The artist and writer Ernst Barlach, denounced by fascists as 'degenerate' and 'unheroic', similarly made no secret of his opposition to the Nazis. Although not officially banned from practising his profession, none of his work was exhibited or published after 1933. Shortly before his death in 1937, Barlach wrote that he had had a 'kind of emigrant existence forced on him' in his own country: 'This gives me a feeling of being ostracised comparable with being abandoned to destruction. . . . My condition is far worse than that of a true emigrant.' Barlach buried in his garden the books he wrote during the fascist era.

The term 'internal emigration' as a designation for literature critical of the regime is also applicable to authors who found themselves at odds with the Nazis for religious or humanitarian reasons. These include chiefly Jochen Klepper, Ernst Wiechert and Werner Bergengruen, who did not come into conflict with the dictatorship by chance. Klepper voluntarily retired from public life with his family in 1942 to save his Jewish wife and daughter from the gas chambers. He was able to entrust his confrontation with the Nazis only to his diaries, which he buried in his garden for fear of the Gestapo.

As a 'troublesome' author, Wiechert was sent for several months to a concentration camp. His courageous 1935 speech against the Nazis was published in 1937 by Brecht, Bredel and Feuchtwanger in the exile journal they edited, *Das Wort* (*The Word*) as a major document of 'internal emigration' in the '*Kulturkampf* of our time'. Wiechert's literary account of his concentration camp experience, *Der Totenwald* (*The Forest of the Dead*), written in 1939, was not published until after 1945.

Lastly, Werner Bergengruen was banned from the Reich Chamber of Literature in 1937. According to information he provided, he had been involved in the resistance work of the 'White Rose', also publishing some of his works anonymously abroad.

All these authors attempted to put up intellectual resistance to the evil ruling spirit of the age. Using the historical novel in particular, also a favourite form among exiled authors, they sought to confront National Socialism (*Der Grosstyrann und das Gericht – The Tyrant and the Judgement; Der Vater – The Father; Las Casas vor Karl V – Las Casas Before Karl V*). In the process they faced the 'five difficulties of writing the truth' of which Brecht had spoken in 1934. Publishing literature overtly critical of the regime was a suicidal undertaking, and in any case futile, since hardly any publisher or printers could be found who would be willing to publish such works. This meant that literature either had to remain 'in the closet', or had to be couched in the 'language of slaves' to dupe the dictatorship and reach the reader, in the hope that the latter would decipher the criticism correctly. In reality this hope was rarely fulfilled. Bergengruen's novel *Der Grosstyrann und das Gericht* (1935), for example, was hailed by the *Völkische Beobachter* as the '*Führer* novel of the Renaissance', and even *Der Vater* (1937), intended by Jochen Klepper as 'criticism, not glorification of the present-day' was well received by the Nazis. These authors did not succeed in making their works 'openly useful as weapons' (Brecht). They were rather the expression of a 'helpless anti-fascism' (W.F. Haug), arising out of the overwhelming supremacy of their authors' political adversary, as well as from the inability of their authors to elaborate a political perspective on fascism from their conservative position.

A reading of the literature that was intended as criticism of the regime reveals that its authors lacked insight into the nature of Nazism. They were unable to see the connection between German history and European fascism. 'Wiechert's Old Prussian pietism, for example, could only offer insipid resistance to Hitler. Although not without its value in the body of resistance to Hitler's barbarism, in itself it was incapable of leading to a renewal of Germany' (Lukács). The widely-held view that Nazism was a matter of 'destiny', a 'German tragedy', or a dictatorship of 'criminals' and 'demons' clearly reveals this lack of any real understanding of fascism, and also helps to explain why the resistance of these authors could never amount to more than a helpless dumb show.

The succeeding generation

Another group of authors made its literary début during the fascist era, or even the Weimar Republic, but did not make a name for itself until after 1945, going on to shape the literary life of the Federal Republic into the 1960s. This group may conditionally be added to the body of 'internal emigrants': Günter Eich, Peter Huchel, Wolfgang Koeppen, Marie Luise Kaschnitz, Max Frisch, Rudolf Hagelstange, Gerd Gaiser, Karl Krolow, Paul Celan, Oskar Loerke and Wilhelm Lehmann.

Eich and Huchel had been successful as radio playwrights during the fascist era, Eich writing fifteen radio plays during this period and regularly supplying German radio stations with plays about life in the provinces.

The real emphasis of literary work among these authors, however, lay in the diary, short prose forms and lyric poetry – forms that gave ample room for their subjectivity. They were also the forms most readily tolerated by the fascist dictatorship, since they posed no threat to the system. There was a marked revival of traditional lyric forms such as the sonnet, the ode, the hymn and the elegy. The strict adherence to form by these authors was integral to their agenda, but was less a matter of deliberate political protest than of an anti-modernist mood, arising out of fundamentally conservative views. This neo-classicist orientation, which persisted after 1945, was devoid of anything approaching resistance, violence or revolution, and yet in view of the diverging varieties of *völkisch* literature and fascist party lyric verse was nevertheless a form that 'was, so to speak, different in and of itself' (Heissenbüttel). Despite being intended as a form of protest, and perceived as such by readers, this retreat by authors into themselves and nature was nevertheless not an act of resistance, but rather an individualistic withdrawal from the here-and-now into the realm of poetry. Brecht's famous complaint about the 'times when a conversation about trees is almost a crime, because it entails a silence about so many

498

misdeeds' (*An die Nachgeborenen – To Those Born After*, 1938), touches on the heart of this dilemma of non-fascist authors.

Nature lyrics

An untold number of nature poems, some of them impressive, were written during the Nazi era (Loerke: *Silberdistelwald – Carline Thistle Wood*, 1934; Lehmann: *Antwort des Schweigens – The Answer of Silence*, 1935). In his *Theorien des deutschen Faschismus* (*Theories of German Fascism*) (1930), Walter Benjamin uncovered the connection between the aggressive forward march of fascism and the regressive literary subjectivity and contemplation that seeks to save itself by retreating into a feeling for nature: 'It should be spelled out with all bitterness. In the face of a totally mobilised country-side, the German feeling for nature has experienced an undreamed-of flowering.' Elisabeth Langgässer's subsequent self-critical comments help explain why the nature poems of Huchel, Loerke and Lehmann probably have such an irritating effect on the modern reader in instances where the 'horror of the age' had penetrated nature or could be associated with it, because as we now know, and authors at the time must at least have guessed, this 'dallying with flowers and blossoms [was taking place] over the horrific, yawning abyss of the mass graves that they covered'.

Nature lyrics are a good example of how 'internal emigration' was for the most part synonymous with 'inward emigration'. Its manifest aversion to political reality, its withdrawal from society and flight into contemplation is a pattern of response not restricted to the 1933–45 period, however. It can be traced back to the eighteenth century, when sections of the literary intelligentsia were not long in reacting to the rise of bourgeois capitalist forms of government with melancholy, escapism and ostentatious individualism. Even Romantic poetry bears the marks of escapism to a considerable degree. These were to be even more emphasised by authors of the Biedermeier era. It was no coincidence that contemplative authors drew on these features, deliberately placing themselves within the tradition, and reviving the concept of poetry as a supra-historical force outside society.

Nevertheless, the critical potential originally contained in this view of poetry, and to some extent even expressed, had proved again and again to be a feeble weapon. Contemplative literature had only the appearance of being able to withdraw from the clutches of totalitarianism. Even where it perceived itself to be evading or circumventing the ambition for power of the regime by escaping into a realm of 'inner freedom', it was ultimately helping to bolster the regime's hegemony by lending the Nazis an appearance of poetic diversity and a flourishing literary scene.

Anti-fascist underground literature

Underground militants

In addition to disguised forms of literary and political dissidence on the part of conservative, Christian and bourgeois authors there was also a militant literature, produced by left-wing, socialist and communist authors. Obviously this literature could only be produced and distributed illegally. The wider reading public only became aware of the existence of an underground literature in 1935 at the international writers' congress in Paris – from a man disguised in a black mask:

> Despite everything there is an underground literature in Germany, for those weeks when German fascism believed it had broken the quill-bearing militants and critics were the hour a new type in anti-fascist literature was born! The young, coming generation left behind in Germany was suddenly faced with an awesome task as it became aware of the huge responsibility that had been placed on its shoulders – the responsibility of showing by literary means the true face of the Third Reich. And it began to fulfil this task, excelling itself and creating the voice from Germany! It is difficult to explain in sober terms the horrific dangers to which each and every one exposes himself in this process. Every line is written literally at the risk of life and limb. There is no safe place to work in this country of spies and Gestapo armies. No place where a typewriter can clatter away without the possibility of the door being flung open and a Gestapo officer asking: 'What are you writing?!'

Jan Petersen

The masked man who gave this account of underground literature in Germany and who wanted to show the world by literary means the 'true face of the Third Reich' was Jan Petersen, Communist Party member since 1923, member of the Union of Proletarian Revolutionary Writers (BPRS) since 1931, and organiser of the underground work of the local BPRS Berlin branch since 1933. Petersen was referring in his now famous statement to the literature written and distributed by himself and his co-militants in the BPRS at risk to their lives. After the Nazi takeover the members of the Berlin branch of the BPRS went underground *en bloc*, immediately beginning to organise and promote political resistance. They saw their duty first in creating a resistance network within the Reich and informing the population about the true nature of the new government, second in alerting countries abroad both about this reign of terror and the resistance to it, and third by means of documentation of this terror in building a bridge between political dissidents within the Reich and in exile outside it. From 1933 until they were rounded up by the Gestapo in 1934 they published their own underground magazine, *Hieb und Stich* (*Cut and Thrust*) while also working on illegal underground factory magazines and participating in the production and distribution of pamphlets and pamphlet and political poster-poetry. Under the slogans 'The Voice from Germany' or 'The Voice of the Underground' they provided regular reports about conditions in Germany in the exile journals *Neue Deutsche Blätter* (Prague) and the *Internationale Blätter* (Moscow). A comprehensive report on what had happened to persecuted and arrested writers was smuggled out of the country at great personal risk and printed in Switzerland under the title *Hirne hinter Stacheldraht* (*Minds behind the Barbed Wire*) (1934). This book also gave an account of the anti-fascist struggle of writers and of the 'new type of writer' who had emerged out of these underground conditions: 'He has become tough and disciplined; today he edits an underground newspaper in a cellar – a dead man on holiday – tomorrow he writes a doggerel verse, the day after tomorrow he writes it or sticks it on to a wall in the street, meanwhile gathering material for a major novel or reportage. There are no theatre premieres giving him thunderous applause, no literary awards, no fees or royalties, no press spreading his fame.'

The burden of illegality

Jan Petersen epitomised this new type of writer. In his novel *Unsere Strasse* (*Our Street*), 'written in the heart of fascist Germany in 1933–4', as the subtitle declares, he gave the first authentic account of the ordeal of the underground struggle, and of the modified view of themselves authors had reached. Petersen recounts as an eyewitness the mounting campaign of terror waged against the working-class quarter of Charlottenburg in Berlin and the resistance put up by the inhabitants. The fears he lived through while writing his chronicle are integral to the book, the literary form itself being an expression of it. Work on the book, as Petersen reports, frequently had to be interrupted:

> I know what will happen to me if I fall into the hands of the Nazis with these records. I didn't write at all this last week. I came close to burning everything. The difficulties just seemed too great. I have been trying to find another place to live where I can write, but it would have to be with comrades, and they are just as involved in underground work as I am. There could be a sudden house search at their homes, too. The place where I keep the written pages is not absolutely safe either. But during this last week when I didn't write I couldn't find inner peace either. I was weighed down by a spiritual urgency that has compelled me to go on writing now. I must write

all this down! We must manage to get this manuscript abroad. It must help to shake people's consciences awake.

Petersen eventually managed to smuggle the manuscript out of Germany in a rucksack, 'baked in two cakes'. An extract appeared in Paris in 1935, in Bern and Moscow in 1936, and in London in 1938, arousing considerable international attention as a document of the resistance in Germany.

Reports from Germany

Besides Petersen's chronicle there were a number of other authentic reports from Germany, such as Heinz Liepmann's 'factual novels' (*Tatsachenromane*) (*Das Vaterland* – *The Fatherland*, 1933; '. . . *wird mit dem Tode bestraft*' – '. . . *will be subject to the death sentence*', 1935). Other important records were by people interned in concentration camps, some written during their period of internment, but most after the authors had escaped and fled to the safety of exile. Willi Bredel wrote down his concentration camp experiences in the novel *Die Prüfung* (*The Test*) (1934), and Wolfgang Langhoff, author of the famous *Moorsoldaten-Lied* (*Song of the Marsh Soldier*), which circulated in his penal camp as a secret camp anthem, recounted his camp experiences in the novel *Die Moorsoldaten* (*The Marsh Soldiers*) (1935). In 1937 the Moscow exile journal *Das Wort* (*The Word*) stressed the importance of these reports of experiences in concentration camps and other places of detention: 'This literature helped tremendously, making fascism visible, if not comprehensible. . . . This literature mobilised people in the cause of peace, against the corrupt fascist culture and the contamination of war.' The enlightening effect of this literature was felt almost exclusively abroad, however. Only in exceptional cases could it be returned to Germany in the form of camouflaged extracts.

Literature for peace

The majority of anti-fascist literature was not published at all, and hence ultimately had no impact. Georg Kaiser, the once famous Expressionist author, dealt in his poems with the uncompromising callousness of the dictatorship, or the 'gas company', as he referred to the Nazi machinery of destruction. There was no chance at all of these being published, so they circulated only among his circle of acquaintances. Similarly, texts written by Haushofer (*Moabiter Sonette* – *Moabit Sonnets*), Apitz (*Esther*, 1944) and Krauss (*PLN*, 1943–4) during their internment in concentration camps did not reach the public until the collapse of the Third Reich. Haushofer, who had been in contact with the conspirators of 20 July, was shot by an SS flying squad shortly before the end of the war. His brother, also under arrest, found the manuscript of the *Moabit Sonnets* in the hands of the dead man. Krauss, a member of the Schulze-Boysen-Harnack resistance group, wrote his book, a coded evaluation of fascism, in the constant expectation that his death sentence would be carried out at any moment, sometimes with handcuffs on.

GERMAN LITERATURE
WRITTEN IN EXILE

The exodus

That writers were obliged to leave their country for political reasons and live in exile is not unique to Nazism. The Jacobin Georg Forster, whose contributions as both politician and writer were crucial for the founding of the Mainz Republic of 1792–3, was compelled to flee to France when this attempt to establish democratic conditions in Germany failed. He died in exile in Paris in 1794. During the 1790s numerous other writers and critical intellectuals like him took refuge in Paris, where they grew into a regular colony of expatriates that tried to organise the literary and political resistance effort against feudal absolutism in their country. At one time there may have been as many as 10,000 of them living in Paris.

Another wave of emigration followed the Karlsbad Resolutions in 1819, which provided the German empire with an ingenious system for monitoring the press, the publishing industry and the universities. A third wave of emigration followed the July Revolution of 1830 in Paris and ensuing attempts at revolution in Germany. This wave encompassed more than intellectuals and writers, escalating into nothing short of a mass exodus of democratically-minded people. By the 1840s there may have been as many as 50–80,000 German exiles living in Paris alone, including such celebrated authors as Marx, Heine, Börne, Ruge and Weitling. Another major author of the day, Georg Büchner, had a warrant issued for his arrest, which he only managed to avoid by fleeing to Strasbourg. His political friends were sentenced to many years imprisonment, and his close friend Weidig died in detention from the after-effects of torture. The fact that these emigrants had good reason to leave Germany is demonstrated not only by what happened to Büchner's friends, but also by the less dramatic fates of Laube and Gutzkow, who were summarily flung into gaol for minor infringements of press legislation.

After the failed 1848 revolution the lives of democratically-minded intellectuals and writers were at risk, and a mass exodus was again the result. Authors such as Freiligrath, Herwegh and Weerth had no option but to leave Germany unless they were prepared to risk their personal liberty. There was a fresh, if smaller, wave of emigration after the promulgation of the 1878 Socialists' Act (*Sozialistengesetz*), and yet another larger wave during World War I, when the convinced pacifists Stefan Zweig, Ernst Bloch, Walter Benjamin and René Schickele all emigrated to Switzerland.

Political exile and emigration hence have a long tradition in Germany. Unlike other European countries, where it was often conservative and reactionary groups who had to emigrate, for example the nobility during the French Revolution, emigration from Germany almost invariably involved democratically-minded dissident movements. There is thus nothing fundamentally new about the exile of authors during the Nazi era. What was new was that it involved a mass expulsion or flight on a scale and over a period that is without parallel in German history.

Emigrants and exiles

It is helpful to distinguish here between emigrants, who included the great majority of Jews driven out of the country (approximately 142,000 up to 1938), and exiles, who were for the most part politicians, creative artists, writers and journalists. The distinction between these two categories, effectively emigrants and outcasts, a distinction also made by Brecht in his famous poem *Über die Bezeichnung 'Emigranten'* (*On the Term 'Emigrant'*), becomes clear from the different ways in which they fled. Whereas the majority of writers, creative artists and journalists fled abroad in 1933 immediately after the Reichstag fire, the mass exodus of Jews did not reach a climax until 1938–9, when the pogroms of 9 November 1938 made it clear to remaining Jewish citizens that the Nazis were serious about wiping them out. Exiles, on the other hand, were

> all those German-speaking persons...who, regardless of their nationality or race, wanted to flee Germany and those countries later annexed to it (Austria and Czechoslovakia) to escape either the threat or the fact of fascism in power, or who did not want to return to it, and who while [they were] abroad in some form, be it politics, journalism or art, either directly or indirectly took up a position against German fascism. This category also includes writers and creative artists who had not been politically active either before or after 1933, but who by the act of leaving Germany and breaking off their relations with publishing houses and other institutions within Germany made it plain that they wanted to have nothing to do with fascist cultural life.
>
> (H. A. Walter)

A definition of this nature rather suggests that exile literature and anti-fascist literature were one and the same thing. This consonance was aimed for by authors with a high political profile, but in reality never came about.

Döblin distinguished among authors gathered in exile between 'conservative', 'Humanist-bourgeois' and 'intellectual revolutionary' authors, hence mapping out those ideological positions that were never to be entirely reconciled. The political spectrum of the Weimar Republic was for the most part recreated in exile.

Stefan George, for example, who had once hailed Hitler as the 'new Fuehrer' ('er heftet / Das wahre Sinnbild auf das völkische Banner' – 'He affixes / The true symbol to the nation's banner'), saw his elitist notions of leadership desecrated by the Nazis, and retired resentfully to Switzerland, rejecting a state prize awarded by Goebbels personally and refusing to be buried on German soil. Despite his unequivocal position, however, George can hardly be ranked among the anti-fascist camp, having too much in common with the fascist ideology. As Brecht realised in 1918, George isolated himself with his 'vanity' and lust for power.

Likewise, the various conservative authors who saw in fascism first and foremost the cultural betrayal of bourgeois Humanism rather than the political perversion of bourgeois society can only conditionally be included in the anti-fascist camp, if at all. Their conviction, that Nazism was best opposed by setting a realm of 'pure mind' against the ruling 'corrupt mind' (*Ungeist*), closely resembled that of authors of the 'internal emigration', who also attempted to offer resistance through a stubborn insistence on 'pure mind' and through 'pure poetry'.

However, representatives of the regressive, escapist stances still espoused by a small number of authors resigned to current circumstances, and who either fell silent as writers or chose to see themselves henceforth in apolitical terms, were in the minority within the broad spectrum of exile literature. Most authors had either taken a deliberate decision against fascism by going into exile, or else arrived later at a more or less consistent anti-fascist position. Important factors in this process were information about Germany, as well as their very role as exiles, which opened the eyes of many authors and strengthened their sense of social commitment. Exile was to prove a major learning process for bourgeois intellectuals especially, who had sought during the Weimar Republic to define themselves as a critical intelligentsia 'above' party politics. One example of this type of bourgeois writer is Thomas Mann, whose *Betrachtungen eines Unpolitischen* (*Observations of a Non-Political Man*) (1918) had set forth his conservative and reactionary world-view. Even during the Weimar Republic, however, he had begun to break free from these conservative stances (*Kultur und Sozialismus*, 1928; *Ein Appell an die Vernunft – An Appeal to Reason*, 1930), and in exile he worked his way towards an anti-fascist position (*Fünfundfünfzig Radiosendungen nach Deutschland – Fifty-five Radio Broadcasts to Germany*, 1940–5). Although not free of contradictions, this was nevertheless remarkable for a writer who had started with fundamentally conservative attitudes.

Living conditions in exile

Exile came first and foremost as a shock, which deepened as the hope for a rapid collapse of Nazism and a speedy return to Germany proved illusory. Uprooted from their habitual milieu, isolated from the familiar language in which they thought and wrote, cut off from the readership on whom they had depended, and deprived of income, exiles suddenly found themselves in countries where they often did not speak the language, with different customs that were alien to them and where people often regarded them with suspicion and complicated their lives as political refugees with red tape.

Goebbels' sneering taunt – 'Let them drivel on a while longer, those ladies and gentlemen in the émigré cafés of Paris and Prague; their life thread is cut off, they are corpses on vacation' – was to become all too oppressive a reality for some exiles. Suicide was alarmingly common among exiles. Their legal position in most of the countries in which they sought asylum was insecure ('Without a passport one cannot live', Klaus Mann), and their financial situation precarious. Only a few prominent authors such as Thomas Mann and Lion Feuchtwanger could rely on a steady income and more or less retain their former living standard. All this threw exiles into a predicament, to which different authors responded in various ways. Those who saw their literary work as part of the anti-fascist struggle usually coped best.

In his seminal novel *Exil* (1940), Feuchtwanger gives a penetrating account of the situation in France, where most refugee writers fled until war broke out. Work opportunities were limited. For a time, some exiled authors still had an income from publications in Germany, or were able to find new sources of income from exile publishing houses and the exile press, or from translations, poetry-readings, talks or lecture tours. The majority, however, were without work permits, and hence dependent on financial support from wealthy writing colleagues or from aid organisations that had been set up in the asylum countries. The most important international aid organisation for writers and journalists was the American Guild for German Cultural Freedom (from 1935 onwards).

'Wir sprechen nun einmal deutsch' – *'We speak German, and that's that'*

Besides their administrative and material problems, authors were made most insecure by the fact that they were only able to obtain temporary residence permits in most of the asylum countries. Those who had initially taken refuge in Austria and Czechoslovakia had to flee again with the annexation of Austria in 1938 and the occupation of Czechoslovakia in 1939, and when war broke out in 1939 had to flee fascist troops in Belgium, Denmark, France and the Netherlands. Not all of them managed to leave in time. Anna Seghers's novel *Transit* (1944) shows how difficult it was to obtain an exit visa and find a ship sailing from Europe. This period marked the beginning of a second phase of exile overseas – mostly to North and South America. This was even harder than the first phase, since it meant being cut off from the European cultural context. Few authors managed to gain a foothold in America. The most important factor in this was the new linguistic milieu, which was often perceived as artificial, resulting in its 'rejection' (Oskar Maria Graf).

> We speak German, and that's that. We have brought this language with us and we work in it. This nevertheless poses the question of what we as German writers can do to keep ourselves alive in a country that speaks a different language from our own. How can we find a niche for ourselves in the economy, and how can we fulfil our political and cultural responsibilities? One cannot destroy language without destroying the culture in oneself. And conversely, one cannot retain and cultivate a culture without speaking in the language in which this culture was formed and through which it lives.
>
> (Bloch)

The living and working conditions of exile were hard – harder than had been foreseen when writers were leaving Germany as fast as they could, often only with what they could carry. The confident mood of the first couple of years was soon deflated when it became clear that the Nazi regime had not in fact collapsed after a brief period of rule, but was stabilising and beginning to show signs of active aggression. This development made a theoretical analysis of the causes and nature of Nazism imperative. There would also have to be discussion of how the anti-fascist struggle was to be organised, and what function authors and literature could have within it.

The struggle for a united front among exiled authors

Out of isolation

The necessity of gathering together the scattered authors who had sought asylum in the countries bordering the German Reich, and rallying them to a joint struggle against fascism, was most clearly perceived by communist and socialist authors. The *Neue Deutsche Blätter*, founded in Prague in September 1933 and edited by Oskar Maria Graf, Anna Seghers, Wieland Herzfelde and Jan Petersen as an outlet for underground literature in the Third Reich, was the first attempt to unite exiled authors behind a coherent joint policy. The *Neue Deutsche Blätter* saw its task as that of 'galvanising its co-workers to joint action and mobilising readers to the same degree', seeking 'to oppose fascism by means of the poetic and critical word'. The editors were concerned from the very outset to keep the alliance they were seeking as broad as possible, thereby opening the way to cooperation with writers who rejected Nazism out of more or less diffuse humanitarian or cultural considerations, and who had reservations about, or were even mistrustful of, socialist and communist positions:

> Many see in fascism an anachronism, an intermezzo, a relapse into medieval barbarity. Others speak of a mental illness among the Germans, or of an anomaly contradicting the 'true' course of history, imagining the Nazis to be a horde of degenerates who have all of a sudden overrun their country. We, on the other hand, do not see in fascism an accidental form, but the organised product of a fatally sick capitalism. Is not every attempt to restore liberal-democratic conditions a refusal to pull up the sickness by the root? Is not every struggle concerned with form alone basically only empty show? Is there any real force capable of achieving lasting victory over want and tyranny other than the proletariat? We are convinced that the correct answers to these questions are of major importance for writers, since authenticity of account, and even the formal quality of literature depend on the depth of knowledge concerning all these events and their causes. This is our opinion. But nothing could be further from our minds than a desire to bring our co-workers 'into line'. . . . We shall allow everyone – even if their convictions are not the same as our own – to have his say, if only he will join us in our struggle.

In the exile journal *Die Sammlung* (*The Gathering*), published like the *Neue Deutsche Blätter* from September 1933 until August 1935, the editor Klaus Mann was likewise concerned with 'gathering' together all manner of dissident writers and focusing them on the joint struggle against fascism: 'We want to gather all with a will towards a future of human dignity, instead of a will to barbarity . . . ; the will towards reason instead of hysterical brutality and a shameless agenda of "Anti-Humanism" '. The slant of the journal, with a much weaker political profile than the *Neue Deutsche Blätter*, enabled it to crystallise a diversity of views. Contributors included convinced Marxists and socialists, as well as people of radical-democratic, Zionist, liberal and conservative views – even authors who saw themselves as apolitical.

These two exile publications, the *Neue Deutsche Blätter* and *Die Sammlung*, anticipated in miniature that anti-fascist alliance that was subsequently to play such a major part in the way exiled authors came to see both themselves and their literary work. They also marked the first step towards a united front that was to become an increasing irritant to the Nazis. Where Goebbels had been able in 1933 to sneer cynically at exiled authors as 'corpses on vacation', by 1935 he saw a 'European danger' in 'the poisonous literary potion of the uprooted émigré clique'.

In 1934 the united front began to put forward more concrete proposals – the formation of a broad anti-fascist alliance, for which Johannes R. Becher appealed to exiled authors in a key platform speech given at the All-Union Congress of Soviet Writers in Moscow. The *Programm zur Verteidigung der Kultur* (*Agenda for the Defence of Culture*) adopted at the 1935 writers' congress in Paris was so broadly formulated that the most widely diverging trends could identify with it. Brecht had already warned in 1933 of the danger that bourgeois and Marxist differences in the analysis of fascism might becoming blurred in the desire to create an alliance, putting those differences beyond the bounds of debate: 'The thesis that they [bourgeois authors] should basically be left alone so as not to forfeit their sympathy was never more false than it is now. They would be more open to real political education now than at any other time.' Brecht insisted that the agenda adopted should form the starting-point for a political and social analysis of fascism, taking criticism beyond that of specific inhuman manifestations of fascism into an analysis of the connection between capitalism, bourgeois society and fascism ('Comrades, let us speak of the question of ownership').

Alliance policy

Authors such as Becher and Brecht, who either belonged to the Communist Party or were sympathetic to it, were not alone in concentrating their efforts on the creation of an international alliance of all anti-fascist writers. There were also socialist and radical-democratic authors. This aim was given a boost in 1935 when the VIIth Comintern World Congress put forward the idea of the People's Front as a solution. Heinrich Mann became the central figure in the People's Front movement, the idea itself shaping his entire literary work during the period of exile. In support of the People's Front campaign he wrote a large number of essays, speeches and appeals, a small number of which even reached Germany illegally to circulate there. Heinrich Mann was convinced that 'only the German People's Front . . . can fulfil the task of uniting the people against Hitler', and that it alone could be the 'creator of a free and happier future for Germany'. As Chairman of the Preparatory Committee for setting up a German People's Front, Heinrich Mann was at pains to keep the political spectrum of the alliance as broad as possible, and above all to involve social democrats. The first call to form a German People's Front, *Bildet die deutsche Volksfront für Frieden, Freiheit und Brot* (*Form the German People's Front for Peace, Freedom and Bread*) (1936), thus proposed an agenda for a democratic revival of Germany based on the nationalisation of big industry, the large banks and extensive landed property, and the democratisation of administration and public life. This agenda did indeed succeed in attracting the signatures not only of communists, but also of social democrats and a number of leading bourgeois authors, such as Feuchtwanger, A. Zweig and Klaus Mann.

Despite the tireless efforts of Heinrich Mann and other authors, however, the work of the People's Front Committee had virtually reached a dead end by the summer of 1937. Lack of consensus on a coherent plan of action between the two workers' parties, the German Communist Party (KPD) and the German Socialist Party (SPD) – the same weakness that had made Hitler's rise to power possible in the first place – effectively crippled the work of the Committee and proved an obstacle to solidarity among its members. Leading social democrats, for example, saw in the People's Front 'not a weakening, but a strengthening of fascism'. The aim of the struggle could not be a 'unified front with communists, but the elimination of the communist parties in Western and Central Europe' (R. Hilferding). The official departure of the social democrats from the People's Front Committee thus marked the sorry end of the People's Front campaign that had been launched with such high hopes.

People's Front?

However, although the People's Front movement failed in the political objectives it set out to achieve, it did mark a significant phase in the political and literary growth of the writers involved in it. As a result of his experience in the People's Front movement, Heinrich Mann, for example, gained an astonishingly clear insight into the connection between fascism and capitalism on the one hand and between fascism and World War II on the other. His analysis of fascism arose out of his revised understanding of the writer as partner and ally of the working class, and his commitment to the idea of the political partisanship of the writer: 'In order to unfold, a talent must first take sides – the right side, that of human welfare.'

The Spanish Civil War

Involvement in the Spanish Civil War of 1936–9 was of no less significance to the way exiled writers came to see themselves. When the Spanish People's Front government was threatened by an army coup led by General Franco, Franco obtained massive military support from German and Italian fascists (the Condor Legion). The People's Front government was for its part backed by the Soviet Union, France and the International Brigades whose ranks included among others many German intellectual volunteers (see Gustav Regler's *Das grosse Beispiel* – *The Great Example*, 1940), including twenty-seven German writers fighting with the word as well as with arms. Erich Weinert, for example, addressed his brothers-in-arms in numerous poems and songs, collected under the title *Camaradas* (1947). Alfred Kantorowicz gives an account of the struggle of socialist and communist intellectuals in his *Spanisches Tagebuch* (*Spanish Diary*) (1948). Other authors supported the struggle indirectly with their literary work. Brecht addressed the Spanish Civil War in his one-act play *Die Gewehre der Frau Carrar* (*Señora Carrar's Rifles*) (1937). Señora Carrar, a Spanish fishwife, wants to save her son from fighting the fascists, and so sends him out to sea fishing. There, however, the unarmed son is shot by the fascists – exactly what his mother had been trying to avoid. Señora Carrar then hands out the rifles she had hidden in the house to the fighting comrades, and joins the struggle herself. Brecht wanted to show in this play that the struggle against fascism is unavoidable, and must be waged in solidarity.

The Expressionism–Realism debate: controversies over a new conception of themselves and literature among exiled authors

'Quality literature' (*Literatur von Rang*)

Behind the apparently self-assured conviction of many exiled authors that 'quality literature [was by definition] anti-fascist' lurked a number of problems. These included the question of the relationship between literature and reality, the function literature should adopt in class relations, what it means to be a political writer, what 'quality literature' is and how it should be recognised, and not least what anti-fascist literature actually was, and what distinguished it in form and content from other literature. The answers to these fundamental questions were sought in three major controversies: the Expressionism debate, discussion surrounding the concept of Realism, and the argument over the historical novel.

The Expressionism debate arose out of the question of whether Expressionism was a forerunner of fascism, or the starting-point for the development of an anti-fascist approach. Gottfried Benn's collaboration with the fascists seemed to speak in favour of the former interpretation, Johannes R. Becher's developing sympathy with Marxism and anti-fascism for the alternative view.

The debate itself was conducted in *Wort* (*Word*), a literary journal that had grown out of the People's Front movement ('*Kind der Volksfront* – *Child of the People's Front*'), and was intended to replace the *Neue Deutsche Blätter* and *Die Sammlung*, both of which had been forced to stop publication in 1935. The People's Front sympathies of this journal, which was published in Moscow, were clear from the make-up of the editorial staff. Besides the independent Marxist Bertolt Brecht there were also the

Communist Party member Willi Bredel and the bourgeois Lion Feucht-wanger. *Das Wort*, which was published from 1936–39, was among the most interesting exile journals and hardly a single leading exiled author did not contribute to it.

The Expressionism debate was precipitated by an essay by Klaus Mann, *Gottfried Benn, die Geschichte einer Verirrung* (*Gottfried Benn: the History of an Error*) and published in the September 1937 issue. The article described Benn's flirtation with fascism as 'self-betrayal' (*Selbstverrat*) and disputed the existence of any connection between Expressionism and fascism. In contrast with this, in the same issue Alfred Kurella asserted that there was a connection between Expressionism and fascism, declaring: 'First, it is obvious today whose spiritual child Expressionism is, and where that spirit leads if taken to its logical conclusion – to fascism. Second, we must all honestly admit that each and every one of us is still somewhat tarred with the brush of that era.' These two contributions established the key note, shifting what had originally been a discussion of Gottfried Benn's personal dilemma to a more general level. The question was no longer one of Benn's relationship with fascism, but the relationship of exiled authors with the literary heritage of Expressionism, making it indirectly a question of their literary and political origins and past. In other words, to what extent did exiled authors, as the literary intelligentsia, feel culpable for the political developments of 1933, and which tradition should they build on? There was a contradiction to be explained: why 'Benn, Bronnen, Heynicke and Johst had become mystics and fascists not in spite of, but because of Expressionism', and why 'Becher, Brecht, Wolf and Zech had become Realists and anti-fascists in spite of Expressionism' (Leschnitzer).

This debate could take up the thread laid by Lukács in 1934 in his essay ' "Grösse" und "Verfall" des Expressionismus' ('The "Greatness" and "Decline" of Expressionism'), published in Moscow in the exile journal *Internationale Literatur* (*International Literature*). In this essay Lukács had been chiefly concerned to take Expressionism to task for its over-abstract opposition to the bourgeoisie, its exaggerated subjective emotional-ism, its intellectual flight from reality, its longing for war as a renewal of the bohemian lifestyle and its rejection of the classical heritage. He likewise dismissed the avant-garde artistic methods of Expressionists as the sterile internal literary forms of a decadent subjectivity, calling on exiled authors to build on the German classical and the great bourgeois Realist tradition of the nineteenth century.

Expressionist elements 'worth passing on'?

Many authors became involved in this debate, some of them former Expressionists seeking to show that Expressionism definitely contained some elements that were 'worth passing on' and should not be condemned out of hand: 'It would be fatalism to assert that poets who took up Expressionism were bound to become fascist poets, or that there was no other alternative for the Expressionist than to become a fascist. One might as well assert that only fascism could have resulted from the Weimar Republic' (Kersten).

Ernst Bloch posed a polemical question: 'Are there no dialectical relationships between rise and fall? Does even the spurned, the immature and the incomprehensible always and inevitably have to be attributed to bourgeois decadence?' He was seeking here to clarify the dialectical connection between the bourgeois heritage, of which Expressionism was undoubtedly a part, and a literature that saw itself as socialist: 'Does the declining bourgeoisie, in the process of declining, contribute elements towards the building of the new world, and if so, what are those elements? It is a purely direct question, one of diabolical utility. As such, it would appear that it has so far been neglected, although it is entirely dialectical. For there may be a dialectically applicable "heritage" not only in the revolutionary rise or vigorous flowering of a class, but also in its decline and in the manifold factors released by its very disintegration.' Bloch was clearly cognisant of the fact that behind the Expressionism debate lay another question concerning the artistic methods of anti-fascist literature, i.e. whether exiled authors should abandon the experimental trends of the modern age in favour of drawing on the artistic methods of eighteenth- and nineteenth-century bourgeois authors.

Even behind the question of 'correct' method, however, lay the more or less tacit political issue of the breadth and diversity of the People's Front movement. Bloch was opposed to the 'black-and-white technique' of the neo-classicists, meaning Lukács and Kurella, of ascribing 'to the ruling class all opposition to the ruling class that is not communist from the outset', thereby irresponsibly limiting the People's Front alliance. Behind the uncompromising toughness in the way Lukács and Kurella conducted their debate on Expressionism, Bloch and others sensed an attempt to impose certain theories and ways of writing on exiled authors, and to implement a leading role for the German Communist Party in this important issue. The effect of the way in which the literary heritage of Expressionism was discussed was to alienate those authors who felt a commitment to Expressionist artistic methods and techniques, and who were open to experimentation with avant-garde formal procedures. All this effectively repelled them from the People's Front alliance. Seeking to wind up the debate formally, Kurella retracted his equation of Expressionism with pre-fascism ('Of course this won't do! The egregious statement is false'), and attempted to mediate between the two opposing sides by attributing to most Expressionists an 'objective reactionary creativity with subjective revolutionary intentions'. This scarcely bridged the gulf that had been created, however. In fact the real issue all along had only peripherally been Expressionism. Lukács's seminal essay *Es geht um den Realismus* (*It's all about Realism*), the final contribution to the debate, made it clear that the true issue was in fact Realism.

The Lukács–Brecht debate

The Expressionism debate itself thus formed part of a more far-reaching debate on Realism. First precipitated by discussion of formalism and Realism in the Soviet Union during the 1930s (at the first All-Union Congress of Soviet Writers, held in Moscow in 1934) this debate went on throughout the exile period. Authoritative contributions were made by Lukács himself, who advocated a conception of Realism based on the classical heritage, and Bertolt Brecht, who was seeking to elaborate a new Realism based on the practical necessities arising out of exile.

Brecht took Lukács's conception of Realism ruthlessly to task in a number of major essays (*Die Expressionismusdebatte – The Expressionism Debate; Praktisches zur Expressionismusdebatte – Some Practical Remarks on the Expressionism Debate; Weite und Vielfalt der realistischen Schreibweise – The Breadth and Diversity of the Realistic Writing Style; Volkstümlichkeit und Realismus – Popularity and Realism*), revealing its formalistic nature. For the sake of the external solidarity of the People's Front, however, Brecht did not publish these essays, originally written for publication in *Das Wort*. Only *The Breadth and Diversity of the Realistic Writing Style* was published in his own lifetime (in 1955) – an article that had failed to be published partly because of a refusal by the publisher of *Das Wort*.

In general terms, Brecht maintained that there could be no question of simply 'extracting' something called 'Realism' from 'certain existing works', such as the novels of Goethe, Balzac or Tolstoy, and then setting it up as a model for the present-day. The realistic writing style, 'of which literature provides many highly divergent examples', was not some supra-historical writing form to which authors could cling, but rather characterised by 'when, how and for which class' it was employed. Brecht tried to use his own definition of Realism to explode the formalistic framework of Lukács's definition: 'Realistic means uncovering the social causal complex / exposing the ruling points of reference as the reference points of the ruling class / writing from the standpoint of the class that has the broadest solutions available / for the most urgent problems in which human society finds itself / emphasising the developmental factor / concretely and enabling abstraction.'

The people versus barbarity

Brecht also combined the call for Realism with the call for a popular approach (*Volkstümlichkeit*), taking up a category that had played a major role among socially critical *Sturm und Drang* and eighteenth-century Jacobin authors: 'To counter increasing barbarism there is only one ally: the people who suffer so greatly under it. Only from them can anything be expected. Our obvious course, therefore, is to turn to the people, which makes it more essential than ever to speak their language.' This effectively combined the watchwords of popularity and Realism in a natural way. For Brecht, 'popular' meant 'comprehensible to the broad masses, adopting and enriching their form of expression / taking their part, securing and correcting it / representing the most progressive section of the people in such a way that it can assume leadership, therefore also being comprehensible to other sections of the people / drawing on traditions, taking them further / mediating the achievements of that section that now leads the people to that section that is striving for leadership.' A writer does not become 'popular' by adopting writing styles that were formerly popular: 'what was popular yesterday is not popular today, because the people are not the same today as they were yesterday'. To be 'popular' consists solely in taking into account the present requirements of the class struggle. For his own day, Brecht recommended authors to employ their inventiveness, originality, humour and imaginative faculties resolutely and regardless of literary convention in the pursuit of new literary techniques in the struggle against fascism. He also tried to put these 'gigantic assignments' into practice in his own writing.

The special role of the historical novel

In comparison with the Realism debate, the dispute surrounding the historical novel might at first glance seem insignificant. In fact, however, it was closely related, giving solid literary form to what would otherwise have been a relatively abstract discussion of how Realism was to be understood. The historical novel genre had enjoyed a high regard even during the Weimar Republic, particularly among conservative and fascist writers. Kolbenheyer's *Paracelsus* trilogy (1917–26), and numerous accounts glorifying Friedrich II might be mentioned in this connection. Besides an endless string of historical novels serving largely to confuse or even misrepresent, there were a few novels that gave an unretouched account, such as Döblin's *Wallenstein* (1920), Feuchtwanger's *Jud Süss* (*Süss the Jew*) (1925) and Neumann's *Der Teufel* (*The Devil*) (1926).

Lack of political instinct?

At first sight the events of 1933 did not seem to stem this flow of historical novels. Thomas Mann took his plan for the *Joseph* novel with him when he left for exile, while his brother Heinrich had already worked out his plan for *Henri Quatre* before 1933. Of Joseph Roth's trilogy on the decline of the Austrian monarchy, the first volume had already appeared in the 1920s, and Alfred Neumann had likewise already worked out the concept of his trilogy on nineteenth-century French history in the Weimar period.

This apparently seamless continuation by exiled authors of the historical novel of the Weimar Republic aroused indignation and antagonism among their contemporaries. Some critics, for example, interpreted the preoccupation with the historical novel on the part of exiled authors in terms of a lack of political instinct: 'The choice of a historical theme in an émigré German writer generally indicates an evasion or flight from present-day problems. Flight and evasion are not signs of strength. This [fact] is bound to come out in the works of evasive or escapist authors, and it does' (Weiskopf). Weiskopf's verdict on exiled authors thus put them on the same plane as the authors of the 'internal emigration', who also had a particularly high regard for the historical novel. Kurt Hiller had even more damning condemnation than Weiskopf, dismissing 'biographitis' as a 'symptom of pathetic procrastination' and describing it as a 'scandal that stinks to high heaven': 'But when this brood of belletrists fills the heads of their readership with all this guff about Catherine of Russia, Christine of Sweden, Josephine of France, Ferdinand I, Phillip II, Napoleon III, the false Nero and the true Peter and all this knowledge of things that are not worth knowing . . . , then this bunch of has-beens deserves the juiciest curse'.

History as refuge

By way of response to this, the authors in question sought to defend the historical novel, as well as to outline the function the genre could have in the struggle against fascism, and to establish how it differed both from the historical novel of the Weimar Republic and that of 'internal emigration'. In his essay *Historie und kein Ende* (*History and No End*) (1936), Döblin offered a vehement defence against the accusation of escapism, instead describing history as a 'refuge', 'something that cannot be lost, a precious thing' to which one could and should hold in the face of fascist distortions of history. He explained the predilection of exiled authors for the historical novel in terms of the 'desire to find historical parallels, to locate themselves in history and justify themselves', the necessity 'of recollecting themselves' and the 'inclination to take comfort, and in their imaginations at least, revenge'. He stressed the 'contemporary content' of the historical novel, as did Ludwig Marcuse, who declared categorically: 'The century or decade to which a fable belongs does not decide its meaningfulness for the present day.'

Similarly, Feuchtwanger saw in the historical novel first and foremost a creative vehicle in the anti-fascist struggle (*Vom Sinn und Unsinn des historischen Romans – On the Sense and Nonsense of the Historical Novel*, 1935). He posed two provocative questions, throwing writing practice open and raising the discussion to a new level: 'If you want to provide contemporary themes, why don't you relate contemporary themes instead of the past?', and 'If a reader is interested in the past, then isn't it better for him to take an exact scholarly account than the fictional invention of a novelist?'

By 1938, the arguments brought by authors against the accusation of escapism were carrying so much weight that a working conference of the SDS was able to take place on the theme of *Der historische Stoff als Waffe im Kampf um die Freiheit* (*Historical Themes as Weapons in the Struggle for Freedom*). The strongest argument of all was in the literary works themselves. The novels *Henri Quatre* (1935–8) by Heinrich Mann, *Der falsche Nero* (*The False Nero*) (1936) by Feuchtwanger, and *Die Saat* (*The Seed*) (1936) by Regler were held up as positive examples, and hailed by critics as 'a topical call to arms, indeed to some extent a direct instruction to enter the battle against fascist tyranny' (Abusch). The historical novel was officially reinstated with the work of Georg Lukács (*Der historische Roman – The Historical Novel*, 1938), who saw in Heinrich Mann's *Henri Quatre* a consummate example of the genre, despite critising a number of details.

Lukács sought to determine the specific anti-fascist substance of the historical novel of exile – as opposed to that of the Weimar Republic or 'internal emigration'. He saw the significance of the medium of the historical novel not so much in its criticism of fascism through the drawing of parallels and contrasts, but rather in the artistic character of the genre:

> The significance of the historical novel of German anti-fascists lies in its very 'poetic' quality: in creating and bringing to life in specific poetic images that Humanistic type of man whose social victory entails at the same time a social and political victory over fascism. That type of man whose universality and supremacy brings with it the cultural salvation of man; that type for whose sake the struggle against fascism becomes a cultural obligation for each and every one of us; that human type under whose banner the struggle against fascism, the struggle of the People's Front, should proceed.

For Lukács the historical novels of the German anti-fascists were a 'reflection of the radical ideological shift among the intelligentsia' caused by having been driven out of their country by the fascists. It had only external generic features in common with the historical novel of the Weimar Republic or of the 'internal emigration'. The historical novel of exile was the medium in which the political orientation of the intelligentsia came about and was dealt with on the artistic level as a 'struggle between the liberal and the democratic world-view in the soul of the Peoples' Front writers'. The most artistically and politically progressive of these novels in his view was *Henri Quatre*, in which Lukács saw 'the beginning of a return to the traditions of the classical historical novel': 'The heroes of the new historical novel are individuals from world history, political leaders, literary geniuses, etc., presented as representatives of historical mass and popular movements.' It was in this new conception of the hero that Lukács saw the feature distinguishing the exile novel from both the nineteenth-century historical novel and that of the Weimar Republic: 'The new historical novel transcends the incoherence of the lonely hero of major historical movements, and restores a long-lost historical connection.'

Despite all this, Lukács still felt an absence in historical novels by exiled authors of the final artistic perfection of the form, which he saw as a political weakness on the part of the author: 'But the artistic composition of these novels is still mostly modern, permeated by the false liberal traditions, hostile to the people, of a bygone age; it is not yet popular, not yet democratic.'

Lukács's plea for the historical novel

Lukács's plea for the historical novel is an expression of the concept of Realism he had already elaborated in the Expressionism debate, and which had provoked strong opposition from Brecht. This controversy between Lukács and Brecht inevitably extended into the historical novel. In his historical novel *Die Geschäfte des Herrn Julius Cäsar* (*The Business Dealings of Mr Julius Caesar*), on which he began work in 1938, fully mindful of the historical novel debate, Brecht offered a counter-image both to the historical novel of his writer colleagues (he gently mocked *Der Neue Cäsar – The New Caesar* by Neumann), and to the 'canonisation' of the type by Lukács. In his Caesar, Brecht sought not to depict 'heroic deeds in the old style' but 'to offer indications of how dictatorships are set up and empires are built'. In Caesar's rise Brecht wanted to show Hitler's last few years before seizing power, showing the SA in the fighting mobs of Catilina, the *Freikorps* (paramilitaries) in the old street clubs and the unions in the professional associations. In the threatened slave uprising he wanted to show the revolutionary situation of Germany in the final years of the Weimar Republic. Brecht was thus concerned not with portraying the 'positive hero' for whom Lukács had called, but rather with a satirical demolition of the type. In his biography of Caesar Brecht erected a monument of irony to writer colleagues fascinated by history and avid to research details of Caesar's private life and gather the 'countless moving traits' of his character so as to pass them on to posterity. Brecht's novel thus contains a 'double lesson': 'The "real" Caesar is what he is in his "dealings", and the chronicler of history has only fulfilled his task when he learns how to chronicle those deeds' (Schröter).

Anti-fascist literary practice

Heinrich Mann's view that 'anti-fascist literature . . . [is] in reality the only German literature' reflected the understanding that many exiled authors had of themselves. Although it was no more than a desire or an agenda, it conferred upon literature the task of waging the struggle against fascism by its own particular means: 'The very fact of emigration is indicative of the facts and correlations. It is the voice of the [German] people who have been struck dumb, and it should remain so before all the world. . . . The emigrant community will insist that the greatest Germans were and are those with that voice, which means at the same time the best Germany' (*Aufgaben der Emigration – The Tasks of Emigration*, 1934).

This ambitious notion of emigration resulted in a dual objective for anti-fascist literary practice:

> On the one hand was the issue of a warning to the world about the Third Reich and making it aware of the true nature of the regime, as well as the issue of keeping in contact with the other, better Germany – the illegal underground Germany with its secret opposition to the regime – and providing the Resistance movement back home with literary material. On the other hand, there was also the task of keeping alive abroad and cultivating with one's own creative contribution the great tradition of the German intellect and the German language – a tradition for which there was no longer any place in the land of its origin.
>
> (Klaus Mann)

These two diverging functions of émigré literature called forth different literary approaches. By drawing on and following traditional bourgeois forms such as the historical novel or the *Gesellschaftsroman*, authors tried to place themselves within a tradition they believed had been broken by fascism. Alternatively, using 'operational' genres such as disguised texts, radio speeches, pamphlets, manifestos, etc., they sought to wage a direct campaign against fascism. These diverging tasks were not distributed among various authors in a division of labour, but were mostly practised side by side in the work of individual authors. The anti-fascist author was indeed defined by the very fact that he combined in a single dialectical unity, in his own person, what were otherwise more often than not two mutually distinct aspects of literary practice – 'non-operational' and 'operational' artistic creation.

Heinrich Mann

The literary practice of Heinrich Mann was not least marked by the fact that he wrote the most important historical novel of the exile period, *Henri Quatre*. He sought through this book above all to clarify in creative literary form his views on the state of the world and the conduct of men by taking an example from history, hoping in this way to support the anti-fascist struggle by presenting a 'true likeness'. At the same time, his exile work in the struggle against fascism was also characterised by prolific direct involvement in political journalism. Between 1933 and 1945 he wrote over 330 essays as part of his tireless efforts to bring about a German People's Front alliance. Some of these essays were successfully smuggled into Germany via the underground to support the local Resistance.

Similarly, his brother Thomas Mann was also active through his traditional work as a writer. It was in exile that he wrote his biblical tetralogy *Joseph und seine Brüder* (*Joseph and his Brothers*) (1933–45), the historical novel *Lotte in Weimar* (1938) and the major contemporary novel *Doktor Faustus* (1947). But he, too, participated directly in the anti-fascist struggle with numerous essays, and most especially with his famous radio speeches.

Literature and politics

Anti-fascist authors represent a type of political writer that had previously only surfaced in exceptional cases and periods of social upheaval, such as the *Vormärz*. Politics and literature are doubly linked, firstly in the combination of journalism with literary creation, and secondly in the aspiration to give a political aspect to literary work – and conversely to achieve a literary quality in political journalism.

Exiled authors not only followed in the tradition of the historical novel of the Weimar Republic, but also creatively developed the *Gesellschaft* (social) and contemporary novels with a view to anti-fascist objectives. Noteworthy in this regard are the novels *Abschied* (*Farewell*) (1940) by Becher, *Die Väter* (*The Fathers*) (1943) by Bredel, *Adel im Untergang* (*Nobility in Decline*) (1944) by Renn, *Pardon wird nicht gegeben* (*Pardon Will Not Be Granted*) (1935) and the *November 1918* trilogy (written 1937–43, published 1948–50) by Döblin, all of which take fascism to task in an authentic manner, giving a penetrating account of both personal and historical experience. Döblin's novel *Pardon wird nicht gegeben* in particular held a mirror up to the 1890–1930 period as a preparatory phase for the fascist takeover. Using numerous autobiographical elements in a highly stylised and typified form in some respects reminiscent of his novel *Berlin*

Alexanderplatz (1929), Döblin relates the story of an entire generation, using the example of the farmer's son Karl, who flees to the city from the horrors of poverty in his class, gains a foothold in middle-class life and becomes a factory-owner, allowing himself to be both politically and morally corrupted by the capitalist system. A massive economic crisis destroys both the family and financial lifestyle that he has established with such effort and inhumanity. At the end of the novel Karl meets his former childhood friend Paul, who is fighting for the rights of the working class, and who retorts laconically 'Pardon will not be granted' to his friend's attempts to justify himself. Karl would like to join his friend in the struggle, but is shot in street fighting that obviously echoes Döblin's own experiences of the 1918 November Revolution.

Anna Seghers

Anna Seghers's novel *Das siebte Kreuz* (*The Seventh Cross*) is better known than Döblin's. The novel was first published in English in 1942, not appearing in German until 1947. Dedicated to 'anti-fascist Germany, dead and alive' it made the author world-famous. Something of a counterpart to Jan Petersen's underground novel *Unsere Strasse* (*Our Street*), *The Seventh Cross* gives a highly differentiated and impressive picture of German reality under the Third Reich, as well as an account of the anti-fascist Resistance. Her familiarity with conditions within Germany and her differentiated assessment of them are all the more remarkable in that Anna Seghers lived in exile from 1933 onwards, cut off from direct experience of everyday life under fascism. She obtained her basic data on everyday fascism from newspapers, documents, archive material, and numerous conversations and interviews with former German concentration-camp prisoners. It was from such reports that she learned of the seven crosses erected for seven escaped prisoners. In her novel these crosses become a symbol of the anti-fascist Resistance. The escape of the seven prisoners, of whom only the communist Georg Heisler manages to evade his pursuers, becomes a touchstone for the personal and political morality of those with whom Georg Heisler comes in contact. Some do not pass the test, while others develop a kind of solidarity through their encounter with the fugitive that transcends personal interests and takes on a political quality. The commitment of the author to the Peoples' Front is the focal point around which her literary material is organised and according to which the actions and attitudes of her characters are judged.

Not as famous as *The Seventh Cross*, which was also made into a film, is Anna Seghers's novel *Transit* (1944), which along with Feuchtwanger's *Exil* (1940) ranks among the most important documents of exile literature. These two novels are concerned neither with analysing the period leading up to the fascist era, nor with ascertaining the element of personal responsibility for it, but rather with the experience of living in exile. Both are still well worth reading today as documents of the period.

Newspapers and journals in exile

In addition to the bourgeois historical, *Gesellschafts-* and contemporary novel genres, a wealth of journalistic forms were used for political ends. These should be seen as both an expression of exile and an attempt to come to terms with it. During the twelve years of the exile period journalism underwent an astonishing upsurge. Well over 400 exile journals, enduring for longer or shorter periods, appeared between 1933 and 1945. As well as expressing the material and idealistic needs of exiled Germans, they also reflected the fragmentation of the Left, which intensified in exile. As early as the summer of 1933 Tucholsky complained of the disordered heterogeneity of the exile press: 'Instead of founding just one good journal, everyone is founding one, and of course they will all fold together. It is a great pity.' Despite this fragmentation, journals were

> virtually the sole means available for combating both the break-up of political groups and the isolation of the individual. Journals were able to bridge the geographical gap separating exiles as a result of their political and material circumstances. In this way, although they exerted hardly any effect at all on the outside world, they were remarkably successful within the exile community itself in preserving or even restoring a reading public. They thus not only verbalised the determination of their editors and publishers, but to a far greater degree acted as instruments whereby readers could reach an understanding of themselves and create a political will, just as in 'normal' times. Journals also assumed organisational functions in the preparation for and implementation of politically and culturally significant movements – functions that they would hardly have been assigned under conditions other than exile. They acted as a stabilising element, an intellectual buttress, to some extent even becoming 'imaginary' centres.

> (H.A. Walter)

Among the most important exile periodicals connected with the People's Front movement were *Die Neue Weltbühne* (*The New World Stage*), a continuation of *Die Weltbühne*, which had been edited by Tucholsky and Ossietzky during the Weimar Republic; *Die Sammlung* (*The Gathering*), edited by Klaus Mann; *Neue Deutsche Blätter*, edited by Anna Seghers, Oskar Maria Graf, Wieland Herzfelde and Jan Petersen; and *Das Wort*, edited by Brecht, Feuchtwanger and Bredel and published in Moscow.

All these journals were partisan in the sense that their anti-fascist editors and contributors saw their journalism as a form of political militancy:

'Wer schreibt, handelt!' ('He who writes, acts!') The age-old contradiction between word and deed, poet and politician, was swept aside by the anti-fascist writer's new understanding of his own role: 'In Germany the National Socialists are on the rampage. We are in a state of war. There is no neutrality. Not for anyone. Least of all for the writer. Even he who is silent is taking part in the struggle. He who flees into a purely private existence, horror-struck and stunned by events, he who uses the weapon of words as a toy or adornment, he who detaches himself and acquiesces, condemns himself to social and artistic sterility and leaves the field to the enemy.'

From the very outset the concept of literature was so broadly construed that not only were 'pamphlets, indictments, outcries' given a place in these journals, but also 'literature of all kinds', i.e. even literature that sought to treat the experiences of the times in traditional literary forms. 'Precisely in this way we hope to demonstrate to the international public that it is no coincidence that virtually all representatives of the German literary scene are resolute opponents of the "Third Reich" ' (*Das Wort*).

Enlightening world public opinion

The role of the anti-fascist exile press in fostering self-understanding among exiles should not be underestimated, but the goals of enlightening world public opinion concerning fascism in Germany and of obtaining support for the Resistance movement in the Third Reich, were only minimally successful. 'Exile journals [have not achieved] visible political success. They have become important and enduring documents of a powerless opposition' (H.A. Walter).

Disguised texts smuggled into Germany at great risk, of which so far well over 500 are known, were intended as direct support for the Resistance movement in Germany. These were printed matter 'containing anti-fascist texts with harmless, innocuous cover titles, sometimes with forged imprints or mastheads (publisher, printer, place and date of publication) as a safe-guard against police seizure, and to protect the distributors and readers of anti-fascist texts' (Gittig). After underground printers still operating in the early years of Nazi rule had been rooted out by the Gestapo, such texts were printed abroad and then smuggled into the country in relatively large numbers of copies (up to 10,000 per edition) and then distributed by Resistance groups. Brecht's essay *Fünf Schwierigkeiten beim Schreiben der Wahrheit* (*Five Difficulties in Writing the Truth*), for example, was smuggled into Germany under the ironic and suggestive title *Praktischer Wegweiser für Erste Hilfe* (*Practical Hints for First Aid*), or *Satzungen des Reichsverbandes Deutscher Schriftsteller* (*Regulations of the Reich Association of German Writers*). Thomas Mann's correspondence with the University of Bonn in 1937 was camouflaged as *Briefe deutscher Klassiker*

(*Letters of Classic German Authors*); an extract from Renn's anti-fascist novel *Krieg* (*War*) was even smuggled into Germany under the name of the fascist author Werner Beumelberg. Well over thirty essays and a large number of proclamations and pamphlets by Heinrich Mann were similarly smuggled into Germany.

The impact of these texts within the Reich is partially documented. It is known, for example, that transcripts of Heinrich Mann's speeches circulated in various concentration camps. A comprehensive anthology of exile literature was even published in 1935 in Leipzig under the title *Deutsch für Deutsche* (*German for Germans*). Compiled by the Paris branch of the SDS (Federation for the Protection of German Writers), it included poems by Brecht, Becher and Weinert, short stories by Seghers, Feuchtwanger, Graf, Bredel, and Scharrer, and essays by Klaus and Heinrich Mann and Toller.

Freiheitssender (*Freedom Radio Station*)

Another way of exerting a direct impact on the German people was through radio broadcasts of speeches by anti-fascist writers. From the famous *Freiheitssender* (Freedom Radio Station) Heinrich Mann broadcast passionate appeals to the German people: 'Do not miss this hour! You can yet rise up against these depraved tormentors of all peoples! (!!!) Sabotage his war! Overthrow Hitler!' Thomas Mann also appealed to the German nation to rise up against fascism in his *Fifty-five Radio Broadcasts to Germany*, broadcast to Germany by the BBC from October 1940 until the capitulation in May 1945. In his *Ansprachen an deutsche Hörer* (*Addresses to German Listeners*), as the series was officially called, Thomas Mann gave political commentaries on current events and the war, exposing the criminal nature of fascism, offering reasons for its inevitable defeat and appealing to the Humanist strengths within his listeners to fight against it. This employment of mass media such as radio was one of the ways Thomas Mann was compelled by circumstances to break out of the esotericism of traditional book production which, compared with radio, was only capable of reaching a negligible literary elite among the German people, and could not possibly hope to combat fascism on an effective mass scale.

'What the Fuehrer Doesn't Know'

Bertolt Brecht wrote satirical poetry for the German *Freiheitssender* (*Was der Fuehrer nicht weiss* – *What the Fuehrer Does Not Know*; *Wörter, die der Fuehrer nicht hören kann* – *Words That the Fuehrer Cannot Hear*; *Die Sorgen des Kanzlers* – *The Worries of the Chancellor*; *Dauer des Dritten Reichs* – *The Duration of the Third Reich*, etc). Lyric poetry in general was a widely-employed 'operational' literary form among exiled writers. The political poem, i.e. a poem with an original political meaning and intended for use in the anti-fascist struggle, was a counterbalance to the nature poem of the 'internal emigration', which could only hope to have an indirect political function. Even during the Weimar Republic Brecht had severely criticised bourgeois authors purporting to write pure, apolitical lyric poetry in the tradition of Rilke, George and Hofmannsthal. He had dismissed them as reprehensible inasmuch as, in his opinion, they either glorified or justified criminal political acts ('Ach, vor eure in Dreck und Blut versunkene Karren / Haben wir noch immer unsere grossen Wörter gespannt!' – Oh, we have always harnessed our great words / Before your carts sunk in filth and blood!'). Alternatively, Brecht had labelled them as disorienting and harmful, insofar as they provided the reader with a purely self-centred pleasure that diverted their attention away from the problems of the here-and-now, rendering them politically defenceless ('Wir haben die Wörter studiert und gemischt wie Drogen / Und haben nur die besten und allerstärksten verwandt / Die sie von uns bezogen, haben sie eingesogen / Und waren wie Lämmer in eurer Hand' – 'We studied and mixed words like drugs / And only used the best and the very strongest / Those they drew from us, they have soaked up / And were like lambs in your hand').

Schlechte Zeit für Lyrik (A Bad Time for Lyric poetry)

In his poem Schlechte Zeit für Lyrik (A Bad Time for Lyric poetry), Brecht deals with the dilemma of the lyric poet confronted with the political realities of his day: 'In mir streiten sich / Die Begeisterung über den blühenden Apfelbaum / Und das Entsetzen über die Reden des Anstreichers / Aber nur das zweite / Drängt mich zum Schreibtisch' ('There is a war inside me / Between my excitement at the blossoming apple-tree / And my revulsion at the speeches of the Dauber [Hitler] / But only the latter forces me to my desk'). In exile, the stimulus to write poems lay for Brecht and other lyric poets, such as Weinert and Becher, in their 'revulsion' at fascism, and in the desire to give expression to that revulsion and shake the reader into action.

However, this could only be achieved by poems dealing with current problems, and structured in such a way as to have an enlightening effect on the reader. In his didactic poems (Was nutzt uns die Güte – What Use is Goodness to Us?; Fragen eines lesenden Arbeiters – Questions of a Reading Worker; An die Nachgeborenen – To Those Born After), and above all in his satirical poems, Brecht aimed to develop a form of political lyric poetry marking a qualitatively new stage in its history. The Svendborger Gedichte (Svendborg Poems) (1939), written in exile in Denmark, contain a wealth of themes, motifs and lyric poetry forms. Besides satire for the purposes of political strategy there are ballads, and didactic poems intended to teach a political world-view, and lyric self-portraits in which the social context is nevertheless ever-present. Even Brecht's love poetry seeks to contribute towards a form of friendly and humane relationships that had inevitably been greatly jeopardised by the 'dark times' of fascism.

Homesickness for the 'better' Germany

The poetry of Erich Weinert was more in conformity with the traditional type of political lyric poetry, most of it being written in connection with the Spanish Civil War (*Camaradas*, 1947), as was that of Johannes Becher, which picked up from the classical traditions of political poetry. Becher's *Tränen des Vaterlands, Anno 1937* (*Tears of the Fatherland, Anno 1937*) was thus a deliberate successor to Gryphius's sonnet *Tränen des Vaterlands*. Becher also wrote nature poems, which were nevertheless fundamentally different from the nature lyric poetry of the 'internal emigration'. Like Brecht's nature poetry (*Frühling – Spring; Vom Sprengen des Gartens – On the Watering of the Garden; Der Pflaumenbaum – The Plum Tree*), Becher's nature poetry was not an expression of flight from political reality, but an articulation of homesickness for Germany, embodied by the landscape of Germany to which he still felt deeply attached.

The role of Bertolt Brecht

The literary work of Bertolt Brecht was one of the high points in anti-fascist literature of the exile period. He was of equal importance as literary theorist, lyric poet and dramatist, and the epitome of what Benjamin described as the 'politically functioning writer' ('operierender Schriftsteller'), in whom there was a functional interdependence of 'progressive literary technique' and 'the right political tendency', thereby doing away with the contradiction between politics and literature. Brecht showed himself superior to most other exiled authors both in his analysis and assessment of fascism and in his development of new literary forms. These he derived from the requirements of the anti-fascist struggle, and not, as Lukács had done, from an abstract concept of Realism: 'For literary forms one must inquire after reality, not aesthetics, not even Realism. Truth can be suppressed in many ways and expressed in many ways. We derive both our aesthetics and our sense of morality from the requirements of our struggle.'

'Die Roheit kommt nicht von der Roheit' ('Brutality does not come from brutality')

The analysis of fascism made by Brecht in his *Aufsätze über den Fascismus* (*Essays on Fascism*) (1933–9) forms the starting-point for his literary theory and practice. Brecht did not see Nazism as error, a natural catastrophe, an unfortunate chain of events, fate or an invasion of evil, as many bourgeois authors frequently did. He offered a materialist explanation to counter the view of bourgeois intellectuals, which saw in fascism merely the general lawlessness and brutalisation of man within modern civilisation: 'Brutality does not come from brutality, but from the businesses that can no longer be run without it. . . . Many of us writers who have experienced the horrors of fascism and are revolted by it have not yet learned this lesson and have failed to uncover the root of the brutality that revolts them. In their case there is still the danger that they will see the atrocities of fascism as unnecessary atrocities.' Holding to the Marxist assessment of fascism, Brecht regarded Nazism as the German variety of fascism: 'Fascism is a historical phase that capitalism has entered, and is to this extent both something new and something old. Fascism now exists in fascist countries only as fascism alone, and can only be combated as capitalism in its most naked, shameless, oppressive and deceptive form.' Brecht likened authors who were against fascism without being against capitalism to people

> who want to eat their share of the calf without the calf having to be slaughtered. They want to eat the calf, but they don't want to see the blood. They are satisfied if the butcher washes his hands before serving the meat. They are not against the conditions of ownership that give rise to barbarity, only against barbarity. They raise their voices against barbarity, doing so in countries in which the self-same conditions of ownership obtain, but where the butchers do wash their hands before serving the meat.

Fascism and capitalism in Brecht's analysis

Brecht saw his task as a writer to consist in clarifying through the medium of art the connection between Nazism, fascism and capitalism, as well as pointing out the prospects for the anti-fascist struggle. He aimed through his works to break apart the indifference and lethargy into which many people had fallen, faced with the horrors of fascism.

> The first time we reported that our friends were being slaughtered, there was a cry of outrage and a great deal of help. Then a hundred were slaughtered. When, however, a thousand were slaughtered and there was no end to the slaughter, a silence fell, and there was very little help. . . . That's the way it is, then. How can this be curbed? Is there no way of stopping a man from turning away from horrors? Why does he turn away? He turns away because he sees no chance for intervention. A man does not linger over the suffering of another if he cannot help him.

In a situation of this kind, literature takes on itself the task of pointing out to readers the chances for intervention, guiding them from the passive role of sympathisers, and mobilising them towards action to bring about change. In order to discover the causes of horror and the prospects for overcoming it, in Brecht's view, the writer needs knowledge above all: 'Apart from conviction, acquirable knowledge is necessary, and learnable methods. For all writers in these times of interconnected events and great changes a knowledge of materialist dialectic, economics and history is necessary. This can be obtained from books and from practical textbooks, provided the necessary desire to work is there.' Brecht had already made an intensive study of Marxism during the Weimar Republic. His *Heilige Johanna der Schlachthöfe* (*St Joan of the Stockyards*) (1927), and above all the plays he wrote during exile, are a testimony to how productive his critical adoption of Marxism and dialectical methods were for his artistic creation.

A didactic play on racism

Brecht's didactic play *Die Rundköpfe und die Spitzköpfe* (*The Roundheads and the Pointedheads*) started out in the 1930s as an adaptation of Shakespeare's *Measure for Measure*. Under the impact of the fascist takeover and exile, however, Brecht set about revising this version, completing it in 1934. His aim was to uncover the function of racist politics for Nazism. Brecht saw Nazi racial persecution, which was a declared element of the Nazi agenda long before 1933, as a political ruse to distract attention from existing class conflicts and the severe economic crisis. In this respect he differed sharply from bourgeois authors such as Ferdinand Bruckner, in whose play *Die Rassen* (*The Races*) (1933) the causes of Nazi racist policy were clouded in mystical obscurity like a kind of 'shadow boxing', and Walter Hasenclever, whose comedy *Konflikt in Assyrien* (*Conflict in Assyria*) (1938) launched an ironic attack on anti-semitism. There were nevertheless points of agreement between Brecht and an author such as Friedrich Wolf, who also dealt with the theme of the fascist racist insanity in his *Professor Mamlock* (1934), which was an attack on fascism as a whole.

A didactic play about fascism

However, this assessment by Brecht almost carelessly underestimated the danger of a Nazi 'racial theory' that ultimately led to the extermination of six million Jews. Faced later with the mass murder of Jews, he himself admitted this and distanced himself from the play. In his didactic play *Der aufhaltsame Aufstieg des Arturo Ui* (*The Resistible Rise of Arturo*) (1941), he dealt with the connection between fascism and capitalism again, in the form of a political parable. The rise of the Nazis is set in the Al Capone milieu of Chicago. He had already set the birth of capitalist business in Chicago in his *Heilige Johanna der Schlachthöfe*. As Brecht writes in his remarks on *Arturo Ui*, he aimed to explain 'to the capitalist world the rise of Hitler by shifting it into a milieu with which it was familiar', while at the same time drawing attention to the structural analogy between fascism and organised crime – an analogy that had already been suggested by theorists such as Max Horkheimer. In an even more powerful way than in *Die Rundköpfe und die Spitzköpfe* (*The Roundheads and the Pointedheads*), *Arturo Ui* is a key political play in which the principal protagonists of German politics from 1929–38 and the main locations of the fascist seizure and stabilisation of power are 'distanced' and presented in a 'great historical gangster show'. The ties between German economic institutions and the Nazis are pointed out through the collaboration between the head of the Cauliflower Trust and the gangster boss Arturo Ui, exposing not only the 'gangster methods' of the Nazis, but also the interest of the economy and of industry in the fascist takeover. One criticism has often been raised against Brecht, that by shifting the action to a gangster milieu he was simplifying history in an unacceptable way, in particular playing down the terrorist character of the fascist regime. This touches on a real weakness of plays of the didactic type. In didactic plays Brecht could only ever deal with and point out one aspect of reality at a time through alienation: the parable character of the didactic play made simplifications inevitable. Complex interconnections within society, such as between fascism and racism in *The Roundheads and the Pointedheads*, or between fascism and capitalism in *Arturo Ui*, could not be dealt with in all their subtlety in the didactic play, nor would they have been compatible with the aim of political agitation proper to this type of play.

The limits of the didactic play

Brecht himself was clearly aware of the limitations of the didactic play, and began to experiment with other dramatic forms during his exile, although without ever abandoning the didactic character of his plays. In the sequence *Furcht und Elend des Dritten Reiches* (*Fear and Misery of the Third Reich*) (1935–8), he made a montage 'table of gestures', as he himself called the play, of twenty-four scenes (in the final version) from everyday life under fascism. Brecht is less concerned here with exposing politico-economic and historical relationships, as in the didactic plays, than with the social psychology of fascism. He shows how fascism penetrates all spheres of life, poisoning and destroying human relationships. On the occasion of the premiere in Paris, Walter Benjamin referred specifically to this social-psychology aspect of Brecht's critique of fascism, namely how unavoidably the reign of terror boasted about before the nations by the

Third Reich subjugates all human relationships to the rule of the lie. The lie takes the form of statements under oath in court (the 'Finding of Justice') and science that teaches statements that are not allowed to be put into practice (the 'Occupational Sickness'); it is that which is ascribed to the public ('Referendum'), and that which is whispered into the ears of the dying (the 'Sermon on the Mount'). It is that which is hydraulically compressed into what a married couple say to each other in the last minutes of their life together (the 'Jewish Wife'); it is the mask put on by sympathy while it still dares to show some sign of life ('Service to the People'). Brecht himself said that he had put the various scenes together on the basis of 'eyewitness accounts and newspaper items'. Among these the four one-act plays *Das Kreidekreuz* (*The Chalk Cross*), *Rechtsfindung* (*Finding of Justice*), *Die Jüdische Frau* (*The Jewish Wife*) and *Der Spitzel* (*The Informer*) have become particularly well known. Brecht exposes in particular the failure of the bourgeois intelligentsia in the face of fascism, as well as the weakness of the petty bourgeoisie and of working people. The fate of individuals, which is often briefly spotlighted, is depicted in these various scenes, but in the total montage of the sequence appears as mass fate. The overall social context is recreated in the perception of the observer.

Brecht on the road to epic theatre

The didactic theatre also includes the exile dramas *Der gute Mensch von Sezuan* (*The Good Woman of Sezuan*) (1938–42), *Mutter Courage und ihre Kinder* (*Mother Courage and her Children*) (1939), *Herr Puntila und sein Knecht Matti* (*Mr Puntila and his Servant Matti*) (1940) and *Das Leben des Galilei* (*The Life of Galileo*) (1938–44, 1945–53), which formed the basis of Brecht's worldwide fame, and established him as one of the classic authors of modern times. Through these plays he created a form of political theatre in which utility and enjoyment formed a dialectic unity: 'Theatre remains theatre, even when it is didactic theatre, and as long as it is good theatre, it is also amusing.' Brecht's theory of epic theatre, most of which he elaborated during his exile and then summarised again after the war in his *Kleines Organon für das Theater* (*Small Organon for the Theatre*) (1949), is derived from the contradiction between 'entertainment theatre' and 'didactic theatre'. Brecht attempted to capture this contradiction with the concepts 'dramatic' and 'epic'. Modern epic didactic theatre, which Brecht both regarded as necessary and tried to bring about in his own theatre work, differs from a 'normal' dramatic production chiefly in that the audience no longer experience an uncritical sympathy with the characters that is effectively without result, but are expected instead to respond critically to what is being presented. This critical attitude, regarded by Brecht as the prerequisite for audiences to be able to transform what they had learned in the theatre into social action and change, was to be achieved by alienation.

The Verfremdungseffekt (the alienation effect)

'An alienated representation is one in which the subject is recognised, but at the same time seems strange.' The alienation effect was a dramatic device that had already been employed in medieval and Asian theatre, where it had had the different aim of 'removing what was represented from the intervention of the spectator'. Brecht's objective, however, was the reverse: to remove from the events depicted on stage 'the stamp of familiarity ... that prevents intervention', thereby enabling the spectator to intervene and giving him the courage to bring about change. Brecht had already experimented with alienation in the *Threepenny Opera* (1927–8) and in his didactic plays of the 1920s, but in his exile dramas it took on a new quality. For Brecht, the question of what the moral of a play could or should be had to be asked anew in face of the threat of fascism.

Later modifications to this didactic concept, compared to the didactic plays, became particularly apparent in *Mother Courage and her Children* (1941). Even when faced with the horrors of war, in which she loses both her livelihood and her children, Mother Courage remains unteachable. The spectator is meant to learn from her inability to learn. Brecht's play *The Good Woman of Sezuan* is likewise based on a highly differentiated understanding of didactic theatre. As in *Mr Puntila and his Servant Matti* (1940), the theme of this play is the antagonistic conditions of life within capitalist society that, despite Puntila's will to be good, do not allow him to be. Through the character of the good woman Shen Te, who in order to survive is obliged to transform herself into the unscrupulous Shui Ta, Brecht impressively recreates the contradictory dilemma of life in capitalist society that destroys and splits the personality. The antagonism that is inherent in capitalist society splits the human being into a human and an inhuman aspect. This makes the conflict between Shen Te and Shui Ta not an accident of personality, but a phenomenon of general importance and expressive power. With this play, Brecht penetrates to the heart of the 'social gearbox of the world' by portraying 'characters and events as historical and alterable' and as 'contradictory', in line with his own envisaged conception, thereby revealing to the spectator the potential for changing reality. Fate is not depicted as inevitable or outside the powers of human intervention. On the contrary, Brecht shows 'that the fate of man is sealed by man'.

Galileo

Galileo is the apotheosis of modern political didactic theatre. In the first
version of 1938, Brecht conceived Galileo as a wily opponent of the
Inquisition, only feigning retraction to those in power, but in reality continuing unwaveringly with his work with his defiant 'and yet it does turn'.
This makes him a potentially symbolic figure for intellectuals under fascism. Brecht's objective was to show how truth can be disseminated even
under the conditions of a dictatorship. This conception nonetheless seemed
to Brecht himself, even while he was still working on the play, problematic,
given that authors of the 'internal emigration' justified their conduct in a
similar way. He therefore regarded the moral of the play as 'too shallow
and cheap'. Even in the first version he prepared, therefore, Galileo did
not appear as an exemplary figure of resistance, as originally planned, but
was still fighting on the side of scientific knowledge and its dissemination,
a distinction being made between Galileo's subjective failure and the objective usefulness of his scientific research. The positive aspects of his character
were modified by the presentation of his 'betrayal'. He comes over as a
fascinating but contradictory character.

The 'Great Bomb'

When the dropping of the atomic bomb over Hiroshima in 1945 plunged
humanity into the nuclear age, Brecht rethought his original conception of
Galileo: 'The "atomic age" made its debut in Hiroshima in the midst of our
work. Overnight I read the biography of the founder of modern physics
in a new light. The infernal effect of the Great Bomb put Galileo's conflict
with the authorities of his time into a new, starker light.' In the revised
1944–5 version of the play, Galileo's retraction becomes a betrayal of both
science and humanity. The wily champion of truth becomes a criminal
scientist who sells out the fruits of his knowledge to those in power. The
core problem of the play is now the responsibility of the scientist for the
results of his research. The second version deals uncompromisingly with
both the human and social failure of Galileo. In a dialogue with his pupil
Andrea, Galileo openly confesses his culpability:

> As a scientist I had a unique opportunity. In my day astronomy
> reached the market-place. Under these very special circumstances the
> steadfastness of one man could have produced shattering results. Had
> I remained steadfast, the natural sciences might have been able to
> elaborate something akin to the Hippocratic oath of physicians, the
> pledge to use their knowledge solely for the benefit of mankind! As
> things now stand, the best one can hope for is a race of inventive
> dwarves who can be hired for anything and everything.

In contrast to his pupil Andrea, who would like to relieve his teacher of this burden of guilt, Galileo holds fast to the notion of the social responsibility of the scientist that he himself has betrayed with his retraction and own conduct:

When scientists, cowed into submission by self-seeking rulers, make do with accumulating knowledge for its own sake, science can be turned into a cripple, and your new machines can only entail fresh affliction. In time you can discover all there is to be discovered, but your progress will still be no more than progress away from humanity. The gulf between you and humanity may one day be so great that your cry of jubilation over a new achievement can only be answered by a universal cry of outrage.

The physicist: twentieth-century angel of death?

In this play Brecht challenges the notions of bourgeois scientists, convinced that they and their 'pure' science are somehow set apart from political responsibility:

The bourgeoisie isolates science in the mind of the scientist, setting it apart as autonomous islands, in order to be able to dovetail it with its policies, its economics and its ideology in practice. The aim of the researcher is 'pure' research, but the result of his research is less pure. The formula $E = mc^2$ is intended as something eternal, apart from everything. This leaves others to make the connection: the city of Hiroshima suddenly proved to be all too ephemeral. Scientists lay claim to the irresponsibility of machines.

(remarks on Galileo)

Brecht employed his literary work in the service of the struggle to a degree matched by virtually no other writer of his day, learning from developments within society and drawing conclusions from them both for the form and content of his drama. Whereas in the first version of *Galileo* the emphasis had been on the traits of resistance in his character, in order to offer a historical parallel to the dictatorship of Hitler, the second version stressed the problems of science in bourgeois society, as seen by Brecht in all their stark reality after the Hiroshima experience. The problem of science was thus not conceived of in metaphysical terms, but was seen by Brecht as rooted in the imperialist policies of capitalist society. To this extent in *Galileo* Brecht shifts his critical attitude towards capitalism on to a new level, whereas in his other exile dramas it had been formulated and presented thematically in terms of a critique of fascism.

POST-1945 GERMAN
LITERATURE

'When the war was over'

A 'last-days' mood

The unconditional capitulation of 8 May 1945 seemed to plunge the whole
of Germany into a political and cultural vacuum. The demise of the Nazi
regime after twelve years of rule led to the collapse of a gigantic, intricate
structure of ideology and propaganda – the dream of a Third, thousand-
year Reich, blind faith in the omnipotence of the *Führer*, and the sense the
latter had inculcated of the superiority of the German nation over other
nations and races. Where institutions had once been politically forced into
line and uniformity by *Gleichschaltung* policy, the chaos of disorientation
now reigned. The previous unreserved fervour for 'total war', drummed
up by militarising public life, now gave way to the sobering reality brought
on by the trauma of collapse in the wake of the utter defeat of Nazi
strategies for subjugation. Long-upheld fascist demagogical notions of salvation and calamity were now suddenly toppled and lay buried under the
rubble of entire cities, or in the millions of war graves, soon to evaporate
into a nightmare of public consciousness out of which the hope for a new
beginning would spring. In a letter dating from around this time, Wolfgang
Borchert writes: 'If I now write that the arrival (*Ankunft*) belongs to us,
I mean not us Germans, but this disappointed, betrayed generation – be
they Americans, Frenchmen or Germans. This statement arose out of
internal opposition to the generation of our fathers, our schoolmasters,
pastors, lecturers and professors. While it must be said that they led us,
blind, into this war, we, who have learned to see, now know that only
arrival on new shores can save us, or to put it more boldly, this hope is
ours alone!'

'Arrival' *(Ankunft)*

The phrase 'arrival on new shores' sums up the hopes of an entire gener-ation for a new beginning that could and should have broken with every-thing that the terror of fascism had brought with it. The inherited conditions of property ownership, private ownership of the means of production, authoritarian and patriarchal social and character structures, alienated modes of consciousness – all these historically unresolved phenomena associated with a highly industrialised capitalist society – were now open to re-examination. Transforming them would have necessitated a willingness on the part of the victorious powers, the Soviet Union, United States, Great Britain and France, to instigate change on a scale tantamount to a revolutionary process from above. It would likewise have required a readiness on the part of the German population to harness the potential of such preconditions for revolution to create a new, radically altered society, a totally new public consciousness and way of life while still under the trauma of what they had just lived through.

Once again, however, this revolution failed to take place. Instead, the German people, incapable of taking the political initiative, became the object of a controversy between the capitalist West and socialist East. The interim result was the founding of two separate states in 1949. These two rump Germanies were then integrated into two respective power blocks locked in the Cold War.

Administration instead of revolution: key features of social and cultural policy in the occupied zones

Socialism from above

From the standpoint of social policy what then took place in East Germany, the Soviet-Occupied Zone, is best described by the formula 'socialism from above' – administration instead of revolution. The true wielders of power in the early years were undoubtedly the Soviet Army, the Soviet Military Administration in Germany (SMAD), and members of the German Com-munist Party (KPD), who after 1946 were organised in the Socialist Unity Party of Germany (SED), most of whom returned to the Soviet-Occupied Zone from exile in the Soviet Union. By order of the Soviet Military Administration, businesses owned by war criminals were confiscated in the Soviet-Occupied Zone, half of whose industrial potential and economic infrastructure (road and rail communications, means of transport, etc.) had been destroyed in the war. This measure effectively nationalised 8 per cent of industrial concerns, accounting for barely 40 per cent of total pro-duction. In addition, two-thirds of rural land was redistributed to some 550,000 landless farm-labourers in land reform. Nazi personnel and their 'cultural appurtenances' were removed from the spheres of culture and education – for example, pro-Nazi books from public libraries.

'Volksdemokratie' ('People's Democracy')

These measures, carried out under the watchword 'establishment of the anti-fascist democratic order on the road to the people's democratic revolution' ('Errichtung der antifaschistisch-demokratischen Ordnung im Wege der volksdemokratischen Revolution'), were ambivalent from the outset. In their utter disregard for basic civil rights they clearly led along the Stalinist road rather than that envisaged by Rosa Luxemburg, and hence in complete contempt for the principles of democracy. Even de-Nazification was a somewhat half-hearted affair, tantamount to a reinstatement of the spirit of subjugation.

Obstacles

In fairness, it should be pointed out that the obstacles to building socialism in any other direction than the one described were almost insuperable. The anti-fascist potential of the population was limited; the economic situation was desperate, and could only improve at a snail's pace given the (justified) reparations being paid to the Soviet Union. East Germany was also faced with an increasingly 'golden' West Germany, whose per capita burden of reparations was much less by comparison with theirs, and which soon began to prosper in the aftermath of the Marshall Plan and other capital imports, to become the *Wirtschaftswunder*, the 'economic miracle'.

Political leaders in those first years may likewise be charged with having from the outset entered into a compromise, consisting of traditional bourgeois parliamentarian and state socialist elements, although passing it off as a long-term (socialist) solution – until recently. As a result of this compromise, socialist theory and the socialist agenda lost their true function, which is to provide the impetus for creative social change. Instead it became an ideology for justifying existing conditions within what was referred to as *realer Sozialismus* (socialism in practice). Marx had known that 'communist society . . . in every respect, economically, morally, intellectually, still bears the birthmarks of the old society out of which it was born'. Despite the manifest persistence of these 'birthmarks' – the payment in goods, payment according to performance, the state apparatus, military expenditures, the 'old' consciousness, etc. – however, this knowledge was largely suppressed.

This was particularly apparent in the officiously propounded view that socialist GDR society no longer contained any 'antagonistic' contradictions, but only 'non-antagonistic' ones, that is, not those that are of a fundamental nature or cannot be resolved in the given context. This meant that dissident voices could not be taken seriously, even if they were truthfully criticising sometimes deeply-rooted, real social injustices. According to the prevailing GDR world view, such criticisms must originate from outside, i.e. manipulated specifically by Western imperialist media and news services.

Literature and the state

One might well ask what this has to do with the history of German literature within the GDR. The answer is that literary developments in the GDR cannot be related too closely to the socio-political development of the country. The reason for this is that literature was both seen and exercised by the Socialist Unity Party, the decisive political force in the country, and by all its literary institutions (publishers, journals, libraries, theatres, schools, etc.), as well as by the overwhelming majority of writers themselves, as having the function of social mobilisation and social pedagogy. Art and literature in the GDR did not lead a separate existence from everyday life, any more than they did in West Germany. With characteristic time-lags, variations and convolutions, they shared the problems, conflicts and tensions that pertained to socio-political development. It would of course be nonsense to suggest that books came about as a result of Party resolutions, or that poets and authors were no more than cogs and screws in the machinery of a Party-dictated literature. All the same, inconsistencies in the overall perception of society are recreated on the level of art. What should emerge spontaneously from below – support for the socially corrective, socialist brief of literature by the reading public, and an active, creative participation in the process of literature (reading, discussing, drama production, writing, etc.), was in the GDR on closer inspection all too often either directed from above and strictly planned, or in reality did not take place at all. The characteristic contrast between state and Party on the one hand and the population on the other, rooted in the political and economic sphere, was thus recreated in the cultural sphere in the GDR.

A mouthpiece for criticism

And yet from its very beginnings, and increasingly in the final years of the state, the literature of the GDR was nevertheless something different as well. Strict as the regulations were, and massive though censorship also was, literature in the GDR did manage to be a mouthpiece for criticism, exposing existing conditions, addressing the issue of rampant suppression and concealment, flouting taboos, awakening new needs and pressing for change. In this sense it was not merely a reflection of or passive witness to the social and historical process, but was also an active agent within it.

It worked in the consciousness of its readers, as well as in the conditions of their existence as delineated by cultural policy.

Capitalism instead of socialism: the factors determining political and cultural restoration in the Federal Republic

Clearly, literary developments in the Federal Republic of Germany are scarcely comprehensible without a sound understanding of the social factors and context in which they came about. Unlike the literature of the GDR, which was closely bound up with state and Party resolutions and with directives from associations and administrative bodies, the literature of the Federal Republic did enjoy a certain degree of autonomy that even ran contrary to the general thrust of the political and economic process in society. Literature was conceived of not merely as a mirror or reflection of reality, but also as a potential critique of it, a vehicle for intervening in it, and a way of changing it, as well as of experiencing reality in alternative ways. Seen in this light, West German literature will be seen to exist in a certain definable relationship to reality, even where it appears to deviate from it. It is this relationship between contemporary literature and the reality that is the Federal Republic, its location within it, and its function for Federal German society, that needs to be constantly re-examined as part of the process of assessing West German literature.

The role of the victorious powers

This is particularly true of the period immediately following World War II. The political intentions of the victorious powers in the respective occupied zones were a decisive factor in literary developments from 1945–8. Only a few months after the military defeat of Germany these intentions were already displaying fundamental and irreconcilable differences. The common struggle of the allies against German fascism, which had at first included a shared vision of a completely de-militarised and de-industrialised Germany in all its parts, failed to outlive the war against the common enemy. After the Allies' victory the disparities between their different social orders began to resurface. Whereas, for example, Soviet policy aimed at effecting far-reaching changes in Germany's social and economic structures, the Western occupying powers, including the economically most powerful one, the USA, were more concerned with restoring the conditions of production and trade relations in order to create and secure export markets for themselves. A plan put forward by the American Secretary of the Treasury, Henry Morgenthau, to transform the whole of Germany into a gigantic agrarian country, was thus no less out of step with this objective than the state socialist plans of the USSR. Backed by a quasi-colonisation of Germany, the interest of the Western powers was concentrated on restoring a capitalist economic and social order, and on securing that order institutionally by means of a bourgeois parliamentarian state system.

'Re-education'

Measures concerned with cultural policy likewise served this interest in the Western zones, albeit linked with the explicit aim of altering the German national character, seen as the chief cause of the rise of Nazism, by means of a fundamental programme of re-education. The German 'national character' was seen as marked by a lust for power, subservience and aggressiveness, with *Preussentum* (the 'Prussian' mentality) and militarism as its historico-social roots.

What was overlooked in all this, however, was the inseparable link between these by no means typically German characteristics, on the one hand, and the conditions of property ownership and the specific social processes and class conflicts that had led to fascism, on the other. Unlike democratisation, which aims at institutional reforms, therefore, 're-education' in this context entailed an attempt to reshape the ideological attitudes of the German population to make them more in keeping with liberal bourgeois, individualistic notions of democracy, based on a largely American model.

This 're-education' programme was augmented by the trial of Nazi war criminals, and by a broad-based, but nevertheless for the most part ineffective 'de-Nazification' campaign, so sarcastically taken to task in Ernst von Salomon's book *Der Fragebogen* (*The Questionnaire*) (1951). The re-education efforts of the Western Allies were also bolstered by a series of measures concerned with literary policy. At least until the 1948 currency reform and the founding of the West German state, these were supported by the prerogative of the occupying powers to intervene in the publishing industry and regulate it politically by means of paper allocation, and the issuing, refusal or revoking of publication licenses.

The Office of Military Government for Germany (OMGUS)

American literary policy may serve to exemplify this. The relevant institution here was the Department of State in Washington, executive power being in the hands of the military offices responsible within the American zone of occupation, known collectively as the Office of Military Government for Germany (US), abbreviated to OMGUS. The office concerned with supervising cultural activities was the Information Control Division (ICD), whose work spanned the entire cultural sphere: publications, radio, film, theatre, and music. It was, in other words, a censorship body. Its mission was to further cultural re-education in two phases. These comprised an initial corrective phase – the banning of Nazi and pro-militarist writings by means of lists prepared for this purpose, as well as removing such writings from libraries, and a second, constructive phrase, whereby licensed translations were to provide the German reading public with a literature in keeping with the aims of re-education. A statistical survey of 1948 reveals that the translations offered to German publishing houses up to that point (some 288 in all) almost all had an educational objective behind them. They comprised mainly biographies, plays, and pieces on the fathers of American democracy, such as Franklin and Jefferson, all intended to fulfil this function, although little heed was paid to them by the German population.

Censorship

In contrast, hardly any socially critical works, literary critiques of capitalism, or problem-oriented novels about the less wholesome aspects of the USA, such as those by Caldwell, Faulkner or Farrell, were able to pass the OMGUS/ICD threshold of censorship. Permission was denied, for example, to perform Arthur Miller's play *All My Sons* (1947), on the grounds of alleged 'anti-business' propaganda. In 1947, Miller himself was moreover summoned before the notorious Committee for Unamerican Activities, accused of communism.

The examples mentioned above make it clear that there was no longer any question of a 'constructive' phase in the sense of American democratic ideals, but rather a steady and lasting cooption of cultural policy to overall anti-communist policy, as differences between the United States and the Soviet Union deepened from about 1947 onwards. As a consequence of this, however, American 're-education' degenerated into nothing more than propaganda for the restoration of capitalist conditions of property ownership.

A good illustration of the manipulation of literature for political ends is the affair surrounding George Orwell's *Animal Farm*. This work was withdrawn by the Americans in the spring of 1947 for fear that it might discredit their Soviet allies, but was then not only put back on sale in 1948, but even broadcast as a radio play with anti-communist tendencies.

In the context of the Berlin blockade in 1948, *Der Monat* (*The Month*), a cultural journal, was founded using funds from the American intelligence service, the CIA. A flood of brochures, totalling over four million copies, distributed in 1948–9 throughout the countries liberated from fascism, ensured the mass dissemination of anti-communist propaganda.

Currency reform, the founding of the Federal Republic of Germany and, lastly, the Occupation Statute that came into force in 1949 marked the definitive end of this brand of restorative cultural policy. From now on, in the absence of institutional jurisdiction, the former occupying power was obliged to further its cultural interests via the 'America houses' it had set up.

Collective culpability

The re-education programme brought with it the accusation of collective culpability, according to which the entire German nation was charged with having brought about and actively supported fascism. Despite this charge, against which the young German intelligentsia especially sought to defend itself (Alfred Andersch, Eugen Kogon, Hans Werner Richter), the Western Allies were still able to rely on a substantial degree of willingness among the newly re-authorised German political parties to commit themselves to a democratic and anti-fascist reconstruction. The feasible alternatives to German fascism now surfaced as 'Christianity and democracy, socialism, pacifism and internationalism' (Ossip K. Flechtheim). Even parts of the Christian Democratic Union declared themselves in favour of economic socialism in the 'Frankfurt Guiding Principles' of September 1945 and the 'Ahlen Economic Programme' of 1947. Christian Democrat politician Jakob Kaiser declared in 1946: 'Let us discern what is necessary: socialism holds the floor.' In fact, of course, this was a socialism of the middle way, a socialism intended to differ both from Western capitalism and from state socialism of the Soviet variety – a 'democratic socialism', as Kurt Schumacher's German Socialist Party (SPD) was to describe its agenda after 1945.

The road to socialism?

The idea of creating not only a socialist Germany, but even a socialist Europe, was widely approved among the German intelligentsia connected with the journals *Merkur, Frankfurter Hefte* and *Der Ruf* (*The Clarion Call*). 'The transformation of socialism – this is the road to the young generation – the transformation of the young generation – that is the road to socialism', declared Hans Werner Richter. The idea was to 'democratise socialism and socialise democracy at the same time'.

This notwithstanding, the genuine feeling with which the 'young generation' discussed and urged a socialist new beginning simultaneously prevented them from seeing that economic reality in the Western zones was already developing in an entirely different direction. The Western occupying powers had long since grasped that their political objectives could not be realised through this thoroughly diffuse 'young generation', but could be materially advanced by a policy furthering the restoration of a capitalist economy and a bourgeois parliamentarian state. For this reason the setting-up of trade unions as mass organisations was suppressed until the autumn of 1946, whereas entrepreneurs obtained prompt opportunities for organisation. Similarly, demands for property confiscation and strikes met with prison sentences. Again, a nationalisation paragraph contained in the constitution of the *Land* of Hesse, and approved by 72 per cent of the population, was suspended by the military authorities. In the view of all major parties the socialism being called for served the interests of a new beginning in Germany.

It did not, however, serve the interests of Western capital and trade at all. The Marshall Plan, which established American capital export, together with the West German currency reform, ushered in a new, capitalist beginning. The more entrepreneur-friendly wing of the Christian Democratic Union was quick to adjust its agenda and jump on the bandwagon.

The function of literature

In this sense, therefore, 1948 may be regarded as the real beginning of the Federal Republic of Germany. It was in this year that the political and economic guidelines were established that have shaped West German reality to this day. In the period that followed literature was not quite so obviously dependent on its social milieu as it had been in the immediate post-war period, and yet it responded to that milieu in a variety of ways. Reactions to the 'economic miracle' and to political restoration, to nuclear armaments, and to the passing of the emergency powers act included protest and criticism, resignation and melancholy. These responses evinced a tension between political representation on the one hand and literary and cultural representation on the other that betrayed a deplorable lack of political culture in the Federal Republic. In broad terms, this is the same tension between mind and power, intelligentsia and political reality, that has for the most part marked the history of German literature throughout the twentieth century.

After World War II, however, this tension was expressed in a particular way. Wherever prevailing policy was publicly questioned by the intelligentsia (ranging from literary loners such as Heinrich Böll, Günter Grass and Martin Walser to whole philosophical schools of thought such as the Frankfurt School of Max Horkheimer and Theodor W. Adorno), intellectuals, creative artists, *literati* and journalists were in turn denounced as politically and morally irrelevant; sometimes communist or terrorist sympathies were even insinuated. A prime example of this attitude is the derogatory term coined by erstwhile Federal Chancellor Ludwig Erhard for opposition intellectuals who criticised his notion of a 'formed society': he called them 'gnomes'.

'One does not burn a Voltaire'

In contrast to the political culture of France, therefore, where radical questioning by journalists and creative artists was taken for granted as an integral part of political and intellectual life, in the Federal Republic of Germany statements of this kind always carried the danger of public

543

defamation. And yet, the very fact that the political commitment of writers continues to this day to be a nuisance factor is in itself an indication of the social function of literature. The sensitivity of its modes of perception and capacity for expression is what gives it that specific aesthetic quality tending towards criticism and controversy, allowing it also to give voice to a type of experience that deviates from the everyday political life of the Federal Republic.

'Zero-point', radical change or continuity? Traditional features of German post-war literature

Revolution failed to occur not only in the political sphere, however, but also in literature. The dilemma of German society after 8 May 1945 – both individually and collectively, as well as of intellectuals and literati in all three Western zones – was often termed 'zero-point' or *Kahlschlag*. Unlike the terms 'disintegration' or 'defeat', used by broad sections of the population to describe the post-war situation, these metaphors implied a challenge to eradicate Nazism – to accomplish a radical and complete social reformation. There was, moreover, a willingness to attempt such reformation, at least among authors returning from exile and younger intellectuals who had lived through war and imprisonment. In special prisoner-of-war camps set up by the Americans during the war with a view to preparing German prisoners of war for a role in the future administration of defeated Germany, for example, there was a widespread desire to build a new Germany free of fascism, militarism and the potential for establishing dictatorship. This Germany was to be based on American concepts of a democratic constitutional state, built up on the basis of peaceful cooperation with the other European states.

Intellectuals in these camps included some writers and journalists who were to make a lasting mark on early post-war German literature: Alfred Andersch, Hans Werner Richter, Walter Kolbenhoff, Walter Mannzen and Gustav Rene Hocke. A variety of journals in the POW camps disseminated their own and American ideas for a new beginning. These included the camp newspaper *Der Ruf* (*The Clarion Call*), later edited by Alfred Andersch and Hans Werner Richter outside the camp as an independent publication. In June 1945 Gustav Rene Hocke voiced the resolve of German prisoners of war to take an active part in a programme for the reconstruction of a democratic Germany: 'These twelve years, this horrendous interregnum, will remain in our memories as a warning against inordinate objectives and unfettered rule by force. They will give us the resolve to return to our true traditions. They make it incumbent on us to rebuild a genuinely free Germany inspired by the desire to cooperate with all nations.'

Coming to terms with the past

This statement typifies the thinking and mood that prevailed among the German younger generation around 1945–6. Side by side with political and moral condemnation of the Nazi regime assessments of the German Resistance could be found in journals, and, side by side with pointers to the freedom-oriented traditions within German literature and journalism, thoughts on the future potential for building a democratic Germany. These ideas are all invoked in an article by Hans Werner Richter written in September 1946, where he asserts: 'Arising out of the displacement of the sense for life, and the violent experiences that the young generation have lived through and been deeply disturbed by, the only way out that seems open to them is one of a spiritual rebirth in the form of an absolute and radical new beginning.'

Aside from good will, agenda statements of this kind also manifest a considerable degree of cultural idealism. Writers and intellectuals of the younger generation were content with the prospect of reinstating morality in political life and formal democracy in West Germany. Their anti-fascist, democratic commitment did bring them into close contact with the handful of writers returning from exile to form a common interest that was to lead to appeals for unity at the (still) all-German Writers' Congress of 1947. In political terms, however, such statements were largely meaningless. Those 'younger generation' authors who nowadays stand out as the leading representatives of the post-war era had virtually no impact at the time either on the dominant social and literary developments, or on tradition.

What persisted in literary terms were poetic positions and forms tracing back to the 1930s. The divergence in German literature that began to take concrete form after 1945 had in fact already begun in 1933 – the year of the fascist seizure of power in Germany. That year saw not only the banning of the major part of German literature, but also the physical exile of writers and intellectuals, of which the repercussions were still to be felt decades later. The final result of this process was the development of two German modes of expression, and two German literatures.

For all its individual peculiarities, exile literature was bound together by the common denominator of exile itself. Its opposition to fascism should be seen as a form of literary solidarity. Meanwhile, within Germany itself, three groups of writers had crystallised: those who sympathised with Nazism, those who distanced themselves from it, for whom the term 'internal emigration' arose as an apt designation, and lastly those who attempted to offer resistance to fascism through literature.

Flight or fight?

After the war, open controversy arose over the various achievements of exile literature and the literary 'internal emigration'. This controversy was chiefly linked with the names of Thomas Mann and Frank Thiess, nominally precipitated by a challenge from the writer Walter von Molo to Thomas Mann to return to Germany *zu Rat und Tat* ('in word and deed'). Thomas Mann rejected this challenge, arguing that twelve years of fascist rule in Germany had made him feel increasingly alienated from his homeland. He added a devastating condemnation, which he later toned down somewhat, of books that had been published in Germany between 1933 and 1945, denouncing them as 'less than worthless and not fit to be handled. There is a stench of blood and shame to them. They should all be pulped.' In a fierce riposte intended as a response to this, Frank Thiess endeavoured first both politically and morally to denigrate the German literature of exile, which he saw embodied in Thomas Mann, and second to uphold his own position as that of a more consequential, and morally untainted Germany.

The continuum of internal emigration

This controversy between exile literature and the literary internal emigration marked the conclusive partition of German literature into two camps, whose political foundations soon became apparent. Thus, the authors of exile literature, notably Anna Seghers, Johannes R. Becher, and Arnold Zweig, returned almost without exception to the Soviet Occupied Zone, later the German Democratic Republic, and were scarcely taken into account in the Federal Republic until well into the 1960s. Within the orbit of the Western zones, later the Federal Republic of Germany, on the other hand, it was the literature of internal emigration that was held in esteem. Analysis of readers and anthologies showed, even as late as 1965, that among sixteen authors arranged in order of their frequency of occurrence in anthologies, the names of Weinheber, Benn, Carossa, Britting, E. Jünger, Bergengruen, Schröder and I. Seidel are all present. The same figures also show just how little exile literature had been absorbed into the official canon: the ratio of the latter's to other literature published concurrently in Germany was a mere 1:6.

This notwithstanding, the very different levels of esteem in which, for example, the brothers Heinrich and Thomas Mann were held in the Federal Republic clearly shows that the key distinction determining whether authors were received into the accepted canon was not that between exile and internal emigration, but that between their political convictions and the forms of literary expression corresponding to them. Against a background of mounting anti-communist feeling in the Federal Republic (the

Communist Party was banned in 1956), authors deemed as being on the 'Left' were defamed, regardless of their literary stature. The split already apparent in German literature had taken on entrenched positions. The boundary in literature no longer ran between exile and internal emigration, but was drawn according to the respective courses of the two Germanies – the socialist-communist and the bourgeois-conservative.

It is not surprising, therefore, that after 1945 only two major works of bourgeois exile literature were widely acclaimed in West Germany. These were Hermann Hesse's *Das Glasperlenspiel* (*The Glass Bead Game*) (1943), a future-oriented perspective on the present aiming at cultural criticism of the 'insecurity and inauthenticity' of educational values in 'the age of the feuilleton', and Thomas Mann's *Doktor Faustus* (1947), a critique of fascism and Nietzsche. The explanation for the success of these two works in post-war West Germany lies in their shared tendency to overstate the critique of civilisation and the present day offered in and through them – a tendency towards an abstraction of social reality. This had the function of relieving the contemporary reader of a burden: he or she could read these works as novels of the 'last days of society', in which the age of fascism had been raised to a time outside time.

Coming to terms with fascism

Thomas Mann's *Doktor Faustus* (1947) is a fascinating literary attempt to come to terms with German fascism. In this book, the Humanist Dr Serenus Zeitblom sets down between 1943 and 1945 the life story of his composer-friend Adrian Leverkühn, who died in 1940. Having abandoned his theology studies, Leverkühn turned to music. Although he knows that musical forms have been exhausted, and can therefore serve as no more than the material with which to play at composing, he nevertheless tries to evade the sterility of such an artistic procedure. He can only do this, however, by entering into a pact with the Devil. The price he pays for this is, on the one hand, a perfect separation of his musical productivity from the world and, on the other, at the end of this productive phase, a cerebral disintegration resulting from syphilis. For his part, the Devil pledges to Leverkühn a 'truly blissful, entrancing, undoubting and believing inspiration' which will enable him to 'break through the crippling difficulties of the times'. Leverkühn does indeed produce a number of musical masterpieces, the culmination of which is the symphonic cantata *Dr Fausti Weheklag* (*The Lament of Dr Faust*). After a creative phase of nineteen years, Leverkühn gathers his friends around him, confesses to them his pact with the Devil, plays to them from his latest work and finally collapses into mental oblivion. Thomas Mann brought to this work a wealth of thematic elements drawn from the widely disparate spheres of philosophy, the history of ideas, theory of music and social history, binding them together to create his own original interpretation of history, made up of the Faust story, theological and mythological sources, the biography and philosophy of Nietzsche, and not least the musical theory of Theodor W. Adorno, and the composition theories of Arnold Schönberg. All these various elements are integrated into the biography of a creative artist whose career takes on features that are increasingly parallel with the rise of fascism in Germany. The connections between these elements, and their application in the novel, were explained in detail by Thomas Mann, likewise in novel form, in *Die Entstehung des Doktor Faustus* (*The Genesis of Doctor Faust*) (1949).

Doctor Faustus acquires its inner tension from the introduction of the fictional narrator Serenus Zeitblom, whose helplessness at the process of development evident in his friend Adrian Leverkühn, a process deriving from his fundamental position as a Humanist, gives expression at the same time to the 'helpless anti-fascism' (W.F. Haug) of a middle class that responded to fascism with rejection, but which had no qualitatively different political position of their own with which to combat it.

At the same time, however, introduction of the Serenus character permits the maintenance of narrative distance, which in turn allows a 'certain brightening of this sombre theme'. In addition to ironic elements, therefore, there are passages of humour and parody that make the novel a pleasure to read, despite the complexity and size of its theme, and despite the oppressive weight of the problems with which it deals. It is a pleasure, however, whose momentous contemporary historical background and topicality, even in the post-war years, emphasises once more the final lines of this lengthy work: 'A lonely old man clasps his hands and pronounces: May God have mercy on your poor soul, my friend, my fatherland.'

Unmistakable as the contemporary historical reference is in this exile novel, the lyric poetry of the post-war years betrays an equally unmistakable escapist character, contemplative and rapturously engrossed in nature. The agenda of this lyric poetry is graphically revealed in the titles of the volumes: *Stern über der Lichtung* (*Star Over the Glade*); *Der hohe Sommer* (*High Summer*); *Die heile Welt* (*The Wholesome World*); *Die Silberdistelklause* (*The Silver Thistle Hermitage*); *Der Laubmann und die Rose* (*The Leafman and the Rose*). The authors of these volumes were the same writers who had sought and found a way of enabling their literature to survive the Third Reich through 'internal emigration'. Besides the authors already mentioned, these also included Friedrich Georg Jünger, Georg von der Vring, Albrecht Goes, and Gertrud von Le Fort. In one poem, for example, by Friedrich Georg Jünger, we find the lines:

In die Geissblattlauben will ich
wo die liebenden sich herzen
um beim Licht des Sichelmondes
mit dem jungen Reh zu scherzen.

> To the honeysuckle bowers would I
> where lovers do caress,
> and in the light of crescent moon
> with the young roebuck jest.

Contemplation, idyll, a blithe spirit in repose, and tranquillity – all qualities echoed in equanimity by the rhythm of this verse – are the hallmarks of a poetry that detaches itself from surrounding reality, withdrawing from it to represent poetic beauty through a retreat into itself.

Resignation?

But wherein lie the reasons for this retreat? Had the end of fascist rule in Germany not offered an opportunity to deal with burning social issues through the medium of literature as well? Is the persistence of 'internal emigration' after 1945 a mark of resignation, or an indication of a deliberate, newly-acquired definition of the function of poetry? The answers to these questions may be discerned both from the way authors saw themselves, and from the characteristic features of their lyric works. The latter show themselves to be not only entirely 'de-historicised', and apparently free of all social references, but also, in line with traditional poetic models such as the sonnet, ballad and elegy, to be pursuing meanings and forms that transcend time (Rudolf Hagelstange, Hans Egon Holthusen). These aspirations, which are their social hallmark, are often accompanied by a discernible increase in religious features and Christian motifs, and sometimes by immersion in a poetry that purports to be autonomous, even above and beyond the world. The self-image of authors reflected this. They saw themselves in the role of heralds of a higher truth that could only be discerned far from empirical reality, a truth accessible only to the few called to it, to poets. Reality, on the other hand, in their view led solely to the realisation that such higher truths – the experience of happiness, love, bliss in nature, or liberty – were not to be found in it. The poet Ina Seidel declares: 'Was bleibt uns in den Trümmern unsrer Welt / Für Zuflucht aus dem Labyrinth der Trauer? Was ist noch da, daran der Mensch sich hält, / Als der Gestirne unberührte Dauer' ('What is left us in the ruins of our world / For refuge from the labyrinth of grief? What is still there for Man to cling to, / If not the stars of virgin timelessness.'

Idyll, contemplation

What emerged, therefore, was a restoration of the lyric, a type of poetry for which an insistence on inherited formal traditions, remoteness from time and the world, idyll and contemplation were as characteristic as its inability to bring about poetic renewal – to create and express a lyric poetry that was discernibly rooted in the here and now. The traditional, hidebound character of this early post-war lyric verse did achieve some kind of social function for itself, but one which was all too typical of the spirit of the age. Widely acclaimed and extolled in prize-giving addresses, this poetry was still being exalted well into the 1950s as exemplary of German literature, officially esteemed as the quintessence of German lyricism. This lyric verse thus served the cosmetic distortion of the here and now by seeming to keep its distance from it.

Nature lyrics

One exception to authors in the tradition of the internal emigration is formed by 'political nature lyric' poets, such as Günter Eich, Peter Huchel, Karl Krolow and Wilhelm Lehmann, who first started writing (in the case of Eich and Huchel) around 1930. Some can be traced back to the literary journal *Kolonne*. This lyric verse was able to effect a renewal in nature poetry as long as it perceived and dealt with reality and the natural world as an inseparable whole, involved in a suggestive interplay and exchange with each other. By the same token, it forfeited substance and poetic credibility to the extent that it evaded reality in order to give a distorted description of natural detail. Krolow, who had once seen in it 'the sole achievement of modern poetry since the demise of Expressionism' acknowledged in 1963 that it, like Expressionism, had suffocated as a result of its own 'narrowness'.

Politico-cultural journalism

Particular importance accrued in the post-war years to the politico-cultural journals that appeared in the four zones of occupation. Given the sparse book production in that period, these journals frequently offered the sole arena for public discussion. This was not without its constraints, however. Like book production, journal production, too, was dependent on the issuing of Allied licenses and journals, like books, were subject to Allied controls, therefore also representing in part the various positions of the Allied powers in their respective zones of occupation. This was equally true, for example, of the journals *Die Wandlung* (*The Change*) (1945–9, American zone), *Lancelot* (1946–51, French zone) or *Aufbau* (*Construction*) (1945–58, Soviet zone/GDR). However, the presentation, communication and implementation of political positions was not the sole concern of early journalism in Germany, which also sought to catch up with literary developments such as the American short story writers and to discuss socialist realism or avant-garde trends that had been banned during the Third Reich.

Between 1945 and 1946 no less than seventeen journals came into existence. Another four appeared in 1947, among them such leading periodicals as *Der Ruf (The Clarion Call)*, *Frankfurter Hefte*, *Ost und West (East and West)* and *Merkur*. These journals may be classified, according to their main content, as political and ideological (*Wandlung, Ruf, Gegenwart*), or literary and cultural (*Die Erzählung – The Narrative Tale, Das Karussell – The Carousel, Das Goldene Tor – The Golden Gate*). In addition, there were even some journals that had survived the Third Reich, such as the *Deutsche Rundschau (The German Panorama)* (from 1874, ceased publication in 1964), *Die neue Rundschau (The New Panorama)* (from 1890), or *Hochland/Neues Hochland – Highland/New Highland* (from 1903 to 1904). From 1949 onwards, their circulation diminished steadily showing that these newly-founded journals had largely fulfilled their function by the time of the currency reforms in West Germany (1948) and the foundation of the two German states (1949). The élan of their founders, and their politico-cultural objectives, which were aimed at building bridges and creating new beginnings as well, however, as criticising the victorious powers, were engulfed and placed in question by the increasing political and economic division between East and West Germany. The readiness for dialogue that had marked the early years of post-war journalism now gave way to resignation in the face of political reality.

Der Ruf (The Clarion Call)

Der Ruf was of central importance in the policy of the victorious powers, as well as for the way politico-cultural journalism saw itself. This journal, founded in 1946, and published by Alfred Andersch and Hans Werner Richter, bore the subtitle: 'Independent newspaper of the young generation', with the accent on 'independent'. This journal of cultural politics adopted a critical stance towards the policy of the victorious powers and a sober approach to the grim ruins that were the reality of the post-war situation, but was also marked by the idealism of the new beginning and of reconstruction that was typical for this time. However, its rejection of a 'German debt account', and its insistence on the 'abundance of suffering' that had been inflicted on the Germans, spurred the Allies to intervene. The American military government banned the journal in April 1947 (from issue no. 17), only permitting its publication again after the former Editor-in-Chief had been replaced by Erich Kuby. His banning and replacement led in 1947 to Hans Werner Richter founding what was perhaps the leading writers' organisation, the *Gruppe 47* (the '47 Group') – an indication that political activities were becoming increasingly more problematic and entrenched in the literary and cultural spheres. *Der Ruf* ceased publication in March 1949.

Gruppe 47

No other institution on the literary scene of the Federal Republic was so maligned and distrusted, or so overestimated and stylised as *Gruppe 47*. Formed as the result of a private initiative by the writer Hans Werner Richter, it remained a loose association to the last (its final conference took place in 1967, by which time it was under attack from student extra-parliamentary opposition). In its heyday at the end of the 1950s and beginning of the 1960s, the group represented modern literature by younger authors – the kind of literature that was 'talked about', and the only kind that carried any weight with the public. Whereas in its early days, however, the group still fully articulated the political aspirations of literature, it soon became institutionalised within the Federal Republican establishment of the 1950s as an exchange of relationships, opinions and tendencies. Only those invited by H. W. Richter could come to any of the 29 conferences. At first writers kept more or less to themselves, the meetings having a workshop character and criticism being the working criticism of colleagues. Later, however, the middle-men of literature (publishers, readers and critics) were in a visible preponderance, redefining the function of their conferences as self-presentations of the literary scene and business. The provocative appearance of Peter Handke at the 1966 Princeton conference was introduced into this set-up seamlessly, not least arousing the interest of the public. From the outset, the main agenda of conferences consisted of readings from still unpublished manuscripts. These readings, like the spontaneous criticism expressed, were soon raised to a ritual status in their own right, as may be seen from the way 'star' critics came to dominate. *Gruppe 47* ultimately disintegrated through its own inconsistencies and lack of inner coherence. The internalisation of literary discourse that it cultivated was bound to run aground against the rising repoliticisation of intellectuals generally in the mid-1960s.

Trümmerliteratur ('literature of the ruins')

For many years, *Trümmerliteratur* and *Kahlschlag* (lit. the 'clear-cutting' of undergrowth) were the key words denoting the newly-emerging litera-ture of the early post-war years. *Trümmerliteratur* denotes the reality that shapes this type of literature – the reality of rubble and ruins, not only of cities and houses, but also of ideals and hopes – the reality of war, death, defeat and survival amid the ruins.

Language and hope

This was the literature in which homecoming authors, provided they did not recoil from the world around them, sought to come to terms with current problems through literature and find solutions for them.

Kahlschlag, on the other hand, denoted the literary aspiration to formu-late a language. The poets, or *Männer des Kahlschlags* (the 'men of the clear-cutting'), were to act as 'foresters', pointing the way 'in the tangled literary undergrowth' of the here and now – post-war literature, in other words. The aim behind this was 'to make a fresh start, a completely fresh start . . . in language, substance and conception' – if necessary, according to Wolfgang Weyrauch, the originator of the *Kahlschlag* postulate, even 'at the price of poetry' itself.

A new beginning was being called for, and hence a forsaking of the traditional phenomena connected with 'internal emigrants', who continued after 1945 to adhere to the literary forms of the German contemplative tradition. At the same time, this call for a new beginning was also linked with an aspiration towards truth – an aspiration that Wolfgang Weyrauch saw persistently threatened by the beauty of poetry: 'Beauty is a fine thing. But beauty without truth is bad. Truth without beauty is better.'

With the benefit of hindsight, this polarisation of beauty and truth must be characterised as a false alternative. What needed to be clarified here was not whether the beauty or truth of poetry should be upheld, but in what the truth of poetry, understood as a literary form, in fact consisted. Even more important than this, however, is to point out the contemporary context in which Wolfgang Weyrauch's *Kahlschlag* postulate was able to unfold. This was an attempt by the homecoming author to put a stop to the dallying with lyric verse that had been going on for years, tacitly bolstering the legitimacy of German fascist rule, and an endeavour to look stark reality squarely in the face. This was an overall poetic undertaking summed up by Wolfdietrich Schnurre in the verse:

> zerschlagt eure Lieder
> verbrennt eure Verse
> sagt nackt
> was ihr müsst.

> smash up your songs
> burn your verses
> say in bare words
> what you must.

A consistent expression of this approach is to be found in Günter Eich's poem *Inventur* (*Inventory*), probably written as early as April/May 1945 in a prisoner-of-war camp, and first published in an anthology edited by Hans Werner Richter entitled *Deine Söhne, Europa* (*Your Sons, Europe*) (1947). 'Making an inventory', subjecting oneself to a stock-taking, enumer-ating one's belongings and keeping one's property together – all this was a key situation for war survivors, prisoners of war and homecomers. It was a situation calling for restriction to the concreteness and location of

the immediate environment, and concentration on the specific conditions
and prerequisites of one's own existence:

> Dies ist meine Mütze,
> dies ist mein Mantel,
> hier mein Rasierzeug
> im Beutel aus Leinen.
>
> Konservenbüchse:
> Mein Teller, mein Becher,
> ich hab in das Weissblech
> den Namen geritzt.
>
> . . . .
>
> Im Brotbeutel sind
> ein Paar wollene Socken
> und einiges, was ich
> niemand verrate,
>
> so dient es als Kissen
> nachts meinem Kopf.
> Die Pappe hier liegt
> zwischen mir und der Erde.
>
> . . . .
>
> Dies ist mein Notizbuch,
> dies ist mein Zeltbahn,
> dies ist mein Handtuch,
> dies ist mein Zwirn.
>
> This is my cap
> this is my coat
> here is my razor
> in a bag made of linen.
>
> A can of food:
> My plate, my beaker,
> I've scratched my name
> in the tinplate.
>
> . . . .
>
> In the bread bag there are
> a pair of woollen socks
> and some things of which
> I will never tell anyone,

And so at night it serves
as a pillow for my head.
The cardboard here lies
between me and the ground.

. . . .

This is my notebook,
this is my tent square,
this is my handkerchief,
this is my twine.

This practical implementation of an agenda of 'naked' language, of a deliberately impoverished poetry, needs to be understood as a reaction to the demolition and abuse of language that took place in the Third Reich. Extreme terseness of form and strict concentration on imparting objective facts are expressions of the mistrust that had grown up under fascism towards the prodigal and insidious use of language. Poetic meaning itself moved to the fore in early post-war literature, its distinguishing characteristic being the crying aloud of what was perceived as being true.

Borchert as a representative

Seen against this background, it will become clear why in the case of one of the younger post-war authors, Wolfgang Borchert, who died as early as 1947, Expressionist and surrealist stylistic and symbolic elements are found side by side with narrative forms clearly developed from American prose models, especially Ernest Hemingway's short stories. In 1946 Borchert published his volume of poems *Laterne, Nacht und Sterne* (*Lantern, Night and Stars*), and in 1947 his short story volumes *An diesem Dienstag* (*This Tuesday*) and *Die Hundeblume* (*The Dogflowers*). These poems and stories express the experiences and complaints not of an individual, but of an entire group – a young generation deceived and betrayed by their parents, who had had to suffer under fascism, robbed of their best years by war, and who now, in the midst of the ruins, were in search of a new understanding of themselves. The Nazis had interned Borchert under various pretexts of 'subversion of military power' i.e. for his pacifist views. It was this radical pacifism, which was inseparable from his idealistic commitment to greater humanity and human sympathy, and more regard for the little things of everyday life, that gave his work the poetic credibility in which his generation was able to find itself again. With their terse, highly exact delineation of situations, and use of precise images to evoke mood, Borchert's short stories revolve again and again around the themes of war, the post-war era, horror and death. It is the stylistic devices of understatement, omission, and seemingly laconic description, allowing him to gain a degree of distance from the immediacy of his experiences, that makes it possible

555

to convey them at all. And yet Borchert's stories also contain suffering, and a heightened sensitivity of perception: his literature and characters after 1945 were open to emotional identification by the reader.

Draussen vor der Tür (The Man Outside)

Wolfgang Borchert created one figure to be identified with in the anti-hero of his best-known work, *Draussen vor der Tür* (*The Man Outside*) (1947), a drama originally planned as a radio play, and to which he added the subtitle 'A play that no theatre wants to perform and no audience wants to see.' This turned out to be a false prognosis: Borchert's drama was the hit of the post-war years. Returning home from the horrors of war, his anti-hero Beckmann is a man betrayed, a victim, and deeply disturbed. He is weary and defeated, subject to the attempts of his fellow men to suppress the past, to the horror of his experiences and memories and to the insinuations of the world around him. Beckmann is an anti-hero not only in terms of Borchert's self-portrayal in the character, but also in the way he gives voice to the scepticism of his generation towards myth, and their weariness of heroes. 'Although this Beckmann had no solutions available, the very fact that he knew a question for every answer exactly matched the disposition of young German people', wrote Peter Rühmkorf. Borchert described this young generation many times, calling them a 'generation without valediction', a 'generation without an aim', a 'generation without commitment' and a 'generation without a self'. Devoid of illusions and full of bitterness though these designations are, they arise from the hope that this generation might be able to bring about some kind of fundamental change. The lack of illusions among this generation and its authors is reflected in the austerity of their language. Its bitterness, however, tended towards the Expressionist scream, with more calculated form being of secondary importance.

Zuckmayer

Wolfgang Borchert's drama *Draussen vor der Tür* can be equated with only one other early post-war play – Carl Zuckmayer's *Des Teufels General* (*The Devil's General*) (written in 1942 in exile in the USA, first performed in Zurich in 1946). It is comparable not only in terms of its theme, which deals with the dilemma of the military in the fascist services, but also in terms of its success. It went on to become the most performed play of the post-war years on German-speaking stages (over 3,000 performances up to 1950).

The reasons for its success, however, were different from those of Borchert's play, deriving above all from a drama that offered relief to contemporary audiences. The central character of the play is General Harras, a heroic type to whose characterisation the contemporary historical background contributes no more than the scenery. Modelled on General Ernst Udet, the 'Devil's' (i.e. Hitler's) general is portrayed as smart and ambitious with youthful charm. His military triumphs allow him to deal with all forms of authority in an affable, easy-going way, an individualist style of behaving and forms of resistance that are all his own (for the sake of a woman friend, for example, Harras saves a Jewish doctor). His conduct towards the ruling Nazis shows little sign of an awareness of right and wrong ('They used me – and they are using me even more so now. But anyway, I couldn't care less'), so that the culminating dramatic conflict offers him little scope for a change of heart. Forced by a Gestapo ultimatum to face the fact that his friend, the idealistic Resistance fighter Oderbruch, is carrying out acts of sabotage on aircraft, Harras sees a suicide mission in one of the defective planes as his only way out.

Problematic dramaturgy

The explanation for the success of this play lies neither in the reality of its content, nor in the conflict with which it deals, but in its dramaturgy. Zuckmayer offers an opportunity to identify with an unbroken hero who, finding himself in a tragic situation modelled on the classic pattern, has no choice but to accept his culpability or go under. This dramaturgy is nonetheless an inappropriate vehicle for dealing with a reality characterised by a machinery of destruction that either forced individual heroism and the individualist capacity for self-sacrifice to absurd lengths, or exploited them for politico-military ends. Since Zuckmayer does not present his protagonist to the audience for critical appraisal using the means of alienation, his play is in constant danger of employing effective dramatic elements solely in order to convey what in spite of everything remains a remarkable individual military career.

The success of this play came in the aftermath of his early folk plays *Der fröhliche Weinberg* (*The Jolly Vineyard*) (1925), *Der Schinderhannes* (1927) and *Der Hauptmann von Köpenick* (*The Captain of Köpenick*) (1931). Zuckmayer's success did not continue, however, after *The Devil's General* with his two other political plays, *Der Gesang im Feuerofen* (*The Song in the Furnace*) (1950) and *Das kalte Licht* (*The Cold Light*) (1955), which present stories from the Resistance in France and the Cold War using obtrusive symbolism and melodramatic effects. His memoirs, however, published in 1966 under the title *Als wär's ein Stück von mir* (*As If It Were a Piece of Myself*), evoked a huge response, bearing witness to Humanist and anti-fascist leanings without denying individual responsibility for processes taking place in history and society. Zuckmayer had already summed up this realisation in 1944 in New York with the words: 'Germany has been found guilty before all the world. We, however, who were unable to prevent it, do not belong among the judges in this great world trial.'

Weisenborn

Günther Weisenborn's play *Die Illegalen* (*The Outlaws*) (first performed in 1946 in Berlin) also dealt with the problems of recent history. Returning from exile in 1937, Weisenborn, who has since unjustly fallen into obscurity, formed the *Rote Kapelle* (*Red Band*) Resistance group. In 1942 he was arrested and sentenced to hard labour. *Die Illegalen* deals with the achievements of the German Resistance movement, whose successes, conflicts, victims and activities are realistically enacted. 'We outlaws are a mute community in this country. We are dressed like everyone else, we have the same customs as everyone else, but we live between betrayal and the grave. The world loves victims, but it also forgets them. The future is forgetful.' This prognosis proved true for Weisenborn himself: his plays, including what was in its day his highly successful *Ballade vom Eulenspiegel, vom Federle und von der dicken Pompanne* (*The Ballad of Eulenspiegel, Featherkin and Fat Pompanne*), are as little known today as his prison memoirs, published in 1948 under the title *Memorial*.

Notwithstanding the stage successes of Zuckmayer, Weisenborn and Borchert, it was lyric poetry rather than drama that became the leading form of literary representation in the early post-war years. The aim of younger authors was to 'anticipate and recognise what is, how it came about, and how the future can be unfolded' (Wolfgang Weyrauch). In lyric verse, they saw a directly accessible opportunity to give voice to their experiences, feelings, and problems. The aim was to develop a poetry combining relevance with reality, an awareness of problems and an orientation towards the future, thus giving lyric verse new avenues in which to unfold. In this way, the *Trümmerlyrik* (lyric of the ruins) of the post-war era became an arena for poetic discussion, concerned with past, present and future alike, and allowing for the full spectrum of contradictions and a diversity of forms. Moulded by the experiences of the immediate past, and sustained by hopes for a liberated future, this lyric verse oscillates between a sense of ruin and the euphoria of a fresh start, between depression and a certain future, resignation and optimism.

The reality of the ruins and reconstruction fervour

This poetry found its themes in and around the war and the end of the war (homecoming, post-war reality), the problem of guilt and collective guilt, and the tension between the reality of ruins and reconstruction fervour. Its formal language nonetheless remained in many ways captive to traditional models. The sonnet, for example, was used without distinction for love and nature poems on the one hand and horrendous war poems on the other. It was so overworked that contemporaries began to speak of a 'frenzy of sonnets'. This predominance of content arranged in literary forms to which it was ill suited derives from the fact that in this period lyric verse was seen to some extent as a 'democratic' vehicle of expression. Available to all, its very availability tended to go hand in hand with a fixation on traditional models, and hence the neglect of a new quality. This revealed even more clearly the legacy of fascist propaganda: language had been largely exhausted through over-emphatic use by the Nazis, through rhetorical emotion and propagandist bombast. This had discredited it and made it virtually impossible to use at all without a sense of alienation. The quality of this early post-war lyric verse was thus in inverse proportion to its quantity. Only weeks after its first issue, the journal *Ulenspiegel* published the following plea: 'We request our contributors where possible to send us no poetry. Or to come to us and seek us out. We hardly exist any longer – we are under a deluge of poems. Write prose, not poetry!'

Prose, however, or prose aimed at renewing language, was hardly written at all in this period. Hermann Kasack's widely-read novel *Die Stadt hinter dem Strom* (*The City Beyond the River*) (1947), Elisabeth Langgässer's *Das unauslösliche Siegel* (*The Indelible Seal*) (1946), Ernst Wiechert's concentration-camp account *Der Totenwald* (*Forest of the Dead*) (1945), and the works of Ernst Kreuder and Emil Barth, if anything evince the continuation of an already existing literary trend extending back beyond 'internal emigration' to the pre-1933 period, rather than the existence of a *Kahlschlag* narrative literature in post-war Germany. The stories of Wolfgang Borchert, Hans Erich Nossack and Wolfdietrich Schnurre, which come closest to the *Kahlschlag* postulate, are, even qualitatively, exceptions to the rule. These authors work with consistently simplified sentence construction, precise description of detail, verbless and broken sentence structure and a literal writing style – in short, with narrative devices aimed at the construction and reconstruction of reality. They remain exceptions to the rule nonetheless: 'It was so incredibly difficult to write even so much as half a page of prose just after 1945', as Heinrich Böll declared, looking back over this period. As in the case of deficient lyrical works, the reason for this lies in the problematic legacy of language from the German fascist era: 'The "young generation" used up the better part of its strength trying to refill the vacuum left by the language policy of the Third Reich' (Urs Widmer).

The brief era of *Trümmerliteratur* thus presents a highly contradictory picture overall. In the poetics envisaged by *Kahlschlag* advocates it was radical, although this could only be put into practice in exceptional cases. There was on the one hand a rediscovery of reality, a desire to come to terms with the past, and an orientation towards the future, but on the other hand a retraction of the sense of reality through the use of traditional literary forms and verbal bombast. Euphoria and the mood for a fresh start were found side by side with resignation and hopelessness. *Trümmerliteratur* is thus an apt illustration of the times that so substantially shaped it. What it was not able to do was to fashion a literary tradition that could set something of poetic substance against the impending social changes and restorative tendencies manifesting themselves in the Federal Republic at that time. What it was not able to do was launch a literary tradition capable of taking a stand against the restorative tendencies at work in the poetic substance of the Federal Republic.

Gathering and reconstruction

The role of the Cultural Alliance (Kulturbund)

The state of affairs in the Soviet-Occupied Zone (at that time usually known as the Eastern Zone), was decidedly different, although even here there was no 'Zero Point'. The dominant political forces in the Eastern Zone, the Soviet Military Administration (SMAD), and the leadership of the Communist Party (the Ulbricht group had returned to Berlin on 29 April 1945), drew on the traditions of the anti-fascist struggle from 1935 onwards, specifically on People's Front policy. From the outset the interzonal, nonpartisan Cultural Alliance for the Democratic Renewal of Germany (Kulturbund zur demokratischen Erneuerung Deutschlands), which had already been planned in exile, was assigned a central role in broad terms for the first three or four years after the war. The alliance made its first public appearance on 4 July 1945 with its founding manifesto, which contained in modified form all the components of the People's Front cultural policy elaborated years earlier. The core of this manifesto reads: 'It is incumbent on the best Germans of all professions and social strata, in this time of severe need in German history, to unite in order to create a movement for German renewal with the aim of destroying the remnants of fascism and reaction in all spheres of life and knowledge, and thereby to build in the intellectual and cultural sphere a new, pure and decent life.'

The text of the manifesto both documents and highlights the vague statements and inconsistencies of an anti-fascist cultural policy conceived in the spirit of the lowest common denominator. Under a broad cloak of anti-fascism and anti-militarism, groups with sharply diverging worldviews could and did gather. Nationalist and conservative Christians, such as the pedagogue Eduard Spranger or the CDU (Christian Democrat) politician Ernst Lemmer, an old liberal such as Ricarda Huch, or an apolitical 'poet-prince' such as Gerhart Hauptmann (who was honorary president in Berlin) were leading members of the Cultural Alliance, as were socialist and communist intellectuals and writers. Johannes R. Becher was its President.

By way of a founding clarion-call, various initiatives by the Cultural Alliance aimed at coming to terms with the fascist past, and at the re-education of formerly convinced fascists, collaborators, and the merely indifferent, into a new anti-fascist, democratic conviction (as long as it was not communist!). Fresh opportunities for anti-fascist literature to exert an impact were sought in meetings, at festivals and on radio. In August 1945 the Aufbau-Verlag publishing house belonging to the Cultural Alliance was established, taking over the publishing programmes and licences of the major exiled publishing houses. Within only two years almost a hundred publications had been produced, with a total circulation level of over two and a half million copies. The most popular work was Theodor Plivier's *Stalingrad*, with over 154,000 copies.

In September 1945 the cultural political journal *Aufbau* (*Construction*) first appeared as a mouthpiece of the Alliance (published until 1959). Contributors included Thomas Mann, Rudolf Hagelstange and Georg Lukács. By 1946 the Cultural Alliance even had a weekly newspaper, *Sonntag* (*Sunday*), whose published texts included works by Hemingway, Jean Cocteau, Erich Kästner and Ernst Wiechert. Having started at the end of 1945 with a membership of 22,000, by the end of 1947 membership of the Alliance had increased to 120,000.

There was an unmistakable trend within the Alliance for the numerically dominant group, communist intellectuals and writers, steadily to increase their influence in the first two or three years, as the Party had envisaged. This gave the Western powers an excuse to ban the Cultural Alliance as 'communist' in their respective zones. This occurred around the time (November 1947) that B.E. Spranger, R. Huch and E. Lemmer, as well as the formerly socialist author Plivier, all emigrated to the West. The first German Writers' Congress of October 1947 also revealed how far apart the Western zones and the Soviet-Occupied Zone had already grown.

The reinstatement of exile literature and a return to the literary heritage

Fascist tyranny had broken continuity in many spheres, including literature. Some of the finest German writers had been murdered by the Nazis (Mühsam, Ossietzky), many had been sent to concentration camps and penal institutions and many had committed suicide for reasons more or less connected with Nazi rule (Tucholsky, Hasenclever, Toller, Benjamin, Stefan Zweig). If not actually involved in the internal Resistance in Germany, the overwhelming majority of democratic and socialist authors had gone, with greater or lesser reluctance, into exile.

561

Homecomers

Of these, the vast majority returned to the Soviet-Occupied Zone, either immediately in 1945 or a short time later. It was to be expected that proletarian revolutionary writers such as Willi Bredel, Eduard Claudius, Otto Gotsche, Karl Grünberg, Hans Lorbeer and others would return from exile and Resistance activity to that part of Germany that promised a socialist future. In fact, however, most other anti-fascist writers also chose to settle in the GDR. Others who returned from Soviet exile, apart from Bredel, were Johannes. R. Becher, Erich Weinert, Friedrich Wolf, Adam Scharrer and Theodor Plivier. From Mexico, the second major centre of exile, came Anna Seghers, Ludwig Renn, Bodo Uhse and Alexander Abusch (later Minister of Culture). From the USA, usually not until around 1947–9, came Marchwitza, Bertolt Brecht, Ernst Bloch, Franz-Carl Weiskopf, Wieland Herzfelde and others. In 1952 Stefan Heym, who had become a US citizen and actually wanted to settle in Prague, also returned to the GDR. Still others came from different countries of exile: Arnold Zweig (Palestine, 1948), the former Expressionist Rudolf Leonhard (France, 1950), Jan Petersen (England, 1946), Erich Arendt (Columbia, 1950), Stephan Hermlin (Switzerland and West Germany, 1947). This list covers the major representatives of East German literature of the late 1940s and early 1950s. They were hesitantly joined by representatives of the younger generation (Erwin Strittmatter, Franz Fühmann, Günter Kunert). And since so many writers gathered in the territory of the Soviet-Occupied Zone, having anti-fascist experiences in common and being of one mind, the literature of 1945–9 is marked by a rare political, and even aesthetic homogeneity.

Motives for return

The reason Anna Seghers gave for deciding to live in the SOZ/GDR could have been given by all the others: 'Because here I can express what I have lived for.' Precisely because these exiles had not withdrawn into an ivory tower, they now enjoyed virtually total support, both spiritual and material, by the Soviet and German authorities in the Soviet-Occupied Zone. Their books were published by the Soviet Military Administration (SMAD), and later by the Aufbau-Verlag. The pages of the journals *Aufbau* (*Construction*), *Ost und West* (*East and West*), *Heute und Morgen* (*Today and Tomorrow*) were available to them, and they were even given help in finding accommodation and food.

Encouragement of the 'critical realists'

The reinstatement of anti-fascist exile literature, however, entailed far more than this. Those in charge of literary policy in the SOZ also promoted the work of some exiles who had not chosen to settle in East Germany with the same zeal as that of those who had. This holds particularly true of the work of Heinrich Mann (who had had every intention of settling in the GDR, but died shortly before his planned departure from the USA in March 1950), Lion Feuchtwanger (who was awarded the National Prize in 1953 and died in the USA in 1958), Leonhard Frank (who returned from the USA to the Federal Republic in 1958) and Thomas Mann (who in 1949, the Goethe Year, gave celebration speeches in both parts of Germany, also being awarded Goethe prizes by both; Mann finally moved from the United States in 1952 to settle in Switzerland). To a lesser extent it also applied to the work of Oskar Maria Graf, still to be discovered. None of the above was a Marxist or a proponent of socialist realism. Instead they were evaluated as bourgeois Humanists and so-called critical Realists, in line with People's Front ideas. In the first few years after 1945 in particular they were even ranked above a large number of consistently socialist authors.

This classification and marked promotion of critical Realists went hand in hand with severe criticism of authors who were in the meantime being hailed in West Germany as classic authors of the modern age, such as Joyce, Proust, Kafka, Faulkner, Beckett and Gide. These and others were soon condemned as representatives of late bourgeois decadence who could scarcely be expected to have a share in the building of a new anti-fascist democratic order, and still less in the building of socialism.

The People's Front heritage

Part of the overall concept of literary policy derived from the spirit of the People's Front was an effort on the part of administrators and people in authority to win over a proportion of authors from the so-called 'internal emigration'. This policy even took in some who had not entirely rejected the Nazi regime, such as Gerhart Hauptmann or Hans Fallada. The former (internal emigration) group included the lyric poet Peter Huchel, the story-writer Ehm Welk and Paul Rilla, who was later to become a leading literary critic. It should be noted that all three had shown an inclination towards the literary left, even in the Weimar Republic.

It may be asserted, therefore, that within the Soviet-Occupied Zone there was certainly no sign of a literary 'Zero Point', although there was a fresh start in the sense of an anti-fascist democratic renewal based on the full spectrum of anti-fascist literary tradition. The result was the formation of a tradition and canon that made literature in the Soviet-Occupied

Zone different from that in West Germany, long before the two separate German states were founded.

The novel takes stock of the age

In 1947 Anna Seghers returned to Germany from exile in Mexico, travelling by way of France and her now ruined home city of Mainz, through the Western zones and on into the Soviet-Occupied Zone. She described what she saw and felt as follows: 'When I returned from exile, I travelled eastward through Germany. The cities lay in ruins, and the people were inwardly just as much in ruins. At that time Germany presented a "unity" of ruins, despair and hunger. And yet there were also people who were not numbed by destitution, and who were for the first time voicing questions that troubled everyone: What happened? How did it happen? This led to the next question: What must happen now to ensure that the horror is never repeated?' Anna Seghers answered this question clearly and unequivocally, both on her own behalf and for her exiled colleagues: 'That was the moment when German writers had to step into the fray to speak and answer as clearly and distinctly as possible. Through their profession they had to help the people to reach an understanding of the situation they had brought on themselves, and to awaken in them the strength to live a different, peaceful life.'

The eradication of fascism (Entfaschisierung)

Their primary concern was the eradication of fascism (*Entfaschisierung*: Brecht, Seghers) in the hearts and minds of those who had had blind faith in the Nazis and followed them with enthusiasm. In Anna Seghers's agenda, the aim was to fill the 'hollow spaces of the emotions' with positive human values, including a new conception of the nation and the Fatherland. Her novel *Die Toten bleiben jung* (*The Dead Stay Young*), begun in exile in Mexico, was her attempt to write a novel taking stock of the age, but also offering even former Nazis among her readers opportunities for self-identification. The book is a comprehensive historical chronicle, beginning with the end of World War I in 1918–19 (and the November Revolution), and concluding with the end of World War II in 1945. The author follows the story of young workers and soldiers (and their courageous wives and children), and that of their persecutors and murderers from among the former military caste and the new SS guard. The honest fighters lose their lives, but live on in their children: such is the dubious promise offered by her novel, which was highly thought of in the GDR.

A glance back at the past

Narrative prose published for the first time between 1945 and 1949 closely followed the themes and tendencies of exile literature, and was almost exclusively concerned with the fascist past. In addition to this, there were a good number of books of an 'enlightening' (*aufklärend*), documentary character, intended to show what had actually happened as well as how the 'green shoots of fact' (*Kräutlein Faktum* – Ernst Bloch) had been disseminated in war reports and Resistance chronicles. Outstanding literary examples of this are Theodor Plivier's novel *Stalingrad*, published in 1945, which is in the tradition of Remarque's *All Quiet on the Western Front*, and *Memorial* (1947), Günther Weisenborn's account of internment. Hans Fallada's neglected novel *Jeder stirbt für sich allein* (*Each Dies For Himself Alone*) (1947), a contrast to his other works, should also be included here.

A whole series of novels visibly blending fact with fiction deal with central characters who manage to overcome the status quo – fellow-travelling – or passive resistance and go through learning processes that are discernible to the reader and ultimately lead them to become politically aware, active anti-fascists. These characters became models for those undecided Germans who were still to be won over to the new anti-fascist democratic order. Bodo Uhse's *Leutnant Bertram* (*Lieutenant Bertram*) (1944), Harald Hauser's *Wo Deutschland lag* (*Where Germany Lay*) (1947), Elfriede Brüning's *Damit du weiterlebst* (*So That You May Live On*) (1949), and Wolfgang Joho's *Die Hirtenflöte* (*The Shepherd's Pipe*) (1948), which deals with the theme of desertion from the German army, are among these works.

Older and more significant prose authors, however, were quick to recognise that restricting literature to the subject of fascism was not good enough. The entire body of German national history, especially the age of imperialism and the two world wars, would have to be opened up to debate to render comprehensible the deeper meaning of the 1945 defeat. In this broader sense four noteworthy authors brought out historical assessments of the age in novel form between 1945 and 1949 – books on which they worked for some years, and in some cases decades. Arnold Zweig was the first author to follow a programme from the early 1920s onwards of exposing the anatomy of the imperialist society on an epic scale, revealing predatory war as a mechanism that was in keeping with imperialist society. His monumental cycle in several volumes, *Der grosse Krieg der weissen Männer* (*The Great War of the White Men*), gives an account of the period from 1913–14 to 1918 in its major historical stages. This was followed after 1945 with the novels *Die Feuerpause* (*The Break in the Firing*) (1954) and *Traum ist teuer* (*Dreams are Dear*) (1962). Zweig's psychological approach to analysing the behaviour of the petty bourgeoisie and intellectuals under fascism in *Das Beil von Wandsbek* (*The Axe of Wandsbek*) (Hebrew 1943, German 1947) is worth pointing out here.

Three authors from the proletarian revolutionary literary movement – Adam Scharrer, Hans Marchwitza and Willi Bredel – had embarked on large-scale period novels (*Epochenromanen*) during their exile, and now brought them to completion. Marchwitza's episodic *Kumiak* trilogy (1959) and Bredel's novel trilogy *Verwandte und Bekannte* (*Family and Friends*) (1953), the proletarian equivalent of the bourgeois family novel, found many readers in the young GDR.

What is troubling about these early post-war years is not so much what *was* published as what was not. Published works consisted almost exclusively of literature about fascism from the pens of older and formerly exiled authors, who anyway had hardly anything suppressed or undisclosed left to reveal. The literary work of middle-aged and young people, on the other hand, devoted as little energy to the Nazi past as German society at large.

The 'work of mourning' the fascist past

Far-reaching psychological and moral analysis, and a settling of accounts – the real work of mourning – was curtailed in favour of an activist attitude of construction with its gaze fixed blindly on the future. Although undoubtedly partly shaped by the contingencies of everyday destitution in an impoverished part of Germany, this attitude was also dictated from above. With a view to the newly-created anti-fascist democratic order, the East Germans were declared to be the 'victors over history' and the final conquerors of fascism in their own country, soon to be called the GDR. This helps to explain why an unreserved confrontation with fascism in respect to those who had been involved in it was such a long time in coming – not until the 1960s, and in some cases the 1970s.

Lyric poetry after dark times

Lyric poetry, too, was faced with the task of overcoming the legacy of twelve years of Nazi rule. This included the songs and ballads of nationalist-racist, fascist bards applauding the Nazi regime, the sterile classicism of Joseph Weinheber and Rudolf Alexander Schröder and, finally, the lyric nature poetry of those who saw themselves as a community of 'internal emigrants'. Such poets gave voice to nature as a magical sphere that was a law unto itself, seeing their putative triumph in the assertion that the barbarity of human history could not touch it. Meant as a protest, nature poetry was in fact a form of flight; purporting to be dissident, it was an expression of elemental helplessness. Intended as a gesture of moral rebuttal, it was actually a noncommittal 'juggling with six balls', an 'anachronistic dallying with flowers and blossoms over the horrific, yawning abyss of the mass graves they covered' (E. Langgässer). Lyric poetry of this sort offered little in the way of a legacy to literature for a new anti-fascist democratic order. And yet even the great authors of the exile found difficulty adapting themselves to their newly assigned poetic role.

Poverty of perception

The years of exile had been 'dark times' indeed, and 'a bad time for lyric poetry', as Brecht pointed out on numerous occasions. Given the severity of the struggle and the 'differentiated nature of the problems', poverty of apprehension and the sacrifice of 'differentiation of feeling' were the order of the day. The very act of writing about the beauty of nature – an apple tree in blossom, or the sea outside the front door in Denmark – seemed to Brecht and others 'almost a crime ... because it entails a silence about so many misdeeds'. How was the wealth of feeling and expression to be retrieved now, after such a long, enforced period of asceticism?

Authors such as Erich Weinert faced quite different problems. Once a leading proponent of militant 'operative' poetry for political agitation in the context of a proletarian revolutionary literary movement, Weinert now found its trenchant satire and militant call to action ill-suited to the more defensive approach of the new anti-fascist democratic order. The political communication system of a class-sensitive workers' movement, of which Weinert's texts, like those of Hans Lorbeer, Wilhelm Tkaczyk and others had once formed part, now no longer existed. In a situation of this kind it was no easy matter to restore the writing and reading of poetry to the status of a productive art form. There were scarcely any poets 'born after' who were going their own way. The propensity for inner contemplation barred the way to the newly-emerging social reality.

Johannes R. Becher

The dominant lyric poet of those years was Johannes R. Becher, who was oriented both towards reality and tradition. This was in contrast to the averred 'modern' lyric poetry of his old antithesis Gottfried Benn, by then living in West Berlin, who was avowedly in favour of 'aestheticism, isolationism and esotericism' (*Berliner Brief – Berlin Letter*, July 1948). Becher's key theme of the 1940s was the plight of Germany and the German people at what he saw as a historical turning-point, and the necessity of 'becoming different' at the end of the fascist reign of terror. No author pinned such high hopes on being able to wrest progress and that 'something different' out of a direct resumption of the Humanist cultural heritage. The issue for him was not a critical eradication of inconsistencies

567

in the history of his nation, but recollection of a Germany and a German culture with its barbaric core elements systematically removed.

The aesthetic structure of the poem seemed to Becher the best way of retrieving the 'dream possession' (*Traumbesitz*) of this obstructed heritage. To this end he aspired both to 'classical' stylistic rendition (particularly in the 'restraining' sonnet form, which he saw as protective, on account of its rigour), and popular (*volkstümlich*) simplicity (the four-line song strophe). He treats stock themes such as the nation, the homeland and liberation in an almost naive and seamless way, even using Christian religious motifs and vocabulary (prayer, the Cross, judgement, redemption, holy, eternal), since they seemed to him, probably rightly, suitable devices for awakening interest, hope and courage among non-proletarian readers. Becher's inflationary, at times non-dialectical poetic treatment of the 'neglected fatherland' (a term borrowed from Hölderlin, and frequently cited by Becher by way of self-justification) in a way that falsely reconciles its inconsistencies makes his lyric poetry about Germany somewhat dubious.

Bertolt Brecht

Recent years have witnessed growing recognition that Brecht the lyric poet is an author of equal stature with Brecht the playwright. The arrival of 1945 brought no interruption in his poetry-writing, and he remained in exile until 1947–8, continuing even then to write mostly satire and poetry warning about fascism. By way of an epilogue to *Furcht und Elend des Dritten Reiches* (*Fear and Misery of the Third Reich*) he cautioned relentlessly: 'The womb is still fertile that gave birth to it' ('Der Schoss ist fruchtbar noch, aus dem das kroch'). Brecht then gradually turned from Nazism as the former main political opponent, re-directing his satire, sometimes caricatured to the point of absurdity, against liberal-democratic capitalism – the system that had survived fascism and now taken its place in Germany. He achieved this in merciless, monumental allegorical images in his poem *Der anachronistische Zug oder Freiheit und Democratie* (*The Anachronistic Procession, or Freedom and Democracy*), modelled on Shelley's ballad *The Mask of Anarchy* (in German: *Der Maskenzug der Anarchie*). This depicts the six scourges – oppression, leprosy, deceit, stupidity, murder and theft, representing twelve years of the past in an ingenious masquerade that is quite up-to-date. Some of the new poems are oriented towards the future, however, their gaze fixed on the historical turning-point as a time of unprecedented opportunity; self-determination and autonomous activity are proclaimed the hallmarks of the new social order. This is the case, for example, with his *Aufbaulied* (*Song of Construction*) (1948).

Among the middle-aged generation following on from older writers such as Becher, Brecht, Weinert, etc., few were able to shape the course of lyric poetry in East German literature in the first five years after the War. Chief among them were Peter Huchel, Stephan Hermlin and Kurt Barthel (KuBa). Poets of the same generation, such as Erich Arendt and Georg Maurer, did not start coming to the fore until the 1950s.

Peter Huchel had been writing poetry since the 1920s, mainly lyric nature poetry in sober, worldly language. His experiences as a soldier brought a new, emphatic use of natural images. In Huchel's post-war work (his volume *Gedichte – Poems* was published in 1948) these images appear as symbols of the old system with its rigidity and death on the one hand, and of the new, life-bringing social order on the other. The landscape and natural world are not a reservation, but a real, live environment on which war (i.e. violent man and the technology of which he makes use) have also made their mark. Huchel's expansion of the nature poem to include 'Stalingrad and the silence of the dead', as Wilhelm Lehmann disparagingly observed, points to one of the key differences between East and West German literature in the years immediately following the collapse of the Nazi regime. This was to have repercussions on lyric poetry in the GDR that can scarcely be overestimated, especially when Huchel's writing began to weave its spell on Johannes Bobrowski and the younger 'landscape' poets, such as Wulf Kirsten and Heinz Czechowski.

Theatre caught between 'major' and 'minor' pedagogy

Franz C. Weiskopf called theatre people who had gone into exile during Nazi rule the 'problem children' of the emigrant community. What he meant by this was that a writer could write for a people without living among them, but that live theatre could not exist in isolation from the theatre-going public. Theatre people were moreover deprived of their equipment in exile – stage, sets, technology, etc. in a much more blatantly obvious way than writers, who 'only' wrote books.

An 'in-between-time'

Inevitably, therefore, playwrights whose plays had hardly any chance at all of being performed in the foreseeable future endured exile as an 'in-between-time' (Brecht) constricting their work, their sights set on a non-fascist and, as many of them hoped, socialist time to come. There was some concern about the literary luggage they would bring back to devastated Germany, and which of the manuscripts in their drawer would be of any use to the post-war theatre. Much more than prose, therefore, a good proportion of the theatre plays written in exile now became the theatre of the present-day.

After the defeat of the fascist regime, the occupying Soviet forces helped to establish a theatrical life with a versatile repertoire. By 1946 there were already seventy-five stages operating full-time. Looking back on this period in 1948, Brecht summed it up with appropriate deference: 'The enemy that had been brought low with such great effort was now invited into the theatre. The first steps by the victors are the provision of food, the supply of water and the opening of theatres! ... One thing is certain: the great change has inaugurated a great time for the arts. How great will they be?' This sceptical concluding sentence suggests that the equipping of theatres was not enough in itself to guarantee the greatness of theatrical art. The central issue was how much political and aesthetic progress was feasible in practice. The first three to four years of post-war theatre in the Soviet-Occupied Zone (when Brecht was still living in exile) were unequivocally marked by a selection of plays, and production methods that was worlds apart both from Brecht's concept of epic dialectic theatre, and from the proletarian revolutionary theatre tradition. The selection of plays was dominated by classic authors and the bourgeois repertoire, including Existentialist plays.

'Perceptual truth'

As regards direction and performance the leading figures of the first few years, Maxim Vallentin and Gustav von Wangenheim, formerly precursors of an 'operative' theatre of political agitation, followed the methods of Stanislavsky. The latter's highest ambition in theatre was to achieve 'perceptual truth', and the presentation of a 'new authenticity' in theatrical art. Applied to the finest plays of classic authors, the idea behind this psycho-physical technique of representing emotions, passions, conflicts and deeds on stage was to reveal social as well as individual truth, and thereby exert an educative effect.

However, the theatres did more than devote themselves to the cultural heritage within the framework of the psychological treatment of the Stanislavsky School. Anti-fascist contemporary plays and historical dramas were also encouraged, and performed when they were written. Günther Weisenborn's play *Die Illegalen* (*The Underground Fighters*) (1938–45/6) was a particular success. The author, who had himself been active in the anti-Nazi Resistance movement (The Schulze-Boysen-Harnack group) and had been interned from 1942 to 1945, portrayed the activities of a Resistance group.

Theatre and the new reality

A striking aspect of the first five or six years of post-war theatre is that not a single author of the younger generation came forward with a play that made any real impact on theatrical life. Theatre was obliged to live in the past in a dual sense. The new and innovative was somehow not yet ready for theatrical presentation, while the teachers from whom younger authors could have learned were either only accepted to a limited degree, or were not yet able to influence them because they had not settled, or had not yet settled, in the Soviet-Occupied Zone, later the GDR. This gave rise to a remarkable situation in which the theatre in the phase of anti-fascist democratic change developed in the absence of, or even counter to the two leading socialist mentors who had shaped the theatrical scene of the 1920s and early 1930s: Friedrich Wolf and Bertolt Brecht. The socialist tradition thus played a subordinate role.

Friedrich Wolf

Friedrich Wolf was quick to return from Soviet exile to East Berlin in the autumn of 1945. He had been the outstanding proponent of *Agitprop* theatre in the Weimar Republic. His plays *Cyankali* (*Cyanide*) and *Die Matrosen von Cattaro* (*The Sailors of Cattaro*) had been both easy to perform and politically effective. The two outstanding plays of his prolific exile output were *Professor Mamlock* and *Beaumarchais*, a play about the 1789 French Revolution. Finding himself alone in the years from 1945 until his death, he had the bitter experience of discovering that there was virtually no demand at all for the proletarian revolutionary tradition of political *Kampftheater* within the democratic construction in the People's Front spirit that was taking place around him. There were a few seasons of *Professor Mamlock* (the story of a conservative Jewish surgeon who is forced to face the untenability of his position after the Nazi takeover). Otherwise, however, Wolf found himself unable to continue in his success-ful vein of the 1920s and 1930s. Yet, as a dispute between him and Brecht in 1949 shows, Wolf was wholly sympathetic to the then dominant theory of poetic immediacy, created by the use of psychological devices. Wolf was a keen proponent of an Aristotelian theatre, aimed at a closed and crafted form of drama, that saw catharsis as an inalienable component. Catharsis, the purification of emotion, was seen as 'one of the major formal elements in the great process of guilt and atonement' that Wolf the socialist moralist saw at work in the most recent social events.

With historical hindsight, Bertolt Brecht is seen to tower head and shoulders above East German theatrical life from the very beginning. He began to live and work in East Berlin from the autumn of 1948. Even there, however, encouragement of his work was not undiluted. In fact, after 1945 his plays were little performed (some not at all), with the exception of the sequence *Furcht und Elend des Dritten Reichs* (*The Fear and Misery of the Third Reich*). A fresh start was called for in all respects, since Brecht realised that even a recourse to his own mode of writing and performing from the pre-1933 years was utopian. In those earlier years, at least in the big cities, there had been a broad, class-conscious, working-class public theatre-goers, an alternative proletarian public with whom Brecht and others had tried to abolish the opposition between theatre-makers and theatre-goers – a 'bridging of the orchestra pit', as Benjamin had called it. Brecht had accomplished this in his didactic plays, which he later called 'major pedagogy', inasmuch as they had abolished the system of performers versus spectators in favour of performers who were also students. Even during his exile, Brecht realised that, given the course of events since 1933, it would be necessary to return to the 'minor pedagogy' of the traditional stage-play performance, and that the traditional communication structure of the theatre was not going to be broken overnight. It was with this theoretical agenda in mind that Brecht set about his practical theatrical work in Berlin.

The authorities allocated him guest nights at the Deutsches Theater, which was under the directorship of Wolfgang Langhoff. Brecht's 'own' former theatre on the Schifferbauerdamm, which had seen the premiere of his *Threepenny Opera*, was still occupied by the *Volksbühne* (People's Stage) company. Finally in July 1949 Brecht and his wife, the actress Helene Weigel, were able to move back there, and he took up the work of the Berliner Ensemble, which is still in existence today.

Ambivalent reception of his *Mutter Courage* (*Mother Courage*) (Zurich premiere 1941, Berlin premiere 1949) indicated clearly enough to Brecht the limitations of progressive theatrical work – limitations among the theatre-going public, but also limitations set by the authorities in charge of cultural policy, who had already caused him to speak angrily of the 'stinking breath of the provinces' in the heart of Berlin. In addition to a series of model productions of his exile plays, continued in the autumn of 1949 with *Herr Puntila und sein Knecht Matti* (*Mr Puntila and his Servant Matti*) as the opening play of the Berliner Ensemble, Brecht was most anxious to produce plays directly concerned with the situation in Germany following the liberation from fascism, and with the chances for socialist revolutionary transformation. In spring 1949, for example, he wrote the play *Die Tage der Commune* (*The Days of the Commune*), which nevertheless proved unsuitable for the post-fascist situation and was not performed until after Brecht's death. The 'efforts of the lowlands', as Brecht once metaphorically described the social process in the post-fascist era, proved hardly less arduous than the previous 'troubles of the mountains'.

LITERATURE OF THE GERMAN DEMOCRATIC REPUBLIC

The 'society of literature' model: life between social pedagogy and censorship

Poets and writers as educators of the people

From its very outset, the GDR ascribed a central and pioneering function to literature in the building and shaping of socialism. 'Literature under real socialism' was no detached sphere of social values with laws of its own (as Max Weber held to be typical for modern societies), but an integral component in the overall strategy for creating socialist conditions and educating the 'socialist personalities' who would sustain them. It would be false, however, to assume from this a 'GDR literature system' consisting of a censorship apparatus that was intrinsically opposed to autonomous literature. It would be truer to say that literature sought from the very outset, and to a high degree, to become integral to the socialist agenda for people's education. It was this that led to what was perhaps the distinguishing feature of the 'GDR literature system', whereby authors were assigned the privileged, if not exaggerated role of people's educators and social pedagogues. They thus resurrected in a new guise the 'great writer' to whom bourgeois society had looked for leadership, prophesy, promises and comfort. Paradoxically, the more the state led by the Socialist Unity Party sank into a crisis of legitimacy and meaning, the truer this became. This was particularly the case when still in their guise as people's educators, writers, by then critical, increasingly took on the task in their works of bridging the gulf between the official state line and the utopian promise of 'true' socialism, and hence compensating for the growing sense of a lack of meaning. It is often difficult to ascertain without undue over-generalisation the role played by the texts of GDR authors – whether it was the above-mentioned role of appeasement, or a genuinely critical one.

The 'democratisation' paradigm

From the very founding of the GDR in 1949 the democratic and socialist aims of its cultural policy stood in stark contradiction of its authoritarian, and indeed repressive character. These were headed by the aspiration to eradicate educational privileges as social privileges. The educational material of the nation, including literature, was to be equally accessible to all members of all social classes. According to one concept of the leading literary policy-maker and first Minister of Culture of the GDR, Johannes R. Becher, literary life was subsumed under the term 'society of literature'. This formula was aimed at the ideal paradigm of a comprehensive 'democratisation' (naturally within an authoritarian socialist context) of literature and its incorporation into society at all levels – authorship, material production, distribution, reception and reading. Specifically, it was aimed at a wider distribution and hence wider socio-political impact of a literature that was automatically envisaged as 'democratic' and progressive. The 'literature of society' model was thus opposed on the one hand to the indisputable ghettoisation of quality literature in non-socialist societies, and on the other to the 'hostility to poetry' (Karl Marx), the ubiquitous subjection of literature to market forces, in Western countries, including the Federal Republic. The GDR 'society of literature' model, at first glance an attractive one, did indeed have its interesting, literature-fostering aspects. These were nonetheless nullified by their authoritarian and doctrinaire overall context, above all censorship. Socialist Unity Party (SED) policy ultimately obliterated virtually all incipient signs of a vital literary life flourishing in freedom by removing the right of self-determination from all groups involved in literary exchange. Authors were told what to write, publishers what to publish, booksellers what to sell, and finally readers told what they could and could not read. The authoritarian practice of controlling and censoring literature led the motto of 'democratisation' *ad absurdum*, thus making a farce of the ideal vision of a 'society of literature'.

Controlled literature

The state apparatus for controlling cultural policy was headed by the Ministry of Culture, backed up by cultural policy steering committees in the various districts, areas and municipalities, etc. Aside from departments for theatre, music, and events, the Ministry of Culture also significantly housed the Central Headquarters for Publishing and Book Sales (formerly the Bureau for Literature and Publishing, 1951–6, and the State Commission for Art Affairs, 1951–4). Its function was 'the licensing of publishing houses, the issuing of directives to the publishers attached to it, and the ensuring of an appropriate division of labour among them. It further steered, coordinated and monitored the carrying out of annual and future publishing programmes, approved manuscripts for book publishers and other products by non-licensed publishers, and issued publishing permits.' The Central Headquarters additionally monitored the professional activity and ideology of the book trade and library administration, approving major titles proposed by publishers for large editions, distributed printing materials and paper quotas and organised publishers' conferences. The Central Headquarters thus formed, it may be said today, the crucial controlling body for a nationwide 'planned literature' (Robert Darnton), working particularly closely with the Cultural Department of the SED Central Committee.

The publishing industry

At first sight, the GDR differed most markedly from other and previous German societies of literature in its mode of book production and conditions of ownership. All the major publishers (over sixty out of seventy-eight) were either 'publicly owned', i.e. state publishing houses, or 'organisation-owned', i.e. in the possession of parties and mass organisations. They were thus completely out of the reach of private owners. The Dietz publishing house thus belonged to the SED, Union-Verlag to the CDU, the Nation publishing house to the NDPD, Der Morgen book publishing house to the LDPD, Tribüne-Verlag to the FDGB, Neues Leben to the Free German Youth, Volk und Welt to the Society for German–Soviet Friendship, and Aufbau to the Democratic Cultural association (now known ultimately to have belonged also to the SED).

Formerly, all these houses were affiliated into a Union of Publicly-Owned Enterprises (VVB publishing houses), and later integrated into a Central Headquarters of Publishing Houses and Book Traders. Obviously, book production was not subject to the principle of the free market economy, with privately-owned, profit-motivated publishers competing with one another, but to a set agenda directed from above by the authorities, and to orders, likewise from above, as to what was to be produced. Publishing houses annually brought out some 6,000 titles amounting to a total of 150 million copies. The average edition of every title was thus nearly 25,000. In terms of per capita output, therefore, the GDR led the world, beside the Soviet Union and Japan. Statistically, each GDR citizen obtained eight to nine new titles annually.

The book trade

The same structure of socialist ownership on the one hand and hierarchical directives on the other obtained for the book trade. One central distribution warehouse in Leipzig, traditionally a book city, despatched the book range directly. There were thus no traders acting as free agents offering books for sale as a commodity under market conditions, as in the Federal Republic. There was still a private book trade, or traders, with state involvement, but the state-owned people's book trade was clearly paramount, selling some 85 per cent of all books in a total of 700 outlets.

Book exhibitions and special sales, 'book weeks', literature festivals, cultural competitions and production 'brigades' were responsible for advertising books, and aimed to increase reading activity among all sections of the population. Books, of course, were loaned as well as sold. The GDR had some 32,000 state, trade union or works libraries housing a total of 110 million volumes, including specialist library stocks. Nearly two-thirds of children able to read were book borrowers, while a quarter of the adult population were library users.

GDR bestsellers

These figures would seem to suggest that the GDR was populated by a nation of readers. Books that in the Federal Republic would have been looked on as too high-brow and/or political, and hence unmarketable, did indeed achieve high sales in the GDR, such as Heinrich Heine's *Deutschland. Ein Wintermärchen* (*Germany: A Winter's Tale*), or Anna Seghers's *Das Siebte Kreuz* (*The Seventh Cross*), of which a total of between one and a half and two million copies were printed. The most successful GDR novel was Hermann Kant's *Die Aula* (*The Hall*), which sold around a million copies. Such large editions, in a country of sixteen million inhabitants, would have been almost inconceivable in the Federal Republic, proving that in the GDR the distance between the reading public and quality literature was narrower. According to 1961 statistics, such literature would only be read by 1 to 2 per cent of the total population in the FRG. Although the working class – the ruling class, according to Party claims, in the GDR – was not fully represented in statistics relating to book ownership and readership, more than 95 per cent of working-class households did have books – generally at least ten or considerably more.

Who read?

Other figures contradict these findings, however. They are incompatible, for example, with a representative sample, in which thirty per cent of respondents asserted that they attached little or no importance to the reading of literature, while 47 per cent admitted to reading either no books at all, or only two a year. The same survey also revealed that both blue-collar and white-collar workers preferred travelogues, adventure and crime fiction, historical novels and biographies. Quality literature in the strict sense of the term, including contemporary GDR literature, lagged far behind in fourth place. Even in the GDR, the correlation between social status and books proved to hold enormous sway. Pupils and students, graduates and intellectuals read a great deal, while industrial and agricultural workers, housewives and pensioners read little.

What was read?

The reading issue was thus ambivalent: while it was true that nowhere in the German-speaking world was more read than in the GDR, this far from justified the assertion that this was a democratic, well-read nation. In the GDR as elsewhere, unequal education and a resulting disadvantaged status in the system of both vertical and horizontal division of labour were impediments to equal opportunity. As in the former Federal Republic, a generation grew up in the GDR for whom a concentrated encounter with cultural phenomena, characterised by the kind of personal initiative and reflection required by reading 'demanding' literature, became increasingly irksome and alien. The prevailing modes of cultural experience, television, radio and records, weaned them away from such habits rather than fostering them. The massive and ever-increasing market for entertainment literature of a trivial nature (science fiction, 'socialist' crime fiction and light novels about everyday themes, etc.) within overall GDR literature production fits into this picture.

A major sector of the GDR 'society of literature' likewise consisted of trivial literature – thrillers for relaxation reading. Monotonous workaday experience, frustrating shortages of goods, lack of travel opportunities, and political chicanery were key experiences for GDR citizens, leading many readers to seek refuge in the pleasant, wholesome, action-packed and, above all, remote worlds of entertainment literature.

The 'nation of readers' before and after the turning-point

The experiences of the 1989–91 turning-point completely debunked the myth of the GDR as a nation of readers. First and foremost, indigenous GDR literature, and for that matter quality literature in general, had assumed a compensatory, auxiliary function that is only imposed on literature in modern, liberal societies in exceptional circumstances. Topical GDR literature by critical authors had to take the place of the public in politics and the media that the authoritarian state would not allow to its citizens. As well, as already mentioned, it offered a (utopian) alternative sense of meaning that helped to compensate for the incalculable deficit of values and meaning of 'real socialism'. Both these compensatory functions of GDR literature are now obsolete. Consequently, the bookshops of the new Federal Länder are empty, their patrons purchasing, if at all, travel literature, guides, specialist books and long-forbidden action novels à la Konsalik.

577

The literary canon

One important authority in the GDR 'society of literature' in its claims to educate the nation was the teaching of German. This played a central role in school education and exerted an early effect on the reading habits of future adults. The literary aspect of this curriculum, which was more extensive than in the FRG, had a dual role. Its first task was to impart a new, socialist picture of humanity when dealing with socialist or Humanist literature. As a rule this involved inculcating party thinking, feeling and action by way of identification with the model literary hero. Its second task was to develop the individual capacity for aesthetic enjoyment by means of imparting linguistic skills.

The reading canon selected for this purpose was quite different from that in Federal curricula. On the one hand it favoured more recent socialist literature (Gorki, N. Ostrovsky, Seghers, Bredel, H. Kant, etc.), and on the other bourgeois Humanist literature (Lessing, Goethe, Schiller, Heine, Heinrich Mann, etc.). The overall effect of this among pupils must have been to produce an impression of an almost exclusively affirmative, optimistic response to given reality. One would have sought in vain in GDR German literature teaching, for example, for a single text by Franz Kafka. Aside from the rigid formality of language teaching, pedagogical practice was imbued with a cliché-ridden style of interpretation that skated over contradictions and tended not to encourage independent thought, and which furthermore went against the grain of many of the texts being taught.

The social responsibility of the author

The production and business of literature, reading habits and German teaching in schools were all major aspects of the 'society of literature'. The crucial question, however, is that of the social responsibilities assigned to authors in the GDR, and their specific living and working conditions. The differences between their status and that of authors in Western countries were huge. In the latter, authors were and are at liberty not only to select their own themes and forms, but also to publish their texts unexpurgated and uncensored – on condition, that is, that they could find a publishing house to do it. For Western authors, the market and the manifest relative interest of the reading public is a decisive factor. This was not the case in the GDR. The SED state fully incorporated authors into the 'real socialist' system – a fact which had its advantages, as well as its decided disadvantages. The high status accorded to educators of the people and authoritative interpreters of social reality, of course along Marxist lines, was associated with a wide range of privileges and opportunities for promotion. On the other hand, the threat of losing all this, and worse, loomed for authors who saw their role as educators and interpreters in terms of expressing criticism and exploding taboos, rather than as an affirmative one.

The Writers' Association

The strict social and political constraints placed on GDR authors was most apparent on the institutional level. Generally members of the Writers' Association, they were obliged by its regulations to be active co-builders of 'advanced socialist society' by means of their creative work. The November 1973 Association constitution further stipulates that 'members of the GDR Writers' Association acknowledge the leading role of the working class and its party in cultural policy. They are committed to the creative method of socialist realism. They are resolutely opposed to all forms of ideological coexistence and the infiltration of reactionary and revisionist ideas into the sphere of literature.' This effectively ascribed a social responsibility to all authors organised in the Writers' Association: along with all creative artists, they were in their own way to foster the building of socialism. The garret poet of Biedermeier days was now a thing of the past, to be replaced by the 'social person of letters' (M. Jäger).

The professional training of writers was not left to chance. In 1955 the Johannes R. Becher Institute of Literature was established in Leipzig, planned along similar lines to the Gorki Institute in Moscow and directed successively by Alfred Kurella, Max Zimmering and M.W. Schulz. The would-be writer could be assigned a place there for a two-year course as a 'creative aspirant', to study the history and theory of literature, Marxism–Leninism, and, not least, how to write. Up to 1969 some one hundred and thirteen budding writers graduated from this institute, including Ralph Giordiano, Erich Loest, Adolf Endler, Karl-Heinz Jacobs, Kurt Bartsch and Rainer and Sarah Kirsch. The Institute enjoyed its cultural political heyday around 1960, when it operated as a nursery for a new type of worker-writer in line with the Bitterfeld Way idea.

The writer's vocation

Membership of the Association, which underpinned the status of authors and which was their sole source of security, bound them to their society in a number of advantageous ways. Chief among these were the manifold opportunities available for financial support of writing projects, such as grants or short-term employment as dramaturgists, readers for publishers or academics. Lyric poets, who were among the lowest-paid writers, were funded out of the cultural budget, making a living from translations – free translations of lyric poetry from foreign languages which they prepared from interlinear translations prepared by professional translators. Writers of high standing had the added security of an honorarium for their membership of the Academy of Arts. It is also worth mentioning that for quality fiction manuscripts GDR publishers paid authors' fees amounting to 10–15 per cent of the retail price – more than the West German author could expect from his or her publisher. Lastly, the GDR ensured the financial support of authors by means of an extensive system of literary prizes. The most coveted of the twelve state and thirty-eight non-state prizes (awarded by parties, mass organisations, academies, city authorities, etc.) were the National Prize, the Heinrich Mann Prize, the Heinrich Heine Prize and the Lessing Prize.

Planning and control

All this might give the impression that the GDR was a promised land for literature and writers, which was not the case. The ultimate fate of books, and hence of their authors, was subject to an often rigid and hierarchical system of planning and control. The Central Headquarters for Publishing and Book Sales was thus an institution without whose authorisation, in the form of a licence, no printed matter could be produced or distributed. This regulation, incidentally, was in violation of the GDR Constitution, in which Article 27 paragraph 1 guaranteed the right to free and public expression of opinion. Even this was not enough, however. According to a law of obligatory submission (*Vorlagepflicht*) introduced in 1965, a Bureau for Copyrights was in charge of issuing copyrights abroad, either to authors or GDR publishing houses, and had the power to refuse copyrights. Every manuscript that an author wanted to publish abroad, for example in the Federal Republic, had first to be submitted to a GDR publishing house, and the latter's decision communicated to the Bureau for Copyrights. These basic regulations, which are tantamount to censorship, were backed by options for legal sanctions that were significantly stepped up in the latter years of the GDR. From 1973 onwards an author could be liable to a fine of up to 10,000 East German marks (prior to 1973 the fine was only 300 marks) for accepting royalties from foreign publishing houses without having them transferred via the Bureau for Copyrights – which was inevitable if the author had not previously obtained a publishing permit. This situation was further exacerbated by the 3rd Criminal Law Amendment Act of 1 August 1979, which permitted the imposition of heavy prison sentences for the free expression of opinion, even in poetic form, on the grounds of 'incitement to subversion' ('staatsfeindliche Hetze'), 'unlawful establishment of contacts' ('ungesetzliche Verbindungsaufnahme') or 'public degradation' ('öffentliche Herabwürdigung'). Even the 'transference' and 'distribution' of such writings was a criminal offence.

Steps against authors who refused to toe the line

Despite innumerable tendencies towards liberalisation and a variety of concessions, the last fifteen years of the GDR's existence, from 1975 to 1989, were a period of increasingly massive encroachment on the sovereignty of authors. The scope of repressive measures ranged from censorship of texts, through the banning of books and plays, the expulsion of authors from the Party and the Writers' Association and publicity campaigns, to secret police surveillance, legal penalties, and direct or indirect deprivation of citizenship. Key moments in this period were the expatriation of Wolf Biermann in 1976 and the expulsion of nine writers from the Writers' Association in the early summer of 1979 (including Adolf Endler, Stefan Heym, Karl-Heinz Jakobs and Klaus Schlesinger. Heym was fined in the same period for publishing his novel *Collin* in the West without official permission). To these measures were added the brutal treatment of younger authors as criminals, among them Jürgen Fuchs, Ulrich Schacht and Lutz Rathenow, and widespread intimidation of all critical authors by means of frequently open spying by the state security services (Stasi).

The true extent of these measures, and how deeply they affected the private lives of authors and their sense of human dignity can now be judged from such documents as Reiner Kunze's *Deckname Lyrik* (*Code Name Lyric Poetry*), Erich Loest's *Der Zorn des Schafes* (*The Wrath of the Sheep*), and Jürgen Fuchs's *Landschaften der Lüge* (*Landscapes of Lies*), or from Christa Wolf's controversial prose work *Was bleibt* (*What Remains*). The controversy unleashed by Wolf Biermann, who alleged informal collaboration by Sascha Anderson with the State Security Service (an allegation since confirmed), revealed that even the literary subculture of the young generation living in Prenzlauer Berg in East Berlin was only relatively exempt from state planning and control.

Censorship

Even before the major recent turning-point, censorship was discernible as the sinister, albeit largely secret, core of the GDR literature system. Since then, its secret nature has been exposed, both through the opening of the archives of the ominous Central Bureau of Publishers and Booksellers, and even more so by a commendable exhibition by the Berlin House of Literature 'Censorship in the GDR'. This has permitted a complete picture to be formed of the everyday practice of censorship in the GDR. It has shown, for example, that its conception and practical functioning were different from censorship in other totalitarian systems or, for example, in the period of historical Absolutism. 'Real socialism' aimed primarily not at direct bans, but rather at the utilisation, or at any rate incorporation of literature within the system of the political enlightenment and education of the people already outlined. Paradoxically, the SED leadership in fact managed to obtain the fundamental consent of most authors, even critical ones, to this system, even though they continued to petition for greater freedom as individuals. This compels us to speak of a partial cooperation (technically denoted by the unattractive loan word 'collaboration') between censors and authors which only a handful, such as Wolfgang Hilbig, refused outright to entertain. One result of all this was a distortion of texts – and some would argue their aesthetic improvement through various devices designed to camouflage or 'write between the lines'. Another was that it treated readers as 'under-age' in literary terms.

Self-censorship

Chief among these results, however, was the pre-emptive internalisation of censorship by authors – self-censorship – perhaps the most disastrous injury of all to the integrity of the creative artist and his or her work. GDR literature operated in a field divided between obedience to the system, incorporation in the system and flouting the system, although there were clearly links between these options.

Even before the recent political turning-point, the list of literary works that had fallen victim to censorship, either definitively or for some years, was known. It was headed by Hanns Eisler's *Johann Faustus* and Bertolt Brecht's *Der Verhör des Lukullus* (*The Interrogation of Lucullus*), followed by Stefan Heym's *5 Tage in Juni* (*Five Days in June*), poetry by Christa Reinig and Helga M. Novak, plays by Heiner Müller and Volker Braun, Fritz Rudolf Fries's novel *Der Weg nach Oobliadooh* (*The Road to Oobliadooh*) and Christa Wolf's *Nachdenken über Christa T.* (*Thoughts About Christa T.*) The publishing ban on Uwe Johnson's early novels (especially *Mutmassungen über Jakob – Speculation About Jacob*) and Wolfgang Biermann's audacious songs was particularly momentous. The latter's deprivation of citizenship in 1976 was followed by another wave of publishing bans, affecting authors such as Reiner Kunze, Stefan Heym, Thomas Brasch, Hans Joachim Schädlich, Jurek Becker, Ulrich Plenzdorf, Klaus Schlesinger and Erich Loest. Volker Braun (*Hinze-Kunze-Roman – Tom, Dick and Harry Novel*), Christa Wolf (the *Cassandra* lectures), and Günter de Bruyn (*Neue Herrlichkeit – New Splendour*) were likewise obliged to accept delays in publication, or modifications to their texts. The procedure for issuing publishing permits, as censorship was euphemistically known, was hardest on younger authors who had not yet established themselves. Some managed to publish here and there in a journal or anthology. Other, highly gifted authors were generally published only in the West, such as Monika Maron (*Flugasche – Flying Ash*), Wolfgang Hegewald or Katja Lange-Müller. All three eventually moved to the Federal Republic.

Authors against censorship

At the tenth Writers' Congress in 1987, something totally unprecedented occurred. Two authors of high standing, Günter de Bruyn and Christoph Hein, made an all-out attack on the whole procedure of issuing publishing permits, calling it by its proper name – censorship. This publicly put an end to the whole principle behind decades of tacit condonement of 'cooperation' between censors and writers. Hein's speech concluded with the words:

> Censorship is the enemy of the people. It is an infringement of the often-invoked and applauded wisdom of the people. The readers of our books are independent enough to be able to judge for themselves. The idea that a bureaucrat can decide what a reader can cope with and what is unsuitable for him betrays no more than the presumption and arrogance of the agencies themselves. Censorship is unlawful because it is unconstitutional. It is irreconcilable with the Constitution of the GDR and is tantamount to 'public degradation'. Authorisation procedures and censorship must disappear as soon as possible and not be replaced, so as to avoid further injury to our culture, and avoid damage to our dignity, our society and our state.

Although the GDR did abrogate the official publishing permission procedure shortly before the major political turning-point, as little remained to be salvaged of the GDR as a 'society of literature' as subsequent events left of 'real socialism' as a whole. Having from the very outset entered into an illicit liaison with the suppression of basic human and civil rights, the utopia of an ideal republic of literati, a pedagogical province, has proved unrealisable.

The 1950s: anti-fascist consensus and coming to terms with new production methods

The foundations of GDR literature, even before the existence of the state itself, was its anti-fascist consensus. This was fostered, authentically and legitimately at first, by authors of the first, older generation who had been in exile, such as Johannes R. Becher, Anna Seghers, Arnold Zweig or Bertolt Brecht. These were then augmented by a few opponents, such as the prose author Werner Krauss (*PLN. Passionen der halykonischen Seele – PLN: Passions of the Halcyon Soul*, 1946), later to become the leading novelist ofthe GDR. Anti-fascism, however, was no more than the covert world-view underpinning the literary work of the second, younger generation of authors. They themselves had lived through the war as part of the Nazi regime in the Hitler Youth and the Union of German Girls, or as SA personnel or soldiers – generally naive pro-Nazi enthusiasts or hangers-on. These authors, born mostly in the 1920s, now exchanged one all-embracing world-view creed for another – the new, potentially totalitarian view of Marxism. This brand of anti-fascism, born of a troubled conscience, became the ideological linchpin that bound such authors as Erwin Strittmatter, Franz Fühmann, Erich Loest, Hermann Kant, Christa Wolf, Heiner Müller, Erik Neutsch, and Dieter Noll together, not only among themselves, but also with their older, convinced anti-fascist colleagues. Only a very few authors, such as Peter Huchel or Günter Kunert, managed to avoid this quasi-informal loyalty to the SED state, which styled itself the 'victor of history', and magnanimously sought to encompass all people of good will and good faith within its victorious alliance.

The victors of history

This basic anti-fascist consensus in GDR literature, which initially seemed so appealing, was nonetheless a disaster from the very outset. It became the cloak under which the first signs of a genuinely new political start within the Soviet Occupied Zone – the establishment of elements of parliamentary and basic democracy – were soon set aside in favour of the implementation of an authoritarian, repressive system, 'socialism from above'.

Socialism from above

The latter's structural similarities with right-wing totalitarian systems were long underestimated, notably by the Western Left. This gave rise to the paradoxical situation in which a great many gifted young authors of good will gave their virtually unconditional support to 'real socialism', producing a literature to go with it, precisely because of their desire to rid themselves entirely of the trauma of the Nazi dictatorship, and make a break with its inhuman system. It was only later, sometimes too late, that authors realised that this alleged break from Nazism demanded elements of continuity with it – authoritarian social and political structures and the submissive mentality that went with them, surveillance and intimidation by the secret services, militarism, and high-handed decision-making in numerous spheres. Some authors refuse to accept this view even now. GDR literature, particularly that of the 1950s, needs to be understood in terms of this deeply-rooted tension between genuine, convinced and emphatic anti-fascism and what was to a greater or lesser extent collusion with the repressive system of 'real socialism'.

Economic constraints

It would be pertinent at this point to call to mind some of the economic and political factors that are equally essential to an understanding of the calculatedly political and largely instrumental role of early GDR literature. The phase known as the anti-fascist democratic New Order of 1945–9, in which genuine signs of a new political beginning were still to be found side by side with massive repression (such as Soviet penal camps, or the enforced unification of pro-labour parties), was characterised chiefly by an immense effort to revive the agricultural and industrial economies, both severely damaged by the war. On the land, this took the form of land reform in the guise of exclusive privatisation through the redistribution, i.e. confiscation, of major land holdings into the hands of *Neubauer* (new farmers). In the industrial sector, some 60 per cent of the means of production had been nationalised by 1950. Clearly a post-war economy with virtually nothing but shortages to administer had no option but to call on the population to forgo consumption and massively increase its work productivity. Some move to this end was made in 1947 when the slogan issued by the 2nd Party Congress of the Socialist Unity Party was 'produce more, distribute more fairly, live better!' An extensive activist and competitive movement was instigated in autumn 1948 by the coal-miner Adolf Hennecke when he exceeded the work norm for his shift by 387 per cent. Meanwhile the continuing nationalisation of factories and their concentration into large-scale enterprises cleared the way for centralised economic planning on the Soviet model. There was a two-year plan for 1949–50 and a five-year plan for 1951–5, giving comprehensive and strict guidelines for both agricultural and industrial production.

The 'building of socialism'

The proclamation of the GDR as a separate state on 7 October 1949 came in response to the founding of the Federal Republic of Germany a short while before. Within that portion of Germany left to the GDR, this made it all the more urgent to proceed apace with the political and economic course already set in motion in a manner that both ensured clear demarcation from the capitalist West, and imitated the people's democracies of the East. National political agitation and rhetoric were nonetheless unabated, and the verbal objective at least of a 'unified, peace-loving, democratic Germany' was likewise retained.

The second Party Congress in 1952 adopted a resolution aimed at the 'construction of socialism' as its 'fundamental task', although obviously the socialism being constructed was of a very distinct type. This 'construction' was in the hands of a single party, the SED, which had in the meantime been reorganised into a political cadre party of the Stalinist type.

Its original principle of leadership parity between the former communists and social democrats was abolished to make way for full implementation of a new organisational principle, known as 'democratic centralism'. The formation of factions was forbidden as the worst form of sacrilege. This principle of centralised planning and management also became, as with the Soviet model, increasingly more rigid in the sphere of production. The result was that the working-class rank-and-file were steadily deprived of their consulting role in major production questions, leaving them with no more than a say in immediate workplace problems in the narrow sense. Although, therefore, the working class was indeed the deciding factor in that period and in that particular policy, its role was purely as an element to be taken account of in economic planning for synchronising the *System-vergleich* (the process whereby socialist Germany was established side by side and in competition with capitalist Germany) – not as a self-determining subject in the historical process.

Brecht once defined socialism as 'large-scale production' (*die grosse Produktion*). This did not just mean that more and better would be produced under socialism than under capitalism. For Brecht it meant the appropriation by mankind not only of an alien natural world, but also the productive, self-determined appropriation of their own nature. Political, cultural and literary developments in GDR society from 1949 onwards need to be examined in terms of whether or not they manifest the qualitatively new human productivity meant by Brecht and others. Literature emerged as an important medium both for posing and resolving these questions.

Culture and literature as planning factors

Culture and literature were soon assigned major tasks within the socialist planning of society. As early as 1948 Alexander Abusch delivered a speech entitled *Der Schriftsteller und der Plan* (*The Writer and the Plan*). A year later, a resolution of the first Party Congress of the SED stated: 'Carrying out cultural work in service of the Two-Year Plan means first and foremost developing the enthusiasm for work among all sections of the population.' The tendency was unmistakable: literature and other cultural activities were not intended to foster human productivity in general or to raise consciousness, but very specifically to stimulate readiness for material work in order to help socialism to victory in the *Systemvergleich*.

The functionalisation of literature

Among writers it was now the Marxists who stood up for what they had always seen as the social function of literature, the direct or indirect 'operative' character of texts. On its own the functionalisation of literature set in motion in the GDR had a constricting, paralysing effect that was ultimately hostile to productivity. The same Becher who had sought to turn all writers into activists was concluding sarcastically only a little later: 'I am making attempts at agitation-rhymes – but a well-known composer of agitation rhymes has proved himself far superior to me in the genre.' Elsewhere he wrote: 'The poet is not a window-dresser. But the art business is flourishing.'

The narrow-mindedness of a 'socialist' functionalism set on a massive proliferation of productive force made itself most keenly felt where the concept was implemented directly in the production of art, as a facet of cultural policy. Writers were urged to seek out the 'basis of society' in a direct way, accumulate experience and convert this into literary form. This was initially an experiment well worth encouraging. The aim was to create 'the new man, the activist, the hero of socialist construction'. What emerged, however, from visits made by writers 'to industrial plants, major construction sites and the now collectivised farms was for the most part no more than slogan literature – tedious, wooden reportage, pamphlet lyric poetry and plays affirming the regime. In 1953 Brecht commented tersely on these events: 'Art is not capable of converting into works of art the notions of art that issue from offices. Only boots can be made to measure.'

The picture, therefore, is one of an oppressive parallel: the use of workers and art as productive forces for raising productivity. The workers of the GDR showed on 17 June 1953 what they thought of this functionalisation. Although there was some loosening of this restrictive (cultural) policy afterwards, the machinery of a centrally-planned, hierarchical, functionalist cultural practice was never entirely shut down in the GDR.

Socialist realism versus formalism

In March 1951 at its fifth Congress, the Central Committee of the Socialist Unity Party (SED) felt compelled to make the cultural development of the young GDR its main theme, issuing clear warnings and proscriptions. The Party now launched an explicit campaign against so-called 'formalism' in art and literature. Formalism was defined as the 'subversion and destruction of art itself. Formalists deny that the central meaning of a work lies in its content, in the idea or thought behind it. In their view the significance of a work of art lies not in its content, but in its form. Wherever the question of form takes on significance in its own right, art loses its humanist and democratic character.'

The underlying causes of these tendencies were rooted in that social form regarded as being opposed to the new socialist order: capitalism and imperialism. As pictured by Stephan Hermlin, 'Formalism is thus the pictorial, musical or literary expression of imperialist cannibalism, an aesthetic accompaniment to the American twilight of the gods.'

Against the 'modern'

Major authors of modern international literature (including Kafka, Joyce and Proust) were now attacked under the alternating labels of 'decadence', 'cosmopolitanism', 'naturalism', 'modernism', and the ever-recurring label of 'formalism'. Above all, however, these labels were used to attack GDR creative artists for whom aesthetic progress was still an important factor in addition to economic progress. The period from 1951 onwards saw a string of publication bans: books were pulped, plays taken off and murals painted over.

One of the more prominent victims of this campaign was Hanns Eisler's 1952 opera libretto *Johann Faustus*. Eisler had conceived the Faust character as a vacillating intellectual (not as one guided by indefatigable Faustian self-exertion), and German history as a succession of miscarried revolutions and defeats in the vein of the 'German calamity'. Since this approach was diametrically opposed to the triumphalist, optimistic notions of the Socialist Unity Party (SED), Eisler's work was banned.

Side by side with the agenda for socialist construction in economic and political life, and as a counter-measure to combat the perils of formalism, a concept known as 'socialist realism' was propounded as a binding strategy for the arts. This concept had first been elaborated in 1932 in the Soviet Union by Stalin and others as an authoritative artistic guideline, later to become a binding rule in 1934 in the formulation devised by Andrei Zhdanov. According to this doctrine it was the duty of the artist 'to know life and to portray it not in a scholastic, dead way as "objective reality", but as an objective reality in the context of its revolutionary development. The authentic and historically concrete artistic portrayal must be combined in this process with the task of ideologically reshaping and educating working people in the spirit of socialism.' Socialist production was a favoured theme. Literary work was to have at its heart a positive, model hero, who was offered to the reader as a potential object for identification.

SED strategy in the arts

The full impact of this agenda of socialist realism was not really felt until it was directly combined with the literary theory of Georg Lukács, who, as was later conceded by critics, enjoyed a 'monopoly position' (Abusch) in this sphere up to 1956. Already fully developed as early as the thirties, Lukács's concept of realism drew theoretically on Hegel, and aesthetically on classical norms and critical realism, which effectively raised the criteria of eighteenth- and nineteenth-century bourgeois artistic creation to the status of quasi-timeless validity. The work of art was to 'reflect in a correct and proportionate context all the essential objective factors that objectively determine the area of life being depicted', in such a way that it appears 'as a totality of life'. In the process of transforming phenomena into types, the 'general', or essence, and the 'legitimacy' of reality should be depicted in the form of 'particularity'. In formal aesthetic terms, the work of art, representing a 'totality of life', should be organic and complete in itself.

Deviation from these principles was seen by Lukács himself and others under the sway of his influence as tantamount to sacrilege – in other words as formalism. Deviation encompassed all aesthetic techniques that ran contrary to these postulates of totality, type, organic wholeness and completeness: forms such as montage, alienation, interrupted narrative, parabolic structure, etc.

To sum up, it may be stated that as a doctrine the GDR version of socialist realism was an odd mixture. In terms of ideological content it followed a schematised version of the materialistic conception of history, while aesthetically sanctioning the formal canon, a specific developmental phase in bourgeois art, as if it were somehow above history. Creative artists and theoreticians who rejected this specific combination found themselves on the defensive and constantly obliged to legitimate themselves (Brecht, Eisler, Dessau and later Heiner Müller, Günter Kunert and others).

Traditionalism

The GDR of the early and mid-1950s was thus dominated thematically by the literature of socialist construction, and aesthetically by a predilection for nineteenth-century tradition. However, by the fourth Writers' Congress in 1956 it was becoming clear that this administrative tutelage and doctrinaire approach to literature could no longer be sustained. Intellectuals such as Hans Mayer were not alone in censuring the 'pan-politicisation' and lack of 'opulence' of literature in their country. By now, even unequivocally socialist authors such as Seghers, Claudius, Heym, and indeed Bredel himself, were voicing severe criticism of the 'dreary, petty bourgeois level' (Claudius), and 'wooden primitiveness' (Heym) of contemporary literature. The twentieth Communist Party Congress in the Soviet Union, at which an attack was launched on the Stalinist personality cult, acted as a spur to such tendencies towards forthright criticism, even appearing to usher in a veritable 'thaw' in the political climate.

This phase from 1953 to 1956, however, usually designated the 'phase of liberalisation', was abruptly cut short. In the aftermath of uprisings in Hungary and Poland in October 1956, previous concessions to the need for intellectual autonomy were largely withdrawn. Even some of the central ideas propagated earlier by the SED were now branded as revisionist. This applied most especially to the by now obligatory criticism of Georg Lukács, now finally following his role as a minister in the 'government of the counter-revolution'.

The Bitterfeld Way

No isolation from everyday life

Initiatives and attempts to eradicate the historically entrenched separation of art from life, and to overcome the division between productive labour and culturally creative work, had already manifested themselves in the 1950s, but had remained sporadic and insubstantial. In 1955, for example, colliers at the Nachterstedt brown coal pits had been directed from above to send an open letter to the writers of their country. This was to go down in literary history as the *Nachterstedter Brief* (*The Nachterstedt Letter*), in which they demanded that art and literature show more solidarity with the people. On the one hand the letter constituted an almost outdated plea for a return to the so-called literature of socialist construction, by now on the wane, and on the other an urgent call to professional writers to abandon their widespread isolation from the everyday lives of production workers – in short, to bring art closer to life.

Later, in 1957, at a plenary session of the Central Committee, Walter Ulbricht called on creative artists to cease being 'infrequent day-trippers' to manufacturing workplaces in town and country, and instead 'to feel at home there, uniting their lives and interests with those of the people'. Finally in July 1958, at the fifth SED Party Congress, the agenda included the aim of 'overcoming the separation between art and life, the alienation between the creative artist and the people'. In Ulbricht's words, 'in state and economy, the working class of the GDR is already in command. It is time now for it to storm the heights of culture and take possession of them.'

Intellectual workers in the factories?

A decisive event for literature came in April 1959 with the Bitterfeld Conference, at which nearly 300 worker-writers and people's correspondents took part, in addition to some 150 professional writers. There was now to be a two-pronged approach to the socialist cultural revolution in the sphere of literature. First, writers, or intellectual workers, were to go into the workplace, work with the brigades and study working conditions on the spot. Second, the 'mates', or manual labourers, were to take up their pens, in the first instance to document the everyday struggles and progress being made in the sphere of production, and in the second instance to improve their own writing abilities and work themselves up to the 'heights of culture' through literary creation.

This agenda proved difficult to implement from the very outset, particularly with regard to the first prong of the approach: few professional writers were prepared to give up their 'head work' in exchange for manual labour for any length of time. Although there were a number of lightning visits by authors, and 'sponsorships' between writers and workplaces (the very term underlines the persistent hierarchical nature of the relationship), the outcome was a great deal of turning-up of noses by authors. There was certainly no question of anything resembling a general movement into the sphere of material production embracing all writers.

The successes of the 'Grab your pen, mate!' ('Greif zur Feder, Kumpel!') movement were quite impressive in the first months and years. Following in the footsteps of the worker-correspondent tradition begun in the Weimar Republic, and side by side with the 'people's correspondents' working for newspapers, of whom there were some 9,500 by 1959, hundreds of writers' circles sprang up at workplaces, and later at borough level. Although predominantly involving workers, there was increasing participation by salaried employees, teachers, and pupils, etc. They were able to transcend the passive, consumer approach to culture by writing texts themselves that arose out of their own interests, and which were intended to have an impact in their own interest, doing this, moreover, collectively rather than as writing individuals.

This was particularly the case with the new genre of the 'brigade diary'. Although kept to record everyday events in the production process, its themes often went far beyond this, dealing with interpersonal relationships or relations between one brigade and another, and making use of such diverse forms as the report, the note or memo, statement, commentary, satire, poetry, portrait, etc. Before long, however, the brigade diary found itself burdened with tasks that were clearly beyond its scope, being called on to contribute to 'personality development', to become a 'nucleus of national German literature', and to work ever more closely towards 'artistic mastery'. The latter requirement was now increasingly and with greater intensity directed at the literary creation of worker-writers' circles.

Art and life

The years between 1960 and 1963–4 witnessed what was initially a scarcely discernible process of revision in cultural policy that revoked the two central aims of the fifth Party Congress and the Bitterfeld movement – eradication of the separation between art and life, and the principle of rapprochement between manual and intellectual workers. The amateur creation of literature in workers' writing circles, of which there continued to be hundreds, now came to be viewed as a 'great school for the formation of artistic abilities and talents of workers, agricultural labourers and the intelligentsia'. Worker-writers were now seen as something of a recruitment pool for professional writers, whose ranks were renewed from it as the need arose, depending on the prevailing criteria of taste (pertaining to 'artistic competence', whatever that might be).

In this way, what had started out as an interesting initiative was soon bogged down. The now firmly entrenched key features of *realer Sozialismus* (socialism in practice), chief among which was the prime imperative of developing a productive labour force, and the orientation towards the bourgeois heritage, proved overwhelming.

Continued writing on Nazi and war themes

Witnesses to the past

The founding of the GDR, and the rapidly ensuing proclamation of a programme of socialist construction, by no means spelled the end of fascism as a theme. The past remained ever-present, and was far from either fully understood or overcome. A number of books by authors of the older and middle generations, e.g. Bodo Uhse, Ludwig Renn and Stephan Hermlin, dealt with the heroic anti-fascist Resistance movement. The question, however, was whether such books, written from the perspective of convinced anti-fascists and Resistance fighters, had the power to persuade the indifferent, the vacillating, the merely naive or the collaborators. Was there, in the virtually wholly positive heroes of such books, any potential for identification that was credible and realistic for the members of this important target group, who for twelve years had taken as reality the attractive outer packaging of an aestheticised politics, and then the apparently unmotivated horrors of the war?

One cannot help but be sceptical about the chances of achieving this desired educative effect. In 1957 the young Christa Wolf pointed out the disquieting reluctance of her older colleagues to make a central literary theme out of the 'deeper conflict of a young person bewitched by the fascist ideology'. An exception to this was Franz Fühmann's novella *Kamaraden* (*Friends*) (1955), which describes in a credible and psychologically tenable way the step-by-step process whereby a young soldier turns his back on fascist war.

A number of other authors, including some ex-Wehrmacht soldiers, wrote prose works about World War II in the second half of the 1950s. As in the case of World War I, the distance of a decade or so was evidently needed before the experiences of war could be made accessible in literary form. These works include Karl Mundstock's story *Bis zum letzten Mann* (*To the Last Man*) (1956) and Harry Thürk's novel *Die Stunde der toten Augen* (*The Hour of the Dead Eyes*) (1957). The dominant motif of their texts, as with Fühmann, is a change of front and a switch to the other side, this moment of decision being placed at the centre of most narratives.

This literature, however, found little favour with the literary critics of the Party apparatus, who deemed it crudely mimetic and objectivist and dismissed it as unable to go beyond the 'naturalist reproduction' of war.

In their view the 'tough writing style' of these authors lacked the required epic distance from this difficult theme. In other words, they were no more than 'critical realists' (i.e. not socialist realists) – or 'war naturalists' as they were known from now onwards.

In 1958, some thirteen years after the end of the war, Bruno Apitz's *Nackt unter Wölfen* (*Naked Among Wolves*) appeared, the most popular concentration-camp novel after Anna Seghers's *Das siebte Kreuz*. Like Ernst Wiechert, whose autobiographical account *Der Totenwald* (*Forest of the Dead*) had appeared in 1947, Bruno Apitz had had long years of experience in the Buchenwald concentration camp in Thuringia. *Naked Among Wolves*, based on a true story, relates in novella form the tale of a 13-year-old Jewish child who is smuggled into Buchenwald by a Pole in an old suitcase following the evacuation of the extermination camp at Auschwitz. The child is not betrayed, and survives. The uprising of the internees shortly before and during the liberation of the camp by the US army is a success. The symbolism of the title, as in Anna Seghers's *The Seventh Cross*, reveals a positive perspective: the human being proves to be stronger than the fascist wolf. The book was also a major success internationally. Even two decades ago it had sold some two million copies in twenty-eight countries, and had been translated into twenty-five languages.

From novel of socialist construction to *Ankunftsliteratur*

Reportage

Literary confrontation with the theme of 'new socialist production' made a slow start, and for some years the theme was hardly even broached by workers themselves. It was 1951–2 before reportage and stories from workplaces emerged to become a force in literary development. And yet these works did not come from construction sites or factories themselves, but were experienced and written from the viewpoint of writers and journalists – intellectuals, in other words – who had changed roles for a while, but for whom the 'proletarian perspective' was often no longer a self-evident one, even if they came from working-class families.

The first stimulus for a whole series of 'novels of socialist construction' between 1952 and 1956 came from Eduard Claudius's book *Menschen an unserer Seite* (*People on Our Side*) (1951), which is still worth reading today. This is the true story of Hans Garbe, a builder of kilns who has great difficulty asserting himself as an activist among his colleagues. The example of Garbe also inspired Brecht to write a play, *Büsching*, which remains a fragment, and later Heiner Müller to write the play *Der Lohndrücker* (*Cheap Labour*).

The novel of socialist construction

Many authors turned their attention to changed conditions on the land, although so-called 'works' and 'production' novels attracted more attention. It is no easy matter to establish the literary merit of these novels. They were burdened with what Claudius once called the tiresome 'application of a sense of obligation to literature'. Again and again one finds in them the beginnings of a working-class perspective and of criticism 'from below', but ultimately they are saturated with a socially integrative tendency to skate over conflicts and appeal for confidence in Party and state.

The 'Bitterfeld Way'

The Bitterfeld Way, proclaimed in 1959 and aimed at effecting a fusion of what had so far been separate – art and life, intellectual and manual labour, material needs and moral maxims – gave a new spurt of life to this 'production literature'. This impetus nevertheless began to flag before it had attained a mass character. At all events the Party wanted to avoid a 'levelling of professional and amateur art'. Progress from the other angle towards eradicating the separation between art and life and the movement of the poet/writer into the production sphere, was likewise hesitant. Although some middle-aged and young authors, such as Regina Hastedt, Franz Fühmann, Christa Wolf, Herbert Nachbar, or Brigitte Reimann, trod this path, the majority of writers did not.

Ankunftsliteratur

The dominant genre of those years was so-called *Ankunftsliteratur*, which was enjoying a revival in the train of the bourgeois novel of education and development. It was concerned with young people who found themselves in a (limited) degree of conflict among themselves and with the requirements of socialism in practice, but who were ultimately allowed to walk into the sunset and arrive at a 'happy end' at the conclusion of a stereotyped socialist learning process. In short, the heroes of *Ankunftsliteratur* arrive at socialism in predictable fashion, to turn their eyes to a better future. Examples of the genre, apart from *Ankunft im Alltag* (*Arrival in the Everyday*) by Brigitte Reimann, after which it takes its name, are novels by Joachim Wohlgemuth, Herbert Nachbar, Werner Bräunig, Joachim Knappe, and Karl-Heinz Jakobs. Related to the prose of the *Ankunftsliteratur* type, but further removed from 'production literature' in the narrow sense of the term, is a group of usually lengthy works latterly known in the GDR as *Entwicklungsromane* (novels of development). It did not seem to strike literary scholars in the GDR at the time as problematic that this genre was a genuinely bourgeois art form in which the essential interest focused on the 'central individual' (*Mittelpunktsin-dividuum* – Brecht). Clearly all the authors involved (the later Anna Segh-ers in her multi-stranded historical and contemporary novel *Die Ent-scheidung* – *The Decision*), 1959; Wolfgang Joho, Erwin Strittmatter with his trilogy *Der Wundertäter* (*The Miracle Worker*), published in 1957, 1973 and 1980, Herbert Jobst, Jurij Brêzan and the earlier Max Walter Schulz, Günter de Bruyn, Dieter Noll, and exponents of *Ankunftsliteratur*) viewed the process of individualisation as entirely shaped by both old and new social conditions, rather than as the organic unfolding of an existing entel-echy. Their unanimous aim was to secure a standpoint that would be of use to a socialist society in the making. The subject-hero of these novels is given more room to develop in his search than was usually the case with the *Betriebsroman*, the 'novel of the workplace'. Yet his attempts to attain maturity are circumscribed by relatively narrow boundaries defining an internalised version of normative, stereotyped perception and thinking that exclude certain aspects of reality.

Stalinism

The central theme of the 1950s in the GDR, the Stalinist, authoritarian shaping of socialism that was only half-heartedly criticised after 1956 and never seriously revised, governed not only the content of prose literature, but also its form. Well into the 1960s, narrative fiction in the GDR was characterised by a crass schematism in storyline, the choice of heroes and of characterisation. The rigid conventionality of this schematism corres-ponded to the parochial, naive world-view of the authors who used it – an object lesson in outwardly-oriented aesthetics.

In a literary landscape governed by the 'famous, notorious theory (and practice) of absence of conflict' and in which the 'great heroic illusion' of a 'socialist nationalist literature' had taken root, the truly significant early narrative work of Uwe Johnson must have arrived on to the scene as if from another planet. Although it could not be discerned as such by his reading compatriots at the time, Johnson's work alone indisputably marks the beginning of the modern age in the narrative prose of the GDR. Johnson's right of the firstborn must be emphatically conceded here, with-out in any way wishing to denigrate the merits of Christa Wolf, Fritz Rudolf Fries or Ulrich Plenzdorf. Conversely, from a Western perspective, today's distance of three decades has also highlighted the surprisingly close links between Johnson's first published novel *Mutmassungen über Jakob* (*Speculations about Jacob*) of 1959 and *Ankunftsliteratur* and the literature of socialist construction. Johnson's novel is in fact a confrontation with the theme of 'new production' in the Marxist sense (including the pro-duction of the 'new man'), as well as representing a contribution to the problem of 'arrival in socialism'. The difference is that Johnson's contribution represents, before the real birth of the affirmative genre, not a confirmation of that arrival, but a questioning of it.

Johnson's first novel, *Ingrid Babendererde. Reifeprüfung 1953* (*Ingrid Babendererde: a Test of Maturity 1953*), written during his student years in Rostock from 1953–6, needs even more to be seen in the context of GDR literature. Johnson offered it in vain to a number of GDR publishing houses, but it was not published at all until after his death, and even then not in the GDR. The novel is about the (historical) conflict between the Christian 'Young Parish' on the one hand and the Party and the Free German Youth organisation on the other in the events leading up to 17 June 1953. The apparently wholesome world of school and first love breaks down, and the two main characters decide to flee to the West. Johnson's first novel is narrated using a highly complex procedure of refraction and multiple layering. At that time, only a few years after the formalism campaign, this met with blank incomprehension in the GDR at the publishing-house reader stage. GDR prose literature in the fifties was compelled to remain a world of clichés, illusory solutions and dreary traditionalism.

'New production' in theatre

In the period from 1949 to 1961 literature for the theatre is virtually all permeated by two characteristics. As far as dramaturgy and writing style is concerned it either followed Brecht, or was at the very least inspired by him, aside from plays in the 'affirmative *Gebrauchstheater*' genre. Plots were mostly drawn directly from new production conditions in the town and country, with a marked preference for the theme of 'socialist life on the land'. Almost every dramatist author wrote an 'Agrodrama' at that time.

By now definitely settled in East Berlin, Brecht worked with theatre in three main directions. He staged various of his older plays with the Berliner Ensemble, adapted texts by other authors, particularly classical, likewise staging them with the Ensemble, and, finally, also produced a few plays by contemporary authors. He completed only one new play, the comedy *Turandot oder Der Kongress der Weisswäscher* (*Turandot, or the Congress of Whitewashers*), written in the summer of 1953, which is a satirical treatment of his intellectual 'colleagues' and the way they accommodated themselves to prevailing conditions. It is striking that Brecht, who hardly ever wrote contemporary plays in the narrow sense of the term, preferring to have his aesthetic domain in history and the realms of parable, became more at home in the contemporary sphere between 1945 and 1956. After settling in the GDR, Brecht worked on only three texts, although these were either not intended as fully-fledged theatre plays (*Herrnburger Bericht* – *The Herrnburg Report*; *Katzengraben* – *Cat-grave* notes), or remained in fragment form, not without reason, as in the case of the *Büsching* draft.

596

A recourse to history

The major emphasis of Brecht's productive work in this period lay in his adaptation of older texts including Shakespeare's *Coriolanus* (1951), Goethe's *Urfaust* (1952), and Molière's *Don Juan* (1954). Läuffer is one in a long list of Brechtian heroes who learn nothing, but who allow the spectator to learn something from them (Mother Courage, Don Juan, Lucullus, Coriolanus, etc.). Characteristically, Brecht draws his model for a didactic play on German history not from the officially-approved cultural heritage of German classicism, but from the marginal *Sturm und Drang* period. Given his pointed interpretation of history, therefore, Brecht's adaptation of *Hofmeister* (*The Tutor*) is anything but remote from the present, as it might at first glance seem. The same holds good for his other adaptations. In the latter, the author gives voice to his scepticism about the semi-official interpretation of history, which sought to smooth over conflicts. Brecht was also indirectly urging a rediscovery and re-adoption of the unclassical, unbourgeois, plebeian elements of German history. His recourse to history is thus a retreat before the ideological climate of *realer Sozialismus*, but also an attempt to justify his own controversial position by the use of historical arguments.

Peter Hacks, who moved from Munich to the GDR in 1955, at first wrote dramas in the Brechtian style. His early plays were all devoted to historical themes (including *Die Schlacht bei Lobositz* – *The Battle of Lobositz*, 1956, which deals with an episode from the Ulrich Bräker story, and the anti-Fredericus-Rex comedy *Der Müller von Sans-souci* – *The Miller of Sans-souci*, 1957), and were entirely in keeping with the tendency manifest in Brecht's adaptations, i.e. reinterpreting history written 'from above' in an ideologically critical way. Towards the end of the 1950s, however, Hacks began to turn to more contemporary subject-matter, including the theme of land reform in his comedy *Moritz Tassow* (1961).

Heiner Müller

Heiner Müller had even more right than either Hacks or Helmut Baierl to claim Brecht as his mentor. Major success eluded Müller, who refused to smooth over conflicts falsely in any shape or form. His first 'production' play, *Der Lohndrücker* (*Cheap Labour*) (1956) was based on an authentic historical event of 1948–9 that had already been adapted and brought to life in literary form by Eduard Claudius and Brecht (the *Büsching* draft). In this play, Müller inquires into the human repercussions of the norms enshrined in the new system ('norms' in both the literal and transferred sense), discovering a discrepancy between individual needs and social exigencies. It is the best and most realistic play about the early years of socialist construction. It asserts unwaveringly the reality that in the given historical conditions the path to socialism was a pre-eminently arduous, painful process hardly likely to bring happiness to individuals, and to which people could initially bring nothing beyond their labour – in other words, that which was most external and abstract to them. Along with Hegel and Marx, Müller located the driving force behind history in negation.

Up until 1961 few other plays from the period can be said to have made their mark on history, or at least literary history. Peter Hacks's audacious 'production play' *Die Sorgen und die Macht* (*The Cares and the Power*), of which the third version was finally performed in 1962, caused quite a stir at the time, but in the main mediocrity reigned. A much-performed witty comedy by Heinar Kipphardt (resident in the GDR until 1959, then in the Federal Republic), captured the essence of the situation in its title: *Shakespeare dringend gesucht* (*Shakespeare Urgently Sought*) (1952–3). It would seem that in Heiner Müller alone the theatre of the GDR found a successor to Brecht, from whom Müller was able to learn without merely copying.

Lyric poetry in the 1950s

Lyric poetry from 1949 to 1961 did not form a homogeneous whole. It would be wrong to speak of 'production lyricism' as a dominant feature of lyric poetry-writing comparable to the 'production' focus manifest in prose and theatre of the same period. One reason for this complex diversity in poetry is that throughout the 1950s some two to three generations of lyric poets were writing and publishing simultaneously, but with very different experiences of life. There were those born before or around the turn of the century (Becher, Brecht, Fürnberg, Arendt, Huchel, Maurer, etc.), those of an in-between generation (KuBa, Hermlin, Bobrowski, etc.), and those who had been born in the 1920s (Cibulka, Fühmann, Wiens, Deicke and Kunert) – a truly motley group. The generation argument does not carry sufficient weight in itself, however, since the same circumstances applied to other literary genres.

The deciding factor was probably that lyric poetry, hitherto a classic vehicle of bourgeois individualist self-expression, even now made no strict break with this tradition, continuing instead to be the preferred literary form for a subjectively-oriented process of coming to terms with reality. For this very reason, however, the politico-ideological anachronisms of authors found their way into lyric poetry in a more direct way than, say, into prose. The idea that belonging to a society is always experienced and expressed on an individual level in literature became firmly entrenched at a much earlier stage in lyric poetry than in prose.

The cult anthem (Hymnik)

This does not mean, of course, that GDR lyric poetry manifested a full-scale, fruitful representation of the new relationship between the individual and society in a way that was authentic and true-to-life, i.e. critical above all. It needs to be borne in mind that the first half of the 1950s was the time of cult anthems to Stalin and Ulbricht, to which even Becher, Brecht and Hermlin made their contributions. As Günther Deicke recently pointed out with trenchant self-criticism, there was an attempt at that time to replace 'the note of the pan-German folk song' of Nazi leaders of the preceding era with 'socialist songs in the folk-song vein' – an attempt that for the most part went awry. The outcome was a marked penchant for the idyllic and the conflict-free, combined with aesthetic dilettantism and adoption of the 'new vernacular' – or 'cadre Latin' (*Kaderwelsch*), as Brecht venomously labelled it.

Brecht's late lyric poetry

Brecht's late lyric poetry differed substantially from that of his exile and immediate post-war periods, almost all of which had been written with the intention of being politically useful, and had, perhaps justifiably, rigidified into an ascetic and scrupulous holding-back from the entire realm of human and natural reality. By contrast, the poetry of Brecht's latter years saw a waning of the usefulness motive, combined with a waxing of the category of beauty, a sphere that had 'embarrassed' the poet in 1938. He ceased to write warning poetry about Germany, the 'pale mother' (1933), propagating instead that 'good Germany' which he saw unfolding in the GDR, despite all his reservations. Whereas the cycle *Neue Kinderlieder* (*New Children's Songs*) (1950) is a transitional work in this sense, his *Buckower Elegien* (*Buckow Elegies*), poems dating from the summer of 1953, after the events of 17 June, exemplify his new writing style. They are neither pure nature poems about the Brandenburg countryside, as the place of their origin might suggest, nor are they elegies in the traditional sense of laments. They are more Brecht's reflections, from the standpoint of his own subjectivity and needs, on what has been achieved and what still remains to be achieved – the changes still to be wrought in his country, a particularly topical theme after 17 June 1953 (this collection includes his famous poem *Die Lösung – The Solution*).

Besides Becher, Brecht, and Weinert, who died in 1953, Louis Fürnberg, and the above-mentioned poets Huchel, Hermlin and KuBa, two other older lyric poets came to the fore during the 1950s. Both came into their own very late, each for quite different reasons: the Romanian-German Georg Maurer, who was at first strongly influenced by Rilke, and Erich Arendt. Arendt was first published in Herwald Walden's journal *Der Sturm*

(*The Storm*), then left Germany in 1933, taking part in the Spanish Civil War from 1936–9 and subsequently emigrating to Columbia. It was 1950 before he returned to the GDR.

Arendt's pre-1933 poetry is strongly reminiscent of that by the Expressionist poet August Stramm – stripped down to bare essentials, gesticulatory, in short lines. Arendt's volumes of poetry from the 1951–6 period neither contain poetry written in exile, nor do they even remotely reflect either his experiences in Columbia, or the realities of the GDR. They are a fusion of traditional lines deriving from Klopstock, Hölderlin, and Expressionism, as well as strands from French (Rimbaud), Spanish (Aleixandre) and South American (Neruda) poetry. Most readily comparable with Paul Celan, Arendt clearly agonises with increasing bitterness and grief at the destructive and self-destructive forces at work in human history, expressing this experience in an extremely terse style, often reduced to single words or isolated metaphors that may strike the less experienced reader as hermetic. Arendt's most important volume of poetry, *Ägäis* (*The Aegean*) (1967) was written during a stay in Greece.

Bobrowski's theme

The lyric poetry of Johann Bobrowski likewise belongs to the 1950s, although it was not available to the public in book form until 1960 onwards. Like Arendt's poetry, it might at first glance seem to be something of a foreign body within East German literary development. Bobrowski came from Tilsit (now Sovetsk) in former East Prussia, and had grown up in Königsberg (Kaliningrad), the home town of Immanuel Kant. After studying art history for a few semesters, he was a soldier for many years. In 1945 he became a Soviet prisoner of war and worked as a miner in the Donets basin before returning to Berlin in 1949. In 1952 Bobrowski wrote his *Pruzzische Elegy* (*Prussian Elegy*) (published in 1955), in 1960 his poetry volume *Sarmatische Zeit* (*Sarmatian Time*) (first published in the Federal Republic, later in the GDR), and in 1962 his *Schattenland Ströme* (*Rivers of the Shadow Country*). In 1966 his posthumous volume *Wetterzeichen* (*Signs of the Approaching Storm*) was published. Bobrowski's theme, in both lyric poetry and prose, was firmly fixed from the outset: the German and European East. Having first-hand experience of fascism and the persecution of Jews and other minorities, the main thrust behind his poetic style was to combat forgetfulness and silence.

Bobrowski's poetic language is unmistakable. His style makes use of intricate imagery and complex inversions of words and phrases, sometimes involving associations that are difficult to follow, interweaving various levels of time, meaning and motive. His procedure reflects the depraved sediment of history in the German memory that needs to be arduously and inquiringly cleared away before it can be dealt with beyond the realm of familiar routine. Bobrowski had learned from Klopstock and Hölderlin to an even greater extent than Arendt or Maurer, and yet he had also left normative ancient verse measures and strophic forms behind, writing almost exclusively in free rhythms, mostly devoid of prescribed strophic forms.

Günter Kunert

Lyric poets born after 1925 or so had enormous difficulty overcoming the limitations of eclecticism and bland enthusiastic affirmation, as can be seen from the innumerable festive and celebratory poems published day after day in GDR newspapers. By contrast, only one author convincingly achieved the required degree of distance and matter-of-factness: Günter Kunert. Although Kunert was obviously indebted to Brecht, Heine, Tucholsky and Ringelnatz, as well as to contemporary American lyric poetry (Edgar Lee Masters, Carl Sandburg), no school ever formed around his own work in the way it did around Bobrowski or Maurer. From his very first small volume in 1950 (*Wegschilder und Mauerinschriften – Signposts and Wall Inscriptions*, 1950), Kunert showed himself to be utterly unpontifical and worldly, and yet not in the prescribed manner. His treatment of his subject-matter was ironic, satirical and aggressive, with an uncompromising refusal to skate over inconsistencies, which if anything he accentuated. He thus evinced a marked and early tendency towards the 'black didactic poem' (called for by Kunert in 1965), bringing him into conflict with the 'blue-eyed' didactic poetry that was current at that time. As the decade proceeded his verse grew ever blacker.

Between affirmation and utopia: the upheaval of the 1960s

The building of the Berlin Wall

On 13 August 1961 the government of the GDR had a fortified wall built between East and West Berlin, thereby abolishing at a stroke the hitherto half-open frontier that had been in operation between the two halves of the city. Over the years, this wall was to acquire the dubious accolade of being one of the most secure frontiers in the world.

The cultural and literary life of the 1960s is more closely related to the closing of the frontier than might at first glance be apparent. This effective 'immurement' of GDR citizens forced them, including intellectuals and writers, to focus much more narrowly on their own local, specific living conditions and circumstances. An outward-directed deflection of thought and imagination was pointless, so that everyone was now compelled to confront everyday problems and inconsistencies on the spot. In literature in particular, this could hardly have led to a less critical relationship between the GDR inhabitant and his country; on the contrary. Semi-official policy proclaimed that there were discrepancies merely 'between the good and the better'. Sensitive authors, however, were becoming aware of epochal incongruities of a 'more persistent and powerful pace' than could be caught up with 'in a single step' (Volker Braun).

GDR literature of the 1960s is thus marked by an increase in critical tendencies, or more precisely the body of texts written at that time is marked by them. Further, the more GDR literature saw the GDR as a country in its own right, and a location of literature, and the Federal Republic as an occasional showcase for literary events, the more frequently GDR texts were published only in the Federal Republic, and not at all in the GDR itself (e.g. Bieler, Biermann, Kunze, Heym, Müller). This split literary existence, that was to persist until the reunification of Germany, began to manifest itself in the phenomenon of an author writing about one Germany, but being published, and hence read (almost) exclusively in the other.

The events of 13 August 1961 similarly sounded the death knell for aspirations towards a homogeneous German culture. Alexander Busch, for three years Minister of Culture, stated flatly in December 1961: 'Assuming that our state of industrial and agricultural workers is the sole legitimate and Humanist German state – the German republic of peace and socialism – we can no longer speak vaguely and stiltedly of German culture in general. No such unified German culture can exist at present in two German states with such mutually exclusive courses of development.' This was the first documented instance of the GDR usurping exclusive rights to the term 'nation', and repudiating all cultural events that took place in the Federal Republic.

The official campaign waged against literary and intellectual tendencies seeking seriously to question *realer Sozialismus* culminated in 1965. The eleventh plenary assembly of the Socialist Unity Party Central Committee in December 1965 ostracised all 'modernist', 'scepticist', 'anarchist', 'nihil-ist', 'liberalist' and 'pornographic' trends in contemporary GDR literature, as well, incidentally, as in film. This was most particularly directed at Wolf Biermann, Manfred Bieler, Werner Bräunig, Peter Hacks, Günter Kunert, Heiner Müller and Stefan Heym, as well as the scientist and philosopher Robert Havemann.

The 1965–71 period as a whole was marked by a further entrenchment of this policy. Since 1962, *Sinn und Form* (*Meaning and Form*) had no longer published Western authors. *Neue Deutsche Literatur* (*New German Literature*), which had hitherto offered works by Walser, Weiss and Böll among others, followed suit from 1966 and ceased to publish Western texts. These were indications of an increased demarcation and self-isolation on the part of a GDR culture purporting to be self-sufficient. After an exciting debate about the meaning and function of lyric poetry 'in this better land' (this being the title of a controversial anthology of lyric poetry edited by A. Endler and K. Mickel), conducted in the summer of 1966 in *Forum*, journal of the Free German Youth organisation, it was chiefly the events of August 1968 in Czechoslovakia that provided new fuel. The ninth plenary session of the Socialist Unity Party Central Committee warned emphatically of the dangers in that country of artistic tendencies towards 'modernism', branded as pointers towards 'counter-revolutionary development'. Wariness of contacts with the New Left in Western countries, particularly the Federal Republic, should also be seen in this context.

The New Economic System of 1963 and literature

Rationalisation and increased efficiency

The sixth Socialist Unity Party Congress of 1963 adopted a far-reaching change of course in economic policy under the heading of the New Economic System (of Planning and Management): *Neues Ökonomisches System (der Planung und Leitung)*, usually abbreviated to *NÖS* or *NÖSPL*. The main aim of the NÖS was to modernise and rationalise the economic system in order to make the economy more effective. The idea was to achieve a qualitatively new level of technological and economic efficiency and an increase in productivity on the basis of a scientific system of control and management (including time and motion studies, and network planning). Those involved in management of the economic process (technicians, scientists, economists) were required to undergo a process of constant requalification, on the assumption that the contribution of planners and managers was absolutely crucial for achieving advances in work productivity.

The 'socialist human community'

After 1967 the Party ceased to refer to the NÖS, the new watchword now being the Economic System of Socialism (*ÖSS*), or more generally the Developed Social System of Socialism (*Entwickeltes gesellschaftliches System des Sozialismus – ESS*). This was intended to indicate that GDR society was no longer trying to construct socialism – because it had already achieved it. Walter Ulbricht coined the euphemism the 'socialist human community' (*sozialistische Menschengemeinschaft*), which was enshrined in the Constitution in 1968. Erich Honecker later spoke more matter-of-factly of 'socialism as it exists in practice' (*real existierender Sozialismus*). This was now no longer presented as a phase in the unfolding of human history to be quickly passed through, but as a 'relatively autonomous socio-economic formation in the historical epoch of transition from capitalism to communism on a world scale'.

Steps taken as part of the New Economic System by leading groups within the state, economy and scholarly circles after 1963 demonstrate their strong fascination for the new potential being opened up by the economic and technological revolution (*wissenschaftlich-technische Revolution*, abbreviated to *WTR*) – first implemented in Western capitalist countries. From this fascination derived their increasing efforts on both the scientific and technological fronts to transform *real existierender Sozialismus* in a systematic way. They saw no danger in what was soon perceived by the Western Left as the possibility of a 'dialectic of enlightenment' (*Dialektik der Aufklärung*) – the capsizing of humane rationality into an absolutism of ratio that reduced human beings to their value as a resource. In the GDR, time (as an economic function of efficiency), performance, planning and management became the fetish-like guiding principles of a calculating socialism that bolstered and raised to a new status the previously upheld prime aim of developing the productive labour force. The historical irony of these efforts is that despite the New Economic System and the technological revolution the GDR never managed to modernise its economy and society effectively. Instead, it produced a poor copy of western modernity that was to entail major damage, both to human beings and to the environment.

Compared with previous years, the cultural sphere especially found itself being transformed into a means to an end that did not stop short of dovetailing it directly into the economy. The objective behind this trend was the 'economic' work of art, i.e. a work with a consciousness-raising tendency, in line with the literary devices employed. The writer was not merely to portray 'socialist personalities' in the context of the 'socialist human community', but, himself a function of economic leverage theory, to be first and foremost a planner and manager promoting the general increase of productivity, in model fashion. In his writing he was to make use of scientifically established 'prognostic' methods, or to put it another way, to forgo all poetry that insisted on the privilege of 'unreasoned dreaming' (Hermlin).

Few writers were quick to discern the potentially dangerous quasi-worship of rationalism and technology inherent in the New Economic System. In 1966, for example, Günter Kunert was still largely on his own in warning of the 'de-emotionalisation' (*Versachlichung*) of human beings taking place under socialism, also pointing out the dangers of a forced credulity in science and technology: 'At the beginning of the technological age we find Auschwitz and Hiroshima, which I mention in the same breath here purely in reference to the socially organised use of technology. It is my belief that only immense naivety is capable of equating technology with social and humanitarian progress.' Some years later this scepticism was reflected in a whole range of literary works, as is vouched for chiefly by Christa Wolf's novel *Nachdenken über Christa T.* (*Reflections about Christa T.*) and Kunert's volumes of poetry.

A self-assured stock-taking of the GDR and the reinstatement of the self in prose

In the prose of the 1960s, too, themes from the past – Germany under fascism – continued to play a major part, up to and including three authors of the young generation, born in 1937 (Jurek Becker, Klaus Schlesinger and Helga Schütz). A wide range of short stories (Franz Fühmann, *Das Judenauto – The Jewish Car*, 1962; Anna Seghers, *Die Kraft der Schwachen – The Strength of the Weak*, 1965; Fred Wander, *Der siebente Brunnen – The Seventh Fountain*, 1971) and novels (by Noll, Bobrowski, Becker, and again Fühmann, *König Ödipus – King Oedipus*, 1966) may be cited in this context. Lively discussion was sparked off by publication of the two-volume novel (originally planned as a trilogy) *Die Abenteuer des Werner Holt* (*The Adventures of Werner Holt*) (1960–3) by Dieter Noll. This work is an attempt to find new, anti-fascist, socially relevant contents for an old vessel: the autobiographically-oriented bourgeois novel of development. The author has his hero live through all the horrors of war and the fascist terror as an eyewitness, to return home at the end of the war sensing a lack of direction. From then on, as befits this form of the novel, his life becomes a search for meaning and self-realisation. Despite this, however, Noll remains bogged down in literary convention, drawing on crass, naturalistic devices.

The most important prose in the 1960s dealing with themes from the past comes from Johannes Bobrowski, whose prose works, like his lyric poetry, stubbornly revolved around his sole theme of 'the Germans and the European East'. At first sight, Bobrowski's prose may seem old-fashioned, cumbersome and naive, but this is deceptive. Bobrowski succeeded in finding such a brilliant writing style, with the power to arouse feelings of grief, pleasure and recognition at the same time, that despite these limitations of theme his works are anything but provincial. This may be judged from his volumes of short stories *Boehlendorff und Mäusefest* (1965) and *Der Mahner* (*The Admonisher*) (published posthumously in 1967), as well as the novels *en miniature*, *Levins Mühle* (*Levin's Mill*) and *Lithauische Claviere* (*Lithuanian Pianos*) (published posthumously in 1966).

Bobrowski's most famous prose work is the novel *Levins Mühle. 34 Sätze über meinen Grossvater* (*Levin's Mill: 34 Sentences about my Grandfather*). As in his other prose works, the *sujet* at first seems antiquated, geographically confined and far from 'earth-shattering'. The novel is set in a village on the Vistula in Western Prussia in the early 1870s. Concerned with a legal case, it is a crime story, and hence in a time-honoured literary tradition (reminiscent of Kleist's *Kohlhaas* and *Der zerbrochene Krug* – *The Shattered Jug*), A. Zweig's *Grischa* novel, or Peter Weiss's *Die Ermittlung* – *The Investigation*).

In Bobrowski's story, the author's German grandfather, a mill-owner, destroys the means of subsistence of a poor Jewish immigrant through criminal machinations. Although the 'little people' are able to bring the truth to light, justice is not done to the Jew, and the culprit remains unrepentant. Bobrowski's major skill lies in his ability to reveal large-scale inadequacies of social structure – a society of masters and servants – through the depiction of everyday, small-scale relationships in miniature. His aim, however, is less to apportion blame than to 'speak clearly', and more 'peacefully' ('lieber schon friedlich'). He accomplishes this not in a few pithy central statements, but in an abundance of hesitant, thoughtful, inquiring subordinate clauses. The narrator involves himself in the story at every turn, interrupting it and conversing with both the reader and his characters, thereby brilliantly overcoming the obstacles to relating his controversial, and thoroughly political theme fairly and justly, and yet without succumbing to the fiction of pretending to be non-partisan.

Jurek Becker, twenty years Bobrowski's junior, was the first to write a prose work on the theme of the past with comparable penetration and artistic brilliance: *Jakob der Lügner* (*Jacob the Liar*) (1968), which is about the fascist terror itself. Becker had grown up in the ghetto, and spent part of his childhood in the Ravensbrück and Sachsenhausen concentration camps. *Jakob der Lügner*, his first novel, thus draws heavily on personal experience. The main character is Jakob Heym, a Jewish ice-cream and potato pancake-maker who tells lies out of human feeling. In the ghetto, now occupied by German fascists, Jakob spreads a report that the Red Army is advancing and will soon liberate the city. He finds himself compelled to fabricate more and more positive news items, quoting as his source a radio that does not actually exist. Jakob thus inspires courage, the will to live and hope, yet ultimately without being able to deliver the goods. The end of the road is the journey to the death camps, which is related by the surviving narrator cheerfully, ironically, wittily, from a distance and suppressing pathos, with psychological precision, and devoid of false heroism.

Literatur des Anwesendseins (*literature of the 'here-and-now'*)

Nevertheless, themes from the past were no longer the hallmark of 1960s prose. 'GDR literature' was now literally just that. Earlier phases of *Abschiedsliteratur* (farewell literature) followed shortly afterwards by *Ankunftsliteratur* (literature of arrival) were now giving way to a *Literatur des Anwesendseins* – a literature of the here-and-now that dealt with authors' experiences of their immediate GDR surroundings.

Far from impoverishing GDR literature, this new phase, particularly towards the end of the 1960s, witnessed a huge diversification of both subject-matter and writing styles. This went hand in hand with the real earnestness and resolve with which a significant number of authors now set about confronting the inconsistencies manifesting themselves in their country.

This tackling of contemporary issues in turn led to an increasing tendency to break out of the idealistic agenda previously set by *Ankunftsliteratur*: the notion of the eternally successful 'arrival' in *realer Sozialismus*. A growing number of heroes now failed to 'arrive'. Alternatively, there was an entirely different interpretation of what 'arrival' actually meant, including the notion of arriving at oneself – self-realisation by an individual over and above his or her integration into society.

The obverse of this literature, in which individual needs were becoming more and more important, was a scarcely-veiled rejection of the Bitterfeld Way of 1959. This earlier call for an eradication of the separation between intellectual and manual work was now, if anything, perceived as an embarrassment. All that remained of this earlier objective was a vague aspiration towards 'ensuring access for writers to the life of the workers'.

Discontinuation of the 'literature of production'

More generally, prose authors of the 1960s were faced with the problem of neither being able nor wanting to continue in the 1950s' vein of 'production literature'. First, the world of production had changed a great deal by this time. Second, directives from above had also changed, and third, this earlier literature offered little that was worth imitating. It gave a contrived, stylised, superficial impression, the predictable positive decision in favour of socialism often striking the reader as forced or just plain boring.

A considerable number of books still dealt with 'socialist' work as their central theme (for example novels by older authors such as Seghers and Selbmann, or younger ones such as Joachim Knappe, Martin Viertel, or Herbert Otto). Nevertheless, penalisation and banning ensued if an author, such as Werner Bräunig, published a prose work that went beyond the usual optimistic clichés and stylised heroes, portraying the harsh realities of working and everyday life that continued to exist, even under socialism. An example of this would be his novel fragment *Rummelplatz* (*Fairground*), published in the *Neue Deutsche Literatur* (*New German Literature*) in 1965. This is set in the uranium-mining region of the western Erzgebirge, the 'Wild West' of the former GDR. The cultural political climate of the 1960s was conducive neither to encouraging authors with mediocre talent and limited powers of self-assertion, nor to the portrayal of literary characters who were not the sought-after 'generation-less, standardised human beings' (Christa Wolf).

Inconsistencies and conflicts

Given this climate, 1960s prose was largely shaped by authors who, either because of their talent, their powers of self-assertion, or their skilful choice of subject-matter, were able to restore its contour, shape, and above all its relevance and realism, even when dealing with contemporary themes. These included Hermann Kant, Christa Wolf, Günter de Bruyn, Fritz Rudolf Fries (although he remained unpublished in the GDR) and, with some reservations, Erik Neutsch and Erwin Strittmatter.

The central theme of novels by these authors published from 1963 to 1968 is the relationship between the individual and (socialist) society, the conflict between individual and social needs and expectations, and the potential for resolving these problems. The individual pursuit of happiness and self-realisation was being taken markedly more seriously than in the literature of the 1950s, while literary heroes are much more psychologically differentiated and individually treated.

What this literature sought to stress was that in socialism not only was society permitted to expect something from the individual, but that, conversely, the individual also had the right to expect something from society. Inconsistencies and contradictions that crop up are no longer artificially resolved in perfect social harmony. An outcome showing persistent dissonance, failure or 'non-arrival' in socialism is now possible.

Erwin Strittmatter

Within the GDR, Erwin Strittmatter was regarded as master of a modern version of village and rural fiction (*Dorf- und Bauernprosa*) that dealt with the transformation of the conditions of production on the land. Even his earlier works, the novel *Ochsenkutscher* (*The Ox-cart Driver*) (1950), his play *Katzgraben* (*Cat-graves*) (1953), his children's story *Tinko* (1954), and his socialist picaresque novel *Der Wundertäter* (*The Miracle Worker*) (vol. 1, 1957) may be classified as remarkable recent publications of their day. His outstanding work, however, is *Ole Bienkopp*, a novel published in 1963.

Set in the transitional phase of land collectivisation in 1952–9, it deals with the clash between the forward-looking *Wegsucher* (pathfinder) and *Spurmacher* (trailblazer) Ole Bienkopp, who wants to found a 'New Farming Cooperative' (LPG) and the people in the village, who 'are not yet ready' for it. The novel closes with the death of Bienkopp, 'tiller of the future' and 'tenacious dreamer', who has exhausted himself in his efforts to turn utopia into reality. Not surprisingly, GDR newspapers chewed this novel over for months, devoting enormous efforts to the attempt to make the violent end of the hero sound plausible.

While Strittmatter's *Bienkopp* is the rural novel of GDR literature *par excellence*, Erik Neutsch's novel *Spur der Steine* (*The Track of the Stones*) (1964) ranks as the authoritative GDR novel on 'new production' in the industrial sphere. Neutsch started as a journalist, making his début with shorter prose chiefly concerned with the formation and everyday activities of socialist work brigades (*Regengeschichte* – *Rain Story*, 1960; *Bitterfelder Geschichten* – *Bitterfeld Stories*, 1961). *Spur der Steine* is an epic-scale novel about life and work on one of the GDR's major construction sites. It also constitutes a practical presentation of the literary agenda of the New Economic System, with planning and management characters at the core of the plot. In fact, however, the 'hero' of the novel as such is the construction brigade leader (*Zimmermannsbrigadier*) Hannes Balla, 'king of the construction site', militant, but a loner and a searcher for happiness after his own fashion. Although he has nothing against socialism, his high work productivity is by no means motivated by altruism. *Spur der Steine* formed the basis for Heiner Müller's play *Der Bau* (*The Construction*) (1965).

An assessment of GDR history up to that point

The novels of Strittmatter and Neutsch are set in a period only slightly before that of the narrator, making them contemporary novels in the strict sense of the term. This is not the case with Hermann Kant's widely-read and much-discussed novel *Die Aula* (*The Hall*) (pre-published in 1964 in the journal *Forum*, and in 1965 in book form), in which the GDR is treated as a historical theme that needs to be assessed. Kant had already published his first work in 1962, the prose volume *Ein bisschen Südsee* (*A Bit of the South*), which had caused quite a stir on account of its narrative skill.

Die Aula dispenses with the convention of individual heroes, replacing them with a collective, or social institution. It deals with the construction phase of the GDR, in which faculties were set up for industrial and rural workers (*Arbeiter- und Bauernfakultäten: ABF*) with the intention of preparing them for university in order to train them as the future leaders of their country. The impetus behind the narrative is a request made to Robert Iswall, a former ABF student, now a journalist, to give a commemorative speech on the occasion of the closing of his former ABF. The speech is never in fact made; in its stead, a novel takes shape under Heine's motto: 'Today is the result of yesterday. We must inquire into what yesterday wanted if we would know what today wants' ('Der heutige Tag ist ein Resultat des gestrigen. Was dieser gewollt hat, müssen wir erforschen, wenn wir zu wissen wünschen, was jener will').

The author seeks in his own work to implement the challenge inherent in this motto by building a network of episodes, anecdotes, associations and reflections from and about the 'age of heroism' of the GDR, with the intention of 'kindling and keeping awake a sense of history'. Although there is some questioning and exploding of myths concerning GDR realities, there is a marked preponderance of praise and a self-assured 'it-has-been-accomplished' attitude. Using the career of the Red October ABF collective as an example, he demonstrates how the working class has become both an educated and the ruling class. The title of the novel, *Die Aula* (*The Hall*), indicates that the working class has claimed as its own this formerly bourgeois symbol of education, i.e. the lecture hall. To this extent, therefore, the novel is indeed representative of the fundamental choice of direction for the GDR as a country. Its very subject-matter makes it *the* GDR novel *par excellence*.

Kant's novel is characterised by his practised use of modern narrative devices: several chronological periods, flashbacks, shifts of perspective, internal monologue, ironic breaks and other similar devices pose no problem to the narrator, giving the novel a strongly Western flavour that contrasts starkly with its content. Kant, a skilful organiser, writes cleverly, smoothly and brilliantly, and with a practised hand. His style is the 'realism' of *realer Sozialismus* that ultimately breaks no taboos.

The same applies to his second novel *Das Impressum* (*The Imprint*) (1972), the story of a GDR career that culminates in a ministerial post. Once again, Kant stirs up the social contradictions in order to smooth them over again all the more securely at the end. Here too he succeeds in cultivating a clever, intellectually demanding, yet easily-digested narrative style.

Christa Wolf

Christa Wolf's début also fell in the early 1960s. No other GDR writer wrote so deeply from her own individual experience, with such authentic subjectivity, or with such an acute awareness that reality could no longer be portrayed as self-evident and complete, without circumlocution. And yet no other writer was capable of such a high degree of pregnant relevance in her comments about GDR society. Her prose works defy vulgarised labels such as *Agroroman*, *Produktionsroman* or *ABF-roman* as used so far. Their whole aim and execution is too complex to allow this. Her works published after 1967 especially raise the major theme of the relationship between the individual and society to an entirely new plane.

Born in Landsberg on the Warthe in 1929, Christa Wolf belonged to a generation that had been only half-aware of living through fascism and war, and who, on the face of it at least, were able to tackle the issue of the construction of socialism unimpeded by prejudice. After taking a degree in German studies she initially worked as a reader and editor for the literary journal *Neue Deutsche Literatur*. In 1961 she published her first book *Moskauer Novelle* (*Moscow Novella*), which she nevertheless later condemned as doctrinaire.

610

Her second prose work *Der geteilte Himmel* (*Divided Heaven*), published in book form in 1963, caused an immediate sensation. Some 160,000 copies were published in one year alone. It was translated into many languages, and later made into a film by Christa Wolf's namesake Konrad Wolf, son of Friedrich Wolf. It was this book that propelled the author to fame.

This short novel relates the love story of a 19-year-old country girl, Rita Seidel, and a chemist called Manfred Herrfurth. Rita follows her boyfriend to a big city, Halle on the Saale, where she takes a degree in education studies, does her teaching practice in the works brigade of a railway carriage works and finally loses Manfred, who remains in West Berlin after the events of August 1961 (the story is set in the two years leading up to 1961). Although she visits Manfred once after his move to West Berlin, she decides against the Western social system, and thus also against Manfred.

The story is narrated from the standpoint of Rita, who is trying to put the pieces of her life together again after a suicide attempt. At the forefront of the novel, as the title suggests, is the fundamental fact of the building of the Berlin Wall and the divided Germany. And yet, as the author states, this is not the central theme of the novel, which is concerned rather with the question of why people must part. Christa Wolf is interested in the potential of the individual to find and realise himself in GDR society, and the obstacles society poses to these processes.

Interestingly, in the GDR the book found itself caught in the cross-fire, not as a work of art, but on political grounds. Although the theme of *Republikflucht* ('escaping' from or leaving the GDR) had already been dealt with by Anna Seghers (*Die Entscheidung – The Decision*) and Brigitte Reimann (*Die Geschwister – The Sisters*), it had never been dealt with in such an unorthodox way as that chosen by Christa Wolf, who to make matters worse combined it with that of a suicide attempt by a positive heroine.

The particular relevance of Christa Wolf's work, aside from its intrinsic value, is the fact that it set signposts and encouraged fresh movement, at the same time clearly indicating new tendencies. This applies not only to its themes, but also to the mode of narration, and poetic reflection on it.

What is Man?

Wolf's 1967 story *Juninachmittag* (*June Afternoon*), and *Nachdenken über Christa T.* (*Reflections about Christa T.*) represent the first examples of a departure from the concept of the auctorial, Olympian, all-knowing narrator, and yet Christa Wolf does not relinquish the right of the narrator to intervene, comment or reflect. She is no proponent of the *Tod der Literatur* (*Death of Literature*) or the *Exekution des Erzählers* (*Execution of the Narrator*) (Kurt Batt on literature in the Federal Republic). On the contrary, what Wolf is concerned with is 'subjective authenticity' as the fourth, in fact real dimension of the work of art. Her essay *Lesen und Schreiben* (*Reading and Writing*) (1968) is a prime example of her stubbornly trenchant, productive work in the discipline of literary theory.

In 1968 *Nachdenken über Christa T.* was published – another book that caused quite a sensation at the time. *Reflections on Christa T.* poses the question of the specific historical form of individuality to which the new mode of production and living has given rise in the GDR. It was inspired by the untimely death of a close friend of the author and narrator, who reflects on the friend and her death in the novel. The content of the book thus revolves around coming to terms with grief. However, it is intended less as an elegy or a helpless song of lament than as a learning process, setting in motion Wolf's personal knowledge of a woman who had lived with great awareness and high aspirations in the best sense of the term, as well as of the society in which this individual life had been lived out. Christa T., who had gone to school and university with the narrator, later marries a veterinary surgeon in the country and has two children. Finally she dies of leukaemia at age 36 – on the face of it a somewhat banal biography, which is nevertheless not exhausted in the recounting of these simple facts. Essentially, it is the story of a woman who, with the intention of living in harmony with the society around her, seeks to develop a new identity, full of impatience, a hunger for the truth and an aspiration towards perfection. She is gradually forced to face the fact that the society around her attaches no value to such an individual, showing a preference for well-adjusted, 'dynamic' 'people of action' as similar in their functioning as peas in a pod and with no imagination – *Hopp-Hopp-Menschen* – people who can 'jump to it'.

In the process of working out her grief, therefore, Christa Wolf is putting on trial a whole social order. Although this order holds aloft on its banner the aspiration of allowing human beings to develop as human beings, in practice their everyday lives reduce them to vehicles for an abstract increase in the productive labour force and 'systems development' (*Systementfaltung*), as set forth in the agendas of the New Economic System and the Developed Social System of Socialism. The scientific and technological revolution has become a fetish, leaving the self-determining individual to fall by the wayside. All this is narrated in an intricate mode of presentation that nevertheless never seeks to be modish – interweaving flashbacks, anticipation, dreams, reflection and other devices serving the narrative interest of reflections with several layers of meaning.

How should one live?

Along with Christa Wolf, a number of other younger and more recent authors from the mid-1960s onwards also posed questions – albeit in a less radical way than Wolf. These included the questions of how one should live, and under what conditions the human being evolved as a moral animal. This effectively shifted an ethical question, rooted in the subjective or inter-subjective level, to the centre of literature, highlighting just how far writers had come since the agenda of the Bitterfeld Way and the proletarian revolutionary tradition.

These authors included writers of such widely varying themes, aesthetic quality and ideological stringency as Karl-Heinz Jakobs (*Beschreibung eines Sommers* – *Description of a Summer*, 1961; *Eine Pyramide für mich* – *A Pyramid for Me*, 1971), Alfred Wellm (*Pause für Wanzka* – *A Break for Wanzka*, 1968), Werner Heiduczek (*Abschied von den Engeln* – *Farewell to the Angels*, 1968; *Marc Aurel oder ein Semester Zärtlichkeit* – *Marcus Aurelius, or a Term of Tenderness*, 1971), and Irmtraud Morgner (*Hochzeit in Konstantinopel* – *Wedding in Constantinople*, 1968). These works deal with romantic and other inter-personal relationships, questions concerned with upbringing and finding an identity, the obstacles to and driving forces behind human self-realisation, and with successful or failed adaptation to life in a given society.

The most important contributions to this new literary tendency were by Günter de Bruyn. His novel *Hohlweg* (*Hollow Passage*), published in 1961, deals with the disparate courses of development of two friends from the final days of the war into the early post-war years, and displays all the 'childhood illnesses' typical of a first novel still in the thrall of 'socialist realism'. Then, in 1968, came his Berlin novel *Buridans Esel* (*Buridan's Donkey*), which is about love, women, marriage, morality, librarianship and contemporary social life. Using the then common device of a love triangle, de Bruyn carries off a brilliant exposure of all the mechanisms of social adaptation, lies and inconsistencies that had by then become widespread in GDR society. The 'successful', conformist Chief Librarian Karl Erp, 'master of self-justification' and his male self-esteem are no match in the long term for the changes necessitated by his love for his emancipated, clever colleague Fräulein Broder. Out of cowardice, he returns to his ostensible family idyll – a decision presented by de Bruyn not as a triumph of socialist morality, but as the very opposite. The story is related in a psychologically precise, highly amusing narrative style that delights in detail – clearly influenced by Jean Paul and Fontane – and which resurfaces in his third novel *Preisverleihung* (*Prize-giving*) (1972).

Modern narrative techniques

To the extent that critical prose writers of the 1960s had ceased to cling nervously to the ideological bannisters, they were able to free themselves from the dogmas of what, in the previous decade, had been an unassailably sacrosanct, outward-oriented aesthetics. In the spirit of the virtuoso example of Bobrowski and the unique style of Christa Wolf, more and more authors now availed themselves of modern narrative techniques: flashbacks, the use of different chronological periods, internal monologue and stream-of-consciousness, the introduction of a narrative character, ironic changes of viewpoint and shifts in narrative perspective.

These devices for enhancing subjectivity, differentiation and richness of perspective, applied to what had hitherto been a static and 'objectively' presented narrative content, now became so commonplace that Max Schulz felt obliged to warn in 1964 of sacrificing 'the requirement that a novel represent a totality', suggesting that the world could 'only be poetically interpreted in various ways'. In the case of one author, Fritz Rudolf Fries, this 'surreptitious adoption' (*verhohlene Aneignung* – H. Küntzel) of modern narrative techniques was carried to such lengths that his first novel was never published in the GDR.

For *Der Weg nach Oobliadooh* (*The Way to Oobliadooh*) (1966) Fries borrowed the model that seemed to him most appropriate to his mode of accommodating reality: the picaresque novel. The *picaro* hero, a frivolous negator and destroyer, an 'abnormal' hero for whom nothing is sacred, should in fact never have made an appearance in GDR literature at all. Despite this, Fries entrusts his interpretation of the GDR and its social order to a *picaro*, a bohemian character named Arlecq, in many respects an autobiographical figure – a translator and novelist living in Leipzig. His friend Paasch, a dentist who is about to become a reluctant father, although no anarchic *picaro*, being more of a meditative pedant, will nevertheless not pass muster as a model character. The two of them stumble their way through the GDR of 1957–8, punctuated by a brief visit to West Berlin with the intention of 'escaping'. This nevertheless ends back in the GDR, where they find themselves inmates of a psychiatric clinic, their capacity to act and to create future prospects considerably deflated. They have lost their dream of the 'distant sunny city', against which their 'own city', the GDR, can only be set as a 'provincial branch and domestic offices'. As indicated in the Jean Paul motto, West Berlin was not the 'sunny city'. All that remains is the Land of Oobliadooh, the world of jazz, a metaphor for a poetic dream-world that lies beyond the reality of the GDR.

However, it is more than the content of Fries's novel that sets it against the norm and the normal. The narrative style also breaks the customary rules and encourages anarchy. Fries is clearly trained in the classical authors of the modern age, above all Marcel Proust, who is bashfully evoked in a number of passages. In this vein, Fries gives his readers a stream of consciousness that blends a wealth of associations, the past, present and future, dream and reality, actual and imagined experience, the near and the far, the private and the public.

The theatre without Brecht: production stories and parable plays

During the 1960s, writing for the theatre took distinct second place to prose in terms of social impact and the part it played in the public awareness, although this is no reflection of its intrinsic merits. A key distinguishing feature of the cultural policy of the GDR's Socialist Unity Party (SED) was that the most important and exciting plays of those years – Peter Hacks's *Die Sorgen und Die Macht* (*The Cares and the Power*) and *Moritz Tassow*, and Braun's *Kipper Paul Bauch* (*Paul Bauch the Tipper*), were either not performed at all, or only in circumstances which more or less excluded the public, thereby inevitably precluding such plays from becoming widely known.

The same period saw an increase in the number of contemporary plays being performed in the GDR (in 1956 GDR authors accounted for only 20 per cent of plays performed, contemporary themes accounting for scarcely 40 per cent; by 1960, these proportions had risen to over a third and almost two-thirds, respectively). The fact is, however, that those plays reaching the stage did not necessarily offer a realistic, illusion-free picture of existing social conditions.

Tendencies

The following tendencies were characteristic for the development of writing for the theatre in the 1960s: unlike the Federal Republic, interesting theatre in the GDR focused on a single city, the capital Berlin, which had three leading houses – the Deutsches Theater (German Theatre) (founded in 1883 and directed for decades by Max Reinhardt before 1933), the Volksbühne (People's Stage), and Brecht's Berliner Ensemble, which was directed after his death by Erich Engel, and later by Helene Weigel. Other major directors of this period were Wolfgang Langhoff, Benno Besson, Manfred Wekwerth and Peter Palitzsch. Brecht's authority, up to that time unquestioned, began to wane somewhat, most especially among the most interesting of his pupils. This process was forcibly encouraged in the 1970s.

The 'production' theme continued to play a major role, albeit adjusted to the new structures laid down by the New Economic System. Some authors showed a marked proclivity for the parable play or mythological texts, which could quite easily symbolise the oppressive here-and-now.

In a public life still straitjacketed and regimented, with journalism and audio-visual media often serving more to hinder than disseminate information, the theatre not infrequently took on the role of an *ersatz* public opinion. The result was a highly alert theatre-going public, astute in picking up veiled references. The majority of ambitious plays, relating to contemporary themes either directly or in historical or mythological guise, either failed to reach the public at all, or did so only after a delay of some years. These were known as 'desk-drawer plays' (*Schubladenstücke* – O.F. Riewoldt), a category that included several works by Heiner Müller and, later, Volker Braun.

The broad theatrical spectrum of that time also comprised a voluminous body of *Gebrauchsdramatik* (utility drama). This abounded in what were usually light-weight dramas applauding socialism. The advent of television in January 1956, which did not nevertheless really take off until around 1965, was accompanied by the rise of the television play and a partial decline of the theatre. By 1966, fifty-four out of every hundred families had a television. Theatre attendance dropped, or at the very least stagnated, and many theatrical playwrights therefore went over to writing for television, or for both theatre and television, producing different versions of the same play for the two media.

Contemporary plays

A major role was played in this period by the *Zeitstück* or contemporary play, by such authors as Helmut Sakowski, Claus Hammel, Armin Stolper, Rainer Kerndl, Horst Kleineidam, Horst Salomon (*Katzengold – Cat Gold*) and, from the end of the decade, Rudi Strahl, by now the most successful writer for the theatre. The same authors also wrote television plays, which were also written by Bernhard Seeger, Benito Wogatzki, Karl Georg Egel (*Dr Schlüter*), Rolf Schneider and Gerhard Bengsch (*Krupp und Krause*). Although here and there a play or two approached honesty and authenticity with respect to detail, as well as being of aesthetic interest, these plays were on the whole of an uncritical, affirmative character.

Most of the 'production' plays written under the banner of the New Economic System share this tendency to skate over disharmonies. Despite criticism of minor points, they fall far short of expressing doubts either about the economic planning and management of the New System (such as the ignorance of those in power, or the interests and needs of the production worker), or about the wisdom of aspiring to a technologised brand of socialism. This can be seen from plays such as Helmut Baierl's *Johanna von Döbeln* (1969) and Erik Neutsch's *Haut oder Hemd* (*Hide or Shirt*) (1966–71).

Over the years, the work of three authors – Peter Hacks, Heiner Müller and Volker Braun – has been an object of sustained and increasing interest for literary historians. During the 1960s, the path taken by Peter Hacks, initially begun in Brecht's footsteps, deviated more and more from realism, veering instead towards a noncommittal brand of classicism (understood by Hacks himself as *Klassik*). His plays *Die Sorgen und die Macht* (*The Cares and the Power*) and *Moritz Tassow* revealed in the clearest possible terms that the GDR was still a place ruled by contingency that impeded, if not actually blocked the happiness of the individual and his free growth.

Somewhere along the way, Hacks shed this viewpoint, so that by 1972 he was able to publish the principles of a 'post-revolutionary dramaturgy'. Here he states: 'In the present condition of socialism, the human being is the master of history to such a sufficient degree that the dramatic author can begin to look on his subject-matter as its master. All he need do is shape it in accordance with the laws of the genre, and give it form, as poetry is bound to do.'

This 'new drama' was to be based 'purely on the essence of art as it relates to man', and to free itself of 'superfluous padding and undigested chance elements' – in other words all those phenomena typical for the 'worst forms of drama' – the 'epic-sociological' dramas. This effectively deposed the erstwhile paradigm, Brecht, although his real defeat had already taken place *de facto* in the plays of the 1960s.

As regards subject-matter, Hacks's plays increasingly sought refuge in history and mythology (*Der Frieden – Peace*, after Aristophanes, 1962; *Die schöne Helena – Helen the Beautiful*, 1964; *Amphytryon*, 1968; *Margarethe von Aix*, 1969; *Omphale*, 1970; *Adam und Eva*, 1972). His histories and parables nevertheless lacked inherent socialist content in the sense demonstrated by Heiner Müller's plays. Hacks became the playwright of the universally human, the quintessential conciliatory genre of the 'post-revolutionary' age.

Dialectic in the theatre: Heiner Müller

For Peter Hacks, the gap between the human longing for happiness and actual living and working conditions in the GDR became less and less significant, and therefore possible to overlook. For Müller, however, there was no vague, positive quantity waiting around the corner. For him, the essence of dialectic was the negation of negation. In specific terms this meant that in the initial phase of socialism the alienation of capitalism was merely replaced by other forms of alienation. A sudden burgeoning of productivity, happiness and humane conduct could not simply be taken for granted.

Müller's conception of dialectic in practice is most apparent in his third 'production' play *Der Bau* (*The Construction*) (based on Erik Neutsch's novel *Spur der Steine – Track of the Stones*, 1963–4; first performed in the GDR in 1979). For a long time, *Der Bau* remained the last play in which Müller clearly dealt directly and without difficulty with the reality of the GDR. In the second half of the 1960s, he wrote plays dealing with ancient mythological subject-matter, side by side with his 'production' plays. Müller was not alone in this: many plays by Peter Hacks, as well as, for example, Karl Mickel's *Nausikaa* (*Nausicaa*) (1968), drew on themes from Greek mythology. In no other author, however, is the range of adaptations so comprehensive or so momentous, beginning with *Philoktet* (*Philoctetes*),

Herakles 5 (*Heracles 5*) (1966; this deals with the fifth Herculean labour of cleaning the stables of Augeas), *Ödipus Tyrann* (*Oedipus Tyrannus*) (1967, based on material by Sophocles and Hölderlin), and a translation of *Prometheus* by Aeschylus (1967–8). His didactic play *Der Horatier* (*The Horatian*) (1968–9), based on an episode from Roman history, is worth mentioning here, the point at issue being whether it denotes a deviation by Müller from the tenets of Marxism, and whether ultimately, as some would have it, this author may be interpreted in existential rather than materialist terms – as the 'Beckett' of the GDR.

Müller's *Philoktet* (*Philoctetes*) (written 1958–64, not performed in the GDR until 1977) is a prime example of why this is not the case. His version of this ancient theme deviates from Sophocles' fable on a number of salient points. The Greeks Odysseus and Neoptolemus, son of Achilles, set sail for the island of Lemnos to bring back Philoctetes, abandoned there years earlier on account of his injured, septic foot. They are in need of Philoctetes and his bow, since without them, or rather the team he commands, they will be unable to conquer Troy. Müller adapts Sophocles' story to make Philoctetes die at the hands of Neoptolemus. Odysseus, whose main weapon is the lie, proves himself better at dealing with the unexpected. Instead of returning to Troy with the live Philoctetes, he brings the dead hero, using Philoctetes' corpse to inspire the team of bowmen to fight.

Written in compact, terse verse form, the heart of Müller's play is a parable about the dialectic relationship between the general – i.e. contingency and reasons of state (in the form of Odysseus, the Machiavellian *Realpolitiker*) – and the specific, i.e. the individual, and the denial of contingency (in the form of Philoctetes, who lives on the periphery of society). This relationship is acted out through the medium of Neoptolemus. Odysseus's thinking is ruled by rational calculation (in its most acute form of subterfuge and deceit), characterised by a complete contempt for individual morality, and devoid of all capacity for sympathy. He also stands as a symbol for the demise of individuality, Humanism and self-generated morality, as evinced by the tactics and reign of terror manifest in more than fifty years of communism in practice, culminating in Stalinism. The latter question was carried still further by Müller again in his 1970 historical piece *Mauser*.

Volker Braun

Volker Braun learned a great deal from Brecht, but belonged to a generation who could no longer know him in person. In Braun's view, Brecht's dramaturgy had marked the final addressing of the issue of class struggle, there being nothing more to be achieved in that direction, since social contradictions were now allegedly of a new, 'non-antagonistic' nature. In line with this view, the new dramaturgy no longer depicted events from the 'class viewpoint. The heroes are friends. They have, in accordance with the political and social position, various interests. The struggle does not have to be to the death. Everyone should live in a more human way. There is no "solution". This must be left to the audience. What is required is comprehensive knowledge about the construction of society.'

This theory of theatre clearly places Volker Braun mid-way between Hacks and Müller, as he himself put it. The 'brilliant Hacks' anticipated so far ahead that 'reality no longer intervene[d]', 'taking off from prosaic reality ... into a poetic future'. The 'magnificent Müller', on the other hand, went back to the 'sharp chains of a prehistory' in which he for the most part perceived reality. Braun preferred to follow in neither of their footsteps to the exclusion of all else. He is stirred, more akin to Müller in this respect, by the 'great conflict ... between the new conditions of production, which call for the development of all forces and authorities – and the grip on workers of traditional capitalist production, which does not require them to be whole men at all'.

His first play, *Die Kipper* (*The Tippers*) (first performed in 1972), on which he worked from 1962 onwards, the first printing of 1967 being entitled *Kipper Paul Bauch* (*Paul Bauch the Tipper*), is about just this conflict. Braun's choice of a hero of gigantic proportions is akin both to Hacks's choice of Moritz Tassow and Heracles (in *Omphale*), and Müller's choice of Bremer (*Die Korrektur* – *The Correction*), Balke (*Der Lohndrücker* – *Cheap Labour*), Barka (*Der Bau* – *The Construction*) and also Heracles (*Herakles 5* – *Heracles 5*). His hero is a worker, a creator, although also a 'Baal' under socialist conditions. It is on the one hand as a result of his human productive force, and his uncompromising rejection of the merely pragmatic and the merely realistic, that socialism grows as 'the great production'. On the other hand, however, this hero impedes 'the great production' as a collective undertaking by being almost entirely unable to think or act beyond his capacity as an individual. By the same token, Braun's *Kipper* play (like, for example, Christa Wolf's prose), is evidence that not even socialist literature can avoid involving itself in the individual sphere.

Braun's second play, whose first version is entitled *Hans Faust* (1968) and second version *Hinze und Kunze* (*Tom, Dick and Harry*) (1973), is a 'production' play. Braun was by no means aiming here for some kind of outward realism. Like Müller's, Braun's texts also incline towards parable. This can be seen from the structure of the plot, as well as its strongly stylised, anti-naturalist language, rich in metaphor and aphorism, that delights in the 'socialist reversal' of figures of speech, using them in the materialistic rather than the formalist sense.

Sensible Wege (Sensitive Paths) in lyric poetry

During the 1960s, lyric poetry became an unprecedented focus of heated debate. This did not revolve around already famous past masters (after Brecht's and Becher's death, these were now Arendt, Huchel, Hermlin, Maurer and Bobrowski).

Disciplinary measures

It was triggered by a group of lyric poets of the younger generation, almost all born during the 1930s. The first major date in this series of events was a reading of lyric poetry by young authors at the Academy of Arts in December 1962 (major disciplinary measures were recorded against its mentor, Stephan Hermlin), which marked the début of a new author, Wolf Biermann, who was to be persecuted from the very outset. By now, Günter Kunert had also been 'exposed' as a Kafka-follower and an unreliable personality. The eleventh plenary session of the SED Party Central Committee in December 1965 launched a fierce attack on both Biermann and Kunert among the lyric poets. Biermann, who had made a tour of the Federal Republic in 1965, was strictly banned from appearing in public in the GDR.

The summer of 1966 saw the beginning of a lyric poetry debate in *Forum*, the journal of the Free German Youth, triggered by the publication of the anthology *In diesem besseren Land* (*In This Better Country*). The position of orthodoxy on this occasion was represented by none other than acting Editor-in-Chief Rudolf Bahro. Previously unpublished poems by Volker Braun, Heinz Czechowski, Karl Mickel, and Sarah and Rainer Kirsch aroused particular official displeasure. Two further anthologies of those 'lyric poetry wave' years also precipitated public discussion: *Sonnenpferde und Astronauten* (*Sun-horses and Astronauts*) (1964) and *Saison für Lyrik* (*Season for Lyric poetry*) (1967). Finally, Reiner Kunze's poetry volume *Sensible Wege* (*Sensitive Paths*) (1969), although published only in the Federal Republic, brought on a fresh, now massive spate of bans. At the sixth Writers' Congress of 1969, Max Walter Schulz arraigned the author with the charge that his lyric poetry, rooted somewhere 'between an inner world-view and anti-communism' displayed a 'crude, action-craving individualism', despite its sensitivity and was hence in league with 'anti-communism, the malicious subversion of the image of the GDR'. The result of this was a ban on the publication of Kunze's works that initially excluded his work as a translator.

The role of the self

What, then, was going on? The derogatory terms 'inner world-view', 'sensibility' and 'individualism' provided key phrases. Since time immemorial, poetry-writing had always been prompted by the desire for micro-cosmic self-expression, a fact which inevitably brought a degree of trenchancy in its wake. Lyric poetry is furthermore also that particular mode of expression that gives the most unfettered voice to subjectivity. These two circumstances were bound to collide with the GDR's 'objectivising' representations of reality under the semi-official heading *Mittel der Wahl* (*means of choice*). Moreover, the lyric poetry and debate of that period was specifically concerned with the role of the self and of subjectivity. In numerous essays Georg Maurer, from whom many of these younger poets had learned, reclaimed for the socialist context the self that had been passed down in modern Western lyric poetry – the individual human being, 'the only being who makes himself a subject, and can then conduct himself freely in relation to himself, who knows what he is doing'.

This process nevertheless entailed a problem that was perceived as surprising. According to Elke Erb, it consisted in the fact that lyric poetry had hitherto been of a 'self-less', affirmative character, 'a didactically arranged identity between (a non-objectively and non-concretely apprehensible) individual and the historical or social subject, which hence rendered the 'individual subject . . . devoid of structure and poetically inactive'. In short, therefore, it was asserted that lyric poetry had hitherto allowed no room for the serious claims of individual subjects. A generation was now beginning to write which was demanding that room be made for this 'disparaged, denounced Self' (Günter Wünsche in his poem *Rehabilitierung des Ich – The Reinstatement of the Self*), and saw in the individual a 'microcosm' full of creative energy – even to a certain extent the legitimate continuation of a God who had been officially put out of business (Uwe Gressmann).

The autonomy of art

As a consequence, the 'attitudes' of lyric poetry also began to change. A personal mode of speech, using the persons I and We, and addressing a You (*Du*), became more commonplace. The desire to instruct continued to abate. This was most apparent in the work of the former 'didactic poet' Günter Kunert. Other poets adhered to the 'operative' character of poetry. Volker Braun, for example, required of a poem that it awaken 'recognition, readiness for action, and appetite'. Despite such differences between these and many other comparable positions, however, they nonetheless shared the desire to close ranks against the idea of direct social utility, as propounded by the cultural policy of the New Economic System.

Adolf Endler, Karl Mickel, Richard Leising, Rainer and Sarah Kirsch, Heinz Czechowski, Reiner Kunze, Wolf Biermann, Volker Braun, Kurt Bartsch, Bernd Jentzsch, Uwe Gressman and Wulf Kirsten may be mentioned as the most important lyric poets of the younger generation. The interesting fact that most of them came from the province of Saxony prompted Endler to refer to a 'Saxon School of Poetry'. Kunze, Biermann, Sarah Kirsch and Braun received the greatest attention, both at that time and since.

Reiner Kunze

At first, Reiner Kunze seemed set to become the archetypal proletarian poet, rising with his class and representing their standpoint with his poetry. A miner's son, he studied journalism, but decided to leave university shortly before graduating. By 1959 he was working as a freelance writer. His first work consisted of acclamatory verses and rhymed aphorisms on such themes as the joy of being a soldier under socialism. It did not differ at all from the lyric poetry of political affirmation that was in vogue at the time. In 1963 he published a volume of poetry entitled *Widmungen (Dedications)* through a West German publishing house, although it was also noted in the GDR as a lyric poetry event of some importance.

Published in 1969 (again only in the Federal Republic), however, *Sensible Wege (Sensitive Paths)* contained a number of poems for which no licence had been issued by the GDR authorities. It thus marked the severing of the cord between the author and the GDR state. *Sensitive Paths* contains poems dating back to 1960, and shows that even then Kunze had lost his blind faith in the GDR (*das ende der fabeln, das ende der Kunst – the end of the tales, the end of art*). Many of his verses were written during or about the Prague Spring of 1967–8 in Czechoslovakia, which had a particularly strong biographical attraction for Kunze. His verses evince an increasing sense of loneliness, scepticism, and despair. His tone grew bitter, even harsh. Communication became more and more sparse, and fewer and fewer clarion calls were issued. This creeping disillusionment was accompanied by an increasing proclivity towards abandoning metaphor, and a poetic style pared down to lucid, epigrammatic terseness.

Wolf Biermann

Similarly, Wolf Biermann, the son of a Hamburg labourer killed by the Nazis in the Auschwitz concentration camp, did not at first seem predestined to become one of the most convincing (socialist) critics of the GDR. He had moved from Hamburg to the GDR in 1953, where he studied philosophy, became an assistant producer, and then towards the end of the 1950s began to sing some of his own songs, accompanying himself on the guitar. The poetry-reading at the Academy of Arts in December 1962 brought his conflict with the Party and state leadership out into the open. From 1965 onwards the stereotype of the eleventh plenary session verdict was to be reiterated many times: 'fundamental opposition to *realer Sozialismus*', 'sensualism', 'pleasure-seeking', and 'anarchistic individualism'. There was far more at stake here than a mere conflict between different opinions and ways of thinking. Here was a total divergence of attitudes, modes of communication and fundamental objectives. The author rejected all those dogmas, rituals, and authorities, which he perceived not merely as the accoutrements, but the structural hallmark of a socialist state convinced of the rightness of its own ways.

Since, moreover, Biermann voiced his criticism volubly, publicly, and with an immense grasp of art in general, he became a severe embarrassment to the Party leadership. At first he published four slender volumes containing ballads, poems and songs: *Die Drahtharfe* (*The Wire Harp*) (1965), *Deutschland – Ein Wintermärchen* (*Germany, a Winter's Tale*) (1965), *Mit Marx- und Engelszungen* (*With the Tongues of Marx and Engels*) (1968) and *Für meine Genossen* (*For My Comrades*) (1972). All four were published only in the Federal Republic: no book by this author was ever published in the GDR. These 'anti-war protest songs', love-songs, 'appeasements and revisions', ballads about everyday conflicts in the GDR and socialist 'encouragements' clearly reveal Biermann's mentors: François Villon, Heinrich Heine and Bertolt Brecht. Although they advocate learning about dialectic, they do so in a pleasing manner; although imparting knowledge, they do not separate it from emotions.

In one and the same song there can be an abrasive discordance between crude effect and surprising delicacy, out-and-out vulgarisms and soft tenderness, exquisite metaphor and bald directness, fury and grief, fear and hope, despair and enthusiasm. It is this that binds his poetry to reality. At one point he will intervene, at another he will seek to galvanise, or change his hearers or readers. And yet he does not forfeit that sensuality, that enjoyment, that is needed in their reading and living by those who would change. In Biermann, the 'operative' poem and song took on a whole new dimension.

Sarah Kirsch

For years, Sarah Kirsch, like Reiner Kunze and others, ranked with the well-meaning writers of the post-war generation who were actively encouraged. Her first major volume of poetry, *Landaufenthalt* (*A Stay in the Country*), was published in 1967, her second volume, *Zaubersprüche* (*Magic Spells*), in 1973. Sarah Kirsch's poetry often gives an impression of spontaneity, naivety or the idyllic. Only repeated close study reveals the painstaking writing process that has gone into it, and the degree of conflict each and every one contains. Many begin with the word 'I'. It is her wish that 'witches, if they existed, could use these poems as their textbooks'. She thus ascribes to lyric poetry powers of sorcery and magic – the power to transform herself, her lover, other people and natural phenomena, and the power to restore through poetry the kind of alienation-free communication that is lacking in an everyday life and language that are devoid of magic.

Volker Braun

Volker Braun is rightly regarded as the epitome of the new lyric poetry style of a generation who consciously lived out their lives solely in the GDR. He no longer troubled himself with the question of whether a specifically political poetry was necessary or not. The dilemma as to whether to be combative or contemplative was for him no longer a matter of discretion for the author. Reality is no longer 'presented' so much as 'broken open'. Braun declared his rejection of the 'bourgeois aesthetics of the representative function of art'. His antithetical-dialectical mode of expression, his 'obsession with change' and his aim of 'working out and not removing conflicts' are a legacy from Brecht. He nevertheless differs from Brecht (and is more akin to Mayakowski) in the tempestuous tone of his poetry – a tone that betrays one who lived through the dark times of fascism and war.

Braun described his first volume of poetry, *Provokation für mich* (*Provocation for Myself*) (1965), as a 'highly personal self-expression on events in which I was involved as a young person'. These poems are indeed provocative, drastic, nonchalant, lacking in inhibition and polemical, as is most apparent in the poem *Kommt uns nicht mit Fertigem* (*Don't Give Us Glib Answers*). Here the poet was not yet interested in a firm structure for his poems.

Wir und nicht sie (*Us and Not Them*) (1970) evinces a changed position that deliberately leaves no room for the personal or intimate, dealing instead with themes concerning the social alternatives available in the two German states, against the backdrop of the fatal historical events leading up to 1945. Obviously, this poetry, like Braun's plays of the same period, betrays a confidence in socialism that nowadays, two decades later, appears remarkably odd, and yet of its time.

Non-modern lyric poetry

None of the major lyric poets of this generation, least of all Braun, started out in an entirely original vein. There are initial signs both of brash, exaggerated stylistic gestures, and emotional, declamatory tendencies. From the Western viewpoint, the new quality in the lyric poetry of Rainer and Sarah Kirsch, Volker Braun, Mickel, Czechowski and Kirsten, Bartsch and Biermann was slow to become apparent, on account of a fixation with the so-called 'structure of modern lyric poetry' (embodied in the poetry of Benn, and described by Hugo Friedrich), which made it impossible for non-hermetic lyric poetry to be perceived as other than imitative.

It was Rainer Kirsch, aiming directly at Mickel's poetry, who first showed what characterised lyric poetry by the best authors of his generation, as well as what distinguished it most sharply from concurrent West German tendencies: 'Precision in the treatment of the subject-matter – the characteristic governs the aesthetic – an astute reflection on the age that was schooled in Marxism, and the deliberate continuation of work using classical aesthetic techniques.'

Older sceptics

In addition to lyric poetry published by twenty-five to thirty-year-olds in the 1960s, there were also, of course, volumes of poetry by older, often resolutely sceptical authors, such as Erich Arendt, Georg Maurer, Franz Fühmann, Johannes Bobrowski (who was only just beginning to exert an influence) and Günter Kunert. Peter Huchel's late lyric poetry, by contrast, was only published in the Federal Republic (*Chausseen, Chausseen – Highways, Highways*, 1963; *Gezählte Tage – Numbered Days*, 1972). Following massive pressure, Huchel resigned in 1962 as Editor-in-Chief of *Sinn und Form* (*Meaning and Form*), thereafter being condemned against his will to nine years of internal emigration. It was 1971 before he was allowed to move to the Federal Republic. Huchel's *nature morte* poetry, with its radically sceptical philosophy of history, expressed in symbols of rigidity, glaciation and ossification, could not be tolerated in the GDR of the 1960s, with its blinkered enthusiasm for progress.

Lastly, mention may be made of three women lyric poets of some stature who for various reasons were not able to be active in the GDR. These were Inge Müller, the wife of Heiner Müller, who committed suicide in 1966 (Her volume *Wenn ich schon sterben muss – If I Must Die* was published posthumously in 1985), Christa Reinig and Helga M. Novak. The latter two left the GDR in the mid-1960s because they could not be published there. In the same decade the GDR 'dispensed' with some of its other leading authors, notably Peter Huchel and Uwe Johnson.

Literature of the 1970s and 1980s: against 'instrumental reason'

More recent GDR literature, whose precursors were already discernible by the end of the 1960s, was characterised by a relinquishing of unreserved avowal of socialism across quite a broad spectrum, and hence also of the previous discourse of affirmative unambiguity. With few exceptions, it continued to pin its hopes on a 'different', 'genuine', i.e. utopian socialism, but at the same time subjected the prevailing system as the civilising structure to increasingly severe and trenchant revision. In short, therefore, in the last two decades of its existence GDR literature became a literature of radical criticism of civilisation. Obviously, until the final collapse of the GDR this new questioning approach remained strangely linked on principle to what was from the Western viewpoint a naive-seeming solidarity with the socialist agenda. In this way, GDR literature, unlike those of other Eastern Bloc countries, only ever became peripherally dissident.

The GDR in the process of deformed modernisation

By the 1960s, the GDR had completed its economic reconstruction and had become, at least by Second World standards, a major industrial nation. It is pertinent to speak of the belated end to this reconstruction period, since it also signified the end of former orientations and attitudes in the intellectual and cultural spheres.

That phase known as the anti-fascist democratic revolution was long a thing of the past, as was the unreserved identification of those involved in culture with the new state and its new production which, far from being interrupted by the building of the Wall in 1961, was if anything reinforced by it. The Bitterfeld Way and 'arrival literature' years (1959–63) were perhaps marked by the closest ever affinity between intellectuals and their country, despite sporadic criticism.

From the implementation in 1963 of the New Economic System that sought, however unsuccessfully, to maintain the primary importance of developing the productive labour force while at the same time combining this with maxims of economic and technical efficiency borrowed from capitalism, this largely naive identification and loyalty was gradually eroded, as well as making such identification by writers appear dubious. The restructuring of the GDR into a socialist industrial society in the wake of the scientific and technological revolution produced negative repercussions that had long been associated exclusively with Western capitalist civilisation in its decadent phase. Many intellectuals failed to the bitter end to acknowledge that the true price of half-hearted, deformed modernisation of the socialist heritage was decidedly higher than that of the much more effective modernisation of Western countries, which was moreover also capable of self-adjustment.

'Genosse Sachzwang' ('Comrade Commercial Exigency')

A comprehensive, forced modernisation of the country was now required by *Genosse Sachzwang*, namely the GDR's need to hold its own as an industrial nation on the international market. In this way, an 'ill thought-out modernity' became the 'vanishing point of development' in the GDR

(Volker Gransow). Robert Havemann described this development as follows: 'The "living standards" striven for by GDR socialism are those already available under capitalism. Whereas, however, capitalism is already beginning to show signs of choking on the after-effects of an explosion in consumerism, the socialist economy, with its own brand of backward technology, struggles in vain to follow capitalist society along more and more senseless paths, and if it were possible, to catch up with it.' Obviously, however, modern Western 'dominance of commercialism' (Winfried Thaa) was blended, almost beyond recognition, in the GDR, right up until its final demise, with the old vices of what was essentially a pre-modern, feudal socialist social and economic order incapable of innovation or changing course. This obliged the GDR population to endure the negative aspects of modernisation without enjoying its benefits, while continuing to suffer under a repressive hierarchical system that often lacked even a passing resemblance to a civil society.

Five cultures

In the wake of these developments, the cultural fabric of the GDR underwent considerable changes during the last fifteen years or so of its existence. In terms of cultural hegemony, there were no longer two, but three dominant cultures. In the view of Volker Gransow, the 'Communist target culture' and 'traditional German culture' (which also comprised age-old authoritarian vices from Prussia to the Nazi regime) were now augmented by a third, 'industrial culture, with its fetishes – growth, security and efficiency, but also characterised by consumerism and alienation'. Based on a similar mode of production, an identical proclivity for technologies and a lifestyle correlating with that of industrial society, symmetrical structures and processes began to develop in East and West alike. This often made the similarities between the two systems seem more relevant than their differences.

An important aspect of this process was that the leadership of the GDR now found itself having to deal not only with a non-dominant Marxist culture of opposition from 'true socialists' (beginning with Havemann, Biermann and Bahro through to Volker Braun), but increasingly with an alternative subculture that was scarcely interested in socialist models at all. In an environment that had been alienated from nature, this culture was seeking alternative ways of living.

The subculture embraced a number of new social movements, which to some extent overlapped: non-institutionalised peace groups, the ecological movement, the anti-nuclear energy movement, the women's movement, and minority movements such as homosexuals and lesbians. The postmodernist orientations of these groups brought them into deep conflict, both with Marxism, and with consumer attitudes observed in the West.

Their call for the conservation of the environment and its rescue from the effects of harmful industrial society could no longer be reconciled with the officially sanctioned 'modern' principles of 'formal rationality' (Max Weber) and 'instrumental Reason' of the GDR (Horkheimer/Adorno).

Misgivings

Authors of the middle and older generations were now seized with misgivings: was this the socialism, the something completely different, for which they had striven? What had become of the alleged upward progression towards the emancipation of all, brought about by an undisputed improvement in the economic situation? What distinguished this new German state from the old one, or from the neighbouring Western one, if the old 'birthmarks' were failing to disappear, and the new criteria of value were economic growth and the rationality of exigency?

A process of rethinking set in as a result, and a turning away from blind faith towards greater reflection. In the course of this process, the notion of (quasi-automatic) historical progress, and ultimately the idea of the Enlightenment as the historical source of modern rationalism, even indeed the Marxist conception of the future itself, were all thrown into doubt. This growing doubt was undoubtedly fed in part by specific events, such as the invasion of Czechoslovakia in August 1968 by troops from the Warsaw Pact countries, including the GDR, the revoking of Biermann's citizenship, or again the Soviet occupation of Afghanistan, all of which incensed young people especially. In general, however, the process was too general and all-embracing in nature to enable its causes to be pinned down to isolated incidents.

The dialectic of enlightenment

Quite independently, the intelligentsia and the literature of the 1970s and 1980s were catching up with insights reached some three or four decades previously by the critical theory of Horkheimer, Adorno and Marcuse – namely that the 'dialectic of enlightenment' and *instrumentelle Vernunft* constituted the unsure ground on which not only Western capitalist, but also Eastern 'real socialist' civilisation was built.

The eighth Party Congress, Biermann's deprivation of citizenship and its consequences

1971: a turning-point?

The eighth Party Congress of the Socialist Unity Party (SED), held in June 1971, has long been regarded as a turning-point not only in GDR policy, but also in the history of the country. It is true that for literature this Party Congress issued creative artists with something akin to a general licence (subject to certain established provisos), thereby clearing the way for a lively, inspired, controversial literary life.

It should nevertheless be noted that the eighth Party Congress did not usher in this new literature itself. It merely authorised it. The literature itself was the creation of authors, and specific living conditions, that had been in existence since around the mid-1960s. The problem then was that writers such as Plenzdorf had had to leave his new *Werther* 'in the drawer'; no theatre was allowed to perform Braun's *Der Kipper* (*The Tipper*), and no wider readership had access to Christa Wolf's *Nachdenken über Christa T.* (*Reflections about Christa T.*). The real significance of 1971, therefore, lies in the fact that it enabled critical GDR literature to reach a wider public.

'No taboos'

The new First Secretary of the Socialist Unity Party Central Committee, Erich Honecker, made a speech to the Central Committee session in December 1971. This gave a signal that was thereafter reiterated, invoked and interpreted incessantly: 'If one is rooted in a firm position of socialism, there can in my judgement be no taboos in the sphere of art and literature. This applies both to the question of structuring content, and to style – in short, questions concerning what is known as artistic mastery.'

This statement appeared to be suggesting that convinced socialists could write about anything, using any and every artistic device, and that they were answerable solely to themselves – not to some other authority, such as a Party official. What, however, was meant by a 'firm position of socialism'? Biermann, who had spoken 'with the tongues of Marx and Engels', and yet continued to be condemned to silence within the GDR, and Reiner Kunze both appeared to lack this position. In the same 'liberal' years, Volker Braun, Stefan Heym, Rainer Kirsch, Günter Kunert and Heiner Müller all likewise fell victim to bans on the publication and/or performance of their works, long before Biermann was deprived of his citizenship, not to mention younger authors such as Thomas Brasch or Stefan Schütz.

Ulrich Plenzdorf's *Die neuen Leiden des jungen W.* (*The New Sufferings of the Young W.*) became something of an acid test for the supposed lifting of taboos. In March 1972, *Sinn und Form* published this story, originally intended as the storyline for a film. From the summer of 1972 onwards the play of the same name was performed in no less than fourteen theatres, proving a huge success.

The fact that many officially sanctioned critics in the GDR responded to Plenzdorf's book brusquely and with rebukes is understandable. From the Party standpoint it contained several not inconsiderable perils: subjectivism, hostility to norms, criticism of the *Vorbildkultur* (the 'model culture') and, not least, criticism of the over-reverent GDR attitude towards its bourgeois-classical literary heritage.

In a survey conducted by *Forum*, journal of the Free German Youth, 40 per cent of respondents claimed to share Edgar Wibeau's criticisms and over 60 per cent could well imagine being good friends with Edgar: there was clearly good cause for alarm that a 'false' figure of identification for young people had been made popular. Despite this, however, neither the prose text nor the stage adaptation were banned.

The debate surrounding Plenzdorf's work nevertheless pointed to the limits that were still in effect with regard to literature on the subject of conflict. These limits were brought home to Stefan Heym when he renewed his attempts to find a publisher for his novel *5 Tage im Juni* (*Five Days in June*). He had been trying to publish the first version of the novel under the title *Der Tag X* (*Day X*) since 1959. The manuscript was passed, without success, from one publishing house to another, also coming to the attention of senior Party authorities. By now, however, there was a completely new, second version (published in the Federal Republic in 1974). This second version can reasonably be construed as an attempt to come to terms with the events of 17 June 1953 from a thorough-going 'firm position of socialism'. A blend of historical documentary reportage and political thriller, punctuated with elements of pulp fiction, it revives a tradition that had been in abeyance since the end of the Weimar Republic – that of the contemporary thriller in the journalistic mould. For his own part, Honecker had seen 'an entirely false account of events' in the novel as early as 1965, and the Party continued to back this view. The theme of 17 June remained taboo.

A plea for literary diversity

This notwithstanding, the seventh Writers' Congress of November 1973 was able to confirm the cultural policy direction introduced by the eighth Party Congress in 1969. The Bitterfeld Way, which had still been upheld at the previous sixth Congress in 1969, was now rejected once and for all. The doctrine whereby planners and managers were the preferred heroes of literature was now officially abrogated, and the notion of a homogeneous 'socialist human community' abandoned. In their place, a diversity of aesthetic positions and writing modes was now welcomed. The dialectical relationship between the individual and society was declared to be the central problem, and a clash between the two as entirely possible.

It must nevertheless be conceded that the 1973–6 period was also marked by the imposition of bans: at the very least it was a period of tension-ridden constraints on literary life. This was most clearly manifested in the way the cultural bureaucracy handled Volker Braun's *Unvollendeter Geschichte* (*Unfinished Story*). Although this appeared in *Sinn und Form* in 1975, it was not allowed to be published in book form. This true-life story written in documentary style was evidently deemed to be all too true-to-life. It was thirteen years before permission was granted to publish the text in book form in the GDR, in 1988.

Biermann's deprivation of citizenship

Scarcely a year after the publication of Braun's controversial story, the painstakingly constructed balance in the literary sphere – between loosening taboos and preserving the state order – simply collapsed like a house of cards. The GDR deprived Biermann of his citizenship, thereby setting off a chain reaction involving out-of-favour literary figures and state sanctions against them that was to persist to the end of the GDR's existence. Obviously, the fuss surrounding the Biermann affair merely acted as a trigger. An open confrontation between critical authors and the state was bound to come sooner or later.

Biermann, who had already been urged to emigrate from the GDR in 1974, obtained permission in 1976 to make a trip to the Federal Republic, where he had been invited by the IG Metall Trade Union to make a concert tour. Following the recording and broadcasting of his concert in Cologne (a programme that could of course be seen on GDR television screens), the Politbüro of the Socialist Unity Party promptly took a step that had undoubtedly been agreed upon earlier. On 17 November 1976 Biermann's citizenship of the GDR was revoked, effectively making it impossible for him to return to the country where he had chosen to live.

The days that followed were to reveal how many leading creative artists in the GDR had resources of civil courage and solidarity with a colleague. Although this support was not surprising, the volume of it was unexpected. Above all, however, it revealed how many writers desired a superior, more tolerant and more democratic socialism in the sense that had been envisaged by Rosa Luxemburg. The very day the measure was announced, 17 November, twelve GDR authors wrote and signed the following open letter:

> Wolf Biermann was and is a troublesome poet – he shares this in common with many poets of the past. Our socialist state, being mindful of the words of Marx's *18 Brumaire*, according to which the proletarian revolution criticises itself continuously, ought, in contrast to anachronistic social forms, to be able to tolerate such troublesomeness with composure and reflection. We identify with every word and action of Biermann, and distance ourselves from attempts to misuse against the GDR the proceedings taken concerning him. Neither in Cologne nor elsewhere has Biermann ever left the slightest

doubt over which of the two German states he stands for, all criticism aside. We protest against his deprivation of citizenship, and request a reconsideration of the measure adopted.

The first signatories were Sarah Kirsch, Christa Wolf, Volker Braun, Franz Fühmann, Stephan Hermlin, Stefan Heym, Günter Kunert, Heiner Müller, Rolf Schneider, Gerhard Wolf, Jurek Becker and Erich Arendt. Over 70 other cultural figures added their names within a few days. Others, such as Reiner Kunze, or Bernd Jentzsch, who was in Switzerland at the time, protested with announcements of their own.

Sanctions

Biermann's deprivation of citizenship was a major step, and proved some years later to have been a historical watershed in the development of GDR cultural policy. Even more momentous, however, was what followed. The relevant Party committees and state authorities now carried out a ramified, precisely calculated programme of sanctions, ranging from arrest, house arrest, expulsion from organisations, Party disciplinary procedure and publication bans to the remarkably swift issuing of travel permits (although only for troublesome intellectuals!).

An exodus of authors

The GDR literary community underwent major changes as a result of the fact that a number of creative artists who had in more or less obvious ways helped to shape it were now no longer part of it. Although there was some hope at first that the phase of emigration would be short-lived and involve only a few of the more capable writers, a decade or so later it was clear that the loss of literary substance to the GDR was considerable, even though not all of the hundred or so writers who had meanwhile gone into exile were necessarily worthy of the name.

One means of intimidating writers was the new or tougher penal statutes, which could be implemented, or withheld, as an effective threat. From 1979 onwards there were isolated cases of implementing legislation pertaining to the handling of foreign currency against writers. This happened in cases where writers had had works published by Western publishing houses without having obtained the legally required permission from the GDR Bureau for Copyrights. Previously, GDR authors had frequently availed themselves of the right to freedom of expression enshrined in their Constitution by having their books published in the Federal Republic if they had not yet obtained permission for publication in the GDR: e.g. Biermann, Heym, Kunert and Heiner Müller. Up to 1979 the GDR had largely turned a blind eye to such infringements. Now, however, they brought the full force of the hard-currency statutes to bear against Robert Havemann and Stefan Heym.

The Writers' Association and state power

Caught up in what had ceased to be merely an ideological struggle and was now a direct attack on literature by the state in the form of intervention and encroachment, the official authors' pressure group, the Writers' Association (Schriftstellerverband), played the somewhat ignominious role of assistant to state power.

At the seventh Writers' Association Congress in May 1978, Hermann Kant replaced Anna Seghers, then 78 years old, as president of the Association. Of the twelve initial signatories to the Biermann declaration, only Hermlin and Braun attended the congress. The other ten had either not been nominated as delegates, chose not to take part or, like Becker and Müller, had long ceased to be Association members.

A fresh clash erupted a year later after criminal proceedings were brought against Havemann and Heym for hard-currency offences. Eight writers wrote a letter to Honecker, including the statement: 'There are increasingly frequent attempts to defame, muffle or ... persecute by means of penal statutes politically-committed critical writers.... The coupling of censorship with penal statues is intended to prevent the publication of critical works.' The authors of this letter, Bartsch, Endler, Poche, Schlesinger, D. Schubert, Heym, Jacobs, R. Schneider and Seyppel, were expelled from the Association. Erich Loest preempted his expulsion in Leipzig by leaving the Association 'voluntarily'. Once again, the Party broke with major authors. All told, the Writers' Association lost over 30 authors through expulsion or resignation from 1976 onwards.

Glasnost in the GDR? Cultural policy in the 1980s

In March 1985 Mikhail Gorbachev became leader of the Soviet Union. We now know that this was to have enormous repercussions, both for the country itself, and for the whole world. The question here is whether it also had an effect on the public life of the GDR, and the arts that formed part of it.

The early 1980s had given little encouragement to literature, as the steady stream of emigrants from the GDR shows. Political functionaries concerned with culture continued to prefer and practise aggressive methods while feigning a wholesome self-awareness. The Director of the Hans-Anselm Theatre in Rostock, for example, asserted at the beginning of 1981 that the GDR did not need to trouble itself over the departure of 'isolated writers and artists': 'A nation that has good politicians has no need of bad poets.' Although the ninth Writers' Congress of 1983 sought to redress the balance – Hermann Kant spoke of the 'painful losses' that had affected the Association – this was no fresh start.

The threat to mankind, and Friedenspolitik (peace policy)

It should be borne in mind that from 1980 to 1983 the 'self-silencing' of GDR literature was pushed into the background by other, more pressing themes. The decision of the West, and specifically of the West German parliament in 1979, to rearm now made the prospect of a Third World War very real for many people – an all too probable, indeed almost inevitable threat. It soon became apparent that neither of the two political systems was capable of putting a stop to the increasing escalation of the arms race. The possible self-destruction of the human race thus became not merely a central theme of literature itself, but also of literary policy.

On 13/14 December 1981 in East Berlin the first 'Berlin Encounter for the Fostering of Peace' (*Berliner Begegnung zur Friedensförderung*) took place, attended by 90 creative artists and scientists from East and West. Authors from both camps were frequently able to find common ground in the realisation that responsibility for this dangerous state of affairs lay not with one but both systems, and that both were also products of one and the same 'terminally ill civilisation' (Christa Wolf).

A second such meeting of writers from East and West took place in May 1982 in The Hague. On this occasion, however, the capacity for reaching consensus between the two parties was limited, given the intensified nuclear threat. Many authors did not even bother to attend.

'New thinking'

The years from 1985 to 1986 in the Soviet Union saw the introduction of Gorbachev's programme of reform, and the concept of *glasnost* – the transparency of all social processes, combined with a new, uninhibited approach to the interpretation of the Soviet Union's history. GDR cultural policy responded to all this with distinct aloofness and caution, if not open rejection. Gorbachev's 'new thinking' was either dismissed as an internal affair of the Soviet Union, or as a 'change of wallpaper' (Kurt Hager) that the GDR had no need to imitate. Critical novels (by Chingiz Aitmatov, Valentin Rasputin or Yuri Trifonov) or films (by Elen Klimov or Abuladze) had a hard time reaching the public, or were even banned, whereas Mikhail Shatrov's play *Dictatorship of the Conscience* was performed.

Reactions

In the last three years of the GDR's existence, more and more voices were raised in favour of applying the *glasnost* concept to the cultural life of the

GDR, or at the very least of approving it. Although books and plays were banned in the latter years of the GDR, three of the most important 'new thinking' books were published in the GDR in 1985: Günter de Bruyn's novel *Neue Herrlichkeit* (*New Glory*), Volker Braun's *Hinze-Kunze-Roman* (*The Tom, Dick and Harry Novel*), and Christoph Hein's *Horns End* (*The End of Horn*), which deals openly with the effects of Stalinism in the GDR during the 1950s.

The year 1986 saw the German–German Cultural Accord, which had some minor positive repercussions, if no momentous ones. These included guest theatre performances on an exchange basis, more readings by authors, special 'days' for GDR books and films in towns in the Federal Republic, friendlier and more intensive contact among scientists, and cooperation between the national libraries in Leipzig and Frankfurt-am-Main. Christa Wolf, Heiner Müller and Volker Braun were awarded the highest literary distinction in the GDR, the National Prize. Finally in 1987, Günter Grass could be published in the GDR, Samuel Beckett performed and Nietzsche at least openly discussed. At the tenth Writers' Congress in November 1987, Christoph Hein and Günter de Bruyn launched an attack on censorship, but an initiative to reinstate writers expelled from the Association in 1979 proved unsuccessful.

The alternative movement

Looking beyond established authors and literary institutions to the way the state dealt with the new pacifist and ecological alternative movements in the GDR, our view of the foothold that 'new thinking' had established becomes a little more sober. This also applies to literature, inasmuch as it was the literature of the new subculture.

In this sphere, official policy was far from disposed to tolerate public criticism and protest, even on a mass scale. Dissension reached an early climax with a number of arrests following a demonstration commemorating Rosa Luxemburg and Karl Liebknecht on 17 January 1988. Among those arrested was the 25-year-old singer-songwriter Stephan Krawczyk and his wife, the director Freya Klier. Krawczyk, once an officially celebrated bard, had been banned from public performance, even on church premises, since November 1987. Under duress, Krawczyk and Klier agreed to leave for the Federal Republic. This was the second occasion (since Biermann's deprivation of citizenship in 1976) that the critical young generation of the GDR had been deprived of a symbolic figurehead. Nevertheless, hasty comparisons between 1976 and 1988 were somewhat misleading. Interestingly, there were no conspicuous statements by distinguished creative artists expressing solidarity with those arrested, as there had been in both 1976 and 1978. The entire affair remained confined to the young alternative movement and civil rights activists.

Fact or fiction? Aspects of narrative critical of civilisation

The execution of the narrator?

Around 1970 the sensitive Rostock literary critic and lecturer Kurt Batt repeatedly arraigned West German prose for having allegedly allowed tradition to wither from neglect, for having internalised (political) revolt and executed the narrator as the responsible subject of narrative. In contrast with this he cited the prose of his own country, the GDR, in a tone of vindication: 'Here, narrative takes the form not of a dumb internal monologue, but of a statement requiring an opposite number – an inherent human characteristic, but one that can only evolve, of course, in a society in which people live *with* one another and not *against* one another, a society in which they communicate.' What Batt is putting forward here is the idea of a society of people living together, free from the 'birthmarks' of the old order, and of a corresponding narrative literature, in which the author is free to communicate with an opposite number. Clearly such an assessment will not hold water today.

It would be more accurate to look at GDR prose of the 1970s and 1980s in terms of catching up, in modified form, with a process that had characterised Western European literary developments between 1910 and 1930. GDR prose became 'modern' and 'contemporary' with the Western world to a degree that heralded the imminent collapse of a social transformation – that of democratic, socialist reform into a politically stultified, *'real socialist'* industrial society. To this extent, GDR literature developed, if not an explosively innovative, then at least a considerable diagnostic and prognostic capacity.

Modernising narrative

As long as there remained an unshakeable faith in the possibility of implementing a humane socialist order, in the inexorable nature of progress and hence in Marxism (understood here as a closed doctrinal system), literary narrative also remained marked by the same credulous faith in totality, the same anti-modernity and the same orthodox notion of realism. GDR narrative is the reflection of a particular world-view: closed, thoroughly positive in outlook and possessing a blind faith in the notion of progress.

This affected not only the structural make-up of 1950s novels, but also the *Ankunftsliteratur* of around 1960 (as propounded by such leading authors as Christa Wolf, Brigitte Reimann, de Bruyn and Jakobs, although they were soon to change). It applies in equal measure to 'novels of development' by Strittmatter, Brêzan, Noll and M.W. Schulz, which betray schematisation in their hidebound storylines, choice of heroes and character depiction. All these were clear signs that such an outwardly-oriented aesthetics was incapable of absorbing open modern forms.

Exceptions to this rule were Uwe Johnson (who nevertheless lived in the Federal Republic from 1959 onwards), Johannes Bobrowski, Christa Wolf, Fritz Rudolf Fries and Erich Köhler, whose works were not published at all at that time, and, with reservations, Hermann Kant and Erwin Strittmatter. Prose by these authors is characterised first and foremost by the intervention of moments of reflection (chiefly through the rediscovery of the narrator), subjectivisation, differentiation and multiple perspectives. It took the first steps away from the one-dimensional into the 'infinitely interwoven surface' of life (Robert Musil), the real texture of society. This prose is distrustful of 'objective' chronology and presentations of causality. It places the onus of narrative on individual example, avoiding generalisations as the work of a faculty of reason that sets itself up as an absolute.

'Power to the imagination'

A specific feature of later GDR narrative prose, and one which distinguishes it from that of the classical modern era, is its opposition to the dictatorship of 'instrumental Reason' – the Reason that sets itself up as the sole 'realistic' world-view, the only one interested in reality. It likewise rejects 'mimesis of the rigid and alienated' (Adorno). It shuns the 'spell of rote-learned reality' (again Adorno) not by fleeing from it, but by setting fantasies, phantasms and fictions against it, as a second, alternative reality. In a place where, as Ernst Bloch had written much earlier, 'imagination is virtually a criminal offence', the watchword of literature now became 'power to the imagination'. In order to combat a coalition of terror made up of male dominance, the use of force, war and undiluted technological rationality, this prose proffers the first fruits of a lively imagination and metaphorical thinking.

Irmtraud Morgner was an author who tried to remedy this process of suppression by attempting a systematic retrieval of metaphorical thinking, the power of the imagination. As part of this process she draws on old myths, fairy tales, sagas and legends. Instead of merely retelling these, she rewrites them, expands them and derives new meanings from them, pursuing her own yearnings and dreams. Using them to aid her, she alienates, enchants, and indeed bewitches the commonplace everyday world, allowing the reader a glimpse of the improbable, wonderful alternatives to life as it is now. Morgner's fantastic works transcend the boundaries of empirical reality – a strictly-calculated, rigid, brutal reality – setting against it a solution made up of the de-(ar)ranged, the dislocated and the fabulous. In a historical and social situation characterised by an excess of system, functionality and order, art has to destroy order, to disorder and be literally anarchic.

Apart from Irmtraud Morgner, Fritz Rudolf Fries (*Alexanders neue Welten – Alexander's New Worlds*, 1983; *Verlegung eines mittleren Reiches – Displacement of a Middle Kingdom*, 1985, written in 1967) and Christa Wolf also helped to restore invention and literary fiction to legitimacy. In 1973, Wolf's volume of stories *Unter den Linden* was published, containing three 'improbable stories' that, among other things, take to task the ubiquitous blind faith in science and technology. The authors of the anthologies *Blitz aus heiterm Himmel* (*Bolt From the Blue*) (1975) and *Die Rettung des Saragossameeres* (*The Rescue of the Sargasso Sea*) (1976), as well as Franz Fühmann with his prose volume *Saiäns Fiktschen* (*Science Fiction*) (1981) and Rainer Kirsch with his four stories in the volume *Sauna oder Die fernherwirkende Trübung* (*Sauna or Long-distance Clouding*) (1985), all point in the same direction. As these books and others show, an increasingly urgent theme is the clash between an (apparently) perfectly-functioning world of technical and political apparatuses and the unpredictable element of human subjectivity, which manifests itself as a 'systems error', causing the whole apparatus to collapse, or at least threatening to do so. In this way, the socialist utopia of a better way of life is transformed into a negative version of itself, a warning utopia.

From about 1975 onwards the tendency towards an expansion of the fictional aspect in GDR prose was increasingly matched by an unmistakable and powerful countertendency towards factual documentary literature. On closer inspection, however, this emerges as more than a mere counterbalance. Here, too, in this hunger for real, true, credible stories, there is a discernible need that cannot be stilled either by the routine of everyday life, or by official newspaper and television reports.

First-hand reports, travelogues, diaries, memoirs, reportage, transcripts and unedited interviews contained a promise of authenticity to a degree that is not commonly attributed to fiction. Moreover, in a country where, in the absence of a normally functioning reading public, literature in general served as a substitute for journalism (Thomas Brasch), still more would have been expected from documentary literature.

Documentary literature

The upsurge of documentary literature in the GDR was a prime example. In 1973, Sarah Kirsch published five tape-recorded stories under the title *Die Pantherfrau* (*The Panther Woman*), in which five GDR women of varying social status give accounts of their lives.

Maxie Wander

Then, in 1975, appeared a volume edited by the Austrian Maxie Wander, *Guten Morgen, du Schöne – Frauen in der DDR: Protokolle* (*Good Morn-*

ing, *My Lovely – Women in the GDR: Transcripts*). This book was to alter the literary landscape of the GDR at a single stroke. Women had never before been heard to speak with such openness and vitality. In these conversations they speak with brilliance and linguistic power about their lives, the way they were brought up (most of them in the GDR era), their new families, work, and sexuality, as well as their unfulfilled longings and aspirations. Through the medium of speech they explore areas of life never explored before, evoking new possibilities of living together or alone by bringing the lives they had lived in the past to the full light of consciousness. Hardly any work says as much about the GDR as Maxie Wander's volume of transcripts.

Maxie Wander's volume of transcripts seemed to break a spell. Documentary literature, already a preferred form in the Federal Republic since the increased politicisation of literature after 1967–8, was now to play an increasingly important role in the GDR. It began with a spate of emancipation-oriented books on women, written in the form of first-hand reports, reportage and transcripts. This was followed by books on men, such as Christine Lambrecht's *Männerbekanntschaften. Freimütige Protokolle* (*Male Acquaintances. Frank Transcripts*) (1986) and Christine Müller's *Männerprotokolle* (*Transcripts on Men*) (1986). In the meantime, however, the spectrum of factual literature had expanded enormously: contemporary GDR society was being sounded out on all fronts for authentic information.

The range of themes

If, instead of the customary examination of modes of writing in GDR prose of the 1970s and 1980s, one looks rather at the subject-matter involved, three main thematic areas emerge. First, narrators were dealing far more emphatically and candidly with everyday GDR life in the immediate present. Second, they were also turning to recent history, chiefly fascism, and even more recently Stalinism. Third, they were also tackling ancient history and myth, examining these as models of real life, rewriting them and drawing analogies with present-day reality. Whatever the subject-matter focused on, however, prose in the latter years of the GDR shared the common aim of questioning the foundations of so-called Western civilisation, including the GDR model.

By the early 1970s, GDR prose was for the most part beginning to turn its back on the postulate of the 'harmonious human community', portraying instead the problem-ridden, even foundering and catastrophic relationship between the individual and the community at large. Narrative fiction was concentrating more and more on the experiences and life-stories of individuals who had been ill-used by other individuals and social institutions, and by an authoritarian and purpose-oriented body of regulations.

Failure under socialism?

The openness of authors to conflict, along with the awareness of conflict in their works, was also growing. Error, failure and culpability were sought and found ever more frequently, not only in the individual, but also in the collective body, the state and the Party. Literary heroes in the mould of a firmly-contoured 'socialist human image' were now less and less frequent – this category became obsolete. As *Nachdenken über Christa T.* showed, heroes were now neither 'typical' nor exemplary, but were for this very reason all the more vital, sensual and real. The individual's yearning for happiness, his grief, failures, dying and death now became almost common themes. A seamless 'arrival' in *realer Sozialismus* was now more the exception than the rule.

'A marred life'

This new narrative fiction did more, however, than simply vaguely lament 'oppressed individuals' and their 'marred lives' (Heinrich Mohr). It inquired actively into their origins and recurrence in order to open them up to literary interpretation. This is evinced perhaps most clearly by the breadth and scientific precision with which more recent prose deals above all with the situation of children and young people in GDR society.

Plenzdorf's prose and play version of *Die neuen Leiden des jungen W.* (1972) is an example of how not only taboos of content, but also of language norms can be violated (with his *Jeanssprache*). Like the 'Old Werther', Plenzdorf's Edgar Wibeau suffers from the burden of rigid expectations and coercion to conform placed on him by a society (like Goethe's around 1770) in which people appear to live only in order to work, and who are ultimately afraid of freedom. Plenzdorf's literary success unleashed a string of works on similar themes, concerned with the difficulties of young people seeking self-realisation. These included Rolf Schneider's *Reise nach Jaroslaw* (*A Trip to Jaroslav*) (1974), and above all Volker Braun's *Unvollendete Geschichte* (*Unfinished Story*) (1975). Evidently perceived as coming too close to the bone, the latter was not cleared for publication for thirteen years. At the end of the story, two young people who love each other become aware of the way their lives are being run for them as if they were on leading-strings, and manage to break out. They are damaged, but not destroyed. 'Here began', the last sentence reads, 'other stories, even before the first had come to an end'.

It is astounding to find in the latter GDR era a genre linking it with the Wilhelmine imperial state of around 1900: the *Schulgeschichte* (school story). This genre shows how school drill fosters conformism, competitiveness and careerism, as can be seen in novels by Alfred Wellm, Günter Görlich and Jurek Becker (*Schlaflose Tage – Sleepless Days*) published only in the Federal Republic), as well as in stories by Erich Loest, Reiner Kunze (*Die wunderbaren Jahre* – *The Wonderful Years*, 1976, again published only in the Federal Republic), or Plenzdorf (*kein runter kein fern* – *not down, not far*, 1978, only published in the Federal Republic).

Even more taboo than the school institution was, of course, the military apparatus, which had so far been dealt with only in works by Jürgen Fuchs, who was forced to move to the Federal Republic in 1977 after a period of imprisonment (*Fassonschnitt* – *Crew-cut*, 1984; *Das Ende einer Feigheit* – *The End of a Cowardice*, 1988).

Women's literature

Besides children and young people, women finally also began to make inroads into GDR literature. Women were now writing about women, making demands of the (male-dominated) society, seeking to reclaim their own nature as they envisaged it, and to see their own life-stories as something open and still to be redeemed. Mention has already been made of Maxie Wanders and Sarah Kirsch in connection with their pathfinding interview books. Further forerunners of a GDR women's literature with its own distinct features were the novels *Franzika Linkerhand* (*Frances Left-hand*) by Brigitte Reimann, *Karen W.* by Gerti Tetzner, and *Leben und Abenteuer der Trobadora Beatriz* (*The Life and Adventures of Beatrice the Troubadour*) by Irmtraud Morgner – all three of which were published in 1974. Prose volumes by Helga Schubert, Helga Königsdorf, Christine Wolter, Charlotte Worgitzky, Brigitte Martin, Angela Stachowa, Rosemarie Zeplin, Helga Schütz, Christine Lambrecht, Gabriele Eckart, as well as Monika Maron, Christa Moog, Katja Lange-Müller and Barbara Honigmann (the latter could only be published in the Federal Republic) were to follow over the next twelve years.

Irmtraud Morgner

The most interesting and remarkable book among this new women's literature was Irmtraud Morgner's montage novel *The Life and Adventures of Beatrice the Troubadour*. The author makes considerable demands on her reader, casting spells, dreaming, fantasising and bounding over world history oblivious of the laws of time, space and probability. Beatrice de Diaz, a *Minne* singer, is awakened in 1968 from an 800-year sleep, like Sleeping Beauty, to see if the world has meanwhile become habitable for women, or whether it is still a 'society for owning women' (*Frauenhaltergesellschaft*). Viewing things through the eyes of a foreign troubadour from another country makes it easier both for the GDR reader to see his or her familiar everyday world with fresh eyes, and to inculcate an awareness that it can be changed. The structural principle of alienation by means of historical treatment, montage, confrontation, and comparison of the apparently incomparable is used repeatedly throughout the book: stories, songs and poems, legends, dreams, newspaper and research reports, passages from an Enlightenment book, factual information from nutritional and behavioural science and contemporary history (the Vietnam War), interviews, and many other items are all worked into the story, partly in documentary and partly in fictional form.

In Morgner's equally inspired sequel *Amanda. Ein Hexenroman* (*Amanda: A Witch Novel*) (1983) she writes of the troubadour's resurrection as a siren, equipped with the body of a bird and a human head. Using secret Blocksberg material, she writes the now complete and true story of her familiar character Laura Amanda, a creature with a dual nature, split, like all women, into a 'usable' (earthly, functioning) and an 'unusable' (witch-like) half. A planned third part of the novel trilogy is intended to deal with the reconciliation of these two separate halves.

The 'hope principle' questioned

Books dating from the early and mid-1970s, especially those by women, are as a rule inspired by a principle of hope – specifically by a faith in the utopia of a better, socialist society. Since that time, however, utopian thinking has sunk into deep crisis, a state reflected with seismographic accuracy by critical narrative literature from the GDR in the last decade and a half of its existence. This proved to be nothing short of a massive paradigm shift in the whole philosophy of history. The progress-oriented thinking propounded by the orthodox version of Marxism was now rejected by creative artists, who also abandoned their faith in an inexorable and certain 'arrival' in socialism, followed by communism. The reasons for this are clear. The horizon of creative artists and intellectuals in the GDR was now increasingly obstructed by a chain of traumatic experiences impossible to dismiss that had long since become part and parcel of the awareness of the Western intelligentsia, but which previous unshakeable faith in socialism had helped to suppress.

One thing that could no longer be ignored, for example, was the self-destructive process unleashed by the Enlightenment and the culmination of rationalist modernisation in an 'industrial culture'. This process had not only reached, but had overstepped its limits, and the price it exacted had escalated beyond calculation – most clearly in the phenomena of the arms race and the destruction of the environment. 'The nightmare', said Heiner Müller at the first Berlin Encounter for the Fostering of Peace in December 1981, is 'that the alternatives of socialism versus barbarity are being replaced by another set of alternatives – destruction or barbarity: the end of humanity as the price for the survival of the planet'.

For a long time, people had agreed with Volker Braun that history was for the time being 'incomplete', but nevertheless capable of completion, despite negative experiences with GDR society. Now, however, people felt confronted in all spheres of life by the inexorable implementation of a purpose-oriented rationality, moreover of a specific, Prussian and *realsozialist* type.

Everyday life as a theme

This shift in perspective is amply demonstrated by the polyphonic character of prose on everyday life in the GDR. This new trend represented both a loss and a gain. Never before had GDR prose offered such a 'real' milieu, authentic modes of speech, or such vivid detail about ordinary everyday events in *realer Sozialismus* as are to be found in works by Klaus Schlesinger, Erich Loest, Ulrich Plenzdorf, Kurt Bartsch, Günter de Bruyn, Christoph Hein or Uwe Saeger. Planner and manager characters now largely gave way to a focus on the 'little man'. Many of these literary figures from the 'ruling class' seek refuge from the corrosive effects of the industrial process that continues to control their lives. They flee into private life, the intimacy of the nuclear family, only to discover that here, too, they are worn down. Either they experience private life as a monotonous treadmill, where the most they can look forward to is a new wardrobe or a colour TV (as in Schlesinger's *Alte Filme* – *Old Films*, or Jurek Becker's *Schlaflose Tage* – *Sleepless Days*), or they find that what was once the joy of family life and a partnership has turned into an arena, a battleground (as in Kurt Bartsch's work, or Christoph Hein's brilliant novella *Der fremde Freund* – *The Stranger-Friend*; title in the West *Drachenblut* – *Dragon's Blood*, 1983). This fiction about everyday life does a superb job of demarcating social and spiritual provinces in the GDR by giving an account of a new, thoroughly Philistine petty bourgeoisie in that country.

From another standpoint, its micro-subject-matter and wealth of detail often provide evidence that authors, through the loss of their own future prospects and their blind faith in the GDR social order, have arrived at a convincing narrative perspective, capable of uncovering root causes and connections. This reduction of totality into everyday life produced prose of the 'most up-to-date relevance' à la Hans Fallada. Its strength lay in its observation of the momentary, rather than in its elucidation of socio-historical connections.

Erich Loest's *Es geht seinen Gang oder Mühen in unserer Ebene* (*It Takes its Course, or Efforts on our Lowlands*) represents perhaps the finest example of this tendency. Loest had made his début in 1950 with his war novel *Jungen, die übrig bleiben* (*Boys Left Over*). Later, after seven years imprisonment in Bautzen from 1957–64, he wrote mainly crime novels. The central character of this novel is the unqualified engineer Wolfgang Wülff – no model socialist, but a truly middle-of-the-road hero. He is friendly, intelligent and hard-working, but utterly devoid of ambition – not at all the 'arrivé' socialist 'planner and manager' that his ambitious wife would have him be.

By showing a segment from the everyday life of this man, the ostensible failure, both at work and politically, that even causes the break-up of his marriage, Loest is able to show GDR society as it to a large extent really was at that time: Philistine, stifling, achievement-oriented, authoritarian and self-righteous. Wülff, an insignificant but appealing Philistine, rebels against all this – not in the grand style of the heroic militant, but simply by shunning total absorption into the system, and refusing to conform or surrender himself – to be 'successful' and 'reasonable' where it is expected of him.

The ecology theme

A new and growing aspect of narrative critical of civilisation is a genre that may be described as ecologically critical literature. The actual development of the GDR economy and society supplied literature with a fresh source of subject-matter: the devastation of the natural environment. For a long time authors had had a relatively problem-free relationship with nature, and contact with it. The increasingly widespread exhaustion of natural resources seemed cause for triumph rather than sorrow. Following the first signs of a more sensitive ecological awareness at the beginning of the 1970s among writers such as Erwin Strittmatter and Jurij Brêzan, and above all in literature for children and young people, the period from the 1980s onwards produced a wealth of prose works taking issue with the dubious achievements of *homo faber, homo oeconomicus*. These ranged from Hanns Cibulka's diary stories *Swantow. Die Aufzeichnungen des Andreas Flemming* (*Swantow: the Notes of Andreas Flemming*) (1981) to Christa Wolf's Chernobyl diary *Störfall. Nachrichten eines Tages* (*Malfunction: Record of a Day*), which is nevertheless somewhat unambitious from the literary viewpoint. Most noteworthy is Monika Maron's novel *Flugasche* (*Flying Ash*) (1981), which no GDR publisher was willing to publish.

Bewältigungsliteratur: coming to terms with the past

A substantial proportion of GDR prose aimed to penetrate beyond the surface of everyday life and to expose the roots of the present-day calamity in history, at the same time doing away with 'sedimented' history. In this way, a third phase of *Bewältigungsliteratur* came about from the mid-1970s onwards, concerned this time not only with fascism, but to some extent with Stalinism on German soil.

No book asks the key question, 'How did we come to be what we are today?' with such precision as Christa Wolf in her novel *Kindheitsmuster* (*Childhood Patterns*) (1976). The author seeks to uncover how 'ordinary', commonplace, everyday fascism came about, with the collusion or tolerance, but not the opposition, of countless human beings. She is concerned neither with the heroes of the Resistance, nor with sadistic Nazi criminals, but with the millions of also-rans. With honesty, the author finds them in her own family, that of the grocer Bruno Jordan. The title *Childhood Patterns* refers to the behavioural patterns acquired and set in childhood: fear, hatred, hardness, dissimulation, false piety, the denial of true feelings, subjection and fidelity and the sense of duty without respect for the person involved. These are all character traits that warp a personality and provide fertile soil for a regime such as the Nazi one. The book is narrated in the form of the reminiscences of real people, chiefly the child character Nelly Jordan, all brought to life again with a wealth of expression and metaphor. A brief trip to a place with childhood memories is the trigger that enables the author to release the forgotten and suppressed images of the past. Through the medium of a kind of trial or court hearing of herself, the narrator confronts her past, her own childhood, marred by the values of the petty bourgeoisie, with her present, the year of her trip, 1971. A third plane of the narrative is formed by a further confrontation of her childhood with the author's everyday experiences at the time of writing: 1972–5. A fourth is constituted by reflection on the 'difficulties associated with writing the truth', arising out of a refusal to avoid a taboo theme. The book, a 'struggle for memory' (A. Mitscherlich), documents the process whereby Christa Wolf unlearns self-censorship and learns how to grieve. It likewise achieves a degree of self-criticism of indigenous authoritarian character structures that were still active in the GDR – a fact that criticism of Wolf in 1990 deliberately overlooked.

Criticism of Stalinism

Narrative fiction acquired a new dimension through the lifting of the taboo that had previously pertained to the Stalinist era. The most successful literary attempt to reinstate the suppressed era of the 1950s in the GDR is Christoph Hein's novel *Horns Ende* (*The End of Horn*) (1985), which confirmed the author as one of the finest narrative fiction writers and stylists of his country. The novel relates the story of a man in the 1940s who has a major function in the Party, is expelled from the Party in 1953, and demoted to become the custodian of a small-town museum. In 1957, the period with which the narrative deals, following an entirely unfounded denunciation, he is interrogated by state security officials and found guilty of subversion. He is later found hanged in the forest.

Horn's death is an unsettling development that no longer permits the continued suppression of individual indifferent or cowardly action. Five inhabitants of a small German town give an account of their role in previous events. What emerges is not one single truth about the past, but a diversity of different perspectives of experience. The disturbing aspect for almost all these characters is the discovery that their behaviour during the 1950s was scarcely different from what it had been in the Nazi era.

A major contribution towards coming to terms with the traumatic events of the past, whether from the 1930s and 1940s or the 1950s and 1960s, was made by a large number of autobiographies and memoirs published from the end of the 1970s onwards. Two outstanding examples are by authors who were convinced Nazis in their youth, rapidly became socialists in 1945, and then at a more advanced age were not spared the 'second realisation' that *real existierender Sozialismus* was yet another doctrinaire system with little sympathy for humanity. These were Erich Loest's *Durch die Erde ein Riss. Ein Lebenslauf* (*A Tear Through the Earth: A Career*) (1981, only published in the Federal Republic), and Franz Fühmann's *Der Sturz des Engels. Erfahrungen mit Dichtung* (*The Fall of the Angel: Experiences with Poetry*) (1982). Former socialists such as Stephan Hermlin, whose short poetic autobiography *Abendlicht* (*Evening Light*) was published in 1979, or Stefan Heym, whose substantial volume of memoirs *Nachruf* (*Obituary*) was published in 1988, again only in the Federal Republic, nevertheless had an easier time. However many conflicts these two latter authors, especially Heym, had to endure with the GDR authorities, at the end of their lives they kept intact an unquestioned identity, in both the political and aesthetic spheres, that was no longer possible for authors of younger generations.

A glance at Klassik and Romantik

This transformed view of history was clearly reflected in a radically altered view of the German *Kunstepoche* – the *Klassik* and the *Romantik*. A diversity of essays and narrative texts now began to rethink the previous view of the Classical era, above all Goethe, which had tended to skate over conflicts. There was now a shift in favour of authors seen as 'outsiders', those who had deviated from classical norms, above all the Romantics. Hölderlin (who went mad), Kleist and Günderode (who entered into a suicide pact), Jean Paul and E.T.A. Hoffmann, who lived and wrote as loners and 'odd' characters, now became a focus of attention. This may be seen in works by de Bruyn (on Jean Paul and others), Fühmann (on Hoffmann and others), Gerhard Wolf (on Hölderlin), Kunert (*Pamphlet für K.*, i.e. Kleist, 1975), Sigrid Damm (on Lenz and Goethe's sister Cornelia), Brigitta Struzyk (on Caroline Schlegel-Schelling), and above all Christa Wolf. Wolf's essays on Kleist, Bettina von Arnim and Karoline von Günderode, and above all her novella *Kein Ort. Nirgends* (*No Place: Nowhere*) (1979), written during the great depression of GDR intellectuals that followed Biermann's deprivation of citizenship, examine the alternative lifestyle and literary concepts of the Romantics with a view to deriving some means of overcoming their own crisis. Quasi-autobiographical works parallel to this period of crisis are Christa Wolf's *Sommerstück* (*Summer Piece*) (published in 1989, although written ten years earlier) and Sarah Kirsch's *Allerleih-Rauh* (*Hotch-potch Galore*) (1988).

Ancient myths

GDR narrators turned in the late 1970s and 1980s not only to history, but also to fairy-tales, legends, and above all ancient myths. Authors sought to decipher myths, first and foremost ancient Greek myths – although Fühmann also dealt with biblical ones – focusing on the history of philosophy. Myths were seen as the original metaphors for a highly conflict-ridden history of Western civilisation, for a questionable means of shaping human reason and 'its other aspect' (*ihres Anderen*) (Hartmut Böhme), namely the body, the senses, and the emotions of human beings. What fascinated them about myth, in the words of Heiner Müller, was 'the return of the Same ... under quite different circumstances ... , and thereby the return of the Same as its other aspect'. What manifests itself in this 'work on myth', to use Hans Blumenberg's term, is the return of suppressed, postponed traumas that have not been dealt with.

This had been discernible in the numerous retold ancient myths of Hermlin, Fühmann and Rolf Schneider, and was now in Fühmann's mythological tales (*Der Geliebte der Morgenröte – The Beloved of the Dawn*, 1978; *Das Ohr des Dionysius – The Ear of Dionysius*, 1985), Morgner's bizarre novels, and above all Christa Wolf's ambitious Cassandra project, consisting of the story *Cassandra* and the Frankfurt lectures *Kassandra: Voraussetzungen einer Erzählung* (*Cassandra: the Pre-Requisites for a Story*) (1983).

Christa Wolf's Cassandra project

Cassandra, daughter of the Trojan King Priam, had had the gift of soothsaying bestowed on her by Apollo, albeit with the accompanying curse that no-one would believe her pronouncements. After the fall of Troy she was captured as a prisoner of Agamemnon and taken to Mycenae, where she became the innocent victim of Clytemnestra's revenge against her husband.

Christa Wolf saw in Cassandra 'one of the first female characters ... whose destiny preempts what was to happen to women for the next three thousand years: she is turned into an object. ... Her inner story is her struggle for autonomy.' For Wolf, the events that take place around Cassandra expose the root causes of the present-day world – the 'mega-machine' of 'destructive irrationality'. Here she sees the formation of that specifically masculine, belligerent, goal-oriented type of civilisation of early Greece and Mycenae that was to prevail both over the Cretan-Minoan culture (envisaged as being of a more matriarchal character), and over Troy. By reconstructing the imaginary internal monologue of the mythological figure Cassandra, the story attempts to find and implement a poetic solution to the ossification of our thought processes and our civilisation. More than this, *Cassandra* contains a palimpsest-like account of the GDR's system of surveillance and spying, already described by Wolf in minute detail and utterly without camouflage in her story *Was bleibt* (*What Remains*), describing the daily routine of the author herself, who was relentlessly observed by the Stasi secret police. Understandably, this text was not published at the time, but only in 1990, unleashing a considerable debate both about her as a person, and about courage and cowardice, toeing the line and resistance among GDR intellectuals – a debate known as the German–German literature debate.

GDR prose at the end of the 1980s evokes a heterogeneous, and above all non-contemporary impression. Some of the best GDR authors were living and working in the West by then, and therefore no longer reaching their original readership. First and foremost, however, a gulf now yawned between proponents of a pre-modern brand of narrative that remained popular in the GDR until its demise, but was scarcely known in West Germany, and a growing vanguard of modern narrative authors. The intellectual and literary scene of the GDR had become one of 'new lucidity' (*neue übersichtlichkeit* – Habermas), and Western readers were right to equate GDR prose with Christa Wolf alone.

Theatre against suppression and forgetting

Facts and figures

From the end of the 1950s, theatre in the GDR was shaped by the contradiction that its most important contemporary plays were either never staged at all, or only after considerable delays. The proponents of orthodox cultural policy were alarmed by the idea that palpable manifestations of dubious circumstances in the country might unsettle audiences, or even lead them to protest. This unfortunate state of affairs persisted, essentially unaltered, well into the 1980s.

After the 1970s, GDR theatre as a whole slid into a crisis already familiar in Western industrial countries. In 1955, its sixty-eight theatres (with some 200 stages), could still boast some 17.4 million theatre-goers. However, from then on attendance figures fell sharply, reaching their lowest point (10.4 million) in 1979. A temporary rise in attendance was recorded in 1980, but thereafter audience figures steadily declined to under 10 million.

In proportion to the population, these were still healthier statistics than those of the Federal Republic, but as elsewhere theatre in the GDR came under increasing competition from audio-visual media to an extent that hit its vital nerve.

In attempting to map out the constellation of major theatre writers and their subject-matter and aesthetic concepts in the 1970s and 1980s, one is bound to record a turn for the worse, and a loss of former lucidity. History, as treated by Brecht's immediate successors, as well as the 'production' play, had long ceased to be major genres. GDR theatre was now dominated by aging former 'anti-aircraft artillery soldiers' and members of the Hitler Youth generation, represented by Heiner Müller on the one hand, and Hacks, Strahl and Helmut Baierl on the other.

Authors who as lyric poets so obviously constituted a generation of uninhibited, ambitious *Stürmer und Dränger* were never even remotely homogeneous in the theatrical sphere. The comedy playwright Armin Stolper (born 1934), Ulrich Plenzdorf, the workers' writer Paul Gratzik, the occasional playwrights Rainer Kirsch and Karl Mickel, or the latecomer Harald Gerlach have to be seen as quite individual authors, who made no lasting impression on GDR theatre. Following the earlier or later departure of Hartmut Lange, Kurt Bartsch and Einar Schleef from the GDR, the sole remaining representative of this generation was Volker Braun, without whom GDR theatre would have been unthinkable.

No noticeable shift in the generation of playwrights took place until the appearance of Christoph Hein, Stefan Schütz, Thomas Brasch and perhaps also Lothar Trolle. For the most part, their personal mentor was no longer Bertolt Brecht, but Heiner Müller, from whom in the most favourable cases (such as Christoph Hein) they then distinctly distanced themselves. From him they learned that theatre calls for subject-matter of real substance, a bold 'operative' strategy and above all a distinctive poetic theatrical language.

By comparison, plays by so-called young playwrights, mostly around forty, seem somewhat irresolute – both dramaturgically and stylistically insipid, despite the fact that these authors were turning to contemporary GDR themes. The most gifted among this group were Jochen Berg, Uwe Saeger, Jürgen Gross, Albert Wedt, Georg Seidel, Heinz Drewniok, and Peter Brasch, one of Thomas Brasch's brothers. Apart from Berg, who wrote pieces set in antiquity, these authors found their themes mostly in the everyday life of *real existierender Sozialismus*, where they located problems also familiar in the Federal Republic: double standards and opportunism, consumerism and coldness in human relationships. Despite criticism with regard to detail, however, most of these plays fail to transcend 'affirmative everyday realism' (Klaus Siebenhaar). A distinctive, provocative theatrical style was rare.

Generally speaking, the emphasis of 1970s drama did not lie on contemporary plays marked by a shift to a more topical approach in the strict sense of the term. Christoph Hein, who emerged during the 1970s and 1980s as a playwright of some stature, stated aptly: 'Plays written in the present day are contemporary plays. It strikes me as important to state this banal fact, because nowadays a contrast is emerging between so-called historical and contemporary plays. . . . The present day is on trial at all events. The theatre is no substitute for the provision of newspaper and correspondence reports.'

Like Hein, Volker Braun, Heiner Müller and the younger authors Thomas Brasch and Stefan Schütz all resisted the burden of replacing a constricted press – a task most often placed on prose (or taken on by prose authors). Instead, with more concerted efforts than during the 1950s and 1960s, they made it their business to come to grips with and open up the confused and suppressed historical process. The latter had sunk into the morass of 'stagnant contradictions' (Fühmann) of the re-ossified, hierarchical, authoritarian and still profoundly inhumane society of their country.

Similar features to those found in prose may also be found in the theatre. The reconstruction of the patently derailed historical development of their own nation, and perhaps even of the entire species, can cover a variety of mid- or long-term periods – fascism, Prussian German history or the history of Western civilisation as a whole, the latter's salient structural elements and metaphorical figures being sought predominantly in early Greek mythology and history.

No other playwright delved so obstinately or so deeply into the 'text of history' as Heiner Müller. He, too, only gradually realised the necessity of elaborating 'historical consciousness as consciousness of self' (Volker Braun), i.e. explaining what is being currently lived out and produced in terms of the deposits left by history. 'Explanation' alone is not enough, however. History, and German history especially, is neither something over and done with, nor something outside us, an historical process that is allegedly objective, ongoing and making progress 'automatically'. It is when seen in this light that history and the present day become fused. For the same reason, Müller takes issue with all those who fail to see the present-day relevance of his play about fascism, *Die Schlacht* (*The Battle*). He wrote to one critic in 1975: 'The very fact that you regard the question as necessary points to the answer: the erosion of historical consciousness by a facile concept of the topical. The theme of fascism is topical, and I fear it will remain so in our lifetime.'

Müller approached the historical process in stages. Scenes and fragments written in the early 1950s already deal with the immediately preceding phase in German history – the Nazi regime and World War II. Müller was to go into these in more depth in *Die Schlacht* and *Germania Tod in Berlin* (*Germania: Death in Berlin*). Later, in the 1960s, he turned to mythical models, in such plays as *Herakles, Prometheus* and *Philoktet*. These seek to analyse the history of Western civilisation as the history of a repressive conquest of Nature by mankind, including our own instinctive drives.

As a consequence of this process, Müller was bound to arrive step by step at German history, and hence Prussia and fascism – always seen from the perspective of his own experience of the present-day GDR. In his plays of the 1970s, therefore, he had 'the historical clock run backwards' (Genia Schulz) to the failed revolution of 1918–19, to Prussia under Friedrich Wilhelm I and Friedrich II, and finally to the 'Germanic heritage' – as far back as Arminius and Flavius and the heroes of the Nibelungen in his *Germania* play. Müller adapts a quotation from Edgar Allan Poe: 'The terror of which I write comes from Germany.'

In *Die Schlacht* (1974), the author is still content to portray the 1945 'zero point' in horrendous, shocking images of war, seen as licensed butchery – without elaborating on the history leading up to these events. All that essentially remains is a collection of butchers, murderers and others contemptuous of humanity, the only people with the will to survive. The inevitable, implicit question behind the play is what kind of socialism is it, and what will it become, that has had to be built on such foundations and with such people?

The history of instinctual drives

Germania Tod in Berlin (completed in 1976) and Müller's play about Prussia, *Leben Gundlings Friedrich von Preussen Lessings Schlaf Traum Schrei* (*The Life of Gundling Frederick of Prussia Lessing's Sleep Dream Shout*) (1977), ultimately decipher German history as the history of instinctual drives – something quite new for the GDR. Müller depicts it as the progressive deformation of the structure of human instinctual drives, leading to the transformation of external, alien urges into self-induced urges ('Every man his own Prussian' is the core statement of the play), the shaping of the authoritarian, sadomasochistic character, and the perversion of the life-enhancing potential for productivity that is inherent to the species into the (fascist) manufacture of death. Müller consequently refuses to provide a positive perspective for the future in his plays, limiting himself instead to what he calls 'constructive defeatism'. Whereas some of his more recent plays are entirely in this vein (such as *Hamletmaschine*, 1978, and *Quartett*, 1981), which made them difficult to perform in the GDR, in other plays Müller strives to achieve a constructive interpretation of the historical process (above all in *Der Auftrag. Erinnerung an eine Revolution – The Mandate: Recollections of a Revolution*, 1980).

Collages without plot

Müller's plays written in the 1980s also show how difficult it is to pin down this dramatist, by now performed all over the world, to a particular world-view or style. He continued to write 'synthetic fragments', collages without plot, as the only form that could do justice to the fragmentary state of history, the modern world and the individuals in it. More recent plays, such as *Verkommenes Ufer Medeamaterial Landschaft mit Argonauten* (*A Ruined Shore of Medea Material: Landscape with Argonauts*) (1983), or *Bildbeschreibung* (*Description of a Picture*) (1985), which set the 'machine of myth' in motion again, dealing above all with the extremely alienated character of male–female relationships in the various stages of patriarchy, seem to owe more to the spirit of Neostructuralism (Foucault, Deleuze, Baudrillard) than to Marxism. Nevertheless, Müller was to surprise his audiences again. His *Wolokolamsker Chaussee* (*Volokolamsky Road*) (1987) deals with the history of the founding of socialism as one of terror and death, and, albeit very obliquely, the age-old vision of a communist utopia.

By this time, Heiner Müller had become something of a mentor to young GDR dramatists. Like the older Müller, Thomas Brasch (particularly with *Rotter*, 1977), Stefan Schütz (e.g. in *Michael Kohlhaas*, 1978), and even Volker Braun, they all either took German history seriously to task as a continuous process of terror, or (like Berg and Schütz) drew from Greek mythology. With his *Simplex Deutsch. Ein Spielkasten für Theater and Schule* (*Simplex German: a Toy-box for Theatre and School*) (1980) and *Siegfried Frauenprotokolle Deutscher Furor* (*Siegfried: Women's Transcripts: German Furore*) (1986), Braun dealt in almost Müller-like fashion with the body of German history. He treats it as a succession of revolutions without revolutionaries, wars and civil wars, with their stereotyped *modus operandi* of murder and manslaughter.

Christoph Hein

Undoubtedly the outstanding figure among younger historical dramatists is Christoph Hein. Hein inquires into history in order to uncover models or model figures from which something could be learned today, even in socialism. In this process he encounters such disparate characters as the leader of the English revolution, Oliver Cromwell, whose 'murderous virtues' interest him (*Cromwell*, 1979), and Ferdinand Lassalle, the intelligent, Philistine, passionate and self-immolating architect of the German workers' movement (*Lassalle fragt Herrn Herbert nach Sonja. Die Szene ein Salon – Lassalle Asks Mr Herbert After Sonya. The Scene a Salon*, 1979). Around these characters he groups stage-plays and plays of ideas (such as the historical and parabolic stories contained in his volume *Einla-*

dung zum Lever Bourgeois (*An Invitation to a Bourgeois Levee*) (1980), which bring the present into focus by exploring history.

Hein's most successful play to date, *Die wahre Geschichte des Ah Q* (*The True Story of Ah Q*) (1983), based on a Chinese novella, develops still further the analysis in earlier plays of intellectuals, who are either excluded from the everyday life of society, or exclude themselves from it. His *chinoiserie*, a blend of realistic passages, parable and clowning, aims to portray the unproductive, reflective, second-hand lifestyle of intellectuals that in case of doubt allows them to fall victim to the powerful, or become their tools – a recurring theme of Marxist dramatists from Brecht's *Turandot* to Müller's *Hamletmaschine*. The period both before and after the major recent political turning-point brought sobering confirmation of the topicality of Hein's parable. His last play, *Die Ritter der Tafelrunde* (*The Knights of the Round Table*) (1989) has proved to be an eloquent metaphor for the final phase of the GDR, marked by the unstoppable disintegration of the *ancien régime*.

Lyric poetry against a symmetrical world

Lyric poetry as breakout

During the 1960s, lyric poetry had a major function as a forerunner in the literary development of the GDR. It was able before other genres to break out of the norms of reflection, representativeness and social activism. Older authors, such as Arendt, Huchel and Bobrowski, were not alone in resisting the appropriation of poetry for the purposes of political pedagogy: younger ones followed suit. Their poetry in practice accomplished something that had thus far seemed impossible. They managed to find a middle way between the Scylla of co-option, hostile to literature (the salient aspect of the 1950s) and the Charybdis of pure aesthetic autonomy. This was a synthesis of social relevance and subjectivity, politics and poetry, acceptance and provocation – a reconciliation of opposites that was to prove extraordinarily fruitful in lyric poetry. The very nature of the genre of lyric poetry allowed it from the outset to adopt a superior position *vis-à-vis* the demand of 'socialist realism' to depict alleged reality (complete with all the 'right' political assessments, of course) – a position far more difficult to achieve in prose. This enabled the lyric poetry of the 1960s to become the driving force behind a self-assured, aesthetically ambitious, modern GDR literature as a whole.

Practice: the 'devourer of utopias'

This lyric poetry of 'working subjectivity' (D. Schlenstedt/G. Maurer) was nevertheless to slide into crisis from the mid-1970s. The increasingly crass

impingement of scientific and technological rationality, the motor of socialist as well as Western industrial society, the doldrums being experienced
in social and political life and the increasing rigidity of cultural policy all
took their toll on poetry, taking the form of grief, fear and despair where
previously hope and the praise of hard work had once reigned. Lyric
poetry of the 1980s and 1980s is similarly marked by the perceptible fading
of former socialist-Humanist dreams. Practice had emerged from its cocoon
as the 'devourer of utopias' (H. Müller). All this affected not only authors
of the older and middle generations, ranging from Arendt and Huchel to
Kunert and Endler, but was especially striking among lyric poets of the
activist awakening that had first made its impact on the reading public at
the beginning of the 1960s.

Losses after Biermann's deprivation of citizenship

Obviously the more or less voluntary resettlement of authors in West
Germany following Biermann's deprivation of his citizenship proved the
heaviest blow to lyric poetry, compared with other genres. The departure
of Huchel (as early as 1971), Biermann, Kunze, Sarah Kirsch, Jentzsch,
Bartsch, Brasch, and Tragelehn removed virtually at a stroke an irreplaceable number of the GDR's leading poets. Others were to follow, mainly
younger poets, such as Frank-Wolf Matthies, Bernd Wagner, Sascha Anderson, Wolfgang Hilbig and Uwe Kolbe. This exodus marked the disintegration of the group consciousness of an entire generation – that of 1960s
GDR lyric poetry.

Changes in writing style

With a more sober world-view among authors on the one hand, and a
state-instigated shift in the function of poetry on the other, not only did
the themes of GDR lyric poetry undergo profound changes from the mid-
1970s onwards, but also writing styles. Both changes are equally remarkable. With respect to changes of theme, Brecht's insight – that the 'troubles
of the mountains' were now passé, and authors must now reorient themselves towards the 'troubles of the lowlands' – now filtered down to the
younger generation. Kunert spoke sarcastically of the 'historical low' in
which they now found themselves.

It did not stop there, however. Historical scepticism and loss of faith in
the notion of progress deepened in the course of the 1970s into an overall
critique of civilisation *per se* that was nothing short of a radical 'last-days'
consciousness. In this respect lyric poetry was no different from prose or
drama. Günter Kunert was not alone now in finally taking leave of 'utopia,
the principle of hope'.

A prime example of this paradigm shift may be seen in the treatment of the mythological figures who now began to people lyric poetry in ever greater numbers. There was a departure not only from embodiments of light and pleasure, such as Apollo and Aphrodite (beloved by Georg Maurer, for example), but also from the heroic founders of civilisation itself, such as Prometheus and Heracles. These were now eclipsed in lyric poetry by the ambivalent, problematic figures of Western civilisation: Sisyphus, Odysseus and, again and again, by Icarus and Daedalus. These were augmented both by female embodiments of suffering, such as Niobe and Cassandra, and suffering representatives of art, chiefly Marsyas and Orpheus. As in other genres, mythological figures from the early history of civilisation symbolised a historical process whose outcome seemed increasingly hopeless and was already present in latent form in the violent proclivities of early history.

'Farewell to lovely nature'

This far-reaching change in GDR lyric poetry in the 1970s and 1980s is most clearly discernible in the nature and landscape poetry that had always played an important role. Almost without exception, a 'farewell to lovely nature' (Ursula Heukenkamp) took place. In the 1950s, Becher, Fürnberg and Maurer had still been able to celebrate 'lovely nature' as revealing true humanity. Now, however, that a symmetry had been discerned between the destructive process of civilisation in West and East alike, nature was portrayed as utterly desolate and condemned, doomed to destruction. This left nothing for nature lyric poetry to work with, in a 'reworked landscape' subjugated to the yardsticks of industrialist rationale. Nature lyrics had no choice now but to become a landscape poetry whose subject-matter was an insoluble fusion of nature, industrial culture and history – all with a strong accent on the imminent danger that nature itself would disappear as a result of its subjugation and invasion by civilisation. In his 1970 poem *Landwüst* (*Landwaste*), Volker Braun had already noted tersely: 'Natürlich bleibt nichts. / Nichts bleibt natürlich' ('Nothing remains natural(ly). / Natural(ly) nothing remains'). His poem *Industrie*, dating from the same period, elaborates on the specific implications of this:

> In der mitteldeutschen Ebene verstreut
> Sitzen wir, hissen Rauchfahnen.
> Verdreckte Gegend. Glückauf
> Und ab in die Wohnhülsen. . . .
> Regen pisst auf Beton. Mensch
> Plus Leuna mal drei durch Arbeit
> Gleich
> Leben.

Scattered over the central German plain
We sit, with smoke-trail flags hoisted.
Filthy landscape. Power to your elbow
And off back to your dwelling-capsule. . . .
Rain pisses on to concrete. Man
Plus *Leuna* times three divided by labour
Equals
Life.

From the mid-1970s, Jürgen Rennert's statement: 'Es stirbt das Land an seinen Zwecken' ('The land is dying from its purposes') likewise became the motto of a critical ecological lyric nature poetry, encompassing proponents of all ages. It spanned a range from still somewhat conventional evocations of the remnants of wholesome nature (for example, by Eva Strittmatter) through the sympathetic but aesthetically imitative warning poems of Hanns Cibulka, to the major historic landscape poems of Volker Braun or Wulf Kirsten. Kirsten's poetry in particular draws on various historical phases, creating a montage of obsolete but still extant aspects of reality and, for example, fragments of perception from the egalitarian industrial present. This permits a clear view of what is being lost in the 'grinding-mill of history', the 'shredder of progress', until in the end 'the homeland decays into a non-district / and no-man's-land'.

Poems by such authors as Kirsten defy the narrow categorisation of 'eco-lyric poetry'. Although, like hundreds of other poems, they deal with the devastation of nature and the destruction of the environment, describing 'refuse landscapes' (Ursula Heukenkamp) and other forms of the *nature morte* phenomenon, these, admittedly dominant, motifs nevertheless, in the better poems, always constitute a protest against a world that has become too neat and tidy – too symmetrical (to use the words of Hölderlin and Braun). This does harm not only to visible nature, but also to the inner nature of man himself, his subjective capacity for life. Lyric poetry of the 1970s and 1980s is hence increasingly marked by a radical, sober reflection on the self, on the basis of an experience evoked by Volker Braun, for example, in his Rimbaud essay (1985). Here he states: 'I'm stuck in the socialist gravel. Province, that is the empty moment. History in the sidings. Status quo. What can make us suffocate: to fall from a time in motion to time stood still.'

In the work of Braun and elsewhere, the outcome of this process of self-recognition is a lyric language that threatens to lose its communicative quality. The montage of disparate fragments, the metaphorical language of 'absolute poetry', the tendency towards radical stylistic terseness (intended to combat the meaning and significance of pretentious verbosity characteristic of official discourse), and experimentation with stylistic material as such, all now made wide inroads into GDR lyric poetry, and finally modernised it. This process took place side by side with that already described in the case of prose. What had hitherto seemed reserved for older authors, such as Arendt or Huchel, now applied to authors such as Mickel, Braun and Wolfgang Hilbig, and even more so to the younger, and youngest, poets, such as Uwe Kolbe, Bert Papenfuss-Gorek and Stefan Döring. Basing themselves on a radical scepticism *vis-à-vis* the official language of watchwords and regulations, these younger authors fundamentally rethought the use of their instrument, language itself. Suspicious of the claims of traditional poetry (not only *realsozialistisch* poetry) to represent reality, they made language itself the subject of their poetic practice. Drawing, consciously or unconsciously, on the diverse traditions of avant-garde literature, the greater part of young GDR lyric poetry now began to reflect on language and experiment with it. Volker Braun continued to fragment existing language with the intention of thereby coming closer to distorted reality, and restoring a profound relationship to it. Most young poets, however, were far removed from such an 'operative' poetics. Their sole aim was the twofold one of destruction, or one might say de-construction, of the fixations that ran over language, and free play with the linguistic elements released by this process. Sascha Anderson's statement: 'apart from my language I have / no means of leaving my language' is a reiteration of Wittgenstein's statement 'The boundaries of my language demarcate the boundaries of my world.' Here, however, Wittgenstein's dictum, critical of perception and sceptical, is applied to bring about an open, innovative aesthetics of poetry. Beyond the discourse of political and other orders, which inclines towards maintaining norms, an unconstrained, malleable language of poetry was discovered. In the given circumstances, this seemed the only productive way of enabling the individual to free himself. The 1989–90 turning-point, however, so thoroughly freed GDR individuals that not only established, but even this alternative GDR literature, too, has been dislocated.

Born into it and dropping out of it: young literature of the GDR

Diversity and critical consensus

If the dogmatic proponents of the pre-modern are excluded, GDR literature of the 1970s and 1980s shares one common denominator, which may be summarised under two aspects. It is against the principle of 'instrumental Reason', and against all the damage and destruction to the individual, society and nature that this principle has wrought. Moreover, it uses aesthetic procedures that have left the doctrines of 'socialist realism' far behind, and evince a confident use of the representational vehicles of modern and avant-garde movements. It may now even be unequivocally asserted that it displays a clear rejection of the 'dictatorship of a single trend in literature'. Diversity, polyphony, experimentation and artistic autonomy were not only heralded, but were actually present in literature itself. 'Self-discovery has now taken its place against being shown, reflection before proof, attitude before insight, practice before imitation', as Robert Weimann, one of the leading literary scholars of the GDR, aptly states.

From out of this critical consensus, which in the meantime united writers of *all* generations, the literary practice of the young generation stands out to such a marked degree from the end of the 1970s that it explodes even the already expanded conception of GDR literature. At first tentatively, and largely outside the well-trodden paths leading to the public, young authors began to emerge who were all 'untainted GDR products' (as Wolf Biermann said of Jürgen Fuchs), inasmuch as their knowledge of the West derived not from direct experience, but solely from television. They had been 'born into' socialism, to quote the title of a volume of poetry by Uwe Kolbe, and had been unable to experience any alternative to it. By the time they had grown up, this socialism could no longer be viewed as a hope, only as a 'deformed reality' (Heiner Müller). They could no longer see themselves as 'those born after' (*Nachgeborene*) the dark times of fascism and war, granted the privilege of moving towards better, friendlier times (as had been Brecht's expectation). The well-meaning idea that it was their turn to take up the baton of the socialist project and hand it on was alien to them. 'By now, anyone who still uses the harmonising metaphor makes himself ridiculous, if anything. Young people today are either not in the handing-on position, or else they have missed the right moment for stretching out their hand. It is no longer worth the effort of taking hold of that dried-out piece of wood being offered them with such ceremony, or to continue running in the direction allegedly destined by the historical process' (M. Jäger).

It was no coincidence that Volker Braun, the former enthusiastic bard of the 1960s, became the contrasting figure in this new-found self-awareness. As early as 1979, Uwe Kolbe had indicated: 'My generation has its arms folded as far as politically-committed action is concerned. No early Braun today. . . . I could go further, and say that this generation is completely at a loss, unable to perceive either the right sense of being at home here, or the existence of alternatives elsewhere.' Fritz-Hendrik Melle, on the other hand, states casually and curtly: 'Volker Braun? All I can say is, the boy is a suffering soul. I've no time for all that any more. I grew up in an already frustrated society. This disappointment is no longer an experience for me. It's a fact of life.'

The Prenzlauer Berg scene

Young authors such as these no longer had their sights set on an official 'career'. On the contrary, they were more inclined to drop out, and in some cases had never been part of the regimented system of *real existierender Sozialismus*. They tended to seek jobs on the periphery of society, contributing in some way to the reproduction, although not the production, of the society they disliked so much, with its growth- and consumer-oriented values. They usually lived in the rear courtyards and basement flats of Prenzlauer Berg in East Berlin, or other such dilapidated old tenement quarters (with very low rents) in large cities such as Dresden, Leipzig, Jena, Weimar or Karl-Marx-Stadt. As Ingrid and Klaus-Dieter Hähnel wrote in 1981, 'Prenzlauer Berg has long ceased to be a mere residential district: it is a state of mind. The cracks in the walls of these rear courtyard tenement buildings not infrequently correlate with the "cracks" and "gaps" in the self.' In the latter days of the GDR an artistic community crystallised in Prenzlauer Berg that in turn formed part of a wider community of people unwilling to be part of mainstream society. This position needs to be understood as a rebellion against the Philistinism of *realer Sozialismus*.

Seen in this light, the young, 'alternative' literature of the GDR is but one facet of a new kind of counter-culture orientation among modern GDR youth – an orientation involving a wholesale rejection of the industrialised world, the new middle class and state-controlled youth culture. At the extreme end of this group are punks, who began to appear in the large cities. Although hardly ever taking the form of confrontation, this counter-culture is, like others, clearly defined. Its 'lowest common denominator' is 'Piss Off' (D. Dahn).

The aspiration towards self-determination pertains not merely to the production and dissemination of literature for an 'alternative' readership, but also to *what* is to be said in that literature. If one refuses allegiance to 'power', its institutions and language, and becomes totally suspicious of ideology *per se*, one then adopts a fundamentally anti-ideological position that flatly refuses to accept any fixed world-view that can be enshrined in dogmas. A representative mode of speech is no longer possible. There is no more mention of progress, optimism, or hope for something entirely different – the truly socialist society. The GDR is experienced as a country in which one is imprisoned, out of which it is scarcely possible to travel, although one can tear oneself out of it once and for all. It is a stagnant pool, a cut-off, 'deadlocked contradiction' with which one has nothing to do as an individual, and from which one no longer expects anything.

A predilection for language

What, however, becomes of a literature that no longer seeks to convey a message – a literature, as Uwe Kolbe puts it, that does not want to replace one faith with another? What it did was to stake its all on language, with a degree of radicalism and exclusiveness that had thus far been foreign to GDR literature. This took place in three ways (usually concomitantly): (1) the predominant mainstream language is criticised, and even de-constructed; (2) Language is discovered as a plaything from which another, liberated language can be generated; (3) Beyond its destructive and merely playful aspects, poetic language develops into a counter-language in opposition to the mainstream, 'ruling' language. To quote Heiner Müller, it seeks to set off a discourse that 'excludes nothing and no-one'. Although this had already been done by members of the now middle-aged generation, such as Elke Erb, Wolfgang Hilbig or Gert Neumann, younger authors, such as Bert Papenfuss-Gorek, Stefan Döring, Sascha Anderson, Rainer Schedlinski, Leonhard Lorek and Jan Faktor took it to new, hitherto unknown bounds of radicalism and, in some cases, virtuosity.

The end of the GDR also spelled the end of this exciting literary subculture. Nevertheless, although a closely-knit group is no longer discernible, there are still a number of interesting individual authors whose future progress is well worth following. The fact that two, or possibly more, of the instigators, Sascha Anderson and Rainer Schedlinski, were secret police informants for many years does nothing to detract from this. The Prenzlauer Berg myth has been tarnished, but the creative output of this 'plantation' (Adolf Endler) is not quite dead. A handful of the gardeners who sowed seeds there were also forces to be reckoned with. The acceptance of this means, once again, acknowledging the authoritarian state of the GDR rather than acquitting it. At all events, the greater or lesser merit of literature, unfortunately, is not measured solely in terms of the strength of character of its originators.

LITERATURE OF THE FEDERAL REPUBLIC

The literary scene

Contemporary German literature does not, of course, exist merely in a definable relationship to political reality in the Federal Republic. Via a diversity of institutions and organisations, it is also an integral part of the social life of the country – of public discussion and of cultural and political issues. At the same time, however, it is also contingent on the given economic conditions prevailing in that cultural life, which also shape the cultural sphere. It is contingent, for example, on the way the publishing industry is organised on a private capital basis, as well as on the public structure of radio and television companies, commercial interests, which reduce books to their commodity character, bestseller lists, sales turnover and publishing strategies and other considerations. All these factors underlying literary life need to be taken into account if one seeks to do justice to the literary work that emerges out of this complex mechanism.

It has become customary to characterise the diverse forms of literary life in the Federal Republic by the critical and apt term *Literaturbetrieb* – the literary scene or business. Used neutrally, it denotes the sphere of production, distribution and consumption of literature. Compared, however, with the model of the *Literaturgesellschaft* (literature society of) fostered in the GDR, the term 'literature business' also designates a spontaneous, disordered, contradictory and thus far more hectic mode of literary production. It denotes the exertion needed to bring out books, the bustle of the book market, book fairs and readings by authors, the competing forms of self-representation by publishers, and the vanities so often evinced in literary criticism, the character of exhibitions, book reviews on radio and television and the star roles increasingly being accorded to prominent authors in the mass-media age. The literary scene or business, understood as the sum total of phenomena that go to make up literary life in the Federal Republic, is, in other words, the diverse and multi-faceted market in which author and work alike are obliged to act and survive.

The status of the author

Seen against this background, the situation of authors in West German society can be more precisely defined. Here the profession is generally practised freelance – a notion that still owes much to an archaic idea of the individual intellectual worker, far removed from the constraints of profession, institution or organisation, diligently behind his desk and pursuing his craft as he chooses.

In reality this image is deceptive, and has been ever since there have been 'freelance' authors. Even Gotthold Ephraim Lessing realised that there was a market to which he as a 'free' poet in the eighteenth century was obliged to pay heed. The potential for authors to make a living – poets no less than translators, textbook writers or journalists, 'word-makers' in the broadest sense – is so limited that they would be unable to do more than eke out a bare living without additional income from the mass media, for lectures and readings, or through other secondary or main professions.

This gives rise to a significant shift of perspective in the currently accepted view of the contemporary author: writers who are able to make a living from their literary works are exceptions to the rule in the literature business. These, for the most part prominent, authors are the very ones who unwittingly create the false impression that it is possible to live as a 'free' writer today. In fact, as the *Autorenreport* (*Authors' Report*) (Fohrbeck/Wiesand 1972) has shown, the number of freelance authors and creative artists is steadily falling, the social security of this professional group up to 1979 being one of the worst of all professional groups in the Federal Republic. Two sets of statistics from the *Autorenreport* give the true picture. Of 1,693 'word-producing' respondents asked, only 40 per cent may be classified in the category of freelance authors, compared with 49 per cent in the category of authors for whom writing is a sideline and 11 per cent in the category of part-time authors. The production of literary works (*belles-lettres* – polite literature), generally regarded as the epitome of literary work, is but one sphere of activity among many in this picture, and quantitatively by no means the most significant.

Radio and television companies as patrons

Seen in this context, it will become clear why the employment of authors in the mass media, and the characteristics of that work, have become permanently differentiated and expanded. Radio and television companies have become the patrons of the modern culture and literature business.

> Freelance employment as an author is above all more diverse in the mass media than traditional, terse employment designations are able to show. It is by no means restricted to 'major' forms such as the novel, radio play or screenplay (creative works in the traditional

sense). It also includes what is nowadays the dominant category (which, in a public-oriented democracy, is at least as important as the above), of topically relevant 'commercial work' – documentary, reportage, commentary, expert opinion, interviews, etc. In addition, a not inconsiderable role is played by popularising and provocative media work (leading discussions, advisory panels, chat shows, etc.). Transitions to other professions (director, announcer, producers, etc.) are smooth.

(Fohrbeck/Wiesand/Woltereck)

'An end to modesty'

On the basis of these altered employment characteristics it also becomes clear that the 'freelance' author in German society is located in an odd hybrid position – as a 'word-producing' small entrepreneur on the one hand and wage-dependent writer on the other. The call for an 'end to modesty' (Heinrich Böll) marked the moment when authors finally drew the necessary conclusions from this hybrid socio-economic position. By demanding an end to their own socio-political modesty, they gave rise to a new self-awareness, and to a consistent set of objectives aimed at finding a new political identity within society that was no longer based on the illusion of the freelance livelihood.

Writers and trade unions

Heinrich Böll proclaimed the 'end of modesty' in 1969 at the inaugural meeting of the German Writers' Association (Verband Deutscher Schriftsteller: VS). His proclamation came in a decade that showed a continuing imbalance between the individual mode of literary production and the industrial evaluation of the product itself. German writers had recognised that their interests within the commercial contingencies of literature marketing needed to be seen in terms of a trade-union model, if market conditions were not to be entirely dictated by their economically more powerful partners – publishers, radio stations, editors and producers. Transcending disparate political positions and literary-aesthetic differences, as well as greater and lesser social reputations, the founders of the VS sought to bring to the fore one key shared factor: the social dependence of the writer, which could only be put right with the aid of an organisation possessing the necessary political capital.

An organisation of loners?

The question of organisation had been unresolved ever since the profession of freelance writer had existed. As early as 1800 the poet and critic

Friedrich Schlegel had urged: 'Like merchants in the Middle Ages, so creative artists should now come together to form a Hanseatic League, so as to be able to protect one another to a certain degree.' It was not until 1842, with the founding of the Leipzig Association of Literati, that the first step in this direction was made. This was soon to be followed by others: in 1878 came the General Federation of German Writers (ADSV), in 1885 the German Writers' Association, and in 1887 the merging of these two associations to form the German Writers' Federation.

It should be pointed out, however, that the objectives of these organisations were far from being of a trade-union nature. They were more organisations of rank, acting on behalf of their members on matters of copyright, but without regarding those members as literary individuals, or even stressing their dependence on fees. It was 1909, with the founding of the Union for the Protection of German Writers, which survived until 1933, before trade union demands as such were raised, albeit still organisationally separate from the associations of wage-earners and salaried employees.

After 1945, the authors' associations of East and West Berlin, which were still briefly able to join to form an all-German association of German authors, attempted jointly to defend the interests of their members. Major differences of political and social outlook soon began to emerge, however. The trade-union aspect dominated among authors who had belonged to the former Soviet Occupied Zone, while the notion of a freelance existence dominated in West Germany. With the division of Germany also came a division of the all-German association, into a German Writers' Association in the GDR and a Confederation of German Writers' Associations in the Federal Republic, which became a member of the Federal Association of Freelance Professions.

This notion of themselves as freelance professionals, however, soon brought writers up against a socio-political issue. Writers were in increasing danger of being lost in the conflict of interests between trade unions and entrepreneur organisations, since they lacked the ability to develop an independent organisational form to further their interests. A survey of the economic situation of the 'intellectual professions' in the mid-1950s showed that 'everywhere a few top earners, box-office hits and star salaries are matched by a thin bracket of medium incomes of between 500 and 1,000 Marks per month, comparable with the earnings of high-ranking salaried employees and skilled labourers. These are then followed by the broad band of the intellectual proletariat and of destitution: young unpaid lecturers and assistant physicians, writers with starvation fees, and out-of-work musicians and actors struggling to eke out a living from their supernumerary fees.'

Demands

Chief among the objectives listed by Dieter Lattmann, first Chairman of the VS, at its inaugural meeting, were to conduct a social survey of the situation of writers in the Federal Republic; to procure pension facilities for their profession in line with social-security legislation; to abrogate 'school textbook clauses' which explicitly permitted the publication of literary works in school textbooks without fees being paid to the authors; and to obtain a share for authors in book loans from libraries. In order to achieve these goals, of course, it was necessary to equip the Writers' Association with the appropriate union backing, to enable it to exert a more powerful influence on organisations, institutions and legislative procedure. This organisational framework was provided by the Federation of German Trade Unions, an umbrella organisation for a number of individual trade unions. Apart from a handful of conservative writers, who formed the more status-oriented Free Association of German Authors (Freier Deutscher Autorenverband), the VS joined the Press and Paper Industry Trade Union in 1973. Subsequently it represented the interests of writers as a specialist group in their own right – with some success, as Lattmann's successor to the VS chairmanship, Bernt Engelmann, was able to confirm in 1979, some ten years after its founding. In Engelmann's view, the VS 'had become a firmly-rooted concept within the Press and Paper Industry Trade Union, and a factor that can no longer be overlooked either in the book publishing sphere, or that of relevant legislation – one increasingly heeded by a democratic public'.

Structural problems

Despite such undeniable success, however, this confident assessment overlooked the structural problems that were to develop for a small specialist group within a large industrial union. These entailed more than disparate political views within the VS itself regarding future policy and topical issues. Towards the end of the 1980s, the more practical realisation drew near of the once so eagerly sought goal of a new, unified trade union – uniting technicians in radio, academics, writers, visual artists, musicians, editors, producers, readers and actors in all spheres of employment within the media – the more ominous it began to appear. Prominent authors such as Günter Grass had forebodings that a comparatively small specialist literary group of 2,400 members, among the total of 150,000 union members, would have little chance either of having their voice heard on the highly specific problems of writers, or of furthering their own interests. For this reason, even some former advocates of the trade union idea were now at pains 'to stop the automatic participation of the VS in the union' (F.C. Delius). A similar motion put forward with an eye to the planned date of entry (April 1989), failed at the 1988 VS congress. And yet there could be no more talk of a 'unity of loners'. The VS committee resigned, and prominent writers (Günter Grass, Anna Jonas, F.C. Delius) announced that they were leaving the union. No-one was now prepared to take on the work of the committee. Two decades after its birth, the end of the VS, shipwrecked on its own objectives, was already close.

Publishing

Although for financial reasons most authors had little choice but to work at least to some extent with the mass media, publishing houses still remained the key organisations by means of which books could finally appear on the book market. Reading, typesetting, printing, bookbinding, distribution and bookselling are all stages that a manuscript accepted by a publisher must go through before reaching the literary readership as a finished product. The decision, however, as to whether it will reach that readership at all is taken at an earlier stage, in the light of considerations of publishing strategy and calculation – a stage hidden from the public gaze. Such considerations by no means defer to the literary, practical or academic quality of a work alone, but arise in an economic context made up of material existence and growth, viability and returns, and the profit and investments of a publishing company. It will be clear from this that a publishing house, regardless of whether it publishes fiction or specialist and technical literature, is first and foremost an economic enterprise that aims to make profits, and organises its strategies, conceptions, and publishing programme according to capitalist principles.

Some data and statistical ratios from 1981 may help to elucidate the kind of level on which publishing houses operate as economic enterprises. In the (West German) Federal Republic as it was then, including West Berlin, there were some 2,044 publishing houses in 1981 (5,100 bookshops). These produced a total of some 67,000 titles, of which 18.5 per cent were accounted for by fiction alone. The number of titles brought out had thus increased over fourfold between 1951 (14,094 titles) and 1981 (67,176), the proportion of paperbacks rising from 4.6 per cent to 11.6 per cent. These production statistics placed the Federal Republic in third place behind the USA and the USSR, both of which produced over 85,000 titles per year. Translations into German accounted in 1981 for some 10 per cent of the total, nearly two-thirds of these being from English. This impressive number of titles, however, was not distributed equally among all existing publishers, as will be clear from the fact that a mere 17 per cent of publishing houses were publishing 80 per cent of all titles. In 1978, book publishers had a turnover totalling 6.6 thousand million DM, and publishers of journals, newspapers, etc. of 8.7 thousand million DM. In terms of overall trends in publishing, ratios within the industry are interesting: a turnover of 6.6 thousand million DM looks decidedly modest when set beside the balance-sheet of Springer-Verlag, which in 1978 alone had a turnover of 1.7 thousand million DM. It may be significant with regard to ratios in the overall economy that despite multiple publications or the issuing of licenses to paperback publishers and book clubs, not even larger publishing houses were able to achieve a market turnover of more than approximately 50 million DM.

The size of businesses

Hardly any other branch of the West German economy is so variegated, motley or stratified as publishing. A media giant such as the Bertelsmann Group, with over 28,000 employees, and a manufacturing concern such as the bustling one-man publishing company Matthes & Seitz have next to nothing in common aside from the fact that both happen to deal with books. Persistent pressure (and coercion) over the years towards mergers and capital concentration has led to the systematic expansion of groups such as Bertelsmann and Holtzbrinck (including the European Educational Union, the German Book Alliance, S. Fischer and Rowohlt) into multi-media giants. This category is matched by the still relatively broad spectrum of small and very small businesses, which are often the most ambitious in literary and political terms (such as Wagenbach-Verlag and Rotbuch-Verlag). In the public awareness, as well as in the shop-windows and display-cases of bookshops, beside the well-known paperback series (Rowohlt, Fischer, dtv, Ullstein, Goldmann), the publishers of fiction have an outstanding role – one which does not in fact accrue to them from the purely economic standpoint. They 'make' literature and authors, often living off high-turnover activities in other spheres which scarcely reach the public attention (e.g. Hanser and Luchterhand from the technical specialist publishing houses incorporated in their group, Suhrkamp/Insel from play distribution agencies, or Rowohlt from paperback publishing). Entirely outside the public interest and awareness, as the press and television phrase has it, are the purely specialist publishing houses, which nevertheless account for the lion's share of total turnover from books.

Marketing

With a view to increasing turnover and raising their share of the market, publishers must of necessity focus on the reader. The latter, however, is influenced as a consumer of books by factors entirely outside literature, for example, the bestseller list, book advertising and above all by the range of books available in bookshops. For this reason, publishers seek to exert through their representatives an influence on the wholesale range and on the retail book trade, to ensure markets for as many copies as possible before the books themselves have even been published. The Frankfurt Book Fair, which was originally intended as a sales exhibition (in 1981 some 5,450 exhibitors took part with a total of 84,000 new publications, including some 1,450 publishing houses from the Federal Republic alone), nowadays scarcely heeds this original function. By the time the Fair is held in autumn, decisions concerning the success of a book have long since been made through direct contacts with publishers, wholesalers and retail outlets. By means of discounts, free copies from publishers, special show-cases, special themes and authors' readings in retail bookshops, 'trends' are launched that are then reflected in the bestseller lists, which in turn exert a motivating influence on consumer interest.

Books as a commodity

It is this traffic in bestsellers, therefore, and the manner in which they are successfully marketed, that permits bookselling to become increasingly a purely commercial trade in commodities. The works of popular authors such as Johannes Mario Simmel and Hildegard Knef are published and marketed in mass editions of hundreds of thousands. In the marketplace itself they are visually dominant, distracting the attention of the buyer from other works. This trend is further augmented by the influence of book clubs (Bertelsmann's *Lesering*, Deutsche Buchgemeinschaft, Europäische Bildungs-Gemeinschaft, Büchergilde Gutenberg), which reach different consumer groups by means of licensed editions. For the most part, more-over, they are able to do so at more favourable prices than the retail book trade, being able to publish on a larger scale, and count on guaranteed sales figures (about 80,000 copies per volume in the case of the Europäische Bildungs-Gemeinschaft) when publishing certain titles as recommended volumes for their members. It must also be conceded that book clubs have done much to popularise reading. In recent years they have also been responsible for publishing programmes that should be taken seriously from the literary viewpoint, as well as for attractively presented works.

Literature and the reader

A country with a reading culture?

What role, however, does reading play within this complex fabric of interests that is largely dependent on economic objectives? Is there such a thing as a reading culture in the Federal Republic? What significance may currently be ascribed to the literary work? If one looks solely at the extent to which libraries are used, interest in reading appears to be quite healthy in the main. Public libraries, excluding academic, church, school and specialist libraries, boast a total stock of some 50 million volumes and make 115 million book loans per year. Of these loans, 60 per cent are accounted for by fiction, children's and young people's literature.

These figures nevertheless reveal little about the actual significance of fiction in overall reading habits. This needs to be seen in relation to other forms of leisure activity, and particularly in terms of media such as television.

Facts and figures

Here too, a few facts and figures help to fill in the picture. A survey conducted in 1973 revealed that the amount of time allocated weekly to the mass media – television, radio, newspapers, and journals – totalled thirty-one hours, whereas the amount of time devoted to books and reading for entertainment as well as for instruction was a mere three hours. Expressed in percentages, therefore, the mass media accounted for 86 per cent, while reading books accounted for only 9 per cent. Television is the clear winner among the public, with 40 per cent, 'entertainment' books accounting for only 6 per cent of leisure time. The degree of control television has over the production sphere in Germany is thus unmistakable.

What is important in this context, however, is the degree to which this proportion persists at the expense of literature. Over half the population are aware of the fact that since the advent of television, or since they have owned a set, their reading has been reduced substantially. Even among 'books', however, a distinction needs to be made, since the term includes fiction magazines (*Romanheftchen*) obtainable at newspaper kiosks for one DM. Such magazines are purchased by a third of the population. Statistically, this means that every adult consumes ten fiction magazines per year, or more precisely, every purchaser of fiction magazines buys thirty-three issues a year, ranging from Mills and Boon novels to Jerry Cotton, and penny dreadfuls about the fighting soldier to science fiction of the Perry Rhodan brand. It is likewise clear from the significance of books in the lives of the German population that differences in levels of education, reflecting class differences, are a key factor in the creation of reading habits. The higher the level of education, the greater the interest in reading books. Nevertheless, the influence of television is exerting a negative effect even among those groups who would traditionally rank among the reading classes in terms of socialisation and education. The value attached to being 'well-read' is falling steadily, especially among the younger generation.

Theatrical plans

In the light of the above, it may seem astonishing that despite the massive interest in television, theatre continues to play a major role on the literary scene. During the 1973–4 theatre season, for example, a total of eighty-five public theatres in the Federal Republic put on some 36,000 performances. Of these, two-thirds were plays, a quarter operas and the remainder operettas and concerts. Allowing for private theatres and festival performances during the same season, this produces a theatre attendance figure of 30 million, with 70–80 per cent full houses – statistics that continue to increase.

Causes for these trends may be sought in two major directions. On the one hand the theatre, as a cultural institution of the middle class, has its faithful adherents, drawn from the educated middle classes. Television will not keep them away from the theatre, since the stage impact of plays, concerts, operas and operettas cannot adequately be conveyed by the medium of television. On the other hand, theatre culture in Germany has become both qualitatively more ambitious in recent years, and more diverse. One need only look at the recent work of theatres such as the Berliner Schaubühne, or at innovations in the sphere of children's and young people's theatre, such as the Munich Rote Rübe (Beetroot) Theatre or the Berlin Grips Theatre.

Programmes are nevertheless still somewhat conventionally structured. The proportion of contemporary authors performed in the last decade was under 10 per cent, despite the fact that such authors have pioneered new directions in experimental theatre, documentary theatre and the theatre of critical realism. Bertolt Brecht continues to enjoy an undisputed paramount position among all authors performed. Favourite classic authors are Lessing, Shakespeare, Molière and Ibsen. Among contemporary authors dominating the 1974–5 scene were the GDR writer Ulrich Plenzdorf, the entertainment writer Curth Flatow, and Franz Xaver Kroetz, author of numerous folk plays with a critical message.

Literary criticism

It will be clear from the above that the Federal Republic of Germany is a media society in which the book, and even more so the work of fiction, is only one 'medium' among many, and from the quantitative viewpoint far from the most important. By the same token, however, discussions conducted on the subject of literature, as well as literary debates and feuds conducted in the *feuilleton* columns of newspapers, journals, and cultural periodicals, reveal that the quality of literary works is very much a subject open to public dispute. Professional literary criticism plays an important role in all this, although a distinction does need to be made both between various forms of literary criticism, and critics themselves.

Form and function

The type of literary criticism provided by radio and television companies, for example, is more akin to a variety of advertisement offering a brief assessment of literature. Some takes the form of regular broadcasts presenting new 'trends' and literary curiosities (e.g. *Aspekte, Bücherjournal*), but there are also extensive 'specials', such as on the Frankfurt Book Fair, combining perfunctory statements about developments in the book market with short items on key works. Equally important as a source of information *en passant* for the reader of daily and weekly newspapers are the special review columns of the press. These, too, give terse appraisals, offering what is inevitably an incomplete survey of developments in contemporary literature at home and abroad.

Literary criticism on the supra-regional level, written by academics or professional critics for national newspapers and journals, is of particular importance. Writers themselves tend to write reviews only sporadically, when special works by colleagues interest them, or to avail themselves of an additional source of income for reasons already touched on. Professional reviewers, on the other hand, and especially the more notable among them, the *Grosskritiker* (Peter Hamm), are the authoritative representatives of literary criticism as a public institution. There can be no doubt that thorough, well-founded and aptly-worded criticism of a literary work in a major journal is a key factor affecting its success or failure on the book market, and hence also the literary future of an author. This does not have to be the case, of course: the enthusiastic praise of a critic is not enough in itself to make a bestseller of a work, any more than total condemnation by literary critics can prevent a book from being distributed. The indisputable influence wielded by critics is reflected from the author's viewpoint in a fundamental distrust of the 'major critics' that may be justified by experience. Martin Walser, for example, was led by such encounters to castigate what he called the 'pope-critics'. The literary critic Marcel Reich-Ranicki had asserted: 'Literary criticism is always polemic. The reviewer disputes for or against a book, a trend, a literature.' Walser's response to this is:

> The bourgeois critic has developed a remarkable facility for throwing everything open to question except the conditions under which he works. He even questions himself constantly, without expecting an answer. His questioning, his doubt, is a Saturday ritual that can hold its own with any Sunday liturgy as a celebration of the *fait accompli*. Such a critic knows full well that his high-handed position produces conceit and megalomania in him. He is only too willing to admit that. Through his personal conduct and writing style he has developed a capacity to savour his own conceit and megalomania.

The writer Peter Schneider has also censured the conduct and writing style of such 'pope-critics', using the examples of Marcel Reich-Ranicki, Hans Mayer and Günther Blöcker to criticise their lack of any firm standpoint, the conceit of their writing style and the scarcely discernible principles behind their judgements.

Impression or solidly-based judgement?

Criticism of this kind is at the same time censure of the conditions and structure of the literary scene and business themselves. The latter's chaotic tangle of mutually competing institutions and spheres of influence often demands and encourages the brilliantly worded impression rather than demonstrable, proven judgement, or its prerequisites.

To this extent, the remarks of Martin Walser and Peter Schneider, although expressed from the point of view of those concerned, i.e. authors, are of particular significance for the reader. As a mediating institution between the author and his book on one side of the literary process, and the reader on the other, literary criticism is only able to fulfil its function when critics are prepared to reflect on and define their own role in that process. Criticism of this kind – criticism being understood here in Ernst Bloch's terms as 'lively controversy in groups for and against, not a non-partisan pleasure, nor a musical chattering, and certainly not contemplation' – could go some way towards the function ascribed to it by Bloch on the basis of its inherent capacities: 'Criticism is analysis; given the right conditions, when confronted with major works, it again becomes commentary and ultimately, as a productive creation, essay.'

Institutions of literary socialisation

If literary criticism may be termed a mediating institution between literature and the reader, then the teaching of German in German schools may be designated an institution of socialisation. This means that children, adolescents and young people become acquainted with literature in the course of their school education, upbringing and learning, as part and parcel of the socialisation process.

The period since the early 1970s has seen a highly contradictory train of events in this regard. In the 1950s and 1960s, German teaching, especially at secondary schools, was still a vehicle for imparting traditional educational patterns and a conservative ideology. It focused on inherited educational values, and was to this extent perfectly suited to the restoration period of the Federal Republic. In line with this, until the late 1960s the canon of school literature in syllabuses was relatively traditionally organised, and more oriented towards classic authors than contemporary literature.

The counterpart of this mode of teaching, and part of the wider agenda, not only in German, but in the arts generally, was the postulate of the 'mature citizen'. This postulate collapsed with the crisis of legitimation in German society, in which traditional values and norms proved fragile. They now gave way to demands for greater inclusion of communication and linguistics issues in German teaching and elsewhere, an incorporation of literature in everyday discussion contexts, an expansion of the concept of 'literature' to encompass other texts, and a new recourse above all to modern literature. This process was not without its problems, giving conservative critics of these developments increasing cause to engage in polemics over the basics. This was because the expansion of the concept of literature to include other texts, and the incorporation of aesthetic phenomena into the very general concept of communication have in many respects caused the unique character of the aesthetic to fade beyond recognition.

One of the consequences of this was that in technocratically justified plans for syllabus organisation (such as in provisions by the Minister of Education and the Arts for the creation of a second fifth form), German teaching since 1972 has been intended to serve 'chiefly the study of the mother tongue'. Literature, on the hand, like music and the visual arts, has been entrusted to 'courses'.

Over and above being an indication of the social context in which it needs to be understood, this ejection of literature from German teaching also pointed to a fundamental difficulty schools had in dealing with poetry. The coercive nature of the school as an institution of socialisation obviously impeded access to a medium that is opposed to all coercion on principle. This may partly help to explain the apathy and unwillingness of pupils to have anything to do with literary texts in school which they might well read voluntarily in their leisure time. It also helps to explain the complaints of teachers about the severe problems they have in expounding to pupils major classic works, and even contemporary literature. It remains open to question whether attempts observable since the end of the 1970s to evaluate administratively the status of literature in schools have been able to encourage its active use. Inculcation of the capacity to read and to take pleasure in reading may derive more from self-determined forms of learning, such as are envisaged by project-oriented teaching.

Cultural policy

Given all that has been said so far about the literary scene and business, and about the mediation of literature, it is reasonable to ask whether the state exerts an influence on literary life in the Federal Republic. This is a difficult question to answer. Such an influence affecting literary life does exist, as do state or state-sponsored institutions, but it is considerably more limited in form than it was in the GDR, for example.

Cultural jurisdiction

In a federative state such as the Federal Republic of Germany, the cultural jurisdiction wielded by the *Länder* allows the federal government to represent the country abroad (via such bodies as the Goethe Institute or Inter Nationes), but little scope for fostering culture within the country itself (festival plays and exhibitions, grants, and associations, the bestowing of prizes and awards and subsidies). The state also has substantial jurisdiction in the sphere of legislation governing copyright questions and commercial law – two key areas for publishing, and hence also for authors.

Promoting culture

The *Länder*, on the other hand, are responsible for legislation governing cultural policy in the Federal Republic, and for promoting culture on the basis of the means available to them, which are in turn partially absorbed by and divided up among local authorities. For this reason, municipal cultural authorities have increasingly become springboards in recent years for cultural initiatives, and above all for literary activities. Public readings by authors have been promoted by them, as have street theatre and song festivals. To some extent, these authorities have themselves provided the impetus for such events.

The means available to them, however, are somewhat meagre: the funds allocated to the promotion of culture by the federation, the *Länder* and the local authorities have remained for decades at a constant one per cent of total expenditure. For this reason, therefore, the backing of authors, either by means of literary prizes (most notably Darmstadt's Georg Büchner Prize and the Bremen literary prize), or grants (such as a study trip to the Villa Massimo German Academy in Rome), are at all events showcase examples rather than evidence of cultural patronage out of the public purse. If anything, the opposite is the case: whenever cuts are advised in finance budgets, heads of cultural departments in German cities complain that the cultural budget is the often the first to be sacrificed. The contribution of the state to the cultural and literary scene in general, therefore, is but one factor among many, having different significance in diverse cultural and institutional pheres, but of limited influence overall.

To sum up, three factors in a state of mutual tension shape the particular character of the literary scene or business: the private capitalist organisation of publishing, the mass media and the aesthetic quality of the literary work. However, the fact that the latter has so far been able to hold its own at all in the midst of the manifold demands and diversions offered by an advanced industrial consumer society says very little about the pro-literature mentality of German society, but a great deal about the import-ance of literature.

The social importance of literature

An attempt at a prognosis will be made here, therefore, in which literary theory is implicit. As long as the literary work is able in both form and content to provide and inspire emotional and intellectual impetus, and is able to convey experiences of social differentiation, and articulate problems, conflicts and mentalities in a unique formal language of its own – as long, in other words, as it possesses an aesthetic identity that cannot be expressed in any other medium, literature will remain irreplaceable in the Federal Republic, and will be perceived as such.

Literature versus politics – the writing style of the 1950s

Restoration and the 'economic miracle'

Literature and politics were never so far removed from each other in the Federal Republic of Germany as they were in the 1950s. The economic reconstruction of the traditional production relations, as well as politico-ideological restoration, formed signposts on the path of the republic that were disowned by intellectuals, creative artists, and writers. The euphoria of the 'economic miracle', the suppression of fascism, the 'demoralis-ation' of the working class that culminated in the banning of the German Communist Party in 1956 by the Federal Constitutional Court, rearma-ment and entry into NATO, and not least the spectre of nuclear armament and the threat from industrialisation and technology – all these factors pertaining to a stabilisation of capitalism, accompanied by the integration of the Federal Republic into the West, were by the same token stages on the road to an increasing distancing and isolation of the intelligentsia. The latter saw themselves being pushed on to the periphery of society with their critical questions. The scepticism, for example, with which the futurologist Robert Jungk confronted the optimistic mood of 'progress' of his day with the self-doubt of the nuclear scientist could not have been more out of step with the times: 'But it is something quite new for our industrial age, perhaps the first symptom of a change in professional ethos, that no longer asks only "What do I produce?", or "How much do I produce?", but "What am I producing for?" and ultimately "What effect does my work have? Is it immoral?" '

The legacy of fascism

Allowing for its various accents, the literature of the 1950s may be termed
a poetic reservoir of such critical and self-critical problems. A sense of
unease pervaded more than the thinking of the future researcher, but was
a key feature of the literature of that time. Reference to recent history
provided an opportunity to discuss contemporary problems. Similarly, the
development of new writing styles and literary perspectives helped contribute to changing forms of perception and ways of looking at things. The
burdensome legacy of fascism proved all-pervasive in this regard. Even
where the literature of the 1950s sought to evade it, this legacy remained
a determining factor influencing even the forms of aesthetic escapism.

The problems of lyric poetry

The continuity of literary history that is characteristic for German lyric poetry
of the post-war era, and especially for nature lyrics, remained a decisive
factor throughout the 1950s. Authors such as Günter Eich and Elisabeth
Langgässer continued as before to shape the discussion of lyric poetry in
those years – authors who even before the era of fascist rule in Germany
had had, despite their individuality of theme and poetic style, many features
in common, and who had been enduringly influenced by the nature lyricists
Oskar Loerke and Wilhelm Lehmann. Karl Krolow, essayist and likewise
a lyric poet in the Loerke tradition, pointed out the common ground of
this nature lyric poetry, referring to a 'process of de-individualisation' at
work in it, a withdrawal of the lyric self that went hand in hand with a
recourse to microcosmic phenomena, a kind of 'mania for detail'.

Nature lyric poets of the 1950s were hence accused of having lost their
sense of reality, and the retreat from reality that pervades this lyric poetry
is indeed a form of withdrawal from a reality that had been rejected. The
central concern of this withdrawal to nature magic and contemplation, to
the microcosmic and to natural detail, is to recreate through poetry an
alternative world that would have nothing more to do with the reality
from which it emerged. What in the 1930s had still been both escape and
protest in the face of fascist rule was now transformed under the changed
social conditions of the 1950s to mere retreat from empirical reality.

Lyric poetry after Auschwitz

It was against this kind of poetry that Theodor W. Adorno directed his
later much misunderstood statement: 'to write a poem after Auschwitz is
barbaric'. Adorno is challenging here a lyric poetry that has failed to open
itself up to the shock and trauma to the poetic spirit of the experience of
death in fascist extermination camps. This trauma is also lacking in the

676

outstanding exponent of lyric as an outward form in the 1950s: Gottfried Benn. Already acclaimed long before 1933 as an Expressionist author, Benn had initially supported the Nazis, finally withdrawing from public life to work as a military doctor in the Wehrmacht, describing this step as an 'aristocratic form of emigration'. Devoid of opportunities for publication after the end of World War II he almost disappeared into obscurity. It was the publication of his volumes *Statische Gedichte* (*Static Poems*) (1948), *Trunkene Flut* (*Drunken Flood*) (1949), *Fragmente* (*Fragments*) (1951) and *Destillationen* (*Distillations*) (1953) that restored him to the awareness of the reading public. These works were augmented by a series of essays, prose works and autobiographical writings (*Doppelleben* – *Double Life*, 1950), in which Benn constantly readdresses the problem of his artistic existence. 'Dualism' is the key word by which this mode of existence is understood – the dualism between a reality that as an empirical phenomenon seems irrelevant to artistic creativity, and an art that obeys its own laws – beauty, style and form – regardless of social context. Benn verbalised this definition of his own existence in his poem *Einsamer nie* (*Never Lonelier*), which was written in the 1930s, but did not reach a wider public until its publication in *Statische Gedichte*:

> Einsamer nie als im August:
> Erfüllungsstunde – im Gelände
> die roten und die goldenen Brände
> doch wo ist deiner Gärten Lust?
> Die Seen hell, die Himmel weich,
> die Äcker rein und glänzen leise,
> doch wo sind Sieg und Siegsbeweise
> aus dem von dir vertretenen Reich?
> Wo alles sich durch Glück beweist
> und tauscht den Blick und tauscht die Ringe
> im Weingeruch, im Rausch der Dinge –
> dienst du dem Gegenglück, dem Geist.

> Never lonelier than in August
> The hour of fulfilment – on the land
> the red and golden fires
> But where is thy garden delight?
> The lakes clear, the heavens soft
> The fields clean and softly gleaming
> But where are victory and its tokens
> From the kingdom you represent?
> When all things prove themselves through joy,
> Exchanging glances, also, rings,
> The scent of wine, and joy of things –
> You serve that other bliss – the Mind.

The dual nature of 'the hour of fulfilment' and the 'other bliss', made here into the theme of poetry itself, and the loneliness that ensues from this dual nature for the lyric self, the creative man, is the agenda of Gottfried Benn the creative artist, for whom history, society, development and personal happiness possess no more than static value, and no quality either even remotely comparable with that of art and poetry, or of any interest to it. 'Thinking and being,' asserts Benn, 'art and the shape of him who makes it, even action and the personal life of private individuals, are entirely separate essences'.

The manner in which Benn was received in the 1950s clearly shows that the issue was one of parallels between states of consciousness. However, recollection of how these came about or could be changed was extinguished in an age and a society doing their best to forget recent history. In both the poetry and the poetics of the 'death-seeking Benn' (Bertolt Brecht), the poetic shock sought by Adorno is at best expressed in sublimated form – through his insistence on a dual nature of art and life that left poetry aloof from challenges.

Clearly, it was not Adorno's intention to deprive all lyric of its right to exist with his dictum on the 'barbaric' character of poetry after Auschwitz. He stated later, self-critically, and by way of modification: 'Perennial suffering has just as much right to expression as the tortured person has to howl. It may, therefore, have been wrong to state that no poem should be written after Auschwitz.'

This right of such suffering to self-expression was sought most of all in the lyric poetry of Paul Celan, through intense concentration on the expressive capacity of a poetic language that increasingly shut itself off from outside reality with the passing years. This shutting-off, however, involved a different approach and objective than was the case in Benn's poetry. In perhaps Celan's best-known poem, *Die Todesfuge* (*Death Fugue*) (written 1945), the realities of fascism and the extermination camps that Celan had experienced first-hand were fully present stylistically as a recollected past with all its atrocity, inexorability and the full force of death. Celan's later lyric verse, however, tends towards a complete representation of immanent stylistic references and their interrelationships. The process whereby Celan shut himself off from the encroaching influences of a reality that remained outside lyric poetry needs to be seen both as a mark of his poetic consistency, and as the existential problem of Paul Celan as a lyric poet. His poetry is thus consistent in its efforts to ward off the unequivocal in all its forms. Celan was made wary by the experience of a poem such as *Die Todesfuge* becoming an obligatory, and hence enforced object of interpretation ritual in German teaching syllabuses, thereby turning it into a kind of commodity in the 1950s business of German–Jewish reconciliation. The lyric verse of his later volumes resolutely defies such categorisation (after *Mohn und Gedächtnis* – *Poppy and Memory*, 1952, *Von*

Schwelle zu Schwelle – From Threshold to Threshold, 1955, and *Sprachgitter – Mesh of Language*, 1959, came *Die Niemandsrose – The Rose of No-one*, 1963, *Atemwende – Turn of Breath*, 1967, *Fadensonnen – Thread Suns*, 1968, and *Lichtzwang – Compulsion of Light*, 1970, all published in Celan's lifetime). With their terseness of style, fluid imagery, and a use of metaphor that defies the equivocal, these poems constitute a hermetically sealed sphere of ambiguity that, as the philologist Peter Szondi showed in his *Celan-Studien* (1972) using the poem *Engführung* as an example, evokes an effect of precise statement: 'Ambiguity, having become the vehicle of perception, reveals the unity of that which had only appeared disparate. It serves precision.' Celan pursued this aim right up to his poetry volume *Schneepart* (*Part of the Snow*), which was published posthumously in 1971. In his eyes, his poetry was 'topicalised language, liberated under the banner of a radical individuation, but one for which language itself has defined the boundaries, and that remains mindful of the potential opened up by language'. Paul Celan took his own life in 1970.

Despite their undoubtedly contradictory and non-comparable natures, Gottfried Benn and Paul Celan may be specified as two major exponents of poetry who made a lasting impact on the German lyric scene after World War II. It should not be overlooked, however, that during the same period, the 1950s, a modern literary trend was also beginning to assert itself, with an unmistakable form of expression of its own. Authors such as Marie Luise Kaschnitz and Nelly Sachs went beyond tradition by the very fact of detaching themselves from post-war nature lyric. The same applies to some early signs of surrealism, to be found in Ernst Meister, Christoph Meckel and Günter Grass (*Die Vorzüge der Windhühner – The Merits of Non-Starting Hens*, 1956). These forms of expression arise out of a new awareness, pertaining to an autonomous lyric style which, having new experiences to impart, seeks to break with conventional models. This also holds good for Peter Rühmkorf and Ilse Aichinger, as well as the lyric poet and radio playwright Ingeborg Bachmann (*Gestundete Zeit – Houred Time*, 1953; *Anrufung des Grossen Bären – Invocation of the Great Bear*, 1956), and above all for Hans Magnus Enzensberger, who caused a stir with his poetry volumes *verteidigung der wölfe* (*defence of the wolves*) (1957), *landessprache* (*land language*) (1960) and *blindenschrift* (*braille*) (1964), for the very reason that his lyric poetry was open to political reality, even that of fascism, without its destroying the identity of his poetry. On the contrary, this reality gives it substance, creates a precondition for it, seeks to be a provocation, brings inconsistencies to the surface, and demands answers, not a collusion in oblivion. The poem *landessprache*, which also forms the title of his 1960 volume, begins with the verses:

was habe ich hier verloren,
in diesem land,

dahin mich gebracht meine älteren
durch arglosigkeit?
eingeboren, doch ungetrost,
abwesend bin ich hier,
ansässig im gemütlichen elend,
in der netten, zufriedenen grube.
was habe ich hier? und was habe ich hier zu suchen,
in dieser schlachtschlüssel, diesem schlaraffenland,
wo es aufwärts geht, aber nicht vorwärts,
wo der überdruss ins bestickte hungertuch beisst,
wo in den delikatessgeschäften die armut, kreidebleich,
mit erstickte stimme aus dem schlagrahm röchelt
und ruft: es geht aufwärts!

what have I lost here,
in this country,
where my forebears brought me
all unsuspecting?
born here, and yet insecure
I am absent here,
settled in a comfortable destitution
in this nice, satisfied grave.
What have I here? And what am I doing here,
in this crucible of battles, this land of Cockaigne,
where we move upwards, but never forwards,
where surfeit bites into the embroidered handkerchief of hunger,
where, in the delicatessens, poverty, pale as death,
rattles with choked voice out of the whipped cream
and cries out: we're moving up!

It will be apparent that by the end of the 1950s a new tone was creeping into lyric poetry, informed by the Brechtian influence, but nonetheless a tone in its own right – political, but not unpoetic. In response to the 'economic miracle' and the affluent society, a political poetry emerged in the transition to the 1960s that was an appropriate expression of the literary theory underpinning it. This theory asserted that the literary work of art also had a political identity and quality, immanent in its poetic structure. This kind of poetry has more in common with the lyric of Paul Celan and the theory of Theodor W. Adorno than with that of Gottfried Benn. It finds its problems as much in a past that it has not yet come to terms with, as in the social conflicts of the here and now. This agenda was a prelude to the political lyric that was to be brought increasingly to the fore in the 1960s and 1970s by such poets as Erich Fried.

Coming to terms with the past and criticising the present: themes and traditions of the novel

The process of withdrawal from the socio-political commitment of the early post-war years in literature, discernible in the founding of *Gruppe 47*, was to have major repercussions, especially in prose. Concentration on the substance of literature itself permitted more concerted efforts towards evolving new modes of writing, an orientation towards contemporary world literature and a greater awareness of subjects, themes and problems from both recent history and the present. Whereas Heinrich Böll's assertion about the difficulty of writing 'even so much as half a page of prose' may be said to sum up the post-war situation, Siegfried Lenz's acknowledgement of his search for models is equally apt for the early 1950s:

> I knew exactly what I wanted to write about, but lacked perspective, among other things, and I found it in Ernest Hemingway. I found it above all in his stories, which represent for me, to some extent even today, an exemplary kind of tension: that is the antagonism between dream and futility, between longing and experience, between rebellion and humiliating defeat. Silence and rebellion – these seemed to be to be the purest form of sanctuary in a world in which death has lost its victorious outward form.

With Paul Schallück and Wolfdietrich Schnurre, Siegfried Lenz was actually an author of the 1950s, sharing with a large number of others the conviction, typical for that decade, that the writer must be morally committed to coming to terms with the past. He made his début in 1951 with the novel *Es waren Habichte in der Luft* (*There Were Hawks in the Air*), followed by *Duell mit dem Schatten* (*Duel with the Shadow*) (1953) and *Stadtgespräch* (*Urban Conversation*) (1963). The novels were regularly punctuated by volumes of short stories, the best-known of which, *So zärtlich war Suleyken* (*So Tender Was Suleyken*), appeared in 1955. His longest novel, *Die Deutschstunde* (*The German Lesson*), did not appear until 1968, by which time it seemed anachronistic in view of the political and literary situation in the Federal Republic at that time. His hero and narrator, Siggi Jepsen, writes from the viewpoint of a youth detained in a borstal. The young Siggi – it is the year 1954 – has to write an essay on the joys of duty. After handing in blank pages, he is placed in solitary confinement, at which point the novel proper begins. Siggi thinks back to 1943, above all to his father, serving in the police force in the village of Rugbüll in Schleswig-Holstein. One day, the police officer has to deliver to his childhood friend, the painter Max Nansen, who has retired to live in the village, a notice issued by Nazi cultural functionaries banning him from practising his profession. He is also responsible for ensuring that the order is complied with. Siegfried Lenz worked aspects of the life-story of Emil Nolde into the plot.

Whereas the father begins to keep the painter under near-paranoid surveillance, the son warns him and becomes his rescuer and protector. Father and son find themselves unable to break out of this enforced pattern of behaviour, even after Nazi rule is over. The reader thus learns the reason for Siggi's detention. He has snatched one of the painter's works from an exhibition, and been imprisoned for theft.

Lenz delineates the circumstances and characters with an obsession for detail and a vast knowledge of his subject – one of the reasons for the popularity of the novel, of which huge numbers of copies were published. And yet the very construction of the story framework, Siggi's detention, has a disjointed, contrived quality about it. During his recollections of the past, he also has difficulty legitimating himself as an omnipresent narrator. Not even memory itself, with its areas of clarity and unclarity, is dealt with by Lenz as a theme.

His playful form of coming to terms with the past is bound to fail because among other things he has segregated provincial conditions too much from the Nazi 'Reich'. This opens up a scope for human decision which, although rendering the malevolence of the father credible, fails to do justice to the actual conditions prevailing at the time.

Like Oskar Maria Graf before him, Lenz is a moralist of the provinces whose characters place themselves in the wrong, and hence set in motion an epic effect. He is a writer who works with devices of film-like immediacy, but not a writer of realistic analysis. The role-like determinism of his characters unfolds in too obvious a way to render comprehensible either the root causes of the authoritarian character of Nazism, or of Jepsen senior. Art, moreover, survived during the Nazi era not in the provinces and the countryside, but in exile.

The antagonisms of which Lenz spoke, having in mind the 1950s, may indeed be designated the structural characteristics of a 'Young German literature of the modern age' (Walter Jens). Authors such as Heinrich Böll and Wolfgang Koeppen, Martin Walser, Alfred Andersch and Max Frisch operated in the electric field between the fascist past and the capitalist present, between refuge and protest, subjectivity and loss of identity. These antagonisms imply that poetic tension between traditionalism and modernity within which German writers of the younger generation were reasserting themselves.

Obviously, of course, narrative fiction of the 1950s also continued to embrace authors who had been of literary importance before 1945, or even before 1933. The outstanding figure among these, and undoubtedly the best-known, is Ernst Jünger. Prior to 1933, Jünger had been the author of reactionary, nationalist works. During the Third Reich he had led the exemplary existence of the literary 'internal emigrant'. With the end of the War, he soon became a talking-point again with his work *Der Friede (Peace)* (1945), which sets forth the idea of a common future for the European nations. Behind these overt transformations, however, an underlying pattern is nevertheless discernible that helps to explain the attraction of Jünger to a conservative reading public across all the decades to the present day. Thus, although Jünger's later writings (above all *Atlantische Fahrt – Atlantic Voyage*, 1947; *Strahlungen – Radiations*, 1949; *Der Gordische Knote – The Gordian Knot*, 1953; and *Gläserne Bienen – Glass Bees*, 1957), define 'liberty' as the 'chief concern of the free man' (*Der Waldgang – The Forest Walk*, 1951), elitism, heroism, the celebration of war and the unknown soldier remain the key factors in this 'free' existence. The vision unfolded in *Der Weltstaat* (*The World State*) (1960) of a 'great and growing uniformity', that could ultimately render even armies superfluous, is bought at a price of victims, sacrifices, and suffering already anticipated in Jünger's essay *Der Arbeiter* (*The Worker*), dating from 1932.

There is thus more to the praise of Jünger as a leading exponent of the German *Geist*, reiterated in various prize-giving speeches until well into the 1980s, than mere celebration of this brilliant stylist who found a new way of combining poetry with the essay. In reality, the honours paid to Jünger (the Goethe Prize of the City of Frankfurt, 1983) are an act of self-glorification on the part of a German conservatism that was unable to admit its own politico-cultural failure in the face of fascism. Even the Vietnam War and the student movement of 1967–9 were seen by the aging Jünger in *Post nach Princeton* (*Post to Princeton*) (1975) as symptoms of an acute 'lack of decision', caused by the strongest political and military power of that period, the USA.

The creation of a tradition

'Young German literature of the modern age', on the other hand, is indebted to a social-critical, realistic narrative tradition. This kind of narrative fiction arises out of the conviction that current processes, experiences of the past, injuries and suffering, shocks and distortions of all kinds can be conveyed as such – that they can be arranged in the form of stories, personality development and successive narrative passages – and that communications of this type can exert an impact among contemporaries, i.e. their readers. Conversely, however, this kind of narrative presumes an ability both to identify its moods, experiences and emotions, to distance itself from them in a literary medium, as well as an effort to discern the self in the non-self, and to transcend one's own experience through that of someone else. Realistic literature of social criticism thus calls for a firm belief in the effectiveness of literature in both directions: with regard to its capacity to give an account of reality, with all its inconsistencies and conflicts, and with regard to the impaired nature of life, in its endeavour to gain experience of the self through what is being narrated. German post-war prose represents this belief in literature in a manner that conveys the overcoming of fascism in the form of a literary accommodation to it.

This observation also applies to the Swiss author Max Frisch, who may be regarded as one of the most important novelists of the 1950s for his *Stiller* (1954) and *Homo Faber* (1957). In that innocuously prosperous society in which everything seems to be as it should, his novels, especially *Stiller*, the most successful book of this period, seem to be the key to the dual character of what is ostensibly so self-evident a reality. 'I'm not Stiller' is the unprecedented circumstance that opens this novel. The American Jim Larkin White is arrested at the Swiss border for allegedly being Anatol Stiller, a sculptor who disappeared six years previously. White strongly denies this, and finds himself detained for interrogation. When his 'lovely' wife Julika was being treated for tuberculosis in a sanatorium, he is alleged to have disappeared to America and attempted suicide in order finally to erase his Anatol Stiller identity. All this comes to light in the form of diary-like entries, written by White and augmented by his comments and distanced approach during his detention. A court order finally finds that White and Stiller are one and the same. White/Stiller passes no comment on this. A 'postscript from the public prosecutor' informs us of what follows. Stiller/White begins a new life with his wife Julika, living by Lake Geneva and trying to make a living as a potter. When Julika's health takes another turn for the worse and she finally dies, Stiller comes to grief yet again as a result of the internal contradictions of his identity and personal responsibility, the root cause of his sense of inner despair.

With *Stiller*, Frisch wrote his most overtly psychological novel. His novels revolve around the themes of loss of the sense of self, the choice of self, the role-playing nature of existence (*Mein Name sei Gantenbein – Let My Name be Gantenbein*, 1964) and identity problems. Frisch came to the conclusion that he had no language with which to express reality, only for what lay behind it, the pre- and unconscious level that exposed reality. It is this that gives his reflective writing style its penetrating quality and his novel of consciousness its form. Frisch ends his novel tersely: 'Stiller stayed in Glion and lived alone.' This hermetic reduction of his character, already seen when the court pronounced its judgement on his identity, discredits all forms of a language that believes itself capable of being equal to reality and literature on the plane of factual statement. With all its echoes of Sartre's screenplay *Les jeux sont faits*, 1947, (*The Game is Up*), Frisch's *Stiller* may have made it clear that the 'reality' of the 1950s was in great need of reflection. Frisch's novel had opened up an inner psychological space that was a shambles.

Heinrich Böll

One of the few works of the 1950s in which the accommodation of the past and criticism of the present are inextricably bound up together is Heinrich Böll's novel *Billard um halbzehn* (*Billiards at Nine-thirty*) (1959). The deliberate simplicity of Böll's earlier works makes the epic construction of this one seem complex by comparison, since his storyline precludes linear, successive narrative modes. Starting with a single day, 6 September 1958, and ultimately returning to it, the development of three generations of the Fähmels, a family of architects, is dealt with in flashbacks, beginning in 1907. The abbey of St Anthony is a symbol of construction and destruction running through the novel. In 1907, Heinrich Fähmel receives a commission to build it. In the final days of World War II, his son Robert destroys it with explosives in order to erect 'a monument to the lambs that no-one shepherded'. Finally, Robert's son Joseph is to help reconstruct it during his own training to become an architect. This development over three generations is concentrated into 6 September 1958, the day on which Joseph Fähmel finds the chalk marks drawn by his father to indicate where to place the explosives. On this day a friend of Robert Fähmel returns from exile, and is forced to realise that while he is still on the wanted list, former Nazis have established themselves as 'democratic' representatives of the Federal German state. On this day too, Johanna Fähmel, Robert's mother and wife of Heinrich Fähmel, leaves a mental home in order to shoot a former fascist on her husband's eightieth birthday. She shoots, however, not him but – by way of a symbol of the overlapping of past and present – a political opportunist seeking to harness former fascists to his bandwagon. The various elements of the story are woven together into a complex fabric. Recollections are presented in the form of both internal and external monologues, as well as actual speech, juxtaposed in time and made to overlap, bound by a diversity of symbols and leitmotifs, associations and citations. These thus form a montage, a variously fractured 'path out of the layers of past transitoriness into a transitory present' (Böll). All the same, this ingenious construction provoked criticism, since the symbolism of the novel in particular does not arise out of the narrative theme in the natural course of events, but discernibly remains the result of an external structuring intervention by Böll in his subject-matter. This charge can be discounted with regard to the central symbol of the book, the abbey of St Anthony, but not with regard to the symbolic pair of opposites around which the novel is structured – the 'sacrament of the buffalo' and the 'sacrament of the lambs', representing persecutor and persecuted, nationalists and pacificists, fascists and anti-fascists. This symbolic pair of opposites in fact transforms a biblical, theological metaphor into a kind of supra-historical, supra-social background against which politico-historical action is assessed. This sums up a fundamental problem with Böll the writer of fiction, who writes from a Catholic standpoint. He does not begin to resolve this problem until his attempt at a fundamental criticism of the Church as an institution, *Ansichten eines Clowns* (*Views of a Clown*) (1963). His radio plays, stories and novels are least convincing from the literary point of view where there is structural intervention using religious elements, metaphors and maxims, or where the latter are even given the function of narrative techniques. *Billard um halbzehn* is not a problematic novel because it was written with high artistic ambitions, or because the author was under the spell of the *nouveau roman* or a 'compulsion to be modern', but because the symbolic structure and elaboration of motifs are not entirely appropriate to the narrative intention.

'Narrated contemporary history' might be a concise designation for this kind of literature. The devices it uses are simplicity, even simplification, of language and syntax. As Heinrich Böll rightly stressed, however: 'Nevertheless, this very process of 'becoming simple' requires an enormous refinement of devices, countless complicated procedures.' Thus it also entailed an accommodation of the past. The pomposity of fascist poetry of legitimation needed to be overcome just as much as the poetic ineptitude of the post-war era and its verbal bombast. This was accomplished by means of a creatively simplified presentation of everyday life during the War and the post-war period, such as is to be found in Böll's early stories and novels (*Der Zug war pünktlich – The Train Was on Time*, 1949; *Wanderer, kommst du nach Spa... – Wanderer, When Should You Come to Spa ...?* 1950; *Wo warst du, Adam – Where Were You, Adam*, 1951; *Und sagte kein einziges Wort – Acquainted with the Night*, 1953; *Haus ohne Hüter – House Without Keepers*, 1954). The same may also be said of Hans Werner Richter, who presents typical life-stories of the World War II and the post-war eras in his novels *Sie fielen aus Gottes Hand* (*They Fell Out of God's Hand*) (1951), and *Linus Fleck oder Der Verlust der Würde* (*Linus Fleck, or Loss of Dignity*) (1959). This narrative style is marked by a definite satirical streak, which for its part indicated the distance of the narrator from what he was narrating. The aim is not to achieve an identification of the reader with events, but rather to make him think, criticise and question. The limitations of narrative fiction of this kind, as may be observed in Martin Walser's first novel *Ehen in Philippsburg* (*Marriages in Philippsburg*) (1957), a social satire on the post-war era, are most clearly apparent where the realistic approach to narration itself is transcended. In Alfred Andersch's autobiographical account *Die Kirschen der Freiheit* (*The Cherries of Liberty*), the existential predicament of flight and liberty is not only depicted using realistic devices, but at the same time objectivised by means of the integration of reflective elements. This creates a narrative atmosphere such as was scarcely attained again in Andersch's later novels, despite similar motifs and thematic elements (*Sansibar oder der letzte Grund – The Flight Afar*, 1957; *Die Rote – The Red One*, 1960).

'Discontemporaneities'

All surveys of literary history are faced with the problem of having to choose from the profusion of material underlying them, and to indicate lines of development which may fail to draw attention to some particular feature or other. The outline offered here is no exception. Attention has been focused so far on authors of the modern Young German era and of an earlier writing tradition. A third strand in the development of literary history has not yet been mentioned: that of writers of the exile era who produced major prose works after the founding of the Federal Republic. Thomas Mann, for example, following his *Doktor Faustus*, published his novel *Der Erwählte* (*The Holy Sinner*) (1951), the story *Die Betrogene* (*The Black Swan*) (1953) and his masterly parody on the German novel of development *Die Bekenntnisse des Hochstaplers Felix Krull* (*Confessions of the Imposter Felix Krull*) (1954). Alfred Döblin, later emphatically acknowledged by Günter Grass as his mentor, published in 1956 his novel *Hamlet oder Die lange Nacht nimmt ein Ende* (*Hamlet, or The Long Night Comes to an End*) in East Berlin – a major late work concerned with psychological issues in the context of the problems of war. Another work to be mentioned in this connection is Joseph Breitbach's novel *Bericht über Bruno* (*Report on Bruno*), published as late as 1962. Here, the author treats political reality as the subject of a thrilling novel, depicting the material driving forces behind political actions (greed, the craving for recognition, fear) using realistic means. In general, the works of exile authors may be summed up as a continuation of paths that had already been trodden. There were no innovations, but there were, in such authors as Thomas Mann, new narrative heights achieved with already familiar literary devices.

Three traditions

There were thus three literary traditions: that of the emigrants, that of authors who had survived the Third Reich and that of the 'young moderns'. In addition to these, however, some authors remained problematic and defied classification, such as Hans-Erich Nossack, or Gerd Gaiser. The latter had a huge success with his fighter pilot novel *Die sterbende Jagd* (*The Dying Pursuit*) (1953), which evinces echoes of Jünger's elitist thinking – the heroic swansong of the heroic lives of the world war, lapped up by a conservative reading public. Conservatism is also evident in Hans-Erich Nossack, but here in a non-conformist sense. His novel *Spätestens im November* (*In November at the Latest*) (1955) depicts people who lose

687

themselves in what from the existential viewpoint is absurd activity. The way out is offered in the form of the self-imposed isolation of the loner, the search for the inner self (*Spirale – Spirals*, 1956; *Der jüngere Bruder – The Younger Brother*, 1958), a theme that Nossack was to take up again and again, with variations, including his novel *Der Fall d'Arthez (The d'Arthez Case)* (1968).

Fresh tones

On the one hand, therefore, the themes and forms of the 1950s show a continuation of narrative traditions that had already been developed. On the other hand, however, there was an unmistakably fresh tone in the choice of subject-matter and narrative devices. Although 'Young German literature of the modern age' drew on models both from Germany (Arnold Zweig, Lion Feuchtwanger) and abroad (Ernest Hemingway), it also drew on such literary inspirations as war themes, the problem of fascism and the conflicts of the post-war era and the present day as thematic pre-requisites that likewise affected style. The repertoire of narrative devices involved contained a broad spectrum of literary techniques, ranging from the limited potential of socially critical, realistic simplicity to the baroque-grotesque narrative monument of Günter Grass. The 1950s in the Federal Republic of Germany saw the emergence of a narrative fiction tradition that was to persist throughout the 1960s into the present, and spill over beyond the frontiers of West Germany. This development was owed, of course, not merely to its literary merits, but also to the indisputable socio-political *engagement* of its leading exponents (Grass, Böll, and above all Walser), who rallied again and again to combat restorative developments and conservative shifts in trend. This is another reason why the tension between literature and politics has persisted to the present day.

Theatre without drama

A difficult fresh start

Max Frisch reports that Bertolt Brecht burst into a fit of rage following their attendance of a theatre performance in the southern German town of Konstanz in 1948. He maintains that Brecht's fury was directed at the naivety, thoughtlessness and lack of feeling with which German playhouses began to perform in the post-war period, as if virtually unscathed by the immediate past: 'The vocabulary of these survivors, however carefree they might be, their affectation on stage, their cheerful obliviousness, the inso-lence with which they simply carried on where they had left off, as if no more than their houses had been destroyed, their salvation through art, their premature reconciliation with their own country, all this was worse than had been feared.' Brecht added with consternation: 'This calls for a completely fresh start.' This bitter anecdote is illustrative on two counts. First, it reveals the expectation with which Bertolt Brecht the theatre-maker and theatre theoretician returned to Germany from the United States – i.e. that people had learned from the experience of fascism, both in the arts and elsewhere. It likewise helps to explain why Brecht saw no chance of making a positive contribution to theatrical life in West Germany. Second, it reveals the sorry state of theatre in the Federal Republic at the end of the 1940s and in the 1950s. Following the irritations of the early post-war years, and the collapse of attempts to make a fresh start, suppression set in with full force. Authors such as Wolfgang Borchert, Carl Zuckmayer and Günther Weisenborn remained exceptions to the rule. Marked by an approach that was strongly critical of the times, their plays were unable to find a point of contact with theatrical developments in Western Europe or the United States, and thus had little prospect of continuation. This is why German post-war theatre was shaped by non-German authors of metaphysical-religious drama, such as Paul Claudel, T.S. Eliot, W.H. Auden, Christopher Fry and Thornton Wilder. In the aftermath of fascism, West German society relished a dalliance with the mood of the 'last days' and general decline, which, in plays such as Wilder's *The Skin of our Teeth* (1942–4), rigidified into a kind of human drama removed from time and obligation, untouched by history. Parallel with these, as part of the trend towards philosophical Existentialism, plays of the absurd theatre became prevalent on West German stages, involving authors such as Eugene Ionesco, Samuel Beckett, Jean-Paul Sartre, Jean Cocteau and Albert Camus.

Existentialism

The topical significance of French Existentialism lay in those ideological vacuums which, both before, and even more so after World War II, grew into feelings of emptiness, powerlessness, despair and fear. As a philosophy of liberty for each and every individual, it offered its German recipients an interpretation of human existence that was interesting in a number of ways. For one thing, it offered the degraded and disoriented war- and post-war generation a model for a philosophy of anthropology, one of 'man without transcendence', into which the experiences of battles, night bombing raids and Nazi terror could be incorporated wholeheartedly. 'There is only one really serious philosophical problem: suicide.' These are the opening words of Albert Camus' essay *The Myth of Sisyphus* (1943, German 1956). Man was faced with a 'preliminary' experience of his own death and his freedom of decision. These are the two focal points that make this uncommonly atheistic non-systematic philosophy, ultimately exclusively concentrated on human existence, so fascinating. Moreover, the confrontation between such writers as Jean-Paul Sartre (*Being and Nothingness*, 1943, German 1962) and the German philosophical tradition, beginning with Kant and Hegel and ending with Husserl and Heidegger, established an intellectual arena that served to divert attention from the fatal developments of the German 'philosophy of existence' up to the Freiburg rectoral address by Heidegger when inaugurating the 1933 summer semester, at which he had effectively handed over the entire philosophical tradition to the new rulers of Germany. Finally, French Existentialism offered a literary model (Sartre, *What is Literature?*, 1947) which, enriched and made politically credible by the experiences of the French Resistance against the Nazi occupation, for the first time placed at the centre of consideration the decision-making process of the author *prior* to writing.

'Why does one write?'

The concept of 'politically committed literature' thus firmly drew the writer into this philosophy of liberty. 'Since critics condemn me in the name of literature, without revealing what they understand by it, the best way to answer them is to say that one examines without prejudice what matters in the art of writing. What does writing mean? Why does one write? For whom? It seems in fact that these questions have never been asked' (Sartre [translated from German]).

Albert Camus and Jean-Paul Sartre, who are comparable despite their differences, and almost all of whose works were translated into German during the 1950s, are important not only as philosophical essayists, but no less so as dramatists and novelists (*romanciers*). Indeed, their chief impact derives from the stage and novel. In *Crime passionnel* (1948), Sartre addresses the attitude of the bourgeois intelligentsia to totalitarianism. Under Communist Party orders to do away with the functionary Hoederer, the middle-class Hugo ultimately does kill him, but out of jealousy and private motives. When the Party swings back in line with Hoederer's way of thinking, and Hugo now stands in their way, however, he seeks to have the murder considered as a political act.

In Albert Camus' first novel *The Outsider* (1942), which was followed by *The Plague* (1947) and *The Fall* (1956), as well as numerous dramas and essays, the clerk Meursault is treated as an alien in society because he feels no sense of grief at his mother's death. When he commits murder and shows no signs of remorse, he is condemned to death. He sums up: 'So that all may be fulfilled, and so I might feel a little less alone, I wish for only one more thing: that on the day of my execution there should be many spectators to greet me with shouts of hatred.' This interpretation of society as an absurd world of wolves also suited the mood of the postwar era. For young university intellectuals in the Federal Republic especially, French Existentialism played a key role in the confrontation between sons and their fathers, who could not be absolved from their share of culpability for the rise of Nazism.

The individual rituals of annihilation and self-destruction of Existentialist drama, such as Sartre's *In Camera* (1944–9), collided with audiences who were trying to comprehend their own socio-historical situation in terms of the categories of immutability and *Geworfenheit*. Bertolt Brecht, however, the sole German author of world renown in this period, was boycotted as a communist until the 1960s as a result of conservative campaigns by West German playhouses.

Contemporary drama

It may be concluded from this that there was no contemporary drama worthy of the name in the Federal Republic in the 1950s. There was, however, a German-speaking drama from Switzerland, notably associated with Max Frisch and Friedrich Dürrenmatt. Most worthy of note in this context are Max Frisch's plays *Biedermann und die Brandstifter* (*Biedermann and the Fire-raisers*) (1959) and *Andorra* (1961), as well as Dürrenmatt's drama *Der Besuch der alten Dame* (*The Visit*) (1956) and *Die Physiker* (*The Physicists*) (1962). These plays are written in a spirit of critical Humanism, and evince a moral rigour that highlights, partly in parable form, the problems of individual and collective intimidation and guilt in the modern world. This shared feature of contemporary criticism, however, should not obscure a substantial difference between the views of these two authors on the theatre – views which had major consequences for their disparate dramatic work. Frisch described his *Biedermann* play as a *Lehrstück ohne Lehre*, a didactic play without a lesson, an idea totally dissimilar from Brecht's pedagogical, didactic motivation. In his speech *The Author and the Theatre* (1964), Frisch expressly stated his distrust of the potential for didactic impact that Brecht sought to attribute to poetry in the context of social processes. This may explain why Frisch frequently indulges in abstract moralising in his plays without imparting insights into the conduct of his characters. His implicit retreat into an idealistic aesthetics that separates art from life in the Schillerian vein makes it impossible for him to argue dramatically in specific contemporary historical circumstances.

Dürrenmatt is different. *The Physicists* is an attempt to make audiences aware of the menace inherent in modern technological advances and in the dubious progress of modern science by, as he states in his twenty-one-point programme to the play, providing them with their 'worst possible future scenario'. The last of these twenty-one points reads: 'Drama can dupe an audience into exposing itself to reality, but it cannot force them to make a stand against it, or even to come to terms with it.' In this respect more sceptical than Brecht the dialectic materialist, therefore, Dürrenmatt wants to confront his audience with the problems presented in his plays, but not to evoke potential solutions through the ruse of dramaturgy. The 'worst possible future scenario' that events can have (in a comedy!) makes fun of horror because it would not otherwise be comprehensible or representable. It leaves that horror, however, in a world that has been unable to come to terms with its own traumas.

Seen from this angle, Dürrenmatt's reflections on drama theory may represent an appropriate response to the situation in the Federal Republic in the transition to the 1960s. The fact, however, that no German drama was found for playhouses in the Federal Republic in the 1950s is indicative not only of a past, but also a present that had not yet been dealt with. It took the traumatic events of the 1960s to rekindle an awareness that the theatre also has a language at its disposal – a language, moreover, capable not only of duping audiences, but also of bringing them to make a stand, and even take action. This hindsight has subsequently vindicated Brecht, rather than Dürrenmatt.

The radio play: between dream and self-destruction

Bertolt Brecht's vision of the social functions of radio may also be cited in such a way as to permit an assessment of post-war developments. In a lecture in 1932, Brecht expounded theses on media politics which in the post-1945 era could still have been surprisingly topical, and formed part of the wider demand for democratisation in other spheres of public life. In the early 1930s, Brecht's idea was to transform radio from a 'distribution apparatus' into a 'communication apparatus'. This would have entailed an involvement by listeners in production and transforming production forms, in accordance with advances in technical standards, by means of 'on-going, continuous suggestions for the improved employment of this apparatus in the public interest'. Clearly, this was not an end in itself: Brecht's main concern was to dislodge 'the social basis of these apparatuses, and to dispute their use in the interests of the few'. This type of agenda seemed at first to be met by the organisational form of radio institutions envisaged under public law in the Federal Republic. Experience in the Third Reich had yielded the lesson that bringing mass media 'politically into line' made them incapable of perceiving more than their propaganda functions, and hardly able to provide stimulus towards innovation. The outcome had been the complete evaporation of whole areas of programming, including the production of radio plays, for example. The organisational form of radio under public law, set beside a press organised on a private business basis, guaranteed programme diversity with a proviso guaranteeing the institutional participation of 'all socially relevant groups'. This potential for exerting influence thus appeared to be available to churches no less than trade unions, and to employers' associations no less than political parties. Media policy in practice, however, soon threw this concept open to doubt. Since 'socially relevant groups' are defined by the political parties represented in the German state parliaments, the degree of influence of such groups in practice reflected the relative strengths of parliamentary factions. What had been intended as an institutional democratisation of radio institutions atrophied into a kind of party proportional representation.

Radio plays and features

After the war, innovation in Brecht's sense of the term signified a close connection between the production of radio plays and the reportage-like form of the 'feature'. Here the focal point was not the pure literary work of art, but the mediation of stylistically ambitious forms of presentation dealing with topical social problems from various spheres (politics, culture, technology, science), such as were undertaken by Alfred Andersch, Axel Eggebrecht, Ernst Schnabel, and later Helmut Heissenbüttel. Listener participation, an integral part of this kind of innovation, was at the same time a feature of radio play production from 1947 to 1950, and shaped its form. In 1947 and 1950, for example, Ernst Schnabel called on listeners to the North-West German radio station (NWDR) to cooperate in his features. His success points to a potential for further work in this sphere that has scarcely been tapped since then: 35,000 and 80,000 listeners respectively took part, with experiences, notes and references, in Schnabel's broadcasts, which in this way became their own. This success contributed to the popularisation of the radio play in a way matched only by Wolfgang Borchert's radio play *Draussen vor der Tür* (*The Man Outside*) (1947).

However, the organisational separation of the radio play and feature production within NWDR in 1950 presaged a narrowing of the radio play concept that was to set in during subsequent years. In line with tendencies already apparent within social developments, listener interest in the 1950s shifted from the politically-motivated feature to the literary work of art. The radio play thus developed into a kind of rhetorical entertainment. Similarly, the manner in which works were received changed from participation to internalisation, while critical activity developed into a consumer attitude.

Günter Eich

Not surprisingly, therefore, the 1950s radio play is marked chiefly by the poetic creation of dream-worlds. A veritable tradition was established with the example set by Günter Eich, who devised a pattern that could be imitated with his radio play *Träume* (*Dreams*) (1951). Whole radio studios were transformed into laboratories producing acoustic dream-worlds.

Günter Eich was the outstanding exponent of West German radio play-writing in the 1950s. He was one of those lyric poets in the tradition of the 1930 *Kolonne* circle who, like Peter Huchel, had already written and produced radio plays during the Third Reich (*Weizenkantate* – *Wheat Cantata* and *Fährten in die Prärie* – *Journeys into the Prairie*, both first performed in 1936). His real breakthrough as an author of radio plays, however, came with *Träume* (*Dreams*), first performed in 1951, which was to exert an enduring influence on radio plays in the ensuing years. None-theless, as a stylistic work of art for radio it followed a somewhat tra-ditional dramaturgical pattern. Over and above, that is, an identification of listeners with dreaming figures from five continents, allowing the play to come over in the form of an existential, nightmarish menace, and beyond a kind of catharsis in the Aristotelian sense, the intention was to convey a sense of deep-rooted, existential peril. The emotional, lyrical style of deliv-ery, the construction of a nightmare world through language, as well as the immediacy and evocative power of Eich's poetic world of words, may have been what evoked the astonishing response to this play among the public. In a world caught up in the economic miracle, Eich aroused pre-dominantly resistance and shock among his listeners, shaking them up with his postulate: 'Everything that happens concerns you.' And yet he also felt a need to give both greater political precision to a radio scene that was increasingly geared to existentialist expectations, and a socially-accentuated, oppositional quality to its emotion, which was imbued with a sense of general menace and peril. Eich attempted to accomplish this with the well-known concluding sequence added on to the end of the play in 1953: 'Do not be complacent. Be sand, not oil, in the machinery of the world.'

Günter Eich, the most prolific and influential post-1945 radio play author, exerting influence not only on his listeners, but also and mainly on other authors, frequently felt a need to add specifying statements of this kind in later revisions of his works. And rightly so, for his aspiration to convey politico-social postulates using the techniques of the modern radio play was sometimes thwarted in his earlier works by a traditional style of dramaturgy that tended towards an existential approach outside the temporal context. His later works, as well as his theoretical obser-vations, thus betray a mounting distrust of conceptions still confident of the ability to fend off social inquiry by means of creating symbols.

Other radio play authors

Other notable writers besides Eich also emerged as radio play authors in the fifties, such as Wolfgang Hildesheimer, Friedrich Dürrenmatt, Ingeborg Bachmann and Ilse Aichinger, Walter Jens, Heinrich Böll and Dieter Wel-lershof, whose works continued to be largely bound up with a literary representation of the experiences and problems of other worlds. From the beginning of the 1960s, however, a new radio play trend emerged, converting this dissatisfaction with the traditional formal language of radio into a radical focus on its acoustic facilities – on the technical resources of radio. This 'new radio play', which also worked with elements of original sound, comes far closer than the 1950s radio play to Brecht's call for innovation, although it still leaves open the question of how it was able to alter the 'social basis' of the mass media. It calls for an active listener, one who cooperates and thinks along with it and who is open to collage, montage techniques and constructive questions rather than glib answers – a listener who is prepared to accept the demolition of preconceived correlations. A noteworthy example of this is Wolf Wondratschek's stereo radio play *Paul oder die Zerstörung eines Hörbeispiels* (*Paul, or the Demolition of a Radio Model*) (first performed 1970). This play involves more than a montage of citations, audio fragments and noises as the sensory impressions and associative fragments of Paul the lorry driver: this montage, and the fictional character of Paul himself, are continually conveyed as fictions. The demolition of radio as a medium using a radio model is itself revealed as no more than a fiction, making it both criticism of 1950s radio, and constructive demontage of the medium by means of its own devices.

Clearly the potential of such a conception, its modes of thinking and arguing, was best able to make use of those authors whose poetic interests already focused on work with language as a material. These were the authors of concrete poetry, such as Franz Mon and Helmut Heissenbüttel, language 'artists' such as Ludwig Harig, and poets of the Vienna group, such as Ernst Jandl and Gerhard Rühm. 'Anything is possible. Anything goes', declared Helmut Heissenbüttel in 1968. This licence was to lead to a complete abolition of interrelationships of meaning, brought on by distrust of the superficial phenomena of reality. Obviously the technical potential of the acoustic demontage of reality was not an end in itself in this newly-developing medium of the 1960s. Rather, it implemented 'innovations' aimed at evoking a constructive sense of unease with regard to the 'social basis' of the medium itself – by changing modes of perception, demolishing the interrelationships of meaning in an environment that had become meaningless and by means of a 'constitutive montage' (Ernst Bloch) of apparently disparate elements.

The politicisation of literature (1961–8)

For the Federal Republic of Germany, the 1960s were a time of profound social crisis. The completion of the period of economic reconstruction, and the onset of an unconstrained, crisis-free, prospering economy that had first begun to appear at the end of the 1950s, were just as important a factor in the developments of the 1960s as the building of the Berlin Wall on 13 August 1961.

These two outward signs of a political policy stretched to its limits rocked German society's view of itself – a society whose belief in the political potency of the West and its own economic growth had up to then been devoid of all self-doubt. This new self-doubt, however, most prevalent among the young generation, intellectuals and the working class, was also awakened and fed by a number of other factors, pertaining to both domestic and foreign policy.

The 'catastrophe of education': a by-word

These factors included the 'catastrophe of German education' (Georg Picht) – which now made this highly advanced industrial nation, the Federal Republic, look very small in terms of its education policy; the social struggles going on in the Third World, and especially of the Vietnamese against the waging of a US war in Vietnam, which outraged the young generation especially; the economic crises of 1966–7, with mass lay-offs and pit closures; the formation of the Great Coalition of Social Democrats and Christian Democrats in 1966, which likewise suggested the onset of a process of political levelling, and a now merely formal understanding of democracy among the established parties; the passing of emergency legislation in 1968 which permitted, in the event of a crisis, the setting aside of a whole range of elementary and basic civil rights; and not least the world-wide student revolts and the emergence of a body of non-parliamentary opposition, which were both a factor in and an expression of this social and political crisis.

In a changing society, these developmental factors had repercussions in the cultural sphere, and literature in particular, that remain discernible to the present day. These pertained chiefly to the way people involved in creating culture saw themselves. Specifically, such people began increasingly to realise that the image of the 'free-floating intellectual' following his own creative impulses removed from the social conflicts of his time was a misleading one. Writers such as Günter Grass and Siegfried Lenz openly committed themselves to social democracy, Martin Walser and Peter Weiss to more socialist positions, and Hans Magnus Enzensberger became a spokesman for the New Left and its Third World commitment. The separation of art from politics that had characterised the 1950s was thus followed by a politicisation of literature in the 1960s.

Vietnam: the watchword

This found its clearest and most unmistakable expression in the political lyrics of the period. Authors such as Erich Fried (*und Vietnam und – and*

Vietnam and, 1966), Yaak Karsunke and F.C. Delius, and song-writers such as Franz Josef Degenhardt and Dieter Sieverkrüpp, took current affairs as the themes for their poetry texts, in order to create a lyric verse, songs, and *Agitprop* poetry that had in common a resolute stand against domination, oppression, and exploitation. Student revolts, class struggle and, again and again, the war in Vietnam, were the focal points of this political lyric poetry. It thereby entailed a change of approach in poetic terms also, since the political quality of poetry was no longer the subject of discussion, as it had been in Enzensberger's postulate. Instead, the deliberate use of poetry as a function of political struggle now came to the fore.

Political theatre: recent history as theatrical event

Similarly, German theatre did not escape the implications of social trends within the Federal Republic. Apart from the Swiss playwrights Max Frisch and Friedrich Dürrenmatt, there had been no sign in the 1950s of any serious efforts on the part of young stage writers to create a new kind of drama in the German-speaking world. The exact opposite was the case in the 1960s, which saw the appearance of numerous stage plays, some of which dealt explicitly with political themes, and indisputably evinced both a sense of social commitment and a style of their own. The reasons for this transformation may be sought in the changing way authors saw themselves. They were now seeking to use the vehicles at their disposal – vehicles for the creative and dramatic adaptation of reality – in order to confront recent developments and the immediate past. They were not concerned here with a mere bald reflection of reality – an effectively elaborated portrayal in terms of theatrical technique. Instead, as Rolf Hochhuth states, they were concerned with the potential for changing that reality: 'Political theatre cannot concern itself with the task of reproducing reality, which is always political. It must concern itself with confronting that reality by projecting a new one.'

On 20 March 1963 Erwin Piscator was responsible for the first performance of a tragedy entitled *Der Stellvertreter* (*The Representative*) by a hitherto completely unknown playwright, Rolf Hochhuth. This play unleashed a literary and political controversy of an intensity probably unmatched by any other play since 1945. His play took up a theme that had so far been taboo in public life – the more or less compliant attitude of the Roman Catholic Church, and in particular of Pope Pius XII, to the extermination of the Jews in the Third Reich. The plot is based on thorough research into contemporary history. For all this, however, Hochhuth's Christian tragedy is not 'documentary' in the sense of the documentary literature that was to develop later. Almost all the characters and their actions are invented, albeit within their historical framework. Hochhuth transposes the reality he has uncovered into fiction, alienating it aesthetically through his use of free rhythms. And yet the extraordinary power of the play derives solely from the political and moral challenge it evokes. Key historical figures are called before a theatrical tribunal to account for their actions. The central character of the play is the Jesuit priest Riccardo Fontana. When all the latter's attempts to influence the attitude of the Church flounder in the face of the power-political calculations of the Pope, he volunteers to go the same way as the victims of the Auschwitz gas chambers. Although Hochhuth highlights the dependence of the Church on the economic and political situation, he ultimately allows only a moral solution, in which the individual is free to choose between good and evil. This outcome permits him to resolve the complex problems of the plot in theatrical terms, but on the other hand also over-simplifies to an unacceptable degree both historical reality and the criminal entanglement of those involved in it.

The problem was that anyone who used the theatre as a sounding-board in this way opened himself in the 1960s to the accusation of abusing the theatre stage and the potential of the play performance in order to propound political ideas in the guise of dramatic illusion.

'Realism'

The provocative aspect of this was the presence of that element in all political theatre that Brecht defined as the hallmark of realism: 'Realism is not [about] how real things are, but how things really are.' This delineation of Realism points to a characteristic device of political theatre, which nevertheless still falls short of a general definition, i.e. the inclusion and adaptation of documentary material from contemporary history and the present day. Plays such as Rolf Hochhut's *Soldaten* (*Soldiers*) and *Der Stellvertreter* (*The Representative*), Peter Weiss's *Die Ermittlung* (*The Investigation*) and *Vietnam Diskurs* (*Vietnam Discourse*) are political plays in the broad sense of the term, with an inclusion of problems from contemporary history. Inasmuch, however, as they deal 'with the documentation of subject-matter', as Peter Weiss put it, they may at the same time be seen as documentary theatre. This blend of explicitly political theatre with documentary elements came to the fore in German theatre of the 1960s. This type of theatre draws its subject-matter as a matter of course from topical or contemporary historical themes. These themes may be grouped around four central issues: peace politics, tyranny, revolution and contemporary problems.

'Peace'

The peace issue encompassed the experiences of World War II, as well as the development of modern means of mass destruction in the age of nuclear fission. The tribulations of war and the nuclear threat are the themes drawn on by authors such as Heinar Kipphardt and Rolf Hochhuth, Leopold Ahlsen (*Philemon und Baukis*, 1961) and Hans Günter Michelsen (*Helm – Helmet*, 1965) in their treatment of these two aspects of the peace issue. The works of Kipphardt and Hochhut are particularly noteworthy in this connection. In *Der Hund des Generals* (*The General's Dog*) (first performed in 1962), Kipphardt uses the devices of epic theatre (songs, open stage structure, actor portraits, and the inclusion of original documents) to show the inhumanity and irrationality of war using an everyday example. The problem of binding orders, presented from various angles, highlights the personal responsibility even of high-ranking military officers, also exposing war as a special form of contempt for humanity. In order to achieve a degree of distance from his audience, Kipphardt chooses the setting of a judicial hearing to provide a dramatic framework from which events during the war are re-enacted in flashbacks.

The inhumanity of war is likewise central to Rolf Hochhuth's *Soldaten (Soldiers)* (1967), although with one distinct difference: Hochhuth is not seeking to do away with war entirely, but only to have it conducted in a 'more humane' way. Using the somewhat conventional structure, from the dramaturgical point of view, of the 'play within a play', the work's success derives mainly from the subjects with which it deals. These were the militarily pointless killing of civilians (the bombing of Dresden), a military operation planned by Churchill and the hypothesis of the murder of members of the Polish exile government by Churchill, which is credibly developed in the play. Heinar Kipphardt's *In der Sache J. Robert Oppenheimer* (*The Case of J. Robert Oppenheimer*) (1964), in contrast, deals with certain of the preconditions for war. Using the historical example of Oppenheimer, the physicist known as the 'father of the American atomic bomb', Kipphardt tackles a problem already broached by Brecht (*Leben des Galilei – The Life of Galileo*, 1938–9) and Dürrenmatt (*Die Physiker – The Physicists*, 1962) before him: the responsibility of the scientist for his discoveries. Against the background of the Communist witch-hunts of the McCarthy era in the USA, Kipphardt relates this problem to technological advances in the military sphere. The tension in the play, which once again uses epic devices, derives from the interplay between military pros and cons and the political background of those years – a structuring principle to which Kipphardt continued to adhere even in his last play *Bruder Eichmann (Brother Eichmann)*, first performed posthumously in 1983.

'Brute force'

The subject of tyranny had already been treated by Max Frisch in *Biedermann und die Brandstifter* and *Andorra* in terms of the problem of individual and collective guilt and intimidation. In the 1960s, it was to be taken up again as a subject for drama adaptations in plays by West German authors, although some of these were in more concrete contemporary historical form, integrating documentary elements. Like Frisch, Siegfried Lenz also uses a parable-like device in his play, intended as a basis for discussion, *Zeit der Schuldlosen* (*Time of the Innocents*) (first performed on stage in 1961; as a radio play in 1960). The play depicts the process whereby guilt is incurred, using two extreme situations that relate to each other in a precise way. In both, an 'ordinary', ostensibly blameless person is confronted with someone who is 'guilty'. The latter incur guilt by succumbing to the power-political contingencies of a dictatorship in a situation of existential danger, saving their own skins in exchange for the destruction of another human being.

Lenz's second stage play of those years is a comparable, parable-like moralising work reminiscent of Erich Kästner's *Die Schule der Diktatoren* (*The School of Dictators*) (1949, first performed 1957): *Das Gesicht* (*The Face*) (1964). Here, too, we find the construction of an extreme situation, the problem of dictatorship, and the problem of the individual incursion of guilt. The difficult aspect about both these plays is the moralising abstractness with which the problem of guilt is removed from its temporal context and presented to a certain degree as an anthropological, existential constant. Although in the case of Lenz these extreme situations have a political foundation, the latter owes nothing to any recognisable social reality. The issue is one of politico-moral abstraction, the discussion of a problem, a kind of theatre of ideas. It is not about transposing these issues into characters, plot and dramaturgy in a manner that is appropriate to the stage medium, as was the case only a little later with Peter Weiss.

Peter Weiss

The period from December 1963 to August 1965 in Hamburg witnessed what was known as the Auschwitz trial, in which charges were brought against eighteen former guards and superintendents from the Nazi extermination camp at Auschwitz. This was the first time a wider public had been made familiar with the massive scale of the crimes committed there. It was also the first time that people found guilty of such offences were sentenced by a West German court. Peter Weiss, himself a Jew who had fled into forced exile, followed both this trial and an on-the-spot investigation in Auschwitz as an observer. In his documentary play *Die Ermittlung* (*The Investigation*) (first performed at seventeen playhouses throughout East and West Germany simultaneously on 17 October 1965), he restricts himself to the model and example of this criminal trial and a delivery of the facts in as unstylised a way as possible. Using his own notes, the records of the trial proceedings, and historical documents, he attempts to uncover the constituent facts that led to these crimes. The play – in the form of a montage of scenes – presents no more than what really happened, and what the trial proceedings were about – the extermination of Jews. The eleven cantos, each subdivided into a further three, making up the play, arrange everyday speech into light rhyme (the subhead also significantly reads: 'Oratorio in eleven cantos'). Through the interplay between the respective addresses and objections of the plaintiffs and the witnesses, the prosecution and the defence, they evoke the mentality of a society in which such crimes had become possible.

In contrast to previous or subsequent attempts to understand Nazism and capture it in literary form, Weiss was not content merely to ask the moral question concerning guilt and its expiation. What *Die Ermittlung* does is to reveal that it was the surrender of the middle class to rampant capitalism, and the entanglement of economic and power-political interests that led to a system which then inevitably morally corrupted the individual also, making Auschwitz possible.

The reason why the relationship between power and guilt became a theme of German drama in the 1960s at all nevertheless requires further explanation. It lies chiefly in the fact that after a long period in which the past was suppressed, during the 1950s and early 1960s, there was now renewed public, and not least academic discussion of fascism. Its ideological version consisted of the thesis of totalitarianism, which made no distinction in principle between communism and fascism, but – and this is where it was akin to parable plays – conceived the problems of power outside time and society, up to a point as essentially identical varieties of oppression. In this light, the works of Hochhuth and Weiss may be understood as concrete ways of addressing the problems of political theatre. They reconstruct situations in which the phenomenon of fascism took specific historical and social form. If one is inclined to draw parallels between the way fascism was dealt with in the arts and in academic inquiry, the progressive discussions of the 1960s pale by comparison with dramas of Hochhuth and Weiss.

'Revolution'

Reflecting German history, the theme of revolution in German drama is presented predominantly in historical guise, or as a problem of the Third World. Against the backdrop of the Cold War, it was a taboo subject. Brecht's *Tage der Commune* (*The Days of the Commune*), written in 1948–9, for example, was not premiered in the Federal Republic until 1970.

Revolutionary topics were thus not aired on the West German stage until the problem of revolution itself had ripened into a subject for public discussion. Once again, the chief exponents were Peter Weiss (*Gesang vom Lusitanian Popanz* – *The Song of the Lusitanian Bogey-man*, 1967; *Vietnam Diskurs* – *Vietnam Discourse*, 1968; *Trotzki im Exil* – *Trotsky in Exile*, 1970; *Hölderlin*, 1972), and Rolf Hochhuth (*Guerillas*, 1970), as well as Hans Magnus Enzensberger (*Das Verhör von Habana* – *The Havana Hearing*, 1970) and Günter Grass (*Die Plebejer proben den Aufstand* – *The Plebeians Rehearse the Uprising*, 1966). These plays primarily discuss the question of whether revolutionary force is justifiable in principle, or whether the perversion of revolutionary methods also discredits the aims of a revolution. The role of artists and intellectuals in revolutionary events has a high profile in these plays. This is the result of a process of self-reflection among authors that forced them to define their own role in the conflicts of their day.

Discussion of 'council communism' (*Rätekommunismus*) at that time, for example, finds expression in Tankred Dorst's drama *Toller* (1968). Here he stages the emergence of the Munich 'Republic of Councils' (*Räterepublik*) of 1919, portraying a historical event by highlighting its topical dimensions in the form of a political revue, 'in parenthesis, fragments and reflections'. Following the success of his play *Die Verfolgung und Ermordung Jean Paul Marats dargestellt durch die Schauspielgruppe des Hospizes zu Charenton unter Anleitung des Herrn de Sade* (*The Persecution and Murder of Jean Paul Marat Presented by the Theatre Company of the Hospice at Charenton Under the Direction of Monsieur de Sade*) (1964), which depicts aspects of the French Revolution using entirely authentic devices of the theatre of illusion, Peter Weiss committed himself emphatically to socialism, protesting publicly against the American war in Vietnam. Weiss realised that politically committed drama of necessity exploded the traditional theatrical area, that he had to depart from the theatre as an institution for bourgeois education, and that a play such as *Vietnam Diskurs* belonged 'in a public place'. In plays and statements of this nature, echoes of the traditions of *Agitprop* theatre and the Piscator revues of the Weimar era are as up-to-date in their way as the impact of street theatre, which was just beginning to emerge in the 1960s. Revolutionary topics went hand in hand with reflection on the revolutionisation of dramatic forms, production, and the social arena in which performances took place. Although Brecht's influence was still discernible everywhere, reflection on the function of theatre itself also points to an attempt to go beyond Brecht's theory of theatre.

The 'present day'

In terms of the problems of the present day, this move away from Brecht could be seen in a number of plays whose themes focus on peripheral existence, and extreme situations and experiences. This departure, however, was not away from the concept of Realism, which continued to underpin them. Here too, things are shown as they 'really are' (Brecht). It is the subject-matter itself, and the way it is unfolded on stage, that point here to a different traditional context in terms of the history of theatre. Authors such as Martin Sperr (*Jagdszenen aus Niederbayern* – *Hunting Scenes from Lower Bavaria*, 1966; *Landshuter Erzählungen* – *Tales from Landshut*, 1968; *Münchner Freiheit*, 1971), Rainer Werner Fassbinder (*Katzelmacher*, 1969), and Franz Xaver Kroetz (*Wildwechsel* – *Wild Animals*, 1971; *Stallerhof*, 1972) draw on the tradition of the socially critical, Realistic folk play devised and implemented by Marieluise Fleisser and Ödön von Horváth prior to the fascist era. The main salient feature of all these plays, besides the fact that they tackle contemporary problems, is their use of (Bavarian) dialect as a hallmark of specific identity, namely that of the authoritarian provincial character. In Fassbinder's *Katzelmacher* and Sperr's *Jagdszenen aus Niederbayern*, a dramatic conflict is built up in a similar manner. An outsider, a homosexual *Gastarbeiter*, is faced with a hostile society in a small village in Bavaria. Sexual envy, anxieties and hatred of anything different drive him into a state of total isolation that ultimately leads to a criminal act. Kroetz's *Wildwechsel* and *Stallerhof* also take the oppressive parochialism of the provinces as their social background. Both plays depict the collapse of a love affair between two underprivileged, dependent human beings as a result of the cruel demands of a social microcosm whose latent brutality erupts into overt inhumanity. The difference between Kroetz on the one hand and Fassbinder and Sperr on the other lies in the divergent functions ascribed to dialect. Whereas in the latter two dialect serves to create a denser atmosphere, in Kroetz it serves as a device for expressing in language the provincial parochialism being portrayed, the 'height of drop between language and obtuseness' (Kroetz). Following his decision to join the German Communist Party (later retracted), Kroetz's method changed as he put into dramaturgical practice his declared intention to move 'away from peripheral manifestations and towards the powerful on the one hand and the average on the other', in *Oberösterreich* (*Upper Austria*) (1972) and *Sterntaler* (1974).

Contemporary issues are also to be found in a number of other plays of the sixties. Martin Walser, for example, wrote a parable of capitalism in his stage play *Überlebensgross Herr Krott* (*Larger than Life Herr Krott*) (1963); in *Eisenwichser* (*Iron-polishers*) (1970) Heinrich Henkel deals with reality in the workaday world of painters and decorators; in *Davor* (*Before*), Günter Grass dramatises crucial discussions during the revolts of school and university students, already dealt with in his novel *örtlich betäubt* (*local anaesthetic*) (1969); in *Die Hebamme* (*The Midwife*) (1972), Rolf Hochhuth brings the problems of the homeless to the stage. In a subhead, Peter Handke described his play *Publikumsbeschimpfung* (*Insulting the Audience*) (written 1965, premiered on 8 June 1966 by Claus Peymann), his first major success, as a *Sprechstück* (a 'spoken play'). Written in the form of a prose-poem (to be divided up among four speakers, in whatever order or length of parts is deemed appropriate), the play proceeds without a plot, characters or props to present various attitudes: 'insult, self-incrimination, confession, statement, question, justification, excuse, prophesy, and the cry for help'. In a play which is a play beyond play(-acting), the audience is confronted with itself. Handke cites, in consistent rhythmical structure and montage, the words, husks of speech, stale jokes and phrases of (theatrical) everyday life, making them palpably discernible by putting them on stage and having them performed. *Sprechstücke*, as the author commented in a later remark on the first edition, 'imitate ironically in the theatre the gestures of the entire accumulated body of natural utterance'. Their initial appearance had an even more provocative impact than had probably been intended. The fact that criticism of speech was made transparent in their surfeit of clichés of speech (a motif taken up by Handke later in his stage play *Kaspar*) tended to be overlooked. *Sprechstücke* present 'the world not in the form of pictures, but in the form of words, and the words of *Sprechstücke* do not present the world as something lying outside, but present the world in the words themselves' (Handke). Nevertheless, the vehement force with which elements of expression drawn from beat and pop music were applied for the first time to bourgeois theatre should not obscure the fact that the protest contained in *Insulting the Audience*, while at all events articulated on the formal level, is not articulated politically: '*Sprechstücke* are prefaces to old plays that have gone independent. They seek not to foment revolution, but to attract attention.'

Overall, therefore, there was an increasing tendency in the theatre not only to take up political and contemporary issues in general, but also to make topical conflicts, burning issues and discussions the subject of stage plays. This involved a staging of strategies for social transformation in a politicised theatre, as well as the world of work and social revolts, and provincial ways of thinking and modes of political conduct. This notwithstanding, the question concerning the impact of this kind of theatre needs to be answered with some scepticism. It is true that Rolf Hochhuth's *Die Hebamme* went on to become the most successful stage hit of the 1972–3 season (with a total audience of some 250,000). It is doubtful, however, whether it achieved anything substantial in terms of changing the attitudes of audiences or the public in general towards the problem of the homeless. It is more realistic to assume that the success of this play (a comedy) is due to its effectiveness on stage, which may, if anything, have obscured the central, distressing problem underneath. The subject-matter, in other words, remains bound by necessity to the aesthetic, social milieu in which it is able to come to light: to the theatre, the space of the stage and the auditorium, the exceptional situation of an evening at the theatre which hardly gives anything away, either about itself or the bourgeois institution that gives it its historical and social context.

The novel: 'Between Realism and the grotesque'

The late 1950s marked the end of a literary era in West German prose. The search for a new autonomous language that had been the hallmark of early post-war literature in particular could now be regarded as at an end, as could the search for themes, subjects, and material that extended beyond the experience of fascism and the war into the present day. By the early 1960s a literary standard had established itself that now permitted reference to a 'literature of the Federal Republic'. A number of authors had also established themselves who were not only to leave an enduring impression on the years that followed, but who were also to become influential figures in their own right. Chief among these were Heinrich Böll, Günter Grass, Siegfried Lenz, Martin Walser and Uwe Johnson. In addition to their literary activities, these writers also constantly and to an unusual degree voiced their opinions in public, in the form of critical journalism. By the same token, they were also focusing more and more on contemporary problems in their literary works.

Wolfgang Koeppen's diagnosis

Wolfgang Koeppen highlights the tension between literary importance on the one hand, and public reputation and the dissemination of works on the other. Koeppen's early works, *Eine unglückliche Liebe* (*Unrequited Love*) (1934) and *Die Mauer schwankt* (*The Teetering Wall*) (1935, reprinted in 1982 under the title *Die Pflicht – The Duty*) had met with resolute opposition from the Nazis. In the 1950s, he published in rapid succession the novels *Tauben im Gras* (*Doves in the Grass*) (1951), *Das Treibhaus* (*The Hothouse*) (1953) and *Der Tod in Rome* (*Death in Rome*) (1954). Influenced by John Dos Passos and James Joyce, these works wrestle with the problems of the present day using avant-garde narrative techniques. So radical and penetrating are they, in fact, that Koeppen's novels contrast sharply from other literary works published at the same time. In *Tauben im Gras*, Koeppen denounced the return of Nazis to West Germany, giving a piercing account of opportunism, restoration, and the well-known developments that took place in post-war West Germany. *Das Treibhaus*, however, provoked nothing short of a scandal. Koeppen was accused of 'cesspit pornography' and 'literary imposture'. Phrases such as 'pseudo-revolution-ary puberty' and 'ruins existentialism' were bandied about. Criticism of this kind, however, was levelled against the motivation to write about contemporary history, not against the literary procedures involved, which were hardly ever appropriately assessed. It is true that in this book, too, Koeppen works with montage, various forms of depicting consciousness, with language association, thought fragments and the most up-to-date literary simulation techniques. What makes this novel different from his others, however, is the fact that the central character is, somewhat conven-tionally, a hero, or more precisely an anti-hero. It is through his experiences that the novel at the same time conveys a particular aspect of West German reality.

The Bonn 'hothouse'

Specifically, that experience is the failure of an opposition, i.e. left-wing, Bundestag representative in the Bonn 'hothouse' to implement a policy aimed at enhancing democracy. He fails in the face of the hopeless tangle of interests, connections, lies, intrigues and hypocrisy that is revealed as the coherent factor underlying the system. This experience, conveyed through the medium of literature, provoked public antagonism. The book responds with hatred and contempt, cynicism and revulsion to the Aden-auer state, rearmament, capitalism, corruption and the industrial lobby, to former Nazis and opportunistic go-getters. All that is left to the anti-hero, Keetenheuve the parliamentary representative, is the freedom of disillusion-ment: 'a jump from this bridge will free him', is the concluding sentence of the book. This is a novel, therefore, with no hope of salvation: no way out, no clarion call for change, but instead a merciless, ruthless view of the realities of the West German state. Radical, indeed, but it is this very quality that makes it credible and authentic in literary terms. Koeppen retained this disillusioning radicalism right up to his prose text *Jugend* (*Young People*) (1976). His critics were nevertheless reconciled to him on account of his apparently apolitical travelogues (*Nach Russland und anderswohin* – *To Russia and Elsewhere*, 1958; *Amerikafahrt* – *A Trip to America*, 1959; *Reisen nach Frankreich* – *Trips to France*, 1961). He suc-ceeded in remaining an object of public discussion mainly because of the distance he kept between himself and the literary business, and his refusal to conform to the prevailing image of the writer who published regularly. The literary merits of his work, however, will guarantee it an enduring value over and above its contemporary historical topicality.

In Heinrich Böll's novel *Ansichten eines Clowns* (1965), the first-person narrator, the clown Hans Schnier, reflects on his release from the insti-tutions of social hypocrisy in a blend of aggression and resignation. Mar-riage, the family, the Church, and Federal German society of the Adenauer era are all objects of a criticism that derives from the perspective of a disillusioned man, an apostate. This apostasy is also the theme of two other major prose works by Böll. In *Entfernung von der Truppe* (*Removal from the Troop*) (1964), desertion is seen as courage: 'You are urgently advised to remove yourselves from the troop', reads the 'moral' heading the epilogue. 'Desertion is advised rather than discouraged.' Similarly, in *Ende einer Dienstfahrt* (*End of an Official Trip*) (1966) the ceremonial burning of a Bundeswehr jeep is presented as an act of resistance against state power. Obviously, however, it is a literary act of resistance. The politicisation of literature manifests itself in Böll's work principally as a shift of accent in theme and subject-matter that replaced the accommodation of the past of the 1950s with conflicts and issues from the present day.

One of the greatest successes of post-war German literature was Günter Grass's novel *Die Blechtrommel (The Tin Drum)* (1959). Over a period of twenty years, this book was printed in a total of three million copies, was translated into twenty languages, and made a virtually unknown author famous overnight. It also caused literature of the Federal Republic to be accorded an esteem hardly ever experienced before. The very first sentence: 'Granted, I'm an inmate of a mental hospital' proclaims the outsider perspective from which the book will be narrated, at the same time emphatically validating the narrative itself. The author Grass reveals his main aim through his hero, Oskar:

> One can begin a story in the middle, reeking havoc both forwards and backwards with daring steps. One can profess modernity, sweeping aside all time and distance, announcing, or having it announced afterwards, that one has finally resolved the time–space problem at the last minute. One can also assert at the very outset that it is impossible to write a novel nowadays, but then, so-to-speak behind one's own back, drop a huge bestseller so as then finally to surface as the last-ever novelist. I too have been persuaded that it looks good and modest to declare at the beginning that there are no heroes of novels any more, because there are no more individualists, because individuality has been lost, because Man is alone, every man equally alone, with no right to individual loneliness, forming a nameless, hero-less, lonely mass. This is all well and good. For me, Oskar and my nurse Bruno, however, I should like to state that we are both heroes, quite different heroes, he behind the peephole, and I in front of it, and when he opens the door, the two of us, in all friendship and loneliness, are not yet a nameless, hero-less mass.

Die Blechtrommel is a picaresque novel, giving an account not of the development of its hero, but rather his observations, trials and experiences in a chaotic string of episodes and images, recorded with baroque stylistic power, from an exemplary place. Danzig (Gdansk) is the setting of the action, the petty bourgeoisie his subject, and the diminutive Oskar the observant, reminiscing inmate of an insane asylum who ignores taboos with blithe self-confidence on the grounds that 'there are things in this world, that, however unwholesome they may be, one cannot afford to leave alone'. These things encompass sexuality and death just as much as the everyday reality of petty bourgeois fears, foibles and aspirations. They encompass the myths of Catholicism, and the reinstatement of history as the living realisation of individuals. Most of all, however, they encompass a narrative procedure. This is sustained by the obsession with detail of the tin-drummer narrator Oskar, who uses traditional narrative models. He both undermines these models and makes use of them in order to draw attention to the narrative itself, invoking extravagant imagination and stylistic power against the much-discussed 'crisis of the novel'.

The grotesque as a stylistic device

It is, moreover, a realistic narrative. Critics have rightly acknowledged that with the absurdity of his narrative inspiration, Günter Grass produced a stylistic compression of the moods and actions of the petty bourgeoisie in the Third Reich that is unequalled. The grotesque, as a genuine vehicle for poetic Realism, says more about the real state of the world under discussion than a Realistic poetics could. In his next novella, *Katz und Maus* (*Cat and Mouse*) (1961) and the novel *Hundejahre* (*Dog Years*) (1963), Günter Grass again made Danzig the setting for his narrative. For this Danzig-born author, that city constituted a microcosm because it is 'precisely in the provinces where everything is reflected and surfaces that – with various tints and shades, of course – could happen or has happened worldwide'.

The 'Danzig Trilogy' was followed by an account of contemporary problems in *örtlich betäubt* (*local anaesthetic*) (1969). The novel takes the reader through the link between political thinking and action, using the example of the school and university student revolts of 1967. Grass is critical of the latter's revolutionary euphoria, using a comparison from his own individual experiences in the Third Reich. On the other hand he asserts its relativity by means of the 'dental treatment' motif, which is elaborated throughout the book. A proclamation by Günter Grass the political reformist, this motif exercises the function of a symbolic corrective of ideas expressed in the extra-parliamentary movement. As an author, Grass is concerned to achieve 'evolution step by step: one jump following another'.

Progress at a snail's pace

This problem of progress as evolution also forms the theme of another of his novels, in which Grass gives an account of experiences from the 1960s – i.e. his autobiographical account *Aus dem Tagebuch einer Schnecke* (*From the Diary of a Snail*), published in 1972. An election campaigner who travelled the country for the SPD voters' initiative, on his return to Berlin Günter Grass describes to his children his experiences and what he has learned from them during these activities. These culminate in the insight that social progress, comparable with the pace of a snail, can only be achieved with patience and fortitude.

As in the case of Böll, therefore, in Grass, too, there is an interplay between public political reflection and a literary account of political and social experience. It may be because of the didactic motivation disclosed by such a narrative aim that Grass's novels of the 1960s did not share the success of his outstanding work, *Die Blechtrommel*. Nevertheless, despite the individuality of their characters and their political views and all the differences in their writing styles, Grass and Böll do nevertheless represent one and the same type of writer: that of the democratically committed intellectual for whom literature and politics, social experience and aesthetic accounts form an inseparable whole – the same type of writer that Heinrich Mann represented in the Weimar era.

Uwe Johnson

Within a very short time, Uwe Johnson also became one of the outstanding narrative fiction writers of the 1960s. From the GDR, he had already published a novel, *Mutmassungen über Jakob* (*Speculation About Jakob*), in 1959. Johnson's writing style itself contains the same confusing aspects as the reality with which it deals. Reality is thus surreptitiously articulated in the form of broken sentence constructions, breaches of syntactic convention and punctuation rules, allowing insecurity, perceptual difficulties and orientation problems to voice themselves. Even before the publication of his first book, Johnson had already developed that unmistakable style that so annoyed literary critics, and that was later to crystallise into an all-encompassing, accumulative obsession with detail in his novels *Das Dritte Buch über Achim* (*The Third Book on Achim*) (1961), and *Zwei Ansichten* (*Two Views*) (1965).

Johnson's theme is the divided condition of Germany. In *Das Dritte Buch über Achim*, for example, a West German journalist by the name of Karsch wants to write a book about a cycling idol in the GDR. He fails, however, because of the impossibility of mediating between these two different worlds, and of creating a language of mutual understanding. Johnson's narrative approach thus points to something over and above the thematic statement in the foreground of the book. The obsession with detail with which this world of cyclists is enccompassed, thereby drawing out the 'fetishist nature of the material world' (Helmut Heissenbüttel), clearly shows that the author's main concern is with the difficulty of communication, of bridging the gulf between separate worlds, and of conveying disparate horizons of experience.

Uwe Johnson produced his *magnum opus* with the tetralogy *Jahrestage (Days of the Year)* (published in 1970, 1971, 1973 and 1980). Although this is a compendium of contemporary history, it nonetheless leaves all contemporary historical constraints behind by fusing three different levels of time: the present day of Gesine Cresspahl, from whose perspective an account of the late 1960s in New York is given; the history of the post-war era in East and West; and the Third Reich era. Through these reminiscences, Johnson succeeds in integrating these three levels into a single temporal, multi-faceted panorama with variously fragmented perceptual angles, revolving around the themes of fascism, socialism and the Vietnam War. His work is concerned with the discrepancy between aspiration and reality – both nowadays and thirty years ago, in both capitalist and socialist reality, and in everyday life and politics alike. Uwe Johnson has outlined the key principles of his poetics lectures *Begleitumstände – Attendant Circumstances* (1980).

Martin Walser

The response of literary critics to the novels of Martin Walser was one of almost unparalleled controversy. Whereas *Ehen in Philippsburg (Marriages in Philippsburg)* (1957) had still largely met with the approval of reviewers, all three parts of Walser's novel trilogy, with its hero and first-person narrator Anselm Kristlein (*Halbzeit – Half-time*, 1960; *Das Einhorn – The Unicorn*, 1966; *Der Sturz – The Drop*, 1973), were highly controversial. Controversy revolved mainly around the question of whether Walser, for all the stylistic virtuosity that was conceded him, was not endangering the readability of his works, and their very identity as novels, with his almost irrepressible poetic torrent of words. Indeed the question of the potential of narrative fiction as the recollection of past reality constitutes the central problem of this literature. Walser's narrator, Anselm Kristlein, already famous since the success of his novel *Halbzeit*, describes in *Das Einhorn* (narrated from the perspective of the bed in which the narrator is lying) his unsuccessful attempts to write a book about love as a commissioned work for a Swiss woman publisher: 'but she thinks like this: the redemption of body and soul, a finer sensuality, getting out of the Christian sack of sins, into greater freedom and all that'. Nevertheless, Anselm Kristlein fails as the author of a 'factual novel' on the theme of love, and it is this failure that forms the theme of this novel. It gives it its subject-matter, plot, pretexts for digressions and associations, narrative licence and escapades, which all serve a single purpose. This is the impossible feat of portraying recalled love as reality through narrative, in a bombardment of words and terminology, an excess of impressions, circumstances, fragments of experience and an accumulation of recollections.

There is a double distance between the narrator and what is being narrated. The author allows his fictitious character Anselm Kristlein to narrate, but Kristlein's relationship with his own narrative and recollecting faculties is obviously also characterised by distance. This dual fragmentation of narrative self-assurance, a feature enhanced still further by wit, irony, and tearfulness, places the novel in explicit contrast with that form of artistic depiction of the past that had still been beyond doubt for Marcel Proust. The poetics of Proust thus form an antitheses to this book. 'Ach du Lieber Proust!' ('For Proust's sake!') is the derisive exclamation that runs through the novel like a leitmotif, resulting from Walser's realisation, elaborated in his essay *Freiübungen* (*Free-standing Exercises*) (1963) into his essential production theory: 'Here Proust is in error. Nothing is salvaged. Not even through art. The model is created and then destroyed. All that art does is to show that nothing is salvaged.... All that remains, at best, is not the model but its destruction.' This process of destruction is revealed in the book through the device of encompassing the theme of love with the power of words – a device that is deliberately erroneous! Walser's novel *Das Einhorn* is thus a book about the failure of a novel, a book that succeeds precisely because it unfolds in literary form the conditions in which that failure occurred. *Das Einhorn* marks a step in Walser's progress as an author towards that writing mode which he himself describes as 'capitalist Realism', and which he later elaborated fully in his novel *Der Sturz* (*The Drop*). Here he conveys the amorphousness and boundlessness arising out of the contradictory nature of countless details, lending them that alien quality that conveys one of the chief characteristic features of alienated capitalist society. To dismiss *Das Einhorn* because of this as a 'product of spleen', therefore, suggests both a misunderstanding of Walser's narrative achievement, and a preconceived notion of what a novel is and should accomplish. No less a figure than Thomas Mann emphatically stresses the diversity inherent in this particular genre: 'The variability of this literary form was always very great. Today, however, it looks almost as if in the sphere of the novel heed is paid only to that which no novel any longer is. Perhaps this was always so.'

The novel *Die Blendung* (*The Subterfuge*) by Elias Canetti constitutes a special case in the literature of the Federal Republic. First published as early as 1936, it was only when reprinted in 1963 that it was accorded the acclaim that its importance deserves. Not without justification, critics have ranked this work beside the prose of Robert Musil and Franz Kafka, James Joyce and Samuel Beckett. It unfolds a pandemonium of poverty of relationship, viciousness and lack of communication that gives expression – without moralising, but equally without any prospects for possible change – to the forms of communication of a petty bourgeoisie that only a little later was to live out its disposition towards fascism. The sinologist Peter Kien, who lives shut away from the world with his vast library, is duped into marriage by a ruse of his housekeeper. From this moment on Kien is caught up in a kind of odyssey, voyaging from one monstrous aspect of the bourgeois world to another, ultimately driven to burn himself to death with his books. The coldness of the narrative approach is a surprisingly appropriate device for expressing the chaos of this world. Canetti narrates with extreme distance and clinical precision, inviting the reader to observe rather than participate inwardly. It is through this narrative device that Canetti succeeds in harnessing the grotesque panorama with which his novel deals. *Die Blendung* (*The Subterfuge*) also first hints at the theme of the 'masses' later pursued by Canetti in his essay *Masse und Macht* (*Power and the Masses*) (1960). As a dramatist, however (*Hochzeit* – *Wedding*, 1932, first performed 1965; *Komödie der Eitelkeit* – *A Comedy of Futility*, 1950 and 1964, first performed 1965; *Die Befristeten* – *The Numbered*, 1956), Canetti has so far made little impact. His autobiographical works, on the other hand, in which he gives an account of the Viennese bourgeois world in the form of a 'history of a young man' (*Die gerettete Zunge* – *The Rescued Tongue*, 1977; *Die Fackel im Ohr* – *The Torch in the Ear*, 1980; *Das Augenspiel* – *The Play of the Eyes*, 1985), have been widely acclaimed.

Although Heinrich Böll and Günter Grass, Martin Walser, Uwe Johnson and Siegfried Lenz were and remain to this day the outstanding individual figures of the 1960s, there were also a number of major literary trends and developments that were of equal importance in shaping the era. One of the key words describing prose between 1961 and 1969, for example, is 'descriptive literature'. Despite the derision that frequently accompanied this term at the time, it is nevertheless a highly apt definition for a broad spectrum of divergent prose texts whose stylistic form shared the common feature of a desire to come close to reality, consciousness, situations and actions. They constitute realistic narrative approaches deriving not from a socially critical perspective, but rather expressing social factuality itself in a critical way, and with extreme density and concentration.

The most systematic and far-reaching attempt to make a breakthrough towards realistic descriptive literature was made from 1964 onwards by the so-called 'Cologne School' of New Realism. Dieter Wellershoff, initiator, mentor and theoretician, as well as literary exponent of this group (*Ein schöner Tag* – *A Lovely Day*, 1966; *Die Schattengrenze* – *The Shadow Frontier*, 1969), defined its agenda by precisely demarcating it from the fictional nature of grotesque and satirical prose: 'Fantastic, grotesque, satirical literature criticised society by confronting it with an exaggerated, distorted picture. New Realism criticises society immanently by means of precise scrutiny. It is a form of criticism deriving not from opinions, but from the production of experience.'

This attempt at self-definition, however, only inadequately encompasses the forms in which New Realism was actually put into practice. Within the domain of Realism, authors such as Günter Herburger (*Eine gleichmässige Landschaft – A Symmetrical Landscape*, 1964; *Die Messe – The Mass*, 1969; *Jesus in Osaka*, 1970), Günter Seuren (*Das Gatter – The Lattice*, 1964; *Lebeck*, 1968), Rolf Dieter Brinkmann (*Die Umarmung – The Embrace*, 1965; *Raupenbahn – The Caterpillar Track*, 1966; *Keiner weiss mehr – No-one Knows Any More*, 1968), as well as Wellershoff himself, represent substantially divergent writing styles that throw into doubt rather than confirm Wellershoff's definition of realistic writing. This is most apparent in the writing methods of Rolf Dieter Brinkmann, which extended into an objectivisation of the objects being narrated whereby the narrative barely stopped short of abolishing itself. Spheres of life and situations of existential importance (birth, love, death, sexuality), are represented by making them represent and express themselves. Rolf Dieter Brinkmann's posthumously published collage volume *Rom Blicke* (*Rome Vistas*), however, clearly shows that he was no longer able to trust language alone with this feat. He therefore expanded his mode of writing to include other possibilities for expression (photos, facsimiles of real documents). A montage of these opened up for him an open and radical idiom.

Works which combined Realistic narrative modes with the devices of the grotesque may be regarded as a parallel and counterdevelopment to the New Realism of the 'Cologne School'. Renate Rasp's *Ein ungeratener Sohn* (*An Undutiful Son*) (1967) ranks among these, as do the later novels of Günter Seurens (*Das Kannibalenfest – The Cannibal Feast*, 1968; *Der Abdecker – The Knacker*, 1970). Provocatively cultivating shocking narrative elements, these works established a new kind of black Realism. In Rasp's novel, for example, a boy is to be changed into a tree through education. The possessive relationships between human beings are exposed with penetrating and meticulous malice against the background of this idea. Much the same is true of Gisela Elsner's novels *Die Riesenzwerge* (*The Giant Dwarves*) (1964), *Der Nachwuchs* (*The Rising Generation*) (1968) and *Das Berührungsverbot* (*Don't Touch*) (1970). These works expose everyday middle-class life in a vision of the terror and horror of the banal – a radical perspective of an order that Gisela Elsner did not regain in her later works (*Der Punktsieg – The Victory on Points*, 1977; *Abseits – Aloof*, 1982).

New Realism – Black Realism

New Realism and Black Realism are two highly divergent narrative modes that nonetheless manifest a striving towards the same goal, which is to make reality open to experience. Neo-realistic narrative forms constitute an effort to achieve such a degree of empathy with reality that it can express itself. Realism that works with the devices of the grotesque, the shocking, and the glaring effect, on the other hand, constitutes in poetic terms a distrust of such an experience of reality. It makes use of elements of alienation, a distortion of reality, and surrealist imagery in order to destroy the surface of reality to such a degree that the middle-class everyday reality of fright and alarm, shock and revulsion is made to stand out from the banality of outward appearances.

The novel, therefore, was 'between Realism and the Grotesque' (Heinrich Vormweg). This very diversity of prose in the 1960s makes it impossible even remotely to lay claim to completeness in a brief account of this kind. Apart from the authors mentioned, for example, other important figures to be considered are those such as Peter Härtling (*Niembsch oder der Stillstand – Niembsch, or Standstill*, 1964) and Hubert Fichte (*Das Waisenhaus – The Orphanage*, 1965; *Die Palette – The Palette*, 1968), Gerhard Zwerenz (*Casanova oder Der Kleine Herr in Krieg und Frieden – Casanova, or The Little Man in War and Peace*, 1966), Ernst Herhaus (*Die homburgische Hochzeit – The Wedding in Homburg*, 1967) and not least Peter Handke who, with his *Die Hornissen* (*The Hornets*) (1966) and *Der Hausierer* (*The Pedlar*) (1967), made his début as, if anything, a traditional narrative fiction writer. There can be no question of giving a full account where it is necessary to show overall contexts. The context of prose at this time, however, was the question concerning the potential and limitations of realistic narrative prose.

The prose of an alienated world

This question also lies behind the prose of two authors who were more inclined to explode rather than affirm traditional definitions of the genre: Alexander Kluge and Jürgen Becker. In *Lebensläufe* (*Careers*) (1962) and *Schlachtbeschreibung* (*Description of a Battle*) (1964, reprinted 1978), Kluge narrates from a distance and apparently without emotion. He reports and records mechanisms, the interplay of which only leads individuals to experience greater dependence. There is no 'story' in the foreground, rather systems of perception and classification – the prose of an alienated world. A radicalised view and deeply penetrating observation are also to be found in Jürgen Becker (*Felder – Fields*, 1964; *Ränder – Edges*, 1968; *Umgebungen – Environments*, 1970). In his texts, however, these qualities derive from an individual sphere of experience expressed with precision and nuance.

'This text', writes Jürgen Becker in his own interpretation of *Felder*, 'dem-onstrates solely the movements of a consciousness through reality, and its transformation into language: i.e. my [consciousness] with its layers, frag-ments and disturbances; reality, i.e. daily, past, imagined [reality]'. The fact that this complex of problems was thematically expanded through a litera-ture that in the 1960s concentrated more and more, and with some exclusiv-ity, on subject-matter concerned with the 'world of work' is particularly indicative of that development that was most typical for the literature of this period as a whole: its politicisation.

The conquest of the world of work by literature

Anyone looking for a literature dealing with the problem of the world of work in the Federal Republic in the period from 1945 to 1960 will be disappointed. There is such a literature, but only in a very restricted, and moreover ideologically defined form.

Traditional lines

During this period, works by older 'worker-poets' (Heinrich Lersch, Karl Bröger, Gerrit Engelke) appeared only sporadically. They went largely unnoticed, and could scarcely be said to bear witness to a living tradition of working-class literature. Literature concerned with the contemporary problems of the working world, on the other hand, spoke of its subject in a transfiguring manner, overlaying the work process with myth and mystification. Seen against the background of a still unaccommodated fascism, and in the context of efforts on the part of conservative politicians and entrepreneurs to achieve harmony and formulas for social partnership, this literature served an ideological function. In the early years when the Federal Republic was being reconstructed, the ideal worker was the one who (as in Martha Schlinkert-Galinsky's novel *Der Schatten des Schlotes –* *The Shadow of the Smoke-stack*, dating from 1947), 'knows that there will always be rich and poor', and who is far from seeking 'to pervert this world order'. Given a literature that is, if anything, hostile to workers and remote from reality, therefore, Walter Jens was right in 1960 to pose the bewildered question: 'Do we not work? Is our daily activity so utterly unimportant? Does nothing really happen between the factory gate and the assembly-line, is the conversation of the officers' mess without mean-ing, does no laboratory experiment on its life-long slaves?'.

A literary vacuum

Searching for the causes for this literary vacuum, one is obliged once again to give socio-political reasons. Writers' associations such as the Union of

Proletarian-Revolutionary Writers (of the German CP), and trade-union book cooperatives in the Weimar era, for example, had seen as one of their major tasks developing and disseminating a working-class literature imbued with class awareness. The demolition of workers' organisations by German fascists in 1933 had not only destroyed their political power-base, but also eliminated their function as cultural organisers of the working class. After 1945, the problems at the forefront of social conflicts were largely of a political rather than a cultural nature, and arose principally from the restrictive trade union policy of the Western occupying powers. Restorative developments in the Adenauer era, culminating in 1956 in the banning of the German CP, and sustained by the reconstruction ideology of the 'economic miracle', ultimately also played a part in the fact that a working-class culture with which the working class could identify was unable to develop. A precondition for this did not arise until the first signs of a changing understanding of society began to manifest themselves with the end of the period of economic reconstruction in 1960–1.

The agenda

An important date for the rediscovery of the world of work for literature came with the founding of the 'Dortmund 61 Group' on Good Friday 1961. The name of the group was not chosen at random. It indicates a deliberate founding of a counter-group to the '47 Group'. The '61 Group' defined its central task as that of 'literary and artistic discussion of the industrial world of work and its social problems'. The forms of this discussion were expected to show an 'individual language and creative power, or to evince signs capable of being developed into a separate form'. This effectively articulates a neo-Realist agenda that feels in no way bound to the class-struggle literature of the Weimar era, but conceives of the 'world of work' primarily in terms of its technological aspects. Its focal point is 'intellectual discussion of the technical age'. Workers and salaried employee are not viewed as potential authors. The emphasis is on 'writers, journalists, lecturers, critics, academics and other personalities whose interests or profession link them with the tasks and work of the 61 Group'.

Wallraff

The writer Günter Wallraff, a member of the '61 Group', attracted attention and had a political impact (*Wir brauchen dich – We Need You*, 1966; *Unerwünschte Reportagen – Undesirable reports*, 1969; *Von einem, der auszog und das Fürchten lernte – Of One Who Set Forth and Learned to Fear*, 1970) from his very first publications. His reportage work concentrates on the reality of the working world, bringing to the public attention its mechanisms of suppression, the brutality and destructiveness inherent in its system and its modes of exploitation and dominance. Time and again, incredulous, stunned amazement at what Wallraff reported on the basis of his observations, and the shaking of heads at corruption, suppression and hypocrisy, have been pushed aside by the stir caused by Wallraff's writing procedure itself, his method. In order to be able to obtain his information in the first place, he mostly poses under a false name in the particular sphere on which he wishes to report. Brought to court on account of this procedure, and charged with false assumption of authority, wilful deceit and underhand journalistic practices, Wallraff defended himself with the remarks: 'I chose the position of collusion so as to be able to obtain a better glimpse behind the masking screen of deceitfulness, official denial and lies. The method I chose was trifling compared to the law-bending measures and illegal testing that I thereby uncovered.'

What we see here, therefore, is a concealment of identity in order to reveal reality. One example of this method was Wallraff's work as an errand-boy for the Gerling conglomerate in Cologne (published with Bernt Engelmann in *Ihr da oben, wir da unten* (*You Up There, Us Down Here*), (1973). Here was the errand-boy who sat down beside the master of the house and ordered select dishes and champagne in the conservatory of the board of directors, in the exclusive, feudal dining wing with its festively laid tables. Here was the errand-boy in the spacious office of the boss, Gerling himself, sitting cross-legged on the desk, holding in his hands the golden globe with the Gerling companies marked around its circumference. His aim was to mock social and internal hierarchies by substituted, revelatory behaviour. On the desk, he discovers Gerling's motto: *Fortes fortuna adjuvat* ('Luck stays with the strong'), and places a note next to it with the comment: 'But not for long!' From a bouquet of two dozen red carnations, the errand-boy breaks off a single bloom and sticks it into his button-hole as a symbol of the Portuguese revolution. When two of the firm's agents finally want to remove him, he sits in the director's seat, eating an apple.

Wallraff's conduct thus contains a social and political goal: the goal of achieving a society with no hierarchies, of thwarting the established fabric of society as a developmental factor in the process of unsettling it. For this reason, Wallraff has been denounced as an 'underground communist'. In fact, however, his method is none other than that of 'sociological experiment' in the sense meant by Bertolt Brecht. From a 'thoroughly subjective, absolutely partisan standpoint', Wallraff reveals 'social antagonisms without resolving them' (Brecht). This method has proved effective right up to his work as 'Ali the Turk' (*Ganz unten – Right at the Bottom*, 1985). It is, moreover, a successful one: more than a million copies of the book were sold in a few months.

Working-class literature: but how?

The issue of the identity of its authors gave rise again and again to tensions within the '61 Group'. It did emphatically distance itself from the emotional working-class writing that surrounded the working process and industrialisation with mystification and myth (Engelke, Lersch, Barthel). And yet the unsolved problem of the social origin of its members remained. In this respect the writer Max von der Grün held a view by no means shared by all members of the group: 'One cannot write about the world of work only if one has been a worker; I believe that with intensive study of this material it is quite possible for the outsider to have something to say on the theme of the world of work.' At the same time, however, Max von der Grün distanced himself from the objectives of the Bitterfeld Way in the GDR which he saw as 'octroi' (i.e. a tax levied on goods from outside): 'I can as a writer obviously go into a factory. . . . I will experience a great deal in that factory – but there is one thing I will most probably never experience, namely that which I would call the basic existential situation. For there is a difference between working in a factory in the certain knowledge that if I don't like it I can go, and working there in the certain knowledge that I must spend my life there because I will never have an opportunity to do anything else.'

The definition of 'working-class literature'

Max von der Grün's postulate of a 'basic existential situation' points to a distinct problem in defining the term 'working-class literature'. Traditionally, a definition of this term is undertaken either on the basis of theme (literature about workers), or on the basis of the origin of authors (literature by workers). Both these, however, have proved inadequate, as they fail to address a more precise definition of the function of such literature (literature for workers). It was critics of the '61 Group' who objected to the latter's openness in principle to all forms of worker literature, on the grounds that this approach could never permit a qualitatively adequate demarcation from the middle-class (bourgeois) literary scene. Although workers, therefore, would often be made the object of accounts in the literary work of the group, they would never appear as active subjects – as writers themselves. These objections, which were to lead later to the departure of a number of group members and the founding of the Werk-kreis Literatur der Arbeitswelt (Working Group on Literature about the World of Work), are nevertheless only of limited validity. In its efforts to draw attention first and foremost to the phenomenon of the working world by literary and artistic means, the '61 Group' could not concern itself in the first years after its founding with implementing a particular political trade union agenda. Its primary concern was to initiate a broad-based process of new literary development.

Max von der Grün

One of the most important authors in the group from its founding was the writer Max von der Grün, who was virtually the only author in that period to make his mark on the public through his work. His novels, such as *Männer in zweifacher Nacht* (*Men in Double Night*) (1962), *Zwei Briefe an Pospischiel* (*Two Letters to Pospischiel*) (1968) and *Stellenweise Glatteis* (*Icy Patches*) (1973), use realistic, and to some extent documentary devices in order to portray the problems of an increasingly industrialised world of work, chiefly in the mining industry. In his second novel, *Irrlicht und Feuer* (*Will-o'-the-Wisp and Fire*) (1963), Max von der Grün incorporated his own experiences as a worker at the coal face (as construction worker, getter and engine driver; he was buried alive twice). Using the development of the miner Jürgen Fohrmann, the novel shows the social problems caused by pit closures, the class struggle from above, the continuing impact of fascism in the present day, and not least the equivocal role played by trade unions in class conflicts.

The furore caused by this novel may be taken as an object lesson in the efficacy of socially critical literature. Industry saw its interests threatened, and attempted to pass an interim order against specific passages of the novel. The mining and energy union likewise felt affronted, and stopped inviting the author to its events until 1967. The firm to which the author was attached as a worker threatened reprisals. In a magazine edition, all passages critical of entrepreneurs were removed for fear of losing advertising revenue. A television version broadcast in the GDR was augmented in the Federal Republic by panel discussions, additional publication of the results of opinion polls and two documentaries on the problems presented, which served to limit its effectiveness and identity as a television film. Nonetheless, the author Max von der Grün could see his views vindicated by these various events: his conception of literature as a specific medium of social action was affirmed by the very actions that were directed against his work. 'Literature', he himself summed up, 'can help to activate people and give them a political consciousness, if that literature makes facts transparent'.

In addition to Max von der Grün, writers such as Bruno Gluchowski, Erwin Sylvanus (*Korczak und die Kinder* – *Korczak and the Children*, 1957) and Josef Reding, as well as younger authors such as Angelika Mechtel, F.C. Delius, Günter Wallraff and Peter-Paul Zahl also affected the development of the '61 Group'. It soon became clear that the open-endedness of the group's agenda, set beside its fixation on 'world of work' subject-matter, was increasingly giving rise to a pattern of conflict that seemed impossible to resolve without a more precise definition of its literary and political functions. In view of the inadequate self-definition of the group 'the best thing would be to disband and start from scratch', wrote F.C. Delius in November 1970. The *Gruppe 61* was 'not actually a location, centre or place of production, but a brand name under which once a year a handful of writers with somewhat diverse interests and ideologies come together ... members of the group seem to have in common more an individualistic sense of literary ambition than a jointly worked-out literary aspiration'.

Working Group

Since, however, it proved impossible to resolve these problems within the group itself, the founding of the Working Group on the Literature of the World of Work (Werkkreis Literatur der Arbeitswelt) ensued in the autumn of 1969. Since then the Working Group has managed, to a greater extent than the '61 Group', to play a major role in the creation of a working-class literature that is at one and the same time a literature by workers and for workers, thus also pursuing political objectives using literary means. An initial set-up phase (up to 1970–1) obtained potential authors from the world of work by means of reportage competition. These authors were subsequently organised in some 25 local working groups with 350 members (trade-union officials, social democrats, communists and independents) with a view to joint discussion of how texts were to be produced, and of political problems and social issues. Up to 1976, the membership of these working groups was divided roughly equally between working-class, white-collar and student members. Books published by the working group – of which over two dozen titles appeared in a paperback series that made a major impact on the reading public – totalled some million copies by the mid-1980s.

A conceptual dilemma

Notwithstanding its impressive progress, however, a decade after its foundation the Working Group was still faced with a crucial problem arising out of its underlying concept of literary policy. Its stated aim was to involve the literary texts it produced, some of them collectively, 'in the day-to-day struggle of the labour movement', in this way developing 'a literature of the world of work as a literature of the working class'. This aim, however, often confronted working writers of literature with the dilemma of having to devise a literary vehicle for, or transpose into literature, some preconceived political notion, idea or specific aim. The result of this was that in the course of planning and writing within the working group modes of writing were propounded in the name of socially critical

Realism that were appropriate to this aim, but which were not infrequently at the expense of the particular aesthetic character of literature. In many cases the imparting of these modes of writing led to no more than naivety and simplicity in character depiction and plot schemes, and to a customising of Working Circle literature. Stagnating sales and a deceleration in the rate of appearance of new titles since the end of the 1970s are an indication of the gradual petering out of this literary concept.

A step further in the direction of the most authentic possible way of capturing reality was taken by Erika Runge, likewise a member of the '61 Group', and later of the Working Circle. In the crisis years of 1966–7, against a background of recession, short-time work, mass lay-offs, pit closures and labour demonstrations, Runge tested out and published with her *Bottroper Protokollen* (*The Bottropp Records*) (1968) a literary procedure whose strengths and weaknesses have since become apparent: the recording of original statements by those people most lastingly affected by social crises. The strength of this working method lay chiefly in the diversity of media spheres of application available to documentary material. The author commented on her working procedure: 'Stories recorded on tape were transcribed by me as faithfully as possible, and then condensed by tidying them up and ordering them dramaturgically. . . . In fact I proceeded in the same manner as in the montage of a documentary film, in which the rough footage is first cut up to create complexes, and only then put together again in the form of a digest.' The *Bottroper Protokolle* was therefore as suitable for use as an authentic text as it was to being adapted into theatre, radio or television plays – able to preserve its identity regardless of the particular medium employed. It remained a collection of statements by social outcasts giving the plain, disillusioning facts about the realities of their lives.

'All literature is bourgeois'

Martin Walser saw in this approach the sole possibility for dealing with the 'world of work' theme without illusions. 'It is ridiculous to expect of writers living the life of "free writers" in a bourgeois society to be able, with the aid of a pinchbeck clemency and so-called artistic talent, to imitate, or even give voice to the lives of working people in the composite of art. All literature is bourgeois here [in West Germany], even though it still gives itself such anti-bourgeois airs.'

Walser's critique of 'bourgeois literature' is nonetheless still unable to resolve the fundamental dilemma of records and documents. The limitations of the latter are identical with those of the reality that is brought 'to expression' in them (Walser). They are denied all opportunity aesthetically to transcend the boundaries of this reality by means of utopia and imagination. Erika Runge conceded this basic problem underlying the documentary method in 1976, referring to her own 'incapacity to express', and her fears of expression: 'Why then did I not include my experiences and cognitions, my imagination and my language? I was unable to, even though I felt the need to do so. I wanted to write, but I lacked the words. I wanted to speak for myself, my wishes and difficulties, but I was afraid to expose myself.' A move towards a 'new subjectivity' in the 1970s is all the more noticeable in the light of the declared aim of trying out 'liberties, imagination, latitude – the self and relationships with others. [I] seek to use the full range of potential open to literature, not only for reasons of political insight, but also as a way of standing up for the human aspiration to self-realisation, individuality, and my own personhood.'

Surface destruction: the theory and practice of concrete poetry

Lyric works from the end of the 1950s onwards, classifiable together under the heading of 'concrete poetry', are also to be seen as a serious attempt, albeit one fraught with problems, to go beyond the theory and practice of literary Realism, as well as the poetics of writers such as Gottfried Benn. This literary trend encompasses highly diverse textual products and theories of text, which nevertheless share the main common feature of opposition. These works are directed against both the content-bound nature of poetry and its traditional verse forms. This common feature in turn links up with a major phenomenon affecting the period of the late 1950s, and even more so the 1960s. This was the growing surfeit of both social and literary conventions – ways of seeing, perceptual forms and customary ways of thinking that were conventional in terms of their proclivity towards social collusion and harmony. To this extent, concrete poetry, for all its separate, unique identity, is entirely comparable with Dadaism and Futurism, the other literary rebellions of this century. It saw a revolutionisation of poetic forms as revolutionary poetry.

The term 'concrete poetry' was coined in 1955 by the text writer and theoretician Eugen Gomringer with reference to developments taking place in the visual arts, already familiar with the concept of 'concrete art' since 1930. Along with Brazilian, Japanese, French and American authors, Gomringer defined concrete poetry as a 'unit of order whose composition is determined by the number of words and letters, and by a new structural method'. In his view, meaning is only a consideration if its 'intellectual and material structure proves interesting and linguistically feasible'. 'Meanings' of this kind were located by Gomringer in words such as 'tree, child, dog, house'.

This move away from the aspect of meaning and from formal traditions was accompanied by reflection on the material character of language, which had a highly evocative and innovative effect in poetic terms. Experimental texts by such authors as Franz Mons, the Vienna group led by Gerhard

Rühm, Friederike Mayröcker and Ernst Jandl, H.C. Hartmann's linguistic
wit and artistry, and the work of Eugen Gromringer and Helmut Heissenbüttel demolish phenomena to do with the surface of language, thereby
also doing away with the traditional character of language, which is to
convey meaning, reconstructing it afresh in uncustomary contexts of use
that often facilitate startling insights. This poetic aim is enhanced by optical
effects, for example a certain typographical arrangement of a text, as well
as by acoustic elements employed during recitations by authors themselves,
on record, or during readings. Changes were thus brought about involving
more than poetic language itself, therefore, extending to the poetic medium
itself, and including audio-visual components. The aim behind this literary
undertaking, however, was to change the reader or hearer's customary ways
of hearing, seeing and thinking. An example from Claus Bremer:

> kann ich allseitig zeigen was ich zeige
> kann ich was ich zeige allseitig zeigen
> allseitig zeigen was ich zeige kann ich
> was ich zeige allseitig zeigen kann ich
> allseitig zeigen kann ich was ich zeige
> was ich zeige kann ich allseitig zeigen

> can I show all round what I show
> can I what I show show all round
> show all round what I show I can
> what I show show all round I can
> show all round I can what I show
> what I show I can show all round

In this text, the three syntagmas (*kann ich* – 'can I' / *allseitig zeigen* –
'show all round' / *was ich zeigen* – 'what I show') are set in such a
relationship to one another and played with in such a way that the question
of meaning posed at the outset, which nevertheless remains abstract, is
answered in the course of the poem itself, and indeed positively so. The
aspect of meaning in this text relates to the statement that underlies it.
The writing procedure used, however, confines this meaning so closely to
form that the two become one. The form of the poem does not merely
transpose or convey its message, but organises it totally by demonstratively
vindicating it. Whereas here, however, the poem remains captive to its
message of meaning, in the example by Konrad Balder Schäuffelen the
meaning aspect is transcended by removing it into the typographical sphere
and transforming it into an optically discernible visual aspect.

Helmut Heissenbüttel, a major exponent of concrete poetry as well as
one of its outstanding theoreticians (various *Textbücher* – *Textbooks* published since 1960), has described the reduction of such texts, their 'return
to linguistic fundamentals', and their 'transcendence of medial limitations'

as their most significant feature. 'The complex syntactic and semantic surface structure of the language in which we customarily make ourselves understood (or try to) is unlocked and infiltrated, reduced to, and at that same extended to include that which supports that surface structure.' Going beyond boundaries into the typographical sphere or into acoustic articulation similarly serves to demolish surfaces: 'they should bear witness to an altered experience in a changing environment, and have at the very least a demonstrative function'. The result of such a poetic operation is total destruction, although not in the nihilistic sense: 'instead it releases language into those elements that go to make up the traditional surface structure: modes, modes of representation, modes of expression, and modes of construction for an altered syntax and an altered semantics'.

In Heissenbüttel's view the achievement of concrete poetry can only be measured and grasped in its entirety if one 'discerns its tendencies not merely as a new idiom, but also as a new mode of linguistic orientation in this world'.

Problems of definition

This remark points to a fundamental problem in concrete poetry, namely that of the inconsistent relationship between theoretical aims and poetic practice or effects. As an 'object for seeing and use – an object of thought – a thought game', as Eugen Gomringer required it to be, the poem calls on the reader to augment and expand on it, as well as demanding an active desire and capacity for playful continuation of it. It thus requires a reader who already concurs with the theoretical postulates of concrete poetry, a reader who brings assumptions to his reading of the texts which the latter have in fact yet to bring into play – according to the aim of their authors. This inconsistency was also pointed out by Peter Schneider:

> Concrete poetry is fraught with one fundamental difficulty. Its openness requires an open reader. The theoretically unprepared reader, however, is not open in this sense. He is unable simply to accept the poem as it is. He comes to the linguistic work of art with expectations shaped by his reading and living habits. He is geared to understand that which he experiences through language in a meaning of his own. He does not ask whether he may do so, he simply does it. If he understands nothing, he does not take this fact as a fact of experience, as the intention of the author, but seeks to reach understanding by means of an unknown key, a secret law, an obscure rule. Finding nothing of the kind, he discards the poem. He does not understand his lack of understanding.

Concrete poetry requires explanation and theoretical explication precisely because it dispenses with all aspects of meaning as part of its critical aim, but without in all cases being able to devise in turn a new, manifest aspect of meaning as pure material for play and utterance. Gomringer's belief in creating a 'universally comprehended common language' out of concrete poetry must therefore be seen as no more than a utopian construction of his own. The real achievements of concrete poetry lie far more in the regenerative and stimulating effects arising out of its 'destructions', as one literary development among others in the German-speaking world of the post-war era. Aside from exceptions such as Ernst Jandl (*Laut und Luise – Loud and Lisa*, 1966), however, the impact of concrete poetry occurred less among a broad reading public than among literary theoreticians and text writers themselves. This was above all the case where, as with Helmut Heissenbüttel, there was a successful development of poetic syntheses, and a productive blending of diverse literary procedures, thus bringing elements of concrete poetry into new, in turn changing contexts of use. This makes it possible to say of concrete poetry what the revolutionary Soviet poet Vladimir Mayakovski asserted of his futuristic colleague Velimir Khlebnikov, namely that the latter was a 'poet for producers'.

> ernst jandl . *lichtung*
> manche meinen
> lechts und rinks
> kann man nicht
> velwechsern.
> werch ein illtum!
>
> some claim that
> reft and light
> cannot be
> foncused.
> Fhat wolly!

Arno Schmidt

In terms of both his personal lifestyle and his work, the writer Arno Schmidt remains a unique literary figure. From the end of the 1950s until his death in 1979, he lived in complete seclusion on the edge of the Lüneberg heath, well away from the 'literature scene'. In addition to his work as translator, essayist and interpreter of unjustly obscure or misunderstood authors (de la Mott-Fouqué, Karl May), Schmidt concentrated exclusively on creative work that came to represent an increasingly unique literary style. His was a combinatory, associative writing mode that dispensed with traditional orthography. It was rich in allusion and multiple meanings, gave ample evidence of wide reading and owed a great deal to the thought of the critical Enlightenment. Narrative technique was frequently punctuated by provincial experiences and elements of science fiction.

Noteworthy works in this regard are his early short stories, published in 1963 under the title *Nobodaddy's Kinder*, his novels *Das Steinerne Herz* (*The Stone Heart*) (1956), *Die Gelehrtenrepublik* (*The Republic of Intellectuals*) (1957), *Kaff auch Mare Crisium* (*Kaff or Mare Crisium*) (1960) and not least his novella comedy *Die Schule der Atheisten* (*The School for Atheists*) (1972).

In the 1960s, however, most of Arno Schmidt's work was devoted to his monumental *Zettel's Traum* (*Card Index Dream*) (1970), a work that defies comparison with any other literary piece. This book was written between 1963 and 1969, and published in a voluminous facsimile edition true to the original. The title is an allusion both to scholarly erudition and sensuality – to the card index of the author and to William Shakespeare's *A Midsummer Night's Dream*. The 'plot' involves a group of four characters: the scholar Daniel Pagenstecher (unquestionably a projection of the author himself), a married couple of translators by the name of Paul and Wilma Jacobi who are seeking advice from Pagenstecher on an Edgar Allan Poe translation, and sixteen-year-old Franziska, their daughter. The work unfolds in the form of three parallel component strands – commentary–action and reflection–digression – comprising 1,330 'index cards', and follows developments in the relationships between these characters. There are conversations full of suspense, as well as reflection and fantasy on literature laden with sexual innuendo and allusion. In relation to the problems of translation and theory, the work of Edgar Allan Poe is central to literary discussion. Schmidt does not restrict himself to the content aspect of plot and theme, however, instead forging a path to the in-depth dimensions of language and literature by uncovering etymological structures and setting them against one another in an equally ambiguous manner. At the same time, the simultaneity of the three component strands affords a mutual demarcation of commentary, plot and digression that calls on the cooperative imagination and intellect of the reader. Nevertheless, Schmidt did not place excessively high hopes on his readers. He supposed that not three hundred readers could be expected to take serious notice of *Card Index Dream*.

The 'death of literature': 1968

'Art is dead!'

The politicisation of German literature, most apparent in the drama and lyric poetry of the 1960s, had much in common with the era's parallel accent on the documentary, as well as its recourse to the facts of everyday reality. Both phenomena evinced an implicit tendency to deny the very right of literature to exist. Discussion of literary theory at the end of the 1960s was dominated by insistent questioning of the purpose of literature.

If on the one hand experiences, situations, problems and frames of mind could be derived directly and authentically from reality, this made what was mediated by literary works of art on the aesthetic plane appear to be little more than a luxurious cultural commodity. If, on the other hand, the significance of literature was determined on the basis of its function within political struggle, then the question of its aesthetic quality was at all events of only secondary interest.

Ideas of these kind were made topical by the worldwide phenomenon of protests against imperialist war and bourgeois social forms – by demonstrations and political action in Italy, France, and the United States. In May 1968 in Paris revolts by French school and university students severely unsettled de Gaulle's French state, involving both a testing and a development of forms of opposition to state power and cultural traditions. Although viewed as aesthetic in nature, these forms nevertheless deliberately sought to debunk inherited concepts of the aesthetic based on notions of the 'beauty of art'. 'Power to the imagination' was one of the slogans of May 1968 in Paris, which saw 'happenings', saucy acts of provocation, the graffiti of cultural revolution, and the building of barricades as the forms of struggle in which the will to revolution manifested itself. All this was accompanied by a leitmotif that cropped up on walls again and again: 'L'art est mort!': 'Art is dead!'

The student movement

In the Federal Republic, these developments abroad, including forms of political action and struggle, were seized on by commentary and analysis and incorporated into the practices of the student movement and extra-parliamentary opposition. The most important locus for discussion of the argumentation of revolutionary theory, and for the elaboration of cultural revolution theory, was the journal *Kursbuch* (*Timetable*), founded by Hans Magnus Enzensberger in 1965. In addition to Vietnam, China and the Third World, the main thematic emphases of this journal revolved around the problems of the labour and student movements, and cultural development. These issues were discussed in the light of the politicisation of everyday life and the revolutionisation of cultural life.

An outstanding document of this discussion is *Kursbuch 15* of November 1968, which both elaborated and defended theoretically an agenda based on the 'death of literature'. 'Writers living today', writes *Kursbuch* Editor-in-Chief Karl Markus Michel in one article, 'find their legitimation through the great dead whose work they carry on, the apparently endless work of art, literature, which reproduces its innumerable molecules by means of glamour and poverty and disputes'. Against the backdrop of events in Paris in May 1968, Michel prophesies a cultural development that will be shaped not 'by a new literature, but by new forms of expression that will make literary avant-gardism seem senile and remind people of the impotence of progressive Western literature in general, which derives from its privileged status'.

The 'cultural revolution'

Peter Schneider pursued these ideas further in an essay entitled *Die Phantasie im Spätkapitalismus und die Kulturrevolution* (*The Imagination in Late Capitalism and the Cultural Revolution*) (*Kursbuch 16*). 'The cultural revolution', asserts Schneider, 'is the conquest of reality by the imagination. Art in late capitalism is the conquest of the imagination by capital. . . . Does this mean that late bourgeois art is dead? Yes, it does.' Schneider is only prepared to entertain two possible functions for 'revolutionary art': 'political agitation and propaganda.'

This did not remain merely an agenda. For a brief period it was put into practice. The shock waves that passed through the Frankfurt Book Fair in 1968, the dissolution of the Germanists' conference in 1968, and mass demonstrations against the Axel Springer conglomerate revealed time and again that the link between political objectives and cultural revolutionary forms of action was insoluble. The expansion of the concept of culture thereby manifesting itself, the liberation of the imagination into social conflicts, and the emergence of political struggle as a field of action for sensuality seemed for one historic moment to be on the point of exploding the social rigidities of the Federal Republic. Herbert Marcuse's assertion about the 'repressive tolerance' of bourgeois society, and the way it defined the function of social minorities, outsiders and peripheral groups, gave intellectuals, school and university students and young workers the identity of a concrete utopia: 'If they use force, they do not set in motion a new chain of violent acts, but break the established one. Since they will be beaten, they are aware of the risk, and if they are of a mind to take it upon themselves, then no third party, and least of all the educator or intellectual, has the right to preach restraint to them.'

Politico-cultural upheaval

Against this background, 1968 can to some extent be justifiably termed a year of politico-cultural upheaval in the Federal Republic. It witnessed a convergence of developments, and a clash of contradictions whose tense interrelationship could in previous years still be balanced. Now, however, with politico-social conventions and the rules of the game declared obsolete, inherited traditions of a cultural or other nature proved fragile and decayed, and were replaced by new, subcultural forms of transaction. Clearly, however, these processes had historical precursors that can be traced back over some years, just as it called forth repercussions that were to be felt well into the 1970s.

Seen in this light, 1968 is also a makeshift construction, providing merely a potential point of orientation in the history of the Federal Republic of Germany and no more representing a watershed in its history than it signified a fundamental new beginning. By the same token, although the scope of literature underwent a process of restriction during the years of revolt, the much-heralded 'death' of literature failed to take place. Literature had not come to an end, nor had it died a politico-social death. As Günter Grass, a critic of these developments, expressed it, literature was merely no longer in a 'boom phase'.

A 'shift of tendency': literature between contemplation and alternative lifestyles (1969–77)

The mood of social upheaval augured by the revolutionary euphoria of 1968, and which took hold of an entire generation seeking to express itself in a desire for political change and new cultural beginnings, evaporated in a brief space of time.

The spectre of boredom

By the mid-1970s the literary yearbook *Tintenfisch* (*Squid*) could observe: 'A *spectre* is on the move in Germany: boredom. Once radical school students now sit sweating over bonus and high risk premiums, and chew over the size of their pensions. Once radical university students now sit freshly-shaven and upright at their clean desks, discovering the old or the new order, but at all events some kind of order. Once radical writers lie in the warm arms of the trade union, and are now docile. The remainder of the population, for fear of dismissal, appears to be living a regulated, unobtrusive life.' A 'shift of tendency' has been suggested in the light of these developments, but what caused it?

For one thing, the extra-parliamentary opposition strategy of a 'long march through institutions' (Rudi Dutschke) had proved to be an illusion. The institutions concerned had remained untouched both in their substance and their independent existence by either personal or politico-administrative attacks. Reforms initiated in the secondary and tertiary educational spheres, for example, arising out of criticism by school and university students of encrusted social institutions, produced minimal changes in terms of either structure or content. The overwhelming majority of such reform moves were taken up purely from the technocratic viewpoint of effectiveness, and converted into regimentation (a points system for the reformed senior grades; structural planning; regulated study periods).

On the other hand, a more serious consequence of the politicisation process of the 1960s was a proliferation of left-wing organisations, and the founding of new parties and political splinter groups whose competitive sectarianism brought about the disintegration of the extra-parliamentary opposition as a whole. This process may be followed to the point where land communes and subcultural groups came about whose common aim was a desire to try out and develop a new social and individual identity through alternative lifestyles.

The Radicals Decree

The West German state responded in an authoritarian manner to the process of politicisation. With the *Radikalenerlass* (*Radicals Decree*) of 1972, the prime ministers introduced political monitoring into the civil service, as a result of which thousands of applicants were vetted, despite protests from the PEN Club, the Writers' Association (Schriftstellerverband) and the Germanists' Association (Germanistenverband). Among the young generation, especially, this fostered a climate of anxiety and resignation that had an intimidating effect on their sense of political commitment. This situation was exacerbated in 1976, in the context of the criminal prosecution of politically motivated crimes of violence, by a stepping-up of censorship regulations that were not rescinded until 1980, and which had repercussions on literature as well as other spheres. This was because the jurisdiction of the state with regard to 'attempts [directed . . .] against the existence or security of the Federal Republic of Germany or against constitutional principles' had to be taken into account as a factor in the assessment of all publications, including literature. The preventive self-censorship of authors and publishing houses was now, therefore, not beyond the bounds of possibility. Heinrich Böll, for example, took the themes of the vetting of (political) views, national security and the prosecution of terrorists as the inspiration for his story *Die verlorene Ehre der Katharina Blum* (*The Lost Honour of Katharina Blum*) (1974), for his satire *Berichte zur Gesinnungslage der Nation* (*Reports on the State of the Nation's Political Mentality*) (1975) and for his novel *Fürsorgliche Belagerung* (*Solicitous Siege*) (1979). Peter Schneider made use of his own experiences in his story *. . . schon bist du ein Verfassungsfeind. Das unerwartete Anschwellen der Personalakte des lehrers Kleff* (*. . . you're a constitutional enemy now. The unexpected enlargement of the personal files of Kleff the teacher*) (1977), and similarly Peter O. Chotjewitz in his novel *Die Herren des Morgengrauens* (*Lords of the Dawn*) (1978), both of which provide examples of a fresh definition of the function of literature, which, following its 'death', was now being rediscovered as a medium for coming to terms with and objectivising personal experience.

To summarise, the outcome of the process of politicisation of the 1960s was a process of de-politicisation that was not apolitical, since it pointed to a move away from social institutions and a mistrust of parties and social hierarchies. At the same time, however, this de-politicisation entailed a strong emphasis on individual interests and motivations, and a deliberate reconquest of personal sensuality that was to have repercussions for literary developments in the seventies. Autobiographies, women's literature, the new dialect poetry and a lyric poetry in which the private and political spheres appeared inseparable evinced a shift in approach to the relationship between reading and writing. This relationship was no longer seen exclusively in terms of the (professional) work of authors and a (consumer) attitude towards reading.

The concept of 'experience'

Instead, set against a concept of 'experience', literature acquired a new character as a reciprocal process of reading and writing that included both the individual processing of and reflection on subjectivity, and its reproduction and expansion within the medium of literature. Writing in the women's movement, and the accent on aesthetic productivity in conceptions to do with the didactics of literature, may be cited as examples of this, as well as the writing experiences of peripheral social groups (such as prisoners), the development of children's and street theatre, and the emergence of the *Autorenfilm*. The last is contingent on the elaboration of new modes of perception, of which it at the same time also bears witness. At the same time, however, the rediscovery of personal subjectivity was unmistakably linked with a deliberate move away from politico-social reality – something which rightly gave rise to critical objections. 'Subjectivity the objective factor' (Rudolf zur Lippe) was thus often reduced to a subjective factor of subjectivity, in other words to individual representation of the self, to introspection and contemplation. The transitions overlap here, the boundaries being difficult to draw, and yet one may still pose the question, by way of assessing this new subjectivity, of the extent to which a social aspect is still present in the forms of its literary treatment.

The discovery of the first person: between autobiography and *Verständigungstext*

'In all branches of literature', noted the writer and critic Reinhard Baumgart in 1973, 'sharp-shooting diaries and intimate short stories have been cropping up again recently, as if hired for the purpose'. This observation refers to a remarkable phenomenon in literary history: in the early 1970s Max Frisch published his *Tagebuch 1966–1971* (*Diary 1966–1971*) (1972), and three years later his autobiographical love story *Montauk*; Peter Rühmkorf produced his 'ideas and reminiscences' under the title *Die Jahre die Ihr kennt* (*The Years You Know*) (1972); with *Kopf und Bauch* (*Head and*

Stomach) (1971), Gerhard Zwerenz published the 'story of a working man who has fallen among intellectuals', i.e. his own, in *Selbstporträt* (*Self-Portrait*) (1970) and *Nahaufnahme (Close-up)* (1973), Jakov Lind gave the story of his own career; likewise Günter Grass (*Aus dem Tagebuch einer Schnecke – From the Diary of a Snail*, 1972) Walter Kempowski (*Tadellöser & Wolf*, 1971; *Uns geht's ja noch gold – We're in Clover*, 1972), Peter Handke (*Der kurze Brief zum langen Abschied – The Short Letter for the Long Goodbye*, 1972; *Wunschloses Unglück – Perfect Misfortune*, 1972).

The reasons for this boom in autobiographies were assumed on the one hand to be a reflex action to popular memoir literature (Hildegard Knef, Peter Bamm), and on the other an exhaustion of poetic invention – a failure of fiction in the face of reality. More convincing, however, is the explanation that after years of thorough-going politico-social commitment, autobiography and the literary treatment of life-story elements marked a necessary return to individuality and personal identity. This was further encouraged by a defence mechanism against tendencies towards technocratic development that were rearing their heads on all sides in the early 1970s. 'The more technocrats exert coercion towards apparent objectivisation in all spheres', wrote Peter Härtling, 'and the more emphatically ideologies polarise, the more subjective literature will be'.

Karin Struck's novel *Klassenliebe* (*Class Love*) (1973) may be termed a thoroughly successful example of such autobiographical literature. Here the author treats her own experiences as an 'upwardly mobile' working woman who finds her way back to her own subjectivity after a period of politicisation during the era of the student movement. The search for political and intellectual identity, and the discovery of primeval commitments in sexuality and motherhood (taken up again and pursued as a problem in *Die Mutter – The Mother*, in 1975) form the substantial focal points of this novel, which is told from the perspective of a first-person narrator who clearly represents the author herself. Karin Struck won admiration for the manifest honesty and frankness with which she documented her life story. This served her as an indication of personal identity and truthfulness: 'To censor oneself is to castrate oneself. Expose contradictions without fear. But fear of being reduced by others: so that's what you are then, this small-minded person?'

Verena Stefan's prose text *Häutungen* (*Skinnings*) (1975) also bears witness to the urge to experience self and the desire for revelation, where a process of detachment may be observed against the background of the women's movement in the Federal Republic – detachment from familiar social commitments and contexts, release from traditional patterns of sexual relationship, and the discovery of a new female identity. This kind of literary reflection is credible, containing as it does 'autobiographical notes poems dreams analyses' (as the subhead reads) that link up with a new form of poetic self-experience, inasmuch as Verena Stefan focuses on that development leading to the statement: 'der mensch meines lebens bin ich' ('I am the person of my life').

These books thus bear witness to a newly discovered, indeed a 'new' subjectivity. Dispensing with neither history nor politics, this nevertheless sets out by ascertaining the self, reflecting on the self, and experiencing the self. Gabriel Wohmann presents this acknowledgement of his own person in a poem that has the character of a policy statement for this literary development. 'Selbstverständlich, sage ich, man kann eine Stellungnahme von mir erwarten / Klar, den Minoritäten und so weiter / Meine Sympathie, klar / ... Aber zuerst muss ich mal dieses nächste Lebenszeichen von mir hinkriegen, dies nächste kleine Herzrhythmusstörung' ('Obviously, I say, a statement can be expected from me / Clearly, on minorities and so on / My sympathy, of course / ... But first I must just get this next sign of life over with, this next little flutter in the heart rhythm').

Günter Grass's novel *Der Butt* (*The Flounder*) (1977) also contains autobiographical elements and contemporary issues, such as the women's movement, relationship problems and the author's trips to Danzig. In this novel these various elements are productively integrated into an expansive, fairytale-like, epic painting relating the history of man from its beginnings to the present day. Allegorised into the flounder figure, the inconsistency of historical processes forms the narrative inspiration for this lengthy novel, which is equal in narrative stature to the *Tin Drum*.

The problems of the egocentric

The egocentric perceptual perspective nevertheless also exhibited a perceptual limitation. Concentration on the states and feelings of an autobiographical first person consciously relies on the possibility of being able to deal with and convey reality in the writing-up and narration of one's own experience. Since, however, the potential for experience and perception of an autobiographically narrative first person are by definition limited, narrative potential is trapped within an agenda of Realism. Reality is not transcended by language, form or structure, and can only at best be adjusted in a structured way. In other words, the measure of quality is no longer the literary quality of the text, but the account of experience it contains.

A consistent, and for this very reason problematic expression of this agenda is represented by a literary genre that found a reading public from the end of the 1970s: the genre known as *Verständigungstexte*. In terms of conception this genre is based on an interest in exchanging the experiences of 'persons concerned'. In terms of content it relates to a diversity of spheres (love, women's problems, or prison, for example). In terms of agenda, *Verständigungstexte* dispense with qualitative literary criteria of comparison. Texts of this kind rely on the effect of recognition, being aimed at readers seeking to encounter themselves again in something that is already familiar. They thereby dispense with the capacity of literature to expand the boundaries of reality instead of merely duplicating them, of provoking instead of confirming experiences and of creating the potential for fresh perceptions instead of offering rehashed ways of seeing.

The fact that such texts do indeed find a reading public, however, may indicate a peripheral oddity. Since 1980 Kristiane Allert-Wybranietz has been publishing lyric poetry with the Fellbach Lucy Körner Verlag (*Trotz alledem, Liebe Grüsse – Despite Everything, Much Love*) that was has been able rapidly to conquer the bestseller lists. Hers are poems about simple things – about feelings, about 'relationships': 'Immer mehr / legen ihre Gefühle / in die / Tiefkühltruhe. / Ob sie glauben, / dadurch / ihre Haltbarkeit / zu verlängern?' ('More and more [people] / are putting their feelings / in the / deep-freeze cabinet. / Do they think / that by so doing / they will prolong their life?') At all events the author achieved total sales of 450,000 within three years – an indication of a widespread need for confirmation, warmth and recognition.

The watchword 'emancipation'

In the second half of the 1970s, women's literature became a label for selling a wide range of diverse texts. Within a few years a large number of women's journals sprang up, of which *Emma* appears to have established itself as a national publication. There are women's music groups (e.g. Schneewittchen – Snow-White), which either exclusively or predominantly perform for women; there are women's theatre groups, and various publishing houses have been founded (Frauenoffensive, Frauenbuchverlag, verlag frauenpolitik, Amazonenverlag, etc.), in which women publish, and sometimes themselves promote and sell in women's bookshops, books by women, about women, and for women – 'women's literature' in the strictest sense of the term. Far removed from the professional literary scene, models for a reading public are tested here that seek to detach themselves from the mechanisms of the male-dominated cultural and literary scenes, often with limited success, and which struggle against the danger of female ghettoisation.

Besides these attempts to create a female counter-public, there are also countless regional centres and initiatives in which, in more or less close connection with the women's movement, women try out forms of cooperation and political activity, and where writing and reading are employed as forms of self-experience and communication. The hope pinned on literature is that it will develop into a medium in which women can reach an understanding both about themselves and with others, and in which the suppressed and constrained creative powers of women can find expression.

One fundamental question that has arisen with increasing clarity in recent years is whether there is such a thing as a female mode of experience and writing, and if so what it consists in and in what ways it differs from the male mode of writing, and what function it might have for women in particular and society in general.

'Mum's Peaches': scholarship and tenderness

Literary journals written and edited by women, *Mamas Pfirsische* (*Mum's Peaches*) (1976–) and *Wissenschaft und Zärtlichkeit* (*Scholarship and Tenderness*) (1978–), have attempted to promote, both theoretically and practically, discussion about the conditions and possibilities for a female aesthetics and scholarship, which form one aspect of a wider issue concerning the possibilities for a women's politics in its own right. They attempt to do this in the same way that individual women are working on the history of women, rediscovering in the process suppressed or obscure female writers and thereby retrieving the historical dimension of women's literature and bringing it into topical discussion.

The surprising success of women's literature (over 100,000 copies of Verena Stefan's *Häutungen* were sold in a short period) led established publishing houses to pay heed to women's literature, too. Rowohlt-Verlag expanded its programme to include a *neue frau* (new woman) series, while other publishing houses likewise seized on so-called women's texts, thereby substantially diminishing the potential livelihoods of women's publishing houses. Many publishing houses also stepped up the sales of works both by earlier and newly discovered female authors by promoting them under the label of 'women's literature' (e.g. Struck, Schwaiger, Plessen). All texts written by women were suddenly ranked among women's literature, thereby watering down the original radical approach of women's literature with bogus conceptual notions and a diversity of modish texts.

The 'literarised' revolt

In terms of theme, a number of works stand out within these new literary trends that were concerned with the assumptions of the time, and in particular with the extra-parliamentary opposition movement and the student revolt. Their authors include Peter-Paul Zahl (*von einem der auszog, GELD zu verdienen – On one who set forth to earn money*, 1970; *Die Glücklichen – The Fortunate Ones*, 1979), Peter Schneider (*Lenz*, 1973), Gerd Fuchs (*Beringer und die lange Wut – Beringer and the Long Fury*, 1973) Uwe Timm (*Heisser Sommer – Hot Summer*, 1974), Roland Lang (*Ein Hai in der Suppe oder das Glück des Philipp Ronge – A Shark in the Soup, or the Fortune of Philipp Ronge*, 1974), Christian Geissler (*Das Brot mit der Feile – The Loaf with the File*, 1976), Bernward Vesper (*Die Reise*

– *The Journey*, written 1969–71, published posthumously 1977), Urs Jaeggi (*Brandeis*, 1978), Jochen Schimmang (*Der schöne Vogel Phönix – The Phoenix, a Beautiful Bird*, 1979) and Jürgen Theobaldy (*Spanische Wände – Screens*, 1981). In terms of life-story and political references these relate closely to a number of autobiographical publications dating from the period of extra-parliamentary revolt, including Bommi Baumann's *Wie alles anfing* (*How It All Began*) (1975); Daniel Cohn-Bendit's *Der grosse Basar* (*The Great Bazaar*) (1975); *Was wir wollten, was wir wurden* (*What We Wanted, What We Became*), edited by Peter Mosler (1977); *Wir warn die stärkste der Partein* (*We Were the Strongest of Parties*) (1977); and Inga Buhmann's *Ich hab mir eine Geschichte geschrieben* (*I've Written a Story*) (1977). These authors wrote novels, short stories, prose texts and autobiographies that all gave an account of developmental processes: politicisation, changes of view, and the link and contradiction between both the private and public spheres, and between theoretical reflection and political action. The subjectivity involved here was thus interwoven with political events around 1968, and their repercussions, and treated and presented in a literary form.

Accounts of failed politicisation

'Today', wrote Peter Schneider in 1975, having proclaimed the 'death of literature' in the days of the student movement, 'today, when even politically active writers have returned to their former workplaces, we are somewhat wiser than we once were. Only now that the movement has been pushed back from the streets into the shared flats are the themes of those years cropping up in literature, in films, and in painting. Suddenly there is again fresh subject-matter in literature, experimentation with new modes of representation – and all this at a time when we find ourselves in a phase of deepening depression and de-politicisation.'

The distinction between political and literary work put forward in this observation entails a withdrawal of the claim to be able to combine literature and politics through writing while being politically active at the same time. 'The longer we write', noted Bernward Vesper, 'the more we remove ourselves, [and] the more we participate in everyday struggles, the less we feel compelled to write'. In the wake of the collapse of the extra-parliamentary opposition there was a growing realisation 'that one cannot instigate a political and a literary revolt at the same time' (Schneider).

With the exception of Vesper's *Die Reise* (*The Journey*) and Zahl's *Die Glücklichen* (*The Fortunate Ones*), however, those novels that dealt with political revolt did not remotely approach a literary revolt. The narrative style of Gerd Fuchs, Uwe Timm and Roland Lang was, if anything, conventional. Their heroes marched a straight road from the phase of politicisation to entry into the German Communist Party, in which, under the leadership of paternal old comrades, they pursued the 'correct' political line: 'Sitting beside Otto, learning what was to be done, what was to go into the leaflet, who would copy it out, pull off the proofs and distribute them, how the factory gazette was to take up ideas, how the housing estate gazette and the next demands were to read, he suddenly realised that he had time. All this was work, clearly defined, cleanly demarcated work, work that was to be done' (Gerd Fuchs, *Beringer und die lange Wut – Beringer and the Long Fury*).

The technique used here, as in the case of Roland Lange and Uwe Timm, is that of psychological Realism. The focal point is a hero whose development is conveyed to the reader by means of empathy. Uwe Timm, for example, fuses the perspective of the narrator with that of the hero, employing the stylistic device of experienced speech throughout, not only to impart to the reader the developmental process of his main character, but at the same time to offer the reader a chance to identify with his learning processes and modes of action. At the forefront, therefore, is a political objective, clothed in a literature designed to convince: 'Out of the all-knowing narrator derives the know-all hero' (Hermann Peter Piwitt).

Fragmentation of the self

The 'hero' perspective likewise communicates actions, realisations, and reflections in the case of Zahl, Schneider, Vesper and Geissler. Here, however, they are not expressed with a view to the reader identifying with them. In the case of Zahl, particularly, this perspective is variously fragmented, being 'realistic' in the sense of capturing reality by means of literary devices – collage, montage, internal monologues and alienation.

The most successful of these prose works was Peter Schneider's *Lenz*, a story so far published in over a hundred thousand copies, and which caused a considerable stir among literary critics, for the most part positive. Using his title character to allude to Georg Büchner's story *Lenz*, Schneider depicts the development and growing sense of unease of a young intellectual. The background to his experience is formed by the break-up of his love affair with a working-class girl, in whom Lenz had seen a chance of being able to overcome 'privately the conflict between class differences in style of perception and life'. However, it is the social, not the private aspect of this relationship and its failure that motivates the story. This is concerned with the failed attempt to build a bridge between students and workers – a bridge across intellectual asceticism and poverty of sensuality, across lack of experience of abstract political concepts and theory formation.

'Escaping' from West Berlin to Italy, Lenz learns that it is possible to combine thought and sensuality, politics and feeling – an experience that makes him realise he is being used. Back in Berlin, he puts great words to the test in the little things of everyday life. Schneider narrates simply, readily and without pretension. His is an account of a learning process whose outcome is open: 'Stay here' is the terse answer Lenz gives to a question put by his departing friend as to what he wants to do now.

The great success of this story is largely attributable to its credibility. Many members of the extra-parliamentary opposition generation could see themselves in the character of Lenz – his sense of unease and his self-doubt in relation to once-believed dogmas.

Bernward Vesper's Die Reise (The Journey)

When Bernward Vesper, son of the prominent Nazi bard and lyric poet of the *Führer*, committed suicide on 15 May 1971, he left behind a substantial book fragment that was published in 1977 under the title *Die Reise. Ein Romanessay* (*The Journey: a Novel Essay*). Vesper describes his 'mental journey into the self and the past', undertaking, in the form of individual archaeology, nothing less than a radical exploration of himself, his origins and his environment, as well as of Federal German reality. Three levels of travel and writing, three tracks of the self, are pursued. One is 'recollection' (described in the book as 'simple report') of the roots of private and political history – self-analysis of his disturbed childhood; exposure of his larger-than-life, authoritarian father, whose image blends with that of the *Führer* to form a figure of negative identification. Another strand is immersion in artificial paradise, the wild transcendence of bodily constraints in the drug trip (related in an extravagant associative language of craziness that exposes the wounds of the damaged psyche). Finally, there is the actual period of writing, 1969–71, the time when the extra-parliamentary opposition, of which Vesper had been a pioneer, was collapsing as a result of internal splits, and when the first signs of political terrorism were beginning to appear. This book makes unmistakably clear how fascism continued to flourish within the institutional political sphere in Germany, and how it permeated the mentality of the entire society. It also shows how the protest movement can only be understood at all by seeing in it an effective denial both of parents' crimes and the crimes of the present day. With a radical approach that does not shrink even from self-destruction, Vesper adhered to a unity of political and psychological liberation. *Die Reise* is a voyage of discovery for the reader into the dispositions of the bourgeois soul.

Everyday lyric poetry: political lyric poetry – no contradiction

'What kind of people are they', asked Günter Herburger provocatively in 1967, 'who write poems – are they still alive? Are they long since dead? Do they use, when working, pure oxygen to breathe, or have they managed to acclimatise to snowflakes, or to the amber inlay of their desk fittings, or what?' Herburger's provocation was aimed at a fresh start in lyric verse, and above all at a departure – a departure from a hermetic poetry that separated art from life, a departure from nature and flower poetry. His intention was a move towards the things of life, the acceptance of everyday life into poetry, a bridging of the gulf between art and life: a poetics directed both against Benn and Celan.

One poet who by the end of the 1960s had already begun to implement such a poetics was Erich Fried. His are for the most part epigrammatic poems, structured dialectically and imparting pointed insights, conveying observations on politics, lifestyles and ways of thinking.

Fried's poetry volume *und Vietnam und* (*and Vietnam and*) marks the beginning of political poetry in the Federal Republic of Germany. The attitude of protest against the war in Vietnam that lends both form and perspective to this volume could obviously not have remained a static, unchanging factor with an author who diagnosed the developments of his time so precisely as Erich Fried. Along with the politico-social events about which he wrote, his themes and mode of expression also changed. In 1974, for example, his poetry volume *Gegengift* (*Antidote*) was published, in which he speaks of doubt, fear and despair, and of self-doubt: 'Zweifle nicht / an dem / der dir sagt / er hat Angst / aber hab Angst / vor dem / der dir sagt / er kenne keine Zweifel' ('Do not doubt / him / who tells you / he is afraid / but fear / him / who tells you / he has no doubts').

Erich Fried is a political poet no less than a satirist, and a moralist in all that he writes. For this reason there is no contradiction in his poetry between politics and life, because life, understood as a stance, a form of thought and perception and a mode of action, is for him always seen in terms of political contexts, being shaped by them and in turn exerting an impact on them.

The poetics of everyday lyric verse, which is also political lyric verse, was taken up by a whole generation of lyric poets, who adopted it in their poetic practice and developed it further. Arnfried Astel, Jürgen Theobaldy, Johannes Schenk, Karin Kiwus and Nicolas Born, for example, all allow details to be voiced in their poems that bear witness to very everyday things. Joy, sorrow, happiness, feelings, and moods are recorded with as much sensitivity as the material world around us, and brought to expression with a simplicity that is artistically precisely calculated. The first person spoken of in this lyric, often extended into a first person plural, deliberately puts something of itself, its own identity and its own sensuality into the poem. It speaks of itself in order to impart itself to others, as in Karin Kiwus's *Glückliche Wendung* (*A Change for the Better*):

Spätestens	Now at the latest
jetzt werden wir	we shall have to
alles vergessen müssen	forget everything

und unauffällig	and go on living
weiterleben wie bisher	unobtrusively as before
hoffnungslos	otherwise
würden wir sonst	we would hopelessly
immer wieder	go on repeating
die Lusttaten bedienen	the same lustful acts
gierig verhungern müssen	having to crave in vain
und uns nie mehr	and never again
erinnern können	be able to remember
an das Glück	the happiness

The drawback of this lyric, of course, was that it was not always able to rise above the banality integral to its theme of the everyday world – a fact that posed a fundamental aesthetic problem. The precise recording of everyday details often led their social character to disappear from view. 'I would wish for my poems', says Jürgen Theobaldy, author and theoretician of everyday lyric, 'that they reveal something of the enduring quality of simple objects, lending these and themselves something that lasts in a society that now only produces so as to discard too soon'. Nevertheless, a poetic method that relates to 'simple objects' in this way runs the risk of having to submit to the same process of change to which those objects are themselves prone, thus falling victim to forgetfulness.

Politics and everyday life

One group sought to avoid this risk by going beyond the precise recording of situations, observations and details to highlight their social and political nature. In this respect they are akin to Erich Fried. These authors include Peter-Paul Zahl, F.C. Delius, Yaak Karsunke and Ludwig Fels. Despite their individuality and the uniqueness of each of their lyric voices, these authors nevertheless have in common a precise synopsis of politics and everyday life, individual experience and social context. An example of this approach would be the poem *Karl Marx im Konzert* (*Karl Marx at the Concert*) by Yaak Karsunke, written on the occasion of a Rolling Stones tour in 1973:

'diese versteinten
verhältnisse dadurch
zum tanzen zwingen
dass man ihnen ihre eigne
melodie vorspielt'
Jagger jault auf der Bühne
You Can't Always Get What You Want
: & dieses Schwein (sagt Andreas)

wiederholt das solange
bis wir zu tanzen anfangen

'To make
these fossilised conditions
dance
by playing them
your own tune'
Jagger howls on stage
You Can't Always Get What You Want
: & that swine (says Andreas)
goes on singing it
until we start dancing

These forms of an everyday lyric verse that is understood in the political sense need to be distinguished from others during the 1970s that propounded a growing awareness of environmental problems and regionalist questions – poetry known as the 'poetry of the provinces'. This was a poetry that presented itself with self-confidence, representing both the urge to intervene and the inwardly reflective dimension of literature, while at the same time preserving the experiences of particular linguistic environments in their respective regional dialects.

These dialects were not employed simply in order to paint a rosy picture of a home region, however, but rather to change those regions in the face of increasing threats from outside. Authors in this category included H.C. Artmann and Herbert Achternbusch, who may be regarded as exemplars for the genre, as well as Thaddäus Troll and Fitzgerald Kusz, for whom playing with the linguistic material of dialect was always at the same time a confrontation with social convention and a criticism of social rigidity – a feature that makes it akin to concrete poetry.

Regional dialect

Authors of the 'Vienna Group' (Gerhard Rühm, Ernst Jandl, Konrad Bayer and Oswald Wiener) are as indicative of this as the Saarländer Ludwig Harig, Oswald Andrae from northern Germany, the Swiss Kurz Mart and the Alsatian André Weckmann. What is being used here is 'dialect as a weapon' (André Weckmann) against metropolitan infiltration of the provinces.

Oswald Andrae: *Riet dien Muul up!*

Riet dien Muul up!
Schree doch ut,
    wat du glöövst,
    wat du meenst,

> wat du denkst,
> wat dien Angst is!
> Schree doch ut,
>   wenn du Courage hest,
> Up de
> Gefahr hen,
> dat dar annern sünd,
>   de di seggt: dat stimmt nich;
> dat dar annern sünd,
>   anner Menen;
> dat dar annern sünd,
>   de geern hisst!
> Schree doch ut!
> Naderhand
>   kann well kamen,
>   kann di sehn,
>   man kiekt weg
>   un will di nich.
> Riet dien Muul up!

Aesthetics fights back: the literature of the 1980s

Whereas the 1970s were unmistakably characterised by a return to individuality and subjectivity in the literature of the Federal Republic, the early 1980s saw a reconquest of literature itself. This development should be seen as a dialectical process: 'new subjectivity' had been a response to the lack of sensuality of the politicisation phase through the discovery of the first person. This response, however, had been in stylistic and perceptual forms that remained entirely confined within the limited horizons of the first person (women's literature, 'Verständigungstexte', 'everyday' lyric).

The reconquest of literature on the threshold of the 1980s was thus in turn a response to the aesthetic deficiencies of 'new subjectivity' – a literary attempt to go beyond the boundaries and constraints of this egocentric horizon of perception, with its defects and experiences of suffering. It also marks a concomitant effort to counteract what was polemically declared from the viewpoint of professional authors to be 'organised dilettantism'. The polemical tone of this declaration derives on the one hand from an impression among professional authors that their works were in danger of being sucked under by a whirlpool of modish subjectivity, and on the other hand from their undoubtedly correct perception that the capacity of literature to impart ideas could not be arbitrarily reduced to the components of 'authenticity' and 'spontaneity'.

Conservative restrictions

Along with all this, a strengthened political, or at the very least social commitment could be observed among writers in the Federal Republic in the early 1980. This, too, was undoubtedly a factor in a dialectical process of development. The 'tendency shift' of the 1970s had led not only to 'new subjectivity' but also to the bolstering of a political conservatism that came to see itself affirmed by the formation of a conservative government in 1983. This was accompanied by restrictive measures in the sphere of cultural policy: in film funding, for example, these were applied to productions by author-film-makers such as Herbert Achternbusch (*Das Gespenst – The Ghost*), Alexander Kluge and Hans Jürgen Syberberg. Financial cuts in the cultural sphere, especially in spending on public libraries, affected a substantial domain of reading culture.

Discussions on representing the Federal Republic culturally abroad likewise brought in their wake a ban on appearances at Goethe Institute events by such *personae non gratae* as Günter Grass and Heinrich Böll. These restrictive tendencies in cultural policy paved the way for protests by those affected by them, and hence the climate for a deterioration in relations between the political and cultural spheres that is reminiscent of the 1950s.

The peace issue

These factors were augmented by another problem that writers in East and West alike felt compelled to discuss – the threat to peace by nuclear rearmament and the arms race. In December 1981, at the personal invitation of the GDR writer Stephan Hermlin, notable authors from the Federal Republic and the GDR, including GDR emigrants such as Jurek Becker and Thomas Brasch, met in East Berlin – the first such joint discussion since 1947. This first meeting had massive media and public involvement and was therefore hailed as a success for being able to manage an exchange of ideas at all. Even then, however, and especially at a second meeting held in The Hague in May 1982, differences of opinion emerged and sharpened to such an extent that the invited GDR writers failed to turn up at all at the Heilbronn meeting held in December 1983. Of greater importance, however, than the dissension that arose in this way, which highlighted official political differences between the two German states, remained the demonstrative effect of their joint appeal for peace. In a resolution from The Hague, participating authors described themselves as 'part of the international peace movement', agreeing 'that the two military blocs should be dissolved, immediately and without reservation'. This public demonstration of the social commitment of writers and intellectuals in the early

1980s reflected their conscious return to the power of poetry to exert resistance.

Transcending the first person

The flood of 'new subjectivity' works, which took on more and more traits of modish dilettantism within the framework of *Verständigungslitera-tur*, makes it necessary to draw careful distinctions using the criteria of aesthetic differences. Against the background of the movements in writing of the 1970s, for example, it is necessary to distinguish works that emerged from them in terms of theoretical and social derivation, but which did not remain constrained by them. These works include Elisabeth Plessens's *Mitteilungen an den Adel* (*Messages to the Nobility*) (1976), Birgit Pausch's *Die Verweigerungen der Johanna Glauflügel* (*The Denials of Johanna Glauflügel*) (1977), Karin Reschke's novel *Verfolgte des Glücks* (*Pursued by Fortune*) (1982), Brigitta Arens's *Katzengold* (*Cat Gold*) (1982), Brigitte Kronauer's novel *Rita Münster* (1983), and Anne Duden's prose text *Über-gang* (*Transition*) (1983). These are all autobiographically motivated works, inasmuch as the women in them tell the stories of women. They are the stories of the authors themselves, written in terms of their politico-social conditioning; the projection of the process of finding themselves on to a fictional character; the story of suffering under the double oppression of women within the fabric of history; the splintering of the experiential context of their life stories into incoherent experiential steps. Different as their literary methods are, and diverse as are the narrative intentions they express, their authors all share a new confidence in the ability of literature to communicate experience by finding a language of its own. This is comparable to the process of self-experience to which the GDR author Christa Wolf submits herself in her *Kinderheitsmuster* (*Patterns of Childhood*). Prose texts of this kind offer a blend of the author's own experience with elements of contemporary history and critical psychologi-cal reflection on it. This prose is concerned not with contemplation, how-ever, but with the critical internal view of an individual being whose social aspect comes the more clearly to the fore the more radically and openly this introspection is pursued.

Searching and testing, rather than knowing all the answers

This is not the case, however, with a novel much praised at the time, Nicolas Born's *Die erdabgewandte Seite der Geschichte* (*The Dark Side of History*) (1976). 'I had no answers to specific historical questions: I was only able at that stage to despise all answers, the more self-assured and correct they sounded', the first-person narrator, a writer like Born, informs us. The motive behind the narrative is thus politico-social irritation, even anger. Capturing moods and landscapes by the use of subtle literary devices, Born tells of himself, his relationship with his girlfriend, and with his daughter, in the certain knowledge that 'stories such as these are what make up real history'. However, this 'real history' does not signify the experience of historical and social identity in the self-experience of individuality. With Born it signifies a rejection of all social aspects of the individual, tending towards another kind of self-assurance and self-righteousness – those of the 'simple life' (Ernst Wiechert), in which the 'individual, torn out of his context' relates to nothing beyond himself.

Born's novel thus marks the transitional boundary between the new subjectivity and the new contemplation. This boundary lies at the point where the 'dark side of history' meets the claim to exclusivity, the right to be 'history' in its own right. We see here the motion of search, of groping in the unknown, feeling one's way forward towards a history of one's own, the unfathomable depths of origins, childhood, and youth, the tracing of individual idiosyncrasies, and aspects of the self that have been suppressed by pedagogy and patriarchy. The searching forms of motion lead to a willingness to accept oneself with all one's inconsistencies, and having reached this point of acceptance in one's personal history, to enter into dialogue with oneself. The forms seem to produce literary orientations precisely because they are not pre-established or dogmatically rigid, instead remaining open to the reader's own realm of experience.

'Findebuch'

The fact that all this can be achieved not only under autobiographical conditions, but also in the form of a life story that has long since been relegated to suppressed and denied history, was demonstrated by Karin Reschke in 1982 in her book *Verfolgte des Glücks* (*Pursued by Fortune*). This *'Findebuch'*, as it is called in the subtitle, tells the life story of Henriette Vogel, a woman scarcely mentioned in biographies and then disparagingly. Only a few of her letters are extant, and there is no mention of her at the place of her voluntary death on 21 November 1811 – the Kleiner Wannsee lake in Berlin. Although there is a gravestone there, its inscription mentions only the name of the man who died with her: Heinrich von Kleist.

Karin Reschke's story is thus not only the life story of a forgotten woman, but also the story of the specifically male form of forgetfulness. The narrative form used is that of a diary – a *'Findebuch'* for more reasons than one: first, because Henriette Vogel finds herself in it; second, because the author is obliged to find or invent her heroine in it; third, because the reader can find in this book a forgotten woman, and thus, in diverse ways a part of him or herself. 'We are pursued by fortune' is the highly paradoxical, ingeniously and dialectically condensed statement expressing the dilemma of a female biography in which the woman was unable to find herself in her own lifetime. Although Karin Reschke adopts the Kleistian style of speech of the day, thus ostensibly lending historical authenticity to her account, the artistic construction of the life story it relates, now history, nonetheless allows it to spill over into the present. This is achieved by beginning the book at the end, by relating the final days and hours: Henriette confides her *Findebuch* to Kleist for final reading. The reader thus reads it with Kleist himself, knowing that when he has finished the actual end of the story, which forms the opening of the novel, will ensue, and so on. It thus forms a never-ending story in the manner of a spiral written across the history of women and of femininity, a history of oppression, forgetting, and suppression that extends to our present day and our own biography: 'Pursued by Fortune'.

Peter Weiss's three-volume work *Ästhetik des Widerstands* (*The Aesthetics of Resistance*), published in 1975, 1978 and 1981, and totalling almost a thousand pages, may be regarded alongside Uwe Johnson's tetralogy *Jahrestage* (*Days of the Year*) as the most significant work published in German in the 1970s and 1980s. It represents an ambitious attempt, going far back into history, to follow the development of the European labour movement from its first beginnings and objectives through its conflicts and aspirations, its declines and failures and its doubts, as well as the continuities and traditions of the struggle against oppression and exploitation in world historical terms.

Weiss relates this history from the viewpoint of a fictitious first-person narrator who, as is revealed in the first volume, lived at first in the communist underground in Berlin in the autumn of 1937, going into exile in Prague, and finally taking part in the Spanish Civil War. The second volume opens after the defeat of the Republicans, in Paris, taking the first-person narrator to Sweden, where he works in a factory, makes contact with communists and becomes part of the Bertolt Brecht group. This volume closes in April 1940. The third volume, a 'roam through Hades', opens with the arrival of the narrator's parents in Sweden, highlighting the problems of dogmatic communism, which are brought out mainly through the 'anti-character' Max Hodann. The story takes us through the Stockholm Party cell and its activities, to Nazi Germany (the crushing of the *Rote Kapelle* resistance organisation and the executions at Plötzensee), showing as well the attrition produced by the intrigues, disputes and terrorisation that heralded fresh evils within the communist and socialist labour movement before the end of World War II.

The fictitious, and yet at the same time in parts minutely detailed and faithfully documented and reconstructed chronicle of the 1937–47 period nevertheless forms only one level of this *roman d'essai* (Alfred Andersch). A second and equally significant level is formed by a discussion of art theory and aesthetics that ranges from the Pergamon altar, through Géricault's *Raft of the Medusa*, to Picasso's *Guernica*, from Kafka through Neukrantz to Brecht. Weiss presents art as the collective memory of humanity, the productive, ongoing ferment of all class struggles, in which the life of man has manifested itself inextinguishably, and which acts as a recollection and expression of historical aspirations that have yet to be fulfilled. Both levels, the contemporary historical level concerned with the anti-fascist struggle, and that concerned with the history and theory of art in relation to aesthetic productivity, are combined by Weiss into a third level, which is that of the work itself. The genre designation 'novel' does not do justice to the book, which is scarcely concerned at all either with plot, or character psychology and development. It is much more akin to a treatise, essay or tract, and more interested in ideas on the theory of art, politics and knowledge than with the narrative development of a social panorama or an individual conflict.

It nevertheless becomes clear as the narrative proceeds that the narrative style sustains and fulfils the task that the author has set himself. The various narrative levels – description, historico-political digression and aesthetic analysis, all increasingly combine as the work moves on, to culminate in a synthesis of essay, report, analysis and reflection. 'Aesthetics is no longer defined using works of art', Weiss comments on the third volume, 'but deposits itself directly'. This remark concerns the communication of the political and the artistic – an aesthetics that is inherently political, and a politics that understands the forms in which it is represented as an expression of its objectives, or alternatively its failure.

Weiss is consequently able to put his finger on the wounds in the communist labour movement – the Moscow show trials, Stalinism and terror within the movement. It is for this reason, in a manner comparable with the pattern of the novel of development, that he has his fictitious narrator work through the cultural history of humanity to its aesthetic potential for resistance: 'You must read, you must educate yourself, you must come to terms with the things that happen to you, you must take a stand, you mustn't sit around and just let everything happen to you, you mustn't give in to everything with the idea that there are more powerful people above you pulling all the strings. These are the basic ideas, and therefore the repeated theme: where, and at what times have men laughed in the face of apparently insuperable obstacles?'

Wunsch-autobiographie: Ideal autobiography

By using the first-person narrator for his work, Weiss avowedly wrote an 'ideal autobiography' – not in the sense of a political whitewashing of his own bourgeois life story, but of a blueprint for a fictional synthesis of aesthetics and resistance, art and politics, whose fictional character is played up rather than down. 'How could all this be told?' is thus the reiterated, stereotyped formula that reveals the organisational principle of the narrative to be that of narrative self-reflection and a poetic framework. The aim behind this is to set against the bourgeois 'inability to mourn' (Alexander Mitscherlich) an 'aesthetics of resistance' that has learned to mourn over its own shortcomings and failures.

This blueprint, the elaboration of which is documented by Peter Weiss in note form (*Notizbücher 1971–1980*, 1981), was highly controversial among professional critics. Writers such as Alfred Andersch and Wolfgang Koeppen, on the other hand, were united in their admiration of the work. 'The novel *The Aesthetics of Resistance*', wrote Wolfgang Koeppen, 'is for me one of the most exciting, courageous and sad books of my time'. In his obituary of Peter Weiss, who died in 1982, Hans Christoph Buch refers to the challenge this work issued: 'The exploration and assessment of this three-volume novel massif, with its heights and depths, peaks and troughs, still remains to be accomplished.'

It is no coincidence that many of the prose works referred to in this chapter as examples of how the boundaries of the self can be transcended were written by women authors. Authors such as Birgit Pausch, Karin Reschke and Anne Duden all follow on from the experiences of the women's movement, putting the idea of female emancipation into effect in their works. They are not, however, straitjacketed by the production and reproduction of experiences and ideological concepts. On the contrary, the most successful passages in these texts represent a counter-blueprint – one of a new world made up of language.

Rita Münster

This may be asserted of Brigitte Kronauer's novel *Rita Münster*, dating from 1983. Here too, individuality and the everyday life of a woman form the starting-point for all perception, but the rhythm and inner tension of this prose texture propel the individual existence of the character into a dynamic that repulses all external references to reality by producing a reality of its own. By disintegrating and dissolving into itself beyond 'authenticity' and 'spontaneity', an identity of the first-person existence emerges – an example of a new, perhaps female writing style. 'But again and again the rippling of the trees, of the cupolas, the vault thrown over broad and narrow shoulders, mighty coats, mourning coats, luxury coats, a circling noise, a rushing sound running along my head as along the horizon, through all my vein pathways and nerve branches, I can feel it in my teeth. A numbness, a dying of complete assent, a dissolving, as if I were being put through a great sieve, nothing but little leaves twitch towards me, pulverised into something of the same kind and still with me, only now completely with me.' This is an experimental discourse with a self that has transcended its boundaries, the articulation of a risk consisting of a lost sense of security and sacrificed certainties.

Lyric of the damaged world

In the prose of female authors in the early 1980s, the loss of a sense of security and of certainties thus found expression among other things in the transcendence of self and the reconstruction of experiential realities. This phenomenon had its counterpart in a lyric poetry that for its part both revealed and tracked down damage. Far removed from the agenda of 'everyday' lyricism, which conveyed its unique character by emphasising the context of life from which it derived, a lyric poetry emerged from the mid-1970s onwards that did not deny, but rather ingeniously exposed its artificial character through its formal language. Its proponents were Sarah Kirsch, Günter Kunert, Michael Krüger and Hans Magnus Enzensberger – its themes, subject-matter, motifs and metaphorical spheres deriving from the Western side of the dividing lines between state and social frontiers.

Expatriation – repatriation?

Sarah Kirsch and Günter Kunert were among those authors who moved to the Federal Republic from the GDR in the late 1970s. Following the expatriation of Wolf Biermann, they were joined by Thomas Brasch, Bernd Jensch, Reiner Kunze, Hans Joachim Schädlich, Jurek Becker and Erich Loest – notable authors even at the time they moved, and not simply as a result of their conspicuous exile. For these writers coming out of the GDR, the essentially politically-motivated interest in them was disturbing. Initially, as Hans Joachim Schädlich expressed it (*Versuchte Nähe – Attempted Nearness*, 1977), it outweighed 'interest in the personal circumstances of authors, because of the state of affairs in the two German states'. Not their literary works but 'living and working conditions in the GDR, or the circumstances [governing] travel to the Federal Republic, or during the first weeks of residence in the Federal Republic,' were the subject of discussion. As Thomas Brasch (*Vor den Vätern sterben die Söhne – The Sons Die Before the Fathers*, 1977; *Kargo oder der 32. Versuch, auf einem untergehenden Schiff aus der eigenen Haut zu kommen – Cargo, Or the 32nd Attempt to Save One's Bacon on a Sinking Ship*, 1978; *Rotter Und weiter – Rotter and so on*, 1978; *Lieber Georg – Dear Georg*, 1979) observed, the Federal German public treated 'people who come from there – at least authors – like very special animals'. Depending on their temperament and political convictions, authors drew various conclusions from this, for them, new experience of public interest. Some remained silent, or at least refused to take part in public discussion in the media (Sarah Kirsch, Hans Joachim Schädlich), some sought to gain a foothold in the literary world of the Federal Republic (Thomas Brasch, Bernd Jentzsch, Günter Kunert), while others deliberately made the realities of life in the Federal Republic their theme (Wolf Biermann).

Sarah Kirsch

Sarah Kirsch had started out in the GDR as a lyric poet writing nature and love poetry. Her choice of subject-matter and motifs remained constant even after her move to the Federal Republic in 1977. Poetry volumes published since then in the Federal Republic (*Wintergedichte – Winter Poems*, 1978; *Katzenkopfpflaster – Cobblestones*, 1978; *Drachensteigen – Flying Kites*, 1979; *La Pagerie*, 1980; *Erdreich – Earth Realm*, 1982) all revolve around the themes of nature, landscape and the animal world. It would be misleading, however, to label her a 'nature lyricist' in the same tradition as Oskar Loerke or Wilhelm Lehmann. The natural conditions, landscapes, animal realms and human relations written about in these poems are disrupted relationships, confused by historical processes, techno-logical advances and social erosion. In this respect too, Sarah Kirsch has remained true to herself. She absorbs these confusions, derived from historico-social developments, into her metaphorical world and formal language, in such a way that they muddle the poetic process in the poem itself, sometimes with an entirely paradoxical intention.

> Auf schwarzen Weiden das Melkvieh
> Suchet den Pferch auf und immer
> Zur nämlichen Zeit. Der zufriedene Landmann
> Sitzt auf dem Schemel am Rande des Wegs
> Raucht eine Marlboro während die Milch
> Wild in den gläsernen Leitungen strömt.

> On blackened meadows the dairy cow
> Searches out the pen, and always
> At the same time. The contented farmer
> Sits on the stool at the side of the path
> Smoking a Marlboro while the milk
> Flows wildly into the glass pipes.

> (from *Erdreich – Earth Realm*, 1982)

The laughter that can be evoked by parody of this kind could neverthe-less hardly give expression to unalloyed pleasure at a lyrically condensed picture of nature. What this lyric seeks to provoke is a laugh of horror, that should not persist for its own sake, but go beyond itself. For this very reason the lyric first person in the poetry of Sarah Kirsch does not appear as captive of the confusions it perceives and conveys. Instead, it sets an alien quality against these threats and damage to life, a quality that at the same time conveys a sense of disruption. Thus, in a highly subtle way, it also conveys the desire for change in the natural and social conditions that have come about.

> ... mir erscheint
> Siebenundzwanzig Rosenstöcke zu retten
> Ein versprengter Engel den gelben Kanister
> Über die stockfleckigen Flügel geschnallt
> Der himmlische Daumen im Gummihandschuh
> Senkt das Ventil und es riecht
> Für Stunden nach bitteren Mandeln.

> ... I see
> So as to save twenty-seven rose-bushes
> A stray angel with yellow canister
> Fastened over his mould-stained wings
> His heavenly thumbs in rubber gloves
> Opens the valve and it smells
> For hours of bitter almonds.

> (from *Erdreich – Earth Realm*, 1982)

Michael Krüger

With a highly sensitive perceptive faculty, Michael Krüger's lyric verse has also recorded and captured in imagery the damage increasingly being done to our social and natural environment. Krüger, who runs a publishing company in Munich, and also edits the journal *Akzente* (*Accents*), made his début as a lyric poet in 1976 with his volume *Reginapoly*, followed in 1978 by *Diderots Katze* (*Diderot's Cat*). In these first two volumes, his lyric poetry is already as artificial as it is reflective, even in relation to its own procedural methods. On the opening pages of Krüger's volume *Aus der Ebene* (*Off the Level*), published in 1982, is the poem *Der Erschrockene Mensch* (*Frightened Man*) – and the question of how to speak nowadays of fright, the way it works and its consequences. This signifies a shift, given the fact of everyday fright, from unfaltering confidence in traditional lyric forms to the question of potential communication. This question become a message in itself: 'Warme Rinde. Warmes Herz. / Und ein Wahnrest, gut verborgen, / der sich durch den Schädel frisst. / Wie soll man diese Operationen / der Seele beschreiben?' ('Warm cortex. Warm heart. / And a remnant of madness, well concealed, / that eats its way through the skull. / How can these operations / of the soul be described?'). Not unlike the confusions in Sarah Kirsch's poetry, running through Krüger's poetry, too, there is a sense of disruption, distance, and a rejection of ways of life in the city and in nature ('Zu viele wollen mitreden, / seit es so billig geworden ist': 'Too many want a say, / since it has become so cheap'). Here too there is a desire for change, but now ironically fragmented by the awareness that the objective of change and the conditions of change are mutually related ('Naturally / a life would be possible: // Naturally, naturally'). And yet Michael Krüger still has confidence in the power of language and its metaphors. He is still committed to the idea that the writing process can allow a kind of communication that would otherwise not find expression, and which could become a language, in both parts of Germany.

Literatur

über den Rand hinaus
ins Freie

Sieh da,   Deutschland.
die Schrift!   Ganz nutzlos
Sie schreibt dich   war es nicht
mühelos   ganz nutzlos

Literature

over the edge and beyond
into Free

See there,   Germany.
The writing!   Entirely pointless
It writes you   it was not
Effortlessly   entirely pointless.

Enzensberger

The career of Hans Magnus Enzensberger provides a good example of the processes of disillusionment within the intellectual Left. In 1968, at the height of the revolt, Enzensberger made *Kursbuch* (*Timetable*), the journal he edited, an outstanding discussion forum for the elaboration of revolutionary theory. Ten years later, in 1978, he declared in the same publication 'that there is no *Weltgeist*; that we do not know the laws of history; that neither social nor natural evolution knows any subject, and that it is unpredictable; that consequently when we act politically we never achieve what we set out to achieve'. This amounts to a refutation of the 1968 movement's convictions about the future, based on Marxism, resting on the personal views and experience of its author. Enzensberger, who had always adopted a critical stance towards *real existierender Sozialismus* of the East European brand, saw his commitment to liberation movements in the Third World permanently undermined by a protracted stay in Cuba. The everyday realities of the Cuban revolution, with its manifest shortcomings, its lack of freedom, its constraints and supervision, shattered the hopes of Western intellectuals for the 'concrete Utopia' (Herbert Marcuse) of a liberated world, at the same time exploding the theoretical assumptions behind those hopes, which derived from Marxism. Enzensberger reflects on this process of disillusionment both in brilliant political essays (*Politische Brosamen – Political Crumbs*, 1982), and in his lyric poetry, written in the same period.

Untergang der Titanic (*The Sinking of the Titanic*) is the title of a verse tale, published in 1978, in which Enzensberger writes of his experiences in Cuba. The title is an allusion to the shipping catastrophe of 1912, in which the *Titanic*, a symbol of technological progress, and regarded as unsinkable, sank after colliding with an iceberg. Enzensberger uses this as an allegory of the sinking of the belief in progress following collision with the 'iceberg' of post-revolutionary Cuba. Thirty-three cantos, alluding to Dante's *Divine Comedy*, correlate Cuba 1968 and Berlin 1977, historical experiences from art and literature ('Apocalypse. Umbrian, around 1490') are expressed and present-day, disillusioned blueprints for continuing life and survival ('unclear, hard to say, why I go on howling and swimming') are communicated. His interweaving of political criticism and laconic arrangement is matched by the juxtaposition of metrical speech, strict metre and precise strophe construction on the one hand, and the colloquial tone of the stale joke ('Who really believes, / that he has to believe it?') on the other.

Enzensberger calls his verse tale a 'comedy', drawing on Dürrenmatt's assertion that 'comedy is all we can cope with nowadays'. Its laconic tone is taken up again in his 1980 volume of poetry, *Die Furie des Verschwindens* (*The Fury of Disappearance*) ('To combat the Ice Age / with matches (you say), that is / a lame business'). After a phase of radical criticism and commitment to revolution, Enzensberger took up again the socially critical and ironic elements of his early lyric poetry, albeit modified by political and social experience, and yet still the same in their rejection of all claims to duty and obligation.

> *Die Furie des Verschwindens*
>
> Eskapismus, ruft ihr mir zu,
> vorwurfsvoll,
> Was denn sonst, antworte ich,
> bei diesem Sauwetter! –,
> spanne den Regenschirm auf
> und erhebe mich in die Lüfte.
> Von euch aus gesehen,
> werde ich immer kleiner und kleiner,
> bis ich verschwunden bin.
> Ich hinterlasse nichts weiter
> als eine Legende,
> mit der ihr Neidhammel,
> wenn es draussen stürmt,

euern Kindern in den Ohren liegt,
damit sie euch nicht davonfliegen.

Escapism, shout out to me,
full of reproach,
What else, I reply,
In this filthy weather! –,
put up my umbrella
and rise up into the air.
From your point of view,
I grow smaller and smaller,
until I disappear.
I leave behind no more
than a legend,
With which its dog in the manger,
when the storm rages outside,
pesters your children,
so that they don't run away from you.

'Iceberg', 'glaciation' and 'ice-age' are all metaphors denoting a wide-spread perception within the lyric poetry of Federal Germany during the transition into the 1980s – that of a social and historical developmental stage signalling both the end of Enlightenment thought and the collapse of all belief in progress. Technology was now perceived as a curse, history as a process of stagnation, or even deterioration and political action as impotent posturing.

This pessimistic view of history probably found its most consistent expression in the lyric poetry of Günter Kunert. In *Abtötungsverfahren* (*Mortification Procedures*) (1980) and *Stilleben* (*Still Life*) (1983), Kunert records visions of the last days and of decline in images of despair.

Erde und Steine
Sand und Geröll
Ziegel und Quader
Zement und Beton
und immer wieder
wir

Earth and stones
Sand and rubble
Bricks and squarestones
Cement and concrete
and again and again
us

This poem, from *Abtötungsverfahren*, bears the evocative title *Evolution*.

It pinpoints a developmental process that is in reality not development at all, but a return of something that is always the same in a guise that is only outwardly changed. Darkness and gloom, caves and blindness, monads and tracks of blood – it is in the auras of meaning around these metaphors that the vision of an apocalypse unfolds, arising out of a consciousness of the inevitability of an ecological catastrophe. Kunert is not trying to invoke collapse – he is convinced of it because the whole of human history has only been pushed forward by the human ideals that accompanied it – including socialist ideals. In this way, Kunert's poetry captures in images, symbols, motifs and metaphors, what the author has also propounded in his articles and essays (*Verspätete Monologe* – *Delayed Monologue*, 1981; *Diesseits des Erinnerns* – *This Side of Memory*, 1982), and in public discussions: 'Those who survive will only be able to retain their life-force, their life substance, by being able to think, and hence also to feel, in a radically different way. And because I do not believe in that, I am not an optimist and have no hope.'

The fact that Kunert nevertheless publicises his views, concentrating his visions of catastrophe in poetry, seems to contradict his sense of hopelessness, but only at first glance. His actual concern is, on the very edge of the abyss, to revive a poetics of 'pure' form in the tradition of Gottfried Benn: 'Without movement / without meaning, without permanence.' In his own estimation, this gives him both the strength and the justification to set the potential of lyric poetry for resistance against the damage of the end-days being done to the world – even if only as a portent:

> Aus blinden Augen
> fällt Finsternis
> bevor die Hand
> ins Leere greift.
>
> Darkness falls
> out of blind eyes
> before the hand
> reaches into emptiness.

'Alternative histories'

Observation of a rediscovery of and return to an idea of the 'unique nature of the aesthetic' (Lukács) as literature moved into the 1980s, and of a strengthened conviction of the capacity of poetry for resistance, is confirmed by a survey of continuities in the work of known authors. Writers such as Peter Weiss, Alexander Kluge, and Herbert Achternbusch, who go back to the 1960s, consistently asserted the ability of literature to capture, deal with and shape reality. Although these authors are scarcely comparable with one another in terms of such details as choice of subject-matter, style, or narrative perspectives and structure, their work does nevertheless stand for a common agenda: to influence, by writing, both the reader and his perception of reality, and thus indirectly to exert an effect on reality itself.

Herbert Achternbusch and Alexander Kluge are highly divergent exponents of this agenda. Achternbusch feels with painful, and yet recurringly ironic and fragmented intensity, the suffering of a subjectivity whose autobiographical traits are not erased, but emphatically depicted in their social and familial character. Compared to this, the stories of Alexander Kluge seem almost like a kind of negative encyclopedia. He shows social diversity and heteronomy in a degree of complexity that threatens individuals to the point of oblivion. Achternbusch's insistence on his own subjectivity, however, clearly differs from the 'new subjectivity' of the 1970s – not only because he found his theme, himself, long before the fashionable discovery of the first person, but also because each and every one of his works presents a new variation on the same theme of Herbert Achternbusch. From *Das Kamel* (*The Camel*) (1970) through *Die Alexanderschlacht* (*The Battle of Alexander*) (1971) and *Der Tag wird kommen* (*The Day Will Come*) (1973) to *Der Neger Erwin* (*Erwin the Negro*) (1981), *Die Olympiasiegerin* (*The Olympic Winner*) (1982) and *Revolten* (*Revolts*) (1982), his first-person theme proliferates into diverse, imaginative metaphors and allegories, spilling over into 'anti'-characters, intermediate and secondary tones, past and future worlds, yet all the while remaining with and returning to the self.

Through this process of self-discovery, which he also continued in the film medium, Achternbusch achieves a comprehensive account of all those processes of suppression that had robbed him as an individual – and not only him – of imagination, feeling, and aesthetic productivity:

> We had to read so many poems unhappily, and yet I knew I had some idea of my own about happiness. But then I was presented with the chance of writing a poem, and there was no more happiness there. Only my ravaged head, my head with 'its' ravaged state. I had just about managed to salvage it from the machinery of alignment and renovation. The fact that I could ascertain that much was my sole remaining happiness. My 'yes' to this unhappiness was my sole happiness. Busying myself with this unhappiness was my sole happiness. Through writing and filming, recollection acquired a utopian radiance.

Achternbusch's solitary existence, far removed from the cultural scene, finds its parallel in a writing style that pays no heed to literary tradition or custom, but which pursues the processes of subjectivisation with which it deals in the subjectivity of its perceptual forms. For this reason, he has never had an easy passage with his public, either as author or film-maker (*Der Depp* – *The Idiot*, 1982; *Das Gespenst* – *The Ghost*, 1982; *Die*

Olympiasiegerin – The Olympic Winner, 1983). He has even had to put up with discriminatory remarks from literary critics and film promoters (the Federal Ministry of the Interior). Nevertheless, it is the consistency with which he answers for no more than himself, as book author, director, producer, performer and distributor of his films, that gives his egocentric literary and film fantasies the credibility and power to convince that are conceded by such as the GDR dramatist Heiner Müller: 'Herbert Achternbusch is the classic author of the anti-colonial liberation struggle within the FRG.'

The literary exorcising of complex international conditions

Alexander Kluge, extremely versatile and broadly-educated (law graduate, church musician, film director, and theoretician) described the agenda of his film and literary work as follows: 'Either social history narrates its *Real-Roman*, without respect to persons, or people narrate their anti-history. They cannot do this, however, unless they do so in the degrees of complexity within reality. This calls literally for an "artificial subject", an aggregate of artificial subjects. Sensuality as a method is not a social product of nature.' This complex theoretical statement contains a number of assumptions that lay behind Kluge's prose from the very outset (*Lebensläufe – Careers*, 1962). Kluge's stories arise out of a reality whose run of events, developments and tendencies are perceived in all their complexity, down to the minutest details of everyday life ('The children are being good, the wife tells them to be quiet') and the finest nuances of feeling ('When he looks at his wife, he grows tired'). The organisation of this material from reality, however, does not exhaust itself in the bald reproduction of reality, in the sense of a replica or likeness. Instead, it condenses and concentrates observed segments of life in a way that produces perplexity, opposition and resistance. The complexity called for by Kluge in his theoretical definition is reflected in the diversity of forms and openness of his texts. The reader can work with these stories, able not only to recognise himself and his reality in them, but also to fill them out with his own experiences. It is from this that the literary uniqueness of these 'anti-stories' by Alexander Kluge derives, as in *Lernprozesse mit tödlichem Ausgang* (*Learning Processes With a Fatal Outcome*) (1973) and *Neue Geschichten. Heft 1–8. 'Unheimlichkeit der Zeit'* (*New Stories, Parts 1–18: 'The Sinister Nature of the Times'*) (1977). Not only do these deal with reality with an appropriate degree of literary complexity, they also modify the reader's view of that reality, from which they themselves have emerged.

Kluge's negative encyclopedia produces the resistance of aesthetics by pointedly and critically projecting as 'science fiction' that which is depicted in our everyday relations as the 'fatal outcome'. The montage character of his narrative method is as little a matter of form in all this as the black humour that underlies it. Like Kluge the director and theoretician, Kluge the story-writer, cognisant of social complexity and heterogeneity, likewise distrusts the purpose and content of a strand that imposes continuities. For the same reason, in his films, too (*Die Patriotin – The Patriot*, 1979; *Die Macht der Gefühle – The Power of Emotion*, 1983) Kluge creates a montage of heterogeneous, contradictory materials from history and the present day, thereby building up complex essays. For the same reason, his theoretical blueprints (*Öffentlichkeit und Erfahrung – The Public and Experience*, 1972; *Geschichte und Eigensinn – History and Obstinacy*, 1981, both with Oskar Negt) refuse to offer so much as a hint of a system-creating line of thought. Kluge is not a 'heartless story-writer' (Hans Magnus Enzensberger), but an educator with a sense for reality.

Hildesheimer

With his biography *Marbot* (1981), Wolfgang Hildesheimer produced an 'anti-story' of quite a different kind – a fictionalisation of fiction. Just as the title may almost be read as an anagram of Hildesheimer's *Mozart* biography (1977), so the character of the title may be seen as a kind of picture-puzzle of aesthetic existence. Hildesheimer's *Marbot* is the biography of a fictitious person drawn from the history of art – a character with something erotically sensational about him as a result of his violation of the incest taboo with his mother, and who at the same time makes use of this quality for his special gifts. The character makes advances in the potential for psychological interpretation in the visual arts and painting by concentrating on reconstructed empathy in both technique and emotion, in the coloration and formal style of nineteenth-century art. Hildesheimer lends life and authenticity to his character in a very careful and ingenious manner, by providing an ostensibly credible background to his existence in the form of documents and photographs, later even citing from the work of this fictitious character in lectures and discussions.

By linking the motifs of incest and the faculty for aesthetic reproduction, Hildesheimer implicitly raises the question of the underlying conditions of artistic production. Similarly, his chosen method of fictionalising fiction also gives rise to the problem of having to redefine the relationship between literature and reality. Wolfgang Hildesheimer himself, successful author of *Lieblose Legenden* (*Loveless Legends*) (1952–62) and *Tynset* (1965), for his part announced his decision to give up writing and to devote himself to painting instead. He has attempted to combine the two art forms in his autobiographical work *Mitteilungen an Max über den Stand der Dinge und anderes* (*Messages to Max About The State of the Art and Other Things*) (1983).

'Anti-stories' by such authors as Alexander Kluge, Herbert Achternbusch and Peter Weiss, as well as younger authors such as Ludwig Fels (*Mein Land – My Land*, 1978; *Betonmärchen – Concrete Fairy-tales*, 1982, Bodo Kirchhoff (*Die Einsamkeit der Haut – The Loneliness of the Skin*, 1981) and Rainald Goetz (*Irre – Crazy*, 1983) are invariably concerned with a critique of reality, a dialectical reference to reality in the sense of an anti-blueprint that points beyond the social status quo – and this through the innovatory elements of its formal language.

This is not the case with another young and highly successful author, Botho Strauss. The success of Strauss's work may be explained not least by the fact that he is gifted with an exceptionally sensitive perceptive faculty, picking up shades of reality that he is able to condense into a stylistic system of equilibrium that can be savoured. The result is cultural and social criticism in the form of an enjoyable reproduction of what is being criticised.

Botho Strauss, who started as a dramaturgist with the theatre director Peter Stein, made his literary début in the early 1970s with his own theatre plays *Die Hypochonder* (*The Hypochondriacs*), (1971); *Bekannte Gesichter, gemischter Gefühle* (*Familiar Faces, Mixed Emotions*), (1974); *Trilogie des Wiedersehens* (*Reunion Trilogy*), (1976); *Gross und Klein* (*Great and Small*) (1977). Besides his works for the theatre, among which his *Kalldewey Farce* (1981) was a huge hit, Strauss also wrote short stories and novels from the mid-1970s onwards (*Die Widmung – The Dedication*, 1977; *Rumor – Unrest*, 1980; *Paare, Passanten – Couples, Passers-by*, 1981).

Strauss also took up in his work the prevalent theme of the 1970s: alienation in our society and the suffering that results from it. Strauss too is concerned with a critique of society and culture. He nonetheless remains captive to that society and culture in a problematic way, seeking, for all his sensitivity and stylistic artistry, to track it down phenomenologically. 'Without dialectic we think *ad hoc* and more stupidly', wrote Strauss with an eye to the Frankfurt School of Theodor W. Adorno *et al.*, 'but it has to be so: without it!' Seen in terms of an agenda, this represents an alternative blueprint to Alexander Kluge's postulate of the 'anti-story': brilliant style, but still no more than 'very beautiful in a transitory way', as Thomas Bernhard has described it – 'like a lilac bush in front of my house'.

If the literary developments of the 1980s in the Federal Republic can be summed up by the formula 'aesthetics fights back', this is undoubtedly because the consciousness of a crisis has found its way into the works of contemporary German literature. The hopes for the future that marked the 1960s have receded into the background, as has the first-person-centred perceptual perspective of 'new subjectivity'. These have been replaced by a knowledge of threatening ecological, nuclear and social catastrophe that has not left authors untouched. The potential of imagination and pro-ductive energies, aimed at changing this abysmal social status quo, find expression not only in political gestures of protest directed at the public, but in the very literary aesthetics of works themselves. The transcendence of the first person, the lyric poetry of a damaged world, the retrieval of sensuality and the reclaiming of historical thought and action are the forms of representation used for contemporary literary opposition. Obviously, in view of the global dimensions of the perceived threat, these could not possibly remain limited to the Federal Republic. They also, for example, had their advocates among authors of the former GDR, such as Irmtraud Morgner and Christa Wolf. To take up a statement made by Heiner Müller at the 1981 writers' convention in East Berlin, they have in common a knowledge of 'the subversion of art, which is necessary in order to make reality untenable'.

1992 UPDATE: THE UNITY AND DIVERSITY OF GERMAN LITERATURE

What is contemporary German literature in the 1990s? Can it be meaning-fully reduced to a common denominator? Has a literary reunification taken place along with the reunification of the German state on 3 October 1990? Was good, significant German literature a homogeneous, coherent literature with both a visible and an invisible fabric even prior to reunification, across state boundaries? Or has there been a counter-process to that of state reunification since the turning-point, exemplified by the German–German dispute over Christa Wolf, whereby intellectuals and creative artists of East and West are becoming increasingly at odds with one another?

What was GDR literature in fact during the forty years of its existence – a midwife of change or an accessory to an ugly dictatorship? Will, as some have asserted, what was formerly a separate literature simply be swallowed up by an already existing one – the West German? Is there indeed a homogeneous entity called 'literature of the Federal Republic'? Or has this itself not long since been fragmented by the tension between the 'conscience of the nation' and the 'postmodern boulevard'?

These and many other topical issues cannot be answered globally, unequivocally and definitively, for all the widely-felt need to do so. In an age in which national, linguistic, and literary boundaries are in any case only of limited conceptual validity, we will have to learn to live with the permanence of contradictions and the contemporary existence of the discontemporaneous. Retrospectively and prospectively, we can do no more than offer a few signposts for literature in the context of this imminent challenge.

How many German literatures?

The first question is: how many German literatures were there prior to the 1989–90 turning point? Even this is not an easy question to answer. German literature was, after all, written not only in the Federal Republic and the GDR, but also in Austria and Switzerland, and, less obviously, in Alsace, Luxembourg and Romania (chiefly in the Banat and Transylvania regions, following the demise of German literature in Bukovina in World War II or its expulsion into exile with such authors as Paul Celan or Rose Ausländer).

It is not only the multi-state character of German literature that confuses the issue, however. Another question that has always been difficult to resolve is that of the criteria – thematic, political, socio-cultural, or aesthetic – according to which distinctions are to be drawn in literature written in the same language. That this is no mere contrived issue is demonstrated by the universality of Spanish literature, which is spread over several continents and whose internal classification raises no objections. Such attempts at internal differentiation should not lead to arrogation or exclusion. A brief review of various East and West German viewpoints is illuminating. Up to 1956 the view prevailed in the GDR that German literature was a unified whole, unaffected by the boundaries of zone, state or social system. The thesis of two German literatures was first put forward by Walter Ulbricht in a message to the fourth Writers' Congress in 1956, reflecting the theory of two states that had been propagated since 1949 in political practice.

Socialist national literature

Henceforth, it became customary in the GDR to assert, or at least encourage, an indigenous, burgeoning 'socialist national literature', which was viewed as being separated by a wide gulf from the bourgeois, capitalist literature of decadence in the West German state. After 1961, the year of the Berlin Wall, this interpretation of German culture and literature was regarded as unassailable, and persisted with only minimal modifications until the demise of the GDR.

The eleven-volume *History of German Literature* issued in the GDR made this view official by assigning to *Literature of the GDR* a separate volume of over 900 pages that treated literary developments in the other German state as something entirely separate and intrinsic.

In the Federal Republic, both this official GDR standpoint and endemic confusion over bewildering internal conditions unleashed an ongoing, and at times polemical, debate as to whether there was one, two, or even more German literatures. Conservative literary criticism in the Adenauer era continued to uphold the idea of a unified German literature comprising the free literature of the West, with the addition of a number of critical and prestigious GDR writers. The rest of GDR literature was viewed as not literature at all, being politically doctrinaire and aesthetically inconsequential.

'Across frontiers'

It was Hans Mayer, first in the GDR, and from 1963 in the Federal Republic, who first questioned this assumption. In 1967 he suggested the existence of 'two fundamentally different structures in literary life ... within Germany', although he also discovered literature 'across frontiers – literature written in East Germany whose intellectual abode was in the West. It is even conceivable for a West German *belles-lettres* to exist for which the reverse would apply.' This statement was tantamount to an acknowledgement that different social structures stimulated different literatures; equally, it was an acknowledgement that the chosen ideological standpoint of an author could be opposed to that of his or her geographical location – leading to overlapping.

The social activist role of literature and its 'popular' quality

In 1964, along with colleagues from East and West alike, Uwe Johnson commented aptly on ideas concerning the socially mediated nature of the emergence of two German languages and literatures:

> I view as dubious the assertion that we all write or express ourselves in a common language. There is a difference of opinion among writers of both currency areas in Germany as to the simple German sentence. They differ as to which sentence is good in the literary sense. ... In my view, it does not lie in the choice of subject-matter. ... It seems very important to me that to these situations, each concerned with an industrial state, a different interpretation is given, so that in one case literature is assigned specific roles, and in the other none. The literature of the GDR, for example, has the role of altering the consciousness of the reader – an expressly socially activist task. West German, West German-speaking literature, lacks this role. This has an effect on aesthetics. This ancient contradiction between progress in artistic form and backwardness in the capacity of the reading public to accept it has been quite radically eliminated in East German literature, both in general and in particular. There, a certain boundary of comprehensibility has been delineated and a unification has taken place. This is the concept of popularity. West German literature, on the other hand, attempts to find appropriate descriptive forms for its subject-matter that do not always pay heed to the capacity of the readership to accept them, or shall we say to a certain sluggishness in receptive consciousness. It can thus come about, at worst, that a West German writer does not understand a sentence written by an East German colleague, or at best asserts that this writing style is outmoded and behind the times.

'Disculturality'

It is clear from Johnson's analysis of the two German literatures and their public functions that it is over twenty-five years old. What he is describing refers to the historical phase lying roughly between 1948 and 1967, a period in the development of the GDR when it was developing not only its own state identity, but also its own cultural identity and a 'disculturality' with regard to the Federal Republic (Jürgen Link). A different set of social experiences was arising in each of the two German states, and along with them diverging cultural and aesthetic norms.

This view has been corroborated repeatedly and from very different standpoints during the last decade. Even in 1979, for example, Hans Mayer pointed to the 'slavish continuity' in GDR literature – that didactic realistic mode of writing, backed by the anti-formalism campaign, that was obliged to go back beyond the discoveries and techniques of creative modernity and remain, or become, provincial.

The provincialism of early GDR literature

A pro-GDR observer such as Günther Diecke has likewise affirmed this provincialism in the GDR literature of the 1950s. Of course this literature did not consist solely of political agitation rhymes and 'tractor' lyric poetry, affirmative plays and schematic novels of development (a form only parodied in the West). Brecht, Müller, Hacks, Arendt, Huchel, and Johnson himself were also active in this period, but the dominant aesthetic feature of this period was that of the literary pre-modern, and one that sacrificed aesthetics to political content, whereas writers in the Federal Republic, when in doubt, did the reverse.

The 'compensatory modernisation' of GDR literature

From the mid- to the late 1960s, a remarkable process was set in motion in GDR literature that might be described as compensatory modernisation. The culmination of this process, in the 1980s, was marked by what was at first a surprising convergence of the literatures of East and West Germany, both thematically and aesthetically. Better GDR literature no longer featured positive heroes and an obligatory happy ending. It became more concerned with the 'afflicted individual', 'damaged life', hence arriving at an 'accessible alienness' (Heinrich Mohr).

All this was not lost either on the publishers or readers of the Federal Republic. Books such as Christa Wolf's *Cassandra* or *Malfunction*, Christoph Hein's *Dragon's Blood*, or Maxie Wander's *Good Morning, My Lovely* were published in large editions. Even Ulrich Plenzdorf, Irmtraud Morgner,

Volker Braun, Reiner Kunze, Erich Loest and Monika Maron reached a wide readership.

What had happened? The fact is that the increasing similarity of literature had had at its roots a similarity in the experience of life.

The hopes pinned on socialism as something quite different became fragile – chiefly with the defeat of the Prague Spring uprising by the Warsaw Pact armies in August 1968 – and separated off as a 'pure utopia' from shoddy reality. To this extent there was a concomitant willingness to pay heed to and describe the shortcomings of 'existing socialism' – the alienation and increasing loneliness of the individual in a hierarchically structured society steeped in rationality, the destruction of the basis of natural life, the triumphant march of what was still no more than 'instrumental reason': in short, the contradictions of an industrial civilisation that had been condemned as pathological. By the same token, as GDR literature was no longer able to close its eyes to the traumatic experiences of the modernism of the civilisation process, it opened itself in a compensatory, and yet creative way to the subversive writing strategies of aesthetic modernism. Of course, pre-modern literature of the 'socialist realism' variety continued to be churned out (e.g. by Erik Neutsch, Dieter Noll, Harry Thürk or Helmut Salkowski). Nevertheless, a substantial proportion of GDR literature by all generations of writers now became modern and on a par with other German literatures. The best GDR authors made skilful use of the literary potential of modern literature, portraying the crisis in the sense of history, of social models, the self, and hence of literature itself, using such techniques as self-reflection, diversity of perspectives, polyphony, intertextuality, montage and collage methods, language destruction and fragmentation, fantastic elements and dream writing, etc.

GDR writers as the conscience of the socialist nation

Authors of this new GDR literature have recently been accused of being so fixated on worldwide issues of civilisation that they closed their eyes to the state repression of their own country, thereby preserving their idealised image of socialism. This accusation cannot be dismissed out of hand, but the true causes of the remarkable delusions of some GDR intellectuals in the midst of the political turning-point – in some cases going as far as subsequent nostalgic distortions of 'existing socialism', particularly with regard to its promotion of the arts – are to be sought elsewhere. They are to be found mainly in the privileged, hypertrophic role ascribed to writers by the socialist system as educators of the people, a role from whose promises and enticements few authors were able to free themselves before the turning-point. It has to be admitted today that the disruptive experience of Biermann's deprivation of citizenship in 1976 and its repressive after-effects were not taken nearly enough to heart by most of the authors who remained in the GDR. Only a handful took on themselves the role of consistent dissidence towards the system as an alternative. This fact is attributable less to a lack of courage on the part of individuals, and cannot in any event be expressed in terms of a moral accusation, than to the internalised, system-conditioned self-view of authors, however critical, as the advocates and conscience of the socialist nation.

The collapse of the GDR and the whole project of 'existing socialism' likewise led to the collapse of this questionable self-view of creative intellectuals, plunging many of them into a state of grief and melancholy, and not infrequently to resentment. However, an era has come to an end, a change of paradigm has occurred and literature is having to readjust. This is as true of the former West German as it is of former East German literature. 'The literature of the Federal Republic is forty-three years old', announced Frank Schirrmacher in an article in the *Frankfurter Allgemeiner Zeitung* on 2 October 1990, on the eve of German reunification. What he meant by this is that a specific literature, written by authors now aged between sixty and seventy-five years – almost all of whom had been organised in the '47 Group' – and once coloured by the war and post-war eras, had finally come to its delayed and deserved end. There are indeed cogent arguments in favour of looking on this literature as outmoded and behind the times, without wishing to take issue with its historical legitimacy. The literature of Böll and Andersch, Lenz and Grass, or Jens and Walser constituted the memory of a generation, obstinately retrieving the question of guilt and returning it to the conscience of the whole nation. This is much to their credit, and should not be denied them. Until 1968, the year of revolt, no other social group or institution paid so much attention to the work of recalling Nazism, the war and the holocaust as did this literature. In effect, however, this function of West German literature in acting as a kind of ersatz public, representing a satiated affluent nation in the process of coming to terms with its own history, came to an end with the student revolts. Political action, however incoherent and incompetent, then took up this issue with the previous generation, its institutions replacing the functions formerly exercised by literature. The latter's moral role was by no means exhausted, but from that time on was firmly relative.

Other notions of literature, ranging from the objectives of extremist political strategy (as in *Kursbuch 15 – Timetable 15*) to playful *l'art pour l'art*, could now establish themselves. Political developments (the Vietnam War, the right-wing putsch in Chile, the arms race and the temporarily increased threat of a world war) in the 1970s and 1980s continued to be of immense importance in constituting the dominant or even exclusive politico-moral definition of the function of literature in the Federal Republic as they had been for its founding fathers, but the end of predominantly morally motivated post-war literature as such came in 1968. Twenty years on, after the turning-point and the collapse of the Second World, this end can no longer be denied.

The older generation of authors in East and West

This same turning-point also revealed the glaring parallels (without losing sight of major differences) between West and East German post-war literature, which were persistent and came to be dominant. What these literatures had in common was that they were the work of one and the same generation, i.e. authors born just before or around the 1920s who either returned home laden with guilt and a bad conscience from the war and imprisonment, or simply shed the shirts of the Hitler Youth and the German Girls' Association. The difference was that whereas in the early Federal Republic young authors and intellectuals defined themselves as the opponents of the conservative country of the economic miracle, in the young GDR they were declared to be the 'victors of history'. They transposed the anti-fascist founding myth of the GDR state into literature, practising their art as a form of belated resistance, albeit with the best of intentions. In the GDR, strengthened by the limited freedom of the press and less media competition, something akin to a Golden Age of literature occurred. Legitimised by its fundamentally anti-fascist approach, GDR literature lent emphatic authenticity to something that had never been achieved, but which at that time still appeared to be achievable – a different, socialist reality and an example of humane self-realisation. Towards the end, in 1989–90, it was the critical creative artists open to reform who ossified into the posture of being the conscience of the nation and *praeceptor Germaniae*. It still remains for them, and for Günter Grass or Walter Jens of the former Federal Republic, to realise what their colleague Hans Magnus Enzensberger realised years ago. First, that the 'tidying-up operation by intellectuals after the demise of fascism, the entire ideological garbage removal, a highly arduous and tedious task', has long since been completed, and second that the former role of intellectuals has been reincorporated into society – 'We have lost Heinrich Böll, but we have gained Amnesty and Greenpeace.'

The diversity of literary models

What is left to literature once its political function has become obsolete? Does the recently revealed involvement of not a few East German and some West German intellectuals in the former power and surveillance structures of the GDR not call for a traditional moral intervention by literature? There is no doubt that it does, and writers can play their part in giving accounts of such involvement. On the other hand, in the presence of a semi-functioning political and media opinion in a civil and open society such as the present Federal Republic, literature cannot devote itself exclusively to this cause, despite possible defamation. Literature throughout Germany is today free to articulate itself in diverse and mutually contradictory ways. As Jochen Vogt has asserted: 'The critical, moralistic function of literature is but one literary option among many', and certainly not the only one. It is indicative of the present situation that no cultural or literary model can establish itself absolutely in Germany today. Indeed, one cannot even speak of a clear hierarchy of diverse models. A miscellany of lifestyles, subjects and writing strategies co-exist among literati themselves and in their texts without crystallising into distinct schools, groups or even institutions.

Two examples may serve to illustrate this. Following Biermann's deprivation of citizenship and the exodus of some one hundred authors from the GDR, there were concerted efforts to group this 'new exile literature' together as a homogeneous form. Erich Loest endeavoured to hold it together, and Fritz J. Raddatz misleadingly spoke of a 'third German literature'. And yet how much was there really in common between Karl-Heinz Jakobs and Wolfgang Hegewald, Thomas Brasch and Erich Loest, or Jürgen Fuchs and Sascha Anderson? Certainly far less than could justify their comprising a single literature.

Similarly, the 'Prenzlauer Berg connection' (Adolf Endler) has recently been revealed as a highly fragile association of diverging tendencies and approaches that has, moreover, been completely exploded in the meanwhile by the proven surveillance activities of some of its protagonists for the GDR intelligence services. To put this 'other' literature forward as a homogeneous enitity – as *the* alternative to the official literary scene, would be tantamount to creating a new literary myth.

'Disorderly plurality'

The time has definitely come to dispense with the idea of compact, clearly definable, institutionalised tendencies and groups in contemporary German literature, and certainly with the notion of a single German literature. There are undoubtedly common features, such as a basically critical attitude towards civilisation, a scepticism with regard to simple perceptual constructions and a refusal to accept the once ubiquitous belief in progress, given a history that has proved to be so unpredictable, volatile and multidimensional, in both the positive and negative senses. All these common features are nonetheless matched by an equal diversity of aesthetic concepts and writing practices, literary regions and social functions, authors' generations and political standpoints which it is beneficial to heed and acknowledge. The international metabolism of these diverging literatures is so diverse that the very descriptive model of 'national literature' is proving more untenable than ever. Contemporary literature in German exists in a variety of scenes that are open to one another, in a lifestyle of 'disorderly plurality', which is a good thing.

FURTHER READING

General reading

Best, O. F. and Schmitt, H. J. (eds): *Die deutsche Literatur. Ein Abriss in Text und Darstellung.* 16 vols. Stuttgart 1974–.

de Boor, H. and Newald, R. (eds): *Geschichte der deutschen Literatur. Von den Anfängen bis zur Gegenwart.* 7 vols. Munich 1949–.

Behrmann, A.: *Einführung in den neueren deutschen Vers. Von Luther bis zur Gegenwart.* Stuttgart 1989.

Geschichte der deutschen Literatur. Various editors. 12 vols. Berlin (East) 1961–.

Gnüg, H. and Möhrmann, R. (eds): *Frauen Literatur Geschichte. Schreibende Frauen vom Mittelalter bis zur Gegenwart.* Stuttgart 1985.

Grimm, R. (ed.): *Deutsche Dramentheorien. Beiträge zu einer historischen Poetik des Dramas in Deutschland.* 2 vols. Frankfurt am Main 1971.

Harth, D. and Gebhardt, P. (eds): *Erkenntnis der Literatur. Theorien, Konzepte, Methoden der Literaturwissenschaft.* Stuttgart 1982.

Hauser, A.: *Sozialgeschichte der Kunst und Literatur.* Munich 1969.

Jens, W. (ed.): *Kindlers Neues Literatur Lexikon.* 20 vols. Munich 1988–.

Killy, W. (ed.): *Die deutsche Literatur. Texte und Zeugnisse.* 7 vols. Munich 1963–.

Killy, W. (ed.): *Bertelsmann Literaturlexikon. Autoren und Werke deutscher Sprache.* 15 vols. Gütersloh and Munich 1988–.

Kissling, W. (ed.): *Deutsche Dichtung in Epochen. Ein literaturgeschichtliches Lesebuch.* Stuttgart 1989.

Lämmert, E. *et al.* (eds): *Romantheorie. Dokumentation ihrer Geschichte in Deutschland.* Vol. 1: *1620–1880*, Cologne and Berlin 1971; vol. 2, *From 1880*, Cologne and Berlin 1975.

Lutz, B. (ed.): *Metzler Autoren Lexikon. Deutschsprachige Dichter und Schriftsteller vom Mittelalter bis zur Gegenwart.* Stuttgart 1986.

Schweikle, G. and Schweikle, I. (eds): *Metzler Literatur Lexikon. Begriffe und Definitionen.* 2nd rev. edn Stuttgart 1990.

Medieval literature

Bertau, K: *Deutsche Literatur im europäischen Mittelalter.* 2 vols. Munich 1972/73.

Bloch, Marc: *Die Feudalgesellschaft.* Frankfurt am Main, Berlin, Vienna 1982.

Bowra, C. M.: *Heldendichtung. Eine vergleichende Phänomenologie der heroischen Poesie aller Völker und Zeiten.* Stuttgart 1964.

Brogsitter, K. O.: *Artusepik.* Stuttgart 1971.

Bumke, J.: *Ministerialität und Ritterdichtung. Umrisse der Forschung.* Munich 1976.

Bumke, J.: *Höfische Kultur. Literatur und Gesellschaft im hohen Mittelalter.* 2 vols. Munich 1986.

Cormeau, C. (ed.): *Deutsche Literatur im Mittelalter. Kontakte und Perspektiven.* Stuttgart 1979.

Curschmann, M. and Glier, I. (eds): *Deutsche Dichtung des Mittelalters.* 2 vols. Munich 1980.

Dronke, P.: *Die Lyrik des Mittelalters. Eine Einführung.* Munich 1973.

Eis, G.: *Mittelalterliche Fachliteratur.* Stuttgart 1967.

Ennen, E.: *Frauen im Mittelalter.* Munich 1984.

Grenzmann, L. and Stackmann, K. (eds): *Literatur und Laienbildung im Spätmittelalter und in der Reformationszeit.* Stuttgart 1984.

Hohendahl, P. U. and Lützeler, P. M. (eds): *Legitimationskrisen des deutschen Adels 1200–1900. Literaturwissenschaft und Sozialwissenschaften* vol 11. Stuttgart 1979.

Kuhn, H.: *Dichtung und Welt im Mittelalter.* Stuttgart 1969.

Kuhn, H.: *Text und Theorie.* Stuttgart 1969.

Kuhn, H.: *Liebe und Gesellschaft.* Stuttgart 1980.

Langosch, K. (ed.): *König Artus und seine Tafelrunde. Europäische Dichtung des Mittelalters.* Stuttgart 1980.

Richter, D. (ed.): *Literatur im Feudalismus. Literaturwissenschaft und Sozialwissenschaften* vol. 5. Stuttgart 1975.

Ruh, K. (ed.): *Abendländische Mystik im Mittelalter. Symposion Kloster Engelberg 1984.* Stuttgart 1986.

Runciman, S.: *History of the Crusades.* New edn London 1990.

Schweikle, G.: *Germanisch-deutsch Sprachgeschichte im Überblick.* 2nd rev. edn Stuttgart 1991.

Schweikle, G.: *Minnesang.* Stuttgart 1988.

Schweikle, G.: *Neidhart.* Stuttgart 1990.

Sowinski, B.: *Lehrhafte Dichtung des Mittelalters.* Stuttgart 1971.

Wapnewski, P. (ed.): *Mittelalterrezeption. Ein Symposion.* Stuttgart 1986.

Wehrli, M.: *Literatur im deutschen Mittelalter. Eine poetologische Einführung.* Stuttgart 1984.

Humanism and Reformation

Anderson, P.: *The Lineages of the Absolutist State*. London 1979.

Batkin, L.M.: *Die italienische Renaissance. Versuch der Charakterisierung eines Kulturtypus*. Basle 1981.

Berger, A.E. (ed.): *Die Sturmtruppen der Reformation. Augsgewählte Flugschriften der Jahre 1520–25*. Leipzig 1931.

Berger, A.E.: *Die Schaubühne im Dienste der Reformation*. 2 parts. Leipzig 1935–.

Bernstein, E.: *Die Literatur des deutschen Frühhumanismus*. Stuttgart 1978.

Beutin, W.: *Der radikale Doktor Martin Luther*. Cologne 1982.

Brackert, H.: *Bauernkrieg und Literatur*. Frankfurt am Main 1975.

Fischer, L. (ed.): *Die lutherischen Pamphlete gegen Thomas Müntzer*. Tübingen 1976.

Guchmann, M.M.: *Die Sprache der deutschen politischen Literatur in der Zeit der Reformation und des Bauernkrieges*. Berlin 1974.

Jäckel, B. (ed.): *Kaiser, Gott und Bauer. Die Zeit des deutschen Bauernkriegs im Spiegel der Literatur*. Berlin 1975.

Kaczerowsky, K. (ed.): *Flugschriften des Bauernkriegs*. Reinbek 1970.

Könneker, B.: *Die deutsche Literatur der Reformationszeit*. Munich 1975.

Laube, A. and Seiffert, H.W. (eds): *Flugschriften der Bauernkriegszeit*. Berlin 1975.

Loewenich, W. von: *Martin Luther. Der Mann und das Werk*. Munich 1982.

Nagel, B.: *Meistersang*. Stuttgart 1978.

Strassner, E.: *Schwank*. Stuttgart 1978.

Weimann, R.: *Renaissanceliteratur und frühbürgerliche Revolution*. Berlin 1976.

Weimann, R.: *Realismus in der Renaissance*. Berlin 1977.

Wohlfeil, R. (ed.): *Reformation oder frühbürgerliche Revolution?* Munich 1972.

Wolf, H.: *Martin Luther*. Stuttgart 1980.

Baroque literature

Alexander, R.J.: *Das deutsche Barockdrama*. Stuttgart 1984.

Barner, W.: *Barockrhetorik. Untersuchungen zu ihren geschichtlichen Grundlagen*. Tübingen 1970.

Barner, W. (ed.): *Der literarische Barockbegriff*. Darmstadt 1975.

Conrady, K.O.: *Lateinische Dichtungstradition und deutsche Lyrik des 17. Jahrhunderts*. Bonn 1962.

Dyck, J.: *Ticht-Kunst. Deutsche Barockpoetik und rhetorische Tradition*. Munich 1969.

Langer, H.: *Kulturgeschichte des Dreissigjährigen Krieges*. Leipzig 1978.

Mannack, E.: *Andreas Gryphius*. Stuttgart 1986.

Mauser, W.: *Dichtung, Religion und Gesellschaft im 17. Jahrhundert*. Munich 1976.

Meid, V.: *Barocklyrik*. Stuttgart 1986.

Meid, V.: *Grimmelshausen. Epoche, Werk, Wirkung*. Munich 1984.

Moser-Rath, E.: *'Lustige Gesellschaft'. Schwank und Witz des 17. und 18. Jahrhunderts in kultur- und sozialgeschichtlichem Kontext*. Stuttgart 1984.

Oestreich, G.: *Geist und Gestalt des frühmodernen Staates*. Berlin 1969.

Otto, K.F.: *Die Sprachgesellschaften des 17. Jahrhunderts*. Stuttgart 1972.

Rötzer, H.G.: *Der Roman des Barock 1600–1700*. Munich 1972.

Schöne, A.: *Emblematik und Drama im Zeitalter des Barock*. Munich 1968.

Segebrecht, W.: *Das Gelegenheitsgedicht. Ein Beitrag zur Geschichte und Poetik der deutschen Lyrik*. Stuttgart 1977.

Steinhagen, H. and Wiese, B. von.: *Deutsche Dichter des 17. Jahrhunderts. Ihr Leben und Werk*. Berlin 1984.

Stoll, C.: *Sprachgesellschaften im Deutschland des 17. Jahrhunderts*. Munich 1973.

Szyrocki, M.: *Die deutsche Literatur des Barock. Eine Einführung*. Stuttgart 1979.

Weisz, J.: *Das deutsche Epigramm des 17. Jahrhunderts*. Stuttgart 1979.

The Enlightenment

Aufklärung. Erläuterungen zur deutschen Literatur. Various editors. Berlin 1971.

Balet, L. and Gerhard, E.: *Die Verbürgerlichung der deutschen Kunst, Literatur und Musik im 18. Jahrhundert*. Ed. and Intro. by G. Mattenklott. Frankfurt am Main, Berlin, Vienna 1973.

Barner, W. *et al*.: *Lessing. Epoche, Werk, Wirkung*. Munich 1987.

Blackall, E.A.: *Die Entwicklung des Deutschen zur Literatursprache*, Stuttgart 1966.

Engelsing, R.: *Der Bürger als Leser. Lesergeschichte in Deutschland 1500 bis 1800*. Stuttgart 1974.

Engelsing, R.: *Analphabetentum und Lektüre. Zur Sozialgeschichte des Lesens in Deutschland zwischen feudaler und industrieller Gesellschaft*. Stuttgart 1973.

Ewers, H.-H. (ed.): *Kinder- und Jugendliteratur der Aufklärung*. Stuttgart 1980.

Fertig, L.: *Die Hofmeister. Ein Beitrag zur Geschichte des Lehrerstandes und der bürgerlichen Intelligenz*. Stuttgart 1979.

Grimminger, R. (ed.): *Deutsche Aufklärung bis zur Französischen Revolution. Hansers Sozialgeschichte der deutschen Literatur vom 16. Jahrhundert bis zur Gegenwart*. vol. 3. Munich 1980.

Guthke, K. S.: *Das deutsche bürgerliche Trauerspiel.* Stuttgart 1984.

Jamme, C. and Kurz, G. (eds): *Idealismus und Aufklärung. Kontinuität und Kritik der Aufklärung in Philosophie und Poesie um 1800.* Stuttgart 1988.

Kiesel, H. and Münch, P.: *Gesellschaft und Literatur im 18. Jahrhundert. Voraussetzungen und Entstehung des literarischen Marktes in Deutschland.* Munich 1977.

Kimpel, D.: *Der Roman der Aufklärung.* Stuttgart 1977.

Leibfried, E.: *Fabel.* Stuttgart 1982.

Martens, W.: *Die Botschaft der Tugend. Die Aufklärung im Spiegel der deutschen Moralischen Wochenschriften.* Stuttgart 1968.

Niggl, G.: *Geschichte der deutschen Autobiographie im 18. Jahrhundert.* Stuttgart 1977.

Sauder, G.: *Empfindsamkeit.* 3 vols. Stuttgart 1974–.

Schings, H.-J,: *Melancholie und Aufklärung. Melancholiker und ihre Kritiker in Erfahrungsseelenkunde und Literatur des 18. Jahrhunderts.* Stuttgart 1977.

Scheuer, H.: *Biographie. Studien zur Funktion und zum Wandel einer literatischen Gattung vom 18. Jahrhundert bis zur Gegenwart.* Stuttgart 1979.

Sørensen, B.A.: *Herrschaft und Zärtlichkeit. Der Patriarchalismus und das Drama im 18. Jahrhundert.* Munich 1984.

The *Kunstepoche*

Bohrer, K.H.: *Der romantische Brief. Die Entstehung ästhetischer Subjektivität.* Munich, Vienna 1987.

Brinkmann, R. (ed.): *Romantik in Deutschland. Ein interdisziplinäres Kolloquium.* Stuttgart 1978.

Bruford, Walter H.: *Kultur und Gesellschaft im klassischen Weimar 1775–1806.* Göttingen 1966.

Conrady, K.O. (ed.): *Goethe. Leben und Werk.* 2 vols Königstein/Ts. 1982/1985.

Conrady, K.O. (ed.): *Deutsche Literatur zur Zeit der Klassik.* Stuttgart 1977.

Klassik. Erläuterungen zur deutschen Literatur. Various editors Berlin 1971.

Lecke, B. (ed.): *Literatur der Klassik I: Dramenanalysen. Projekt Deutschunterricht* vol. 7. Stuttgart 1974.

Lecke, B. (ed.): *Literatur der Klassik II: Lyrik Epik, Ästhetik. Projekt Deutschunterricht* vol. 9. Stuttgart 1975.

Lutz, B. (ed.): *Deutsches Bürgertum und literarische Intelligenz 1750–1800. Literaturwissenschaft und Sozialwissenschaften* vol. 3. Stuttgart 1974.

Mandelkow, K.R.: *Goethe in Deutschland. Rezeptionsgeschichte eines Klassikers.* 2 vols. Munich 1980.

Mandelkow, K.R.: *Goethe im Urteil seiner Kritiker. Dokumente zur Wirkungsgeschichte Goethes in Deutschland.* 4 vols. Munich 1975/1977/1979/1984.

Müller-Seidel, W.: *Die Geschichtlichkeit der deutschen Klassik. Literatur und Denkformen um 1800.* Stuttgart 1983.

Ott, U. (ed.): *'O Freyheit! Silberton dem Ohre . . .' Französische Revolution und deutsche Literatur 1789–1799. Marbacher Kataloge 44.* Marbach/N. 1989.

Richter, K. and Schönert, J. (eds): *Klassik und Moderne. Die Weimarer Klassik als historisches Ereignis und Herausforderung im kulturgeschichtlichen Prozess.* Stuttgart 1983.

Schlaffer, Hannelore: *Wilhelm Meister. Das Ende der Kunst und die Wiederkehr des Mythos.* Stuttgart 1980.

Schlaffer, Heinz: *Faust zweiter Teil. Die Allegorie des 19. Jahrhunderts.* Stuttgart 1981.

Schön, E.: *Der Verlust der Sinnlichkeit und die Verwandlung des Lesers. Mentalitätswandel um 1800.* Stuttgart 1987.

Stephan, I.: *Literarischer Jakobinismus in Deutschland.* Stuttgart 1976.

Ueding, G.: *Klassik und Romantik. Deutsche Literatur der Französischen Revolution 1789–1815. Hansers Sozialgeschichte der deutschen Literatur* vol. 4. Munich, Vienna 1987.

Vormärz

Adler, H. (ed.): *Literarische Geheimberichte. Protokolle der Metternich-Agenten.* 2 vols. Cologne 1977/78.

Adler, H.: *Soziale Romane im Vormärz. Literatursemiotische Studien.* Munich 1980.

Bock, H. *et al.*: *Streitpunkt Vormärz. Beiträge zur Kritik bürgerlicher und revisionistischer Erbeauffassungen.* Berlin 1977.

Denkler, H.: *Restauration und Revolution. Politische Tendenzen im deutschen Drama zwischen Wiener Kongress und Märzrevolution.* Munich 1973.

Deuchert, N.: *Vom Hambacher Fest zur badischen Revolution. Politische Presse und Anfänge deutscher Demokratie 1832–1848/49.* Stuttgart 1983.

Estermann, A.: *Die deutschen Literaturzeitschriften 1815–1850. Bibliographien, Programme, Autoren.* 10 vols. Nendeln 1978–1981.

Feudel, W.: *Lyrik im deutschen Vormärz.* Halle 1985.

Hinderer, W. (ed.): *Geschichte der politischen Lyrik in Deutschland.* Stuttgart 1978.

Hohendahl, P.U.: *Literarische Kultur im Zeitalter des Liberalismus 1839–1870.* Munich 1985.

Höhn, G.: *Heine-Handbuch. Zeit, Person, Werk.* Stuttgart 1987.

Köster, U.: *Literatur und Gesellschaft in Deutschland 1830–1848. Die Dichtung am Ende der Kunstperiode.* Stuttgart 1984.

McInnes, E.: *Das deutsche Drama des 19. Jahrhunderts.* Berlin 1983.

Minder, R.: 'Deutsche und französische Literatur – inneres Reich und Einbürgerung des Dichters'. In: *Kultur und Literatur in Deutschland und Frankreich.* Frankfurt am Main 1962.

Möhrmann, R.: *Die andere Frau. Emanzipationsansätze deutscher Schriftstellerinnen im Vorfeld der Achtundvierziger Revolution.* Stuttgart 1977.

Obenaus, S.: *Literarische und politische Zeitschriften 1830–1848.* Stuttgart 1986.

Pech, K.-U. (ed.): *Kinder- und Jugendliteratur vom Biedermeier bis zum Realismus.* Stuttgart 1985.

Reisner, H.P.: *Literatur unter der Zensur. Die politische Lyrik des Vormärz.* Stuttgart 1975.

Rosenberg, R.: *Literaturverhältnisse im deutschen Vormärz*, Munich 1975.

Ruckhäberle, H.-J. (ed.): *Frühproletarische Literatur. Die Flugschriften der deutschen Handwerksgesellenvereine in Paris 1832–1839.* Kronberg 1977.

Seidler, H.: *Österreichischer Vormärz und Goethezeit. Geschichte einer literarischen Auseinandersetzung.* Vienna 1982.

Sengle, F.: *Biedermeierzeit. Deutsche Literatur im Spannungsfeld zwischen Restauration und Revolution* 1815–1848. 3 vols. Stuttgart 1971/72/80.

Stein, P.: *Epochenproblem Vormärz.* Stuttgart 1974.

Steinecke, H.: *Romantheorie und Romankritik in Deutschland.* 2 vols. *Die Entwicklung des Gattungsverständnisses von der Scott-Rezeption bis zum programmatischen Realismus.* Stuttgart 1975/76.

Weigel, S.: *Flugschriftenliteratur 1848 in Berlin. Geschichte und Öffentlichkeit einer volkstümlichen Gattung.* Stuttgart 1979.

Werner, H.G.: *Geschichte des politischen Gedichts in Deutschland von 1815 bis 1840.* East Berlin 1969.

Wülfing, W.: *Schlagworte des Jungen Deutschland.* Berlin 1982.

Realism and the *Gründerzeit*/Under the banner of imperialism

Anz, T.: *Literatur der Existenz. Literarische Psychopathographie und ihre soziale Bedeutung im Expressionismus.* Stuttgart 1977.

Anz, T. and Stark, M. (eds): *Expressionismus. Manifeste und Dokumente zur deutschen Literatur 1910–1920.* Stuttgart 1982.

Aust, H.: *Literatur des Realismus.* Stuttgart 1977.

Brauneck, M.: *Literatur und Öffentlichkeit im ausgehenden 19. Jahrhundert. Studien zur Rezeption des naturalistischen Theatres in Deutschland.* Stuttgart 1974.

Brauneck, M. and Müller, Chr. (eds): *Naturalismus. Manifeste und Dokumente zur deutschen Literatur 1880–1900.* Stuttgart 1987.

Brinkmann, R.: *Expressionismus. Internationale Forschung zu einem internationalen Phänomen.* Stuttgart 1980.

Bucher, M. *et al.* (eds): *Realismus und Gründerzeit. Manifeste und Dokumente zur deutschen Literatur 1848–1880.* 2 vols. Stuttgart 1975/76.

Emmerich, W.: *Proletarische Lebensläufe. Autobiographische Dokumente zur Entstehung der 'Zweiten Kultur' in Deutschland.* 2 vols. Reinbek 1975.

Fohrmann, J.: *Das Projekt der deutschen Literaturgeschichte.* Stuttgart 1989.

Haas, W.: *Die Belle Epoque.* Munich 1967.

Hagen, W.: *Die Schillerverehrung in der Sozialdemokratie. Zur ideologischen Formation proletarische Kulturpolitik vor 1914. Literaturwissenschaft und Sozialwissenschaften* vol. 9. Stuttgart 1977.

Hamann, G. and Hermand, J.: *Epochen deutscher Kultur von 1870 bis zur Gegenwart.* 5 vols. Berlin 1965–.

Ketelsen, U.K.: *Völkisch-nationale und nationalsozialistische Literatur in Deutschland 1890 bis 1945.* Stuttgart 1976.

Knilli, F. and Münchow, U. (eds): *Frühes deutsches Arbeitertheater 1847–1918. Eine Dokumentation.* Munich 1970.

Kreuzer, H.: *Die Boheme. Analyse und Dokumentation der intellektuellen Subkultur vom 19. Jahrhundert bis zur Gegenwart.* Stuttgart 1971.

Martini, F.: *Deutsche Literatur im bürgerlichen Realismus 1848–1898.* Stuttgart 1974.

Melchinger, S.: *Geschichte des politischen Theaters.* 2 vols. Frankfurt am Main 1974.

Mayer, H.: *Deutsche Literaturkritik.* 4 vols. Frankfurt am Main 1978.

Ott, U. (ed.): *Literatur im Industriezeitalter. Marbacher Kataloge 42.* 2 vols. Marbach/N. 1987.

Peschken, B. and Krohn, C.D. (eds): *Der liberale Roman und der preussische Verfassungskonflikt. Analysematerialien und Skizzen. Literaturwissenschaft und Sozialwissenschaften* vol. 7. Stuttgart 1976.

Ruprecht, E. and Bänsch, D. (eds): *Jahrhundertwende. Manifeste und Dokumente zur deutschen Literatur 1890–1910.* Stuttgart 1970.

Sagarra, E.: *Tradition und Revolution. Deutsche Literatur und Gesellschaft 1830–1890.* Munich 1972.

Scherer, H.: *Bürgerlich-oppositionelle Literaten und sozialdemokratische Arbeiterbewegung nach 1890.* Stuttgart 1974.

Schlawe, F.: *Literarische Zeitschriften 1885–1933.* 2 vols. Stuttgart 1965/74.

Selbmann, R.: *Dichterdenkmäler in Deutschland.* Stuttgart 1988.

Stark, M.: *Für und wider den Expressionismus. Die Entstehung der Intellektuellendebatte in der deutschen Literaturgeschichte.* Stuttgart 1982.

Trommler, F.: *Sozialistische Literatur in Deutschland. Ein historischer Überblick.* Stuttgart 1976.

Ueding, G.: *Die anderen Klassiker. Literarische Porträts aus zwei Jahrhunderten.* Munich 1986.

Widhammer, H.: *Die Literaturtheorie des deutschen Realismus*. Stuttgart 1977.

Zerges, K.: *Sozialdemokratische Presse und Literatur. Empirische Untersuchungen zur Literaturvermittlung in der sozialdemokratischen Presse 1876 bis 1933*. Stuttgart 1982.

Literature in the Weimar Republic

Berg, J. *et al.*: *Sozialgeschichte der deutschen Literatur von 1918 bis zur Gegenwart*. Frankfurt am Main 1980.

Fähnders, W.: *Proletarisch-revolutionäre Literatur der Weimarer Republik*. Stuttgart 1977.

Fähnders, W. and Rector, M.: *Linksradikalismus und Literatur. Untersuchungen zur Geschichte der sozialistischen Literatur in der Weimarer Republik*. 2 vols. Reinbek 1974.

Film und revolutionäre Arbeiterbewegung in Deutschland 1918–1932. 2 vols. Berlin 1975.

Gallas, H.: *Marxistische Literaturtheorie. Kontroversen im Bund proletarisch-revolutionärer Schriftsteller*. Neuwied and Berlin 1971.

Hörburger, C.: *Das Hörspiel der Weimarer Republik. Versuch einer kritischen Analyse*. Stuttgart 1975.

Hoffmann, L. and Hoffmann-Ostwald, D.: *Deutsches Arbeitertheater 1918–1932*. 2 vols. 3rd edn Berlin 1977.

Kaes, A. (ed.): *Weimarer Republik. Manifeste und Dokumente zur deutschen Literatur 1918–1933*. Stuttgart 1983.

Klein, A. (ed.): *Aktionen, Bekenntnisse, Perspektiven. Berichte und Dokumente vom Kampf um die Freiheit des literarischen Schaffens in der Weimarer Republik*. Berlin 1966.

Klein, A.: *Im Auftrag ihrer Klasse. Weg und Leistung der deutschen Arbeiterschriftsteller 1918 bis 1933*. Berlin and Weimar 1972.

Knopf, J.: *Brecht-Handbuch*. vol. 1 (*Theater*); vol. 2 (*Lyrik, Prosa, Schriften*). *Eine Ästhetik der Widersprüche*. Stuttgart 1980/84.

Lethen, H.: *Neue Sachlichkeit 1924–1932. Studien zur Literatur des 'Weissen Sozialismus'*. Stuttgart 1975.

Mennemeier, F.N.: *Modernes deutsches Drama. Kritiken und Charakteristiken*. Vol. 1: *1918 bis 1933*. Munich 1973.

Möbius, H.: *Progressive Massenliteratur? Revolutionäre Arbeiterromane 1927–1932*. Stuttgart 1977.

Rothe, W. (ed.): *Die deutsche Literatur in der Weimarer Republik*. Stuttgart 1974.

Vogt, J. *et al.*: *Einführung in die deutsche Literatur des 20. Jahrhunderts*. Vol. 2: *Weimarer Republik, Faschismus und Exil*. Opladen 1977.

Weimarer Republik. Ausstellungskatalog. Ed. Kunstamt Kreuzberg, Berlin, and the Institut für Theaterwissenschaft der Universität Köln. Berlin and Hamburg 1977.

Literature in the Third Reich

Brenner, H.: *Die Kunstpolitik des Nationalsozialismus*. Reinbeck 1963.

Denkler, H. and Prümm, K. (eds): *Die deutsche Literatur im Dritten Reich. Themen, Traditionen, Wirkungen*. Stuttgart 1976.

Gittig, H.: *Illegale antifaschistische Tarnschriften 1933–1945*. Leipzig 1972.

Loewy, E.: *Literatur unterm Hakenkreuz. Das Dritte Reich und seine Dichtung. Eine Dokumentation*. Frankfurt am Main 1966.

Schnell, R.: *Literarische Innere Emigration 1933 bis 1945*. Stuttgart 1976.

Schnell, R. (ed.): *Kunst und Kultur im deutschen Faschismus. Literaturwissenschaft und Sozialwissenschaften* vol. 10. Stuttgart 1978.

Stollmann, R.: *Ästhetisierung der Politik. Literaturstudien zum Subjektiven Faschismus*. Stuttgart 1978.

Wulf, J.: *Literatur und Dichtung im Dritten Reich*. Gütersloh 1964.

Wulf, J.: *Presse und Funk im Dritten Reich*. Gütersloh 1964.

Zeller, B. (ed.): *Klassiker in finsteren Zeiten 1933–1945*. Marbacher Kataloge 2 vols. Marbach/N. 1983.

German literature in exile

Arnold, H. L. (ed.): *Deutsche Literatur im Exil 1933–1945*. 2 vols. Frankfurt am Main 1974/75.

Dahlke, H.: *Geschichtsroman und Literaturkritik im Exil*. Berlin and Weimar 1976.

Durzak, M. (ed.): *Die deutsche Exilliteratur 1933 bis 1945*. Stuttgart 1973.

Grimm, R. and Hermand, J. (eds): *Exil und Innere Emigration I*. Frankfurt am Main 1972.

Heeg, G.: *Die Wendung zur Geschichte: Konstitutionsprobleme antifaschistischer Literatur im Exil*. Stuttgart 1977.

Hohendahl, P.U. and Schwarz, E. (eds): *Exil und Innere Emigration II*. Frankfurt am Main 1973.

Schmitt, H.-J. (ed.): *Die Expressionismusdebatte. Materialien zu einer marxistischen Realismuskonzeption*. Frankfurt am Main 1973.

Schmitt, H.-J. and Schramm, G. (eds): *Sozialistische Realismuskonzeptionen. Dokumente zum 1. Allunionskongress der Sowjetschriftsteller*. Frankfurt am Main 1974.

Loewy, E. (ed.): *Exil. Literarische und politische Texte aus dem deutschen Exil 1933–1945*. Stuttgart 1979.

Walter, H.A.: *Deutsche Exilliteratur 1933–1950*. 7 vols. Vol. 2: *Europäisches Appeasement und überseeische Asylpraxis*. Stuttgart 1984– vol. 3: *Internierung, Flucht und Lebensbedingungen im Zweiten Weltkrieg*.

Stuttgart 1988– vol. 4: *Exilpresse*. Stuttgart 1978–. Other volumes forthcoming.

Winckler, L. (ed.): *Antifaschistische Literatur*. 2 vols. Kronberg/Ts. 1977.

Winkler, M. (ed.): *Deutsche Literatur im Exil 1933 bis 1945. Texte und Dokumente*. Stuttgart 1977.

Literature of the German Democratic Republic

Albrecht, R.: *Das Bedürfnis nach echten Geschichten. Zur zeitgenössischen Unterhaltungsliteratur in der DDR*. Frankfurt am Main, Berne, New York, Paris 1987.

Anz, T. (ed.): *'Es geht nicht um Christa Wolf'. Der Literaturstreit im vereinten Deutschland*. Munich 1991.

Arnold, H.L. (ed.): *Literatur in der DDR. Rückblicke* (Text & Kritik. Sonderband). Munich 1991.

Arnold, H.L. and Wolf, G. (eds): *Die andere Sprache. Neue DDR-Literatur der 80er Jahre* (Text & Kritik. Sonderband). Munich 1990.

Behn, M.: *DDR-Literatur in der Bundesrepublik Deutschland. Die Rezeption der epischen DDR-Literatur in der BRD 1961–1975*. Meisenheim 1977.

DDR-Handbuch. Wissenschaftliche Leitung: H. Zimmermann. Edited by the Bundesministerium für Innerdeutsche Beziehungen. 2 vols. 3rd rev. edn. Cologne 1985.

Deiritz, K. and Krauss, H. (eds): *Der deutsch–deutsche Literaturstreit. Analysen und Materialien*. Hamburg and Zurich 1991.

Dokumente zur Kunst-, Literatur- und Kulturpolitik der SED. Vol. 1: 1949–1970, ed. E. Schubbe, Stuttgart 1972; vol. 2: 1971–1974, ed. G. Rüss, Stuttgart 1976; vol. 3: 1975–1980, ed. P. Lübbe, Stuttgart 1984.

Emmerich, W.: *Kleine Literaturgeschichte der DDR*. 1945–1988. Rev. edn. Frankfurt am Main 1989.

Franke, K.: *Die Literatur der DDR (Kindlers Literaturgeschichte der Gegenwart*, Vol. 2). 3rd rev. edn. Frankfurt am Main 1980.

Greiner, B.: *Literatur der DDR in neuer Sicht. Studien und Interpretationen*. Frankfurt am Main, Berne, New York 1986.

Hanke, I.: *Alltag und Politik. Zur politischen Kultur einer unpolitischen Gesellschaft. Eine Untersuchung zur erzählenden Gegenwartsliteratur in der DDR in den siebziger Jahren*. Wiesbaden 1986.

Herminghouse, P. and Hohendahl, P.U. (eds): *Literatur und Literaturtheorie in der DDR*. Frankfurt am Main 1976.

Herminghouse, P. and Hohendahl, P.U. (eds): *Literatur der DDR in den 70er Jahren*. Frankfurt am Main 1983.

Jäger, M.: *Kultur und Politik in der DDR. Ein historischer Abriss*. Cologne 1982.

Köhler-Hausmann, R.: *Literaturbetrieb in der DDR. Schriftsteller und Literaturinstanzen*. Stuttgart 1984.

Langenbucher, W.R., Rytlewski, R. and Weyergraf, B. (eds): *Handbuch zur deutsch–deutschen Wirklichkeit. Bundesrepublik Deutschland/Deutsche Demokratische Republik im Kulturvergleich (Kulturpolitisches Wörterbuch)*. Stuttgart 1883/1988.

Laschen, G.: *Lyrik in der DDR. Literatur und Reflexion*. Frankfurt am Main 1971.

Mittenzwei, E. (ed.): *Theater in der Zeitenwende. Zur Geschichte des Dramas und des Schauspieltheaters in der DDR 1945–1968*. 2 vols. Berlin 1972.

Naumann, M. *et al.*: *Gesellschaft – Literatur – Lesen. Literaturrezeption in theoretischer Sicht*. Berlin and Weimar 1973.

Profitlich, U.: *Dramatik der DDR*. Frankfurt am Main 1987.

Raddatz, F.J.: *Traditionen und Tendenzen. Materialien zur Literatur der DDR*. Rev. edn. Frankfurt am Main 1976.

Scherpe, K. and Winckler, L. (eds): *Frühe DDR-Literatur* (Argument Sonderband 149). Berlin 1987.

Schivelbusch, W.: *Sozialistisches Drama nach Brecht. Drei Modelle: Peter Hacks – Heiner Müller – Hartmut Lange*. Darmstadt, Neuwied 1974.

Schlenker, W.: *Das 'Kulturelle Erbe' in der DDR. Gesellschaftliche Entwicklung und Kulturpolitik 1945–1965*. Stuttgart 1977.

Schlenstedt, D.: *Die neuere DDR-Literatur und ihre Leser. Wirkungsästhetische Analysen*. Berlin 1979; Munich 1980.

Schmitt, H.-J. (ed.): *Einführung in Geschichte, Theorie und Funktion der DDR-Literatur. Literaturwissenschaft und Sozialwissenschaften* Vol. 6. Stuttgart 1975.

Schmitt, H.-J. (ed.): *Die Literatur der DDR. Hansers Sozialgeschichte der deutschen Literatur* vol. 11. Munich, Vienna 1983.

Sommer, D. *et al.*: *Funktion und Wirkung. Soziologische Untersuchungen zur Literatur und Kunst*. Berlin and Weimar 1978.

Staritz, D.: *Geschichte der DDR 1949–1984*. Frankfurt am Main 1984.

Walther, J. *et al.* (eds): *Protokoll eines Tribunals. Die Ausschlüsse aus dem DDR-Schriftstellerverband 1979*. Reinbek bei Hamburg 1991.

Wichner, E. and Wiesner, H. (eds): *Zensur in der DDR. Geschichte, Praxis und 'Ästhetik' der Behinderung von Literatur*. Berlin 1991.

Zimmermann, P.: *Industrieliteratur der DDR. Vom Helden der Arbeit zum Planer und Leiter*. Stuttgart 1984.

Literature of the Federal Republic

Arnold, H.L. (ed.): *Literaturbetrieb in Deutschland*. 2nd rev. edn. Munich 1981.

Arnold, H.L. (ed.): *Kritisches Lexikon zur deutschsprachigen Gegenwartsliteratur*. Munich 1978–.

Batt, K.: *Revolte intern. Betrachtungen zur Literatur in der Bundesrepublik Deutschland*. Munich 1975.

Baumgärtner, A.C. (ed.): *Lesen. Ein Handbuch*. Wiesbaden 1974.

Born, N. and Manthey, J. (eds): *Literaturmagazin 7. Nachkriegsliteratur*. Reinbek 1976.

Braunbeck, M. (ed.): *Autorenlexikon deutschsprachiger Literatur des 20. Jahrhunderts*. Reinbek 1984.

Buch, H.C. (ed.): *Literaturmagazin 4. Literatur nach dem Tod der Literatur*. Reinbek 1975.

Durzak, M. (ed.): *Deutsche Gegenwartsliteratur. Ausgangspositionen und aktuelle Entwicklungen*. Stuttgart 1981.

Endres, E.: *Autorenlexikon der deutschen Gegenwartsliteratur 1945–1975*. Frankfurt am Main 1975.

Engelmann, B. (ed.): *VS vertraulich*. 3 vols. Munich 1977–1979.

Geschichte der deutschen Literatur. Von den Anfängen bis zur Gegenwart. Edited by an author-collective, headed by A. Thalheim. Vol. 12: *Geschichte der Literatur der Bundesrepublik Deutschland*. East Berlin 1983.

Fohrbeck, K. and Wiesand, A.J.: *Der Autorenreport*. Reinbek 1972.

Fischer, L. (ed.): *Literatur in der Bundesrepublik Deutschland bis 1967. Hansers Sozialgeschichte der deutschen Literatur* vol. 10. Munich, Vienna 1986.

Glaser, H. (ed.): *Bundesrepublikanisches Lesebuch. Drei Jahrzehnte geistiger Auseinandersetzung*. Munich, Vienna 1978.

Hamm, P. (ed.): *Kritik/von wem, für wem, für wen, wie. Eine Selbstdarstellung der Kritik*. Munich 1970.

Imayr, W.: *Politisches Theater in Westdeutschland*. Meisenheim 1977.

King, Janet K.: *Literarische Zeitschriften 1945 bis 1970*. Stuttgart 1974.

Kröll, F.: *Die Gruppe 47. Soziale Lage und gesellschaftliches Bewusstsein literarischer Intelligenz in der Bundesrepublik*. Stuttgart 1977.

Kröll, F.: *Die Gruppe 47*. Stuttgart 1979.

Lattmann, D. (ed.): *Die Literatur der Bundesrepublik. Autoren, Werke, Themen, Tendenzen, seit 1945*. Frankfurt am Main 1986.

Lüdke, W.M. (ed.): *Nach dem Protest. Literatur im Umbruch*. Frankfurt am Main 1979.

Lützeler, P.M. and Schwarz, E. (eds): *Deutsche Literatur seit 1965. Untersuchungen und Berichte*. Königstein/Ts. 1980.

Rutchsky, M.: *Erfahrungshunger. Ein Essay über die siebziger Jahre*. Cologne 1980.

Schnell, R.: *Die Literatur der Bundesrepublik. Autoren, Geschichte, Literaturbetreib*. Stuttgart 1986.

Schuhmann, K.: *Weltbild und Poetik. Zur Wirklichkeitsdarstellung in der*

Lyrik der BRD bis zur Mitte der siebziger Jahre. Berlin and Weimar 1979.

Schwenger, H.: *Literaturproduktion*. Stuttgart 1979.

Vaterland, Muttersprache. Deutsche Schriftsteller und ihr Staat von 1945 bis heute. Berlin 1979.

Wehdeking, V.C.: *Der Nullpunkt. Über die Konstituierung der deutschen Nachkriegsliteratur (1945–1948) in den amerikanischen Kriegsgefangenenlagern*. Stuttgart 1971.

Würffel, S.B.: *Das deutche Hörspiel*. Stuttgart 1978.

Zürcher, G.: *Trümmerlyrik. Politische Lyrik 1945 bis 1950*. Kronberg/Ts. 1977.

INDEX